Fodor's 89 Europe

Fodor's Travel Publications, Inc.
New York and London

Fodor's Europe

Editor: Sean Connolly
Contributors: Judy Allen, Carmen Anthony, Hilary Bunce, Victoria Clark, Lisa M. Cussans, Robin Dannhorn, Nigel Fisher, Asgeir Fridgeirsson, Birgit Gericke, Geoffrey Graham-Bell, Simon Hewitt, Alannah Hopkin, Kenneth Loveland, Susan Lowndes-Marques, Carol Martin, Sylvie Nickels, Gillian O'Meara, Christopher Pick, Witek Radwanski, Philip Ray, Peter Sheldon, Caroline B. D. Smith, Linda Stout, Judy Tither, Peter Urgent, Barbara Walsh-Angellilo
Art Director: Fabrizio La Rocca
Cartographer: David Lindroth
Illustrator: Karl Tanner
Cover Photograph: Owen Franken

Design: Vignelli Associates

the Saronic Gulf islands and resorts on the eastern Peloponnese.

One luxury sea option in the eastern Mediterranean is the **Orient-Express,** owned by the same company that operates the *Venice Simplon-Orient-Express* train. The ship connects with the train at Venice, sails to Piraeus, Istanbul, and Kusadasi (Turkey); returns via Patmos and Katakolon in Greece, then meets the train again in Venice. For details, contact: **Venice Simplon-Orient-Express,** Suite 2565, 1 World Trade Center, New York, NY 10048. **British Ferries Orient-Express,** 8th Floor, Sea Containers House, 20 Upper Ground, London SW1 1JL.

River Travel Major river systems crisscross Europe. Among the many attractive river trips available are a number of luxury cruises on the Rhine and Danube rivers.

The Danube passes through seven European countries in western and eastern Europe, and international cruises are possible. Contact the **German National Tourist Office** for details. There is also an international hydrofoil service that operates several times a day on the Danube between Budapest in Hungary and Bratislava in Czechoslovakia. Information and booking are available through **Ibusz,** the Hungarian state travel agency, or **Cedok,** its Czech equivalent, in New York or London. For details of Rhine trips, contact **K.D. German Rhine Line,** 170 Hamilton Ave., White Plains, NY 10601; or **G.A. Club Rhine Cruise Agency Ltd.,** 80/81 St. Martin's Lane, London WC2N 4AA.

Though a great deal less spectacular than either the Rhine or the Danube, the smaller rivers of Belgium, Holland, France, and other western European countries can also provide a relaxed and fascinating vacation. **Floating Through Europe** (271 Madison Ave., New York, NY 10016) specializes in these kinds of tours.

By Bicycle

Bicycling in Europe can be sheer pleasure or unadulterated torment—depending on when you go, where you go, and what you try to do.

If you're planning a European bike trip, you are probably experienced enough not to need advice on equipment and clothing. But it needs to be said that some European countries are far more user-friendly than others toward bicyclists. In countries like Holland, Denmark, and Belgium, bikes are very much part of the landscape—mainly because the landscape tends to be uniformly flat and presents no challenges to even the wimpiest rider. City streets and many main roads in these countries (as well as in the Federal Republic of Germany) have special bike lanes set aside, and car drivers are used to coping with large numbers of bicycle riders.

Cyclists also get a good deal in the Eastern Bloc countries, where, for economic reasons, the bicycle is still the everyday form of transport. In France, bicycling can be a pleasure, but there are few cycle lanes, and French drivers can be taxing on the nerves.

Northern Scandinavia and Iceland, with their steep terrain, are destinations only for the serious cyclist. The Scandinavian countries have plenty of excellent-value campsites. Ireland has emptier roads and a gentler landscape than Sweden or Norway and is a pleasant country to bicycle in, though the temptation to sample just one more Guinness at each wayside pub can be a hazard in itself.

Of the wealthier European countries, Britain has the most shameful record when it comes to providing facilities for bicyclists or considering their interests. Riding in London traffic is a stomach-churning experience requiring nerves of steel. Except in remoter areas—such as the north of Scotland—main roads are overcrowded and often dangerous to bicycle on.

Bicycle Transport Transporting your bicycle from the United Kingdom to Europe holds no big problems—some ferry lines transport bicycles free, others charge a nominal fee. Shop around. Surprisingly, you may transport your bicycle by air as checked baggage—you won't have to pay extra so long as you are within the 44-pound (20-kilogram) total baggage allowance.

Most European rail lines will transport bicycles free of charge or for a nominal fee, though you may have to book ahead. Check with the main booking office. One of the joys of biking in Europe is being able to bike one way, and to return by train; or to board a train with your bike when you need to cover long distances, or simply when you need to take a rest. Transporting your bike by bus is also possible but may tax your powers of persuasion, as the bus lines don't seem to have any hard and fast rules but leave the decision to the driver or guide.

Renting Bicycles Bicycles can be rented by the day or week in most European capitals and are most readily available in cities like Amsterdam and Copenhagen, where cycling is part of the way of life. Local tourist boards are the best source of information on reliable rental agencies with safe bicycles to rent; remember to check on local traffic rules and make sure your insurance covers you in case of an accident. **GermanRail (DB)** rents bicycles at selected stations in summer—get further information from GermanRail or the German National Tourist Office in New York.

Contents

Maps

Maps

Foreword

This is an exciting time for Fodor's, as it begins a three-year program to rewrite, reformat, and redesign all 140 of its guides. Here are just a few of the exciting new features:

★ Brand-new computer-generated maps locating all the top attractions, hotels, restaurants, and shops

★ A unique system of numbers and legends to help readers move effortlessly between text and maps

★ A new star rating system for hotels and restaurants

★ Restaurant reviews by major food critics around the world

★ Stamped, self-addressed postcards, bound into every guide, that give readers an opportunity to help evaluate hotels and restaurants

★ Complete page redesign for instant retrieval of information

★ ITINERARIES—The experts help you decide where to go and how to organize your time

★ FODOR'S CHOICE—Our favorite museums, beaches, cafés, romantic hideways, festivals, and more

★ HIGHLIGHTS '89—An insider's look at the most important developments in tourism during the past year

★ TIME OUT—The best and most convenient lunch stops along the shopping and exploring routes

★ Exclusive background essays that create a powerful portrait of each destination

★ A minijournal for travelers to keep track of their own itineraries and and addresses

While every care has been taken to assure the accuracy of the information in this guide, the passage of time will always bring change, and consequently, the publisher cannot accept responsibility for errors that may occur.

All prices and opening times quoted here are based on information available to us at press time. Hours and admission fees may change, however, and the prudent traveler will avoid inconvenience by calling ahead.

Fodor's wants to hear about your travel experiences, both pleasant and unpleasant. When a hotel or restaurant fails to live up to its billing, let us know and we will investigate the complaint and revise our entries where the facts warrant it.

Send your letters to the editor of Fodor's Travel Publications, 201 E. 50th Street, New York, NY 10022. European readers may prefer to write to Fodor's Travel Publications, 30–32 Bedford Square, London WC1B 3SG, England.

Highlights '89 and Fodor's Choice

Highlights '89

It is an ironic reflection of the times that while the European Common Market (EEC) puts the finishing touches on its plans to remove all travel barriers for residents in and between member countries by 1992, the same countries are simultaneously working hard to improve border security.

Of course, *their* aim is to tackle the worldwide problem of terrorism, and there are clear signs that the security emphasis is beginning to pay off. In Europe, 1987 and most of 1988 were free of the kind of major terrorist incidents that, in 1985 and 1986, had scared off many prospective visitors from North America.

The problem hasn't gone away, but anyone who travels throughout Europe today can see the way things are being made safer, particularly at airports. There are more checks and more monitoring of people and baggage. There is, of course, a price to pay in longer lines and longer waits to pass through the various controls. Inevitably, too, this means more restrictions, such as the tiresome visa requirements for U.S. visitors to France.

Scandinavia has remained free of major terrorist incidents, with the assassination of Swedish Premier Olaf Palme seen as an isolated incident. **Sweden, Denmark,** and **Norway** remain among the world's most stable nations, and **Finland** has experienced an encouraging warming of relations with the Soviet Union that, in turn, has opened up more options for the traveler.

Politics Elsewhere in Eastern Europe, the effects of *glasnost* are expected to spread to some of the Soviet Bloc nations. **Hungary** and **Bulgaria** are already well on the road, following **Yugoslavia's** more open, restriction-free approach to tourists from the West. The easing of Poland's own political tensions should make it more accessible and enjoyable to visit, but **Romania** and **Albania** will remain political hardliners while the current leaders remain in power.

Fortunately, visitors can usually remain untouched by political rows—even serious ones—within Western European countries. Rarely do these disagreements have much impact on tourism. One exception could be in **Gibraltar,** where a newly elected administration has thrown the plans for closer links with Spain—down to the sharing of the airport—into some doubt. It is unlikely, though, that the border between the two, only recently opened after much squabbling, will be closed again.

Perhaps the major exception of relatively recent times was the partitioning of **Cyprus** following the Turkish invasion. Tensions still run high there periodically, but current signs are of a new resolve by the Greek and Turkish communities to settle their differences without military involvement. Last August saw the formal meeting of leaders of the two communities in a series of UN-sponsored discussions.

Spain, too, has survived some threats to its hard-won democracy, and the government is now strong enough to have had major success—with the cross-the-border help of the French—in controlling the Basque separatists.

After a period of dramatic unpopularity as taxes on wealth and—even more contentious—on eating out were introduced, the socialist administration of **France** under François Mitterrand has been reelected, and fears of a polarized society have receded.

Even **Italy** has had governments lasting years rather than the usual weeks or months, as in the past, although a joke candidate (a soft-porn actress) won a seat in parliament during recent elections, adding the usual whimsical element to Italian politics.

For the future, the key date is 1992, when Barcelona hosts the summer Olympics and the EEC is due to knock down all travel barriers. This could also mean the end of duty-free concessions among member countries and the imposition of the Value-added Tax (or sales tax) on a wider range of goods and travel. Prices could rise by up to 15%. Experts say, though, that it will be well after 1992 before all the intended measures take effect.

In the meantime, a word of warning for all smokers. It's **Europe's Anti-Cancer Year** (1989). Expect to find even more places where smoking is forbidden.

At the same time, **Great Britain** has made life a little easier for those who like a pint of ale or those who just want to rest their feet over a soft drink in the late afternoon. Last year, England and Wales liberalized their licensing laws to allow pubs to stay open from 11 to 11 every day except Sunday. (Scotland has operated on this more liberal basis for several years.)

New Attractions Europe is beginning to pay more attention to leisure time, with better service, better-quality accommodations, and better entertainment facilities firmly on the agenda.

When the Disney Corporation decided on a European Disneyland, the countries battled it out to attract Mickey, Donald, & Co. **France** battled hardest—and won. Work has already started on a site that is a short drive from Paris.

Elsewhere in Europe, **Spain** and **Portugal** are awash in watery pleasure domes. Outdoor and indoor amusement complexes are dominated by scary-but-safe water chutes and rides. The favorite family sunshine destinations on Spain's Costa del Sol and Portugal's Algarve have the biggest and best examples so far.

In **Holland,** the concept of holiday camps has been taken to a new level by Center Parcs, which offers a comprehensive range of sports and entertainment facilities to go with its upscale family apartments and stylish restaurants. Most of the facilities (including an elaborate water playground complex) are under a transparent dome, making it an all-weather destination. The idea has spread to **Great Britain** and there are plans for more Center Parcs in the rest of Europe.

Italy has increased the number of pedestrian-only zones in the historic centers of many cities, making it a pleasure to walk around without climbing over double-parked cars or diving away from teenage motorcyclists.

All over Europe, countries are vying with each other to keep tourists entertained. The lack of a vibrant nightlife has been one of **Yugoslavia's** disadvantages (or benefits, depending on your point of view), and this year, the authorities there have extended the opening hours of bars in the tourist resorts from midnight to 2 AM.

Gibraltar is even tapping its famous asset to keep visitors entertained. Deep inside the Rock itself is the new Laser Experience, a spectacular audio-visual display highlighting the area's history.

Portugal has stepped up its Sportugal campaign, encouraging hotels to add sports—mainly tennis, squash, and golf—facilities.

New Accommodations In **Greece,** the limit of 300 rooms put on new hotel buildings has been lifted to allow for the introduction of resort-style hotel complexes that are so much in favor in the United States and the Caribbean.

The number of hotel beds in **Turkey** has quadrupled in the past five years, but the development of sports and entertainment facilities has not kept pace. Club Mediterranné has solved this problem by providing entertainment at its new center near Antalya. For anyone staying in a conventional hotel, though, Turkey is a country for quiet days and even quieter nights.

One major trend in European tourism has been the demand for a more independent style of vacation. That staple of North American vacations, the motor home, is now an increasingly popular choice for visitors to **West Germany.** Americans want to see more of the countries they visit, and European governments have responded by creating new "authentic" options for accommodations. In **Portugal,** they call it agro-tourism. The government has given country farmhouse owners financial inducements to open up their homes to foreign visitors. At the same time, the *pousadas* (like the paradors in Spain) grow more popular every year. These are government-run restorations of historic palaces, monasteries, and castles turned into high-quality, relatively inexpensive, hotels.

In **France,** the wealth tax introduced by the incoming Socialist government had at least one beneficial effect—it "encouraged" the owners of the many châteaux to open up to guests under the *Château Acceuil* (Château Welcome) scheme. France also now has its own bed-and-breakfast network, which it attractively markets as *Café-Couette* (coffee-quilt).

More positive news is on the accommodations front. Effective government action has been taken against a plague of timeshare salespeople, who have been using the hard sell on unwary tourists in popular coastal resorts. The problem reached a peak in Spain and Portugal in 1986, but both governments have since created laws to limit the number of "Outside Personal Canvassers." The upside to the growth of timeshares, though, is the high quality of most of the new resorts. There are attractive new developments in Portugal's Algarve, for example, notably Four Seasons at Quinto do Lago.

European cities are upgrading their facilities for conventions, leading to an increased demand for five-star hotel rooms. Hilton opened new hotels in **Vienna** and **Ankara** late last year and in Munich this year. A new Sheraton opened in Limassol (**Cyprus**) in 1987 and one will open on the **Turkish Riviera** next year. The Meridien and Marriott groups have plans for hotels on that Turkish coast, too.

The first hotel with the Orient Express name opens in **Portugal's** Quinta do Lago this year. The owners are also in their third year of operating the sea extension of the London–Venice Orient Express train. The eponymous car ferry/cruise ship makes regular round trips between Venice and Istanbul throughout the summer.

Also leaving European ports this summer are substantially more cruise ships, now returned to the Mediterranean after a couple of summers cruising in Scandinavia or the Caribbean following the *Achille Lauro* hijack.

Pollution This return to the Mediterranean may also be a result of the efforts that several European nations have been putting into trying to protect this important natural resource. It was estimated several years ago that there were 27 diseases carried in one pint of sea water off the French Riviera coast; swimming off the Spanish coast was deemed equally hazardous. Since then, the Spanish and French governments have been leading the way in the cleanup of the Mediterranean. Results have been better and faster than expected, and although the Mediterranean is not 100% pollution free, conditions are improving.

Unfortunately, the efforts to save **Venice** from the encroaching waters have been less well rewarded, and that beautiful city remains in serious long-term peril. Equally, **Greece** has a long way to go before it solves the pollution problems of Athens, although the restrictions on private cars using the city's roads are a step in the right direction.

More important to Greece's tourism—and to people looking for new places in Europe—has been the expansion of air services to the **Greek islands.** There are now international flights into 25 Greek airports, including those on lesser-known islands such as Kos.

Dining The new fashions in food have led to the expected backlash against nouvelle cuisine. Restaurants in **France** are still serving colorful concoctions, but the portions are markedly more substantial.

Scandinavia In 1989, **Scandinavia** is looking to recover some of the visitors
Update who were put off by worries about the aftereffects of Chernobyl. **Sweden,** for example, saw the number of U.S. visitors drop by 31% immediately after the 1986 Soviet disaster. Its tourism officials are confident that the impact will be short-lived, and there is a substantial amount of investment committed to tourism projects. Sweden's largest sports and leisure complex, with self-catering accommodations, opened in 1987 at Tanum Strand near the port of Gothenburg; and the

Scandic Hotels group has opened the first of six "Active" hotels, offering comprehensive sports facilities in Sweden's major ski resorts, starting with Dalarna. The SARA group has also opened a new hotel in a ski resort, a 200-room property at Are. Both groups are opening more conventional city hotels in Gothenburg, Stockholm, and Malmö.

There are twice the number of hotel beds in **Norway** today as eight years ago—not that they have become any cheaper to stay in—and the country's tallest, a 34-story, 700-bed building, is being built in Oslo while the country's second largest, the Royal Garden, has recently opened in Trondheim. The largest hotel chain in the country, Rica, has opened hotels in Kristiansand and the ominously named Hell, near Trondheim. There is a new ski resort called Snowland opening between Stryn and Grotli. At the northernmost settlement in Europe, Mageroya, at the North Cape, a restaurant complex incorporating a videographic theater has been extended into the cliff rock face, with windows looking out into the Arctic Ocean. The first phase was completed last year, with phase two due in 1990.

Next year a new technology center aimed at entertaining children opens in Oslo. Motorists who haven't driven in Norway for several years will find the roads much improved, with new tunnels obviating the need to negotiate some of the worst mountain roads.

There has also been a breakthrough for drivers in **Finland,** with the Soviet Union having opened its border to visitors who want to drive to Leningrad. The Soviets are even providing details of where gas stations are located and when they are open. The **Lapland** province of Finland has been officially designated (at least by the Finnish authorities) as Santa Clausland, and a whole industry has been built up with post offices, banks, and information centers all operating in Santa's name. The Finns have clearly beaten the Swedes and the Danes to it, since both those nations previously claimed Santa for their own.

The emphasis on fantasy is true for all of **Denmark,** with the Tivoli pleasure gardens attracting over 4 million visitors a year and Legoland nearly a million. The country is also seeing its first water playground this year with the opening of Vandland in Aalborg.

Eastern Europe Eastern Europe (including the Balkan countries), like Scandi-
Update navia, was also less visited by foreign tourists following Chernobyl. Although this seems likely to be short term in its effect as well, the countries have other problems to face. In **Poland,** there remains a shortage of hotel rooms, particularly in the four- and five-star categories. The major chain Orbis has 10 establishments under construction, which should ease the problem in the next couple of years. There is also raging inflation that, for western visitors, is just about offset by the falling exchange value of the złoty.

There is a similar financial situation in **Yugoslavia,** with inflation at 100%-plus but a rapidly devalueing dinar.

There are also shortages, particularly in the food department, in both countries, but they are considerably better off than **Romania,** although the deliberate restriction on the import of foreign alcohol by the latter has now been eased.

After Yugoslavia, **Hungary** and **Bulgaria** are doing the most to attract visitors from outside the Eastern Bloc. The Danube link between Budapest and Vienna (Austria) is being strongly promoted. The country's "westernization" has been acknowledged with the decision to award the hosting of the first Grand Prix motor race to be held in Eastern Europe to Hungary last year.

In **Bulgaria,** there is now a casino in the capital Sofia. It is only open for foreign visitors using hard currency and it is operated by the New Otani Hotel. The country's ski resorts are also being developed, with a Sheraton hotel planned for Borovets. A new resort has just opened at Bansko in the Pirin Mountains.

Unlikely to get off the ground is the plan by a West German to convert the POW camp at Colditz in **East Germany** into a hotel. This will leave **Albania** as still perhaps the most forbidding of the Eastern European countries for the Western visitor. The Albanians have stopped insisting that visitors crossing into the country at land borders take a disinfectant bath and shave off beards and long hair, yet Albania remains a difficult place in which to stay and travel, and the ban on U.S. visitors remains.

Overall, Europe is set to welcome record numbers of visitors after a few relatively lean years. Anyone returning after a few years' absence is likely to find higher standards across the board.

Fodor's Choice

No two people will agree on what makes a perfect vacation, but it's fun and it can be helpful to know what others think. In compiling this list, we've included choices from each of the 33 countries covered in the book, and we hope that you'll have a chance to experience some of them yourself. For more detailed information about each entry, refer to the appropriate chapters within this guidebook.

Sights to Remember

Austria	The Wachau Valley at dawn or dusk
Belgium	Dusk in Bruges
Bulgaria	The panorama from the ramparts of Veliko Tarnovo
France	Mont St-Michel at high tide
Iceland	The midnight sun on Eyjafjordur
Ireland	A jaunting car ride along the lakefront at Killarney
	Slea Head (near Dunquin) after a storm
Italy	Venice Grand Canal at dawn
Malta	The fishing fleet on Valetta Harbor
Norway	The view of the Sør and Hardanger Fjords from Utne
Poland	Wawel Castle and Cathedral in Cracow
Spain	The perched white villages of Andalusia
Turkey	Istanbul skyline at sunset from Camliça Hill
Yugoslavia	The medieval walled city of Dubrovnik

Hotels

Austria	Schlosshotel, Dürnstein (*Very Expensive*)
Denmark	Falsled Kro, Falsled (*Very Expensive*)
France	Château d'Artigny, Montbazon (*Very Expensive*)
	The Ritz, Paris (*Very Expensive*)
	Any Logis et Auberges (Country Hotels and Inns) de France hotel (*Inexpensive*)
Great Britain	Connaught or Claridge's, London (*Very Expensive*)
	Royal Crescent, Bath (*Very Expensive*)
Holland	Pulitzer, Amsterdam (*Very Expensive*)
	De l'Europe, Amsterdam (*Expensive*)
Ireland	Park, Kenmare (*Very Expensive*)
Italy	Hassler-Villa Medici, Rome (*Very Expensive*)
	Monna Lisa, Florence (*Expensive*)
Portugal	The pousadas, particularly at Estremoz (*Moderate*)
Spain	Parador Conde de Orgaz, Toledo (*Expensive*)
Sweden	Clas på Hörnet, Stockholm (*Expensive*)

Switzerland Fischerzunft, Schaffhausen (*Very Expensive*)

West Germany Vier Jahreszeiten, Munich (*Very Expensive*)

Restaurants

Austria Zu den Drei Husaren, Vienna (*Very Expensive*)

Belgium Comme Chez Soi, Brussels (*Very Expensive*)

France Jamin, Paris (*Very Expensive*)

Great Britain Popjoy's, Bath (*Very Expensive*)

Hungary Kis Buda, Budapest (*Expensive*)
Legradi testvérek, Budapest (*Expensive*)

Monaco Louis XV in the Hôtel de Paris (*Very Expensive*)

Spain El Caballo Rojo, Córdoba (*Expensive*)

Sweden Johanna, Gothenburg (*Expensive*)

Switzerland Veltliner Keller, Zürich (*Moderate*)
Kronenhalle, Zürich (*Expensive*)

West Germany Aubergine, Munich (for lunch)

Monuments

Belgium The Atomium, Laeken, near Brussels

Czechoslovakia U Stareho Hrbitova (Old Jewish Cemetery), Prague

France The battlefields of Verdun
The Arc de Triomphe, Paris

Great Britain The original Prime Meridian marker, Greenwich

Ireland The Rock of Cashel

Italy The Pantheon, Rome

Luxembourg The Devil's Altar, Diekirch

Norway The Vigeland Monument, Oslo

Poland The Solidarity Monument, Gdańsk

Spain The Valley of the Fallen, near Madrid

Museums and Galleries

East Germany Pergamon Museum, East Berlin

France Toulouse-Lautrec Museum, Albi

Great Britain Wallace Collection, London

Holland Kröner-Müller Museum, Otterlo

Leichtenstein Prince's Art Gallery, Vaduz

Norway Munch Museum, Oslo

Portugal Gulbenkian Foundation, Lisbon

Spain Prado Museum, Madrid

Switzerland Villa Favorita, Lugano

Turkey	Topkapı Saray (Palace) and Harem, Istanbul
West Germany	Alte and Neue Pinakotheks, Munich

Festivals

Austria	Spring Festival, Salzburg
Denmark	Århus Festival
Finland	International Opera Festival, Savonlinna
Great Britain	Edinburgh International Festival
Holland	Holland Festival of Opera and Ballet, Amsterdam
Italy	Venice Carnavale
Spain	Easter Celebrations, Seville The Horse Fair, Jerez
Turkey	Istanbul Art Festival
West Germany	Oktoberfest, Munich
Yugoslavia	Dubrovnik Festival

Churches, Temples and Mosques

Austria	Karlskirche, Vienna
France	Chartres Cathedral
Great Britain	Salisbury Cathedral York Minster
Hungary	The medieval synagogue, Budapest
Italy	The two-level Basilica, Assisi San Lorenzo, Florence
Norway	Medieval stave church, Heddal
Portugal	Jeronimos Monastery, Belem
Spain	The 10th-century Mezquita (Mosque), Córdoba
Turkey	Santa Sofia, Istanbul
West Germany	Assamkirche, Munich

Classical Sights

Albania	Butrint
Cyprus	Curium
Greece	Delphi
Italy	Herculaneum and the temples of Paestum
Portugal	Conimbriga
Romania	Istria
Turkey	Ruins of Ephesus
Yugoslavia	Diocletian's Palace, Split

Parks and Gardens

Czechoslovakia	Vrtba Zahrada, Prague
France	Monet's "Water Lily" garden, Giverny
Great Britain	Hidcote Manor Garden, near Chipping Campden
	Regent's Park and Queen Mary's Gardens, London
Holland	Het Loo, Apeldoorn
Portugal	Estufa Fria, Lisbon
Spain	Generalife, Granada
Sweden	Linné Gardens, Uppsala
West Germany	Alpine Garden, Pforzheim

For Children

Austria	Cable car from Innsbruck to the mountains
Denmark	Legoland, Billung
	Tivoli Gardens, Copenhagen
Finland	Santa Claus's Workshop, Arctic Circle, near Rovaniemi
France	Le Jardin d'Acclimatation, Paris
	Ride to the top of the Eiffel Tower, Paris
Gibraltar	The Barbary Apes in the Apes' Den
Great Britain	The Whispering Gallery of St Paul's, London
Italy	The view from the roof of St Peter's, Rome
Spain	Snowflake, the albino gorilla, Barcelona zoo
West Germany	Zoologischer Garten (Zoo), Berlin

Shopping

East Germany	Classical LPs from East Berlin
France	Chocolates from the Maison du Chocolat, Paris
Great Britain	Cashmere sweaters from Edinburgh
Greece	Natural sponges from Athens
Iceland	Hand-woven woolen goods from Reykjavik
Ireland	Donegal tweeds from Dublin
Sweden	Crystal from Växjö
Turkey	Hand-woven carpets from Bodrum

Europe

World Time Zones

Numbers below vertical bands relate each zone to Greenwich Mean Time (0 hrs.).
Local times frequently differ from these general indications,
as indicated by light-face numbers on map.

+11 +12 - -11 -10 -9 -8 -7 -6 -5 -4 -3 -2

MONDAY
SUNDAY

International Date Line

Auckland, **1**	Denver, **8**	New York City, **16**	Rio de Janeiro, **23**
Honolulu, **2**	Chicago, **9**	Washington, DC, **17**	Buenos Aires, **24**
Anchorage, **3**	Dallas, **10**	Miami, **18**	Reykjavik, **25**
Vancouver, **4**	New Orleans, **11**	Bogotá, **19**	Dublin, **26**
San Francisco, **5**	Mexico City, **12**	Lima, **20**	London (Greenwich), **27**
Los Angeles, **6**	Toronto, **13**	Santiago, **21**	Lisbon, **28**
Edmonton, **7**	Ottawa, **14**	Caracas, **22**	Algiers, **29**
	Montreal, **15**		Paris, **30**
			Zürich, **31**

Prime Meridian

Prime Meridian

+7 +8 +9 +10 +11 +12

+1 +2

+3 +4 +5 +6

+3:30 +4:30

+5

+5:30 +6:30

+8

+8

+9

+8

+7

+8

+9

-1 0 +1 +2 +3 +4 +5 +6 +7 +8 +9 +10
Greenwich
Mean Time

0 +1 +2 +3 +2 +3 +44

Stockholm, **32**
Copenhagen, **33**
Berlin, **34**
Vienna, **35**
Warsaw, **36**
Budapest, **37**
Madrid, **38**

Rome, **39**
Istanbul, **40**
Athens, **41**
Jerusalem, **42**
Nairobi, **43**
Johannesburg, **44**
Moscow, **45**
Baghdad, **46**

Mecca, **47**
Delhi, **48**
Rangoon, **49**
Bangkok, **50**
Saigon, **51**
Singapore, **52**
Djakarta, **53**
Beijing, **54**
Shanghai, **55**

Hong Kong, **56**
Manila, **57**
Perth, **58**
Seoul, **59**
Tokyo, **60**
Sydney, **61**

Ten Great Itineraries

Austria: Salzburg to Vienna

Leaving the musical city of Salzburg, take route 158 east, through the delightful Lake Country to Bad Ischel. Visit the Kaiservilla, where Emperor Franz Josef held his summer court. Turning northward, stop off at Gmunden, with its double castle—a Landschloss on the shore and the picturesque Seeschloss on an island in the lake—connected by a causeway. This is an excellent water sports center. From Gmunden, go northeast to Wels, a convenient center for trips into the Danubian hinterland but with its own Romanesque, Baroque, and Renaissance delights. Linz is the capital of Upper Austria, sitting on the banks of the Danube, and is a city of great contrasts —with Austria's largest medieval square, on the one hand, and the country's most modern multipurpose hall, the Brucknerhaus, used for concerts, conventions, and all kinds of gatherings, on the other.

One of the finest examples of Baroque architecture in Austria is to be found at St. Florian, a few miles east of Linz. Among its important art treasures is the Sebastian Altar, painted by Albrecht Altdorfer, one of the masters of the Danube school. Follow the Danube to Melk, which sits on a rocky crag above the great river. The Baroque abbey dominating the town was originally built as a fortress in the 10th century and was taken over by the Benedictines in the 12th. The route between Melk and Krems is through the glorious Wachau Valley—56 kilometers (35 miles) of the most romantic scenery in Austria, with fairytale castles perched upon misty hilltops and charming villages dedicated to wine and fruit growing dotted along the banks. Be sure to visit Weissenkirchen and Dürnstein, two of the most attractive villages on the Danube. You're now only 90 minutes away from Vienna, and as you proceed southeastwards the mountains recede and the scenery becomes far less dramatic.

Length of Trip 9 to 14 days.

Transportation The best way to see this area is by car, though if you have the time, take a boat trip on the Danube, down the Wachau Valley between Melk and Krems.

The Main Route **Two nights: Bad Ischl.** Excursions to Hallstatt and Ebensee en route to Gmunden.

Two nights: Gmunden. Relax along the tree-lined promenade, visit the theaters and concert hall, and enjoy the water sports and magnificent scenery. Excursion to Wels en route to Linz.

Three nights: Linz. Visit the old town and its cathedral. Walk along the city ramparts. Excursions to St. Florian and Melk en route to Krems.

Two nights: Krems. Excursions to the medieval towns of Weissenkirchen and Dürstein.

Further Information: *See* Austria.

Danube Cruise

Once the northern border of the Roman Empire, the river Danube is a main artery through Europe's history and geography.

Cruises begin either in Passau or Vienna; choose the former and you'll see the beautiful Wachau region of Austria, characterized by steeply terraced vineyards and craggy castles. Beyond Vienna—one of Europe's most gracious and musical cities—you enter waters shared by Czechoslovakia and Hungary at Bratislava.

There's a stretch of watery wilderness before you round the hilly section of the Danube Bend and, then, the river swings south to divide Hungary's capital into the two towns, Buda and Pest, which form the city of Budapest.

The scene changes as the Danube flows across the vast Hungarian plains that once were exposed to the Mongol warriors sweeping in from the East. The Danube, broader now, crosses the Hungarian frontier into Yugoslavia, where it wends by the imposing fortress of Petrovaradin at Novi Sad before it reaches the country's capital, Belgrade.

Now the dramatic section begins. The river squeezes through a series of gorges that it has carved from the Carpathian mountains. On route, you pass the archaeological site of a Neolithic fishing settlement at Lepenski Vir. This is also the site of Roman military victories, marked by a 2nd-century inscription. While once the fearsome waters rushed through these gorges, the Danube's rush to get to the Black Sea is now controlled by the Iron Gates Hydroelectric Dam on the Yugoslav–Romanian border. This requires the cruise ship to be floated through locks before it continues onward.

The final journey of the Danube is through flat farmland—first in Romania, then Bulgaria, and then back into Romania—until the magnificent wilderness of the delta is reached and the Danube enters the Black Sea.

Length of Trip One or two weeks.

Transportation Soviet Danube Shipping Company is the only cruise company to offer a cruise along the length of the Danube from Passau. Its 10-day trips start at Frankfurt and include a continuation to Istanbul for the flight back. The agents for the Soviet Danube Shipping Company are **United States:** International Cruise Center, 185 Willis Avenue, Mineola, NY 11501, tel. 516/747–8880. **United Kingdom:** CTC Lines, 1 Regent Street, London SW1Y 4NN, tel. 01/930–5833.

Local tour companies in Vienna and Budapest also offer cruises along shorter stretches of the Danube.

Further Information: *See* Austria, Hungary, Romania, Yugoslavia.

France: Châteaux of the Loire

Châteaux are all over France, but often they are no more than undistinquished manor houses. That's not so in the Loire valley. Here, not only is there a profusion of châteaux, but they are often architectural masterpieces. Besides the splendid châteaux, the area has old and noble fortresses, such as the castles at Angers and at Chinon. Let us not forget, either, the various and excellent wines of the Loire valley that help to make a picnic on the banks of the Loire or its tributaries a memorable experience.

Start at Angers, with its 13th-century castle-fortress, and head east along the Loire to Saumur and its Renaissance château on a hill overlooking the river. Visit the Cavalry Museum and the curious *maisons troglodytes*, hillside cave dwellings that now serve as mushroom farms and tasting centers for the famous local wines.

Farther east is Chinon, where the large château-fortress perches above the town on a steep hill. Its inside is bare, thanks to Cardinal Richelieu's henchmen in the 17th century. The castle dates from the 12th century and the age of Henry II of England, who died here and is buried, along with Richard the Lionhearted, in the medieval abbey of Fontevraud, a few miles away.

Several miles south of the Loire, on the banks of the little river Indre, lies Azay-le-Rideau, the white fairytale château that is a pure Renaissance pleasure palace with its whimsical turrets. The elegance of its exterior is reflected in the still waters of the moat, and the surrounding park makes an ideal picnic stop. Six miles northeast of Azay-le-Rideau is Villandry, with its château and famous gardens: 1,500 linden trees line the avenue to the terrace in the back.

Amboise is farther along the Loire, beyond the bustling city of Tours and the famous vineyards of Vouvray. The château was a royal palace in the 15th and 16th centuries. Its terrace and park look down on the town, and it is a good base for excursions.

Seven miles from Amboise is Chenonceau, usually described as the most beautiful château of them all. Unlike many châteaux, Chenonceau has an interior that has been undisturbed by the passage of time. It is a showcase of splendid ceilings, huge fireplaces, and famous paintings. These reflect the tastes of some of its famous owners, including Catherine de Medici.

The château of Blois dominates the busy city below: Its construction shows the changing styles from the 13th to the 17th centuries. Inside there are hidden rooms and narrow passages that were conducive to the intrigue that swept the region during the Wars of Religion in the 16th century.

Chambord, on the road east, was built by Francois I in 1519 and, with 440 rooms, is easily the largest of the Loire châteaux. You can wander freely through 3,000 acres of the adjacent forest, formerly the royal hunting grounds. Finish your itinerary in Orléans, with its memories of Joan of Arc.

Length of Trip One week.

Transportation **By Car.** Driving is the best way to explore the châteaux and countryside, particularly because the roads are well marked.

By Public Transportation. Fast trains and buses link all the major towns, from where you can take local buses to visit the sights in the rural areas.

The Main Route **One night: Saumur.** Explore the château, Cavalry Museum, and local cave dwellings. Excursion to Fontevraud en route to Chinon.

Two nights: Chinon. Excursion to Azay-le-Rideau and Villandry en route to Amboise.

Two nights: Amboise. Excursion to Chenonceau en route to Blois.

Two nights: Blois. Excursion to Chambord en route to Orléans.

Further Information: *See* France.

Great Britain: Royal Roads from London

Less than half an hour west of London is Windsor, the home town of the queen of England. Her house is the castle, which sits on a high bluff above the town and overlooks the playing fields of Eton. The castle itself is fascinating, but make sure you see the paintings on exhibit, which represent only a small fraction of the royal collection.

Winchester, an hour west of Windsor, was the capital of England from the 9th to the mid-11th century, and several Saxon kings are buried within its Gothic cathedral. Nearby is the 13th-century Great Hall, the meeting place of medieval parliaments; in it is the supposed Round Table of Arthurian legend.

Farther west is Salisbury. As you approach, you'll see the 404-foot steeple of its 13th-century cathedral, said to be the most complete and perfect English cathedral. On route from Salisbury to Warminster, pay homage to the druids at Stonehenge. Close to Warminster is Longleat House, the best surviving Elizabethan house in the Italianate Renaissance style.

Wells, with England's first completely Gothic cathedral, is the farthest point west on the itinerary. Have a look at one of the few surviving medieval clocks, whose figures strike every quarter hour, then unwind in the peaceful setting amid ancient trees and lawns. A few miles away is Glastonbury, a cradle of early Christian faith and the traditional burial place of King Arthur.

Elegant Bath is north of Wells; handsome Georgian streets run alongside (and above) remains of the Roman occupation. Bath was revitalized in the 18th century when it became the fashion to take the waters in its famous spa.

Head north to Cirencester in the Cotswolds, the region of honey-colored stone villages and rolling pasture land, where rural pleasures are staunchly maintained and nothing changes except the seasons.

Stratford-upon-Avon is the northernmost point on the itinerary; the town of Shakespeare's birth is now England's second most popular tourist destination, after London. Visit the houses and museums related to the great playwright and take in a play at the Royal Shakespeare Theatre. Nearby, you can visit the 14th-century castle at Warwick and Charlecote Park, an Elizabethan mansion where, it is said, Shakespeare poached deer on its estate.

Oxford is your last stop on the way south to London. Some of the most attractive college chapels and courtyards are open to the public, and the Ashmolean Museum has one of the world's foremost collections of antiquities from Greece, Crete, and the Near East. Close to Oxford is Woodstock, the estate village of Blenheim Palace, home of the Dukes of Marlborough and of Churchill. Visit the church at Bladon, on the southeast of the estate, where Churchill is buried.

Length of Trip 10–14 days.

Transportation **By Car.** A rented car is the best way to appreciate the leafy country lanes and smaller villages.

By Public Transportation. Bus and train service between some of the smaller towns is sporadic at best, but recommended overnight stops are well served by trains and buses.

The Main Route **Two nights: Winchester.** Excursion to Salisbury en route to Warminster.

Two nights: Warminster. Excursions to Stonehenge and Longleat House.

One night: Wells. Excursion to Glastonbury.

Two nights: Bath. Explore the Roman and Georgian features of the city.

Three nights: Cirencester. Make this the base for a leisurely discovery of the attractive Cotswold villages and countryside.

Two nights: Stratford-upon-Avon. Visit all the Shakespeare shrines and take in a performance at the Royal Shakespeare Theatre. Excursions to Warwick Castle or Charlecote Park.

Two nights: Oxford. Visit the colleges and the Ashmolean Museum. Excursion to Woodstock and Blenheim Palace.

Further Information: *See* Great Britain.

Ireland: Dingle and the Ring of Kerry

Go south and west from Dublin past the stables and paddocks of Kildare. Beyond Cork City, the scenery grows wilder and, as the shore is washed by the Gulf Stream, the climate becomes appreciably milder. The roads are rarely crowded, and you will enjoy the novelty of almost traffic-free driving. Killarney's lakes are best explored by bicycle or jaunting car (pony and cart) and rowboat; serious climbers will find challenging peaks in the sandstone mountains that encircle the blue island-studded lakes. You'll rarely see greener greens than those on the championship golf courses by the lakes.

The circular coastal road, known as the Ring of Kerry, provides dramatically contrasting views of Dingle Bay and the wide estuary of the Kenmare River. Offshore, the Skellig Rocks, containing early Christian monks' cells, protrude in conical shapes from the pounding Atlantic. Fishing for wild salmon or trout or a day trip afloat in search of shark and other deep-sea specimens tempts many fishermen to the area. The wild, unspoiled Dingle Peninsula is a Gaelic-speaking region, where some of the country's best traditional musicians can be heard giving impromptu concerts in whitewashed pubs. The area is known for its generous hospitality and the spontaneity of its way of life.

Length of Trip One week.

Transportation **By Car.** 815 miles round trip from Dublin.

By Public Transportation. Make your base in Killarney. The train from Dublin to Killarney takes about four hours. From here, you can take local buses or sign up for daily excursions to all points, including the Ring of Kerry and the Dingle Peninsula. Rented bikes are handy in the Killarney area.

The Main Route **One night: Cork.** Day excursion to the Blarney Stone or Gougane Barra National Park.

Two nights: Killarney. Day excursion by bicycle or jaunting car to Muckross House and the Gap of Dunloe; drive through the mountain passes to Kenmare and Glengarriff.

One night: Waterville (Ring of Kerry). Day excursion around the Ring, deep-sea fishing offshore, or (weather permitting) boat trip from Valentia to the Skellig Rocks.

One night: Dingle. Day excursion to Dunquin, the cliffs of Slea Head, and across the Connor Pass to Brandon Bay.

One night: Cashel. Drivers can break the 300-mile Tralee–Dublin journey here to visit the monastic remains on the Rock of Cashel.

Further Information: *See* Ireland.

Italy: Tuscany's Art Treasures

A week's tour of Tuscany will make you want to come back next year for another visit to the famous works of art and architecture, the timeless hill towns, and the glorious scenery of the Tuscan landscape. From Renaissance Florence, home to the works of such masters as Michelangelo and Donatello, head west through sometimes ochre, sometimes green countryside to Lucca. On the way, stop and visit the fine medieval cathedrals of Prato and Pistola. As if defended by its mighty brick walls, Lucca is still free from the tourist hordes. Here you will see magnificently carved churches in this gracious city with tree-shaded promenades that is set in a luxuriant plain surrounded by hazy blue hills.

On your way to Sienna, drop down to the coast to see Pisa's architectural curiosity, the Leaning Tower, and its white marble companions. Turning inland from Pisa and leaving the flat, coastal plain, proceed through the ageless beauty of the Tuscan countryside and there, awaiting you, will be the Middle Ages, the town of Siena. Gothic palaces and churches are everywhere. Wander through the narrow streets, explore their curves and slopes, and discover for yourself the beauties of the past. For present enjoyment, sip on the local Chianti.

On the way back to Florence, travel up to the hill town of San Gimignano, where turrets were built for noblemen to establish their status in society. Then, while driving through the rolling countryside, blanketed with vineyards, to Florence, plan your return visit to Tuscany.

Length of Trip One week.

Transportation **By Car.** Driving this itinerary makes a 250-kilometer (150-mile) round trip. Connections between most of the main towns can also be made by train or bus.

By Public Transportation. There are no direct trains between Pisa and Siena, but you can take a train from Pisa to Empoli (frequent service) and then from there on to Siena.

The Main Route **Three nights: Florence.** Excursions to Prato and Pistoia en route to Lucca.

Two nights: Lucca. Excursion to Pisa en route to Siena.

Two nights: Siena. Day excursion to San Gimignano.

Further Information: *See* Italy.

Norwegian Coastal Cruise

Every day since 1893, a passenger and car vessel has headed north out of the old Hanseatic port of Bergen for the 4,000-kilometer (2,500-mile) round trip over "the top of Europe" to Kirkenes. The route is called the *Hurtigrute*, and is an adventurous way to explore this northern coast. Scenically, it's of almost unrelieved splendor, reaching its peak north of the Arctic Circle in the fish-rich waters round the Lofoten Islands (where Trollfjord is barely wide enough for the ship to turn around).

Scores of fishing communities cling to the shore of this intricately indented coast, some now also bustling hubs for another harvest: the black gold of North Sea oil. Trondheim, first Viking and royal capital, is the place for history—its glorious medieval Nidaros Cathedral showing striking similarities to England's Lincoln Cathedral. In contrast, Tromsø's Arctic Ocean Cathedral explodes with light from modern stained glass. Farther north, you might see reindeer herds massing across straits and fjords on summer migration. And at Kirkenes, you'll be offered an eight-kilometer (five-mile) bus excursion to the Soviet border.

Each season offers a different thrill: the mists and opening blossoms of the spring, the long days of summer when darkness remains hidden, the blazing colors of the autumn, and the white winter snows contrasting with the long black nights. But the most popular time to make the cruise is between mid-May and July to see the midnight sun at the barren cliffs of the North Cape. Bird life is fascinating throughout the trip, and a pair of binoculars is a priority for the best enjoyment of the ever-passing scene.

Length of Trip Two weeks.

Transportation Daily departures from Bergen for the 4,000-kilometer (2,500-mile) round trip, largely through sheltered waters, with 11 nights on board. The vessels vary in size (142–228 berths) and age (1952–1983) and are cozy rather than luxurious; restaurants are licensed for beer and wine. In season, from mid-May through August, shore excursions can be prebooked before you board the cruise ship; at other times, you make the booking on board. Substantial reductions apply in the off-season, with additional discounts if you're 67 years or older.

Further Information: *See* Norway.

Moorish Spain

Heading north from Madrid, your destination is Segovia, but first stop off at the tiny village of San Lorenzo de El Escorial, with its austere monastery, the Escorial, burial place of Spanish monarchs. Then, on route to Segovia, visit the Valle de los

Caídos (Valley of the Fallen), a memorial to the dead of the Spanish Civil War and the final resting place of General Franco.

At Segovia, you will encounter the monumental Roman aqueduct, one of the best-preserved Roman remains in the world, and the fairy-tale fortress-palace of the Alcázar. Visit Avila for its imposing city walls, which date from the Middle Ages, and for its shrines to Saint Teresa. The road southeast from Avila leads you to Toledo, in the spectacular setting of the river Tagus. It was once the home of El Greco, and there are many examples of his work in this ancient city.

Heading farther south across the vast plains of La Mancha, following the trail of Don Quixote, and across the infinite vineyards of Valdepeñas, you enter Andalusia, its ancient white villages and great southern cities a living memorial to the 800 years of Moorish occupation. Córdoba is the ancient city of the caliphs: Nowhere else in Europe will you find an 8th-century mosque and a medieval synagogue within a few paces of each other.

South of Córdoba is Seville, on the banks of the Guadalquiver. This was the river from which, downstream at Sanlucar de Barrameda, Columbus sailed his galleons across the Pacific. There are memorabilia from his epic voyage and his tomb is in the cathedral. But the highlight of this Andalusian tour will probably be the magical Alhambra Palace and Royal Chapel in Granada. Complete your tour by returning north to Madrid.

Length of Trip One week.

Transportation This itinerary is best followed by car, but with careful planning, it is possible to go by bus, although it may take more than seven days. The winding route to Granada covers 1,000 kilometers (620 miles), but there is a more direct route back to Madrid, only 430 kilometers (260 miles).

The Main Route **Two nights: Segovia.** Stop at the Escorial on your way to Segovia. Excursion to Avila on the way to Toledo.

One night: Toledo. Wander the ancient streets and go to the cathedral.

One night: Córdoba. Visit the 8th-century Moorish mosque.

Two nights: Seville. Visit the huge cathedral and climb the Giralda Tower. Explore the Alcázar or fortress.

One night: Granada. Explore the Alhambra, seat of the caliphs and kings.

Further Information: *See* Spain.

West Germany's Romantic Road

The 420-kilometer (260-mile) Romantischestrasse (part of it over 1,000 years old) is a north–south procession through a continuous pageant of history, art, and architecture. In this itinerary, start at the northern end of the road and work southward, though you could easily do it the other way around. The first stop after leaving the ancient town of Würzburg, Franconia, is Rothenburg ob der Tauber, an imperial free city and the best-preserved medieval town in Germany. It is renowned for its Pentecost and September festivals. Follow the road south through Feuchtwangen, with its attractive monastery church used as a backdrop for plays in summer, to Dinkelsbühl, another imperial free city, complete with medieval city walls, a moat, bastions, gate, and towers.

Farther south, Nördlingen is described as "the living medieval city." At night, you'll hear the watchman's eerie call echoing through the narrow streets, as it has for centuries. Stop off at the small town of Harburg, Swabia, with its imposing 13th-century hilltop fortress, now a museum of surprising treasures: Romanesque ivory carvings, a fine collection of Gobelin tapestries, and a huge library. Its near neighbor, Donauwörth, is another medieval showpiece.

Venturing into Bavaria, you come to Augsburg, a town founded by the Romans, which grew in status in the early Middle Ages and claims to have been the richest town in Europe during the 15th and 16th centuries. The cathedral, dating from 995, has the oldest stained glass in the world (11th century). It was also the birthplace of both Holbeins and Mozart's father. A little farther south, Landsberg is famous for the Rococo wonders of architect Dominikus Zimmermann. Beyond that is the quiet rural center of Schongau, also known as "The Town in Front of the Mountains." The Alps provide a dramatic backdrop on the horizon and made this town an important staging post in the Middle Ages on the busy trade route between Augsburg and Italy. The city walls, towers, and historic buildings from this era still survive. Complete your journey at the restful spa town of Füssen; the area is dotted with beautiful lakes and spectacular views from Hohenschwangau and Neuschwanstein, the fairy-tale castles built in the 19th century by King Ludwig of Bavaria.

Length of Trip   7 to 10 days.

Transportation   **By Car.** The Romantic Road is a specially designated tourist road and is well maintained and marked.

By Public Transportation. The Europabus route 190/190A runs along the Romantic Road via Frankfurt, Augsburg, and Munich from June to September.

The Main Route   **Two nights: Rothenburg ob ter Tauber.** Excursions to Feuchtwangen and Dinkelsbühl.

Two nights: Nördlingen. Excursions to Harburg and Donauwörth.

Three nights: Augsburg. Excursions to Landburg, Schongau, and Füssen.

Further Information: *See* West Germany.

Crossroads in Yugoslavia

From Roman Pula on the coast, you head toward the towering massif of the Julian Alps, pausing on the way at Postojna for a train ride into Europe's grandest limestone caverns. Ljubljana, with its castle and Mestnitrg market, and the Upper Town of Zagreb introduce you to the medieval Slav communities that expanded into major Habsburg cities. Beyond, there are glimpses of the plains that spill over from Hungary before you plunge south into more mountains, this time those of Bosnia, rent by deep, dramatic river gorges.

Huddled at a valley head is Sarajevo. Here, oriental sights and sounds fill the *baščaršija* (bazaar) area threaded by labyrinthine alleys between old mosques and caravansaries, a few blocks from high-rise suburbs and the installations built for the 1984 Winter Olympics. The old town that surrounds Mostar's famous 16th-century bridge echoes over 400 years of Ottoman rule.

From Sarajevo, it's on to the coast for mellow, walled Dubrovnik, which, situated between the rival interests of Venice and the Ottoman Empire, maintained centuries of independence against all odds. From Dubrovnik northward, along the magnificent coast, the road twists and turns between steep mountains and the island-studded sea. The medieval town of Split was built within the walls of Roman Emperor Diocletian's massive palace, and there are more Roman and medieval treasures to be seen in Zadar before you turn inland. At Plitvice, 16 terraced lakes set in beautiful forests spill into each other through a myriad of cascades. From here, you complete the circuit via Rijeka back to Pula.

Length of Trip Two weeks.

Transportation **By Car.** A rented car is recommended for this round trip of approximately 1,930 kilometers (1,200 miles).

The Main Route **Two nights: Kranjska Gora.** Day excursion to explore the Julian Alps.

Two nights: Sarajevo. The *Baščaršija* (bazaar) and trip to the Olympic resort area of Jahorina.

Three nights: Dubrovnik. Walk the walls, explore the old town, take an excursion to the islands.

Two nights: Split. Explore the Diocletian palace (old town) and neighboring medieval Trogir.

Two nights: Plitvice. Ramble along marked forest paths round picturesque terraced lakes.

Further Information: *See* Yugoslavia.

1 Planning Your Trip

Before You Go

Government Tourist Offices

Austria Austrian National Tourist Office. In the United States: 500 Fifth Ave., 20th Floor, New York, NY 10110, tel. 212/944–6880; 500 N. Michigan Ave., Suite 544, Chicago, IL 60611, tel. 312/644–5556; 11601 Wilshire Blvd., Suite 2480, Los Angeles, CA 90025, tel. 213/477–3332; 4800 San Felipe, Suite 500, Houston, TX 77056, tel. 713/850–9999.
In Canada: 1010 Sherbrooke St. W., Suite 1410, Montreal, Quebec H3A 2R7, tel. 514/849–3709; 736 Granville St., Suite 1220–1223, Vancouver Block, Vancouver, British Columbia V6Z 1J2, tel. 604/683–5808; 2 Bloor St. E., Suite 3330, Toronto, Ontario M4W 1A8, tel. 416/967–3381.
In the United Kingdom: 30 George St., London W1R OAL, tel. 01/629–0461.

Belgium Belgian National Tourist Office. In North America: 745 Fifth Ave., Suite 714, New York, NY 10151, tel. 212/758–8130.
In the United Kingdom: 38 Dover St., London W1X 3RD, tel. 01/499–5379.

Bulgaria Bulgarian National Tourist Office. In North America: Balkan Holidays (authorized agent), 161 E. 86th St., New York, NY 10028, tel. 212/722–1110.
In the United Kingdom: 18 Princes St., London W1R 7RE, tel. 01/499–6988.

Cyprus Cyprus Tourist Office. In North America: 13 E. 40th St., New York, NY 10016, tel. 212/213–9100.
In the United Kingdom: 213 Regent St., London W1R 8DA, tel. 01/734–9822; North Cyprus Tourist Office, 28 Cockspur St., London SW1Y 5BN, tel. 01/930–5069.

Czechoslovakia Czechoslovak Travel Bureau and Tourist Office (Cedok). In North America: 10 E. 40th St., New York, NY 10016, tel. 212/689–9720.
In the United Kingdom: 17–18 Old Bond St., London W1X 4RB, tel. 01/629–6058.

Denmark Danish Tourist Board. In the United States: 655 Third Ave., New York, NY 10017, tel. 212/949–2333.
In Canada: Box 115, Station N, Toronto, Ontario M8V 3S4, tel. 416/823–9620.
In the United Kingdom: 169–173 Regent St., London W1R 8PY, tel. 01/734–2637.

Finland Finnish Tourist Board. In the United States: 655 Third Ave., New York, NY 10017, tel. 212/949–2333.
In Canada: 1200 Bay St., Suite 640, Toronto, Ontario M5R 2A5, tel. 416/964–9159.
In the United Kingdom: 66–68 Haymarket, London, SW1Y 4RF, tel. 01/839–4048.

France French Government Tourist Office. In the United States: 610 Fifth Ave., New York, NY 10020, tel. 212/315–0888; 645 N. Michigan Ave., Chicago, IL 60611, tel. 312/337–6301; World Trade Center No. 103, 2050 Stemmons Frwy., Dallas, TX 75258, tel. 214/742–7011; 9401 Wilshire Blvd., Beverly Hills, CA 90212, tel. 213/272–2661; 1 Hallidie Plaza, Suite 250, San Francisco, CA 94102, tel. 415/986–4174.

In Canada: 1981 McGill College, Suite 490, Montreal, Quebec H3A 2W9, tel. 514/288–4264; 1 Dundas St. W., Suite 2405, Box 8, Toronto, Ontario M5G 1Z3, tel. 416/593–4723.
In the United Kingdom: 178 Piccadilly, London W1V OAL, tel. 01/491–7622.

Germany **German National Tourist Office. In the United States:** 747 Third Ave., New York, NY 10017, tel. 212/308–3300; 444 S. Flower St., Suite 2230, Los Angeles, CA 90017, tel. 213/688–7332.
In Canada: Box 417, 2 Fundy, Place Bonaventure, Montreal, Quebec H5A 1B8, tel. 514/878–9885.
In the United Kingdom: (Federal Republic) 61 Conduit St., London W1R OEN, tel. 01/734–2600; (Democratic Republic) Berolina Travel Ltd., 22 Conduit St., London W1R 9TB, tel. 01/629–1664.

Gibraltar **Gibraltar Government Tourist Office. In the United Kingdom:** Arundel Great Court, 179 The Strand, London WC2R 1EH, tel. 01/836–0777.

Great Britain **British Tourist Authority. In the United States:** 40 W. 57th St., New York, NY 10019, tel. 212/581–4700; John Hancock Center, Suite 3320, 875 N. Michigan Ave., Chicago, IL 60611, tel. 312/787–0490; World Trade Center, 350 S. Figueroa St., Suite 450, Los Angeles, CA 90017, tel. 213/628–3525; Cedar Springs Rd., Suite 210, Dallas, TX 75201, tel. 214/720–4040; 2580 Cumberland Pkwy., Suite 470, Atlanta, GA 30339, tel. 404/432–9635.
In Canada: 94 Cumberland St., Suite 600, Toronto, Ontario M5R 3N3, tel. 416/925–6326.
In the United Kingdom: Thames Tower, Black's Rd., London W6 9EL, tel. 01/846–9000.

Greece **Greek National Tourist Organization: In the United States:** 645 Fifth Ave., New York, NY 10022, tel. 212/421–5777; 611 W. 6th St., Suite 1998, Los Angeles, CA 90017, tel. 213/626–6696; 168 N. Michigan Ave., Chicago, IL 60601, tel. 312/782–1084.
In Canada: 233 Rue de la Montagne, Montreal, Quebec H3G 1Z2, tel. 514/871–1535; 68 Scollard St., Lower Level, Unit E, Toronto, Ontario M5R 1G2, tel. 416/968–2220.
In the United Kingdom: 195–197 Regent St., London W1R 8DL, tel. 01/734–5997.

Hungary **Hungarian Travel Bureau (IBUSZ). In North America:** 630 Fifth Ave., New York, NY 10111, tel. 212/582–7412.
In the United Kingdom: Danube Travel Ltd. (authorized agent), 6 Conduit St., London W1R 9TG, tel. 01/493–0263.

Iceland **Iceland Tourist Board. In North America:** 655 Third Ave., New York, NY 10017, tel. 212/949–2333.
In the United Kingdom: 73 Grosvenor St., London W1X 9DD, tel. 01/499–9971.

Ireland **Irish Tourist Board. In the United States:** 757 Third Ave., New York, NY 10017, tel. 212/418–0800; Peachtree Summitt, Suite 1970, 401 W. Peachtree, Atlanta, GA 30308, tel. 800/223–6470.
In Canada: 10 King St. E., Toronto, Ontario M5C 1C3, tel. 416/364–1301.
In the United Kingdom: Ireland House, 150 New Bond St., London W1Y OAQ, tel. 01/493–3201.

Italy **Italian Government Travel Office (ENIT). In the United States:** 630 Fifth Ave., New York, NY 10111, tel. 212/245–4822; 500 N. Michigan Ave., Chicago, IL 60611, tel. 312/644–0990; 360 Post St., Suite 801, San Francisco, CA 94108, tel. 415/392–6206.

In Canada: 3 Place Ville Marie, Montreal, Quebec H3B 2E3, tel. 514/866–7667.
In the United Kingdom: 1 Princes St., London W1R 8AY, tel. 01/408–1254.

Luxembourg **Luxembourg Tourist Information Office. In North America:** 801 Second Ave., New York, NY 10017, tel. 212/370–9850.
In the United Kingdom: 36–37 Piccadilly, London W1V 9PA, tel. 01/434–2800.

Malta **Malta National Tourist Office. In North America:** Maltese Consulate, 249 E. 35th St., New York, NY 10016, tel. 212/725–2345.
In the United Kingdom: College House, Suite 207, Wrights Lane, London W8 5SH, tel. 01/938–2668.

Monaco **Monaco Government Tourist and Convention Bureau. In North America:** 845 Third Ave., New York, NY 10022, tel. 212/759–5227.
In the United Kingdom: 25 Whitehall, London SW1A 2BS, tel. 01/930–4699.

Netherlands **Netherlands Board of Tourism. In the United States:** 355 Lexington Ave., New York, NY 10017, tel. 212/370–7367; 255 N. Michigan Ave., Suite 326, Chicago, IL 60601, tel. 312/819–0300; 605 Market St., Suite 401, San Francisco, CA 94105, tel. 415/543–6772.
In Canada: 25 Adelaide St. E., Suite 710, Toronto, Ontario M5C 1Y2, tel. 416/363–1577.
In the United Kingdom: 25–28 Buckingham Gate, London SW1E 6LD, tel. 01/630–0451.

Norway **Norwegian Tourist Board. In North America:** 655 Third Ave., New York, NY 10017, tel. 212/949–2333.
In the United Kingdom: 20 Pall Mall, London SW1Y 5NE, tel. 01/839–2650.

Poland **Polish National Tourist Office (Orbis). In North America:** 500 Fifth Ave., New York, NY 10110, tel. 212/391–0844; 333 N. Michigan Ave., Chicago, Il 60601, tel. 312/236–9013.
In the United Kingdom: 82 Mortimer St., London W1N 7DE, tel. 01/637–4971.

Portugal **Portuguese National Tourist Office. In the United States:** 548 Fifth Ave., New York, NY 10036, tel. 212/354–4403.
In Canada: 2180 Yonge St., Toronto, Ontario M4S 2B9, tel. 416/487–3300.
In the United Kingdom: 1–5 New Bond St., London W1Y ONP, tel. 01/493–3873.

Romania **Romanian National Tourist Office. In North America:** 573 Third Ave., New York, NY 10016, tel. 212/697–6971.
In the United Kingdom: 29 Thurloe Place, London SW7 2HP England, tel. 01/584–8090.

Spain **Spanish National Tourist Office. In the United States:** 665 Fifth Ave., New York, NY 10022, tel. 212/759–8822; 845 N. Michigan Ave., Chicago, IL 60611, tel. 312/944–0215; San Vicente Plaza Bldg., 8383 Wilshire Blvd., Suite 960, Beverly Hills, CA 90211, tel. 213/658–7188.
In Canada: 60 Bloor St. W., Suite 201, Toronto, Ontario MW4 3B8, tel. 416/961–3131.
In the United Kingdom: 57–58 St. James's St., London SW1 1LD, tel. 01/499–0901 or 0903.

Sweden   **Swedish Tourist Board. In North America:** 655 Third Ave., New York, NY 10017, tel. 212/949–2333.
In the United Kingdom: 3 Cork St., London W1X 1HA, tel. 01/437–5816.

Switzerland   **Swiss National Tourist Office. In the United States:** 608 Fifth Ave., New York, NY 10020, tel. 212/757–5944; 250 Stockton St., San Francisco, CA 94108, tel. 415/362–2260.
In Canada: Commerce Court W., Box 215, Commerce Court Postal Station, Toronto, Ontario M5L 1E8, tel. 416/868–0584.
In the United Kingdom: Swiss Center, New Coventry St., London W1V 8EE, tel. 01/734–1921.

Turkey   **Turkish Culture and Information Office. In North America:** 821 UN Plaza, New York, NY 10017, tel. 212/687–2194.
In the United Kingdom: 170 Piccadilly, London W1V 9DD, tel. 01/734–8681.

Yugoslavia   **Yugoslav National Tourist Office. In North America:** 630 Fifth Ave., Suite 280, New York, NY 10111, tel. 212/757–2801.
In the United Kingdom: 143 Regent St., London W1R 8AE, tel. 01/734–5243.

Tour Groups

The range of tours to Europe is immense, with everything from fully escorted to almost entirely independent trips available, and at prices to suit almost every pocketbook. Whatever your budget, package tours often add value to your trip by providing lower airfares and hotel rates than you would get on your own. There can be trade-offs, of course—you may find yourself dining with 20 strangers and marching to the beat of a tour director's drum.

When considering a tour, be sure to find out: (1) exactly what expenses are included (particularly tips, taxes, side trips, additional meals, and entertainment); (2) government ratings of all hotels on the itinerary and the facilities they offer; (3) cancellation policies for both you and for the tour operator; (4) the number of travelers in your group; and (5) the single supplement cost, should you be traveling alone.

It is beyond the scope of this book to provide a full listing of the many hundreds of tours to Europe currently catalogued. The following is only a sampling of packages from some of the most established, experienced operators. For more information, contact your travel agent. (Most tour operators request that bookings be made through a travel agent—there is no additional charge for this.)

General-Interest Tours   **American Express Vacations** (Box 5014, Atlanta, GA 30302, tel. 800/241–1700 or, in Georgia, 800/282–0800) offers a veritable supermarket of tours. At last count, it had about 100 ways to see Europe, including nearly 20 tours under the general title "Europe in Depth." *"Tempo,"* for example, is a classic grand tour stopping in England, France, Switzerland, Italy, Austria, Germany, and Holland over a frenetic 15 days.
Cosmos/Globus Gateway (150 S. Los Robles Ave., Suite 860, Pasadena, CA 91101, tel. 818/449–0919 or 800/556–5454) has a wide variety of quality tours from the mind-boggling "Super European"—a Globus Gateway tour of 14 countries in 43 days —to regional and city tours. Cosmos is generally the more budget-minded of the affiliated companies.

Caravan Tours (401 N. Michigan Ave., Chicago, IL 60601, tel. 312/321–9800 or 800/621–8338) weighs in with four grand tours and a variety of regional tours. Caravan's "Two Week Slow and Easy" is a welcome change of pace with only four countries—England, France, Switzerland, and Italy—over 17 days.

If you are willing to pay for luxury, **Hemphill/Harris** (16000 Ventura Blvd., Suite 200, Encino, CA 90024, tel. 818/906–8086 or 800/421–0454) and **Abercrombie & Kent International** (1420 Kensington Rd., Oak Brook, IL 60521, tel. 312/954–2944) each offers some posh programs. Other popular operators include **Maupintour** (Box 807, Lawrence, KA 66044, tel. 913/843–1211 or 800/255–4266) and **Olson-Travelworld** (5855 Green Valley Circle, Culver City, CA 90230, tel. 213/670–7100 or 800/421–2255).

In the United Kingdom, **Thomas Cook** (Box 36, Thorpe Wood, Peterborough PE3 6SB, tel. 0733/502200) offers a massive range of European vacations, either escorted tours or packages for the independent traveler, but with a representative on site to help out if needed.

Thomson Holidays (Greater London House, Hampstead Rd., London NW1 7SD, tel. 01/435–8431), another market leader, offers vacations in almost every resort in Europe. A similar company with a wide range of packages is **Horizon Holidays Ltd.** (Broadway, Edgbaston, Birmingham B15 1BB, tel. 021/616–6222). Check out the brochures from these companies, particularly for fly/drive deals, which are often the best-value options for getting around Europe.

Special-Interest Tours
Adventure

If trekking through the Pyrenees in Spain, France, and Andorra, or a breathtaking (in more ways than one) Alpine pass in Switzerland is your idea of fun, investigate **Sobek's International Explorers Society** (Angels Camp, CA 95222, tel. 209/736–4524). Various cycling, skiing, backpacking, hiking, and walking tours are also available.

In the United Kingdom, **Top Deck Travel** (131–133 Earl's Court Rd., London SW5 9RH, tel. 01/244–8641) offers 15 tours to central Europe, with activities including flotilla sailing, a variety of water sports, and rafting.

Art/Architecture

Esplanade Tours (581 Boylston St., Boston, MA 02116, tel. 617/266–7465) and **Exprinter Tours** (500 Fifth Ave., New York, NY 10110, tel. 212/719–1200) concentrate on Europe's rich heritage. **Olson-Travelworld's** *(see* General-Interest Tours) "From the Rijksmuseum to the Louvre" covers a staggering range of artistic treasures.

In the United Kingdom, **Prospect Art Tours Ltd.** (10 Barley Mow Passage, London W4 4PH, tel. 01/995–2163) offers a comprehensive range of art and architecture tours including Great Britain, France, Spain, Italy, Austria, Holland, and East and West Germany.

Ballooning

Buddy Bombard Balloon Adventures (6727 Curran St., McLean, VA 22101, tel. 703/448–9407 or 800/862–8537), offers fine dining and gentle breezes in and above France, Austria, Italy, Switzerland, and England.

Christmas/Culture

"Christmas in Europe and the Kaiserball" is one of **Olson-Travelworld's** *(see* General-Interest Tours) unique packages. The program includes a traditional white Christmas in the

Swiss Alps, a performance at the marionette theater in Salzburg, and the exclusive Kaiserball in Vienna.

In the United Kingdom, **Page & Moy Ltd.** (136–140 London Rd., Leicester LE2 1EN, tel. 0533/552521) offers nine Christmas tours, including ones with traditional Christmas festivities in the Lake District or the Highlands of Scotland.

Health/Fitness **DER Tours** (11933 Wilshire Blvd., Los Angeles, CA 90025, tel. 213/479–4140 or 800/421–4343) offers a menu of Europe's most heralded spa resorts. Some maintain surprisingly sophisticated medical facilities, others are simply beautiful and healthy places to relax.

In the United Kingdom, **Serena Holidays** (40 Kenway Rd., London SW5 ORA, tel. 01/244–8422) has vacations to a health farm on Malta for one, two, three weeks, or for as long as it takes!

Music **Dailey-Thorp Travel** (315 W. 57th St., New York, NY 10019, tel. 212/307–1555) transforms the traditional grand tour into the *"Grand Opera Tour of Europe."* Stops on the deluxe program generally include Paris, Milan, Vienna, and London, although itineraries vary according to available performances. "Musical Heartland of Europe" features musical performances in Berlin, Dresden, and Prague, while "Prague, Budapest, Vienna" highlights the historic capitals of the Hapsburg Empire. All tours are deluxe, with generally excellent seats for performances.

In the United Kingdom, **Brompton Travel Ltd.** (206 Walton St., London SW3, tel. 01/584–6143) will arrange tickets and book your flights and accommodations for any musical event in Europe that takes your fancy.

Nature **Questers Tours and Travel** (257 Park Ave. S., New York, NY 10010, tel. 212/673–3120) has an exciting program of worldwide nature tours. Rare birds and animals as well as the ancient sites are the tour stars.

In the United Kingdom, **Ramblers Holidays Ltd.** (Longcroft House, Fretherne Rd., Welwyn Garden City, Herts. AL8 6PQ, tel. 0707/331133) arranges walking tours within Europe with walk leaders to point out natural features of interest.

Rail Climb aboard the *Istanbul Train* with **Olson-Travelworld** *(see* General-Interest Tours) and follow the route of the *Orient-Express* from London's Victoria Station through France, Austria, Hungary, Romania, Bulgaria, and into Istanbul, Turkey.

Singles and **Trafalgar Tours** (21 E. 26th St., New York, NY 10010, tel. 212/
Young Couples 689–8977 or 800/854–0103) offers *Club 21–35*, faster paced tours for travelers unafraid of a little physical activity—from bike riding to discoing the night away.

In the United Kingdom, **Club 18–30 Holidays Ltd.** (Academic House, Oval Rd., London NW1 7EA, tel. 01/485–4141) offers much the same activities as Trafalgar Tours, with beach parties, discos, sports, and lots more for those with plenty of energy.

Sports **Travel Concepts** (373 Commonwealth Ave., Suite 601, Boston, MA 02115, tel. 617/266–8450) gives you the choice of the British Open Golf Tournament, the Henley Royal Regatta, or, if you prefer to play rather than sit, the Rangitiki Polo School in Windsor, England, or the SAS Bjorn Borg Tennis Clinic in Stockholm.

In the United Kingdom, **Caravela Tours** (38–44 Gillingham St., London SW1V 1JW, tel. 01/630–9223) has tennis and golf vacations in Austria and Portugal. If you prefer to watch rather than participate, **Page & Moy Ltd.** *(see* Christmas/Culture) arranges vacations to see the international motor racing competitions in Europe.

Wine/Cuisine   **Travel Concepts** *(see* Sports) serves up some exceptional food and drink in France, Germany, Italy, Switzerland, Scandinavia, England, and Ireland. Gracious living (and dining) is also available from **Floating Through Europe** (271 Madison Ave., New York, NY 10016, tel. 212/685–5600), with deluxe barge cruises on inland waterways in England, France, Germany, Belgium, and Holland.

In the United Kingdom, **World Wine Tours Ltd.** (4 Dorchester Rd., Drayton St. Leonards, Oxon OX9 8BH, tel. 0865/891919) has a six-night wine tasting tour of Germany, along the Rhine, and France in the region of Alsace.

Package Deals for Independent Travelers

Cosmos/Globus Gateway, DER Tours, American Express, and **Abercrombie & Kent** *(see* General-Interest Tours) all offer packages for independent travelers, with choices of hotels, air, ground transportation, and sightseeing. The international airlines are also good sources, particularly **TWA Getaway Vacations** (800–GETAWAY) and **Pan Am Holidays** (800–THE-TOUR). **CIE Tours** (122 E. 42nd St., New York, NY 10168, tel. 212/972–5735) specializes in "fly/drive" tours, as does DER Tours.

In the United Kingdom, the companies mentioned in General-Interest Tours are good for the independent traveler as well as for those who prefer to have their activities organized for them. These companies offer flights and accommodations; tours and activities are offered as optional extras once you arrive at your destination. Company representatives usually are on hand to help you organize anything that may not be covered in their programs.

Festivals and Seasonal Events

The following is just a sampling of the special events in Europe throughout the year; a complete list would fill an entire book. A good overall guide—*Major Events in Europe*—is available from the **European Travel Commission,** 630 Fifth Ave., Suite 565, New York, NY 10111, tel. 212/307–1200.

January   **Austria.** Carnival begins in Vienna, continuing until Shrove Tuesday. Mozart Week is held in Salzburg. The World Cup Skiing Competition usually takes place in Kitzbühel.
Belgium. National Opera of Brussels, Royal Opera of Wallonia, and the Flanders Opera all begin their seasons.
France. International Circus Festival is held.
Great Britain. London International Boat Show is staged at Earl's Court Exhibition Centre.
Greece. Epiphany celebrations (January 6) occur throughout the country. Greek Carnival is festive at Patras, Iraklio, Thebes, and on the islands of Lesbos, Skyros, and Hios.
Iceland. Reykjavik concert season opens.

Italy. Epiphany celebrations (January 6) occur throughout the country.

Monaco. Monte Carlo Rally takes place.

Norway. Kristiansund Opera Festival features original productions, art exhibits, and concerts.

Poland. Warsaw hosts the Golden Washboard Traditional Jazz meet.

Portugal. St. Sebastian Festival in Aveiro—dating from the 16th century—includes a procession and food fair.

Switzerland. International Hot Air Balloon Week takes off at Château d'Oex, just east of Montreux.

Turkey. Camel Wrestling Festival tests the strength of young men in Selçuk.

West Germany. *Fasching* season, or Carnival, is celebrated throughout the country. International Green Week Agricultural Fair is in Berlin. World Cup Downhill Ski competition takes place in Garmisch-Partenkirchen.

February **Belgium.** Carnival of the Gilles attracts thousands to Binche.

Finland. Finlandia Ski Race is a mass cross-country marathon covering 47 miles from Hameenlinna to Lahti.

France. Carnival is celebrated in Nice.

Great Britain. The Jorvik Viking Festival takes place all month in York. Cruft's Dog Show is at Earl's Court, London.

Holland. Carnival celebrations are held throughout The Netherlands and Luxembourg.

Hungary. The Gypsy Festival is held in Budapest.

Iceland. Feast of Thorri is a month-long celebration throughout the country.

Italy. Carnival is celebrated in Venice and Viareggio.

Malta. Feast of St. Paul's shipwreck takes place on February 10.

Portugal. Carnival of Portugal is celebrated throughout the country, with the most famous festivities in the southern Algarve, in Aveiro, and on the island of Madeira.

West Germany. International Toy Fair takes place in Nuremberg. Black Forest Ski Marathon takes off in Schonach-Hinterzarten.

Yugoslavia. Film festival takes place in Belgrade.

March **Austria.** Easter Festival is held in Salzburg; the Annual Spring Fair in Graz.

Belgium. Festivals of Flanders and Wallonia bring the arts to several cities and towns.

Finland. Lady Day Church Festival, with traditional Lapp dancing and reindeer driving, takes place in Enontekio. Ounasvaara Winter Games unfold in Rovaniemi.

France. Prix du Président de la République horse race is run at Auteuil Racecourse in Paris.

Great Britain. Shakespeare Season opens in Stratford-upon-Avon. Edinburgh International Folk Festival begins. Grand National Steeplechase takes place at Aintree Racecourse, Liverpool. The Devizes to Westminster International Canoe Race takes off along the Kennet and Avon Canal and the Thames.

Hungary. Budapest celebrates its Spring Festival.

Ireland. St. Patrick's Week is celebrated with the grandest festivities in Dublin, Cork, Galway, and Limerick. International Marching Band Competition and Choral festival takes place in Limerick.

Italy. Explosion of the Cart, a folklore event, is held in Florence on Easter. Good Friday procession is held in Rome.

Portugal. The Tertiary Procession by the Franciscans makes its way through Ovar. St. Joseph's Festival means street dancing and fireworks in Braga.

Romania. The Kiss Fair takes place in Arad.

Spain. The Fallas de San José are towering papier-mâché caricatures that help celebrate a week-long festival in Valencia. Holy Week processions are held nationwide, but especially in Seville.

Switzerland. Lucerne Easter Festival lasts a week.

West Germany. Frankfurt Music Fair is held and spring fairs take place throughout the country. Munich Fashion Week introduces the latest fashions.

April **Denmark.** Tivoli Gardens open in Copenhagen.

France. Sound and light shows begin at several Loire châteaux.

Great Britain. Camden Festival and London Marathon take place in London. Eastbourne hosts an International Folk Festival. The Oxford and Cambridge boat race is rowed on the Thames.

Greece. Sound and light shows begin in Athens and Rhodes.

Holland. Tulips blooming at Keukenhof Gardens in Lisse are cause for local celebrations.

Italy. Florence May Music Festival is the oldest and most prestigious Italian festival of the performing arts.

Monaco. The Monte Carlo Open Tennis Championship takes place at the Monte Carlo Country Club.

Spain. April Fair in Seville transforms the Andalusian capital with colorful tents, wreaths, and paper lanterns.

Sweden. Walpurgis Night celebrations take place nationwide on April 30.

West Germany. Stuttgart Jazz Festival occurs. Munich Ballet Days open. The Mannheim May Fair celebrates spring. The Walpurgis Festivals in the Harz Mountains commemorate the night before May Day.

May **Austria.** International Music and Drama Festival is held in Vienna.

Belgium. The Cat Festival in Ieper venerates felines with parades and costumes. The Holy Blood Procession in Bruges celebrates the vial of holy blood brought by the Count of Flanders from the Second Crusade. Golden Chariot Procession and Battle of the Lumecon in Mons commemorates that city's delivery from the plague in 1349.

Bulgaria. Sofia Music Weeks and the Festival of Arts, Roman Theater, Plovdiv, are held.

Denmark. Ballet and Opera Festival are staged at the Royal Theater in Copenhagen.

Finland. May Day is celebrated throughout the country.

France. Cannes Film Festival draws movie stars to the Riviera; the International Marathon of Paris brings runners to the City of Light. In Paris, the French Open Tennis Championship takes place. In Bordeaux, it's the May Musical de Bordeaux.

Great Britain. The Chichester Festival Theatre Season opens in West Sussex. The Glyndebourne Festival Opera Season begins. In Home Park, Windsor, it's the Royal Windsor Horse Show. Late May brings the Chelsea Flower Show to London, as well as marking the Bath International Festival and the Nottingham Festival.

Italy. The Palio of the Archers is a medieval crossbow contest in Gubbio. The Sardinian Cavalcade in Sassari is a traditional costumed procession.

Luxembourg. Procession of St. Willibrod is a medieval celebration in Echternach. Genzefest celebrates the golden blossoms of the gorse, in Wiltz.

Malta. May sees the Valetta Carnival.

Monaco. Formula One racers hit the streets of Monaco for the Grand Prix of Monaco.

Poland. Chopin celebrations take place in several locations. International Chamber Music Festival is held in Lancut.

Portugal. Pilgrimage to Fatima is one of the largest in the world.

Spain. Horse Fair takes place in Jerez de la Frontera.

Sweden. Drottningholm Court Theater season opens outside Stockholm.

Turkey. Ephesus Festival of Culture and Art features folk dances, concerts, exhibits in Selçuk. Kirpinar Wrestling Matches in Edirne date back six centuries.

Yugoslavia. Moreska Sword Dance takes place on the island of Korcula.

June **Austria.** Graz hosts Styriarte Music Festival. Midsummer's Day features bonfires nationwide. International Youth Music Festival is held in Vienna.

Bulgaria. The Festival of the Roses takes place in Karlovo and Kazanlak.

Denmark. Midsummer's Eve festivals are commemorated with bonfires throughout the country.

Finland. Kuopio Dance and Music Festival of Central European Dance features classical ballet and modern dance performances and seminars.

France. Festival du Marais is held in Paris. Strasbourg International Music Festival takes place. Grand Steeplechase de Paris and Grand Prix de Paris are two major horse races in Paris. The 24-hour Endurance Race is in Le Mans.

Great Britain. Major June sports events include Derby Day at Epsom Racecourse, Royal Ascot Horse Race, Wimbledon Lawn Tennis Championships, and the Henley Royal Regatta at Henley-on-Thames, Oxfordshire. June also means Trooping the Colour at Whitehall in London, and the Aldeburgh Festival of Music and the Arts in Suffolk.

Greece. Arts festivals are held in Athens, Epidaurus, Patras, Iraklion, and Ioannina.

Holland. The month-long Holland Festival of International Performing Arts programs takes place in Amsterdam.

Hungary. Two musical events are the Sopron Festival Weeks and the Chamber Music Festival, Veszprém.

Iceland. Seamen's Day is celebrated in Reykjavik and every other Icelandic fishing port. Iceland National Day (June 17) means parades, sports competitions, and dances throughout the country.

Ireland. Festival of Music in Great Irish Houses is heard in stately homes in several counties.

Italy. The Flower Festival takes place in Genzano. A medieval Battle of the Bridge is staged in Pisa. Keen competition unfolds in Venice during the Regatta of the Great Maritime Republics. The legendary performing arts Festival of Two Worlds, in Spoleto, begins toward the end of the month.

Luxembourg. International Festival of Classical Music is held at several churches and theaters in Echternach and Luxembourg City.

Poland. Cracow Art Festival is held. Midsummer Wianki celebrations occur nationwide on June 23.

Portugal. St. Anthony's Eve means colorful lantern processions in Lisbon dedicated to the patron saint of young lovers.

Spain. The Rocio Pilgrimage takes place across the countryside from Heulva, Cadiz, and Seville, meeting at Almonte. The art of flamenco is celebrated in Cordoba during the Patio Festival. The San Isidro Festival brings internationally known musicians and dancers to Madrid.

Sweden. The Stockholm marathon attracts 16,000 runners from 30 nations. Midsummer celebrations, with folk music and dancing around the Maypole, take place throughout the country.

Turkey. The Izmir International Culture and Art Festival means concerts, exhibits, and theatrical presentations, as does the Istanbul International Festival.

West Germany. Frankfurt Summertime Festival, Franco-German Folk Festival in Berlin, and Nymphenburg Summer Festival are among the many summer festivals in June. Castle Concerts, many with castle illuminations, begin throughout the country. Kiel Week is an international sailing regatta. Late in the month is the Munich Film Festival.

Yugoslavia. Summer Fair is an international exhibition of consumer goods, handicrafts, fashion, and music in Budva.

July **Austria.** Bregenz Festival brings opera and concerts to this Boden See resort. The Salzburg Music Festival is Austria's most famous musical event.

Belgium. The medieval Ommegang Pageant takes place in Brussels's Grand' Place.

Czechoslovakia. There's a Music Summer, through August, held in Bratislava.

Denmark. Rebildfest, since 1912, has been the largest celebration of America's independence (July 4) outside the United States. Copenhagen stages a Jazz Festival. Other festivities are in northern Jutland.

Finland. The works of Verdi, Wagner, and Mozart are performed at the Savonlinna Opera Festival. Pori Jazz Festival attracts performers from the world over.

France. Major festivals include Festival of Avignon, Festival of Lyric Art and Music in Aix-en-Provence, and Festival Estival of Paris. Of course, Bastille Day (July 14) is celebrated throughout the country. Cyclists in the Tour de France finish along the Champs-Elysées.

Great Britain. City of London Festival takes place. The Royal Tournament at Earl's Court features displays and pageantry. Cowes Week is a yachting festival off Isle of Wight.

Greece. Wine festivals take place in Daphni and Alexandroupolis.

Hungary. Haydn and Mozart concerts are held at the Esterházy Palace in Fertöd through August. Debrecen has a Bartók Choral Festival.

Italy. Palio Horse Race is run in Siena. Verona begins its outdoor opera season in Ravena. Gondolas gather in Venice during the Feast of the Redeemer. The Festa de Noantri in the Trastevere section of Rome includes processions, a parade of boats, and fireworks.

Luxembourg. Remembrance Day honors General George Patton, liberator of the Grand Duchy, in Ettelbruck.

Norway. Molde International Jazz Festival is Norway's oldest.

Exhibitions and parades highlight the Peer Gynt Festival in Vinstra.

Portugal. Estoril Handicrafts Fair attracts artisans and folk dancers from across the country. Bulls are turned loose in the ring during the Festival of the Red Waistcoat, Vila Franca de Xira.

Spain. San Fermin Festival features bulls and young men running through the streets of Pamplona. The St. John Bonfires bring three days of fireworks, bullfights, and religious celebrations. Early in the month is the International Music and Dance Festival of Granada.

Sweden. Arbro and other towns host the Folk Dance Festival.

Turkey. International Bursa Folklore and Music Festival takes place.

West Germany. Folk festivals take place throughout the country. Munich stages an Opera Festival. The major musical event is the Richard Wagner Festival in Bayreuth.

Yugoslavia. Balkan Festival of Original Folk Dances and Songs is held outdoors in Ohrid. The Dubrovnik Summer Festival takes place throughout the city. The International Summer Cultural Events take place in Ljubljana.

August **Austria.** Grand Prix auto racing takes place in Zeltweg and Styria.

Belgium. Planting of the Mayboom Tree takes place at the Grand' Place in Brussels. The Wedding of the Giants, in Ath, pairs a 12-foot image of the patron of crossbowmen with an equally large bride.

Czechoslovakia. Karlovy Vary holds a Dvořák Festival.

Finland. A Goldpanning Competition is held in Tankavaara. Classical and chamber music is presented during the Turku Music Festival. The Helsinki Festival runs the gamut from art and cinema to opera and theater.

Great Britain. There's the Battle of Flowers in the Channel Island of Jersey. The huge Edinburgh International Festival includes the colorful Edinburgh Military Tattoo.

Greece. In Poros, during the Trireme, 170 oarsmen sail a replica of an ancient war galley. The Athens Festival includes performances at the foot of the Acropolis. International car racers compete at the Chalkidikis Rally.

Iceland. The Westman Islands Festival includes outdoor entertainment and bonfires on these volcanic islands.

Ireland. Dublin Horse Show is the premier event of the Irish social calendar. In Tralee, the Rose of Tralee Festival keeps celebrants busy for a week.

Italy. The Joust of the Quintana is a historical pageant in Ascoli/Piceno, and the Venice Film Festival takes place on the Lido. Musical events include the Stresa Musical Weeks and Siena Music Week.

Luxembourg. The Luxembourg City Kermesse has been held since 1340.

Switzerland. Swiss National Day, August 1, celebrates the foundation of the Swiss Confederation.

West Germany. The Castle Festival in Heidelberg means month-long open-air theater presentations. Wine Festivals begin throughout Rhineland. Grand Baden-Baden Week includes horse racing at Iffezheim in Baden-Baden.

September **Andorra.** National festivities and pilgrimage to the shrine of Meritxell happen on September 8.

Austria. Harvest and wine festivities take place in many villages.

Bulgaria. The Plovdiv International Arts Festival takes place.

Denmark. Aarhus Festival Week is Denmark's most comprehensive program of concerts, sports, theater, and exhibitions.

France. The Festival of Autumn occurs throughout Paris. A series of chamber music concerts make up the Music Festival of Besançon and Franche-Comte.

Great Britain. Burghley Horse Trials are run in Stamford, Lincolnshire. The Chelsea Antiques Fair takes place in London.

Holland. The Boulevard of Broken Dreams is a potpourri of theatrical offerings in tents on Amsterdam's Museumplein. Parliament opens during Prinsjesdag at The Hague.

Hungary. September sees the start of the Budapest Music Weeks.

Ireland. Dublin Theatre Festival is a major event involving all of Dublin's major theaters.

Italy. The Piedigrotta brings fireworks and parades to Naples. Two-oar gondolas compete during the Historic Regatta in Venice. The Joust of the Saracen is a tilting contest in Arezzo.

Luxembourg. A two-day Grape and Wine Festival takes place in Grevenmacher.

Romania. The Bucharest Folklore Festival starts.

Spain. Blessings of the grapes and the first wine are bestowed, along with flamenco dancing and bullfights, in Jerez de la Frontera.

Switzerland. The Knabenschiessen includes a shooting contest and other festivities in Zurich.

West Germany. Munich's Oktoberfest attracts millions of visitors.

October **Austria.** The Styrian Autumn Festival takes place in Graz.

France. The Prix de l'Arc de Triomphe at Paris's Longchamp Racecourse is run.

Great Britain. The Cheltenham Festival of Literature takes place in Gloucestershire. The world's top show jumpers compete at the Horse of the Year Show in London's Wembley Arena.

Greece. Athens's Marathon re-creates the original route of Phidippides from Marathon to Athens. The Demetria Festival brings the arts to Thessaloniki.

Iceland. Leif Erikson's Day is celebrated on October 9 to mark his discovery of North America in AD 1000.

Italy. The Feast of St. Francis is celebrated in Assisi. Alba hosts a Truffle Fair.

Poland. International Jazz Festival is held in Warsaw.

Portugal. The second yearly pilgrimage to Fatima, about 95 miles from Lisbon, begins.

Spain. The Barcelona International Music Festival attracts top performers in a wide range of music and theater. The Saffron Rose Festival is held in the shadow of the Castle of Consuegra in Toledo.

Switzerland. The Chestnut Festival is celebrated in Locarno.

Turkey. Turkish Republic Day (28–29) is commemorated throughout the country.

West Germany. The Frankfurt Book Fair is a popular literary event. The Berlin International Marathon takes place.

Yugoslavia. BEMUS—Belgrade Music Festival—attracts a number of well-known artists.

November **Austria.** St. Leopold's Day and Vintage Festival is celebrated in Klosterneuburg. Advent brings special markets and exhibits in Vienna and Salzburg as well as performances by the Vienna Boys' Choir.

France. *Les Trois Glorieuses* is a wine auction, with considerable merriment throughout Burgundy.

Great Britain. The London-to-Brighton Veteran Car run starts at Hyde Park. The Lord Mayor's Procession and Show accompanies the Lord Mayor's inauguration in the City of London.

Portugal. Horse lovers from all the world over gather in Golega during the São Martinho Fair.

West Germany. The Six-Day Cycle Race takes off in Munich. St. Martin's Festival celebrations are held throughout the Rhineland. Berlin hosts an Antiques Fair.

December **Austria.** The Imperial Ball at the Imperial Palace is a leading event on Europe's social calendar.

France. The Shepherd's Festival is a Christmas celebration in Les Baux, Provence.

Great Britain. The Olympia International Show Jumping Championships take place in London.

Italy. Opera Season opens at Milan's La Scala. The Feast of St. Ambrose celebrates Milan's patron saint.

Norway. Nobel Peace Prize is awarded in Oslo.

Sweden. In Stockholm, Santa Lucia Day celebrates the Queen of Light and the coming of longer days. Nobel Prize ceremonies take place.

Switzerland. Klausjagen is a venerable custom surrounding St. Nicholas in Kuessnacht am Rigi.

Turkey. Festival of Mevlana honors the founder of the order of the Whirling Dervishes in Konya.

West Germany. Christmas markets are set up in Munich, Hamburg, Berlin, Frankfurt, and many other cities.

Climate

Current weather information on 235 cities around the world is only a phone call away. Call 800/247–3282 to obtain the Weather Trak telephone number for your area. When you reach that number, a taped message will tell you to dial the three-digit access code to any of the 235 destinations. The code is either the area code (in the United States) or the first three letters of the foreign city. For a list of all access codes send a stamped, self-addressed envelope to Cities, Box 7000, Dallas, TX 75209. For further information, phone 214/869–3035 or 800/247–3282.

For the average daily maximum and minimum temperatures of the major European cities, *see* When to Go in each individual country chapter.

What to Pack

Pack light—porters and baggage trolleys are scarce. The luggage restrictions imposed on international flights help limit what you pack. *(See* Getting to Europe.)

What you pack depends more on the season than on any particular dress code. In general, northern and central Europe have cold, snowy winters, and the Mediterranean countries have mild winters, though parts of southern Europe can be bitterly cold, too. In the Mediterranean resorts you may need a warm jacket for mornings and evenings, even in summer. The mountains usually are warm on summer days, but the weather, especially in the Alps, is unpredictable, and the nights are generally cool. The Pyrenees don't have much snow except in the higher elevations, but they have extremely damp, foggy weather and lots of rain year-round.

For European cities, pack as you would for an American city: formal outfits for first-class restaurants and nightclubs, casual clothes elsewhere. Jeans are as popular in Europe as they are in the rest of the world and are perfectly acceptable for sightseeing and informal dining. Sturdy walking shoes are appropriate for the cobblestone streets and gravel paths that fill many of the parks and surround some of the historic buildings. For visits to churches and cathedrals, especially in southern Europe, avoid shorts and immodest outfits. Italians are especially strict, insisting that women cover their shoulders and arms (a shawl will do). Women, however, no longer have to cover their heads in Roman Catholic churches.

To discourage purse snatchers and pickpockets, take a handbag with long straps that you can sling across your body, bandolier-style, and with a zippered compartment for money and other valuables.

You'll need an electrical adapter for hair dryers and other small appliances. The voltage in most parts of Europe is 220, with 50 cycles. If you stay in budget hotels, take your own soap: Many do not provide soap, and those that do often give guests only one tiny bar per room.

Taking Money Abroad

Traveler's checks and major U.S. credit cards—particularly Visa—are accepted throughout the major cities and resorts of Western Europe and in some cities of Eastern Europe. Even in Western Europe you'll need cash for some of the smaller cities and rural areas and for small restaurants and shops in the major cities. Although you won't get as good an exchange rate at home as abroad, it's wise to change a small amount of money into the currency of the country you're visiting (or the one you'll visit first) to avoid long lines at airport currency exchange booths. Most U.S. banks will exchange your money into foreign currency. If your local bank can't provide this service, contact **Deak International**, 630 Fifth Ave., New York, NY 10011, tel. 212/635–0515.

For safety and convenience, it's always best to take traveler's checks. The most recognized traveler's checks are American Express, Barclay's, Thomas Cook, and those issued through major commercial banks such as Citibank and Bank of America. Some banks will issue the checks free to established customers, but most charge a 1% commission fee. Buy some of your traveler's checks in small denominations to cash toward the end of your trip. This will avoid having to cash a large check and ending up with more foreign money than you need. You can also buy traveler's checks in foreign currency, a good idea if the U.S. dollar is falling and you want to lock in the current rate. Remember to take along addresses of offices where you can get refunds for lost or stolen traveler's checks.

Banks and bank-operated exchange booths at airports and railroad stations are the best places to change money. Hotels and privately run exchange firms will give you a significantly lower rate of exchange.

Getting Money from Home

There are at least three ways to get money from home: (1) Have it sent through a large commercial bank with a branch in the European country you're visiting. The only drawback is that you must have an account with the bank; if not, you'll have to go through your own bank and the process will be slower and more expensive. (2) Have it sent through American Express. If you are a cardholder, you can cash a personal check or a counter check at an American Express office for up to $1,000; $200 will be in cash and $800 in traveler's checks. There is a 1% commission on the traveler's checks. American Express has a new service, American Express MoneyGram, that will be available in most major European cities by January 1989. Through this service, you can receive up to $5,000 cash. To find out the American Express MoneyGram location nearest your home and the addresses of offices in Europe, call 800/543–4080. You do not need to be a cardholder to use this service. (3) Have it sent through Western Union (tel. 800/988–4726). If you have a MasterCard or Visa, you can have money sent for any amount up to your credit limit. If not, have someone take cash or a certified cashier's check to a Western Union office. The money will be delivered in two business days to a bank in the town where you're staying. Fees vary with the amount of money sent. For $1,000 the fee is $67; for $500, $57.

Passports and Visas

Americans All U.S. citizens need a **passport** to enter the 33 countries covered in this guide. Applications for a new passport must be made in person; renewals can be obtained in person or by mail *(see* below). First-time applicants should apply well in advance of their departure date to one of the 13 U.S. Passport Agency offices. In addition, local county courthouses, many state and probate courts, and some post offices accept passport applications. Necessary documents include: (1) a completed passport application (Form DSP–11); (2) proof of citizenship (either birth certificate with raised seal or naturalization papers); (3) proof of identity (driver's license, employee ID card, or any other document with your photograph and signature); (4) two recent, identical, two-inch-square photographs (black and white or color); (5) $42 application fee for a 10-year passport (those under 18 pay $27 for a five-year passport). Passports are mailed to you in about 10 working days.

To renew your passport by mail, you'll need completed Form DSP–82, two recent, identical passport photographs, and a check or money order for $35.

At press time, U.S. citizens need **visas** to enter Andorra, Bulgaria (if traveling alone but not if part of a group of six or more), Czechoslovakia, France, East Germany, Hungary, Monaco, Poland, Romania, and Yugoslavia. Many countries require visas for stays of three months or longer; apply at the country's embassy in Washington, DC. Since the United States does not have diplomatic relations with Albania, visa applications must go through the Albanian Mission in Paris or Rome; visas are currently issued only to business representatives and to groups of 10 or more.

Canadians All Canadians need **passports** to enter the 33 countries in this guide. Send the completed application (available at any post office or passport office) to the Bureau of Passports, Complexe Guy Favreau, 200 Dorchester W., Montreal, Quebec H2Z 1X4. Include $25, two photographs, a guarantor, and proof of Canadian citizenship. Applications can be made in person at the regional passport offices in Edmonton, Halifax, Montreal, Toronto, Vancouver, or Winnipeg. Passports are valid for five years and are nonrenewable.

Visas are required by Canadian citizens traveling to Albania, Bulgaria, Czechoslovakia, East Germany, France, Hungary, Poland, Romania, and Yugoslavia. Obtain them from the nearest embassy.

Britons All British citizens need **passports;** applications are available from travel agencies or a main post office. Send the completed form to your nearest regional Passport Office. The application must be countersigned by your bank manager or by a solicitor, barrister, doctor, clergyman, or justice of the peace who knows you personally. In addition, you'll need two photographs and the £15 fee. The occasional tourist might opt for a British Visitor's Passport. It is valid for one year and allows entry into most European countries (Yugoslavia and Eastern European countries currently excepted). It costs £7.50 and is nonrenewable. You'll need two passport photographs and identification. Apply at your local post office.

Visas are required for British citizens entering Albania, Czechoslovakia, East Germany, Hungary, Poland, and Romania. Apply at the nearest embassy or consulate.

Customs and Duties

On Arrival Arrival formalities vary from country to country and are detailed in each chapter. In addition to specific duty-free allowances, most countries allow travelers to also bring in cameras and a reasonable amount of film and electronic equipment; most do not allow fresh meats, plants, weapons, and narcotics. Eastern European countries generally restrict the importation of Western newspapers, tape and video cassettes, and medicines except those for personal use.

On Departure If you are bringing any foreign-made equipment from home, such as a camera, it's wise to carry the original receipt with you or to register such equipment with U.S. Customs before you leave (Form 4457). Otherwise you may end up paying duty on your return.

U.S. residents may bring home duty-free up to $400 worth of foreign goods, as long as they have been out of the country for at least 48 hours. Each member of the family is entitled to the same exemption, regardless of age, and exemptions may be pooled. For the next $1,000 worth of goods, a flat 10% rate is assessed; duties vary with the merchandise for anything over $1,400. Included for travelers 21 or older are one liter of alcohol, 100 cigars (non-Cuban), and 200 cigarettes. Only one bottle of perfume trademarked in the United States may be brought in. However, there is no duty on antiques or art over 100 years old. Anything exceeding these limits will be taxed at the port of entry and may be taxed additionally in the traveler's home state. Unlimited amounts of goods from designated "developing" or GSP countries also may be brought in duty-free; check with the U.S. Customs Service, Box 7407, Washington, DC 20044. Gifts valued at under $50 may be mailed to friends or relatives at home duty-free, but not more than one package per day to any one addressee and not including perfumes costing more than $5, or tobacco or liquor.

Canadian residents have a $300 exemption and may also bring in duty-free up to 50 cigars, 200 cigarettes, 2 pounds of tobacco, and 40 ounces of liquor, provided these are declared in writing to customs on arrival and accompany the traveler in hand or checked-through baggage. Personal gifts should be mailed as "Unsolicited Gift—Value under $40." Request the Canadian Customs brochure "I Declare" for further details.

British residents, *see* Customs and Duties in Great Britain.

Traveling with Film

If your camera is new, shoot and develop a few rolls before leaving home. Pack some lens tissue and an extra battery for your built-in light meter. Invest about $10 in a skylight filter; it will protect the lens and also reduce haze.

Film doesn't like hot weather. If you're driving in summer, don't store film in the glove compartment or on the shelf under the rear window. Put it behind the front seat on the floor, on the side opposite the exhaust pipe.

On a plane trip, never pack unprocessed film in check-in luggage; if your bags get X-rayed, you can say good-bye to your pictures. Always carry undeveloped film with you through security and ask to have it inspected by hand (carry your film in a plastic bag for quick inspection). Inspectors at American airports are required by law to honor requests for hand inspection; abroad, you'll have to depend on the kindness of strangers.

The old airport scanning machines use heavy doses of radiation that can turn a family portrait into an early-morning fog. The newer models—used in all U.S. airports—are safe for anything from five to 500 scans, depending on the speed of your film. The effects are cumulative; you can put the same roll of film through several scans without worry. After five scans, though, you're asking for trouble.

If your film gets fogged and you want an explanation, send it to the National Association of Photographic Manufacturers, 600 Mamaroneck Ave., Harrison, NY 10528. Experts will try to determine what went wrong. This service is free.

Photographing trains, junctions, or railway stations can land you in *serious* trouble in Eastern Europe. Turkish and, to a lesser extent, Greek authorities can also be sensitive. This is equally true of airports. Don't take pictures without making sure it is permitted.

Staying Healthy

There are no serious health risks associated with travel in Europe. However, the Centers for Disease Control (CDC) in Atlanta cautions that most of southern Europe is in the "intermediate" range for risk of contracting traveler's diarrhea. Part of this may be due to an increased consumption of olive oil and wine, which can have a laxative effect on stomachs used to a different diet. The CDC also advises that international travelers swim only in chlorinated swimming pools if there is any question about contamination of local beaches and freshwater lakes.

If you have a health problem that might require purchasing prescription drugs while in Europe, ask your doctor to prescribe the drug by its generic name. Brand names vary widely from country to country.

The International Association for Medical Assistance to Travelers (IAMAT) is a worldwide association offering a list of approved English-speaking doctors whose training meets British and American standards. Contact IAMAT for a list of European physicians and clinics that belong to this network. **In the United States:** 736 Center St., Lewiston, NY 14092, tel. 716/754–4883. **In Canada:** 188 Nicklin Rd., Guelph, Ontario N1H 7L5. **In Europe:** Gotthardstrasse 17, 6300 Zug, Switz. Membership is free.

Shots and Medications Inoculations are not needed for Europe. The American Medical Association (AMA) recommends Pepto-Bismol for minor cases of traveler's diarrhea.

Insurance

Travelers may seek insurance coverage in three areas: health and accident, lost luggage, and trip cancellation. Your first step is to review your existing health and home-owner policies; some health insurance plans cover health expenses incurred while traveling, some major medical plans cover emergency transportation, and some home-owner policies cover the theft of luggage.

Health and Accident Several companies offer coverage designed to supplement existing health insurance for travelers:

Carefree Travel Insurance (Box 310, 120 Mineola Blvd., Mineola, NY 11501, tel. 516/294–0220 or 800/645–2424) provides coverage for medical evacuation. It also offers 24-hour medical phone advice.

Health Care Abroad, International Underwriters Group (243 Church St. W., Vienna, VA 22180, tel. 703/281–9500 or 800/237–6615), offers comprehensive medical coverage, including emergency evacuation for trips of 10–90 days.

International SOS Insurance (Box 11568, Philadelphia, PA 19116, tel. 215/244–1500 or 800/523–8930) does not offer medical insurance but provides medical evacuation services to its clients, who are often international corporations.

Travel Guard International, underwritten by Cygna (1100 Centerpoint Dr., Stevens Point, WI 54481, tel. 715/345–0505 or 800/782–5151), offers medical insurance, with coverage for emergency evacuation when Travel Guard's representatives in the United States say it is necessary.

Lost Luggage Airlines are responsible for lost or damaged property only up to $1,250 per passenger on domestic flights, and $9.07 per pound (or $20 per kilo) for checked baggage on international flights, and up to $400 per passenger for unchecked baggage on international flights. If you're carrying valuables, either take them with you on the airplane or purchase additional insurance for lost luggage. Some airlines will issue additional luggage insurance when you check in, but many do not. Insurance for lost, damaged, or stolen luggage is available through travel agents or directly through various insurance companies. Two that issue luggage insurance are **Tele-Trip** (tel. 800/228–9792), a subsidiary of Mutual of Omaha, and the **Travelers Insurance Co.** (Ticket and Travel Dept., 1 Tower Sq., Hartford, CT 06183, tel. 203/227–0111). Tele-Trip operates sales booths at airports, and also issues insurance through travel agents. Tele-Trip will insure checked luggage for up to 180 days and for $500 to $3,000 valuation. For 1–3 days, the rate for a $500 valuation is $8.25; for 180 days, $100. The Travelers Insurance Co. will insure checked or hand luggage for $500 to $2,000 valuation per person, and also for a maximum of 180 days. Rates for 1–5 days for $500 valuation are $10; for 180 days, $85. Other companies with comprehensive policies include **Access America, Inc.,** a subsidiary of Blue Cross-Blue Shield (Box 807, New York, NY 10163, tel. 800/851–2800); **Near, Inc.** (1900 N. MacArthur Blvd., Suite 210, Oklahoma City, OK 73127, tel. 800/654–6700); and **Travel Guard International** *(see* Health and Accident Insurance).

Before you go, itemize the contents of each bag in case you need to file an insurance claim. Be certain to put your home or business address on each piece of luggage, including carry-on bags. If your luggage is lost or stolen and later recovered, the airline must deliver the luggage to your home free of charge.

Trip Cancellation Flight insurance is often included in the price of a ticket when paid for with American Express, Visa, and other major credit cards. It is usually included in combination travel insurance packages available from most tour operators, travel agents, and insurance agents.

Renting, Leasing and Purchasing Cars

Renting It's best to arrange a car rental before you leave. You won't save money by waiting until you arrive in Europe, and you may find the type of car you want is not available at the last minute. If you're flying into a major city and planning to spend some time there before using your car, save money by arranging to pick it up on the day of your departure. You'll have to weigh the added expense of renting a car from a major company with an airport office against the savings on a car from a budget company with offices in town. You could waste precious hours trying to locate the budget company in return for only a small financial saving. If you're arriving and departing from different airports, look for a one-way car rental with no return fees. If you're traveling to more than one country, make sure your rental contract permits you to take the car across borders and that the insurance policy covers you in every country you visit. Be prepared to pay more for a car with an automatic transmission; because they are not as readily available as those with manual transmissions, reserve in advance.

Rental rates vary widely and depend on size and model, number of days you use the car, insurance coverage, and whether special drop-off fees are imposed. In most cases, rates quoted include unlimited free mileage and standard liability protection. Not included are Collision Damage Waiver (CDW), which eliminates your deductible payment should you have an accident; personal accident insurance; gasoline; or local taxes. European Value-Added Taxes (VAT) vary from country to country, ranging from zero in Switzerland to a whopping 33.3% in France.

Rental companies usually charge according to the exchange rate of the dollar at the time the car is returned or when the credit card payment is processed. Three companies with special programs to help you hedge against the falling dollar, by guaranteeing advertised rates if you pay in advance, are: **Budget Rent-a-Car,** 3350 Boyington St., Carrollton, TX 75006, tel. 800/527–0700; **Connex Travel International,** 983 Main St., Peekskill, NY 10566, tel. 800/333–3949; and **Cortell International,** 770 Lexington Ave., New York, NY 10021, tel. 800/223–6626 or, in New York, 800/442–4481.

Other budget rental companies serving Europe include **Europe by Car,** One Rockefeller Plaza, New York, NY 10020, tel. 800/223–1516 or, in California, 800/252–9401; **Foremost Euro-Car,** 5430 Van Nuys Blvd., Van Nuys, CA 91404, tel. 800/423–3111; and **Kemwel,** 106 Calvert St., Harrison, NY 10528, tel. 800/678–0678. Other major firms with European rentals include **Avis,** tel. 800/331–1212; **Hertz,** tel. 800/223–6472 or, in New York, 800/522–5568; and **National** or **Europcar,** tel. 800/Car–Rent.

In the United Kingdom, there are offices of **Avis** (Hayes Gate House, Uxbridge Rd., Hayes, Middlesex UB4 0NJ, tel. 01/848–8733); **Hertz** (Radnor House, 1272 London Rd., London SW16 4XW, tel. 01/679–1799); and **Europcar** (Bushey House, High St., Bushey, WD2 1RE, tel. 01/950–4080).

Driver's licenses issued in the United States and Canada are valid in Europe. Non-EEC nationals must have Green Card insurance. You might also take out an International Driving Permit before you leave in order to smooth out difficulties if you have an accident or as an additional piece of identification. Permits are available for a small fee through local offices of the **American Automobile Association** (AAA) and the **Canadian Automobile Association** (CAA), or from their main offices: AAA, 8111 Gatehouse Rd., Falls Church, VA 22047–0001, tel. 703/AAA–6000; and CAA, 2 Carlton St., Toronto, Ontario M5B 1K4, tel. 416/964–3170.

Britons driving in Europe should have a valid driver's license. Green Card insurance is a wise buy, though not compulsory for EEC nationals. All drivers must carry their car registration documents and a red warning triangle.

Leasing For trips of 21 days or more, you may save money by leasing a car. With the leasing arrangement, you are technically buying a car and then selling it back to the manufacturer after you've used it. You receive a factory-new car, tax-free, with international registration and extensive insurance coverage. Rates vary with the make and model of car and length of time used. Car leasing programs are offered by Renault, Citroën, and Peugeot in France, and by Volkswagen, Ford, Audi, and Opel, among others, in Belgium. Delivery can be arranged outside of

France and Brussels for an additional fee. Before you go, compare long-term rental rates with leasing rates. Remember to add taxes and insurance costs to the car rentals, something you don't have to worry about with leasing. Companies that offer leasing arrangements include Kemwel and Europe by Car, listed above.

Purchasing Given the weakness of the dollar on the international market and the logistical complexities of shipping a car home, the option of purchasing a car abroad is less appealing today than it was a decade ago. The advantage of buying a car in Europe is that you'll get what amounts to a free car rental during your stay in Europe. If you plan to purchase a car in Europe, be certain the prices quoted are for cars built to meet specifications set down by the U.S. Department of Transportation. If not, you will have to go through considerable expense to convert the car before you can legally drive it in the United States. You will also be subject to a U.S. Customs duty. For more information, contact Kemwel or Europe by Car, both listed above, or ask your local car dealer to put you in touch with an importer.

Student and Youth Travel

The **International Student Identity Card** (ISIC) entitles students to youth rail passes, special fees on local transportation, Intra-European student charter flights, and discounts at museums, theaters, sports events, and many other attractions. If purchased in the United States, the $10 card also entitles the holder to $2,000 in emergency medical insurance, plus $100 a day for up to 60 days of hospital coverage. Apply to the **Council on International Educational Exchange** (CIEE), 205 E. 42nd St., New York, NY 10017, tel. 212/661–1414. In Canada, the ISIC is also available for $10 from the **Association of Student Councils,** 187 College St., Toronto, Ontario M5T 1P7.

The **Youth International Educational Exchange Card** (YIEE), issued by the **Federation of International Youth Travel Organizations** (FIYTO), 81 Islands Brugge, DK–2300 Copenhagen S, Denmark, provides similar services to nonstudents under 26 years of age. In the United States, the card costs $10 and is available from CIEE (*see* above) or from **ISE,** Europa House, 802 W. Oregon St., Urbana, IL 61801, tel. 217/344–5863. In Canada, the YIEE card is available from the **Canadian Hostelling Association** (CHA), 333 River Rd., Vanier, Ottawa, Ontario K1L 8H9, tel. 613/476–3844.

An **International Youth Hostel Federation** (IYHF) membership card is the key to inexpensive dormitory-style accommodations at thousands of youth hostels around the world. Hostels provide separate sleeping quarters and are situated in a variety of locations, including converted farmhouses, villas, restored castles, and specially constructed modern buildings. IYHF membership costs $20 a year and is available in the United States through **American Youth Hostels** (AYH), Box 37613, Washington, DC 20013, tel. 202/783–6161. AYH also publishes an extensive directory of youth hostels around the world. Economical bicycle tours for small groups of adventurous, energetic students are another popular AYH student travel service. The 16-day tour of England for $1,300 (from New York) is typical. For information on these and other AYH services and publications, contact the AYH at the address above.

Council Travel, a CIEE subsidiary, is the foremost U.S. student travel agency and specializes in low-cost charters and serves as the exclusive U.S. agent for many student airfare bargains and student tours. The 80-page *Student Travel Catalog* and *Council Charter* brochure are available free from any Council Travel office in the United States (enclose $1 postage if ordering by mail). Contact CIEE headquarters at the address above, or Council Travel offices in Amherst, Austin, Berkeley, Boston, Cambridge, Chicago, Dallas, La Jolla, Long Beach, Los Angeles, Portland, Providence, San Diego, San Francisco, and Seattle.

The **Educational Travel Center,** another student travel specialist worth contacting for information on student tours, bargain fares, and bookings, may be reached at 438 N. Frances St., Madison, WI 55703, tel. 608/256–5551.

Students who would like to work abroad should contact CIEE's **Work Abroad Department,** at the address given above. The council arranges various types of paid and voluntary work experiences overseas for up to six months. CIEE also sponsors study programs in Europe, Latin America, and Asia, and publishes many books of interest to the student traveler, including *Work, Study, Travel Abroad: The Whole World Handbook* ($8.95 plus $1 postage), *Work Your Way Around the World* ($10.95 plus $1 postage), and *Volunteer! The Comprehensive Guide to Voluntary Service in the U.S. and Abroad* ($5.50 plus $1 postage).

The Information Center at the **Institute of International Education** (IIE), 809 UN Plaza, New York, NY 10017, tel. 212/981–5413, has reference books, foreign university catalogues, study-abroad brochures, and other materials that may be consulted by students and nonstudents alike, free of charge. The Information Center is open weekdays 10 to 4, Wednesdays 10 to 7.

IIE administers a variety of grant and study programs offered by U.S. and foreign organizations, and publishes a well-known annual series of study-abroad guides, including *Academic Year Abroad, Vacation Study Abroad,* and *Study in the United Kingdom and Ireland.* The institute also publishes *Teaching Abroad,* a book of employment and study opportunities overseas for U.S. teachers. For a current list of IIE publications, along with prices and ordering information, write to the IIE Publications Service at the address given above. Books must be purchased by mail or in person; telephone orders are not accepted. General information on IIE programs and services is available from its regional offices in Atlanta, Chicago, Denver, Houston, San Francisco, and Washington, DC.

For information on the Eurail Youthpass, *see* Rail Passes.

Traveling with Children

Publications   *A Capital Guide for Kids: A London Guide for Parents with Small Children* by Vanessa Miles (Allison & Busby, 6a Noel St., London W1V 3RB; £1.95).
Children's Guide to London by Christopher Pick (Cadogan Books, 16 Lower Marsh, London SE1 7RJ; $8.50).
Europe with Children by K. Appler (Alexandria Press, Alex-

andria, VA; $4.95) is less a planning guide than an account of one family's trip.

Family Travel Times is an 8- to 12-page newsletter published 10 times a year by TWYCH (Travel with Your Children, 80 Eighth Ave., New York, NY 10011, tel. 212/206–0688). Subscription includes access to back issues and twice-weekly opportunities to call in for specific advice.

Kids' London by Elizabeth Holt and Molly Perham (St. Martin's Press).

Young People's Guide to Munich is a free pamphlet available from the German National Tourist Office (747 Third Ave., New York, NY 10017, tel. 212/308–3300).

Family Travel Organizations
American Institute for Foreign Study (AIFS; 102 Greenwich Ave., Greenwich, CT 06830, tel. 203/869–9090) offers family vacation programs in England, France, Switzerland, and Austria specifically designed for parents and children.

Families Welcome! (1416 Second Ave., New York, NY 10021, tel. 212/861–2500 or 800/472–8999) is a travel agency that arranges England and France tours brimming with family-oriented choices and activities.

Paris Accueil (485 Madison Ave., New York, NY 10022, tel. 212/838–2444) and **The French Experience** (171 Madison Ave., New York, NY 10016, tel. 212/683–2445) are two organizations that understand family needs.

Getting There
On international flights, children under two years not occupying a seat pay 10% of the adult fare. Various discounts apply to children 2–12. Reserve a seat behind the plane's bulkhead, where you'll have more leg room and can usually fit a bassinet (supplied by the airline). At the same time, inquire about special children's meals or snacks, offered by most airlines. (For a rundown on children's services offered by 46 airlines, see TWYCH's "Airline Guide," in the February 1988 issue of *Family Travel Times*.) Ask the airline in advance if you can bring aboard your child's carseat. (For the booklet "Child/Infant Safety Seats Acceptable for Use in Aircraft," contact Community and Consumer Liaison Division, APA–400 Federal Aviation Administration, Washington, DC 20591, tel. 202/267–3479.)

Hotels
Novotel hotels in Europe permit up to two children to stay free in their parents' room and get a free breakfast, too. Many Novotel properties have playgrounds. (International reservations, tel. 800/221–4542.)

Sofitel hotels in Europe offer a free second room for children during July and August and over the Christmas holiday. (International reservations, tel. 800/221–4542.)

Happy Family Swiss Hotels are 22 properties in Switzerland that have joined together to welcome families, offering outstanding programs for children at reduced prices. A brochure on these hotels is available from the Swiss National Tourist Office (608 Fifth Ave., New York, NY 10020, tel. 212/641–0050).

Club Med (40 W. 57th St., New York, NY 10019, tel. 800/CLUB–MED) has "Baby Clubs" (from age four months), "Mini Clubs" (for ages four to six or eight, depending on the resort), and "Kids Clubs" (for ages eight and up during school holidays) at many of its resort villages in France, Italy, Switzerland, and Spain.

In Germany, families should consider any one of the **Schloss** ("castle") hotels, many of which are located on parklike

grounds. United States representatives: **Europa Hotels and Tours** (tel. 800/523–9570 or, in Washington, 206/485–6985); **DER Tours, Inc.** (tel. 800/421–4343 or, in California, 213/479–4411).
CIGA hotels (Reservations, tel. 800/221–2340) has 22 properties in Italy, all of which welcome families.

Villa Rentals   **At Home Abroad, Inc.**, 405 E. 56th St., Suite 6H, New York, NY 10022, tel. 212/421–9165
Villas International, 71 W. 23rd St., New York, NY 10010, tel. 212/929–7585 or 800/221–2260
Hideaways, Inc., Box 1464, Littleton, MA 01460, tel. 617/486–8955
B. & D. de Vogue, 1830 S. Mooney Blvd., #113, Visalia, CA 93277, tel. 209/733–7119 or 800/338–0483
Meeting Points, 5515 S.E. Milwaukee Ave., Portland, OR 97207, tel. 503/233–1224
Vacances en Campagne/Vacanze in Italia/Heritage of England, 153 W. 13th St., New York, NY 10011, tel. 212/242–2145 or 800/553–5405
Italian Villa Rentals, Box 1145, Bellevue, WA 98009, tel. 206/827–3694

Home Exchange   See *Home Exchanging: A Complete Sourcebook for Travelers at Home or Abroad* by James Dearing (Globe Pequot Press, Box Q, Chester, CT 06412, tel. 800/243–0495 or in CT 800/962–0973).

Baby-sitting Services   To find out about recommended child-care arrangements, first ask your hotel concierge. Also call the American Embassy or Consulate for a listing of child-care agencies with English-speaking personnel. Local tourist offices, especially in Germany, maintain an updated list of local baby-sitters.

Pen Pals   For names of children in Europe to whom your children can write before your trip, send a self-addressed, stamped envelope to: **International Friendship League**, 55 Mt. Vernon St., Boston, MA 02108, tel. 617/523–4273; **Student Letter Exchange**, 308 Second St. NW, Austin, MN 55912.

Hints for Disabled Travelers

The Information Center for Individuals with Disabilities (20 Park Plaza, Room 330, Boston, MA 02116, tel. 617/727–5540) offers useful problem-solving assistance, including lists of travel agents who specialize in tours for the disabled.
Moss Rehabilitation Hospital Travel Information Service (12th St. and Taber Rd., Philadelphia, PA 19141, tel. 215/329–5715) provides information on tourist sights, transportation, and accommodations in destinations around the world. The fee is $5 for each destination. Allow one month for delivery.
Mobility International (Box 3551, Eugene, OR 97403, tel. 503/343–1284) has information on accommodations, organized study, and so forth, around the world.
The Society for the Advancement of Travel for the Handicapped (26 Court St., Brooklyn, NY 11242, tel. 718/858–5483) offers access information. Annual membership costs $40, or $25 for senior travelers and students. Send a stamped, self-addressed envelope.
The Itinerary (Box 1084, Bayonne, NJ 07002, tel. 201/858–3400) is a bimonthly travel magazine for the disabled.

Access to the World: A Travel Guide for the Handicapped by Louise Weiss is useful. Though out of date, it is available from Facts on File, 460 Park Ave. S., New York, NY 10016, tel. 212/683-2244.

Frommer's Guide for Disabled Travelers is also helpful but dated.

Hints for Older Travelers

The American Association of Retired Persons (AARP, 1909 K St. NW, Washington, DC 20049, tel. 202/662-4850) has two programs for independent travelers: (1) the **Purchase Privilege Program**, which entitles members to discounts on hotels, airfare, car rentals, and sightseeing; and (2) the **AARP Motoring Plan**, which offers emergency aid and trip routing information for an annual fee of $29.95 per couple. The AARP also arranges group tours, including apartment living in Europe, through two companies: *Olson-Travelworld* (5855 Green Valley Circle, Culver City, CA 90230, tel. 800/227-7737) and *RFD, Inc.* (4401 W. 110th St., Overland Park, KS 66211, tel. 800/448-7010). AARP members must be 50 or older. Annual dues are $5 per person or per couple.

Elderhostel (80 Boylston St., Suite 400, Boston, MA 02116, tel. 617/426-7788) is an innovative 13-year-old program for people 60 and older. Participants live in dorms on some 1,200 campuses around the world. Mornings are devoted to lectures and seminars; afternoons, to sightseeing and field trips. The all-inclusive fee for trips of 2–3 weeks, including room, board, tuition, and round-trip transportation, is $1,700–$3,200.

Travel Industry and Disabled Exchange (TIDE, 5435 Donna Ave., Tarzana, CA 91356, tel. 818/343-6339) is an industry-based organization with a $15 per-person annual membership fee. Members receive a quarterly newsletter and information on travel agencies and tours.

Travel Tips for Senior Citizens (U.S. Dept. of State Publication 8970, revised September 1987) is available for $1 from the Superintendent of Documents, U.S. Government Printing Office, Washington, DC 20402.

The Discount Guide for Travelers over 55 by Caroline and Walter Weintz (Dutton, $7.95) lists helpful addresses, package tours, reduced rate car rentals, and so forth, in the USA and abroad.

Getting to Europe

Because the air routes between North America and Europe are among the world's most heavily traveled, the passenger has many airlines and fares to choose from. But fares change with stunning rapidity, so consult your travel agent on which bargains are currently available.

From North America by Plane

Be certain to distinguish among (1) nonstop flights—no changes, no stops; (2) direct flights—no changes but one or more stops; and (3) connecting flights—two or more planes, two or more stops.

The Airlines The U.S. airlines that serve the major cities in Europe are **TWA,** tel. 800/892–4141; **Pan Am,** tel. 800/221–1111; **American Airlines,** tel. 800/433–7300; **Northwest,** tel. 800/447–4747; and **Delta,** tel. 800/241–4141.

Many European national airlines fly directly from the United States to their home countries. The biggest advantage in arriving on a home airline is that the landing privileges are often better, as are the facilities provided at main airports. Here are the U.S. telephone numbers of those airlines that have representation in the States; most of the numbers are toll-free.

Austria: Austrian Airlines, tel. 800/533–0369
Belgium: Sabena Belgian World Airlines, tel. 800/632–8050
Cyprus: Cyprus Airways, tel. 212/714–2190
Czechoslovakia: Czechoslovak Airlines (CSA), tel. 212/682–5833
Denmark: Scandinavian Airlines (SAS), tel. 800/221–2350
Finland: Finnair, tel. 800/223–5700
France: Air France, tel. 800/237–2747
Great Britain: British Airways, tel. 800/247–9297; Virgin Atlantic, tel. 800/862–8621
Greece: Olympic Airways, tel. 800/223–1226
Holland: KLM Royal Dutch Airlines, tel. 800/777–5553
Hungary: Malev Hungarian Airlines, tel. 212/757–6446
Iceland: Icelandair, tel. 800/223–5500
Ireland: Aer Lingus, 800/223–6537
Italy: Alitalia, tel. 800/442–5860
Malta: Air Malta, tel. 415/981–8581
Norway: Scandinavian Airlines (SAS), tel. 800/221–2350
Poland: LOT Polish Airlines, tel. 212/869–1074
Portugal: TAP Air Portugal, tel. 800/221–7370
Romania: Tarom Romanian Airlines, tel. 212/687–6013
Spain: Iberia Airlines, tel. 800/221–9741
Sweden: Scandinavian Airlines, tel. 800/221–2350
Switzerland: Swissair, tel. 800/221–4750
Turkey: THY Turkish Airlines, tel. 212/986–5050
West Germany: Lufthansa, tel. 800/645–3880
Yugoslavia: JAT Yugoslav Airlines, tel. 800/752–6528

Flying Time From New York: 6½ hours to London and 7–8 hours to Scandinavian capitals. From Chicago: 8½ hours to London, 10–11 hours to Scandinavian capitals. From Los Angeles: 10 hours to London, 12–13 hours to Scandinavian capitals.

Discount Flights The major airlines offer a range of tickets that can increase the price of any given seat by more than 300%, depending on the day of purchase. As a rule, the further in advance you buy the ticket, the less expensive it is and the greater penalty (up to 100%) for canceling. Check with airlines for details.

The best buy is not necessarily an APEX (advance purchase) ticket on one of the major airlines, because these tickets carry certain restrictions: They must be bought in advance (usually 21 days), they restrict your travel, usually with a minimum stay of seven days and a maximum of 90, and they also penalize you for changes—voluntary or not—in your travel plans. But if you can work around these drawbacks (and most travelers can), they are among the best-value fares available.

Charter flights offer the lowest fares but often depart only on certain days, and seldom on time. Though you may be able to arrive at one city and return from another, you may lose all or most of your money if you cancel your trip. Travel agents can make bookings, though they won't encourage you, since commissions are lower than on scheduled flights. Checks should, as a rule, be made out to the bank and specific escrow account for your flight. To make sure your payment stays in this account until your departure, don't use credit cards as a method of payment. Don't sign up for a charter flight unless you've checked with a travel agency about the reputation of the packager. It's particularly important to know the packager's policy concerning refunds should a flight be canceled. One of the most popular charter operators is **Council Charter** (tel. 800/223–7402), a division of CIEE (Council on International Educational Exchange). Other companies advertise in Sunday travel sections of newspapers.

Somewhat more expensive—but up to 50% below the cost of APEX fares—are tickets purchased through consolidators, companies that buy blocks of tickets on scheduled airlines and sell them at wholesale prices. Here again, you may lose all or most of your money if you change plans, but at least you will be on a regularly scheduled flight with less risk of cancellation than on a charter. Once you've made your reservation, call the airline to confirm it. Among the best-known consolidators are **UniTravel** (tel. 800/325–2222) and **Access International** (250 W. 57th St.; Suite 511, New York, NY 10107, tel. 212/333–7280). Others advertise in newspaper Sunday travel sections.

A third option is to join a travel club that offers special discounts to its members. Three such organizations are **Moments Notice** (40 E. 49th St., New York, NY 10017, tel. 212/486–0503); **Discount Travel International** (114 Forrest Ave., Narberth, PA 19072, tel. 215/668–2182); and **Worldwide Discount Travel Club** (1674 Meridian Ave., Miami Beach, FL 33139, tel. 305/534–2082). These cut-rate tickets should be compared with APEX tickets on the major airlines.

Enjoying the Flight If you're lucky enough to be able to sleep on a plane, it makes sense to fly at night. Many experienced travelers, however, prefer to take a morning flight to Europe and arrive in the evening, just in time for a good night's sleep. Because the air on a plane is dry, it helps, while flying, to drink a lot of nonalcoholic beverages; drinking alcohol contributes to jet lag. Feet swell at high altitudes, so it's a good idea to remove your shoes at the beginning of your flight. Sleepers usually prefer window seats to curl up against; those who like to move about the cabin ask for aisle seats. Bulkhead seats (adjacent to the exit signs) have more legroom, but seat trays are attached to the arms of your seat rather than to the back of the seat in front.

Smoking If smoking bothers you, ask for a seat far from the smoking section. If a U.S. airline representative tells you there are no seats available in the nonsmoking section, insist on one: Government regulations require airlines to find seats for all nonsmokers.

Luggage Regulations Airlines allow each passenger two pieces of check-in luggage and one carry-on piece on international flights from North America. Each piece of check-in luggage cannot exceed 62 inches (length + width + height) or weigh more than 70 pounds. The carry-on luggage cannot exceed 45 inches (length + width + height) and must fit under the seat or in the overhead luggage compartment. On flights within Europe, you are allowed to check a total of 44 pounds, regardless of luggage size. Requirements for carry-on luggage are the same as for those on transatlantic flights.

For information on luggage insurance, *see* Insurance in Before You Go.

Labeling Luggage Put your home or business address on each piece of luggage, including hand baggage. If your lost luggage is recovered, the airline must deliver it to your home, at no charge to you.

From North America by Ship

Cunard Line (555 Fifth Ave., New York, NY 10017, tel. 800/221–4770 or 212/661–7777) operates four ships that make transatlantic crossings. One is the *Queen Elizabeth 2*, the only ocean liner that makes regular transatlantic crossings. The others make repositioning crossings twice a year, as one cruise season ends in Europe and another begins in North America. The *QE2* makes regular crossings April through December, between Baltimore, Boston, and New York City, and Southampton, England. Arrangements for the *QE2* can include one-way airfare. The *Sea Goddess I* and *Sea Goddess II* sail to and from Madeira, Portugal, and St. Thomas, the U.S. Virgin Islands, for their repositioning crossings. The *Vistafjord* sails to and from Marseilles, France, and Fort Lauderdale, Florida, on its repositioning crossings. Cunard Line offers fly/cruise packages and pre- and post-land packages. For the European cruise season, ports of call include Southampton; Madeira, Marseilles, Hamburg, Genoa, Rome, Venice, Naples, Monte Carlo, Malaga, Piraeus (Athens), Copenhagen, and Stockholm. Ports of call vary with the ship.

Royal Viking Line (750 Battery St., San Francisco, CA 94111, tel. 800/634–8000) has four ships that cruise out of European ports. Two of the ships make repositioning crossings to and from Fort Lauderdale and Lisbon, Portugal. Fly/cruise packages are available. Major ports of call, depending on the ship, are Copenhagen, Stockholm, Bergen, Hamburg, Leningrad, Barcelona, Venice, Dubrovnik, Villefranche, Corfu, and Lisbon.

American Star Lines (660 Madison Ave., New York, NY 10021, tel. 800/356–7677 and, in New York, 212/644–7900) makes transatlantic crossings in spring and fall to and from Greece and Barbados (in the British West Indies). The crossings are regular cruises, with ports of call in Portugal, Italy, Turkey, and the Greek islands. Summer cruises are from Piraeus (Athens), to the Greek islands, and Turkey. Fly/cruise packages are available.

Check the travel pages of your Sunday newspaper for other cruise ships that sail to Europe.

From the United Kingdom by Plane

Air travel from Britain to continental Europe has become much cheaper, more convenient, and more competitive in recent years, thanks largely to the British government's determination to break down the cozy system of intergovernmental fare setting. This system, which has only begun to break up in the 1980s, was aimed at protecting the earnings of national, government-owned airlines. Increasingly, however, while air travel in Europe is still substantially more expensive than in the States, airlines are being given more freedom to compete without government interference. Britain sold its national carrier, British Airways, almost two years ago, and since then BA has pioneered lower fares and better consumer service.

More governments are beginning to let airlines compete—good news for the traveler—and this applies not just to competition between state- and privately owned carriers but also to competition between scheduled and charter airlines. From Britain, for example, rules against "seat-only" charters—that is, tickets for charter flights that are not sold as part of a package tour including pre-booked accommodation—have been lifted, and these can be a very cost-effective way of getting to some European destinations, particularly those Mediterranean ones popular with British vacationers.

Scheduled Airlines If time rather than money is your main consideration, then scheduled flights are a better option than charters. London, with its two main airports—Heathrow and Gatwick—and three subsidiary airports—Luton and Stansted farther away from the city, and London City Airport only six miles from the City of London—is Europe's biggest air hub, and frequent scheduled services connect it with virtually every other European capital, most major regional cities, and most resort destinations. Generally speaking, the smaller the city, the less frequently it is likely to be served, but most European cities have daily service by BA and at least one other airline.

New competition by up-and-coming airlines like British Midland and Air Europe, both privately owned, are determined to grab up customers from BA, meaning that there are many options to choose from. Travelers can make substantial savings if they are prepared to accept certain conditions.

These smaller airlines have pioneered routes to European capitals from regional British airports. Manchester, for instance, has become a busy northern hub for several carriers, with shuttle flights to London and several flights a day to Amsterdam and other European points. From Scotland, there are daily flights from Edinburgh to Paris by Air France and to Copenhagen by SAS. Both Glasgow and Edinburgh are linked to London by frequent shuttle flights by BA, British Midland, and others.

Most airline schedules in Europe cater mainly to business travelers who want to fly at clearly defined peak times. But the airlines offer lower fares to leisure travelers who can use off-peak flights. Look for better fares on mid-day flights and ask about cheaper weekend fares. Some of these—called PEX and Super PEX—can be less than half the normal coach-class fare. Most of these bargain rates require a mandatory Saturday night at your destination.

Remember, few flights over Europe last more than four hours; most are less than two hours long. For such short flights, you may feel that flying first or business class, even if it's within your budget, is an unnecessary luxury. Remember, too, that on most European airlines, business class is open to anyone traveling on a normal coach-class fare (called full economy in Europe).

Fares between London and Amsterdam are the cheapest in Europe. Amsterdam's Schiphol Airport also has excellent onward connections to other European cities. Fares from London to Brussels are also lower than the European average, mile for mile, and there is an increasing range of competitive service to Frankfurt and to Paris.

The rule of thumb is that the cheaper the fare, the more likely it is to carry a burden of restrictions. *Always* make sure you know what these are—ask the airline or travel agent before you buy the ticket.

Some of the more common conditions include a mandatory overnight stay at your destination; no refund, or reduced refund, if you cancel your reservation; no change of itinerary allowed once you have booked; full payment at time of booking; and, most commonly, a minimum stay requirement.

Charter Airlines Charter airlines offer much cheaper fares to Europe than the scheduled carriers, but the rules that bind them are even more restrictive. While the British government turns a blind eye to sales of "seat-only" charter tickets, some European governments still require proof that you have bought an inclusive package vacation rather than just a flight.

Most of the seat-only agencies will therefore give you a voucher stating that you have accommodations at a certain hotel. This is to comply with the rules—it won't get you a bed, even if you can find the hotel in question!

Greece specifically has expressed its determination to stamp out seat-only traffic this year by threatening passengers using such tickets with fines or deportation under international rules on charter sales.

Charter flights are by far the cheapest form of air transport to main vacation destinations—particularly in the Mediterranean—and some of the charter fares available to last-minute buyers compare favorably even with bus or rail fares. To such destinations as Spain, Greece, Turkey, or Italy, charter flights represent big savings over scheduled fares because these countries are zealously protective of their national carriers and oppose the introduction of cheap scheduled fares by BA or other British carriers.

The main drawback of traveling by charter is its rigid timetabling. Your return flight will be seven, 14, or 21 days from your departure date. The cheapest flights leave at inconvenient times—mainly in the early hours of the morning—and from airports a long way from the city center, such as Luton. Another disadvantage to charter flights is that they can be seriously unreliable timekeepers. Delays of several hours are quite common, and a vacation can easily be ruined by the frustration of having to hang around a crowded airport that has inadequate facilities for handling large crowds for long periods.

Arrival airports are often resorts rather than capital or major cities. In Spain, most charters fly to the Mediterranean coast rather than to Madrid or Seville; in Portugal, most flights arrive in the Algarve resort area rather than Lisbon. In Greece, this system can be an advantage rather than a drawback—most flights go to the islands rather than to Athens, so if your destination is, for example, Mykonos or Crete, you can fly there direct by charter without having to transfer to domestic flights or ferries at Athens.

Charters bought at the last minute can be extremely cheap—check in travel agents' windows or in the classified sections of the *London Evening Standard* for cheap late-booking deals. Some of these may be so inexpensive that you may consider discarding the return half of the ticket and traveling onward in Europe from your arrival point, rather than coming back to London.

From the United Kingdom by Car

Traveling by car in Europe has outstanding advantages, not the least of which is freedom from dependence on public transport networks, and the ability to explore off the beaten track and away from major cities.

For advice on whether to bring your own car, or to buy or rent one on your trip, *see* Renting, Leasing and Purchasing Cars in Before You Go.

Most people's reason for traveling by car is to see as much as possible, and for that reason the shortest sea routes—from Dover to Calais and Boulogne—will be the best bet, especially for first-time visitors to Europe. However, if you plan to tour Scandinavia, you may find it worthwhile to travel by sea to Esbjerg in Denmark, or Gothenburg in Sweden; similarly, if your target is the Iberian Peninsula (Spain and Portugal), sailing to Santander cuts out a long drive through France.

Ferries are "ro-ro"—roll-on, roll-off—and you must book ahead if you are traveling by car; rates vary according to the length of your vehicle, the time of your crossing, and whether you plan to travel in peak, shoulder, or low season. Morning and evening crossings in the summer months are most expensive, and national holidays should be avoided where possible.

Both the **Automobile Association** (Fanum House, Basingstoke, Hants. RG21 2EA) and the **Royal Automobile Club** (RAC Motoring Services Ltd., 49 Pall Mall, London SW1Y 5JG) operate on-the-spot breakdown repair services and have tow facilities to get you and your car to your destination within the United Kingdom in case of serious breakdown. Cost of full membership is around $60.

Customs and immigration checks at most entry points are routine, and you will frequently be waved through without inspection of your vehicle. European customs officials do, however, have the authority to randomly spot-check vehicles and documents. If you are driving a rented car, the rental company will have provided you with all necessary papers; if the vehicle is your own, you will need proof of ownership, certificate of roadworthiness (known in the United Kingdom as a Ministry of Transport road vehicle certificate, "MOT" for short), up-to-date vehicle tax, and a Green Card proof of insurance, available from the AA or RAC for a fee of £15.

From the United Kingdom by Ferry/Ship

Ferry routes for passengers and vehicles link the British North Sea, English Channel, and Atlantic ports with almost all of Britain's maritime neighbors.

The Fast Routes By far the busiest and for most visitors the most convenient routes are those connecting the English Channel ports with France and Belgium. The fastest services are the Hovercraft routes between Dover and Calais, making the 22-mile crossing in around 40 minutes with both passengers and cars. Another high-tech route is the passengers-only Dover–Ostend Jetfoil service operated by the Belgian company RTM that is timed to connect with London–Brussels trains.

While making the crossing in less than half the time of conventional ferry vessels, both the Hovercraft and the Jetfoil are more expensive and more likely to be canceled or delayed by bad weather, especially in winter.

To France Travelers to France have a choice of crossings, ranging from the **Sally Lines** service between Ramsgate and Dunkirk in the north, to the **Brittany Ferries** route between Portsmouth and St. Malo in Brittany. If Paris is your final destination, Calais and Boulogne are the most convenient entry ports; they are linked by an excellent freeway *(autoroute)* to Paris, and ferries connect with trains at the port for travelers without cars.

Sailing to St. Malo cuts out the rather dull drive through northern France and delivers you directly to Brittany. The crossing, however, takes about 20 hours as compared with two or three hours for the shortest Channel ferry crossings. Furthermore, sailings are much less frequent (every two days as opposed to several times a day), and for passengers without cars the rail connections onward into France are not as good as those at Calais, Boulogne, or Dieppe.

To Spain and Portugal Brittany Ferries, which runs the St. Malo service, also sails three times a week from Plymouth in the west of England to Santander in northern Spain. The crossing takes 24 hours and the line's "cruise ferries" offer economy and luxury cabins as well as entertainment facilities that include a cinema and restaurants. If you are traveling by car and plan to tour Spain, this route offers you the option of looping back through France and returning to Britain without retracing your tracks. Onward travel into Spain without a car, however, will be time-consuming and is really an option only for those with plenty of time to spare.

To the Northern Countries For travelers heading north to Germany, the Netherlands, or Scandinavia, there are ferry routes linking British east coast ports with Europe's North Sea coast. Crossings are longer than English Channel routes, and most North Sea ferry lines have adopted the "ferry-cruise" concept, with cabins in varying degrees of comfort, and on-board facilities that can include duty-free shopping, bars, restaurants, discos, and casinos.

Main operators between the United Kingdom and the Netherlands are **Olau Line,** which sails from Sheerness; **North Sea Ferries,** sailing from Hull; and **Sealink,** sailing from Harwich. The main Dutch ports are Rotterdam, Hook of Holland, and Vlissingen. All three Dutch ports have excellent connections to Amsterdam by road and rail.

DFDS Seaways sails from Harwich and Newcastle to the Danish west coast port of Esbjerg and onward to Gothenburg in Sweden. The sea voyage to Gothenburg takes just under 24 hours, and the port is an excellent jumping-off place for a tour of

Northern Scandinavia—Sweden, Norway, and Finland—by car.

To Germany If northern Germany is on your itinerary, sail to either Esbjerg or the Dutch ports. For southern Germany and Austria, sail to a northern French port and cut across France to Strasbourg.

Passengers without cars will have little trouble finding berths at short notice at any time of year. Peak traffic is in the summer months and during British school breaks, but the ferry lines increase services accordingly. If you are traveling with a car, book ahead—either directly with the ferry line or through a travel agent. Times to avoid if possible are British national holidays, and the school summer vacation period from late July until early September.

To Ireland Ferry lines also link British west coast ports with the Republic of Ireland and with Northern Ireland. Motorists traveling within the British Isles can cross from Stranraer in Scotland to Larne in Northern Ireland, drive through the Republic, and re-enter the United Kingdom via the Cork–Swansea route—or vice versa. Cork has a ferry connection to St. Malo as well, so motorists can use this French connection to travel to the Continent.

Cruises Fewer cruise ships proper, as opposed to luxury ferries, now sail from British ports for European waters. However, **CTC Lines** operates a winter cruise from Southampton, England, to Australia, with stops at Naples and Piraeus (Athens). It is possible to book these sectors and travel on independently, or fly back to the United Kingdom as part of the fare package.

Useful Addresses For information on the services mentioned above, contact:
Brittany Ferries, Brittany Ferry Centre, Wharf Rd., Portsmouth, Hants. P02 8RU, tel. 0705/819416.
DFDS Seaways, Scandinavia House, Parkeston Quay, Harwich, C012 4QG, tel. 0255/554681.
Hoverspeed, Maybrook House, Queens Gdns., Dover, Kent CT17 7UQ, tel. 01/5547061.
North Sea Ferries, King George Dock, Hedon Rd., Hull HU9 5QA, tel. 0482/796145.
Olau Line, Ferry Terminal, Sheerness, Kent ME12 1SN, tel. 0795/666666.
P&O European Ferries, Channel View Rd., Dover, Kent CT17 9TJ, tel. 0800/456456.
Sealink, 163/203 Eversholt St., London NW1 1BG, tel. 01/3871234.

From the United Kingdom by Train

Air travel may offer the fastest point-to-point service, car travel the greatest freedom, and bus transportation the lowest fares, but there is still an unparalleled air of romance about setting off for Europe by train from one of the historic London stations.

Boat trains timed to meet ferries at Channel ports leave London/Victoria station and connect with onward trains at the main French and Belgian ports. Calais and Boulogne have the best quick connections for Paris (total journey time about six to seven hours using the cross-Channel Hovercraft); the Dover-Ostend Jetfoil service is the fastest rail connection to Brussels (about 5½ hours, station to station) with good rail connections to Germany, northern France, the German Democratic Republic, Poland, and the U.S.S.R.

Boat trains connecting with ferries from Harwich to the Dutch and Danish North Sea ports leave from London/Liverpool Street; there are good rail connections from the Dutch ports to Amsterdam and onward to Germany and Belgium, and south to France.

For the Republic of Ireland, trains connecting with the ferry services across the Irish Sea leave from London/Paddington.

One-way and return city-to-city tickets, including rail and ferry fares, can be booked in the United States through **BritRail**, either directly or through your travel agent. If you are traveling on one of the European rail passes bookable in the States or in Britain, you may be entitled to free or discounted ferry crossings *(see* Getting Around Europe By Train).

If all international rail journeys have a certain glamor, the *Venice Simplon-Orient-Express*, leaving London/Victoria for the Channel crossing and arriving in Venice 32 hours later after a spectacular journey over the Alps, must be the most glamorous of all. This reconditioned vintage train leaves twice weekly and costs upward from £620.

Useful Addresses For European rail information, contact: **InterCity Europe,** the international wing of **BritRail,** at London/Victoria station. Information tel. 01/834–2345; reservations tel. 01/828–9892. Bookings can be made by phone using American Express, MasterCard, and Visa.

From the United Kingdom by Bus

Excellent freeways (motorways) in the United Kingdom link London with the English Channel ferry ports and make bus travel—connecting with fast ferry, Jetfoil, or Hovercraft crossings—only a little slower than rail travel on the shorter routes into Europe.

Bus travel to cities such as Paris, Brussels, Amsterdam, Rotterdam, and Bruges is by fast and comfortable modern buses with reclining seats, air-conditioning, video entertainment, and airplane-style refreshment carts. There are frequent departures from central London pickup points. Fares by bus are a good deal less than the equivalent rail fare.

Eurolines—a consortium of bus operators that includes the British companies **Wallace Arnold, National Express,** and **Grey Green,** as well as Dutch, Belgian, and French lines—offers a range of day and night services linking London with Amsterdam, Paris, Antwerp, Brussels, and other points en route. Night services to Paris take about 10¼ hours; overnight journey time to Amsterdam is a little more than 13 hours.

Faster **Citysprint** daytime crossings use the Dover–Ostend Jetfoil service en route to Amsterdam, reducing journey time to a little more than eight hours. The fast Hoverspeed crossing to France cuts the day trip time to Paris to just under seven hours. There are also one-day round-trips to Antwerp and Brussels and **Eurobreakaway** holiday packages with accommodations for 2–3 nights in Paris, Amsterdam, and Brussels.

National Express uses Sealink British Ferries connections to the Republic of Ireland. A connecting bus service in Ireland is operated by **Bus Eireann.** Sailings are from Fishguard to Rosslare—a 3½-hour crossing. The onward service goes via Waterford and Cork to Killarney and Tralee.

There are summer coach tours to the Spanish vacation resorts, aimed mainly at British families on a tight vacation budget. If you, too, are on a budget, these can be an inexpensive way of getting to Spain. The same is true for the winter coaches that run to Europe's less expensive ski destinations, notably Andorra and some Italian resorts.

Longer-haul coaches operate to Greece, aiming mainly at the student and backpacker market, but these tend to be less comfortable and, to a certain extent, less safe. Roads deteriorate rapidly once you leave Western Europe, and the overused and narrow main highway through Yugoslavia is to be avoided. Coach travel to Greece and Turkey is only for the really budget-conscious, and even then the savings on the lowest charter airfare are not very great; return bus fare to Athens, costing about £90 to £100, or to Istanbul at £120 to £150 (1988 prices), is only £30 or so cheaper than the lowest airfare.

Getting Around Europe

By Car

Touring Europe by car has tremendous advantages over other ways of seeing the Continent. You can go where you want, when you want, traveling at your own pace, free of the petty restrictions of timetables. But there are pitfalls too. For the American driver, used to a uniform system of signs and traffic rules from coast to coast, and accustomed to being able to ask directions in English, Europe can be a bewildering experience. On the excellent freeways of northern and central Europe, it's quite possible to drive through three or four countries in less time than it would take to cross one of the larger of the U.S. states—which means that in one day you may have to cope with perhaps four different languages and four sets of traffic rules!

Road Conditions In general, the richer European countries—Germany, Holland, Denmark, the Benelux countries, the United Kingdom, and Italy—all have excellent national highway systems. In Spain, freeway building is proceeding rapidly and roads are much better than they were even 10 years ago.

By contrast, Greece has just two stretches of freeway-type road—the Odos Ethnikos, or National Road, between Athens and Salonika, and the main road between Athens and Patras.

Portugal, of the western European countries, still lags furthest behind in freeway building, but the factor that holds it back—it is the poorest country in western Europe—also means that far fewer people own cars, so its relatively poor roads are also less crowded.

Traffic Conditions On the freeway, U.S. drivers may find the pace of European traffic alarming. Speed limits in most countries are set much higher than those in the States. Even on British motorways, where the upper limit is a conservative 70 mph (113 kph), it is not uncommon to be passed by vehicles traveling 15–20 mph (24–32 kph) faster than that. On German *autobahns*, French *autoroutes*, or Italian *autostrade*, cars in the fast lane are often moving at 100 mph (160 kph). Much of the time traffic is heavier than is common on U.S. freeways outside major city rush hours.

That said, most tourists will find it more rewarding to avoid the freeways and use the alternative main routes—"A" roads on British road maps, or *routes nationales* in France. On these roads, where traffic moves more slowly, driving at a more leisurely pace is possible, and stopping en route is easier. This can also save money; many European freeways (such as those of France, Spain, Italy, and Greece) are toll roads, and a day's drive on them can be expensive. If you break down on any of the European highways, you can expect to pay a hefty fee for towing unless you have prudently joined one of the motorist plans offered by one of the many national associations such as the AA or RAC in Britain (*see* From the United Kingdom by Car in Getting to Europe).

As in many U.S. states, traffic officers in most European countries (with a few exceptions, such as the United Kingdom) are empowered to fine you on the spot for traffic violations. The language barrier will not make your case any easier.

In Spain, make sure you carry insurance that provides bail bond in case of an accident. This advice also holds good for Greece. When driving a rental car in Greece, beware of damaging the underside of the vehicle on Greek roads, which are among the worst in Europe. Normal collision damage waiver, even from one of the major international chains, may not cover such damage, and you could face a crippling fine.

In Eastern Europe, police and frontier officials will pay much closer attention to your papers than in the West, but roads are emptier and foreign drivers still a novelty. The language barrier may be greater, but the novelty value has been known to lead to foreigners being let off with a warning where local drivers might be fined for minor offenses.

Road Signs In some European countries—Bulgaria, Greece, and parts of Yugoslavia—the language barrier is compounded by an alphabet barrier. Main road signs in Greece for example, are written in the Greek alphabet. The only solution is to carry a good map.

Rules of the Road In the United Kingdom, the Republic of Ireland, Cyprus, and Gibraltar, cars drive on the left. In other European countries, traffic is on the right. Beware the transition when coming off ferries from Britain or Ireland to the Continent (and vice versa)!

Dangerous Times During peak vacation periods, main routes can be jammed with holiday traffic. In the United Kingdom, try to avoid driving during any of the long "Bank Holiday" (public holiday) weekends, when motorways, particularly in the south, can be totally clogged with traffic. In France, where huge numbers of people still take a fixed one-month vacation in August, avoid driving during *le depart*, the first weekend in August, when vast numbers of drivers head south; or *le retour*, when they head back.

Many German families drive to the Yugoslavian or Greek beaches for their summer vacations and, in the months of June and July, the main highways of Yugoslavia—which are at any time among Europe's worst roads—can also be horrendously overcrowded.

Frontiers You may be surprised at the relatively casual approach many European countries have toward border controls for drivers. At many frontiers, you may simply be waved through; it is quite possible, for example, to drive from Amsterdam to the Federal Republic of Germany, via Belgium and France, without once being stopped for customs or immigration formalities. There are, however, spot checks at all borders, and at some— particularly those checkpoints used by heavy commercial truck traffic—there can be long delays at peak times. Ask tourist offices or motoring associations for latest advice on ways to avoid these tie-ups. Remember that, when crossing from western Europe into Eastern Bloc countries, papers are likely to be rigorously inspected at all times.

By Train

European railway systems vary from the sublime to the ridiculous in terms of comfort and convenience. France, Germany, and the United Kingdom have led the field in developing high-speed trains. The **French National Railroads'** (SNCF's) *Train à Grande Vitesse* (TGV), for example, takes just 4½ hours from Paris to the Mediterranean. The TGV also runs to Grenoble (3 hrs., 10 mins.) and Geneva (3½ hrs.).

BritRail operates high-speed InterCity 125 trains—with a top speed of 125 mph (202 kph)—on its north-south routes between London and Scotland. Normal fares apply on the BritRail high-speed services, but there is a supplementary fare for travel on French TGV services.

The Federal German rail system **Deutsche Bundesbahn** (DB, known in the States as GermanRail) last year wrested the world rail speed record from the French, and its high-speed InterCity trains make rail travel the best public transport option within Germany.

International trains link most European capital cities, including those of Eastern Europe; service is offered several times daily. Generally, customs and immigration formalities are completed on the train by officials who board when it crosses the frontier.

Most European systems operate a two-tier, sometimes three-tier, class system, with first class substantially the most expensive. The only outstanding advantage of first class is that it is likely to be less crowded on busier routes. Train journeys in Europe tend to be shorter than in the States—trains are much faster and distances much shorter—so first-class rail travel is usually a luxury rather than a necessity. Some of the poorer European countries retain a third class, but avoid it unless you are on a rock-bottom budget.

A number of European airlines and railways operate fast train connections to their hub airports, and these can sometimes be booked through the airline's computer reservation service. The **Lufthansa Express** connects Frankfurt and Cologne/Bonn airports and is a splendid two-hour scenic journey along the Rhine valley.

Trains in Sweden and Norway offer supreme comfort, but greater distances and the more rugged terrain make for longer journey times; if you are on a tight schedule you may prefer to take internal flights.

In Italy, there are some excellent rail services between major cities—but be sure that the train you book *is* a main intercity service, not one that stops at every minor station. Off the major lines, Italian rail services are slower and less frequent.

Trains are generally to be avoided in Spain and Portugal as point-to-point transportation—though there are some attractive scenic routes and special tourist trains. In Greece and Turkey anyone but the most fanatical rail traveler will find the more frequent, modern, and comfortable buses preferable to the trains, which are slow, unreliable, crowded, and dirty.

Rail travel is vital to most Eastern Bloc countries, and services within and between them are better and more comfortable than you might expect. Though usually much slower than the more modern western European trains, service is frequent and reliable.

Scenic Routes While the high-speed expresses are an ideal and comfortable way of getting from one place to another, travelers who delight in train travel for its own sake will find plenty to please them in Europe's smaller rail lines.

In Norway and Sweden, almost any train journey offers a superb view of some of Europe's most grandiose scenery. The trains of Switzerland, Austria, and Czechoslovakia are also a comfortable way to view impressive mountain vistas.

In Portugal, rail travel is not ideal, but there are some charming journeys to be made on small local trains. For instance, the rail line north from Oporto to Viana do Castelo and the Spanish border, passes through picturesque small towns and crosses over two remarkable river bridges built by Gustav Eiffel, designer of Paris's famed landmark. Branch lines from the same route run through some of Europe's prettiest and least-developed rural countryside.

Special tourist trains operate in many countries in Europe, a number of them using historic rolling stock or original steam engines. The **Venice Simplon-Orient-Express** uses the original sleeping and dining cars and coaches of Europe's most romantic train (*see* From the United Kingdom by Train in Getting to Europe). In Scotland, the **Royal Scot** travels the spectacular glens of the Highlands with antique cars from the heyday of rail travel. In southern England, the **Bluebell Railway** is a private line only a few miles in length run by a group of steam enthusiasts and using an old-time coal-fired steam engine and matching cars; it makes a pleasant day trip from London.

In Spain, a "tourist" special runs in the summer months through the pretty north coast country of Cantabria and Asturias, leaving from Santander. From Seville, the luxurious **Andalus Express** uses four vintage cars built in the 1920s and operates five-day rail cruises via Cordoba and Granada to Málaga. The train features its own bar—open to 3 AM—with live music and dancing, restaurant cars, and a video and game room.

National tourist offices in the United States or in London, and national rail network offices, are the best sources of information on these tourist specials, some of which may operate for one season only.

Rail Passes Almost all European countries offer discount rail passes; details are given in the appropriate country chapter. Here is a listing of the rail passes available before you leave.

The **EurailPass,** valid for unlimited first-class train travel through 16 countries (Austria, Belgium, Denmark, Finland, France, West Germany, Greece, Holland, Ireland, Italy, Luxembourg, Norway, Portugal, Spain, Sweden, and Switzerland), is the best value ticket for visitors from outside Europe. The ticket is available for 15 days ($298), 21 days ($370), one month ($470), two months ($650), and three months ($798). For visitors 26 and under, there is the **Eurail Youthpass,** for one or two months' unlimited second-class train travel, at $320 and $420. The EurailPass does not cover Great Britain and is available only to those who live outside Europe or North Africa. The pass must be bought from an authorized agent before you leave home. Apply through your travel agent, or one of the following: **French National Railroads, GermanRail,** or **Italian State Railways**—for details *see* Useful Addresses below.

For those who want to spread out their train journeys, there's the new **Eurail Flexipass,** which gives travelers unlimited first-class train travel on any nine days in a 21-day period. The Flexipass costs $310.

For European travelers under 26, the **Inter-Rail card** is an unbeatable value. It is available to people who have been resident in Europe for at least six months, and for one calendar month gives unlimited rail travel in 21 countries—the same as the EurailPass with the addition of Hungary, Morocco, Romania, European Turkey, and Yugoslavia. It also gives half-price travel within the United Kingdom and discounts of up to 50% on some ferry services to and from the United Kingdom. The card costs around £145 and is available from rail stations.

Useful Addresses Full information on rail services within the countries listed here is available from the addresses below. Otherwise, contact the national tourist office of the country concerned.

In the United States and Canada **Belgian National Railroads,** 745 Fifth Ave., New York, NY 10151.
BritRail Travel International Inc., 630 Third Ave., New York, NY 10017; 800 S. Hope St., Los Angeles, CA 90017; Cedar Maple Plaza, 2305 Cedar Springs, Dallas, TX 75201; 94 Cumberland St., Toronto, Ontario M5R 1A3; 409 Granville St., Vancouver, BC V6C 1T2.
French National Railroads, 610 Fifth Ave., New York, NY 10020; 9465 Wilshire Blvd., Beverly Hills, CA 90212; 11 E. Adams St., Chicago, IL 60603; 2121 Ponce de Leon Blvd., Coral Gables, FL 33114; 360 Post St., Union Sq., San Francisco, CA 94108; 1500 Stanley St., Montreal, Quebec H3A 1R3; 409 Granville St., Vancouver, BC V6C 1T2.
GermanRail, 747 Third Ave., New York, NY 10017; 625 Salter Office Bldg., Boston, MA 02116; 95–97 W. Higgins Rd., Suite 505, Rosemont, IL 60018; 112 S. Ervay St., Dallas, TX 75201; 11933 Wilshire Blvd., Los Angeles, CA 90025; 442 Post St., 6th Floor, San Francisco, CA 94102; 8000 E. Girard Ave., Suite

518S, Denver, CO 80231; 1290 Bay St., Toronto, Ontario M5R 2C3.

Italian State Railways, 666 Fifth Ave., New York, NY 10103.

In the United **Belgian National Railways,** 22–25A Sackville St., London W1X
Kingdom 1DE.

DFDS (Danish) Seaways, Scandinavia House, Parkeston Quay, Harwich CO12 4QG.

French Railways, French Railways House, 179 Piccadilly, London W1V 9DB.

Netherlands Railways, 25–28 Buckingham Gate, London SW1E 6LD.

Norwegian State Railways Travel Bureau, 21–24 Cockspur St., London SW1Y 5BN.

Swiss Federal Railways, Swiss Center, 1 New Coventry St., London W1V 8EE.

By Plane

Getting around Europe by air is complicated by the fact that almost every country—with the exception of Britain—has its own state-owned airline, and despite moves toward a more liberal policy, many governments are still bent on protecting the earnings of their pet carrier. Licences to operate on a given international or internal route are issued by governments, and international route licences are in most cases still issued on the basis of bilateral agreements between the two countries in question. This means that bus stop-style services, like those so common in the States, do not yet exist in Europe, though they may begin to appear in the near future. So-called "fifth freedom" licences, which grant airlines the right to land and pick up passengers at intermediary points on a given route, are jealously guarded by governments and consequently are hard to come by. This makes touring Europe entirely by air a costly process, and the best bet, if you plan to visit a number of European countries, is to combine air travel with other transport options.

Hub Airports As in the USA, airlines are developing 'hub and spoke'-style services within Europe. The idea is that you take a transatlantic flight to an airline's hub, then continue on its intra-European services to other European cities. Thus, **SAS** is actively developing Copenhagen as a Scandinavian hub; **KLM** is doing the same at Schiphol; **BA** at London Heathrow and Gatwick; and **Lufthansa** at Frankfurt. If you plan to fly to other European cities, one of these hubs is your obvious choice.

Domestic Services Most western European countries have good internal services linking the capital city with major business and industrial centers, and with more remote communities. In West Germany, France, and Spain, regional flights tend to connect major business cities rather than areas of touristic interest—though in Spain there is a considerable overlap between the two.

In such countries as Sweden, Norway, Greece, and to some extent the United Kingdom, however, air services are a vital link between remote island and mountain communities and are often subsidized by the central government. In Greece, for example, you can fly very inexpensively between Athens and the islands—though not *between* islands.

Before booking an internal flight, consider the alternatives. Flights from London to Edinburgh take about one hour—airport to airport—while the competing BritRail InterCity train takes 4½ hours. But if you factor in the hour needed to get from central London to the airport, the need to check in as much as one hour before departure, the inevitable flight delays, the time spent waiting for luggage on arrival, and the transfer time back into town from Edinburgh Airport—you'll find you may not have saved any more than an hour in travel time for a considerably higher fare. When looking into air travel as an option, remember that distances between European cities can be deceptively short to an eye accustomed to U.S. routings.

Formalities For scheduled flights, you will be asked to check in at least one hour before departure; for charter flights, generally two hours. These are guidelines; if you are traveling with just hand luggage, it is possible to check in as late as 30 minutes before takeoff time. European luggage allowances are based on total weight of your checked luggage, not, as in the United States, on the number of bags. The usual allowance is 44 pounds (20 kilograms).

You may be pleasantly surprised by the Green Channel/Red Channel customs system in operation at most western European airports and at other international frontier posts. Basically, this is an honor system: If you have nothing to declare, you walk through the Green Channel without needing to open your bags for inspection. There are, however, random spot checks, and penalties for abusing the system can be severe. If in doubt, go through the Red Channel.

Eastern Europe Eastern European countries need hard Western currency so badly that they try not to set airfares at intolerably high levels. Most routes are operated in tandem with Western carriers, however, and anyone with an eye to comfort and safety will prefer the latter.

By Bus

If you have opted for land rather than air travel, the choice between rail and bus is a major decision. In countries such as Britain, France, Germany, and Holland, bus travel was, until recently, something of a poor man's option—slow, uncomfortable, and cheap. Today, though, fast modern buses travel on excellent highways and offer standards of service and comfort comparable to those on a train—but still at generally lower fares. Between major cities and over long distances, trains are still preferable, but buses will take you to places that trains often do not reach.

In several southern European countries—including Portugal, Greece, much of Spain, and Turkey—the bus has supplanted the train as the main means of public transportation, and is often quicker, more frequent, and more comfortable than the antiquated rolling stock of the national rail system. Choose the bus over the rail in these countries unless there is a particular scenic rail route or a special tourist train you want to use. But be prepared to discover that the bus is now more expensive than the lowly railway. Competition among lines is keen, so compare services such as air-conditioning or reclining seats before you buy.

Information Information on bus transportation in most countries is available from national or regional tourist offices. For reservations on major bus lines, contact your travel agent at home. For smaller bus companies on regional routes, you may have to go to a local travel agency or to the bus line office.

Note that travel agencies may be affiliated with a certain line and won't always tell you about alternative services—you may have to do some legwork to be sure of getting the best service.

By Ferry/Ship

Bounded by the sea on three sides and crossed by a number of major rivers, Europe offers an abundance of choice for anyone who loves water travel.

The Baltic In the north, ferries ply daily between most of the major Baltic ports in western Europe as well as between Finnish ports and those of the Soviet Union. Baltic crossings are not for those in a hurry—several of them last overnight—and shipping lines operate luxury cruise-ferry vessels with all kinds of entertainment facilities and duty-free shopping.

Local ferries ply the Norwegian fjords and are an excellent way of seeing the country, whether you are traveling by car or on public transportation; a fjord trip in mid-summer, the time of the Midnight Sun in north Norway, should not be missed.

Main international Baltic ports are Copenhagen, Gothenburg, Malmö, Stockholm, Helsinki, Kristiansand, and Oslo—also Stavanger and Bergen on Norway's Atlantic coast, Hamburg and Travemunde in West Germany, and Leningrad in the Soviet Union.

Scotland Ferry services are important, too, in the Scottish Western Isles, where the **Caledonian Macbrayne Ltd.** (The Ferry Terminal, Gourock, Renfrewshire PA19 1QP, Scotland) has enjoyed a virtual monopoly for many years on its services linking the islands to the mainland port of Oban. The northern Scottish islands of the Orkney and Shetland groups are served by sea from Scrabster on the north coast of mainland Scotland—near John O'Groats.

Greece Interisland ferries play an important part in the Mediterranean, too, particularly among the Greek islands. Many island communities have formed cooperative companies to operate services linking their island with others and with Piraeus, the port of Athens. While all Baltic ferries offer high standards of comfort, even luxury—at commensurately high fares—Mediterranean ferry lines observe widely differing standards. On Greek ships, for example, you can travel in a first- or second-class cabin, or rough it in deck class for a much lower fare. The same is true for the international ferries plying between the Italian ports of Bari and Brindisi, and the Greek ports of Corfu, Igoumenitsa, and Patras. The age of Greek ferry boats varies widely too. Some are of pre-World War II vintage, while others —like the *Naxos*, which sails between Piraeus and Crete—are modern vessels. For Greek ferry information, contact the **National Tourist Organization of Greece** in New York or London.

Flying Dolphin Lines operates fast hydrofoil service from Piraeus to points popular with Athenian vacationers, including

2 Albania

Introduction

At a time when the Soviet Union is testing the waters of change with *glasnost* and *perestroika* and China has had its first tastes of free enterprise, Albania remains resolutely Marxist. It is a country where the name Stalin is still held in esteem and where the hard line of the '40s has hardly wavered in more than four decades of strict Communist power. True, Enver Hoxha, the founder of the modern Albanian system and contemporary of his neighbor Marshal Tito of Yugoslavia, has been dead four years, but there is little sign of his influence waning in the near future. Albania is officially skeptical of the "deviationist" leanings of its former mentors, the Soviet Union and China, and considers itself untainted by challenges to its collectivist ideology.

An important aspect of Albania's hard line has been a *total ban on visitors from the United States*, and this is still in effect. People from Canada and Britain can visit—on guided tours. Travel and accommodations are strictly organized, and there is little scope for exploring the country beyond the prearranged itinerary.

Despite all these restrictions—and perhaps because of Albania's self-imposed isolation—the country is a fascinating place to visit. On one level, it can be seen as almost a time capsule, a safe, quiet retreat from the frenetic pace of modern life, where private cars are unknown and crime seems not to exist. There are no tourist traps; medieval mosques and churches still dominate the traditional architecture of many villages, although these are now secular buildings in this officially atheistic state. On another level, Albania is a grim monument to social engineering, an authoritarian nightmare-come-true for many visitors.

Albania has the same rugged countryside as its neighbors, Greece and Yugoslavia. It also has long stretches of beach, but while these would be prime sites for modern hotels and tourist facilities in either of these other two countries, in Albania they remain deserted. From parts of Albania you can look across only three miles (five kilometers) of water to the popular Greek island of Corfu, which, for all its nearness, is inaccessible from Albania.

Before You Go

When to Go Most tours to Albania are scheduled from April to October, but midsummer is likely to be very hot and surprisingly humid at times. It's best to visit in spring or fall, or go in summer and arrange to spend part of the time in the cooler mountains.

The following are the average daily maximum and minimum temperatures for Tirana.

Jan.	53F	12C	May	74F	23C	Sept.	81F	27C
	36	2		53	12		58	14
Feb.	54F	12C	June	82F	28C	Oct.	73F	23C
	36	2		60	16		50	10
Mar.	59F	15C	July	87F	31C	Nov.	63F	17C
	41	5		63	17		47	8
Apr.	65F	18C	Aug.	89F	31C	Dec.	56F	14C
	47	8		62	17		40	5

Albania

Currency The Albanian unit of currency is the lek, divided into 100 qindarkas. There are bills of 1, 3, 5, 10, 25, 50, and 100 leks; coins are for 5, 10, 20, 50 qindarkas, and 1 lek. At press time (fall 1988), there were 14 leks to the pound sterling. Albania insists that no one take leks out of the country, so remember to change your unwanted local currency before leaving. Like the countries of the Eastern bloc, Albania has a number of hard currency stores, where local currency is not accepted. Don't expect to get your change in the same currency, though.

What It Will Cost With travel, food, and accommodations already paid for as part of most package tours to Albania, the cost while there is low. Dining and drinking—outside your hotel—are cheap, and stores tend to be understocked, making it difficult to spend very much anyway.

Sample Prices Cup of coffee, 3 leks; bottle of beer, 3 leks; bottle of mineral water, 2 leks; meat risotto, 5 leks.

Visas Visas are required for all visits to Albania; these are arranged by the tour operator, who will include your name on a group visa. You will need to pay a fee (about £11 for Canadians, £7 for Britons) and have four passport-style photographs. The visa process takes time to arrange, so apply early. It is also essential that your passport be valid for the duration of your stay in Albania.

Customs on Arrival You should be on safe ground if you pack as if the customs official is a puritanical atheist with an overriding sense of nationalism. It would be impossible to list all the publications considered offensive, but it is safe to assume that Albanian customs sheds are full of Bibles, political books, Superman comics, and even Fodor's guides.

Because you will be judged by your appearance, women should dress modestly and bearded men should shave or trim their beards. There are stories of unappreciated hair being removed on the spot.

Many consumer items—watches, electric razors, calculators—are registered when you arrive; keep track of them, so you won't face a charge of disposing of them while in the country.

Language Albanian is a beautiful but very difficult language. It uses the Roman alphabet and seems to have borrowed more words from other Western languages than have Finnish or Hungarian, for example. Albanian-English and Albanian-French dictionaries are available, but get them before leaving home. You may find some young Albanians who speak a few words of English, which has replaced Russian as the primary foreign language studied in school.

Getting Around

By Bus Because you will almost certainly be in Albania on a group tour, you will usually have no choice but to travel by tour bus. These are comfortable and air-conditioned, but even their strong suspensions cannot cushion against every pothole and rut in roads more accustomed to heavy industrial transport or donkey carts. It is best to be as cheerful as possible about these travel arrangements and to be at meeting points at the right time. Delays can occur, partly because itineraries are subject to last-minute changes by the authorities, but complaining will only make things worse and sometimes lengthen the delay.

On Foot Guides discourage visitors from going around on their own, even in centers where you are likely to be staying for several days. Still, you will probably be able to find some spare time for a little individual exploring. This is best done on foot because the combined difficulties of language and timetables could make it hard to judge the return times for public transport—mainly buses and occasional taxis.

Essential Information

Arriving and Departing *By Plane*	**Voyages Jules Verne** is the only tour company offering direct London–Tirana flights; these, like all other arrangements to Albania, are part of a group tour, since individual travel is not allowed. There are weekly flights from other European capitals, including Pakistan International Airlines's direct flight from Paris and Alitalia's Rome–Bari–Tirana connection. All tours include bus connections from the airport to the center of Tirana.
By Bus	Nearly every tour goes via Yugoslavia, ending in Titograd for the bus trip over the border to Shkoder in Albania.
Guided Tours	Since there is no individual travel to Albania, you must go with a package tour company. Tours include all fares and airport taxes, accommodations with full board, entrance fees to archaeological sites and museums, the services of a tour leader, and the assistance of an English-speaking Albanian guide. The following companies all operate from Britain: **Regent Holidays (U.K.) Ltd.**, 13 Small St., Bristol BS1 1DE, tel. 0272/211711. **Serenissima Travel Ltd.**, 21 Dorset Sq., London NW1 6QG, tel. 01/730–9841. **Swan-Hellenic Tours**, 77 Oxford St., London WC1A 1PP, tel. 01/831–1616. **Voyages Jules Verne**, 10 Glentworth St., London NW1 5PG, tel. 01/486–8080.
Telephones	Public telephones are located in post offices, which are open daily from 8 AM to 10 PM. International calls can be made, although these may take a long time. A three-minute call (minimum) to the United Kingdom costs about 50 leks; each additional minute costs 16 leks. You can also make calls from some of the larger hotels. Inquire at the desk to see if the rates are competitive.
Mail *Postal Rates*	It costs 1 lek to mail a letter to Britain and a bit more to the United States or Canada. It is a good idea to take advantage of the cheap postal rates to send locally purchased books home, especially if you are returning via Yugoslavia, where these could be confiscated.
Shopping	With a bit of effort and perseverance, you can find some good buys in gifts or souvenirs. Traditional crafts reflect the influences of former trading partners or invaders. Carpets and goods made of silver can be of very high quality, as are some silk and cotton goods. Local department stores, called Ma-Po, reinforce the preconceived notion of drab life in a state with little choice of goods; these accept leks only. Other stores in or around the major hotels accept Western currencies and have a correspondingly wider range of products for sale. The town of Gjirokastër sports a bustling old-style bazaar.
Photography	Do not take pictures of docks, military establishments, or military personnel. Because Albanians, particularly in rural areas, are not used to tourists with cameras, ask their permission before you take their pictures; they seldom object, however. If necessary, ask your guide to translate your request.
Opening and Closing Times	**Banks.** Banks are usually open 7:30–11:30 AM. **Museums.** Museum opening times are very peculiar by Western standards. Some are open evenings, 6–8, and some, mornings 10–12. Check locally. **Shops.** Most shops are open 9–12 and 4–7.

National Holidays January 1 (New Year's Day); January 2 (New Year's Observance Day); January 11 (Republic Proclamation Day); May 1 (May Day); November 28 (Independence Proclamation Day); November 29 (Liberation Day).

Dining All meals are included in the cost of an organized tour, but it is worth indulging your curiosity and venturing farther afield if you get a chance. Hotel breakfasts are uneven, although some include a substantial spread of omelet, jam, rolls, and coffee. Lunch is the main meal, usually four courses, starting with soup and finishing—if you are lucky—with fresh fruit. Dinner, a less lavish affair, is usually only three courses, with salad. Outside the hotel, try the meat and cheese pies at a *byrektore*, or pie shop. Cafés are good places for local beers, brandies, fruit juices, or excellent mineral water. Prices are uniformly low.

Lodging Accommodations in Albania are surprisingly comfortable. Many rooms have their own bath or shower, but it is a good idea to pack a rubber stopper or plug. Not all hotels are modern; some are rather frayed at the edges.

Avoid drinking hotel tap water; stick to mineral water, which is excellent and cheap.

Tipping Never tip with cash. If you want to acknowledge good service—from your driver or guide, for example—cigarettes or stockings will be well received.

Emergencies Contact your tour leader or hotel reception personnel first. Through them you can reach either the French or Italian embassies in Tirana; France and Italy are the only major Western countries with full diplomatic relations with Albania.

Medical attention is free, although you will be expected to pay for prescriptions.

Exploring Albania

It would be fruitless even to suggest an itinerary, with travel in Albania so structured and—at times—arbitrary. Still, the following places figure on most tours.

Tirana, the capital, has a population of 300,000. The absence of any real traffic gives the spacious streets an eerie silence at times. Tirana is a capital created in this century, rather like a Balkan Brasília, centrally located in a country divided by mountainous terrain. The old part of town remains attractive, however, and its **mosque** is one of the finest in the country.

Durrës is the country's main port, a popular place for Albanians in search of the beach—the one here is magnificent. A **Roman amphitheater** is still being excavated, and a visit to a local **dairy farm** is a popular choice for tour groups.

Gjirokastër, the birthplace of Enver Hoxha, is the chief town of southern Albania. It spills over deep ravines, with narrow, picturesque streets leading into an attractive—and surprisingly colorful—**bazaar.** The town is dominated by the 13th-century **fortress** on its southwest edge, renovated in the last century under Ali Pasha.

Shkodër, another important town, is on the Yugoslavian border. Dominated by the brooding **fortress of Rozafat,** it was built by the Venetians in the 15th century. Shkodër was once the center of the Roman Catholic Church in Albania, but now it is known for its **Atheist Museum.** The center of town has an interesting market and a **Museum of Albanian Folk Art.**

Saranda is an important port that offers good swimming—but sometimes rough seas—and excellent coastal scenery. You can look across the channel to the Greek island of Corfu several miles away. Nearby are the ruins of the classical city of **Butrint,** with a **Roman theater** and a **baptistery** with vivid mosaics.

Vlorë, farther up the coast, is a port with a good natural harbor and a history that stretches back to the ancient Greeks and includes the Romans, Normans, Venetians, and Ottomans along the way. It is not surprising that it was here, in 1912, that Albania's independence was proclaimed. Vlorë is now the main base for Albania's navy (you run a terrible risk taking photographs of anything remotely naval here).

The medieval town of **Kruja,** perched atop a mountain, is the birthplace of Albania's national hero, Skanderbeg, who led the national resistance against the Turks in the 15th century. The restored castle is now a **museum** devoted to Skanderbeg.

Between these cities the scenery varies dramatically, considering the relatively small distances involved: Albania is about the size of Maryland. Dusty plains give way to rocky coastline on the one side and to rugged mountains on the other. It is worth pointing out again that summer temperatures can soar, and in the absence of air-conditioning, the only respite during that season will be in the mountains.

3 Andorra

Andorra

FRANCE

Pic de Siguer

Pic de Serrera

El Serrat

Pic de l'Estanyó

Coma Pedrosa

Valira del Norte

Sant Joan de Caselles

La Cortinada

Soldeu

Arinsal

Canillo

Ordino

Erts

Valira del Orient

Pal

La Massana

Sanctuary of Meritxell

Port de'Envalira

Encamp

Sant Roma de les Bons

Pas de la Casa

CG-3

Pont de St. Antoni

Alt del Griu

Sant Miguel d'Engolasters

Andorra la Vella ☆

Les Escaldes

Pic de Pessons

Santa Coloma

Ramio

CG-1

Certers

Valira River

SPAIN

Sant Julia de Loria

Juverri

| 0 | | 10 miles |
| 0 | | 15 km |

N

Introduction

Anyone would be forgiven for not pinpointing Andorra immediately on the map, where it resembles a tiny pea pressed between the hulking flanks of southern France and northeastern Spain. Andorra is only 16 miles (25 kilometers) long and 18 miles (29 kilometers) wide—about a quarter the size of the state of Rhode Island. It's situated right in the midst of the Pyrenees, and within the past few years these mountains have provided a major source of tourist income, as Andorra has been hailed as the budget European skiing capital for those whose means can't stretch as far as the more prestigious Alpine resorts. Andorra has another claim to tourist fame—as a bargain basement, whose prices are often as little as half of what you'd expect to pay at home.

The principality's capital, Andorra la Vella, is turning into a nightmare of hurriedly erected high-rise hotels, but outside the capital nothing has disturbed the tranquil medieval atmosphere that hovers about the numerous Romanesque churches, bridges, and shrines dotted throughout the landscape. And the mountain backdrop is nothing short of superb.

Before You Go

When to Go   Winter months bring a huge influx of ski buffs, though any time of year suits those with an eye on Andorra's tax- and duty-free shopping status. Hikers and nature lovers would do best to come in summer, or in the spring, when the mountains are covered with wild orchids and poppies. Be warned that even in summer the nighttime temperatures can drop to freezing.

The following are the average daily maximum and minimum temperatures for Andorra.

Jan.	43F	6C	May	62F	17C	Sept.	71F	22C
	30	−1		43	6		49	10
Feb.	45F	7C	June	73F	23C	Oct.	60F	16C
	30	−1		39	10		42	6
Mar.	54F	12C	July	79F	26C	Nov.	51F	10C
	35	2		54	12		35	2
Apr.	58F	14C	Aug.	76F	24C	Dec.	42F	6C
	39	4		53	12		31	−1

Currency The Spanish peseta is the major Andorran currency, though French francs are also widely accepted. For exchange rates and coinage information, *see* Currency in the France and Spain chapters.

What It Will Cost
Sample Prices Andorra's prices are refreshingly easy on the wallet. At press time, some sample costs were as follows: Coca-cola, 60 ptas.; cup of coffee, 35–40 ptas.; ham sandwich, 200 ptas.; glass of beer, 75 ptas.; one-mile taxi ride, 125 ptas.

Customs Andorra is unusually lax in the matter of customs, duties, visas, and suchlike. Non-Europeans can get in with only a passport. Europeans need only an identity card but as visitors are usually just waved in; the card is almost an irrelevance. (On the way *out* of the country, however, be prepared for mega-traffic jams: The French and Spanish customs officers take their jobs far more seriously than do their Andorran counterparts.)

Language Catalan is the official language, though Spanish and French are heard just as often. English is spoken in most hotels, shops, and ski resorts.

Getting Around

By Car The major road network is very simple and lies in the basic shape of the letter Y, with Andorra la Vella at the crossroads. Most roads are in fine condition and provide beautiful views of the woods, trees, and mountains.

By Bus Minibuses connect the towns and villages; the basic fare is about 60 ptas. Ask at the Sindicat d'Iniciativa for details.

On Foot Two excellent trails traverse the country and are dotted with mountain refuges specifically for hikers' use.

Essential Information

Telephones For local inquiries, tel. 11.

Mail Both French franc and Spanish peseta denominations of Andorran stamps are used, though the postal service within the country is free. The Spanish post office in Andorra la Vella is at Joan Maragall; the French post office is at Avenida Meritxell 39.

Opening and Closing Times **Banks.** Open weekdays 9–1 and 3–5, Saturday 9–noon.

Churches. Most chapels and churches are kept locked around the clock, with the key being left at the closest house. Check with the tourist office for further details.

Shops. Open daily 9–8, though some close 1–3.

National Holidays September 8 (La Verge de Meritxell). Shops open throughout republic except in Meritxell itself, where festival is celebrated.

Local Holidays At *Canillo*, 3rd Saturday in July and following Sunday and Monday; at *Les Escaldes*, July 25–27; at *Sant Julià de Lòria*, last Sunday in July and following Monday and Tuesday at Andorra la Vella, first Saturday, Sunday, Monday in August; at *Encamp* and *La Massana*, August 15–17; at *Ordino*, September 16, 17.

Dining Andorran cooking is a judicious blend of French, Spanish, and Catalan influences. Like so many homespun cuisines, it is both satisfying and delicious. Meats, notably pork and ham, as well as freshly caught fish, are staples; if it's on the menu, try *rostes amb mel* (ham prepared with honey). True to its Spanish heritage, Andorrans eat late: Dinners don't usually get underway until 8:30 at least, and lunch is a substantial meal often followed by an afternoon siesta.

Ratings The following ratings are for a three-course meal for one person. Best bets are indicated by a star ★. At press time, there were 110 pesetas to the dollar.

Category	Cost
Expensive	over 1,700 ptas
Moderate	1,000–1,700 ptas
Inexpensive	under 1,000 ptas

Credit Cards The following credit card abbreviations are used: AE, American Express; DC, Diners Club; MC, MasterCard; V, Visa.

Lodging Most hotels are open year-round. Reservations are necessary during July and August. Hotel rates often include at least two meals.

Ratings As a general guide, the following price ratings apply for a double room. Best bets are indicated by a star ★. At press time, there were 110 pesetas to the dollar.

Category	Cost
Very Expensive	over 7,000 ptas
Expensive	5,000–7,000 ptas
Moderate	3,000–5,000 ptas
Inexpensive	under 3,000 ptas

Credit Cards The following credit card abbreviations are used: AE, American Express; DC, Diners Club; MC, MasterCard; V, Visa.

Tipping Restaurants and cafés almost always tack on a 10–15% service charge; if they don't, it's customary to leave a similar amount.

Andorra la Vella

Arriving and Departing *By Plane*	The closest airport to Andorra la Vella is the Seo de Urgel–Andorra airport (tel. 973/351826), 12 miles (20 kilometers) south over the border in Spain. It is linked to Barcelona International Airport by three daily flights.
Between the Airport and Downtown	A regular bus service shuttles visitors back and forth; the one-way fare is 3,000 ptas. Taxis are available, too.
By Train	From Barcelona, take the train to Puigcerdá, then the bus to Seo de Urgel and Andorra la Vella; from Madrid, a train to Lérida and then a bus to Seo de Urgel and Andorra la Vella; from Toulouse, take the train to Ax-les-Thermes or Tour de Carol (on the route to Perignan), then the bus to Seo de Urgel and Andorra le Vella.
By Bus	A bus service runs twice daily from Barcelona (Ronda Universidad 4).
By Car	There are only two possible routes—the CG-1, which links Andorra with Spain, or the CG-2, which crosses the French border at the Pas de la Casa. (A third route, CG-3, runs due north from Andorra la Vella and dead-ends a few miles short of the combined French and Spanish borders.)
Getting Around	In this tiny capital, buses head down the main street on their way to the next village. Everything in town is accessible by foot.
Important Addresses and Numbers	**Sindicat d'Iniciative** (National Tourist Office), c/o Dr. Vilanova, tel. 628/20214. Open daily year-round, Monday–Saturday 10–1 and 3–7, Sunday and holidays 10–1.
Consulates	**U.S.,** Via Layetana, Barcelona, tel. 93/319–9550; **Canadian,** Nunez de Balboa 35, Madrid, tel. 91/225–9119; **U.K.,** Apartado de Correos 12111, Barcelona, tel. 93/322–2151.
Emergencies	**Doctor,** tel. 628/21905; **Police,** tel. 628/21222; **Ambulance and Fire,** tel. 628/20020.
English Bookstores	American and English newspapers and magazines are widely available at most newsstands and bookstores in the capital.
Travel Agency	**American Express,** in the Relax travel agency, Roc dels Escolls 12, tel. 628/22044.
Guided Tours	Tours of the capital and surrounding countryside are offered by several firms; check with the tourist office for details.

Exploring Andorra

Overlooking Andorra la Vella's main square is the stone bulk of the **Casa de la Vall** (House of the Valleys), a 16th-century medieval building that today acts as the seat of the Andorran government. A charmingly rustic spot, the Casa contains many religious frescoes of note, some of which were carefully transported here from village churches high up in the Pyrenées. The kitchen is particularly interesting, with a splendid array of ancient copper pots and other culinary implements. *Vall St. Free. Open Mon.–Fri. 9–10 and 3–4, Sat. 9–10.*

The spa town of **Escaldes** and the Romanesque church of **Sant Miguel d'Engolasters** are northeast of the capital; the church's tall tower is visible from afar, but you'll have to walk at least half an hour from Escaldes to reach it. Just beyond Encamp, four miles (six kilometers) northeast, is the 11th-century church of **Sant Roma de les Bons,** situated in a particularly picturesque spot of medieval buildings and mountain scenery.

Midway between Encamp and Canillo is the **Sanctuary of Meritxell,** the focal point of the country's prodigious religious fervor. The Blessed Virgin of Meritxell is the principality's patron saint, though oddly enough for such a religious country this patronage was declared only in the late 19th century. The original sanctuary was destroyed by fire in 1972; the new gray stone building looks remarkably like a factory, but the mountain setting is superb. *Free. Open weekdays 10–1, 3:30–6:30, Sat. 10–1; closed Sun.*

Another two miles (three kilometers) farther, just before reaching the town of Canillo, you will see an old stone six-armed cross (actually, five-armed as one has broken off). A mile or so beyond is the Romanesque church of **Sant Joan de Caselles,** whose ancient walls have mellowed with age. The bell tower is stunning, three stories of weathered stone punctuated by rows of arched windows. Inside, the main building is a good example of a *reredos* (a wall or screen positioned behind an altar) dating from 1525 and depicting the life of St. John the Apostle.

Retrace your way back to Andorra la Vella, and this time take the CG-3 due north out of the capital. After just a few miles you'll come to an ancient stone bridge, the **Pont de St. Antoni,** which spans a narrow river. Two miles (three kilometers) farther is the picturesque mountain town of **La Massana;** take some time to stroll along its quaintly rustic streets. Another three miles (five kilometers) on is the tiny village of **Ordino.** Its medieval church is exceptionally pretty; to see it properly, go at night between 7 and 8 when mass is celebrated.

In **La Cortinada,** a mile or so farther, is the **Can Pal,** another fine example of medieval Andorran architecture. This time the building is a privately owned manor house (strictly no admittance), with a pretty dovecote attached. Note the turret perched high up on the far side.

Backtrack once more to Andorra la Vella, then take the CG-1 south. Within a few miles you'll come to the church of **Santa Coloma,** in the village bearing the same name; parts of the church date from the 10th century.

Shopping

Andorra is a dedicated shopper's dream-come-true: Almost every brand-name item will be substantially cheaper, often by as much as 40%. Shopping is also virtually tax-free. The only drawback are the very long lines at the French and Spanish borders, as customs officials check to see what goods you may be trying to smuggle out beneath your floppy sun hat.

Dining and Lodging

For details and price category definitions, *see* Dining and Lodging in Essential Information.

Andorra la Vella **Chez Jacques.** The varied menu in this cozy eatery dwells main-
Dining ly on both classical and nouvelle French dishes, though other international cuisines are handled with flair. It's very popular

with the locals. *Av. Tarragona, tel. 628/20395. No jeans. Reservations accepted. AE, DC, MC, V. Expensive.*

Moli del Fanals. This excellent-value restaurant is atmospherically set in an old windmill and serves mainly classic French dishes. *C/o Dr. Vilanova, Borda Casadet, tel. 628/21387. Dress: casual. Reservations accepted. AE, V. Moderate.*

★ **Versailles.** A tiny and authentic French bistro with only a handful of tables, Versailles is always packed. *Cap del Carrer 1, tel. 628/21331. Dress: casual. Reservations advised. DC, MC, V. Moderate.*

Lodging **Andorra Palace.** The large and modern Palace is widely consid-
★ ered one of the capital's best hotels. The outdoor terrace is a pleasant spot in which to relax and watch the bustle below. *Prat de la Creu, tel. 628/21072. 140 rooms with bath. Facilities: restaurant, private parking, bar, sauna, pool. AE, DC, MC, V. Expensive.*

Andorra Park. The Park ranks with the Palace as one of Andorra la Vella's two top hotels. There's a pretty garden, as well as a terrace and private balconies. *Roureda de Guillemo, tel. 628/ 20979. 75 rooms with bath. Facilities: restaurant, tennis, private parking, bar, pool. AE, DC, MC, V. Expensive.*

President. This modern hotel is clean and tidy and offers good value rather than charm. The restaurant commands a particularly dramatic mountain view. *Avda. Sta. Coloma 40, tel. 628/ 22922. 88 rooms with bath. Facilities: bar, sauna, pool. DC, MC, V. Moderate.*

Florida. This is a cheerful, inexpensive hotel. There's no restaurant, but there are several nearby. *Carrer la Llacuna 11, tel. 628/20105. 35 rooms, 32 with bath. Facilities: bar, lounge. DC, MC, V. Inexpensive.*

Les Escaldes **1900.** Andorra's top restaurant has only eight tables, so be sure
Dining to make reservations. The food is nouvelle French. *Carrer de la
★ Unioll, tel. 628/26716. Jacket and tie. AE, DC, MC, V. Closed July. Expensive.*

Lodging **Roc Blanc.** Sleek, modern, and luxurious trappings—and a
★ wealth of facilities to pamper the body—are what the Roc Blanc is all about. This is not so unusual in a spa town, where healthy bodies are big business. El Pi, the hotel's restaurant, has set consistently good standards. *Placa Coprinceps 5, tel. 628/21486. 240 rooms with bath. Facilities: 2 pools, sauna, tennis, health club, restaurant, bar, terrace. AE, DC, MC, V. Very Expensive.*

Encamp **Belvedere.** An ex-patriate English couple runs this friendly lit-
Lodging tle inn, which is set in the midst of some amazing mountain scenery. The exceptionally clean rooms tend toward the small side. *Carrer Ballàvista, tel. 628/31263. 10 rooms, 1 with bath. Facilities: restaurant, bar, garden, terrace. No credit cards. Closed mid-Oct.–mid-Dec. Moderate.*

Santa Julia **Pol.** Gracefully modern surroundings and friendly staff are just
de Loria two reasons why this hotel is so popular. *Av. Verge de Canolich
Lodging 52, tel. 628/41122. 71 rooms with bath. Facilities: restaurant, bar, garden, terrace. AE, MC, V. Moderate.*

4 Austria

Introduction

What Austria lacks in size, it more than makes up for in diversity. Its Alps and mountain lakes in the central and southern provinces rival those of neighboring Switzerland; the vast Vienna Woods remind some of the Black Forest; the steppes of the province of Burgenland blend with those across the border in Hungary; and the vineyards along the Danube rival those of the Rhine and Mosel river valleys. In addition, nobody else has a Vienna or a Salzburg—or such pastry shops!

Austria has become considerably more expensive in recent years. There are bargains still to be found, however, and one of the diversions of a vacation in Austria can be their discovery.

The country is highly accessible. There are virtually no outposts that are not served by public transport of one form or another. The rail network has been maintained, and trains are fast, comfortable, and on time. Highways are superb and well-marked. Public transportation in the cities, although not cheap, is safe, clean, and convenient. In short, the visitor spends more time in Austria enjoying himself than coping with the logistics of getting from A to B.

The Austrians are, for the most part, friendly and welcoming. They are an outdoor people, given at a moment's notice to head off to the ski slopes, the mountains, the lakes, and the woods. At the same time, they can be as melancholy as some of the songs of their wine taverns would suggest. Communicating with them is not too difficult, since most speak another language beside their native German, and English is the usual choice.

What you'll discover in conversation with Austrians is that they are more for evolution than revolution, so change is gradual and old values tend to be maintained. Graceful dancers do execute the tricky "left waltz" on balmy summer evenings in Vienna, and you may find an entire town celebrating some event, complete with brass band in Lederhosen.

Before You Go

When to Go Austria has two main tourist seasons. The summer season starts at Easter and runs to about mid-October. The most pleasant months weather-wise are May, June, September, and October. June through August are the peak tourist months, and aside from a few overly humid days when you could wish for wider use of air conditioning, even Vienna is pleasant; the city literally moves outdoors in summer. The winter cultural season starts in October and runs into June; the winter sports season gets underway in December and lasts until the end of April, although you can ski in selected areas well into June and on some of the highest glaciers year-round. Some events—the Salzburg Festival is a prime example—make a substantial difference in hotel and other costs. Nevertheless, bargains are available in the (almost nonexistent) off-season.

Climate Summer can be warm; winter, bitterly cold. The southern region is usually several degrees warmer in summer, several degrees colder in winter. Winters north of the Alps can be

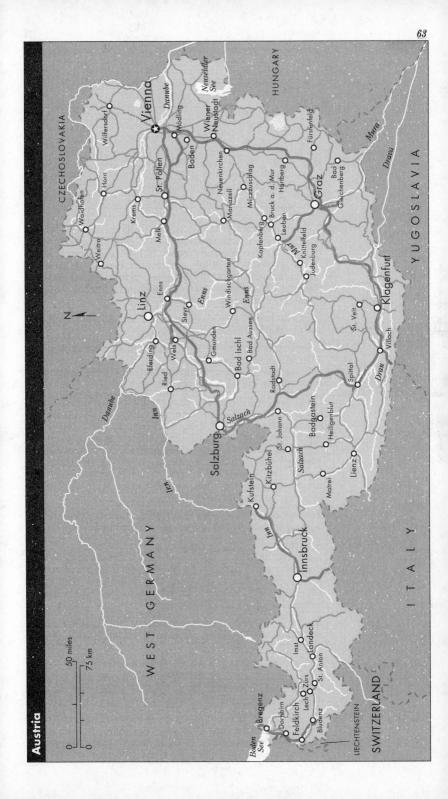

Austria

overcast and dreary, whereas the south basks in winter sunshine.

The following are the average daily maximum and minimum temperatures for Vienna.

Jan.	34F	1C	May	67F	19C	Sept.	68F	20C
	25	−4		50	10		53	11
Feb.	38F	3C	June	73F	23C	Oct.	56F	14C
	28	−3		56	14		44	7
Mar.	47F	8C	July	76F	25C	Nov.	45F	7C
	30	−1		60	15		37	3
Apr.	58F	15C	Aug.	75F	24C	Dec.	37F	3C
	42	6		59	15		30	−1

Currency The unit of currency is the Austrian schilling (AS), divided into 100 groschen. There are AS 20, 50, 100, 500, and 1,000 bills; AS 1, 5, 10, and 20 coins; and groshen 1, 2, 10, and 50 coins. The 1- and 2- groschen coins are scarce, and the AS 20 coins are unpopular—though useful for some cigarette machines. The 500- and 100-schilling notes look perilously similar; confusing them can be an expensive mistake:

At press time (fall 1988), there were about AS 12 to the dollar, and about AS 22 to the pound sterling.

Credit cards are widely used throughout Austria, although not all establishments take all cards. American Express has money machines in Vienna at Parkring 10 (actually in Liebenberggasse, off Parkring) and at the airport.

Cash traveler's checks at a bank, post office, or American Express office to get the best rate. All charge a small commission; some smaller banks or "change" offices may give a poorer rate *and* charge a higher fee. All change offices at airports and the main train stations in major cities cash traveler's checks. Bank-operated change offices in Vienna with extended hours are located on Stephansplatz and in the Opernpassage. The Zentralsparkasse machine on Stephansplatz will change bills in other currencies into schillings.

You may bring in any amount of foreign currency or schillings; legally, only AS 50,000 in currency may be taken out.

What It Will Cost Austria is not inexpensive, but since inflation is negligible, costs remain fairly stable. Vienna and Salzburg are the most expensive cities, along with the fashionable resorts such as Kitzbühel, Seefeld, Badgastein, Bad Hofgastein, Velden, Zell am See, and Pörtschach. Many smaller towns offer virtually identical facilities at half the price.

Drinks in bars and clubs are considerably higher than in cafés or restaurants. Austrian prices are inclusive; that is, service and tax are included.

Sample Prices Cup of coffee, AS 22; half-liter of draft beer, AS 26; glass of wine, AS 32; Coca-Cola, AS 20; open sandwich, AS 18; theater ticket, AS 120; concert ticket, AS 170; opera ticket, AS 500; one-mile taxi ride, AS 25.

Customs on Arrival Austria's duty-free allowances are as follows: 200 cigarettes or 100 cigars or 250 grams of tobacco, two liters of wine and one liter of spirits, one bottle of toilet water (about 300-mililiter size); 50 mililiters of perfume for those age 18 and over arriving

from other European countries. Visitors arriving from the
USA, Canada, or other non-European points may bring in
twice the above amounts.

Language German is the official national language. In larger cities and
most resort areas, you will have no problems finding those who
speak English; hotel and restaurant staff, in particular, speak
English reasonably well. Most younger Austrians speak at
least passable English, even if fluency is relatively rare.

Getting Around

By Car The highway system is excellent, and all roads are well main-
Road Conditions tained and well marked. Secondary mountain roads may be
narrow and winding, but traffic is generally light. Check the
condition of mountain roads in winter before starting out:
Many mountain passes are closed, though tunnels are kept
open.

Rules of the Road Drive on the right. Seat belts are compulsory in front. Speed
limits are as posted; otherwise, 130 kph (80 mph) on express-
ways, 100 kph (62 mph) on other main roads, 50 kph (31 mph) in
built-up areas. The right-of-way is for those coming from the
right (especially in traffic circles) unless otherwise marked. A
warning triangle, standard equipment in rental cars, must be
set up in case of breakdown.

Parking Observe signs; tow-away in cities is expensive. Overnight
parking in winter is forbidden on city streets with streetcar
lines.

Gasoline Prices—AS 9–AS 10 per liter—are fairly consistent throughout the country. Unleaded ("Bleifrei")—regular and premium
—is now available almost everywhere.

Breakdowns Emergency road service is available from ARBÖ (tel. 123 nationwide) or ÖAMTC (tel. 120). Special phones are located
along autobahns and major highways.

By Train Trains in Austria are fast and efficient, and most lines have now
been electrified. Hourly express trains run on the key Vienna-
Salzburg route. All principal trains have first- and second-class
cars, and smoking and nonsmoking areas. Overnight trains
have sleeping compartments, and most trains have dining cars.
If you're traveling at peak times, a reserved seat—available for
a small additional fee—is always a good idea.

Fares If you're visiting other European countries, a **Eurail Pass** *(see
Getting Around Europe, in Planning Your Trip, for details),*
valid throughout most of Europe, is the best deal. Austria has
only two discount tickets. The **Austria Ticket** offers unlimited
travel for those under 26. The **"kilometerbank"** is of value only
to natives or visitors planning to travel 2,000 kilometers (1,250
miles) in any one year. Full details are available from travel
agents or from the Austrian National Tourist Office.

By Plane Domestic service is expensive. **Austrian Airlines** flies between
Vienna and Linz, Salzburg, Graz, and Klagenfurt. **Tyrolean
Airlines** has service from Vienna to Innsbruck.

By Bus Service is available to virtually every community accessible by
highway. Winter buses have ski racks. Vienna's central bus
terminal (Wien–Mitte/Landstrasse Hauptstrasse, opposite
the Hilton) is on the international bus route; in most other cities
the bus station is adjacent to the train station.

By Boat Boats ply the Danube from Passau in West Germany all the way to Vienna and from Vienna to Bratislava (Czechoslovakia), Budapest (Hungary), and the Black Sea. Only East European boats run beyond Budapest. Overnight boats have cabins; all have dining. The most scenic stretches in Austria are from Passau to Linz and through the Wachau valley (Melk, Krems). From Vienna, there are day trips you can take upstream to the Wachau and downstream to Budapest. There are also special moonlight dancing and jazz excursions. Make reservations from DDSG in Vienna (tel. 0222/266536) or travel agents.

By Bicycle Bicycles can be rented at many train stations; return them to any other station or the same. Most trains and some postal buses will take bikes as baggage. Bikes can be taken on the Vienna subway on weekends. Marked cycling routes parallel most of the Danube.

Essential Information

Telephones
Local Calls Pay telephones take AS 1, 5, 10, and 20 coins. A three-minute local call will cost AS 1. Emergency calls are free. Instructions are in English in most booths. Add AS 1 when time is up to continue the connection. If you will be phoning frequently, get a phone "credit card" at a post office. This works in all "Wertkartentelefon" phones; the cost of the call will be deducted from the card automatically. Card costs are AS 95 for AS 100 worth of phoning.

Phone numbers within Vienna and Innsbruck are being changed. A sharp tone indicates no connection or that the number has been changed.

International Calls It costs more to telephone *from* Austria than it does to telephone *to* Austria. Calls from post offices are least expensive. Hotels time all calls and charge a "per unit" fee according to their own tariff, which can add AS 100 or more to your bill. To avoid this charge, call overseas and ask to be called back. To make a collect call—you can't do this from pay phones —dial the operator and ask for an "R" (pronounced "err")-Gespräch.

International Information Dial 09. Most operators speak English; if yours doesn't, you'll be passed to one who does.

Mail
Postal Rates Airmail letters to the United States and Canada cost AS 9.50; postcards cost AS 7.50. Airmail letters to the United Kingdom cost AS 6; postcards cost AS 5.

Receiving Mail American Express offices in Vienna, Linz, Salzburg, and Innsbruck will hold mail at no charge for those carrying an American Express credit card or American Express traveler's checks.

Shopping Austria is known for handicrafts, lace and embroidery, petitpoint, glassware, ceramics, and jewelry. These, together with traditional clothing (dirndls for women, lederhosen for men), are available throughout the country. Prices can be high, but quality is generally tops.

VAT Refunds VAT at 20% (in certain cases, 32%) is charged on all sales and is automatically included in prices. If you purchase goods worth AS 2,000 or more, you can claim back the tax as you leave or once you're back home. Ask shops where you buy the goods to fill out and give you the necessary papers. Get them stamped at the airport or border by customs officials (who may ask to see the goods). You can get an immediate refund of the VAT at the airport or at main border points, less a service charge, or you can return the papers by mail to the shop(s), which will then deal with the details. The VAT refund can be credited to your credit card account or paid by check.

Opening and Closing Times **Banks.** Doors open weekdays 8–12:30 and 1:30–3. Principal offices in cities stay open during lunch.

Museums. Opening days and times vary considerably from city to city and depend on season, the size of the museum, budgetary constraints, and assorted other factors. Your hotel or the local tourist office will have current details.

Shops. These open weekdays from 8 or 9 until 6, Saturday until noon or 1 only. Many smaller shops close for one or two hours at midday.

National Holidays January 1 (New Year's Day); January 6 (Epiphany); March 24, 27 (Easter); May 1 (May Day); May 4 (Ascension); May 14, 15 (Whitsun); May 25 (Corpus Christi); August 15 (Assumption); October 26 (National Day); November 1 (All Saints); December 8 (Immaculate Conception); December 25, 26.

Dining Take your choice of sidewalk "Wurstl" (frankfurter) stands, quick-lunch stops (Imbisstube), cafés, Heuriger wine restaurants, self-service restaurants, modest Gasthäuser neighborhood establishments with local specialties, and full-fledged restaurants in every price category. Most establishments post their menus outside. Shops selling coffee beans (such as Eduscho) also offer coffee by the cup at considerably lower prices than those in a café.

Mealtimes Austrians often eat up to five meals a day—a very early Continental breakfast of rolls and coffee; a slightly more substantial breakfast *(Gabelfrühstück)* with egg or cold meat, possibly even a small goulash, at mid-morning (understood to be 9, sharp); a main meal at noon; afternoon coffee *(Jause)* with cake at teatime; and, unless dining out, a light supper to end the day. Cafés offer breakfast; most restaurants open somewhat later. Lunches usually cost more in cafés than in restaurants.

Ratings Prices are per person and include soup and a main course, usually with salad, and a small beer or glass of wine. Meals in the top-price categories will include a dessert or cheese and coffee. Prices include taxes and service (you may wish to leave small change, in addition). Best bets are indicated by a star ★. At press time, there were 12 schillings (AS) to the dollar.

Category	Cost: major city	Cost: other areas
Very Expensive	over AS 800	over AS 600
Expensive	AS 500–AS 800	AS 400–AS 600
Moderate	AS 200–AS 500	AS 170–AS 400
Inexpensive	under AS 200	under AS 170

Credit Cards The following credit card abbreviations are used: AE, American Express; DC, Diners Club; MC, MasterCard; V, Visa.

Lodging Austrian hotels and pensions are officially classified from one to five stars. These gradings broadly coincide with our own four-way rating system. No matter what the category, standards for service and cleanliness are high. All hotels in the upper three categories will have bath or shower in the room; even the most inexpensive accommodations will have hot and cold water. Accommodations include castles and palaces, conventional hotels, country inns *(Gasthof)*, motels (considerably less frequent), and the more modest pensions.

Ratings All prices quoted here are for two people in a double room. Though exact figures will vary, a single room will generally cost more than 50% of the price of a comparable double room. Breakfast—which can be anything from a simple roll and coffee to a full and sumptuous buffet—is always included in the room rate. Best bets are indicated by a star ★. At press time, there were 12 schillings (AS) to the dollar.

Category	Cost: major city	Cost: other areas
Very Expensive	over AS 2,300	over AS 1,800
Expensive	AS 1,250–AS 2,300	AS 1,000–AS 1,800
Moderate	AS 850–AS 1,250	AS 700–AS 1,000
Inexpensive	under AS 850	under AS 700

Credit Cards The following credit card abbreviations are used: AE, American Express; DC, Diners Club; MC, MasterCard; V, Visa.

Tipping Railroad porters get AS 10 per bag. Hotel porters or bellhops get AS 5 per bag. Doormen get AS 10 for hailing a cab and assisting. Room service gets AS 10 for snacks and AS 20 for full meals. Maids get no tip unless your stay is a week or more, or special service is rendered. In restaurants, 10% service is included. Add anything from AS 5 to AS 50, depending on the restaurant and the size of the bill.

Vienna

Arriving and Departing

By Plane All flights use **Schwechat Airport,** about 10 miles (16 kilometers) southwest of Vienna (tel. 0222/77702231).

Between the Buses leave every half-hour from 6 to 8:30 AM, and every 20 min-
Airport and utes from 8:50 AM to 10:10 PM from the airport to the city air
Downtown terminal by the Hilton on Wien Mitte-Landstrasse Hauptstrasse. Buses also run every hour from the airport to the Westbahnhof (west train station) and the Südbahnhof (south train station). Be sure you get on the right bus! The one-way fare for all buses is AS 50. A taxi from the airport to downtown Vienna costs about AS 330; agree on the price in advance. Cabs (legally) do not meter the drive, as fares are more or less fixed (legally again) at about double the meter fare. A seat in a limousine will cost less; book at the airport. If you are driving from the airport, follow signs to "Zentrum."

By Train Vienna has four train stations. The principal station, **Westbahnhof,** is for trains to and from Linz, Salzburg, and Innsbruck. Trains from Germany and France arrive here, too. The **Südbahnhof** is for trains to and from Graz, Klagenfurt, Villach, and Italy. **Franz–Josefs–Bahnhof** is for trains to and from

Prague, Berlin, and Warsaw. Go to **Floridsdorf Station** for local trains to and from the north of the city.

By Bus If you arrive by bus, it will probably be at the central bus terminal, **Wien Mitte,** opposite the city air terminal (and the Hilton).

By Boat All Danube river boats dock at the DDSG terminal on Mexicoplatz. There's an awkward connection with the U–1 subway from here. Some boats also make a stop slightly upstream at Heiligenstadt, Nussdorf, from where there is an easier connection to the U–4 subway line.

By Car Main access routes are the expressways to the west and south (Westautobahn, Südautobahn). Routes to the downtown area are marked "Zentrum."

Getting Around

Vienna is fairly easy to explore on foot; as a matter of fact, the heart of the city—the area within the Ring—is largely a pedestrian zone. The Ring itself was once the city ramparts, torn down just over a century ago to create today's broad, tree-lined boulevard. Public transportation is comfortable, convenient, and frequent, though not cheap.

Tickets for bus, subway, and streetcar are available in most stations. Tickets in multiples of five are sold at cigarette shops, known as Tabak-Trafik, or at the window marked "Vorverkauf" at central stations such as Karlsplatz or Stephansplatz. A block of five tickets costs AS 65, a single ticket AS 19. If you plan to use public transportation frequently, get a three-day tourist ticket (cost AS 93). Maps and information are available at Stephansplatz, Karlzplatz, and Praterstern U-Bahn stations.

By Bus or Streetcar Inner City buses are numbered 1A through 3A, and operate weekdays to 7:40 PM, Saturday until 2 PM. Lower fares (buy a Kurzstreckenkarte; it gives four trips for AS 26) cover these routes as well as designated shorter stretches (roughly two to four stops) on all other bus or streetcar lines. Streetcars and buses are numbered according to route, and run until about midnight. Night buses marked N follow special routes every hour; the fare is AS 25. The central terminal point is Schwedenplatz. The "1" and "2" streetcar lines run the circular route around the Ring, clockwise and counterclockwise respectively.

By Subway Subway lines (U-Bahn; stations are marked with a huge blue U) are designated U-1, U-2, and U-4 and are clearly marked and color-coded. Additional services are provided by the city railroad, the Stadtbahn, indicated by a brown S symbol, and by fast suburban train, the S-Bahn, indicated by a stylized blue "S" symbol. Both are tied into the general city fare system.

By Taxi Cabs can be flagged on the street if the "Frei" (free) sign is illuminated. Alternatively, dial 60160 '9101, or 4369 to call for one. All rides are metered. The basic fare is AS 22, but expect to pay AS 60 for an average city ride. There are additional charges for bags.

Important Addresses and Numbers

Tourist Information City Tourist Office, Opernpassage, tel. 0222/431608. Open daily 9–7.

Embassies **U.S.** Gartenbaupromenade (Marriott Bldg.), tel. 0222/51451. **Canadian.** Dr. Karl Lueger-Ring, tel. 0222/633691. **U.K.** Reisnerstr. 40, tel. 0222/756117.

Emergencies **Police,** tel. 122; **Ambulance,** tel. 144; **Doctor,** American Medical Society of Vienna, Lazarettegasse 13, tel. 0222/424568; **Pharmacies,** open weekdays 8–6, Sat. 8–noon.

English Bookstores **Big Ben Bookshop,** Porzellangasse 24, tel. 0222/316412; **British Bookshop,** Weihburggasse 8, tel. 0222/5121945; **English Book Shop,** Plankengasse 7, tel. 0222/5123701; **Shakespeare & Co.,** Sterngasse 2, tel. 0222/5354376.

Travel Agencies **American Express,** Kärntnerstr. 21–23, tel. 0222/51540; **Parkring** 10, tel. 0222/5151180; **Austrian Travel Agency,** Kärntnerring 3–5, tel. 0222/588000; **Wagons-Lits/Thomas Cook,** Kärntner Ring 2, tel. 0222/50160.

Guided Tours

Orientation Tours **Vienna Sightseeing Tours** (tel. 0222/7124683) offers a short highlights tour or a lengthier one to the Vienna Woods, Mayerling, and other areas surrounding Vienna. Tours start in front of or beside the opera house. **Cityrama** (tel. 0222/53413) provides city tours with hotel pickup; tours assemble opposite the Intercontinental Hotel. All hotels and travel agencies have details.

Special-Interest Tours Tours are available to the Spanish Riding School, the Vienna Boys Choir, operettas, and concerts, the wine suburb of Grinzing, nightclubs, and Vienna by night. Check with the city transit office for details.

Walking Tours "Vienna from A to Z" (in English) is available at most bookstores; it explains the numbered plaques attached to all major buildings in Vienna. "Vienna: Downtown Walking Tours" by Henriette Mandl outlines suggested routes and provides information on sights. For organized walking tours with English-speaking guides, check with your hotel or the tourist office.

Excursions Day bus trips are organized to the Danube valley, the Hungarian border, the Alps south of Vienna, Salzburg, and Budapest; get information from the city tourist office.

Exploring Vienna

Vienna has been described as an "old dowager of a town," not a bad description for this one-time center of empire. It's not just the aristocratic and courtly atmosphere, with monumental doorways and stately facades of former palaces at every turn. Nor is it just that Vienna has a higher proportion of middle-aged and older citizens than any other city in Europe, with a concommitant sense of stability, quiet, and respectability. Rather, it's these factors combined with a love of music, a discreet weakness for rich food (especially cakes), an adherence to old-fashioned and formal forms of address, a high, if unadventurous, regard for the arts, and a gentle mourning for lost glories that combine to produce a stiff but elegant, slightly other-worldly, sense of dignity.

Most main sights are in the inner zone, the oldest part of the city, encircled by the Ring, once the city walls and today a broad boulevard. Before setting out, be sure to check opening times of museums carefully; they can change unpredictably. Carry a ready supply of AS 10 coins, too; many places of interest have coin-operated tape machines providing English commentaries. As you wander around, train yourself to look upward; some of the most memorable architectural treasures are on upper stories and roof lines.

The Main Attractions

Vienna's role as imperial city is preserved in the complex of buildings that makes up the former royal palace. Start your tour at Albertinaplatz, behind the opera house. Head down Augustinerstrasse. On your left is the **Albertina,** home to the world's largest collection of drawings, sketches, engravings, and etchings. There are works here by Dürer—these are perhaps the highlight of the collection—Rembrandt, Michelangelo, Corregio, and many others. The holdings are so vast that only a limited number can be shown at one time. Some original works are so delicate that they can only be shown in facsimile. *Augustinerstr. 1, tel. 0222/534830. Admission: AS 30. Open Mon., Tues., Thurs. 10–4; Wed. 10–6; Fri. 10–2; Sat. and Sun. 10–1; closed Sun. in July and August.*

Next door is the 14th-century **Augustinerkirche,** a favorite on Sundays, when the 11 AM mass is sung in Latin. Nearby is the **Nationalbibliothek** (the National Library), with its stunning Baroque great hall. *Josefsplatz 1, tel. 0222/5337026. Admission: AS 15. Open May–Oct., Mon.–Sat. 10–4; Nov.–Apr., Mon.–Sat. 11–12.*

Josefsplatz is where much of *The Third Man* was filmed, specifically in and around the Palais Pallavicini across the street. The entrance to the **Spanische Reitschule,** the Spanish Riding School, is here, too, though the famed white horses are actually stabled on the other side of the square. For tickets, write the Austrian Tourist Office (Friedrichstr. 7, A–1010 Vienna) *at least* three months in advance. There are performances on Sunday at 10:45 and Wednesday at 7 PM year-round. Mid-April through October, there are additional performances on Saturday at 9 AM.

Above the stables is the **Neue Galerie,** housing mainly Impressionist and other 19th- and early 20th-century paintings and sculptures. It's a compact collection, though it contains nothing of outstanding interest. *Reitschule 1, tel. 0222/5336045. Admission: AS 15. Open Wed.–Mon. 10–4; closed Tues.*

From here you're only a few steps from Michaelerplatz, the little square that marks the entrance to the **Hofburg,** the royal palace. On one side of the square, opposite the entrance, on the corner of Herrengasse and Kohlmarkt, is the **Loos building** (1911), designed by Adolf Loos. It's no more than a simple brick-and-glass structure, but architectural historians point to it as one of the earliest "modern" buildings in Europe—a building where function determines style. In striking contrast is the Baroque **Michaelertor** opposite, the principal entrance to the Hofburg.

Time Out   Some insist that no visit to Vienna is complete without a visit to **Demel,** just down Kohlmarkt to the left. Others find the café-

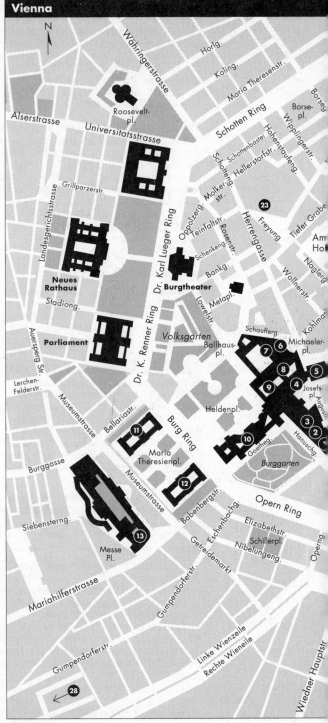

Vienna

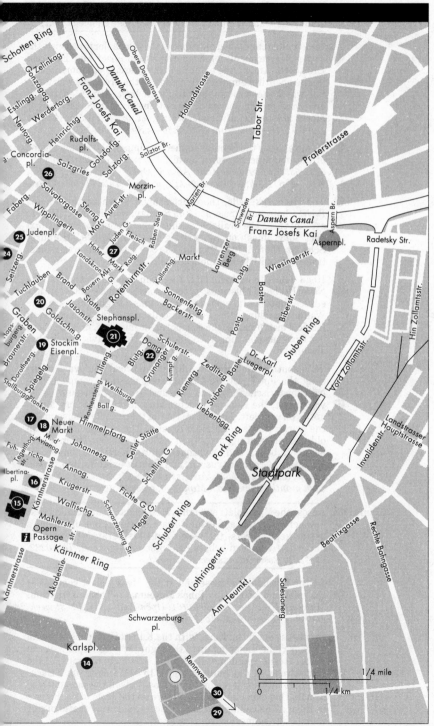

pastry shop overpriced—it is expensive even by Vienna standards—and complain of the service. The choice is yours.

 Head under the domed entrance of the Michaelertor to visit the **imperial apartments** of Emperor Franz Josef and Empress Elizabeth. Among the exhibits is the exercise equipment used by the beautiful empress. Here, too, is the dress she was wearing when she was stabbed to death by a demented Italian anarchist on the shores of Lake Geneva in 1898; the dagger marks are visible. *Michaelerplatz 1, tel. 0222/5875554. Admission: AS 15. Open Mon.–Sat. 8:30–4, Sun. 8:30–12:30.*

⑧ Be sure to see the **Schatzkammer,** the imperial treasury, home of the magnificent crown jewels. *Hofburg, Schweizerhof, tel. 0222/5337931. Admission: AS 45. Open Nov.–Mar., Mon., Wed.–Fri. 10–4, weekends 9–4; Apr.–Oct. until 6; closed Tues.*

⑨ The **Hofburgkapelle,** the court chapel, is where the Vienna Boys' Choir sings mass at 11 on Sunday. You'll need tickets to attend; these are available at the chapel from 5 PM Friday (expect long lines) or by writing to Burgkapelle, Hofburg, Schweizerhof, A-1010 Vienna. The city tourist office can sometimes help with ticket applications.

⑩ Head south to Heldenplatz, the open square in front of the **Neue Hofburg Museums,** a ponderously ornate 19th-century edifice housing a series of museums. Highlights are the Waffensammlung (the weapons collection), the collections of musical instruments, the ethnographic museum, and the exciting Ephesus museum, with finds from the excavations at that ancient site.

⑪
⑫ Walk south again across the Ring, the broad boulevard encircling the inner city, to the imperial museum complex. The **Naturhistorisches Museum** (Natural History Museum) is on your right, the **Kunsthistoriches Museum** (Art History Museum) is on your left. The latter is one of the great art museums of the world; this is not a place to miss. The collections focus on old-master painting, notably Brueghel, Cranach, Titian, Canaletto, Rubens, and Velazquez. But there are important Egyptian, Greek, Etruscan, and Roman exhibits, too. *Burgring 5, tel. 0222/934541. Admission: AS 45; free the 1st Sun. of each month. Open Wed.–Mon. 9–6; closed Tues.*

Time Out Across the Messeplatz stretches Messepalast, the building that now serves as fair and exhibit space. Inside is one of Vienna's better-kept secrets, the **Glacis-Beisl** restaurant. The garden under the vine-clad arbors has to be experienced. *Tel. 0222/9307374. Reservations recommended.*

⑬ At the Mariahilferstrasse end of the Messepalast complex is the small and fascinating **Tabak Museum,** the Tobacco Museum. *Mahriahilfstr., tel. 0222/961761. Open Wed.–Fri. 10–3; weekends 9–1; Tues. 10–5; closed Mon.*

⑭ Head east down the Ring, with the Kunsthistoriches Museum on your right. Looming up to the right, over Karlsplatz, is the heroic facade and dome, flanked by vast twin columns, of the **Karlskirche.** It was built around 1715 by Fischer von Erlach. The oval interior is surprisingly small, given the monumental facade: One expects something more on the scale of St. Peter's in Rome. The ceiling has airy frescoes, and stiff shafts of gilt radiate like sunbeams from the altar.

Take the pedestrian subway (the city **tourist office** is here) and walk back under the Ring to Opernplatz. This is the site of the **(15) Staatsoper,** the opera house, one of the best in the world and a focus of Viennese social life. Tickets are expensive and rare, so you may have to settle for a backstage tour. They are given five times daily in July and August, and once daily in June and September.

Head up Kärntnerstrasse, Vienna's main thoroughfare, now an elegant and busy pedestrian mall. On your left is the creamy **(16)** facade of the **Sacher Hotel.** Take a look inside at the plush red-and-gilt decor, a *fin de siècle* masterpiece. The hotel is also the home of the original Sachertorte—the ultimate chocolate cake. Leading off Kärntnerstrasse, to the left, is the little street of **(17)** Marco d'Aviano-Gasse. Follow it to **Kapuzinerkirche,** in whose crypt, called the **Kaisergruft** or the imperial vault, the serried ranks of long-dead Hapsburgs lie. The oldest tomb is that of Ferdinand II; it dates from 1633. The most recent tomb is that of Franz Josef, dating from 1916.

(18) In the center of the square is the ornate 18th-century **Donner Brunnen,** the Providence Fountain. The figures represent main rivers that flow into the Danube; Empress Maria Teresa thought the figures obscene and wanted them removed or properly clothed.

Time Out Coffee or tea and what are said, even by the French and Belgians, to be the best pastries in the world are available in staggering quantity at the **Konditorei Oberlaa.** *Neuer Markt 16.*

Continue north through Neuer Markt to reach pedestrians-**(19)** only Graben. The **Pestsäule,** or Plague Column, shoots up from the middle of the street, looking like a geyser of whipped cream touched with gold. It commemorates the Black Death of 1697; look at the graphic depictions of those who fell victim to the ravages of the terrible disease. A small turning to the right, **(20)** just past the column, leads to the Baroque **Peterskirche.** The little church, the work of Johann Lukas von Hildebrandt, finished in about 1730, has probably the most theatrical interior in the city. The pulpit is especially fine, with a highly ornate canopy; but florid and swirling decoration is everywhere. Many of the decorative elements are based on a tent form, a motif suggested by the Turkish tents camped outside the city walls during the great siege of Vienna at the end of the 17th century.

Walk back to Graben and along to Stephansplatz, site of the **(21) Stephansdom** (St. Stephen's Cathedral). Its towering Gothic spires and gaudy 19th-century tiled roof are still the dominant feature of the Vienna skyline. The oldest part of the building is the 13th-century entrance, the soaring **Riesentor,** or Giant Doorway. Inside, the church is mysteriously dark, filled with an array of monuments, tombs, sculptures, paintings, and pulpits. Despite extensive wartime damage—and numerous Baroque additions—the building radiates an authentically medieval atmosphere. Climb up the 345 steps of **Alte Steffl,** Old Steve, the south tower, for a stupendous view over the city. An elevator goes up the north tower to **Die Pummerin,** the Boomer, a 22-ton bell cast in 1711 from cannon captured from the Turks. Take a 30-minute tour of the crypt to see the entrails of the Hapsburgs, carefully preserved in copper jars.

On a narrow street east of the cathedral, is the house where
22 Mozart lived from 1784 to 1787. Today it's the **Mozart
Erinnerungsräume,** the Mozart Museum. It was here that he
wrote *The Marriage of Figaro,* and here, some say, that he
spent the happiest years of his life. *Domgasse 5, tel. 0222/
5240722. Admission: AS 15. Open Tues.–Sun. 10–12:15 and 1–
4:30.*

Exploring Other Corners of Vienna

Walk back down the Graben and the narrow Naglergasse, and
turn left into the Freyung. On your left is the **Palais Ferstl,** now
a stylish shopping arcade. At the back is the skillfully restored
Café Central, once headquarters for Vienna's leading literary
23 figures. Cross the Freyung to the dominant **Schottenkirche.**
The monks brought to found it were actually Irish, not Scottish. They started a school as well, which shares the courtyard
to the left with a pleasant garden restaurant in summer. Turn
back through the Freyung to **Am Hof,** a remarkable square with
the city's Baroque central fire station, possibly the world's
24 most ornate. Cross the square to the **Kirche am Hof.** The interi-
or is curiously reminiscent of many Dutch churches.

Time Out For a typical meal or just a beer or coffee, stop at **Gustlbauer.**
The restaurant is a regular stop for the Fiaker coachmen, who
leave their livery and passengers briefly for a quick Schnapps.
The waiter will help you decipher the handwritten menu.
Vienna's mayor, who lives nearby, often appears. *Am Hof,
Drahtgasse 2, tel. 0222/635889.*

Continue to Judenplatz and turn right into Parisergasse to the
25 **Uhrenmuseum** (Clock Museum), located in a lovely Renaissance
house. *Schulhof 2, tel. 0222/5332265. Admission: AS 15; free
Fri. morning. Open Tues.–Sun. 9–12:15, 1–4:30.*

Turn down the Kurrentgasse and, via Fütterergasse, cross the
Wipplingerstrasse into Stoss im Himmel (literally, a "thrust
26 to heaven"). To your left down Salvatorgasse is **Maria am
Gestade,** originally a church for fishermen on the nearby canal.
Note the ornate "folded hands" spire. Return along Wip-
27 plingerstrasse, across Marc Aurel-Strasse, to **Hoher Markt,**
with a central monument celebrating the betrothal of Mary and
Joseph. Roman ruins are displayed in the museum on the south
side of the square. *Hoher Markt 3, tel. 0222/5355606. Admission: AS 15; free on Fri. morning. Open Tues.–Sun. 10–12:15,
1–4:30.*

On the north side of Hoher Markt is the amusing **Anker-Uhr,** or
clock that tells time by figures moving across a scale. The figures are identified on a plaque at the lower left of the clock; it's
well-worth passing by at noon to catch the show. Go through
Judengasse to the **Ruprechtskirche** (St. Rupert's). The oldest
church in Vienna is small, damp, dark, and, unfortunately, usually closed, though you can peek through a window.

Vienna Environs

It's a 15-minute ride from center city on subway line U-4 (stop
28 either at Schönbrunn or Hietzing) to **Schönbrunn Palace,** the
magnificent Baroque residence built between 1696 and 1713 for
the Hapsburgs. Here Kaiser Franz Josef I was born and died:

His "office" (kept as he left it in 1916) is a touching reminder of his spartan life; other rooms, however, reflect the elegance of monarchy. The ornate public rooms are still used for state receptions. A guided tour covers 45 of the palace's 1,441 rooms; among the curiosities are the Chinese room and the gym fitted out for Empress Elisabeth, where she exercised daily to keep her figure. *Schönbrunner Schlosstr, tel. 0222/833646. Admission: AS 50. Open daily, Oct.–Apr. 9–noon, 1–4; May–Sept. 9–noon, 1–5.*

Once at the grounds, don't overlook the **Tiergarten** (Zoo). It's Europe's oldest menagerie and, when established in 1752, was intended to amuse and educate the court. It contains an extensive assortment of animals, some of them in their original Baroque enclosures. (Tel. 0222/821236. Admission: AS 30. Open daily 9–dusk, 6 PM latest.) Follow the pathways up to the **Gloriette** (open May–Oct., 8–6. Admission: AS 10), that Baroque ornament on the rise behind Schönbrunn, and enjoy superb views of the city. Originally this was to have been the site of the palace, but projected construction costs were considered too high.

The **Wagenburg** (Carriage Museum), near the entrance to the palace grounds, holds some splendid examples of early transportation, from children's sleighs to funeral carriages of the emperors. *Admission: AS 30. Open Apr.–Oct., Tues.–Sun. 10–4, May–Sept. 10–5.*

㉙ Take the D streetcar toward the Südbahnhof to reach **Schloss Belvedere** (Belvedere Palace), a Baroque complex often compared to Versailles. It was commissioned by Prince Eugene of Savoy and built by Johann Lukas von Hildebrandt in 1721–22. The palace is made up of two separate buildings, one at the foot and the other at the top of a hill. The lower tract was built first as residential quarters; the upper buildings were reserved for entertaining. The gardens in between are among the best examples anywhere of natural Baroque ornamentation. The buildings hold contemporary significance: The State Treaty that gave Austria its independence in 1955 was signed in the great upper hall. The composer Anton Bruckner lived in an apartment to the north of the upper building until his death in 1896. Both sections now house outstanding art museums: the gallery of 19th- and 20th-century art in the Upper Belvedere (Klimt, Kokoschka, Schiele, Waldmüller, Markart), and the Baroque museum (including medieval Austrian art) in the Lower Belvedere. *Prinz-Eugen-Str. 27, tel. 0222/784158. Admission: AS 30. Open Tues.–Sun. 10–4.*

㉚ Continue across the Gurtel southward to the **20th Century Museum,** containing a small but extremely tasteful modern art collection. *Schweizer Garten, tel. 0222/782550. Admission: AS 30. Open Thurs.–Tues. 10–4; closed Wed.*

You can reach a small corner of the **Vienna Woods** by streetcar and bus: Take a streetcar or the subway U-2 to Schottentor/ University and, from there, the no. 38 streetcar (Grinzing) to the end of the line. Grinzing itself is out of a picture book; alas, much of the wine offered in the taverns is less enchanting. (For better wine and ambience, try the village of Nussdorf, reached by streetcar D. To get into the Woods, change in Grinzing to the no. 38A bus. This will take you to Kahlenberg, which provides a superb view out over the Danube and the city. You can take the bus or hike to Leopoldsberg, the promontory over the Danube from which Turkish invading forces were repulsed in the 16th and 17th centuries.

What to See and Do with Children

The **Prater** amusement park (Praterstern, subway U-1) offers something for all, from pony and horseback rides for smallest children to the *Riesenrad*, or giant ferris wheel. Older children may enjoy the **Technisches Museum** (Technical Museum), which includes the first typewriter, plus airplanes, locomotives, and other attractions. *Mariahilfer Str. 212, tel. 833618. Admission: AS 30. Open Tues.–Fri., Sat. 9–1, Sun. 9–4; streetcar 52 or 58.*

Off the Beaten Track

Vienna's **"Bermuda Triangle"** (around Judengasse/Seitenstettengasse) is jammed with everything from good bistros to jazz clubs. Also check the tourist office's museum list carefully: There's something for everyone, ranging from Sigmund Freud's apartment to the Funeral and Burial Museum. The **Hundertwasserhaus** (Kegelgasse/Löwengasse; streetcar N), an astonishing apartment complex designed by artist Friedenreich Hundertwasser, with turrets, towers, odd windows, and uneven floors, will be of interest to those who think architectural form need not follow function.

Shopping

Antiques The best (and most expensive) shops are in the inner city, but there are good finds in some of the outer districts, particularly among the back streets in the Josefstadt district.

Boutiques Name brands are found along the Kohlmarkt and the side streets off the Kärntner Strasse.

Folk Costumes A good selection at reasonable prices is offered by the **NÖ Heimatwerk** (Herrengasse 6); try also Trachten Tostmann (Schottengasse 3a) or Loden-Plankl (Michaelerplatz 6).

Shopping Districts Tourists gravitate to the **Kärntner Strasse,** but the Viennese do most of their shopping on the **Mariahilfer Strasse.**

Department Stores **Steffl** (Kärntner Str.) **Gerngross, Herzmansky,** and **Stafa** Mariahilfer Str.)

Food and Flea Markets The **Naschmarkt** (between Rechte and Linke Wienzeile. Weekdays 5–6 AM to mid-afternoon, Sat. to noon–1) is a sensational open food market, offering specialties from around the world. The **Flohmarkt** (flea market) operates year-round beyond the Naschmarkt (subway U-4 to Kettenbrückengasse) and is equally fascinating (Sat. 8–4). Bargaining here goes on in any number of languages. One of the best seasonal local markets for handicrafts is in Spittelberggasse.

Dining

In contrast to many cities, the leading Viennese hotels are in competition for the country's best cooks and so offer some of the city's best dining. Even the chain hotels have joined in the effort to see which can win over the leading chefs. The results are rewarding; you may not even have to leave your hotel to enjoy outstanding food and service.

The following price categories are given per person and usually cover a three-course meal including wine, tax, and service charge, though a tip will normally be added as extra. Best bets are indicated by a star ★. At press time, there were 12 schillings (AS) to the dollar.

Category	Cost
Very Expensive	over AS 800
Expensive	AS 500–800
Moderate	AS 200–500
Inexpensive	under AS 200

Very Expensive

★ **Zu den Drei Husaren.** This is one of Vienna's enduring monuments to tradition, complete with candlelight and live piano (except on Sundays). Casual visitors (as opposed to the "regulars") may have to settle for more atmosphere than service, however. The hors d'oeuvre trolleys are intentionally enticing and can easily double the dinner bill. *Weihburggasse 4, tel. 0222/5121192. Jacket and tie. Reservations essential. AE, DC, MC, V.*

★ **Korso.** You'll find outstanding food and atmosphere at this gourmet temple of "New Vienna Cuisine." Not all agree with the kitchen's approach to experiments—some say the restaurant really was created for the cook—but few are disappointed. *Mahlerstr. 2, tel. 0222/51516546. Jacket and tie. Reservations recommended. AE, DC, MC, V. Closed Sun., Sat. lunch.*

Expensive

da Conte. The newest Italian restaurant on the scene is also the best, set in a series of charming, arched-ceilinged rooms. The same management is responsible for the cheaper, smaller restaurant next door, as well as the Italian gourmet deli on the corner. *Kurrentgasse 12, tel. 0222/636464. Jacket and tie. Reservations recommended. AE, DC, MC, V. Closed Sun.*

Le Salut. This intimate restaurant offers the best French cuisine in town, with a price tag to match. In summer, the tables outside add to the pleasure. *Wildpretmarkt 3, tel. 0222/633581. Dress: studied casual at noon; jacket and tie evenings. Reservations advisable. AE, DC, MC, V. Closed Sun., also Sat. in July and Aug.*

★ **Rotisserie Prinz Eugen.** "New Vienna Cuisine" is combined successfully with more usual dishes at the Hilton's Rotisserie Prinz Eugen, which has managed to sustain its initial reputation for outstanding decor, service, and food. Piano accompaniment in the evening. *Hilton Hotel, Am Stadtpark, tel. 0222/752652. Jacket and tie. Reservations advisable. AE, DC, MC, V. Closed Sat. lunch.*

Steirereck. Steirereck boasts the 1988 Chef of the Year, although not all would agree. Some of the standard dishes are more successful than the forays into the "New Vienna Cuisine." No one denies the elegance of the ambience, however. The garden outside in summer is pleasant in the later evening when traffic lets up. *Rasumofskygasse 2, tel. 0222/733168. Dress: studied casual noon and outside in summer; evenings jacket and tie. Reservations advisable. AE. Closed Sat., Sun., Hols.*

★ **Vier Jahreszeiten.** This restaurant effortlessly manages to achieve that delicate balance between food and atmosphere. The service is attentive without being overbearing. The lunch buffet offers both excellent food and value. Evening dining includes grill specialties and live piano music (except on Sunday). *Hotel Intercontinental, Johannesgasse 28, tel. 0222/75050. Jacket and tie. Reservations recommended. AE, DC, MC, V.*

Moderate **Bastei-Beisl.** A comfortable, wood-paneled restaurant offering good traditional Viennese fare. Outdoor tables are particularly pleasant on summer evenings. *Stubenbastei 10, tel. 0222/524319. Casual dress. Reservations usually not necessary. AE, DC, MC, V. Closed Sun.*

★ **Franchi's.** This place has become a hot favorite, particularly for lunch and after concerts. The food is imaginative, with French overtones; the ambience inside is pleasant, and service is attentive—at least until the later hours. Nobody seems to mind the traffic, so the tables outside in summer are always packed. *Schwarzenbergplatz 3, tel. 0222/755334. Dress: studied casual noon and outside; jacket and tie for dinner inside. Reservations recommended for dinner and outside lunch. AE, DC, MC, V.*

★ **Gigerl.** It's hard to believe you're right in the middle of the city at this imaginative and charming wine restaurant that serves hot and cold buffets. Rooms are small and cozy but may get smoky and noisy when the place is full—which it usually is. The food is typical of wine gardens on the fringes of the city: roast meats, casserole dishes, cold cuts, salads. The wines are excellent. The surrounding narrow alleys and ancient buildings add to the charm of the outdoor tables in summer. *Rauhensteingasse 3, tel. 0222/5134431. Dress: casual. Reservations useful. DC, V.*

Zur Himmelpforte. This quality restaurant has a deserved reputation for reasonably priced gourmet meals. Standards may not reach the heights of some other Viennese establishments, but then neither do the prices! The house offers the *real* Budweiser beer as well. *Himmelpfortgasse 24, tel. 0222/5131967. Dress: informal. Reservations not essential. AE, DC, MC, V. Closed Sun.*

Melker Stiftskeller. This is one of the city's half-dozen genuine wine taverns, or kellers; the food selection is limited but good, featuring pig's knuckle. House wines from the Wachau are excellent. *Schottengasse 3, tel. 0222/635530. Dress: casual. Reservations usually not needed. No credit cards. Evenings only; closed Sun.*

★ **Ofenloch.** This place is always packed, which speaks well not only of the excellent specialties from some Viennese grandmother's cookbook but also of the atmosphere. Waitresses are attired in appropriate period costume, and the furnishings add to the color. If you like garlic, try *Vanillerostbraten*, a rump steak with as much garlic as you request. *Kurrentgasse 8, tel. 0222/637268. Dress: studied casual or jacket and tie. Reservations essential. No credit cards. Closed Sun.*

Stadtbeisl. Good standard Austrian fare is served up at this popular eatery, which is comfortable without being pretentious. Service gets uneven as the place fills up, but if you are seated in the garden outside in summer, you probably won't mind. *Naglergasse 21, tel. 0222/633323. Dress: informal. Reservations useful.*

Zu ebener Erde und erster Stock. Ask for a table upstairs in this

exquisite, tiny, utterly original Biedermeier house; the downstairs space is really more for snacks. *Burggasse 13, tel. 0222/
936254. Jacket and tie. Reservations advisable. AE, DC, MC,
V. Closed Sun.*

Inexpensive   **Demel.** One of Vienna's most famous pastry shops offers magnificent snacks of delicate meats, fish, and vegetables, as well
as the expected cakes and other goodies. The stuffed mushrooms and vegetable-cheese combinations are especially nice;
so is the hot chocolate. *Kohlmarkt 14, tel. 0222/6355160. Dress:
casual. No reservations. AE. Closed Sun.*

★ **Figlmüller.** Known for its Schnitzel, Figlmüller is always
packed. Guests share the benches, the long tables, and the experience. Food choices are limited, but nobody seems to mind.
Only wine is offered to drink, but it is good. The small garden
outside in summer is just as popular as the tables inside.
*Wollzeile 5 (passageway), tel. 0222/526177. Dress: casual. No
reservations. No credit cards. Closed Sat. dinner, Sun.*

Ilona-Stüberl. Head to Ilona-Stüberl for a cozy Hungarian atmosphere—without the gypsy music. Be prepared to douse
the fire if you ask for a dish with hot peppers! The tables outside in summer are pleasant but somewhat public. *Bräunerstr.
2, tel. 0222/526191. Dress: casual. Reservations useful. AE,
DC, MC, V. Closed Sun.*

Zu den drei Hacken. This is one of the few genuine Viennese
Gasthäusen in the city center; like the place itself, the fare is
solid if not elegant. Legend has it that Schubert dined here; the
ambience probably hasn't changed much since. There are tables outside in summer, although the extra seating capacity
strains both the kitchen and the service. *Singerstr. 8, tel. 0222/
525895. Dress: casual. No reservations. No credit cards.
Closed Sat. dinner, Sun.*

Lodging

Vienna's inner city is the best base for visitors because it's so
close to most of the major sights, restaurants, and shops. This
accessibility translates, of course, into higher prices.

Our price categories are based on prices for a double room and
include breakfast. Best bets are indicated by a star ★. At press
time, there were 12 schillings (AS) to the dollar.

Category	Cost
Very Expensive	over AS 2,300
Expensive	AS 1,250–AS 2,300
Moderate	AS 850–AS 1,250
Inexpensive	under AS 850

Very Expensive   **Bristol.** Opposite the opera house, the Bristol is classic Vien-
★ nese, preferred by many for the service as well as the location.
The bar is comfortable, though not overly private; the restaurants associated with the hotel are outstanding, especially
Korso. Back and upper guest rooms are quieter. *Kärntner
Ring 1, tel. 0222/515160. 152 rooms with bath. Facilities: bar,
fax, newsstand. AE, DC, MC, V.*

★ **Imperial.** This former palace represents elegant old Vienna at
its best, with such features as heated towel racks in some

rooms. The location could hardly be better, although being on the Ring, the front and lower rooms can be noisy. The bar is intimate and pleasant. Lunch in the café is both reasonable and good; the hotel restaurant is superb. *Kärntner Ring 16, tel. 0222/501100. 151 rooms with bath or shower. Facilities: hair stylist, beauty parlor, conference rooms, newsstand.*

★ **InterContinental.** Vienna's modern InterContinental has the reputation of being one of the chain's very best. Rooms are spacious, the main restaurant exceptional. But whereas the hotel succeeds in acquiring some Viennese charm, the bar fails hopelessly, as does the Brasserie. Rooms in front overlooking the park are quieter, particularly in winter when the ice-skating rink to the back is in operation. *Johannesgasse 28, tel. 0222/ 711220. 500 rooms with bath. Facilities: sauna, health club, laundry, dry cleaning service, barber, hair stylist, complimentary limo, tennis, skating. AE, DC, MC, V.*

Palais Schwarzenberg. Rooms are incorporated into a quiet wing of a Baroque palace, a 10-minute drive from the opera. The restaurant enjoys a good reputation. *Schwarzenbergplatz 9, tel. 0222/784515. 38 rooms with bath. Facilities: bar. AE, DC, MC, V.*

Sacher. The hotel's reputation has varied considerably over recent years, but it remains one of the legendary addresses in Europe, with its opulent decor highlighted by original oil paintings, sculptures, and objets d'art. The Blue and Red bars are intimate and favored by nonguests as well, as is the café, particularly in summer when tables are set up outside. Guest rooms are spacious and elegantly appointed. *Philharmoniker Str. 4, tel. 0222/514560. 117 rooms with bath or shower. Facilities: coffee shop, bar. No credit cards, but personal checks accepted.*

Expensive

★ **Astoria.** Though the Astoria is one of Vienna's traditional old hotels, the rooms are considerably modernized. The paneled lobby has been preserved, however, and retains an unmistakable Old World patina. The location is central, but because of the street musicians and the late-night crowds in the pedestrian zone, rooms overlooking the Kärntner Strasse tend to be noisy in summer. *Kärntner Str. 32–34, tel. 0222/515770. 108 rooms with bath or shower. Facilities: restaurant. AE, DC, MC, V.*

Capricorno. Overlooks the Danube Canal in a fairly central location. Although its facade is modern and somewhat short on charm, the hotel nonetheless represents good value. *Schwedenplatz 3–4, tel. 0222/633104. 46 rooms with bath or shower. AE, DC, MC, V.*

Europa. The location—midway between the opera house and the cathedral—is ideal, but rooms on the Kärntner Strasse side are noisy in summer; ask for a room overlooking Neuer Markt. The building is postwar modern and lacks the charm of older hotels, but the staff is friendly and helpful. The café is popular for people-watching year-round, particularly in summer when tables are put outdoors. *Neuer Markt 3, tel. 0222/515940. 102 rooms with bath. Facilities: coffee shop, bar, restaurant. AE, DC, MC, V.*

★ **König von Ungarn.** This utterly charming, centrally located hotel is tucked away in the shadow of the cathedral. The historic facade belies the modern efficiency of the interior, from the atrium lobby to the guest rooms themselves. The restaurant (just next door in a house that Mozart once lived in) is excellent, though not inexpensive, and is always packed at noon.

Schulerstr. 10, tel. 0222/5265200. 32 rooms with bath or shower. AE, DC, MC, V.

Mailberger Hof. This is a favorite of opera stars, conductors, and those who want a central but quiet location. Some rooms have limited kitchenette facilities. The arcaded courtyard is very pretty. *Annagasse 7, tel. 0222/5120641. 80 rooms with bath or shower. AE, DC, MC, V.*

Hotel Ring am Gestade. Rooms here are small to miniscule but offer good value; the location is within walking distance of the downtown area. Vienna's oldest Gothic church, Maria am Gestade, is just next-door. *Am Gestade 1, tel. 0222/637701. 23 rooms with bath or shower. Facilities: bar. AE, DC, MC. V*

Moderate **Austria.** This older hotel is on a quiet side street in an historic area. It is popular with tourists. *Wolfengasse 3/Fleischmarkt, tel. 0222/51523. 51 rooms, 40 with bath or shower. Facilities: bar. DC, MC.*

Pension Christina. This one is gaining a solid reputation, due in part to its central yet quiet location in the inner city. *Hafnersteig 7, tel. 0222/632961. 32 rooms with bath or shower. MC.*

Kärntnerhof. Though tucked away in a tiny, quiet side street, Karntnerhof is nevertheless centrally located. It's known for its particularly friendly staff. Rooms are functionally decorated but clean and serviceable. *Grashofgasse 4, tel. 0222/5121923. 45 rooms, 34 with bath or shower. AE, DC, MC, V.*

★ **Post.** The hotel takes its name from the city's main post office, opposite. An older but updated hotel that offers fine location, friendly staff, and a good café. *Fleischmarkt 24, tel. 0222/515830. 77 rooms with bath or shower. AE, DC, MC, V.*

Schweizerhof. This is more of a pension than a hotel, but the location is excellent and the smallish rooms are certainly adequate. *Bauernmarkt 22, tel. 0222/5331931. 55 rooms with bath or shower. AE, DC, MC, V.*

Wandl. The house is old and the rooms small, but the Wandl's location and reasonable prices compensate for most deficiencies. *Petersplatz 9, tel. 0222/636317. 134 rooms with bath or shower. No credit cards.*

★ **Pension Zipser.** This has become a favorite with regular visitors to Vienna. It is slightly less central than some others on our list, but very comfortable. *Lange Gasse 49, tel. 0222/420228. 46 rooms with bath or shower. Facilities: bar. AE, DC, MC, V.*

Inexpensive **Central.** This older hotel doesn't have quite the downtown location its name suggests, but it is reasonably central, although across the canal. *Taborstr. 8a, tel. 0222/21105. 60 rooms, 41 with bath or shower.*

The Arts

Theater and Opera Check the monthly program published by the city; posters also show opera and theater schedules. Tickets for the **Opera, Volksoper,** and the **Burg** and **Akademie** theaters are available at the central ticket office to the left rear of the Opera (*Bundestheaterkassen,* Hanuschgasse 3, tel. 0222/514440; open weekdays 9–5, weekends 9–1). Tickets go on advance sale a week before performances. Unsold tickets can be obtained at the evening box office. Plan to be there at least one hour before the performance; students can buy remaining tickets at lower prices, so they are usually out in force. Theater is offered in English at **Vienna English Theater** (Josefsgasse 12, tel.

0222/421260) and **International Theater** (Porzellangasse 8, tel. 0222/316272).

Music Most classical concerts are in either the **Konzerthaus** (Loth-ringerstr. 20, tel. 0222/721211) or **Musikverein** (Dumbast-rasse 3, tel. 0222/658190). Tickets can be bought at the box of-fices. Pop concerts are scheduled from time to time at the **Austria Center** (Am Hubertusdamm 6, tel. 0222/2369150; U-4 subway to VIC stop).

Film Films are shown in English at **Burg Kino** (Opernring 19, tel. 0222/5878406) and **Film Museum** (Augustinerstra. 1, tel. 0222/5337054). To find English-language movies, look for "OF" ("Originalfassung") or "OmU" (original with subtitles) in the newspaper listings.

Entertainment and Nightlife

Cabarets Most cabarets are expensive and unmemorable. Two of the best are **Cassanova** (Dorotheergasse 6, tel. 0222/5129845), which emphasizes striptease, and **Moulin Rouge** (Walfischgasse 11, tel. 0222/5122130).

Discos The **Splendid** (Jasomirgottstr. 3, tel. 0222/5331515) is the city's oldest dance-bar, open daily to 4 AM. The refurbished **Scotch** (Parkring 10, tel. 0222/5129417) is going upscale in its efforts to regain its one-time legendary popularity, though it still hasn't quite made it yet. **Queen Anne** (Johannesgasse 12, tel. 0222/5120203) is central, popular, and always packed. Live bands, dancing, and snacks are offered at **Chattanooga** (Graben 29, tel. 0222/524218).

Nightclubs A casual '50s atmosphere pervades the popular **Café Volks-garten** (Burgring 1, tel. 0222/630518), situated in the city park of the same name; tables are set outdoors in summer. The more formal **Eden Bar** (Liliengasse 2, tel. 0222/527450) is consid-ered one of Vienna's smartest nightspots; don't expect to be let in unless you're dressed to kill.

Wine Taverns For a traditional Viennese night out, head to one of the city's atmospheric wine taverns, which sometimes date as far back as the 12th century. You can often have full meals at these tav-erns, but the emphasis is mainly on drinking. **Melker Stiftskeller** (*see* Dining) is one of the friendliest and most typi-cal of Vienna's wine taverns. Other well-known ones: **Anti-quitäten-Keller** (Magdalenenstr. 32, tel. 0222/5669533; closed Aug.), which has a backdrop of classical music; **Augustiner-keller** (Augustiner Str. 1, tel. 0222/5331026), open at lunch well as evenings, in the same building as the Albertina collection; **Esterhazykeller** (Haarhof 1, tel. 0222/5333482), a particularly mazelike network of rooms; **Piaristenkeller** (Piaristengasse 45, tel. 0222/429152), with zither music; and **Zwölf-Apostelkeller** (Jonnenfelsgasse 3, tel. 0222/526777), near St. Stephen's Cathedral.

The Danube Valley

The Danube valley stretches about 80 kilometers (55 miles) west of Vienna, and many visitors enjoy it as part of an ex-cursion from the country's capital. What this region offers is magnificent countryside, some of Austria's best food and

The Danube Valley

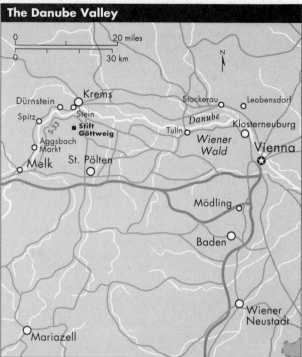

wines, and comfortable, in some cases elegant, accommodations. Above the river are the ruins of ancient castles; the one at Durnstein was where the 12th-century English king Richard the Lionhearted was held captive. The abbeys at Melk and Göttweig, with their magnificent libraries, dominate their settings. Vineyards sweep down to the river, which is lined with fruit trees that burst into blossom every spring. People here live close to the land, and at certain times of year vintners open their homes to sell their own wines and produce. Roadside stands offer flowers, fruits, vegetables, and wines. And this is an area of legend: The Danube as well as the Rhine shares the story of the mythical Niebelungen, defenders of Siegfried, hero of German myth.

Getting Around

By Car   If pressed for time, take the Áutobahn to St. Pölten, turn north onto Route 333, and follow signs to Melk. For a more scenic route, leave Vienna via Klosterneuburg, take S-33 along the south shore of the Danube, cross the Danube at Melk, and then return to Vienna along the north bank of the river.

By Train   Depart from the Westbahnhof for Melk; then take the bus along the north bank of the Danube to Dürnstein and Krems. Side bus trips can be made from Krems to Göttweig.

By Boat   Travel upstream, with stops at Krems, Dürnstein, Melk, and points between. Return to Vienna by boat or by train from Melk (combination tickets available).

Guided Tours

Vienna travel agencies offer tours of the Wachau, as the Danube valley is known. These range from one-day outings to longer excursions. For details contact the Vienna tourist office at Heidenschauss 2, tel. 0222/5333114.

Tourist Information

Dürnstein. Im Rathaus, tel. 02711/219.
Klosterneuburg. Neidermarkt, Postfach 6, tel. 02243/2038.
Krems. Wichnerstr. 8, tel. 02732/2676 (covers **Stein an der Donau** as well).
Melk. Im Rathaus, tel. 02752/2307.
Tulln. Nussallee 4, tel. 02272/4285.

Exploring

North of Vienna lies **Klosterneuburg,** whose huge **abbey** dominates the market town. The abbey's extensive vineyards offer excellent wines; the abbey itself is a major agricultural landowner in the region. *Open Mon.–Sat. 9:30–11 and 1:30–4, Sun. 1:30–4.*

If you are driving, you have the choice of following the river bank or heading up over the village of St. Andrae and down to the river plain again. At **Tulln,** the **town hall** dominates the town square.

You will see **Stift Göttweig** long before you reach it. This impressive, 11th-century Benedictine abbey affords sensational views of the Danube valley; walk around the grounds and view the impressive chapel. *Ronte 303, on the right bank of the Danube, opposite Krems.*

Farther along the valley is the abbey of **Melk,** holding a commanding position over the Danube. The library is rich in art as well as books; the ceiling frescoes are particularly memorable. *Open Palm Sunday–Oct., Mon.–Sat. 9–11:30 and 1–4, Sun. 9:30–11:30 and 1–4; June–Aug. daily 1–5; Nov.–Palm Sunday, daily 11–2.*

Time Out   Pay a visit to the Abbey's **Stiftskeller.** The local wines are excellent. Open daily from April through October.

Cross to the north of the river and head back downstream. The beautiful Medieval town of **Dürnstein** is known for keeping Richard the Lionhearted imprisoned in its now-ruined castle for 13 months. The town is also known for its fine hotels, restaurants, and wines. Virtually next door is **Stein,** with its former **Imperial Toll House. Stein** and **Krems** sit at the center of Austria's foremost winegrowing area and are two towns that have grown together.

The road back to Vienna now wanders away from the Danube, crossing through some attractive woodlands. When you reach Leobensdorf you'll spot **Burg Kreuzenstein,** perched to the left upon a nearby hilltop. The castle includes a small museum of armour. *Regular tours daily to 4 PM.*

Dining and Lodging

For details and price category definitions, *see* Dining and Lodging in Essential Information.

Dürnstein
Lodging
★

Schlosshotel. This early-Baroque castle has been luxuriously converted. Try for a room overlooking the Danube. Eat in the celebrated restaurant and don't miss out on the house wines. *Dürnstein 2, tel. 02711/212. 37 rooms with bath or shower. Facilities: sauna, pool. Closed Nov.–Mar. AE, DC, MC, V. Very Expensive.*

Klosterneuburg
Lodging

Schlosshotel Martinschloss. The Martinschloss—a circa 1766 Baroque castle—is romantically set on the banks of the Danube, in the midst of some rolling park land. The real Trapp family lived here until just before the outbreak of World War II. Try for a room overlooking the river. *34–36 Martinstr., tel. 02243/7426. 54 rooms, 24 with bath. Facilities: pool, sauna. AE, DC, MC, V. Expensive.*

Krems
Lodging

Alte Post. A 16th-century house with an arcaded courtyard, the Alte Post is conveniently positioned right in the center of town. In good weather the courtyard is used for dining. *Obere Landstr. 32, tel. 02732/2276. 20 rooms, most with bath. No credit cards. Inexpensive.*

Langelebarn
Dining
★

Zum Roten Wolf. This outstanding, elegant country restaurant serves traditional local foods. *Bahnstr. 58, tel. 02272/2567. Dress: studied casual. Reservations advisable. Closed Tues. AE, DC, MC, V. Moderate.*

Mautern
Dining
★

Bacher. The Bacher is one of Austria's best restaurants, elegant but entirely lacking in pretension. Dining in the garden in summer adds to the experience. *Südtirolerplatz 208, tel. 02732/2937. Dress: studied casual. Reservations recommended. Closed Mon. May–Oct., Mon. and Tues. Nov.–Apr. Expensive.*

Salzburg

Arriving and Departing

By Plane For information, phone Salzburg airport, tel. 0662/851204.

Between the Airport and Downtown Buses leave for the Salzburg train station in Europaplatz every 15 minutes during the day, every half-hour at night. Journey time is 18 minutes. Taxi fare runs about AS 150.

By Train Salzburg's main train station is at Europlatz. Train information, tel. 0662/1717; telephone ticket orders and seat reservations, tel. 0622/1700.

By Bus The central bus terminal (tel. 0662/72150) is in front of the train station.

By Car Salzburg has several autobahn exits; study the map and decide which one is best for you. Parking is available in the cavernous garages under the Mönchsberg.

Getting Around

By Bus and Trolleybus Service is frequent and reliable; route maps are available from the tourist office or your hotel.

By Taxi At Festival time, taxis are too scarce to hail on the street, so order through your hotel porter or phone 0662/74400 or 0662/17611.

By Fiaker Fiakers, or horsedrawn cabs, are available at Residenzplatz.

By Car Don't even think of it!

Guided Tours

Sightseeing Tours Guided bus tours of the city and its environs are given by **Autoreisebüro Salzkraft** (Mirabellplatz 2, tel. 0662/72656); **Albus** (Markartplatz 9, tel. 0662/73445); and **Albus Kiosk** (Mirabellplatz, tel. 0662/71773). **Salzburg Panorama Tours** (Mirabellplatz, tel. 0662/74029) organizes chauffeur-driven tours for up to eight people.

Tourist Information

Salzburg's official tourist office, **Stadtverkehrsbüro,** has its headquarters at Auerspergstr. 7, tel. 0662/80720. There's also an **information center** at Mozartplatz 5, tel. 0662/847568, and at the main train station, tel. 0662/71712.

Exploring Salzburg

Salzburg is best known as the birthplace of Wolfgang Amadeus Mozart and receives its greatest number of visitors during the annual Mozart Festival in July and August. Dominated by a fortress on one side and a minimountain (Mönchsberg) on the other, this Baroque city is best explored on foot. Many areas are pedestrian precincts. Some of the most interesting boutiques and shops are found in the dozens of alleys and passageways that link streets and squares. Parking anywhere near the center is all but impossible, so if you're driving, leave your car at your hotel or in the vast parking garage under Mönchsberg. And take an umbrella: Salzburg is noted for sudden brief downpours that stop as abruptly as they start.

The Salzach river separates the old and new towns; for the best perspective on the old, climb the **Kapuziner** hill (pathways from the Linzer Strasse or Steingasse). Once back down at river level, walk up through Markartplatz, to the **Landestheater,** where light opera and operettas are staged outside at Festival time; the larger houses used during the Festival are closed most of the year. Wander through the **Baroque Mirabell** gardens in back of the theater and enjoy a dramatic view of the Old City, with the castle in the background. If you are pressed for time, pass up the **Baroque Museum,** but be sure to look inside **Schloss Mirabell.** It houses public offices, including that of the city's Registrar's Office; many couples come here to be married in such a sumptuous setting. The foyer and staircase, decorated with cherubs, are good examples of Baroque excess. Chamber music concerts are given in the Baroque hall upstairs in summer. *Baroque Museum, Mirabelgarten, tel. 0662/74432. Admission: AS 20. Open Tues.–Sat. 9–noon and 2–5, also Mon. in July and Aug.; Sun. 9–noon. Schloss Mirabell, Mirabellplatz, tel. 0662/80722258. Open Mon.–Thurs. 8–4, Fri. 8–1.*

Head down Schwarzstrasse, back toward the center of the city. On your left is the famed **Mozarteum,** a music academy

Alter Markt, **14**

Baroque Museum, **2**

Bürgerspital, **6**

Carolino Augusteum
Museum, **5**

Dom, **10**

Festspielhaus, **7**

Festung
Hohensalzburg, **11**

Franzikanerkirche, **9**

Kollegialitätskirche, **8**

Landestheater, **1**

Mozarteum, **4**

Mozart's Birthplace, **15**

Residenz, **13**

Schloss Hellbrunn, **16**

Schloss Mirabell, **3**

Stiftskirche
St. Peter, **12**

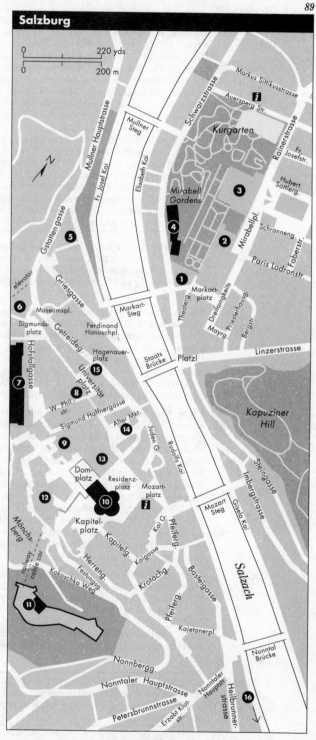

(Schwarstr. 26, tel. 0662/74492) whose courtyard encloses the summer house in which Mozart wrote his opera *The Magic Flute*. Cross over the Markart-Steg footbridge to the "Old City" side of the Salzach river. Turn right and walk a short distance up the Kai to the **Carolino Augusteum Museum.** This is the city museum, whose collections include art, archaeology, and musical instruments. *Museumsplatz 1, tel. 0662/843145. Admission: AS 20; combined ticket with toy museum in Bürgerspital (see below). Open Tues.–Sun. 9–5.*

Time Out From the Carolinum, as the museum is called, turn the corner into Gstattengasse. On your right is the Monchsberg elevator that will take you to the top of the promontory. Once here, go to the **Café Winkler** (Am Monchsberg 32, tel. 0662/841215), which is rather commercial but offers superb views of the city, with the fortress in the background. It's a delightful hike over the ridge to the fortress from here (making the trip in reverse, however, will save you an uphill climb).

Down again at city level, follow the Gsattengasse to the **Bürgerspital,** which houses a toy museum within its Renaissance arcades. *Bürgerspitalplatz 2, tel. 0662/847560. Admission: AS 20; combined ticket with Carolino Augusteum. Open Tues.–Sun. 9–5.*

Ahead is Sigmundsplatz, whose central Pferdeschwemme (Horse Fountain) is its most notable feature. Built into the side of the mountain itself is the **Festspielhaus,** a huge complex where Salzburg's annual Festival, the Festspiel, is held. *Hostallgasse 1, tel. 0662/842541. Admission: AS 25. Guided tours in May, June, and Sept. weekdays at 11 and 3, Sat. at 11; Oct.–Apr. weekdays 3, Sat. 11; during Easter festival, weekdays at 2. No tours in July and August.*

From the Festspeilhaus, turn left into the Wiener-Phil-harmoniker-Strasse. The **Kollegialitätskirche** (Collegiate Church) on the left is the work of Fischer von Erlach and is one of the best examples of Baroque architecture anywhere; be sure to look inside. On weekday mornings, the Univers-itätsplatz, in front of the church, is crowded with market stands. Cut under the covered passageway and turn left into Sigmund Haffner-Gasse. At the corner on the left stands the 13th-century **Franzikanerkirche** (Franciscan Church), an eclectic mix of architectural styles, with Romanesque and Gothic accents. Nearby, at Domplatz, is the Salzburg **Dom** (cathedral), a magnificently proportioned building; note the great bronze doors as you enter.

To reach the fortress on the hill above, walk under the arcade to the right side of the church and up the narrow Festungsgasse at the back end of Kapitalplatz. From here, you can either follow the footpath up the hill or take a five-minute ride on the Festungsbahn, the inclined railway cable car. On a sunny day, a far more pleasurable—and strenuous!—route is to hike up the Festungsgasse, turning frequently to enjoy the changing panorama of the city below.

Time Out **Stieglkeller** (Festungsgasse 10, tel. 0662/842681) offers a wide choice of good Austrian fare, served outdoors in summer. The local beer is superb. Try their *Salzburger Nockerln,* a heavenly meringue dessert.

⑪ Once at the **Festung Hohensalzburg** itself, you can wander around on your own (admission: AS 10) or take a tour (AS 30). The views in all directions from the 12th-century fortress are magnificent. The main attraction is **St. George's Chapel**, built in 1501. A year later, in 1502, the Festung acquired the 200-pipe barrel organ, which plays daily in summer at 7 AM, 11 AM, and 6 PM. *Mönchsberg, tel. 0662/8438213. Open daily, May–Sept. 9–5:30, Oct.–Apr. 9–4:30.*

⑫ Back down in the city, follow the wall to **Stiftskirche St. Peter** (St. Peter's Abbey). The cemetery lends an added air of mystery to the monk's caves cut into the cliff. The catacombs attached to the church can be visited by guided tour. *Just off Kapitelplatz, tel. 0662/844578. Admission: AS 10. Tours daily May–Sept. 10–5, Oct.–Apr. 11–12 and 1:30–3:30.*

⑬ Head around the cathedral to the spacious Residenzplatz, a vast and elegant square. The **Residenz** itself includes the Bishop's living quarters and representative rooms. *Residenzplatz 1, tel. 0662/80422693. Admission: AS 20. Tours Sept.–June 10, 11, 2, 3; July–Aug. every 20 mins. from 10–4:40.*

The **Residenzgalerie,** in the same building complex, has an outstanding collection of 16th- to 19th-century European art. *Residenzplatz 1, tel. 0662/80422270. Admission: AS 20. Open daily 10–5.*

⑭ From the lower end of Residenzplatz, cut across into the **Alter Markt** which still serves as an open market. Salzburg's narrowest house is squeezed into the north side of the square. Turn left into Griesgasse, a tiny street packed with boutiques and fascinating shops. At the head of the tiny Rathausplatz is **⑮** **Mozart's birthplace,** now a museum. *Getreidegasse 9, tel. 0662/844313. Admission: AS 35. Open May–Sept. 9–7, Oct.–Apr. 9–6.*

Wander along Getreidegasse, with its ornate wrought-iron shop signs and the Mönchsberg standing sentinel at the far end. Don't neglect the warren of interconnecting side alleys: These include a number of fine shops and often open onto impressive inner courtyards that, in summer, are guaranteed to be filled with flowers.

⑯ One popular excursion from Salzburg is to **Schloss Hellbrunn,** about five kilometers (three miles) outside the city. The castle was built in the 17th century, and its rooms have some fine *trompe l'oeil* decorations. The castle's full name is Lustschloss Hellbrunn—Hellbrunn Pleasure Castle. It was designed for the relaxation of Salzburg's prince bishops and includes the **Wasserspiele,** or fountains, conceived by someone with an impish sense of humor. Expect to get sprinkled as water shoots up from unlikely spots, such as the center of the table at which you're seated. The Baroque fountains are also fascinating. Both castle and fountain gardens can be included on a tour. (Tel. 0662/841696. Admission: AS 39. Tours Apr. and Oct. 9–4:30; May and Sept. 9–5; June 9–5:30; July and Aug. 9–6.) The **Tiergarten** (zoo) here is outstanding because of the way in which the animals have been housed in natural surroundings. (Tel. 0662/841169. Admission: AS 30. Open Oct.–Mar. 9–4; Apr.–Sept. 9–6.) The Hellbrunn complex also includes a small **folklore museum** (Admission: AS 10. Open Easter–Oct. 9–5).

Dining

Some of the city's best restaurants are in the leading hotels. This is a tourist town, and popular restaurants are always crowded, so make reservations well ahead, particularly during Festival time. For details and price category definitions, *see* Dining in Essential Information.

Expensive **Alt Salzburg.** One of the city's most acclaimed dining spots, Alt Salzburg has elegant red-and-white rooms and fine service. Try the traditional *tafelspitz* (Austrian pot roast). *Bürgerspitalgasse 2, tel. 0622/841476. Jacket and tie. Reservations essential. AE, DC, MC. Closed Sun. and Feb.*

Goldener Hirsch. Outstanding creative cuisine is served in a chic atmosphere. Service can be slow, but the grilled hare is well worth any wait. *Getreidegasse 37, tel. 0662/848511. Jacket and tie. Reservations essential. AE, DC, MC, V.*

Mirabell. Although it's housed in a chain hotel (the Sheraton), some will argue that the Mirabell is the city's top restaurant. The menu mixes international dishes with adventurous versions of local specialties such as wiener schnitzel and wildschwein (wild boar). *Auerspergstr. 4, tel. 0662/79321. Jacket and tie. Reservations advisable. AE, DC, MC, V.*

★ **Zum Eulenspiegel.** The intimate rooms of an old city house contribute to the charm of this city restaurant. *Hagenauerplatz 2, tel. 0662/843180. Jacket and tie. Reservations advisable. AE, DC, MC, V.*

Moderate **Domstueben.** Good, solid Austrian fare and the comfortable and cozy dining rooms are the strengths of the Domstueben. It's equally popular with locals and visitors. *Goldgasse 17, tel. 0662/844681. Dress: studied casual. Reservations advisable. DC.*

Moser Weinstube. This favorite of Festival musicians offers less atmospheric charm than the Domsteuben, but the food is what counts. *Wiener-Philharmoniker-Str. 3, tel. 0662/841136. Dress: casual. Reservations advisable on festival evenings. DC.*

Inexpensive **Sternbräu.** If you're not looking for anything too fancy, try the hearty sausages and roasted meats at this vast complex, which has a pleasant garden in summer. *Griesgasse 23, tel. 0662/842140. Dress: casual. No credit cards.*

Ratzka. Visitors from all corners of the world come to this café for a taste of Herr Ratzka's *Zwetschkenfleck,* or apple wine cake. His pastries, *torten,* and petit fours are all of unsurpassed quality. *Imbergstr. 45, tel. 0662/70919. Dress: casual. Closed Mon. and Tues. No credit cards.*

Lodging

Reservations are always advisable and are essential at Festival time (both Easter and summer). For details and price category definitions, *see* Lodging in Essential Information.

Very Expensive **Bristol.** The attractive Belle Epoque facade of the Bristol will prepare you for the comfortable rooms and period furnishings inside. One of Austria's classic hotels. *Markartplatz 3, tel. 0662/73557. 90 rooms with bath or shower. AE, DC, MC, V. Closed Jan.–Mar.*

★ **Goldener Hirsch.** This old-timer—800 years old and an inn since

1564—is conveniently set right in the heart of the old city. Arched corridors, vaulted stairs, rustic furniture, and antiques provide a medieval atmosphere; the essential modern appliances stay ingeniously hidden. The restaurant (*see* above) is excellent. *Getreidegasse 35–37, tel. 0662/848511. 75 rooms with bath. AE, DC, MC, V.*

Österreichischer Hof. Salzburg's *grande dame* occupies a lovely riverside location, and some of the rooms give views of the fortress and the old city. All four restaurants are excellent, but reservations are essential. *Schwarzstr. 5–7, tel. 0662/72541. 120 rooms, 118 with bath or shower. AE, DC, MC, V.*

Sheraton. A Sheraton is a Sheraton, but this one has a superior restaurant. The location, beside the Mirabell Gardens, is a plus. *Auerspergstr. 4, tel. 0662/793210. 165 rooms with bath. Facilities: indoor pools, valet, room service, laundry, health spa adjacent. AE, DC, MC, V.*

Expensive   **Bayrischer Hof.** Not as close to the downtown area as visitors may want but only two blocks from the train station. The modern rooms are very comfortable—which may explain why they're almost always full. *Elisabethstr. 12, tel. 0662/54170. 60 rooms with bath or shower. Facilities: 3 restaurants. AE, DC, MC, V.*

Gablerbräu. A country inn transported to town, the Gablerbräu is cheerful and friendly and an obvious favorite with repeat visitors. *Linzer Gasse 9, tel. 0662/73441. 51 rooms with bath or shower. AE, DC, MC, V.*

Pitter. Close to the train station, the Pitter is a favorite with business people. The inexpensive restaurant is a definite plus. *Rainerstr. 6–8, tel. 0662/78571. 220 rooms with bath and shower. AE, DC, MC, V.*

Moderate   **Markus Sittikus.** This one is reasonably priced and more than reasonably comfortable. The train station is just a stone's throw away. *Markus-Sittikus-Str. 20, tel. 0662/71121. 35 rooms with bath or shower. AE, DC, MC, V.*

The Arts

Festivals   Tickets for the festival performances are almost impossible to get once you are in Salzburg. Write ahead to Salzburger Festspiele, Postfach 140, A-5010 Salzburg.

Opera, Music, and Art   Theater and opera are presented in the **Festspielhaus;** opera and operetta at the **Landestheater;** concerts at the **Mozarteum.** Chamber music—in costume—is performed in Schloss Mirabell. Special art exhibits in the **Carolinum** are often outstanding.

Innsbruck

Arriving and Departing

By Plane   The airport is three kilometers (two miles) to the west of the city. For flight information, phone 5222/81777.

Between the Airport and Downtown	Buses go to the main train station; journey time is about 20 minutes. Taxis should take no more than 10 minutes.
By Train	All trains stop at the city's main station. Train connections are available to Munich, Vienna, Rome, and Zurich. For train information, phone 5222/1717. Ticket reservations, tel. 5222/1700.
By Bus	The terminal is in front of the main train station.
By Car	Exit from the east-west autobahn, or from the Brenner autobahn running south to Italy. Much of the downtown area is paid-parking only; get parking vouchers at tobacco shops.

Getting Around

By Bus and Streetcar	Most bus and streetcar routes begin or end at Südtiroler Platz, site of the main train station. The bus is the most convenient way to reach ski slopes outside the city. Schedules are available at the tourist office or any hotel.
By Taxi	Taxis are not much faster than walking, particularly along the one-way streets and in the Old City. To order a radio cab, phone 5222/27711 or 45500.

Guided Tours

Sightseeing Tours	Hour-long bus tours of the city's most important sights leave from the Hofburg at 10:15, noon, 2, and 3:15. Longer tours (about two hours) leave from Bozner Platz at 10 and 2.

Tourist Information

The city's two main tourist offices are at Bozner Platz 6, tel. 5222/2077; and Burggraben 3, tel. 5222/760500.

Exploring Innsbruck

At the center of the province of Tirol lies the quaint and well-preserved capital city of Innsbruck. Squeezed by the mountains and sharing the valley with the Inn river, Innsbruck is compact and very easy to explore on foot. The ancient city—it received its municipal charter in 1239—no doubt owes much of its fame and charm to its unique situation. To the north, the steep, sheer sides of the Alps rise like a shimmering blue-and-white wall from the edge of the city, an awe-inspiring backdrop to the mellowed green domes and red roofs of the picturesque Baroque town.

Modern-day Innsbruck retains close associations with three historical figures: Emperor Maximilian I and Empress Maria Theresa, both of whom are responsible for much of the city's architecture, and Andreas Hofer, a Tirolean patriot. You will find repeated references to these personalities as you tour the city. A good starting point is the **Goldenes Dachl** (the Golden Roof), which made famous the ancient mansion whose balcony it covers (it's actually made of gilded copper tiles). The building now houses an **Olympic Museum,** which features videotapes of the Innsbruck winter Olympics. *Herzog-Friedrich-Str., tel. 5222/575. Admission: AS 20. Open daily 10–5:30.*

 A walk up the Hofgasse brings you to the **Hofburg,** the Rococo

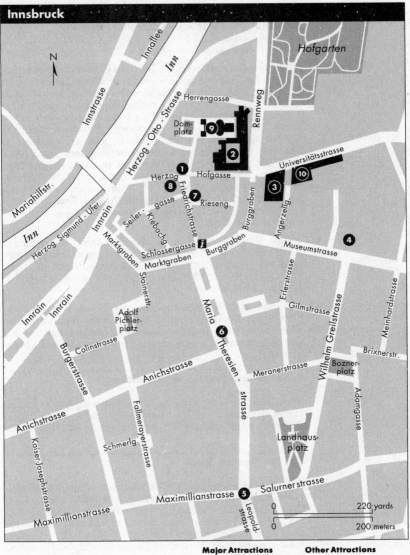

Innsbruck

Major Attractions
Annasäule, **6**
Ferdinandeum, **4**
Goldenes Dachl, **1**
Hofburg, **2**
Hofkirche, **3**
Triumphpforte, **5**

Other Attractions
Dom St. Jakob, **9**
Helblinghaus, **8**
Stadtturm, **7**
Tiroler
Volkskunstmuseum, **10**

imperial palace, with its ornate reception hall decorated with portraits of Maria Theresa's ancestors. *Rennweg 1, tel. 5222/ 22186. Admission: AS 20. Open mid-May–mid-Oct. daily 9–4; mid-Oct.–mid-May, Mon.–Sat. 9–4.*

❸ Close by is the **Hofkirche,** the Imperial Church, built as a mausoleum for Maximilian. The emperor is surrounded by 24 marble reliefs portraying his accomplishments, as well as 28 oversize statues of his ancestors, including the legendary King Arthur. The above-mentioned Andreas Hofer is also buried here. Don't miss the silver chapel with its ornate altar. The **Tiroler Volkskunstmuseum** (Tirolean folk art museum) is housed in the Hofkirche, too, and shows costumes, rustic furniture, and farmhouse rooms decorated in styles ranging from Gothic to Rococo. *Universitätsstr. 2, tel. 5222/24302. Admission: AS 18 (Hofkirche), AS 15 (Volkskunstmuseum); combined ticket AS 25. Hofkirche open daily May–Sept. 9–5, Oct.– Apr. 9–12 and 2–5; Volkskunstmuseum open Mon.–Sat. 9–12 and 2–5, Sun. 9–12.*

❹ Follow Museumstrasse to the **Ferdinandeum,** which houses Austria's largest collection of Gothic art, as well as paintings from the 19th and 20th centuries. *Museumstr. 15, tel. 5222/ 22003. Admission: AS 20. Open Tues.–Sat. 10–noon and 2–5, Sun. 9–noon and 2–5.*

❺ Cut back down Wilhelm-Greil-Strasse to the **Triumphpforte**
❻ (Triumphal Arch), built in 1765, and walk back up Maria-Theresien-Strasse past the **Annasäule** (Anna Column) for a classic "postcard" view of Innsbruck with the Alps in the background.

What to See and Do with Children

The **Alpine Zoo** is usually good for an hour's enjoyment and includes an aquarium with both alpine fish and aquatic animals. *Weiherburg, tel. 5222/36775. Admission: AS 32. Open daily 9–6.*

Off the Beaten Track

Just three kilometers (two miles) southeast of the city and easily reached by either bus or streetcar, is **Schloss Ambras,** one of the country's finest and best-preserved castles. Originally dating from the 11th century, it was later rebuilt as a residence for the Archduke Ferdinand of Tirol (from 1564 to 1582), so most of what you now see is in German Renaissance style. The collection includes numerous pictures, weapons, armor, *objets d'art,* and furniture. *In the village of Ambras (streetcar lines 3 or 6), tel. 5222/48446. Admission: AS 30. Open May–Sept., Wed.– Sun. 10–4.*

Shopping

Shopping Districts Many shops are found in the historic streets of Maria-Theresienstrasse, Museumstrasse, Brixnerstrasse, Meranerstrasse, and among the arcades of Herzog-Friedrichstrasse.

Gift Ideas The best-known and best-loved local specialties include Tirolean hats (those little pointed green felt ones, garnished with a feather), Loden cloth, lederhosen, dirndls, wood-carvings, and mountain and skiing equipment.

Dining

For details and price category definitions, *see* Dining in Essential Information.

Expensive   **Belle Epoque.** Cut-glass chandeliers, heavy swagged curtains, and impressively thick linen tablecloths set an opulent tone at this restaurant in the Hotel Clima. Chef Friedrich Wolf's deftly prepared dishes lean toward the French; try the venison ragout. *Zeughasgasse 7, tel. 5222/588361. Jacket and tie. Reservations essential. AE, DC, MC, V. Closed lunch and Sun.*

Domstub'n. The family-run Domstub'n provides a sophisticated variation on the traditionally jolly Austrian theme: Leave the lederhosen at home for this one! *Pfarrgasse 3, tel. 5222/573353. Jacket and tie. Reservations recommended. DC.*

Philippine Welser. Regional specialties and swift service are two reasons why the Hotel Europa's restaurant is highly regarded by locals and visitors. *Brixner Str. 6, tel. 5222/5931648. Jacket and tie. Reservations recommended. DC.*

Schwarzer Adler. This place drips with atmosphere, its massive-beamed rooms a perfect backdrop to typical Austrian dishes like *Knödeln* (dumplings) and *Tafelspitz* (a type of pot roast). *Kaiserjagerstr. 2, tel. 5222/587109. Jacket and tie. Reservations useful. AE, DC, MC, V.*

Moderate   **Hirschenstuben.** Old-fashioned hospitality and dark-wood trimmings are found in force at this charming local favorite. *Kiebachgasse 5, tel. 5222/582979. Dress: casual. Reservations recommended. AE, DC, MC, V. Closed Sun.*

Ottoburg. A rabbit warren of rooms, in a 13th-century building, the Ottoburg is exactly right for an intimate, cozy lunch or dinner. It's packed with Austriana and 100% genuine. Go for the trout if it's available. *Herzog-Friedrich-Str. 1, tel. 5222/574652. Dress: casual. Reservations useful. AE, DC, MC, V.*

Inexpensive   **Goethestube.** The wine tavern of the city's oldest inn, the Goldener Adler (*see* Lodging), is one of Innsbruck's best. It was here that Goethe (who lent his name to the tavern) used to sip quantities of red South Tirolean wine during his stays in 1786 and 1790. *Herzog-Friedrich-Str. 6, tel. 5222/26334. Dress: informal. Reservations not required. AE, DC, MC, V.*

Stieglbrau. Lovers of good beer will be delighted to find this popular rustic spot, which, in addition to its thirst-quenching ales, provides good, solid Austrian fare. Portions are huge, the garden exceptionally pleasant. Wilhelm-Greil-Str. 25, tel. 5222/24338. Dress: casual. Reservations not required. No credit cards.

Lodging

For details and price category definitions, *see* Lodging in Essential Information.

Very Expensive   **Europa.** The Europa is a postwar building blessed with a considerable amount of charm. Some rooms have period furnishings; others are 20th-century modern. The restaurant, Philippine Welser (*see* above), is highly regarded. *Sudtiroler Platz 2, tel. 5222/5931. 132 rooms with bath. Facilities: bar, hair and beauty salon. AE, DC, MC, V.*

Sheraton. Innsbruck's newest major hotel is one of the reliable international chain. Rooms are modern plush, and, as with all Sheratons, facilities are extensive. The train station is nearby. *Salurner Str. 15, tel. 5222/571079. 191 rooms with bath. Facilities: restaurant, bar, health club, pool. AE, DC, MC, V.*

Innsbruck. The city's namesake hotel is modern, comfortably appointed, and the proud possessor of fantastic views of the old city and Nordkette mountains. Its central location is another plus. *Innrain 3, tel. 5222/59868. 90 rooms with bath. Facilities: restaurant, bar, pool, sauna. AE, DC, MC, V.*

Expensive **Clima.** The Belle Epoque restaurant (*see* above) is the Clima's major trump card; unfortunately, the rest of the hotel is decorated in a faintly antiseptic modern style. It's comfortable enough, though, and central as well. The disco is popular and sophisticated. *Zeughausgasse 7, tel. 5222/588361. 60 rooms with bath. Facilities: bar, coffee shop, disco. AE, DC, MC, V.*

★ **Goldener Adler.** The Golden Eagle has been an inn since 1390, and over the centuries has welcomed nearly every king, emperor, duke, or poet who passed through the city. The facade looks suitably ancient, and inside passages and stairs twist romantically and rooms crop up when least expected. The restaurant offers well-prepared seasonal and local dishes, and a good selection of wines from the Tirol. *Herzog-Friedrich-Str. 6, tel. 5222/586334. 40 rooms. 31 with bath or shower. Facilities: restaurant, bar, coffee-shop. AE, DC, MC, V.*

Union. A well-known favorite of many visitors to Innsbruck, the Union commands a loyal following. Very close to the station. *Adamgasse 22, tel. 5222/583313. 60 rooms with bath or shower. Facilities: restaurant, bar. AE, DC, MC, V.*

Moderate **Weisses Kreuz.** Occupying an honored position just next to the famous Goldenes Dachl (*see* Exploring), Weisses Kreuz is itself a lovely old historic building. The staff is unusually welcoming. *Herzog-Friedrich-Str. 31, tel. 5222/594790. 39 rooms, 28 with bath or shower. AE.*

Inexpensive **Binder.** A short bus trip from the center of town shouldn't be too high a price to pay for the less costly comfort at this small, friendly hotel a little ways out from the city's beating heart. *Dr.-Glatz-Str. 20, tel. 5222/42236. 32 rooms, some with bath or shower. AE, DC, MC, V.*

The Arts

Most hotels have a monthly calendar of events (in English). The **Central Ticket Office** is on Central Street, tel. 5222/32882. Opera, operetta, musicals, and concerts take place at the **Tiroler Landestheater** (Rennweg 2, tel. 5222/21771) and **Kongresshaus.**

Entertainment and Nightlife

Innsbruck is not known for its nightlife, if by nightlife you have in mind cabaret and Las Vegas-style floor shows. Most locals repair to one of the city's wine taverns or cafés for an evening of conversation and perhaps a yodelling competition or two. Some of the most atmospheric ones are the **Goethestube** in the Goldener Adler (*see* Dining); **Happ** (Herzog-Friedrich-Str. 12, tel. 5222/22980), which offers good local delicacies while you quaff your beer; and the traditional, century-old **Munding** café (Kiebachgasse 16, tel. 5222/24118). For dancing cheek-to-cheek, check out **Dorian Gray,** which has a live orchestra and an Italian restaurant overlooking the dance floor (Valiergasse 10, tel. 5222/47928). If it's disco you crave, try the **Kaiserstube** (Museumstr. 31, tel. 5222/29889).

5 Belgium

Introduction

Belgium covers a strip of land just under 200 miles (320 kilometers) long and 100 miles (160 kilometers) wide bordering the North Sea between France and Holland. With more than 10 million people, Belgium is the second most densely populated country in the world. It is a divided nation, populated by two distinct peoples. The Flemish, who speak Dutch (Flemish), inhabit the northern half of the country and account for 56% of the population. The French-speaking Walloons live in the other half. The capital, Brussels, is officially designated a dual-language area.

Belgium is the world's most heavily industrialized country with only 5% of the working population engaged in agriculture (though they still manage to produce two of Europe's greatest pâtés and any number of fine sausages). Besides being good businessmen, the Belgians also work very hard—partly to make up for what has so long been denied them. In the course of history, the Belgians have been ruled by the Romans, Vikings, French, Spanish, Austrians, Dutch, English, and Germans. Many of Europe's greatest battles have been fought on Belgian soil—from Waterloo and earlier, to the long-slogging encounters of World War I. During World War II, this territory witnessed both the initial *Blitzkrieg* of Nazi Panzer units and Hitler's final desperate counterattack against the advancing Allies in the Ardennes—an offensive that has gone down in history as the Battle of the Bulge.

The south of the country is a wild wooded area, with mountains rising to more than 2,000 feet (610 meters). In the Dutch-speaking north, on the other hand, the land is flat and heavily cultivated, much as in neighboring Holland. Here stand the medieval Flemish cities of Ghent and Bruges, with their celebrated carillons and canals—not to mention the 50 miles (80 kilometers) of sandy beaches that make up the country's northern coastline. To the northeast lies Antwerp, the country's main seaport. This city, where the painter Rubens lived, is now the world's leading diamond-cutting center.

Brussels stands in the very center of the country. A booming, expanding, and often very expensive city, it is now the capital of Europe. Here the Common Market (EEC) has its headquarters, as does NATO. The city boasts more ambassadors than any other in the world—approximately 160. Partly as a result of this concentration of power and partly because of the Belgians' celebrated love of good food, Brussels has become one of the most renowned gastronomic cities in the world. Those without expense accounts, beware! Belgian cuisine adds French flare to Dutch-size portions—which means that you seldom have to order very much.

Perhaps in order to work off all this good living, the Belgians are fanatical bicyclists. Several of the great legendary figures of the *Tour de France* have been Belgians. And despite its name, this annual race (the world's greatest and most grueling) usually has a stage or two running through Belgium.

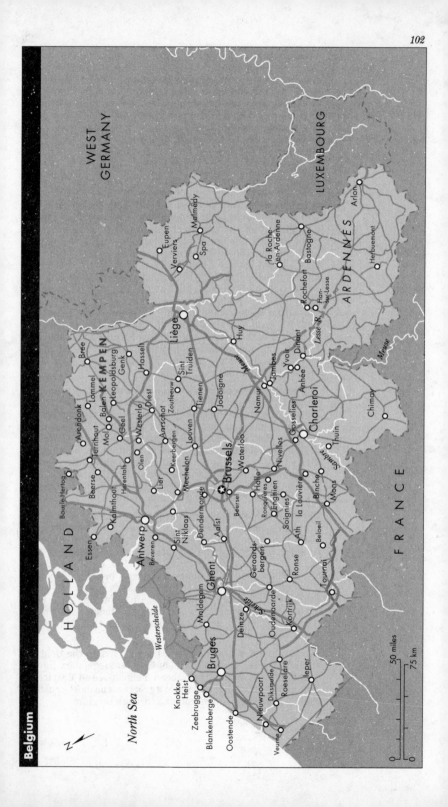

Before You Go

When to Go   The tourist season runs from early May to late September and peaks in July and August, when the weather is best. In recent years, however, off-season travel has become increasingly popular. Air and hotel rates are considerably cheaper, trains are less crowded, and advance reservations for hotel rooms are not always essential. In the coastal resorts, some hotels and restaurants remain open all year.

Climate   Temperatures range from around 65 F in May to an average 73 F in July and August. In winter, temperatures drop to an average of about 40 to 45 F. Snow is unusual except in the mountains of the Ardennes, but rain is frequent throughout the year. Bring a raincoat or an umbrella.

The following are the average daily maximum and minimum temperatures for Brussels.

Jan.	40F	4C	**May**	65F	18C	Sept.	69F	21C
	30	−1		46	8		51	11
Feb.	44F	7C	**June**	72F	22C	Oct.	60F	15C
	32	0		52	11		45	7
Mar.	51F	10C	**July**	73F	23C	Nov.	48F	9C
	36	2		54	12		38	3
Apr.	58F	14C	**Aug.**	72F	22C	Dec.	42F	6C
	41	5		54	12		32	0

Currency   The unit of currency in Belgium is the franc. There are bills of 100, 500, 1,000, and 5,000 francs; 50-franc bills are now being taken out of circulation and are being replaced by 50-franc coins. There are also 1.5- and 20-franc coins, and 50-centime pieces (100 centimes = 1 franc). At press time (fall 1988), the exchange rate was about BF35 to the dollar and BF65 to the pound sterling.

Traveler's checks and credit cards are the safest and simplest ways to carry money. American Express, Bank of America, Barclays, and Thomas Cook traveler's checks are all honored in Belgium. American Express and Visa cards are widely accepted, too. Avoid exchanging money on weekends or at hotels and restaurants unless you're prepared to pay a big premium.

What It Will Cost   The cost of a hotel stay in Brussels is higher than in many other European cities, largely because of the international role that the city plays. The rates are about the same as in London. Restaurants, however, are less expensive than in surrounding countries. Sales tax on most items ranges from 6% to 33% on luxury items, including jewelry, furs, and a wide selection of electronic goods. Many shops advertise goods "for export"; they provide documents you can use to reclaim the sales tax or VAT when you leave the country. (*See* Shopping below). If you're making substantial purchases, ask the shop to provide the export papers.

Sample Prices   A cup of coffee in a café will cost about BF50; a glass of beer, about BF65; and a glass of wine, about BF100. Train travel averages BF6 per mile; the average bus ride costs BF35; theater tickets cost about BF400, and movie tickets, about BF150.

Customs on Arrival   Visitors from EEC countries can bring in 300 cigarettes or 75 cigars or 400 grams of tobacco; 5 liters of still wine and 1½ liters of spirits or 3 liters of liqueur wine; and 75 grams of perfume. Other goods imported from the EEC may not exceed BF15,800 in value. Visitors from non-EEC countries can bring in 200 cigarettes or 50 cigars or 250 grams of tobacco; 2 liters of still wine and 1 liter of spirits or 2 liters of liqueur wine; 50 grams of perfume. Other goods from non-EEC countries may not exceed BF2,000 in value. There are no restrictions on the import or export of currency.

Language   There are two national languages in Belgium: French, spoken primarily in the south of the country, and Dutch or Flemish, spoken in the north. Brussels is bilingual, with both languages officially recognized.

Many people speak English in Brussels and in the north. Fewer speak it in smaller towns, particularly in the south.

Getting Around

By Car   Belgium has an excellent system of expressways, and the main
Road Conditions   roads are generally very good. Road numbers for main roads have the prefix N; expressways, the prefix A or E.

Rules of the Road   Drive on the right and pass on the left (passing on the right is forbidden). Seatbelts are compulsory in front seats. Each car must have a warning triangle to be used in the event of a breakdown or accident. At intersections, particularly in cities, traffic on the right has priority. Adhere strictly to this rule because there are few stop or yield signs. Cars within a traffic circle have priority over cars entering it. Buses and streetcars have priority over cars. Maximum speed limits are 120 kph (70 mph) on highways, 90 kph (55 mph) on major roads, and 60 kph (35 mph) in cities.

Parking   Most cities have metered on-street parking (parking meters take 1-, 5-, or 20-franc coins) and parking lots.

By Train   Fast and frequent trains connect all main towns and cities. If you intend to travel frequently, buy a **Tourrail Ticket,** which allows unlimited travel for 16 days, or on 5 days during a 16-day period. Cost for the five-day pass is BF2,400, first class or BF1,600, second class; for the 16-day pass, BF4,380, first class or BF2,920, second class.

There are special discount prices for round-trips on weekends starting at 4 PM on Thursday and ending at midnight on Sunday. You can also buy reduced-fare excursion tickets to places of interest. Ask at train stations for the best fare and buy your tickets there.

By Bus   There is a wide network of local and regional buses throughout Belgium. Details of services are available at train stations and tourist offices.

By Bicycle   You can rent a bicycle from Belgian railways at 48 stations throughout the country; train travelers get reduced rates. A special brochure is available at most stations. Bicycling is especially popular in the north and on the coast, where the land is flat. Bicycle lanes are provided in many Flemish cities.

Essential Information

Telephones   Pay phones work with 5- and 20-franc coins or with Telecards,
Local Calls   available in a number of denominations starting from BF200.

The Telecards can be purchased at any post office and at many newsstands. Most phone booths that accept Telecards have a list indicating where these cards are sold. An average local call costs 10 or 20 francs.

International Calls The least expensive method is to buy a high-denomination Telecard and make a direct call from a phone booth. A five-minute phone call to the United States at a peak time will cost about BF650 by this method. International calls can also be made at most hotels, but nearly all have a service charge that may double the cost. It's always wise to ask what the service charge is before placing the call. Operator-assisted international calls can also be made at most post offices.

Operators The numbers for operator assistance and information vary from city to city; it's best to ask at a hotel or post office or to consult a telephone directory.

Mail
Postal Rates Airmail letters to the United States cost BF36 for the first 20 grams; postcards, BF30. Airmail letters to the United Kingdom are BF13 for the first 20 grams. Stamps can be purchased at all post offices and at many larger hotels.

Receiving Mail You can have mail forwarded direct to your hotel. If you're uncertain where you'll be staying, have mail sent in care of **American Express** (1 pl. Louise, B-1000 Brussels). Cardholders are spared the $2 per letter charge.

Shopping Antwerp is a world-famous diamond center, and there are also a number of diamond and other jewelry shops in Brussels and Kortrijk. Val Saint-Lambert crystal is available in stores throughout the country. Bruges is famous for its lace, and you can still see women practicing this traditional craft in many places in the city. Brussels and Mechelen are also famous for their lace work and linen. For centuries, Huy has been known for its pewter ware. Spa specializes in wood carvings.

There are only a few large department stores in the country, and smaller shops tend to specialize in leather goods, crystal, jewelry, and the like.

The shopping districts in most cities, often in the center of the city, are usually in pedestrian-only streets. These areas usually have the widest selection and, frequently, the lowest prices.

VAT Refunds When you buy goods for export, you can ask most shops to fill out special forms covering VAT (value-added tax) or sales tax. When you leave Belgium, you must declare the goods at customs and have the customs officers stamp the forms. Once back home, you send the stamped forms back to the shop, and your VAT or sales tax will be refunded. This facility is available in most boutiques and large stores and covers most purchases of more than BF2,000.

Opening and Closing Times **Banks.** Banks are open weekdays from 9 to 4; some close for an hour at lunch. Exchange facilities are usually open on weekends, but you'll get a better rate during the week.
Museums. Most museums are open from 10 to 5 every day except Monday. Check individual listings.
Shops. Stores are open weekdays and Saturday from 10 to 6 and generally stay open later on Friday. Hours vary from store to store, so it's best to check in advance. Some small places, mostly food stores, remain open on Sunday.

National Holidays January 1 (New Year's Day); March 27 (Easter Monday); May 1 (May Day); May 4 (Ascension); May 15 (Whit Monday); July 1 (Flanders only); July 21 (National Holiday); August 15 (Assumption); September 27 (Wallonia only); November 1 (All Saints); November 11 (Armistice); November 15 (king's birthday, but stores, banks, etc., not closed; some schools are); December 25.

Dining Visitors have a choice of restaurants, sandwich bars, cafeterias, cafés, and fast-food shops. Most restaurants do not serve breakfast, are open for lunch from about noon, and for dinner from about 6:30. Delis (sandwich bars) and cafeterias are open only at lunchtime, from about noon until 3. Some fast-food shops are open for breakfast, but others open only at about 11 and stay open until late at night.

Mealtimes Most hotels serve breakfast until 10 AM. Belgians usually eat lunch between 1 and 3 PM, some making it quite a long, lavish meal. However, the main meal of the day is dinner, which most Belgians eat between 7 and 10 PM; peak dining time is about 8.

Precautions Most tap water and food served at restaurants is perfectly safe.

Ratings Prices are per person and include a first course, main course, and dessert but no wine or tip. Best bets are indicated by a star ★. At press time, there were 35 Belgian francs to the dollar.

Category	Cost
Very Expensive	over BF2,000
Expensive	BF1,600–BF2,000
Moderate	BF850–BF1,600
Inexpensive	under BF850

Credit Cards The following credit card abbreviations are used: AE, American Express; DC, Diners Club; MC, MasterCard; V, Visa.

Lodging You can trust Belgian hotels, almost without exception, to be clean and of a high standard. The more modern hotels in city centers can be very expensive, but there are smaller, well-appointed hotels, offering lodging at excellent rates. The family-run establishments in out-of-the-way spots, such as the Ardennes, can be surprisingly inexpensive, especially if you are visiting them out of season. Check in advance, however, since many country hotels close in the off-season.

Pensions Pensions offer a single room with bath or shower and full board from BF900 to BF1,100 in Brussels, BF500 to BF700 in other areas. These terms are often available only for a minimum stay of three or more days.

Youth Hostels For information about youth hostels, contact **Fédération Belge des Auberges de la Jeunesse** (tel. 02/215–31–00). In the United States: **American Youth Hostels, Inc.,** Box 37613, Washington, DC 20013. In the United Kingdom: **Camping and Caravan Club Ltd.,** 11 Lower Grosvenor Pl., London SW1; **Youth Hostels Association International Travel Bureau,** 14 Southampton St., London WC2.

Camping Belgium is well supplied with camping and caravan sites. Details from the **Royal Camping and Caravaning Club of Belgium,** rue Madeleine, 31, B-1000 Brussels, tel. 02/513–12–87.

Ratings Hotel prices are inclusive and are usually listed in each room. All prices are for two people in a double room. Best bets are indicated by a star ★. At press time, there were 35 Belgian francs to the dollar.

Category	Cost
Very Expensive	over BF3,700
Expensive	BF2,600–BF3,700
Moderate	BF1,600–BF2,600
Inexpensive	under BF1,600

Credit Cards The following credit card abbreviations are used: AE, American Express; DC, Diners Club; MC, MasterCard; V, Visa.

Tipping Tipping has been losing its hold in Belgium over the past few years because a service charge is often figured into the bill. For example, a tip of 16% is included in all restaurant and café bills, and you do not have to leave more than that! The tip is also included in taxi fares. If you want to give more, you could round the amount up to the nearest 50 or 100. Porters in railway stations ask a fixed per-suitcase price, usually around BF35–BF40. For moderately priced hotels, BF50 should be an adequate tip for bellhops and doormen; in the very expensive hotels, though, BF100 will usually be more appropriate. At the movies, tip the usher BF20, whether or not he or she shows you to your seat. In theaters, tip about BF50 for programs and BF50 for checking your coat. In restaurants, cafés, cinemas, theaters, train stations, and other public places, you should tip the washroom attendant BF7. Sometimes there is no attendant but simply a plate on which you are expected to leave BF7.

Brussels

Arriving and Departing

By Plane All international flights arrive at Brussels's Zavetem Airport, about a 30-minute drive or a 16-minute train trip from the city center. For information on arrival and departure times, call the individual airlines.

Between the Airport and Downtown There is regular train service from the airport to the Gare du Nord (North Station) and the Gare Centrale (Central Station), which leaves every 20 minutes, takes 16 minutes, and costs BF120; you can buy a ticket on the train. A taxi to the city center will take about half an hour and costs about BF800.

By Train There are three main stations in Brussels: the Gare du Nord, Gare Centrale, and Gare du Midi (South Station). There is also a Gare du Quartier Léopold on the east side of the city. The Gare Centrale is most convenient for the downtown area, which includes the Grand' Place. For train information, telephone 02/219–26–40 or inquire at any station.

By Bus There is no central bus depot, but most tour buses stop near the Gare Centrale, a short walk from the Grand' Place.

By Car   All main roads into Brussels link up with the outer Ring road, a beltway surrounding the city. You will see exit signs for downtown and for the north and south of the city.

Getting Around

By Metro, Tram, and Bus   The Metro, trams (streetcars), and buses run as part of the same system. All three are clean and efficient, and a single ticket costs BF40. Best buy is a 10-trip ticket, which costs BF250. You can purchase these tickets in any Metro station or at newsstands. Single tickets can be purchased on the bus. All services are few and far between after 10 PM.

Detailed maps of the entire public transport network are available in most Metro stations and at the Tourist Office (rue Marché-aux-Herbes 61, tel. 02/513–89–40).

By Taxi   Taxis are expensive, but—as a small plus—the tip is included in the fare. To call a taxi, phone **Taxis Verts** (tel. 02/347–47–47) or **Taxis TUP** (tel. 02/640–40–40), or catch one at one of the many taxi stands (it is nearly impossible to pick up cruising taxis in Brussels). Hotels and restaurants will phone for taxis for you.

Important Addresses and Numbers

Tourist Information   The main tourist office for Brussels is in the Hôtel de Ville on the Grand' Place (tel. 02/513–89–40), open Mon.–Sat. 9–6. The main tourist office for the rest of Belgium is near the Grand' Place (rue Marché-aux-Herbes 61, tel. 02/512–30–30) and has the same opening hours.

Embassies   U.S. Blvd. du Regent 27, B-1000 Brussels, tel. 02/513–38–30. **Canadian.** Rue de Loxum 6, B-1000 Brussels, tel. 03/513–79–40 **U.K.** Britannia House, rue Joseph II 28, B-1040 Brussels, tel. 02/217–90–00

Emergencies   **Police,** tel. 101; **Ambulance/Fire,** tel. 100; **Doctor,** tel. 02/479–18–18; **Dentist,** tel. 02/426–10–26; **Pharmacy,** to find out which one is open on a particular night or on weekends, tel. 02/479–18–18.

English Bookstores   **House of Paperbacks,** chaussées de Waterloo 813, Uccle, tel. 02/343–11–22. Open Tues.–Sat. 10–6, Sun. 10–1. **The Strathmore,** rue St. Lambert 131, tel. 02/771–92–00. **W. H. Smith,** rue Adolf Max 71–75. Open Mon.–Sat. 10–6.

Travel Agencies   **American Express,** pl. Louise 1, B-1000 Brussels, tel. 02/512–17–40. **Wagons-Lits,** blvd. Adolphe Max 52, tel. 02/217–62–40.

Guided Tours

Guided tours of Brussels are organized by **Sightseeing Tours,** rue de Colline 8, Grand' Place, tel. 02/513–77–44; and **Panorama Tours,** rue Marché-aux-Herbes 105, tel. 02/5143–61–54.

Special-Interest Tours   Walking tours of the city center are organized by **Brussels at a Glance,** tel. 02/217–49–85.

Personal Guides   Qualified guides for individual tours are available from the **Tourist Center,** tel. 02/513–89–40.

Exploring Brussels

Brussels is now the capital of Europe, the home of the Eurocrats with their legendary expense accounts. This means that, at the highest level, Brussels is as well equipped as any other city in Europe. But, side by side with this bureaucratic boomtown lies the old traditional capital, the heart of ancient Brabant. As a duchy, it was once the buffer state between the Lotharingian empire and the marauding counts of Flanders. Now it is where the two separate cultures of Belgium meet—a true mixture of the Walloon and Flemish cultures.

In many respects, Brussels is a thoroughly modern city. Shining steel-and-glass structures dominate the skyline, while nattily dressed Eurocrats patronize the elegant shops or brightly lighted places of entertainment. The city has an impressive network of expressways and road tunnels, and the metro trains are fitted with some of the world's most comfortable public transport seats. But within the city there are still cobbled streets that even the most experienced motorist will have problems navigating, canals where old barges still discharge their freight, and forgotten spots where the city's eventful and romantic past is plainly visible through its 20th-century veneer.

The Main Attractions

1 The best way to explore Brussels is to start at the **Grand' Place,** close to the Bourse, one of the most ornate market squares in Europe. On Sunday morning there is a colorful bird market in the center. On summer nights, the entire square is flooded with colored lights. If weather permits, you can sit in one of the many outdoor cafés and soak up the atmosphere.

2 The highlight of the Grand' Place is the **Hôtel de Ville** (Town Hall), which dates from the 15th century. At the top of the 315-foot (96-meter) tower stands a statue of St. Michael, the patron saint of Brussels. Among the magnificent rooms are the **Salle Gothique,** with its beautiful paneling; the **Salle Maximilienne,** with its superb tapestries; and the **Council Chamber,** with a ceiling fresco of the *Assembly of the Gods* painted by Victor Janssens in the early 15th century. *Free. Open Tues.–Fri. 9–5; Sun. 10–4.*

3 Opposite the Town Hall is the **Maison du Roi**—though no king ever lived there—a 16th-century palace housing the **City Museum.** The collection includes important ceramics and silverware—Brussels is famous for both—church sculpture, and statues removed from the facade of the Town Hall. *Grand' Place, tel. 02/511–27–42. Admission: BF50. Open weekdays Apr.–Sept., 10–5, Oct.–Mar., 10–4; weekends and holidays 10–noon.*

4 Southwest of the Town Hall, on the corner of the rue de l'Etuve and rue du Chêne, stands the famous **Manneken Pis,** a fountain with a small bronze statue of a chubby little boy peeing. Made by Jerome Duquesnoy in 1619, the statue is known as "Brussels' oldest citizen" and is often dressed in costumes that are kept in the City Museum. He has quite a wardrobe!

Keeping the Grand' Place on your right, head east along the rue du Marché-aux-Herbes and the rue de la Madeleine until you

Brussels

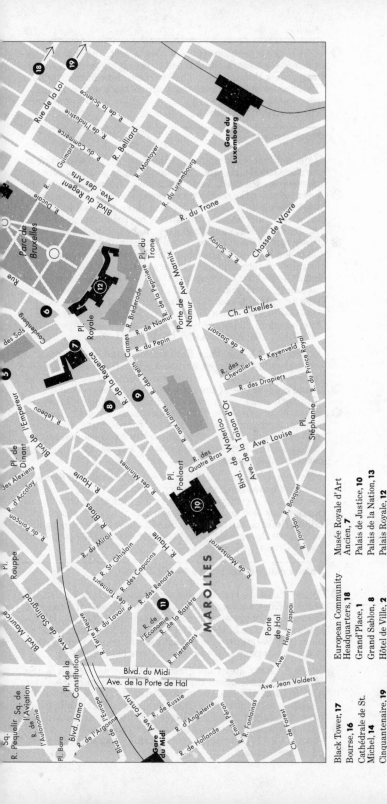

Black Tower, **17**
Bourse, **16**
Cathédrale de St. Michel, **14**
Cinquantenaire, **19**
Equestrian Statue of King Albert, **5**

European Community Headquarters, **18**
Grand'Place, **1**
Grand Sablon, **8**
Hôtel de Ville, **2**
Maison du Roi, **3**
Manneken Pis, **4**
Musée d'Art Moderne, **6**

Musée Royale d'Art Ancien, **7**
Palais de Justice, **10**
Palais de la Nation, **13**
Palais Royale, **12**
Petit Sablon, **9**
Place du Jeu de Balle, **11**
Place des Martyrs, **15**

⑤ come to the **equestrian statue of King Albert.** To the left of the statue is the Central Station and to the right, the **National Library.** Walk through the formal gardens next to the National Library and look back at the very **ornate clock** with moving figures over the lower archway. Try to hear—and see—it at noon, when it strikes the hour.

Place Royale

If you continue walking through the gardens, you will arrive at the **place Royale,** the site of the Coudenberg palace, where the sovereigns once lived. Here you have a superb view over the **⑥** lower town. On the northwest corner of the square is the **Musée d'Art Moderne** (Museum of Modern Art), with an important sculpture collection and paintings by such famous Belgian painters as Delvaux and Magritte. On the western corner is the **⑦** **Musée Royale d'Art Ancien** (Royal Museum of Fine Arts). Here the collection is of Flemish and Dutch paintings, ranging from magnificent 15th- and 16th-century works—Cranach, Matsys, and Brueghel the Elder among them—to Rubens (several fine canvases), Van Dyck, and David. There are concert and lecture halls here, too. *Musée d'Art Moderne, place Royale 1, tel. 02/ 513–96–30. Free. Open Tues.–Sun. 10–5. Musée Royale d'Art Ancien, place Royale. Free. Open Tues.–Sun., Rooms XV– XVI: 10–1, 2–5; Rooms XVII–IX: 10– 12, 1–5.*

As you stand in the place Royale facing back the way you've come, the rue de la Regence runs on your left up to the Palais de Justice. The Sablon lies along this street, on the right. The **⑧** **Grand Sablon,** one of the pleasantest squares in Brussels, is alive with cafés, restaurants, and antique shops. Across the **⑨** street is an attractive little garden square called the **Petit Sablon,** surrounded by 48 statues representing Brussels's medieval guilds. Each craftsman carries an object that reveals his trade: The furniture maker holds a chair, the wine merchant, a goblet, and so on.

Immediately beyond the Petit Sablon is the **Palais d'Egmont,** now used by the Belgian Ministry of Foreign Affairs for official meetings. If security allows, you can enter yet another small park on this side and walk through it to the coffee shop at the Hilton Hotel on the boulevard de Waterloo. If the Petit Sablon entrance is closed, cut through the garden from the entrance on rue de Grand Cerf.

Palais de Justice to the Black Tower

⑩ At the end of the rue de la Regence is the **Palais de Justice.** Often described as the ugliest building in Europe, the palais is designed to impress upon you the majesty of justice. It's located on the site of the former Gallows Hill. If you climb the more than 500 steps to the cupola, you will get an excellent view of the countryside around Brussels, weather permitting.

Down a rather steep hill from the Palais de Justice is the **Marolles district,** where the artist Pieter Brueghel the Elder died in 1569. His tomb is in the Eglise de Nôtre Dame de la Chapelle, in the place de la Chapelle at the foot of the hill. From here, turn right along rue Blaes and head back toward the **⑪** Sablon. You will pass the spacious **place du Jeu de Balle,** where there is a lively flea market every morning (especially interesting on weekends).

Return via the Sablon to the place Royale. Directly ahead of
⑫ you is the **Parc de Bruxelles** with the **Palais Royale** (Royal Palace) at the end closest to you. (The palace is usually open
during August and a few days before and after. Dates vary
⑬ from year to year.) You can walk through the park to the **Palais
de la Nation** at the opposite end, where the two houses of the
Belgian Parliament meet. When Parliament is not sitting, you
can visit the building. *Guided tours 10–4, closed weekends and
public holidays.*

Surrounding the park are elegant turn-of-the-century houses.
The prime minister's office is next to the Parliament building.
A walk downhill (rue des Colonies) toward the downtown area
⑭ and a short right-hand detour brings you to the **Cathédrale de
St. Michel.** The cathedral's chief treasure is the beautiful
stained-glass windows designed by Bernard van Orley, an early 16th-century painter at the royal court. In summer the great
west window is floodlit from inside to reveal its glories.

⑮ Continue downhill to the **place des Martyrs,** an attractive
square over a mass grave for local patriots who died in the 1830
battle to expel the Dutch. Along one side of the place des Martyrs runs the rue Neuve, a busy shopping street. Cross the rue
Neuve and continue on to the boulevard Adolphe Max. Turn
⑯ left and then right, in front of the **Bourse,** to place Sainte Cath-
⑰ erine. The 13th-century **Black Tower** here is part of the city's
first fortifications. Today the square holds the city's best seafood restaurants.

Parc du Cinquantenaire and Bois de la Cambre

Another walk takes you from the Palais de la Nation down the
rue de la Loi toward the Cinquantenaire (if the walk is too long
for you, take the metro). On the way, you pass in front of the
⑱ **European Community Headquarters** at the Rond Point Schu-
man. The vast 13-story cruciform building houses the
European Commission. The council offices are located nearby.
⑲ The **Cinquantenaire** is a huge, decorative archway, built in 1905
in a pleasant park. The buildings on either side of the archway
house the Royal Museums of Art and History. Displays include
Greek, Roman, and Egyptian artifacts and toys. Some galleries are closed on even dates, some on odd dates—check locally.
*Parc du Cinquantenaire 10, tel. 02/733–96–10. Admission:
BF5. Open weekdays 9:30–12:30, 1:30–4:45; weekends 10–
4:45.*

The **Bois de la Cambre,** a public park with open-air cafés at the
end of avenue Louise, is also worth a visit. Take the tram for a
pleasant 20-minute ride. Just before the Bois is the former **Abbey of La Cambre,** a 14th-century church with cloisters, an
18th-century courtyard, and a terraced park. Beyond the Bois
is the **Boitsfort race course,** and eastward lies the **Forêt de
Soignes,** 17 square miles (44 square kilometers) of forest, mostly beech trees, with walking and riding paths.

Waterloo

No history buff can visit Brussels without making the pilgrimage to the site of the **Battle of Waterloo,** where Napoleon was
finally defeated on June 18, 1815. It is easily reached from the
city and lies 12 miles (19 kilometers) to the south of the Forêt de
Soignes; take a local W bus. **Wellington's Headquarters** is now a
museum. There is also a **Battle Panorama Museum,** near the

Lion Monument, where you can get a good idea of how the battle was fought. **Napoleon's Headquarters** (the **Musée de Caillou**), on the Charleroi road, is also worth visiting for an ampler view of events. Tours of the site are led by official guides who are multilingual. *Wellington's Headquarters open Tues.–Sun. 10–noon, 2–7 (winter 4–6 only); Battle Panorama Museum open Tues.–Sun. 9:30–noon, 1:30–4:30; Napoleon's Headquarters open Wed.–Mon. 9–5.*

Time Out Try the **Bivouac de l'Empereur,** an attractive 1720s farmhouse close to the Lion Monument, for a satisfying lunch of authentic Belgian cuisine. *Route de Lion 315, tel. 02/384–67–40. Moderate.*

What to See and Do with Children

Children love the **Bois de la Cambre,** which offers pony rides, boat rides, an outdoor roller skating rink, and a puppet theater. In late July and August, a huge **fair** with games and rides is held in front of the Midi train station. For rainy days, try the children's museum, **Musée des Enfants** (rue du Bourgemestre 15, tel. 02/640–01–07. Open Wed., Sat., and Sun. 2:30–5). Children also enjoy the **Museum at the Atomium,** a 336-foot (102-meter) model of an iron crystal molecule, the symbol of the 1958 World's Fair in the nearby town of Laeken. *Admission: BF80. Open daily 9:30–4.*

Off the Beaten Track

Musée Instrumental (Musical Instrument Museum) houses a unique collection of more than 5,000 instruments, with about 1,000 on display. The instruments date from many centuries and come from a wide variety of countries. *Place du Petit Sablon 17, tel. 02/511–04–27. Free. Open Thurs. and Sat. 2:30–4:30; Sun. 10:30–12:30; Wed. 5–7 PM.*
Musée Horta contains photos of the works of the famous early 20th-century art nouveau architect, Baron Victor Horta (1861–1974). *Rue Americaine 25, St. Gilles. Admission: BF40. Open Tues.–Sun. 2–5:30; closed Nov.*
Visit the **Midi Market** on Sunday mornings in front of the Midi Station. It sells everything from vegetables to live plants, with clothes and shoes thrown in to boot. It's a great outdoor bazaar, packed with different nationalities. There's always something to see, but be careful of pickpockets.

Shopping

Lace Handmade lace is one of the great souvenirs from Brussels, and there are plenty of shops selling it around the Grand' Place, particularly in the area between the Grand' Place and the Mannekin Pis.

Antiques Along the rue du Midi, which leads down from the Grand' Place toward the Gare du Midi, there are a variety of shops selling old prints, stamps, coins, and antiques. But the best areas for antiques are around the Grand Sablon and along the rue Blaes.

Shopping Districts For designer clothes, leather goods, crystal, or china, go to the boulevard de Waterloo, the place Louise, and the place Stephanie. For a variety of goods at moderate prices, try **Inno**

—one of Brussels's few department stores—or other shops along the rue Neuve. Mouth-watering Belgian chocolates are sold here and throughout the city.

Dining

Prices are per person and include a first course, main course, and dessert, but no wine or tip. Best bets are indicated by a star ★. At press time, there were 35 Belgian francs to the dollar.

Category	Cost
Very Expensive	over BF2,000
Expensive	BF1,600–BF2,000
Moderate	BF850–BF1,600
Inexpensive	under BF850

Very Expensive
★ **Comme Chez Soi.** This small, intimate restaurant, with elegant turn-of-the-century decor, is famous for its traditional Walloon cuisine, especially for its seafood. *Pl. Rouppe, tel. 02/512–19–21. Dress: formal. Reservations required. AE, DC. Closed Sun., Mon., and July.*

La Maison du Cygne. A town house on the Grand' Place is the setting for this world-renowned restaurant serving exquisite French-Belgian cuisine. It has a view of the square and live piano music every evening. *Grand' Place, tel. 02/511–82–44. Dress: formal. Reservations required. AE, DC, MC, V. Closed Sun., Sat. lunch, and 2 weeks in Aug.*

Expensive
La Belle Maraîchère. Try the fricassee of lobster or the sole meunière at this famous fish and seafood restaurant. Though newly decorated, the style remains traditional. *Pl. St. Catherine, tel. 02/512–97–59. Jacket and tie. Reservations advised. AE, DC, MC, V. Closed Wed. eve. and Thurs.*

★ **Chez François.** Popular and bustling, this delightfully Old World fish and seafood restaurant is close to place Sainte Catherine. Try the North Sea shrimp, smoked eel, or sole cardinal. *Quai au Brigues 2, tel. 02/511–60–89. Jacket and tie. Reservations advised. AE, DC, MC, V. Closed Mon.*

Comtes de Flandre. This is hotel dining in the Sheraton, in plush and elegant surroundings with soft piano music in the background. Try smoked bass, rabbit pâté, or traditional lamb chops with all the trimmings. *Pl. Rogier 3, tel. 02/219–34–00. Dress: formal for dinner. Reservations advised. AE, DC, MC, V. Closed weekends.*

Moderate
Bon Vieux Temps. In a setting of wood paneling and stained-glass windows, try traditional specialties such as duck or ice cream flavored with *kriek*, the famous Belgian cherry-flavored beer. *Rue Marché-aux-Herbes 12, tel. 02/218–15–46. Jacket and tie for dinner. Reservations advised. AE, DC, MC. Closed Sun. lunch and Aug.*

Inexpensive
Ainsi-Soit-Il. Younger diners like the small candle-lit rooms in this cheery restaurant near the university. Try the meats grilled with a variety of sauces. *Av. Adolphe Buyl 104, tel. 02/649–39–25. Dress: come as you are. Reservations not necessary. Closed Sun. and Sat. lunch.*

★ **Le Grain de Sel.** The young couple who run this restaurant near the Ixelles ponds serve simple but excellent home-style food at reasonable prices. Try their roasts with vegetables, grilled goat cheese, or chicken livers. *Chaussée de Vleurgot 9, tel. 02/698-18-58. Dress: informal. Reservations not always necessary. No credit cards. Closed Sat. lunch and Sun.*

Maison d'Attilla. This is slightly out of town, but the young in spirit will enjoy coming here as much for the fun as for the food. There's always plenty of activity, and you get all you can eat for BF690. Kebabs are particularly recommended; you make them up from a large selection of meats and vegetables and grill them yourself. *Av. du Prince de Ligne, tel. 02/375-05-70. Dress: informal. No reservations. No credit cards.*

La Tsampa. This is a vegetarian restaurant, but nonvegetarians will also enjoy the informality, lively conversation, and leafy plants. Try the fried *seitan* and cauliflower with a nutty dressing and follow it with one of the excellent desserts. *Rue de Livourne 109, tel. 02/647-03-67. Dress: informal. AE, DC, MC, V. Closed Sat. dinner and Sun.*

Lodging

Brussels has a wide variety of hotels in every category and catering to every taste.

Ratings Hotel prices are inclusive and are usually listed in each room. Our grading system is divided into four categories, and all prices are for two people in a double room. Best bets are indicated by a star ★. At press time, there were 35 Belgian francs to the dollar.

Category	Cost
Very Expensive	over BF3,700
Expensive	BF2,600–BF3,700
Moderate	BF1,600–BF2,600
Inexpensive	under BF1,600

Very Expensive **Amigo.** This world-famous hotel was built in the 1950s, but it
★ has the charm of an older age. It's located just off Grand' Place not far from the Mannekin Pis. Each room is individually decorated; all have color TV and minibar. Apartment suites have terraces. Service is first class, and there is an excellent French restaurant. *Rue d'Amigo 1, tel. 02/511-59-10. 183 rooms with bath. Facilities: bar, parking. AE, DC, MC, V.*

Astoria. In the heart of the ministerial quarter and close to the Parc de Bruxelles, this circa 1908 building has rooms sumptuously furnished in Louis XV or Empire style. It was renovated in 1986. *Rue Royale 103, tel. 02/217-62-90. 114 rooms with bath. Facilities: restaurant, bar, parking. AE, DC, MC, V.*

Hilton International. This imposing 27-story tower has light, airy modern rooms equipped with color TV and minibar. The top-floor restaurant—**Plein-Ciel**—has a terrific view over the city. Centrally located, it is next to the main luxury shopping area and overlooks the quiet Parc d'Egmont. Everyone on the staff speaks English. *Blvd. de Waterloo 38, tel. 02/513-88-77. 365 rooms with bath. Facilities: health club, sauna, 2 restaurants, coffee shop, bar, solarium. AE, DC, MC, V.*

Hyatt Regency. The Brussels link in this reliable chain is a modern, sophisticated hotel next to the Botanical Gardens and close to the rue Neuve shopping area. All rooms have color TV and minibar, and there's a good French-style restaurant on the premises. *Rue Royale 250, tel. 02/217–12–34. 315 rooms with bath. Facilities: piano bar, indoor parking. AE, DC, MC, V.*

★ **Hotel Metropole.** The Metropole's lobby is grandly furnished, and most guest rooms are in Art Deco or Art Nouveau style. Every room is different, so try to see several before choosing one. Some rooms do not have TV. The hotel is centrally located near Grand' Place and the Bourse, with a good restaurant and an elegant popular sidewalk café worth visiting even if you're not staying here. The hotel was built in 1895 but was recently renovated. *Pl. de Brouckère 31, tel. 02/217–23–00. 400 rooms with bath. Facilities: tavern, sauna. AE, DC, MC, V.*

Expensive **Arenberg.** This is an older hotel close to St. Michael's Cathedral. All rooms have color TV and radio. Its restaurant can accommodate special dietary requirements. *Rue d'Assaut 15, tel. 02/511–07–70. Facilities: coffee shop, bar, secretarial service. AE, DC, MC, V.*

Bedford. All rooms in this 1920s building have been completely renovated and now have modern decor, color TV, and minibar. The hotel is located halfway between Grand' Place and the Gare du Midi. Its restaurant can accommodate special diets. *Rue du Midi 135, tel. 02/512–78–40. 275 rooms with bath, Facilities: 2 restaurants, bar, gift shop, art gallery, indoor parking. AE, DC, MC, V.*

Delta. This modern hotel has a bar but no restaurant. It is located off avenue Louise and close to the place Stéphanie. *Chaussée de Charleroi 17, tel. 02/539–01–60. 256 rooms with bath. AE, DC, MC, V.*

New Siru. This Golden Tulip hotel is housed in a completely renovated (1988) older building and offers good value in its category. For even better value, take a room with a shower rather than a bath. Every room is decorated in a different style, and all have color TV. There are two decent restaurants. *Pl. Rogier 1, tel. 02/217–75–80. 100 rooms with bath. Facilities: bar, parking nearby. AE, DC, MC, V.*

Moderate **Arcade Sainte Catherine.** This good, reasonably priced hotel is just a few blocks from the Grand' Place. Decor leans toward the motelish, but every room has a shower and a TV. *Rue Joseph Plateau 2, tel.02/513–76–20. 234 rooms with bath or shower. Facilities: coffee shop, bar, MC, V.*

★ **Charlemagne.** Near the European Community headquarters, the Charlemagne is undistinguished but offers good value. All rooms have TV. *Blvd. Charlemagne 25, tel. 02/239–21–35. 61 rooms with bath. Facilities: bar, parking. AE, DC, MC, V.*

Inexpensive **Aux Arcades.** This hotel is well situated on one of the city's best restaurant streets, in a very lively part of town. Rooms are basic, but all have showers. There is a bar. *Rue des Bouchers, tel. 02/511–28–76. 18 rooms with bath. AE, DC, MC, V.*

Congrès. In the ministerial quarters, this place is conveniently close to the museums and the Parc de Bruxelles. There is a restaurant and a choice of shower or bath. *Rue de Congrès 42, tel. 02/217–18–90. 38 rooms, 22 with bath or shower. AE, DC, MC, V.*

★ **The Derby.** Good value is the calling card at this hotel, located farther out on the other side of Parc Cinquantenaire. Guest rooms are fairly basic, but all have either bath or shower. *Av.*

de Tervuran 24, tel. 02/733–08–19. 28 rooms with bath. Facilities: restaurant. AE, DC, MC, V.

★ **Marie-José.** Each room is decorated in a different style, most with antiques, in this bargain hotel that is just a five-minute walk from the Parc de Bruxelles. The restaurant, **Chez Callens,** moderately priced and great for seafood dishes. *Rue du Commerce, tel. 02/512–08–42. 17 rooms with bath or shower. Facilities: restaurant. AE, DC, MC, V.*

The Arts

The traditional performing arts—ballet, opera, theater—are well-represented in Brussels. There is also a wide range of English-language entertainment, including movies, and, on occasion, theater. The best way to find out what's going on is to buy a copy of the English-language weekly magazine *The Bulletin.* It's published every Thursday and sold at newsstands for BF60.

Entertainment and Nightlife

Nightclubs The best floor shows can be seen at the **Show Point** (pl. Stephanie 14, tel .02/511–53–64).

For **disco dancing,** try the **Crocodile Club** at the Royal Windsor Hotel (rue Duquesnoy 6, tel. 02/511–42–15) or the **Golden Gate** at the Galerie Louise 98.

Jazz The **Brussels Jazz Club** (Grand' Place 13, tel. 02/512–40–93) is open every night except Wednesday and Sunday.

American Bar At **Rick's Café American,** (av. Louise 344, tel. 02/647–75–30) you can have a meal and a drink and sit around talking all evening.

Antwerp

Arriving and Departing

By Plane **Antwerp International Airport** lies just two miles (three kilometers) southeast of the city. For flight information, phone 03/2181211.

Between the Airport and Downtown Buses bound for Antwerp's Central Station leave about every 20 minutes; travel time is around 15 minutes. Taxis are readily available as well.

By Train Express trains run between Antwerp and Brussels; the trip takes 35 minutes. The Antwerp Central Station is at Koningin Astridplein 27, tel. 03/2317690. Four trains leave every hour from Antwerp's Central and North stations.

By Car Several major highways converge on Antwerp's inner-city Ring expressway. It's a 10-lane racetrack, so be sure you maneuver into the correct lane well before you exit. Antwerp is an easy 28-mile (45-kilometer) drive from Brussels on A1/E19.

Getting Around

By Streetcar In the downtown area, the streetcar (or tram) is the best, and most usual, means of transportation. Some lines have been rebuilt underground (look for signs marked "Metro"); the most useful line runs between the Central Station (metro stop Diamant) and the Groenplaats (for the cathedral). For detailed maps of the transport system, stop in at the tourist office at Koningin Astridplein, tel. 03/2330570.

On Foot   Unlike Brussels, Antwerp is flat and therefore much easier to navigate on foot.

Guided Tours

The tourist office opposite Central Station operates a **Guide's Exchange** and is able to meet most requirements for city guides. A week's advance notice is needed, however.

Tourist Information

Antwerp's main **tourist office** is just opposite Central Station on Koningin Astridplein, tel. 03/2330570. It's open weekdays from 8:30 to 6, weekends from 9 to 5. Another office is at Gildekamersstr. 9, tel 03/2322284.

Exploring Antwerp

Antwerp, the fifth-largest port in the world, is the main city of Belgium's Flemish region. Its inhabitants, the Flemings, speak Dutch. Lying on the Schelde River, Antwerp is a bustling, wealthy city and contains one of Europe's largest Jewish quarters. With its 500-year tradition of diamond cutting, Antwerp has its own diamond exchange market. Most of the world's diamond dealing, and much of the cutting and polishing, takes place here.

❶ Antwerp's **Central Station** is a good place to start exploring the city. An elegant building dating from the early 1900s, and only a few blocks from the downtown area, it is surrounded by cafés and movie theaters. To the east of the station, there is a 25-acre
❷ (102,000-square meter) **zoo,** one of Europe's most modern, and well worth a visit for both children and adults. It has a pleasant open-air café. *Koningin Astridplein 26, tel. 03/231-16-40. Admission: BF260 adults, BF160 children. Open daily 8:30-6:30 (depending on time of year).*

Near Central Station, along the Pelikaanstraat and the streets running off it, lies the **Diamond Quarter.** You can visit the diamond exhibition and see diamond cutters at work at the
❸ **Veiligheidsmuseum.** *Jesusstr. 28-30. Free. Open Wed. to Sun. 10-5.*

The broad De Keyserlei, on the south side of Central Station, leads west toward the main shopping area, the **Meir.** South of
❹ the Meir, on Rubensstraat, is the **Rubens house.** The artist lived here from 1610 until his death in 1640. It's an atmospheric place, very much a patrician's home of the period, enriched with paintings by Rubens and his contemporaries. *Wapper 9. Admission: BF50. Open daily 10-5.*

❺ One of Europe's earliest skyscrapers, the 24-story **Torengebouw,** stands at the end of the Meir. Pass to the left of this building, down the Schoenmarkt, and into the wide
❻ Groenplaats, with its statue of Rubens. The towering **Onze-Lieve-Vrouw** (Cathedral of Our Lady) stands at the opposite

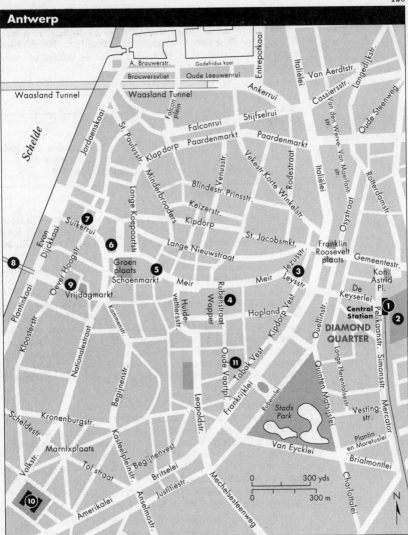

Antwerp

Central Station, **1**

Koninklijk Museum
Voor Schone
Kunsten, **10**

Nationale
Scheepvaartmuseum, **7**

Onze-Lieve-Vrouw, **6**

Plantin-Moretus
Museum, **9**

Rubens House, **4**

St. Annatunnel, **8**

Torengebouw, **5**

Veiligheidsmuseum, **3**

Vogelmarkt, **11**

Zoo, **2**

end of the square. Built in Gothic style, it has seven naves and 125 pillars and is the largest church in Belgium as well as Holland. It also has three masterpieces by Rubens. *Admission: BF20. Open weekday afternoons until 5.*

From the cathedral, walk the short distance along the Suikerrui to the river. To your right is the fortresslike **Steen,** the oldest building in Antwerp. Dating from the 12th century, the Steen now houses the **Nationale Scheepvaartmuseum** (Maritime Museum), which has many beautiful ship models, especially of the East India clippers. *Steenplein 1. Admission: BF50. Open daily 10–5.*

From the terraces around the Steen, you can see the main port installations. For a close look, a boat excursion around the port leaves from Quay 13 on weekdays and from Steen Landing stage on Sunday. *Cost: BF300 adults, BF180 children. Information from n.v. Flandria, Steenplein 1, tel. 03/233–74–22.*

Walking along the river south of the Steen, you come to a foot tunnel (the **St. Annatunnel**) leading to the left bank of the river (the entrance is close to the Plantin-Moretus Museum, *see* below). From the riverside park, you get the best view of the city's great spires and wharves.

Return through the tunnel and walk east until you come to the **Plantin-Moretus Museum,** a famous printing works founded in the 16th century. The building is a fine example of Renaissance architecture and is magnificently furnished. Among its treasures are many first editions, engravings, and a copy of Gutenberg's 36-line Bible, the *Biblia Regia. Vrijdagmarkt 22. Admission: BF50. Open daily 10–5.*

From the Plantin walk through the Vrijdagmarkt, where there is a **furniture and antiques market** every Wednesday and Friday morning. Continue up the Oude Koornmarkt to the Groenplaats and catch a tram to the Royal Museum of Fine Arts. The **Koninklijk Museum Voor Schone Kunsten** lies in the southern part of the city and houses more than 1,000 paintings by old masters, including a magnificent array of works by Rubens, Van Dyck, Hals, and Brueghel. The second floor houses one of the best collections of the Flemish school anywhere in the world. The first floor is given over to more modern paintings. The neoclassical building also has an adequate snack bar. *Leopold de Waelplaats 1–9. Free. Open Tues.–Sun. 10–5.*

On Sunday morning you can see the famous **vogelmarkt,** or bird market, on the south side of the city on the Oude Vaartplaats. Here is everything from birds and domestic pets to plants, clothes, and food.

Dining

For details and price category definitions, *see* Dining in Essential Information.

Very Expensive **La Perouse.** Seafood is an Antwerp specialty, and here you can sample it in style on a moored ship. It's small, so you *must* reserve ahead. *Steenplain, tel. 03/232–35–28. Dress: formal. Closed Sun., Mon., and May–mid-Sept.*

★ **Sir Anthony von Dijck.** The Sir Anthony is a superb seafood restaurant on an ancient lane near the cathedral. The antiques make dining here a pleasure. *Oude Koornmarkt 16, tel. 03/231–61–70. Dress: formal. Reservations required. AE, DC, MC, V. Closed Sun. and Mon., most of Aug., and Christmas.*

Expensive **Het Fournis.** There's a heavily country touch in the decor here, and the food matches the ambience, with traditional local dishes and large helpings, all of it cooked with a master's touch. *Reydersstraat 24, tel. 03/233–62–70. Dress: neat casual. Reservations advised. AE, DC, MC, V. Closed Sat., Sun., most of Aug., and Christmas.*

Vateli. It's not fish that rules here (although it is on the menu) but duck—a great favorite in Belgium. One of the special versions that Vateli offers is duck *à la Rouennaise*, as done in Rouen. The cooking is classical and excellent, and the service friendly. *Kidporpvest 50, tel. 03/233–17–81. Dress: formal but not excessive. Reservations advised. AE, DC, MC, V. Closed Sun., Mon., July, and Christmas.*

Moderate **Rooden-Hoed.** Seafood is featured in this restaurant that's said
★ to be Antwerp's oldest. Specialties include eels and mussels, in season. *Oude Koornmarkt 25, tel. 03/233–28–44. Dress: casual. Reservations advised. AE. Closed Wed. and Thurs.*

Sawadee. Evoking a long-standing Far East connection, the menu here is well-stocked with delicious Thai dishes. The restaurant operates on an upper floor of an old house, worth seeing in itself. *Britselei 16, tel. 03/233–08–59. Dress: informal. Reservations advised. AE, DC, MC, V. Closed Tues.*

Inexpensive **In de Schaduw van de Kathedraal.** As the name plainly states,
★ this good budget restaurant serves traditional food "in the shadow of the cathedral." *Handshoemarkt 17, tel. 03/232–40–14. Dress: relaxed. Reservations not required. AE, DC, MC, V. Closed Tues.*

Lodging

For details and price category definitions, *see* Lodging in Essential Information.

Very Expensive **De Keyser.** This well-maintained deluxe hotel is handily situ-
★ ated only 150 yards (50 meters) from the Central Station and near the Diamond Center. It has a restaurant that prides itself on its selection of local dishes. *De Keyserlei 66, tel. 03/234–01–35. 117 rooms. Facilities: airport express bus that stops opposite the hotel, café, bar, nightclub, parking, videos available. AE, DC, MC, V.*

Expensive **Novotel.** As with most members of this French chain, this one is thoroughly modern and efficient, but a bit anonymous. It lies on the north side of town, next to a network of highways, so it's convenient only for visitors with cars. *Luiten-Haven 6, tel. 03/542–03–20. 119 rooms, all with bath. Facilities: Pool, tennis. AE, DC, MC, V.*

Moderate **Columbus.** The main attraction of this hotel is its central location—convenient for sightseeing. It has no restaurant. *Frankrijklei 4, tel. 03/233–03–90. 27 rooms, most with bath or shower. AE, DC, MC, V.*

Inexpensive **Tourist.** Situated next to the Central Station, the Tourist is a
★ long-term budget stalwart—built in 1930—and has been popular for a long while. It has no restaurant, but there is a

breakfast room. *Pelikaanstr. 22, tel. 03/232–58–70. 148 rooms, most with bath. AE, V.*

Bruges

Arriving and Departing

By Train Trains run hourly at 46 minutes past the hour from Brussels to Bruges; the London–Brussels service stops here as well. The train station is south of the canal that surrounds the downtown area; for information, tel. 050/38–58–71 or 38–23–82. Travel time from Brussels is 70 minutes.

By Bus National buses do not connect with Bruges, but individual bus tours from Brussels stop here on day excursions.

By Car Bruges lies 61 miles (97 kilometers) northwest of Brussels. The most direct route between the two cities is the A10/E40.

Getting Around

On Foot By far the easiest way of exploring the city is on foot because the downtown sights are fairly close together.

By Horse-Drawn Cab An expensive means of seeing the sights is provided by the horse-drawn cabs that congregate in the market square daily March through November from 10 to 6. A 35-minute trip will cost BF450, and the cabs take up to four people.

Guided Tours

Boat Trips Boat trips along the city canals are run by several companies and depart from five separate landings. Boats ply the waters from March through November, from 10 to 6. There is no definite departure schedule; boats leave when enough people have gathered, but you'll never have to wait more than 15 minutes or so. The following are just two of the companies operating: **P. C. B. Stael** (tel. 050/33–27–1) and **Coudenys** (tel. 050/33–51–03). During summer months, special evening cruises can be arranged.

Orientation Tours Three-hour bus trips of Bruges and its environs are available from July through September. One of the major companies is **Gidsenkring** (tel. 050/82–32–02). Buses leave from Beursplein at 10 and 2:30 on Tuesday, Thursday, and weekends. For further information and a full list of companies, check with the tourist office.

Tour Guides Individual guides can be arranged through the tourist office. Be sure to make your request at least a week in advance.

Tourist Information

The **Bruges Tourist Office** is at Burg 11, tel. 050/44–80–80.

Exploring Bruges

A magnificent medieval town crossed by canals, Bruges is often called the Venice of the North—other cities are, too, but with much less reason. In any case, Bruges is one of Europe's loveliest towns, both because of its water-haunted location and its superb medieval architecture.

①② The best place to start a walking tour is the **Grote Markt** or Grand' Place (Market Square). From the top of the **Beffroi** (Belfry)—"Thrice destroyed and thrice rebuilded," as Longfellow tells us—there's a panoramic view of the town. The belfry has a carillon notable even in Belgium, where they are a matter of civic pride. On summer evenings, the Markt is brightly lighted. *The Beffroi. Admission: BF50. Open daily 9:30–12:30 and 1:30–6. Carillon concerts Oct.–mid-June, Sun., Wed., and Sat. 11:45–12:30; mid-June–Sept., Mon., Wed., and Sat. 9–10 PM.*

③ On the eastern side of the Markt stands the **Provinciaal Hof** (the neo-Gothic Provincial Government building), and next to it is the attractive **Post Office.** Walk east from the Markt along Breidlestraat, to the Burg, another square, this one at the cen-
④ ter of ancient Bruges. On the left is the **Landshuis,** built in 1622. Across the square is a row of magnificent buildings—the
⑤ **Stadthius** (Town Hall), dating from the 14th century, its won-
⑥ derfully ornate facade covered with statues; **Oude Griffie,** the former Recorder's House dating from the 1530s, and also ornate,
⑦ with impressive windows; and the **Heilig Bloedbaziliek** (the Basilica of the Holy Blood), built to enshrine the vial containing Christ's blood, and a building so fascinating that it alone would warrant a visit to Bruges. Here, too, is a **Museum of the Holy Blood,** with many treasures associated with the cult. *Stadthius—Admission: BF30. Open daily 9:30–12 and 2–6. Heilig Bloedbaziliek—Worship of the Blood, Fri. 8:30–11:45 and 3–4. Free guided visits daily 2–5. Museum—Admission: BF20. Open daily 9:30–12 and 2–4.*

⑧ Walk through a passage between the town hall and the Oude Griffie and you come to the **Dijver,** the City Canal. Canal boat trips leave from here during the day and in the evening from June to September. *Boats leave on demand. Average trip 30 minutes. Cost: BF110.*

⑨ Walking south along the Dijver soon takes you to a group of museums. The **Gruuthuse Museum,** in the 15th-century former palace of the aristocratic Gruuthuse family, contains archaeological exhibitions and a display of lace from all over Belgium. *Dijver 17. Admission: BF80; combined ticket for BF200 covers the Groeninge, Gruuthuse, Memling, and Brangwyn museums (see below). Open daily 9:30–noon and 2–6.*

⑩ The **Groeninge Museum,** on the Dijver Canal, has a very rich, wide-ranging collection of Flemish masterpieces, with works by van Eyck, Memling, Bosch, and Brueghel, among many others, plus some contemporary works. *Dijver 17. Admission: BF80. Open daily 9:30–6.*

⑪ Here, too, is the **Memling Museum,** dedicated to the work of one of Bruges's most famous sons, Hans Memling (1430–90), and housed in the former Sint Jans Hospitaal (Hospital of St. John), where the artist was nursed back to health after being wounded in France. *Mariastraat 38. Admission: BF80. Open daily Apr.–Dec. 9–12:30 and 2–6; Jan.–Mar. 10–noon and 2–5.*

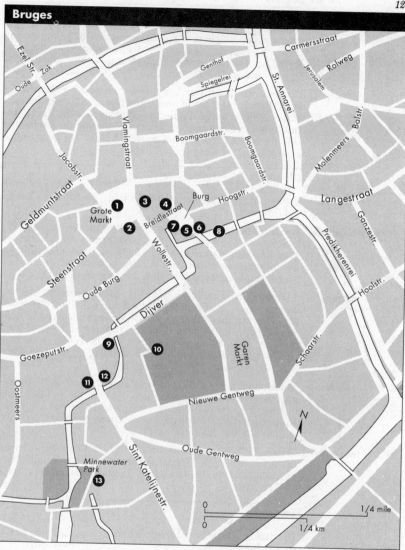

Beffroi, **2**

Dijver, **8**

Groeninge Museum, **10**

Grote Markt, **1**

Gruuthuse Museum, **9**

Heilig Bloedbaziliek, **7**

Landshuis, **4**

Memling Museum, **11**

Minnewater Park, **13**

Onze Lieve
Vrouwekerk, **12**

Oude Griffie, **6**

Provinciaal Hof, **3**

Stadthius, **5**

⓬ Next to the Memling Museum is the **Onze Lieve Vrouwekerk** (Church of Our Lady), with, at 375 feet (114 meters), the highest tower in Belgium, a notable collection of paintings and carvings—especially a *Madonna* by Michelangelo—and some splendidly colorful tombs. *Mausoleums—Admission: BF30. Open weekdays 10–11:30 and 2:30–5, Sun. 2:30–5.*

⓭ Continue east, past Our Lady, to the enchanting **Minnewater Park** (Park of the Lake of Love) for a rest, and then take a tour of the medieval ramparts. Retrace your steps to the Markt, and this time dawdle as much as you can, exploring the fascinating side streets and enjoying the ancient houses, the busy shops, and the churches along the quay.

Dining

For details and price category definitions, *see* Dining in Essential Information.

Very Expensive   **De Witte Poorte.** The fish here, fresh from the North Sea, is in a class by itself; so is the game in season. Family run, and housed in an old, vaulted warehouse, the de Witte Poort is *the* place for a meal you'll remember. *Jan Van Eyckplein 6, tel. 050/33–08–83. Dress: elegantly casual. Reservations advised. AE, DC, V.*

Expensive   **'t Pandreitje.** Here's the place to go for nouvelle cuisine, Belgian-style, in distinctly elegant surroundings. "Belgian-style" means that helpings are larger than one expects from nouvelle dining. It's handily located just across the canal from the Burg complex. *Pendreitje 6, tel. 050/33–11–90. Dress: elegantly casual. Reservations advised. AE, DC, MC, V. Closed Sun., Mon., most of Mar., and end of Dec.*

Moderate   **Oud Brugge.** Many of the city's restaurants are found in atmospheric ancient buildings, and this is one of them. Tasty local dishes are served under yet more vaulted ceilings. *Kuiperstraat 33, tel. 050/33–54–02. Dress: casual chic. Reservations advised. No credit cards.*

Inexpensive   **Gistelhof.** The Gistelhof serves hearty fish stews and other local dishes in historic Flemish surroundings. *West Gistelhof 23, tel. 050/33–62–90. Dress: casual. Reservations not necessary. AE, DC, MC, V.*

Lodging

For details and price category definitions, *see* Lodging in Essential Information.

Very Expensive   **Duc de Bourgogne.** Set in a stunning location at the bend of a canal. The Duc has rooms that are all tastefully furnished in 17th-century style. There is also a fine restaurant—try the many fish dishes—with a truly remarkable view. *Huidenvettersplein 12, tel. 050/33–20–38. 19 rooms with bath. AE, DC, MC, V.*

Expensive
★   **Die Swaene.** The Swan, sitting right in the center of town, is a real find. The 15th-century building, lovingly restored by the Hessels-Dutoit husband-and-wife team, has many original features preserved. An ugly former courtyard, for example, is now a pleasant garden. There's no restaurant, but a copious breakfast buffet is available. *Steenhouwersdijk 1, tel. 050/34–27–98. 26 rooms with bath and shower. AE, DC, MC, V.*

Moderate   **Ter Brughe.** If it's atmosphere and period charm you want, you won't be disappointed by this delightful canalside hotel, a 15th-century survival, with friendly service and a cozy atmosphere. There's no restaurant. *Oost-Gisthelhof 2, tel. 050/34-03-24. 19 rooms. DC, MC, V. Closed Jan.–Feb. and mid-Nov.–Christmas.*

Inexpensive   **Van Eyck.** This small, modest hotel, a stone's throw from the market square, makes a fine base for exploring. There's a simple restaurant that gives hearty helpings. *Kotre Zilverstraat 7, tel. 050/33-52-67. 8 rooms, 5 with bath or shower. AE, MC, V.*

6 Bulgaria

Introduction

Although Bulgaria is the Soviet Union's most faithful client and supporter, it has many westernized traits, with simplified passport and visa formalities, sophisticated hotels, well-equipped spas, and burgeoning winter sports resorts. It also has a fairly open and tolerant attitude toward the foibles of Western guests and a great deal to offer them—a splendid coastline on the Black Sea; a lovely hinterland of forested ridges; lakes and swift rivers; a diverse flora and fauna; picturesque monasteries and towns; a colorful folk culture; a high standard in religious art, crafts, and music; and an equable climate.

The earliest known inhabitants, the Thracians, were absorbed by Alexander the Great and his armies. Then came the Romans, who established the cities of Serdica (Sofia) and Trimontium (Plovdiv). The vacuum they left when they departed in AD 395 was gradually filled by invading Slavs, though it was a rival Turkish race that appointed the first actual king, Khan Asparukh, in 681. The emergent kingdom adopted Christianity and launched a monastic tradition that was responsible for the first Slavic alphabet, Cyrillic. In 1393 the Byzantines conquered the country and maintained an iron grip for the next five centuries. The fortified monasteries became refuges for works of art as well as people.

Uprisings against the Turks grew steadily more frequent. Two prominent freedom fighters, Vassil Levsky (1837–73) and Hristo Botev (1848–76) are remembered in the names of streets, lakes, and mountains. The April Uprising of 1876, in Koprivštica, was crushed with a savagery that shocked the civilized world. The following year the Russians earned Bulgaria's eternal gratitude by going to war with Turkey.

In 1879 a German princeling, Alexander of Battenburg, was placed on the throne by the European powers, who thought, mistakenly, that a German would ensure peace. He was succeeded by another princeling, Ferdinand of Saxe-Coburg-Gotha, who abdicated after World War I—in which he had taken the German side and thus lost a lot of territory. In 1923 a military dictatorship under his son Boris stamped out Europe's first antifascist rising. One of the leaders of the revolt, Georgi Dimitrov, lived to be first secretary of Socialist Bulgaria after 1945, when the Russian armies had driven out Hitler's occupying forces.

Despite all these past upheavals, Bulgaria remains a society made up largely of farmers and shepherds, its economy enriched by attar of roses. "Roses are our golden currency," says the school sign in a village in the Valley of Roses. In fact, ounce for ounce, rose oil has risen above the price of gold on the international market.

Before You Go

When to Go The weather is generally pleasant throughout the year, with warm summers and cold, crisp winters. The coastal areas enjoy considerable sunshine. Even when the thermometer climbs, the Black Sea breezes and the cooler mountain air prevent the heat from being overpowering.

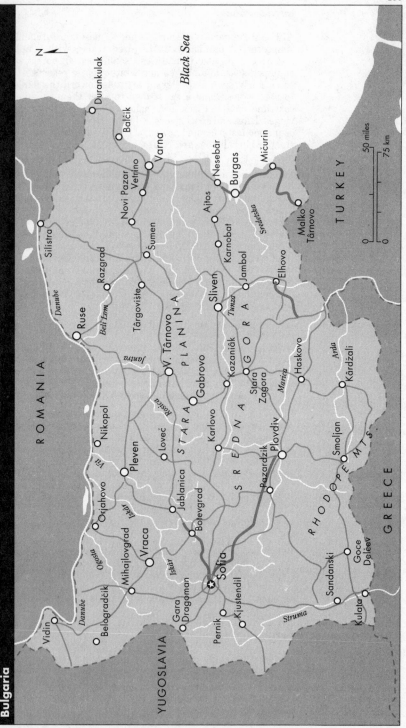

Bulgaria

Climate The skiing season lasts from mid-December through March, while the Black Coast season runs all the way from May to October, reaching its crowded peak in July and August. March and April are the wettest months inland. April and May are the times to see the fruit trees in blossom; in May and early June the blooms are gathered in the Valley of Roses (you have to be up early to watch the harvest); in September the fruit is picked, and in October the fall colors are at their richest.

The following are the average daily maximum and minimum temperatures for Sofia.

Jan.	35F	2C	May	69F	21C	Sept.	70F	22C
	25	−4		50	10		52	11
Feb.	39F	4C	June	76F	24C	Oct.	63F	17C
	27	−3		56	14		46	8
Mar.	50F	10C	July	81F	27C	Nov.	48F	9C
	33	1		60	16		37	3
Apr.	60F	16C	Aug.	79F	26C	Dec.	38F	4C
	42	5		59	15		28	−2

Currency The unit of currency in Bulgaria is the lev (plural leva), divided into 100 stotinki. There are bills of 1, 2, 5, 10, and 20 leva; coins of 1, 2, and 5 leva, and of 1, 2, 5, 10, 20, and 50 stotinki. At press time (fall 1988), the rate of exchange was approximately 0.8 lev to the dollar and 1.45 to the pound sterling.

You may import any amount of foreign currency, including traveler's checks, and exchange it at branches of the Bulgarian State Bank, Balkantourist hotels, airports, and border posts. Always try to exchange it through a Balkantourist office, which will add a generous currency bonus, provided that you have prepaid a minimum of two nights' hotel accommodation. Always hold on to your official exchange slips. Avoid the active black market in foreign currency—there are heavy penalties, including imprisonment, for being caught.

It is forbidden either to import or export Bulgarian currency. Unspent leva must be exchanged at frontier posts on departure, before going through passport control. You will need to present your official exchange slips to prove that the currency was legally purchased.

The major international credit cards are accepted in the larger stores, hotels, and restaurants.

What It Will Cost Prices in Bulgaria, as in most Eastern European countries, are generally low and reasonably stable. Bulgaria is best geared to prepaid arrangements, which can be flexible. If you choose the more moderate of the Balkantourist hotels and restaurants, Bulgaria is inexpensive, and it is possible to cut costs still further by staying in a private room in a Bulgarian house or apartment—also arranged by Balkantourist—or by camping. The currency bonus *(see* Currency) can significantly expand your spending power and so can seeking out the duty-free Corecom shops *(see* Shopping in Essential Information).

Sample Prices Museum entry, .20–.90 leva; trip on tram, trolley, or bus, .60 leva; theater ticket, 1.20–6 leva; coffee in a moderate restaurant, 1–2 leva; bottle of wine in a moderate restaurant, from 4 leva.

Visas All visitors need a valid passport; some require a visa as well. Many package tours are exempt from the visa requirement; check with the tour operator or travel agent at the time of purchase.

American travelers needing visas should apply at least two or three weeks in advance to the Embassy of the People's Republic of Bulgaria, 1621 22nd St. NW, Washington, DC 20008. Applicants will need to submit a valid passport, a visa application, one passport-size photo, a self-addressed envelope, and $4–$19 for postage and handling, and the $15 fee.

Canadians in need of visas should apply to the Consulate General of the People's Republic of Bulgaria, 100 Adelaide St. W., Suite 1410, Toronto, Ontario MYH 163.

British travelers should apply for visas to the Embassy of the People's Republic of Bulgaria, 186 Queen's Gate, London SW7 5HL. The cost is £10.

Customs on Arrival You may import duty-free into Bulgaria 250 grams of tobacco products, plus one liter of alcohol and two liters of wine. You should declare all items of value—cameras, tape recorders, etc.—so there will be no problem with Bulgarian customs officials when you leave.

Language The official language is Bulgarian—a Slavic language written in the Cyrillic alphabet. English is spoken in the hotels and restaurants, and fairly widely elsewhere, but it is essential to remember that, in Bulgaria, a nod of the head means "no" and a shake of the head means "yes."

Getting Around

By Car
Road Conditions Main roads are generally well engineered, although some routes are narrow for the volume of traffic they have to carry. A large-scale beltway construction program has begun to link main towns. Completed stretches run from Kalotina—on the Yugoslav border—to Sofia, and from Sofia to Plovdiv. Highways are free of tolls, but be prepared for delays at border points (open 24 hours) while documents are checked and stamped.

Rules of the Road Traffic drives on the right, as it does in the USA. The speed limits are 60 kph (36 mph) in built-up areas, 80 kph (50 mph) elsewhere, except on highways, where it is 120 kph (70 mph). The limit for a car towing a trailer is 10–20 kph (6–10 mph) less in each case. If you do not have a Green Card, you will need a Blue Card, and you must also take out insurance providing third-party cover—this you can do at the border checkpoints (Balkantourist recommends Casco Insurance). You are required to carry a first-aid kit in the vehicle and must not sound the horn after dark or in towns. The drinking-driving laws are extremely strict—you are expressly forbidden to drive after consuming any alcohol at all.

Parking Park only in clearly marked parking places. If in any doubt, check with the hotel or restaurant.

Gasoline Stations are regularly spaced on main roads but may be few and far between off the beaten track. All are marked on Balkantourist's free motoring map. Gas can be bought only with vouchers, issued at reduced prices at all border checkpoints, large hotels, and Balkantourist roadside facilities.

Breakdowns In case of breakdown, telephone 146. The Road Air Service trucks carry essential spares, but it's wise to carry your own spare parts kit.

Car Rental The Rent-a-Car organization has offices in most of the major hotels and at Sofia Airport. Rental cars and fly/drive arrangements can be prebooked through Balkantourist agents abroad.

By Train Buy tickets in advance at a ticket office—there is one in each of the major centers—and avoid long lines at the station. Trains are very busy; seat reservations are obligatory on expresses. All medium- and long-distance trains have first- and second-class carriages and limited buffet services; overnight trains between Sofia and Black Sea resorts have first- and second-class sleeping cars and second-class couchettes. From Sofia there are five main routes—to Varna and to Burgas on the Black Sea coast; to Plovdiv and on to the Turkish border; to Dragoman and the Yugoslav border; and to Kulata and the Greek border. Large sections of the main line are powered by electricity. Plans to electrify the rest are under way.

By Plane Balkan Bulgarian Airlines (**Balkanair**) has services from Sofia to Varna and Burgas, and limited services elsewhere within the country. Book through Balkantourist offices, though this can take time, and overbooking is not unusual.

By Bus The routes of the crowded buses are mainly planned to link towns and districts not connected by rail. Within the cities a regular system of trams and trolley buses operate for a single fare of 6 stotinki. Ticket booths, at most tram stops, sell single or season tickets; you can also pay the driver. The tourist information offices have full details of routes and times.

By Boat Hydrofoils link main communities along the Bulgarian stretches of the Danube and the Black Sea, and there are coastal excursions from some Black Sea resorts. A ferry from Vidin to Calafat links Bulgaria with Romania.

Essential Information

Telephones Calls can be made from hotels or from public telephones in the post office in each major town or resort. There is direct dialing throughout Europe (the code for the United Kingdom is 0044), but calls to the United States must be placed through the operator.

Mail Letters and postcards cost 60 stotinki to the USA, 45 stotinki to the United Kingdom.

Shopping The state commercial organization **Corecom** runs a network of shops in which Bulgarian and imported articles are sold for hard currency at favorable prices. There are branches at most major hotels and at border checkpoints. Look for the famous Attar of Roses, replicas of antique jewelry, copies of icons and medieval frescoes, embroidery and weaving, ceramics, metalwork, woodcarving, and leatherwork. Balkanton records are widely available. Many bookshops sell English translations of modern Bulgarian literature.

Opening and **Banks.** The Foreign Trade Bank is open weekdays 8–noon.
Closing Times **Museums.** Museums are usually open 8–6:30, but are often closed Monday or Tuesday.
Shops. Shops are open Monday–Saturday 9–1 and 2–7.

National Holidays January 1; May 1, 2 (Labor); May 24 (Bulgarian Culture); September 9, 10 (Liberation); November 7 (October Revolution).

Dining There is a choice of hotel restaurants with their "international" menus, Balkantourist restaurants, or the inexpensive restaurants and cafeterias run by local authorities. The best bets are the small folk-style restaurants that serve national dishes and local specialties. The word *picnic* in a restaurant name means that the tables are outdoors. Standards are improving, but food is still rarely served piping hot, and visitors should be prepared for loud background music.

Balkantourist operates a prepaid voucher scheme under which you can eat in any Balkantourist restaurant at no extra cost even if you have booked full board in a specific hotel.

Precautions Tap water is safe in large cities, not always so elsewhere. The local mineral water is excellent, and so are the bottled fruit juices.

Specialties Balkan cooking revolves around lamb and pork, potatoes, peppers, eggplant, tomatoes, onions, carrots, and spices. Fresh fruit, vegetables, and salads are particularly good, and so are the soups. Bulgaria invented yogurt *(kišalo mleko)* with its promise of good health and longevity, and there are rich cream cakes and syrupy *baklava* to round out a meal.

Bulgarian wines are good, usually full-bodied and inexpensive. The national drink is *slivova*—plum or grape brandy—but vodka is popular, too, and you should try the local rose petal liquor. Coffee is strong; tea is taken with lemon instead of milk.

Ratings Prices are per person and include first course, main course, dessert, and tip, but no alcohol. Best bets are indicated by a star ★. At press time, there were 0.8 leva to the dollar.

Category	Cost
Expensive	over 15 leva
Moderate	10–15 leva
Inexpensive	under 10 leva

Credit Cards The following credit card abbreviations are used: AE, American Express; DC, Diners Club; MC, MasterCard; V, Visa.

Lodging There is a wide choice of accommodations, ranging from hotels —most of them dating from the '60s and '70s—to apartment rentals, rooms in private homes, hostels, and campsites. Although hotels are improving, they still tend to suffer from erratic plumbing and temperamental wiring, and it is worth it to pack a rubber drain cover.

Hotels Most hotels used by Western visitors are owned by Balkantourist (Interhotels are of the deluxe variety). Others are run by municipal authorities or organizations catering to specific groups (Šipka for motorists, Orbita for young people, Pirin for hikers). Most have restaurants and bars; the large, modern ones have swimming pools, shops, and other facilities. Some coastal resorts have complexes where different categories of hotels are grouped, each with its own facilities.

Reservations If you arrive in Sofia without reservations, go to Interhotels Central Office, 4 Sveta Sofia St. (Interhotels only); Balkantourist, 37 Dondukov Blvd.; Bureau of Tourist Information and Reservations, 35 Eksarh Josif St. (near Lenin Square), at the Palace of Culture (off Vitoša Blvd.), and the Central Rail Station.

Rented Accommodations Rented accommodations are a growth industry, with planned, modern complexes as well as picturesque cottages. Cooking facilities tend to be meager and meal vouchers are included in the deal. An English-speaking manager is always on hand.

Private Accommodations Staying in private homes, arranged by Balkantourist, is increasingly popular. Some offer bed and breakfast only, some full board.

Hostels Hostels are basic, but clean and cheap. Contact **Orbita**, 45a Stambolij St., Sofia.

Campsites There are more than 100 campsites, many near the Black Sea coast. They are graded one, two, or three stars, and the best of them offer hot and cold water, grocery stores, and restaurants. Balkantourist provides a location map.

Ratings The following hotel categories are for two people in a double room with half-board (breakfast and a main meal). Best bets are indicated by a star ★. Prices are given in dollars, since the rooms are usually prepaid.

Category	Cost: Sofia	Cost: Other Areas
Very Expensive	over $115	over $90
Expensive	$70–$115	$50–$90
Moderate	$50–$70	$35–$50
Inexpensive	under $50	under $35

Credit Cards The following credit card abbreviations are used: AE, American Express; DC, Diners Club; MC, MasterCard; V, Visa.

Tipping Tipping is officially discouraged but nevertheless acceptable. A safe bet is to tip 10%; foreign coins, which the recipient can spend in foreign currency shops, are particularly welcome.

Sofia

Arriving and Departing

By Plane All international flights arrive at Sofia airport. For information on international flights, tel. 2/72–24–14; domestic flights, tel. 2/54–11–13.

Between the Airport and Downtown Bus 84 and long-distance bus 284 both serve the airport, but if you don't know the area, it's safest to take a taxi. There is a stand at the airport; be prepared to be patient.

By Train The Central Station is at the northern edge of the city. For information, tel. 2/3–11–11. The ticket offices in Sofia are at Lyudmila Zhivkova National Palace of Culture or the Rila International Travel Agency, 5 Gurko St., tel. 2/87–07–77. There is a taxi stand at the station.

By Car Heading to or from Yugoslavia, the main routes are E80, going through the border checkpoint at Kalotina on the Nis—Sofia road, or E870 going through the checkpoint at Gyueshevo.

Traveling from Greece, take E79, passing through the checkpoint at Kulata, and from Turkey, take E80, passing through checkpoint Kapitan-Andrevo.

Getting Around

By Bus Buses and trolleys run fairly often. Buy a ticket from the ticket stand near the streetcar stop and punch it into the machine as you board. (Watch how the person in front of you does it.) For information, tel. 2/59–71–83.

By Taxi Taxis are cheap but rather rare. Hail them in the street or at a stand—otherwise, ask the hotel to call one.

By Rented Car You may rent a car through Balkantourist and hotel reception desks.

On Foot The main sites are centrally located, so the best way to see the city is on foot.

Important Addresses and Numbers

Tourist Information Balkantourist Head Office (tel. 2/43–331) is at 1 Vitoša Blvd.; the tourist and accommodation office (tel. 2/88–44–30) is at 37 Donduvkov Blvd. It also has offices or desks in all the main hotels.

Embassies **U.S.** 1 Stamboliiski Blvd., tel. 2/88–48–01. **U.K.** 65 Tolbukhin Blvd., tel. 2/88–53–61.

Emergencies **Police,** Sofia City Constabulary, tel. 166; **Ambulance,** tel. 150; **Fire,** tel. 160; **Doctor,** Clinic for Foreign Citizens, Mladost 1, 1 Eugeni Pavlovski St., tel. 2/75–361; **Pharmacies,** tel. 178 for information about all-night pharmacies.

Guided Tours

Orientation Tours Guided tours of Sofia and environs are arranged by Balkantourist from either of the main Sofia offices or from the Balkantourist desks at the major hotels. Among the possibilities are 3–4 hour tours of the principal city sights by car or minibus; or a longer 4–5 hour tour that goes as far as Mount Vitoša.

Excursions Balkantourist also arranges day trips to the Rila Monastery, to the "museum town" of Koprivshtitsa, Plovdiv, or the Valley of Roses.

Evening Tours Balkantourist has a number of these, from a night out eating local food and watching folk dances to an evening at the National Opera.

Exploring Sofia

Sofia is set on the high Sofia Plain, ringed by mountain ranges: the Balkan range to the north, Ljulin Mountains to the west, part of the Sredna Gora Mountains to the southeast and, to the southwest, Mount Vitoša, the city's playground, which rises to 7,500 feet (2,286 meters). The area has been inhabited for about 5,000 years, but the visitor's first impression is of a modern city with broad streets, light traffic, spacious parks, and open-air cafés. As recently as the 1870s, it was a Turkish capital, and

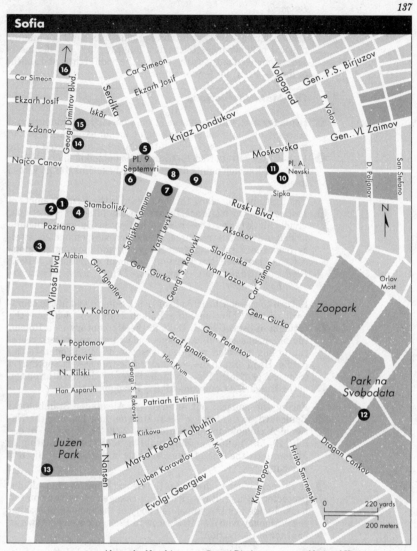

Alexander Nevski
Memorial Church, **10**
Banja Basi Mosque, **15**
Bulgarian Communist
Party Headquarters, **5**
Central Department
Store, **14**
Central Market Hall, **16**

Georgi Dimitrov
Mausoleum, **7**
Lenin Square, **1**
Ljudmila Zivkova
National Palace of
Culture, **13**
National Archaeological
Museum, **6**
National Art Gallery
and National
Ethnographic
Museum, **8**

National History
Museum, **3**
Park Na Svobodota, **12**
St. Nikolaj, **9**
St. Sofia, **11**
Sveta Nedelja Church, **2**
Sveti Georgi Rotunda, **4**

two mosques still remain; but most of the city was planned after 1880. There are enough intriguing museums and high-quality musical performances to merit a lengthy stay, but if time is short, you need only two days to see the main sights, and another day, at least, for Mount Vitoša.

The Main Attractions

① **Lenin Square,** with its statue of the Russian revolutionary and statesman, is a good starting point for an exploration of the main sights. The south side of the square is dominated by the **②** 19th-century **Sveta Nedelja Church.** Go behind it to find Vitoša Boulevard, which points directly to the beautiful Mount Vitoša itself.

The first building along this boulevard is the former Courts of Justice, now the **National History Museum.** Its vast collections, **③** vividly illustrating the creative history of Bulgaria, include priceless Thracian treasures, Roman mosaics, enameled jewelry from the First Bulgarian Kingdom, and glowing religious art that survived the years of Ottoman oppression. *Vitoša Blvd., tel. 2/88–41–60. Open Tues.–Thurs., weekends 10:30–6:30; Fri. 2–6:30.*

Return to the southeast side of Lenin Square and in the courtyard of the Sheraton Sofia Balkan Hotel you will see the **④** rotunda of **Sveti Georgi.** Built in the 4th century as a Roman temple, it has served as mosque and church, and recent restoration has revealed medieval frescoes. It is not open to the public. Head east to the vast and traffic-free Deveti Septemvri (September Ninth) Place, watched over by the red star on top **⑤** of the **Bulgarian Communist Party Headquarters.**

Facing the square, but entered via Alexander Stambolijski **⑥** Boulevard, is the former Great Mosque, now housing the **National Archaeological Museum,** (tel. 2/88–24–05, open Wed.–Sun. 10–5). The 15th-century building itself is as fascinating as its contents, the best of which are now in the National History Museum.

⑦ In the next block to the east is the **Georgi Dimitrov Mausoleum,** protected by a military guard that changes every hour on the hour. Inside lies the embalmed body of the famous Bulgarian revolutionary who died in Moscow in 1949 and is now known as "Father of the Nation."

⑧ Across the street is the **National Art Gallery** and **National Ethnographic Museum** (tel. 2/88–35–59, open Wed.–Mon. 10:30–**⑨** 6:30). Next to it stands the ornate Russian Church of **St. Nikolaj,** or St. Nicholas, erected 1912–14.

From here you enter Ruski Boulevard, with its monument to the liberators, topped by the equestrian statue of Russian Czar Alexander II. It stands in front of the National Assembly. At last you are confronted by the neo-Byzantine structure with glittering onion domes whose image looks out from almost every piece of tourist literature and which really does dominate **⑩** the city. This is the **Alexander Nevski Memorial Church** built by the Bulgarian people at the beginning of this century as a mark of gratitude to their Russian liberators. Inside are alabaster and onyx, Italian marble and Venetian mosaics, and space for a congregation of 5,000. Attend a service to hear the superb choir, and don't miss the fine collection of icons in the **Crypt Museum**. *Open Wed.–Mon. 10:30–6:30.*

⑪ Cross the square to the west to pay your respects to the much older church of **St. Sofia,** which dates back to the 6th century, though remains of even older churches have been found during excavations. Its age and simplicity are in stark contrast to its more glamorous neighbor.

⑫ Return to Ruski Boulevard and continue east to the **Park Na Svobodota** (Freedom or Liberty Park), with its lake and fountains, woods and lawns, huge sports stadium, and open-air theater. From the park take Dragan Cankov west (back toward Lenin Square) briefly, before going left on Patriarh Evtimij, toward Juzen Park. The formal gardens and extensive woodlands here are to be extended as far as Mount Vitoša.

⑬ At the entrance to the park stands a large modern building, the **Ljudmila Zivkova National Palace of Culture,** with its complex of halls for conventions and cultural activities. Its underpass, on several levels, is equipped with shops, restaurants, discos, and a bowling alley.

⑭ Back at Lenin Square, follow Georgi Dimitrov Boulevard to the train station. The large building on the right is the recently refurbished **Central Department Store** (open Mon.–Sat. 8–8).
⑮ Just beyond is a distinctive building, a legacy of Turkish domination, the **Banja Basi Mosque** (closed to visitors). Closeby you will see the Public Mineral Baths. Across the boulevard is the
⑯ busy **Central Market Hall** with its foodstuffs and household goods.

Time Out Anyone doing the full tour is going to need at least one refreshment stop. There are several eating places on the northern length of Vitoša Boulevard. Across from Lenin's Monument the underpass leading toward the Central Department Store has a café (and the little 14th-century church of Sveta Petka Samardzijska). Or take a break in a café in the underpass at the Palace of Culture, or on Lenin Square itself at the Complex Roubin.

Off the Beaten Track

The little medieval church of **Bojana,** about six miles (10 kilometers) south of the city center, is well worth a visit. The church itself is closed for restoration, but a replica, complete with copies of the exquisite frescoes, is open to visitors.

The **Dragalevci Monastery** stands in beechwoods above the nearby village of Dragalevci, and here you can see the real 14th-century church and its frescoes. From here take the chair lift to the delightful resort complex of Aleko, and another nearby chair lift to the top of Malak Rezen. There are well-marked walking and ski trails in the area.

Shopping

Gifts and Souvenirs There is a good selection of arts and crafts at the shop of the **Union of Bulgarian Artists,** (6 Ruski Blvd.). You will find a range of souvenirs at **Sredec** (7 Legue St.), **Souvenir Store** (7 Stambolijski Blvd.), and **Prizma Store,** (2 Ruski Blvd). If you are interested in furs or leather, try **4 Slavjanska St., 7 Car Kalojan St.,** or **2 Ruski Blvd.** For recordings of Bulgarian music, go to **Maestro Atanassov** (8 Ruski Blvd.).

Shopping Districts The latest shopping center is in the subway of the modern **Palace of Culture,** where stores sell fashions, leather goods, and all forms of handcrafts. The pedestrians-only area along **Vitoša Blvd.** features many new, small shops.

Department Stores The biggest is the newly renovated **Central Department Store** at 2 Georgi Dimitrov Blvd.

Food Markets All kinds of foods are on sale at the **Central Market Hall,** 25 Georgi Dimitrov Blvd., including excellent fruit and vegetable preserves, local wines, and spirits.

Dining

Eating in Sofia can be enjoyable and even entertaining, if the restaurant has a nightclub or folklore program. Be prepared to be patient and make an evening of it, as service can be slow at times. If you are in a hurry, try a *mehana*, or tavern, where the atmosphere is informal and service is a bit quicker.

Ratings Prices are per person and include first course, main course, dessert, and tip, but no alcohol. Best bets are indicated by a star ★. At press time, there were 0.8 leva to the dollar.

Category	Cost
Expensive	over 15 leva
Moderate	10–15 leva
Inexpensive	under 10 leva

Expensive **Berlin.** German food is the specialty in this sophisticated restaurant in the Serdika Hotel. *2 General Zaimov Blvd., tel. 2/44–34–11. AE, DC, MC, V.*

★ **Budapest.** This place enjoys a reputation as one of the best restaurants in Sofia for good food, wine, and live music. As the name suggests, Hungarian food takes pride of place. *145 G.S. Rakovski St., tel. 2/82–27–50. AE, DC, MC, V.*

Havana. Cuban food is featured in this popular restaurant near the center of town. *27 Vitoša Blvd., tel. 2/87–01–31. AE, DC, MC, V.*

Moderate **Bojanske Hanche.** Local and national specialties are the main features in this restaurant and folklore center six miles (10 kilometers) from downtown. *Near Bojanske church, tel. 2/56–30–16. No credit cards.*

Gorubljana. Attached to the motel of the same name about six miles (10 kilometers) southeast of the center, Gorubljana is recommended for a combination of local specialties and folklore presentations. *On E80 southeast of Sofia, tel. 2/72–37–20. No credit cards.*

Rubin. This eating complex in the center of Sofia has a snack bar and an elegant restaurant serving Bulgarian and international food. A full meal can sometimes push the cost into the Expensive bracket. *4 Lenin Sq. No credit cards.*

Inexpensive **Ropotamo.** With its central location, and reasonable prices, Ropotamo is a good bet for visitors on a budget. *73 Lenin Blvd., tel. 2/72–25–16. No credit cards.*

Vodanicarnski Mehani. The English translation is "Miller's Tavern," which is appropriate, since it's made up of three old mills linked together. It is at the foot of Mount Vitoša and features a folklore show and a menu of Bulgarian specialties. *Dragalevci District. No credit cards.*

Zlatnite Mostove. This restaurant on Mount Vitoša has live music in the evenings. *Vitoša District, 12 mi. (19 km.) from center. No credit cards.*

Lodging

The following hotels all meet a high standard of cleanliness, and are open year-round unless otherwise stated. If you arrive in Sofia without a reservation, the following offices can be useful: Interhotels Central Office, 4 Sveta Sofia St.; Balkantourist, 37 Dondukov Blvd.

Ratings The following hotel price categories are for two people in a double room with half-board (breakfast and one main meal). Best bets are indicated by a star ★. Prices are given in dollars since rooms are prepaid.

Category	Cost
Very Expensive	over $115
Expensive	$70–$115
Moderate	$50–$70
Inexpensive	under $50

Very Expensive **Novotel Europa.** This member of the French Novotel chain is near the train station and not far from the center of the city. *131 Georgi Dimitrov Blvd., tel. 2/3–12–61. 600 rooms with bath. Facilities: restaurant, cocktail bar, nightclub, shops (including Corecom shop). AE, DC, MC, V.*

★ **Sheraton Sofia Hotel Balkan.** The former Grand Hotel Balkan has been recently done up to Sheraton standards. It is now a first-class hotel with a central location that is hard to match. *1 Lenin Sq., tel. 2/87–65–41. 188 rooms with bath. Facilities: fitness center, nightclub, bars, 3 restaurants. AE, DC, MC, V.*

★ **Vitoša-New Otani.** There is a distinct Oriental flavor to this towering, trim Interhotel, which is not surprising, since it was designed by the Japanese. It is hard to match the range of services and activities available here. *100 Anton Ivanov Blvd., tel. 2/62–41–51. 454 rooms with bath. Facilities: Japanese restaurant, health center, pool, nightclub, casino. AE, DC, MC, V.*

Expensive **Grand Hotel Sofia.** This five-story, centrally located Interhotel conveys an atmosphere of relative intimacy, compared with some of its larger rivals in the capital. *1 Nrodno Sobranie Sq., tel. 2/87–88–21. 172 rooms with bath or shower. Facilities: coffee shop, folk tavern, nightclub, shops. AE, DC, MC, V.*

Park Hotel Moskva. The pleasant park setting makes up for the fact that this hotel is not as centrally located as some other comparable hotels. The Russian restaurant has a nightly floor show. *25 Nezabravka St., tel. 2/7–12–61. 390 rooms with bath. Facilities: restaurants, coffee shop, cocktail bar, nightclub, shops. AE, DC, MC, V.*

Rodina. Sofia's newest high-rise hotel is not far from the center and boasts the latest in modern facilities. *8 General Totladen*

Blvd., tel. 2/53–31. 536 rooms with bath. Facilities: restaurants, coffee shop, summer and winter gardens, pool, gym, nightclub. AE, DC, MC, V.

Moderate **Bulgaria.** Despite its central location, this small hotel is quiet and a bit old-fashioned. *4 Ruski Blvd., tel. 2/87–19–77. 72 rooms, some with bath or shower. No credit cards.*

Hemus. This is a smaller place near the Vitoša-New Otani. Guests can take advantage of the facilities of its larger neighbor while saving money for the casino or nightclub. *31 Georgi Traikov Blvd., tel. 2/66–13–13. 240 rooms, most with bath or shower. Facilities: folk tavern, nightclub. No credit cards.*

Inexpensive **Serdika.** The centrally located Serdika has an old Berlin-style restaurant serving German specialties. *2 General Zaimov St., tel. 2/44–34–11. 140 rooms, most with bath or shower. No credit cards.*

Slavia. The Slavia is in the southwest, some distance from the center. *2 Sofijski Geroi St., tel. 2/52–55–51. 75 rooms, some with bath or shower. No credit cards.*

The Arts

The standard of music in Bulgaria is high, whether it takes the form of opera, symphonic, or folk music, which has just broken into the international scene with its close harmonies and colorful stage displays. Contact Balkantourist or the **Concert Office,** (2 Ruski Blvd., tel. 2/87–15–88).

Entertainment and Nightlife

Nightclubs The following hotel bars have floor shows and a lively atmosphere: **Bar Sofia,** Grand Hotel Sofia, Narodno Sobranie Sq., tel. 2/87–88–21; **Bar Variety Ambassador,** Vitoša-New Otani Hotel, 100 Anton Ivanov Blvd., tel. 2/62–41–51; **Bar Variety,** Park Hotel Moskva, 25 Nezabrauka St., tel. 2/7–12–61; **Bar Variety,** Grand Hotel Balkan, 2 Lenin Sq., tel. 2/87–65–41.

Discos There is a disco, nightclub, and bowling alley at the **Lyudmila Zhivkova National Palace of Culture.**

Casino Gamblers can try their luck at the casino in the **Vitoša-New Otani Hotel.**

The Black Sea Golden Coast

Bulgaria's most popular resort area attracts visitors from all over the Eastern bloc and, increasingly, from Western countries. Its sunny, sandy beaches are backed by the last hills of the Balkan range and the Strandja Mountains. Although the tourist centers tend to be huge state-built complexes, with a somewhat lean feel, they have modern amenities. Sunny Beach, the largest of the resorts with 112 hotels, is known as "the children's paradise"—the availability of baby-sitters may make parents feel they are in paradise, too.

The busy port of Varna is a good center for exploration. It is a focal point of land and sea transport and has museums, a variety of restaurants, and some nightlife. The fishing villages of Nesebar and Sozopol are more attractive. Lodgings tend to be scarce in these villages, so private accommodations, arranged by Balkantourist, may be the answer. Whatever resort you choose, all offer facilities for water sports and some have instructors. Tennis and horseback riding are also available.

Getting Around

Bus service is frequent and inexpensive. Buy your ticket in advance. **Cars** and **bicycles** can be rented; bikes are particularly useful for getting around such spreading resorts as Sunny Beach. A **hydrofoil** service links Varna, Nesebar, Burgas, and Sozopol. A regular **boat** service travels the Varna–Druzba–Golden Sands–Albena–Balcik route.

Guided Tours

A wide range of excursions are arranged from all resorts. Check with your hotel information desk or with the Balkantourist office.

Tourist Information

There is a Balkantourist office in most towns and resorts. In Varna the main office is at 3 Moussala St. (tel. 52/22–55–24), and the private accommodations office is at 3 Lenin Boulevard.

Exploring

Varna Varna, Bulgaria's third-largest city, is easily reached by rail (about 7½ hours by express) or road from Sofia. If driving, allow time to see the Stone Forest (Pobiti Kamuni) just off the Sofia–Varna road between Devnya and Varna. The unexpected groups of monumental sandstone tree trunks are thought to have been formed when the area was the bed of the Lutsian Sea. There is plenty to see in the port city of Varna. The ancient Greek city of Odessos became a major Roman trading center and is now an important shipbuilding and industrial city. The main sights can be linked by a planned walk.

Begin with the **Museum of History and Art,** one of the great—if lesser known—museums of Europe. The splendid collection includes finds from the Varna necropolis of the 4th millennium BC, as well as Thracian, Greek, and Roman treasures, and richly painted icons. *41 Dimitar Blagoev Blvd., tel. 52/23–70–57. Open Tues.–Sun. 10–5.*

Near the northeastern end of Dimitar Blagoev Boulevard are numerous shops and cafés; the western end leads to Varnenska Komouna Square and the monumental **Cathedral** (1880–86), whose lavish murals are worth a look. Running north from the cathedral is Karl Marx Street, with shops, movie theaters, and eateries. Opposite the cathedral, in the City Gardens, is the **Old Clock Tower,** built in 1880 by the Varna Guild Association. On the south side of the City Gardens, on September 9th Square, stands the Baroque magnificence of the **Stoyan Bucharov National Theater.**

Leave the square to the east, and walk past the Moussala Hotel. The Tourist Information Office is at 3 Moussala Street. Nearby, on the corner of Lenin Boulevard and Shipka Street, are the remains of the **Roman fortress wall** of Odessos. Lenin Boulevard is another of Varna's shopping streets. At No. 44 you

The Black Sea Coast

SOVIET UNION

Galaţi

Danube

Danube Delta

Sulina

Brăila

Tulcea

Dunavatu

Sfîntu Gheorghe

Băbadag

Lake Razelm

Giurgeni

Hirşova

Lake Sinoe

Crişan

Istria

Slobozia

Feteşti

Black Sea

Danube

Cernavodă

Mamaia

Medgidia

Constanţa

Călăraşi

Techirgiol

Eforie

N

Mangalia

0   20 miles

0   30 km

BULGARIA

can buy handcrafted souvenirs from one of the outlets of the Union of Bulgarian Artists.

Walk south along Odessos Street to Khan Krum Street. Here you'll find the Holy Virgin Church of 1602, and the substantial remains of the **Roman Thermae**—the public baths, dating from the 2nd–3rd centuries AD. Buy the excellent English guidebook here to get the most out of your visit.

Not far from the baths, moving west, is old Druzki Street, recently restored and comfortingly lined with restaurants, taverns, and coffee houses.

Head toward the sea and November 8 Street. The old prison building at No. 5 houses the **Museum of the Revolutionary Movement,** (open Tues.–Sun. 10–5). Continue to Cervenoarmejski Boulevard and follow it, with the sea on your right, to No. 2 for the **Naval Museum** (open daily 8–6:30), with its displays of the early days of navigation on the Black Sea and the Danube. The museum is at the edge of the extensive and luxuriant **Marine Gardens,** which enjoy wide views over the bay, and have restaurants, an open-air theater, and the fascinating **Copernicus Astronomy Complex** (open weekdays 8–noon and 2–5) near the main entrance.

Druzba A few miles north along the coast from Varna is Druzba (Friendship), the smallest and most intimate of the Black Sea resorts, spread through a wooded park near a series of sandy coves. Warm mineral springs were discovered here in 1947, and the five-star Grand Hotel Varna, the most luxurious on the coast, offers all kinds of hydrotherapy under medical supervision.

In contrast to the sedate atmosphere of Druzba is lively **Zlatni Pjasaci** (Golden Sands), a mere five miles (eight kilometers) north, with its extensive leisure amenities, mineral spring medical centers, and sports and entertainment facilities. Just over two miles (four kilometers) inland from Golden Sands is **Aladji Rock Monastery,** one of Bulgaria's oldest, cut out of the cliff face and made accessible to visitors by sturdy iron stairways.

From Druzba, if time permits, take a trip 10 miles (16 kilometers) north to **Balcik,** part of Romania until just before World War II, now a relaxed setting where Bulgaria's writers, artists, scientists, and trade unionists can enjoy state-sponsored R and R. The beautiful **Botanical Gardens** are dotted with curious buildings, including a small Byzantine-style church.

Slancev Brjag Another popular resort, this time south of Varna, is Slancev Brjag (Sunny Beach). It is enormous, and especially suited to families because of its safe beaches, activities for children beachside restaurants, and plenty of gardens and green spaces.

Nesebur is close to Slancev Brjag, and accessible by regular excursion buses. It would be hard to find a town that exudes a greater sense of age than this ancient settlement founded by the Greeks 25 centuries ago on a rocky peninsula reached by a narrow causeway. Among its vine-covered houses are richly decorated medieval churches. Don't miss the frescoes.

Still traveling south along the coast, the next place of any size is **Burgas,** Bulgaria's second main port on the Black Sea. Burgas is rather industrial, with several oil refineries, though it does have a pleasant **Maritime Park** with an extensive beach below.

For a more appealing stopover, continue for another 20 miles (32 kilometers) south to **Sozopol,** a fishing port with narrow cobbled streets leading down to the harbor. This was Apollonia, oldest of the Greek colonies, and is now a popular haunt for Bulgarian and, increasingly, foreign writers and artists who find private accommodations in the pretty stone and wood houses, and sustenance in the restaurants and inns.

Six miles (ten kilometers) to the south is the vast, modern resort village of **Djuni,** where visitors can stay in up-to-date cottages, in the modern Monastery Compound, or in the Seaside Settlement. The wide range of amenities—cafés, folk restaurants, a sports center, shopping center, yacht club, and marina—make it another attractive spot for families.

Dining and Lodging

For details and price category definitions, *see* Dining and Lodging in Essential Information .

Burgas **Starata Gernia.** The name of this restaurant translates as "old
Dining boat," appropriate for a beachfront restaurant featuring fish specialties. *Purvai Mai St. No credit cards. Moderate.*

Lodging **Bulgaria.** The Bulgaria is a high-rise Interhotel in the center of town, with a restaurant set in a winter garden. *21 Parvi May St., tel. 56/4–28–20. 200 rooms, most with bath or shower. AE, DC, MC, V. Moderate.*

Druzba
Dining

Bulgarska Svatba. This folk-style restaurant with dancing is on the outskirts of the resort; charcoal-grilled meats are especially recommended. *Druzba Resort. No credit cards. Moderate.*

Manastirska Izba. Centrally located, this eatery is a modest but pleasant restaurant with a sunny terrace. *Druzba Resort, tel. 56/6–11–77. No credit cards. Moderate.*

Lodging
★

Grand Hotel Varna. This Swedish-built hotel has a reputation as the best hotel on the coast. It is set conveniently near the beach and offers a wide range of hydrotherapeutic treatments featuring the natural warm mineral springs. *Druzba Resort, tel. 52/6–14–91. 325 rooms, all with bath or shower. Facilities: 3 restaurants, nightclub, 2 swimming pools, sports hall, tennis courts, bowling alley. AE, DC, MC, V. Expensive.*

Caika. Caika means "sea gull" in Bulgarian, and this hotel has a bird's-eye view of the whole resort, from its perch above the northern end of the beach. *Druzba Resort. 130 rooms, most with bath or shower. No restaurant. No credit cards. Moderate.*

Slancev Brjag
Dining

Hanska Satra. Situated in the coastal hills behind the sea, this combination restaurant and nightclub has been built to resemble the tents of the Bulgarian khans of old. It has entertainment well into the night. *3 mi (5 km) west of Slancev Brjag. No credit cards. Moderate.*

Ribarska Hiza. This lively beachside restaurant specializes in fish and has music until 1 AM. *Northern end of resort. No credit cards. Inexpensive.*

Lodging

Burgas. Large and comfortable, this hotel lies at the southern end of the resort. *Slancev Brjag Resort, tel. 0554/23–58. 250 rooms, all with bath or shower. Facilities: restaurant, 2 pools, sports hall. AE, DC, MC, V. Moderate.*

★

Globus. Considered by many to be the best in the resort, this hotel combines a central location with modern facilities. *Slancev Brjag Resort, tel. 0554/22–45. 100 rooms, all with bath or shower. Facilities: indoor pool, restaurant, sports hall. AE, DC, MC, V. Moderate.*

Kuban. Near the center of the resort, this large establishment is just a short stroll from the beach. *Slancev Brjag Resort, tel. 0554/23–09. 210 rooms, most with bath or shower. AE, DC, MC, V. Moderate.*

Caika. This hotel offers the best location at a low cost. *Slancev Brjag Resort, tel. 0554/23–08. 85 rooms, some with bath or shower. No credit cards. Inexpensive.*

Varna
Dining

Starata Kusta. This restaurant's name means "the old house." Part of a new catering complex along with several bars and restaurants, it provides national specialties in a pseudo old-time atmosphere. *14 Druzki St., tel. 52/23–90–65. No credit cards. Moderate.*

Lodging
★

Cerno More. One of the best things about this modern Interhotel is the panoramic view from the 22nd floor; another is the modern facilities. *35 Georgi Dimitrov Blvd., tel. 52/22–01–67. 230 rooms, all with bath or shower. Facilities: 3 restaurants, ground floor café with terraces, nightclub. AE, DC, MC, V. Expensive.*

Inland Bulgaria: Mountains and Ancient Cultures

Inland Bulgaria is not as well known to tourists as the capital and coast, and the adventurous traveler, willing to put up with limited hotel facilities and unreliable transportation, will find plenty to photograph, paint, or simply savor. Wooded and mountainous, the interior is dotted with attractive "museum" villages and ancient towns; the folk culture is a strong survivor from the past, not a tourist-inspired re-creation of it. The foothills of the Balkan Range, marked Starat Planina or "old mountains" on most maps, lie parallel with the lower Sredna Gora mountains, with the verdant Valley of Roses between them. In the Balkan range is the ancient capital of Veliko Tarnovo; south of the Sredna Gora stretches the fertile Thracian plain and Bulgaria's second city of Plovdiv. Between Sofia and Plovdiv is the enchanting old town of Koprivštica. To the south, in the Rila Mountains, is Borovec, first of the mountain resorts. A round-trip covering all of these towns, with a side excursion to Rila Monastery, could be made in four or five days, although more time is recommended.

Getting Around

Rail and bus services cover all parts of inland Bulgaria, but the timetables are not easy to follow and there are frequent delays. The best bet is to rent a car; Balkantourist can arrange this.

Guided Tours

Organized tours set out from Sofia, each covering different points of interest. Check with your Sofia hotel information desk or with Balkantourist for specific information.

Tourist Information Plovdiv: 34 Moskva Blvd., tel. 32/5–38–48.
Veliko Tarnovo: 2 Vasil Levski St., tel. 62/2–02–36.

Exploring

Koprivštica Koprivštica, one of Bulgaria's showpiece villages, is set in mountain pastures and pine forests, about 3,000 feet (914 meters) up in the Sredna Gora range. It is 62 miles (103 kilometers) from Sofia, reached by a minor road south from the Sofia–Kazaluk expressway. Founded in the 14th century, it is now a living museum of the carved wood architecture of the National Revival period, or Renaissance, of the 18th and 19th centuries. Many of the houses—several belonging to artists and poets—may be visited. Visually, nothing much has changed since the first shots of the tragic April 1876 uprising against the Turks were fired here. A place of pilgrimage for Bulgarians, Koprivštica attracts Western visitors because of its setting and its brightly painted houses, with their distinctive overhanging eaves and broad verandas, their courtyards glimpsed through studded wooden gates.

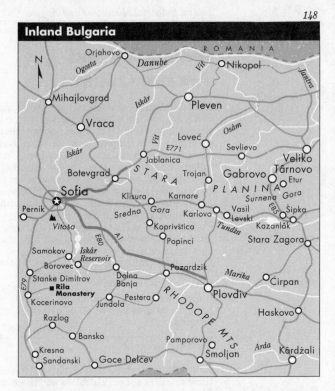

Inland Bulgaria

Return to the main road and turn right. After nine miles (15 kilometers) you reach **Klisura** and the beginning of the Valley of Roses. Another 11 miles (17 kilometers) turn, at the village of Karnare, take the winding scenic road north over the Balkan range to the town of Trojan, and, a few miles away, **Trojan Monastery**, set in the heart of the mountains. Trojan Monastery Church was painstakingly rebuilt in the 19th century, and its icons, wood carvings, and frescoes are classic examples of National Revival art. Back at Trojan, continue north on the mountain road until it meets highway E771, where you turn right for Veliko Tarnovo, 50 miles (82 kilometers) away.

Veliko Tarnovo Veliko Tarnovo, a town of panoramic vistas, rises up against steep mountain slopes through which the River Jantra runs its jagged course. During the 13th and 14th centuries, this was Bulgaria's capital, cradle of its history and consequently the focus of repeated Ottoman attack—not to mention an earthquake in 1913. Fortunately as much effort has gone into restoring old buildings as into constructing new ones, and it is now a museum city of marvelous relics. The town warrants two or three days of exploration, but even in a short visit some sights should not be missed. Ideally, begin at a vantage point above town to get an overview of its design and character. Next, seek out **Tsaravec** to the west (Caravec on some maps), protected by a river loop. This is where medieval czars and patriarchs had their palaces. The area is under restoration, with steep paths and stairways for easier viewing of the extensive ruins of the Patriarchite and the royal palace.

The prominent feature to the south is **Baldwin's Tower,** the 13th-century prison of Baldwin of Flanders, one-time Latin Emperor of Constantinople. Nearby are three important churches: the 13th-century church of the **Forty Martyrs,** with its frescoes of the Tarnovo schools and two inscribed columns, one dating back to the 9th century; the church of **Saints Peter and Paul,** with vigorous murals both inside and out; and, across the river, reached by a bridge near the Forty Martyrs, the restored church of **Saint Dimitus,** built on the spot where the Second Bulgarian Kingdom was launched in 1185.

Back toward the center of town, near the Yantra Hotel, is Samovodene Street, lined with restored craft workshops—a fascinating place to linger and a good place to find souvenirs, Turkish candy, or a charming café. On nearby Rakovski Street are a group of buildings of the National Revival period. One of the finest is **Nikoli Han,** a museum that was once an inn (tel. 62/2–17–10 for opening times).

Leave Veliko Tarnovo by E85, and head toward Plovdiv, allowing for three stops en route. The first, near the industrial center of Gabrovo—interesting in itself for its House of Humor Museum—is the museum village of **Etur,** five miles (eight kilometers) to the southeast. Its mill is still powered by a stream, and local craftsmen are even today trained in traditional skills. Second is the **Sipka Pass,** with its mighty monument on the peak to the 200,000 Russian soldiers and Bulgarian volunteers who died here in 1877, during the Russo-Turkish Wars. Third is **Kazanlak,** at the eastern end of the Valley of Roses, where you can trace the history of rose production, Bulgaria's oldest industry. There is also a highly decorated replica of a Thracian tomb of the 3rd or 4th century BC, set close to the original, which remains closed for its preservation.

Plovdiv   From Kazanlak, take the road west through the **Valley of Roses,** at its fragrant best in May and June, although lavender, sunflowers, vines, and fruit trees are also impressive in season. At either Vasil Levski or Karlovo, turn south for Plovdiv, Bulgaria's second-largest city, one of the oldest in Europe, and a major industrial center. The old town, on the hillier southern side of the Marica River, is worth a visit.

Begin at the **National Ethnographical Museum** in the House of Arghir Kovyoumidjioglu, an elegant example of National Revival style that made its first impact in Plovdiv. The museum is full of artifacts from that important period. *2 Comakov St. Open Tues.–Sun. 9–noon and 1:30–5.*

Below the medieval gateway of Hissar Kapiya is the attractive **Georgicdi House** on Starina Street, and the steep, narrow Strumna Street, lined with workshops and boutiques, some reached through little courtyards. Follow Maxim Gorki Street westward to its junction with the pedestrians-only Vasil Kolarov Street; here are the remains of a **Roman stadium.** The **Kapana District** of restored and traditional shops and restaurants is nearby. Turn east off Vasil Kolarov Street and walk to the fine hilltop **Roman Amphitheater,** sensitively renovated and frequently used for dramatic and musical performances. On the other side of the old town, toward the river, is the **National Archaeological Museum** (open Tues.–Sun. 9–12:30 and 2–5:30) at 1 Suedinie Square, which holds a replica of the 4th century BC Panagjuriste Gold Treasure—the original of which is in Sofia.

Travel west along the E80 Sofia Road. At Dolna Banja, turn off to **Borovec,** about 4,300 feet (1,300 meters) up the northern slopes of the Rila Mountains. This is an excellent walking center and winter sports resort, well-equipped with hotels, folk taverns, and ski schools. The winding mountain road leads back to Sofia from here, past Lake Iskar—largest in the country.

On the way back to Sofia, you should consider a visit to the **Rila Monastery,** founded by Ivan of Rila in the 10th century. Cut across to E79, travel south to Kocerinovo, and then turn east to follow the steep forested valley past the village of Rila. The monastery has suffered so frequently from fire that most of it is now a grand National Revival reconstruction, although a rugged 14th-century tower has survived. The atmosphere in this mountain retreat, populated by many storks, is still heavy with a sense of the past—although much of the complex has been turned into a museum and the monks' cells are now guest rooms. The visitor can see 14 small chapels with frescoes from the 15th and 17th centuries, a lavishly carved altarpiece in the new Assumption church, the sarcophagus of Ivan of Rila, icons, and ancient manuscripts, a reminder that this was a stronghold of art and learning during the centuries of Ottoman rule. It is well worth the detour—or a special trip from Sofia.

Dining and Lodging

For details and price category definitions, *see* Dining and Lodging in Essential Information.

Koprivština **Djedo Liben Inn.** This attractive folk restaurant is built in the
Dining traditional style of the area—with half-timbered, high stone walls. The menu reflects a similar attention to traditional detail. *Koprivština (no tel.). No credit cards. Moderate.*

Lodging **Koprivština.** This good-value hotel is popular with Bulgarians themselves, and is just over the river from the center of town. *Koprivština, tel. 21–18. No credit cards. Inexpensive.*

Plovdiv **Pldin.** This is an attractive folk restaurant in the center of town.
Dining A video presentation in the lobby highlights the city's past. *3 Knyaz Tseretelov St., tel. 032/23–17–20. AE, DC, MC, V. Expensive.*

Alafrangues. A restored 19th-century house with wood-carved ceilings and a vine-covered courtyard is the location of this charming folk-style restaurant. *15 Nektariev St., tel. 032/22–98–09. No credit cards. Moderate.*

Rhetora. This coffee bar is in a beautifully restored old house near the Roman amphitheater in the old part of the city. *8A G. Samodoumov St., tel. 032/22–20–93. No credit cards. Moderate.*

Lodging **Novotel Plovdiv.** The large, modern, and well-equipped Novotel is across the river from the main town, near the fairgrounds. *2 Zlatju Boyadjiev St., tel. 032/4–45–95. 322 rooms with bath. Facilities: restaurant, folk tavern, nightclub, sports hall, pools. AE, DC, MC, V. Expensive.*

Trimontium. This centrally located Interhotel built in the '50s is comfortable and ideal for exploring the old town. *2 Kapitan Raico St., tel. 032/2–55–61. 163 rooms, all with bath or shower.*

Facilities: folk tavern, restaurant. AE, DC, MC, V. Expensive.

Marica. This is a large, modern hotel that offers a less expensive alternative to its neighbor, the Novotel. *5 Georgi Dimitrov St., tel. 032/5–27–35. 171 rooms, all with bath or shower. Facilities: bar, restaurant. No credit cards. Inexpensive.*

Veliko Tarnovo
Dining

Boljarska Izba. In the center of the busy district just north of the river, this place is a folk tavern. *Dimiter Blagoev St. (no tel.). No credit cards. Moderate.*

Lodging

Veliko Tarnovo. Located right in the middle of the most historic part of the town, this modern Interhotel boasts some of the best facilities for this class of hotel. *2 Emile Popov St., tel. 062/ 2–05–71. 195 rooms, all with bath or shower. Facilities: 2 restaurants, coffee shop, disco, sports hall, indoor pool. AE, DC, MC, V. Expensive.*

Yantra. The Yantra has some of the best views in town, looking across the river to Tsaravec. *1 Velchova Zavera Sq., tel. 062/ 20–30–91. 60 rooms, most with shower. Facilities: restaurant, coffee shop, bar. No credit cards. Moderate.*

Etur. This moderate-size hotel has an address near the more expensive Veliko Tarnovo, making it a good base for sightseeing within town. *I. Ivailo St., tel. 062/2–68–51. 80 rooms, most with shower. Facilities: restaurant, coffee shop, bar. Inexpensive.*

7 Cyprus

Introduction

The Mediterranean island of Cyprus was at one time a center for the cult of Aphrodite, who is said to have risen naked and perfect from the sea near Paphos. Wooded and mountainous, with a 400-mile (640-kilometer) coastline, Cyprus lies just off the southern coast of Turkey. Oranges, olives, lemons, grapes, and cherries grow here, and fish are plentiful. The summers are hot and dry, the spring, gentle. Snow covers the Troodos Mountains in winter, making it possible to ski in the morning and sunbathe on a beach in the afternoon.

Cyprus's strategic position in the eastern Mediterranean has made it subject to regular invasions by powerful countries. Greeks, Phoenicians, Assyrians, Egyptians, Persians, Romans, and Byzantines—all have ruled here. In the Middle Ages, the English King Richard I took it by force from the Byzantine Empire and gave it to Guy of Lusignan. Guy's descendants ruled until the late 15th century, when it was annexed by the Venetians.

This tragic history adds to the island's appeal—at least for tourists. Many fortifications built by the Crusaders and the Venetians still stand. The tomb of the Prophet Muhammad's aunt (Tekke of Hala Sultan), located on the shores of the great salt lake near Larnaca, is one of Islam's most important shrines. A piece of the true cross is said to exist in the Monastery of Stavrouni, and Paphos has the remains of a pillar where St. Paul is said to have been tied and beaten for preaching Christianity.

The upheavals are not over. At press time (summer 1988), the island consists, politically, of two states. The southern two-thirds, inhabited mainly by Greek Cypriots, form the Republic of Cyprus, the only part of the island to receive international recognition. The northern third, whose population is almost entirely Turkish Cypriot, is recognized only by Turkey as the Turkish Republic of North Cyprus. The two sections are divided by the UN Green Line, or "Attila Line," which cuts right through the capital city of Nicosia.

Talks aimed at uniting the communities into one bizonal federal state have been going on for years, lately under the auspices of the United Nations secretary-general. At press time, the talks have not made much progress, and there is still virtually no communication between north and south. It is possible to visit the north of the island from the south, on a day trip through the checkpoint in Nicosia, but visitors *must* return to the south by 6 PM. It is not possible to visit the south from the north.

In general, tourism is more thoroughly developed in the south than in the north, though the north is trying to catch up. The south has more and better facilities, more nightlife, and better beaches. The north shows fewer signs of foreign influence, with an exotic, Eastern flavor. The noticeable military presence shouldn't bother visitors who refrain from taking photographs where the signs forbid it and who avoid areas they are asked to stay out of.

Cyprus

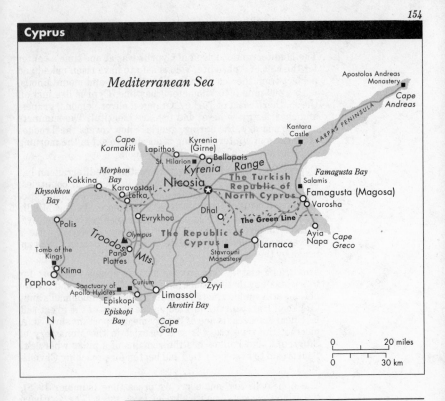

Before You Go

When to Go The tourist season runs throughout the year, though prices tend to be lower from the beginning of November through March.

Climate The rainy season lasts from December through February, and there is snow on the Troodos Mountains from January through March. January and February can be very cold and wet; July and August, very hot and dry.

The following are the average daily maximum and minimum temperatures for Nicosia.

Jan.	59F	15C	May	85F	29C	Sept.	92F	33C
	42	5		58	14		65	18
Feb.	61F	16C	June	92F	34C	Oct.	83F	28C
	42	5		65	18		58	14
Mar.	66F	19C	July	98F	37C	Nov.	72F	22C
	44	7		70	21		51	10
Apr.	75F	24C	Aug.	98F	37C	Dec.	63F	17C
	50	10		69	21		45	7

Visas No visas are necessary for holders of valid passports from the United States, Canada, and the United Kingdom.

Customs on Arrival Customs regulations are minimal, but the export of antiques and archaeological treasures is strictly forbidden.

Language English is spoken—to a greater or lesser degree—in hotels, *tavernas*, and other tourist haunts. Off the beaten track, sign language may have to do.

Credit Cards Credit cards are not widely accepted in either the north or the south, though major hotels such as the Hilton will take them. Banks, however, usually allow you to draw cash upon your credit card account, so payment is rarely a problem.

The Republic of Cyprus (Greek)

Currency

The monetary unit in the Republic of Cyprus is the Cyprus pound (C£), which is divided into 100 cents. There are notes of C£10, C£5, C£1, and 50 Cyprus cents and coins of 20, 10, 5, 2, 1, and ½ Cyprus cents. Because of the high rate of inflation of the Turkish lire (the currency of North Cyprus), we have quoted most prices in this chapter in dollars.

What It Will Cost

A cup of coffee or tea costs about US 30¢; a kebab around $2; a bottle of local wine, $1–$1.50.

Arriving and Departing

There are no direct flights from the USA. **Cyprus Airways** and **British Airways** fly direct from London, Birmingham, and Manchester to Larnaca and Paphos. There are ferries from Greek and Egyptian ports. An inclusive tour is probably the cheapest and most convenient approach.

Getting Around

By Car International and British driving licenses are acceptable for driving in Cyprus. Roads are generally good, though narrow and winding. Drive on the left. Gas costs around $2.75 a gallon. Cars are available for rent from $18 a day with unlimited mileage.

By Bus This is the cheapest form of transportation; bus fares are only about 3¢ a mile.

By Service Taxi These taxis cost about twice as much as buses, where you book seats. (**Note:** No buses or service taxis operate after 6:30 or 7 P.M.)

By Private Taxi Private taxis are usually available, very cheap, and always metered.

On Foot The only way to enjoy nature trails and archaeological sites is on foot. Comfortable shoes are essential. It is unwise to explore remote areas alone—ask the tourist office to recommend safe footpaths.

Essential Information

Telephones Pay phones take 2¢, 10¢, and 20¢ coins. Hotels will add a small service charge for placing a call for you.

Mail Airmail postal rates are always subject to change. At press time, a 10-gram letter to the United States costs Cyprus 25¢, a postcard, 17¢. To the United Kingdom, a 10-gram letter cost Cyprus 18¢, and a postcard, 15¢. Check at your hotel for the latest rates.

Shopping Handmade lace, embroidery, filigree silver, and leather goods make excellent gifts or souvenirs.

Opening and Closing Times **Banks.** Banks are open Monday–Saturday 8:30–noon. Some will cash traveler's checks weekdays 4–6 PM.
Museums. Museums are open from about 8 to 1:30; afternoon hours vary according to the time of year. Most ancient monuments are open from dawn to dusk.
Shops. Shops are open Monday–Saturday 7:30–1. Afternoon hours vary, but many shops close on Wednesday and Saturday afternoons.

National Holidays January 1; January 6 (Epiphany); February 22; March 25 (Independence); April 28, 31 (Greek Easter); May 1; June 29 (Pentecost); August 15 (Assumption); October 28 (Oxi); December 25, 26 (Christmas).

Tipping A service charge of 10% is usually added to all bills. If service has been especially good, add 5%.

Important Addresses and Numbers The head **tourist information office** is at 18 Theodotou St., Nicosia, tel. 02/43374. There are local offices at all major resorts.

Embassies or High Commissions **U.S. Embassy,** Dossitheos and Therissos Sts., Nicosia, tel. 02/465151. **British High Commission,** Alexander Pallis St., Nicosia, tel. 02/473131.

Emergencies **Ambulance, Fire Brigade,** and **Police,** tel. 199. **Doctor: Nicosia General Hospital,** tel. 061/32364; **Limassol Hospital,** tel. 051/63111; **Paphos Hospital,** tel. 061/32364. **Pharmacies:** A list, with opening times, appears in the English-language *Cyprus Mail.*

Guided Tours Bus tours and boat trips are run by companies based in Nicosia, Limassol, and Lanarca. Tourist offices have lists of operators and detailed brochures of organized visits to archaeological sites.

Exploring the Republic of Cyprus

Nicosia, the capital, is twice divided. The picturesque Old City is contained within 16th-century Venetian fortifications, which separate it from the wide tree-lined streets, large hotels, and high rises of the modern section. The second division is political and more noticeable. The so-called Green Line, set up by the United Nations, that divides the island is frustrating to the visitor, because many of the more interesting ancient monuments are in the, northern, Turkish sector. As mentioned above, it is possible, at the time of writing, to arrange a day trip from the Greek to the Turkish sector through the official checkpoint in Nicosia, though it is essential to return by 6 PM. Visits in the other direction are not permitted.

There is, however, plenty to see in the Greek sector. A good starting point is **Laiki Gitonia** at the southern edge of the Old City, an area of tree-shaded cafés and restaurants, craft workshops, and the Tourist Information Center. Just to the west lies

Ledra Street, where modern shops alternate with yet more craft shops.

Within the walls to the east of the Old City is a cluster of museums. The new **Archbishopric-Makarios Foundation** houses the **European Art Gallery**, with its collection of undistinguished 17th- and 18th-century works; the **Byzantine Art Museum**, with fine displays of icons spanning 1,000 years; and the **Greek War of Independence Gallery**, with a collection of maps, paintings, and mementoes of 1821. *Admission charged. Open weekdays 9:30–1 and 2–5:30, Sat. 9–1.*

Next door, the **Museum of the National Struggle** has dramatic displays on the country's resistance to British occupation. *Admission charged. Open Mon.–Sat. 7:30–1:30.*

Close by is the **Cyprus Folk Art Museum** (housed in the old part of the Bishopric, dating from the 14th century), which offers demonstrations of ancient weaving techniques and displays of farm implements, olive and wine presses, and Cypriot costumes. *Admission charged. Open weekdays 8–4, Sat. 8–1.*

Before going outside the walls, visit the **Cathedral of St. John** and look for the paintings depicting the discovery on Cyprus of St. Barnabus's tomb. Outside the walls, to the west, stands the small **Cyprus Museum.** Its archaeological displays range from prehistory to the Romans. A pretty park and café are nearby. *Museum St. Admission charged. Open Mon.–Sat. 7:30–1:30 and 4–6 (winter afternoons 3–5), Sun. 10–1.*

Many visitors choose to stay in the seaside resorts. Both Larnaca and Paphos, each with its airport, make excellent centers. **Larnaca** is famous as the burial place of Lazarus and for its flamboyant Whitsuntide celebration, *Kataklysmos.* It has fine beaches, palm trees, and a modern harbor and marina, the starting point for boat trips. The tourist office is right at the marina, open mornings only, and just a short walk from **Larnaca Museum,** with its displays of finds from the island's archaeological sites. *Admission charged. Open weekdays 7:30–1:30 and 4–6 (in winter 3–5), Sat. 7:30–1 and 3–5, Sun. 10–1.*

A short walk north from the museum, along Kyman Street, will bring you to the site of Biblical **Kittim,** where the excavations may be observed from specially constructed walkways.

Southward from the marina is the 17th-century **Turkish fort,** open the same hours as the museum and with similar, though not as extensive, displays. Walk inland from the fort to one of the island's more important churches, **Ayios Lazarus,** resplendent with icons, and with a fascinating crypt containing Lazarus's sarcophagus.

Paphos, in the west of the island, has superb sea bathing and numerous historical sights. Begin at the tourist office in Gladstone Street in Upper Paphos.

Don't miss the elaborate mosaics in the **Roman Villa of Theseus** and in the **House of Dionysos,** both in New Paphos. The town bus stops nearby. Also worth seeing are the **Tombs of the Kings,** an early necropolis dating from 300 BC. Natural caves have been extended and linked by passages, and though the coffin niches are empty, a powerful sense of mystery remains.

Limassol, commercial port and wine-making center, is also a thriving tourist spot. The modern buildings may be plain and oppressive, but facilities are plentiful and the nightlife is the liveliest on Cyprus. If you're interested in wine making, seek out the KEO Winery, just west of town, which welcomes visitors daily. The tourist office is on Spyros Araouzos Street, only a short walk from the **Castle**, now restored as a museum of medieval armor and relics. *Admission charged. Open Mon.– Sat. 7:30–1:30.*

Ayia Napa is a fishing village whose extensive sandy beaches led to its development as a tourist center. Its 16th-century **Monastery**, now an Ecumenical Conference Center, is in distinct contrast to the plethora of tavernas, bars, and discos and to the tennis, putting, and diving facilities.

The **Troodos Mountains**, north of Limassol, are sought in summer for the shade of their cedar and pine forests and the coolness of their lakes and mineral spas. In winter, skiers take over. **Platres**, in the foothills of Mount Olympus, is the principal resort. Be sure to visit the **Kykko Monastery**, whose prized icon of the Virgin is reputed to have been painted by St. Luke. Though founded in the 12th century, the monastery buildings and lavish church were added in the 19th-century.

Off the Beaten Track

Stavrouni Monastery stands on a mountain west of Larnaca. It was founded by St. Helena (mother of the Emperor Constantine) in AD 326, though the present buildings date from the 19th century. Ideally, it should be visited in a spirit of pilgrimage rather than sightseeing, out of respect for its monks, though the views of the island are splendid. The monks have decreed that female visitors are admitted only on Monday, Wednesday, Friday, and Sunday.

Curium (Kourion), west of Limassol, has numerous Greek and Roman ruins. There is an **amphitheater**, where modern-day actors occasionally present classical drama. Next to the theater is the **Villa of Eustolios,** a summer house that belonged to a wealthy Christian; its mosaic floors are still in good condition. A nearby **Roman stadium** has been partially rebuilt. Farther along the main Paphos road is the **Sanctuary of Apollo Hylates** (of the woodlands), an impressive site when viewed through an archaeologist's eye.

Dining

Most hotels have restaurants, but these tend to serve bland international-style food garnished with french fries. Visitors with a sense of adventure will want to dine in local restaurants or in one of the formal, family-run tavernas featuring live music. Meals start with a variety of *mezes* (snacks). Kebabs are popular, as are *dolmas*—stuffed grape leaves or cabbage leaves—stews, fresh fish, and various lamb dishes. End with fruit or honey pastries and Turkish coffee, so-named throughout Cyprus. Moderate establishments display a menu; in the Inexpensive ones it is the custom to go into the kitchen and choose your meal.

Prices are for a three-course meal for one person, not including drinks or tip.

Category	Cost
Expensive	over $12
Moderate	$6–$12
Inexpensive	under $6

Larnaca   **Kellari.** Tournedos is the specialty of the house at this informal seaside taverna, which serves both Cypriot and French foods. There's often live musical accompaniment in the evening. *85 Athens Ave., tel. 041/5166. Inexpensive.*

Nicosia   **The Corner.** This full-fledged restaurant features a pleasant, traditional decor. Stephanos steak is a favorite of the chef. *Dem. Severi Ave., tel. 02/465735. Closed lunch and Sun. Moderate.*

Plaka. Lovers of hefty lamb dishes will be happy with the *souvla* and *kleftiko* at this large taverna. Tables spill out onto the sidewalk in front. *Archbishop Makarios Sq., Engomi, tel. 02/446498. Closed lunch and Sun. Inexpensive.*

Paphos   **Britannia.** Eat right on the beach at this small restaurant, which provides a wide range of Cypriot and international dishes. *75 Poseidon Ave., tel. 061/36032. Closed Dec.–Mar. Moderate.*

Nautical Club. This huge seaside restaurant seats more than 180. Fresh fish is your best bet. *St. Paul's Ave., tel. 061/33745. Moderate.*

Lodging

Most hotels listed below have private bath or shower, but check when making reservations. Most have at least partial air-conditioning.

Our prices are per person sharing a double room, with breakfast and dinner.

Category	Cost
Expensive	over $27
Moderate	$18–$27
Inexpensive	under $18

Ayia Napa   **Nissi Beach.** This modern, fully air-conditioned, family-style hotel is set in magnificent gardens overlooking a white sandy beach. *Box 10, Ayia Napa, tel. 037/21021. 251 rooms. Facilities: pool. Expensive.*

Pernara Beach. Those on a budget should enjoy this hotel with a view of the beach. All rooms are air-conditioned. *Tel. 037/21011. 92 rooms. Inexpensive.*

Larnaca   **Golden Bay.** Comfort is high on the list at this beach hotel. The extensive range of sports facilities makes it ideal for summer or winter vacations. *Larnaka-Dheklia Rd., Box 741, tel. 041/23444. 194 rooms. Expensive.*

Four Lanterns. Local color, homey atmosphere, and modern comfort are much in evidence at this seafront hotel. There's also a good restaurant. *19 Athens Ave., Box 150, tel. 041/502011. 52 rooms. Moderate.*

Cactus Hotel. This recent addition to Larnaca's hotels is 20 minutes from the seafront, with all its tavernas. *6–8 Shakespeare St., Box 744, tel. 041/27400. 56 rooms. Inexpensive.*

Limassol **Apollonia Beach.** This is a luxury hotel on the beach in the main resort area. The restaurant has an excellent reputation. *Potamos Yermassoyias, Box 594, tel. 051/23351. 204 rooms. Expensive.*

Pamevar. Among this refurbished hotel's attractions are its beach-side setting. *28th October Ave., Box 263, tel. 051/24535. 65 rooms. Facilities: pool. Moderate.*

Nicosia **Cyprus Hilton.** This is among the island's best hotels, with standards you'd expect from a Hilton. It has its own pool, sports facilities, dancing, and more. *Archbishop Makarios Ave., Box 2023, tel. 02/46040. 230 rooms. Expensive.*

Philoxenia. This is a smallish hotel that still has plenty to offer, with its own pool and a variety of sports options, as well as a handy central location. *Eylenia Ave., Box 5466, tel. 02/499700. 35 rooms. Moderate.*

Nicosia Palace. Those seeking a budget option should consider the Nicosia Palace. Located just inside the city walls, it makes an ideal base for exploring the Old City. There is partial air-conditioning. *4–6 Pantelides Ave., tel. 02/463718. 42 rooms. Inexpensive.*

Paphos **Paphos Beach.** There are many facilities at this popular hotel surrounded by attractive gardens. Accommodations are either in the main hotel or in spacious bungalows on the grounds. *Posidonos St., Box 136, tel. 061/33091. 190 rooms. Expensive.*

Aloe. On the same street as the Paphos Beach, Aloe has ocean views, a swimming pool, and sports facilities. *Posidonos St., Box 190, tel. 061/34000. 113 rooms. Moderate.*

The Arts

Information on theater, concerts, and movies is published in the English-language *Cyprus Time Out.*

Nightlife

Most of the large hotels have dance floors; some also have cabarets and discos. Tavernas may also have live music.

North Cyprus (Turkish)

Currency

The monetary unit in North Cyprus is the Turkish lire (TL). There are bills for 10,000, 5,000, 1,000, 500, 100, 50, 20, and 10 TL, and coins for lesser sums. The Turkish lire is subject to considerable inflation, so most prices in this chapter are quoted in dollars.

What It Will Cost

Prices for food and accommodations tend to be lower than in the Republic of Cyprus, and standards dip as well. Wine and spirits, on the other hand, are imported from Turkey and drinks will be slightly more expensive.

Arriving and Departing

Turkish Airlines and **Cyprus Turkish Airlines** run flights, usually with a change of plane at Istanbul. There are also direct flights via Izmir to Ercan Airport near Nicosia. Ferries run from Mersin and Tasucu in Turkey to Famagusta and Kyrenia, respectively, but in both cases the journey is long and tiring. *It is not possible to enter North Cyprus from the Republic except for a day trip from Nicosia.*

Getting Around

By Car *See* By Car in the Republic of Cyprus.

By Bus Buses and the shared taxi *(dolmush)* are the cheapest forms of transportation. Services are frequent on main routes.

Fares A bus from Nicosia to Kyrenia costs about 40¢, and to Famagusta about 70¢. A seat in a dolmush for the same trips would cost about 90¢ and $1.70, respectively.

Essential Information

Mail Postal rates vary with the rate of inflation; check at your hotel for the latest rates.

Shopping Look for lace, pottery and metalwork, and leather shoes, made to order, at low prices.

Opening and Closing Times **Banks.** Banks are open Monday–Saturday 8:30–noon. Some will cash traveler's checks weekdays 4–6 P.M.
Museums. Museums are open from about 8 to 1:30; afternoon hours vary according to the time of year. Most ancient monuments are open from dawn to dusk.
Shops. Shops are open Monday–Saturday 7:30–1. Afternoon hours vary, but many shops close on Wednesday and Saturday afternoons.

National Holidays January 1, April 23, May 19, August 30, October 29, and various Moslem religious holidays, which vary from year to year.

Tipping A service charge is usually added, but an additional small tip is expected in better hotels and restaurants.

Important Addresses and Numbers The main **tourist information office** is at Mehmet Akif Ave., Nicosia. There are local offices at major resorts.

Embassies or High Commissions **The British High Commission** has an office in the Turkish section of Nicosia.

Emergencies Same as for the Republic of Cyprus.

Exploring North Cyprus

There are two important things to bear in mind in North Cyprus. One is to obey the "no photographs" signs wherever they appear. The other is to note that Turkish names have now been given to all towns and villages. These new names appear on the signposts—not always with the Greek version alongside—so it helps to know that **Nicosia** is known as **Lefkosa, Kyrenia** as **Girne,** and **Famagusta** as **Magosa.** A useful map showing these and other Turkish names is available free from tourist offices.

The **Turkish half of Nicosia** is the capital of North Cyprus. In addition to the Venetian walls already mentioned (*see* Exploring the Republic of Cyprus), it contains the **Selimiyre Mosque,** formerly the 13th-century Cathedral of St. Sophia, and a fine example of Gothic architecture to which a pair of minarets has now been added. Near the Girne Gate is the former **"Tekke"** of the Mevlevi Dervishes, a Sufi order popularly known as Whirling Dervishes. The building now houses a museum of Turkish history and culture. *Admission charged. Open Mon.–Sat. 8–1, Sun. 10–1.*

A walk around the **Old City,** within the encircling walls, is rich with glimpses from the Byzantine, Lusignan, and Venetian past. There is a great deal of restoration and reconstruction work going on, especially in the parts of the city beyond the walls.

Of the coastal resorts, **Kyrenia,** with its yacht-filled harbor, is the most appealing. There are excellent beaches to the east and west of the town. **Kyrenia Castle,** overlooking the harbor, is Venetian, though on the site of a much older Byzantine defensive structure. It now houses the **Shipwreck Museum,** whose prize possession is the remains of a ship that sank around 300 BC. *Admission charged. Open Mon.–Sat. 8–1, Sun. 10–1.*

Famagusta, the chief port of North Cyprus, has massive and well-preserved Venetian walls and the late 13th-century Gothic Cathedral of St. Nicholas, now **Lala Mustafa Pasha Mosque.** The **Old Town,** within the walls, is the most intriguing part to explore. Elsewhere, many of the hotels lie empty and desolate in a sort of "no-man's land" between Greek and Turk, where the military presence cannot be ignored.

Off the Beaten Track

It is well worth making two short excursions from Kyrenia, to **St. Hilarion** and to **Bellapais.** The fantastic ruins of the **Castle of St. Hilarion** stand on a hilltop seven miles (11 kilometers) to the southwest. It's a strenuous walk, but the views are breathtaking. The ruins of the former **Abbey of Bellapais,** built in the 12th century by the Lusignans, are just as impressive. They lie on a mountainside four miles (six kilometers) to the northeast. The showpiece is the refectory, but there are also dormitories, storerooms, and a church with frescoes.

Salamis, north of Famagusta, is an ancient ruined city, perhaps the most dramatic archaeological site on the island. Founded in the 12th century and once the capital of Cyprus, it was devastated by earthquakes, but the signs of its Roman past are still much in evidence. The setting is beautiful, and some of the ruins are sufficiently overgrown to give the visitor a satisfying sense of discovery.

Dining

There is not a great deal of difference between Greek and Turkish cooking on Cyprus, though the Turks don't eat pork and are more sparing in their use of oil. As in the Republic of Cyprus, the larger hotels have dining rooms, but individual restaurants have more local atmosphere. Travelers in North Cyprus should also consider army-run **Mucahitler** restaurants, which offer excellent value. Try the **Otello** in Famagusta (opposite the

Othello Tower), the **Istanbul** along the Bogaz Road, or the **Alsancak** near Kyrenia.

Our ratings reflect prices per person for a three-course meal and do not include drinks.

Category	Cost
Expensive	over $10
Moderate	$5–$10
Inexpensive	under $5

Famagusta **Kemal's Fish Restaurant.** This family-run restaurant specializes, of course, in fresh fish. *Moderate.*
Patek Pastanesi. This is the place to go if you're in the mood for Turkish coffee and honey-drenched cakes. *Opposite Famagusta's Sea Gate. Inexpensive.*

Kyrenia **Harbor Bar.** Surprisingly high-quality French cooking is offered at this little eatery right on the harbor. *Moderate.*
Kyrenia Taverna. This traditional taverna, near the harbor, features fish. *Inexpensive.*

Lodging

There is very little difference between the hotels of North Cyprus and those of the Republic. Again, our prices are based on one person sharing a double room, including breakfast and dinner.

Cost	Category
Expensive	over $27
Moderate	$18–$27
Inexpensive	under $18

Famagusta **Park.** Just outside Famagusta, the Park is handy for those who plan to visit the ruins at Salamis. It has its own private beach and a variety of sports facilities. The restaurant is noted for its excellent cuisine. *Tel. 036/65511. 93 rooms. Expensive.*
Rebecca. This family hotel is situated on the edge of Salamis Forest, five minutes from the sea. The restaurant serves good Turkish and Continental food, and there's an outdoor café in the large shaded courtyard. *Tel. 036/58000. 42 rooms. Moderate.*
Mimosa. This beach front hotel, best known for its restaurant, specializes in local and Turkish food. Tables are set under a big mimosa tree on the terrace a few yards from the sea. *Tel. 036/56460. 51 rooms. Inexpensive.*

Kyrenia **Dome.** Close to the harbor and within easy distance of Kyrenia is this hotel with a private swimming and sunbathing area built out into the sea. Bedrooms have views of either the bay or the Kyrenia Mountains. *Tel. 081/52453. 161 rooms. Facilities: restaurant, casino. Expensive.*
Club Acapulco Village. Six miles (10 kilometers) east of town, these simple bungalow-style accommodations are ideal for independent travelers. There's a restaurant and beach bar in the village. *Tel. 081/53510. Moderate.*

Dorana. Located close to the main shopping area and only 300 yards (90 meters) from the sea, the Dorana is a pleasant modern hotel with a bar, restaurant, and 24-hour room service. *Tel. 081/53521. 33 rooms. Moderate.*

Nicosia **Saray.** This hotel overlooks Atatürk Square in the town center. The ninth-floor restaurant has excellent views over the city. There's a casino and live music on weekends. *Tel. 020/71115. 72 rooms. Moderate.*

Picnic. This small hotel, in a quiet area of town, offers a good restaurant and a disco. Snacks are served in the vine-shaded garden. *Tel. 020/72001. 10 rooms. Inexpensive.*

8 Czechoslovakia

Introduction

No country is more centrally European than Czechoslovakia, ringed as it is by Austria, Germany, Poland, the Soviet Union, and Hungary. This central position is a fact of life that has made Czechoslovakia both a cultural crossroads and a wearyingly frequent political pawn. It has also bred in the Czechs a certain artistic flair and stoic endurance, a good measure of guile, and a neat sense of the ridiculous. This is indeed the land of Kafka and the Good Soldier Švejk.

Invaders and traders have come and gone. Twice an empire was ruled from here. Revolutionary movements have been born and quelled. Above all, the arts have found fertile ground on which to flourish, as did democracy between the two world wars.

In 1938, the British and French sold Czechoslovakia out to Nazi Germany in exchange for a hollow "peace in our time." Thirty years later, Soviet tanks rumbled into Prague and thwarted a brave political experiment combining Communist ideology with democratic rights. Whatever your views, when visiting here it's wise to keep an open mind and to respect the considerable achievements of these intelligent and talented people in this sensitive corner of Europe.

Socialist Czechoslovakia has certain bureaucratic requirements, detailed in the following pages. But you're free to travel where you will and, in the process, may welcome such advantages as streets that are safe to walk at night and a refreshing lack of commercial hype.

Tourist amenities sometimes lack polish, and service can be ungracious. But it is by no means always so, and the loveliness of the countryside and the heritage of history, art, and architecture go a long way to make up for it.

Before You Go

When to Go Organized sightseeing tours run from April or May through October. Some monuments, especially castles, either close or open for shorter hours in winter. Hotel rates drop in the off-season except during festivals. May, the month of fruit blossoms, is the time of the Prague Spring Music Festival. During the fall, when the forests are glorious, Bratislava and Brno hold their music festivals.

The following are the average daily maximum and minimum temperatures for Prague.

Jan.	49F	10C	May	82F	28C	Sept.	84F	29C
	7	−13		36	2		38	4
Feb.	53F	11C	June	88F	31C	Oct.	71F	22C
	10	−12		44	7		29	−2
Mar.	64F	18C	July	91F	33C	Nov.	57F	14C
	18	−8		49	9		24	−5
Apr.	73F	23C	Aug.	89F	32C	Dec.	50F	10C
	29	−2		47	8		14	−10

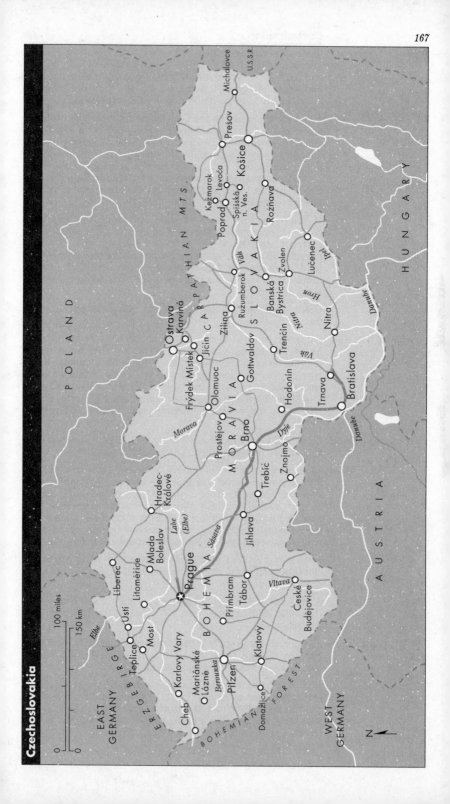

Currency The unit of currency is the crown, or koruna, written as Kčs., and divided into 100 haler. There are bills of 10, 20, 50, 100, 500, and 1,000 Kčs., and coins of 5, 10, 20, and 50 halers and 1, 2, and 5 Kčs. At press time (fall 1988), the exchange rate was about 5.03 Kčs. to the dollar and 15 Kčs. to the pound sterling.

If you visit the country on a Čedok tour or prebook hotel accommodations with breakfast and dinner, you'll get a 36% bonus when you cash your traveler's checks or special bonus currency vouchers (buy them from Čedok before you leave) at Čedok offices, Interhotels, Balnea spa hotels or sanatoriums. This bonus is *not* available at other exchange offices. Note also that Czech currency acquired in this way can't be reconverted into foreign currency.

If you're visiting Czechoslovakia independently, you must change approximately $15 every day you're in the country. All currency exchanges will be noted on your visa and only amounts *above* the required minimum can be reconverted into hard currencies on departure—and even then there can be problems. Avoid the temptations of the black market: The penalties are severe.

Credit cards are widely accepted in establishments used by foreign tourists.

What It Will Cost Some services and items—hotels or tours, for example—may be less expensive if you haven't paid for them in advance in foreign currency. But in these cases, you lose the advantage of the currency bonus, added to which there's no doubt that vouchers smooth the way. Costs are highest in Prague and only slightly less in the High Tatra resorts and main spas. The least expensive areas are southern Bohemia and central and eastern Slovakia.

Sample Prices Cup of coffee, 6 Kčs.; beer (½ liter), 6–10 Kčs.; Coca-Cola, 6–9 Kčs.; ham sandwich, 4 Kčs.; one-mile taxi ride, 10 Kčs.

Visas Visas are required by all visitors. You can get one by sending or bringing a completed visa application form, two photographs, and your passport either directly to one of the Czech embassies, or, in the United Kingdom, to Čedok. Visas are valid for a specified period within three months of the date of issue and are linked with exchange regulations (*see* Currency). They are *not* issued at the border, but can be extended during your stay.

Note that if you're staying with friends or relatives in Czechoslovakia, you must register with the local police within 48 hours.

In the United States American citizens pay $16 for a visa. Apply to the **Embassy of the ČSSR,** 3900 Linnean Ave., NW, Washington, DC 20008, tel. 202/363–6308.

In Canada Canadians should apply to the **Embassy of the ČSSR,** 50 Rideau Terrace, Ottawa, Ontario K1M 2AL, tel. 416/234–6581, or 1305 ave. de Pins Ouest, Montreal H3G 1B2, tel. 849–4495.

In the United Kingdom Britons who have booked a Čedok tour can have visa applications processed by Čedok for £14. For independent travelers, the visa fee is £20 plus a £3 service charge through Cedok. The visa section of the **Czech Embassy** is at 28 Kensington Palace Gardens, London N8 4QY, tel. 01/727–3966.

Customs on Arrival Valuable items should be entered on your customs declaration. You can bring in 250 cigarettes (or their equivalent in tobacco), two liters of wine, one liter of spirits, ½ liter of eau de cologne, and gifts to the value of 600 Kčs.

On Departure You can take out gifts and souvenirs to the value of 600 Kčs., as well as goods bought at Tuzex hard-currency shops (keep the receipts). Crystal and some other items not bought at hard-currency shops may be subject to a tax of 100% of their retail price. Only antiques bought at Tuzex or specially appointed shops may be exported.

Language English is spoken fairly widely among both the young and those associated with the tourist industry. Elsewhere, you will come across English speakers, though not frequently. German is sometimes spoken by older Czechs. Whether a knowledge of German will win you friends is a different matter.

Getting Around

By Car
Road Conditions Czech roads are usually good, if sometimes narrow, and traffic is light, especially away from main centers. An expressway links Prague, Brno, and Bratislava. Other highways are single lane only.

Rules of the Road Drive on the right. Speed limits are 60 kph (37 mph) in built-up areas, 90 kph (55 mph) on open roads, and 110 kph (68 mph) on expressways. Seatbelts are compulsory outside built-up areas; drinking and driving is strictly prohibited.

Parking The center of Prague is banned to all cars except those belonging to hotel guests. In other parts of the city, parking is limited to a few specially reserved places. Parking times are limited, however, and you will have to pay for the privilege. If you park anywhere else in Prague, you risk having your car towed away, and getting it back will prove time-consuming and expensive. Elsewhere in the country there's little problem.

Gasoline Gasoline costs about 9 Kčs. per liter. Gas stations are rarer than in the West, but a free map from Čedok shows locations throughout the country. You can buy nonrefundable coupons for gas from Čedok before you go, which you can use at all gas stations; cost is about 60¢ a liter. If, however, you are entitled to the currency bonus (*see* Currency above), gas coupons are of little benefit.

Breakdowns **Autotourist** (head office: Na rybnicku, Prague, tel. 02/203355) operates a patrol service on main highways. The emergency telephone number for motorists is 154; for ambulances, 155; for police (traffic accidents) 02/242424.

By Train There is an extensive rail network throughout the country. As elsewhere in Eastern Europe, fares are low and trains are always crowded. Also, you have to pay a supplement on all express trains (this does not apply if you bought your ticket outside Czechoslovakia). All long-distance trains have dining cars; overnight trains between main centers have sleeping cars.

Fares Eurail pass and Eurail Youthpass tickets are not valid in Czechoslovakia unless you are merely passing through the country.

By Plane Czechoslovakia has a remarkably good internal air service linking Prague with eight other towns, including Brno, Bratislava, Poprad (for the High Tatras), Karlovy Vary, and Piestany.

Make reservations at Čedok offices or direct with CSA, Czechoslovakia Airlines (tel. 02/2146).

By Bus There's a wide-ranging bus network, though much of it operates only where there are no trains. Fares are comparable to those on trains. Buses are always full, and, on long-distance routes especially, reservations are essential.

Essential Information

Telephones These cost 1 Kčs. from a pay phone. Lift the receiver, insert the
Local Calls coin, and dial.

International Calls You'll pay through the nose if you make calls from your hotel. There's automatic dialing to many countries, including North America and the United Kingdom. Special international pay booths in central Prague will take 5 Kčs. coins, but your best bet is to go to the main post office (Jindřišská 24, near Wenceslas Square). For international inquiries, dial 0132 for the United States, Canada, or United Kingdom.

Mail Airmail letters to the United States cost 6 Kčs. up to 10 grams,
Postal Rates postcards 5 Kčs. Airmail letters to the United Kingdom cost 4 Kčs. up to 20 grams, postcards 3 Kčs.

Receiving Mail Mail can be sent to Poste Restante at the main post office in Prague (Jindřišská 24), or to any other main post office. There's no charge. The American Express office in Prague will hold letters addressed to cardholders or holders of American Express traveler's checks for up to one month free of charge.

Shopping Most tourists gravitate to **Tuzex** shops, where only hard currency or its equivalent in Tuzex coupons is accepted. There are branches all over Czechoslovakia; Čedok can give you a list of outlets. Here you can buy many goods imported from the West, as well as some of the best national products. These include Bohemian glass and crystal, peasant pottery, porcelain, wooden toys, hand-embroidered clothing, and charming corn-husk dolls. You may pay less in shops taking only local currency, but these goods may be liable to 100% tax on departure. Other good buys are records—most of excellent quality—and costume jewelry. Czechoslovakia imposes no sales tax.

Opening and **Banks.** Banks are open weekdays 8–2.
Closing Times **Museums.** Museums are usually open from Tues. to Sun. 10–5, but there are many variations. Museum admission fees range from 3 to 5 Kčs.
Shops. Shops are generally open weekdays 9–6 (9–8 on Thurs.); some close between noon and 2. Many are also open Sat. 9–noon (department stores, 9–4).

National Holidays January 1 (New Year's Day); March 27 (Easter Monday); May 1 (Labor Day); May 9 (Liberation); December 25, 26.

Dining Independent travelers with prepaid meal vouchers (nonrefundable) are now able to use these at any Čedok hotel or restaurant in the city or region where they are staying. For meals not limited by vouchers, you can choose among restaurants, wine cellars *(vinárna)*, the more down-to-earth beer taverns *(pivnice)*, cafeterias, and a growing number of coffee shops and snack bars. Eating out is popular, and it's wise to make reservations whenever possible.

Prague ham makes a favorite first course, as does soup, which is less expensive. The most typical main dish is roast pork (or duck or goose) with sauerkraut and dumplings. Dumplings in various forms, generally with a rich gravy, accompany many dishes. Fresh green vegetables are rare, but there are plenty of the pickled variety.

Mealtimes Lunch is usually from noon to 2 or 3; dinner from 6 to 9:30 or 10.

Ratings Prices are reasonable by American standards, even in the more expensive restaurants. Czechs don't normally go in for three-course meals, so the following prices apply only if you're having a first course, main course, and dessert (but they exclude wine and tip). Best bets are indicated by a star ★. At press time, there were 5.03 Korunas (Kčs). to the dollar.

Category	Cost: Prague	Cost: Other Areas
Very Expensive	over 150 Kčs.	over 90 Kčs.
Expensive	100–150 Kčs.	60–90 Kčs.
Moderate	50–100 Kčs.	30–60 Kčs.
Inexpensive	under 50 Kčs.	under 30 Kčs.

Credit Cards The following credit card abbreviations are used: AE, American Express; DC, Diners Club; MC, MasterCard; V, Visa.

Lodging There's a choice of hotels, motels, some private accommodations, and campsites. Many older properties are gradually being renovated and the best have great character and style. There remains an acute shortage of rooms in the peak season, so make reservations well in advance. The standard of facilities and services hardly match those in the West, so don't be surprised by faulty plumbing or indifferent reception clerks. The prices at least compare favorably.

Hotels These are officially classified from one to five stars. Prices include obligatory half-board, except for five-star hotels, where only breakfast is included. Most hotels used by foreign visitors —Interhotels—belong to Čedok and are mainly in the three- to five-star categories. These will have all or some rooms with bath or shower. Čedok can also handle reservations for some non-Čedok hotels, such as those run by Balnea (the spa treatment organizations), CKM (the Youth Travel Bureau), and municipal organizations, some of which are excellent.

Čedok prices are quoted in hard currency. If you haven't reserved in advance, you'll have to pay in hard currency at Interhotels, but not at others, though you may need to produce evidence that your Kčs. were legally acquired.

Private Accommodations Pragotur has the biggest selection in Prague. Čedok can offer some in Prague (minimum stay is three nights) and more in the High Tatras (minimum stay is seven nights).

Camping Campsites are run by a number of organizations. A free map and list are available from Čedok.

Ratings Prices are for double rooms and obligatory half-board for two, except for the Very Expensive and Expensive places, most of which include breakfast only. Prices at the lower end of the scale apply to low season. At certain periods, such as Easter or during festivals, there may be an increase of 15–25%. Best bets are indicated by a star ★. We've listed prices in dollars, since most visitors will prebook their rooms.

Category	Cost: Prague	Cost: Other Areas
Very Expensive	over $150	over $100
Expensive	$100–$150	$80–$100
Moderate	$66–$100	$55–$80
Inexpensive	under $66	under $55

Credit Cards The following credit card abbreviations are used: AE, American Express; DC, Diners Club; MC, MasterCard; V, Visa.

Tipping Czechs are not usually blatant about the fact that tips are expected. Small sums of hard currency, though not officially encouraged, will certainly be most welcome. Otherwise, in moderate or inexpensive restaurants, add a few Kčs; in more expensive ones, add 10%. For taxis, add 5 Kčs. In the better hotels, doormen should get a 2 Kčs. for each bag they carry to the check-in desk; bellhops get up to 5 Kčs. for taking them up to your rooms. In Moderate or Inexpensive hotels, you'll have to lug them yourself.

Prague

Arriving and Departing

By Plane All international flights arrive at Prague's **Ruzyně** Airport, about 20 kilometers (12 miles) from downtown. For arrival and departure times, tel. 02/367814 or 367760.

Between the Airport and Downtown ČSA provides bus services linking the airport with Town Terminal Vltava (Revoluční 25). Departures depend on aircraft schedules. The trip costs 6 Kčs. and takes about 30 minutes. A special shuttle service serves main hotels and costs 50 Kčs.; buy the ticket before boarding. The cheapest way to get into Prague is by regular bus 119; the cost is 1 Kčs., but you'll need to change to the subway for the last leg of the trip. By taxi, expect to pay 70–100 Kčs.

By Train The main station for international and domestic routes is **Hlavni nádraží** (tel. 02/244441), not far from Wenceslas Square.

By Bus The main bus station is **Florenc** (at Na Florenci, tel. 02/221445), not far from the train station.

Getting Around

Public transportation is a bargain. Some subway stations sell a one-day ticket for 8 Kčs., giving unlimited use of all public transportation. Otherwise, tickets cost 1 Kčs. and should be obtained before boarding at newsstands, tobacco shops, various stores and hotels, or subway stations. Punch your ticket in the machine as you board.

By Subway Prague's three modern subway lines are easy to use and spotlessly clean. They provide the simplest and fastest means of transport, and most new maps of Prague mark the routes.

By Tram/Bus You need to buy a new ticket every time you change vehicles. Express buses (marked with green badges) serve the suburbs and cost 2 Kčs.

By Taxi Taxis (tel. 02/202951 or 203941) are inexpensive, but can be difficult to find. The basic charge of 6 Kčs. is increased by 3 Kčs. per kilometer (surcharge at night). Rates are a little higher from the airport and some Interhotels.

Important Addresses and Numbers

Tourist Information Čedok (Na příkopě 18, tel. 02/212711) is very near Wenceslas Square. For its **Department of Accommodation Services,** go to Panská 5 (tel. 02/227004) just around the corner. Almost next-door to Čedok is the **Prague Information Service** (Na příkopě 20, tel. 02/544444). Across the road, **Pragotur** (U Obecního domu 2, tel. 02/2317281), near the Powder Tower, provides a variety of services, including reservations in non-Čedok hotels and private accommodations.

Embassies U.S. Tržiště 15, Malá Strana, tel. 02/536641. **Canadian.** Mickiewiczova 6, tel. 02/326941. **U.K.** Thunovská 14, Malá Strana, tel. 02/533347.

Emergencies Police, tel. 158; **Ambulance,** tel. 155; **Doctor,** Fakultní poliklinika, Karlovo náměstí 32, Prague 2, tel. 02/299381. **24-Hour Pharmacy,** Na příkopě 7, near Wenceslas Square.

English Bookstores Try Štěpánska 42 or Na příkopě 27. Except in a few top hotels, English-language newspapers are limited to left-wing publications such as *The Morning Star.*

Travel Agencies **American Express** and **Thomas Cook** are both located at the Čedok Foreign Travel Division, Na příkopě 18, tel. 02/224251.

Guided Tours

Čedok arranges a variety of tours in and around Prague; they can be arranged before you leave or can be booked in Prague. Call 02/2318255 or 2316619 for any of the following:

Orientation Tours The **Prague City tour,** departing from three central points, covers the main monuments, including Prague Castle and St. Vitus Cathedral, in half a day.

Special-Interest Tours The **"U Fleků" Brewery and Beer-tasting Tour** starts at Wenceslas Square 24 and lasts two hours. For cultural tours, call Čedok (*see* above). These include performances of folklore, Laterna Magika (*see* The Arts), opera, and concerts. You can save money by buying tickets—if any are available—at box offices, but this will take time.

Walking Tours A three-hour walk starts at Čedok (Wenceslas Sq. 24) at 8:45 daily, lasts 2¼ hours, and ends at Prague Castle.

Excursions Čedok's one-day tours out of Prague cover main historic and scenic sights, and include lunch. The **Czech Garnet Jewelry and Czech Paradise Tour** should yield attractive buys as well as good scenery. The **Beauty Spots of South Bohemia Tour** focuses on history and medieval architecture among woods and lakes.

Personal Guides Contact **Čedok,** Panská 4, tel. 02/224404.

Exploring Prague

Like Rome, far to the southwest, the city of Prague is built on seven hills, sprawling within the confines of a broad loop of the Vltava River. This riverside location makes a great setting for two of the city's particular features: its extravagant architecture and its memorable music. Mozart claimed that no one understood him better than the citizens of Prague, and he was only one of several great masters who lived or lingered here.

It was under Charles IV (Karel IV) in the 14th century that Prague briefly became the seat of the Holy Roman Empire—virtually the capital of western Europe—and acquired its distinctive Gothic imprint. At times, you'll need to look quite hard for this medieval inheritance; it's still here, though, under the overlays of graceful Renaissance and exuberant Baroque buildings.

Prague escaped serious wartime damage, but it didn't escape neglect. A long-term restoration program now under way always leaves some part of the city under scaffolding. But what's completed—which is nearly all that's described in the following itineraries—is hard to fault as an example of sensitive and painstaking restoration.

The Nové Mĕsto and Staré Mĕsto (New and Old Towns)

① **Václavské námĕstí** (Wenceslas Square) is the Times Square of Prague. Confusingly, it's not actually a square at all, but a
② broad boulevard sloping down from the **National Museum** and
③ the equestrian **statue of Wenceslas** (who has yet to fulfill the legend that he will again lead his people in their time of greatest need). The lower end is where all the action is. **Na příkopĕ**, once part of the moat surrounding the Old Town, is now an ele-
④ gant pedestrian mall. **Čedok's** main office and Prague In-
⑤ formation Service are along here, on your way to the **Powder Tower,** a 19th-century neo-Gothic replacement of the medieval original.

⑥ Turn into Celetná and you're on the old **Royal Route,** once fol-
⑦ lowed by coronation processions through **Staromĕstski námĕstí**
⑧ (Old Town Square), Karlova, across **Karlŭv most** (Charles Bridge), and up to the castle. Along this route, you can study every variety or combination of Romanesque, Gothic, Renaissance, and Baroque architecture. Two good examples are **12 Celetná** and **8 Karlova.** On Staromĕstske námĕstí, the crowds regularly gather below the famous **Clock Tower,** where, on the hour, the complex 16th-century mechanism activates a procession that includes the Twelve Apostles. Note the skeleton figure of Death that tolls the bell.

⑨ In U Starého Hřbitova (the Old Jewish Cemetery) in the **Prague Ghetto,** ancient tombstones lean and jostle each other; below them, in a dozen layers, are 12,000 graves. As you stand by the tomb of the scholar Rabbi Low, who died in 1609, you may see, stuffed into the cracks, scraps of paper bearing prayers and requests. It's said that many Jews hid their valuables here before being transported to the concentration camps. Their story, and many aspects of the culture of one of the oldest ghettos in Europe, is told in several nearby synagogues that now form part of

⑩ the **State Jewish Museum.** *Jachymova 3. Admission charged. Open weekdays, 9–4:30.*

When you stand on **Charles Bridge,** you'll see views of Prague that would still be familiar to the 14th-century architect Peter Parler and to the sculptors who added the 30 Baroque statues in the early 18th century (a few have been replaced). They're worth a closer look, especially the 12th on the left (St. Luitgarde, by Matthias Braun, circa 1710), and the 14th on the left (in which a Turk guards suffering saints, by F. M. Brokoff, circa 1714).

⑪ The **museum** devoted to Prague composer **Bedřich Smetana,** located nearby at Novotného lávka, is small, and its exhibits mainly documentary. But it's a lovely quiet oasis in which to listen to tapes of Smetana's music—music that must have been inspired by the views across the Vltava and up to the Castle. *Novotného láuka. Open Wed.–Mon. 10–5. Admission charged.*

⑫ **Bethlehem Chapel** has been completely reconstructed since Jan Hus thundered his humanitarian teachings from its pulpit in the early 15th century to congregations that could number 3,000. But the little door through which he came to the pulpit is original, as are some of the inscriptions on the wall. *Betlémské Náměstí. Open daily 9–6.*

Mala Strana and Hradcany (Lesser Town and Castle)

Cross Charles Bridge and follow Mostecká up to Malostranské náměstí. After the turbulence of the Counter-Reformation at the end of the 16th century, Prague witnessed a great flowering of what became known as Bohemian Baroque. The
⑬ architects (Dienzenhofer, father and son) of the **Church of St. Nicholas** were among its most skilled exponents. If you're in Prague when a concert is being given in this church, fight for a ticket. The lavish sculptures and frescoes of the interior make for a memorable setting. *Malostranské náměstí. Open daily 9–6.*

⑭ The monumental complex of **Prague Castle** has witnessed the changing fortunes of the city for more than a thousand years. The scaffolding has only recently been removed from the latest restoration on the castle's **Cathedral of St. Vitus.** It took from 1344 to 1929 to build, so you can trace the whole gamut of styles from Romanesque to 19th-century. This is the final resting place for numerous Bohemian kings. Charles IV lies in the crypt. Good King Wenceslas has his own chapel in the south transept, studded with semiprecious stones. Knightly tournaments often accompanied coronation ceremonies in the castle; consequently, the broad **Riders' Staircase** leading up to the grandiose Vladislav Hall off the Third Courtyard. Oldest of all the buildings, though much restored, is the Romanesque complex of **St. George's Church and Monastery.** Now in a Baroque dress, it houses a superb collection of Baroque and earlier Bohemian art. *Hradčanské náměstí. Admission charged. All museum buildings in the castle are open Tues.–Sun. 10–5.*

Time Out At the small, pleasant snack bar of U Ševce Matouše (At the Cobblers) on Loretánské náměstí, you can get your shoes repaired while you take refreshment.

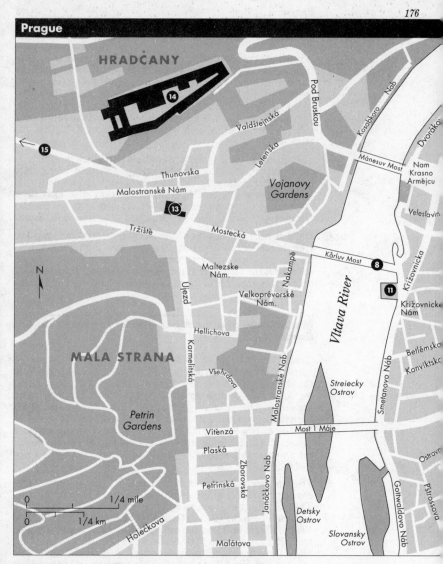

Prague

HRADČANY

Pod Bruskou
Kosabkaro Nab
Dvorako
Valdštejnská
Letenská
Mánesuv Most
Nam Krasno Armějcu
Thunovska
Vojanovy Gardens
Malostranské Nám
Veleslavin
Tržiště
Mostecká
Kârluv Most **8**
Maltezske Nám.
Nakampě
11
Křižovnicka
Velkoprévorské Nám.
Křižovnicke Nám
Újezd
Vltava River
Hellichova
Betlémska
MALA STRANA
Karmelitská
Všehrdova
Malostranské Nab
Streiecky Ostrov
Smetanovo Náb
Konviktsko
Petrin Gardens
Vitěnzá
Most 1 Máje
Plaská
Zborovská
Ostrov
Petřinská
Janáčkovo Nab
Pstrossova
Detsky Ostrov
Gottwaldovo Náb
Holečkova
Slovansky Ostrov
Malátova

N

0 _____ 1/4 mile
0 _____ 1/4 km

Bedřich Smetana Museum, **11**
Bethlehem Chapel, **12**
Čedok, **4**
Church of St. Nicholas, **13**

Karlův most, **8**
Loretto Church, **5**
National Museum, **2**
Powder Tower, **5**
Prague Castle, **14**
Royal Route, **6**
Staroměstski náměstí, **7**

State Jewish Museum, **10**
Statue of Wenceslas, **3**
U Starého Hřbitova, **9**
Václavské náměstí, **1**

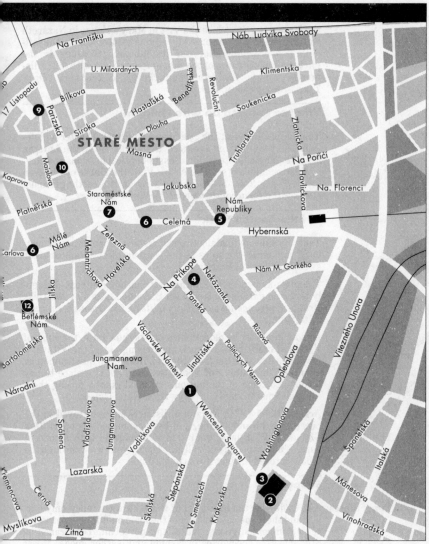

⑮ The Baroque church and shrine of the **Loretto** is named after the Italian town to which the Virgin Mary's House in Nazareth was supposedly transported by angels to save it from the infidel. The crowning glory of its fabulous treasury is the glittering monstrance of the *Sun of Prague*, set with 6,222 diamonds. *Loreta 12. Admission charge to Treasury. Open Tues.–Sun. 9–noon, 1–5.*

What to See and Do with Children

The puppet shows at the **Špejbl and Hurvínek Theater** will delight the young of any age. (*see* The Arts). Go to the **Laterna Magika** (Magic Lantern) for a feast of optical illusions and clever film techniques (*see* The Arts). Visit the **House of Children** (*open Tues.–Sun. 10–noon and 3–5*) on the castle grounds. *One adult may accompany each child of 6–15 years.*

Off the Beaten Track

Take the subway to Malostranská metro station, cross a courtyard, and climb the steps to the **Gardens** on the Ramparts for sweeping views of Prague.

The little-known **Vrtba Zahrada** is a charming retreat of steeply terraced gardens dotted with Baroque statues by Matthias Braun. *Entrance through Karmelitská 25. Open in summer until 9* PM.

Almost as old as the oldest parts of Prague Castle, the ruins of **Vyšehrad castle** crown a rock bluff rising out of the Vltava, a few miles downstream from the Old Town. The quiet cemetery adjoining the **Church of Sts. Peter and Paul** is a place to pay homage to some of the nation's cultural giants, among them Bedřich Smetana and the playwright Karel Čapek.

Across the river, in Prague 5 district, Mozart stayed in the peaceful **Bertramka Villa,** and here composed his opera *Don Giovanni*. With luck, your trip will coincide with a concert here. If not, taped music will accompany your walk through the villa, restored to what it was in his day.

Shopping

Tuzex Stores Ask Čedok for the latest list of these hard-currency-only outlets and their specialties. One of the main ones is at Železná 18, selling imported goods, glass, and porcelain. The branch at Štěpanská 23 specializes in fashion and leather goods. **Moser** (Na příkopě 12) is the most famous for glass and porcelain.

Specialty Shops Look for the name **Dilo** for objets d'art and prints; ULUV or UVA for folk art. At Na příkopě 12 you'll find excellent costume jewelry.

Shopping Districts Many of the main shops are in and around Wenceslas Square (Václavské náměstí) and Na příkopě and along Celetná and Pařížská.

Department Stores Three central ones are **Bilá Labut** (Na poříčí 23), **Družba** (Wenceslas Square 21), and **Kotva** (nám. Republiky 8).

Dining

Eating out in Prague is a very popular pastime, so it's advisable to make reservations whenever possible, especially for dinner.

Prices for our categories are for a three-course meal for one person, excluding wine and tip. Best bets are indicated by a star ★. At press time, there were 5.03 Korunas (Kčs.) to the dollar.

Category	Cost
Very Expensive	over 150 Kčs.
Expensive	100–150 Kčs.
Moderate	50–100 Kčs.
Inexpensive	under 50 Kčs.

Very Expensive **Klášterní Vinárna.** You'll find this wine restaurant in a former Ursuline convent in the city center. The emphasis is on Czech home cooking—try the "house" goulash. *Národní 8, tel. 02/290596. Jacket and tie. Reservations accepted. No credit cards. Closed Sun.*

U Labuti. Located in tastefully remodeled stables in the castle area, "At the Swans" has a stylish—if slightly rich and heavy—menu (haunch of venison, goose liver with ham and almonds). The place is rich in atmosphere, too. *Hradčanské náměstí 11, tel. 02/536962. Jacket and tie. Reservations required. AE, DC, MC, V. Closed lunch.*

★ **U Malířů.** This is one of Prague's most picturesque wine taverns, popular with the artist set (the name means "At the Painters"). *Maltézské náměstí 11, Lesser Town, tel. 02/531883. Tie and jacket. Reservations required. No credit cards. Closed lunch and all day Sun.*

U Mecenáše. This wine restaurant manages to be both medieval and elegant despite the presence of an ancient gallows! Try and get a table in the back room. Moussaka is one of the specialties from an international menu. *Malostranské náměstí 10, Lesser Town, tel. 02/533881. Jacket and tie. Reservations required. AE, DC, MC, V. Closed lunch and all day Sat.*

Expensive **U Zlaté Hrušky.** Careful restoration has returned this restaurant to its original 18th-century style. It specializes in Moravian wines, which go down well with fillet steaks and goose liver. *Nový Svět 3, Castle area, tel. 02/531133. Jacket and tie. Reservations required. No credit cards. Closed lunch.*

Moderate **Opera Grill.** Though called a grill, this is one of the most stylish
★ small restaurants in town, complete with antique Meissen candelabra and Czech specialties. *K. Světlé 35, Old Town, tel. 02/265508. Jacket and tie. Reservations required. AE, DC, MC, V. Closed lunch and weekends.*

U Lorety. Sightseers will find this an agreeable spot—peaceful except for the welcoming carillon from neighboring Loretto Church. Venison and steak are specialties. *Loretánské náměstí 8, near the Castle, tel. 02/531395. Jacket and tie. Reservations advised. AE, DC, MC, V. Closed Mon. and Tues. in winter.*

U Pastýřky-Koliba. It's worth the trek from the center to enjoy the folk-style decor and specialty dishes of Slovakia here, complete with open fire for spit roasts. *Bělehradská 15, tel. 02/434093. Dress: informal. Reservations required. No credit cards. Closed lunch and all day Sun.*

Vikárka. This was an eating house beside St. Vitus Cathedral as far back as the 16th century. It offers good-value local cooking in a historic setting. *Vikářská 6, in the Castle, tel.*

02/535150. Dress: informal. Reservations accepted. AE, DC, MC, V. Closed Mon. in winter.

Inexpensive **U Medvídků.** Enjoy South Bohemian and old Czech specialties here in a noisy but jolly atmosphere. *Na perštýně 7, tel. 02/2358904. Dress: casual. Reservations unnecessary. No credit cards. Closed Sun.*

U Pinkasů. The two great attractions here are the draught beer and the goulash—you can also add your signature to the wall with the countless others before you. *Jungmannovo náměstí 15, tel. 02/265770. Dress: informal. Reservations unnecessary. No credit cards.*

★ **U Sv. Tomáše.** This restored ancient tavern overflows with atmosphere. Try the famous dark ale and the good down-to-earth fare like roast pork with cabbage and dumplings. *Letenská 12, Lesser Town, tel. 02/530064. Dress: informal. Reservations advised. No credit cards. Closed Sun.*

U Zlatého Tygra. This is a favorite with not-so-young beer connoisseurs—a typical no-frills Prague pub. The pork fillet in potato pancake with sauerkraut salad makes a good foundation for the beer. *Husova 17, tel. 02/265219. Dress: informal. Reservations unnecessary. No credit cards. Closed Sun.*

Lodging

Many of Prague's older hotels—some having great style—have recently been or are due to be renovated. If you haven't prebooked, go to Čedok or Pragotur when you arrive *(see* Tourist Information in Important Addresses and Numbers). Hotels designated *Interhotels* belong to the Čedok network.

Prices are for double rooms and obligatory breakfast and dinner for two. Most Very Expensive and Expensive hotels include breakfast only. Best bets are indicated by a star ★. We've listed prices in dollars since most visitors will prebook their rooms.

Category	Cost: Prague
Very Expensive	over $150
Expensive	$100–$150
Moderate	$66–$100
Inexpensive	under $66

Very Expensive **Forum** (Interhotel). Prague's latest high rise is near ancient Vyšehrad castle. Prices include half-board. *Štětkova ul, tel. 02/410111. 531 rooms with bath. Facilities: saunas, pool, bowling alleys, miniature golf, gym, nightclub, roulette. AE, DC, MC, V.*

InterContinental (Interhotel). A fine riverside position in the Old Town makes this an attractive choice. It opened in 1975 and is a favorite with U.S. visitors. *Náměstí Curiových 5, tel. 02/2899. 395 rooms with bath. Facilities: saunas, health club, nightclub. AE, DC, MC, V.*

★ **U Tří Pštrosů.** "The Three Ostriches" has a magical location at the Lesser Town end of Charles Bridge: The river views are superb. It's very popular, so you'll need to make reservations well ahead. Prices include half-board. *Dražického 12, tel. 02/536151. 18 rooms with bath. AE, DC, MC, V.*

Expensive **Alcron** (Interhotel). This stylish old town house just around the
★   corner from Wenceslas Square is a favorite with Americans
who prefer traditional decor over modern. *Štěpánská 40, tel.
02/2359216–30. 149 rooms with bath. Facilities: 3 restaurants.
AE, DC, MC, V.*

Esplanade (Interhotel). Facing a park near the National Museum, this is another favorite with Americans looking for a
traditional atmosphere. An old town house, it was last renovated in 1980. The nightclub, Est Bar, has a good local
reputation. *Washingtonova 19, tel. 02/222552–4. 65 rooms with
bath. AE, DC, MC, V.*

Jalta (Interhotel). The Jalta has a plum location on Wenceslas
Square. Despite its five-star status, it's on the shabby side, but
comfortable, nevertheless. *Vaclavské náměstí 45, tel. 02/
265541. 90 rooms with bath. Facilities: 2 nightclubs. AE, DC,
MC, V.*

Panorama (Interhotel). Near Vyšehrad castle, with good subway connections to the center, this hotel makes a practical
exploring base. Prices include half-board. *Milevska 7, tel. 02/
416111. 432 rooms with bath. Facilities: saunas, pool, solarium, nightclub. AE, DC, MC, V.*

Moderate **International** (Interhotel). Situated about 3 miles (5 kilometers) from the center, the International is known as the Russian
Ritz for its 30-year-old architectural pretensions! High season
prices can edge this one up into the Expensive category. *Náměstí družby 1, tel. 02/321051. 327 rooms with bath. Facilities:
garden, miniature golf, nightclub. AE, DC, MC, V.*

★   **Paříž** (Interhotel). This is the pick of the Moderate hotels, de-
spite some small rooms. Its turn-of-the-century Art Nouveau
style was tastefully restored in 1985, while the hotel's Old
Town location is ideal. Rooms without bath are Inexpensive. *U
Obecního domu 1, tel. 02/2322051. 86 rooms, 75 with bath. AE,
DC, MC, V.*

Zlatá Husa (Interhotel). This is another oldie from the turn of
the century and was renovated in 1983. It's right on Wenceslas
Square. *Václavské náměstí 7, tel. 02/221351. 62 rooms with
bath. Facilities: disco. AE, DC, MC, V.*

The Arts

Prague's cultural life is one of its top attractions and its citizens
like to dress up for it, but performances are usually booked far
ahead. You can get a monthly program of events from the
Prague Information Service, Čedok, or many hotels. **Čedok**
(Bílkova, tel. 02/2318255) is the main ticket agency for foreigners, but there's a wider choice through **Sluna** (Pasáž Černa
Růže, off Na příkopě).

Concerts Performances are held in the **National Gallery** in Prague Castle; the **National Museum;** the **Gardens** below the castle (where
music comes with a view; the **Church of St. Nicholas** in the
Lesser Town; and **St. James's Church** on Malá Stupartská (Old
Town), where the organ plays amidst a flourish of Baroque
statuary.

Year-round concert halls include the **House of Artists, Smetana
Hall,** and the **Palace of Culture.**

Opera and Ballet Opera is of an especially high standard in Czechoslovakia. The
main venues in the grand style of the 19th century are the beau-

tifully restored **National Theater** and **Smetana Theater**. The
even older **Týl Theater** is still under restoration.

Theater You won't need to know the language at **Divadlo na Zabradlí**
(Theater on the Balustrade, Anenské náměstí 5), home of the
famous Black Theater mime group when it is (rather rarely) in
Prague. **Laterna Magika** (Magic Lantern, Národní 40) is a popular extravaganza combining live actors, mime, and
sophisticated film techniques.

Puppet Shows These are brought to a high art form at the **Špejbl and Hurvínek
Theater** (Římská 45).

Nightlife

Cabaret The **Alhambra** (Václavské náměstí 5) has a three-part floor
show. More moderately priced is **Variete Praha** (Vodičkova 30).
You'll find plenty of fellow foreigners at both.

Discos The best-known and most crowded is at the **Zlatá Husa** hotel
(see Lodging). There's one at each of the three hotels on the
Vltava River: **Amirál** (Hořejši nábřeží), **Albatros** (nábřeží L.
Svobody), and **Racek** (Dvorecká louka).

Bohemian Spas and Castles

The Bohemian countryside is a restful world of gentle hills and
thick woods. It is especially beautiful during fall foliage or in
May, when the fruit trees that line the roads are in blossom. In
such settings lie the two most famous of Czechoslovakia's
scores of spas: **Karlovy Vary** and **Mariánské Lázně**. In the 19th
and early 20th centuries, the royalty and aristocrats of Europe
who came to ease their over indulged bodies (or indulge them
even more!), knew these spas as Karslbad and Marienbad.

To the south, the higher wooded hills of Šumava, bordering
West Germany, have their own folklore and give rise to the
headwaters of the Vltava. You'll follow its tortuous course toward Prague as you enter South Bohemia, which has spawned
more castles than any other region of comparable size. The
medieval towns of South Bohemia are exquisite, though be prepared to find them in varying stages of repair or decay. In such
towns was the Hussite reformist movement born in the early
15th century, sparking off a series of religious conflicts that
eventually embroiled all Europe.

Getting Around

Though there are bus connections throughout the area, you
may have problems sorting out the timetables. The most convenient way to follow the whole of this itinerary is by car.

Guided Tours

Many of the attractions on this itinerary, and some additional
ones in Moravia, are covered by Čedok's escorted seven-day
Short Tour of Czechoslovakia out of Prague. Most can also be
visited on a series of day trips from the capital.

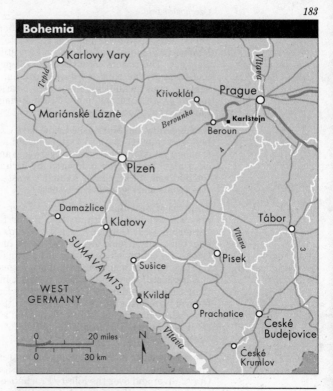

Bohemia

Tourist Information

České Budějovice. Hroznova 21, tel. 038/32381.
Český Krumlov. Gottwaldovo náměstí, tel. 0337/2062.
Domažlice. Náměstí Míru 129, tel. 0189/2713.
Karlovy Vary. Tržiště 23, tel. 017/27798.
Mariánské Lázně. Odboránřů 48, tel. 0165/2500.
Tábor. Tř. 9 května 1282, tel. 0361/144585.

Exploring

If you're traveling by car, the best—though not fastest—route is to head south from Prague on Highway 4, then west along minor roads up the Berounka Valley, taking in the castles of **Karlštejn** and **Křivoklát**. The first is an admirable restoration of the 14th-century castle built by Charles IV, but not worth the uphill slog unless the stunning Chapel of the Holy Rood is re-opened, its walls covered with 128 Gothic paintings and encrusted with 2,000 gems. **Křivoklát's** main attractions are its glorious woodlands, a favorite royal hunting ground in times past. *Admission charged. Both castles open Tues.–Sun. 9–6; closed the day after public holidays.*

Karlovy Vary, or Karlsbad, was named after Charles IV who, while out hunting, was supposedly led to the main thermal spring of Vřídlo by a fleeing deer. In due course, the spa drew not only many of the crowned heads and much of the blue blood of Europe but also leading musicians and writers. The same parks, promenades, and colonnades still border the little river Teplá, beneath wooded hills. For all its later buildings and proletarian patients, Socialist Karlovy Vary still has a great deal of elegance. The waters from the spa's 12 springs are uniformly foul-tasting. The thing to do is sip them from traditionally shaped cups while nibbling rich Karlovy Vary wafers (*oplatky*), then resort to the "13th spring," Karlovy Vary's tangy herbal liqueur called *Becherovka*.

Karlovy Vary and **Mariánské Lázně** have Czechoslovakia's two best golf courses. As a spa, Mariánské Lázně is younger and smaller, yet its more open setting gives it an air of greater spaciousness. It was much favored by Britain's Edward VII, though from all accounts, he didn't waste too much time on strict diets and rigorous treatments.

The spas of west Bohemia have long catered to foreign travelers. As you head south to the higher Šumava mountains bordering West Germany, you'll be following much less frequented trails. **Domažlice** is the heart of the region of the Chods, for centuries guardians of Bohemia's frontiers, a function that earned them a number of privileges. Their special folk culture is still very much alive, not least in their pottery and their contagious dances accompanied by local bagpipes (main festival in mid-August). It is a beautiful little town with a lovely arcaded square, old fortifications, and a castle that houses the **Chod Museum** of local folk culture. *Admission charged. Open Tues.–Sun. 8–noon and 1–4:30.*

From Domažlice runs a tortuous but extremely pretty route, mainly along minor roads, through **Sušice** along the upper Otava River and over the hills to **Prachatice** and **Kvilda,** where the road joins the young Vltava River. Downstream, the Vltava has been trapped to form the great reservoir and recreational area of **Lipno.** You skirt part of it before turning northeast to Český Krumlov.

The whole of this part of South Bohemia has strong associations with feudal families such as the Rožmberks, who peppered the countryside with their castles and created lake-size "ponds" in which to breed highly prized carp, still the main feature of a Czech Christmas dinner. Once the main seat of the Rožmberks, **Český Krumlov** will be a magic place when all the scaffolding has finally been removed. The Vltava River snakes through the town, which is steeply stacked on either bank, with flights of steps linking various levels and with twisting narrow lanes converging on **Gottwaldovo náměstí,** the main square of the Old Town. There are arcades and courtyards and, of course, a Rožmberk Castle, this one with an 18th-century theater.

České Budějovice is on a much larger scale, and here your main stop should be the massive but handsome **Žižka Square.** The town, originally called Budweis, produces Budvar beer. The townsfolk will be happy to express their own colorful views on its American near-namesake!

Farther north along Highway 3 is **Tábor,** the very cradle of the Hussite movement. Its twisting streets were designed to confuse the enemy. A labyrinth of tunnels and cellars below the town were used both as living quarters and as links with the outer defenses. Their story is told in the **Hussite Museum** in the 16th-century Town Hall on Žižka Square. *It should be open daily 9–5 following restoration in 1988.*

Dining and Lodging

For details and price category definitions, *see* Dining and Lodging in Essential Information.

Český Krumlov **Krumlov** (Interhotel). This 19th-century town house will be a
Lodging charmer, once it—and the rest of this town—has been restored. It's in the center of the old town. *Gottwaldovo náměstí 14, tel. 0337/2255–8. 36 rooms, 13 with bath. AE, DC, MC, V. Inexpensive.*

Karlovy Vary **Grand Hotel Pupp-Moskva** (Interhotel). Founded in the early
Lodging 18th century, the Moskva still features a fine 18th-century hall,
★ Slavností sál. It's one of the oldest surviving hotels in Europe, with a glittering list of guests, both past and present. *Mírové náměstí 2, tel. 017/22121–5. 170 rooms with bath. Facilities: saunas, tennis, golf, riding, 2 nightclubs, several restaurants and taverns. AE, DC, MC, V. Very Expensive.*
Parkhotel (Interhotel). This grande dame will soon celebrate its first centenary. One of its two restaurants specializes in Oriental foods, a rarity in this country. Prices decrease to Moderate in low season. *Mírové náměstí 2, tel. 017/22121–5. 117 rooms with bath. Facilities: saunas, nightclub. AE, DC, MC, V. Expensive.*

Mariánské Lázně **Golf** (Interhotel). Built around 1930 and renovated in 1982, this
Lodging hotel is located a bit out of town by the golf course. The decor is
★ traditional and the restaurant serves good regional dishes such as dumplings. *Zadub 55, tel. 0165/2651–6. 26 rooms with bath. Facilities: pool, tennis, golf, riding. AE, DC, MC, V. Very Expensive, but Moderate in low season.*
Palace Praha (Interhotel). Built in 1875 during the spa's heyday, this elegant building is conveniently situated just within the resort center. French foods are the specialty at one of the hotel's two restaurants. *Třída Odborářů 67, tel. 0165/2222. 35 rooms, 23 with bath. Facilities: nightclub. AE, DC, MC, V. Moderate.*

Highlights of Slovakia

Even if it had not developed quite separately for nearly a millenium under Hungarian or Hapsburg rule, Slovakia would be different from Bohemia in a great many aspects. Its mountains are higher and more rugged, its veneer less sophisticated, its people more carefree. Their talent for spinning a good yarn and their independent spirit have led many to compare them with the Irish. And as with the Irish, Slovakia's folk culture is particularly rich.

Most visitors head for the great peaks of the High Tatras, with their excellent tourist facilities; and this is where most tours will take you. The mountains *are* spectacular, but also worth seeing are the exquisite medieval towns of Spiš in the plains and valleys below the High Tatras and the beautiful 18th-century country churches farther east. Away from main centers, these areas are short on tourist amenities; so if creature comforts are important to you, stick to the High Tatras.

Getting Around

ČSA's flights from Bratislava to Poprad (for the High Tatras) connect with services from Prague once or twice daily; the journey takes about 40 minutes. From Bratislava to Poprad by bus takes 5–6 hours; by train 6–7 hours. The bus from Poprad to Prešov takes 2½ hours; from here it takes about 40 minutes by train, a little longer by bus, to Bardejov. You can then return directly by bus from Bardejov to Poprad.

Guided Tours

Čedok's **Seven-day Tour of Slovakia** leaves from Bratislava and takes in most of the places on this itinerary, plus a few more. From the High Tatras resorts, day trips include either some of the Spiš towns or Červený Kláštor and the Pieniny National Park.

Tourist Information

Bardejov. Námestie osvoboditelov 46, tel. 0935/2134.
Bratislava. Štúrova 13, tel. 07/55280.
Prešov. Ul. Slov. Republiky rád 1, tel. 091/24040.
Smokovec. Starý Smokovec V/22, tel. 0969/2417.
Žilina. Hodžova 9, tel. 089/23347.

Exploring

It may come as a surprise that for 300 years **Bratislava** was the capital of Hungary (after Buda and Pest fell to the Turks in the 15th century). The Hungarians knew it as Pozsony and the Hapsburgs, who subsequently took it over, as Pressburg. It wasn't until 1918 that it regained its Slavic name.

In the 18th century, royal and noble families built patrician houses that still add much charm to the narrow streets of the old town, currently undergoing restoration below the **castle.** The castle has been virtually rebuilt since World War II, and is a good point from which to get your bearings as you look down on the broad waters of the Danube, the Gothic spire of the **Cathedral of St. Martin**—where Hungarian kings and queens were crowned—and the huddled roofs of the old town.

Down in the old town there's architectural interest on almost every street, particularly on the square of Primaciálne námestie, with its Gothic-Renaissance **Old Town Hall** and its elegant **Primate's Palace.** The palace has some lovely 17th-century tapestries (made in the royal workshops at Mortlake near London), depicting the legend of Hero and Leander. *Primaciálne námestie. Admission charged. Open Tues.–Sun. 9–5.*

Whether you travel by car, bus, or train, your route will follow the Váh valley for most of the way to **Poprad,** a transit point for the High Tatras, and, unfortunately, a dreary place. Its suburb of **Spišská Sobota,** however, is a little gem. It was one of 24 small Gothic towns in a medieval region known as Spiš. Steep shingled roofs, high timber-framed gables, and brick-arched door ways are the main features of the rich merchants' dwellings, usually grouped around a main square domi-

Slovakia

nated by a Gothic church, often with a separate Renaissance bell tower. Keep in mind the name Pavol of Levoča, one of the great woodcarvers of the 16th century. The main altar in **Sv. Juraj** (the Church of St. George) is his work.

An electric train network and the so-called Freedom Road link the resorts strung out on the lower slopes of the High Tatras. **Štrbské Pleso** is the highest of the towns and the best launching point for mountain excursions. **Smokovec** is really three resorts in one (Starý, Nový, and Horný) and has the most varied amenities. For the most effortless high-level trip, though, go to **Tatranská Lomnica,** from where a two-stage cable car will take you via Skalnaté pleso (lake) to Lomnický štít, which is 8,635 feet (2,632 meters) high. The upper stage is being reconstructed but should reopen in 1989. The **Museum of the Tatra National Park** at Tatranská Lomnica offers an excellent introduction to the area's natural and human history. *Admission charged. Open weekdays 8–noon and 1–5, weekends 8–noon.*

Leave Poprad on Highway 18 east. Restoration work on **Levoča,** the most famous of the Spiš towns, is well under way, and the overlays of Renaissance on Gothic are extremely satisfying to the eye (note especially **Nos. 43, 45, 47, and 49** on the main square). Pavol of Levoča's work on the main altar of **Sv. Jakub** (the Church of St. James) on the main square is both monumental in size and exquisite in its detail.

The surrounding countryside is dotted with more Spiš towns. About 10 miles (16 kilometers) to the east, the massive, partly restored ruins of **Spiš Castle,** above Spišské Pohradie, dominate the surrounding pastures, orchards, and strawberry fields.

Some of **Prešov's** fortifications survive and its spindle-shaped main square is lined with buildings in the Gothic, Renaissance, and Baroque styles. You are now out of Spiš and into Šariš, a region whose proximity to the Orthodox east has left a unique legacy of both Orthodox and Greek Catholic (Uniat) churches. The latter are particularly interesting because, though acknowledging the pope's supremacy, their clergy retain their own liturgy and are permitted to marry.

Bardejov is a splendid walled town and makes the best center from which to set out on a journey of exploration, as long as you're prepared to get lost along some minor roads while seeking out the 17th- and 18th-century wooden churches of **Bodružal, Mirola,** and **Šemetkovce**—and the right person to open them up for you. You'll find these churches east and northeast of **Svidník,** near the border with Poland.

Dining and Lodging

For details and price category definitions, *see* Dining and Lodging in Essential Information.

Bardejov
Lodging

Minerál. This recently renovated modern hotel lies in a quiet location in the spa town of Bardejovské kúpele, 3½ miles (5 kilometers) from Bardejov. *Bardejovské kúpele, tel. 0935/4122. 60 rooms with shower. Facilities: tennis. No credit cards. Inexpensive.*

Bratislava
Dining

Kláštorna vináren. Old town dining can be a delight in the vaulted cellars of an old monastery. Slovak specialties include pork fillet *Liptovsky Hradok,* wrapped in cheese pastry. *Pugačevova 2, tel. 07/330340. Dress: informal. Reservations advised. No credit cards. Closed Sun. Expensive.*

Rybársky cech. The name means "Fishermen's Guild," and this restaurant is in the guild's house on the river embankment below the castle. It has its own aquarium, and, as you'd expect, the emphasis is on fish specialties, prepared by two award-winning chefs. Try the carp. *Žižkova 1, tel. 07/313049. Dress: informal. Reservations advised. No credit cards. Closed Mon. Expensive.*

Stará sladovna. The Old Malthouse has been converted into a series of taverns on three floors, serving the best of Czech beers. The main restaurant is on the top floor. *Cintopinska 32, tel. 07/51151. Dress: informal. Reservations unnecessary. No credit cards. Moderate.*

★ **Slovenská reštaurácia–Luxor.** This is one of the city's best places to try Slovak specialties, prepared by its award-winning chef, Gašpar Fukas. The folk art decor adds to the atmosphere. Try the *pastierska pochút'ka,* spicy potato pancakes filled with diced meat, mushrooms, and onions. *Štúrova ul. 3, tel. 07/52881. Dress: informal. Reservations advised. AE, DC, MC, V. Closed Sun. Moderate.*

Lodging

Forum Bratislava (Interhotel). The Forum should open early in 1989 in downtown Bratislava, offering top facilities. It will house a French as well as a Slovak restaurant and several cafés and bars. *Mierove námestie 2. 219 rooms with bath. Facilities: saunas, pool, solarium, health club, nightclub. AE, DC, MC, V. Very Expensive.*

Devin (Interhotel). Many American visitors stay at this recently renovated modern building on the Danube bank, near the old town. *Riečna 4, tel. 07/330851–4. 93 rooms, 87 with bath. Facilities: nightclub, French, Slovak, and Asian restaurants. AE, DC, MC, V. Expensive.*

Juniorhotel Sputnik. This modern hotel occupies a scenic lakeside position about 3 miles (5 kilometers) outside the city. The best rooms in the house are 211, 311, and 411, all with terrific views. *Drieňova 14, tel. 07/288084. 95 rooms with bath. Facilities: disco. No credit cards. Moderate.*

Smokovec
Dining

Tatranská kúria. The Tatranská's rustic decor and Slovak specialties, prepared by award-winning chef Jan Rogoz, will provide some insight into local life. Dishes include *rezeň kúria* (pork cutlets with a cheese and ham filling in a cheese pastry) and *bryndzove pirohy* (a ravioli-like pastry served with cream and bacon). *Starý Smokovec, tel. 0969/2806. Dress: informal. Reservations unnecessary. No credit cards. Moderate.*

Lodging

Bellevue (Interhotel). This modern high rise lies 200 yards (183 meters) from the resort center, with well-appointed rooms. Rates include breakfast and dinner. *Horný Smokovec, tel. 0969/2941–3. 103 rooms, 63 with bath. Facilities: saunas, pool. AE, DC, MC, V. Very Expensive.*

Grand Hotel (Interhotel). The town's oldest hotel has maintained its fin de siècle atmosphere through frequent renovation. It's right in the resort center, with an excellent restaurant. Rooms without bath are Moderate. *Starý Smokovec, tel. 0969/2154. Some rooms without bath. Facilities: pool, nightclub. AE, DC, MC, V. Expensive.*

Tatranski Lomnica
Dining

Zbojnícka koliba. Slovak specialties are prepared over an open fire, accompanied by folk music. The rustic atmosphere is so thick you can cut it with a knife. *Near Grandhotel Praha, tel. 969/967630. Dress: casual. Reservations unnecessary. No credit cards. Closed lunch and weekends. Expensive.*

Lodging

Grandhotel Praha (Interhotel). A renovated turn-of-the-century building, the Grandhotel has large, comfortable rooms decorated with a traditional touch. A short walk brings you to the downtown area. Rates include breakfast and dinner. *Tatranská Lomnica, tel. 969/967941–5. 92 rooms with bath. Facilities: nightclub. AE, DC, MC, V. Very Expensive.*

9 Denmark

Introduction

The Danes are sometimes called "the Italians of Scandinavia." The title sums up the easy ebullience and sense of humor of a nation with a long tradition of welcoming visitors, and none of the Scandinavian reputation for melancholy. Denmark is the only Scandinavian country that does not have wild tracts of forest and lake. This is a land of well-groomed agriculture, where every acre is rich in orchard and field. Nor does Denmark have any mountains. (The name Himmelbjerget, or "Sky Mountain," in Jutland, which glorifies one of the country's highest hills—at about 450 feet (140 meters)—illustrates the Danes's ability to laugh at themselves.) But despite this lack of grandeur, no one who has seen the colorful wildflowers that line the straight, empty roads in early summer would describe Denmark as boring or unappealing.

It is easy, too, to see why the Danes of long ago were magnificent seamen, Vikings who explored most of the then-known world. Nowhere are you far from the sea, as you drive on and off ferries and bridges that link the three regions: Jutland, Funen, and Zealand. In summer, the Danes like to spend their weekends and vacations along the 2,800 miles (4,500 kilometers) of coastline, where the pink and green of the wild roses spread out like fingers over the edge of the sand, or among the islands and archipelagos of the Great Belt or the Kattegat.

Yet Copenhagen is the liveliest Scandinavian capital, a city that enjoys itself for most of the 24 hours of the day, and does not mind coming out onto the street to do so. All over the city, the squares and alleyways are full of people at sidewalk cafés, drinking coffee, beer, and sometimes aquavit, all minding their own business and watching the people go by.

At night, there are dozens of tempting restaurants. Danes claim to provide the best Scandinavian food of all, and few who have supped at a lavish cold table (*det store kolde bord*) would dispute the claim. It is an appealing spread of herring, fish, meat, pâté, salads, and desserts, which, despite the name, also includes warm dishes. Danes love jazz, so music clubs and cafés proliferate.

Perhaps Denmark's greatest charm is its manageable size, making for easy driving, reasonable distances, and no strain. The journey from the ferry at Esbjerg to Copenhagen takes around five hours, and from there, you can make comfortable, unhurried expeditions by boat and car or train and bus to cover what is one of the world's most civilized countries.

Before You Go

When to Go Those who expect Scandinavia to be constantly chilly are surprised at the warmth of the Danish summer. Most visitors arrive in July and August, but there are advantages to coming in May, June, or September, when places are less crowded and many establishments offer off-season discounts. Danish school vacations last from mid-June to mid-August, so children's favorites, such as the Legoland park at Billund, are thronged with youngsters and their families. But few places in Denmark are ever unpleasantly crowded, and with so many away at the beach, the cities have even more breathing space.

Denmark

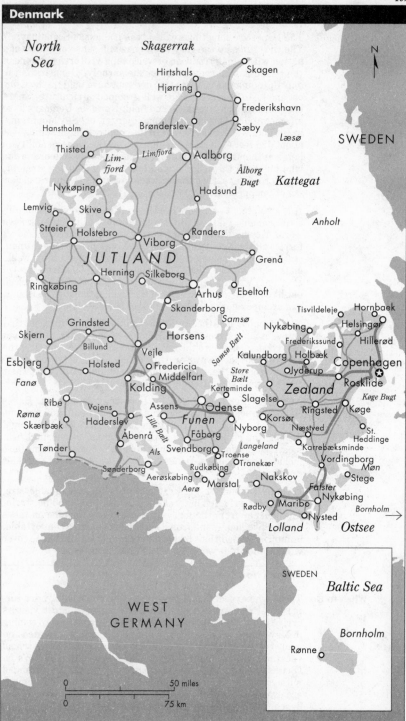

North
Sea

Skagerrak

SWEDEN

Hirtshals
Hjørring
Skagen
Frederikshavn
Brønderslev
Sæby
Læsø

Hanstholm
Thisted
Limfjord
Limfjord
Aalborg
Ålborg
Bugt
Kattegat

Nykøping
Hadsund

Lemvig
Skive
Anholt
Streier
Holstebro
Randers
Viborg
JUTLAND
Grenå

Herning
Silkeborg
Ringkøbing

Århus
Ebeltoft
Skanderborg
Samsø
Tisvildeleje
Hornbaek
Nykøbing
Helsingør
Horsens
Frederikssund
Hillerød
Skjern
Grindsted
Vejle
Samsø Bælt
Kalundborg
Holbæk
Copenhagen
Billund
Esbjerg
Holsted
Fredericia
Store
Bælt
Jyderup
Roskilde
Fanø
Middelfart
Zealand
Kolding
Kerteminde
Slagelse
Køge Bugt
Ribe
Vojens
Assens
Odense
Ringsted
Køge
Rømø
Haderslev
Funen
Nyborg
Næstved
St.
Skærbæk
Åbenrå
Lille Bælt
Fåborg
Korsør
Heddinge
Tønder
Als
Svendborg
Karrebæksminde
Sønderborg
Troense
Langeland
Vordingborg
Aerøskøbing
Rudkøbing
Tranekær
Møn
Aerø
Marstal
Nakskov
Stege
Falster
Rødby
Maribo
Nykøbing
Bornholm →
Nysted
Lolland
Ostsee

SWEDEN
Baltic Sea

WEST
GERMANY

Bornholm

Rønne

0   50 miles
0   75 km

Climate   The following are the average daily maximum and minimum temperatures for Copenhagen.

Jan.	36F	2C	May	61F	16C	Sept.	64F	18C
	28	−2		46	8		51	11
Feb.	36F	2C	June	67F	19C	Oct.	54F	12C
	28	−3		52	11		44	7
Mar.	41F	5C	July	71F	22C	Nov.	45F	7C
	31	−1		57	14		38	3
Apr.	51F	10C	Aug.	70F	21C	Dec.	40F	4C
	38	3		56	14		34	1

Currency   The monetary unit in Denmark is the krone (kr. or DKK), which is divided into 100 øre. At press time (fall 1988), the krone stood at 6.45 to the dollar and 12.18 to the pound. Most well-known credit cards are accepted in Denmark. Traveler's checks can be changed in banks or in many hotels, restaurants, and shops.

What It Will Cost   Denmark's economy is stable and inflation reasonably low, without wild fluctuations in exchange rates. But, as in the rest of Scandinavia, both the standard and the cost of living are high, especially for luxuries such as alcohol. Do as the Danes do; concentrate on beer and wine but don't forget to bring in your duty-free goods. The least expensive areas are Funen and Jutland.

Sample Prices   Cup of coffee, 9–13 kr.; bottle of beer, 13–15 kr.; Coca-Cola, 10 kr.; ham sandwich, 24 kr.; one-mile taxi ride, 20 kr.

Customs on Arrival   Coming from an EEC country, people of all nationalities may import duty-free 1½ liters of liquor or three liters of strong wine (under 22%) plus four liters of other wine. U.S. residents may import 300 cigarettes or 75 cigars or 400 grams of tobacco; U.K. residents may import 300 cigarettes or 75 cigars or 400 grams of tobacco. Other articles may be brought in up to a maximum of 2,800 kr.; also, 75 grams of perfume.

All nationalities entering from all other countries may import duty-free one liter of liquor or two liters of strong wine plus two liters of other wine. U.S. tobacco regulations are the same as above; U.K. residents may import 200 cigarettes or 50 cigars or 250 grams of tobacco. Other articles (including beer), up to a maximum of 375 kr.; 50 grams of perfume.

Language   The joke about Danish is that it is not as much a language as "a disease of the throat." It is difficult for foreigners to understand, let alone speak, but this causes few problems. Danes are good linguists, the main foreign languages are taught in schools, and almost everyone, except elderly people in rural areas, speaks English well.

Getting Around

By Car   Roads here are good, and mainly traffic free (except around Co-
Road Conditions   penhagen); you can reach many islands by toll-free bridges. The driver needs a valid national driver's license and, if you're driving your own car, it must have a certificate of registration and national plates. A hazard-warning triangle is compulsory and comes with a rented car. The driver and front-seat passengers must wear seat belts. (Motorcyclists must wear helmets and use low-beam headlights always.)

Rules of the Road Drive on the right and give way to traffic from the right. A red-and-white triangular "yield" sign, or a line of white triangles across the road, means you must give way to traffic on the road you are entering. Do not turn right on a red light, even if the road is clear, unless a green arrow indicates otherwise. Use the horn only in case of danger, otherwise flash headlights. Low-beam headlights are compulsory in the dark, mist, or fog; parking lights are not enough. Speed limits are 50 kph (30 mph) in built-up areas; on highways, 100 kph (60 mph); and on other roads, 80 kph (50 mph). If towing a trailer, you must not exceed 70 kph (40 mph). Speeding and, even more, drinking and driving, are treated very severely, even if no damage is caused.

Parking You can normally park on the right-hand side of the road, though not on main roads and highways. *Parkering/Standsning Forbudt* means no parking and no stopping, though you get three minutes' grace to load and unload. Parking disks are used in towns, except where there are parking meters. Get disks from gas stations, post offices, police stations, most tourist offices, and some banks, and set them to show your time of arrival.

Gasoline Gas costs around 6.60 kr. a liter.

Breakdowns Before you leave home, consult your own insurance company. Members of organizations affiliated with AIT can get technical and legal assistance from the **Danish Motoring Organization** (FDM, at Blegdamsvej 124, DK–1200 Copenhagen Ø, tel. 01/38–21–12). All highways have emergency phones, and you can even phone the car rental company. If you cannot drive your car to a repair shop, the rescue corps, Falck (tel. 01/14–22–22), can help anywhere, night or day. Mechanics will either tow the car away or repair it on the spot, in either case charging a fee.

By Train and Bus Traveling by train or bus is easy because Danish State Railways (DSB) and a few private companies cover the country with a dense network of services, supplemented by buses on quieter stretches. Hourly Intercity trains connect the main towns with Copenhagen and Zealand with high-speed diesels or Lyntog, used on the most important stretches. Since all these trains have to cross the Great Belt, between the islands of Funen and Zealand, which takes about an hour, you get a break on board the ferry. You can reserve seats on Intercity trains and Lyntog, and you *must* have a reservation if you plan to cross the Great Belt. Buy tickets at stations for trains, buses, and connecting ferry crossings. As a rule, you can also buy bus tickets on the bus itself, which will be modern and comfortable. Children under age four travel free and those between four and 12 go half-price. Ask about discounts for the over-65s and for groups.

Fares Nordic Tourist Tickets (**Nordpass**) are a good buy for 21 days of unlimited travel by rail and on some sea routes in Denmark, Norway, Sweden, and Finland. The price for an adult going first class is 2,325 kr., second class 1,550 kr.; young adults (12–26) first class 1,740 kr.; second class 1,160 kr.

By Boat Denmark is connected by sea with Germany, Poland, Sweden, Norway, and the Faroes, as well as with Britain. Services across the sea between the three areas of Jutland, Funen, and Zealand are provided by a network of domestic ferries that also connect many smaller islands (100 are inhabited). There are good views as you thread your way between the islands. Danish State Railways and several private shipping companies publish timetables in English, and you should reserve on domestic as well as overseas routes. Ask about special discounts that some companies offer at various times of the year.

By Bicycle One of the best ways to savor the gentle countryside and meet the Danes is by bicycling. Bikes can be rented at some train stations and many tourist offices, as well as from private firms. Further information on cycling can be supplied by the **Danish Cyclists' Association** (*Dansk Cyklist Forbund*, Kjeld Langes Gade 14, DK-1367, Copenhagen). Danish tourist offices in some countries produce a pamphlet entitled "Cycling Holiday in Denmark."

Essential Information

Telephones Pay phones take 25 øre and 1, 5, and 10 kr. coins. Do not put
Local Calls money into the phone until the called number answers. Area codes are now needed even *within* the individual telephone areas.

International Calls Dial 009 plus international code plus area code plus the number. Calls dialed from hotel rooms may be very expensive, so it is better to find a pay phone. For collect calls, dial 0015.

Operators and To speak to an operator, dial 0033; for an international opera-
Information tor, dial 0039.

Mail Surface and airmail letters to the USA cost 4.10 kr. for
Postal Rates 20grams; postcards 3.20 kr. Letters to the United Kingdom and EEC countries cost 3.10 kr., postcards 3 kr. You can buy stamps at post offices or from shops selling postcards.

Receiving Mail If you do not know where you will be staying, have mail sent on to American Express or Poste Restante at any post office. American Express charges noncardholders $2 for each letter.

Shopping Danish design is world famous; good buys are glass, gold- and silverwork, fur, furniture, woodwork, porcelain, knitwear, pipes, embroidery, and arts and crafts of every type. While Copenhagen is naturally the showcase, other towns offer their own particular specialties, often made by local craftworkers who open their workshops to visitors.

VAT Refunds Visitors from a non-EEC country can save 18% by obtaining a refund of the Value Added Tax. Either have the shop send your purchase direct to your home address and pay only the sale price, exclusive of VAT, plus dispatch and insurance costs or if you want to take the goods home yourself, pay the full price in the shop and get a VAT refund at the Danish Duty-Free Shopping Center at Copenhagen Airport (Europe's largest duty-free shop). Look for the Tax-Free sign on shop windows and inquire there.

Opening and **Banks.** In Copenhagen, banks are open weekdays from 9:30 to
Closing Times 4, Thursday until 6; several *bureaux de change* stay open until 10 PM. Outside Copenhagen, banking hours vary, so check locally.

Museums. As a rule, museums are open from 10 to 3 or 11 to 4, but times and days vary. Look at the local papers or ask at tourist offices for the latest times.

Shops. Shops are usually open from 9 to 5:30, stay open on Friday until 7 or 8, and close on Saturday at 1 or 2.

National Holidays January 1 (New Year's Day); March 23–27 (Easter); Apr. 21 (Common Prayer); May 4 (Ascension); May 15 (Pentecost Monday); June 5 (Constitution Day; shops close at noon); December 25, 26.

Dining Danes love their food, and you can find eating places in every price range, from the luxury manor houses, where the proprietor may well do the cooking for you, to the familiar fast-food outlets. Where you see the *Danmenu* sign, you can be certain of a good two-course meal, either lunch or dinner, for 75 kr. Cheapest of all are sausages and hamburgers from sidewalk vans (*pølsvogn*), which provide excellent filling fare.

All Scandinavian countries have their versions of the Scandinavian cold table, but Danes claim that theirs, *det store kolde bord*, is the original, and the best. This is a celebration meal, and the setting of the long table is a work of art, often with paper sculpture, silver platters, and the food itself a miracle of design and decoration. In hotels and restaurants, the cold table is served at lunch only, though you will find a more limited version at hotel breakfasts—a good bet for budget travelers because you can eat as much as you like.

As you would expect, both fish and meat are top quality in this fishing and farming country, and Danish pork is really tasty. Open sandwiches have been elevated to an art form and often look too good to eat. Another specialty, of course, is Danish pastry (*Wiener Brod*), and this original is far superior to anything that dares call itself "Danish pastry" anywhere else.

Mealtimes The Danes start work early, which means they generally eat lunch at noon. Evening meals are also taken early, but visitors can be certain of being able to eat and drink well into the small hours.

Ratings Meal prices vary little between town and country. The difference comes more from the standards than from the restaurant location. While we give approximate gradings below, remember that even a Very Expensive restaurant can provide a Moderate meal if you select carefully. It is essential to study the menu outside *before* you go in, and don't forget the possibility of the *Danmenu*. Prices are per person and include a first course, main course, and dessert, plus taxes and tip, but not wine. Best bets are indicated by a star ★. At press time, there were 6.45 krone to the dollar.

Category	Cost
Very Expensive	over 300 kr.
Expensive	170–300 kr.
Moderate	90–170 kr.
Inexpensive	under 90 kr.

Credit Cards The following credit card abbreviations are used: AE, American Express; DC, Diners Club; MC, MasterCard; V, Visa.

Lodging Accommodations in any category are rarely less than good and always clean. Even inexpensive hotels offer simple designs in good materials and comfortable beds. Many Danes prefer a shower to a bath, so if you particularly want a bath, ask for it, but be prepared to pay more. While the quality and service in city hotels are noteworthy, farmhouse and inn (*kro*) accommodations are better for getting to know the friendly inhabitants of rural parts. Except in the case of rentals, breakfast and taxes are usually included in prices, but check when making a reservation.

Hotels Luxury hotels in the city or countryside offer a very high standard of room, and in a manor house hotel, you could find yourself sleeping in a four-poster bed. Less expensive accommodations can also be found in cities.

Inns (kro) These are the old stagecoach inns scattered throughout Denmark, and they are much less expensive than hotels. Though well modernized, they have the charm of the past and have sometimes added motel-style rooms. You can save money by buying a book of Inn Checks, valid at 66 inns, and offering a discount. These are available from travel agents, or contact **Dansk Kroferie** (Horsens Tourist Office, Søndergade 26, DK-8700 Horsens, tel. 05/62–38–22).

Farm Vacations These are perhaps the best way to see how the Danes live and work. You stay on a farm and share meals with the family; you can even get out and help with the chores. Children love this type of visit, and there is usually some form of children's discount. Contact local tourist offices for information and reservations.

Youth Hostels There are 95 youth hostels in Denmark, all clean and well run, and open to all, regardless of age. If you have an International Youth Hostels Association card (obtainable before you leave home), the average rate is 50 kr. Without the card, the fee is 18 kr. more.

Rentals Another good way to see the countryside on your own terms is to rent a house for a week or more. The chances are that you will be staying in a Danish family's summer home, which is rented out only occasionally, so it will not be impersonal, and, however basic, will have the same high standards of most Danish homes. A simple house with room for four will cost from 1,000 kr. a week. Contact the Danish Tourist Board for details on reservations and payment.

Camping Denmark has more than 500 approved campsites, with a rating system giving them three, two, or one star. All are clean, and three-star sites provide a full range of facilities. You need an International Camping Carnet or Danish Camping Pass (available at any campsite and valid for one year). For more details on camping and discounts for groups or families, contact Campingradet (Skjoldsgade 10, DK-2100 Copenhagen, tel. 01/32–32–22).

Ratings Prices are for two people in a double room and include service and taxes and usually breakfast. Best bets are indicated by a star ★. At press time, there were 6.45 krone to the dollar.

Category	Cost—Copenhagen	Cost—Other Areas
Very Expensive	over 1,100 kr.	over 700 kr.
Expensive	800–1,100 kr.	550–700 kr.

| Moderate | 670–800 kr. | 345–550 kr. |
| Inexpensive | under 670 kr. | under 345 kr. |

Credit Cards The following credit card abbreviations are used: AE, American Express; DC, Diners Club; MC, MasterCard; V, Visa.

Tipping The egalitarian Danes do not expect to be tipped. Service is included in bills for hotels, bars, and restaurants. Taxi drivers round up the fare to the next krone but expect no tip. The exception is hotel porters, who get around 5 kr. a bag; you should also leave 1 or 2 krones for the use of a wash basin in a public rest room.

Copenhagen

Arriving and Departing

By Plane The main airport for both international flights and the domestic network is **Copenhagen Airport,** six miles (10 kilometers) from the center of town.

Between the Airport and Downtown There is frequent bus service to the city; the airport bus to Central Station leaves every 15 minutes, costs 20 kr., and takes around 25 minutes. You pay on the bus. For information, call 01/25–24–20. At around 75 kr. to the center, taxis are more expensive but may be more practicable for groups. A taxi ride takes around 15 minutes.

By Train Copenhagen's **Central Station** is the hub of the train networks. Express trains leave every hour on the hour 6 AM–10 PM for principal towns in Funen and Jutland. Find out more from **DSB Information,** at Central Station (tel. 01/14–17–01); **reservations** at Central Station (tel. 01/14–88–00) and most stations and travel agents. At Copenhagen, for the use of Inter-Railers, there is an Inter-Rail Center that offers rest and a bath, and where you can cook a meal. Open day and evening.

Getting Around

By Bus and Suburban Train A joint fare system, with optional transfers, covers buses and suburban trains (S-trains) in Copenhagen and the surrounding region. A one-hour ticket for three zones costs 7 kr. from bus drivers and train stations. Buy discount tickets from 60–170 kr., depending on the length of travel, from train stations or in some hotels. You can also get a "stamp" card for nine trips per card (valid each trip for a minimum of three zones). This system covers an area that includes Køge, Roskilde, Hillerød, and Elsinore. Buses and S-trains start at 5 AM (Sunday 6 AM). The last bus and S-train leave central Copenhagen around 12:30 AM, but night buses cover certain city routes. Get zone system details from the 24-hour information service, tel. 01/14–17–01 or 01/95–17–01.

In and around Copenhagen you can save by buying a **Copenhagen Card,** a ticket that costs 80 kr. (one day), 140 kr. (two days), or 180 kr. (three days). It also provides free admission to more than 40 museums and other places of interest, including Tivoli Gardens, and a reduction of up to 50% on the ferry crossing to Sweden. You buy the card at tourist offices, hotels, and from travel agents.

By Car   Try not to use your car in Copenhagen: The charm of its pedestrian streets is paid for by a complicated one-way system and difficult parking. Driving out of town is relatively easy, with well-marked roads in all directions.

By Taxi   Taxis are not cheap, but all are metered. The basic charge is 12 kr., plus 8–10 kr. per kilometer. A cab is available when it displays the sign *Fri* (free), and it can be hailed, picked up at taxi stands, or called, tel. 01/35–35–35.

By Bicycle   More than half the Danish population is said to ride bikes, and bikes are popular with visitors, too. Bike rental costs around 25–50 kr. a day, with a deposit of 100–200 kr. Contact **Danwheel-Rent-a-bike**, Colbjørnsengade 3, tel. 01/21–22–27; **Rent-a-Bicycle, Jet-Cycles**, Istegade. 71, tel. 01/23–17–60; or **Københabns Cyclebørs-Velonia**, Gothersgade 157, tel. 01/14–07–17.

Important Addresses and Numbers

Tourist Information   The main information office is **Danmarks Turistråd** (The Danish Tourist Board), H.C. Andersens Boulevard 22, (opposite City Hall), DK-1553 Copenhagen, tel. 01/11–13–25. Open May–Sept. weekdays 9–6, Sat. 9–2; Sun. 9–1; Oct.–Apr., weekdays 9–5, Sat. 9–noon, closed Sun. In summer there are also offices at Elsinore, Hillerød, Køge, Roskilde, Gilleleje, Hundersted, and Tisvildeleje.

Embassies   U.S. Dag Hammarskjöldsallé 24, tel. 01/42–31–44. **Canada.** Kr. Bernikowsgade 1, tel. 01/12–22–99. **U.K.** Kastelsvej 40, tel. 01/26–46–00.

Emergencies   **Police, Fire, Ambulance,** tel. 000 (free from pay phones). **Doctor,** tel. 0041 (fees paid in cash only; night fees around 250 kr.). **Dentist,** Dental Emergency Service, Oslo Plads 14, near Østerport Station (no telephone; emergencies only; cash only). **Pharmacies,** central Copenhagen: *Steno Apotek*, Vesterbrogade 6C, tel. 01/14–82–66; Amager area: *Sønderbro Apotek*, Amagerbrogade 158, (tel. 01/58–01–40; Glostrup area: **Glostrup Apotek,** Hovedvegen 101, tel. 02/96–00–20.

English Bookstores   English-language publications can be found at the Central Station newsstand and in most bookstores around town.

Travel Agencies   **American Express,** Dagmarhus, Amagertorv 18, tel. 01/12–23–01. **Wagon-Lits/Thomas Cook,** Vesterbrogade 2, tel. 01/14–27–47. **Tiaereboro Rejser,** Rådhus Pladsen 75, tel. 01/11–41–00 (can arrange charter flights and accommodations all over Europe).

Guided Tours

Orientation Tours   There are a number of ways to get acquainted with Copenhagen. The following tours leave from Rådhus Pladsen (City Hall Square) at the Lur Blower Column. All are monitored by the tourist office, where you can get full details of their cost. You can buy tickets on board the boat or bus or from travel agencies. The "Harbor and Canal Tour" takes you on a trip around the harbors, passing the Amalienborg Palace, exploring the canals of Christianshavn, and floating under bridges. Bus tours with guide include the short "City Tour" (daily in summer) and "Grand Tour of Copenhagen" (daily all year), covering the major attractions, and the "Royal Tour of Copenhagen" (Tues., Thurs., Sat., and Sun., May through mid-Sept.) taking in

Christiansborg and Amalienborg palaces and Rosenborg Castle. For a combined boat and bus tour, take the good, short "City and Harbor Tour," which includes Copenhagen highlights.

Special-Interest Tours "Under Sail on the Sound": This trip on Denmark's oldest schooner, *Isefjord*, takes around four hours and includes lunch or dinner on board. It leaves from Amaliehaven (behind Copenhagen's Admiral Hotel, Toldbodgade 245) and takes groups of up to 24 people. For details and reservations, phone 01/15–17–29. "Carlsberg Brewery Tour": Meets at the Elephant Gate, Ny Carlsbergvej 140, weekdays at 9, 11, and 2:30 or by arrangement for groups, tel. 01/21–12–21, ext. 1312. Tuborg Breweries also provides brewery tours (Strandvejen 54, bus 1 or 21) weekdays 8:30–2:30 or by arrangement for groups, tel. 01/29–33–11, ext. 2212. Or take the "Royal Copenhagen Porcelain" tour (Smallegade 45, tel. 01/88–48–48), which is given on Tuesday and Thursday at 9:30 for groups of more than five people.

Walking Tours Two-hour guided walking tours, organized by the Copenhagen Tourist Information Center, operate all year (English-speaking guide July and August only). Or set your own sightseeing pace with a taped cassette guide to take you around; the information office will tell you where to buy one. The useful magazine *Copenhagen This Week* (which actually gives information for a month!) also suggests a walking tour or two in each issue.

Regional Tours The Copenhagen Tourist Information Center has full details of tours outside the city, including special visits to castles (including Hamlet's castle), the Viking Ship Museum, and even Sweden.

Personal Guides You can hire a guide and limousine; travel agents have details of price and availability. The Tourist Information Center can recommend multilingual guides for individual needs.

Exploring Copenhagen

When Denmark ruled Norway and Sweden, back in the 15th century, Copenhagen was the capital of all three countries. Today it is still the liveliest Scandinavian capital, with around a million inhabitants. It is a city meant for walking, the first in Europe to realize the value of pedestrian streets in creating a friendly and unthreatening town.

Nor are you ever far from water, be it sea or canal, as you stroll through this jumble of cobbled streets and modern thoroughfares. You should linger, too, in the five main pedestrian streets collectively known as "Strøget," with shops, cellar galleries and craft workshops, and street musicians and vendors by the dozen. Copenhagen is also the great European capital of jazz and rock, with dozens of music cafés and pubs, open until the wee hours.

In summer, Copenhagen moves outside, so sit at one of the sidewalk cafés in the shady squares and get a feel of the city and its people. Somehow, the Danes have managed to combine one of the most democratic societies in the world with a sensible amount of royal pomp—the Changing of the Royal Guard has all the grandeur of high ceremony.

Prices are reasonable by Scandinavian standards and, for a quick snack, it's hard to beat the streetside sausage vans (*pølsevogn*) selling sausages and hamburgers. If you get lost, remember it was the Danish entertainer Victor Borge who said, "The shortest distance between two people is a smile." A passerby will always help.

Rådhus Pladsen and Slotsholmen

1 The area around Strøget is Copenhagen's downtown area. The best place to start a stroll is the **Rådhus** (City Hall) in **Rådhus Pladsen** (City Hall Square). The redbrick Rådhus has a tower, and a statue of Copenhagen's founder, Bishop Absalon, rises above the entrance. Inside is the World Clock—the brainchild of Jens Olsen—as well as the official-function rooms and the council chamber. If you feel energetic, take a guided tour up the 350-foot (106-meter) tower for a panoramic view. *Rådhus Pladsen, tel. 01/15-38-00. Admission: 5 kr. adults, 3 kr. children. Open Mon.–Thurs. 9:30–3, Fri. 9:30–4. Tower: several conducted tours daily, except Sun.*

2 On the right of Rådhus Square is **Lur Blower's Column**—a *lur* is an ancient bronze trumpet—starting point for sightseeing buses, near the Tourist Information Center. If you continue to the square's northeast corner and turn right, you are in Frederiksberggade, the first of the five streets that make up **3** **Strøget.** Walk down this section, and cross the double square of Gammel and Nytorv. The fountain here celebrates the queen's birthday on April 16, when golden apples (really gilded metal balls) dance on the water jets to the delight of the local children.

4 Look right from Nytorv and turn down to Rådhusstraede toward Frederiksholms Canal. This is the entrance to the **National Museet** (National Museum), which includes collections from the Ice Age, superb runic stones from the Viking era, and the Hingdsgavl Dagger. *Frederiksholms Kanal 12, tel. 01/13-44-11. Free. Open Tues.–Sun. (Phone for opening times, which differ according to the exhibit.)*

5 Across from the National Museum is the **Folketing** (Parliament House), in **Christiansborg Slot,** an impressive building on what is said to be the site of the first fortress built by Bishop Absalon in 1167. You can visit these remains under the present building. *Slotsholmen, tel. 01/92-64-92. Admission: 17 kr. adults, 6 kr. children for conducted tours. Tours in English at 11, 1, 3. Closed Mon.*

6 This whole area is an island in the heart of the city, with a cluster of fascinating places to see. There is **Det Kongelige Bibliotek** (Royal Library), with the country's largest collection of books, newspapers, and manuscripts. Look for early records of the Viking journeys to America and Greenland and the statue of the philosopher Kierkegaard in the garden. *Christians Brygge 8. Free. Open weekdays 9–7, Sat. 9–6.*

7 Close to the library is the **Theater Historisk Museet** (Theater History Museum), in the Royal Court Theater of 1766. Also at this address are the **Royal Stables,** which display vehicles used by the Danish monarchy from 1776 to the present day. *Christiansborg Ridebane 18, tel. 01/11-51-76. Admission: 10*

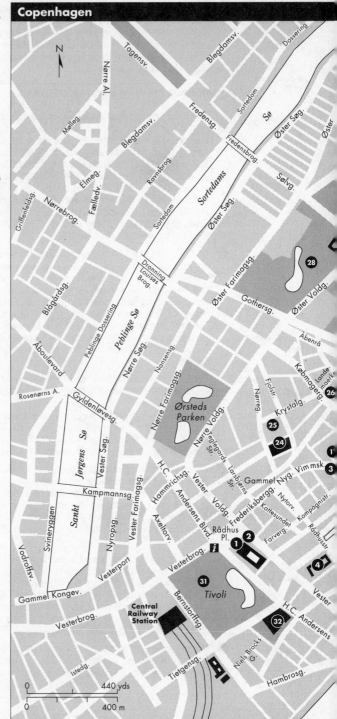

Copenhagen

kr. adults, 5 kr. children. Open June–Sept. Wed., Fri., Sun. 2–4; Oct.–May Wed., Sun. 2–4.

8 Across the street that bears its name is **Tøjhuset Museum** (Royal Armory), with impressive displays of uniforms, weapons, and armor in an arched hall 200 yards (180 meters) long. *Tøjhusgade 3, tel. 01/11–60–37. Free. Open May–Sept. Tues.–Sat. 1–4, Sun. 10–4; Oct.–Apr. Tues.–Sat. 1–3, Sun. 11–4.*

9 A few steps from Tøjhuset is the old Stock Exchange, **Børsen,** said to be the world's oldest one still in use—though only on special occasions—for its original purpose.

That most prolific builder, King Christian IV, was the inspiration behind this beautiful Renaissance structure, and he is said to have had a hand at twisting the tails of the four dragons that form the distinctive spire. With its steep roofs, tiny windows, and many gables, this is one of Copenhagen's treasures. *Closed to the public, unfortunately.*

10 From Børsen, look south across the drawbridge (**Knippelsbro**) that connects Slotsholmen with Christianshavn, one of the oldest parts of Copenhagen, and to the green-and-gold spire of **Vor Frelsers Kirke** (Our Savior's Church), with its curious exterior spiral staircase curling around it. Though you'll need to make a special detour, the view from the top is well worth the climb. *Skt. Annaegade, tel. 01/57–27–98. Admission to steeple: 10 kr. adults, 4 kr. children. Open June–Aug. Mon.–Sat. 9–4:30, Sun. noon–4:30; Sept.–May Mon.–Sat. 10–2, Sun. noon–2.*

Back on Strøget, turn right along the Vimmelskaftet section.
11 Toward the end and to the left is the circa 1730 **Helligånds Kirken** (Church of the Holy Ghost), in its own little world behind a wrought-iron railing. In Amagertorv, the first thing to catch your eye is the Stork Fountain, and in Østergade, the last of the streets that make up Strøget, you cannot miss the tower-
12 ing spire of **Nikolaj Kirke** (Nikolaj Church), one of Copenhagen's landmarks, though now its role is secular—as an exhibition center.

Time Out **Cafe Nikolaj,** inside the old Nikolaj Kirke, is a good place to sample a Danish pastry or light meal. Its long opening hours (noon–midnight) and central location make it a popular choice for meeting or for recharging your batteries. *Closed Mon. and holidays.*

Strøget's greatest attraction is its shops, but it's also fun to stroll and watch the colorful streetlife—guitar players, flower stalls, and peddlars selling balloons, jewelry, and novelty toys.

Around the Royal Palace

Kongens Nytorv (the King's New Market) is the square marking the end of Strøget. On the south side of Kongens Nytrov is
13 the **Kongelige Teater** (Danish Royal Theater), the home of Danish opera, ballet, and drama. The Danish Royal Ballet is one of the world's great companies, with long history and a repertoire ranging from classical to modern productions. The street leading southeast from Kongens Nytorv is *Nyhavn.* Turn right and stroll along beside the far side of **Nyhavn Canal,** with its fleet of old-time sailing ships and well-preserved 18th-century buildings, many of which are now restaurants. Nearer the har-

bor are old shipping warehouses, including two—71 Nyhavn and the Admiral—now converted into comfortable hotels.

Along the harbor front, your constant companions are the hopeful gulls, ready to swoop at the slightest hint of food. Turn

(14) left into Sankt Anna's Plads, there is the **Admiral Hotel,** a charming converted granary overlooking the harbor and one of the city's best-value hotels (*see* Lodging). Turn right into

(15) Amaliegade and go straight ahead for **Amalienborg Palace,** since 1794 the principal royal residence, four identical buildings arranged with geometric precision around an equestrian statue of King Frederik V. Queen Margarethe lives in the palace immediately to the right, while the Dowager Queen Ingrid's home is the building diagonally right. When the Royal Family is in residence during the fall and winter, the Royal Guard and Band march through the city at noon to change the Palace Guard. *The palace interior is closed to the public.*

Rest and linger for a moment on the palace's harbor side, under

(16) the trees and fountains of the **Amaliehavn Gardens.** Across the

(17) square, it is just a step to Bredgade and the **Marmorikirken** (Marble Church), with a dome that looks several sizes too large for the building.

Bredgade is also home to the exotic onion domes of the **Russiske Ortodoxe Kirke** (Russian Orthodox Church), and as you walk to

(18) the right, you soon come to **St. Ansgar's** Roman Catholic

(19) Church, which celebrates Mass daily, and the **Kundindustrimuseet** (Museum of Decorative Art), with a large collection of European and Oriental handicrafts—ceramics, silverware, and tapestry—and an eclectic selection of musical instruments. *Bredgade 68, tel. 01/14–94–52. Admission: free, except 12 kr. July and Aug. Open Tues.–Sun. 1–4.*

A little farther on and into Esplanaden, you come to

(20) **Frihedsmuseet** (Liberty Museum), which, though small, gives an evocative picture of the heroic Danish Resistance in World War II. Appropriately, it is situated at Churchill Parken. *Esplanaden, tel. 01/13–77–14. Free. Open Tues.–Sun. 10–4.*

(21) At the entrance to the park stands the English church, **St.**

(22) **Alban's,** and in the center, the **Kastellet** (Citadel), with two rings of moats. This was the city's main fortress in the 18th century but it suffered a grim reversal in World War II, when the Germans used it as the focal point of their occupation of Denmark. (Free. Open year-round, 6 AM–sunset.) Continue on to the Langelinie, which on Sunday is thronged with promenading

(23) Danes, and at last to **The Little Mermaid,** one of the world's most loved statues, commemorating the character from the story by Hans Christian Andersen.

Around the Strøget

From Langelinie, take the train or bus from Østerport station back to the center. Most of the remaining sights are within

(24) striking distance of the Strøget. **Vor Frue Kirke** (The Church of Our Lady), which is just north of the Strøget, has been Copenhagen's cathedral only since 1924, but a place of worship since the 13th century, when Bishop Absalon, the father of Copenhagen, is said to have built a chapel here. Inside, look particularly at Thorvaldsen's marble sculptures of *Christ and*

the Apostles and Moses and David in bronze. *Fjol Straede, tel. 01/14–41–28. Free. Closed during services.*

㉕ Head north up Fjolstraede until you come to the main **university** building, built in the 19th century on the site of the medieval bishops' palace. Past the university, turn right into Krystal Gade. On the left is the **synagogue,** which has a daily service.

㉖ Just across Købmagergade is the **Runde Tårn,** a round tower built as an observatory in 1642 by Christian IV, a scholar, warrior, and architect of much of the city. It is said that Peter the Great of Russia drove a horse and carriage up the 600 feet (180 meters) of the inner staircase. You'll have to walk, but it's worth it for the view. *Købmagergade, tel. 01/14–86–08. Admission: adults 10 kr., children 4 kr. Tower open May–Sept., daily 10–8; Oct.–Apr., daily 11–4. Observatory open Oct.–Mar., Wed. 7–10 PM if the weather is clear.*

Turn right at Runde Tårn into Landemaerket and then left into Åbenrå. If your appetite for museums is not yet exhausted, turn right out of Åbenrå until you reach Gothersgade
㉗ and then right into Øster Voldgade and **Rosenborg Slot.** This Renaissance castle was built by the ubiquitous Christian IV and is the home of the collection of Crown Jewels, costumes, and royal memorabilia. Don't miss Christian IV's pearl-studded saddle. *Øster Voldgade 4a, tel. 01/15–32–86. Admission: 20 kr. adults, 5 kr. children. Open daily 10–3.*

㉘ The palace is surrounded by gardens, and just across Øster Voldgade is **Botansk Have,** Copenhagen's Botanic Gardens, with 25 acres (102,000 square meters) of plants, plus an observatory and Geological Museum. Taken together with Rosenborg Slot, these gardens could easily occupy a whole day.

㉙ Leave the garden through the north exit to get to **Statens Museum for Kunst** (National Art Gallery), where the official doorman greets you in an old-fashioned outfit with buckle shoes and a cocked hat. The collection inside is impressive and wide ranging: Danish art is well represented, but many come to see the works of Rembrandt, Rubens, Dürer, the French Impressionists, and—in particular—Matisse. *Sølvgade, tel. 01/11–21–26. Free. Open Tues.–Sun. 10–5.*

Time Out | The small, but very good cafeteria in the museum makes an excellent stop for lunch or just a coffee—and to see some of the Matisses on its walls.

㉚ An adjacent building houses the **Hirschprung Collection** of 19th-century Danish art. The Danish school made its name with its evocative representations of the play of light and water that characterizes so much of the Danish countryside. *Stockholmsgade, tel. 01/42–03–36. Free. Open Wed.–Sun. 1–4, closed Mon., Tues.*

From Stockholmsgade, turn right on Sølvgade and then left on Øster Søgade just before the bridge. Continue past two bridges and you eventually reach the head of the harbor. Continue straight until you turn left onto Vesterbrogade.

Your exertions will be rewarded because you'll find Copenhagen's best-known asset just ahead on the right. The
㉛ **Tivoli Gardens** were laid out in 1843 by Georg Carstensen, a Danish architect who managed to persuade King Christian

VIII that if people were well entertained, they would be less likely to talk politics. In the comparatively short season, from May to September, around four million people come through the gates. With its Pantomime Theater and open-air stage, Tivoli is more than an amusement park. It attracts international musical stars of all sorts—soloists and ensembles—with many classical concerts as well as jazz and rock music. Weekends see elaborate fireworks displays and maneuvers by the Tivoli Guard, a youthful (age limit 17) version of the Queen's Royal Guard. Try to see Tivoli at least once by night, when the trees are illuminated, along with the Chinese Pagoda and the main fountain.

32 At the southern end of the gardens, on Hans Christian Andersens Boulevard, is the **Ny Carlsberg Glypotek.** This elaborate neoclassical building houses a collection of works by Gauguin, Degas, and the Impressionists, as well as sculpture—Egyptian, Greek, Roman, and French. The Egyptian hippopotamus is particularly famous. Carl Jacobsen, the founder of Carlsberg, gave Glypotek to Copenhagen, and it is supported by the Carlsberg Foundation. *Dantes Plad, tel. 01/91–10–65. Admission: 12 kr. adults, free for children (adults free on Wed., Sun). Open Tues.–Sun. 10–4.*

What to See and Do with Children

Tivoli is tops with kids, but they also love the hustle of **Strøget.** Take a trip to the **Aquarium** at Strandvejen in Charlottenlund, and don't forget the **Benneweis Circus,** a cavalcade of beautiful, well-cared-for animals, clowns, and other circus *artistes* (leave Tivoli by the Vesterbrogade exit and head straight up Axeltorv). Don't miss the children's zoo, at the **Copenhagen Zoo** on Roskildevej, where children may pet and hold harmless animals. Anyone with a sweet tooth will love **Sømod's Bolcher**, on a passage just off of Nørrgade; it's an old factory that turns out handmade candy. And, at least once, you must treat the family to the Danish specialty, a homemade waffle ice cream.

Off the Beaten Track

A lot of Copenhagen's private galleries are hidden away in small out-of-the-way cellars. Two not to be missed are the **Gallerie Peder Oxe,** attached to the restaurant of the same name (*see* Dining), and **Galerie Asbaek,** a combination café and exhibition of Danish modern painting. **Illum's Bolighus** (the famous store) often has a design exhibition, and its lunch restaurant is an oasis of quiet. Dating from the late 16th century, Hamlet's castle of **Kronborg** in Elsinore (Helsingør), is about 600 years younger than the fortress we imagine from the setting of Shakespeare's tragedy. It boasts a 200-foot-long (61 meters) dining hall and powerful ramparts demonstrating its role as a coastal bulwark (Sweden is only a few miles away). *50 minutes by train from Copenhagen. Admission: 10 kr. Open daily, May–Sept. 10–5, Apr. and Oct. 11–4, Nov.–Mar. 11–3.*

Shopping

Gift Ideas Shopping in Copenhagen is rarely cheap (though you almost always get good value for the money), but inexpensive ideas for gifts include handmade glass spheres and shapes, which you hang inside a window to catch the light; pretty table decorations; and long-lasting candles, often handmade, for which Scandinavia is famous.

Specialty Shops Shopping here is synonymous with Strøget's pedestrian streets. For glass, there's **Holmegaard** at Østergade. Just off the street is **Pistolstraede,** a typical old courtyard that has been lovingly restored and is full of intriguing shops. Another idea for an easy souvenir is **PosterLand,** home of the largest collection of art prints and posters in northern Europe. There are specialists such as **Royal Copenhagen Porcelain,** which has a small museum attached, as has one of Denmark's most famous silversmiths, **Georg Jensen.** Off the eastern end of Strøget in Ny Østergade, the **Pewter Center** has a large pewterware collection, and on Gammel Strand there's another pewter designer, **Selangor Designer,** which started in 1885. Back along Strøget, **Birger Christensen** will offer you a glass of sherry while you look at the furs, while **FONA** is the place to buy Bang & Olufsen stereo systems, so renowned they are on display in the permanent design collection of New York's Museum of Modern Art. B & O is expensive but as a tourist, you get favorable prices and can reclaim the Value-Added Tax (*see* Shopping in Essential Information).

Dining

Some things to bear in mind: Lunch is often the Danes's main meal; in many restaurants and cafés, a salad is included in the price of the main dish and a second cup of coffee is often free, which halves the cost of what may seem an expensive cup.

Price categories are figured per person and include a first course, main course, and dessert, plus tax and tip, though not wine. Best bets are indicated by a star ★. At press time, there were 6.45 krone to the dollar.

Category	Cost
Very Expensive	over 300 kr.
Expensive	170–300 kr.
Moderate	90–170 kr.
Inexpensive	under 90 kr.

Very Expensive **L'Alsace.** This gourmet restaurant is set in an ancient courtyard bedecked with paintings and sculptures by famous artists, among them Ernst, Braque, and Chagall. The art is set off by sparkling white walls and fresh flowers. The Alsatian cuisine is by a talented chef, Franz Stockhammer. *Ny Østergade 9, tel. 01/14–57–43. Dress: informal. Reservations advisable. AE, DC, MC, V. Closed Sun.*

★ **Den Gyldne Fortun–Fiskkaelderen.** You are surrounded by fish here as you eat seafood fresh from the waters around Denmark and Greenland. This is Copenhagen's number-one seafood restaurant. *Ved Stannden 18, tel. 01/12–20–11. Dress: informal. Reservations essential. AE, DC, MC, V. Closed lunch on weekends.*

Kong Hans Kaelder. Superb French cooking is the fare here in one of Copenhagen's oldest buildings (it dates from the 12th century). *Vingardsstraede 6, tel. 01/11–68–68. Tie required. AE, DC, MC, V. Dinner only; closed Sun. and mid-July–mid-Aug.*

Pakhusaeldere. Situated in the basement of 71 Nyhavn Hotel, with old Pomeranian beams along the ceilings, this is principally a grill house, serving fish as well as meat dishes—both French and Danish style. Look for *det store kolde bord* (Danish cold table) at lunchtime. *Nyhavn 71, tel. 01/11–85–85. Dress: informal. Reservations recommended. AE, DC, MC, V.*

★ **Skt. Gertrude's Kloster.** Chef Even Nielsen prepares an international cuisine in this 700-year-old cloister, where you dine by the light of hundreds of candles, among vaults, spiral stairways, and ecclesiastical antiques. *Hauser Plads 32, tel. 01/14–66–30. Jacket and tie. Reservations essential. AE, DC, MC, V.*

Expensive **Els.** The Els is a small, intimate restaurant in an attractive 19th-century building, with the original 1853 decorations and antique murals. Chef Ole Mathiesen specializes in nouvelle French/Danish cuisine and changes his menu daily. *Stora Strandstaede 3, tel. 01/14–13–41. Dress: casual chic. Reservations strongly advised. AE, DC, MC, V.*

Gilleleje. Danish-international cooking is served here on 100-year-old tables made from the wood of a royal ship. The house specialty is Indonesian Rijstafel—it's been on the menu for nearly half a century! *Nyhavn 10, tel. 01/12–58–58. Tie required. Reservations advisable. AE, DC, MC, V. Closed Sun. and July.*

★ **Langelinie Pavillonen.** Pick the right table, and you can watch the Little Mermaid as you eat. The food here is either French or Danish, and the location very attractive—between the old wooded ramparts and the waterfront. There's dancing many evenings. *Langelinie 2100, tel. 01/12–12–14. Jacket and tie, except in summer. Reservations advisable. AE, DC, MC, V.*

Moderate **Copenhagen Corner.** This is a modern restaurant, with excellent international dishes. Eating is outside in summer. *Rådhus Pladsen, tel. 01/14–45–45. Dress: informal. Reservations accepted. AE, DC, MC, V.*

Hereford Beefstouw. If you like tender steaks cooked to order, this is the place for you. There's a large branch at Vesterbrogade 3 (in Tivoli), and another smaller, more intimate one, at Åbenrå. *Vesterbrogade 3, tel. 01/12–74–41; Åbenrå 3, tel. 01/11–91–90. Dress: informal. Reservations handy. AE, DC, MC, V. Closed lunch on weekends.*

★ **Peder Oxe.** The Peder Oxe is located in an 18th-century square in the old center of town, with whitewashed walls, wooden floors, an open fireplace, and crisp damask tablecloths. It's usually crowded with diners from every walk of life. All main courses include a self-service salad bar. *Graabrøde Torv 11, tel. 01/11–00–77. Dress: informal. It's safer to reserve. DC, MC, V.*

Inexpensive **Café Asbaek.** This is, in fact, a picture gallery, with light meals and lunchtime specialties—a relaxed spot. *Ny Adelgade 8, tel. 01/12–24–16. Dress: casual. Reservations accepted. No credit cards. Closed dinner.*

The Cedars. An excellent-value Lebanese restaurant, the Cedars offers Oriental dishes, too. The chef is a Lebanese, Abdo Noujain, and his authentic cooking is served in an Oriental decor. *Lavendelstraede 6, tel. 01/13–55–08. Dress: relaxed. Reservations accepted. DC, MC, V.*

Det Gronne Køkken. The "Green Kitchen" is a vegetarian restaurant with a very popular buffet. *Larsbjornstraede 10, tel. 01/12–70–88. Dress: casual. Reservations not required. No credit cards. Closed Sun.*

Lodging

Copenhagen is well served by a wide range of hotels. Steer clear of those in the red-light district behind the train station, though otherwise you can expect your accommodations to be clean, comfortable, and well run. Most Danish-run hotels include a substantial breakfast in the room rate, but this isn't always the case with foreign chains: Inquire when making reservations. During summer, reservations are always recommended but if you should arrive without one, try booking through Room Service at the airport or at Central Station, Kiosk P. Young travelers should head for "Use It" *(Huset)* at Magstraede 14 (tel. 01/15–63–18); after hours , you can check the bulletin board outside for accommodations suggestions.

Prices are for two people in a double room, including service and taxes and usually breakfast. Best bets are indicated by a star ★. At press time, there were 6.45 krone to the dollar.

Category	Cost
Very Expensive	over 1,100 kr.
Expensive	800–1,000 kr.
Moderate	670–800 kr.
Inexpensive	under 670 kr.

Very Expensive

★ **D'Angleterre.** Copenhagen's most gracious grande dame also ranks as one of Europe's best. Over the years, the late 18th-century D'Angleterre has been frequented by royalty and other famous people. Aristocratic and spacious, it exudes a faultlessly Old World elegance, and service is impeccable. *Kongens Nytorv 34, tel. 01/12–00–95. 139 rooms, 125 with bath. Facilities: restaurant, bar, barber, beauty salon. AE, DC, MC, V.*

★ **Nyhavn 71.** This imposing hotel started life in 1804 as a humble harbor warehouse, though its subsequent metamorphosis has won several design awards. Ask for a room overlooking the harbor—the quaint, porthole-style windows add to the charm. *Nyhavn 71, tel. 01/11–85–85. 82 rooms with bath. Facilities: restaurant, bar. AE, DC, MC.*

SAS Scandinavia. A modern, cloud-scraping tower, the Scandinavia is the city's tallest building. It's set midway between the airport and downtown, facing the old city moats. The prevalent atmosphere is of efficiency and functionality, tempered with expensive plush. *Amager Blvd. 70, tel. 01/11–23–34. 542 rooms with bath. Facilities: sauna, pool, restaurant, bar, coffee shop. AE, DC, MC, V.*

Expensive

City. American tourists love this place, partly because of its convenient downtown location, but also because of its traditional atmosphere and gracious architecture. The hotel restaurant provides only breakfast, but there are many eateries nearby. *Peder Skramsgade 24, tel. 01/13–06–66. 88 rooms with bath. AE, DC, MC, V.*

Savoy. A surprising oasis of peace in a small garden courtyard off Vesterbrogade, the Savoy dates from 1906 and was beautifully renovated a few years ago by a team advised by experts from the Danish National Museum. American guests are here in abundance. *Vesterbrogade 34, tel. 01/31–40–73. 72 rooms with bath. Facilities: restaurant (breakfast only). AE, DC, MC, V.*

Webers. Housed in a century-old building, Webers is yet another American favorite: Try for a room overlooking the attractive courtyard with its pretty fountain. *Vesterbrogade 11B, tel. 01/31–14–32. 80 rooms with bath. Facilities: restaurant (breakfast only), solarium, hairdresser, perfume and film shops. AE, DC, MC, V.*

Moderate

Ascot. A charming old building in the city's downtown area, the Ascot features an elegant wrought-iron staircase and many original features. Guests will appreciate the excellent breakfast buffet. *Studiestraede 57, tel. 01/12–60–00. 70 rooms, 6 apartments, all with bath. Facilities: restaurant. AE, DC, MC.*

★ **Copenhagen Admiral.** A converted 18th-century granary, the Admiral has a massive and imposing exterior that disguises considerable interior comforts. Sturdy wooden beams throughout harmonize with an ultramodern decor. Located at the southern end of Nyhavn, it's just down the street from the Amalienborg Palace, and some windows look out onto the passenger ship terminal. A few duplex suites are in the Expensive category. *Toldbrogade 27–28, tel. 01/11–82–82. 366 rooms with bath. Facilities: restaurant, bar, café, shop, sauna. MC, V.*

Excelsior. Guests here enjoy relaxing—long, cool drink in hand—in the pleasant atrium garden. The circa-1890 building has comfortable, relatively spacious bedrooms and is decorated throughout with sturdy Swedish and Danish pieces. *Colbjørnsgade 4, tel. 01/24–50–85. 55 rooms, 42 with bath. Facilities: restaurant, bar. AE, DC, MC, V. Closed Dec. 19–Jan. 3.*

Neptun. The centrally situated Neptun has been in business for nearly 150 years and shows no signs of flagging. Guest rooms are prettily decorated with mahogany touches and are usually reserved well in advance by American visitors. *Skt. Annae Plads 18, tel. 01/13–89–00. 66 rooms, 11 apartments, all with bath. Facilities: restaurant, café, travel agency. AE, DC, MC, V. Closed Dec. 24–Jan. 2.*

Vestersøhus. This family hotel facing the lakes is heavily patronized by the U.S. Embassy. It features large rooms with balconies from which to take in the wonderful views. The best bet here is a two-room suite, complete with kitchen and balcony. *Vestersøgade 58, tel. 01/11–38–70. 44 rooms, 34 with bath; 15 apartments. Facilities: restaurant (breakfast only), roof garden, laundromat. AE, DC, MC, V.*

Inexpensive

Skovshoved. A charming hotel about 5 miles (8 kilometers) from the center of town, the Skovshoved has as neighbors a few old fishing cottages beside the yacht harbor. Licensed since 1660, it has retained its Old World charm, though fully modernized. Individual rooms vary from very large ones overlooking the sea to smaller rooms overlooking the courtyard. The restaurant provides gourmet international dishes but ranks in the Expensive category. *Strandvejen 257, Charlottenlund, tel. 01/64–00–28. 20 rooms with bath. Facilities: function room. AE, DC, MC.*

Viking. A comfortable, century-old former mansion close to Amalienborg Castle, Nyhavn, and the Little Mermaid, the Viking is convenient to most sights and to public transportation. Rooms are surprisingly spacious. *Bredgade 65, tel. 01/12–45–50. 90 rooms, 19 with bath. Facilities: restaurant on premises (not under same management). AE, DC, MC.*

The Arts

Copenhagen This Week has good information on musical and theatrical events, as well as on films and exhibitions. Concert and festival information is available from **DMIC,** the Dansk Musik Information Center (Vimmelskaftet 48, tel. 01/11–20–86). Copenhagen's main theater and concert season runs from September through May, and tickets can be obtained either directly from theaters or concert halls or from ticket agencies (ask your hotel concierge for advice).

Music   **Tivoli Concert Hall** (Vesterbrogade 3, tel. 01/15–10–12), home of the Zealand Symphony Orchestra, offers more than 150 concerts (many free of charge) each summer, featuring a host of Danish and foreign soloists, conductors, and orchestras.

Theater, Opera, The **Royal Theater** (tel. 01/15–22–20) regularly holds perfor-
and Ballet   mances alternating between theater, ballet, and opera. For English-language theater, attend a performance at the **Mermaid Theater** (Ny Vestergade 7, tel. 01/11–43–03).

Film   The Danes rarely dub films or television imports, so you can often see original American and British movies and TV shows.

Entertainment and Nightlife

Many of the city's restaurants, cafés, bars, and clubs stay open after midnight, some as late as 5 AM. Copenhagen is famous for jazz, but you'll find nightspots catering to musical tastes ranging all the way from bop to ballroom. Younger tourists should make for the **Minefield,** the district around the Nikolaj Kirke that holds scores of trendy discos and dance spots, with admission only the price of a beer.

Nightclubs Some of the most exclusive ones are in the biggest hotels: **Fellini's** in the SAS Royal (Hammerichsgade 1, tel. 01/14–14–12); **After Eight** at SAS Scandinavia (*see* Lodging); and the **Penthouse** at the Sheraton (Vester Søgade 6, tel. 01/14–35–35).

Jazz   Copenhagen has a worldwide reputation for sophisticated jazz clubs. The following are a few of the best: **De Tre Musketerer** (Nikolaj Plads 25); **Jazzhus Monmartre** (Noregade 1), widely held to be one of the best on the Continent; **Jazzhus Slukefter** (Tivoli); and **La Fontaine** (Kompagnistraede 11).

Folklore   For a rousing Danish-style evening, try **Vin & Olgod** (Skindergade 45), which puts on Viking dinners, with dancing and singing, plus demonstrations of an ancient trumpetlike instrument, the lur.

Funen and the Islands

Hans Christian Andersen is said to have given the island of Funen its name "The Garden of Denmark." It's a mixture of orchard and farmland in a rolling landscape that makes it ideal for bicycling as well as driving. There are two main towns: Odense in the north is the birthplace of the fairy tale writer and is devoted to his memory; to the south lies Svendborg, the gateway to the islands of Tåsinge and Langeland, which in turn are connected by road bridges and ferry to the island of Ærø. (Ærø's main town, Ærøkøbing, with its twisting cobbled street and tiny half-timbered houses, has scarcely changed through the centuries. The local people speak their own dialect and claim it as the tongue spoken by angels on Sundays!) Funen is also an island of manors and country houses where, until 1788, peasants were tied to a particular landowner and worked as feudal tenants. The abolition of villenage is one of the major events in Danish history, the start of Denmark's system of social rights, which today makes the country one of the world's most liberal.

Getting Around

The best starting point from Copehangen is over the Great Belt, by train or car, to Nyborg on Funen's east coast. From there, though public transport is good, the easiest way is undoubtedly by car. (Get details of rentals from local tourist offices.) Distances in Funen and its islands are short, but there is much to see and you could easily spend two or three days here. The choice is to circle the islands from Nyborg or to base yourself either in Odense or Svendborg and make excursions. The itinerary that follows can be used for either.

Guided Tours

There are few organized tours of any of area Denmark outside Copenhagen. The Funen town of Odense has a two-hour tour that operates Monday through Saturday during July and August only, however, and it takes in all the town's major sights. Expect to see anything and everything to do with native son Hans Christian Andersen.

There's also a day trip to Odense from Copenhagen each Sunday from mid-May to mid-September. Lasting about 11 hours, the trip includes stops at several picturesque villages and a lightning visit to Egeskov Castle. Departure is at 8:30 AM from Copenhagen's City Hall Square.

Tourist Information

Nyborg: Torvet 9, tel. 09/31–02–80.
Odense: Rådhuset, tel. 09/12–75–20.
Syendborg: Møllergade 20, tel. 09/21–09–80.

Exploring

Before heading north out of Nyborg for Kerteminde, take a look at the 12th-century **Nyborg Slot** (Nyborg Castle), one of the country's royal castles; the first Danish constitution, the Great Charter, was granted here by Erik Glipping in 1282. The castle has a fine interior with a magnificent view from the battlements. *Slotspladsen. Admission: 10 kr. adults, 3 kr. children. Open Mar., Apr., Oct., and Nov., Tues.–Sun. 10–3; May and Sept., Tues.–Sun. 9–6; June–Aug., daily 9–6.*

Just south of Kerteminde lies the village of Ladby. Stop here to see the **Ladbyskibet,** the 1,100-year-old underground remains of a Viking chieftain's burial, complete with his 72-foot-long (22 meters) ship. The warrior was equipped for his trip to Valhalla with his weapons, four hunting dogs, and 11 horses. *Vikingsvej 12. Admission: 10 kr. adults, 3 kr. children. Open May–Sept., daily 10–6; Oct.–Apr., daily 10–3.*

Kerteminde itself is the island's most important fishing village as well as a picturesque summer resort. If old half-timbered houses are your passion, stroll down **Langegade.**

Back on the road to Odense, stop off at **Bjørnholt Keramik** in Munkebo to see a Danish potter hard at work. Visitors are always welcome, and you can buy what you like. *Risingavej 12. Open weekdays.*

Odense Odense is one of Denmark's best-known cities; it celebrated its thousandth year in 1988; Hans Christian Andersen is big news every year. Try to spend at least one night in Odense. Go first to **H. C. Andersens Barnsdomshjem** (Andersen's childhood home), which contains mementos of his childhood as well as letters from Charles Dickens and Swedish soprano Jenny Lind. *Munkemøllestraede 3. Admission: 2 kr. adults, 1 kr. children. Open daily, Apr.–Sept. 10–5; Oct.–Mar. noon–3.*

Your next stop must be the **H. C. Andersens Hus** (Hans Andersen Museum), which houses a large collection devoted to the writer's life, with pictures, letters, manuscripts, and personal belongings. Among the most evocative rooms is one furnished exactly as his Copenhagen study was; you can get a feel for the height of the man from the immense size of his long, narrow boots, casually tossed into a corner. *Hans Jensenstraede 37. Admission: 15 kr. adults, 3 kr. children. Open June–Aug., daily 9–7, rest of year 10–5 or 10–3; it's best to check.*

Don't neglect **Den Fynske Landsby** (Funen Village), two miles (three kilometers) south; an enjoyable way of getting there is to travel down the Odense River by boat. The open-air museum-village is made up of 20 farm buildings, including workshops, a vicarage, a watermill, and a windmill. There's a little open-air theater, too, which in summer puts on adaptations of you-know-who's classic tales. *Sejerskovvej 20. Admission: 10 kr., adults, 2 kr. children. Open Apr.–Oct., daily 9 until dusk; Nov.–Mar., Sun. and holidays only.*

Assens Head southwest once again, all the way to Funen's west coast and the town of Assens. The town is home to a nautical museum, housed in a 17th-century building that was the home of Danish naval hero Peter Willemoes. *Østergade 36. Admission: 6 kr. adults, 3 kr. children. Open daily June–Aug.*

Take a picnic with you when heading out south of town. Outdoors-loving Tove and Gunner Sylvest have created some outstanding gardens, **De 7 Haver** (The Seven Gardens), where you can park yourself and your lunch at special vantage points dramatically overlooking the sea. *Å Stradndvej 62, tel. 09/74–12–85. Admission: 20 kr. adults, 5 kr. children. Open daily, May–Oct.*

Continue south to **Millinge,** where shoppers can stop in at **Grete Hjort Design** (Hornegyden 16; open May–Sept.), which sells hats, clothes, and handbags. On the left, just before you reach

Funen and the Islands

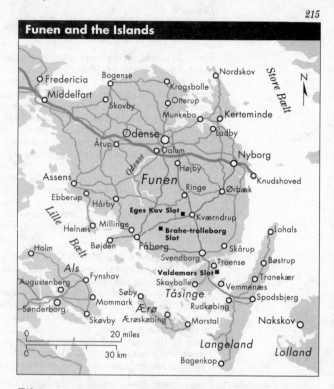

Fåborg, you can't miss the impressive gates of **Steensgårds Herregård,** a magnificent three-wing manor house-hotel with an excellent restaurant (*see* Dining and Lodging).

Fåborg   Fåborg is a lovely little town that four times a day echoes to the dulcet chiming of the **Klokketårnet's** (belfry's) carillon, the largest in Funen. Dating from 1725, **Den Gamla Gård** (the Old Merchant's House) is worth a stop, having been set up as a historical museum in 1932. *Holkegade 1, tel. 09/61-33-38. Admission: 10 kr. adults, free for children. Open daily May–Sept.*

Anyone who enjoys art should take time out to visit the **Fåborg Museum for Fynsk Malerkunst** (Art Gallery for Funen Artists), which has a charming collection of paintings and sculpture by "the Funen Artists," mainly dating from 1880–1920. The gallery does full justice to painters such as Peter Hansen, Fritz Syberg, and Johannes Larsen, whose works are full of the special light that so often illuminates Scandinavian painting. *Grønnegade 75. Admission: 10 kr. adults, 5 kr. children. Open Apr.–Sept., daily 10–4; Oct.–Mar., daily 11–3.*

Ærøskøbing   From Fåborg, take the car ferry to Søby at the northern tip of **Ærø** Island. To get the full flavor of this charming place, whose roads wend through fertile fields and past picturesque thatched farmhouses, you could leave your car at Fåborg and rent a bicycle for the short trip from Soby to Ærøskøbing, the main town, and the old naval port of Marstal in the southeast (no more than 12 miles or 20 kilometers away). When you've spent an hour walking through the cobbled 17th- and 18th-century streets of Ærøskøbing, you will see why it draws visitors back year after year.

From Ærøskøbing, the ferry takes just a tad more than an hour to return to Svendborg, Funen's southernmost town, which has some noteworthy manors and country houses nearby. Svendborg is also the gateway to the country's southern islands, so leave it for the moment and cross over the bridge into the tiny island of Tåsinge. Dating from around 1640, **Valdemars Slot** is one of Denmark's oldest privately owned castles, now a sumptuously furnished naval museum, and has a wonderful view of Svendborsund. Most interesting, however, is the castle church, illuminated only by candlelight, and the castle restaurant (*See* Dining and Lodging) situated beneath the church. The Tea Pavilion is now a café looking over Lunkebugten Bay to one of south Funen's best stretches of beach. *Slotsalleen 100, Troense, tel. 09/22–61–06. Admission: 20 kr. adults, 10 kr. children. Open May–Sept., daily 10–5; Oct.–Apr., weekends 10–5.*

Troense Pretty Troense is one of Denmark's best preserved villages, with its rows of half-timbered houses. Once the home port for many sailing ships, commercial and Viking, today the harbor is more likely to be stuffed with the pencil-slim masts of pleasure yachts. Tåsinge is connected with the island of **Langeland** by a causeway-bridge. The largest island in the southern archipelago (in this itinerary, only Funen is larger), Langeland is rich in relics of the past, and the beaches are worth scouting out. Langeland's main town is **Rudkøbing**, whose native son H. C. Ørsted is remembered as the discoverer of electromagnetism.

Svendborg Head back now, passing through Tåsinge, to Funen's Svendborg. Lying just north of town is **Eges Kov Slot,** one of Denmark's most famous castles. Egeskov means "oak forest," and an entire one was felled around 1540 to form the piles on which the castle was built. It ranks as the best-preserved island castle in Europe, with gardens that attract even the professionals. Unfortunately, few sections of the castle are open to the public. There is also a **Veteran Museum,** which displays a collection of old cars, aircraft, motorcycles, and horse-drawn carriages. *Kvaerndrup. Admission (combined ticket for castle, park, and museum): 48 kr. adults, 28 kr. children. Open May–Sept., daily 9–6; Oct.–Apr., daily 10–5.*

From Egeskov, turn briefly toward Fåborg and drive past **Brahe-trolleborg Slot,** once a Cistercian abbey (circa 1170) and later a baronial castle. Here, at the end of villenage, Denmark's 18th-century high chancellor, John Ludvig Reventlow, allowed his peasants to burn a wooden horse to symbolize his granting their freedom. *Park open daily 9–5.*

Dining and Lodging

Most hotels maintain prices throughout the year, but it's worth asking about off-season rates (October through May). Many hotels and inns have special weekend rates. Inquire about the **Funen Combi Pension,** a flexible package that allows visitors to stay at one place but lunch and dine en route. The islands are also endowed with numerous campsites and youth hostels, all of which are clean and attractively set; for information, contact the local tourist office.

For details and price category definitions, *see* Dining and Lodging in Essential Information.

Ærøskøbing
Lodging
★

Ærøhus. Close to the beach and the harbor, the Ærøhus is a large, half-timbered building with a steep red roof; from the outside, at least, it bears more than a passing resemblance to a huge barn. Inside it's decorated with a lot of comfort and much rural simplicity. The five cottages in the garden all come equipped with little terraces. *Vertergade 38 (AErø), tel. 09/ 52–10–03. 35 rooms, 12 with bath; 5 cottages. Facilities: restaurant, garden, terrace. AE. Closed end of Dec. and first 3 weeks in Jan. Moderate.*

Assens
Dining and Lodging

G1. Brydegard. This popular inn lies about 6 miles (10 kilometers) south of Assens, near Ebberup, and is within a stone's throw of the sea. The converted old farmhouse serves up excellent Danish fare, in surroundings that are suitably atmospheric. Rooms are available as well for visitors who want to prolong their stay. *Helnaesvej 4, Hårby (Funen), tel. 09/77–14–75. 17 rooms, 3 apartments, all with bath. No credit cards. Moderate.*

Falsled
Dining and Lodging
★

Falsled Kro. The very picture of a cozy Danish roadside inn back in the 15th century, this long, low, thatched building was a smugglers' hideaway. Guest rooms overlook either the garden or the harbor and are furnished with a mix of antique and modern pieces; most are divided with a sitting area and fireplace. The Falsled's restaurant is superb and enjoys a considerable reputation (reservations are a must). The menu is weighted toward local seafood (try the mussels from a bed just a short row away), though game is often featured. The wine list is pretty exceptional as well. *Assensvej 513, just north of Millinge on the Assens–Fåborg highway (Funen), tel. 09/68–11–11. 14 rooms with bath. AE, DC, MC. Closed mid-Dec.–Feb. Very Expensive.*

Millinge
Dining and Lodging
★

Steensgård Herregårdspension. A really magnificent manor house dating from the early 1300s, the Steensgård Herregårdspension (the Manor House Hotel) is one of Denmark's most memorable places to stay. The interior is an elegant symphony of wood paneling, tile and parquet floors, carved antique furniture, and porcelain stoves—there's even a resident ghost. The parklike grounds contain a shelter for deer and wild boar, ancient chestnut trees, and a flower-bedecked terrace. The candle-lit restaurant is, as you'd expect, top-notch; try the game if it's on the menu. *Steensgård 4 (Funen), tel. 09/61–94–90. 15 rooms, 13 with bath. Facilities: tennis, horseback riding, restaurant. AE, MC, V. Closed Jan.*

Monkebo
Dining

Rudolf Mathis. Expect delectable seafood specialties and a splendid view of Kerteminde harbor at this traditional Danish restaurant. *Dosseringen 13 (Funen), tel. 09/32–32–33. Dress: casual. Reservations accepted. No credit cards. Closed Mon. Moderate.*

Dining and Lodging

Munkebo Kro. The half-timbered and thatched Monkebo Kro has been in business as an inn since 1816. The decor is traditional, with lots of pewter goblets, hanging lamps, and polished wood. The restaurant is locally famous for its fried eels. *Fjordvej 56–58 (Funen), tel. 09/97–40–30. 20 rooms with bath. Facilities: restaurant. Dress: casual. Reservations advised. DC, MC. Closed Dec. 21–Jan. 5. Expensive.*

Nyborg
Lodging

Nyborg Strand. A seaside location adds to the charm of this typical Danish hotel, parts of which have been softened with age. It's clean, bright, and popular. *Østerøvej 2 (Funen), tel. 09/31–31–31. 247 rooms with bath. Facilities: pool, sauna, game room, restaurant, bar, garden. AE, DC, MC, V. Moderate.*

Odense
Dining

Under Lindetraet. This award-winning restaurant has collected praise both for its excellent culinary concoctions and extensive wine cellar. *Just opposite Hans Christian Andersen's house, Ramherred 2 (Funen), tel. 09/12–92–86. Dress: informal. Reservations advised. DC, MC, V. Closed July. Expensive.*

Hereford Beefstouw. If herring and caviar are beginning to wear thin, or if you're simply a steak-and-potatoes person, give this popular chain restaurant a try. The steaks here are among the best you'll find in this fish-oriented country and come grilled any way you like them. *Vestergade 13 (Funen), tel. 09/12–02–22. Dress: casual. Reservations accepted. AE, DC, MC, V. Moderate.*

Dining and Lodging

Den Gamle Kro. Antique-filled bedrooms and an atmospheric, brick-vaulted restaurant are the main pull at this delightful inn, which dates back to 1683. It's just a few minutes walk from Andersen's house. There's patio dining, weather permitting. *Overgade 23 (Funen), tel. 09/12–14–33. 8 rooms with bath. DC, MC, V. Expensive.*

Svendborg
Dining

Borgen. Good local fare at reasonable prices is what you'll find at this cozy corner overlooking the harbor. Try the shellfish (particularly the mussels) or the eel. *Faergevej 34 (Funen), tel. 09/21–29–76. Dress: casual. Reservations handy. No credit cards. Moderate.*

Troense
Dining

Valdemars Slot. Situated in the ancient vaults beneath the church of Valdemar Castle, this restaurant provides a cool retreat and an excellent meal. Arched ceilings, tiled floors, and candlelight set the elegant tone. *Slotsalleen 100 (Tåsinge), tel. 09/22–59–00. Dress: casual chic. Reservations advised. MC. Closed Mon. Expensive.*

Jutland and the Lakes

The peninsula of Jutland is the only part of Denmark that is attached to the continent of Europe; its southern boundary is the frontier with Germany. A tenth of the peninsula consists of moors and sand dunes, though the latter are almost entirely confined to the western coast. Jutland's other nine-tenths are devoted to agriculture and, to a lesser extent, forestry. To the east of the region, facing Funen, lie the deeply indented and well-wooded fjords, which run for miles inland.

Getting Around

If you follow this itinerary directly after the tour around Funen, the best route is to head northwest from Odense through Middelfart, and then on to Vejle. By train, either from Odense or Copenhagen, the starting point is Kolding, to the south of Vejle. There are good train and bus services between all the main centers, but our tour is best taken by car. Delightful though they are, the offshore islands are suitable only for those with a lot of time, since many involve a night's stay.

Guided Tours

Guided tours are scarce in these parts, the tourist office having ascertained that most visitors prefer to rent cars and take in the sights at their own pace. However, several Jutland towns— such as Århus, Aalborg, and Silkeborg—offer recorded taped tours, à la Walkman, from May to August. Ribe even goes so far as to have a "nightwatchman" wander around the town center telling traditional stories and expounding on the town's historical exploits (*see* Exploring). Århus also offers an excursion giving a quick overview of the surrounding countryside, including lightning visits to a few well-chosen castles. Tours last about 2½ hours; tours to the north of town are given on Sunday, while everything to the south is covered each Tuesday.

Tourist Information

Aalborg: Øster 8, tel. 08/12–60–22.
Århus: Rådhuset, tel. 06/12–16–00.
Billund: c/o Legoland A/S, tel. 05/33–19–26.
Herning: Bregade 35, tel. 07/12–44–70.
Kolding: Torvet 5, tel. 05/53–21–00.
Randers: Hellingåndshuset, Erik Menveds Plads 1, tel. 06/42–44–77.
Silkeborg: Torvet 9, tel. 06/82–19–11.
Skanderborg: Biblioteket, Biulbiotekstorvet 2, tel. 06/52–09–33.
Vejle: Den Smidske Gard, Søndergade 14, tel. 05/82–19–55.
Viborg: 5 Nytorv, tel. 06/62–16–17.

Exploring

If **Kolding** is your starting point, you might first like to look at the impressive and much restored **Koldinghus** castle (open May–Sept., daily 10–5; Oct.–Apr., Mon.–Sat. noon–3, Sun. 10–3), built in 1208, and **Den Geografiske Have** (Geographical Garden, open daily, June and Aug. 9–7; July 9–8; Sept.–May 10–6), which includes some 2,000 plants from all parts of the world, arranged geographically.

Vejle But our Jutland tour really starts in Vejle, about 12 miles (20 kilometers) to the north of Kolding. Vejle is beautifully positioned on the fjord amid forest-clad hills, looking toward the Kattegat, the strait that divides Jutland and Funen. You can hear the time of day chiming on an old Dominican monastery clock; the clock remains, but the monastery has long since given way to the town's imposing 19th-century **Rådhuset** (Town Hall). Vejle's tourist office is part of **Den Smidske Gård,** a merchant's house dating from 1799; the building also houses the town's local history exhibition.

Leaving Vejle, take the road north to Jelling through the **Grejs valley,** which has an abundance of plants and birdlife. In **Jelling,** you'll find two enormous **burial mounds** marking the ancient seat of King Gorm the Old and his wife Thyra. Between the mounds are the **Jelling runic stones,** one of which is known as "Denmark's Certificate of Baptism" because it shows the oldest known figure of Christ in Scandinavia. In a curious mixture of paganism and Christianity, the inscription explains that the

Jutland and the Lakes

0 ——————————— 40 miles
0 ——————————— 60 km

Skagerrak

Skagen
Hirtshals
Hjørring
Frederikshavn
Sæby
Brønderslev
Hanstholm
Nørresundby
Thisted
Limfjord
Aalborg
Lim-
fjord
Løgstør
Nibe
Nykøping
Djursland
Peninsula
Hadsund
Lemvig
Hobro
Mariager Fjord
Limfjord
Venö
Bugt
Skive
Mariager
Streier
Holstebro
Viborg
Randers
Nissum
Fjord
Gudenå
Auning
Djursland
Peninsula
Grenå
Ringkøbing
Silkeborg
Ebeltoft
Storå
Herning
Århus
Ringköbing
Fjord
Skjernå
Brande
Skanderborg
Samsø
Skjern
Grindsted
Givskud
Jelling
Horsens
Varde
Billund
Vejle
Esbjerg
Vardeå
Vejle Fjord
Fredericia
Store Bælt
Fanø
Vejnes
Middelfart
Holsted
Kolding
Funen
Ribe
Kongeå
Fladså
Christiansfeld
Odense
Rømø
Haderslev
Nyborg
Skærbæk
Fåborg
Åbenrå
Svendborg

N

stone was erected by Gorm's son, King Harald, who brought Christianity to the Danes in AD 960.

A few miles to the north is **Loveparken** (the Lion Park) at Givskud, where about 40 lions live in open surroundings. Other animals can be seen as well, including baboon, elephants, and, oddly enough, camels. *Admission: 40 kr. adults, 25 kr. children. Open end of Apr.–last Sun. in Sept. daily 10–6:30.*

Silkeborg   Head north toward Silkeborg, set on the banks of the River Gudenå in Jutland's Lake District. The district stretches from Silkeborg in the west to Skanderborg in the east and has some of the loveliest scenery in Denmark, plus one of Denmark's "mountains" (a decent-size hill in just about any other country)—**Himmelbjerget,** measuring 483 feet (147 meters) above sea level. The best way to explore the area is by water because the Gudenå winds its way some 100 miles (160 kilometers) through lakes and wooded hillsides down to the sea. You can take one of the excursion boats or, best of all, the world's last coal-paddle steamer, *Hjejlen,* based at Silkeborg. Since 1861, it has paddled its way through narrow stretches of fjord, where the treetops meet overhead, to the foot of the mighty Himmelbjerget in the Lake of Julsø. From that point, you may clamber up the narrow paths through heather and trees to the top, where an 80-foot (24-meter) tower stands sentinel, placed there on Constitution Day in 1875 in memory of King Frederik VII.

Silkeborg's other attraction is housed in the **Silkeborg Kulturhistoriske Museum** (Museum of Culture and History): the 2,200-year-old **Tollund Man,** one of the so-called bog-people whose corpse was preserved, strangely, by natural ingredients in the soil and water. *Admission: 10 kr. adults, 5 kr. children. Open mid-Apr.–mid-Oct., daily 10–5; mid-Oct.–mid-Apr., Wed., Sat., and Sun. 10–noon and 2–4.*

Århus   On the coast, lying directly east from Silkeborg, is Århus, Denmark's second-largest city. The town is at its liveliest during the 10-day **Århus Festival** in September, which brings together everything from classical concerts to clowning, jazz and folk music, theater, exhibitions, street entertainers, beer tents, and a lot of sports and children's events. The festival began as a greeting to the university students at the start of their new academic year. Now, however, it has become an international event and makes use of the fine early 18th-century organ in the 13th-century **Domkirke,** Scandinavia's longest church. For a fine view of the town and its surroundings, take a trip up the 200-foot (61-meter) tower of the **Rådhuset** (Town Hall). The Rådhuset was built between 1938 and 1942 as a showpiece of Danish architecture and makes lavish use of glass and murals; it features an immense carpet depicting the city map. In front of the Rådhuset is the *Pig's Well,* a charming study of a sow and her piglets by Danish sculptress Mogens Bøggild, and, at the foot of the tower, is the fountain called *Agnete and the Merman.*

Make every effort to see the town's open-air museum, known as **Den Gamle By** (The Old Town). It features 65 half-timbered houses, a mill, and a millstream. The period interiors let visitors feel they are seeing a Danish market town as Hans Christian Andersen might have seen it. *Købstadsmuseet. Admission: 25 kr. adults, 10 kr. children. Open Apr. and Oct.,* *daily 10–4; May–Sept., daily 10–5; Nov.–Mar., weekdays 11–1, weekends 11–3.*

Randers Heading north again toward Aalborg, you come first to the medieval town of Randers, where, in 1340, the Danish patriot Niels Ebbesen killed Count Gert the Bald of Holstein, whose army was then occupying most of Jutland. Ebbesen's statue stands in front of the Rådhus (Town Hall). To the east of Randers is the **Djursland peninsula**, a popular vacation area with many fine Jutland manor houses open to the public. If your time is limited, you can feel safe in choosing to visit only **Gammel Estrup**, a grand 17th-century manor in the tiny village of Auning, containing the Jutland Manor House Museum, full of rich period furnishings, including an alchemist's cellar. There's also an agricultural museum. *Admission: 10 kr. adults, 2 kr. children. Manor and farm open May–Oct., daily 10–5; Nov.– Apr. (manor), Tues.–Sun. 11–3, (farm) weekends 11–4.*

Aalborg Aalborg is set at the narrowest point of the great waterway of northern Jutland, the Limfjord, the gateway between east and west. You'll find charming combinations of new and old; twisting lanes filled with medieval houses run side by side with broad modern boulevards. **Jomfru Ane Gade** is a tiny cobbled street in the center of Aalborg, with a number of restaurants, inns, and sidewalk cafés. Major sights include the magnificent **Jens Bangs Stenhus** (Jens Bang's stone house), a five-story building dating from 1642; it has a remarkably atmospheric restaurant and an excellent wine cellar (*see* Dining and Lodging). The best way to see this historic city is to take a guided walking tour (in English), which takes in the 16th-century cathedral, the **Budolfi Kirke**, dedicated to the English saint Botolph, and the early 15th-century **Helligandsklosteret** (Monastery of the Holy Ghost). *Cost: 15 kr. adults, 10 kr. children. Tours start at 1:30 each Thurs. from end of June–1st week in Aug., starting at the tourist office.*

Just to the north, at Nørresundby, is **Lindholm Høje,** a Viking and Iron Age burial place, where stones placed in the shape of a ship enclose 150 of the site's 682 graves.

Skagen Aalborg is the turning point for this itinerary, though if you have some extra time to spare, head north right up to the tip of Jutland to Skagen. Many artists and writers have been inspired by Skagen's picturesque streets and its luminous quality of light. The 19th-century Danish artist Drachmann and his friends actually founded the Skagen school of painting; you can see their efforts on display in the local **Skagens Museum.** *Admission: 25 kr. adults, free for children. Open Apr.–Oct., daily 10–5; Nov.–Mar., weekends 11–3.*

Viborg Heading south once more, you next come to Viborg, whose history goes back to the 8th century when it was a trading post and a place of pagan sacrifice. Later it became a center of Christianity, with many monasteries and even an episcopal residence. The 1,000-year-old **Haervejen,** the old military road that starts near here, was once Denmark's most important connection with the outside world. Legend has it that in the 11th century King Canute set out from Viborg on his way to conquer England. Today, in the town, you can buy cuff links made with reproductions of the silver coin minted by the king (*before* he achieved his goal) with the inscription "Knud, Englands Konge" (Canute, King of England).

Built in 1130, Viborg's **Domkirke** (cathedral) was once the largest granite church in the world. Today only the crypt remains of the original building, restored and reopened in 1876. The early 20th-century biblical frescoes are by Danish painter Joakim Skovgaard.

Viborg is near some terrific walking country, beside **Hald Sø** (Hald Lake) and on the heatherclad **Dollerup Bakker** (Dollerup Hills); the area is particularly well suited for fishing. Next head southwest to **Herning,** an old moorland town whose flourishing knitwear industry is based on original farmhouse knitting. Painting and sculpture are important to the town, and, as if to prove the point, Henry Moore's *Sitting Woman* does her stuff outside the Congress Center. Don't miss the remarkable circular house, with its 400-foot (122-meter) outer frieze by Carl-Henning Pedersen; it houses the **Carl-Henning Pedersen and Else Afelt's Museum,** set within a sculpture park artistically strewn with modern iron sculptures. *Admission: 20 kr. adults, free for children. Open daily 10–4.*

Ribe Much farther south, but well worth the extra driving time, is Ribe, Denmark's oldest town, whose medieval town center is preserved by the Danish National Trust. From May to mid-September, a nightwatchman goes around the town telling of its ancient history and singing traditional songs. Visitors can accompany him nightly by gathering at the main square at 10 PM. The town's present cathedral stands on the site of one of Denmark's earliest wooden churches, built around AD 860. The present cathedral was erected between 1117 and 1225 but has undergone many alterations. Its tower dates from the 14th century, the bell serving as an alarm and storm warning (making use of the tower's wide view of the surrounding marshland). Note the "Cat Head Door": It's said to be for the exclusive use of the devil.

Time Out Hospitality is the rule of the house at the old inn known as **Weis' Stue,** on Ribe's market square. Stop in for a meal—or even stay the night in one of the nine bedrooms—and admire the 400-year-old clock in the parlor, a carved cupboard dated 1500, and a candelabrum from 1599.

Devotees of the half-timbered house can get their fill on Sønderportsgade, Puggårdsgade, and Sortebrødregade, dating mainly from the 16th century. Ribe's **Black Friars Abbey** (Kloster) is the best preserved and most beautiful monastery in Denmark, barring that at Helsingør.

Before heading back to Vejle, stop off at **Billund** to see the country's most famous tourist attraction. **Legoland** is a park whose makers have re-created cities, towns, and villages from all over the world, as well as the Pyramids, a statue of Sitting Bull, Mount Rushmore, a safari park, even a Wild West saloon—all constructed entirely of millions of tiny plastic Lego bricks. The park alone could keep visitors—especially children—occupied for days, but there are also exhibitions inside the main building, where the highpoint is undoubtedly **Titania's Palace,** a sumptuous dollhouse built in 1907 by Sir Neville Wilkinson for his daughter. *Admission: 36 kr. adults, 18 kr. children. Open May–mid-Sept., daily 10–8; last 2 weeks in Sept., daily 10–5. Indoor displays open Easter–3rd Sun. in Dec., daily 10–5.*

Dining and Lodging

For details and price category definitions, *see* Dining and Lodging in Essential Information.

Aalborg
Dining
★
Duus Vinkiaedler. Occupying part of Jens Bang's house, and with 300 years of tradition behind it, Duus Vinkiaelder is one of Aalborg's best-known eateries, with a reputation that makes reservations a prudent move. The wine cellar is phenomenal, a legacy of the days when Bang himself would barter timber for wine and spices in Spain and France. *9 Østerå, tel. 08/12–50–56. Dress: casual. Reservations required. No credit cards. Closed Sun. Expensive.*

Lodging
Phønix. A centrally located hotel in an attractive historic building, the Phønix is discreet, traditional, and exceptionally popular. Guest rooms are comfortable and as spacious as you could wish; as with so many Danish hotels, the staff is extremely pleasant and helpful. One of the restaurants, the Halling, is highly recommended. *Vesterbro 77, tel. 08/12–00–11. 185 rooms, 180 with bath. Facilities: sauna, solarium, game room, 2 restaurants, bar, café. AE, DC, MC. Very Expensive.*

Scheelsminde. A pleasantly austere manor house built in 1808, the Scheelsminde was for a time run as a farm before some enterprising soul long ago decided to try his hand in the hotel business. The venture has been a success. A traditional atmosphere prevails in the public rooms, while bedrooms are Danish-modern. The restaurant has made a name for itself for both its food and wine offerings. *Scheelsmindevej 35, tel. 08/18–32–33. 70 rooms with bath. Facilities: sauna, Jacuzzi, solarium, garden, restaurant. AE, DC, MC, V. Very Expensive.*

Århus
Dining
★
De 4 Årstider. Mouth-watering French food is served here at the Four Seasons, which ranks as one of Scandinavia's finest restaurants. And it's almost always crowded. *Åboulevarden, tel. 06/19–96–96. Jacket and tie. Reservations required. DC, MC, V. Closed Sun. Expensive.*

Randers
Dining and Lodging
★
Randers. Top marks to this Danish institution: Anyone who enjoys a bit of pampering would do well to come here. Service is friendly, efficient, and prompt (are they psychic?), decor is as plush as Denmark ever gets, and the Grill Room restaurant regularly produces memorable meals. *Torvegade 11, tel. 06/42–34–22. 82 rooms with bath. Facilities: restaurant. Dress: casual chic. Reservations advised. AE, DC, MC, V. Closed Dec. 23–Jan. 1. Expensive.*

Ribe
Dining and Lodging
★
Dagmar. Right in the center of town, and occupying a building that dates from 1581, the Dagmar is a cozy place with lots of period atmosphere. It encapsulates all the charm of the 16th century—stained-glass windows, frescoes, sloping floors, carved chairs. The restaurant has a delightful central fireplace, and the food is first-class: Try the fillet of veal à la Dagmar. *Torvet 1, tel. 05/42–00–33. 50 rooms with bath. Facilities: restaurant. Dress: casual chic. Reservations advised. AE, DC, MC, V. Expensive.*

Skagen
Lodging
★
Brøndums. With an attractive beach-side location, the Brøndums is a decidedly friendly hotel, a nice place to return to after a long day of sightseeing. It's decorated throughout with paintings by 19th-century artists of the "Skagen School." The restaurant puts on a terrific cold table and has lots of fish spe-

cialties. There's often music in the evening, while the garden is a good spot in which to admire the town's uniquely luminous light. *Anchersvej 3, tel. 08/44–15–55. 14 rooms with bath. Facilities: restaurant. Dress: casual. Reservations are a good idea. AE, MC, V. Expensive.*

Vejle
Lodging
★

Munkebjerg. On the outskirts of Vejle, the Munkebjerg was founded in 1880 by a nature lover who chose the site for the marvelous scenery: As recently as 1933, guests' luggage had to be hauled up to the hotel on the back of a donkey because there was no road. The original building has long since gone, but the spectacular view over beech woods and fjord remains. Guest rooms are modern and light, with fresh colors and stripped-pine decor. The Munkebjerg has two fine restaurants, both of which specialize in first-class French dishes. *Munkebjergvej 125, tel. 05/72–35–00. 148 rooms with bath. Facilities: 2 restaurants, pool, sauna, solarium, game room, biking, jogging and walking trails, tennis, heliport, nearby riding school and golf course. AE, DC, MC, V. Very Expensive.*

10 Finland

Introduction

If you like majestic open spaces, fine architecture, and civilized living—and can afford the prices—Finland is for you. It is a land of lakes, 187,888 at the last count, and of trees. It is a land where nature is so prized that even the design of city buildings reflects the soaring spaces of the countryside.

The music of Sibelius, Finland's most famous son, tells you what to expect from this Nordic landscape. Both can swing from the somber nocturne of mid-winter darkness to the tremolo of sunlight slanting through pine and bone-white birch or from the crescendo of a sunset before it fades into the next day's dawn. Similarly, the Finnish people reflect the changing moods of their land and climate. They can get annoyed when described as "children of nature," but the description is apt. Their affinity with nature has produced some of the world's greatest designers and architects. Many American cities have buildings designed by Alvar Aalto and the Saarinens, Eliel and son Eero. In fact, Eliel and his family moved to the United States in 1923 and became American citizens—but it was to a lonely Finnish seashore that Saarinen had his ashes returned.

Until 1917, Finland (the Finns call it *Suomi)* was under the domination of its nearest neighbors, Sweden and Russia, who fought over it for centuries. After more than 600 years under Swedish rule and 100 under the tsars, the country inevitably bears many traces of these two cultures, including a small (6%) Swedish-speaking population and a scattering of Russian Orthodox churches.

But the Finns themselves are neither Scandinavian nor Slavic. All that is known of their origins—they speak a Finno-Ugrian tongue, part Finnish, part Hungarian—is that they are descended from wandering groups of people who probably came from west of Russia's Ural mountains before the Christian era and settled on the swampy shores of the Gulf of Finland.

There is a tough, resilient quality in the Finn. No other country that shared its border with the Soviet Union in 1939 now retains its independence. Indeed, no other country has fought the Soviets to a standstill, as the Finns did in the Winter War of 1939-40. This resilience, in part, stems from the turbulence of the country's past but also comes from the people's strength and determination to work the land and survive the long winters. No wonder there is a poet-philosopher lurking in most Finns, one who sometimes drowns his melancholic, darker side in the bottle. For the Finn is in a state of constant confrontation —against the weather, the land, and the Russian bear breathing down his neck. The Finn is stubborn, patriotic, and insular, yet he is not aggressively nationalistic. On the contrary, rather than being proud of past battles, the Finn is proud of finding ways to live in peace with the Soviet Union. His country's neutrality and his own personal freedom are what he tenaciously holds on to and will never easily relinquish.

The average Finn doesn't volunteer much information, but that's due to reserve, not indifference. Make the first approach and you may have a friend for life. Finns like their silent spaces, though, and won't appreciate back-slapping familiarity

Finland

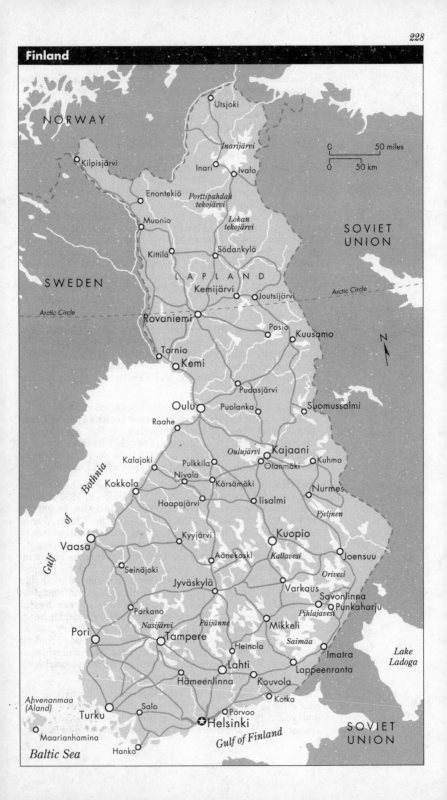

NORWAY

Utsjoki

Inarijärvi

Kilpisjärvi

Inari Ivalo

Enontekiö *Porttipahdan tekojärvi*

Muonio *Lokan tekojärvi*

SOVIET UNION

SWEDEN

Kittilä Sodankylä

L A P L A N D

Kemijärvi

Arctic Circle

Rovaniemi Joutsijärvi

Arctic Circle

Posio Kuusamo

Tornio

Kemi

Pudasjärvi

Oulu Puolanka Suomussalmi

Raahe

Oulujärvi Kajaani

Kalajoki Pulkkila Otanmäki Kuhmo

Nivala Kärsämäki

Kokkola

Haapajärvi Iisalmi Nurmes

Pjeljnen

Kyyjärvi Kuopio

Vaasa Aänekoski *Kallavesi* Joensuu

Seinäjoki *Orivesi*

Jyväskylä Varkaus

Savonlinna

Parkano Punkaharju

Pihlajavesi

Pori *Nasijärvi* *Päijänne* Mikkeli

Tampere *Saimaa*

Heinola Imatra Lake Ladoga

Lahti Lappeenranta

Hämeenlinna Kouvola

Ahvenanmaa (Aland) Salo Kotka

Turku Porvoo

Maarianhamina ★Helsinki SOVIET UNION

Hanko *Gulf of Finland*

Baltic Sea

Gulf of Bothnia

0   50 miles

0   50 km

N

—least of all in the sauna, still regarded by many as a spiritual, as well as a cleansing, experience.

Before You Go

When to Go The tourist summer season runs from mid-June until mid-August. Outside this period, many amenities and attractions close or operate on much reduced schedules. But there are advantages to visiting Finland off-season, not the least being that you avoid the mosquitoes, which can be fearsome, especially in the north. Also, hotel rates, especially in vacation villages, may drop by 15% to 40%, and the fall colors (from early September in the far north, October in the south) are spectacular—they even have a special name, *ruskaa*. January through March (through April in the north) is the main cross-country skiing season, and in the lengthening spring days you can get a great suntan. Spring is brief but magical, as the snows melt, the ice breaks up, and nature explodes into life almost overnight.

Climate Generally speaking, the spring and summer seasons begin a month earlier in the south of Finland than they do in the far north. You can expect warm (not hot) days in Helsinki from mid-May, in Lapland from mid-June. The midnight sun can be seen from May to July, depending on the region. In mid-winter there is a corresponding period when the sun does not rise at all but when there can be magnificent displays of the Northern Lights. Even in Helsinki, summer nights are brief and never really dark, whereas in mid-winter daylight lasts only a few hours.

The following are average daily maximum and minimum temperatures for Helsinki.

Jan.	26F	− 3C	**May**	56F	14C	**Sept.**	59F	15C
	17	− 9		40	4		46	8
Feb.	25F	− 4C	**June**	66F	19C	**Oct.**	47F	8C
	15	−10		49	9		37	3
Mar.	32F	0C	**July**	71F	22C	**Nov.**	37F	3C
	20	− 7		55	13		30	−1
Apr.	44F	6C	**Aug.**	68F	20C	**Dec.**	31F	−1C
	30	− 1		53	12		23	−5

Currency The unit of currency in Finland is the Finnmark (FIM), divided into 100 penniä. There are bills of FIM 10, 50, 100, 500, and 1,000. Coins are 5, 10, 20, and 50 penniä, and FIM 1 and FIM 5. At press time (fall 1988), the exchange rate was about FIM 4 to the dollar and FIM 6.8 to the pound. Credit cards are widely accepted. Traveler's checks can be exchanged in banks and at bureaux de change at international airports, major train stations, seaports, and hotels.

What It Will Cost The cost of hotels and restaurants in Finland matches the standard of living: Both are high! Expect to spend about 50% more on lodging than in southern Europe, and even more for meals. Prices are highest in Helsinki; otherwise they vary little throughout the country. Taxes are already included in hotel and restaurant charges, and there is no airport departure tax. However, the price of many goods includes an 11% sales tax (*see* Shopping in Essential Information).

Sample Prices Cup of coffee, FIM 5; bottle of beer, FIM 12; Coca-Cola, FIM 5; ham sandwich, FIM 10.50; one-mile taxi ride, FIM 13.50.

Customs on Arrival Europeans aged 16 and over entering Finland may bring in 200 cigarettes or 250 grams of other tobacco; visitors from outside Europe may bring in twice as much. All visitors aged 20 or over may also bring in two liters of beer, one liter of alcohol under 18% volume, and one liter over 18% volume. Visitors aged 18 or over may import two liters of beer and two liters of alcohol under 18% volume. Goods up to a value of FIM 1,000 may be imported, but be sure to check restrictions on the amount and type of foodstuffs allowed.

Language The official languages of Finland are Finnish and Swedish, though only a small minority (about 6%) speak Swedish. English is widely spoken among people in the travel industry and by many younger Finns, though they're often shy about using it. Nearly all tourist sites and attractions provide texts in English.

Getting Around

By Car Finland has no superhighways, but there is an expanding net-
Road Conditions work of efficient, major roads. In some areas, however, especially in the north, you can expect long stretches of dirt road. These are usually adequate to good, although during the spring thaw they become difficult to negotiate. Away from the larger towns, traffic is light, but take moose and reindeer warning signs seriously.

Rules of the Road Drive is on the right. At intersections, cars coming from the right have priority. Speed limits (usually marked) are 50 kph (30 mph) in built-up areas, 80 kph (50 mph) in the country, and 110 kph (70 mph) on main roads. Drunk-driving laws are strictly enforced. Low-beam headlights must be used at all times outside city areas, seat belts are compulsory, and you must carry a warning triangle in case of breakdown.

Parking This is a problem only in some city centers. Major cities offer multistory garages; most towns have on-street meters. Make sure that you are legally parked, or your car may be towed away.

Breakdowns and The **Automobile and Touring Club of Finland** (ACTF, tel. 90/
Accidents 694–0022) operates a road patrol service on main roads, where you'll also find a limited number of emergency telephones. If you're involved in an accident, report it without delay to the **Finnish Motor Insurers' Bureau** (tel. 90/19251) as well as to the police.

By Train Finland's extensive rail system reaches all main centers of the country and offers high standards of comfort and cleanliness.

Fares A special **Finnrail Pass** entitles you to unlimited travel for eight, 15, or 22 days. A 15-day second-class ticket costs $118; first class, $177. Children pay half fare. These tickets are available in the USA from **Holiday Tours of America** (tel. 212/832–9072) or **Scantours** (tel. 213/451–0911); in the U.K., from **Finlandia Travel** (tel. 01/839–4741). Other reductions apply to children, groups of three or more, and senior citizens. Reservations are essential on special fast trains.

By Plane Finnair (tel. 90/410411) operates an elaborate network of flights linking 21 towns in Finland. For $250, **Holiday Ticket**

guarantees you unlimited travel for 15 days; visitors aged 12–23 can get a **Youth Holiday Ticket** for $200. Other discounts apply to family groups, children, and senior citizens.

By Bus Bus travel plays a leading role in Finland, and the country's bus system provides the most extensive travel network of all; it can take you virtually anywhere. A **Coach Holiday Ticket,** available from bus stations and travel agencies, entitles you to 1,000 kilometers (621 miles) of bus travel for 220 FIM. Additional discounts apply for children, family groups, and senior citizens (*see* Helsinki: Getting Around).

By Boat Helsinki and Turku have regular sea links with the Åland Islands in the Baltic Sea. From mid-June to mid-August you can cruise the labyrinthine lakes of the Finnish interior. Try to include at least one of these trips in your itinerary. Full timetables are available from the Finnish Tourist Board.

By Bicycle Planned bicycle routes, generally following old country roads, are provided in many areas. The main advantages to the cyclist are the lack of hills and the absence of heavy traffic. Bikes can be rented in most tourist centers. The Finnish **Youth Hostel Association** (tel. 90/694–0377) offers accommodation packages of four, seven, or 14 days to tie in with visitors' cycling tours.

Essential Information

Telephones
Local Calls Hotels charge a substantial fee for all calls. You can avoid this by using the pay phones provided in most lobbies. Have some FIM 1 and FIM 5 coins ready. Note that the Finnish letters *a*, *ä*, and *o* come at the end of the alphabet; this may be useful when looking up names in the telephone book.

International Calls The least expensive way to make an international call is to go to a telegraph office; these are marked *Lennätin* and usually adjoin the post office. An operator will assign you a private booth and collect payment at the end of the call. Except in a few remote areas, there is direct automatic dialing to Britain and the USA.

Operators and Information For information about telephone charges, dial 09; for number inquiries in the Helsinki area, 012; for other areas, 020.

Mail
Postal Rates Airmail rates to North America are FIM 3 for a letter of up to 10 grams and FIM 2.40 for postcards. Letters and postcards to the United Kingdom cost FIM 2.40.

Receiving Mail If you're uncertain about where you'll be staying, ensure that mail sent to you is marked "Poste Restante" and addressed to the Main Post Office, Mannerheimintie 11,00100 Helsinki, or to major post offices in other towns. American Express offers a free Clients' Mail Service and will hold mail for up to one month (*see* Helsinki: Important Addresses). The Finland Travel Bureau also provides a free mail service for foreigners: Mail should be addressed to its Mail Dept., Box 319, 00101 Helsinki, and collected from the office at Kaivokatu 10A.

Shopping Finnish products are known for their cool, crisp, modern designs. Ceramics, glass, handwoven textiles, fashions, furs, stainless steel, metal and semiprecious jewelry, and wooden toys are some of the items to look for.

VAT Refunds If you purchase goods worth more than FIM 150 in any of the many shops marked "tax-free for tourists," you can get an 11%

refund when you leave Finland. Show your passport and the store will give you a check for the appropriate amount, which you can cash at most departure points.

Opening and Closing Times

Banks. Open weekdays 9:30–4.

Museums. Opening hours vary considerably, so check individual listings. Most close one day a week, usually Monday.

Shops. Usually open weekdays 9–6, Saturday 9–2. Department stores and supermarkets often stay open until 8 on Monday and Friday.

National Holidays January 1 (New Year's Day); January 7 (Epiphany); March 24, 27 (Easter); April 30 (May Day Eve); May 1 (May Day); May 4 (Ascension); May 13, 14 (Whitsun); June 23, 24 (Midsummer's Eve and Day); November 4 (All Saints'); December 6 (Independence); December 24, 26 (Christmas).

Dining You can choose among restaurants, taverns, coffee houses, and snack bars. As in other parts of Scandinavia, the cold table *(voileipäpöytä)* is often a work of art as well as a feast. It's usually available at lunchtime. Special Finnish dishes include reindeer casserole *(poronkä*ristys; superb in Lapland); salmon, herring, and various fresh-water fish; and meat balls *(lihapullia)* with a tasty sauce. Crayfish parties are popular between the end of July and early September. For a delicious dessert, try cloudberries (related to blackberries) and other forest fruits. And if you're heading north and want to find out where you can sample Lapland specialties, get the *Lappi à la Carte* booklet from the Finnish Tourist board.

Mealtimes The Finns eat early: lunch runs from 11 or noon to 1 or 2, dinner from 4 to 7. Fixed-price menus, available at these times, are far more moderately priced than the à la carte choices served outside these hours.

Ratings Prices are per person and include first course, main course, dessert, and service charge—but not wine. Most restaurant checks include a service charge *(sisältää palvelupalkkion)*. If you want to leave an additional tip—and it really isn't necessary—it's enough to round the figure off to the nearest 5 or 10 FIM. Best bets are indicated by a star ★. At press time, there were 4 finnmarks (FIM) to the dollar.

Category	Helsinki	Rest of Country
Very Expensive	over FIM 200	over FIM 180
Expensive	FIM 160–200	FIM 140–180
Moderate	FIM 100–160	FIM 85–140
Inexpensive	under FIM 100	under FIM 85

If one selects the fixed-price menu, which usually covers two courses and coffee, the cost of the meal will be substantially less.

Credit Cards The following abbreviations are used: AE, American Express; DC, Diners Club; MC, MasterCard; V, Visa.

Lodging The range of accommodations available in Finland includes hotels, motels, boarding houses, private homes, rented chalets and cottages, farmhouses, youth hostels, and campsites. There is no official system of classification, but standards are generally high. If you haven't reserved a room in advance, you can make reservations at the **Hotel Reservation Center** at Helsinki Train Station (tel. 90/171133) or through a travel agency.

Hotels Nearly all hotels in Finland are modern or will have been recently renovated; a few occupy fine old manor houses. Most have rooms with bath or shower. Prices normally include breakfast and often a morning sauna and swim. The Finncheck voucher system, operating in many hotels from June through August, offers good discounts. Only the first night can be reserved, but subsequent reservations can be made free from any Finncheck hotel. Ask at the Finnish Tourist Board for further details.

Several hotel groups, such as Rantasipi and Arctia, offer special packages, and some hotels drop their prices substantially in July, unless there's a festival going on.

Summer Hotels University students' accommodations are turned into "Summer Hotels" from June through August; these offer modern facilities at slightly lower-than-average prices.

Boarding Houses and Private Homes These provide the least expensive accommodations. Local tourist offices have lists.

Rentals The choice is huge, and the chalets and cottages are nearly always in delightful lakeside or seashore settings. For comfortable (not luxurious) accommodations, count on paying FIM 800–FIM 1500 for a four-person weekly rental. A central reservations agency is **Lomarengas** (tel. 90/441346).

Farmhouses These are located in attractive settings, usually near water. A central reservations agency is **Suomen 4H-liitto** (tel. 90/642233).

Youth Hostels These range from empty schools to small manor houses. There are no age restrictions. You can get a list from the Finnish Tourist Board.

Camping There are about 350 Finnish campsites, all classified into one of three grades. All offer showers and cooking facilities, and many include cottages for rent. A list is available from the Finnish Tourist Board.

Ratings Prices are for two people in a double room, and include breakfast and service charge. Best bets are indicated by a star ★. At press time, there were 4 finnmarks (FIM) to the dollar.

Category	Helsinki	Rest of Country
Very Expensive	over FIM 700	over FIM 600
Expensive	FIM 500–700	FIM 400–600
Moderate	FIM 300–500	FIM 250–400
Inexpensive	under FIM 300	under FIM 250

Credit Cards The following credit-card abbreviations are used: AE, American Express; DC, Diners Club; MC, MasterCard; V, Visa.

Tipping The Finns are less tip-conscious than other Europeans. For restaurant tips, *see* Dining, above. You can give taxi drivers a few small coins, but it's not essential. Train and airport porters have a fixed charge. It's not necessary to tip hotel doormen for carrying bags to the check-in counter, but give bellhops FIM 2–FIM 5 for carrying bags to your room. The obligatory check-room fee of FIM 3–FIM 4 for restaurant doormen is usually clearly indicated; if not, give FIM 3–FIM 10, depending on the number in your party.

Helsinki

Arriving and Departing

By Plane All international flights arrive at Helsinki's **Vantaa Airport,** 20 kilometers (12 miles) north of the city. For arrival and departure information, phone 90/829–2451.

Between the Airport and Downtown Finnair buses leave two to four times an hour for the City Terminal, located at the Inter-Continental hotel (Töölönkatu 21, tel. 90/410111) and the main train station. The trip takes about 25 minutes and costs FIM 12. A local bus service (no. 615) operates on a similar frequency to the train station and costs FIM 10. Expect to pay about FIM 100 for a taxi into the city center. If you are driving, the way is well marked to Highway 137 and *Keskusta,* downtown Helsinki.

By Train Helsinki's main train station is in the heart of the city. For train information, phone 90/659411.

By Bus The terminal for many local buses is the Train Station Square *(Rautatientori).* The main bus station is located off Mannerheimintie between Salomonkatu and Simonkatu. For information phone 90/602122.

By Sea The Silja Line terminal for ships arriving from Stockholm is at Olympialaituri, on the west side of the South Harbor. The Finnjet-Silja Line and Viking Lines terminal for ships arriving from Travemünde and Stockholm is at Katajanokka, on the east side of the South Harbor.

Getting Around

The center of Helsinki is compact and best explored on foot. However, the **Helsinki City Tourist Office** provides a free Helsinki route map that shows all public transportation. As far as public transportation tickets go, your best buy is the **Helsinki Card,** which gives unlimited travel on city public transportation, as well as free entry to many museums, a free sightseeing tour, and a variety of other discounts. It's available for one, two, or three days (FIM 60, 80, and 95; half-price for children). You can buy it at most hotels and at the Helsinki City Tourist Office. Another option is a special **Tourist Ticket** (FIM 40), valid for 24 hours of unlimited public transportation on vehicles marked with two black arrows on a yellow background. You can buy it at the Helsinki City Tourist Office.

By Subway One subway line links the train station with Itäkeskus, in the eastern suburbs. It runs from 6 AM to 11 PM and each ride costs FIM 6.

By Streetcar These run from 5:30 or 6 AM to 10:30 PM or 1 AM, depending on the line. The fare is the same as for the subway. The 3T streetcar follows a figure-eight circuit around the city center, and, during summer, provides commentary in several languages.

By Taxi Taxis are all marked *taksi*. The meters start at FIM 10.20, with the fare rising on a kilometer basis. There is a surcharge after 6 PM and on weekends.

By Boat In summer there are regular boat services from the South Harbor market square to the islands of Suomenlinna and Korkeasaari.

Important Addresses and Numbers

Tourist Information The **Helsinki City Tourist Office** is near the South Harbor, at Pohjoisesplanadi 19, tel. 90/1693757; open weekdays 8:30–6, Sat. 8:30–1. The **Finnish Tourist Board's Tourist Information Office** (covering all of Finland) is nearby at Unioninkatu 26, tel. 90/144511; open weekdays 9–1 and 2–3:30.

Embassies U.S. Itäinen Puistotie 14A, tel. 90/171931. **Canadian.** Pohjoisesplanadi 25B, tel. 90/171141. **U.K.** Uudenmaankatu 16–20, tel. 90/647922.

Emergencies Police, tel. 000; **Ambulance,** tel. 000; Doctor, tel. 008; **Dentist,** tel. 90/736166; **Pharmacy,** *Yliopiston Aptekki,* Mannerheimintie 96 (always open).

English Bookstores You'll find a good selection of books in English at **Akateeminen Kirjakauppa** (Keskuskatu 1) and **Suomalainen Kirjakauppa** (Aleksanterinkatu 23). English newspapers are on sale at the train station and in major hotels. For news in English, dial 040.

Travel Agencies **American Express,** Travek Travel Bureau, Katajanokan Pohjoisranta 9–13, tel. 90/661631. **Thomas Cook,** Finland Travel Bureau, Kaivokatu 10A, tel. 90/18261.

Guided Tours

Orientation Tours **Suomen Turistiauto** (tel. 90/585166) runs a "City Tour" (one and a half hours, starting 1 PM) that covers the main city-center sights and a "Daughter of the Baltic" tour (two and three-quarter hours, starting 10:15 AM) that extends out to the modern suburbs and the island of Suomenlinna. Both start from Asema-aukio, across from the main post office, and you can buy tickets on the bus 15 minutes before departure. **Ageba Travel Agency** (tel. 90/669193) offers a similar but longer combination tour (four hours) including lunch, starting from the Olympic Harbor at 10 AM. **Royal Line Rautakorpi** (tel. 90/652088) operates "Helsinki by Sea" boat tours (one and a half hours, starting at 11, 1, and 3) from the South Harbor market square. The same agency runs "Lunch Cruises" to several island restaurants, departing from the South Harbor market square at noon.

Walking Tours You can get an excellent free booklet, *See Helsinki on Foot,* detailing six walking tours of various lengths, from the Helsinki City Tourist Office.

Personal Guides Contact the **Guide Reservation Center** (tel. 90/601966).

Excursions **Finland Travel Bureau** (tel. 90/18261) offers a four-hour trip on Wednesdays to Hvitträsk, for a tour of historic homes of Finnish artists and architects. On Sundays there is a six-hour trip to Sibelius's home at Ainola and the beautiful old town of Porvoo. No-visa trips by sea to the Soviet Union (Leningrad or Riga, three nights) are offered by **Finnsov Tours** (tel. 90/6942011).

Saimaa Lines offers one-day cruises (with visa) to Tallinn (tel. 90/6587330).

Exploring Helsinki

Helsinki is a city of the sea. It was built on peninsulas that stab into the Baltic, and streets and avenues curve around bays, bridges arch over to nearby islands, and ferries reach out to islands farther off shore. Sweet-tasting salt air hovers over the city, and the sounds from the vessels steaming into port resonate off the city's buildings.

Like other European capitals, Helsinki has expanded its boundaries to absorb a quarter of the Finnish population, and the suburbs sprawl from one peninsula to another. The Helsinki resident must know the peninsulas in order to know his city. However, most of the city's sights, hotels, and restaurants cluster on one peninsula, thus forming a compact hub of special interest for the traveler.

Unlike most other European capitals, Helsinki is "new." About 400 years ago, King Gustav Vasa of Sweden decided to woo trade from the Estonian city of Tallinn and thus challenge the monopoly of the Hanseatic League. To do this, he commanded the peoples of four Finnish towns to pack up their belongings and relocate at the rapids on the river Vantaa. This new town became Helsinki.

For three centuries, Helsinki had its ups and downs as a trading town. Turku, to the west of Helsinki, remained the capital and the center of the country's intellectual pursuits. Ironically, not until Finland was thrust under the dominance of Russia did Helsinki's fortunes improve. Tsar Alexander wanted Finland's political center closer to Russia and, in 1812, selected Helsinki as the new capital. Shortly after the capital was moved from Turku to Helsinki, Turku suffered a monstrous fire. Such was the inferno that the university left Turku in its ashes and moved to Helsinki. From then on Helsinki's future was secure.

Another fortuitous event, at least for the future of Helsinki, was the fire that occurred just before the tsar named the city the capital. The fire swept through the city, permitting the construction of new buildings suitable for a nation's capital. The German-born architect Carl Ludvig Engel was commissioned to rebuild the city, and, as a result, Helsinki has some of the purest neo-Classical architecture in the world. Add to this foundation the modern buildings designed by talented Finnish architects and you have a European capital city that is as architecturally eye-catching as it is different from its Scandinavian neighbors or the rest of Europe.

Helsinki is an easy city to visit on foot. Not only are the key sights on one peninsula but most of them are also contained in the area between the railway station and the central **Market Square** (Kauppatori). Let's start exploring at Kauppatori, since every morning, except Sunday, it is the liveliest place in town.

❶ If you have not already done so, you may first want to call in at the **City Tourist Office** to collect maps, brochures, and the latest information about what's on and where.

Across from the City Tourist Office and beside the South Harbor is the **Kauppatori.** Sometimes it seems that every Helsinki wife is here seeking the best buys for the day or simply catching up on the gossip. All around are stalls selling everything from colorful, freshly cut flowers to ripe fruit, from vegetables trucked in from the hinterland to handicrafts made in small villages. Look at the fruit stalls—mountains of strawberries, raspberries, blueberries, and, if you're lucky, cloudberries *(suomuurain)*, which grow above the Arctic Circle in the midnight sun. Closer to the dock are fresh fish, caught that morning in the Baltic Sea and still flopping. The market is a hive of activity and, in a sense, the heartbeat of everyday life in Helsinki. Stop at one of the food stalls and, as you sip your coffee, notice the **statue of Havis Amanda** standing in the square. This beautiful lady is loved by all Finns, and every May Day eve she is crowned by students with their white caps who wade through the protective moat to embrace her.

The market ends about 1 PM and, in the summer, the fruit and vegetable stalls are replaced with arts and crafts. This happens at about 3 PM and lasts until about 8 PM.

Another heartbeat of Helsinki is across the street, on the other side of Pohjoisesplanadi. The uniformed guards will prevent you from entering, but the building is the **Presidential Palace** and next to it is City Hall and various administrative offices. Across from the palace is the waterfront, where ferries and sightseeing boats set out into the bay. On a summer's day it is a sailor's vision: sails hoisted and taut to the wind, yacht clubs beckoning, and island waters to explore. In the winter, the cold winds off the Baltic make you scurry away from this exposed waterfront and perhaps take shelter at Orthodox **Uspenski Cathedral,** the red-brick edifice perched above the west side of the market.

Just behind the cathedral is the district of **Katajanokka.** Here the 19th-century brick warehouses are slowly being renovated to form a complex of boutiques, arts and craft studios, and restaurants. One can find innovative designs at these shops, and the restaurants tend to offer lighter fare, which can make this a tempting area to stop for lunch.

A five-minute stroll north of City Hall brings you into **Senaatintori** (Senate Square), the heart of neo-Classical Helsinki and one of the most graceful squares in Europe, dominated by the domed **Lutheran Cathedral** (Tuomiokirkko). The square is the work of Ludvig Engel. The harmony created with the Tuomiokirkko, the university, and the State Council Building places you amidst one of the purest styles of European architecture. In the past, Senaatintori used to have a dignified, stately air, but now, in the summer, sunworshippers gather on the wide steps leading up to Tuomiokirkko and, throughout the year, there is always a bustle around the relatively new **Senaati Shopping Center** on the square's south side.

Most of the streets leading off Senaatintori contain government and administrative offices. Worth noting is **Snellmaninkatu** (street), named after J. V. Snellman. Known for awakening the Finnish national spirit, he was instrumental in persuading the Russian overlords to officially recognize the Finnish language and accept the idea of a separate Finnish currency. It is Snellman's statue that stands in front of the Bank of Finland.

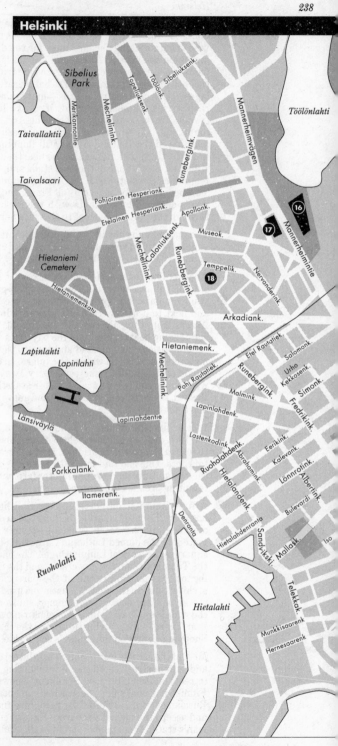

Helsinki

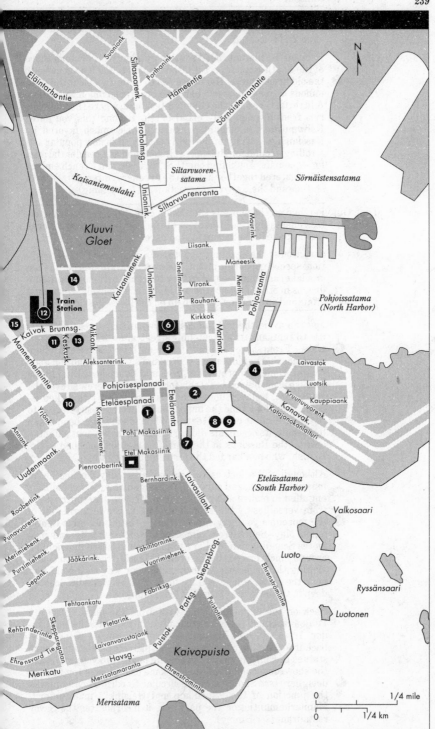

N

Eläintarhantie
Suoniank.
Sillasaarenk.
Porthonink.
Hämeentie
Sörnäistenrantatie

Broholmsg.

Kaisaniemenlahti

Unionink.

Siltavuoren-
satama

Siltavuorenranta

Sörnäistensatama

Kluuvi
Gloet

Kaisaniemenk.

Unionink.

Liisank.

Maurink.

Maneesik.

Meritullink.

Snellmanink.

Vironk.

Rauhank.

Kirkkok.

Mariank.

Pohjoisranta

Pohjoissatama
(North Harbor)

14

12 Train
Station

15

Kaivok. Brunnsg.

Keskusk.

11 **13**

Miktonk.

Aleksanterink.

Mannerheimintie

6

5

3

4

Laivastok.

Luotsik.

Kruunuvuorenk. Kauppiaank.

Kanavak.

Kalajanokanlaituri

Pohjoisesplanadi

2

Eteläesplanadi

1

Eteläranta

10

Yrjönk.

Korkeavuorenk.

8 **9**

7

Ammank.

Pohj Makasiinik.

Etel Mokasiinik.

Eteläsatama
(South Harbor)

Pienroobertink.

Bernhardink.

Uudenmaank.

Laivasillank.

Valkosaari

Roobertink.

Luoto

Punavuorenk.

Merimiehenk.

Pursimiehenk.

Sepank.

Jääkärink.

Tähtitorink.

Vuorimiehenk.

Ryssänsaari

Luotonen

Fabriksg.

Tehtaankatu

Skeppsbrog.

Pietarink.

Parkg.

Puistotie

Ehrenströmintie

Rehbinderintie

Skepparegatan Tie

Laivanvarustajank.

Puistok.

Ehrensvard Tie

Havsg.

Kaivopuisto

Merikatu

Merisatamaranta

Ehrenströmintie

Merisatama

0   1/4 mile

0   1/4 km

If you continue walking along Snellmaninkatu, you will reach the ferry that runs over to **Korkeasaari** Island where the **Helsinki Zoo** is located.

Back on the market, head southward along the western shore of the South Harbor on Eteläranta Street. You'll soon come to the old brick **Market Hall**—it's worth taking a look at the voluminous displays of meat, fish, and other gastronomic goodies. A little farther on is the **Olympia Terminal,** where the huge ferries from Sweden and Poland berth. Beyond this you enter **Kaivopuisto,** the elegant parkland district much favored by Russian high society in the 19th century. It is now popular as a strolling ground for Helsinki's citizens and as a residential area for diplomats. You'll find the U.S., British, and French embassies clustered together among the greenery, interspersed with statues and the Kaivohuone restaurant (*see* Dining).

Time Out Perched on the shore is the **Ursula café.** However good the refreshments may be, the view of the harbor and water-borne traffic make it the reason to stop here.

Just around the headland you'll spot a peculiarly Finnish tradition: special platforms jutting out over the water (either the sea or a lake) on which people gather to scrub their carpets. Laundry, as in other parts of the world, becomes a lively, communal affair and an occasion to catch up on the latest gossip.

You can avoid the long walk back by cutting across Kaivopuisto to Tehtaankatu and catching streetcar no. 3T to the marketplace. From here, there's frequent ferry service to **Suomenlina.** Suomenlina means "Finland's Castle," and for good reason. Under its protection, Helsinki flourished. In 1748 the Finnish army helped build this fortress, which grew so over the years that, today, Suomenlinna is a series of interlinked islands. For a long time the impregnable fortress was referred to as the "Gibraltar of the North." While it has never been taken by assault, its occupants did surrender twice without a fight—once to the Russians in the war of 1808–1809 and then to the British, who bombarded the fortress, causing fires.

Although still a fortress, Suomenlina is today a collection of museums, parks, and gardens. In early summer, Suomenlina is engulfed in mauve and purple mists of lilacs, trees introduced from Versailles by the Finnish architect, Ehrensvard. One of the museums you may care to visit is the **Nordic Arts Center** (open May–Sept.; free admission), which exhibits and promotes Scandinavian art. Try to plan your visit to Suomenlina around lunchtime so that after investigating the ramparts and visiting the museums you can make your way to the old fort near the historic King's Gate for a meal at **Walhalla,** located deep in the bastions of the fort (*see* Dining).

Back on the mainland, head west from the marketplace up **Pohjoisesplanadi** (North Esplanade). To your left, the leafy linden trees in the Esplanade gardens provide a peaceful backdrop for daily concerts at the Esplanade bandstand where statues of Finnish writers grace the lawns. On your right are the showrooms and boutiques of some of Finland's top fashion designers (*see* Shopping). The circular **Swedish Theater** marks the junction of the Esplanade and Helsinki's main artery, Mannerheimintie; on the park side it incorporates the **Savoy** restaurant (*see* Dining).

⑪ If you take a right up **Keskuskatu,** you come to **Stockmann's,** Helsinki's most famous store, well-worth a shopping stop.

⑫ Next you come to the **train station** and its square, the bustling commuting hub of the city. The station's huge red-granite figures are by Emil Wikström, but the solid building they adorn was designed by Eliel Saarinen, one of the founders of the early

⑬ 20th-century National Romantic Style. The **Ateneum,** Finland's central art museum, is on the south side of the square

⑭ facing the **National Theater.** *Open June–Aug. weekdays 9–5, weekends 11–5; Sept.–May, Mon.–Sat. 9–5, Sun. 11–5; open Wed. year-round to 8 PM.*

Time Out Café Socis, in the **Sourahuone Hotel** opposite the train station, provides a restful turn-of-the-century atmosphere for a fixed-price lunch or afternoon tea.

⑮ In front of the main **post office,** west of the station, is the equestrian statue of Marshal Mannerheim gazing down Mannerheimintie, the major thoroughfare named in his honor. Perhaps no man in Finnish history is so revered as Marshal Baron Carl Gustaf Mannerheim, the great leader who guided Finland through much of the turbulent 20th century. When he died in Switzerland on January 28, 1951, his body was flown back to his native land to lie in state in the cathedral. For three days, young war widows, children, and soldiers with caps in hand filed past his bier by the thousands. Never in Finland's history has there been such an expression of national feeling.

About half a mile along, past the colonnaded red-granite Parliament House, stands **Finlandia Hall,** one of the last creations
⑯ of Alvar Aalto. If you can't make it to a concert there, take a guided tour. Behind the hall lies the inland bay of Töölönlahti
⑰ and, almost opposite, the **National Museum,** another example of National Romantic exotica in which Eliel Saarinen played a part. *Admission: 5 FIM (free on Tues.). Open daily 11–4, also Tues. 6 PM–9 PM.*

Tucked away in a labyrinth of streets to the west is the strik-
⑱ ingly modern **Temppeliaukio Church.** Carved out of solid rock and topped with a copper dome, this Helsinki landmark is a center for religious activities, church services, concerts, and lectures. *Lutherinkatu 3. Open 10–8, Sun. 12–2 and 5–8.* From here it's only a short distance back to Mannerheimintie, where you can pick up any streetcar for the downtown area.

What to See and Do with Children

Take a **boat trip** from the South Harbor to **Suomenlinna** (*see* Exploring Helsinki) for a scramble over its 18th-century ramparts; or ride the ferry to **Korkeasaari Island** and visit Helsinki **Zoo;** visit the **Sports Museum** and take the elevator up to the **Olympic Stadium Tower** (open weekdays 9–8, weekends 9–6); or go to the **Linnanmäki Amusement Park** (open weekdays 4–10, Sat. 1–10, Sun. 1–9).

Off the Beaten Track

Located in Espoo, Helsinki's next door neighbor, is Tapiola Garden City, one of Finland's architectural highlights. Designed by Aalvar Aalto, the urban landscape of alternating high and low residential buildings, fountains, gardens, and swimming pools blends into the natural surroundings. What began as an experiment in communal, affordable housing has now lost its radical appeal, but Tapiola still holds interest for anyone interested in urban planning. Guides and sightseeing tours are available from the Espoo City Tourist Office, tel. 467-652 or 467-692.

Askeli Gallen Kallela (1865–1931) was one of Finland's greatest artists. His studio-home can be seen at Gallen-Kallelantie 27, Tarvaspää (open Tues.–Thurs. 10–8, Fri.–Sun. 10–5).

Shopping

Shopping Districts and Specialty Shops   You should find everything you need on **Pohjoisesplanadi** (North Esplanade) and **Aleksanterinkatu;** in the **Forum Shopping Mall** at Mannerheimintie 20; or on the pedestrian mall **Iso Roobertinkatu.** You can make purchases until 10 PM, seven days a week, in the shops along the Tunneli underpass leading from the train station.

The shops in **Senaatti Center** and along Pohjoisesplanadi are open on Sundays from noon to 4 in summer. Along the latter you'll find some of Finland's top design houses: **Metsovaara** fashions at No. 23; **Arabia-Nuutajärvi** ceramics and glass at 25; **Pentik** leather, **Aarikka** accessories, and wooden toys at 27; **Iittala** glass at 27A; **Marimekko** fashions at 31; and **Studio Tarja Niskanen** furs at 33.

Helsinki's three top jewelry boutiques are almost adjacent: **Galerie Björn Weckström,** Unioninkatu 30; **Kalevala Koru,** Unioninkatu 25; and **Kaunis Koru,** Senaatti Center.

Department Stores   Stockmann's, a huge store that fills an entire block between Aleksanterinkatu, Mannerheimintie, and Keskuskatu, is your best bet if you want to find everything under one roof.

Markets   The **South Harbor market** (*see* Exploring Helsinki) is an absolute "must." Also try to find time for the **Hietalahti flea market** located at the southwest end of Bulevardi. Stallholders here include everyone from junk merchants to socialites clearing out their attics, and there is a corresponding variety of goods on offer. *Open Mon.–Sat. 6:30 AM–2 PM.*

Dining

Prices quoted here are per person and include first course, main course, dessert, and service charge, but not wine. Best bets are indicated by a star ★. At press time, there were 4 finnmarks (FIM) to the dollar.

Category	Cost
Very Expensive	over FIM 200
Expensive	FIM 160–200
Moderate	FIM 100–160
Inexpensive	under FIM 100

Very Expensive
★   **George.** George was voted "Restaurant 1987" by a Finnish gourmet club. It is centrally located and offers continental cuisine with soft lights and quiet corners. Try the grilled fillet of

lamb with fennel and garlic-butter sauce. *Kalevankatu 17, tel. 90/647662. No jeans. Reservations advised. AE, DC, MC, V. Closed Sun., Christmas, Easter, and Midsummer.*

★ **Kaivohuone.** Red plush and crystal chandeliers set the mood in this elegant 19th-century restaurant once favored by the Russian aristocracy. Award-winning chef Juha Niemiö adds to its reputation with specialties such as smoked salmon loaf in puff pastry with white-wine butter sauce. *Kaivopuisto, tel. 90/ 177881. Jacket and tie recommended in the evenings. Reservations required. AE, DC, MC, V. Closed Sun., Mon., Christmas, and Easter; in winter, open evenings only.*

Savoy. With its airy dining room overlooking the Esplanade gardens, the Savoy is a favorite for business lunches. It was Finnish statesman Marshal Mannerheim's favorite, too, and he introduced the *Vorschmack* (minced lamb meat and anchovies) hors d'oeuvre. *Eteläesplanadi 14, tel. 90/176571. Jacket and tie recommended. Reservations necessary for lunch, advisable for dinner. AE, DC, MC, V. Closed Christmas, Easter, and Midsummer.*

Walhalla. Deep inside the granite ramparts of Suomenlinna fortress is a restaurant well worth the 20-minute boat ride from South Harbor. Specialties include whitefish from the stone grill. *Suomenlinna, tel. 668552. Dress informal. Reservations vital. AE, DC, MC, V. Closed mid-Sept.–mid-May.*

Expensive   **Amadeus.** Situated in an old town house near the South Harbor, Amadeus specializes in game dishes, such as baked ptarmigan and reindeer fillets. *Sofiankatu 4, tel. 90/626676. Dress: informal. Reservations advised. AE, DC, MC, V. Closed Christmas.*

★ **Bellevue.** Despite its French name, the Bellevue is Russian both in decor and cuisine. Filet à la Novgorod and chicken à la Kiev are the authentic articles here. *Rahapajankatu 3, tel. 90/ 179560. Dress: informal. Reservations advised. AE, DC, MC, V. Closed Sun., Christmas, and Midsummer.*

Kultainen Sipuli. The "golden onion," located in an old brick warehouse in the central Katajanokka district, is one of Helsinki's newest restaurants. The decor is an imaginative combination of timber and leather. Be sure to sample the outstanding crayfish soup. *Kanavaranta 3, tel. 90/179900. No jeans. Reservations advised. AE, DC, MC, V. Closed Sun., Christmas, and New Year's Eve.*

Troikka. The Troikka takes you back to Tsarist times in decor, paintings, and music, and offers exceptionally good food. If you're reluctant to try bear steak cooked in a clay pot, try the Siberian *pelmens* (small meat pasties). *Caloniuksenkatu 3, tel. 90/445229. Dress: casual. Reservations vital in the evening. AE, DC, MC, V. Closed Sun., Christmas, Easter, and Midsummer.*

Moderate   **Omenapu.** This cozy family restaurant set in the midst of a busy shopping district features special dishes for weight watchers. *Keskuskatu 6, tel. 90/630205. Dress: informal. Reservations advisable for lunch. AE, DC, MC, V.*

Perho. This is the restaurant connected to Helsinki's catering school. Visitors are served by friendly students, and in summer the emphasis is on Finnish food, particularly salmon and reindeer. *Mechelininkatu 7, tel. 90/493481. Dress: informal. Reservations advised. AE, DC, MC, V. Closed Christmas and Midsummer.*

Wellamo. The decor at this restaurant draws upon changing exhibitions by new artists. The small, subdued dining area extends outside to the shore of the North Harbor where, in the summer, you may enjoy the chef's cooking outside. Try the lamb steak in garlic butter. *Vyökatu 9, tel. 90/663139. Dress: informal. No reservations. AE, MC, V. Closed Mon., Christmas, and Midsummer.*

Inexpensive **Chez Marius.** This cozy French-style bistro is an established favorite, especially for lunch. It's located in the city center, so be prepared for crowds. *Mikonkatu 1, tel. 90/669697. Dress: informal. No reservations. No credit cards. Closed weekends, Christmas, and Midsummer.*

Kynsilaukka. The rustic decor suits the menu, which includes juniper-smoked beef. *Fredrikinkatu 22, tel. 90/651939. Dress: informal. No reservations. MC, V.*

Lodging

Standards of service and amenities in nearly all Helsinki hotels are reliable. The main criteria for inclusion here are price and location. Our price categories are for a double room and almost always include breakfast and service charges. Best bets are indicated by a star ★. At press time, there were 4 finnmarks (FIM) to a dollar.

Category	Cost
Very Expensive	over FIM 700
Expensive	FIM 500–700
Moderate	FIM 300–500
Inexpensive	under FIM 300

Very Expensive **Hesperia.** Enlarged and redecorated in 1986, the Hesperia is modern in the best Finnish tradition and just a short stroll from the center of the city. *Mannerheimintie 50, tel. 90/43101. 384 rooms with bath. Facilities: sauna, pool, golf simulator, nightclub, helicopter service. AE, DC, MC, V. Closed Christmas.*

★ **Inter-Continental.** This is the most popular hotel in the city—with American visitors, at least. It's modern and close to Finlandia Hall, although its rooms are on the small side. Restaurant noise may disturb guests staying on the top floor. *Mannerheimintie 46–48, tel. 90/441331. 55 rooms with bath. Facilities: sauna, pool, disco, AE, DC, MC, V.*

Palace. The Palace has a splendid situation overlooking the South Harbor—but make sure you ask for a room with a view. All such here are on the 9th floor. *Eteläranta 10, tel. 90/171114. 59 rooms with bath. Facilities: sauna, renowned Palace Gourmet restaurant. AE, DC, MC, V. Closed Christmas.*

Rivoli Jardin. Rivoli Jardin is a central town house, with all rooms overlooking a quiet courtyard. Rooms are rather small but well equipped and attractively designed. Breakfast is served in the winter garden, but there's no restaurant. *Kasarmikatu 40, tel. 90/177880. 54 rooms with shower. Facilities: sauna. AE, DC, MC, V. Closed Christmas.*

Expensive **Merihotelli Cumulus.** Located on the seafront, the Merihotelli Cumulus is a 10-minute walk from the center of town. Rooms are somewhat small but modern; those with a sea view get some traffic noise. *Hakaniemenranta 4, tel. 90/711455. 87 rooms with bath. Facilities: sauna, pool. AE, DC, MC, V.*

Rantasipi Airport Hotel. Just two miles from the airport, the Rantasipi was built in 1981 and expanded in 1986. Although the rooms are rather small, they have forest views. Airport shuttle service is provided, and the hotel features an entire floor for nonsmokers. *Takamaantie 4, Vantaa, tel. 90/826822. 300 rooms with shower. Facilities: sauna, pool, nightclub. AE, DC, MC, V. Closed Christmas.*

★ **Seurahuone.** This is a traditional town house from 1914, renovated in 1982, facing the station. Room decor ranges from sleek modern to crystal chandeliers and brass bedsteads, so specify your preference. Streetside rooms get some traffic noise. *Kaivokatu 12, tel. 90/170441. 118 rooms with bath. Facilities: sauna, disco. AE, DC, MC, V.*

Vaakuna. Located close to the train station, the Vaakuna offers light, airy rooms featuring high-back easy chairs. *Asemaaukio 2, tel. 171811. 288 rooms, 194 with bath, rest with shower. Facilities: sauna, solarium, nightclub. AE, DC, MC, V.*

Moderate **Anna.** The Anna, a circa 1935 town house, has light, cheerful rooms well-insulated against traffic noise. It's within easy reach of the town center but has no restaurant (breakfast room only). Nonsmokers will appreciate the designated nonsmoking floor and smoke-free public areas. *Annankatu 1, tel. 90/648011. 58 rooms with shower. Facilities: sauna. AE, DC, V. Closed Christmas and New Year's.*

Helka. The Helka is a town house built in 1925 and extended and renovated in 1985–86. It's convenient to the city center but rooms are rather small. *Pohjoinen Rautatiekatu 23A, tel. 90/440581. 153 rooms, most with shower. Facilities: sauna, solarium. AE, DC, MC, V. Closed Christmas.*

Hospiz. The Hospiz is located on a quiet, central street and is unpretentious but comfortable. *Vuorikatu 17, tel. 90/170481. 163 rooms, 33 with bath, 106 with shower. Facilities: sauna. AE, DC, MC, V.*

Inexpensive **Academica.** The Academica is a town house with simple but adequate rooms; 10 minutes' walk from the town center. *Hietaniemenkatu 14, tel. 90/440171, reservations 90/4020580. 216 rooms, most with shower. Facilities: sauna, pool, indoor tennis, disco. AE, V. Closed Sept.–May.*

Clairet. This is a small, modest, old-fashioned hotel centrally located close to the train station. There's no restaurant, but breakfast is served in your room. *Itäinen Teatterikuja 3, tel. 90/669707. 15 rooms with hot water, bathrooms in corridor. MC, V. Closed Christmas.*

★ **Finn.** Occupying the two top floors of a circa 1913 town house, the Finn is the best (and most expensive) hotel in this category. Some rooms are unusually large, but there's no restaurant— breakfast is served in your room on request. *Kalevankatu 3B, tel. 90/640904. 28 rooms, most with bath. Facilities: sauna and pool. V. Closed Christmas, Easter, and Midsummer.*

The Arts

For a list of events, pick up the free publications *Helsinki This Week* or *Helsinki Today* available in hotels and tourist offices. For recorded program information in English, dial 058. A central reservations office for all events is **Lippupalvelu** (Mannerheimintie 5, tel. 90/643043).

Theater Although all performances are in Finnish or Swedish, summertime productions in bucolic settings such as **Suomenlinna Island, Kekuspuisto Park, Mustikkamaa Island,** and the **Rowing Stadium** (operettas) make enjoyable entertainment. The splendid new **Opera House** opens in 1990 in a waterside park by **Töölönkahti.**

Concerts The two main locations for musical events are **Finlandia Hall** (tel. 90/40241) and **Temppeliaukio Church** (*see* Exploring). Free organ recitals are given on Sundays at 8 PM in the cathedral, and there's daily entertainment at the bandstand in the **Esplanade** gardens.

Nightlife

Nightclubs **Pressa,** the most popular club in town, is in the Ramada Presidentti Hotel (Eteläinen Rautatiekatu 4, tel. 90/6911). The nightclub in the **Hotel Hesperia** (tel. 90/431010) is more intimate and has the prettiest showgirls in town.

Discos The liveliest and most popular is **Ky Exit** (Pohjoinen Rautatiekatu 21, tel. 90/407238), followed by **Club Anna and Erik** (Eerikinkatu 3, tel. 90/6944204).

The Lakelands

This is a region of lakes, forests, and islands in southeastern Finland. The light in these northern latitudes has a magical softness, and the vistas are constantly changing.

For centuries the lakeland region was a buffer between the warring empires of Sweden and Russia. After visiting the people of the lakelands, you should have a basic understanding of the Finnish word *sisu* (guts), a quality that has kept Finns independent, fiercely guarding their neutrality.

Getting Around

Savonlinna is the most accessible town in the Lakelands and can make a convenient base from which to begin exploring. You can fly to the Savonlinna area from Helsinki in 40 minutes; a connecting bus takes you the remaining 16 kilometers (10 miles) into town. By train, the journey takes five-and-a-half hours, by bus, six hours.

If you travel by car, most of the lake can be explored on separate excursions. The alternative is to take advantage of the excellent network of air, rail, bus, and boat transportation. Take the boat from Savonlinna to Kuopio in 12 hours (**Roll Ships,** tel. 971/126744). From Kuopio, take the 320-kilometer (200-mile) cross-country bus ride via Jyväskylä to Tampere. Continue by boat to Hämeenlinna in seven hours (**Silver Line,** tel. 931/124803). The final leg by bus or train back to Helsinki takes about one and a half hours.

Guided Tours

A program of **Friendly Finland Tours,** available through a number of travel agencies, offers escorted lakeland packages from two to 11 days, starting from Helsinki. Brochures are available

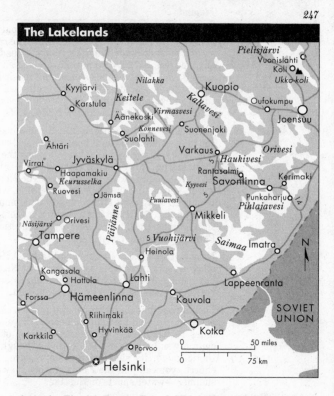

The Lakelands

from the **Finnish Tourist Board,** Unioninkatu 26, Helsinki, tel. 90/144511.

Tourist Information

Hämeenlinna. Raatihuoneenkatu 15, tel. 917/202388.
Kuopio. Haapaniemenkatu 17, tel. 971/182584.
Savonlinna. Puistokatu 1, tel. 957/13492.
Tampere. Verkatehtaankatu 2, tel. 931/126652.

Exploring

Savonlinna   The center of Savonlinna is a series of islands linked by bridges. First, stop in at the tourist office for information; then cross the bridge east to the open-air **market** which flourishes alongside the main passenger quay. It's from here that you can catch the boat to Kuopio. In days when water-borne traffic was the major form of transport, Savonlinna was the central hub of the Saimaa lake network, the largest such network in Europe. Now the lake traffic is dominated by sightseeing boats, but the drama of friends and relatives arriving and departing still prevails.

A ten minute stroll from the quay to the southeast brings you to Savonlinna's most famous sight, the castle of **Olavinlinna.** First built in 1475 to protect Finland's eastern border, it retains its medieval character and is one of Scandinavia's best preserved historic monuments. Still surrounded by water that once formed part of its defensive strength, the fortress rises out of the lake as a shimmering mirage. In the courtyard each July is held the International Opera Festival. The combination of music and scenery is spellbinding. You will need to reserve well in advance (tel. 957/22-684) both for tickets and for hotel rooms, since Savonlinna becomes a mecca for music lovers. And music is not the only activity; arts and crafts are also strongly featured in exhibits around town. *Castle open June–Aug. 9–5; Aug.–May 10–3. Admission: FIM 10.*

The most popular excursion from Savonlinna is to **Retretti.** You can take either a two-hour boat ride or a 30-minute, 18-mile bus trip. The journey by bus takes you along the five-mile ridge of **Punkaharju.** This amazing ridge could be a modern dyke, but its existence pre-dates the Ice Age. The ridge rises out of the water, separating the lakes on either side. At times it narrows to only 25 feet, yet it still manages to accommodate a road and train tracks. At Retretti is a modern art complex of unique design, which includes a new cavern section built into the Punkaharju ridge. *Open 10–8.*

Near Retretti is the **Punkaharju National Hotel.** The building started as a gamekeeper's lodge for Tsar Nicholas I in 1845 but has been subsequently enlarged and restored, and is now a restful spot for a meal or an overnight visit.

Should you want to see the largest wooden church in the world, one that can hold up to 5,000 people, drive or take the bus 14 miles to **Kerimaki,** situated to the east of Savonlinna. The church was built in the 1840s, and although not of great aesthetic value, its sheer size is impressive. After seeing the church, you can join the Finns in what they enjoy most in the summer—water sports on the lake.

From Savonlinna, there are many options for exploring. One is to begin a leisurely return trip to Helsinki. Take the Helsinki-bound steamer that runs through the Saimaa lake network to **Lappeenranta.** From this lively resort town on the southern shores of Saimaa, trips are available on the Saimaa Canal. The canal crosses into the Soviet Union to Viipuri (Viborg), but for the moment this route, which leads eventually to Leningrad via the Gulf of Finland, is not open to non-Scandinavian visitors. The old fortress area of Lappeenranta is of particular interest. A half-hour drive from here is **Imatra,** whose magnificent rapids, tamed and diverted to help power the considerable local industry, are released as a tourist attraction on certain Sundays each summer.

The other main alternative is to head north to **Kuopio,** a trip that can be made by car or an enjoyable 12-hour boat trip. This trip, perhaps more than any other, gives a deep sense of the region so dominated by interlocking lakes, with soft northern light shimmering on their waters.

If you have a car, rather than drive straight to Kuopio on highways 14, 464, and 5 via Rantasalmi and Varkaus, make the detour to **Joensuu** through the long and immensely intricate system of lakes, canals, and narrow channels, all of which are part of the Saimaa network.

Joensuu is the only town of any size in the vast area known as North Karelia. Its chief claim to distinction is a town hall that, like the one at Lahti, was designed by Eliel Saarinen. Our objective, however, is **Koli** on the western shore of Lake Pielinen

(Pielisjärvi), nearly 64 kilometers (40 miles) due north of Joensuu. By boat, three times a week, the journey takes a leisurely six to seven hours, but you can also go by train to Vuonislahti, on the lake's eastern shore, and take a motorboat across to Koli. Alternatively, there is a bus service from Joensuu to Koli.

As we mentioned earlier, Finland is relatively flat; thus, in comparison with the hills found in most parts of the country, Koli is mountainous. This is its great appeal. From the rocky summit of Ukko-Koli, more than 300 meters (1,000 feet) up, there are some of the most magnificent views to be found anywhere in the country. There is a modern tourist hotel near the hilltop and holiday villages on the lake shore. Much has been done for the visitor to Koli in the way of well-marked footpaths for the hiker and other facilities. On the Pielisjoki river the canoeing is excellent. But it is for winter sports that this region is particularly noted.

The region to the east of Joensuu is little known to foreign visitors, though of special interest as a traditional stronghold of the Orthodox church. The summer calendar features a number of Pradznik festivals and traditional Orthodox church and folk celebrations, the most important being at Ilomantsi in July.

From Joensuu, it is less than three hours by major highway to Kuopio.

Kuopio Whether you arrive in Kuopio by boat or by car, you may want to take advantage of the Kuopio Card, which allows you unlimited local transportation and free entrance to museums. It is available from the **Kuopio Tourist Office,** located close to the **Tori** (market place). The Tori should be one of the places you visit first, for it is one of the most colorful outdoor markets in Finland. *Open weekdays 7-3, Sat. 7-2.*

Other sights worth seeing are the Orthodox Church Museum and the view from the tower on Puijo hill.

The **Orthodox Church Museum** has one of the most interesting and unusual collections of its kind in the world. When Karelia was ceded to the Soviet Union after World War II, the religious art was taken out of the monasteries and brought to Kuopio. The collection is eclectic and, of its type, one of the rarest in the world. *Karjalankatu 1, Kuopio, tel. 971/122-6111. Open Tues.- Sun. 10-4.*

Visitors who are fascinated by the treasures in the museum will want to visit the Orthodox **convent of Lintula** and the **monastery of Ursi-Valamo.** Both can be reached by boat on scenic day-excursion.

Pulio Tower is best visited at sunset, when the lakes shimmer with reflected light. The slender tower is located three three kilometers (two miles) northwest of Kuopio. It has two observation decks and a revolving restaurant on top where one can enjoy the marvelous views. *Open 8 AM–11 PM.*

From Kuopio, there are three major alternatives. First, one can return to Helsinki, a five-hour journey. Second, one can travel north through Central Finland to Rovaniemi—on the edge of the Arctic Circle—and Lapland. Third, one can cross to Tampere, in the southwestern part of Finland, and then travel south to Turku before returning along Finland's southern shore to Helsinki.

The 320-kilometer (192-mile) journey from Kuopio to **Tampere** will take four to five hours, whether you travel by car or bus. The trip can also be made by train, with changes at Varkaus and Parkano. The train ride from Helsinki to Tampere takes about two hours.

Tampere Almost every guide will inform you that Tampere, the country's second largest city, is Finland's Pittsburgh. However, the resemblance begins and ends with the concentrated presence here of industry—the settings themselves have little in common.

From about the year 1,000, this part of Finland was a base from which traders and hunters set out on their expeditions to northern Finland and even to Lapland. But it was not until 1779 that a Swedish king actually founded the town of Tampere. Forty-one years later, a Scotsman by the name of James Finlayson came to the infant city and established a factory for spinning cotton. This was perhaps the beginning of "big business" in Finland. The firm of Finlayson exists today and is still one of the country's leading industrial enterprises.

Artful location is the secret of Tampere's many factories. An isthmus little more than a kilometer wide at its narrowest point separates the lakes Näsijärvi and Pyhäjärvi, and at one spot the **Tammerkoski Rapids** provide an outlet for the waters of one to cascade through to the other. Called the "Mother of Tampere," these rapids provide the power on which the town's livelihood depends. Their natural beauty has been preserved in spite of the factories on either bank, and the well-designed public buildings of the city grouped around them enhance their general effect. Also in the heart of town is **Hämeensilta Bridge**, with its four statues by the well-known sculptor Wäinö Aaltonen.

Close to the **Hameensilta bridge**, near the high-rise Hotel Ilves, are some warehouses which have been restored as shops and boutiques. Nearby at Verkatehtaankatu 2, is **the city tourist office**, where you can buy a 24-hour **Tampere Service Card** that allows unlimited travel on local city transportation, entrance to museums, and a variety of discounts.

The high ridge of **Pyynikki** separating the two lakes forms a natural park on the Särkänniemi peninsula, about a 20-minute walk to the northwest of the city center. On the way there, visit one of Tampere's best small museums, **The Workers' Museum of Amuri**. The exhibit consists of a block of old timber houses, with descriptions and illustrations of how the original tenants lived. *Makasiininkatu 12, Tampere. Open 12-6, closed Monday.*

At Särkänniemi is Finland's tallest structure, the 560-foot **Nasinnuela Observation Tower** (open daily 10–8). On top is an observatory as well as a revolving restaurant. The views are magnificent, commanding the lake, forest, and town. The contrast between the industrial maze of Tampere at your feet and the serenity of the lakes stretching out to meet the horizon is unforgettable.

The same building complex houses the first **planetarium** in Scandinavia and a well-planned aquarium, which includes a separate dolphinarium. Near this complex, landscaped walkways lead to another striking example of Finnish architecture, the **Sarah Hilden Art Museum,** where modern Finnish and international artists (including Miro, Leger, Picasso, and Chagall) are on display. *Admission: FIM 30. Open 11-6.*

At the foot of the Pyynikki Ridge is the **Pyynikki Open Air Theatre** with a revolving auditorium that can be moved, even with a full load of spectators, to face any one of the sets, ready prepared by nature.

On the east side of the town is the modern **Kaleva Church.** What appears from the outside to be a grain elevator is in fact, as seen from the interior, a soaring monument to space and light. *Open 10-6.*

Most buildings in Tampere, including the cathedral, are comparatively modern. However, though the cathedral was built only in 1907, it is worth a visit to see some of the best known masterpieces of Finnish art, including Magnus Encknell's frescoes, "The Resurrection," and two works by Hugo Simberg, "Wounded Angel" and "Garden of Death."

Just outside of town, in **Kaukajärvi,** is the charming *Haihara Doll Museum* (open noon-6 PM). Also near Tampere is the *Lenin Museum* (Hallituskatsu 19; open Tues.-Sat. 11–3; Sun. 11–4), with displays of photos and momentos. It was in Tampere that Lenin and Stalin first met.

The **Silver Line's** white motor ships leave for **Hämeenlinna** from the **Laukontori terminal.** If you're traveling by car, take Highway 3 and stop en route at the famous **Iittala Glassworks,** which offers guided tours and has a museum and shop. The magnificent glass is produced by top designers, and the "seconds" are real bargains that you won't find elsewhere. *Open 9–8.*

Hämeenlinna's secondary school has educated many famous Finns, among them composer Jean Sibelius. The only timber house surviving in the town center is the **birthplace of Sibelius,** a modest dwelling built in 1834. Here you can listen to tapes of his music and see the harmonium he played when he was a child. *Hallituskatu 11. Open daily 10–4.*

One of the most popular excursions from Tampere is the **"Poet's Way"** boat tour along Lake Näsijärvi. The boat passes through the agricultural parish of Ruovesi, where J. L. Runeberg, Finland's national poet, used to live. Shortly before the boat docks at Virrat you pass through the **straits of Visuvesi,** where many artists and writers today spend their summers. Not far north of Virrat is Ähtäri, where Finland's first **wildlife park** has been established in a beautiful setting, with a holiday village, a good hotel, and recreation facilities.

Kangasala, southeast of Tampere, is the center of a region considered by some to be even more beautiful than the "Poets' Way." It lies on one of the routes of the Finnish Silver Line, through Lakes Roine and Vanajavesi to Aulanko and Hämeenlinna.

Turku Should you have the time, consider making a detour to Turku before returning to Helsinki. It will add only a few hours to your trip, either by train or by car, and Turku has a very special meaning for the Finns.

Finland's oldest city, founded in the 13th century—and its capital until 1812—Turku is situated on both banks of the Aura River. With a population of 162,000, it is the country's third largest city and is sometimes called "the cradle of Finnish culture." Commercially, its great importance is that its harbor is easy to keep open throughout the winter (the word *turku* means trading post). It is also widely known for its shipyards and for its two universities, one Finnish, the other Swedish.

Called Åbo by the Swedish-speaking Finns, Turku is the center of the southwest part of the country, whose land is fertile and whose winters are relatively mild. With a **cathedral** over 700 years old, the city is still the seat of the archbishop of Finland. Although gutted by fire in 1827, the cathedral has been completely restored. In the choir can be seen R. W. Ekman's frescoes portraying Bishop Henry (an Englishman) baptizing the heathen Finns and Mikael Agricola offering the Finnish translation of the New Testament to Gustav Vasa of Sweden.

Where the Aura flows into the sea stands **Turku Castle** (open daily 10–6), the city's second most important historical monument. The oldest part of the fortress was built at the end of the 13th century; the newer part dates back to the 16th century. Once a prison, it has been attractively restored and today contains the **Historical Museum,** with collections of furniture, portraits, arms, and implements covering 400 years.

Like Helsinki, Turku has a lively open-air morning market, which in summer reopens 4–8 PM. Among the other main sights is the **Handicraft Museum** (open daily 10–4)—a street of wooden homes that survived the 1827 fire and now houses workshops where comb-makers, weavers, and potters demonstrate equipment and techniques that date back a century and a half. In summer, visitors may also try their hand under expert guidance.

Notable, too, is the **Resurrection Chapel** (open by appointment only), one of the outstanding creations of modern Finnish architecture. Also well worth visiting in Turku are the **Sibelius Museum** (Piispankatu 47; open daily 11–3, Wed. 6–8 PM) and the **Wäinö Aaltonen Museum,** the latter devoted to the works of Finland's great sculptor and also featuring changing exhibitions of contemporary art. Both are on the banks of the Aura.

The **Ruissalo National Park,** located on an island three miles from Turku and accessible by road, has the largest oak woods in the country. The park has a pleasant sandy beach, modern accommodations, and good sports facilities.

One of the greatest attractions in the vicinity of Turku is the beach at the coastal resort of **Naantali** (Naådendal), where the president of Finland has his summer residence. Finland's oldest known author, Jöns Budde, was a monk in the 15th-century monastery whose chapel now serves as the church. There are water-bus trips on certain summer evenings from Turku to Naantali. Other good excursions from Turku include the **Tour of Seven Churches,** covering some of the delightful medieval churches of the area.

Dining and Lodging

For details and price category definitions, *see* Dining and Lodging in Essential Information.

Hämeenlinna
Dining

Hame Castle. Situated on the lake shore half a mile from the town center, Hame Castle is sometimes the setting for medieval banquets. It also has a pleasant coffee house. *Linnantie 6, tel. 917/25928. Jacket and tie. Reservations essential for banquets. No credit cards. Restaurant Expensive; coffee house Moderate.*

Piiparkakkutalo. Located in a renovated old timber building, Piiparkakkutalo has a restaurant upstairs, a tavern downstairs. The menu offers fine Finnish fare. *Kirkkorinne 2, tel. 917/121606. Dress: casual. Reservations advised. AE, DC, MC, V. Moderate.*

Lodging
★

Rantasipi Aulanko. One of Finland's top hotels sits on the lake shore in a beautifully landscaped park four kilometers (two miles) from town. *Aulanko, tel. 917/29521. 216 rooms with bath. Facilities: saunas, pool, squash, tennis, golf, riding, boating, swimming beach, nightclub, and tax-free shop. AE, DC, MC, V. Very Expensive (Moderate in July).*

Kuopio
Dining

Mustalammas. Located near the passenger harbor, Mustalammas has been attractively adapted from a beer cellar and features steaks and basic fish dishes. *Satamakatu 4, tel. 971/123494. Dress: casual. Reservations advised. AE, DC, MC, V. Expensive.*

Sampo. Situated in the town center, Sampo specializes in vendace (*muikku*) a kind of whitefish. Try the smoked variety. The atmosphere is unpretentious and lively. *Kauppakatu 13, tel. 971/114677. Dress: casual. MC, V. Inexpensive.*

Lodging

Rauhalahti. About five kilometers (three miles) from the town center, Rauhalahti is set near the lake shore and has a number of amenities catering to sportsmen and families. The hotel has three restaurants, including the tavern-style Vanha Apteekkari—a local favorite. *Katiskaniementie 6, tel. 971/311700. 126 rooms with bath or shower. Facilities: saunas, swimming pool, solarium, gymnasium, children's playroom, disco, tennis, horseback riding, squash, boat rental. AE, DC, MC, V. Expensive.*

Rivoli. Completed in 1987, the Rivoli is the most modern and best equipped of local hotels. It also has all the advantages of a lakefront location, and is close to the center of town. *Satamaktu 1, tel. 971/195111. 141 rooms with bath or shower. Facilities: sauna, swimming pool, Jacuzzi, solarium, tennis, boat rental. AE, DC, MC, V. Expensive.*

Sport Hotel Puijo. Located next to Puijo Tower, the Sport Hotel Puijo is only four years old but built in the traditional timber style. Rooms are large and very quiet. *Puijo, tel. 971/114841. 20 rooms with shower. Facilities: saunas. AE, DC, MC, V. Moderate.*

Savonlinna
Dining

Rauhalinna. This romantic turn-of-the-century timber villa was built by a general in the Imperial Russian Army. It's 16 kilometers (10 miles) by road, 40 minutes by boat, from town. Both food and atmosphere are old Russian, but some Finnish specialties are also available. *Lehtiniemi, tel. 957/523119. Dress: casual. Reservations necessary during Festival season. DC. Closed Sept.–mid-June. Expensive.*

Snellman. This small 1920s-style mansion is in the center of town. Meals are served against a quiet background of classical music. *Olavinkatu 31, tel. 957/13104. Dress: casual. Reservations advised. AE, DC, MC, V. Expensive in evenings; Moderate lunches upstairs.*

Majakka. Centrally located, Majakka goes in for home cooking and a family atmosphere. *Satamakatu 11, tel. 957/21456. Casual dress. Reservations necessary during Festival season. DC, MC, V. Moderate.*

San Martin. A steak house with a pleasant open courtyard in summer. *Olavinkatu 46, tel. 957/13004. Dress: casual. AE, DC, MC, V. Moderate.*

Musta Pässi. Located near the bus station, Musta Pässi serves fresh fish, meatballs, potatoes, and other homemade dishes in a tavern setting. *Tulliportinkatu 2, tel. 957/22228. Dress: casual. DC, MC, V. Inexpensive.*

Lodging **Tott.** This is an old favorite, located in the downtown area opposite the passenger harbor. It was completely renovated in 1987/88. *Satamakatu 1, tel. 957/22925. 60 rooms with bath or shower. Facilities: saunas, pool, nightclub. AE, MC, V. Expensive (Very Expensive in July).*

Casino Spa. Built in the 1960s and renovated in 1986, the Casino Spa has a restful lakeside location on an island linked by a pedestrian bridge to the center of town. *Kasinonsaari, tel. 957/22864. 79 rooms with bath or shower. Facilities: saunas, pool, nightclub, marina, spa treatment. AE, DC, MC, V. Expensive.*

Seurahuone. This old town house is located near the market and passenger harbor. A new extension is opening in 1989. Some older rooms are small. *Kauppatori 4, tel. 957/22267. 32 rooms with shower, plus new extension. Facilities: saunas, disco. AE, MC, V. Moderate.*

Vuorilinna Summer Hotel. Guests at this modern hotel use the facilities, including the restaurant, of the nearby Casino Spa Hotel. *Kasinonsaari, tel. 957/24908. 160 rooms, with shower for every two rooms. AE, DC, MC, V. Open June 1–August 31. Inexpensive (Moderate in July).*

Tampere **Finlayson Palatsi.** Set in its own gardens about one kilometer
Dining (one-half mile) from the town center, this elegant restaurant still has many of the original furnishings from the turn of the century, when it was a private residence. *Kuninkaankatu 11, tel. 931/125905. Dress: casual. Reservations advised. AE, DC, MC, V. Very expensive.*

Natalie. Russian in atmosphere, cuisine, and background music, Natalie is housed in the old Workers' Theater near the center of town. *Hallituskatu 19, tel. 931/32040. Dress: casual. Reservations advised. AE, DC, MC, V. Moderate.*

Salud. Salud has a well-earned reputation for Spanish specialties, though it also features some Finnish dishes. *Otavalankatu 10, tel. 931/35996. Casual dress. Reservations advised. AE, DC, MC, V. Moderate. Closed weekends in July.*

Silakka. Although its atmosphere is casual and unpretentious, Silakka has earned a great name for its Finnish fish specialties. *Vuolteenkatu 20, tel. 931/149740. Dress: casual. MC, V. Closed Sun. in summer. Inexpensive.*

Lodging **Ilves.** The city's newest hotel soars above a newly gentrified area of old warehouses near the city center. It is favored by Americans. *Hatanpään valtatie 1, tel. 931/121212. 336 rooms with bath or shower, special floor for nonsmokers. Facilities: saunas, pool, Jacuzzi, nightclub. AE, DC, MC, V. Very Expensive.*

Cumulus. Overlooking the tamed rapids of Tammerkoski, Cumulus is central and modern. The Finnair terminal is in the

same building. *Koskikatu 5, tel. 931/35500. 230 rooms with
shower. Facilities: saunas, pool, nightclub. AE, DC, MC, V.
Expensive.*
Domus Summer Hotel. The drawing cards are its location—
near the center of town, in the Kaleva district—and good value. *Pellervonkatu 9, tel. 931/550000. 200 rooms, 85 with
shower. Facilities: saunas, pool, disco. MC, V. Closed Sept.-
May. Inexpensive.*

Finnish Lapland

Nature has fashioned a wilderness of endless forests, fells, and
great silences. So often the arrival of settlers has obliterated
all that came before, but here man has walked gently and left
the virgin solitude of this country almost unspoiled. Now easily
accessible by plane, train or bus, this Arctic outpost offers comfortable hotels and modern amenities, yet you won't have to go
very far to find yourself in an almost primordial solitude.

The oldest traces of human habitation in Finland have been
found in Lapland, and hoards of Danish, English, and even Ara-
bian coins indicate the existence of trade activities many
centuries ago. The origins of the Lapps themselves are lost in
the mists of history. There are only about 3,500 pure Lapps still
living here; the remainder of the provinces' population of
220,000 are Finns. Until the 1930s, Lapland was still largely
unexploited, still a region where any trip was an expedition.
Then the Canadian-owned Petsamo Nickel Company (now in
Soviet hands) completed the great road that connects Rovaniemi with the Arctic Sea. Building activities increased along
this route (later to be known as the Arctic Highway), the land
was turned and sown, and a few hotels were built to cater to increasing numbers of visitors.

In September 1944, in conformity with the terms of the Armistice Treaty with the Soviet Union, the Finns began driving
out considerable numbers of German troops then stationed in
Lapland. The retreating Germans destroyed all they could; the
capital, Rovaniemi, was leveled, and almost every farmhouse,
cottage, and cattle-shed was burned down or blown up.

Before the ruins ceased smoking, the Finns were already back
working to create new communities out of the desolation. Certain areas of Lapland had to be ceded to the Soviet Union (the
Arctic coastline, Petsamo, and part of the Salla district on the
eastern frontier), but their inhabitants were resettled within
the new Finnish boundaries. Among them were 250 Skolt
Lapps, a unique tribe who were settled at Sevettijärvi on the
northern shores of Lake Inari.

Summer has the blessing of daylight up to 24 hours long and often beautiful weather to go with it—but beware of the
mosquitoes. In early fall the colors are so fabulous that the
Finns have a special word for it: *ruska*. If you can take the intense but dry cold, winter is also a fascinating time in Lapland,
not only for the Northern Lights but for experiences such as
the unique reindeer roundups.

Depending how far north of the Arctic Circle you go, the sun
might not rise for several weeks around midwinter. Don't
imagine it is pitch dark, though. There is reflected light from

the invisible sun below the horizon during the middle of the day and a luminosity from the ever-present snow.

In December and January, reindeer owners round up their herds from all over the country and corral them by the thousands. Sometimes dressed in colorful costumes, the Lapps (and also many Finns) lasso the reindeer in true Wild West fashion, recognizing their own animals by brand marks on the ears. The roundups are attended by many buyers, for reindeer meat is considered quite a delicacy and is exported to the south and abroad.

To get to some of the remoter roundups you may have to travel by taxi plane, though other corrals are near the road, especially around Ivalo, Inari, and Enontekiö. Most Lapps and northern Finns get there or by one of those motorized sledges that rather sadly have almost entirely replaced the much more attractive (and silent) reindeer-drawn *pulkka* (a kind of boat-shaped sleigh on one runner). In southern Lapland especially, an increasing number of roundups occur in the fall. Finding out exactly when and where a roundup is taking place is not easy, for much depends on the whims of the weather and the reindeer, so you must check locally. The information offices in Rovaniemi, however, will be able to give some guidance.

A few words should be said about the Lapps—a proud, sensitive, and intelligent people—some of whom, with justification, resent the attitude of those visitors who regard them as a tourist attraction put there for their benefit. Modern influences (and intermarriage) have rather regrettably changed many aspects of their traditional way of life; for example, the attractive costumes are less frequently seen, except on festive occasions. The young, especially, have been affected by the changes, and many of them are far more interested in becoming teachers, lawyers, or engineers than in breeding reindeer or hunting from their remote homesteads. Yet others have found profit from selling souvenirs to the tourists. But most prefer to go about their daily life minding their own business. The Lady Day Church Festival in Enontekiö in March is a particularly colorful event, attended by many Lapps in their most brilliant costumes, and usually feature reindeer racing or lassoing competitions.

The new and the old intermingle in this remote northern corner of Europe. The new Lapland is a place of modern techniques where careful management is gradually driving back the wilderness and creating cornfields beyond the Arctic Circle. The forests are being exploited and managed with expert care, and light industry and hydro-electric projects have added their mark to the Lapland map. Yet gold-panners cut off from the world except for occasional visitors and the aircraft that swoop down with their mail and provisions, still wash the gravel of the Lemmenjoki river, and the rhythm of the seasons still governs the life of all those connected with reindeer. And the experienced traveler who would like to roam through the wilds for days on end without meeting a fellow human being can still do so without any problem at all. Be warned, however, that climatic conditions change rapidly and often unpredictably, especially on those lonely Arctic fells. Always seek local advice and let your hotel and friends know where you are heading and how long you intend to be away. An attractive alternative is provided by organized canoeing or hiking trips with nights in huts or tents in the wilderness.

Getting Around

Rovaniemi is the best base for traveling around the Arctic area. It connects with Helsinki and the south with road, rail, and air links; there is even a car-train from Helsinki. Within the area, driving is the best way to get around, although a regular bus service connects most towns. There are also daily flights from Rovaniemi to Ivalo.

Guided Tours

Friendly Finland Tours features the itinerary (*see* Exploring Lapland below) on an escorted **Three-Day Arctic Lapland Tour** out of Helsinki. Contact the Helsinki office of the Finnish Tourist Board, Unioninkatu 26, tel. 90/144511.

Tourist Information

Ivalo. Bus Station, Piiskuntie 5, tel. 9697/12521.
Rovaniemi. Aallonkatu, tel. 960/16270; in summer, also at the train station, tel. 960/22218. For further information on the region, contact Lapland Travel, Maakuntakatu 10, tel. 960/16052.
Sodankylä. Jäämerentie 9, tel. 9693/13474.

Exploring Lapland

To explore Lapland, you could base yourself in Kemi, the southernmost town of the province, but this is somewhat south of the Arctic Circle, on the coast of the Gulf of Bothnia. It would be preferable to stay closer to the Arctic Circle, in the town of **Rovaniemi,** where the Ounas and Kemi rivers meet. Rovaniemi is the so-called "Gateway to Lapland" and the administrative hub and communications center of the province.

If you're expecting an Arctic shanty town, you're in for a surprise. Rovaniemi was nearly razed by the retreating German army in 1944, so what you'll see today is a modern city strongly influenced by Aalvar Aalto's architecture. The old way of life is preserved in museums. During the process of rebuilding, the population rose from 8,000 to more than 32,000, so be prepared for a contemporary city on the edge of the wilderness, with various amenities and some incredible architecture—notably **Lappia Hall,** the concert and congress center that also houses the world's northernmost professional theater, designed by Aalto. Rovaniemi also has the best collection of shops in the region.

After collecting information from the **tourist office,** find a window table in the restaurant of the nearby **Pohjanhovi Hotel,** and plan your itinerary while gazing out at the fast-flowing Kemi River. Short river cruises are conducted daily in summer.

You can get a good instant introduction to the region and its natural history at the **Museum of the Province of Lapland** at Lappia House. The collection also includes exhibits of *Same* culture. *Admission: FIM 5. Open Tues.–Sun. 10–6.*

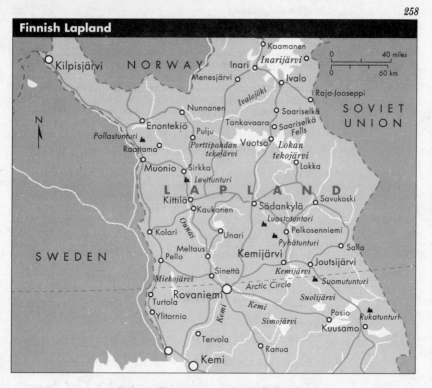

Finnish Lapland

But you'll get more of a feel for the living past from the **Pöykkölä Museum,** located in 18th-century farm buildings five kilometers (two miles) from the town center. *Admission: FIM 5. Open daily 12–4; bus service available.*

Although interesting, Rovaniemi is by no means typical of Lapland. To explore the province in summer, you have two main alternatives. The first is to fly or to take the Arctic Highway north to Ivalo. This is the main artery of central and northern Lapland, and an important postbus route. The second alternative is to head west via Pello to the Swedish border and drive north to the border with Norway and Sweden near Kilpisjärvi. Let's look at the Arctic Highway route first.

Eight kilometers (five miles) north of Rovaniemi, right on the Arctic Circle, is **Santa Claus's Workshop,** where gifts can be bought in midsummer for shipping at any time of year, with a special Santa Claus Land stamp. There are some reindeer here and a museum devoted to North Polar exploration, but most visitors seem to come only to say they've been to the Arctic Circle and to mail postcards home from the special post office. Though there's a decent souvenir shopping complex, the most impressive sight is the mountains of mail that pour in from children all over the world. Yes, all of it gets answered. *Free. Open daily 9–8.*

Much farther north, at **Södankylä,** there is a **Northern Lights Observatory** and an ancient **wooden church.**

Continue north, through the small village of **Vuotso,** to **Tankavaara,** the southernmost Lapp region. This is also the most accessible and the best developed of several gold-panning areas, where you can try your hand at sifting gold dust. The **Gold Museum** (admission: FIM 5; open daily 9–6) tells the century-old story of Lapland's hardy fortune seekers. For a small fee, authentic prospectors will show you how to sift gold dust and tiny nuggets from the dirt of an ice-cold stream. You can keep what you find but don't expect to be able to retire early.

Thirty kilometers (18 miles) north of Tankavaara is the holiday center of **Saariselkä,** which has a variety of accommodations and makes a sensible base from which to set off on a trip (alone or in a group) into the true wilderness. There are marked trails through forests and over fells, where virtually nothing has changed since the last Ice Age, and where you can experience the timeless silence of the Arctic landscape. More than 965 square miles of this magnificent area has been named the **Urho Kekkonen National Park.**

Just south of the village of Ivalo, the highway passes the **Ivalojoki River.** This is an excellent canoeing river, and you can rent canoes to paddle down to Lake Inari and return by bus.

The village of **Ivalo** is the main center for northern Lapland. However, except for a first-class hotel, an airport, and many of the amenities of a modern community, it has little to offer the tourist in search of a wilderness experience.

The huge island-studded expanses of **Lake Inari** (Inarijärvi), north of Ivalo, offer endless possibilities for wilderness exploration. It is a beautiful 40-kilometer (24-mile) drive west from Ivalo, along the lakeshore, to **Inari.** This is a good base for summer boat excursions. The *Same Museum,* on the village outskirts, covers all facets of Lapp culture. *Admission: FIM 5. Open daily 8 AM–10 PM.*

In recent years, a growing number of small holiday villages have blossomed near Inari and to the north of it, usually with a small restaurant and shop attached. Amenities are simple, but the locations are often magnificent and bring you very close to the true pulse of Lapland. Usually there will be a boat at your disposal, fishing possibilities, and the experience of preparing your own sauna. From Kaamanen, north of Inari, a side road leads to **Sevettijärvi,** home of the Skolt Lapps, and eventually into Norway.

Further north still is **Utsjoki,** a village on the Norwegian border. This is in the country's northernmost parish, where you can travel by boat on the **Teno**—famed for its salmon waters and considered Finland's most beautiful river. Should you wish to take a trip into Norway, you can drive over the border at Nuorgam, northeast of Utsjoki, or from Karigasniemi, over the Norwegian Arctic Highway, and eventually return to Finland at Kilpisjärvi, in the far northwest. Utsjoki and Karigasniemi are now linked by a minor road following the Teno river, a road that continues south along the border with Norway to Angel from where you can return east to Inari.

It is an attractive drive back south from Inari to Menesjärvi through a wilderness of forest and swamp. Take every opportunity to leave your car and do some walking; it's the only way to experience the vastness of these Arctic spaces. The hills gets gentler and the ride less dramatic as you continue south to

Levitunturi, the last of the gently sloping fells before you reach the banks of the Ounas River and return to Rovaniemi.

On our other suggested route—west from Rovaniemi to the border—the fells are higher and the scenery more impressive than along the Arctic Highway.

The fell group of **Pallastunturi** and the villages of **Enontekiö** and **Kilpisjärvi** are particularly recommended. A superb wilderness trail, about 96 kilometers (60 miles) long, links Pallastunturi and Enontekiö across the fells, with unattended huts along the way in which to overnight. To the east of the fells, a relatively recent minor road passes through **Raattama** and other hamlets whose remoteness has protected them from war devastation; a number of farm buildings survive from quite ancient times. Enontekiö straggles along a lake shore, and from it a road leads to Kautokeino in Norway, eventually linking up with the rest of the Norwegian road network.

The road from Muonio to Kilpisjärvi, paralleling the Swedish border, is known as the **Way of the Four Winds** (after the four points of the male Lapp headgear). Along this route, **Karesuvanto** is well placed for excursions into the wilderness and trips into Sweden. From **Kilpisjärvi** itself, a popular excursion is to the simple granite **Stone of the Three Countries** that marks the boundary of Sweden, Norway and Finland. There are marvelous views for those with energy to climb **Saana fell,** looming over Kilpisjärvi. To the northwest rise more fells including the highest in Finland, **Halti,** at over 4,000 feet.

Dining and Lodging

For details and price category definitions, *see* Dining and Lodging in Essential Information.

Inari
Lodging

Kultahovi. This recently renovated old inn is located on the wooded banks of a swiftly flowing river. *Inari, tel. 9697/51221. 29 rooms with shower. Facilities: saunas. AE, MC, V. Moderate.*

Ivalo
Lodging

Hotel Ivalo. Right on the riverside about a kilometer (half a mile) from the village center, Ivalo is modern and well-equipped. One of its two restaurants serves Lapland specialties, including *poronkaristys,* a reindeer casserole. *Ivalontie 34, tel. 9697/21911. 62 rooms with bath or shower. Facilities: saunas, swimming pool, boating, disco. AE, DC, MC, V. Expensive.*

Levitunturi
Lodging

Levitunturi. Built in traditional log style at the foot of the fells, Levitunturi is a particularly well-equipped and modern tourist complex. *Sirkka, tel. 9694/81301. 82 rooms with shower. Facilities: special nonsmoking floor, saunas, swimming pool, Jacuzzi, squash, gymnasium, tennis, boating, cross-country skiing, spa facilities. AE, DC, MC, V. Expensive.*

Luostotunturi
Lodging

Kantakievari Luosto. Situated amid the fells southeast of Sodankylä, this small-scale hotel is modern and comfortable. It is built in traditional timber style. *Sodankylä, tel. 9693/44214. 32 rooms with shower. Facilities: saunas, boating, disco, cross-country skiing. AE, MC, V. Moderate.*

Rovaniemi
Dining

Bel Giovanni. Northern Finland may be the last place you'd expect to find a lively little Italian restaurant, but the atmosphere here is authentic and friendly. The emphasis is on pizzas, pastas, and grills. *Valtakatu, tel. 960/16406. Dress: casual. No reservations. MC, V. Moderate.*

Pinja. Quiet and intimate, Pinja offers good home cooking in a relaxed atmosphere. *Valtakatu 19, tel. 960/14272. Dress: casual. No reservations. No smoking. No credit cards. Moderate.*

Lodging **Rantasipi Pohjanhovi.** With its pleasant location overlooking the Kemi River, this hotel is an old favorite with travelers to the north. It has been extended and modernized over the years. The hotel offers guests free raft trips. *Pohjanpuistikko 2, tel. 960/313731. 212 rooms with bath or shower. Special floor for nonsmokers. Some rooms in neighboring building. Facilities: saunas, swimming pool, raft trips, boating, disco. AE, DC, MC, V. Very Expensive.*

Ounasvaara. Located on a hilltop three kilometers (two miles) from the center, Ounasvaara is the top choice for views and a tranquil atmosphere, but it's best if you have a car. *Ounasvaara, tel. 960/23371. 52 rooms with bath or shower. Facilities: saunas, cross-country skiing. AE, DC, MC, V. Expensive.*

Gasthof. Built in 1986, the Gasthof is a comfortable small hotel with a restaurant featuring Russian specialties. *Koskikatu 41, tel. 960/23222. 28 rooms with shower. Facilities: special nonsmoking floor, saunas, swimming pool. No credit cards. Moderate.*

Oppipoika. This hotel belongs to the Hotel School of Rovaniemi. Rooms are spacious and comfortable, but the real reason to come here is the food: Chef Tapio Sointu has created the *Lapland à la Carte* program, featuring a variety of Lapland specialties. *Korkalonkatu 33, tel. 960/20321. 40 rooms with bath or shower. Facilities: saunas, swimming pool. AE, MC, V. Moderate.*

Saariselkä **Riekonlinna.** The latest and best-equipped addition to this de-
Lodging veloping tourist complex on the fringes of the wilderness fells, Riekonlinna makes best use of its location. *Saariselkä, tel. 9697/81601. 66 rooms with shower. Facilities: saunas, tennis, boating, squash, cross-country skiing, AE, DC, MC, V. Very Expensive.*

Tankavaara **Wanhan Waskoolimiehen Kahvila.** Lapland specialties are fea-
Dining tured in this attractive café and restaurant; try the braised reindeer with creamed potatoes and lingonberries. Accommodations are limited in the vicinity. *Tankavaara Gold Village, tel. 9693/46158. Dress: casual. No reservations. No credit cards. Moderate.*

11 France

Introduction

The French are different. They don't have the "Anglo-Saxon" outlook you may find reassuring in, say, Germany or Scandinavia. They are a Mediterranean people—temperamental and spontaneous, closer to the Spanish and Italians than to northern Europeans. At the same time, they are heirs to the Cartesian tradition of logic ("I think, therefore I am"), as well as being inveterate theorizers. Their reluctance to take a shortcut to an obvious solution often frustrates English-speaking pragmatists.

One thing the French do well—probably because it's instinctive and they don't need to think about it—is live. The essence of French *savoir vivre* is simplicity. Everyday things count: eating, drinking, talking, dressing, shopping. Get in the mood: Daily rituals are meant to be enjoyed. Food is the best example. The French don't like rushing their meals. They plan them in advance, painstakingly prepare them, look forward to them over an *apéritif*, admire the loving presentation of each dish, savor each mouthful. The pace is unhurried and the wine flows steadily.

Make the most of the simple pleasure to be had from basking in the sunshine outside a café. Admire the casual elegance of the passersby or the old men in their time-honored berets. Even the most mundane things can become objects of beauty in French eyes. The daily market is a festival of colors and textures, with fruit and vegetable stalls artistically and imaginatively composed. Shop windows are works of art.

Most French towns and villages are quietly attractive and historic. Chances are that the ornate *Mairie* (town hall) has been there since the Revolution, and the church or cathedral since the Middle Ages. The main streets tend to be lined with sturdy trees planted before living memory. The 20th century is kept firmly at bay. Modern buildings—such as supermarkets—are banished to the outskirts or obliged to fit in with the architecture of the town center.

At the hub of nearly every town you can expect to find an "eternal triangle" of buildings. The church and Mairie, representing God and the State, are the first two. The third—representing the tourist—is the Syndicat d'initiative. The Syndicat d'initiative (marked on signs with an *i* and sometimes more helpfully known as the Office de tourisme) should be your first stop when visiting any French town. At the very least, you'll come away with a street map and list of hotels—if you're lucky, reservations can be made for you on the spot—plus plenty of brochures about other towns and regions.

There is a bewildering variety of man-made marvels in France. Southern France is rich in Roman remains: Try not to miss the triumphal arch in Orange, the amphitheater in Arles, or the Pont du Gard aqueduct near Nîmes. Western France is dotted with Romanesque churches from the 10th and 11th centuries, with some of the best examples in Poitiers.

Gothic architecture was born in the Ile de France around Paris: The huge cathedrals of Amiens, Rheims, Bourges, or Chartres—not to forget Notre-Dame in the capital—rank among the world's finest. The Renaissance yielded the sumptuous Loire

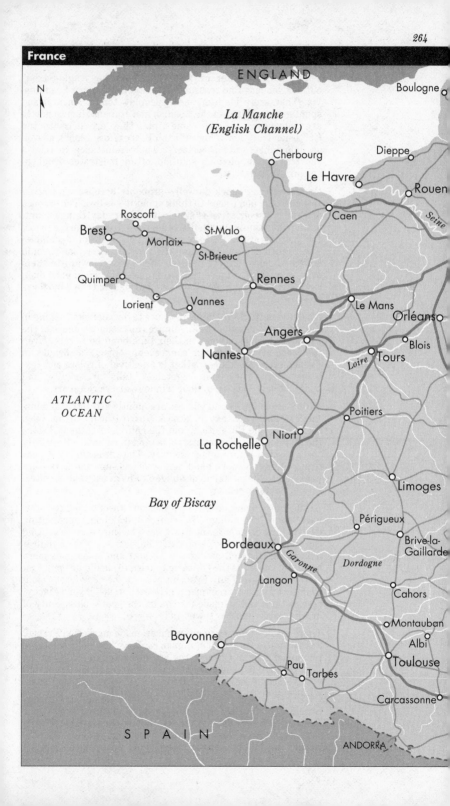

Calais

BELGIUM

Lille

Arras
Amiens
Cambrai
St. Quentin

Beauvais

LUXEMBOURG

Reims

Paris
Châlon-sur-Marne

Metz

Nancy
Strasbourg

Troyes

GERMANY

Mulhouse
Belfort

Bourges
Nevers
Beaune
Dijon
Besançon

SWITZERLAND

Montluçon
Macon
Bourg-en-Bresse

Saône

Clermont-Ferrand
Lyon
Rhône

Chambéry

Aurillac
Le Puy
Grenoble

Rhône

ITALY

Rodez
Millau
Montélimar

Nîmes
Avignon
Monte Carlo

Montpellier
Aix en Provence
Nice
Cannes

Narbonne
Marseilles
Toulon

Perpignan

0   50 mi

0   75 km

Mediterranean Sea

Corsica

Corsica

Calvi
Bastia

Corte

Ajaccio

châteaux and the Palace of Fontainebleau, paving the way for the haughty Baroque of Versailles.

Bordeaux is an elegant example of the more restrained Classicism prevalent in the 18th century. Paris contains masterly demonstrations of 19th-century architecture and city planning. The 20th century has been as productive as its predecessors— take the futuristic steel and glass of La Défense, west of Paris, the space age Pompidou Center, or the glass pyramid of the Louvre.

France boasts as much natural as man-made variety. There's just about every type of landscape except desert. You'll find ski slopes and towering peaks in the Alps or Pyrenees; beaches and cliffs in Brittany or along the Mediterranean; extinct volcanoes in Auvergne; limitless horizons beyond the golden grain fields of the Beauce or the misty plains of the north; haunting evergreen forests stretching from the Ardennes, near Belgium, down to the Midi (south); marsh and canals in the Marais Poitevin, the "Green Venice" of the west; barren, rock-strewn wilderness in the southern Causses; lush, sofly lit valleys along the Seine or Loire; steep-climbing terraces above the Rhône; and wherever you go, the swirl and sway of ripening vines.

Although its regional differences are tangible, France remains a well-knit nation. Its boundaries are largely natural and undisputed. It is a manageable size and a sensible shape (Frenchmen refer to their country as the Hexagon). Not that all Frenchmen are the same. Along the south coast, exuberant Latins live in tune with the sun-and-siesta rhythms of the Mediterranean. Nice, after all, was an Italian city until 1860. The southwest of France looks toward Spain: Basque territory extends on either side of the Pyrenees. The wine regions of Bordeaux and Cognac have centuries-long links with Britain, and it is no coincidence that their inhabitants are comparatively calm and "phlegmatic" (a Frenchman's favorite adjective for the average Englishman). The people of Brittany proudly defend their Celtic heritage and feel as much affinity with the Cornish and Welsh as with their fellow-French. Don't forget the Viking origins of the Normans who conquered England or the historical German influence on Alsace. And the French of the north have plenty in common with their Belgian neighbors, beginning with a mutual craving for beer and french fries.

Whatever you may have been led to believe, France is a welcoming country. Don't be misled by the superficial coldness of the French: They are a formal people who don't go out of their way to speak to strangers (except in anger). Above all, don't suppose that all Frenchmen are like Parisians—it's not true. Most of the French are more approachable and friendly. One of the reasons is that a great many have foreign origins themselves. France has always attracted immigrants from less affluent countries: Italy, Spain, Portugal, Poland, and North Africa. More than a million Frenchmen were brought up in Algeria and came "home" only in the early 1960s after Algerian independence.

Despite the parochial inertia you may find in rural areas, many of the French can be remarkably outward looking. Their unique geographical position has a lot to do with that. France considers itself to be, above all, a European power. It borders seven countries (Belgium, Luxembourg, West Germany, Switzerland, Italy, Spain, Andorra) and looks across the Channel at an eighth (Great Britain). France played a crucial role in the creation of the European Economic Community and, since the admission of Spain and Portugal, can claim more than ever to be the crossroads of Western Europe. Everywhere you go you will hear talk of 1992—the date when internal trade barriers between members of the EEC will be abolished, an event anticipated by the French as a watershed in modern history. The French cannot understand why the British cling to their insularity and have dragged their feet so long over the Channel Tunnel.

Still, deep down, most of the French are chauvinists who are proud of *La douce France,* worship Napoleon, and feel that the Liberty-Equality-Fraternity motto of the French Revolution confers moral superiority upon their country. You can be sure that exuberant patriotism will be very much on display during the Bicentennial of the Revolution in 1989.

Before You Go

When to Go
On the whole, June and September are the best months to be in France. Both months are free of the mid-summer crowds. June offers the advantage of long daylight hours, while slightly cheaper prices and frequent Indian summers (often lasting well into October) make September an attractive proposition. Try to avoid the second half of July and all of August, or be prepared for inflated prices and huge crowds on the beaches. Don't travel on or around July 14 or August 1, 14, or 31 (national holidays). In addition, July and August heat can be stifling in southern France. Paris can be stuffy in August, too. But, on the other hand, it's pleasantly deserted (although many restaurants, theaters, and small shops are closed).

The skiing season in the Alps and Pyrenees lasts from Christmas through Easter—steer clear of February (school vacation time) if you can. Anytime between March and November will offer you a good chance to soak up the sun on the Riviera. If you're going to Paris or the Loire, remember that the weather is unappealing before Easter. If you're dreaming of Paris in the Springtime, May (not April) is your best bet.

Climate
Be prepared for changes in climate if you wish to visit different parts of France. North of the Loire (including Paris), France has a northern European climate—cold winters, pleasant if unpredictable summers, and frequent rain. Southern France has a Mediterranean climate: mild winters, long, hot summers and sunshine throughout the year. The more continental climate of eastern and central France is a mixture of these two extremes: Winters can be very cold and summers very hot. France's Atlantic coast has a temperate climate even south of the Loire, with the exception of the much warmer Biarritz.

The following are the average daily maximum and minimum temperatures for Paris.

Jan.	43F	6C	May	68F	20C	Sept.	70F	21C
	34	1		49	10		53	12
Feb.	45F	7C	June	73F	23C	Oct.	60F	16C
	34	1		55	13		46	8
Mar.	54F	12C	July	76F	25C	Nov.	50F	10C
	39	4		58	15		40	5
Apr.	60F	16C	Aug.	75F	24C	Dec.	44F	7C
	43	6		58	14		36	2

The following are the average daily maximum and minimum temperatures for Marseille.

Jan.	50F	10C	May	71F	22C	Sept.	77F	25C
	35	2		52	11		58	15
Feb.	53F	12C	June	79F	26C	Oct.	68F	20C
	36	2		58	15		51	10
Mar.	59F	15C	July	84F	29C	Nov.	58F	15C
	41	5		63	17		43	6
Apr.	64F	18C	Aug.	83F	28C	Dec.	52F	11C
	46	8		63	17		37	3

Currency The unit of French currency is the franc, subdivided into 100 centimes. Bills are issued in denominations of 20, 50, 100, and 500 francs (frs); coins are 5, 10, 20, and 50 centimes, and 1, 2, 5, and 10 francs. The small, copper-colored 5-, 10-, and 20-centime coins have considerable nuisance value but can be used for tips in bars and cafés.

International credit cards and traveler's checks are widely accepted throughout France, except in rural areas. At press time (fall 1988), the dollar was worth 5.7 frs, and the pound was worth 10.3 frs.

What It Will Cost Gasoline prices are above the European average, and there are tolls on major highways. Train travel, though, is a good buy.

Hotel and restaurant prices compensate for travel expense. Prices are highest in Paris, on the Riviera, and in the Alps during the ski season. But even in these areas, you can find pleasant accommodations and excellent food for surprisingly reasonable prices.

All taxes must be included in posted prices in France. The initials TTC *(toutes taxes comprises*—taxes included) are sometimes included on price lists but, strictly speaking, they are superfluous. Restaurant and hotel prices must *by law* include taxes and service charges: If they are tacked on your bill as additional items, you should complain.

Sample Prices Cup of coffee, 4–6 frs; bottle of beer, 6–8.5 frs; Coca-Cola, 6–10 frs; ham sandwich, 12–15 frs; one-mile taxi ride, 20–25 frs.

Visas Citizens of the United States and Canada—but not Britain—need a visa as well as a passport to visit France. Completed application forms should be submitted along with your passport to the nearest French consulate. U.S. citizens must pay $3 for a 72-hour transit visa, $9 for a three-month multiple-entry visa, and $15 for a five-year multiple-entry visa. Canadians must go through the same process. Check with travel agents for the latest costs.

Customs on Arrival Travelers from the United States and Canada may bring into France 400 cigarettes or 100 cigars or 100 grams of tobacco, one liter of liquor of 22% volume and two liters of wine, 0.50 liters of perfume and 0.25 liters of toilet water, and other goods to the value of 300 frs.

Adults traveling from the United Kingdom may bring into France 300 cigarettes or 150 cigarillos or 75 cigars or 400 grams of tobacco; 1.5 liters of liquor over 22% volume or three liters of liquor under 22% volume or three liters of fortified/sparkling wine, plus four liters of still wine; 0.9 liters of perfume and 0.375 liters of toilet water; plus other goods to the value of 2,400 frs.

Language The French study English for a minimum of four years at school, but few are fluent in their conversation. English is widely understood in major tourist areas, and in most tourist hotels there should be at least one person who can converse with you. Be courteous, patient, and speak slowly: France, after all, has visitors from many countries and is not heavily dependent for income on English-speaking visitors as, for example, Spain is.

Even if your own French is rusty, try to master a few words: The French are more cooperative when they think you are at least making an effort to speak their language.

Getting Around

By Car France's roads are classified into five types, numbered and pre-
Road Conditions fixed A, N, D, C, or V. Roads marked A *(Autoroutes)* are expressways. There are excellent links between Paris and most French cities, but poor ones between the provinces (the principal exceptions being A62 between Bordeaux and Toulouse and A9/A8 the length of the Mediterranean coast). It is often difficult to avoid Paris when crossing France—this need not cause too many problems if you steer clear of the rush hours (7–9:30 AM and 4:30–7:30 PM). A toll *(péage)* must be paid on most expressways: The rate varies but can be steep. The N *(Route Nationale)* roads—which are sometimes divided highways—and D *(Route Départementale)* roads are usually wide and fast, and driving along them can be a real pleasure. Don't be daunted by smaller (C and V) roads, either. The yellow regional Michelin maps—on sale throughout France—are an invaluable navigational aid.

Rules of the Road You may use your own driver's license in France but must be able to prove you have third-party insurance. Drive on the right. Be aware of the French tradition of yielding to drivers coming from the right. Seat belts are obligatory, and children less than 12 may not travel in the front seat. Speed limits are 130 kph (80 mph) on expressways, 110 kph (70 mph) on divided highways, 90 kph (55 mph) on other roads, 60 kph (40 mph) in towns. French drivers break these limits and police dish out hefty on-the-spot fines with equal abandon.

Parking Parking is a nightmare in Paris and often difficult in other large towns. Meters and ticket machines (pay and display) are common: Make sure you have a supply of 1-fr coins. In smaller towns, parking may be permitted on one side of the street only—alternating every two weeks—so pay attention to signs. The French sometimes ignore them, but don't follow their example; if you're caught, your vehicle may unceremoniously be hauled off to the dreaded compound (from where it will cost you 500 frs to retrieve it).

Gasoline Fuel is more expensive on expressways and in rural areas. Don't let your tank get too low—you can go for many miles in the country without passing a gas station—and keep an eye on pump prices as you go. These vary enormously; anything from

4.50 to 5.30 frs per liter. Be careful to choose the right gas for your automobile: *"Super"* is high-test and *"essence"* is regular.

Breakdowns If you break down on an expressway, go to the nearest roadside emergency telephone and call the breakdown service. If you break down anywhere else, find the nearest garage or contact the police.

By Train France's SNCF is generally recognized as Europe's best national train service: fast, punctual, comfortable, and comprehensive. The high-speed TGVs, with a top speed of 160 mph (250 kph) are the best domestic trains, operating between Paris and Lyon, the Riviera, and Switzerland, with a new link to Nantes and Bordeaux scheduled for 1990. As on other express trains, you may need to pay a small supplement when taking a TGV at peak hours. Also, you need a seat reservation—easily obtained at the ticket window or from an automatic machine. Seat reservations are reassuring but seldom necessary on other French trains, except at certain busy holiday times.

You need to punch your train ticket in one of the waist-high orange machines you'll encounter alongside platforms. Slide in your ticket face up and wait for a "clink" sound. If nothing happens, try another machine. (The small yellow tickets and automatic ticket barriers used for most suburban Paris trains are similar to those in the metro/RER).

It is not necessary to take an overnight train, even if you are traveling from one end of France to the other; but if you take one, you have a choice between *wagons-lits* (sleeping cars), which are expensive, and *couchettes* (bunks), which sleep six to a compartment (sheet and pillow provided) and are more affordable (around 75 frs). Ordinary compartment seats do not pull together (as in West Germany) to enable you to lie down. There are special summer night trains from Paris to Spain and the Riviera geared for a younger market, with discos and bars to enable you to dance the night away.

Fares Various reduced-fare passes are available from major train stations in France and from travel agents acting as agents for SNCF. If you are planning a lot of train travel, we suggest you buy a special France Vacances card (around 1,350 frs for nine days). Families and couples are also eligible for big discounts. So are senior citizens (over 60) and young people (under 26), who qualify for different discount schemes. Having paid for your pass, you can get 50% reductions during blue periods (most of the time) and 20% most of the rest of the time (white periods: noon Friday to noon Saturday; 3 PM Sunday to noon Monday). On major holidays (red periods) there are no reductions. A calendar showing the red, white, and blue periods is available at any station. Note there is no reduction for booking a round-trip *(aller-retour)* ticket rather than a one-way *(aller simple)*.

By Plane Air France operates France's domestic airline service, called Air Inter. Most domestic flights from Paris leave from Orly. Contact your travel agent or Air Inter (tel. 45–39–25–25). Train service may be faster, though, particularly when you consider the time it takes to travel between the airport and center city, so check train schedules before commiting yourself to a flight.

By Bus   Because of excellent train service, long-distance buses are rare and found mainly where train service is inadequate. Bus tours are organized by the SNCF and other tourist organizations, such as Horizons Européens: Ask for their brochures at any major travel agent, or contact France-Tourisme at 214 rue de Rivoli, 75001 Paris, tel. 42–60–30–01.

By Boat   France has Europe's busiest inland waterway system. Canal and river vacations are popular: Visitors can either take an organized cruise or rent a boat and plan their own leisurely route. Contact a travel agent for details or ask for a *Tourisme Fluvial* brochure in any French tourist office. Some of the most picturesque stretches are to be found in Brittany, Burgundy, and the Midi. The Canal du Midi between Toulouse and Sète, constructed in the 17th century, is an historic marvel. Further information is available from French national tourist offices; **France-Anjou Navigation,** Quai National, 72300 Salbé-sur-Sarthe; or **Bourgogne Voies Navigables,** Maison du Tourisme, 89000 Auxerre.

By Bicycle There is no shortage of wide empty roads and flat or rolling countryside in France suitable for bike riding. The French themselves are great cycling enthusiasts—witness the Tour de France. Bikes can be rented from many train stations for around 30 frs a day; you need to show your passport and leave a deposit of about 200 frs (unless you have a Visa or MasterCard). You do not always need to return the bike to the same station. Bikes may be sent as accompanied luggage from any station in France; some trains in rural areas don't even charge to transport bikes. Tourist offices will supply details on the more than 200 local shops that have bikes for rent, or obtain the SNCF brochure "Guide du Train et du Velo."

Essential Information

Telephones   The French telephone system is modern and efficient. Phone
Local Calls   booths are plentiful; they are nearly always available at post offices and cafés. A local call in France costs 12 centimes per minute (minimum tariff 73 centimes); half-price rates apply between 9:30 PM and 8 AM and between 1:30 PM Saturday and 8 AM Monday.

Pay phones work with 1- and 5-fr coins (1 fr minimum). Lift the receiver, place the coin(s) in the appropriate slot, and dial. Unused coins are returned when you hang up. Many French pay phones are now operated by cards *(télécartes)*, which you can buy from post offices and some shops (cost: 40 frs for 50 units; 96 frs for 120). These cards save money and time.

All French phone numbers have eight digits; a code is required only when calling the Paris region from the provinces (dial 16–1 and then the number) and for calling the provinces from Paris (dial 16, then the number). Note that the number system was changed in 1985 and that you may come across some seven-digit numbers in Paris and some six-digit ones elsewhere. Add 4 to the front of such Paris numbers and the former two-digit area code to provincial ones.

International Calls Dial 19 and wait for the tone, then dial the country code (1 for the United States and Canada, 44 for the United Kingdom), area code (minus any initial), and number. If you make phone calls from your hotel room, expect to be greatly overcharged.

Operators To find a number within France, or to request other information, dial 12. For international information, dial 19–33 plus the country code.

Mail Airmail letters to the United States cost 4.20 frs for 5 grams, to
Postal Rates Canada 2.80 frs for 5 grams; these prices increase by 60 centimes per 5 grams up to 20 grams total. Letters to the United Kingdom cost 2.20 frs for up to 20 grams, as they do within France. Postcards cost 2.00 frs within France and if sent to Canada and EEC countries; 2.80 francs to the United States and elsewhere. Stamps can be bought in post offices and cafés sporting a red *Tabac* sign outside.

Receiving Mail If you're uncertain where you'll be staying, have mail sent to American Express, Thomas Cook, or Poste Restante at most French post offices. American Express has a $2 service charge per letter.

Shopping Local wines are always a favorite but, after adding in shopping charges, you may discover that you can pay less through a liquor store or importer at home. As for food, *foie gras* (goose liver) is sold in the southwest, mussels and oysters on the Channel and Atlantic coasts, olives and herbs in Provence, sausages and sauerkraut in Alsace, and nougat in Montelimar. Most regions also have their own cheeses.

As for clothes, Paris is the firm fashion capital; traditional regional strongholds (Lille for textiles, Calais for lace) have little clout these days, although good clothes can be bought everywhere and are invariably cheaper outside Paris.

VAT Refunds A number of shops, particularly large stores in cities and holiday resorts, offer VAT refunds to foreign shoppers. You are entitled to an export discount of 13% or 23%, depending on the item purchased, though this often applies only if your purchases in the same store reach a minimum 2,400 frs (for residents of EEC countries) or 1,200 frs (all others, including Americans and Canadians).

Bargaining Shop prices are clearly marked and bargaining is not a way of life. Still, at outdoor markets, flea markets, and in antiques stores, you can try your luck. If you're thinking of buying several items in these places, you have nothing to lose in cheerfully suggesting to the proprietor, *"Vous me faites un prix?"* ("How about a discount?").

Opening and **Banks.** In general, banks are open weekdays 9:30 AM–4:30 PM,
Closing Times but times vary.

Museums. Most museums are closed one day a week (usually Tuesday) and on national holidays. Usual times are from 9:30 to 5 or 6. Many museums close for lunch (noon–2); many are open afternoons only on Sunday.

Shops. Large shops in big towns are open from 9 or 9:30 AM to 6 or 7 PM without a lunch break. Smaller shops often open earlier (8 AM) and close later (8 PM), but take a lengthy lunch break (1–4 PM). This siesta-type schedule is more typical in the south of France. Corner grocery stores, often run by immigrants, frequently stay open until around 10 PM.

National Holidays January 1 (New Year's Day); March 27 (Easter Monday); May 1 (Labor Day); May 8 (VE Day); May 4 (Ascension); May 14 (Pentecost Monday); July 14 (Bastille Day); August 15 (Assumption); November 1 (All Saints); November 11 (Armistice); December 25.

Dining   Eating in France is a serious business, at least for two of the three meals each day. For a light meal, try a *brasserie* (steak and french fries remain the classic), a picnic (a *baguette* loaf with ham, cheese, or pâté makes a perfect combination), or one of the fast-food places that have sprung up in urban areas over recent years.

French breakfasts are relatively modest—strong coffee, fruit juice if you insist, and croissants. International chain hotels are likely to offer American or English breakfasts, but in cafés you will probably be out of luck.

Mealtimes   Dinner is the main meal and usually begins at 8 PM. Lunch begins at 12:30 or 1.

Precautions   Tap water is perfectly safe, though not always very appetizing (least of all in Paris). Mineral water—there is a vast choice of plain *(eau plate)* as well as fizzy *(eau gazeuse)*—is a palatable alternative.

Ratings   Prices are per person and include a first course, main course, and dessert plus taxes and service (which are always included in displayed prices), but not wine. Best bets are indicated by a star ★. At press time, there were 5.7 francs to the dollar.

Category	Cost
Very Expensive	over 400 frs
Expensive	250–400 frs
Moderate	150–250 frs
Inexpensive	under 150 frs

Credit Cards   The following credit card abbreviations are used: AE, American Express; DC, Diners Club; MC, MasterCard; V, Visa.

Lodging   France has a wide range of accommodations, from rambling old village inns to stylishly converted châteaux. Prices must, by law, be posted at the hotel entrance and should include taxes and service. Prices are always by room, not per person. Ask for a *grand lit* if you want a double bed. Breakfast is not always included in this price, but you are usually expected to have it and often are charged for it whether you have it or not. In smaller rural hotels, you may be expected to have your evening meal at the hotel, too.

The quality of rooms, particularly in older properties, can be uneven; if you don't like the room you're given, ask to see another. If you want a private bathroom, state your preference for shower *(douche)* or bath *(baignoire)*—the latter always costing more. Tourist offices in major train stations can reserve hotels for you, and so can tourist offices in most towns.

Hotels   Hotels are officially classified from one-star to four-star-deluxe. France has—but is not dominated by—big hotel chains: Examples in the upper price bracket include Frantel, Holiday Inn, Novotel, and Sofitel. The Ibis and Climat de France chains are more moderately priced. Chain hotels, as a rule, lack atmosphere, with the following exceptions:

Logis de France. This is a group of small, inexpensive hotels that can be relied on for comfort, character, and regional cuisine. Look for its distinctive yellow and green sign. The Logis de France paperback guide is widely available in bookshops (cost: around 45 frs) or from Logis de France, 25 rue Jean-Mermoz, 75008 Paris.

France-Accueil is another chain of friendly low-cost hotels (free booklet from France-Accueil, 85 rue Dessous-des-Berges, 75013 Paris).

Relais et Châteaux. You can stay in style at any of the 150 members of this prestigious chain of converted châteaux and manor houses. Each hotel is distinctively furnished, provides top cuisine, and often stands in spacious grounds. A booklet listing members is available in bookshops or from Relais et Châteaux, 10 pl. de la Concorde, 75008 Paris.

Rentals **Gîtes Ruraux** offers families or small groups the opportunity for an economical stay in a furnished cottage, chalet, or apartment. These can be rented by the week or month. Contact either the **Fédération Nationale des Gîtes Ruraux,** 34 rue Godot de Mauroy, 75009 Paris (indicate the region that interests you), or the French Government Tourist Office in New York or London.

Bed and Breakfast These are known in France as *chambres d'hôte* and are increasingly popular in rural areas. Check local tourist offices for details.

Youth Hostels With inexpensive hotel accommodations in France so easy to find, you may want to think twice before staying in a youth hostel—especially as standards of French hostels don't come up to those in neighboring countries. Contact **Fédération Unie des Auberges de Jeunesse,** 6 rue Mesnil, 75016 Paris.

Villas The French Government Tourist Offices in London and New York publish extensive lists of agencies specializing in villa rentals. You can also write to *Rent-a-Villa Ltd.*, 3 W. 51st St., New York, NY 10019; or, in France, **Interhome,** 88 blvd. Latour-Maubourg, 75007 Paris.

Camping French campsites have a good reputation for organization and amenities but tend to be crowded in July and August. More and more campsites now welcome advance reservations, and if you're traveling in summer, it makes sense to book in advance. A guide to France's campsites is published by the **Fédération Française de Camping et de Caravaning,** 78 rue de Rivoli, 75004 Paris.

Ratings Prices are for double rooms and include all taxes. Best bets are indicated by a star ★. At press time, there were 5.7 francs to the dollar.

Category	Cost
Very Expensive	over 850 frs
Expensive	450–850 frs
Moderate	250–450 frs
Inexpensive	under 250 frs

Credit Cards The following credit card abbreviations are used: AE, American Express; DC, Diners Club; MC, MasterCard; V, Visa.

Tipping The check in a bar or restaurant will include service, but it is customary to leave some small change unless you're dissatisfied. The amount varies, from 30 centimes for a beer to a few francs after a meal. Tip taxi drivers and hairdressers about 10%. Give ushers in theaters 1–2 frs. Cloakroom attendants will expect nothing if there is a sign saying *Pourboire interdit*—no tip; otherwise give them 5 frs. Washroom attendants usually get 5 frs—a sum that is often posted.

Bellhops should get 10 frs per item.

If you stay more than two or three days in a moderately priced hotel, it is customary to leave something for the chambermaid—perhaps 10 frs per day. Expect to pay 10 frs for room service—but nothing is expected if breakfast is routinely served in your room. If the chambermaid does some ironing or laundering for you, leave an additional 5 frs in the room.

Service station attendants get nothing for giving you gas or oil, and 5 or 10 frs for checking tires. Train and airport porters get a fixed sum (6–10 frs) per bag. Museum guides should get 5–10 frs after a guided tour. It is standard practice to tip guides (and bus drivers) after an excursion.

Paris

Arriving and Departing

By Plane International flights arrive at either Charles de Gaulle Airport (Roissy), 15 miles (24 kilometers) northeast of Paris, or at Orly Airport, 10 miles (16 kilometers) south of the city. For information on arrival and departure times, call individual airlines.

Between the Airport and Downtown **From Charles de Gaulle:** Buses leave every 12 minutes from 5:45 AM to 11 PM. The fare is 35 frs and the trip takes 40 minutes (up to 1½ hours during rush hour). You arrive at Porte Maillot, on the Right Bank by the Hotel Concorde-Lafayette, a half-mile (one kilometer) west of the Champs-Elysées (two stops by métro).

From Orly: Buses leave every 12 minutes from 5:50 AM to 11 PM and arrive at the Air France terminal near Les Invalides on the Left Bank. The fare is 28 frs, and the trip takes between 30 and 60 minutes, depending on traffic.

Both airports provide bus shuttles (fare about 10 frs) to the nearest train stations, where you can take the RER service to Paris. The advantages of this are speed, price (25 frs to Paris from Charles de Gaulle in Roissy, 20 frs from Orly) and the fact that the RER trains link up directly with the métro system. The disadvantage is having to lug your bags around. Taxi fares from airports to Paris range from 150 to 200 frs).

By Train Paris has five international stations: **Gare du Nord** (for northern France, northern Europe, and England via Calais or Boulogne); **Gare de l'Est** (for Strasbourg, Luxembourg, Basle, and central Europe); **Gare de Lyon** (for Lyon, Marseille, the Riviera, Geneva, Italy); **Gare d'Austerlitz** (for the Loire Valley, southwest France, Spain); **Gare St-Lazare** (for Normandy, England via Dieppe). The **Gare Montparnasse** currently serves only western France (mainly Nantes and Brittany) but is scheduled as the terminus for the new TGV Atlantic service that should link Paris to Bordeaux and Spain by 1990. For train information, phone 45–82–50–50. You can reserve tickets at any Paris station regardless of the destination. Go to the **Grandes Lignes** counter for travel within France or to the **Billets Internationaux** (international tickets) desk if you're heading out of France.

By Bus Long-distance bus journeys within France are rare compared with train travel, and Paris has no central bus depot. The two leading Paris-based bus companies are **Eurolines Nord** (7 av. de la Villette, 19e, tel. 42–05–12–10) and **L'Autobus** (4 bis rue St-Sauveur, 2e, tel. 42–33–86–72).

By Car It is no surprise in a country as highly centralized as France that the highway system fans out from Paris. You arrive from the north (England/Belgium) via A1; from Normandy via A13; from the east via A4; from Spain and the southwest via A10; from the Alps, the Riviera, and Italy via A7. Each of these expressways connects with the beltway *(Periphérique)* that encircles Paris. Note that exits here are named by "Porte," not numbered. The *"Périphe"* can be extremely fast—but it gets very busy and is best avoided between 8 and 10 AM and between 5 and 7:30 PM.

Getting Around

Paris is relatively small as capital cities go, and most of its prize monuments and museums are within walking distance of one another. A river cruise is a pleasant way to get an introductory overview. The most convenient form of public transportation is the métro, with stops every few hundred yards; buses are a slower alternative, though they do let you see more of the city. Taxis are not expensive but not always easy to hail, either. Car travel within Paris is best avoided because parking is chronically difficult.

By Métro There are 13 métro lines crisscrossing Paris and the near suburbs, and you are seldom more than 500 yards or meters from the nearest station. It is essential to know the name of the last station on the line you take, since this name appears on all signs within the system. A connection (you can make as many as you please on one ticket) is called a *correspondance*. At junction stations, illuminated orange signs, bearing the names of each line terminus, appear over the corridors leading to the various correspondances. Illuminated blue signs, marked *sortie*, indicate the station exit.

The métro service starts out from each terminus at 5:30 AM and continues until 1:15 AM—when the last métro on each line reaches its terminus. Some lines and stations in the seedier parts of Paris are a bit risky at night—in particular Line 2 (Porte-Dauphine–Nation) and the northern section of Line 13 from St-Lazare to St-Denis/Asnieres. The long, bleak corridors at Jaurès and Stalingrad are a haven for pickpockets and purse snatchers. But the Paris métro is a relatively safe place, as long as you don't walk around with your wallet hanging out of your back pocket or (especially women) travel alone late at night.

The métro network connects at several points in Paris with RER trains that race across Paris from suburb to suburb: RER trains are a sort of "supersonic métro" and can be a great time-saver. All métro tickets and passes are valid for RER and bus travel within Paris. Second-class métro tickets cost 4.70 frs, each, though a carnet (10 tickets for 30 frs) is a far better value. Alternatively, you can buy a weekly *(coupon jaune)* or monthly *(carte orange)* ticket, sold according to zone. Zones 1 and 2 cover the entire métro network (cost: 46 frs per week or 162 frs per month). If you plan to take a suburban train to visit monuments in the Ile-de-France, you should consider a four-zone ticket (Versailles, St-Germain-en-Laye; 81 frs per week) or five-zone ticket (Rambouillet, Fontainebleau; 98 frs per week). For these weekly or monthly tickets, you need to obtain a pass (available from train and major métro stations) and provide two passport-size photographs.

There are also so-called *Sesame* tickets valid for two, four, or seven days (cost: 57, 85, and 141 frs, respectively) entitling you to first-class travel on the métro, buses, and RER A and RER B (south of the Gare du Nord only).

Access to métro and RER platforms is through an automatic ticket barrier. Slide your ticket in flat and pick it up as it pops up farther along. Keep your ticket; you'll need it again to leave the RER system.

By Bus Most buses run from around 6 AM to 8:30 PM; some continue until midnight. Night buses operate from 1 AM to 6 AM between Châtelet and nearby suburbs. They can be stopped by hailing them at any point on their route. The buses and the métro use the same tickets, but they must be bought either from métro stations or tobacco shops. You need to show weekly/monthly/Sesame tickets to the driver as you get on; if you have individual yellow tickets, you should state your destination and be prepared to punch one or more tickets in the red and gray machines on board the bus.

By Taxi There is no standard vehicle or color for Paris taxis, but all offer good value. Daytime rates (6:30 AM to 9 PM) within Paris are about 2.50 frs per kilometer, and nighttime rates are around 3.75 frs, plus a basic charge of 10 frs. Rates outside the city limits are slightly higher. It is best to ask your hotel or restaurant to ring for a taxi, since cruising cabs can be hard to find. There are numerous taxi stands, but you have to know where to look. Note that taxis seldom take more than three people at a time.

Important Addresses and Numbers

Tourist Information Paris Tourist Office, 127 av. des Champs-Elysées, tel. 47–23–61–72. Open daily 9 AM–8 PM. (Closed Dec. 25, Jan 1.) Offices in major train stations are open daily 8–8.

Embassies U.S. 2 av. Gabriel, 75008 Paris, tel. 42–96–12–02. **Canadian.** 35 av. Montaigne, 75008 Paris, tel. 42–25–99–55. **U.K.** 35 rue du Faubourg St-Honoré, 75008 Paris, tel. 42–66–91–42.

Emergencies **Police,** dial 17 for emergencies. Automatic phone booths can be found at various main crossroads for use in police emergencies (Police-Secours) or medical help (Services Medicaux); **Ambulance,** tel. 18 or 43–78–26–26; **Doctor,** tel. 47–07–77–77; **American Hospital,** 63 blvd. Victor-Hugo, Neuilly, tel. 47–47–53–00; **British Hospital,** 48 rue de Villiers, Levallois-Perret, tel. 47–58–13–12; **Dentist,** tel. 47–07–77–77 weekdays 8 AM–8 PM, 24-hour 43–37–51–00 8 PM–8 AM on weekdays, all day on

Paris Metro

Gabriel Péri
(Asnières-Genneviliers) **13**

Carrefour Pleyel
Mairie de
St-Ouen
St-Denis
Porte de Paris

Mairie de Clichy

Garibaldi

**Porte de
Clignancourt 4**

Porte de St-Ouen

Porte de Clichy

Guy Môquet

Jules Joffr
Lamarck-
Caulaincourt

Brochant

Abbesses

**Pont de Levallois-
Bécon 3**

Pigalle

La Fourche

Anvers

Anatole-
France

Blanche

Place de Clichy

Notre-
Dame-
de-Lorette

Saint-
Georges

Louise-Michel

Périere

Wogram

Malesherbes

Rome

Villiers

Liège

Trinité

Le Peletier

Cadet

**Richelieu-
Drouot**

R.
Montma

Porte de
Champerret

**St-
Lazare**

Europe

**Chaussée-
d'Antin**

**Havre-
Caumartin**

R. Montmart

Monceau

4 Septembre

Courcelles

St-
Augustin

Auber

Opéra

Bours

Pont de Neuilly

Ternes

St-Philippe-
du-Roule

Miromesnil

Madeleine

Pyramides

**Charles de Gaulle/
Etoile**
SUBURBAN RAIL LINE A

1

Les Sablons
Porte Maillot
Argentine
Victor
Hugo

6

George V

**F.D.
Roosevelt**

**Champs
Elysées
Clemenceau**

Concorde

Tuileries

Kléber

Alma-Marceau

Seine

Porte Dauphine

2

Boissière

Iéna

Invalides

Quai d'Orsay

Chambre des Députés

Trocadéro

Pont de
l'Alma

Varenne

Solférino

St-Germain
des-Prés

Rue de la Pompe
La Muette

Passy

Latour-
Maubourg

Rue du Bac

Ranelagh

St-François
Xavier

**Sèvres-
Babylone**

Mabillo

Jasmin

Champ-de-Mars

Bir-Hakeim

Duroc

Rennes

Vaneau

St-
Sulpic

Porte d'Auteuil

**Michel-
Ange-
Auteuil**

Eglise
d'Auteuil

Dupleix

Ecole
Mil.

Ségur

Saint-
Placide

Boulogne-
Jean-Jaurès

Sèvres-
Lecourbe

Falguière

10

**Michel-Ange-
Molitor**

Chardon
Lagache

Mirabeau

Javel

Charles
Michels

Emile
Zola

Cambronne

**La Motte-
Picquet**

Pasteur

**Montparnasse
Bienvenüe**

Edg
Quir

Boulogne-
Pt. de St-Cloud

Exelmans

Commerce

Volontaires

Gaîté

Boulevard
Victor

Félix Faure

Vaugirard

Pernety

SUBURBAN RAIL LINE C

Porte de
St-Cloud

Boucicaut

Plaisance

Lourmel

Convention

Porte de Vanves

Marcel Sembat

8

Balard

Porte de Versailles

Malakoff-
Plateau de Vanves

Bilancourt

Malatoff-
Rue Etienne Dolet

9 Pont de Sèvres

12

Mairie d'Issy

Corentin Celton

**Châtillon-
Montrouge**

13

weekends and holidays; 24-hour **Pharmacies,** *Dhéry*, Galerie des Champs, 84 av. des Champs-Elysées, tel. 45–62–02–41; *Drugstore*, corner of blvd. St-Germain and rue de Rennes, 6e (open until 2 AM), *Pharmacie des Arts*, 106 blvd. Montparnasse 6e (open until midnight).

English Bookstores **W. H. Smith,** 248 rue de Rivoli; **Galignani,** 224 rue de Rivoli; **Brentano's,** 37 av. de l'Opéra; **Marshall's Bookshop,** 26 rue de Brey; **Shakespeare & Co.,** rue de la Bûcherie.

Most newsstands in central Paris sell *Time, Newsweek*, and the *International Herald Tribune*.

Travel Agencies **American Express,** 11 rue Scribe 75009 Paris, tel. 42–66–09–99. **Thomas Cook,** 32 rue du 4 Septembre 75002 Paris, tel. 42–63–48–48.

Guided Tours

Orientation Tours Bus tours of Paris offer a good introduction to the city. The two largest operators are **Cityrama** (tel. 42–60–30–14) and **Paris Vision** (tel. 42–60–30–01). Tours start from their respective offices, 4 pl. des Pyramides and 214 rue de Rivoli. Both addresses are in the first arrondissement, opposite the Tuileries Gardens (toward the Louvre end). Tours are generally in double-decker buses with either a live guide or tape-recorded commentary (English, of course, available). They last three hours and cost about 140 frs). The same operators also offer a variety of other tours with a theme (Historic Paris, Modern Paris, Paris by night, etc.) lasting from 2½ hours to all day and costing between 110 and 270 frs.

Boat Trips Boat trips along the Seine are a must for first-time Paris visitors. The two most famous services are the **Bâteaux Mouches,** which leaves from the Pont de l'Alma, at the end of the Avenue George V, and the **Vedettes du Pont-Neuf,** which sets off from the square du Vert Galant, on the western edge of the Ile de la Cité. Price per trip is around 25 frs. Boats depart in season every half-hour from 10:30 AM to 5 PM (slightly less frequently in winter). Evening cruises are available most of the year and, thanks to the boats' powerful floodlights, offer unexpected views of Paris's riverbanks.

Canauxrama (tel. 46–07–13–13) organizes canal tours in flat-bottom barges along the picturesque but relatively unknown St-Martin and Ourcq Canals in East Paris. Departures from 5 bis quai de la Loire, 19e (métro Jaurès), or the Bassin de l'Arsenal, opposite 50 blvd. de la Bastille, 12e (métro *Bastille)*. Times vary, so phone to check hours. Cost: from 60 frs, depending on the time of day and length of trip.

Walking Tours There are numerous special-interest tours concentrating on historical or architectural topics. Most are in French, however. Charges vary between 25 and 50 frs, depending on fees that may be needed to visit certain buildings. Tours last about two hours and are generally held in the afternoon. Details are published in the weekly magazines *Pariscope* and *L'Officiel des Spectacles* under the heading "Conférences."

Excursions The **RATP** (Paris Transport Authority) organizes many guided excursions in and around Paris. Ask at its Tourist Service on the place de la Madeleine (north of place de la Concorde), or at the RATP office at St-Michel (53 quai des Grands-Augustins).

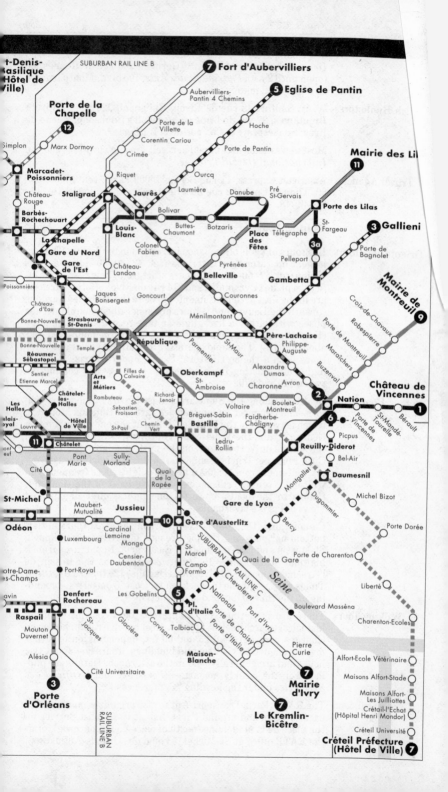

Cityrama and **Paris Vision** *(see* Getting Around By Bus) organize half- or full-day trips to Chartres, Versailles, Fontainebleau, the Loire Valley, and the Mont St-Michel at a cost
of between 140 and 750 frs.

Personal Guides **International Limousines,** (182 blvd. Péreire 17e, tel. 45–
74–77–12) has luxury cars and minibuses that take up to seven
passengers around Paris or to surrounding areas for a minimum of three hours. The cost is about 200 frs per hour. Phone
for details and reservations.

Exploring Paris

Paris is a compact city. With the possible exception of the Bois
de Boulogne and Montmartre, you can easily walk from one
sight to the next. Paris is divided in two by the River Seine,
with two islands (Ile de la Cité and Ile St-Louis) in the middle.
The south—or Left—Bank has a more intimate, Bohemian flavor than the haughtier Right Bank. The east–west axis from
Chatelet to the Arc de Triomphe, via the rue de Rivoli and the
Champs-Elysées, is the principal thoroughfare—for sightseeing and shopping on the Right Bank.

Monuments and museums are sometimes closed at lunchtime
(usually noon–2) and one day a week (Monday or Tuesday):
Check before you make the trip. And remember that cafés—
unlike British pubs, for example—stay open all day, making
them the goal of foot-weary tourists in need of coffee, a beer, or
a sandwich. Bakeries are another reliable source of sustenance.

Though attractions are grouped in four logical touring areas,
there are several "musts" that most first-time visitors will not
want to miss: the Eiffel Tower, the Champs-Elysées, the Louvre, and Notre-Dame. If time is a problem, you can explore
Notre-Dame and the Latin Quarter; head to place de la
Concorde and enjoy the vista from the Champs-Elysées to the
Louvre; then take a *bateau mouche* along the Seine for a waterside rendezvous with the Eiffel Tower and a host of other
monuments. You could finish off with dinner in Montmartre
and consider it a day well spent.

Notre-Dame and the Left Bank

❶ The most enduring symbol of Paris, and its historical and geographical heart, is **Notre-Dame Cathedral,** around the corner
from *Cité* métro station. This is the logical place to start any
tour of the city—especially as the tour starts on the Ile de la
Cité, one of the two islands in the middle of the Seine, where
Paris's first inhabitants settled around 250 B.C. Notre-Dame
has been a place of worship for more than 2,000 years; the present building is the fourth on this site. It was begun in 1163,
making it one of the earliest Gothic cathedrals, although building dragged on until 1345. The facade seems perfectly
proportioned until you notice that the north (left) tower is
wider than the south.

The interior is at its lightest and least cluttered in the early
morning. Bay-by-bay cleaning is gradually revealing the original honey color of the stone. Window space is limited and filled

Paris

Arc de Triomphe, **20**
Arènes de Lutèce, **7**
Aux Trois Quartiers, **30**
Bois de Boulogne, **19**
Centre Pompidou, **39**
Eglise de la
Madeleine, **28**

Eglise St-Séverin, **3**
Eiffel Tower, **17**
Fauchon's, **29**
Grand Palais, **21**
Les Grands
Magasins, **34**
Les Halles, **38**
Hôtel de Cluny, **4**
L'Hôtel des
Invalides, **15**

Hôtel de Ville, **44**
Jardin des Plantes, **8**
Jardin des Tuileries, **23**
Louvre, **24**
Louvre des
Antiquaires, **36**
Moulin Rouge, **27**

Musée Marmottan, **18**
Musée d'Orsay, **13**
Musée Picasso, **40**
Musée Rodin, **16**
Notre-Dame
Cathedral, **1**
Opéra, **33**
Palais Bourbon, **14**
Palais de Justice, **46**
Palais du
Luxembourg, **10**

with shimmering stained glass; the circular rose windows in the transept are particularly delicate. The 387-step climb up the towers is worth the effort for a perfect view of the famous gargoyles and the heart of Paris. *Towers open 10–5:30. Admission: 10 frs. Treasury (religious and vestmental relics) open 10–6 (Sun. 2–6). Admission: 15 frs.*

The pretty garden to the right of the cathedral leads to a bridge that crosses to the city's second and smaller island, the **Ile St-Louis,** barely 400 yards (366 meters) long and an oasis of inner-city repose.

② The rue des Deux Ponts bisects the island. Head left over the Pont de la Tournelle. To your left is the **Tour d'Argent,** one of the city's most famous restaurants.

③ Continue along quai de la Tournelle past Notre-Dame, then turn right at rue St-Jacques. A hundred yards ahead, on the right, is the back end of the **Eglise St-Séverin,** an elegant and unusually wide 16th-century church. Note the unique spiraling column among the forest of pillars behind the altar.

④ Turn left out of the church, cross the bustling boulevard St-Germain and take rue de Cluny to the left. This leads to the **Hôtel de Cluny.** Don't be misled by the name. This is a museum devoted to the late Middle Ages and Renaissance. Look for the *Lady with the Unicorn* tapestries and the beautifully displayed medieval statues. *6 pl Paul-Painlevé. Admission: 15 frs (Sun. 8 frs). Open Wed.–Mon. 9:45–12:30 and 2–5:15.*

⑤ Head up rue de la Sorbonne to the **Sorbonne,** Paris's ancient university. Students here used to listen to lectures in Latin, which explains why the surrounding area is known as the *Quartier Latin.* The Sorbonne's pompous 17th-century buildings hardly foster a campus atmosphere, as a quick stroll into the main courtyard (off place de la Sorbonne) will bear out.

⑥ Walking up rue Victor-Cousin and turning left into rue Cujas, you come to the **Panthéon.** Its huge dome and elegant colonnade are reminiscent of St. Paul's in London but date from a century later (1758–89). The Panthéon was intended to be a church, but during the Revolution was swiftly earmarked as a secular hall of fame. Its crypt contains the remains of such national heroes as Voltaire, Rousseau, and Zola. The interior is empty and austere, with principal interest centering on Puvis de Chavanne's late 19th-century frescoes, relating the life of Geneviève, patron saint of Paris. *Admission: 10 frs. Open 10–6.*

Behind the Panthéon is **St-Etienne du Mont,** a church with two claims to fame: Its ornate facade and its curly Renaissance rood-screen (1521–35) separating nave and chancel—the only one of its kind in Paris.

⑦ Take the adjoining rue Clovis, turn right into rue Descartes, then left at the lively place de la Contrescarpe down rue Rollin. Cross rue Monge to rue de Navarre. On the left is the **Arènes de Lutèce** (always open, free admission) a Gallo-Roman arena rediscovered only in 1869 and since parkscaped and excavated to reveal parts of the original amphitheater. It counts as one of the least-known points of interest in Paris.

⑧ Rue de Navarre and rue Lacépède lead to the **Jardin des Plantes** (Botanical Gardens), which have been on this site since the 17th century. The gardens have what is reputedly the oldest tree in Paris, a robinia planted in 1636 (allée Becquerel), plus a zoo, Alpine garden, hothouses, aquarium, and maze. Natural science enthusiasts will be in their element at the various museums, devoted to insects *(Musée Entomologique)*, fossils and prehistoric animals *(Musée Paléontologique)*, and minerals *(Musée Mineralogique)*. *Museums open Wed.–Mon. 2–5. Admission: 10–16 frs.*

Head back up Rue Lacépède from the Jardin des Plantes. Turn left into rue Gracieuse, then right into rue Ortolan, which soon crosses the rue Mouffetard—site of a colorful market and many restaurants. Continue along rue du Pot-de-Fer and rue Rataud. At rue Claude-Bernard, turn right; then make your first left up rue St-Jacques.

9 Set slightly back from the street is the **Val de Grâce,** a domed church designed by the great architect Jules Hardouin Mansart and erected in 1645–67 (after the Sorbonne church but before the Invalides). Its two-tiered facade, with capitals and triangular pedestals, is directly inspired by the Counter-Reformation Jesuit architectural style found more often in Rome than in Paris. The Baroque of the interior is epitomized by the huge twisted columns of the baldachin (ornamental canopy) over the altar.

Time Out If you're feeling thirsty (and rich), continue to the **Closerie des Lilas** along nearby boulevard de Port-Royal. This celebrated brasserie retains more style than some of its cousins farther down the once bohemian, now unexciting, boulevard Montparnasse, whose modern landmark, the 656-foot (200-meter) Tour Montparnasse, is visible in the distance. *171 blvd. Montparnasse, tel. 43–26–70–50. Dress: casual. Reservations advised. AE, DC, V.*

---

10 The view down the tree-lined avenue de l'Observatoire toward the gardens and **palais du Luxembourg** is more enticing. The palace was built by Queen Maria de' Medici at the beginning of the 17th century in answer to Florence's Pitti Palace. It now houses the French Senate and can be visited only on Sunday. In the surrounding gardens, mothers push their baby carriages along tree-lined paths among the majestic fountains and statues. *Palace visits: Sun. 9:30–11:30 and 2–4:30. Admission: 5 frs.*

Head through the gardens to the left of the palace into rue de Vaugirard. Turn left, then right into rue Madame, which leads **11** down to the enormous 17th-century church of **St-Sulpice.** Stand back and admire the impressive, though unfinished, 18th-century facade, with its unequal towers. The interior is overwhelmingly impersonal, but the wall paintings by Delacroix, in the first chapel on the right, are worth a visit.

12 Rue Bonaparte descends to boulevard St-Germain. You can hardly miss the sturdy pointed tower of **St-Germain-des-Prés,** the oldest church in Paris (begun around 1160, though the towers date back to the 11th century). Note the colorful nave frescoes by the 19th-century artist Hippolyte Flandrin, a pupil of Ingres.

Time Out The spirit of writers Jean-Paul Sartre and Simone de Beauvoir still haunts the **Café de Flore** opposite, though this, and the neighboring **Aux Deux Magots,** have more tourists than liter-

ary luminaries these days. Still, you can linger over a drink
while watching what seems to be all of Paris walking by. *Café
Flore and Aux Deux Magots, blvd. St-Germain. No credit
cards.*

Rue de l'Abbaye runs along behind St-Germain-des-Prés to
place Fürstenberg, a charming little square where fiery Romantic artist Eugène Delacroix (1798–1863) had his studio. If
you go there on a summer evening you'll usually find young
Frenchmen singing love songs, to guitar accompaniment. Turn
left into rue Jacob and continue along rue de l'Université. You
are now in the heart of the Carré Rive Gauche, the Left Bank's
district of art dealers and galleries.

About 250 yards (230 meters) along rue de l'Université, turn
⑬ down rue de Poitiers. Ahead is the sandstone bulk of the **Musée
d'Orsay.** Follow it around to the left to reach the main entrance.
The new Musée d'Orsay—opened in late 1986—is already one
of Paris's star tourist attractions, thanks to its imaginatively
housed collections of the arts (mainly French) spanning the
period 1848–1914. Exhibits take up three floors, but the visitor's immediate impression is one of a single, vast hall. This is
not surprising: The museum was originally built in 1900 as a
train station. The combination of hall and glass roof with narrow, clanky passages and intimate lighting lends Orsay a
human, pleasantly chaotic feel. You may get lost inside, but you
won't mind too much.

The chief artistic attraction, of course, is the Impressionist collection, transferred from the inadequate Jeu de Paume museum across the river. Other highlights include Art Nouveau furniture, a faithfully restored Belle Epoque restaurant (formerly
part of the station hotel), and a model of the Opéra quarter beneath a glass floor. *Musée d'Orsay. 62 rue de Lille, tel. 45–49–
48–14. Admission: 23 frs, 11 frs Sun. Open Tues., Wed., Fri.,
Sat. 10:30–5:30; Thurs. 10:30–9; Sun. 9–5:30.*

If the lines outside Orsay prove daunting, take a peek into the
Légion d'Honneur museum opposite, a stylish mansion with a
collection of French and foreign medals and decorations. *Admission: 10 frs. Open Tues.–Sun. 2–5.*

⑭ Return to the Seine and follow its bank to the 18th-century **Palais Bourbon** home of the French National Legislature
(Assemblée Nationale). The colonnaded facade commissioned
by Napoleon is a sparkling sight after a recent cleaning program (jeopardized at one stage by political squabbles as to
whether cleaning should begin from the left or right). There is
a fine view from the steps across to place de la Concorde and the
Madeleine.

Follow the Seine down to the exuberant **Pont Alexandre III.** The
Grand and Petit Palais are to your right, across the river. To the
⑮ left, the silhouette of **L'Hôtel des Invalides** soars above expansive if hardly manicured lawns. The Invalides was founded by
Louis XIV in 1674 to house wounded (or "invalid") war veterans. Although only a few old soldiers live here today, the
military link remains in the form of the **Musée de l'Armée**—a
vast collection of arms, armor, uniforms, banners, and pictures. The **Musée des Plans-Reliefs** contains a fascinating
collection of scale models of French towns made by military architect Vauban in the 17th century.

The museums are far from being the only reason for visiting the Invalides. It is an outstanding Baroque ensemble, designed by Bruand and Mansart, and its church possesses the city's most elegant dome as well as the tomb of Napoleon, whose remains are housed in a series of no less than six coffins within a tomb of red porphyry. *Open 10–6 (10–5 in winter). Admission to museums and church: 21 frs. A son-et-lumière performance in English is held in the main courtyard on evenings throughout the summer. Admission: 30 frs.*

🔟 Alongside is the **Musée Rodin.** Together with the Picasso Museum in the Marais, this is the most charming of Paris's individual museums, consisting of an old house (built 1728) with a pretty garden, both filled with the vigorous sculptures of Auguste Rodin (1840–1917). The garden also has hundreds of rosebushes, with dozens of different varieties. *77 rue de Varenne. Admission: 15 frs (7.5 frs Sun.). Open Wed.–Mon. 10–5:15.*

Take avenue de Tourville to avenue de La Motte-Picquet. Turn left, and in a few minutes you will come face to face with the
🔟 **Eiffel Tower.** It was built by Gustave Eiffel for the World Exhibition of 1889 and is in good shape to celebrate its 100th birthday. Recent restorations haven't made the elevators any faster —long lines are inevitable—but decent shops and two good restaurants have been added. Consider coming in the evening, when every girder is lit in glorious detail. Such was Eiffel's engineering precision that even in the fiercest winds the tower never sways more than 4½ inches (11½ centimeters). Today it is the foremost Parisian landmark and exudes a feeling of permanence. Standing beneath it, you may have trouble believing that it nearly became 7,000 tons of scrap-iron when its concession expired in 1909. Only its potential use as a radio antenna saved the day; it now bristles with a forest of radio and television transmitters. If you're full of energy, stride up the stairs as far as the third floor. But only the elevator goes right to the top. The view from 1,000 feet (305 meters) up will enable you to appreciate the city's layout and proportion. *Admission: on foot, 7 frs; elevator, 12–44 frs, depending on level. Open July, Aug. daily 10 AM–midnight, Sept.–June, Sun.–Thurs. 10 AM– 11 PM, Fri., Sat. 10 AM–midnight.*

West Paris and the Louvre

🔟 Our second itinerary starts at the **Musée Marmottan.** To get there, take the métro to *La Muette*, then head down chaussée de la Muette, through the small Ranelagh park to the corner of rue Boilly and avenue Raphaël. The museum is a sumptuous early 19th-century mansion, replete with many period furnishings, and probably is the most underestimated museum in Paris. It houses a magnificent collection of paintings by Claude Monet—including some of his huge, curving *Waterlily* canvasses—along with other Impressionist works and some delicately illustrated medieval manuscripts. *2 rue Louis-Boilly. Admission: 18 frs. Open Tues.–Sun. 10–5:30.*

Continue along rue Boilly and turn left on boulevard Suchet.
🔟 The next right takes you into the **Bois de Boulogne.** Class and style have been associated with "Le Bois" (The Woods) ever since it was landscaped into an upper-class playground by Haussmann in the 1850s. The attractions of this sprawling 2,200-acre (nine square kilometers) wood include cafés, restau-

rants, gardens, waterfalls, and lakes. You could happily spend a day or two exploring, but for the moment we suggest you pass Auteuil racetrack on the left and then walk to the right of the two lakes. An inexpensive ferry crosses frequently to an idyllic island. Rowboats can be rented at the far end of the lake. Just past the boathouse, turn right on the route de Suresnes and follow it to Porte Dauphine, a large traffic circle.

Cross over to avenue Foch, with the unmistakable silhouette of the Arc de Triomphe in the distance. Keep an eye out for the original Art Nouveau iron-and-glass entrance to *Porte Dauphine* métro station, on the left. Then continue along Foch, the **20** widest and grandest boulevard in Paris, to the **Arc de Triomphe.** This 164-foot (50-meter) arch was planned by Napoleon to celebrate his military successes. Yet when Empress Marie-Louise entered Paris in 1810, it was barely off the ground, and an arch of painted canvas had to be strung up to save appearances. Napoleon had been dead for more than 20 years when the Arc de Triomphe was finally finished in 1836. It has some monumental sculpture, but has recently been showing signs of decay: the netting is there to stop crumbling masonry from injuring those on the ground.

Place Charles de Gaulle, referred to by Parisians as **L'Etoile,** is one of Europe's most chaotic traffic circles. Short of a death-defying dash, your only way to get over to the Arc de Triomphe is to take the pedestrian underpass from either the Champs-Elysées (to your right as you arrive from avenue Foch) or avenue de la Grande Armée (to the left). France's Unknown Soldier is buried beneath the archway; the flame is rekindled every evening at 6:30.

From the top of the Arc you can see the "star" effect of Etoile's 12 radiating avenues and admire two special vistas: One, down the Champs-Elysées toward place de la Concorde and the Louvre, and the other, down avenue de la Grande-Armée toward La Tête Défense, a severe modern arch surrounded by imposing glass and concrete towers. Halfway up the Arc there is a small museum devoted to its history. *Museum and platform. Admission: 10 frs. Open 10–5:30.*

The Champs-Elysées is the site of colorful national ceremonies on July 14 and November 11; its trees are often decked out with French tricolors and foreign flags to mark visits from heads of state. It is also where the cosmopolitan pulse of Paris beats strongest. The gracefully sloping 1¼-mile (two-kilometer) boulevard was originally laid out in the 1660s by André Le Nôtre as a garden sweeping away from the Tuileries. There is not much sign of that as you stroll past the cafés, restaurants, airline offices, car showrooms, movie theaters, and chic arcades that occupy its upper half. Farther down, on the right, is **21** the **Grand Palais,** which plays host to Paris's major art exhibitions. Its glass roof makes its interior remarkably bright. *Admission varies. Usually open 10:30–6:30.*

The Grand Palais also houses the **Palais de la Découverte,** with scientific and mechanical exhibits and a planetarium. Entrance is in the avenue Franklin-Roosevelt. *Admission: 15 frs, additional 11 frs for planetarium. Open Tues.–Sun. 10–6.*

Directly opposite the main entrance to the Grand Palais is the **22** **Petit Palais,** built at the same time (1900) and now home to an attractively presented collection of French painting and furniture from the 18th and 19th centuries. *Admission: 12 frs. Open Tues.–Sun. 10–5:40.*

The flowerbeds, chestnut trees, and sandy sidewalks of the lower section of the Champs-Elysées are reminders of its original leafy elegance. Continue down to place de la Concorde, built around 1775 and scene of more than a thousand deaths at the guillotine, including those of Louis XVI and Marie-Antoinette. The obelisk, a gift from the viceroy of Egypt, was erected in 1833.

23 To the east of the place de la Concorde is the **Jardin des Tuileries:** formal gardens with trees, ponds, and statues. Standing sentinel on either side are the **Jeu de Paume**—former home of the Impressionist collection and now the home of temporary exhibitions—and the **Orangerie,** recently restored to contain some early 20th-century French works by Monet, Renoir, Marie Laurencin, and others. *Admission: 15 frs, 8 frs Sun. Open Wed.–Mon.*

Pass through the Tuileries to the Arc du Carrousel, a rather small triumphal arch erected more quickly (1806–08) than its big brother at the far end of the Champs-Elysées. Towering before you is the **Louvre,** with its controversial glass pyramids. **24** The Louvre, originally a royal palace, is today the world's largest and most famous museum. I. M. Pei's controversial pyramids are the highlight of a major modernization program, providing a new entrance vestibule and becoming the easternmost landmark of a majestic vista stretching through the Arc du Carrousel, Tuileries, place de la Concorde, the Champs-Elysées, and the Arc de Triomphe all the way to the giant arch of La Défense, 2½ miles (four kilometers) west of the capital.

The Louvre was begun as a fortress in 1200 (the earliest parts still standing date from the 1540s) and completed under Napoleon III in the 1860s. The apparent harmony of its buildings belies their various construction dates. The Louvre used to be even larger; a wing facing the Tuileries Gardens was razed by rampaging revolutionaries during the bloody Paris Commune of 1871.

Whatever the aesthetic merits of Pei's new-look Louvre, the museum has emerged less cramped and more rationally organized. Yet its sheer variety can seem intimidating. The main tourist attraction is Leonardo da Vinci's *Mona Lisa* (known in French as *La Joconde),* painted in 1503. The latest research, based on Leonardo's supposed homosexuality, would have us believe that the subject was actually a man! The *Mona Lisa* may disappoint you; it's smaller than most imagine, it's kept behind glass, and it's invariably encircled by a mob of tourists.

Turn your attention instead to some of the less-crowded rooms and galleries nearby, where Leonardo's fellow-Italians are strongly represented: Fra Angelico, Giotto, Mantegna, Raphael, Titian, and Veronese. El Greco, Murillo, and Velasquez lead the Spanish; Van Eyck, Rembrandt, Frans Hals, Brueghel, Holbein, and Rubens underline the achievements of northern European art. English paintings are highlighted by works of Lawrence, Reynolds, Gainsborough, and Turner. Highlights of French painting include works by Poussin, Fragonard, Chardin, Boucher, and Watteau—together with

David's *Coronation of Napoleon*, Géricault's *Raft of the Medusa*, and Delacroix's *Liberty Guiding the People.*

Famous statues include the soaring *Victory of Samothrace* (3rd century BC), the celebrated *Venus de Milo* (end of 2nd century BC), and the realistic Egyptian *Seated Scribe* (C. 2000 BC). Be sure to inspect the Gobelins tapestries, the Crown Jewels (including the 186-carat Regent diamond), and the 9th-century bronze statuette of Emperor Charlemagne. *Admission 20 frs, free Sun. Open Wed.–Mon. 9:45–6:30.*

Montmartre

If you start at the Anvers métro station and head up rue de Steinkerque, with its budget clothing shops, you will be greeted by the most familiar and spectacular view of the Sacré Coeur basilica atop the *Butte of Montmartre*. The **Sacré-Coeur** was built in a bizarre, mock-Byzantine style between 1876 and 1910. It is no favorite with aesthetes, yet it has become a major Paris landmark. It was built as an act of national penitence after the disastrous Franco-Prussian War of 1870—a Catholic show of strength at a time when conflict between Church and State was at its most bitter.

The large, rather gloomy interior is short on stained glass but long on golden mosaics; *Christ in Glory*, above the altar, is the most impressive. The basilica's many cupolas are dominated by a dome and a 260-foot (80-meter) belltower that contains the *Savoyarde*, one of the world's largest bells, cast in Annecy, Savoy, in 1895. The view from the dome is best on a clear day: All the sights of Paris are spread out before you.

Around the corner is the **place du Tertre**, full of would-be painters and trendy, overpriced restaurants. The painters have been setting up their easels on the square for years; don't be talked into having your portrait done unless you really want to—in which case, check the price first.

Despite its eternal tourist appeal and ever-growing commercialization, Montmartre has not lost all its traditional Bohemian color. Walk down rue Norvins and descend the bustling rue Lepic to place Blanche to one of the favorite haunts of Toulouse-Lautrec and other luminaries of the Belle Epoque—the legendary **Moulin Rouge** cabaret.

Montmartre is some distance from the rest of the city's major attractions, so go left up boulevard de Clichy as far as **place Pigalle,** then take the métro (direction Marie d'Issy) to Madeleine.

Central Paris

The **Eglise de la Madeleine,** with its array of uncompromising columns, looks like a Greek temple. The only natural light inside comes from three shallow domes; the walls are richly but harmoniously decorated, with plenty of gold glinting through the dim interior. The church was designed in 1814 but not consecrated until 1842, after efforts to turn the site into a train station were defeated. The portico's majestic Corinthian colonnade supports a huge pediment with s sculptured frieze of the *Last Judgment*. From the top of the steps you can admire the vista down rue Royale across the Seine. Another vista leads up boulevard Malesherbes to the dome of St-Augustin, a mid-19th-century church notable for its innovative use of iron girders as structural support.

Place de la Madeleine is in the heart of Paris's prime shopping
㉙ district: Jewelers line rue Royale; **Fauchon's,** behind the
㉚ Madeleine, is a high-class delicatessen; **Aux Trois Quartiers,** at the start of boulevard de la Madeleine, is a stylish department store.

Continue down boulevard de la Madeleine and turn right into boulevard des Capucines. This nondescript street leads to rue de
㉛ la Paix. Immediately to the right is **place Vendôme.** This is one of the world's most opulent squares, a rhythmically proportioned example of 17th-century urban architecture that shines in all its golden-stoned splendor since being sandblasted a few years ago. Other things shine here, too, in the windows of jewelry shops that are even more upscale (and discreet) than those in
㉜ rue Royale—fitting neighbors for the top-ranking **Ritz** hotel. The square's central column, topped by a statue of Napoleon, is made from the melted bronze of 1,200 cannons captured at the Battle of Auschwitz in 1805.

Time Out Rue de la Paix leads, logically enough, to the **Café de la Paix** on the corner of the place de l'Opéra. There are few grander cafés in Paris, and fewer places where you can perch with as good a tableau before you.

㉝ Dominating the northern side of the square is the imposing **Opéra,** the first great work of the architect Charles Garnier, who in 1860 won the contract to build the opera house, at the intersection of the *grands boulevards*. He used elements of neoclassical architecture—bas reliefs on facades and a fondness for columns—in an exaggerated combination that borders on parody. The lavishly upholstered auditorium, with its delightful ceiling painted by Marc Chagall in 1964, seems small—but this is because the stage is the largest in the world, accommodating up to 450 players. *Admission: 18 frs. Open Mon.–Sat. 10–5.*

㉞ Behind the Opéra are **les grands magasins,** Paris's most venerable department stores. The nearer of the two, the **Galeries Lafayette,** is the more outstanding because of its elegant turn-of-the-century glass dome. But **Printemps,** farther along boulevard Haussmann to the left, is better organized and has an excellent view from its rooftop cafeteria.

Take the métro at Chaussée d'Antin, near the Galeries Lafayette, and travel three stops (direction Villejuif) as far as
㉟ **Palais-Royal.** This former royal palace, built in the 1630s, has a charming garden, bordered by arcades and boutiques, that many visitors overlook.

㊱ On the square in front of the Palais-Royal is the **Louvre des Antiquaires,** a chic shopping mall full of antiques dealers. It deserves a browse whether you intend to buy or not. Afterward, head east along rue St-Honoré and left into rue du Louvre. Skirt the circular Bourse du Commerce (Commercial Ex-
㊲ change) and head toward the imposing church of **St-Eustache,** (1532–1637), an invaluable testimony to the stylistic transition between Gothic and Classical architecture. It is also the "cathe-
㊳ dral" of **Les Halles**—the site of the central market of Paris until

the much-loved glass-and-iron sheds were torn down in the late '60s. The area has since been transformed into a trendy shopping complex *(Le Forum)*.

Head across the topiary garden and left down rue Berger. Pass the square des Innocents, with its Renaissance fountain, to boulevard de Sébastopol. Straight ahead lies the futuristic, 39 funnel-topped **Centre Pompidou**—a must for lovers of modern art. The Centre Pompidou, also known as the Beauborg, was built in the mid-1970s and named in honor of former French president Georges Pompidou (1911–74). This "cultural Disneyland" is always crowded, housing a **Museum of Modern Art,** huge library, experimental music and industrial design sections, children's museum, and a variety of activities and exhibitions. Musicians, magicians, fire-eaters, and other street performers fill the large forecourt near the entrance. *Admission: Museum of Modern Art, 20 frs, free Sun.; 40 frs for daily pass covering all sectors of the centre. Open Mon., Wed.–Fri. noon–10, weekends 10–10; closed Tues.*

Continue east to the **Marais,** one of the most historic quarters of Paris. The spacious affluence of its 17th-century mansions, many restored to former glory, contrasts with narrow winding streets full of Jewish shops and restaurants. Rue de Rambuteau leads from the Centre Pompidou into rue des Francs-Bourgeois. Turn left on rue Elzivir to rue Thorigny, where you 40 will find the Hôtel Salé and its **Musée Picasso.** This is a convincing experiment in modern museum layout, whether you like Picasso or not. Few of his major works are here, but rather, many fine, little-known paintings, drawings, and engravings. *5 rue Thorigny. Admission: 21 frs. Open Thurs–Mon. 9:15–5:15, Wed. 9:15 AM—10 PM; closed Tues.*

Double back down rue Elzivir and turn left along rue des 41 Francs-Bourgeois until you reach the **place des Vosges.** Built in 1605, this is the oldest square in Paris. Its harmonious proportions, soft pink brick, and cloisterlike arcades give this square a feel of real calm. In the far corner is the **Maison de Victor Hugo,** containing souvenirs of the great poet's life and many of his surprisingly able paintings and ink drawings. *6 pl. des Vosges. Admission: 9 frs. Open Tues.–Sun. 10–5:40.*

Time Out The shops on nearby rue St-Antoine (see below) have all the makings for a first-class picnic, which you can have in the shade of the square inside pl. des Vosges.

Rue Birague leads from the middle of the place des Vosges, down to rue St-Antoine. About 100 yards (90 meters) down on 42 the left is the **place de la Bastille.** Unfortunately, there are no historic vestiges here; not even the soaring column, topped by the figure of Liberty, commemorates the famous storming of the Bastille in 1789. Only the new *Opéra de la Bastille,* opening in 1989, can be said to mark the bicentennial.

Retrace your steps down rue St-Antoine as far as the large Baroque church of **Saint-Paul-Saint-Louis** (1627–41). Then con-
43
44 tinue down the rue de Rivoli to the **Hôtel de Ville.** This magnificent city hall was rebuilt in its original Renaissance style after being burned down in 1871, during the violent days of the Paris Commune. The vast square in front of its many-statued facade is laid out with fountains and bronze lamps.

Avenue de Victoria leads to place du Châtelet. On the right is
45 the **Tour St-Jacques.** This richly worked 170-foot (52-meter)
stump is all that remains of a 16th-century church destroyed in
1802.

From Châtelet take the pont-au-Change over the Seine to the
46 Ile de la Cité and the **Palais de Justice** (law courts). Visit the
turreted **Conciergerie,** a former prison with a superb vaulted
14th-century hall *(Salles des Gens d'Armes)* that often hosts
temporary exhibitions. The **Tour de l'Horloge** (clock tower)
near the entrance on the quai de l'Horloge has a clock that has
been ticking off time since 1370. Round the corner in the boulevard du Palais, through the imposing law court gates, is the
Sainte-Chapelle, built by St-Louis (Louis IX) in the 1240s to
house the Crown of Thorns he had just bought from Emperor
Baldwin of Constantinople. The building's lead-covered wood
spire, rebuilt in 1854, rises 250 feet (76 meters). The somewhat
garish lower chapel is less impressive than the upper one,
whose walls consist of little else but dazzling 13th-century
stained glass. *Conciergerie and Sainte-Chapelle. Admission:
joint ticket 17 frs; single ticket 10 frs. Open daily 10–6.*

From boulevard du Palais turn right on quai des Orfèvres. This
47 will take you past the quaint place Dauphine to the **square du
Vert Galant** at the westernmost tip of the Ile de la Cité. Here,
above a peaceful garden, you will find a statue of the *Vert
Galant*—gallant adventurer Henry IV.

What to See and Do with Children

Children will enjoy a trip to the **Eiffel Tower** *(see* Exploring).

An hour on the Seine with a *bateau mouche* is good fun; so is a
ride in a rented rowboat in the Bois de Boulogne.

The Jardin d'Acclimation in the Bois de Boulogne, (métro Les
Sablons) has a children's amusement park and a zoo. Paris's
biggest zoo is in the **Bois de Vincennes** (métro Porte Dorée).

The two **Musée Grévin** waxworks museums are good on a rainy
afternoon. *10 blvd. Montmartre, 9e—métro rue Montmartre;
and Forum des Halles, 1er, métro Les Halles. Admission: 32
frs.*

Names of baby-sitting agencies can be found in *L'Officiel des
Spectacles* under "Gardes d'Enfants'." Basic rate is 25 frs per
hour. Free baby sitting for disabled children is provided by the
Fondation Claude Pompidou. *42 rue du Louvre, 1er, tel. 45–08–
45–15. Call between 2 and 6 PM.*

Off the Beaten Track

Few tourists venture into east Paris, but there are several
points of interest tucked away here. The largest is the **Bois de
Vincennes,** a less touristy version of the Bois de Boulogne,
with several cafés and lakes. Rowboats can be taken to the two
islands in Lac Daumesnil or to the three in Lac des Minimes.
There is also a zoo, cinder racetrack *(hippodrome)*, and an extensive flower garden *(Parc Floral, route de la Pyramide)*. The
Château de Vincennes (avenue de Paris) is an imposing, high-
walled castle surrounded by a dry moat and dominated by a
170-foot (52-meter) keep. It contains a replica of the Sainte-
Chapelle on Ile de la Cité and two elegant classical wings added

in the mid-17th century. *Best métro access to the woods is at Porte Dorée; to the flower garden and castle (admission: 10 francs; open 10–6), at Château de Vincennes.*

Cemeteries aren't every tourist's idea of the ultimate attraction, but **Père Lachaise** is the largest, most interesting, and most prestigious in Paris. It forms a veritable necropolis with cobbled avenues and tombs competing in pomposity and originality. Steep slopes and lush vegetation contribute to a powerful atmosphere; some people even bring picnic lunch. Leading incumbents include Chopin, Molière, Proust, Oscar Wilde, Sarah Bernhardt, Jim Morrison, and Edith Piaf. Get a map at the entrance and track them down. *Avenue du Père-Lachaise, 20e; métro Gambetta.*

The **Canal St-Martin** starts life just south of the Place de la Bastille but really comes into its own during the three-quarter-mile (1¼-kilometer) stretch north across the 10th *arrondissement*. It has an unexpected flavor of Amsterdam, thanks to its quiet banks, locks, and footbridges. *Closest métro stations: Jaurès to the north and Jacques Bonsergent to the south.*

If you're intrepid and don't mind the smell, a glimpse—and a good whiff—of subterranean Paris can be had in the sewers, **Les Egouts.** *Meet at the angle of quai d'Orsay and place de la Résistance on the Left Bank just east of Pont de l'Alma in the 7th arrondissement. Admission: 8 frs. Open Mon., Wed., and last Sat. of the month; 2–5; métro Alma-Marceau.*

Hidden away in a grid of narrow streets not far from the Opéra is Paris's central auction house, the **Hôtel Drouot.** It is open six days a week (except at Christmas, Easter, and midsummer), and its 16 salesrooms make a fascinating place to browse, with absolutely no obligation to bid—though you may well wish to do so! Everything from stamps and toy soldiers to Renoirs and 18th-century commodes is available. The mixture of fur-coated ladies with money to burn, penniless art lovers desperate to unearth an unidentified masterpiece, and scruffy dealers trying to look anonymous, make up Drouot's unusually rich social fabric. *Viewing takes place 11–noon and 2–6, with auctions starting at 2 PM (entrance at the corner of rue Rossini and rue Drouot, 9e; métro Richelieu-Drouot).*

Shopping

Gift Ideas Paris is the home to fashion and perfumes. Old prints are sold in stalls along the Left Bank of the Seine. For state-of-the-art home decorations, the shop in the **Musée des Arts Décoratifs** in the Louvre (107 rue de Rivoli) is worth visiting.

Antiques Antique dealers proliferate in the **Carré Rive Gauche** between St-Germain-des-Prés and the Musée d'Orsay. There are also several dealers around the Drouot auction house near Opéra (corner of rue Rossini and rue Drouot, 9e; métro: Richelieu-Drouot). The **Louvre des Antiquaires,** near the Palais-Royal (*see* Exploring), and the **Village Suisse,** near the Champ de Mars (78 av. de Suffren), are stylish shopping malls dominated by antiques.

Boutiques Only Milan can compete with Paris for the title of capital of European chic. The top shops are along both sides of the Champs-Elysées and along the avenue Montaigne and the rue du Faubourg St-Honoré. If you're on a tight budget, search for bargains along the shoddy streets around the foot of Montmartre (*see* Exploring), or near **Barbès-Rochechouart** métro station. The streets to the north of the Marais, close to **Arts-et-Métiers** métro, are historically linked to the cloth trade, and many shops offer garments at wholesale prices.

Department Stores The most famous department stores in Paris—*les grands magasins* on boulevard Haussmann—are mentioned above (*see* Exploring). Others include *Au Bon Marché* (near *Sèvres-Babylone* métro on the Left Bank); the *Samaritaine*, overlooking the Seine east of the Louvre (métro *Pont-Neuf*); and *Aux Trois Quartiers*, near the Madeleine (*see* Exploring).

Food and Flea Markets The sprawling *Marché aux Puces de St-Ouen*, just north of Paris, is one of Europe's largest flea markets. Best bargains are to be had early in the morning (open Sat.–Mon.; métro Porte de Clignancourt). There are smaller flea markets at the Porte de Vanves and Porte de Montreuil *(weekends only)*.

Dining

Eating out in Paris should be a pleasure, and there is no reason why choosing a less expensive restaurant should spoil the fun. After all, Parisians themselves eat out frequently and cannot afford five-star dining every night either.

Ratings Prices are per person and include a first course, main course, dessert, and all taxes and services (these are always included in the displayed prices), but no wine. Best bets within each category are indicated by a star ★. At press time, there were 5.7 francs to the dollar.

Category	Cost
Very Expensive	over 400 frs
Expensive	250–400 frs
Moderate	150–250 frs
Inexpensive	under 150 frs

Credit Cards The following credit card abbreviations are used: AE, American Express; DC, Diners Club; MC, MasterCard; V, Visa.

Left Bank
Very Expensive **Jules Verne.** The sensational view from this restaurant on the third floor of the Eiffel Tower is a fitting accompaniment to the subtle flavors of Louis Grondard's cuisine. The elegant gray-and-black decor is at its best at night, but prices are most accessible on a weekday at lunch, when there is a good fixed-price menu. *Eiffel Tower, 7e, tel. 45–55–61–44. Jacket. Reservations essential. AE, DC, V.*

★ **Tour d'Argent.** Discretion is the key at this temple of French gastronomy, on the Left Bank opposite the Ile St-Louis. The restaurant's exterior is plain, yet inside, a plush elevator whisks you to the top and to a memorable view of Notre-Dame and the Ile de la Cité. Waiters materialize in anticipation of your slightest wish. Parisians are hoping that the food will maintain its high standards under new chef Manuel Martinez. The prices will do so, without doubt, although there is a fixed-price lunch menu every day except Sunday. *15 quai de la Tournelle, 5e, tel. 43–54–23–31. Jacket and tie. Reservations essential. AE, DC, V. Closed Mon.*

Expensive **Le Coupe-Chou.** This is a rickety old town house at the foot of Montagne Ste-Genevieve, near the Pantheon. Uneven floors, bare stone walls, and candlelit alcoves make this many-roomed restaurant popular for its atmosphere. The service can seem desultory, but the competent cuisine and magical setting compensate. Coffee amid the cushions and flickering shadows of the after-dinner lounge makes a romantic end to the evening. *9 rue Lanneau, 5e, tel. 46-33-68-69. Jacket and tie. Reservations advised. V. Closed Sun. lunch.*

Moderate **Petit Zinc.** This is a long-established haunt on the lively rue du Buci. Its imperturbable white-aproned waiters and unpretentious Belle Epoque decor lend it an authentically Parisian atmosphere, especially on the bustling, green-walled first floor; the room upstairs is larger but more discreetly lit. The seafood is good here; game and poultry (the guinea-fowl— *pintade*—is recommended) are served up in robust sauces. It is open until 3 AM. *25 rue de Buci, 6e, tel. 43-54-79-34. Dress: informal. Reservations advisable. AE, DC, MC, V.*

Suffren. Next to the Ecole Militaire at the far end of the Champ de Mars, is this archetypal brasserie: lively, good value, with oysters, fish, and other seafood in abundance. The fast-speaking, nonstop waiters rush you into ordering, promptly forget about you for half an hour, then inquire anxiously if you're enjoying your meal. Foreigners are treated with a welcome lack of condescension. *84 av. de Suffren, 15e, tel. 45-66-97-86. Dress: informal. Reservations not needed. V. Closed Mon.*

Vagénende. Dark wood, gleaming mirrors, and obsequious waiters take the Vagénende dangerously close to turn-of-the-century pastiche. It claims to be a bustling brasserie, but don't believe it: Service is far too unhurried and the dining room far too cozy (despite the efforts of the mirrors to make it seem huge). Get over all these contradictions and you can be sure of having a copious and enjoyable meal (foie gras, oysters, and chocolate-based desserts outstanding), with a stroll outside along the cheerful boulevard St-Germain to walk it off. *142 blvd. St-Germain, 6e, tel. 43-26-68-18. Dress: informal. Reservations advisable. AE, DC, MC, V. Closed Feb. 1–8.*

West Paris **Maxim's.** Eating here is a once-in-a-lifetime experience for two
Very Expensive reasons: First, the plush velvet interior, with its curly riot of Art Nouveau furnishings; second, Maxim's international reputation for luxurious abandon. Unfortunately, the check—and not the cuisine—is the most lasting reminder of a dinner here, but that seems not to bother most customers. *3 rue Royale, 8e, tel. 42-65-27-94. Jacket and tie. Reservations essential. AE, DC, V. Closed Sun. in July, Aug.*

★ **Robuchon.** Virtuoso chef Joël Robuchon is a cult figure in epicurean circles and a worthy successor to the great Jamin, previous owner of this elegant restaurant near the Trocadero. To get a table here—there are only 45 seats—you need to make a reservation well in advance, but it is worth it: The menu changes constantly as Robuchon concocts new works of edible art. *32 rue de Longchamp, 16e, tel. 47-27-12-27. Jacket and tie. Reservations essential. AE, DC, V. Closed Sat., Sun., Aug.*

Expensive **Chez Edgard.** Some come here for the reliable French cuisine, accompanied by a fine wine list. But most are eavesdroppers, picking up the crumbs from the whispered conversations of senior politicians and journalists amid the discreet warmth of its deep red decor. It is a place to watch Paris power brokers in action—and a handy address close to the Champs-Elysées. *4 rue Marbeuf, 8e, tel. 47–20–51–15. Jacket and tie. Reservations advisable. AE, DC, MC, V. Closed Sun.*

Inexpensive **Relais de la Sabretèche.** It's worth traveling deep into the residential 16th arrondissement, near the Porte de St-Cloud, for a restaurant that offers both unbeatable value and appealing, country-house decor. We suggest you consider the four-course set menu (served lunchtimes and at dinner until 9 PM) for about 90 frs. For double the price, you can wash the meal down with a St-Estèphe or Châteauneuf-du-Pape (ask for a bottle from the cellar or it will be too warm). The service is discreet to the point of forgetfulness. *183 blvd. Murat, 16e, tel. 46–47–91–39. Dress: informal. Reservations advised. V. Closed Sun. dinner, Mon.*

Montmartre and **Au Quai des Ormes.** Sometimes you're better off at a restaurant
Central Paris that seems to make no concessions to tourists. Au Quai des
Expensive Ormes is one of these. Most of its business comes from Parisians who put the quality of food—particularly the game entrées—before strained attempts at atmosphere. A special low-calorie menu (rare in Paris) indicates a further concern for the customer. An attractive and convenient setting on the Right Bank, by the Ile St-Louis, adds to its popularity. *72 quai de l'Hotel de Ville 4e, tel. 42–74–72–22. Jacket. Reservations essential. V. Closed Sat., Sun.*

Escargot Montorgueil. Traditional French favorites—such as snails, of course—help the Escargot Montorgueil maintain its reputation as one of the most reliable restaurants in Les Halles. The extravagant turn-of-the-century decor—with mirrors and traditional wall sofas—recalls the time before this area underwent its dramatic face-lift. *38 rue Montorgueil, 1er, tel. 42–36–83–51. Jacket. Reservations essential. AE, DC, MC, V. Closed for one week in mid-Aug.*

Moderate **Brasserie Flo.** Flo is an authentic, bustling brasserie that effortlessly recaptures the spirit of 1900. Sausages and sauerkraut are served with large glasses of Alsatian beer. The atmosphere gets livelier—some would say noisier—through the evening. Closing time is 1:30 AM. *7 cour des Petites-Ecuries, 10e, tel. 47–70–13–59. Dress: informal. Reservations essential. AE, DC, V.*

Clodenis. A small, elegant restaurant down the slope from the Sacré Coeur, Clodenis serves excellent fish dishes and has some fixed-price menus for less than 200 frs. The decor—soft lighting, small tables, and salmon-pink wallpaper—is easy on the eye. *57 rue Caulaincourt, 18e, tel. 46–06–20–26. Jacket. Reservations advised. AE, DC, V. Closed Sun., Mon.*

Inexpensive **Chartier.** This is the down-to-earth Belle Epoque cousin of the Vagénende (*see* Left Bank). Again, there are mirrors and fancy lamps, but here you'll be rushed and crowded; the waiter's white apron will be stained, and your check will be written on the tablecloth. This is the gastronomic equivalent of roughing it, but as this is Paris, you can have steak, fries, and a glass of wine for the same price as the burger meal at the fast-food places nearby. The good food belies the price. *7 rue du Faubourg-Montmartre, 9e, tel. 47–70–86–29. Dress: informal. No reservations. No credit cards. Closes 9:30 PM.*

★ **Jo Goldenberg.** The doyen of Jewish eating places in Paris, Jo Goldenberg is in the heart of the most Jewish district, the Marais. Its two-level restaurant, with modern paintings, is always good-natured and crowded. The food is solid and cheap and heavily influenced by Central Europe (ground beef and salami). This makes it a great place to dine on a winter evening, but a bit heavy going in summer. The Israeli and Eastern European wines are rarely available elsewhere in France. *7 rue Rosiers, 4e, tel. 48–87–20–16. Dress: informal. Reservations advised. AE, DC, V.*

Lodging

Paris is popular throughout the year, so make reservations early. The cost of renovating many hotels for the bicentennial celebrations has been passed on to the consumer, so be prepared for higher prices.

Ratings Prices are for double rooms and include all taxes. Best bets in each of the price categories are indicated by a star ★. At press time, there were 5.7 francs to the dollar.

Category	Cost
Very Expensive	over 850 frs
Expensive	450–850 frs
Moderate	250–450 frs
Inexpensive	under 250 frs

Credit Cards The following credit card abbreviations are used: AE, American Express; DC, Diners Club; MC, MasterCard; V, Visa.

Left Bank and Ile St-Louis
Very Expensive

Lutetia-Concorde. Looking across a leafy square at the Bon Marché department store, the Lutetia-Concorde maintains its excellent reputation for old-fashioned service. The building was renovated from top to bottom only four years ago, under the eagle eye of top fashion designer Sonia Rykiel. The facade shines again, and the elegant interiors are full of Art Deco touches. *45 blvd. Raspail, 6e, tel. 45–44–38–10. 300 rooms with bath. Facilities: air-conditioning. AE, DC, MC, V.*

Expensive
★

Hôtel d'Angleterre. Some claim the Hôtel d'Angleterre is the ultimate Left Bank hotel: a little shabby, but elegant, small, and perfectly managed. The 18th-century building was originally the British ambassador's residence; later, Ernest Hemingway made it his Paris home. Room sizes and rates vary greatly, and all rooms are individually decorated. Some are imposingly formal, others are homey and plain. Ask for one overlooking the courtyard. There's no restaurant, but a small bar has been installed. *44 rue Jacob, 6e, tel. 42–60–34–72. 30 rooms with bath. Facilities: bar. AE, DC, MC, V.*

Moderate

Esmeralda. You'll find this delightful 17th-century inn just across from Notre-Dame. The rooms are small but full of character: Don't be afraid to ask for one with a view of the cathedral. There are also three inexpensive singles in the eaves. *4 rue St-Julien-le-Pauvre, 5e, tel. 43–54–19–20. 19 rooms, all doubles with bath or shower. Facilities: sauna. No credit cards.*

Marroniers. There are few better places in Paris for great value and great atmosphere. Located on appealing rue Jacob, the hotel is reached through a small courtyard. All the rooms are light and full of character. Those on the top floor have sloping ceilings, uneven floors, and terrific views over the church of St-Germain-des-Prés. The vaulted cellars have been converted into two atmospheric lounges. There's a bar but no restaurant. *21 rue Jacob, 6e, tel. 43–25–30–60. 37 rooms with bath. Facilities: bar. No credit cards.*

St-Louis. This is another of the Ile-St-Louis's elegantly converted 17th-century town houses, and antique furniture and oil paintings decorate the public areas. The bedrooms are elegantly simple, with exposed beams and stone walls. Blue-gray or light brown tiles add a classy accent to the bathrooms. Breakfast is served in the ancient cellar, but there's no restaurant or bar. *75 rue St-Louis-en-Ile, 4e, tel. 46–34–04–80. 21 rooms with bath. No credit cards.*

Inexpensive **Vieux Paris.** Low rates and a handy location on a side street leading to the Seine make the Vieux Paris a winner. The hotel is tiny and is set in a late 15th-century building. You won't find great comfort in the rooms—some of them are *very* small—but the combination of age and slightly musty French charm is hard to resist. *9 rue Gît-le-Coeur, 6e, tel. 43–54–41–66. 21 rooms, 11 with bath. MC, V.*

West Paris
Very Expensive
★

Le Bristol. Luxury and discretion are the Bristol's trump cards. The understated facade on rue du Faubourg St-Honoré might mislead the unknowing, but the Bristol ranks among Paris's top four hotels. The spaciously elegant and air-conditioned rooms all have authentic Louis XV and Louis XVI furniture. Moreover, the management has filled the public room with paintings, sculptures, sumptuous carpets, and tapestries. The marble bathrooms are magnificent. Nonguests can have tea in the vast garden or dine in the summer restaurant; the piano bar is open till 1 AM. For hotel guests, there's a pool on the roof, complete with solarium and sauna. Service throughout is impeccable. *112 rue du Faubourg St-Honoré, 8e, tel. 42–66–91–45. 200 rooms and 45 suites with bath. Facilities: 2 restaurants, bar, pool, sauna, solarium, parking, conference facilities for 400. AE, DC, MC, V.*

Crillon. There can surely be no more sumptuous hotel than this regal mansion overlooking place de la Concorde. The Crillon was founded in 1909—and is still run—by the Champagne family Taittinger, with the express intention of creating the best hotel in the city. They chose as their setting two adjoining town houses built by order of Louis XV. Renovations in the '80s have seen great additional comfort—all rooms are air-conditioned—though not at the expense of the original imposing interior. Mirrors, marbles, tapestries, sculptures, great sprays of flowers, and glistening floors are found in all the public rooms. The expansive bedrooms have judicious mixtures of original and reproduction antiques and are hung with beige velvet. The bathrooms are, of course, marble. If you want to enjoy the amazing view over place de la Concorde to the National Assembly, you'll have to reserve one of the palatial suites. Of the three restaurants, the best is Les Ambassadeurs, housed in what was originally the Grand Salon and offering the best hotel food in the city. *10 place de la Concorde, 8e, tel. 42–65–24–24. 189 rooms and suites with bath. Facilities: 3 restaurants, bars, private reception rooms. AE, DC, MC, V.*

George V. Some say that the George V lacks the style of its super deluxe Parisian counterparts. Others value its unashamedly international atmosphere. There's no lack of authentic period furniture or of excellent, highly trained staff, but the stylishness of the Crillon, say, or the Bristol, is noticeably absent. Nonetheless, all the rooms are impeccably decorated and imposing, though the penthouse suites are the only ones to enjoy a commanding view over the city. There are a number of restaurants, the best of which is Les Princes; in summer, you can eat on the leafy patio. *31 av. George V, 8e, tel. 47–23–54–00. 250 rooms and 42 suites with bath. Facilities: 3 restaurants, bars, shopping mall, hairdresser, conference facilities. AE, DC, MC, V.*

Moderate **Bradford.** The Bradford prides itself on providing slightly old-fashioned, well-polished service in an appealing, fusty atmosphere, the kind that has guests coming back year after year. It's no surprise to learn that this is a family-run hotel. An old wooden elevator takes you up from the flower-filled lobby to the rooms. Some are vast, with brass beds and imposing fireplaces. None has TV; that's not the Bradford style. Drinks are served in the soothing Louis XVI-style lounge on the first floor; there's no restaurant. *10 rue St-Philippe-du-Roule, 8e, tel. 43–59–24–20. 49 rooms with bath, 12 with shower. MC, V.*

Queen's Hotel. Queen's is one of only a handful of hotels located in the desirable residential district around rue la Fontaine, within walking distance of the Seine and the Bois de Boulogne. The hotel is small and functional, but standards of comfort and service are high. Flowers on the facade add an appealing note. *4 rue Bastien-Lepage, 16e, tel. 42–88–89–85. 7 rooms with bath, 22 with shower. MC, V.*

Montmartre and Central
Very Expensive
Grand. The restoration in 1988 of the Grand's honey-colored facade put the final touch to a three-year renovation program that has transformed this 19th-century palace on place de l'Opéra. All rooms have been lavishly redecorated in Art Nouveau style and are air-conditioned. The hotel prides itself on its exemplary business facilities, not the least of which are its three restaurants. The Opéra is the most formal and imposing, while the Relais Capucines offers less intimidatingly grand meals. Le Patio serves buffet lunches and breakfast. *2 rue Scribe, 9e, tel. 42–68–12–13. 515 rooms and suites with bath. Facilities: 3 restaurants, 2 bars, 13 conference rooms, secretarial services, travel agency, shops, parking for 2,000 cars. AE, DC, MC, V.*

Ritz. The Paris Ritz is one of the world's most famous hotels, located on the most famous and elegant square in the city. Millions of dollars have been lavished on the hotel by Egyptian-born owner Mohammed al-Fayed (the owner of Harrods in London). The building is a sumptuous 18th-century town house, a delightful combination of elegance and comfort. The luxurious suites are named after just some of the guests who have stayed here—Coco Chanel, Marcel Proust, and Edward VII among them. The two restaurants—L'Espador and the Vendôme—maintain the luxurious note. *15 pl. Vendôme, 1er, tel. 42–60–38–30. 187 fully equipped rooms and 46 suites. Facilities: health and sports complex, 2 restaurants. AE, DC, MC, V.*

Expensive **Bretonerie.** You'll find this small, three-star hotel on a tiny street in the Marais, a couple of minutes' walk from the Beaubourg. Rooms are decorated in elegant Louis XIII-style but vary considerably in size. The largest is room 1, a duplex; others are definitely cramped. The bar and breakfast rooms in the vaulted cellar have been completely renovated, but there is no restaurant. *22 rue Ste-Croix-de-la-Bretonnerie, 4e, tel. 48–87–77–63. 27 rooms with bath, 5 with shower. Facilities: bar. MC, V.*

Regina. The historic place des Pyramides is the location of this late 19th-century hotel. The building is somewhat old-fashioned and formal, but the rooms are spacious and the service is excellent—friendly but efficient. There is a restaurant and a bar. Ask for a room overlooking the Louvre and the Tuileries Gardens. *2 pl. des Pyramides, 1er, tel. 42–60–31–10. 130 rooms and 15 suites with bath. AE, DC, MC, V. Restaurant usually closed in Aug.*

Moderate **Family.** A few minutes' walk from the Tuileries Gardens will get you to this small two-star hotel near the Madeleine. It was entirely renovated in 1988, but the rooms have kept their stylish '30s look. There's no restaurant, but breakfast and snacks can be served in your room. Service is exceptionally friendly. *35 rue Cambon, 1er, tel. 42–61–54–84. 24 rooms and 1 suite with bath. MC, V.*

Place des Vosges. A loyal American clientele swears by this historic little hotel, located on a charming street just off the exquisite square of the same name. The grand entrance hall is decorated in Louis XIII style; some of the rooms, however, are little more than functional, and a number of the smaller ones fall into the inexpensive category. There's no restaurant, but there's a welcoming little breakfast room. *12 rue de Birague, 4e, tel. 42–72–60–46. 11 rooms with bath, 5 with shower. AE, DC, MC, V.*

Regyn's Montmartre. Despite small rooms (all currently being renovated), this small, owner-run hotel in Montmartre's place des Abbesses is rapidly gaining an enviable reputation for simple but stylish accommodation. A predominantly young clientele and a correspondingly relaxed atmosphere have made the hotel very popular. Try for one of the rooms on the upper floors for great views over the city. *18 pl. des Abbesses, 18e, tel. 42–54–45–21. 14 rooms with bath, 8 with shower. DC, MC, V.*

The Arts

The monthly magazine *Passion* (in English) and the weekly magazines *Pariscope, L'Officiel des Spectacles* and *7 à Paris* give detailed entertainment listings. The best place to buy tickets is at the place of performance. Otherwise, try hotels, travel agencies (try *Paris-Vision* at 214 rue de Rivoli), and special ticket counters (in the FNAC stores at 26 av. de Wagram, near the Arc de Triomphe and the Forum des Halles). Half-price tickets for same-day theater performances are available at the ticket stand at the west side of the Madeleine church.

Theater There is no Parisian equivalent to Broadway or the West End, although a number of theaters line the grands boulevards between Opéra and République. Shows are mostly in French; classical drama is at the distinguished **Comédie Française** (by Palais-Royal). A completely different charm is to be found in the tiny **Théâtre de la Huchette,** near St-Michel, where Ionesco's short modern plays make a deliberately ridiculous mess of the French language.

Concerts The principal place for classical music is the *Salle Pleyel* (252 rue du Faubourg St-Honoré), near the Arc de Triomphe; leading international orchestras play here regularly. You can also attend one of the many inexpensive organ or chamber music concerts in churches throughout the city.

Opera   The Opéra itself is a splendid building, and, with Rudolf Nureyev as artistic director, its dance program has reached new heights. Getting a ticket for an opera or ballet performance is not easy, though, and requires either luck, much preplanning, or a well-connected hotel receptionist. The **Opéra Comique** (the French term for opera with spoken dialogue), close by in the rue Favart, is more accessible. The new **Opéra de la Bastille** was in the throes of completion at press time; it should open in 1989 and stage both traditional opera and symphony concerts.

Films   There are hundreds of movie theaters in Paris and some of them, especially in principal tourist areas such as the Champs-Elysées or the boulevard des Italiens near Opéra, run English films marked "V.O." *(version original,* i.e., not dubbed). Admission is around 30–35 frs, with reduced rates on Monday. Movie fanatics should check out the **Centre Pompidou** and **Musée de Cinéma** at Trocadéro, where old and rare films are often screened.

Entertainment and Nightlife

Cabaret   This is what Paris is supposed to be all about. Its nightclubs are household names—more so abroad than in France, it would seem, judging by the hefty percentage of foreigners present at most shows. Prices range from 150 frs (basic admission plus one drink) up to 500 frs (dinner included). For 250–350 frs, you can get a good seat plus half a bottle of Champagne.

The **Crazy Horse** (12 av George V, tel. 47–23–32–32) is one of the field leaders in pretty women and dance routines: It features lots of humor and a lot less clothes. The **Moulin Rouge** (place Blanche, tel. 46–06–00–19) is an old favorite at the foot of Montmartre. Nearby is the **Folies-Bergère**, (32 rue Richer, tel. 42–46–77–11), not as it once was but still renowned for its glitter and vocal numbers. The **Lido** (116 bis av. des Champs-Elysées, tel. 45–63–11–61) is all razzle-dazzle.

Bars and   Upscale nightclubs are usually private, so, unless you have a
Nightclubs   friend who is a member, forget it. A good bet, though, for drinking and dancing the night away, is the **Club 79** (79 av. des Champs-Elysées). For a more leisurely evening in an atmosphere that is part bar and part gentlemen's club, try an old haunt of Hemingway, Fitzgerald, and Gertrude Stein— **Harry's Bar** (5 rue Danou), a cozy wood-paneled spot for Americans, journalists, and sportsmen.

Jazz Clubs   The Latin Quarter is a good place to track down Paris jazz, and the doyen of clubs is the **Caveau de la Huchette,** where you can hear Dixieland in a hectic, smoke-filled atmosphere. *5 rue de la Huchette. Open Sun.–Thurs. 9:30 PM–2:30 AM, Fri. 9:30 PM–3:30 AM, Sat. 9:30 PM–4 AM. Admission: 45–55 frs.*

Le Slów Club, another favorite, tries to resurrect the style of early Bourbon street, and nearly succeeds. *130 rue de Rivoli. Open Tues.–Sat. 9:30 PM–2:30 AM. Admission: 50–60 frs.*

Rock Clubs   **Le Sunset** is a small, whitewashed cellar with first-rate live music and a clientele that's there to listen. *60 rue des Lombards. Open from 11 PM. Admission varies.*

New Morning is a top spot for visiting American musicians and good French bands. *7 rue des Petites Ecuries. Open from 9:30 PM. Admission varies.*

Discos **Club Zed** is the best place for lively dancing. *2 rue des Anglais. Open 10:30–dawn. Admission: 50–85 frs.*

Memphis boasts some impressive lighting and video gadgetry. *3 impasse Bonne Nouvelle. Open 10:45 PM–dawn. Admission: 80–100 frs.*

Ile de France

The area surrounding Paris is called the Ile (island) de France, reflecting the role it has played over the centuries as the economic, political, and religious center of the country. For many visitors to Paris, it is the first taste of French provincial life, with its slower pace and fierce devotion to the soil.

Parts of the area are fighting a losing battle to resist the encroaching capitol, but you can still see the countryside that was the inspiration for the Impressionists and other 19th-century painters, and a wealth of architecture dating back to the Middle Ages. The most famous buildings are Chartres—for many the most beautiful of French cathedrals—and Versailles, the monumental château of Louis XIV, the Sun King.

Before the completion of Versailles, King and Court resided in the delightful château of St-Germain-en-Laye, west of Paris. This is within easy day-trip range from Paris, as are the châteaux of Vaux-le-Vicomte, Rambouillet, and Fontainebleau.

Getting Around

The attractions below can all be reached easily from Paris by car and by regular suburban train (RER) services. But you might find it convenient to group some of them together: Versailles, Rambouillet, and Chartres are all on the Paris–Chartres train line; Fontainebleau, Barbizon, and Vaux-le-Vicomte are all within a few miles of each other.

By Car Expressway A13, from the Porte d'Auteuil, followed by A12, will take you from Paris to Versailles. Alternatively, you can get to Chartres on A10 or N10 south from Porte d'Orleans. For Fontainebleau, take A6 from Porte d'Orleans or, for a more attractive route through the forest of Senart and the northern part of the forest of Fontainebleau, take N6 from Porte de Charenton via Melun. Vaux-le-Vicomte is four miles (six kilometers) northeast of Melun via N36 and D215.

By Train Three lines connect Paris with Versailles; on each, the trip takes about 30 minutes. Best for the château is RER C2 (Express métro line) to Versailles Rive Gauche station. Trains from Gare St-Lazare go to Versailles Rive Droite. Trains from Gare Montparnasse go to Versailles Chantiers and then on to Rambouillet and Chartres. Fontainebleau is served by 20 trains a day from Gare de Lyon; buses for Barbizon leave from in front of the main post office in Fontainebleau.

Guided Tours

Two private companies, **Cityrama** and **Paris Vision,** organize regular half-day and full-day tours from Paris with English-speaking guides. Times and prices are identical. Cityrama tours depart from 4 place des Pyramides 1e, tel. 42–60–30–14. Paris Vision leaves from 214 rue de Rivoli 1e, tel. 42–60–31–25.

Versailles and Les Trianons. Daily excursions starting at 9:30 include a complete tour of Paris in the morning followed by an afternoon at Versailles. Half-day excursions of Versailles leave mornings and afternoons daily (9:30 and 1:30. Admission: 160 frs) and include a guided tour of the château, Hall of Mirrors, and Queen's Suite. On Thursday only, a daylong excursion (280 frs) extends the tour to include an afternoon visit (starting 1:30) to Les Trianons. Separate afternoon visits to Les Trianons, again on Thursday, start at 1:30 (140 frs).

Chartres. Both companies organize half-day tours to Chartres on Tuesday and Saturday afternoons (departure at 1. 180 frs), but if you're short of time or cash, you'd be better off taking the **Versailles-Chartres** day trips, also on Tuesday and Saturday (departure at 9:30).

Fontainebleau and Barbizon. Half-day trips (departure at 1:30. 160 frs) on Wednesday, Friday, and Sunday run to Fontainbleau and nearby Barbizon (which is otherwise difficult to reach), but can be linked to a Versailles tour leaving at 9:30 AM on the same days.

Tourist Information

Barbizon. 41 rue Grande, tel. 60–66–41–87.
Chartres. 7 Cloitre Notre-Dame, tel. 37–21–54–03.
Fontainebleau. 31 pl. Napoleon Bonaparte, tel. 64–22–25–68.
Rambouillet. Pl. de la Libération, tel. 34–83–21–21.
Versailles. 7 rue des Réservoirs, tel. 39–50–36–22.

Exploring

Versailles Versailles is the location of one of the world's grandest palaces and one of France's most popular attractions. Wide, tree-lined avenues, broader than the Champs-Elysées and bordered with massive 17th-century mansions, will lead you directly to the Sun King's château. From the imposing place d'Armes in front of the château, you enter the Cour des Ministres, a sprawling cobbled forecourt. Right in the middle, the statue of Louis stands triumphant, surveying the town that he built from scratch to house those of the 20,000 noblemen, servants, and hangers-on who weren't lucky enough to get one of the 3,000 beds in the château.

The building of the château took 50 years. Hills were flattened, marshes drained, forests transplanted, and water for the magnificent fountains was channeled from the Seine several miles away. Visit the **Grands Appartements,** the six salons that made up the royal living quarters, and the famous **Galerie des Glaces** (Hall of Mirrors). Both can be visited without a guide, but you can get a cassette in English. There are also guided tours of the **petits appartements,** where the royal family and friends lived in relative intimacy, and the miniature opera house—the first

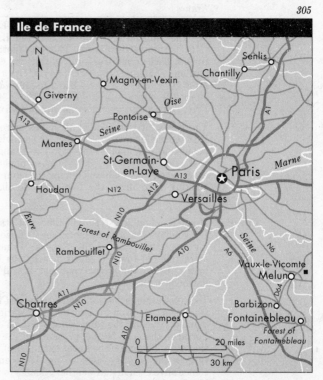

Ile de France

oval room in France, built on the north wing *(aile du Nord)* for Louis XV in 1770. *Grands Appartements and Galerie des Glaces. Admission: 20 frs, 10 frs Sun. Open Tues.–Sun. 9:45–5. Guided tour of Petits Appartements. Admission: included in initial cost. Open Tues.–Sun. 9:45–3:30.*

The château's vast grounds (Free. Open 8:30–dusk.) are masterpieces of formal landscaping. At one end of the Petit Canal, which crosses the Grand Canal at right angles, is the **Grand Trianon,** a scaled-down pleasure palace built in the 1680s. The **Petit Trianon,** nearby, is a sumptuously furnished 18th-century mansion, commissioned by Louis XV for Marie-Antoinette, who would flee here to avoid the stuffy atmosphere of the court. Nearby, she built the village, complete with dairy and mill, where she and her companions would dress as shepherdesses and lead a make-believe bucolic life. *Grand Trianon. Admission: 10 frs. Open 9:45–5:30. Petit Trianon. Admission: 10 frs. Open 9:45–noon and 2–5:30.*

Rambouillet Just a little more than 12 miles (20 kilometers) southwest of Versailles is the small town of Rambouillet, home of a château, adjoining park, and 34,000 acres (138 square kilometers) of forest. Since 1897, the château has been a summer residence of the French president; today, it is also used as a site for international summits. You can visit the château only when the president is not in residence—not very often.

French kings have lived in the château since it was built in 1375. Highlights include the **Appartements d'Assemblée,** decorated with finely detailed wood paneling, and Napoleon's bathroom, with its Pompeii-inspired frescoes. The park stretches away behind the château. Beyond the **Jardin d'Eau** (Water Garden) lies the English-style garden and the **Laiterie de la Reine** (Marie-Antoinette's Dairy). This was another of her attempts to "get back to nature"—but within the confines of a formal garden. *Château. Admission: 16 frs. Open Apr.–Sept., Wed.– Mon. 10–12 and 2–6; Oct.–Mar., 10–12 and 2–5. Park. Admission: free. Open sunrise–sunset. Marie-Antoinette's Dairy. Free. Open same hours as Château, closes at 4 in winter.*

The **Forest of Rambouillet** stretches more than 34,000 acres (138 square kilometers). By car, you can visit the 20 attractive ponds and small lakes *(étangs)*. The **Etang de Hollande,** near St-Leger-en-Yvelines, is the most popular but gets overcrowded on weekends and during the summer. There is a good walking route from the town; get details from the tourist board.

Chartres From Rambouillet, N10 will take you straight to Chartres. Long before you arrive you will see its famous cathedral towering over the plain of the Beauce, France's granary. The attractive old town, steeped in religious history and dating back to before the Roman conquest, is still laced with winding medieval streets.

Today's Gothic cathedral, **Notre-Dame de Chartres,** is the sixth Christian church on the site; despite a series of fires, it has remained virtually the same since the 12th century. The **Royal Portal** on the main facade, presenting "the life and triumph of the savior," is one of the finest examples of Romanesque sculpture in the country. Inside, the 13th-century rose window comes alive even in dull weather, thanks to the deep "Chartres blue" of the stained glass: Its formula remains a mystery to this day. *Cathedral tours available: Ask at the Maison des Clercs, 18 Cloître Notre-Dame.*

The rest of the tour is on another side of Paris, and it is probably easier to return to the capital to continue (*see* Getting Around).

Fontainebleau In the early 16th century, the flamboyant Francis I transformed the medieval hunting lodge of Fontainebleau into a magnificent Renaissance palace. His successor, Henry II, covered the palace with his initials, woven into the *D* for his mistress, Diane de Poitiers. When he died, his queen, Catherine de Médici, carried out further alterations, which were extended under the patronage of Louis XIV. Napoleon preferred the relative intimacy of Fontainebleau to the grandeur of Versailles. Before he was exiled to Elba, he bade farewell to his Old Guard in the courtyard, now known as the **Cour des Adieux** (Farewell Court). The emperor also harangued his troops from the **Horseshoe Staircase.** Ask the curator to let you see the **Cour Ovale** (Oval Court), the oldest and perhaps most interesting courtyard. It stands on the site of the original 12th-century fortified building, but only the keep remains today.

The **Grands Appartements** (royal suites and ballroom) are the main attractions of any visit to the château. The **Galérie de Francois I** is really a covered bridge (built 1528–30) looking out over the Cour de la Fontaine. The overall effect inside the Galérie—and throughout Fontainebleau—is one of classical harmony and proportion, combining to create a sense of Renaissance lightness and order. Francis I appreciated the Italian artistic resurgence, and the ballroom is decorated with frescoes by Primaticcio and his pupil, Niccole dell'Abbate. If you're there on a weekday, you will also be able to join a guided tour of the Petits Appartements, used by Napoleon and Josephine, *Fontainebleau. Admission: 23 frs. Open 9:30–12:30 and 2–5. Closed Tues. and public holidays.*

The huge **Forest of Fontainebleau** is a favorite spot for walkers, horseback riders, and climbers. The French Alpine club started using the famous *rochers* (outcrops) for training back in 1910 and still climb the best known: Plutus and Gargantua. There are more than 90 miles (144 kilometers) of paths, so before you go, invest in a Touring Club map at the Tourist Office. One of the best views in the forest is from the **Hauteurs de la Solle,** within easy walking distance of Fontainebleau itself.

Barbizon   The **Rochers des Demoiselles,** just south of the town, are also good for an afternoon stroll. The **Gorges d'Apremont,** which offer the best views of the rocks, are located near Barbizon, on the edge of the forest, 10 kilometers (six miles) northwest of Fontainebleau. This delightful little village is scarcely more than a main street lined with restaurants and hotels, but a group of landscape painters put it on the map in the mid-19th century. Théodore Rousseau and Jean-François Millet both had their studios here. Sculptor Henri Chapu's bronze medallion, sealed to one of the famous sandstone rocks in the forest nearby, pays homage to the two leaders of what became known as the Barbizon group.

Drop in at the **Ancienne Auberge de Père Ganne** (Pere Ganne's Inn), where most of the landscape artists ate, drank, and slept while in Barbizon. They painted on every available surface, and even now you can see some originals on the walls and in the buffet. Today, the back room is devoted to modern landscape artists. *Rue Grand, tel. 60–66–46–73. Free. Guided visits mid-Mar.–Oct., Wed.–Mon. 9:45–6; Nov.–mid-Mar., Fri. 2–6, weekends 10–6.*

Next to the church, in a barn that Rousseau used as a studio, you'll find the **Musée de l'Ecole de Barbizon** (Barbizon Group's Museum), containing documents of the village as it was in the 19th century as well as a few original works by Rousseau, Diaz, Troyon, and Charles Jacque. *Rue Grande, tel. 60–66–22–38. Admission: 7 frs, children free. Open Apr.–Sept., weekdays 10:30–12:30 and 2–6, weekends 2–6, closed Tues.; off-season, weekdays 10:30–12:30 and 2–5, weekends 2–5, closed Tues.*

From Barbizon, D64 offers a pleasant shortcut to Melun and then on to the château of **Vaux-le-Vicomte,** one of the greatest monuments of 17th-century French architecture. It was to be Nicolas Fouquet's pride and joy, but turned out to be his downfall. This superintendent of France's finances under Louis XIV tended to use state resources for his own benefit—the château itself is damning evidence—and the Sun King eventually had him imprisoned for life. From the visitor's point of view, though, Fouquet's *folie de grandeur* is a treat. He had excellent taste (and a large budget) and knew how to choose the best-qualified team to build Vaux-le-Vicomte. Louis liked the results enough to reemploy them all when he built Versailles. Visit the kitchens, which have been preserved just as they were in the 17th century. The **gardens** (admission: 13 frs) are open all day and are good examples of that type of French garden that imposes an exact formality on what nature has provided. *Guided tours of château. Admission: 40 frs. Open Apr.–Oct., daily 10–6; off-season, daily 11–5. Candlelit visits. Admission: 50 frs. Open May–Sept., Sat. 8:30–11:30.*

Dining and Lodging

For details and price category definitions, *see* Dining and Lodging in Essential Information.

Barbizon **Le Relais.** The delicious specialties—particularly the trout and
Dining the game (in season)—are served in large portions and there is a good choice of fixed-price menus. The Relais is spacious, with walls covered with paintings and hunting trophies, and there is a big open fire. The owner is proud of the large terrace where you can eat in the shade of lime and chestnut trees. *2 av. Charles de Gaulle, tel. 60–66–40–28. Jacket and tie. Reservations essential weekends. MC, V. Closed Tues., Wed., Aug. 20–Sept. 5, Dec. 18–Jan. 6. Expensive.*

Lodging **Auberge des Alouettes.** The delightful Auberge des Alouettes, a family-run 19th-century inn, is set on two acres (8,100 square meters) of grounds, with its own tennis court and parking lot. The interior has been redecorated in '30s style, but many rooms still have their original oak beams. The restaurant, with a large open terrace, features nouvelle cuisine in sizable portions. *4 rue Antoine Barye, tel. 60–66–41–98. 23 rooms with bath or shower and TV. Jacket and tie for restaurant. Reservations essential for restaurant. AE, DC, MC, V. Moderate.*

Chartres **Vielle Maison.** Located in a 14th-century building only 50 yards
Dining (46 meters) from the cathedral, Vielle Maison serves excellent nouvelle cuisine as well as more traditional dishes. Try the regional *menu Beauceron* for the homemade *foie gras* and duck dishes, or the mouth-watering *menu gourmand*, if the wallet allows. *5 rue au Lait, tel. 37–34–10–67. Jacket and tie. Reservations essential. AE, DC, MC, V. Closed Jan. 1–15, July 15–31. Expensive.*

Buisson Ardent. Set in an attractive old oak-beamed building opposite the cathedral's south portal, Buisson Ardent is a popular restaurant providing inexpensive fixed-price menus (especially good on weekdays) and a choice of imaginative *à la carte* dishes with delicious sauces. The wine list is comprehensive. *10 rue au Lait, tel. 37–34–04–66. Jacket and tie. Reservations advised. AE, DC, MC, V. Closed Sun., Tues. evening, Wed. Moderate.*

Lodging **Grand Monarque.** The Monarque is an 18th-century coaching inn that has had a recent face-lift: 11 rooms were added in 1988 and the entrance hall was completely renovated. The rooms have the level of comfort and consistency you would expect from a Best Western. It also has a moderately priced restaurant. *22 pl. des Epars, tel. 37–21–00–72. 57 rooms, 52 with bath or shower. AE, DC, MC, V. Moderate.*

Fontainebleau **Le Dauphin.** Prices are reasonable in this homey, rustic restau-
Dining rant located near the Town Hall and just five minutes from the château. Specialties include snails, *confit de canard*, and a variety of homemade desserts. *24 rue Grande, tel. 64–22–27–04. Dress: informal. Reservations advised, especially on Sun. Closed Tues. evening, Wed., Feb., Sept. 1–8. Inexpensive.*

Lodging **Londres.** The balconies of this tranquil, family-style hotel look out over the palace and the Cour des Adieux; the 19th-century facade is preserved by government order. Inside, the decor is dominated by the Louis XV-style furniture. The Londres has its own restaurant and tea room as well as bar and parking lot. *1 pl. Général de Gaulle, tel. 64-22-20-21. 22 rooms, most with bath or shower. AE, MC, V. Closed Dec. 20–Jan. 31. Moderate.*

Rambouillet **La Poste.** Traditional, unpretentious cooking is the attraction
Dining of this former coaching inn, right in the center of Rambouillet. Until 1988, it could seat only 36 people, but a new upstairs dining room has been opened, doubling the capacity. The service is good, as is the selection of fixed-price menus, even on Sunday. *101 rue du Général-de-Gaulle, tel. 34-83-03-01. Jacket and tie. Reservations advised. AE, MC, V. Moderate.*

Versailles **Trois Marches.** This, the best-known restaurant in Versailles, is
Dining also recognized as one of the best in France for its nouvelle cuisine. Don't miss Gerard Vie's bisque of lobster, salmon with fennel, or turbot *galette*, served in this magnificent *hôtel particulier* (town house) decorated with Old Masters. *3 rue Colbert, tel. 39-50-13-21. Jacket and tie. Reservations essential. AE, DC, MC, V. Closed Sun., Mon. Expensive.*

Boule d'Or. Built in 1696, this restaurant claims to be the second-oldest house in Versailles, as well as the oldest inn. Its friendly owner, Claude Saillard, loves to reproduce 17th- and 18th-century dishes in the appropriately oak-beamed surroundings. His specialty is the "Trilogy" (served evenings only); it includes sole in a sauce introduced in 1733; braised beef, created in 1742; and a duck fricassé first served in 1654. There are simpler lunchtime fixed-price menus. *25 rue du Maréchal Foch, tel. 39-50-22-97. Jacket and tie. Reservations essential. AE, DC, MC, V. Closed Sun. evening, Mon. Moderate.*

Potager du Roy. There is excellent value in this restaurant run by Philippe Letourneur, former colleague of Gerard Vie (*see* Trois Marches). The cuisine gets better each year, yet the prices remain reasonable. It is hardly surprising that this bistro and the enclosed terrace are often crowded and that reservations are a must. *1 rue Marechal Joffre, tel. 39-50-35-34. Jacket and tie. Reservations essential. MC, V. Closed Sun., Mon. Moderate.*

Normandy

Jutting out into the Channel, Normandy probably has more associations with the English-speaking world than any other part of France. The association continues to this day, with visitors flocking not just to see historic monuments but to relax in the rich countryside, with its apple orchards, lush meadows, and sandy beaches.

The historic cities of Rouen and Caen, capitals of Upper and Lower Normandy, respectively, are full of churches, well-preserved buildings, and museums. The Seine Valley is lined with abbeys and castles from all periods: St-Wandrille, for example, dates back to the 7th century. Richard the Lion-hearted's 12th-century Château Gaillard, at Les Andelys, is still imposing. Normandy also has one of France's most enduring tourist attractions, Mont St-Michel, a remarkable Gothic

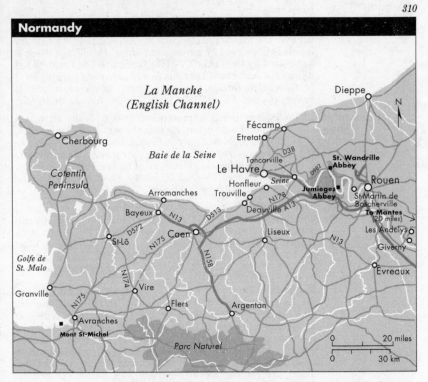

La Manche (English Channel)

Cherbourg

Dieppe

Fécamp

Etretat

Baie de la Seine

Tancarville

D38

St. Wandrille Abbey

Cotentin Peninsula

Le Havre

D982

Rouen

Honfleur

Seine

Arromanches

Trouville

Jumieges Abbey

St Martin de Boscherville

Bayeux

N13

D513

Deauville

A13

N178

To Mantes (20 miles)

St-Lô

D572

N175

Caen

Liseux

N13

Les Andelys

Golfe de St. Malo

N158

Giverny

Granville

N174

Vire

Evreaux

N175

Flers

Argentan

Avranches

Mont St-Michel

Parc Naturel

N

0   20 miles

0   30 km

abbey perched on a rocky mount off the coast of the Cotentin peninsula.

Etretat and Fécamp on the Alabaster coast and Deauville, Trouville, and Honfleur on the *Côte Fleurie* (Flowered Coast) are among Normandy's many seaside resorts. Hotels, restaurants, and beaches cater to the simpler pleasures of life, while casinos make the rich poor—and sometimes the other way around, too. Normandy is also recognized as one of France's finest gastronomic regions; try some of the local cheeses washed down with local cider or apple brandy (Calvados), as well as the wide range of seafood dishes.

Getting Around

Normandy is best visited by car, although there are regular daily trains from Paris to Rouen, Caen, and other large towns in the area. Limited train connections make cross-country traveling difficult. Many historic monuments and some towns—such as Honfleur, which has no train station—are off the beaten track.

Guided Tours

Cityrama and **Paris Vision** organize identical one-day excursions to Mont St-Michel from Paris, leaving at 7:15 Saturday morning and taking you by bus to Mont St-Michel in time for lunch at the Terrasse Poulard restaurant (*see* Mont St-Michel). There is a guided tour of the mount and the abbey, and you return by first-class train from Laval to Gare Montparnasse. Cost: 750 frs.

Cityrama. 214 rue de Rivoli, Paris ler, tel. 42–60–31–25.
Paris Vision. 4 pl. des Pyramides, Paris ler, tel. 42–60–30–14.

Tourist Information

Regional Centers Caen (Lower Normandy). Pl. du Canada, tel. 31–86–53–30.
Rouen (Upper Normandy). 2 rue du Petit Square, tel. 35–88–61–32.

Local Offices Les Andelys. Rue Philippe Auguste, tel. 32–54–41–93.
Bayeux. 1 rue des Cuisiniers, tel. 31–92–16–26.
Caen. Pl. St-Pierre, tel. 31–86–27–65.
Deauville. Pl. de la Mairie, tel. 31–88–21–43.
Etretat. Pl. de la Mairie, tel. 35–27–05–21.
Fécamp. Front de Mer, tel. 35–29–16–34.
Honfleur. 33 cour des Fosses, tel. 31–89–23–30.
Mont St-Michel. Corps de Garde des Bourgeois, tel. 33–60–14–30.
Rouen. Pl. de la Cathedrale, tel. 35–71–41–77.

Exploring

Take Expressway A13 from Paris (Porte d'Auteuil) as far as Meulan or Nantes and cross the Seine to the right (north) bank. Then follow D913 or make a short stop in the little village of **Giverny**, where you can visit the house and gardens where the Impressionist painter Claude Monet lived and worked. *Admission: 10 frs. Open Apr.–Oct., 10–noon and 2–6; closed Mon.*

D313 goes to **Les Andelys**, a small town on the banks of the Seine, dominated by the imposing *Château Gaillard*, a fortress built in 1196 by English king and duke of Normandy, Richard the Lionhearted. *Admission: 10 frs. Open mid-Mar.–mid-Nov. 10–12:30 and 2–5, Wed. 2–5, closed Tues.*

Rouen, the capital of Upper Normandy, has a remarkable number of historic churches, from the city's **Cathédrale Notre-Dame,** dating from the 12th century, to the modern, fish-shaped **Eglise Jeanne d'Arc** on the old market square, where Joan of Arc was burned at the stake in 1431. The tourist office organizes a guided tour leaving from the place de la Cathédrale and visiting the city's main churches, the **Palais de Justice,** and the lively old quarter around the rue du Gros-Horloge, where you can see the giant Renaissance clock that was built in 1527. The most noteworthy churches are located on the right bank, around the old quarter, and can be visited on foot. Try to visit **Eglise St-Maclou,** with its five-gabled facade; **Eglise St-Ouen,** a beautifully proportioned 14th-century abbey; and the **Eglise St-Godard,** with well-preserved stained-glass windows.

One ticket will get you in to several of Rouen's best museums, notably the **Musée des Beaux Arts** (Fine Art Museum), near Eglise St-Godard. This specializes in 17th- and 19th-century French paintings, with a particular emphasis on artists who lived and worked locally. There is an outstanding collection of macabre paintings by Romantic painter Géricault. Nearby museums include **Musée Le Secq des Tournelles,** which has an unusual collection of wrought iron; the **Musée de la Ceramique,** which now houses Rouen's porcelain collections; and the **Musée du Gros-Horloge,** where you can study the mechanism of the Renaissance clock that gives its name to the museum. *Museums. Admission: 10 frs. Open 10–noon and 2–6, Wed. 2–6; closed Tues.*

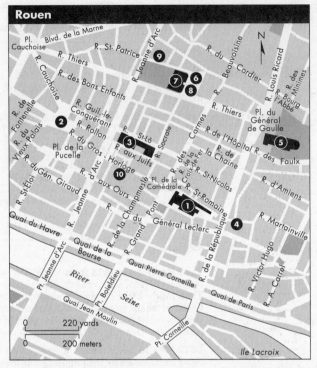

Rouen

Follow D982 across the Forest of Romare and along the Seine
via St-Martin de Boscherville, with its mighty 11th-century
Romanesque abbey church of St-Georges, to the **Jumieges Abbey,** once a powerful Benedictine center. The abbey was
dismantled during the Revolution, but you can still wander
through the remains of the chapter house and several of the
chapels. *Admission: 15 frs. Open Apr.–Sept. daily 10–noon
and 2–6; Oct.–Mar., daily 10–noon and 2–4.*

The nearby **St-Wandrille Abbey,** on D982, was founded a few
years before—in 649—and still has a Benedictine community.
Arrive early in the morning to hear the Gregorian chants at
Mass. *Morning Mass Mon.–Sat. at 9:30; Sun. and holidays at
10.*

Fécamp, at the foot of the highest cliffs in Normandy, was the
region's first place of pilgrimage. (Legend has it that in the
first century, an abandoned boat washed ashore here with a
bottle containing Christ's blood.) The 11th-century **Eglise de la
Trinité** was built to accommodate all the pilgrims. *Guided
tours. Admission: 10 frs. Tours May–Oct., Sun. at 11, 3, and 5.*

Fécamp is also home of the famous Benedictine liqueur. The
museum devoted to its production—rebuilt in 1892 after a
fire—is one of the most popular attractions in Normandy.
*Musée de la Benedictine. 110 rue Alexandre-le-Grande. Ad-
mission: 17 frs. Open Easter–Nov., daily 9:30–11:30 and
2–5:30.*

Follow the pretty coast road about seven miles (12 kilometers) to **Etretat**, where the sea has cut into the cliff to create two immense archways that lead to the neighboring beaches at low tide. For a view over the bay and the **Aiguille**, which is an enormous rock towering in the middle, take the little path up the Falaise d'Aval cliff.

To avoid doubling back to Fécamp, take D39 to the Tancarville Bridge, which links Upper with Lower Normandy. Have some small change ready for the toll. Turn right on D178 and drive south for nine miles (14 kilometers) to a major crossroads. Turn right and drive the same distance to Honfleur.

Once an important port for maritime expeditions, **Honfleur** became a favorite spot for painters, including the Impressionists. Today, Honfleur's lively cobbled streets, inland harbors full of colorful yachts, and the Eglise Ste-Catherine, a little 15th-century wooden church, make it very popular with tourists. In the summer or on weekends, be prepared for lines at restaurants and cafés.

The popular resorts of **Trouville** and **Deauville** are 10 miles (16 kilometers) along the Côte de Grace, on D513. Deauville is the swankier of the two, with its palaces, casino, horse racing, and film festival: But its more modest neighbor, Trouville, with its active fighting fleet, is a better place to get a feel for traditional Normandy.

Caen, slightly inland from these resorts, is the capital of Lower Normandy. It was badly bombed in 1944 but has been rebuilt with care and imagination. William the Conqueror was responsible for Caen's large **fortress** perched on a hill behind the town: Its ramparts now encircle the public garden. William and his queen, Mathilde, also built Caen's "his and hers" abbeys— **Abbaye aux Hommes** and **Abbaye aux Femmes.** The city hall is in the Abbaye aux Hommes, which has hourly guided tours (Admission: 5 frs); Abbaye aux Femmes is now a hospital and therefore closed to visitors.

Bayeux, a few miles inland from the D-Day beach via N13, was the first French town freed by the Allies in June 1944. But it is known primarily as the home of **La Tapisserie de la Reine Mathilde** (known to us as the Bayeux Tapestry), telling the epic story of William's conquest of England in 1066. It is on show at the **Centre Culturel Guillaume le Conquerant** (William the Conqueror Cultural Center). *Rue St-Exupère. Admission: 20 frs. Open June–Sept., daily 9–7; Oct.–May, daily 9–noon and 2–7. Closed Dec. 25, Jan. 1.*

The new **Musée de la Bataille de Normandie** (Museum of the Battle of Normandy) traces the history of the Allied advance against the Germans in 1944. It overlooks the British Military Cemetery. *Blvd. Général-Fabian-Ware. Admission: 15 frs. Open summer, daily 9:30–7; off-season, daily 10:30–12:30 and 2–6:30.*

Bayeux is a good starting point for excursions to the coast. In **Arromanches** harbor, you can see the remains of **Mulberry B,** an artificial port built for the British D-Day landings. Mulberry A, where American troops landed farther up the coast on what is now known as **Omaha Beach,** was destroyed by a storm a few months after the landings. The **Musée du Debarquement** (Landings Museum) on Arromanches seafront shows the landing plan and a film (in English) on the operation. *Admission: 16 frs. Open June–mid-Sept., daily 9–6:30; mid-Sept.–mid-Apr., daily 9–11:30 and 2–5:30. Closed Dec. 25, Jan. 1–18.*

Drive through the fertile heartland of Normandy, among the rolling hills and orchards that produce Calvados and cider. Take D972 to St-Lô and then N174 and N175 to **Avranches,** where you will have your first view of **Mont St-Michel,** the Gothic abbey and village rising up from the sea. The mount's fame comes not just from its location—it's cut off from the mainland at high tide—but from the dramatic nature of its construction in the 8th century, when tons of granite were brought from the nearby Chausey Islands and Brittany and hauled up the 265-foot (81-meter) peak. It has been a pilgrimage center ever since.

For most of the year, Mont St-Michel is surrounded by sandy beach. The best time to see it is during the high tides of spring and fall, when the sea comes pounding in—dangerously fast—and encircles the mount. **La Mervaille** (the Wonder) is the name given to the collection of Gothic buildings on top. What looks like a fortress is in fact a series of displays that trace the evolution of French architecture from Romanesque to late-Gothic. You can join a guided tour (in English). *Admission: 25 frs. Open mid-May–Sept., daily 9–11:30 and 1:30–6; Oct.–mid-May, 9–11 and 1:30–4; closed Tues.*

The **village,** with its narrow and steep streets, is best visited off-season when the souvenir sellers and tourists have departed. The ramparts, and the North Tower in particular, offer the best views over the bay.

Dining and Lodging

For details and price category definitions, *see* Dining and Lodging in Essential Information.

Bayeux
Lodging

Lion d'Or. Flower-filled balconies and a courtyard full of palm trees adorn this '30s property in the center of Bayeux. The rooms are all well equipped—good news for those who want to watch color TV—and the restaurant was recently redecorated and serves Norman specialties. *71 rue St-Jean, tel. 31–92–06–90. 28 rooms with bath or shower. Facilities: indoor garage. AE, DC, MC, V. Closed mid-Dec.–mid-Jan. Moderate.*

Caen
Dining

Bourride. Michel Bruneau, owner and chef of this famous restaurant set in one of the oldest streets near the castle, bases his inventive recipes almost exclusively on local and regional produce. Specialties include skate caramelized in honey and cider and meat pastry cooked in cider vinegar. *15 rue Vaugueux, tel. 31–93–50–76. Jacket and tie. Reservations advised. AE, DC, MC, V. Closed Sun.; Mon. in Jan. Aug. 15–31. Expensive.*

Lodging

Le Dauphin. Although small, the rooms in this old priory near the citadel are clean and renovated. Many of them overlook the quiet hotel courtyard. Le Dauphin also has an excellent restaurant serving Norman dishes topped by unusually light sauces, with an emphasis on seafood. *29 rue Gémare, tel. 31–86–22–26. 21 rooms with bath or shower. Facilities: parking lot, color TV in most rooms. AE, DC, MC, V. Closed mid-July–mid-Aug.; restaurant closed Sat. Inexpensive.*

Deauville   **Spinnaker.** Here is a handy—and affordable—restaurant in
Dining   the center of this chic resort. The atmosphere is informal and
the food is local, with special emphasis on seafood. Try the delicious fresh pasta and crab salad. *52 rue Mirabeau, tel. 31–88–
24–40. Jacket and tie. Reservations advised. MC, V. Closed
Wed. in summer; Thurs. Moderate.*

Etretat   **Roches Blanches.** A warm welcome is the rule in this family-run
Dining   seafood restaurant near the ocean. The restaurant is particularly popular on Sunday. Try the fixed-price menus or the *plat
du terroir* (veal escalope *flambée* with Calvados). *Rue Abbé
Cochet, tel. 35–27–07–34. Jacket and tie. Reservations essential. MC, V. Closed Wed. in summer; Tues.–Thurs. in winter.
Moderate.*

Fécamp   **Martin.** This is the sort of unpretentious restaurant that only
Dining   the French seem to know how to run. The food—seafood is a
good bet—is of a high standard. For dessert try the *soufflé a la
Benedictine* or the *soufflé au Calvados. 18 pl. St-Etienne, tel.
35–28–23–82. Dress: informal. Reservations not necessary.
Closed Sun. evening, Mon.; Mar. 1–15, Sept. 1–15. Inexpensive.*

Lodging   **Hotel d'Angleterre.** Oak beams and wood paneling set the tone
in the lobby of this comfortable hotel near the sea, glowing
now, thanks to the 1988 renovations carried out by the new
owners. Its restaurant is good and has four fixed-price menus.
*93 rue Plage, tel. 35–28–01–60. 30 rooms, 23 with bath or
shower. Facilities: garage. AE, DC, MC, V. Closed Dec.
Inexpensive.*

Honfleur   **Absinthe.** The magnificent 17th-century dining room domi-
Dining   nates the ground floor, where you will also find the pub-style
bar, the Ivanhoe. But in warm weather, the place to be is on the
sunny terrace on the quayside. The menu features both
nouvelle and traditional cuisines, with the accent on seafood. *10
quai de la Quarantaine, tel. 31–89–39–00. Jacket and tie. Reservations advised. AE, DC, MC, V. Moderate.*
Ancrage. Vast seafood platters are the specialty in this charming old restaurant overlooking the *Vieux Bassin* (old harbor),
but meat dishes are good, too, particularly the calf sweetbreads braised in cider. *12 rue Montpensier, tel. 31–89–00–70.
Jacket and tie. Reservations advised in summer. MC, V.
Closed Tues. evening, Wed.; Jan.–Feb. 15. Moderate.*

Lodging   **Ferme St-Simeon.** One of the most luxurious hotels in Normandy, St-Simeon is set in an impressive 17th-century farmhouse
on the edge of Honfleur, overlooking the Seine estuary. There
are several rooms in the nearby manor house and in a recently
converted cider press. Its restaurant is known for its fresh seafood, sophisticated desserts, and excellent wine list. *Route
Adolphe-Marais, tel. 31–89–23–61. 38 rooms with bath, 4 with
Jacuzzi. Jacket and tie in restaurant. Reservations essential
in restaurant. MC, V. Very Expensive.*

Mont St-Michel   **Terrasses Poulard.** This delightful, 19th-century hotel was com-
Lodging   pletely renovated in 1986; each room was given the name of a
famous local Norman personality and decorated accordingly.
Several rooms have breathtaking views of the bay, while others
look out onto a little garden. The restaurant, with superb fresh
lobster, has its best views upstairs. *Rue Principale, tel. 33–
60–14–09. 29 rooms with bath. Facilities: color TV, minibars.
AE, DC, MC, V. Expensive.*

Rouen
Dining

La Couronne. Built in 1345, La Couronne claims to be the oldest inn in France. The oak beams, leather upholstery, and woodwork provide an attractive setting for a collection of sculptures. The traditional cuisine features homemade foie gras, duck *à l'orange*, and turbot in flaky pastry. *31 pl. du Vieux Marché, tel. 35-71-40-90. Jacket and tie. Reservations essential. AE, DC, V. Expensive.*

Lodging

Hotel de Dieppe. A 19th-century hotel opposite the train station, Hotel de Dieppe offers two types of room: modern or period-style. The buffet-style breakfast is substantial—unlike most in France—and the popular restaurant serves a range of grilled meats as well as *canard au sang* (duck cooked in its own blood). *Pl. Bernard Tissot, tel. 35-71-96-00. 42 rooms with bath or shower. AE, DC, MC, V. Moderate.*

Burgundy and Lyon

For a region whose powerful medieval dukes held sway over large tracts of Western Europe and whose current image is closely allied to its expensive wine, Burgundy is a place of surprisingly rustic, quiet charm.

Despite the mighty Gothic cathedrals of Sens and Auxerre, Burgundy's leading religious monument is the Romanesque basilica at Vézelay. Once one of Christianity's most important pilgrimage centers, Vézelay is today a tiny village hidden in the folds of rolling, verdant hills. In its time, the abbey of Cluny farther south was equally important, but few of its buildings remain.

The heart of Burgundy consists of the dark, brooding Morvan Forest. Dijon is the region's only city and retains something of its medieval opulence. Its present reputation is essentially gastronomic, however; top-class restaurants abound, and local "industries" involve the production of mustard, *cassis* (blackcurrant liqueur), snails, and—of course—wine. The vineyards extending down toward the ancient town of Beaune are among the world's most distinguished and picturesque.

The vines continue to flourish as you head south along the Saône Valley, through the Mâconnais and Beaujolais, toward Lyon, one of France's most appealing cities. The combination of frenzied modernity and unhurried *joie de vivre* give Lyon a sense of balance. The only danger is temptation to overindulge in its rich and robust cuisine.

Burgundy's winters are cold, its summers hot. The ideal times to come are late May, when the countryside is in flower, and September or October, for the wine harvest.

Getting Around

Burgundy is a region best visited by car. Its meandering country roads invite leisurely exploration. There are few big towns, and traveling around by train is unrewarding, especially since the infrequent cross-country trains steam along at the speed of a legendary Burgundy snail.

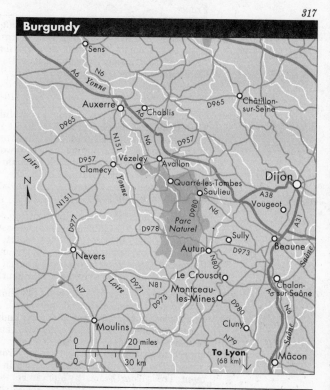

Guided Tours

The Dijon branch of the regional tourism office organizes a series of tours using Dijon as a base. These include wine tastings and historic tours of the famous religious centers. Write to Comité Régional de Tourisme, 4 rue Nicolas-Berthot 21000 Dijon.

Tourist Information

Auxerre. 1 quai de la République, tel. 86–52–06–19.
Beaune. Rue de l'Hotel-Dieu, tel. 80–22–24–51.
Dijon. Pl. Darcy, tel. 80–43–42–12.
Lyon. Pl. Bellecoeur, tel. 78–42–25–75.
Sens. Pl. Jean-Jaures, tel. 86–65–19–49.

Exploring

It makes sense for **Sens** to be your first stop on the way down to Burgundy, since it lies just 70 miles (120 kilometers) from Paris on N6—a fast, pretty road that hugs the Yonne Valley south of Fontainebleau. Sens is home to France's senior archbishop and is dominated by the 12th-century **Cathédrale de St-Etienne.** This is one of the oldest cathedrals in France and has a foresquare facade topped by towers and an incongruous little Renaissance campanile. The vast, harmonious interior contains outstanding stained glass of various periods.

The 13th-century **Palais Synodal** alongside, now a local museum, provides a first encounter with Burgundy's multicolored tiled roofs; from its courtyard, there is a fine view of the cathedral's south transept, constructed in the fluid Flamboyant Gothic style of the 16th century. *Rue des Déportés de la Résistánce. Admission: 10 frs. Open Mar.–mid-Dec. daily 10–noon and 2–5; mid-Dec.–Feb., Thurs.–Tues. 10–noon and 2–5.*

N6 continues to **Auxerre,** a small, peaceful town with its own **Cathédrale St-Etienne,** perched on a steepish hill overlooking the Yonne. The muscular cathedral, built between the 13th and 16th centuries, has a powerful north tower similar to that at Clamecy. The former **abbey of St-Germain** nearby contains an underground church dating from the 9th century. *Rue Cochois. Guided tour of crypt. Admission: 8 frs. Open Wed.–Mon. 10–noon and 2–5.*

Chablis, famous for its dry white wine, makes an attractive excursion 10 miles (16 kilometers) to the east of Auxerre, along N65 and D965. Beware of village tourist shops selling local wines at unpalatable prices. The surrounding vineyards are dramatic: Their towering, steeply banked hills are in marked contrast to the region's characteristic gentle slopes.

From Auxerre, take N151 27 miles (43 kilometers) south along the Yonne to **Clamecy.** This sleepy town is not on many tourist itineraries, but its tumbling alleyways and untouched, ancient houses epitomize *La France profonde*. The many-shaped roofs of Clamecy, dominated by the majestic square tower of the **church of St-Martin,** are best viewed from the banks of the Yonne. The river played a crucial role in Clamecy's development: Trees from the nearby Morvan Forest were cut down and floated in huge convoys to Paris. The history of this curious form of transport *(flottage)*, now extinct, is detailed in the town **museum.** *Rue Bourgeoise. Admission: 4 frs. Open July–Sept. Wed.–Mon. 10–noon and 2–5; rest of the year by appointment.*

Vézelay lies 15 miles (24 kilometers) east of Clamecy, along D951. The **Basilica** is perched on a rocky crag, with commanding views of the surrounding countryside. It rose to fame in the 11th century as the resting place of the relics of St. Mary Magdalene and became a departure point for the great pilgrimages to Santiago de Compostela in northwest Spain. The church was rescued from decay by the 19th-century Gothic Revival architect Eugène-Emmanuel Viollet-le-Duc and counts as one of the foremost Romanesque buildings in existence. Its interior is long and airy, with superbly carved column capitals; the facade boasts an equally majestic tympanum.

Avallon is eight miles (13 kilometers) farther along from Vézelay, via D957. Its site, on a promontory, is spectacular, and its old streets and ramparts agreeable places to stroll. The imagination of medieval stone carvers ran riot at the portals of the venerable church of **St-Lazarus.**

The expressway passes close by Avallon and can whisk you along to Dijon, 60 miles (96 kilometers) away, in less than an hour. If you're in no rush, take the time to explore part of the huge **Morvan Regional Park:** The road twists and turns through lakes, hills, and forests. Take D10 south to **Quarré-les-Tombes**—so called because of the empty prehistoric stone tombs discovered locally and eerily arrayed in a ring around the church—before continuing southeast toward Saulieu. The

Rocher de la Pérouse, five miles (eight kilometers) from Quarré-les-Tombes, is a mighty outcrop worth climbing for the view of the Cousin Valley. Continue to **Saulieu** via the D6, D264, and D977.

Saulieu's reputation belies its size (just 3,000 inhabitants). It is renowned for good food (Rabelais, that 16th-century authority, extolled its hospitality) and Christmas trees (a million are harvested each year). The **Basilica of St-Andoche** is almost as old as Vézelay's, though less imposing and much restored. The adjoining town **museum** (Admission: 5 frs. Open Wed.–Mon., 10–noon and 2–5) contains a room devoted to François Pompon, a sculptor whose smooth, stylized creations smack of state-of-the-art yet predate World War II.

N6 and then D977 link Saulieu to the Dijon-bound A38 expressway to the east. **Dijon** is capital of both Burgundy and gastronomy. Visit its restaurants and the **Palais des Ducs** (Ducal Palace), testimony to bygone splendor and the setting for one of France's leading art museums (Admission: 8 frs. Open Wed.–Mon. 10–noon and 2–5). The tombs of Philip the Bold and John the Fearless head a rich collection of medieval objects and Renaissance furniture. Outstanding features of the city's old churches include the stained glass of **Notre-Dame,** the austere interior of the **cathedral of St-Bénigne,** and the chunky Renaissance facade of **St-Michel.** Don't miss the exuberant 15th-century gateway at the **Chartreuse de Champmol**—all that remains of a former charterhouse—or the adjoining **Puits de Moïse,** a "well" with six large, compellingly realistic medieval statues on a hexagonal base.

A31 connects Dijon to Beaune 25 miles (40 kilometers) to the south, but you may prefer a leisurely trip through the vineyards. Take D122, then N74 at Chambolle-Musigny; just to the south is the Renaissance **Château du Clos de Vougeot,** famous as the seat of Burgundy's elite company of wine tasters, the *Confrérie des Chevaliers du Tastevin,* who gather here in November at the start of the three-day festival *Les Trois Glorieuses*—which includes a wine auction at the **Hospices de Beaune.** *Château du Clos de Vougeot. Admission: 10 frs. Guided tours daily 10–noon and 2–4:30. Closed Dec. 24–Jan. 3.*

The Hospices (or Hôtel-Dieu) owns some of the finest vineyards in the region yet was founded in 1443 as a hospital. Its medical history is retraced in a **museum** that also features Roger van der Weyden's medieval Flemish masterpiece *The Last Judgment,* plus a collection of tapestries, though a better series (late 15th century, relating the *Life of the Virgin*) hangs in Beaune's main church, the **Collégiale Notre-Dame** (begun 1120). *Musée des Beaux-Arts. Rue Hôtel de Ville. Admission: 13 frs. Open daily 10–noon and 2–5.*

The history of local wines can be explored at the **Musée du Vin de Bourgogne,** housed in a mansion built in the 15th and 16th centuries (Admission: 6 frs. Open daily, 9:30–noon and 2–5) The place to drink the stuff is in the candle-lit cellars of the **Marché aux Vins** (wine market), on rue Nicolas Rolin, where you can taste as much as you please for around 30 frs.

Autun is 30 miles (48 kilometers) west of Beaune along D973 but is worth a detour, if only for the Renaissance **château of Sully**

on the way (Admission: 5 frs. Visits to grounds only, daily in summer, 10–noon and 2–5). The leading monument in Autun is the church of **St-Lazarus**, a curious Gothic cathedral redone in the Classical style by 18th-century clerics trying to follow fashion. The building actually dates back to the first half of the 12th century. Note the majestic picture by Ingres, the *Martyrdom of St-Symphorien*, in one of the side chapels. Across from the cathedral is the **Musée Rolin** (Admission: 7 frs. Open 10–noon and 2–5; Sun. 2–5; closed Tues.), with several fine paintings from the Middle Ages, although the town's importance dates back to Roman times, as you can detect at the **Porte St-André**, a well-preserved archway, and the **Théâtre Romain**, once the largest arena in Gaul.

From Autun, head southeast along N80 and D980, via industrial Montceau-les-Mines, to **Cluny**, 50 miles (80 kilometers) away. The **Abbey** of Cluny, founded in the 10th century, was the biggest church in Europe until Michelangelo built St. Peter's in Rome in the 16th century. The ruins give an idea of its original grandeur. Note the **Clocher de l'Eau-Bénite** (a majestic bell-tower) and the 13th-century **Farinier** (flour mill) with its fine chestnut roof and collection of statues, *Guided tours of ruins. Admission: 15 frs. Open 9–noon and 2–5.*

A model of the original abbey can be seen in the **Musée Ochier**, the 15th-century abbot's palace. *Rue Conant. Admission: 4 frs. Open 10–noon and 2–5. Closed Tues.; Jan. 1–15.*

Cluny is a mere 16 miles (28 kilometers) northwest of **Mâcon**, a bustling town best known for its wine fair in May and for its stone bridge across the Saône; the low arches are a headache for large river barges. At Mâcon take N6 or A6 due south to Lyon, where the River Rhône runs parallel to the Saône before the two converge south of the city center.

Lyon In recent years, Lyon has solidified its role as one of Europe's leading commercial centers, thanks to France's policy of decentralization and the TGV train that puts Paris at virtual commuter distance (two hours). Much of the city has an appropriate air of untroubled prosperity, and you will have plenty of choices when it comes to good eating.

❶ The clifftop silhouette of **Notre-Dame de Fourvière** is the city's most striking symbol: an exotic mish-mash of styles with an interior that's pure decorative overkill. Climb the Fourvière heights for the view instead and then go to the nearby Roman remains. *Théatres Romains. Admission: 10 frs. Open Mar.–Oct. 8–noon and 2–5, Sat. 9–noon and 3–6, Sun. 3–6; Nov.–Feb. 8–noon and 2–5, closed Sat., Sun.*

❷ The medieval **Primatiale St-Jean** (closed noon–2) is Lyon's disappointing cathedral. Note the Romanesque chancel, the 14th-century astronomical clock in the north transept (chimes at 3 PM), and the variety of styles of window and vaulting in the lateral chapels. Lyon's oldest sectors—St-Jean, St-Paul, and St-Georges—run north of the cathedral along the west bank of the Saône. Their narrow streets and medieval/Renaissance houses throb with cheap restaurants and cafés.

❸ The pick of Lyon's museums is the **Musée des Beaux-Arts** (open Wed.–Mon. 11–6). It houses sculpture, classical relics, and an extensive collection of Old Masters and Impressionists. Don't miss local artist Louis Janmot's 19th-century mystical cycle

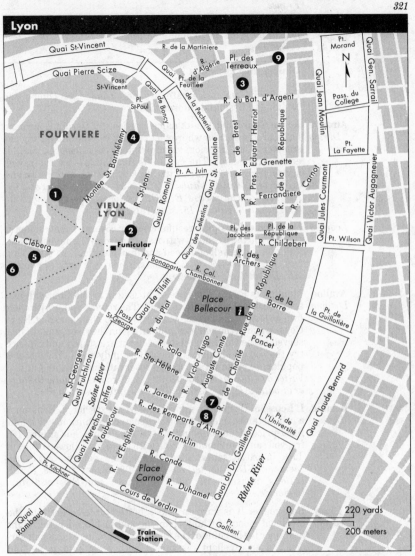

Lyon

Major Attractions

Musée des Beaux-Arts, **3**

Notre-Dame de Fourvière, **1**

Primatiale St-Jean, **2**

Other Attractions

Hôtel de Ville, **9**

Musée des Arts-Decoratifs, **8**

Musée Gallo-Romain, **5**

Musée Historique de Lyon, **4**

Musée Historique des Tissus, **7**

Théâtres Romains, **6**

The Poem of the Soul, 18 canvases and 16 drawings that took nearly 50 years to complete. *Admission: 10 frs. Open 11–6, closed Tues.*

Dining and Lodging

For details and price category definitions, *see* Dining and Lodging in Essential Information.

Auxerre **Jardin Gourmand.** As its name implies, the Jardin Gourmand
Dining has a pretty garden where you can eat *en terrasse* during the summer. The interior, dominated by light-colored oak, is equally congenial. The cuisine is innovative—try the ravioli and *foie gras* or the duck with black currants—and the service is discreet. *56 blvd. Vauban, tel. 86–51–53–52. Jacket and tie. Reservations advised. AE, DC, V. Closed Sun. evening (winter), Feb. 1–7, Nov. 1–15. Moderate.*

Lodging **Normandie.** This picturesque creeper-covered construction is right in the town center, with its own garden but no restaurant. The rooms are well equipped and unpretentious. *41 blvd. Vauban, tel. 86–52–57–80. 48 rooms, some with bath or shower. AE, DC, MC, V. Inexpensive.*

Avallon **Moulin des Ruats.** The hotel is housed in an old flour mill just
Lodging southwest of Avallon along D427. The rooms, many with their own balcony, are rustic. Most look onto the sparkling River Cousin, and in the summer you can eat on the riverbank. Dishes served in the wood-paneled restaurant are sturdy and copious; try the *coq au vin* done in local Burgundy wine. This hotel is popular, so make sure to have a reservation in July or August. *Vallée du Cousin, tel. 86–34–07–14. 20 rooms, some with shower or bath. AE, DC, MC, V. Closed winter. Inexpensive.*

Beaune **L'Ecusson.** Despite its unprepossessing exterior, L'Ecusson is
Dining a comfortable, friendly, thick-carpeted restaurant, with four fixed-price menus offering outstanding value. For around 160 frs, you can have rabbit terrine with tarragon followed by leg of duck in oxtail sauce; then cheese, and dessert. *2 rue du Lieutenant-Dupuis, tel. 80–22–83–08. Jacket and tie. Reservations advised. AE, DC, V. Closed mid-Feb.–mid-Mar. Moderate.*

Cluny **Bourgogne.** It is hard to find a better place to get into the
Lodging medieval mood of Cluny than this old-fashioned hotel, right next door to the ruins of the famous abbey. There is a small garden and an excellent restaurant with sober pink decor and refined cuisine (*foie gras*, snails, and fish with ginger are specialties). *Pl. de l'Abbaye, tel. 85–59–00–58. 14 rooms with bath or shower. AE, DC, V. Closed mid-Nov.–mid-Mar.*

Dijon **Jean-Pierre Billoux.** M. Billoux is a good-enough chef to have
Dining given his name to his restaurant, which is reputedly the best of the many in this most gastronomic of French cities and magnificently situated in a spacious, restored town house with garden, bar, and stone-vaulted restaurant. Service is charming. Specialties include frogs' legs steamed and served with cress pancakes, and guinea fowl with *foie gras*. *14 pl. Darcy, tel. 80–30–11–00. Reservations essential. AE, DC, MC, V. Closed Sun. evening, Mon., mid-Feb.–mid-Mar. Expensive.*

Lodging **Chapeau Rouge.** This is a good choice if you want to be sure of getting a quiet, well-appointed room in the center of town—it's close to Dijon cathedral. It is even a better choice for its restaurant, renowned as a haven of regional cuisine. New chef Bernard Noël, formerly of the top-ranking Tour d'Argent in Paris, creates a marvelous, saucy menu. *22 blvd. de la Marne, tel. 80–72–31–13. 30 rooms with bath or shower. Jacket and tie in restaurant. Reservations essential. AE, DC, MC, V. Moderate.*

Lyon
Dining

Léon de Lyon. A mixture of regional tradition (dumplings, hot sausages) and eye-opening innovation keep Léon de Lyon at the forefront of Lyon's restaurant scene. It consists of two floors in an old house full of alcoves and wood paneling. The blue-aproned waiters melt into the old-fashioned decor, and dishes such as fillet of veal with celery or leg of lamb with fava beans will linger in your memory. *1 rue Pléney, tel. 78–28–11–33. Jacket and tie. Reservations essential. V. Closed Sun., Mon. lunch, Dec. 24–Jan. 6. Expensive.*

A Ma Vigne. Here is a restaurant that's popular with readers; it provides straightforward meals as a break from too much gourmet Lyonais dining. French fries, mussels *(moules),* roast ham, and tripe lead the menu. Locals appreciate this, too, so get there early, especially at lunchtime. *23 rue Jean-Larrivé, tel. 78–60–46–31. Dress: informal. Reservations not needed, but arrive early. V. Inexpensive.*

Lodging

Royal. The Royal is located on the spacious and elegant place Bellecoeur in the very heart of Lyon. Beware of the huge range in room prices (250–700 frs); many rooms have been stylishly renovated and some of the most expensive are positively luxurious. The hotel has its own garage, and most rooms have television. *20 pl. Bellecoeur, tel. 78–37–57–31. 90 rooms, most with bath or shower. AE, DC, MC, V. Moderate.*

Sens
Lodging

Paris et Poste. This is a newly modernized hotel and makes a pleasant stopping point on the way to Burgundy from Paris. The helpful service and sumptuous breakfasts (rare in France) confirm a sense of well-being created by the robust evening meal (with fixed-price menus including duck, snails, and steak) served in the large, solemn restaurant, whose decor can be described as rustic Burgundian. *97 rue de la République, tel. 86–65–17–43. 34 rooms with bath or shower. AE, DC, MC, V. Moderate.*

Vézelay
Dining

L'Esperance. Located in the small neighboring village of St-Père-sous-Vézelay, L'Esperance is one of France's premier restaurants. Chef Marc Meneau is renowned for the subtlety and originality of his cuisine. Parisian gourmets think nothing of driving down to Burgundy to eat here: Madame Meneau is a charming hostess, and the setting—by a park and stream with Vézelay's hill and basilica in the background—makes even a long trip worth it. *St-Père-sous-Vézelay, tel. 86–33–20–45. Jacket and tie. Reservations essential. AE, V. closed Tues., Wed. lunch. Very Expensive.*

Loire Valley

The Loire is the longest river in France, rising near Le Puy in the east of the Massif Central and pursuing a broad northwest curve on its 630-mile (1,000-kilometer) course to the Atlantic Ocean near Nantes. The region traditionally referred to as the Loire Valley—château country—is the 140-mile (225-kilome-

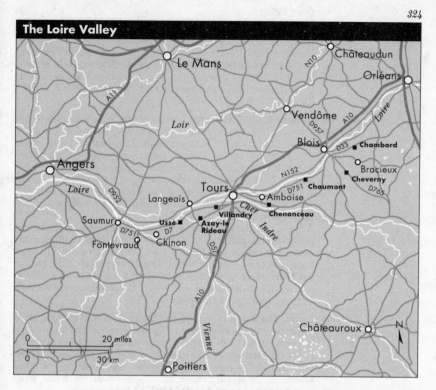

The Loire Valley

ter) stretch between Orléans, 70 miles (110 kilometers) south of
Paris, and Angers, 60 miles (100 kilometers) from the Atlantic
coast. Thanks to its mild climate, soft light, and lush mea-
dowland, this area is known as the Garden of France. Its leading actor—the wide, meandering Loire—offers two distinct
faces: fast-flowing and spectacular in spring, sluggish and
sandy in summer.

To the north lies the vast grain plain of the Beauce, to the
southeast the marshy, forest-covered Sologne, renowned for
mushrooms, asparagus, and game. The star attractions along
the rocky banks of the Loire and its tributaries—Rivers Cher,
Indre, Vienne, and Loir (with no *e*)—are the famous châteaux:
stately houses, castles, or fairy-tale palaces. Renaissance elegance is often combined with fortresslike medieval mass: The
Loire Valley was fought over by France and England during
the Middle Ages. It took the example of Joan of Arc, the
"Maid of Orléans" (scene of her most rousing military successes), for the French finally to expel the English.

The Loire Valley's golden age came under Francis I (1515–47),
France's flamboyant contemporary of England's Henry VIII.
He hired Renaissance craftsmen from Italy and hobnobbed
with the aging Leonardo da Vinci, his guest at Amboise. His
salamander emblem is to be seen in many châteaux, including
Chambord, the mightiest of them, begun in 1519.

The best months to come are June to October, though the
weather can sometimes be hot and sticky in midsummer. Nature in the region is at its best in late spring and early fall, when

there are fewer crowds. In peak season (especially August), it is essential to have your accommodations reserved.

Getting Around

The easiest way to visit the Loire châteaux is by car; N152 hugs the riverbank and offers excellent sightseeing possibilities. Trains run along the Loire Valley every two hours, supplemented by local bus services. A peaceful way to explore the region is to rent a bicycle at one of the SNCF train stations. (Some trains even transport bikes for nothing.)

Guided Tours

Bus tours for the main châteaux leave daily in summer from Tours, Blois, Angers, Orléans, and Saumur: Ask at the relevant tourist office for latest times and prices. Most châteaux insist that visitors follow one of their own tours anyway, but try to get a booklet in English before joining the tour, as most are in French only.

Tourist Information

Angers. Pl. du Président Kennedy, tel. 41–88–12–43.
Blois. 3 av. du Docteur Jean-Laigret, tel. 54–74–06–49.
Orléans. Blvd. Aristide-Briand, tel. 38–53–05–95.
Tours. Pl. du Maréchal Leclerc, tel. 47–05–58–08.

Exploring

Orléans Orléans, little more than an hour away by expressway (A10) or train, is the most obvious gateway to the Loire Valley if you're coming from Paris. Apart from its arts museum and august Sainte-Croix cathedral, however, Orléans has little going for it. We suggest instead that you take the expressway from Paris to Chartres, then N10 along the undisturbed Loir valley to **Châteaudun,** whose colossal château stands resplendent on a steep promontory and houses graceful furniture and lavish tapestries. Its chapel contains 15 statues produced locally in the 15th century. *Admission: 18 frs. Guided tours 9:30–11:45 and 2–6; winter 2–4:45. Closed Tues.*

Vendôme Continue along N10 to Vendôme, 25 miles (10 kilometers) to the southwest, where the Loire splits into many arms, lending the town a canallike charm that harmonizes with its old streets and bridges. Architecture buffs will pinch themselves as they inspect the large but little-known main church, **Eglise de la Trinité,** an encyclopedia of different styles with brilliantly carved choir stalls and an exuberant west front—the work of Jean de Beauce, best known for his tower and spire at Chartres Cathedral. Vendôme also has a ruined **castle** with ramparts and pleasant, uncrowded gardens. *Admission: 5 frs. Open Mar.–June 10–noon and 2–6, closed Tues.; July, Aug., daily 10–noon and 2–6.*

Blois Blois lies 20 miles (32 kilometers) southeast of Vendôme along D957. It is the most attractive of the major Loire towns, with its tumbling alleyways and its château. The **château** is a mixture of four different styles: Feudal (13th-century); Gothic-Renaissance transition (circa 1500); Renaissance (circa 1520);

and Classical (circa 1635). *Admission: 20 frs. Open May–Aug. 9–6:30; Sept.–Apr. 9–noon and 2–6:30.*

Chambord Blois makes an ideal launching pad for a visit to the châteaux of Chambord and Cheverny. Chambord (begun circa 1520) is 11 miles (20 kilometers) east of Blois along D33 and near Bracieux. It stands in splendid isolation in a vast forest and game park. There's another forest on the roof: 365 chimneys and turrets, representing architectural self-indulgence at its least squeamish. Grandeur or a mere 440-room folly? Judge for yourself, and don't miss the superb spiral staircase or the chance to saunter over the rooftop terrace. *Admission: 24 frs. Open mid-June–Aug. 9:30–11:45 and 2–6:30; winter 9:30–11:45 and 2–4.*

Cheverny A pleasant 12-mile (20-kilometer) drive through the forest leads you southwest to Cheverny, which can also be reached along D765 from Blois. This white, symmetrical château in the disciplined Classical style (built 1620–34) has ornate painted and gilded paneling on its walls and ceilings. Hunting buffs will thrill at the sight of the antlers of 2,000 hapless stags in the Trophy Room. Hordes of hungry hounds lounge around outside dreaming of their next kill. *Admission: 20 frs. Open June–Sept. 9–6:30; Oct.–May 9:30–noon and 2:30–5.*

Chaumont About 12 miles (20 kilometers) south of Blois, along D751, stands the sturdy château of Chaumont, built between 1465 and 1510—well before Benjamin Franklin became a regular visitor. There is a magnificent Loire panorama from the terrace, and the stables—where Thoroughbreds dined like royalty—show the importance attached to fine horses, for hunting or just prestige. *Admission: 24 frs. Open Apr.–Sept. 9:30–11:45 and 2:15–5:45; winter 9:30–11:45 and 2:15–4.*

Amboise Downstream (westward) another 10 miles (16 kilometers) lies the bustling town of Amboise, whose château, with charming grounds, a rich interior, and excellent views over the river from the battlements, dates from 1500. It wasn't always so peaceful: In 1560, more than 1,000 Protestant "conspirators" were hanged from these battlements during the Wars of Religion. *Admission: 22 frs. Open July, Aug. 9–6:30; Sept.–June 9–noon and 2–6:30.*

The nearby **Clos-Lucé,** a 15th-century brick manor house, was the last home of Leonardo da Vinci, who was invited to stay here by Francis I. Da Vinci died here in 1519, and his engineering genius is illustrated by models based on his plans and sketches. *Admission: 26 frs. Same hours as château.*

Chenonceau The early 16th-century château of Chenonceau, 10 miles (16 kilometers) south of Amboise along D81 and then D40, straddles the tranquil river Cher like a bridge. It is surrounded by elegant gardens and a splendid avenue of plane trees. Inside, note the fine paintings, colossal fireplaces, and richly worked ceilings. A waxworks museum lurks in an outbuilding. *Admission: 26 frs. Open Mar.–Oct. 9–6; winter 9–noon and 2–4.*

Tours Tours, 15 miles (25 kilometers) farther on, and equidistant from Orléans and Angers, is the unofficial capital of the Loire. It retains a certain charm despite its sprawling size (250,000 inhabitants) and extensive postwar reconstruction. Its **Cathe-**

dral of St-Gatien (1239–1484) numbers among France's most impressive. The influence of local Renaissance sculptors and craftsmen is much in evidence on the ornate facade, and the stained glass in the choir is particularly delicate: Some of it dates from 1320.

Villandry The château of Villandry, 10 miles (16 kilometers) southwest of Tours along the river Cher, is known for its painstakingly re-laid 16th-century gardens, with their long avenues of 1,500 manicured lime trees. The château interior, restored like the gardens in the mid-19th century, is equally beguiling. Note the painted and gilded ceiling from Toledo and the collection of Spanish pictures. *Admission: 24 frs. Open daily 9–6; gardens open 8–dusk.*

Langeais Langeais is just nine miles (14 kilometers) west of Villandry: Keep on D7 to Lignières before turning right onto D57 and crossing the Loire. A massive castle, built in the 1460s and never altered, dominates this small town. Its apartments contain a superb collection of tapestries, chests, and beds. *Admission: 18 frs. Open summer 9–6:30; winter 9–noon and 2–6:30. Closed Mon.*

Azay-le-Rideau Azay-le-Rideau (1518–29), one of the prettiest of the Loire châteaux, lies on the River Indre six miles (10 kilometers) south of Langeais along D57. It has harmonious proportions and exquisite grounds, with a domesticated moat that is really a lake. This graceful ensemble compensates for the château's spartan interior, as does the charm of the surrounding village. *Admission: 20 frs. Open summer 9:30–12 and 2–6:30; winter 9:30–12 and 2–4:45.*

Ussé A short ride down the Indre Valley (on D17 and then D7) from Azay will help you judge whether Ussé really is, as the brochures claim, the fairy-tale setting that inspired *Sleeping Beauty*. Its bristling roofs and turrets, flowered terraces, and forest backcloth have undeniable romance. Don't forget the chapel in the park, built 1520–38 in purest Renaissance proportions. *Admission: 30 frs. Open mid-Mar.–Nov. 9–noon and 2–6.*

Chinon Chinon, eight miles (13 kilometers) from Ussé via D7 and D16, is an ancient town nestled by the River Vienne, with a rock-of-ages castle patrolling the horizon. This 12th-century fortress, with walls 400 yards (366 meters) long, is mainly in ruins, though small museums are installed in the Royal Chambers and sturdy Tour de l'Horloge (clock tower). There are excellent views from the ramparts over Chinon and the Vienne Valley. *Admission: 15 frs. Open June–Sept. 9–6; winter 9–noon and 2–5. Closed Wed.; Dec., Jan.*

Fontevraud From just south of Chinon, D751 heads off up the Vienne Valley toward Fontevraud, 13 miles (21 kilometers) away. This quiet village is dominated by its medieval abbey, where English kings Henry II and Richard the Lionhearted are buried. The church, cloisters, Renaissance chapter house, long-vaulted refectory, and octagonal kitchen are all still standing. The guided tours are in French, but you can get a brochure in English to keep track of where you are. *Admission: 20 frs. Open summer 9–noon and 2–6:30; winter 10–noon and 2–4.*

Saumur Saumur, 10 miles (16 kilometers) west along the Loire from Fontevraud along D947, is a prosperous town famous for its riding school, wines, and château—a white 14th-century castle that towers above the river and contains two outstanding museums: the **Musée des Arts Décoratifs** (Decorative Arts Museum), featuring porcelain and enamels; and the **Musée du Cheval** (Equine Museum) with saddles, stirrups, skeletons, and Stubbs engravings. *Admission: 18 frs. Open July–mid-Sept. 9–6:30 and 8:30–10:30; winter 10–5, closed Tues.*

Angers Angers is a large, historic town on the River Maine just to the north of the Loire. D952 runs along the Loire Valley from Saumur, 28 miles (45 kilometers) away. The feudal château was built by St-Louis (1228–38) and has a dry moat, drawbridge, and 17 round towers along its half-mile (1-kilometer) long walls. A modern, well-integrated gallery houses an exquisite tapestry collection, notable for the enormous *Tapestry of the Apocalypse*, woven in Paris around 1380. *Admission: 22 frs. Open summer 9:30–6; winter 9:30–noon and 2–6.*

The substantial 12th–13th century **St-Maurice Cathedral** has early Gothic vaulting and masterly stained glass of various eras. Also of interest is the **Musée David d'Angers,** where works by the distinguished local 19th-century sculptor are displayed in a ruined church with a modern glass roof. *33 rue Toussaint. Admission: 10 frs. Open 10–noon and 2–6, closed Mon.*

Dining and Lodging

For details and price category definitions, *see* Dining and Lodging in Essential Information.

Angers **Le Quéré.** Despite a curious upstairs setting (in a former bar-
Dining bershop), Le Quéré is rated one of the region's finest eating places. The large dining room has brass chandeliers and lace tablecloths. Fish from the Loire and foie gras with asparagus can be admirably accompanied by any of a vast selection of local wines. *9 pl. du Ralliement, tel. 41–87–64–94. Jacket and tie. Reservations advised. AE, DC, V. Closed Fri. evening, Sat., part of Feb., July 1–20. Expensive.*

Lodging **Hôtel d'Anjou.** An old friend of a hotel, this has spacious, well-modernized rooms and is handily situated by the Jardin du Mail, a pleasant park. It has its own parking facilities and a good restaurant, La Salamandre (tel. 41–88–99–55), with a Renaissance-style dining room. *1 blvd. du Mal-Foch, tel. 41–88–24–82. 51 rooms with bath or shower. AE, DC, V. Restaurant closed Sun. Moderate.*

Blois **Bocca d'Or.** The old 14th-century stone vaults at this restau-
Dining rant, in the heart of Blois, provide a historical atmosphere that contrasts with its nouvelle cuisine, though both are refined. Fish, shellfish, and poultry figure prominently, and the wine list is comprehensive. *15 rue Haute, tel. 54–78–04–74. Jacket and tie. Reservations advised. AE, V. Closed Sun., Mon. lunch; Mar. 1–8. Moderate.*

Lodging **Anne de Bretagne.** An unpretentious hotel without a restaurant, Anne de Bretagne is conveniently situated on a broad avenue close to the tourist office and château. Parking is less of a headache here than it can be in the narrow streets of old Blois, but you may feel cheated of some of the atmosphere here. *31 av.*

du Dr Jean-Laigret, tel. 54–78–05–38. 29 rooms, some with bath or shower. AE, MC, V. Closed mid-Feb.–mid-Mar. Moderate.

Chambord
Lodging

Hôtel St-Michel offers good value, considering its location—right opposite the château. Some of its rooms afford splendid views of the château, its lawns, and the forest backcloth, as does the conveniently sited terrace just outside, an ideal place for summer morning coffee before the tourist hordes arrive. The hotel has its own tennis courts, garage, and restaurant. *Bracieux, tel. 54–20–31–31. 38 rooms, some with bath or shower. MC, V. Closed Nov. 12–Dec. 19. Moderate.*

Chinon
Lodging

Auberge du Haut Clos. Situated 3 miles (5 kilometers) south of Chinon (via D751), this hotel stands on a steep hill. You will enjoy the views from the terrace—a great place for an aperitif—before moving inside to the large dining hall with its huge fireplace and vast serving table festooned with salads and cuts of meat. The hotel is something of a letdown, being inexpensive and adequate, rather than memorable, although the flowered wallpaper in some rooms is overpowering. *La Roche-Clermault, tel. 47–95–94–50. 15 rooms, some with shower. Dress: casual for restaurant. Reservations not needed. MC, V. Closed Jan., Feb. Restaurant closed Sun. evening, Mon. off-season. Inexpensive.*

Saumur
Lodging

Le Prieuré. Five miles northwest of Saumur via D751, Le Prieuré is a neo-Renaissance manor house perched high above the south bank of the Loire. It has its own restaurant overlooking the river, a heated swimming pool, and vast park. The rooms are large and luxuriously furnished, most with a view of the Loire. A reservation is advisable, or you may find yourself in one of the less attractive houses in the park. *Chênehutte-les-Tuffeaux, Gennes, tel. 41–50–15–31. 35 rooms with bath. V. Closed Jan., Feb. Expensive.*

Tours
Dining

Jean Bardet. The restaurant takes its name from the chef, one of the finest in France, who moved from Châteauroux to Tours in 1987. His new restaurant is situated just north of the Loire in an early 19th-century mansion. The dining room overlooks a large garden (planted by a previous English owner) and is decorated with colorful chairs and carpets. There is a superb wine list and each dish is a work of art and originality: Try the eel fricassée or lobster in wine spiced with lime and ginger. Doing it all justice doesn't come cheap—but you can get a glimpse with a set menu for around 200 frs. *57 rue Groison, tel. 47–41–41–11. Jacket and tie. AE, DC, V. Expensive.*

Lodging

Domaine de la Tortinière, six miles (10 kilometers) due south of Tours along N10, this turreted restaurant dates from the mid-19th century. It stands proudly on a hill amid vast fields and woodland. The bedrooms are individually decorated in styles ranging from conventionally old-fashioned to brash ultramodern. The airy restaurant (closed Wed. lunch and Tues. out of season) looks out over the gardens. Salmon, pigeon, and rabbit with truffles are menu highlights. *Les Gués de Veigné, 37250 Montbazon, tel. 47–26–00–19. 14 rooms with bath. MC, V. Closed mid-Nov.–mid-Mar. Expensive.*

Vendôme
Lodging

Hôtel Vendôme. Near the banks of the Loir, Hôtel Vendôme makes a handy base for exploring the pedestrian streets of the old town. It is stylish and appropriately priced, with excellent, modernized rooms, though lacking a little in character. There is a garage and a trustworthy restaurant with quietly efficient English-speaking service. *15 Faubourg Chartrain, tel. 54–77–02–88. 35 rooms with bath or shower. MC, V. Closed Dec. 23–Jan. 6. Restaurant closed Sun. evening in winter. Moderate.*

The Riviera

Few places in the world have the same pull on the imagination as France's fabled Riviera, the Mediterranean coastline stretching from St-Tropez in the west to Menton on the Italian border. Cooled by the Mediterranean in the summer and warmed by it in winter, the climate is almost always pleasant. Avoid the area in July and August, however—unless you love crowds. To see the Riviera at its best, plan your trip in the spring or fall, particularly in May or September.

The Riviera is a land of contrasts. While the coastal resorts seem to live exclusively for the tourist trade and have often been ruined by high-rise blocks, the hinterlands remain relatively untarnished. The little villages perched high on the hills behind medieval ramparts seem to belong to another century. One of them, St-Paul de Vence, is the home of the Maeght Foundation, one of the world's leading museums of modern art.

Artists, attracted by the light, have played a considerable role in popular conceptions of the Riviera, and their presence is reflected in the number of modern art museums: the Musée Picasso at Antibes, the Musée Renoir and the Musée d'Art Moderne Mediterranéan at Cagnes-sur-Mer, and the Musée Jean Cocteau near the harbor at Menton. Wining and dining are special treats on the Riviera, especially if you are fond of garlic and olive oil. *Bouillabaisse*, a spicy fish stew, is the most popular regional specialty.

Getting Around

By Train The train line follows the coast from Marseille to the Italian border, providing excellent access to the seaside resorts and some inland towns such as Grasse, but you will have to take local buses (marked *Gare Routiere*) or guided tours to visit the perched villages.

By Car Expressway A8 is the only way to get around the Riviera quickly, but for the drama of mountains and sea, take one of the famous Corniche roads.

Guided Tours

SNCF, the French national railroad company, runs the greatest number of organized tours. For information, contact the Nice Tourist Office (*see* Tourist Information). Tours are most valuable to areas otherwise impossible to reach by public transport: St-Paul-de-Vence, Upper Provence, or the spectacular Verdon Gorges.

Boats operate from Nice to Marseille; from St-Tropez to the charming Hyeres islands; and from Antibes, Cannes, or Juan-les-Pins to the Lerins islands.

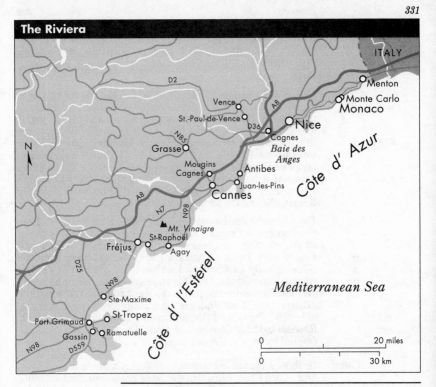

The Riviera

Menton
Monte Carlo
Monaco
Nice
Vence
St.-Paul-de-Vence
Cagnes
Baie des Anges
Grasse
Mougins
Cagnes
Antibes
Juan-les-Pins
Cannes
Mt. Vinaigre
St-Raphaël
Fréjus
Agay
Côte d' Azur
Côte d' l'Estérel
Ste-Maxime
St-Tropez
Port Grimaud
Gassin
Ramatuelle
Côte d' Azur
Mediterranean Sea
ITALY

0   20 miles
0   30 km

Tourist Information

Antibes. Pl. du Général de Gaulle, tel. 93–33–95–64.
Cagnes-sur-Mer. 26 av. Renoir, tel. 93–20–61–64.
Cannes. Palais des Congrès, La Croisette, tel. 93–39–24–53.
Fréjus. Blvd. de la Liberation, tel. 94–51–48–42.
Grasse. 3 pl. Foux, tel. 93–36–03–56.
Menton. Palais de l'Europe, tel. 93–35–77–23.
Nice. Av. Thier, tel. 93–87–07–07; av. Gustave Flaubert, tel. 93–87–60–60.
St-Paul-de-Vence. Maison Tour, rue Grande, tel. 93–32–86–95.
St-Tropez. Quai Jean-Jaurès, tel. 94–97–45–21.
Vence. pl. du Grand Jardin, tel. 93–58–02–02.

Exploring

St-Tropez   St-Tropez was just another pretty fishing village until it was "discovered" in the 1950s by the "beautiful people," a fast set of film stars, starlets, and others who scorned bourgois values while enjoying bourgois bank balances. Today, its summer population swells from 6,000 to 60,000. In season, its top hotels, restaurants, nightclubs, and chic little shops are jammed. In the winter, it's hard to find a restaurant open. The best times to visit, therefore, are early summer or fall. May and June are perhaps the best months, when the town lets its hair down during two local festivals.

The **old port** is the liveliest part of town. You can kill time here at a café terrace, watching the rich and famous on their gleaming yachts. Between the old and new ports is the **Musée de l'Annonciade**, set in a cleverly converted chapel, which houses paintings by artists drawn to St-Tropez between 1890 and 1940—including Paul Signac, Matisse, Derain, and Van Dongen. *Quai Gabriel-Péri. Admission: 15 frs. Open June-Sept., 10–noon and 3–7; Oct.–May, 10–noon and 4–6. Closed Tues.*

Across the place de l'Hôtel de Ville lies the old town, where twisting, narrow streets, designed to break the impact of the terrible mistral wind, open on to tiny squares and fountains. A long climb up to the **citadel** is rewarded by a splendid view over the old town and across the gulf to **Ste-Maxime,** a quieter, more working-class family resort with a decent beach and reasonably priced hotels. St-Tropez is also a good base for visiting **Port Grimaud,** a pastiche of an Italian fishing village (take D559) and the nearby hilltop villages—the old Provençal town of **Ramatuelle** and the fortified village of **Gassin.**

The **Corniche des Issambres** (N98) runs along the coast from Ste-Maxime to **Fréjus,** a Roman town built by Julius Caesar in 49 BC, standing on a rocky plateau between the Maures and Esterel hills. Two main roads link Fréjus and Cannes. Tortuous N7, originally a Roman road, skirts the northern flank of the rugged Esterel hills. Look for an intersection called the *carrefour du Testannier* and follow the signs to **Forêt Domaniale de l'Esterel** and **Mont Vinaigre** for a magnificent view over the hills. The **Corniche d'Or** coast road (N98) takes you past **St. Raphaël** to the little resort of **Agay,** whose deep bay was once favored by ancient Greek traders.

Cannes In 1834, a chance event was to change Cannes's lifestyle forever. Lord Brougham, Britain's lord chancellor, was en route for Nice when an outbreak of cholera forced the authorities to freeze all travel to prevent the disease from spreading. Trapped in Cannes, he fell in love with the place and built himself a house there as an annual refuge from the British winter. The English aristocracy, czars, kings, and princes soon caught on, and Cannes became a community for the international elite. Grand palace hotels were built to cater to them, and Cannes came to symbolize dignified luxury. Today, Cannes is also synonymous with the **International Film Festival,** which celebrated its 40th anniversary in 1987 in the controversial **Palais des Festivals,** often known by its critics as the "Bunker."

Cannes is for relaxing—strolling along the seafront on the **Croisette,** and getting tanned on the beaches. Almost all the beaches are private, but that doesn't mean you can't use them, only that you must pay for the privilege. The Croisette offers splendid views of the **Napoule Bay.** Only a few steps inland is the old town, known as the **Suquet,** with its steep, cobbled streets and its 12th-century watchtower.

Grasse is perched in the hills behind Cannes. Take N85 or just follow your nose to the town that claims to be the perfume capital of the world. A good proportion of its 40,000 inhabitants work at distilling and extracting scent from the tons of roses, lavender, and jasmine produced here every year. The various perfumiers are only too happy to guide visitors around their fragrant establishments. Fragonard is the best known. *20 blvd. de Fragonard, tel. 93–36–44–65.* The old town is attractive, with its narrow alleys and massive, somber **cathedral.** Three of the paintings inside the cathedral are by Rubens and one is by Fragonard, who lived here for many years.

Take N85 back down to the coast, but fork left at **Mougins,** an attractive fortified hilltop town, famous for one of France's best restaurants, **Le Moulin de Mougins.** D35 takes you to **Antibes** and **Juan-les-Pins,** originally two villages that now form one town on the west side of the **Baie des Anges** (Angels' Bay).

Antibes Antibes, the older village, dates back to the 4th century BC, when it was a Greek trading port. Today, it is renowned throughout Europe for its industrial flower and plant production. Every morning, except Monday, the market on the Cours Masséna comes alive with the colors of roses, carnations, anemones, and tulips. The Grimaldis, the family that rules Monaco, built **Château Grimaldi** here in the 12th century on the remains of a Roman camp. Today, the château's main attraction is the **Musée Picasso**—a bounty of paintings, ceramics, and lithographs inspired by the sea and Greek mythology. *Admission: 15 frs. Open summer 10–noon and 3–7; winter, 10–noon and 3–6. Closed Tues., Nov.*

The 13-mile (20-kilometer) stretch of flat coast between Antibes and Nice lacks charm, but the hinterland makes up for it. The picture-book medieval village of **St-Paul-de-Vence** (via D2 and D7) stands hidden behind its ramparts. A prosperous town in the Middle Ages, it was only "rediscovered" in the 1920s by a group of painters who met at the **Colombe d'Or,** now a popular inn with its walls covered with their paintings. Today, the village is full of artists' studios, antiques shops, and craft galleries, and is one of the most visited in France. The **Fondation Maeght** is less than a mile away. This temple of modern art is an attractive ensemble in a pinewood setting. Giacometti's figures stride the courtyard between the white concrete and rose-colored brick buildings, housing an excellent collection of modern art and sculpture, studios, a library, cinema, and auditorium. *Admission: 30 frs. Open July–Sept., daily 10–7; June and Oct., daily 10–12:30 and 2:30–7; winter, daily 10–12:30 and 2:30–6.*

The larger village of **Vence** lies farther along D2. Like St-Paul, it has its share of artists' studios and galleries, but its major contribution to modern art is the **Chapelle du Rosaire,** the Rosary Chapel designed and decorated by Henri Matisse in the late 1940s. *Free. Open Tues. and Thurs., 10–11:30 and 2:30–5:30.*

Nice Take D36 back down to the coast and join A8 or N7 into Nice. With its population of 400,000, its own university, new congress hall, and nearby science park, Nice is the undisputed capital of the Riviera. Founded by the Greeks as Nikaia, it has lived through several civilizations and was attached to France only in 1860. It consequently boasts a profusion of Greek, Italian, British, and French styles. Tourism may not be the main business of Nice, but it is a deservedly popular center with much to offer. The double blessing of climate and geography puts its beaches within an hour-and-a-half's drive of the nearest ski resorts. There is an eclectic mixture of old and new architecture, an opera house, museums, flourishing markets, and regular concerts and festivals, including the Mardi Gras festival and the Battle of Flowers.

 The **place Masséna** is the logical starting point for an exploration of Nice. This fine square was built in 1815 to celebrate one of Napoleon's most successful generals and a local hero. The

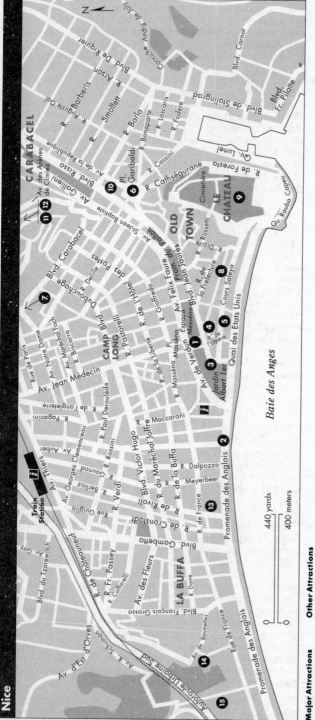

Nice

Major Attractions
Jardin Albert 1er, **3**
Musée Chagall, **7**
Opera House, **5**
Place Garibaldi, **6**
Place Masséna, **1**
Promenade des
Anglais, **2**
St-François-de-Paul, **4**

Other Attractions
Arènes de Cimiez, **12**
Castle Ruins, **9**
Flower Market, **8**
Musée d'Art Naïf, **15**
Musée J. Chéret, **14**
Musée d'Histoire
Naturelle, **10**
Musée Masséna, **13**
Musée Matisse, **11**

2 **Promenade des Anglais,** built by the English community here in
3 1824, is only a short stroll past the fountains and the **Jardin Al-bert ler.** It now carries heavy traffic but still forms a splendid
strand between town and sea. The narrow streets in the old
town are the prettiest part of Nice: Take the rue de l'Opéra to
4 **5** see **St-François-de-Paul** church (1750) and the **opera house.** At
the northern extremity of the old town lies the vast **place**
6 **Garibaldi**—all yellow-ocher buildings and formal fountains.

7 The **Musée Chagall** is on the boulevard de Cimiez, near the Roman ruins. The museum was built in 1972 to house the Chagall
collection, including the 17 huge canvases of *The Message of the
Bible,* which took 13 years to complete. *Admission: 15 frs.
Open July–Sept., 10–7; Oct.–June, 10–12:30 and 2–5:30.*

Menton Menton also once belonged to the Grimaldis and, like Nice, was
attached to France only in 1860. Because of its popularity
among British visitors, the western side of the town was
developed at the turn of the century to cater to the influx of the
rich and famous, with spacious avenues, first-class hotels, and
the inevitable casino. The eastern side of town long remained
the domain of the local fishermen but has more recently been
developed to cater to the needs of tourists. A large marina was
built and the **Sablettes,** once a tiny beach, has been artificially
extended.

Down by the harbor stands a small 17th-century fort, where
Jean Cocteau, the artist, writer, and filmmaker once worked.
It now houses the **Musée Jean Cocteau,** with a collection of his
work. *111 quai Napoléon. Admission: 5 frs. Open mid-June–
mid-Sept., Wed.–Sun. 10–noon and 3–6; winter 10–noon and
2–5:30.*

Menton's Lemon Fair in February celebrates the town's vast
production of excellent citrus fruits. In August, its popular
chamber music festival holds concerts in the attractive Italianate churches in the old town.

Dining and Lodging

For details and price category definitions, *see* Dining and
Lodging in Essential Information.

Antibes **Auberge Provençale.** André Martin is rightly proud of his con-
Lodging verted abbey in the old town near the harbor, with its gardens
in the former cloisters. The rooms and service are sunny, partly a reflection of the manageable size of the hotel. Its popular
restaurant serves lobster and shellfish as well as *boudin de
rascasse,* a minced fish shaped into a sausage. *61 pl. Nationale,
tel. 93–34–13–24. 6 rooms with bath or shower. Jacket and tie
and reservations for restaurant. AE, DC, MC, V. Closed mid-
Nov.–mid-Dec. Restaurant closed Mon., Tues. lunch. Moderate.*

Cagnes **Cagnard.** This hotel is in an attractive 15th-century building in
Lodging the old village. The restaurant—once the Grimaldi Château
Guards's Room—dates back to the early 14th century. The hotel has several suites in two houses in the garden and a third up
the road. The view from them all—over the Cap d'Antibes—is
memorable. *Rue Pontis-Long, tel. 93–20–73–21. 19 rooms and
suites with bath. AE, DC, MC, V. Closed Nov.–Dec. 20. Restaurant closed Thurs. lunch. Expensive.*

Cannes
Dining

Mirabelle. For many, this is a favorite restaurant in the Suquet. Mirabelle was entirely redecorated in 1988 and now has a more countrified atmosphere, reflecting the new menu with specialties from all over France. The cuisine is inventive, the sauces light, and the desserts special. *24 rue St-Antoine, tel. 93–38–72–75. MC, V. Closed Tues., Dec., Mar. 1–15. Expensive.*

Lodging

Majestic. Unlike most of its neighbors among the luxury hotels lining the Croisette on the seafront, the Majestic has a discreet atmosphere. The rooms are spacious and traditional but refreshingly decorated in pastels. It also offers a reasonably priced evening meal in winter. *6 blvd. Croisette, tel. 93–68–91–00. 262 rooms with bath. Facilities: private beach, swimming pool, air-conditioning, parking lot, access to tennis, golf, and horseback riding. AE, DC, MC, V. Closed Nov. 20–Dec. 20. Very Expensive.*

Roches Fleuries. A pretty little hotel near the Suquet and the old port, Roches Fleuries is set on several levels, with stairs leading up from its garden to two terraces, where you can have breakfast while looking down on the sea. Rooms vary in size and style: Some are genuinely Provençal, and several have balconies. *92 rue George Clemenceau, tel. 93–39–28–78. 24 rooms, 15 with bath or shower. No credit cards. Closed Nov. 15–Dec. 27. Inexpensive.*

Grasse
Lodging

Panorama. The excellent views of the Massif d'Esterel and right across to Cannes are the vindication of this hotel's name. It is modern and well run and has ample parking. Most rooms have good views, but there is no restaurant. *2 pl. du Cours, tel. 93–36–80–80. 36 rooms with bath. AE, DC, MC, V. Moderate.*

Menton
Lodging

Chez Mireille l'Ermitage. Best known for its restaurant, this elegant yet cozy hotel stands on the promenade du Soleil, overlooking the beach. Each room has its own style and all are different, although many have good views. The restaurant is a favorite for local specialties: *bourride* and *bouillabaisse*, salmon, and bass fillets. *1080 promenade du Soleil, tel. 93–35–77–23. 21 rooms with bath or shower. AE, DC, MC, V. Restaurant closed Mon. evening, Tues. mid-Nov–mid-Apr. Moderate.*

Mougins
Dining

Le Moulin de Mougins. Roger Vergé has created one of France's finest restaurants in a converted mill about 1½ miles from the village along D3. The cuisine ranges from some apparently simple salads to some rich, complicated sauces for lobster, salmon, or turbot. Considering that it is a gourmet favorite, the restaurant has a surprisingly informal atmosphere. *Quartier Notre-Dame-de-Vie, tel. 93–75–78–24. Jacket and tie. Reservations essential. AE, DC, MC, V. Closed Mon. (except summer), Thurs., lunch, Feb.–Mar. 20. Expensive.*

Nice
Dining

Ane-Rouge. Famous for generations as *the* place for Nice's best fish and seafood, this tiny, family-run restaurant is popular with locals, not least for the Vidalots, the pleasant couple who run it. *7 quai des Deux-Emmanuels, tel. 93–89–49–63. Jacket and tie. Reservations advised. MC, V. Closed Sat., Sun., mid-July–mid-Aug. Expensive.*

Lodging

Negresco. Opened in 1912, the Negresco is officially listed as a historic monument and is a byword for Old World elegance. The public rooms have antique coffered ceilings and magnificent fireplaces. No two bedrooms are alike, but they all have antique furniture and paintings. Its main restaurant, Le Chanteclerc, is, without doubt, the best in Nice: Chef Jacques Maximin is one of France's leading advocates of nouvelle cuisine. He also presides over the Rotonde, which serves a cheaper version of the same fare. *37 promenade des Anglais, tel. 93–88–39–51. 140 rooms with bath. Jacket and tie and reservations for restaurants. AE, DC, MC. Restaurants closed Nov. Very Expensive.*

St-Tropez **Byblos.** This hotel is unique. Its luxury rooms and suites are
Lodging built around tiled courtyards, fragrant with magnolia and orange trees, like a miniature Provençal village. Each room is different, with amusing touches and subtle lighting. Les Caves du Roy, one of its two nightclubs, and Le Chabichon, an independent restaurant within the complex, are considered among the best in town. Chef Michel Rochedy is famous for his delicate, inventive touches. Specialties include foie gras and lobster. The more adventurous should try the baby squid stew with pigs' feet and fava beans. La Braiserie, the hotel's other restaurant, offers more moderately priced meals. *Av. Paul Signac, tel. 94–97–00–04. 70 rooms and 37 suites with bath. Facilities: sauna, pool, hairdresser. AE, DC, MC, V. Closed Nov.–Feb. Very Expensive. Le Chabichou, tel. 94–54–00–04. Jacket and tie. Reservations essential. AE, DC, MC, V. Closed Nov.–Apr. Very Expensive.*

12 East Germany

Introduction

East Germany, or the German Democratic Republic, divides a nation otherwise united by language and cultural heritage. Though the standard of living here is the highest of all the Communist countries, the urban centers are unmistakably "Eastern bloc," with drab apartment blocks housing a populace exhorted by banner and slogan to do its best for the development of socialism and "the common good." Outside the cities, however, villages and their residents appear to the casual visitor to be not much different from their Western counterparts. East Germany, however, has been spared most of the worst aspects of modernization that have blighted so much of West Germany. The countryside is attractive, and great effort has been put into removing the devastating effect of the last war.

The Prussian mentality that in past centuries built disciplined armies that swept across Europe is still evident in the determination with which the government has placed East Germany among the top-ranking industrial nations in the world. The same purposeful effort has gone into creating world champions in various sports, rebuilding whole sections of cities, and carrying subsidies to such extremes that the prices of some goods and services are so low they bear no relationship to their real cost.

These are the features that make East Germany both interesting and a challenge to the tourist. Every corner offers a contrast—or a mirror reflection—when seen against the rest of Europe, whether the Europe of today or that of an elegant past.

Before You Go

When to Go The main tourist season runs from late April to early October. Berlin, however, is active year-round. The weather is best in the spring and fall; summer can be muggy, except along the Baltic coast or in the southern mountains. Avoid Leipzig around the first weeks in March and September; the trade fair commandeers all accommodations and prices soar. Off-season prices are not substantially lower.

The following are the average daily maximum and minimum tempertures for Berlin.

Jan.	35F	2C	May	66F	19C	Sept.	68F	20C
	26	−3		47	18		50	10
Feb.	37F	3C	June	72F	22C	Oct.	56F	13C
	26	−3		53	12		42	6
Mar.	46F	8C	July	75F	24C	Nov.	45F	7C
	31	0		57	14		36	2
Apr.	56F	13C	Aug.	74F	23C	Dec.	38F	3C
	39	14		56	13		29	−1

Currency The monetary unit of East Germany is the mark der DDR (M), divided into 100 pfennigs. There are banknotes of 100, 50, 20, 10, and 5 marks and coins of 20, 10, 5, 2, and 1 mark and 50, 20, 10, and 1 pfennig. The exchange rate for the East German mark is the same as that for the West German deutschmark. At

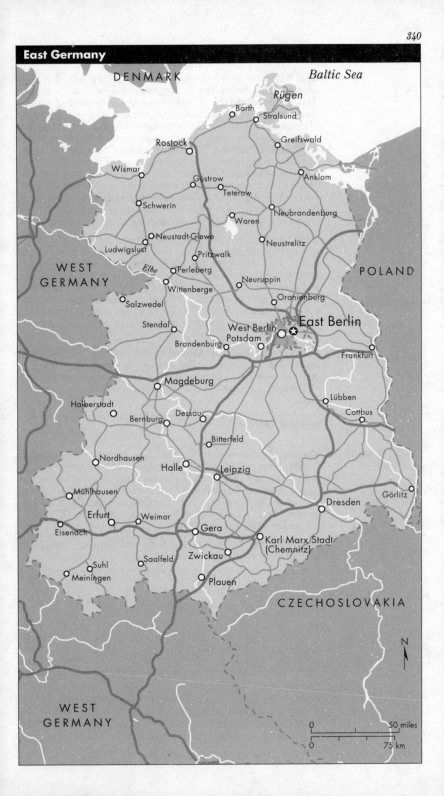

East Germany

DENMARK

Baltic Sea

Rügen

Barth

Stralsund

Greifswald

Rostock

Wismar

Güstrow

Teterow

Anklam

Schwerin

Waren

Neubrandenburg

Neustadt-Glewe

Ludwigslust

Neustrelitz

Pritzwalk

Elbe

Perleberg

Neuruppin

WEST
GERMANY

Wittenberge

Oranienburg

POLAND

Salzwedel

Stendal

West Berlin

East Berlin

Potsdam

Brandenburg

Frankfurt

Magdeburg

Halberstadt

Lübben

Cottbus

Bernburg

Dessau

Bitterfeld

Nordhausen

Halle

Leipzig

Mühlhausen

Dresden

Görlitz

Erfurt

Weimar

Gera

Eisenach

Karl Marx Stadt
(Chemnitz)

Suhl

Saalfeld

Zwickau

Meiningen

Plauen

CZECHOSLOVAKIA

N

WEST
GERMANY

0   50 miles

0   75 km

press time (fall 1988), it was M1.67 to the dollar and M3.16 to the pound sterling.

You may bring in as much foreign currency as you wish, but you must declare it upon arrival. What you fail to declare, you may not be able to take out. East German currency may not be exported.

Currency and traveler's checks can be exchanged at nearly all banks and larger hotels; airports and main train stations also have money-changing facilities. Resist any offers for unofficial exchange by private individuals: If caught, you not only lose the money but run the risk of fine and arrest.

Visitors are required to change DM25, or its equivalent in another Western currency, per day per person; DM7.50 for children 6–15 years of age. If you have prepaid hotel or camping vouchers, you probably have already met the minimum exchange requirement. When changing currency or paying in Western currency, or with a credit card, get a receipt. This will serve as proof that you have met the minimum exchange requirement.

Credit Cards All Interhotels, Intershops, and some independent shops and restaurants accept American Express, Diners Club, MasterCard, or Visa. These cards are also valid for car rentals. Save all charge slips as evidence of currency exchange.

What It Will Cost By Western standards, East Germany is not an expensive country to visit. The major exception is hotel lodging. The main hotels in the larger cities are very much up to Western standards and are priced accordingly. Off the beaten track, prices drop, but accommodations are more modest.

Sample Prices Cup of coffee in a cafe, M1.50–M2; draft beer in a Bierkeller, M2–M3; vodka or schnapps, M2.50–M4; half-bottle of wine in a restaurant, M20–M30; Coca-Cola, M1–M2; movie ticket, M3–M4; theater ticket, M5–M10; concert or opera ticket, M5–M15; one-mile taxi ride, M.70–M1.10; streetcar, bus, subway or city railway ticket, M.20–M.50.

Visas Visas are required of all visitors to East Germany. East German consulates in the United States and the United Kingdom do not issue visas to individuals, only to accredited travel agencies. The procedure takes 6–8 weeks and costs the equivalent of DM15. A travel agent in the USA will charge $16–$20 for the visa and handling, $26–$30 for rush service. You will also need a voucher confirming your hotel reservations; this can be arranged with the travel agent at the same time.

Visitors from the USA or Canada can find out the names and addresses of accredited travel agencies by writing the **East German Consulate** (1717 Massachusetts Ave. NW, Washington, DC 20036). In the United Kingdom, East German tourist affairs, including visa assistance, are handled by **Berolina Travel** (20 Conduit St., London W1R 9TD, tel. 01/629–1664).

Upon entering East Germany, you will be given a small form to fill out that will be stamped with the entry date. This form must be surrendered when you leave the country, so be careful not to lose it.

You can visit East Berlin from West Berlin on a daily pass card good for a 24-hour stay. The visa costs DM5 or its equivalent and can be extended for up to a week, either by an Interhotel or by the *Reisebüro der DDR* once you are in the country. Note that the minimum currency exchange requirement applies to shorter visits as well (*see* Currency). Transit visas for stays of up to 72 hours are available at border crossing points, provided you have a valid visa for the country to be visited next (usually Poland or Czechoslovakia). Obtaining a day pass from West Berlin into East Berlin is no major problem but may take time at the border. It is far preferable to make arrangements in advance and have the visa and other papers ready when you reach the border. You can obtain a visa (day pass) directly from the East German consulates in Washington, DC (*see* above) or London (34 Belgrave Sq., SW1X 8QZ, tel. 01/235–4465); usually only two or three days are required. Visas are included as part of the half-day tour packages operated by travel agencies from West Berlin.

If you are staying in East Germany, you must be registered with the police; your hotel management will normally take care of this, but it's best to check.

Customs
On Arrival Customs procedures vary from casual to meticulous, but it is wisest to follow the rules and not take chances. You may import any amount of tobacco, spirits, or wine. You may also bring in gifts to the value of M200 duty-free per person for visits of up to five days. If your visit will last longer than five days, this amount is increased to M100 for each day of your stay, to a maximum of M1,000. Note that the value of the goods brought in is based on their price in East Germany, not necessarily on what you paid for them. Customs regulations have now been somewhat relaxed regarding publications, but some Western magazines and newspapers may not be allowed, and officials may hesitate over tape- and videocassettes. If you are carrying such valuables as a video recorder, special photo equipment, or a fur coat, avoid possible problems when leaving the country by having these items noted in your passport when you arrive.

On Departure When you leave, duty may be charged on goods you take out beyond the value of M20 per person per day's stay for up to five days, or M100 for a longer stay. This regulation is rarely enforced and is designed mainly to keep Poles from coming across the border and buying up East German goods "on the cheap." If you buy antiques or anything else of substantial value, you will get an official receipt (assuming you bought it from an authorized source), which will solve any export problems, should customs officials ask. For regulations covering the import and export of money, *see* Currency.

Language English is widely spoken in the main city centers, but is far less common in other areas than it is in West Germany.

Getting Around

By Car
Road Conditions Nearly 1,000 miles (1,600 kilometers) of expressway and 7,000 miles (11,000 kilometers) of secondary roads crisscross the country. Highways are constantly being improved, but many roads other than main routes are in poor condition.

Rules of the Road Drive on the right-hand side of the road. Traffic regulations, from parking rules to speed limits, are strictly enforced. The police levy fines—in West German currency, for foreigners—for the slightest offense. Driving while intoxicated is strictly forbidden, and fines are heavy. If not otherwise indicated, cars coming from the right have the right-of-way. Speed limits on the autobahn (expressway) are 100 kph (62 mph); on other roads, 80 kph (50 mph); and in towns, 50 kph (30 mph).

Gasoline Gas is available at either **Minol** or **Intertank** stations; both chains sell regular and premium grades by the liter. Diesel fuel is not available at all stations, and distribution of unleaded fuel is limited to expressways and main centers. Minol stations supply gasoline for either East German marks (you may be asked to show your currency exchange receipt) or coupons, which may be bought at a discount at the border. Otherwise, the Intertank stations sell gasoline at reduced prices for West German deutschmarks.

Road Tax Foreign drivers must pay a tongue-twisting *Strassenbenutzungsgebühr*, or road-users' tax, at the rates of M5 for up to 200 kilometers (125 miles), M15 for up to 300 kilometers (190 miles), M20 for up to 400 kilometers (250 miles), or M25 for up to 500 kilometers (310 miles). The tax must be paid in equivalent foreign currency.

By Train The government runs three types of trains: express, the fastest, shown as *IEx* or *Ex* in timetables; fast, shown as *D;* and slightly slower services, indicated with an *E*. These categories have varying supplementary fares; local trains do not. Most long- and medium-distance trains have both first- and second-class cars, and many have either dining or buffet cars, although these may be open only to and from specific destinations. Trains are usually full, so reservations—made either via the *Reisebüro der DDR* travel agency or at any major train station—are recommended.

By Boat "White Fleets" of inland boats, including paddleboats, ply the inland lakes around Berlin and on the Elbe river. Dresden is the major starting point; from there, boats go upstream to Meissen or downstream and on into Czechoslovakia.

Essential Information

Telephones Pay phones require a 20-pfennig coin. Long-distance calls are not possible from a pay phone, but may be made from your hotel or from any post office. Connections within Europe are immediate; overseas calls may take longer. Some hotels have international direct dialing. To call the USA or Canada, dial 012–1 followed by the area code and number. For the United Kingdom, dial 0644 plus the city code and the number.

Mail Airmail letters to the USA and Canada cost M1.40, postcards, *Postal Rates* 90 pfennig. Airmail letters to the United Kingdom cost 80 pfennig, postcards, 60 pfennig. Some hotels may ask for West German currency in payment for stamps; post offices deal only in local currency.

Receiving Mail Hotels will hold mail for visitors who have reservations; envelopes should indicate the date of expected arrival.

Shopping East Germany produces attractive dolls, wooden toys, Christmas ornaments, excellent lace, pewter, ceramics, glass, crystal ware, and, of course, Meissen porcelain. Sheet music is a real bargain, either in the shops on East Berlin's Unter den Linden or opposite the Thomaskirche in Leipzig. Books, too, are a bargain, but, of course, are mainly in German. As a rule, prices in stores are fixed and no bargaining is possible. For general shopping, the **Centrum** department stores (the largest is in Berlin) offer a wide selection at low prices. Western goods—even some East German products not otherwise available—can be found in **Intershops** in virtually every Interhotel.

Opening and Closing Times

Banks. Banks are generally open Monday to Saturday from 8 to 11:30. Some have afternoon hours.

Museums. Museums are generally open from 10 to 6 daily except Monday. Most have a small admission fee of around M1.

Shops. Most Berlin shops are open weekdays from 10 to 7 (8 on Thursday); shops outside Berlin, from 9 to 6. Only department stores and other large shops are open on Saturday, and then mornings only.

National Holidays

January 1 (New Year's Day); March 24 (Good Friday); May 1 (Labor Day); May 15 (Whitmonday); October 7 (Republic); December 25, 26.

Dining

Dining possibilities range from the street stands offering frankfurters and various types of very tasty sausages; the "quick lunch" stops (mainly stand-up snack bars), called *Imbiss-stube*, which specialize in local favorites such as knuckle of pork; cafés, most of which have at least a limited lunch menu; *Bierkellers*, which offer hearty local fare and tankards of beer; and restaurants, which can be divided between *SB (Selbstbedienung,* or self-service cafeterias) and the more traditional establishments in all price ranges. If not eaten in a hotel, breakfast is a café affair; restaurants generally do not open until about 10 AM. The country's Eastern Bloc ties are reflected in national restaurants featuring the cuisines of other socialist states, although such exotica as Japanese, Chinese, Indonesian, and French dishes are now appearing.

Specialties

National favorites include *Eisbein mit Sauerkraut,* knuckle of pork with pickled cabbage; *Rouladen,* rolled stuffed beef; *Berliner Schüsselsülze,* potted meat in aspic; and *Kartoffelpuffer,* fried potato cakes. Regional specialties are finding wider acceptance. Typical dishes are *Thüringer Sauerbraten mit Klössen,* roast corned beef with dumplings; *Bärenschinken,* cured ham; and *Harzer Köhlerteller mit Röstkartoffeln,* charcoal-grilled meat with roast potatoes.

Mealtimes

The main meal of the day is traditionally taken at noon. Restaurants are crowded then and reservations are necessary. Evening dining usually begins at 7 or 7:30.

Ratings

Prices are per person in the lower-priced establishments. They include a main course and a small beer or possibly a glass of wine. In the top two categories, meals will be at least three courses. Prices include tax and tip, but it is customary to leave a small extra tip of M1–M3. In Very Expensive establishments, double this tip. Best bets are indicated by a star ★. At press time, there were 1.67 East German marks to the dollar.

Category	City	Country
Very Expensive	over M40	over M30
Expensive	M30–M40	M25–M30
Moderate	M20–M30	M15–M25
Inexpensive	under M20	under M15

Credit Cards	The following credit card abbreviations are used: AE, American Express; DC, Diners Club; MC, MasterCard; V, Visa.
Lodging	Western visitors to East Germany are effectively obliged to stay in the hotels of the state-run **Interhotel** chain; these include the major hotels in all cities and other tourist centers. Interhotels such as the Grand, Palast, and Metropol in Berlin, Merkur in Leipzig, and Bellevue in Dresden measure up to the highest international standards, including prices. Tourists seeking more moderate accommodations may try the **H-O** chain or the hostels run by the Evangelical church. The few private hotels are real bargains but are almost impossible for a Western visitor to book. East German travel officials will try to steer you to one of the best hotels; if you want more moderate accommodations, be prepared to argue your point at some length.
Ratings	Prices indicated here are for double rooms, with full bath in the top two categories. A single room with bath will cost about M5–M10 more than half the double rate shown. Breakfast is included in room rates. Best bets are indicated by a star ★ . At press time, there were 1.67 East German marks to the dollar.

Category	Cost
Very Expensive	over M250
Expensive	M170–M250
Moderate	M130–M170
Inexpensive	under M130

Credit Cards	The following credit card abbreviations are used: AE, American Express; DC, Diners Club; MC, MasterCard; V, Visa.
Tipping	The official line on tipping is *nein*, but tips are generally accepted, indeed expected, in major hotels and better restaurants. Tip in West German deutschmarks if possible, otherwise in U.S. currency. When paying by credit card, leave the tip in cash. Tip porters and doormen DM1, $1, or, as a last resort, M1 if you don't have any deutschmarks left. Taxi drivers do not expect a tip, but round up the fare to the nearest mark or to the next M.50.

East Berlin

Arriving and Departing

By Plane	All flights arrive at Schönefeld airport, about 15 miles (24 kilometers) outside the downtown area. For information on arrival and departure times, tel. 02/6724031.
Between the Airport and Downtown	A shuttle bus (fare M20) leaves every 10–15 minutes for the nearby S-Bahn train station. S-Bahn trains (fare M30) leave every 20 minutes for the Friedrichstrasse station. The trip takes about 30 minutes, and you can get off at whatever stop is nearest your hotel. Taxis are usually available at the stops from Ostbahnhof onward. You can also take a taxi from the airport; fare to your hotel will be about M30–35, and the trip will take about 40 minutes. By car, follow the signs for *Stadtzentrum Berlin*.

By Train International trains arrive at Friedrichstrasse or the Ost-bahnhof. For train information, phone 02/49541 for international trains, 02/49531 for domestic services. Trains coming from or via West Berlin arrive at the Friedrichstrasse station.

By Bus Berlin has no scheduled intercity or international bus service.

By Car Expressways lead to Berlin via Magdeburg, Leipzig, Rostock, Dresden, and Frankfurt-Oder. Road crossings also go to and from West Berlin. The downtown is marked *Stadtzentrum.*

Getting Around

Most tourist goals are easily reached on foot, and walking is recommended as the best way to see the city. That said, public transportation is good and wonderfully cheap.

By Bus and Streetcar Buses and streetcars are often crowded, and route maps, posted at each stop (marked H or HH), are not particularly clear to the uninitiated. Fares on buses and streetcars are a uniform M.20 within the main city area, allowing transfer from one line or from one form of transport to another. Get a ticket by dropping coins into the dispenser on the bus or tram; you'll have to pull the lever several times until the machine produces your ticket. If you transfer, put the first ticket into the dispenser and get yourself a new one for the next leg. A one-day tourist ticket *(Touristenkarte,* dated for any day you want; you can get several in advance) is available for M2; it's good on all transportation, including the trip to Schönefeld airport.

By U-Bahn and S-Bahn All city guides and maps show the subway (U-Bahn) and city train (S-Bahn) routes and stops. The system is simple to understand. The U-Bahn ticket system is the same as for the trams and buses (see above). The elevated electric line (S-Bahn) is fast and frequent. Tickets are issued from a dispenser (exact change!) for M.20, good for most destinations (fares are posted). The ticket is validated by poking it into a stamping device at the end of each platform: Take your cue from other passengers. The M2 full-day *Touristenfahrkarte* avoids all the hassle.

By Taxi Finding a taxi in Berlin can be an adventure, but try the ranks at such busy points as the Friedrichstrasse and Alexanderplatz stations. Taxis can be flagged on the street and are nearly always available around major hotels. If the "Taxi" light is on, the cab is available. Order a cab by phoning 02/3646 for immediate or same-day reservations, 02/3654176 for service during the coming week. Taxi fares are low, with a typical downtown fare costing M2–M4.

By Car Arrangements can be made through any of the Interhotels. Rental headquarters is at the **Metropol Hotel** (tel. 02/2204695); cars can be rented at **Schönefeld airport** as well (tel. 02/6722418).

Important Addresses and Numbers

Tourist Information **Reisebüro der DDR,** Alexanderplatz 5, tel. 02/2154328; special service office for foreign visitors on second floor (tel. 02/2154402); Schönefeld airport, tel. 02/6788248.

Embassies U.S. Neustädtische Kirchstr. 4–5, tel. 02/2202741. **U.K.** Unter den Linden 32–34, tel. 02/2202431. **Canadian.** There is no Canadian Embassy in East Berlin at present. If circumstances demand, call the Canadian Embassy in Warsaw (from East Berlin, phone 064822/0298051; address: Ulica Matejika 1–5, PL-00481 Warsaw, Poland). Alternatively, try the Canadian Military Mission in West Berlin (tel. 849/2611161). If that fails, the British Embassy will help, provided the people know that you have made an effort to contact the other two.

Emergencies **Police,** tel. 110; **Ambulance,** tel. 115; **Doctor, Dentist,** tel. 1259, or call the U.S. or U.K. Embassy for assistance; **Pharmacies,** tel. 160; **Motorist's assistance,** tel. 02/5243565, 6 AM–10 PM.

Guided Tours

Eleven different guided city tours, lasting from one hour to nearly four hours, can be booked through your hotel or the Reisebüro der DDR; fares range from M3 to M12. Taxi sightseeing tours of the city cover six fixed routes, starting and ending at Alexanderplatz. Tours last from 40 minutes to 2½ hours and cost M16.50–M55, depending on the route, for up to four persons; tel. 02/2462255 for details.

Exploring East Berlin

The infamous wall seems ever-present, but bear in mind it surrounds West, not East, Berlin, much as you may have a slightly claustrophobic feeling when you're in the eastern sector of the city. Stark contrasts exist between West and East. In the latter, discipline, orderliness, and the lack of traffic are immediate impressions, as is the overall subdued tone. The stately buildings of the city's past are not as overwhelmed by new high-rise construction as in West Berlin, but East Berlin's postwar architectural blunders are just as monumental in their own way. These will be obvious—along with the sad shabbiness of years of neglect—as you explore the side streets together with the main thoroughfares.

The Main Attractions

❶ As you head up the Friedrichstrasse from **Checkpoint Charlie,** your initial impression will be that the differences between East and West Berlin are minimal: Both sides of the street are lined with attractive new shops and trendy restaurants. Turn right into Johann-Dieckmann-Strasse and you'll arrive at the Platz der Akadamie, with its beautifully reconstructed **❷** **Schauspielhaus**—built in 1818, and now the city's main concert hall—and the rebuilt **German and French cathedrals.** In the lat- **❸** ter, you'll find the **Huguenot Museum,** which has some interesting collections of the history and art of the French Protestant Huguenots who took refuge in Germany after being expelled from Catholic France in 1685. *Platz der Akadamie. Admission charge. Open weekdays 10–5.*

Time Out The **Arkade Café** on the northwest corner of the plaza (Französischer Str. 25) is perfect for a light snack, some excellent pastry, and a beer, coffee, or tea.

❹ Continue east along the Französischer Strasse to Babelplatz. The peculiar round shape of **St. Hedwigskathedrale** (St. Hedwig's Cathedral) calls to mind Rome's Pantheon. The tiny

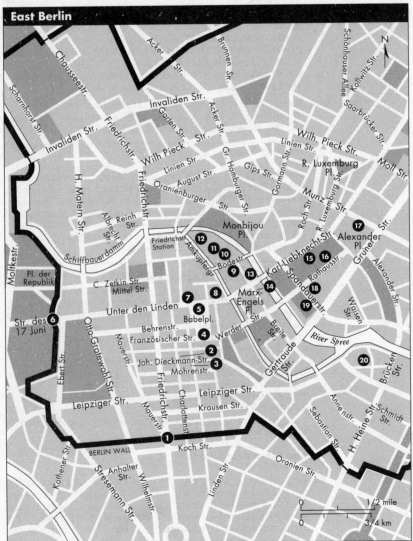

East Berlin

Altes Museum, **9**

Berlin Cathedral, **13**

Bodemuseum, **12**

Brandenburger Tor, **6**

Centrum department
store, **17**

Checkpoint Charlie, **1**

Huguenot Museum, **3**

Humboldt University, **7**

Marienkirche, **15**

Markisches Museum, **20**

Museum für Deutsche
Geschichte, **8**

Nationalgalerie, **10**

Nikolaikirche, **19**

Palast der Republik, **14**

Pergamon Museum, **11**

Rathaus, **18**

Schauspielhaus, **2**

St. Hedwigskathedrale, **4**

State Opera, **5**

TV Tower, **16**

street named Hinter der Katholische Kirche (Behind the Catholic Church) is a reminder that though Berlin was very much a Protestant city, St. Hedwig's was built (about 1747) for Catholics.

⑤ Walk north on Unter den Linden, the elegant central thoroughfare of old Berlin, to the **State Opera,** the great opera house of Berlin, now with an entirely new interior. Next door is the former crown prince's palace, the **Palais Unter den Linden,** now restored and used to house official government visitors.

⑥ Look back down to the western sector and you'll see, just inside the wall, the monumental **Brandenburger Tor** (Brandenburg Gate), its chariot-and-horses sculpture now turned to face the east. Cross Unter den Linden and look into the courtyard of **⑦** **Humboldt University:** It was built as a palace for the brother of Friedrich II of Prussia but became a university in 1810, and today is the largest in East Germany. Marx and Engels were its two most famous students. Next door, housed in a one-time ar- **⑧** senal (1695–1705) is the **Museum für Deutsche Geschichte** (Museum of German History), which traces events from 1789 to the present—with a pronounced Marxist bias. *Unter den Linden 2. Admission charge. Open Mon.–Thurs. 9–7, weekends 10–5; closed Fri.*

Turning left along the Spree canal will bring you to East Berlin's museum complex, at the northern end of what is known as **Museumsinsel** (Museum Island). The first of the Big Four that **⑨** you'll encounter is the **Altes Museum** (entrance on Lustgarten), an austere neoclassical building just to the north of Marx-Engels-Platz. The collections here include postwar art from some of East Germany's most prominent artists, and numerous etchings and drawings from the Old Masters. Next comes the **⑩** **Nationalgalerie,** on Bodestrasse, which features 19th- and **⑪** 20th-century painting and sculpture. The **Pergamon Museum** on Am Kupfergraben, is one of Europe's greatest. Its name derives from the museum's principal exhibit and the city's number-one attraction, the **Pergamon Altar,** a monumental Greek temple dating from 180 B.C. that occupies an entire city block. Almost as impressive is the **Babylonian Processional Way.** The Pergamon Museum also houses vast Egyptian, early-Christian, and Byzantine collections, plus a fine array of sculpture from the 12th to the 18th centuries. To the north is the **⑫** **Bodemuseum** (also on Am Kupfergraben, but with its entrance on Monbijoubrücke), with an outstanding collection of early-Christian-Byzantine and Egyptian art, as well as special exhibits of Italian Old Masters. *Museum complex open Wed., Thurs., weekends 9–6, Fri. 10–6; closed Mon. and Tues. (except Pergamon Museum, whose Pergamon Altar and architectural rooms remain open 9–6). Admission charge.*

From the museum complex, follow the Spree canal south to **⑬** Unter den Linden and the vast and impressive **Berlin cathe-** **⑭** **dral.** The hideous modern building across the way is the **Palast der Republik** (Palace of the Republic), a postwar monument to socialist progress, also housing restaurants, a theater, and a dance hall.

Time Out The cafeteria-style **Quick restaurant** in the Palast Hotel, although mobbed at noon, is a good spot for lunch or a snack (entrance on Karl-Liebknecht-Strasse).

Cross the street for a closer look at the 13th-century
⑮ Marienkirche (Church of St. Mary), especially noting its late-
Gothic *Dance of Death* fresco. You are now at the lower end of
Alexanderplatz, easy to find from any part of the city: just head
⑯ in the direction of the massive **TV tower**, an East Berlin land-
⑰ mark. A focal point for shopping is the **Centrum department
store,** alongside the Hotel Stadt Berlin, at the very top of the
plaza.

⑱ The area adjacent to the **Rathaus** (City Hall)—itself somewhat
of a marvel for its red-brick design and the frieze depicting
scenes from the city's history—has been handsomely rebuilt.
⑲ Nikolaikirche (on Spandauerstrasse), dating from about 1200,
is Berlin's oldest building. It was heavily damaged in the war,
but has been beautifully restored. The quarter surrounding
the church is filled with delightful shops, cafés, and restaurants. Wander back down Muhlendamm into the area around
the Breite Strasse—there are some lovely old buildings here—
and on over to the **Fischerinsel** area. The throbbing heart of Old
Berlin of 750 years ago, Fischerinsel retains a tangible
medieval flavor.

Time Out   The **Alt-Kollner Schankstuben,** overlooking the Spree canal
(Friedrichsgracht 50), is as charming and friendly a café as
you'll find in East Berlin. On a sunny day, enjoy a glass of beer
at an outdoor table.

⑳ Nearby is the **Markisches Museum** (Museum of Cultural History), which has an amusing section devoted to automaphones—
"self-playing" musical instruments. *Am Kollnischen Park 5.
Admission charge. Open Wed. and Sun. 9–6, Thurs. and Sat.
9–5, Fri. 9–4; closed Mon. and Tues.*

Shopping

Shopping Districts   Good shops in Berlin are found along the Friedrichstrasse,
Unter den Linden, and around Alexanderplatz. Shops run by
other socialist countries along the north side of Alexanderplatz
may have some interesting offerings. The Palast and Grand hotels both contain small shopping malls.

Department Stores   For basic local goods, including souvenirs, try the Centrum department store at the north end of Alexanderplatz. The
subsidized prices for some items make them very cheap,
though style is not a strong point.

Dining

Most menus are translated into English. In general, the smaller the establishment, the more limited the choice. Unfortunately, the custom of posting a menu outside seems to be disappearing, but no one will mind if you ask to see a menu before
being seated—even if you then decide to go elsewhere.

Ratings   Prices are per person. In the lower-priced restaurants, they include a main course, a small beer, or possibly a glass of wine.
Meals in the Expensive and Very Expensive categories will be
at least three courses. Best bets are indicated by a star ★. At
press time, there were 1.67 East German marks to the dollar.

Category	Cost
Very Expensive	over M40
Expensive	M30–M40
Moderate	M20–M30
Inexpensive	under M20

Very Expensive
★

Ermeler Haus. The wine restaurant in a series of upstairs rooms reflects the elegance of this restored patrician house, which dates from 1567 (it was moved to its present location in 1969, however). The atmosphere is subdued, the wines are imported, and the service matches the excellent German specialties. There's dancing on Saturday evening. *Märkisches Ufer 10–12, tel. 02/2794036. Jacket and tie. Reservations advisable. AE, DC, MC, V.*

Ganymed. Velvet draperies, oil paintings, and brass chandeliers adorn this particularly attractive restaurant, whose choice of dishes ranges from cold plates to cordon bleu, with even a few Indonesian specialties thrown in. The front room has piano music in the evening. *Schiffbauerdamm 5, tel. 02/2829540. Dress: casual chic for lunch; jacket and tie for dinner. Reservations essential. No credit cards. Closed Mon. lunch.*

Expensive
★

Schwalbennest. This is a fairly new restaurant on the edge of the Nikolai quarter, overlooking the Marx-Engels-Forum. Both food and service are outstanding; the choice is wide for both main dishes and wines. The grilled meats are wonderful, but note that no additional price is indicated on the menu for the flambéed dishes—ask about this, or you could be in for a surprise when the bill arrives! *Am Marstall, Rathausstr. at Marx-Engles-Forum, tel. 02/2124569. Dress: formal. Reservations essential, even for lunch. AE, DC, MC, V.*

Moderate

Moskau. Some may mutter that Moskau is overpriced for what it offers—superb Soviet dishes like chicken Kiev, and real Russian vodka—but it has nevertheless been voted top choice among Berliners for several years running. That said, it is undeniably less central and offers considerably less in the way of atmosphere than many other city eateries. *Karl-Marx-Allee 34, tel. 02/2794052. Dress: casual. Reservations advised. No credit cards.*

Ratskeller. This is actually two restaurants in one—a wine and a beer cellar, both vast, atmospheric, and extremely popular. Menus are limited, but what's here is good, solid Berlin fare. The beer cellar is guaranteed to be packed at main dining hours, and attempts at reservations may be ignored (locals simply line up and wait). *Rathausstr. 14, in basement of the City Hall, tel. 02/2124464. Dress: informal. Reservations advisable, though not always possible. No credit cards.*

Wernesgrüner Bierstube. Wernesgrüner beer is considered one of the city's best, and this cozy, pine-paneled beer cellar serves plenty of it alongside heaping portions of *Eisbein* (knuckle of pork) and *Schlachteplatte* (a variety of grilled meats). Lunchtime brings a ban on smoking in the right-hand room. *Karl-Liebknecht-Str. 4, tel. 02/2824268. Dress: casual. Reservations advisable, especially at lunch. No credit cards.*

Inexpensive

Alt-Cöllner Schankstuben. A charming and genuine old Berlin house is the setting for this conglomerate of no less than four tiny restaurants, all of which provide exceptionally friendly service. *Friedrichsgracht 50, 02/2125972. Dress: casual. No reservations. No credit cards.*

★ **Zur letzten Instanz.** Established in 1525, this place combines the charming atmosphere of Old-World Berlin with a limited (but tasty, nonetheless) choice of dishes. Napoleon is said to have sat alongside the tiled stove in the front room. The emphasis here is on beer, both in the recipes and in the mug. Service can be erratic, though engagingly friendly. *Waisenstr. 14–16 (U-Bahn Klosterstrasse), tel. 02/2125528. Dress: informal. Reservations essential for both lunch and dinner. No credit cards.*

Lodging

All of the newer hotels in Berlin are in the Very Expensive category; if you prefer more modest and less expensive accommodations, you will have to argue for it. Travel officials will encourage bookings in the fancier Interhotels and often tell you that the less expensive hotels are fully booked. If you name a particular establishment and are patient, you may win out.

You cannot get into East Germany–other than on a 24-hour pass from West Berlin–without a hotel reservation, but should you find yourself needing a hotel room, check with the **Reisebüro der DDR** at Alexanderplatz 5, tel. 02/2124328, and ask for the *Zimmervermittlung.*

Ratings   Prices indicated are for double rooms, with private bath in the top two categories. A single room with bath will cost about M5–M10, more than half the double rate shown. Best bets are indicated by a star ★. At press time, there were 1.67 East German marks to the dollar.

Category	Cost
Very Expensive	over M250
Expensive	M170–M250
Moderate	M130–M170
Inexpensive	under M130

Very Expensive   **Grand Hotel** (Interhotel). Berlin's newest is also its most expensive. There's nothing of Eastern Europe here: Facilities range from the plush atrium lobby, four restaurants, winter garden, beer stube, bars, and a concert café to a swimming pool, sauna, and squash courts. *Friedrichstr. 158–164, corner Behrenstr., tel. 02/20920. 350 rooms with bath. Facilities: shopping arcade, hairdresser, theater ticket office, car and yacht rental. AE, DC, MC, V.*

★ **Metropol** (Interhotel). This is the businessperson's choice, not least for its excellent location opposite the Friedrichstrasse train station and the Internation Trade Center. The staff is particularly helpful and friendly. Best rooms are those in front, with a view toward the north. While none of the three restaurants is especially notable (except for price), the nightclub is excellent. *Friedrichstr. 150–153, tel. 02/22040. 320 rooms with bath. Facilities: pool, sauna, health club, shops, car, horse-drawn carriage, and yacht rental. AE, DC, MC, V.*

Palast (Interhotel). This is another of Berlin's mega-facility hotels. Ask for a room overlooking the Spree river; those on Alexanderplatz can be noisy if you like your windows open. The shopping arcade includes an antiques gallery and the main central theater ticket office. *Karl-Liebknecht-Str. 5, tel. 02/2410. 600 rooms with bath. Facilities: 6 restaurants, 4 bars, beer stube, nightclub, pool, sauna, health club, bowling, car and yacht rental. AE, DC, MC, V.*

Expensive **Stadt Berlin** (Interhotel). With its 40 stories (it's the city's largest hotel), the Stadt Berlin, at the top end of Alexanderplatz, competes with the nearby TV tower for the title of City Landmark. The roof dining room, Panorama, features not only good food and service but stunning views as well; reservations are essential. *Alexanderplatz, tel. 02/2190. 975 rooms with bath. Facilities: 4 restaurants, beer garden, 3 bars, sauna, shops. AE, DC, MC, V.*

★ **Unter den Linden** (Interhotel). The class may be missing, but the location couldn't be better. The restaurant is known for the best food on what was once Berlin's most elegant boulevard. *Unter den Linden 14, corner Friedrichstr., tel. 02/2200311. 307 rooms with bath. Facilities: souvenir shop. AE, DC, MC, V.*

Moderate **Adria** (H-O). This hotel tends to be fully booked well in advance, attesting to its less expensive prices rather than to any particular charm. Rooms in back are quieter, if you have any choice. *Friedrichstr. 134, tel. 02/2825451. 70 rooms with bath. Facilities: restaurant. No credit cards.*
Newa (H-O). The Newa—an older hotel just a 10-minute streetcar ride from downtown—is popular, but, as with the Adria, this is mainly due to the price. Rooms in front can be noisy. *Invalidenstr. 115, tel. 02/2825461. 57 rooms, some with bath. No credit cards.*

Inexpensive **Hospiz am Bahnhof Friedrichstrasse.** For reasons of both price and convenience, this Evangelical church-run hostel tends to be heavily booked months in advance. It appeals to families, so public rooms are not always restful. *Albrechtstr. 8, tel. 02/2825396. 110 rooms, some with bath. Facilities: restaurant. No credit cards.*
Hospiz Augustrasse. Another church-run hostel, this one with comfortable rooms and a particularly friendly staff. It's about a 10-minute streetcar ride to the downtown sights. Only breakfast is served. *Auguststr. 82, tel. 02/2825321. 70 rooms, some with bath. No credit cards.*

The Arts

The quality of opera and classical concerts in Berlin is impressively high. Tickets are available at the separate box offices, either in advance or an hour before the performance. Tickets are also sold at the central tourist office of the Reisebüro der DDR (Alexanderplatz 5), at the ticket offices in the Palast and Grand hotels, or from your hotel service desk. Check the monthly publication *Wohin in Berlin?*

Concerts **Schauspielhaus,** Platz der Akadamie, tel. 02/2272156; **Palast der Republik,** Marx-Engels-Platz, tel. 02/2382354.

Opera and Ballet **Deutsche Staatsoper,** Unter den Linden 7, tel. 02/20540; **Komische Oper,** Behrenstr. 55–57, tel. 02/2202761; **Metropol Theater,** Friedrichstr. 101, tel. 02/2000651.

Entertainment and Nightlife

The nightlife here is more modest than in West Berlin—but the prices are less extravagant, too. An evening of dancing, entertainment, and wine at the Stadt Berlin hotel can cost as little as DM25 (payable in hard currency or with a credit card). Other Interhotels offer dinner-dancing as well, but are more expensive. Music in the hotels is generally live; clubs have discos with DJs. For nightclubs with music and atmosphere, try one of the following: **Club Metropol** in the Metropol Hotel; **Panorama Bar** atop the Hotel Stadt Berlin; **Hafenbar,** Chauseestr. 20; **Haifishbar,** Unter den Linden 5, in the Opern Café complex; **Sinusbar** in the Palast Hotel.

Dresden

Arriving and Departing

By Plane Dresden Airport (tel. 051/589141) lies about six miles (10 kilometers) north of the city. Buses are available into the downtown area, leaving 45 minutes to an hour after each flight arrives; travel time is half an hour. Taxis are available as well.

By Train Dresden is easily reached by direct train connections with East Berlin; travel time is anywhere from 2½ to 3 hours.

By Car Dresden is about 100 miles (160 kilometers) south of Berlin. Leave Berlin on the E22. Exit at Lübbenau for the E15, which leads directly to Dresden.

Getting Around

Local public transport in the form of buses and streetcars is both cheap and efficient. Taxis, too, are inexpensive, but the city is small and walking is the best way to discover its hidden surprises.

Guided Tours

Dresden tours are often reserved well in advance by groups, so their availability will vary. In general, **walking tours** of the city sights depart daily (check with the tourist office for details). **Streetcar tours** leave from Postplatz Tuesday to Sunday, at 9, 11, and 1:30. **Bus tours** leave from Dr.-Kulz-Ring on Tuesday, Wednesday, and Thursday at 11.

Tourist Information

For information and reservations on city tours, contact the Dresden Tourist Office, **Reisebüro der DDR,** Prager Str. 11, tel. 051/4955025. Open Monday–Wednesday 9–6, Thursday 9–6:30, Friday 9–7, and weekends and holidays 9–2.

Exploring Dresden

Dresden, splendidly situated on the banks of the Elbe river, was devastated during World War II but has been lovingly rebuilt. Italianate influences are everywhere, most pronounced in the city's glorious Rococo and Baroque architecture.

The **Semper Opera House,** at *Theaterplatz,* in the center of Dresden, is a mecca for music lovers. Named for its architect, Gottfried Semper, and opened in 1850, its conductors have included Wagner and von Weber. The original building was destroyed in the 1945 bombings, but Semper's architectural-drawings had been preserved and it was rebuilt following his plans and reopened in 1985. Tickets are in great demand and hard to come by. Try booking through your travel agent before you go or ask at your hotel.

The city's other main attraction is the **Zwinger Palace,** with its wonderful portrait gallery. The building itself, like most of old Dresden, is a restored masterpiece, dating from 1710. It now contains a brilliant collection of paintings (few other museums can match its collection of 16th- and 17th-century Italian and Dutch masterpieces by Raphael, Rembrandt, Rubens, and Tintoretto), weapons, coins, armor, and Meissen china. *Postplatz. Admission charge. Art gallery open Tues.–Sun. 10–5; Porcelain collection open Mon.–Thurs. 9:30–4, weekends 9–4; closed Fri.; Gallery of New Masters open Fri.–Wed. 10–5, Tues. 10–6; closed Thurs.*

An unusual attraction is the **Deutches Hygene-Museum** (German Museum of Health), reflecting Dresden's position of importance in medicine. *Lingnerplatz 1. Admission charge. Open Sat.–Thurs. 9–6.*

Two fine examples of Baroque architecture, both built by Pöppelman, designer of the Zwinger Palace, are the Oriental-influenced **Schloss Pillnitz** and the hunting lodge at Moritzburg, which now houses an excellent **Baroque Museum.** Both places can be reached by streetcar of river boat.

Dining

For details and price category definitions, *see* Dining in Essential Information.

Moderate **Café Pöppelmann.** There's a splendid Baroque atmosphere in
★ this restored old city house, now cleverly incorporated into the Hotel Bellevue. Try the hearty *Eisbein mit sauerkraut* (knuckle of pork, accompanied by Germany's favorite side dish). *Grösse Meissner-Gasse 15, tel. 051/56620. Dress: informal. Dinner reservations advised. AE, DC, MC, V.*

Sekundogenitur. This wine restaurant is situated right on the bank of the Elbe. If the weather allows, ask for an outside table so you can observe the tranquil flow of the river while you eat. The Wiener schnitzel is great. *Brühlsche Terrasse, tel. 051/4951435. Dress: informal. Reservations advised. No credit cards. Closed Mon.*

Inexpensive **Kügeln Haus.** Actually a combination grill-coffee shop-restaurant-and-beerkeller, Kügeln Haus is extremely popular, so either get there early or reserve your table in advance. You'll find the usual local hefty dishes, but prepared with a deft touch. *Str. der Befreiung 14, tel. 051/52791. Dress: informal. Reservations advised. No credit cards.*

Lodging

For details and price category definitions, *see* Lodging in Essential Information.

Very Expensive **Hotel Bellevue** (Interhotel). A modern hotel opened in 1985, but combining new sections with some older city architecture, the Bellevue is just across the river from the Zwinger Palace and the Semper Opera House; the views are terrific. One of the hotel's five restaurants, Café Pöppelmann (*see* Dining), is recommended both for its atmosphere and its hearty dishes. *Kopckestr., tel. 051/56620. 328 rooms with bath. Facilities: 5 restaurants, wine cellar, café, bars, nightclub, shops, pool, sauna, solarium jogging course. AE, DC, MC, V.*

Expensive **Newa** (Interhotel). A sleek, ultramodern construction close to the train station, the Newa is a good choice for comfort, though slightly anemic in decoration. Its main restaurant accepts only hard currency or credit cards. The hotel is on the package tour route and is often booked well in advance. *Leningrader Str. 34, tel. 02/4967112. 314 rooms with bath. Facilities: restaurant, café, 2 bars, sauna, shops, AE, DC, MC, V.*

Moderate **Astoria** (Interhotel). Close to the Dresden zoo, the Astoria is a modern, five-story, cream colored hotel with a garden terrace. You'll find nothing fancy as far as decor (Minimalist would describe it best), but the hotel staff is pleasant. *Ernst-Thälmann-Platz, tel. 051/4755851. 84 rooms, most with bath. Facilities: 2 restaurants, bar, shop. AE, DC, MC, V.*

13 West Germany

Introduction

West Germany is a challenge to the visitor. At first glance, it is the most American of European countries, with an efficient network of highways linking cities with modern shopping complexes, chain hotels, and extensive sports facilities. Work seems to be taken more seriously than in France or Italy, where long lunches are still the norm, or in Great Britain, where a busy day at the office begins sometime around 9:30 AM. Americans can also understand a country where the capital concentrates on federal administration but is overshadowed by regional giants in other areas, such as commerce and industry.

At the same time, though, West Germany is steadfastly European. Officially the Bundesrepublic Deutschland, it was a founding member of the European Common Market, now the European Economic Community (EEC), and its government has always championed efforts to expand the "club." Bordered by more countries than any other EEC member, West Germany has led the way to the dismantling of trade frontiers— now set to take effect in 1992.

A fact of life about West Germany is its sometimes daunting prosperity. Look at the taxis lined up outside a major train station and you'll think you've found the assembly line of the Mercedes-Benz factory. Top-flight restaurants in Munich (München) and Frankfurt turn away customers every night. Electronics shops are full of expensive gadgets geared for the spoiled child or pampered business executive. The economy is healthy, and it shows.

Luckily, the Germans also know the importance of good value and a good time. Like a rich person who still clips shopping coupons, the prosperous West German will insist on attractively priced travel, food, and accommodations, which are there for the visitor as well. Always check to see if your train ticket or overnight stay in a hotel falls within the boundaries of some special deal. And, as in other countries, exploring the out-of-the-way regions has the bonus of turning up the real bargains. Remember, too, that inflation has long been held in check in West Germany, and domestic prices haven't really risen in years.

There's no question about "All work and no play makes Johann a dull boy," either. A series of holidays and festivals throughout the country and the calendar helps see to that. Moreover, apart from the five weeks of vacation that a typical West German white-collar worker can expect, there is often an extra two weeks of "rest" time to be spent in the revivifying air of a spa or mountain resort. While you're likely to see groups of Germans being put through their paces in the exercise trail through a forest, you're just as likely to see some others toning up their drinking arms in preparation for the next *Oktoberfest* in Munich.

The great outdoors have always been an important escape hatch for the Germans, and *lebensraum* (living space) is even more highly prized in the era of high technology and pressurized urban life. West Germany does its best to meet the needs of its hardworking inhabitants. A Bavarian mountain inn, the glow of its lights reflected on the blanket of snow outside, may be only a short drive from Munich. The busy industrial city of Stuttgart lies at the gateway to the Black Forest (Schwarzwald), the popular region of spas, hiking trails, and its tempting cake. Even West Berlin, a hectic enclave well inside East Germany, is surrounded by its own lakes and green parklands. The Green Party is a political expression of this environmental concern.

West Germany's size—less than half that of France—belies its social and geographical diversity. Everyone knows that Germany was divided into West and East after World War II, but few realize that the prewar state of unity was in fact only recent and was preceded by a long period of fragmentation and bitterness. Semiautonomous states were political and economic rivals, united—only to an extent—by a shared language and culture. A trip down the now peaceful Rhine (Rhein) would have meant having to pay a series of tolls to anyone who felt he could collect it. Religious differences were often settled by the sword.

Things are a lot quieter now, but you'll still meet cold stares if you sing the praises of Rhine wines in beer-drinking Munich or tell a Berliner that you intend to visit the "capital": To him Bonn is a sleepy provincial town in the middle of nowhere. Instead, make the most of each city or region and welcome the differences you'll find up the river, across the lake, or farther along the mountain road.

The transportation system needed to link these important regions is a godsend to the visitor. West German trains are fast, clean, and punctual, and a drive on a speed limit-free autobahn will give you an idea of just how fast all those BMW and Mercedes sports cars are meant to go. Maybe the best way to soak in the flavors and sights of West Germany is to float along the Rhine, past the vineyards and medieval castles, viewing it all from the deck of a steamer. Whichever way you go, take some time to reflect on the achievements of this hardworking people, who have produced an economic miracle on a grand scale, while at the same time nurturing one of the most vigilant environmental pressure groups in the world. Anomalies like this are typical of a country that has made a selling point of its diversity and turned conflict into consensus.

Before You Go

When to Go The main tourist season in Germany runs from May to late October, when the weather is naturally at its best. In addition to many tourist events, this period has hundreds of folk festivals. The winter sports season in the Bavarian Alps runs from Christmas to mid-March. Prices everywhere are generally higher during the summer, so you may find considerable advantages in visiting out of season. Most resorts offer out-of-season *(Zwischensaison)* and "edge-of-season" *(Nebensaison)* rates, and tourist offices can provide lists of hotels offering special low-price inclusive weekly packages *(Pauschalangebote)*. Similarly, many winter resorts offer lower rates for the periods immediately before and after the high season (*Weisse Wochen,* or "white weeks"). The other advantage of out-of-season travel is that crowds, which in major destinations are often thick on the ground, are very much less in evidence. The disadvantages of visiting out of season, especially in winter, are that the

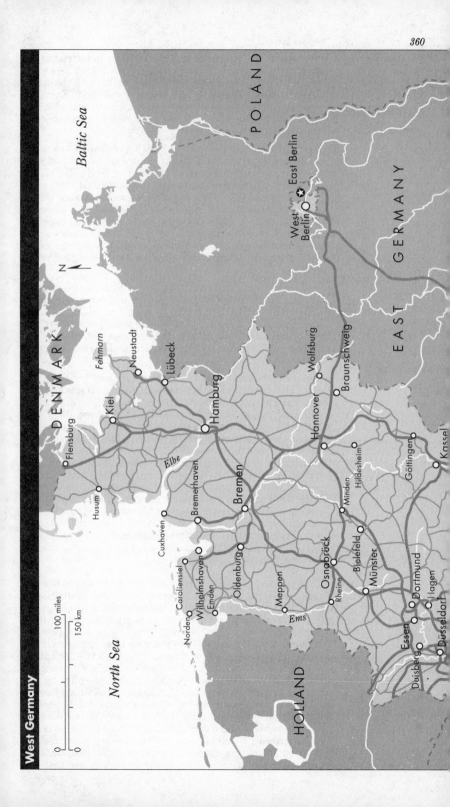

West Germany

North Sea

Baltic Sea

DENMARK

POLAND

HOLLAND

EAST GERMANY

West Berlin
East Berlin

N

0   100 miles
0   150 km

Flensburg
Husum
Kiel
Neustadt
Fehmarn
Lübeck
Hamburg
Elbe
Cuxhaven
Bremerhaven
Bremen
Wolfsburg
Braunschweig
Hannover
Hildesheim
Göttingen
Kassel
Minden
Norden
Carolensiel
Wilhelmshaven
Emden
Oldenburg
Meppen
Ems
Osnabrück
Rheine
Bielefeld
Münster
Dortmund
Hagen
Essen
Duisberg
Düsseldorf

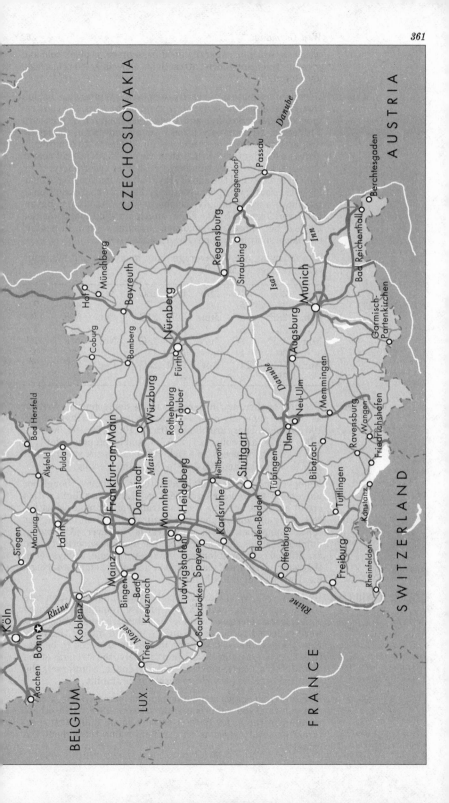

weather, which is generally good in summer, is often cold and gloomy, and many tourist attractions, especially in rural areas, are closed.

Climate   Germany's climate is generally temperate. Winters can be dull though never particularly cold, except in the Alps, the Harz region of Lower Saxony, and the higher regions of northern Franconia. Summers are usually sunny and warm, though be prepared for a few cloudy and wet days. The south is normally always a few degrees warmer than the north. As you get nearer the Alps, however, the summers get shorter accordingly, often not beginning until the end of May. Fall is sometimes spectacular in the south: warm and soothing. The only real exception to the above is the strikingly variable weather in southern Bavaria (Bayern) caused by the *Föhn*, an Alpine wind that gives rise to clear but oppressive conditions in summer and, in winter, can cause snow to disappear overnight.

The following are the average daily maximum and minimum temperatures for Munich.

Jan.	35F	1C	May	64F	18C	Sept.	67F	20C
	23	−5		45	7		48	9
Feb.	38F	3C	June	70F	21C	Oct.	56F	13C
	23	−5		51	11		40	4
Mar.	48F	9C	July	74F	23C	Nov.	44F	7C
	30	−1		55	13		33	0
Apr.	56F	14C	Aug.	73F	23C	Dec.	36F	2C
	38	3		54	12		26	−4

Currency   The unit of currency in Germany is the deutschmark, written as DM and generally referred to as the mark. It is divided into 100 pfennigs. There are bills of 5 (rare), 10, 20, 50, 100, 500, and 1,000 marks, and coins of 1, 2, 5, 10, and 50 pfennigs and 1, 2, and 5 marks. At press time (fall 1988), the mark stood at DM 1.67 to the dollar and DM 3.16 to the pound sterling.

Major credit cards are widely accepted in Germany, though not universally so. You can buy a seat on a Lufthansa flight with a credit card but not on a German train, for example. Most hotels, a significant number of restaurants, and all leading car rental companies accept credit cards, however. A growing number of shops also honor them, but don't be surprised if you are offered a discount for cash. As a general rule, always check that your own piece of plastic will be accepted before ordering a meal or checking into a hotel.

What It Will Cost   By early 1988, West Germany had cut its annual inflation rate to practically zero, just 0.2% to be precise, though it was hinted that sales tax increases and higher public transportation fares were expected to nudge the figure upward during the year. Nonetheless, the cost of living in 1989 is expected to be less than 2% above that in 1988. Unfortunately, the strength of the deutschmark, particularly against the dollar, counteracts the potential benefits for visitors of this price stability.

Although some cities and municipalities increased bus, streetcar, subway, and suburban train fares in 1988, with others planning increases for 1989, rises were small. Public transportation generally remains an excellent value throughout the country.

The most expensive areas to visit are the major cities, notably Düsseldorf, Hamburg, and Munich. Out-of-the-way rural regions, such as north and east Bavaria, the Saarland on the French border, and parts of central Germany, offer the lowest prices.

The only tax occasionally levied on visitors is the modest Kurtax, a nominal DM 1 or DM 2 per person per night; because only a handful of spas and resorts levy the tax in the first place, however, it is unlikely to upset your vacation budgeting.

Sample Prices Cup of coffee in a café, DM 2.50, in a stand-up snack bar DM 1; bottle of beer in a beer hall, DM 3, from a supermarket, DM 1.5; Coca-Cola, DM 2; ham sandwich, DM 3; one-mile taxi ride, DM 7.

Customs on Arrival There are three levels of duty-free allowance for visitors to West Germany.

Entering West Germany from a non-European country, the allowances are (1) 400 cigarettes or 100 cigars or 500 grams of tobacco, plus (2) one liter of spirits more than 22% proof or two liters of spirits less than 22% proof, plus (3) two liters of wine, plus (4) 50 grams of perfume and a quarter-liter of toilet water, plus (5) other goods to the value of DM 115.

Entering West Germany from a country belonging to the EEC, the allowances are (1) 200 cigarettes (300 if not bought in a duty-free shop) or 75 cigars or 400 grams of tobacco, plus (2) one liter of spirits more than 22% proof (1.5 liters if not bought in a duty-free shop) or three liters of spirits less than 22% proof, plus (3) five liters of wine, plus (4) 75 grams of perfume and one-third of a liter of toilet water, plus (5) other goods to the value of DM 780.

Entering Germany from a European country not belonging to the EEC (Austria or Switzerland, for example), the allowances are (1) 200 cigarettes or 50 cigars or 250 grams of tobacco, plus (2) one liter of spirits more than 22% proof or two liters of spirits less than 22% proof, plus (3) two liters of wine, plus (4) 50 grams of perfume and one-quarter of a liter of toilet water, plus (5) other goods to the value of DM 115.

Tobacco and alcohol allowances are for visitors aged 17 and over. Other items intended for personal use may be imported and exported freely. There are no restrictions on the import and export of West Germany currency.

Language English is a compulsory subject in German high schools other than those in the Saarland (where pupils can study French instead). As a result, most Germans under age 40 can speak passable English, though a staggering number are practically fluent. Older people in rural areas are less likely to speak English, but there are few hotels and restaurants anywhere in Germany where English is not spoken, in however rudimentary a fashion. For the most part, however, the German cab driver who can discuss Shakespeare with his English-speaking passenger is not an exception.

If you speak some German, you may find some regional dialects hard to follow, particularly in Bavaria. At the same time, however, all Germans can speak "high," or standard, German; even in the backwoods of Bavaria, the locals can alternate between dialect and standard German at will. Don't be shy about trying out whatever German you can muster. Your efforts will be appreciated by your *Gesprächspartner* (literally, "conversation partner").

Getting Around

By Car
Road Conditions

West German autobahns (turnpikes) are marked either A (on blue signs), meaning inter-German highways, or E (on green signs), meaning they form part of the Europe-wide *Europastasse* network. All autobahns are toll-free. Local roads are called *Bundestrassen* and are marked by their number on a yellow sign. All local roads are single lane and slower than autobahns.

Rules of the Road

Drive on the right, as in the United States. Always give way to traffic from the right unless traffic signs indicate otherwise. There is no speed limit as such on autobahns—Germans like to drive fast, and speeds over 160 kph (100 mph) are common—but there is a recommended limit of 130 kph (80 mph). The speed limit on Bundestrassen is 100 kph (60 mph). In built-up areas, speed limits vary between 30 kph (18 mph) and 80 kph (50 mph). Limits are shown on the side of the road.

Parking

Daytime parking in cities is almost impossible. If you can find one, use a parking lot or you'll risk having your car towed. Parking restrictions are not always clearly marked, but can be hard to understand anyway. At night, parking meter spaces are free.

Gasoline

Leaded, low-octane gas is no longer available in Germany, so if you have an older model car, you'll have to fill it with high-octane gas. In summer 1988, a liter of gas cost DM 1.8.

Breakdowns

The **ADAC,** the major West German automobile organization, gives free help and advice to tourists, though you have to pay for any spare parts and labor you need. All autobahns have regularly spaced telephones with which you can call for help. The contact address for the ADAC is Am Westpark 8, 8000 Munich 70 (tel. 089/76760).

By Train

West Germany has one of the most comprehensive and efficient rail systems in Europe. All German cities are linked by fast Inter-City trains; principal services run hourly. In addition, the domestic network is fully integrated with the Europe-wide Euro-City system, which joins most major cities in 13 European countries. Both services have first- and second-class cars, though some Euro-City trains have first-class cars only. A supplement of DM 6 (DM 10 for first class) is payable on Euro-City trains, but this includes the seat-reservation charge. Overnight trains have sleeping cars. These range from private compartments in first class to six-bunk "couchette" (sleeper) cars. All overnight Euro-City services depart before midnight and arrive after 6 AM, meaning you're assured of a good night's sleep. There are no nighttime stops, and any frontier formalities are handled by sleeping car attendants. All daytime trains have dining or buffet cars, while light refreshments, drinks, and breakfast are available on night trains.

Other trains are D trains (regular express services); E trains (short-distance services); local trains, sometimes supplemented by buses; and FD trains, which connect some German cities with resort areas like the Alps.

Fares German Railways offers a bewildering range of special fares. If you're visiting other European countries, a **EurailPass** *(see* Planning Your Trip, in Getting Around Europe), valid for most other rail systems in Europe, too, is the best deal. If you're visiting West Germany only, German Railways' **Tourist Card** offers the simplest and most inexpensive way of traveling around the country. The card is available for four, nine, or 14 days and allows unlimited travel on virtually all trains, most long-distance buses, and riverboats on the Rhine, Moselle, and Main. The cost at press time was DM 164 for the four-day card and DM 339 for the 14-day card. If you plan to visit West Berlin using the card, a supplement is payable (on the other hand, you do get a complementary tour of the city).

By Bus Long-distance bus services in Germany are part of the Europe-wide Europabus network. Services are neither as frequent nor as comprehensive as those on the rail system, so make reservations. Be careful in selecting the service you travel on: All Europabus services have a bilingual hostess and offer small luxuries that you won't find on the more basic, though still comfortable, regular services. For details and reservations, contact **Deutsche Touring Gesellschaft** (am Römerhof 17, 6000 Frankfurt/Main 90, tel. 069/79030). Reservations can also be made at any of the Deutsche Touring offices in Cologne (Köln), Hanover, Hamburg, Munich, Nuremberg (Nürnberg), and Wuppertal and at travel agents.

Rural bus services are operated by local municipalities and some private firms, as well as by German Railways and the post office. Services are variable, however, even when there is no other means to reach your destination by public transportation.

By Plane West Germany's national airline, **Lufthansa,** serves every West German city other than Berlin. Services are frequent and efficient, if expensive by U.S. standards. Check out the *Flieg und Spar* ("fly and save") round-trip tickets; you can save between 35% and 40% on the full fare. Contact Lufthansa at Frankfurt International Airport, 6000 Frankfurt 65 (tel. 069/6961).

By Bicycle Bicycles can be rented at more than 280 train stations throughout Germany. Cost is DM 10 per day, or DM 5 if you have a train ticket. You can return your bike at any other train station. Bicycles can be carried free on all trains except Inter-City services and some local trains. Most cities also have privately run bike rental companies; ask at local tourist offices for details.

By Boat For a country with a small coastline, West Germany is a surprisingly nautical nation: You can cruise rivers and lakes throughout the country. The biggest fleet, and most of the biggest boats, too, belongs to the Cologne-based KD line, the Köln-Düsseldorf Rheinschiffahrt. It operates services on the rivers Rhine, Moselle, and Main, ranging from luxurious five-day trips from Amsterdam or Rotterdam in Holland all the way down the Rhine to Basel in Switzerland, to short "riverboat shuffles" with jazz bands and freely flowing wine. For details, write **Rhine Cruise Agency**, Dietrich Neuhold Corp., 170 Hamilton Ave., White Plains, NY 10601, or **KD Line,** Frankenwerft 15, 5000 Köln 1.

Services on the 100-mile (160-kilometer) stretch of the Danube (Donau) between the spectacular Kelheim gorge and Passau on the Austrian border are operated by **Donauschiffahrt Wurm & Köck** (Höllgasse 26, D-8390 Passau). The company has daily summer cruises on the rivers Danube, Inn, and Ilz, which meet at Passau; some two-day cruises are also offered. Bodensee (Lake Constance), the largest lake in Germany, located at the meeting point of Germany, Austria, and Switzerland, has up to 40 ships crisscrossing it in summer, the so-called Weisse Flotte, or white fleet. Write **Deutsche Bundesbahn,** Bodensee-Schiffsbetriebe, D-7750 Konstanz. Bavaria's five largest lakes —Ammersee, Chiemsee, Königsee, Tegernsee, and Starnbergersee—have regular summer cruises and excursions. Details are available from local tourist offices.

Essential Information

Telephones Local calls cost a minimum of 23 pfennigs. Public phones take *Local Calls* 10 pfennigs, 50 pfennigs, and DM 1 coins. If you plan to make an out-of-town call, take along a good supply of DM 1 coins. Most phone booths have instructions in English as well as German; if yours doesn't, simply lift the receiver, put the money in, and dial.

International Calls These can be made from public phones bearing the sign "Inlands and Auslandsgespräche." They take 10 pfennigs, DM 1, and DM 5 coins; a four-minute call to the United States costs DM 15. To avoid weighing yourself down with coins, however, make international calls from post offices; even those in small country towns will have a special booth for international calls. You pay the clerk at the end of your call. Never make international calls from your hotel room; rates will be at least double the regular charge.

Operators and The West German telephone system is fully automatic, and it's *Information* unlikely that you'll have to employ the services of an operator. If you do, dial 1188, or 00118 for international calls. If the operator doesn't speak English (also unlikely), you'll be passed to one who does.

Mail Airmail letters to the United States and Canada cost DM 1.40; *Postal Rates* postcards cost 90 pfennigs. Airmail letters to the United Kingdom cost 80 pfennigs; postcards cost 60 pfennigs.

Receiving Mail You can arrange to have mail sent to you in care of any West German post office; have the envelope marked "Postlagernd." This service is free. Alternatively, have mail sent to any American Express office in Germany. There's no charge to cardholders, holders of American Express traveler's checks, or anyone who has booked a vacation with American Express. Otherwise, you pay DM 2 per collection (not per item).

Shopping The range of German-made goods that you may want to take home is as large and as varied as the country itself. Curiously, regional differences are not a significant factor in finding goods: Bavarian beer mugs are available in Hamburg, as much as Hamburg tugboat skippers' caps are stocked in most Munich hat shops. But a dirndl bought in an Alpine village will naturally have that bit more flavor and appeal than a pair of lederhosen bought in Düsseldorf, say. So we have suggested good-value local shops in all the "Shopping" sections that follow. Prices can be high, but quality is generally tops.

VAT Refunds German goods carry a 14% value added tax. You can claim this back either as you leave the country or once you're back home. When you make a purchase, ask the shopkeeper for a form known as an "Ausfuhr-Abnehmerbescheinigung"; he or she will help you fill it out. As you leave the country, give the form, plus the goods and receipts, to German customs. They will give you an official export certificate or stamp. In the unlikely event that there's a branch of the Deutsche Bank on the spot, you can take the stamped form to it, where you will receive the refund on the spot. Otherwise, send the form back to the shop, and it will send the refund.

Opening and **Banks.** Times vary from state to state and city to city, but
Closing Times banks are generally open weekdays from 8:30 or 9 to 3 or 4 (5 or 6 on Thursday). Branches at airports and main train stations open as early as 6:30 AM and close as late as 10:30 PM.

Museums. Most museums are open from Tuesday to Sunday 9–6. Some close for an hour or more at lunch, and some are open on Monday.

Shops. Times vary, but are generally Monday to Saturday from 8:30 or 9 until 5:30 or 6; some close at 2 or 2:30 Saturday. On the first Saturday of each month, larger shops and department stores are open until 7:30 or 8.

National Holidays January 1; March 24, 27 (Easter); May 1 (May Day); May 4 (Ascension); May 15 (Pentecost Monday); May 25 (Corpus Christi, southern Germany only); June 17 (German Unity Day); August 15 (Assumption Day, Bavaria and Saarland only); November 1 (All Saints); November 22 (Day of Prayer and Repentance); December 25, 26.

Dining It's hard to generalize about German food beyond saying that it's nearly always good and nearly always hearty. In fact, the range of dining experiences is vast: everything from highly priced nouvelle cuisine to hamburgers. As a visitor, you should search out local restaurants if atmosphere and regional specialties are your priority. Beer restaurants in Bavaria, *Apfelwein* taverns in Frankfurt, *Kneipen*—the pub on the corner cum local café—in Berlin nearly always offer best value and atmosphere. But throughout the country you'll find *Gaststätten* and/or *Gasthöfe*—local inns—where atmosphere and regional specialties are always available. Likewise, just about every town and many villages, too, will have a *Ratskeller,* a cellar restaurant in the town hall, where exposed beams, huge fireplaces, sturdy tables, and immense portions are the rule.

The most famous German specialty is sausage. Everyone has heard of frankfurters, but if you're in Munich, try *Weisswurst,* a delicate white sausage traditionally eaten only between midnight and noon. Nuremberg's sausage favorite is the *Nürnberger Bratwurst;* its fame is such that you'll find restaurants all over Germany serving it. Look for the "Bratwurststube" sign. Dumplings (*Knödel*) can also be found throughout the country, though their natural home is probably Bavaria; farther north, potatoes often take their place.

The natural accompaniment to German food is either beer or wine. Munich is the beer capital of Germany, though there's no part of the country where you won't find the amber nectar. Say "Helles" if you want light beer; "Dunkles" if you want dark beer. In Bavaria, try the beer brewed from wheat, called *Weissbier*. Germany is a major wine-producing country, also, and much of it is of superlative quality. You will probably be happy with the house wine in most restaurants or with one of those earthenware pitchers of cold Moselle wine. If you want something more expensive, remember that all wines are graded in one of three basic categories: *Tafelwein* (table wine); *Qualitätswein* (fine wines); and *Qualitätswein mit Prädikat* (top-quality wines).

Mealtimes Lunch is served from around 11:30 (especially in rural areas) to around 2; dinner from around 8 to 10:30 (and sometimes later in cities). Lunch tends to be the main meal, a fact reflected in the almost universal appearance of a lunchtime *Tageskarte*, or suggested menu; try it if you want maximum nourishment for minimum outlay. This doesn't mean that dinner is a rushed or skimpy affair, however; the Germans have too high a regard for food for any meal to be underrated. Breakfast, served anytime from 6:30 to 10, is often a substantial affair, with cold meats, cheeses, rolls, and fruit.

Ratings Prices are per person and include a first course, main course, dessert, and tip and tax. Best bets are indicated by a star ★. At press time, there were 1.67 deutschmarks to the dollar.

Category	Cost: Major Cities and Resorts	Cost: Other Areas
Very Expensive	over DM 95	over DM 90
Expensive	DM 65–DM 95	DM 55–DM 90
Moderate	DM 45–DM 65	DM 35–DM 55
Inexpensive	under DM 45	under DM 35

Credit Cards The following credit card abbreviations are used: AE, American Express; DC, Diners Club; MC, MasterCard; V, Visa.

Lodging The standard of German hotels, from top-notch luxury spots (of which the country has more than its fair share) to the humblest pension, is generally excellent. Prices can be high, but not disproportionately so in comparison to other northern European countries. You can expect courteous service, clean and comfortable rooms, and, in rural areas especially, considerable old-German atmosphere.

In addition to hotels proper, the country also has numerous *Gasthöfe* or *Gasthäuser* (country inns); pensions or *Fremdenheime* (guest houses); and, at the lowest end of the scale, *Zimmer*, meaning, quite simply, rooms, normally in private houses. Look for the sign "Zimmer frei" or "zu vermieten," meaning "for rent." A red sign reading "besetzt" means there are no vacancies.

Lists of hotels are available from the German National Tourist Office and from all regional and local tourist offices. Tourist offices will also make reservations for you—they charge a nominal fee—but may have difficulty doing so after 4 PM in peak season and on weekends. A reservations service is also operated by **ADZ** (Beethovenstr. 61, 6000 Frankfurt/Main, tel. 069/740767). The reservation fee is DM 3 per person.

Most hotels have restaurants, but those describing themselves as *Garni* will provide breakfast only.

Romantik Hotels Among the most delightful places to stay and eat in Germany are the aptly named Romantik Hotels and Restaurants. All are in historic buildings—this is a precondition of membership—and are personally run by the owners. The emphasis generally is on solid comfort, good food, and style. Prices vary from moderate to very expensive, but you can often find special weekend deals and lower rates for stays of three or more days, especially if you have one main meal a day at the hotel. A detailed listing of all Romantik Hotels is available from **Romantik Hotel Reservations,** Box 1278, Woodinville, WA 98072, tel. 800/826–0015.

Castle Hotels This is a similar hotel association, though you may find that some of the simpler establishments lack a little in the way of comfort and that furnishings can be basic. But most can be delightful, with antiques, imposing interiors, and out-of-the-way locations setting the tone. Prices are mostly moderate. Ask the German National Tourist Office or your travel agent for the "Castle Hotels in Germany" brochure. It details a series of good-value packages, most for stays of four to six nights.

Rentals Apartments and hotel homes, most accommodating from two to eight guests, can be rented throughout Germany. Rates are low, with reductions for longer stays. Charges for gas and electricity, and sometimes water, are usually added to the bill. There is normally an extra charge for linen, but not if you bring your own. Local and regional tourist offices have lists of apartments in their areas; otherwise write the **German Automobile Association** (ADAC), Am Westpark 8, 8000 Munich 70, tel. 089/76760.

Farm Vacations *Urlaub auf dem Bauernhof,* as the Germans know them, have increased dramatically in popularity over the past four or five years. Almost every regional tourist office has listings of farms by area offering bed and breakfast, apartments, or whole farmhouses to rent. Alternatively, write the **German Agricultural Association** (DLG), Rüsterstr. 13, D-6000 Frankfurt/Main 1. It produces an annual listing of more than 1,500 farms, all of them inspected and graded, that offer accommodations.

Camping There are more than 2,000 campsites in Germany, about 1,600 of which are listed by the **German Camping Club** (DCC), Mandlstr. 28, D-8000, Munich 40. The German National Tourist Office also publishes an annually updated listing of sites. Most are open from May through October, with about 400 staying open year-round. They tend to become crowded during the summer, so it's always worthwhile to make reservations a day or two ahead. Prices range from DM 10 to DM 15 per night for two adults, a car, and trailer (less for tents). If you want to camp away from an official site, you must get permission beforehand; if you can't find the owner, ask the police. You're allowed to spend no more than one night in parking lots on roadsides if you're in a camper, and you may not set up any camping equipment.

Youth Hostels Germany's youth hostels—*Jugendherbergen*—are probably the most efficient, up-to-date, and proportionately most numerous of those in any country in Europe. There are 600 in all, many located in castles, adding a touch of romance to otherwise utilitarian accommodations. There's an age limit of 27 in Bavaria; elsewhere, there are no restrictions, though those under 20 take preference if space is limited. You'll need an International Youth Hostel card to stay in a German youth hostel; write **American Youth Hostels Association,** Box 37613, Washington DC 20013, or **Canadian Hostelling Association,** 333 River Rd., Ottawa, Ontario K1L 8H9. For full listings, write **Deutsches Jugendhergerbswerk Hauptverband,** Bülowstr. 26, D-4930 Detmold, tel. 05231/74010, or contact the German National Tourist Office.

Ratings Service charges and taxes are included in all quoted room rates. Similarly, breakfast is usually, but not always, included—large breakfasts are always extra—so check before you book in. Rates are often surprisingly flexible in German hotels, varying considerably according to demand. Major hotels in cities often have lower rates on weekends or other periods when business is quiet. If you're lucky, you can find reductions of up to 60%. Likewise, rooms reserved after 10 PM will often carry a discount, on the basis that an occupied room at a reduced rate is better than an empty one. Although it's worthwhile asking if your hotel will give you a reduction, don't count on finding rooms at lower rates late at night, especially in the summer. Prices are for two people in a double room. Best bets are indicated by a star ★. At press time, there were 1.67 deutsch marks to the dollar.

Category	Cost: Major Cities or Resorts	Cost: Other Areas
Very Expensive	over DM 200	over DM 180
Expensive	DM 160–DM 200	DM 120–DM 180
Moderate	DM 100–DM 160	DM 80–DM 120
Inexpensive	under DM 100	under DM 80

Credit Cards The following credit card abbreviations are used: AE, American Express; DC, Diners Club; MC, MasterCard; V, Visa.

Tipping The Germans are as punctilious about tipping as they are about most facets of life in their well-regulated country. Overtipping is as frowned upon as not tipping at all, though the kind of abuse you risk in some countries for undertipping is virtually unknown here. Nonetheless, tips are expected, if not exactly demanded. Follow these simple rules and you won't go wrong.

In restaurants, service is usually included (under the heading *Bedienung,* at the bottom of the check), and it is customary to round out the check to the next mark or two, but never to more than 5% of the total. In cafés and beer halls, where it may not always be clear if service is included, give 10%. Taxi drivers also get 10%. Railway and airport porters (if you can find any) have their own scale of charges, but round out the requested amount to the next mark. Hotel porters get DM 1 per bag. Doormen are tipped the same amount for small services, such as calling a cab. Room service should be rewarded with at least DM 2 every time you use it. Maids should get about DM 1 per day. Double all these figures at luxury hotels. Service station attendants get 50 pfennigs or DM 1 for filling the tanks, checking oil and tires, or cleaning windshields.

Munich

Arriving and Departing

By Plane Munich (München) airport, Riem, is located about six miles (10 kilometers) from downtown. Conditions can be chaotic in summer and around Christmas, and the airport authorities are periodically driven to appeal to overseas visitors for patience. (A new, much larger, airport is scheduled to open in 1991.)

Between the Airport and Downtown Buses leave Riem for Munich every half hour between 6 and 8 AM and every 15 minutes between 8 AM and 9 PM. Thereafter, buses run according to aircraft arrivals. Buses to Riem leave from the north of the main train station in Munich, opposite the hotel Deutscher Kaiser, every 15 minutes between 5 AM and 9 PM. The 30-minute ride costs DM 5. At rush hours, a taxi can take just as long as the bus; other times, the trip should take about 15 minutes. The one-way fare is around DM 20. If you're picking up a rental car from the airport, simply take the main road out of the airport and follow the "Stadtmitte" signs (meaning downtown). The autobahn will take you right into Munich.

By Train All long-distance services arrive at and depart from the main train station, the Hauptbahnhof. Trains to and from destinations in Bavaria use the adjoining Starnbergerbahnhof. For information on train times, call 089/592991; English is spoken by all the railroad staff. For tickets and information, go to the station or to the ABR travel agency right by the station on Bahnhofplatz.

By Bus Munich has no central bus station. Long-distance buses arrive at and depart from the north side of the train station. A taxi stand is 20 yards (18 meters) away.

By Car From the north (Nuremberg, Frankfurt), leave the autobahn at the Schwabing exit and follow the "Stadtmitte" signs. The autobahn from Stuttgart and the west ends at Obermenzing; again, follow the "Stadtmitte" signs. The autobahns from Salzburg and the east, from Garmisch and the south, and from Lindau and the southwest all join up with the city beltway, the Mittlere Ring. The city center is well posted.

Getting Around

Downtown Munich is only about one mile square, so it can easily be explored on foot. Other areas—Schwabing, Nymphenburg, the Olympic Park—are best reached on the efficient and comprehensive public transportation network. Munich's public transportation system is, in fact, a model of its kind: clean, fast, and ultra-reliable. It incorporates buses, streetcars, subways (U-Bahn), and suburban trains (S-Bahn). Tickets are good for the entire network, and you can break your journey as many times as you like using just one ticket, provided you travel in one direction only and within a given time limit. If you plan to make only a few trips, buy individual tickets; the cost is DM 2.40 (DM 2 for children under 15) for a single-zone ride. Otherwise, buy the 24-hour (24-Stunden) ticket, which allows unlimited travel on all public transportation in any 24-hour period. Costs are DM 6.50 (children under

15 DM 2) for an inner-zone card and DM 12 (children under 15 DM 4) for the entire network. Holders of a EurailPass, a Youth Pass, an Inter-Rail Card, or a DB Tourist Card travel free on all S-Bahn trains.

By Taxi Munich's cream-colored taxis are numerous. Hail them in the street or call 089/2161 (there's an extra charge for the drive to the pickup point). Rates start at DM 2.90 and rise by DM 1.70 per kilometer (about DM 2.75 per mile). There are additional charges of 50 pfennigs for each piece of luggage. Figure on paying DM 7 to DM 10 for a short trip within the city.

Important Addresses and Numbers

Tourist Information The main tourist information office is in the heart of the city at Sendlingerstrasse 1, tel. 089/23911. It's around the corner from Marienplatz. Open Monday–Thursday 8:30–3, Friday 8:30–2. Longer opening hours are kept by the city tourist office at the Hauptbahnhof, tel. 089/239–1256. Open Monday–Saturday 8:30–10 PM, Sunday and holidays 1 PM–9:30 PM.

Consulates US, Königinstrasse 5, tel. 089/23011. **Canadian,** Maximiliansplatz 9, tel. 089/558531. **UK,** Amalienstrasse 62, tel. 089/394015).

Emergencies Police, tel. 089/110. **Ambulance** and **emergency medical attention,** tel. 089/558661. **Dentist,** tel. 089/723–3093. **Pharmacies:** The Internationale Inter-Apotheke, corner of Luisenstrasse and Elisenstrasse, stocks American and British products; tel. 089/595444. Open weekdays 8–5:30, Saturday 8–1. Outside these hours, call 089/594475.

English Bookstores The **Anglia English Bookshop,** Schellingstrasse 3, tel. 089/283642, has the largest selection of English-language books in Munich. A library of English-language books is kept in **Amerika Haus,** Karolinenplatz 3, tel. 089/595369.

Travel Agencies **American Express,** Promenadenplatz 6, tel. 089/21990. **ABR,** the official Bavarian travel agency, has outlets all over Munich; tel. 089/12040 for information.

Guided Tours

Orientation Tours City bus tours are operated by **Münchner Fremden-Rundfahrten.** Contact them at the ABR office at the train station (tel. 089/12040). Tours run daily and take in the city center, the Olympic Park, and Nymphenburg. Departures are at 10 AM from outside the Hertie department store across from the train station, and the cost is between DM 13 and DM 23 per person, depending on the duration of the tour.

Walking Tours The Munich tourist office (see above) organizes guided walking tours, for either groups or individuals, on demand; no regular walking tours are offered. Tours will be tailored to suit individual requirements, and costs vary accordingly.

Excursions **Münchner Fremden-Rundfahrten** organizes bus trips to most leading tourist attractions outside the city. A tour of the royal palaces of Ludwig II, for example, costs DM 46 per person. All tours leave from outside the Hertie department store. See above for contact address. Other tours are offered by **Reisebüro Autobus Oberbayern,** Lenbachplatz 1, tel. 089/558061. Among the offerings is a "Late Riser's Excursion," which departs at 10

AM. All tours leave from Elisenstrasse, in front of the Old Botanical Garden.

Exploring Munich

Even in Bonn—the real capital of Germany—they grudgingly call Munich the nation's "secret capital." This sly compliment may reflect the importance of Munich—it's far and away the most important tourist destination in Germany, as well as being probably the most attractive major German city—but there's nothing "secret" about the way the Münchner makes this brave claim. Indeed, the noise with which the people of Munich trumpet the attractions of their city could be dismissed as so much Bavarian bombast were it not for the fact that it is so enthusiastically endorsed by others. Flamboyant, easygoing Munich, city of beer and Baroque, is light-years away from the dour Prussian glumness of Berlin, the gritty industrial drive of Hamburg, or the hardheaded commercial instincts of high-rise Frankfurt. This is a city to visit for its good-natured and relaxed charm—*Gemütlichkeit* they call it here—and for its beer halls, its museums, its malls, its parks, and its palaces.

Munich has been described as a mixture of corn and class, a juxtaposition epitomized by the fanciful and extravagant buildings of its most famous 19th-century son, the "Dream King," Ludwig II, ruler of Bavaria from 1864 to 1886, champion of Wagner and builder of fantasies. By turns elegant, opulent, and just a little bit vulgar, Munich is a city that's easy to like.

The Main Attractions

 Begin your tour of Munich at the **Hauptbahnhof,** the main train station and an important orientation point. The city tourist office is here, too, ready with information and maps. Cross the street and you're at the start of a mile and a half of pedestrian shopping malls. Facing you are **Hertie,** Munich's leading department store, and **Karlsplatz** square, known locally as Stachus—though no one seems to know why for certain—and one of Europe's busiest traffic intersections.

Head down into the pedestrian underpass—it's another extensive shopping area—to reach the other side and one of the original city gates, **Karlstor.** The city's two principal shopping streets—**Neuhauserstrasse** and **Kaufingerstrasse**—stretch away from it on the other side. Two of the city's major churches are here, too: the **Bürgersaal** and the **Michaelskirche.** The latter is one of the most magnificent Renaissance churches in Germany, a spacious and handsome structure decorated throughout in plain white stucco. It was built for the Jesuits in the late 16th century and is closely modeled on their church of the Gesù in Rome. The intention was to provide a large preaching space, hence the somewhat barnlike atmosphere. Ludwig II is buried here; his tomb is in the crypt. The large neoclassical tomb in the north transept is the resting place of Eugène de Beauharnais, Napoleon's stepson. The highly decorated Rococo interior of the Bürgersaal makes a startling contrast with the simplicity of the Michaelskirche.

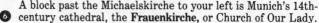 A block past the Michaelskirche to your left is Munich's 14th-century cathedral, the **Frauenkirche,** or Church of Our Lady.

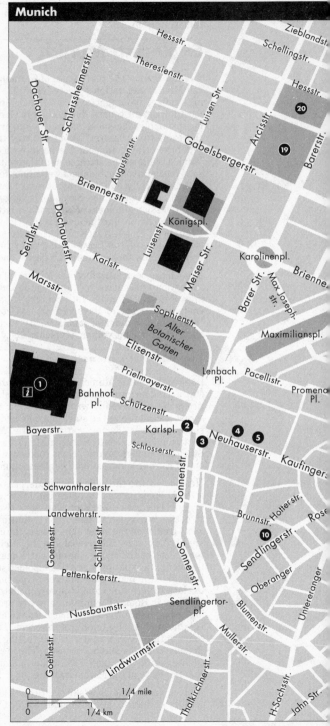

Munich

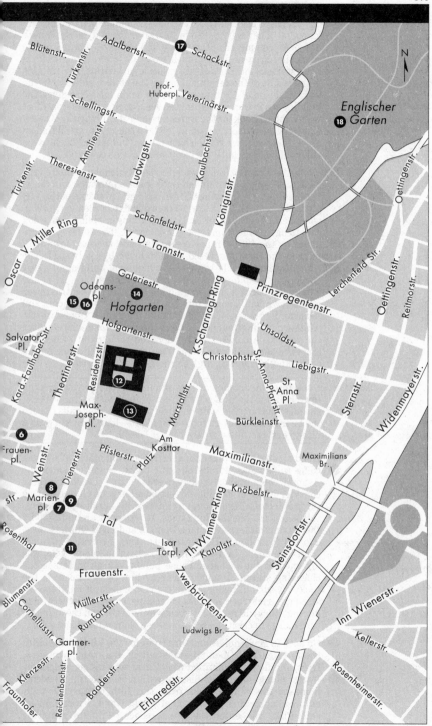

Towering above it are two onion-shaped domes, symbols of the city (perhaps because they resemble brimming beer mugs, cynics claim). They were added in 1525 after the body of the church had been completed. Step inside and you'll be amazed at the stark simplicity of the church; it's very different from the darkly mysterious interiors of other Gothic cathedrals. In part, this is the result of the terrible damage the church suffered in the war: A series of photographs at the main entrance show the building as it was just after the war, a gaunt skeleton filled with rubble. Look for the Baroque tomb of Ludwig the Bavarian by the west door, put up in 1662. In the crypt, you'll find an assortment of other Wittelsbach tombs (the Wittelsbachs were rulers of Bavaria until the early years of this century).

7 From the Frauenkirche, walk to the **Marienplatz** square, the heart of the city, surrounded by shops, restaurants, and cafés. It takes its name from the 300-year-old gilded statue of the Virgin in the center. When it was taken down to be cleaned in 1960, workmen found a small casket containing a splinter of wood said to have come from the cross of Christ. The square is domi-
8 nated by the 19th-century **Neues Rathaus**, the new town hall, built in the fussy, turreted style so loved by Ludwig II. The
9 **Altes Rathaus**, or old town hall, a medieval building of great charm, sits, as if forgotten, in a corner of the square. At 11 and 5 daily the **Glockenspiel**, or chiming clock, in the central tower of the town hall, swings into action. Two tiers of dancing and jousting figures perform their ritual display. It can be worthwhile scheduling your day to catch the clock. Immediately after the war, an American soldier donated some paint to help restore the battered figures and was rewarded with a ride on one of the knight's horses, high above the cheering crowds.

Time Out Duck into the arcades at **Donisl,** on your left as you face the town hall, for the first beer of your Munich visit. This is one of the most authentically Bavarian of the city's beer halls, where the beer flows freely all day—and night—long. You can grab a bite to eat, too. *Weinstrasse 1.*

Heading south down Sendlingerstrasse from Marienplatz, you
10 come to the **Asamkirche** on your right. Some consider the Asamkirche a preposterously overdecorated jewelbox; others consider it one of Europe's finest late-Baroque churches. One thing is certain: If you have any interest in church architecture, this is a place you shouldn't miss. It was built around 1730 by the Asam brothers—Cosmos Damian and Egid Quiran—next door to their home, the Asamhaus. They dedicated it to St. John Nepomuk, a 14th-century Bohemian monk who was drowned in the Danube. Pause before you go in to see the charming statue of angels carrying him to heaven from the rocky riverbank. Inside, there is a riot of decoration: frescoes, statuary, rich rosy marbles, billowing clouds of stucco, and gilding everywhere. The decorative elements and the architecture merge to create a seamless sense of movement and color.

11 Go back to Marienplatz and turn right for the **Viktualienmarkt,** the food market. Open-air stalls sell cheese, wine, sausages, fruit, and flowers. Fortified with Bavarian sausage and sauer-
12 kraut, plunge into local history with a visit to the **Residenz,** home of the Wittelsbachs from the 16th century to their enforced abdication at the end of World War I. From Max-Joseph-Platz you enter the great palace, with its glittering

Schatzkammer, or treasury, and gloriously Rococo theater, designed by court architect François Cuvilliès. Also facing the square is the stern neoclassical portico of the **Nationaltheater,** built at the beginning of the 19th century and twice destroyed. *Residenz and Residenz Museum, Max-Joseph-Platz 3. Admission: DM 2.50, children free. Open Tues.–Sat. 10–4:30, Sun. and holidays 10–1.*

To the north of the Residenz is the **Hofgarten,** the palace gardens. Two sides of the gardens are bordered by sturdy arcades designed by Leo von Klenze, whose work for the Wittelsbachs in the 19th century helped transform the face of the city. Dominating the east side of the Hofgarten are the bombed-out ruins of what was once the War Museum. Next to its gaunt silhouette, work is proceeding apace on one of the most controversial building projects Munich has seen for many years, the new State Chancellery.

Time Out Munich's oldest café, the **Annast,** is located on Odeonsplatz, right by the west entrance to the Hofgarten. Sit at one of the tables under the Hofgarten trees, and the downtown bustle can seem miles away.

Odeonsplatz itself is dominated by two striking buildings. One is the **Theatinerkirche,** built for the Theatine monks in the mid-17th century, though its handsome facade, with twin eye-catching domes, was added only in the following century. Despite its Italian influences, the interior, like that of the Michaelskirche, is austerely white. The other notable building here is the **Felderrennhalle,** an open loggia built by Ludwig I and modeled on the Loggia dei Lanzi in Florence. Next to it is the site of Hitler's unsuccessful *putsch* of 1923, later a key Nazi shrine.

The Felderrennhalle looks north along one of the most imposing boulevards in Europe, the **Ludwigstrasse,** which in turn becomes the **Leopoldstrasse.** Von Klenze was responsible for much of it, replacing the jumble of old buildings that originally stood here with the clean, high-windowed lines of his restrained Italianate buildings. The state library and the university are located along it, while, halfway up it, is the **Siegestor,** or Arch of Victory, modeled on the Arch of Constantine in Rome. Beyond it is **Schwabing,** once a sort of combination Latin Quarter and Greenwich Village. It's much glossier these days, but still has an unmistakable vigor and spontaneity. Explore the streets around Wedekindplatz to get the feel of the place.

Back on Leopoldstrasse, wander down to the university, turn on to Professor-Huber-Platz (he was a Munich academic executed by the Nazis for his support for an anti-Hitler movement), and take Veterinärstrasse. It leads you to Munich's largest park, the magnificent **Englischer Garten.** You can rent a bike from Dr. Buss's stand at the entrance to the park on summer weekends. Cost is DM 5 per hour and DM 15 for the day.

The Englischer Garten, three miles (five kilometers) long and more than a mile (1½ kilometers) wide, was laid out by Count Romford, a refugee from the American War of Independence. He was born in England, but it wasn't his English ancestry that determined the park's name as much as its open, informal nature, a style favored by 18th-century English aristocrats. You can rent boats, visit beer gardens—the most famous is at the foot of a Chinese Pagoda—ride your bike (or ski in winter), or simply stroll around. Ludwig II used to love to wander incognito along the serpentine paths. What would he say today, now that so much of the park has been taken over by Munich's nudists? This is no misprint. Late 20th-century Germans have embraced nature worship with almost pagan fervor, and large sections of the park have been designated nudist areas. The biggest is behind the Haus der Kunst, Munich's art gallery, one of the few Hitler-era buildings left in the city. If you prefer the idealized version of the human body to the real thing, head inside. Unusually, the museum also houses one of the city's most exclusive discos, the PI. *Hans der Kunst, Prinzregentenstr. 3. Admission: DM 3, Sun. and holidays free. Open Tues.–Sun. 9–4:30; also open Thurs. 7 PM–9 PM.*

You'll find more culture in Munich's two leading picture galleries, the Alte (meaning "old") and the Neue (meaning "new") Pinakothek. They are located on Barerstrasse, just to the west of the university. The **Alte Pinakothek** is not only the repository of some of the world's most celebrated old masters, but an architectural treasure in its own right, though much scarred from wartime bomb damage. It was built by von Klenze at the beginning of the 19th century to house Ludwig I's collections. Early-Renaissance works, especially by German painters, are the museum's strongest point, but there are some magnificently heroic works by Rubens, too, among much else of outstanding quality. *Barerstr. 27. Admission: DM 4, children free; free Sun. and holidays. Open Tues.–Sun. 9–4:30; Tues. and Thurs. 7 PM–9 PM.*

The **Neue Pinakothek** was another of Ludwig I's projects, built to house his "modern" collections, meaning, of course, 19th-century works. The building was destroyed in the last war, and today's museum opened in 1981. Whatever you think of the low, brick structure—some have compared it with a Florentine palazzo—it is an unparalleled environment in which to see one of the finest collections of 19th-century paintings in the world. *Barerstr. 29. Admission: DM 4, children free; free Sun. and holidays. Open Tues.–Sun. 9–4:30; Tues. and Thurs. 7 PM–9 PM.*

There are two trips you can take to attractions just out of Munich. One is to the **Olympic Park**, a 20-minute U-Bahn ride north of the city; the other is to Nymphenburg, four miles (six kilometers) northwest and reached by the No. 12 streetcar or the 41 bus.

Schloss Nymphenburg was the summer palace of the Wittelsbachs. The oldest parts date from 1664, but construction continued for more than 100 years, the bulk of the work being undertaken in the reign of Max Emmanuel between 1680 and 1730. The gardens, a mixture of formal French *parterres* (trim, ankle-high hedges and gravel walks) and English parkland, were landscaped over the same period. The interiors are exceptional, especially the Banqueting Hall, a Rococo masterpiece in green and gold. Make a point of seeing the Schönheits Galerie, the **Gallery of Beauties.** It contains more than 100 portraits of women who had caught the eye of Ludwig I; duchesses rub shoulders with butchers' daughters. Among them is Lola Montez. Seek out the **Amalienburg,** or Hunting Lodge, on the grounds. It was built by Cuvilliès, architect of the Residenz Theater in Munich. That the hunting the lodge was designed for was often the indoor variety can easily be guessed by the sumptuous silver and blue stucco and the atmosphere of courtly high life. The palace also contains the **Marstallmuseum** (the Museum of Royal Carriages), containing a sleigh that belonged to Ludwig II, among the opulently decorated vehicles, and, on the floor above, the **Nymphenburger Porzellan,** where examples of the gorgeous porcelain produced here between 1747 and the 1920s, when the factory closed, can be seen. *Schloss Nymphenburg. Admission: DM 5, children free. Open Tues.–Sun. 9–12:30 and 1:30–5.*

Of all the controversial buildings that mark Munich's skyline none outdoes the circus tent-shaped roofs of the **Olympic Park.** Built for the 1972 Olympics, the park, with its undulating, transparent tile roofs and modern housing blocks, represented a revolutionary marriage of technology and visual daring when first unveiled, though it all seems a little bit dated now. Sports fans might like to join the crowds in the Olympic stadium when the local soccer team, Bayern Munich, has a home game. Call 089/3061–3577 for information and tickets. There's an amazing view of the stadium, the Olympic Park, and the city from the Olympic tower. An elevator speeds you to the top in seconds. *Admission: DM 4 adults, DM 2.50 children. Open mid-Apr.–mid-Oct., daily 8 AM–midnight; mid-Oct.–mid-Apr., daily 9–midnight.*

What to See and Do with Children

The **Hellabrunn Zoo,** in the southern suburb of Thalkirchen, is a must. *Admission: DM 4.50. Open Apr.–Oct., daily 8–6; Nov.–Apr., daily 9–6.* Children love the **Deutsches Museum,** the world's largest science museum. It's located on the Museum Island in the river Isar, a 10-minute walk from the city center. *Admission: DM 5 adults, DM 2 children. Open daily 9–5.* For the very young (and their parents), the **Munich Children's Theater** is a delight, even if you can't speak German. *Dachauerstr. 46, tel. 089/595484.* In summer, seek out the 100-year-old **carousel** at the edge of the Englischer Garten beer garden; it's just a beer mug's throw from the Chinese Pagoda.

Off the Beaten Track

Even though the Olympic Tower is higher, romantics say the best view of Munich and the Alps is from the top of the **Alter Peter** church tower; it's just off Marienplatz. Check that a white disk is hanging on the wall outside the entrance: It means that visibility is good. There are 302 steps to climb to the top. For the most inexpensive sightseeing tour of the center, take a No. 19 streetcar from outside the train station at Bahnhofplatz and ride it to **Wienerplatz,** itself located in Haidhausen, one of Munich's most interesting areas. On a fine day, join the chess players at their open-air board in Schwabing's **Münchner Freiheit** square. On a rainy day, pack your swimsuit and splash around in the Art Nouveau setting of the **Müllersches Volksbad** pool; it's located on the corner of the Ludwigsbrücke, one of the bridges over the Isar.

Shopping

Gift Ideas Munich is a city of beer, and beer mugs and coasters make an obvious gift to take home. There are many specialist shops in downtown Munich, but **Ludwig Mory,** located in the town hall on Marienplatz, is about the best. Munich is also the home of the famous Nymphenburg porcelain factory; its major outlet is on Odeonsplatz.

Shopping Districts From Odeonsplatz you are poised to plunge into the heart of the huge pedestrian mall that runs through the center of town. The first street you come to, **Theatinerstrasse,** is also one of the most expensive. In fact, it has only one serious rival in the money-no-object stakes: **Maximilianstrasse,** the first street to your left as you head down Theatinerstrasse. Both are lined with elegant shops selling desirable German fashions and other high-priced goods from around the world. Leading off to the right, you'll find **Maffeistrasse,** where **Loden-Frey** has Bavaria's most complete collection of traditional wear, from green "loden" coats to Lederhosen. Maffeistrasse. runs parallel to Munich's principal shopping streets: **Kaufingerstrasse** and **Neuhausenstrasse,** the one an extension of the other.

Department Stores All the city's major department stores are here. **Kaufhof** and **Oberpollinger** are probably the best. Both have large departments stocking Bavarian arts and crafts, as well as clothing, household goods, jewelry, and other accessories.

Antiques Antique hunters should make for **Karlstrasse** and **Türkenstrasse,** or to the flea markets held on weekends on **Dachauerstrasse,** beyond Leonrodplatz.

Dining

If it's generally true that the Germans take their food seriously, then it's unquestionably true that it's the Müncheners who take it most seriously of all. In fact, you can probably eat as well here as in any other city in Europe, Paris perhaps excepted. It's no surprise that Munich boasts what, by common consent, are generally held to be the two best restaurants in the country. If you're interested in haute cuisine, however, don't come expecting to find it dressed in Bavarian garb. The best Bavarian food has unmistakable Teutonic elements, but otherwise has much more in common with the sort of sophisticated nouvelle offerings you find in Paris than with wholesome and hearty German specialties. It would be wrong, though, to give the impression that the only food you'll find in Munich is light and sophisticated. Those with a taste for the kind of time-honored, traditional eating places that have been pulling in the crowds for years will not be disappointed. The city's beer and wine restaurants offer great atmosphere, low prices, and as much wholesome German food as you'll ever want. If there's one specialty you shouldn't miss it's *Weisswurst,* a delicate white sausage traditionally eaten only between midnight and noon. Wash it down with a large glass of cold beer. *Leberkäs,* meat loaf made with pork and beef, is another celebrated favorite.

Prices are per person for a three-course meal, excluding drinks. Best bets are indicated by a star ★. At press time, there were 1.67 deutschmarks to the dollar.

Category	Cost
Very Expensive	over DM 95
Expensive	DM 65–DM 95
Moderate	DM 45–DM 65
Inexpensive	under DM 45

Credit Cards The following credit card abbreviations are used: AE, American Express; DC, Diners Club; MC, MasterCard; V, Visa.

Very Expensive **Aubergine.** German gourmets swear by the upscale nouvelle cuisine of Eckart Witzigmann, chef and owner of the most sophisticated, if not exactly the most elegant, restaurant in town. The decor is streamlined modern—white and glittery. The service is appropriately polished. If you want a gastronomic experience on the grand scale, try the turbot in champagne or the breast of pigeon with artichoke and truffle salad. *Maximilianplatz 5, tel. 089/598171. Jacket and tie. Reservations essential. MC. Closed Sun., Mon., Christmas and New Year's Day, and first 3 weeks of Aug.*

Boettner's. This is the oldest of Munich's classy restaurants, in business since 1905 and still going strong. There's a time-honored and quiet quality to its gracious bar and dark, wood-paneled dining room. They provide a welcome contrast to the bustle of the city center outside. Seafood dominates the menu; try the lobster and sole served on a bed of tomato-flavored pasta. *Theatinerstr. 2, tel. 089/221210. Jacket and tie. Reservations essential. AE, DC, MC, V. Closed Sat. for dinner, Sun., and public holidays.*

Sabitzer's. Further evidence of upscale Munich's love affair with nouvelle cuisine, though with Bavarian influences, is provided by the classy offerings at Sabitzer's. Within its elegant gold-and-white 19th-century interior, you dine on specialties such as wild salmon with stuffed goose livers and lamb with venison. *Reitmorstr. 21, tel. 089/298584. Jacket and tie. Reservations essential. AE, DC, MC. Closed Sat., Sun., July and Aug.*

★ **Tantris.** Chef Heinz Winkler presides almost regally over what most consider Munich's top restaurant. Here, too, nouvelle cuisine, served with great panache, reigns supreme. Try the pigeon breast for a remarkable gastronomic experience. The downside is the setting, which bears an uncanny resemblance to an airport departure lounge, albeit one for VIPs. The restaurant is located in glitzy Schwabing. *Johann-Fichter-Str. 7, tel. 089/362061. Jacket and tie. Reservations essential. AE, DC, MC. Closed Sat. lunch, Sun., Mon., 1st week in Jan., and 3 weeks in Aug.*

Expensive **Austernkeller.** The nautical decor of this centrally located,
★ vaulted cellar-restaurant provides an appropriate setting for the classy seafood specialties of the Austernkeller. Oysters—*Austern* in German—dominate the menu, but there's a wide range of other shellfish featured, too. *Stollbergstr. 11, tel. 089/298787. Jacket and tie. Reservations advised. AE, DC, MC, V. Closed Mon. and Christmas.*

Bouillabaisse. There's little point eating here if your tastes run to Bavarian and other German specialties. As its name makes clear, this is a restaurant that makes no bones about the fact that pungent and rich *bouillabaisse*, the garlicky fish stew from Provence in the south of France, is the star attraction. The decor is striking, with imposing chandeliers to lighten up the otherwise somber and heavy-beamed dining room. *Falkenturmstr. 10, tel. 089/297909. Jacket and tie. Reservations advised. AE, DC, MC, V. Closed Sun., Mon. lunch, and Aug.*

Le Gourmet. Imaginative combinations of French and Bavarian specialties have won the little Gourmet substantial praise from local critics. Try chef Otto Koch's oxtail in champagne sauce or his zucchini and truffle salad. *Ligslazstr. 46, tel. 089/503597. Jacket and tie. Reservations advised. AE, DC, MC. Closed Sun. and 1st week in Jan.*

Käferschanke. Fresh fish, imported daily from the south of France, is the attraction here. Try the grilled prawns in a sweet-sour sauce. The rustic decor, complemented by some fine antique pieces, is a delight. The restaurant is located in the classy Bogenhausen suburb, a 10-minute taxi ride from downtown. *Schumannstr. 1, tel. 089/41681. Jacket and tie. Reservations advised. AE, DC, MC. Closed Sat. and public holidays.*

★ **Preysing Keller.** Devotees of all that's best in modern German food—food that's light and sophisticated but with recognizably Teutonic touches—will love the Preysing Keller, the best hotel-restaurant in the city. The restaurant is in a 16th-century cellar, though this has been so overrestored that there's practically no sense of its age or original character. Never mind; it's the food, the extensive wine list, and the perfect service that make this somewhere special. Try the fixed-price seven-course menu—a bargain at DM 100 per person—for best value and an all-around taste of the most underrated restaurant in Munich. *Innere-Wiener-Str. 6, tel. 089/481015. Jacket and tie. Reservations essential. No credit cards. Closed Sun., Christmas, and New Year's Day.*

Moderate **Bistro Terrine.** The name may make you think that this is no more than a humble, neighborhood French-style restaurant. In fact, excellent classic French dishes are served within its appealing Art Nouveau interior. Order the fixed-price menu to keep the check low; *à la carte* dishes are appreciably more expensive. *Amalienstr. 40, tel. 089/281780. Jacket and tie. Reservations advised. AE, MC. Closed Sun.*

Goldene Stadt. Named for the "Golden City" of Prague, capital of Czechoslovakia, this is the place to find authentic Bohemian specialties. Try roast duck or goose with dumplings. *Oberanger 44, tel. 089/264382. Dress: informal. Reservations advised. AE, DC, MC. Closed Sun.*

Kasak. Among the numerous ethnic restaurants in Munich, this one really stands out. Chef Anastatious Pistolas presides over the best Greek food in town. Try the three-course lunch menu for exceptional value for your money. *Friedrichstr. 1a, tel. 089/391771. Dress: informal. Reservations advised. AE, DC, MC, V.*

★ **Nürnberger Bratwurstglockl.** This is about the most authentic old-time Bavarian sausage restaurant in Munich, and it's always crowded. Wobbly chairs, pitch-black wooden paneling, tin plates, monosyllabic waitresses, and, downstairs, some seriously Teutonic-looking characters establish an unbeatable mood. If you want undiluted atmosphere, try for a table downstairs; if you want to hear yourself speak, go for one upstairs.

The menu is limited, with *Nürnberger stadtwurst mit kraut*—finger-size Nürnberg sausages—taking pride of place. The beer, never in short supply, is served straight from wooden barrels. The restaurant is right by the Frauenkirche—the entrance is set back from the street and can be hard to spot—and makes an ideal lunchtime layover. *Frauenplatz 9, tel. 089/220385. Dress: informal. Reservations advised. No credit cards.*

Inexpensive **Donisl.** Ranking high among the beer restaurants of Munich, Donisl is located just off Marienplatz, and in summer, its tables spill out onto the sidewalk. But the real action is inside. The large central hall, with garlands of dried flowers and painted and carved booths lining the walls, is animated night and day with locals and visitors alike. The atmosphere, like the food, is rough and ready. The beer flows freely. *Weinstr. 1, tel. 089/220184. Dress: informal. No reservation. AE, DC, MC, V.*

Dürnbräu. A fountain plays outside this picturesque old Bavarian inn. Inside, the mood is crowded and noisy. Expect to share a table; your fellow diners will range from millionaires to students. The food is resolutely traditional. Try the cream of spinach soup and the boiled beef. *Dürnbräugasse 2, tel. 089/222195. Dress: informal. Reservations advised. AE, DC, MC, V.*

Franziskaner. Vaulted archways, cavernous rooms interspersed with intimate dining areas, bold blue frescoes on the walls, long wooden tables, and a sort of spic-and-span medieval atmosphere—the look without the dirt—set the mood. This is the place for an early morning *Weisswürst* and a beer; the Bavarians swear it will banish all trace of that morning-after feeling. The Franziskaner is located near the State Opera. *Peruastr. 5, tel. 089/645548. Dress: informal. No reservations. No credit cards.*

★ **Haxnbauer.** This is about the most sophisticated of the beer restaurants. There's the usual series of interlinking rooms—some large, some small—and the usual sturdy/pretty Bavarian decoration. But there is much greater emphasis on the food than in other similar places. Try *Leberkäs*, meat loaf made with pork and beef, or *Schweinshaxe*, pork shank. *Munzstr. 2, tel. 089/221922. Dress: informal. Reservations advised. MC, V.*

Hofbräuhaus. The heavy stone vaults of the Hofbräuhaus contain the most famous of the city's beer restaurants. Crowds of singing, shouting, swaying beer drinkers—make no mistake; this is a place where beer takes precedence over food—fill the atmospheric and smoky rooms. Picking their way past the tables are hefty waitresses in traditional garb bearing frothing steins. Some people love it. Others deplore the rampant commercialization and the fact that the place is now so obviously aimed at the tourist trade. It's just north of Marienplatz. *Platzl 9, tel. 089/221676. Dress: informal. No reservations. No credit cards.*

Hundskugel. This is Munich's oldest tavern, dating back to 1640; history positively drips from its crooked walls. The food is surprisingly good. If *Spanferkel*—roast suckling pig—is on the menu, make a point of ordering it. This is simple Bavarian fare at its best. *Hotterstr. 18, tel. 089/264272. Dress: informal. Reservations advised. No credit cards.*

Max Emanuel Bräuerei. Folk music and theater are featured in this time-honored Munich institution, located just by the university. The clientele is predominantly young, and the atmosphere is always lively. In summer, you can eat in the delightful little beer garden. The food is wholesome Bavarian, with some Greek and French touches. *Adalbertstr. 33, tel. 089/271–5158. Dress: informal. Reservations advised. DC, MC.*

★ **Pfalzer Weinprobierstube.** A warren of stone-vaulted rooms of various sizes, wooden tables, glittering candles, dirndl-clad waitresses, and a vast range of wines add up to an experience as close to your picture of timeless Germany as you're likely to get. The food is reliable rather than spectacular. Local specialties predominate. *Residenzstr. 1, tel. 089/225628. Dress: informal. No reservations. No credit cards.*

Lodging

Make reservations well in advance and be prepared for higher-than-average rates. Though Munich has a vast number of hotels in all price ranges, most are full year-round; this is a major trade and convention city as well as a prime tourist destination. If you plan to visit during the "fashion weeks" (Mode Wochen) in March and September or during the Oktoberfest at the end of September, make reservations at least two months in advance. The tourist office at Rindermarkt 5 has a reservations office, but note that personnel will not accept telephone reservations. There's also a reservations office at the airport. Your best bet for finding a room if you haven't reserved in advance is the tourist office at Bayerstrasse by the train station. The staff will charge a small fee, but are supremely well organized.

The closer to the city center you stay, the higher the price. Consider staying in a suburban hotel and taking the U-Bahn or S-Bahn into town. Rates are much more reasonable, and a 15-minute train ride is no obstacle to serious sightseeing. Check out the city tourist office "Key to Munich" packages. These include reduced-rate hotel reservations, sightseeing tours, theater visits, and low-cost travel on the U- and S-Bahn. Write to the tourist office at Rindermarkt 5.

Prices are for two people in a double room, including tax and service. Best bets are indicated by a star ★. At press time, there were 1.67 deutschmarks to the dollar.

Category	Cost
Very Expensive	over DM 200
Expensive	DM 160–DM 200
Moderate	DM 100–DM 160
Inexpensive	under DM 100

Credit Cards The following credit card abbreviations are used: AE, American Express; DC, Diners Club; MC, MasterCard; V, Visa.

Very Expensive **Arabella.** If you love traditional Bavarian styles, this is not the place for you. The Arabella occupies the 22nd and 23rd floors of a high-rise apartment building in Bogenhausen, a suburb east of the city about 4 miles (6 kilometers) from the airport. The main feature is a "tropical island" leisure center ranged around a palm-fringed pool and the obligatory Caribbean bar. Room styles range from Teutonic rustic to crisp, modern town house. *Arabellastr. 5, tel. 089/92320. 56 rooms and suites with bath.*

Facilities: restaurant, bar, sauna, solarium, pool, garage.
AE, DC, MC, V.

Bayerischer Hof. This is one of Munich's most traditional luxury
hotels. It's set on a ritzy shopping street, with a series of exclusive shops right outside the imposing marble entrance. Public
rooms are decorated with antiques, fine paintings, marble, and
painted wood. Old-fashioned comfort and class abound in the
older rooms; some of the newer rooms are rather functional.
Promenadenplatz 2–6, tel. 089/21200. 440 rooms with bath. Fa-
cilities: 3 restaurants, nightclub, rooftop pool, garage, sauna,
masseur, hairdresser. AE, DC, MC, V.

★ **Vier Jahreszeiten.** The Vier Jahreszeiten—it means the Four
Seasons—has been playing host to the world's wealthy and titled for more than a century. It has an unbeatable location, on
Maximilianstrasse, Munich's premier shopping street, and is
only a few minutes' walk from the heart of the city. Elegance
and luxury set the tone throughout; many rooms have handsome antique pieces. Dine in one of Munich's finest restaurants, the Walterspiel. *Maximilianstr. 17, tel. 089/230390.*
(Reservations in the USA from Kempinski International, tel.
800/426–3135). 341 rooms with bath, 25 apartments, presiden-
tial suite. Facilities: restaurant, nightclub, rooftop pool,
garage, sauna, car rental, Lufthansa check-in desk. AE, DC,
MC, V.

Expensive **Eden Hotel Wolff.** Chandeliers and dark wood paneling in the
public rooms underline the old-fashioned elegance of this downtown favorite. It's located close to the train station and the
fairgrounds of Theresienwiese. Rooms are comfortable, and
most are spacious. Dine on excellent Bavarian specialties in the
intimate Zirbelstube restaurant. *Arnulfstr. 4, tel. 089/551150.*
210 rooms with bath. Facilities: restaurant. No credit cards.

Excelsior. It's no surprise that the Excelsior is very much a
businessperson's hotel. A sense of functional comfort pervades
this modern hotel, while the pedestrian mall location, close by
the train station, makes it ultraconvenient for downtown. Renovations in 1986 have helped maintain the Excelsior's reputation for efficiency and good service. *Schützenstr. 11, tel.*
089/551370. 116 rooms with bath or shower. Facilities: restau-
rant, bar. AE, DC, MC, V.

Palace. The Palace is a modern hotel that opened in 1986. Decor
and mood lean toward old-fashioned elegance, with the accent
firmly on Louis XVI styles and plush luxury. Most rooms overlook the little courtyard. The hotel is located in Alt-
Bogenhausen, 4 miles (6 kilometers) from the airport. Downtown Munich is a 10-minute tram ride away (the tram stop is
right by the door). *Trögerstr. 21, tel. 089/4705091. 73 rooms*
and suites with bath. Facilities: bar, roof garden, Jacuzzi, sau-
na, gym. AE, DC, MC, V.

Prinzregent. An air of slightly functional Bavarian rusticity
pervades this small, new hotel. Carved wood, gilt angels,
Rococo-style sconces and mirrors, and rough white plaster
walls predominate. There's no restaurant, but the breakfast
room, decked out with woods taken from an old farmhouse,
makes for a soothing start to the day. The small bar off the lobby is a discreet rendezvous. The hotel is just a 10-minute ride
from downtown. *Ismaningerstr. 42–44, tel. 089/4702081. 70*
rooms with shower. Facilities: sauna, pool, bar. AE, DC,
MC, V.

★ **Splendid.** Chandelier-hung public rooms, complete with antiques and Oriental rugs, give the small Splendid something of the atmosphere of a spaciously grand 19th-century hotel. Service is attentive and polished. Have breakfast in the small courtyard in summer. There's no restaurant, but the bar serves snacks as well as drinks. The classy shops of the Maximilianstrasse are a 5-minute stroll in one direction; in the other, an equally brief walk brings you to the Isar river. *Maximilianstr. 54, tel. 089/2966606. 37 rooms with bath and 1 suite. Facilities: bar. AE, MC, V.*

Trustee Park Hotel. Located close to the exhibit grounds, the newly opened Trustee Park is first and foremost a businessperson's hotel (and correspondingly functional in decor); high season coincides with trade fairs and conventions. Check out weekend rates: Special family deals are often available. Rooms are spacious, and many have balconies or terraces. *Parkstr. 31, tel. 089/5195421. 40 rooms with bath. Facilities: restaurant, bar. AE, DC, MC, V.*

Moderate **Adria.** A modern and comfortable hotel, the Adria is located on the edge of Munich's museum quarter, in the attractive Lehel district, a short walk from the Isar river and the Englischer Garten. There's no restaurant, but there's a large and bright breakfast room. *Liebigstr. 8, tel. 089/293081. 51 rooms with bath. AE, DC, MC, V. Closed Dec. 24–Jan. 6.*

Braüfpanne. The plain concrete exterior of the Braüfpanne belies the considerable if functional comforts within. Though the rooms are sparsely furnished, they are intelligently designed, with writing desks and sofas. The restaurant offers excellent local specialties at affordable prices. Don't stay here if you want to be close to the center of things; the Braüfpanne is located a 25-minute tram ride from downtown in the northeast suburbs. *Oberföhringerstr. 107, tel. 089/951095. 25 rooms with bath. Facilities: restaurant, bar, skittle alley. AE, DC, MC, V.*

Domus. Head here for home comforts and friendly, personal service. All rooms have balconies. There's no restaurant, but drinks and snacks are available in the Tyrolean Room bar, decked out in appropriately rough-hewn and snug Alpine style. The hotel is located in the Lehel district, close to many museums and the Englischer Garten. *St. Anna-Str. 31, tel. 089/ 221704. 45 rooms with bath. Facilities: bar, garage. AE, DC, MC, V. Closed Christmas.*

★ **Gästehaus am Englischer Garten.** Not so long ago, only a handful of lucky initiates knew about this converted, 200-year-old watermill. Today, despite the still slightly basic rooms, its fame is such that you need to reserve well in advance to be sure of getting a room. The hotel, complete with ivy-clad walls and shutter-framed windows, stands right on the edge of the Englischer Garten, no more than a 5-minute walk from the bars and shops of Schwabing. There's no restaurant, but who needs one with Schwabing's numerous eating possibilities so close? Be sure to ask for a room in the main building; the modern annex down the road is cheaper but charmless. In summer, breakfast is served on the terrace. *Liebergesellstr. 8, tel. 089/ 392034. 34 rooms, some with bath. No credit cards.*

Intercity. Despite a location no more than a whistle-stop from the train station, double-glazing in all rooms ensures peace in this longtime downtown favorite. Try for one of the Bavarian-style rooms; others are basic and little more than adequate. There's an excellent restaurant offering good-value Bavarian specialties. *Bahnhofplatz 2, tel. 089/558571. 208 rooms and 4 apartments with bath. Facilities: restaurant, bar, skittle alley. DC, MC, V.*

Inexpensive **Ariane.** Make reservations well in advance for this small pension; it's located a 5-minute walk due south of the train station. Standards of comfort are high, and many appreciate the excellent central location. *Pettenkoferstr. 44, tel. 089/535529. 12 rooms, most with bath. No credit cards.*

Kriemhild. If you're traveling with children, you'll appreciate the low rates of this welcoming, family-run pension in the western suburb of Nymphenburg. It's located just a few minutes' walk from the palace itself and from the Hirschgarten park, site of one of the city's best beer gardens. It's a 30-minute tram ride from downtown. There's no restaurant, but there is a small bar. An extensive breakfast buffet is included in the room rate. *Guntherstr. 16, tel. 089/170077. 40 rooms, half with bath. Facilities: bar. MC.*

★ **Monopteros.** There are few better deals in Munich than the little Monopteros. It's located just south of the Englischer Garten, with a tram stop for the 10-minute ride to downtown right by the door. Rooms may be basic, but the excellent service and warm welcome, coupled with the great location, more than compensate. There's no restaurant. *Oettingenstr. 35, tel. 089/292348. 11 rooms, 3 with shower. No credit cards.*

The Arts

Details of concerts and theater performances are available from the "Vorschau" or "Monatsprogramm" booklets obtainable at most hotel reception desks. Some hotels will make ticket reservations; otherwise use one of the ticket agencies in the city center, such as Radio-Rim or the Residenz Bücherstube, both on Theatinerstrasse.

Concerts Munich's Philharmonic Orchestra has a new home, the concert hall of the **Gasteig Cultural Center.** Tickets can be bought directly at the box office (the Gasteig center is on Rosenheimerstrasse, on a hill above the Ludwigsbrücke bridge). The Bavarian Radio Orchestra performs Sunday concerts here. In summer, concerts are held at two Munich palaces, **Nymphenburg** and **Schleissheim,** and in the open-air interior courtyard of the **Residenz.**

Opera Munich's **Bavarian State Opera** company is world famous, and tickets for major productions in its permanent home, the State Opera House, are difficult to obtain. Book far in advance for the annual opera festival held in July and August. The box office, (at Maximilianstr. 11, tel. 089/221316) takes reservations one week in advance. It's open Monday–Friday 10:30–1:30 and 3:30–5:30, Saturday 10–12:30.

Dance The ballet company of the Bavarian State Opera performs at the **State Opera House.** Ballet productions are also staged at the attractive late 19th-century **Gärtnerplatz Theater.**

Movies Munich has an annual film festival, usually held in June. English-language films are shown regularly at the **Atlantic Palast** (Schwantalerstr. 2–6), **Cinema** (Nymphenburgerstr. 31), the **Filmuseum** (St. Jakobs Platz), and the **Museum Lichtspiele** (Ludwigsbrücke).

Theater There are two state theater companies, one of which concentrates on the classics. More than 20 other theater companies (some of them performing in basements) are to be found throughout the city. An English-speaking company, called the **Company** (tel. 089/343827) presents about four productions a year.

Nightlife

Bars, Cabaret, Nightclubs Although it lacks the racy reputation of Hamburg, Munich has something for just about all tastes. For spicy striptease, explore the regions south of the train station (Schillerstr., for example), or in the neighborhood of the famous Hofbräuhaus (Am Platzl). **Sexyland**, just up the street, combines high-class striptease and a relatively low check, if you're careful.

Jazz The best jazz can be heard at the **Allotria** (Türkenstr. 33), the **Domicile** (Leopoldstr. 19), and the **Podium** (Wagnerstr. 1). **Jenny's Place** (Georgenstr. 50) is run by an English actress-singer who has a great voice and a warm welcome for any visitor from the United States or Britain.

Discos Schwabing is disco-land. Try the **Circo Valentino** on Occamstrasse (a fun street at all times of day).

For singles Every Munich bar is singles territory. Three you might like to try are: **Schumann's** (Maximilianstr. 36) any time after the curtain comes down at the nearby opera house; **Alter Simpl** (Türkenstr. 57) but not before midnight, and **Harry's New York Bar** (Falkenturmstr. 9), which offers an escape from the German bar scene *and* serves genuine Irish Guinness.

Frankfurt

Arriving and Departing

By Plane **Frankfurt airport,** the busiest in central Europe, is about six miles (10 kilometers) southwest of the city.

Between the Airport and Downtown There are several ways to get into town. Two suburban (S-Bahn) lines connect the airport and the center. The S-14 runs between the Hauptwache Station and the airport, and the S-15 from the main train station, the Hauptbahnhof. The S-14 runs every 20 minutes and takes 15 minutes; the S-15 leaves every 10 minutes and takes 11 minutes. The trip costs DM 3.10 (DM 4.20 in rush hour). Inter-City trains also stop at Frankfurt airport train station on hourly direct runs to Cologne, Dortmund, Hamburg, and Munich. A No. 61 bus runs from the airport to the Sudbahnhof station in Sachsenhausen, where there is access to the U-Bahn (subway) lines U-1 and U-3; the fare is DM 3.10. Taxi fare from the airport to downtown is DM 35. By rented car, follow the signs to Frankfurt ("Stadtmitte") via the B-43 main road.

By Train Frankfurt's main train station, the Hauptbahnhof, and the airport station are directly linked with all parts of the country by fast Euro-City and Inter-City services. For train information, tel. 069/230333. For tickets and general information, go directly to the station or to the DER travel office at the Hauptbahnhof.

By Bus Long-distance buses connect Frankfurt with more than 200 European cities. Buses leave from the south side of the Hauptbahnhof. Tickets and information are available from **Deutsche Touring GmbH.** (Am Römerhof 17, tel. 069/79030).

By Car From the north, leave autobahn A5 at the Nordwestkreuz, join A66 and follow it to its end, in the Nordend district. From the east, A66 brings you into Enkheim, from where you follow the signs to the downtown area, the "Stadtmitte." From the west, leave autobahn A3 at the Frankfurt-south ("Frankfurt-Süd") exit and enter the city on B43/44. From the south, leave the autobahn at the Offenbach exit (the "Anschlusse-stelle Offenbach") and enter the city on B459.

Getting Around

By Public Transportation A combination of subway and suburban train, streetcar, and bus services provides speedy and efficient public transportation. Tickets cover travel on the complete network, which is divided into two tariff zones. A 24-ticket booklet costs DM 7, less than the cost of four single tickets in the inner (city) tariff zone. The 24-hour ticket is available at all ticket-selling points; single tickets from the blue automatic dispensing units are at all major stops. For further information or assistance, call 069/26940.

By Taxi Taxi meters start at DM 3.60, and the fare is DM 1.80 per kilometer (about DM 2.90 per mile). Count on paying DM 10 to DM 12 for a short city ride. Taxi drivers charge 50 pfennigs for each piece of luggage carried. To order a taxi, call 069/250001, 069/230023, or 069/545011.

Guided Tours

Orientation Tours Bus tours of the city, with English commentary, start at the north side of the main train station, at 10 and 2 daily from March through October; at 2 only from November to mid-December and from mid-January through February. The tour takes about three hours and costs DM 26 (half-price for children and over-60s). A tour that takes in not only the main city sights but also some of the Taunus countryside starts at 11 daily from January through November (DM 34, half-price for children and over-60s). On weekend afternoons, a gaily painted old streetcar ("The Ebbelwei Express") trundles around the city and Sachsenhausen, on the south side of the Main. The 40-minute ride—starting and ending at the Ostbahnhof train station, at Danzigerplatz in Frankfurt's Ostend district—includes a glass of apple cider ("Ebbelwei") and a pretzel in the DM 3 fare. Further information and tickets can be obtained from the Stadtwerke, Rathenauplatz 3, tel. 069/13682425.

Excursions Bus tours of the surrounding countryside, as far as the Rhine, are offered by the **Reisebüro Wagon-Lits** (Kaiserstr. 72, tel. 069/2687214); the **Deutsche Touring GmbH** (Am Römerhof 17, tel. 069/79031); and **DEMA Reisen GmbH** (Tour Center, Karlsruhestr. 18, tel. 069/231322). One-day excursions are also offered by German Railways, the Bundesbahn. These are described in a brochure, "Der Schöne Tag," obtainable from the main train station and the DER tourist office. A *Casino-Express* bus service runs daily from Frankfurt (departing from Baselerplatz) to the casino at Bad Homburg in the Taunus mountains. The fare is deducted from the entrance charge to the casino. The *Casino-Express* makes the trip hourly, from 2:15 to 11:15 PM.

Tourist Information

The main tourist information office is at the Hauptbahnhof, across from platform 23 (tel. 069/2128849). It's open 8 AM–10 PM (until 9 PM Nov.–Mar.), Sunday and holidays 9:30 AM–8 PM. Another information office is at the Hauptwache (tel. 069/2128708). It's open weekdays 9–6, Saturday 9–2. There are three information offices at the airport (in departure hall B, arrival hall B, and transit hall B). For information in advance of your trip, contact the **Verkehrsamt Frankfurt/Main** (Gutleutstr. 7–9, 6000 Frankfurt, tel. 069/2128849).

Exploring Frankfurt

At first glance, Frankfurt-am-Main doesn't seem to have much to offer the tourist. Virtually flattened by bombs during the war, it now bristles with skyscrapers, the visible sign of the city's role as West Germany's financial capital. Yet the inquisitive and discerning visitor will find many remnants of Frankfurt's illustrious past (besides being well placed for excursions to other historic cities, such as Heidelberg and Würzburg, and within easy reach of the Rhine).

Originally a Roman settlement, Frankfurt was later one of Charlemagne's two capitals (the other being Aachen). Still later, it was for centuries the site of the election and coronation of the emperors of that unwieldy entity, the Holy Roman Empire, which was the forerunner of a united Germany. It was also the birthplace of the poet and dramatist Goethe (1749–1832). The house in which he was born is one of many restored and reconstructed old buildings that inject a flavor of bygone days into the center of this busy modern city.

Although the true center of Frankfurt is its ancient **Römerberg Square,** where the election of Holy Roman emperors was traditionally proclaimed and celebrated, this tour of the city begins

❶ slightly to the north, at the **Hauptwache,** an 18th-century guardhouse that today serves a more peaceful purpose as a café, with a city information center on the lower ground floor. The printed material you can pick up here is in English and includes a recommended tour of the city, which is followed on these pages for much of its route.

❷ Head south along Kornmarkt, passing on the left the **Church of St. Catherine**—historic center of Frankfurt Protestantism. After crossing Berlinerstrasse, and still heading south, you'll

❸ pass the **Paulskirche,** (Church of St. Paul): It was here that the first all-German parliament convened in 1848, and the church is therefore an important symbol of German unity and democracy. Continue down Buchgasse and within a few minutes you're on the north bank of the river **Main.** Turn left toward the great iron bridge known as the **Eiserne Steg** and at the **Rententurm,** one of the city's medieval gates, bear left again and you'll arrive

❹ at the massive **Römerberg,** center of Frankfurt civic life over the centuries. In the center of the square stands the 16th-century **Fountain of Justitia** (Justice): At the coronation of Emperor Matthias in 1612, wine instead of water spouted from the stonework. The crush of people was so great, however, that the Germans have not repeated the trick since.

⑤ Compared with many city halls, Frankfurt's **Römer** is a modest affair, with a gabled Gothic facade. It occupies most of one side of the square and is actually three patrician houses (the Alt-Limpurg, the Römer—from which it takes its name—and the Lowenstein). The mercantile-minded Frankfurt burghers used the complex not only for political and ceremonial purposes, but for trade fairs and commerce.

The most important events to take place in the Römer, however, were the elections of the Holy Roman emperors. The **Kaisersaal** (banquet hall) was last used in 1792 to celebrate the election of Emperor Francis II, who was later forced to abdicate by arch-egomaniac Napoleon Bonaparte. (A 16-year-old Goethe smuggled himself into the banquet celebrating the coronation of Emperor Joseph II in 1765 by posing as a waiter.) Today, visitors can see the impressive full-length 19th-century portraits of the 52 emperors of the Holy Roman Empire that line the walls of the banqueting hall. *Admission: DM 1 adults, 25 pfennigs children. Open Mon.–Sat. 9–5, Sun. 10–4.*

Charlemagne's son, Ludwig the Pious, established a church on the present site of the Römerberg in AD 850. His church was replaced by a much grander Gothic structure, one used for im-
⑥ perial coronations; it became known as the **Kaiserdom**, the Imperial Cathedral. The cathedral suffered little damage in World War II, and it still contains most of its original treasures, including a fine 15th-century altar.

On the south side of the square stands the 13th-century church
⑦ of **Nikolaikirche** (St. Nicholas's Church). It's worth trying to time your visit to the square to coincide with the chimes of the Glockenspiel carillon, which ring out three times a day. *Carillon chimes daily at 9, noon, and 5.*

From the Römerberg, stroll back down to the river, but turn
⑧ right this time, past the riverside **Leonhardskirche**, (St. Leonhard's Church), which has a fine 13th-century porch and a beautifully carved circa 1500 Bavarian altar, then into the nar-
⑨ row Karmelitergasse to the **Carmelite Monastery.** Within its quiet cloisters is the largest religious fresco north of the Alps, a 16th-century representation of the birth and death of Christ. *Open weekdays 8–4.*

⑩ From here, it's only a short way to the **Goethehaus und Goethemuseum** (Goethe's House and Museum). It was here that the poet was born in 1749, and though the house was destroyed by Allied bombing, it has been carefully restored and is furnished with pieces from Goethe's time, many belonging to his family. The adjoining museum contains a permanent collection of manuscripts, paintings, and memorabilia documenting the life and times of Germany's most outstanding poet. *Grosser Hirschgraben 23, tel. 069/282824. Admission: DM 3 adults, DM 1.50 children. Open Mon.–Sat. 9–6, Sun. 10–1.*

From the Goethehaus, retrace your steps to the Hauptwache via Rossmarkt. From there, take a window-shopping stroll past the elegant boutiques of Goethestrasse, which ends at Opernplatz and Frankfurt's reconstructed opera house, the
⑪ **Alte Oper.** Wealthy Frankfurt businessmen gave generously for the construction of the opera house in the 1870s (provided

Frankfurt

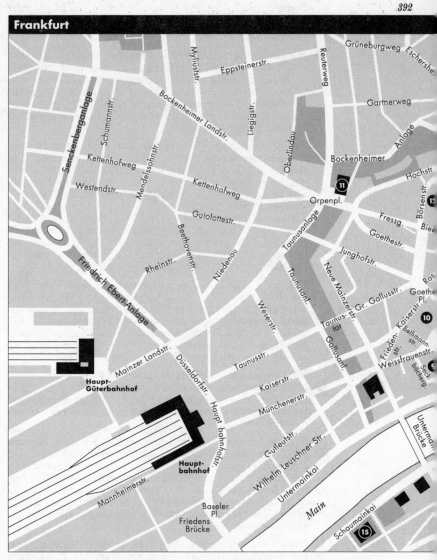

Myliusstr.
Eppsteinerstr.
Grüneburgweg   Eschershe
Reuterweg
Gartnerweg
Anlage
Bockenheimer Landstr.
Liegigstr.
Bockenheimer
Senckenberganlage
Schumannstr.
Hochstr.
Oberlindau
Kettenhofweg
Mendelssohnstr.
Kettenhofweg
Börsenstr.
Westendstr.
Orpenpl.
Fressg.
Bie
Guiolottestr.
Taunusanlage
Goethestr.
Beethovenstr.
Junghofstr.
Ros
Rheinstr.
Niedenau
Taunusanl.
Neue Mainzer str.
Goethe
Pl.
Friedrich Ebert-Anlage
Weserstr.
Taunus-
tor
Gr. Gallusstr.
Frieden- Kaiserstr.
Bethmann-
str.
str.
Weissfrauenstr.
Gallusanl.
Taunusstr.
Seck-
bacherIg.
Mainzer Landstr.
Düsseldorfstr.
Taunusstr.
Haupt bahnhofstr.
Kaiserstr.
Haupt-
Güterbahnhof
Münchenerstr.
Unterman.
Brücke
Haupt-
bahnhof
Gutleutstr.
Wilhelm Leuschner Str.
Untermainkai
Mannheimerstr.
Baseler
Pl.
Main
Friedens
Brücke
Schaumainkai

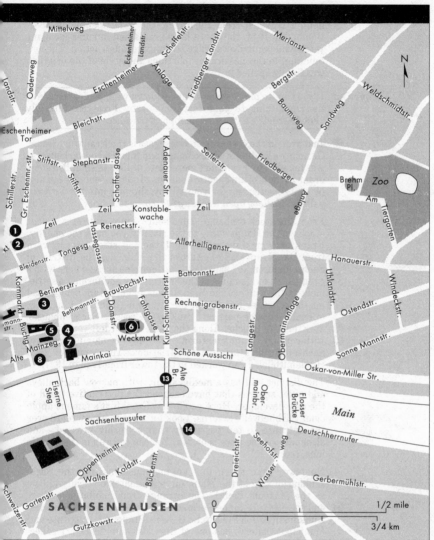

Mittelweg

Eckenheimer Landstr.

Scheffelstr.

Friedberger Landstr.

Merianstr.

Oederweg

Eschenheimer Anlage

Bergstr.

Baumweg

Sandweg

Weldschmidtstr.

Landstr.

Bleichstr.

Eschenheimer Tor

Seilerstr.

Friedberger

Brehm Pl.

Zoo

Stiftstr.

Stephanstr.

Schaffer-gasse

K. Adenauer Str.

Anlage

Am Tiergarten

Schillerstr.

Gr. Eschenhr.-str.

Stiftstr.

Zeil

Konstable-wache

Zeil

Hanauerstr.

Windeckstr.

Zeil

Reineckstr.

Allerheiligenstr.

Uhlandstr.

Ostendstr.

Bleidenstr.

Tongesg.

Hassegasse

Battonnstr.

Obermainanlage

Sonne Mannstr.

Berlinerstr.

Braubachstr.

Rechneigrabenstr.

Langestr.

Kurt-Schumacherstr.

Oskar-von-Miller Str.

mann-str.

Buchg.

Bethmannstr.

Domstr.

Fahrgasse

Weckmarkt

Mainzeg.

Alte

Mainkai

Schöne Aussicht

Alte Br.

Ober-mainbr.

Flosser Brücke

Main

Eiserne Steg

Sachsenhausufer

Deutschherrnufer

Dreieichstr.

Seehofstr.

Wasser weg

Oppenheimstr.

Walter

Koldstr.

Bückenstr.

Gerbermühlstr.

Schweizerstr.

Gartenstr.

SACHSENHAUSEN

Gutzkowstr.

0   1/2 mile

0   3/4 km

they were given priority for the best seats), and Kaiser Wilhelm I traveled from Berlin for the gala opening in 1880. Bombed in 1944, the opera house remained in ruins for many years while controversy raged over its reconstruction. The new building, in the classical proportions and style of the original, was finally opened in 1981.

Time Out   If you think a picnic lunch would go down well, you're certain to find something to your taste in nearby **Fressgass** (literally "Food Street"), a gourmet shopper's paradise.

⑫   Just around the corner from Fressgass is the Frankfurt **Börse**, Germany's leading stock exchange and financial powerhouse. It was founded by Frankfurt merchants in 1558 to establish some order in their often chaotic dealings. Today's dealings can also be quite hectic; see for yourself by slipping into the visitors' gallery. *Gallery open weekdays 11:30–1:30.*

From the stock exchange, turn south again and retrace your steps via the Hauptwache to the river (if you have the energy, Frankfurt's main shopping street, the **Zeil**, stretches eastward from the Hauptwache). Across the Main lies the district of **Sachsenhausen**. It's said that Charlemagne arrived here with a group of Saxon families in the 8th century and formed a settlement on the banks of the Main. It was an important bridgehead for the crusader Knights of the Teutonic Order, and, in 1318, officially became part of Frankfurt. Cross to Sachsenhausen
⑬   over the **Alte Brücke**. Along the bank to your left you'll see the
⑭   15th-century **Kuhhirtenturm**, the only remaining part of Sachsenhausen's original fortifications. The composer Paul Hindemith lived and worked in the tower from 1923 to 1927.

The district still has a medieval air, with narrow back alleys and quiet squares that have escaped the destructive tread of the city developer. Here you'll find Frankfurt's famous apple cider ("Ebbelwei") taverns. Look for a green pine wreath over the entrance to tell passersby that a freshly pressed—and alcoholic—apple juice is on tap. You can eat well in these little inns, too.

No fewer than seven top-ranking museums line the Sachsenhausen side of the Main, on **Schaumainkai** (locally known as the Museum Bank). These range from exhibitions of art
⑮   and architecture to the German Film Museum. The **Städelsches Kunstinstitut und Städtische Galerie** (Städel Art Institute and Municipal Gallery) has one of the most significant art collections in Germany, with fine examples of Flemish, German, and Italian old masters, plus a sprinkling of French Impressionists. *Schaumainkai 63. Admission: DM 2. Open Tues.–Sun. 10–5 (Wed. until 8); closed Mon.*

Dining

Several Frankfurt restaurants close for the school summer vacation break, a six-week period that falls between mid-June and mid-September. Always check to avoid disappointment.

For details and price category definitions, *see* Dining in Essential Information.

Expensive   **Brückenkeller.** "Keller" is German for cellar, and that's where the Brückenkeller is situated, underground but above reproach. The ancient vaulted interior (the restaurant has been in business since 1652) is set off by carefully selected antiques. The wine-list choice of 180 different labels is supported by an extraordinary stock of 85,000 bottles. Ask for a look at the wine cellar—and ask, too, for *Tafelspitz* (a version of pot roast) with *grüner* sauce. *Schützenstr. 6, tel. 069/284238. Jacket and tie. Reservations handy. AE, DC, MC, V. Dinner only. Closed Sun. and 3 weeks in July.*

Gourmet. The restaurant of the Hotel Gravenbruch Kempinski is a 7-mile (11-kilometer) drive to the southern suburb of Neu Isenburg, but this is no hindrance to the regulars who say its style and quality are hard to match. The extensive menu is French nouvelle, which complements the restaurant's subdued French decor. *Hotel Gravenbruch Kempinski, 6078 Neu Isenburg 2, tel. 06102/5050. Jacket and tie. Reservations necessary. AE, DC, MC, V. Dinner only. Closed weekends and summer school vacation.*

Gutsschanke Neuhof. About 8 miles (13 kilometers) south of Frankfurt (take the A661 to the Dreieich exit), Gutsschanke Neuhof is part of a country estate. Sheep graze within sight of the elegant dining room, which offers an eclectic mix of German and international dishes. The estate farm supplies the restaurant with home-cured meats, which can be bought and taken home as well as ordered from the extensive menu. *6072 Dreieich-Götzenhain, tel. 06102/3214. Jacket and tie. Reservations advised. AE, DC, MC, V.*

Humperdinck. The nouvelle dishes of chef Willi Tetz depend on what he finds in the market each morning; everything, from salads to soup, is of guaranteed freshness. Engelbert Humperdinck—the 19th-century composer *(Hänsel und Gretel)*, not the ruffle-shirted crony of Tom Jones and Andy Williams—used to live and work in the Grüneburg house it occupies. *Grüneburgweg 95, tel. 069/722122. Jacket and tie. Reservations advised. AE, DC, MC, V. Closed Sat. lunch, Sun., and summer school vacation.*

Moderate **Bistrot 77.** Mainly Alsatian specialties are served at this bright,
★ light, and cheerful French restaurant in Sachsenhausen. Ask chef/owner Dominique Mosbach for her advice on what to order, and you won't go wrong. *Ziegelhüttenweg 1–3, tel. 069/614040. Dress: casual. Reservations accepted. AE, DC, MC, V. Closed Sat. lunch, Sun., and mid-June–mid-July.*

Börsenkeller. French dishes dominate the menu of this centrally located eatery, which is on a pedestrian-only street close to the stock exchange. *Schillerstr. 11, tel. 069/281115. Dress: casual. Reservations accepted. AE, DC, MC, V. Closed Sun.*

Casa Nova. The inviting exterior is fully matched by the cozy interior of this superior Italian restaurant, in an attractive Sachsenhausen house. Fish is prepared with imagination and skill, and if the pasta proves too plentiful, half-portions are willingly served. *Stresemannallee 38, tel. 069/632473. Dress: casual. Weekend reservations essential. MC. Closed Sat. and 2 weeks in Aug.*

Inexpensive **Atschel.** A blackboard announces specialties of the day at this former apple-cider tavern in Sachsenhausen. If fish soup is chalked up, you're in luck—it's delicious. Atschel is not for the shy. Expect to eat at one of the long tables that retain the tavern style of this friendly restaurant. *Wallstr. 7, tel. 069/619201. Dress: casual. Reservations not needed. No credit cards. Closed until 6 PM and Mon.*

★ **Zum Gemalten Haus.** This is the real thing, a traditional wine tavern in the heart of Sachsenhausen. Its name means "At the Painted House," a reference to the frescoes that cover the place inside and out. In the summer and on fine spring and autumn days, the courtyard is the place to be (the inner rooms can get a bit crowded). But if you can't at first find a place at one of the bench-lined long tables, order an apple cider and hang around until someone leaves: It's worth the wait. *Schweizerstr. 67, tel. 069/614559. Dress: casual. Reservations not needed. No credit cards. Closed Mon. and Tues.*

Zur Eulenburg. Take the subway or a streetcar to Seckbacher Landstrasse, in the district of Bornheim, to visit this popular apple-cider tavern. You'd better be hungry, though: portions are on the caveman side. Meat dishes cram the menu—try the Frankfurt-style *Rippchen* (ribs). *Eulengasse 46, tel. 069/451203. Dress: casual. Reservations not needed. No credit cards. Dinner only. Closed Mon. and Tues.*

Zum Rad. Another apple-cider tavern serving inexpensive but tasty local dishes is the 19th-century Zum Rad, in the picturesque village of Seckbach on the outskirts of Frankfurt (take the subway line 4 to Seckbacher Landstrasse and then bus No. 43 or 12). In summer and on fine spring and autumn days, the tree-shaded courtyard is a delight. *Leonhardtsgasse 2, tel. 069/479128. Dress: casual. Reservations not needed. No credit cards. Closed lunch.*

Lodging

For details and price category definitions, *see* Lodging in Essential Information.

Very Expensive **Gravenbruch Kempinski.** A spacious, elegant hotel, Graven-
★ bruch Kempinski retains the atmosphere of the manor house that once stood on its parkland site in leafy Neu Isenburg (a 15-minute drive south of Frankfurt). Some of its luxuriously appointed rooms and suites are arranged as duplex penthouse apartments. Make sure you get a room overlooking the lake. *6078 Neu Isenburg 2, tel. 06102/5050. 317 rooms with bath. Facilities: restaurant, indoor and outdoor pools, tennis, health spa, hairdresser, Lufthansa check-in service, limo service to airport and city (both 15 minutes away). AE, DC, MC, V.*

Hessischer Hof. This former palace is still owned by a prince of Hesse, and fine antiques are deftly positioned in many guest rooms. A daily supply of fresh fruit delivered to all rooms is part of the outstanding service. One of the two bars, Jimmy's, numbers among Frankfurt's best, and the hotel restaurant is highly prized both for its gourmet cuisine and refined ambience (the fine Sèvres porcelain display is a particularly elegant touch). *Friedrich-Ebert-Anlage 40, tel. 069/75400. 167 rooms with bath. Facilities: restaurant, 2 bars. AE, DC, MC, V.*

Steigenberger Hotel Frankfurter Hof. The presidential suite here is as spacious as a house, while the other guest rooms and suites are by no means cramped. All are impeccably furnished in teak and cherry wood. A majestic building in true "grande dame" style, the hotel stands in the downtown area. *Am Kaiserplatz 17, tel. 069/20251. 359 rooms with bath. Facilities: restaurant, shopping arcade. AE, DC, MC, V.*

Expensive **Palmenhof.** The city's West end houses this turn-of-the-century hotel that has recently been renovated to a very high standard.

In the basement is a cozy restaurant, the Bastei, which has an expensive nouvelle menu. *Bockenheimer Landstr. 89–91, tel. 069/7530060. 50 rooms with bath. Facilities: restaurant. AE, DC, MC, V.*

Moderate **Arcade.** The modern Arcade is situated on the north bank of the Main river, just 5 minutes' walk from the train station. Rooms are furnished basically, though all have TV, and 2 are specially equipped for disabled guests. *Speicherstr. 3–5, tel. 069/273030. 193 rooms with bath. Facilities: restaurant, bar. MC, V.*

Liebig. A comfortable, family-run hotel, the Liebig has spacious, high-ceilinged rooms and a friendly feel. Be sure to ask for a room at the back—they're much quieter. The Weinstube restaurant serves an excellent Hessen wine. *Liebigstr. 45, tel. 069/727551. 20 rooms with bath. Facilities: restaurant. DC, MC, V.*

★ **Maingau.** This excellent-value hotel is in the city's Sachsenhausen district, within easy reach of the downtown area and just a stone's throw from the lively Altstadt quarter, with its cheery apple-cider taverns. Rooms are spartanly furnished, though clean and comfortable, and some even have TV. *Schifferstr. 38–40, tel. 069/617001. 100 rooms with bath. Facilities: restaurant. AE, MC.*

Neue Kräme. This small, friendly hotel is located on a pedestrians-only street right in the downtown area, so along with being very central to most of the sights, shops, and restaurants, it has the additional plus of being exceptionally quiet. Rooms are basic, but all have TV and minibar. There's no restaurant, but drinks and snacks are available. *Neue Kräme 23, tel. 069/284046. 21 rooms with bath. AE, DC, MC, V.*

Inexpensive **Diana.** A pleasant residential area is the location of this family-run pension, convenient both for the Frankfurt fairground and the downtown area. *Westendstr. 83, tel. 069/747007. 29 rooms, 9 with bath. AE, DC, MC, V.*

Pension Uebe. This one occupies the top three floors of an office building on a street favored with some excellent restaurants. The elevator stops at the fourth floor, though by walking up just one extra flight of steps, you'll find yourself on the top floor, whose rooms are cozily and atmospherically set under the inclined eaves. *Grüneburgweg 3, tel. 069/591209. 18 rooms with bath. AE, DC, MC, V.*

Hamburg

Arriving and Departing

By Plane Hamburg's international airport, **Fuhlsbüttel,** is seven miles (11 kilometers) northwest of the city. Lufthansa flights connect Hamburg with all other major German cities.

Between the Airport and Downtown A bus service between Hamburg's central bus station and the airport (stopping also at the hotels Atlantic and Plaza and the Schauspielhaus Theater) operates daily at 20-minute intervals between 5:15 AM and 9:30 PM. The first bus leaves the airport for the city at 6:30 AM. It takes about 25 minutes. One-way fare, including luggage, is DM 7. There is also an **Airport Express** bus, No. 110, which runs between the airport and the Ohlsdorf S-Bahn (suburban line) and U-Bahn (subway) station. The fare is DM 2.80. **Taxi** fare from the airport to the downtown area is about DM 25. By **rented car,** follow the signs to "Stadtmitte" (Downtown), which appear immediately outside the airport area.

By Train Hamburg is a terminus for mainline services to northern Germany; trains to Schleswig-Holstein and Scandinavia also stop here. There are two principal stations: the main train station **(Hauptbahnhof)** and **Hamburg-Altona.** Euro-City and Inter-City services connect Hamburg with all German cities and the European rail network. For train information, tel. 040/339911.

By Bus Hamburg's bus station, the **Zentral-Omnibus-Bahnhof,** is in Adenauerallee, behind the Hauptbahnhof. For tickets and information, contact the **Deutsche Touring Gesellschaft** (Am Romerhof 17, 6000 Frankfurt/Main, tel. 069/79030).

By Car Hamburg has proportionately fewer cars than most other German cities and an urban road system that is the envy of many of them. Incoming autobahns end at one of Hamburg's three beltways, which then connect easily with the downtown area ("Stadtmitte").

Getting Around

By Public Transportation The comprehensive city and suburban transportation system includes a subway network (U-Bahn), which connects efficiently with S-Bahn (suburban) lines, and an exemplary bus service. Tickets cover travel by all three, as well as by harbor ferry. A ticket costs DM 1.70 and can be bought at the automatic machines found in all stations and most bus stops. A 24-hour ticket for the central city zone costs DM 7 (free for children under 12). A 24-hour ticket covering the entire Hamburg urban area is DM 13 (under-12s free). The all-night buses (Nos. 600–640) tour the downtown area, leaving the Rathausmarkt and the Hauptbahnhof every hour. Information can be obtained from the **Hamburg Passenger Transport Board** (HHV), tel. 040/322911.

By Taxi Taxi meters start at DM 3, and the fare is DM 1.60 per kilometer (or about DM 2.55 per mile), plus 50 pfennigs for each piece of heavy luggage. To order a taxi, phone 040/441011, 040/656211, or 040/682001.

Guided Tours

Orientation Tours Bus tours of the city, with an English-speaking guide, leave from Kirchenallee (across from the Hotel Europäischer Hof and next to the Hauptbahnhof) at 11 and 3, from late March until the end of October, and at 2 during the winter months. The two-hour tour costs DM 18 for adults, DM 9 for children. A 2½-hour tour, taking in more of the city, starts at 10 and 2 daily from the same place. The fare is DM 22 for adults, DM 11 for children. A night tour of the city sets off from the Kirchenallee at 8 and returns shortly after midnight. The fare of DM 80 includes a drink at each stop and a short boat ride.

Boat Tours Hamburg is a city dominated by water, and one of the best ways of getting a feel of the place is by taking one of the many boat trips offered. From mid-March through November, tours of the harbor (with English-speaking guides) start twice a day (11:15 and 3:15) from pier 1 on the Landungsbrücken; the one-hour tour costs DM 11 for adults, DM 5.50 for children. During the winter months, tours with an English-speaking guide can be organized in advance (tel. 040/564523).

From Easter to Christmas, you can combine a nighttime cruise on the harbor, a lavish buffet, and a shuffle around the dance floor of the party boat, which leaves the HADAG pavilion on the Landungsbrücken every evening at 8 (tel. 040/313687). Cost is about DM 50.

Cruises of the Binnenalster and Aussenalster leave from the Jungfernstieg every half hour between 10 and 6, April through October. The fare is DM 9 for adults, DM 4 for children. A tour including canals leaves every 40 minutes (DM 15 and DM 7, respectively). For information, tel. 040/341141.

For general information on boat tours of Hamburg, phone 040/2201201.

Excursions Bus tours of the surrounding countryside are offered by **Jasper-Reisebüro** (Colonnaden 72, tel. 040/343751).

Tourist Information

The principal Hamburg tourist office is at Bieberhaus, Hachmannplatz, near the Hauptbahnhof. It's open weekdays from 7:30 to 6, Saturday from 7:30 until 3 (tel. 040/248700). There's also a tourist information center inside the Hauptbahnhof itself (open daily from 7 AM to 11 PM, tel. 040/24870240) and in the arrivals hall of Hamburg Airport (open daily from 8 AM to 11 PM, tel. 040/24870240). The last two centers will reserve hotel accommodations. **Hafen Tip** (at the St. Pauli-Landungsbrücken, tel. 040/313977) provides information about the harbor and sells cruise tickets. It's open weekdays 9–6.

Exploring Hamburg

The comparison that Germans like to draw between Hamburg and Venice is—like all such comparisons with the *Serenissima*—somewhat exaggerated. Nevertheless, Hamburg is, like Venice, a city on water: the great river Elbe, which flows into the North Sea; the small river Alster, which has been dammed to form two lakes, the Binnenalster and Aussenalster; and many canals. Once a leading member of the Hanseatic League of cities, which dominated trade on the North Sea and the Baltic during the Middle Ages, Hamburg is still a major port, with 33 individual docks and 500 berths for oceangoing vessels.

Apart from its aquatic aspects, the most striking thing about Hamburg is its contradictions. Within the remaining traces of its old city walls, Hamburg combines the seamiest, steamiest streets of dockland Europe with the sleekest avenues to be found anywhere between Biarritz and Stockholm. During World War II and afterward, Hamburg was wrecked from without and within—by fire, then by Allied bombing raids, and finally by philistine town planners, who tore down some of the remaining old buildings to make way for modernistic glass-and-steel boxes. The result is a city that is, in parts, ugly, but still a fascinating mixture of old and new.

It is also a city in which escaping the urban bustle is relatively easy, since it contains more than 500 miles (800 kilometers) of riverside and country paths within its boundaries. The follow-

Hamburg

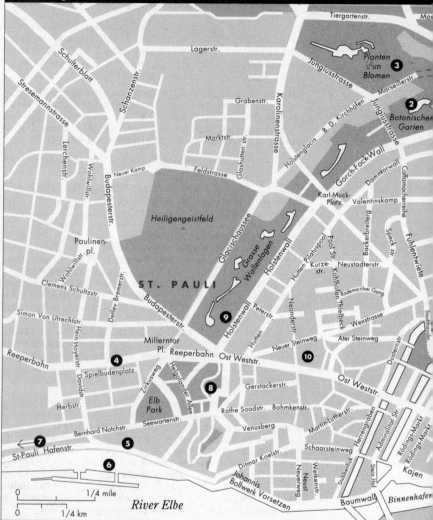

Schulterblatt
Stresemannstrasse
Lagerstr.
Schanzenstr.
Lerchenstr.
Wohlwillstr.
Neuer Kamp
Budapesterstr.
Grabenstr.
Marktstr.
Feldstrasse
Glashütten str.
Karolinenstrasse
Holstenglacis
B. D. Kirchhöfen
Tiergartenstr.
Mo
Jungiusstrasse
Planten un Blomen
Marseillerstr.
Jungiusstrasse
Botanischer Garten
Gorch-Fock-Wall
Dammtorwall
Caffamachereihe
Karl-Muck-Platz
Valentinskamp
Speck str.
Fuhlentwiete
Heiligengeistfeld
Paulinen-pl.
Wohlwillstr.
Clemens Schultzstr.
Simon Von Utrechtstr.
Hein Hoyerstr.
Davidstr.
Detlev Bremerstr.
Budapesterstr.
ST. PAULI
Glacischaussee
Grasse Wallenlagen
Holstenwall
Holstenwall
Peterstr.
Hütten
Pilatuspool
Kurze-str.
Neustadterstr.
Kohlhöfen
Bäckerbreitergang
Neander str.
Rademacher Gang
Thielbeck
Wexstrasse
Alter Steinweg
Neuer Steinweg
Düsternstr.
Stadthausb.
Reeperbahn
Spielbudenplatz
Millerntor Pl. Reeperbahn
Ost Weststr.
Ost Weststr.
Herbstr.
Zirkusweg
Elb Park
Helgoländer Allee
Gerstackerstr.
Rothe Soodstr.
Bohmkenstr.
Venusberg
Martin-Lutherstr.
Herrengraben
Admiralität Str.
Rödings-Markt
Rödings-Markt
Bernhard Notchstr.
Seewartenstr.
Ditmar Koelstr.
Schaarsteinweg
Stubbenhuk
Stein Hof
Kajen
St-Pauli Hafenstr.
Johannis Bollwerk Vorsetzen
Neust Neuerweg
Werkenstr.
Baumwall
Binnenhafen

River Elbe

1/4 mile

1/4 km

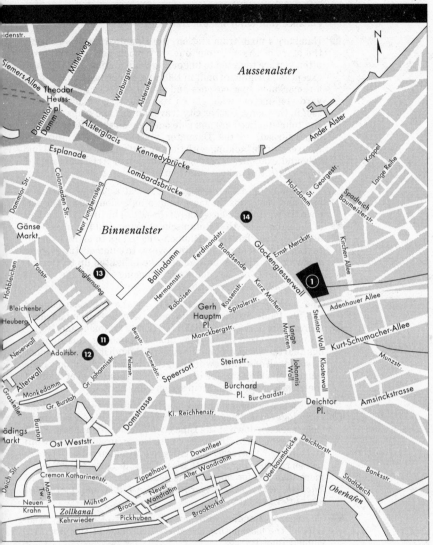

N

Aussenalster

idenstr.

Siemers Allee
Theodor
Heuss-
pl.

Mittelweg

Warburgstr.

Alsterufer

Dammtor Damm

Alsterglacis

Kennedybrücke

Ander Alster

Koppel

Lange Reihe

Esplanade

Lombardsbrücke

Spadteich
Baumeisterstr.

Dammtor Str.

Colonnaden Str.

Neuer Jungfernstieg

Binnenalster

Holzdamm

St. Georgstr.

Ernst Merckstr.

Kirchen Allee

Gänse
Markt.

14

Glockengiesserwall

1

Höhbleichen

Poststr.

Jungfernstieg

13

Ballindamm

Hermannstr.

Raboisen

Ferdinandstr.

Brandsende

Kurz Murhen

Adenauer Allee

Steintor Wall

Bleichenbr.

Heuberg.

Neuerwall

Adolfsbr.

11

12

Gerh
Hauptm
Pl.
Monckbergstr.

Rossenstr.

Spitalerstr.

Lange
Murhen

Kurt-Schumacher-Allee

Johannis
Wall

Munzstr.

Alterwall

Monkedamm

Bergstr.

Gr. Johannistr.

Pelzerstr.

Schmiedstr.

Speersort

Steinstr.

Amsinckstrasse

Grasteller

Burstah

Gr. Burstah

Domstrasse

Kl. Reichenstr.

Burchard
Pl.
Burchardstr.

Klosterwall

Deichtor
Pl.

ödings
Markt

Ost Weststr.

Dovenfleet

Deichtorstr.

Deich Str.

Marten
Tw.

Cremon Katharinenstr.

Mühren

Zippelhaus

Neuer
Wandrahm

Brook

Alter Wandrahm

Oberbaumbrücke

Banksstr.

Stadtdeich

Oberhafen

Neuen
Krahn

Zollkanal
Kehrwieder

Pickhuben

Brocktortal

ing itinerary includes a few detours, some by boat, which will enhance your enjoyment of Hamburg.

❶ Hamburg's main train station, the **Hauptbahnhof,** is not only the start of the city tour but very much part of it. It's not often you are tempted to linger at a train station, but this is an exception. Originally built in 1906 and modernized since, it has a remarkable spaciousness and sweep, accentuated by a 160-yard (146-meter) wide glazed roof, the largest unsupported roof in Germany. Gather city travel guides and maps from the city tourist office here and ride one stop on the S-Bahn (suburban railroad) to the Dammtor station. Compare this Art Nouveau-style building with the one you've just left. You'll find splendid examples of Germany's version of Art Nouveau, the *Jugendstil,* throughout your tour of Hamburg.

The Dammtor station brings you out at a narrow stretch of parkland that runs for more than a mile alongside what was once the western defense wall of the city. The first two sections
❷ of the park—the **Alter Botanischer Garten** (Old Botanical Gar-
❸ den) and the **Planten un Blomen**—have lots to attract the attention of gardeners and flower lovers. In summer, the evening sky over the Planten un Blomen lake is lighted up by the colored waters of its fountain, dancing what the locals romantically call a "water ballet."

The park is interrupted abruptly by the northern edge of the **St. Pauli** district and its most famous—or infamous—
❹ thoroughfare, the **Reeperbahn** *(see* Entertainment and Nightlife). Unlike other business sections of Hamburg, this industrious quarter works around the clock; although it may seem quiet as you stroll down its tawdry length in broad daylight, any male tourist who stops at one of its bars will discover that many of the girls who work this strip are on a day shift.

If it's a Sunday morning, join the St. Pauli late revelers and the
❺ early joggers and dog walkers for breakfast at the **Fischmarkt** (fish market), down at the Elbe riverside between the St. Pauli Landungsbrücken (the piers where the excursion boats tie up) and Grosse Elbstrasse. The citizens of Hamburg like to breakfast on raw herring, but if that's not to your taste, there's much more than fish for sale, and the nearby bars are already open. *The fish market is held every Sun., 5 AM–9:30 AM, starting an hour later in winter.*

❻ The nearby **Landungsbrücken** is the start of the many boat trips of the harbor that are offered throughout the year *(see* Guided Tours).

Along the north bank of the Elbe is one of the finest walks Hamburg has to offer. The walk is a long one, about eight miles (13 kilometers) from the St. Pauli Landungsbrücken to the at-
❼ tractive waterside village of **Blankenese,** and that's only three-quarters of the route. But there are S-Bahn stations and bus stops along the way, to give you a speedy return to the downtown area. Do, however, try to reach Blankenese, even if you have to catch an S-Bahn train from downtown to Blankenese station and walk down to the riverbank from there.

Blankenese is another of Hamburg's surprises—a city suburb that has the character of a fishing village. If you've walked all the way from St. Pauli, you may not be able to face the 58 flights of stairs (nearly 5,000 individual steps) that crisscross through

Blankenese between its heights and the river. But by all means attempt an exploratory prowl through some of the tiny lanes, lined with the retirement retreats of Hamburg's sea captains and the cottages of the fishermen who once toiled here.

Time Out For a fine view and fine refreshment to accompany it, stop in at **Sägebiel's Fährhaus,** a former farmhouse, where Kaiser Wilhelm once celebrated his birthday. If you're lunching, fish is the natural choice. *Blankenese Hauptstr. 107, tel. 040/861514.*

A ferry connects Blankenese with Hamburg's St. Pauli, although the S-Bahn ride back to the city is much quicker. Back at St. Pauli, resume your tour at the riverside and head back toward the downtown area through the park at the side of the Helgolander Allee, to the **Bismarck Memorial**—an imposing statue of the Prussian "Iron Chancellor," the guiding spirit of the 19th-century unification of Germany. Cross the square ahead of you and make for the **Museum für Hamburgische Geschichte** at Holstenwall 24. This fascinating display of Hamburg's history has a feature of great interest to American descendants of German immigrants, who can arrange to have called up from the microfilm files information about any ancestors who set out for the New World from Hamburg. *Holstenwall 24, tel. 040/30050050. Admission: DM 2 adults, 70 pf. children. Open Tues.–Sat. 10–1 and 2–5.*

Cross Holstenwall to Peterstrasse, where you'll find a group of finely restored, 18th-century half-timbered houses. Turn right down Neanderstrasse and cross Ost-West-strasse to Hamburg's principal Protestant church, **St. Michaelis,** decorated in a florid Baroque style. Twice in its history, this well-loved 17th-century church has given the people of Hamburg protection—during the Thirty Years' War and again in World War II. From its 440-foot (134-meter) tower, there is a magnificent view of the city and the Elbe, and twice a day the watchman blows a trumpet solo from up there. *Cost for the elevator up to the tower: DM 2.50 adults, DM 1.50 children.*

From St. Michaelis, recross Ost-West-strasse and turn left down Brunnenstrasse to Wexstrasse. At the end of Wexstrasse, cross the Bleichenbrücke and Adolphsbrücke bridges, over two of Hamburg's canals (known as the Fleete), turn left into Alter Wall, and you'll come to the **Rathausmarkt,** the town hall square. The designers of the square deliberately set out to create a northern version of the Piazza San Marco in Venice and, to a certain extent, succeeded. The 100-year-old **Rathaus** is built on 4,000 wooden piles sunk into the marshy ground beneath. It is the home not only of the city council but of the Hamburg state government, for Hamburg is one of West Germany's federal, semiautonomous states. The sheer opulence of its interior is hard to beat. Although visitors can tour only the state rooms, the tapestries, huge staircases, glittering chandeliers, coffered ceilings, and gilt-framed portraits convey forcefully the wealth of the city in the last century and give a rich insight into bombastic municipal taste. *Marktplatz. Admission: DM 1. Guided tours weekdays every hour from 10:15 to 3:15; weekends 10:15–1:15.*

If you've had enough sightseeing by this time, you've ended up at the right place, for an arcade at the western edge of the Rathausmarkt signals the start of Europe's largest undercover **shopping area,** nearly a mile of airy arcades, cool in summer and warm in winter, bursting with color and life. Three hundred shops, from cheap souvenir stores to expensive fashion boutiques, are crammed into this consumer-age labyrinth. There are expensive restaurants and cozy cafés, and one of the rare opportunities in Germany (or anywhere) to eat lobster and sip good wine at a fast-food outlet. It's easy to get lost here, but all the arcades lead at some point to the wide, seasidelike promenade, the **Jungfernstieg,** which borders Hamburg's two artificial lakes, the **Binnenalster** and the **Aussenalster.** Although called lakes, they are really dammed up sections of the Alster River, which rises only 35 miles (56 kilometers) away in Schleswig Holstein. The river was originally dammed up at the beginning of the 13th century to form a millrace before it spilled into the Elbe. The original muddy dam wall is today the elegant Jungfernstieg promenade. From the Jungfernstieg, you can take a boat tour of the two Alster lakes and the canals beyond *(see* Guided Tours), passing some of Hamburg's most ostentatious homes, with their extensive grounds rolling down to the water's edge (the locals call it "Millionaires' Coast").

Hamburg has its share of millionaires, enriched by the city's thriving commerce and industry. But they, in turn, can claim to have enriched the artistic life of Hamburg. For example, it was a group of wealthy merchants who, in 1817, founded the Kunstverein, from which grew Hamburg's famous Kunsthalle collection. The **Kunsthalle** is well placed at the end of our Hamburg tour, next to the Hauptbahnhof, and its collection of paintings is one of Germany's finest. You'll find works by practically all the great northern European masters from the 14th to the 20th centuries, as well as by painters such as Goya, Tiepolo, and Canaletto. For many visitors, the highlight of the entire collection is the *Grabow Altarpiece,* painted in 1379 by an artist known only as Master Bertram; the central scene is the Crucifixion, but numerous side panels depict the story of man from genesis to the nativity. *1 Glockengiesserwall, tel. 040/248251. Admission: adults DM 4, children DM 1. Open Tues.–Sun. 10–5, closed Mon.*

Dining

For details and price category definitions, *see* Dining in Essential Information.

Expensive   **L'Auberge Française.** Generally regarded as Hamburg's most authentic French restaurant, L'Auberge Française specializes in traditional seafood dishes and fine wines. *Rutschbahn 34, tel. 040/4102532. Jacket and tie. Reservations required. DC, MC, V. Closed weekends in summer.*

Landhaus Dill. Situated in a former coaching inn on the road to Blankenese *(see* Exploring), Landhaus Dill is an informal restaurant with an imaginative and varied menu. In summer, specialties include lobster salad, prepared at your table; in fall, wild duck with port wine sauce. *Elbchaussee 404, tel. 040/828443. Jacket and tie. Reservations advised. AE, DC, MC, V. Closed Mon.*

Landhaus Scherrer. A popular, country house-style restaurant located in the city's Altona district, Landhaus Scherrer specializes in fine regional cuisine and prides itself on its extensive wine list. It offers a separate bistro for lunches. *Elbchaussee 130, tel. 040/8801325. Reservations required. AE, DC, MC. Closed Sun.*

La Mer. Located in the elegant Hotel Prem, on the southwest bank of the Aussenalster, La Mer offers a fine and varied menu. Chef Rainer Wolter, Germany's 1986 New Chef of the Year, serves a host of sumptuous specialties. Try the marinated inoki mushrooms with imperial oysters and salmon roe or the spring venison with elderberry sauce. *An der Alster 9, tel. 040/241726. Jacket and tie. Reservations advised. AE, DC, MC, V. Closed Sat. and Sun. lunch.*

Peter Lembcke. This formal, traditional restaurant offers the best of German cuisine. The imaginative menu features such Hamburg delicacies as eel soup and *Rote Grütze*, a melange of sweet and sour berries. Steaks are another specialty. *Holzdamm 49, tel. 040/243290. Jacket and tie. Reservations advised. AE, DC, MC. Closed Sun.*

Moderate   **Ahrberg.** Located on the river in Blankenese, the Ahrberg has a pleasant terrace for summer dining, and, for a warm retreat on cooler days, a cozy, wood-paneled dining room. The menu features a range of traditional German dishes and seafood specialties—often served together. Try the shrimp and potato soup and fresh carp in season. *Strandweg 33, tel. 040/860438. Jacket and tie. Reservations advised. AE, DC, MC.*

★ **Le Château.** Visitors to this traditional French restaurant, located in a modernized, 19th-century mansion in fashionable Poseldorf, can enjoy cuisine prepared by a former chef at Maxim's in Paris—for a fraction of the price. *Milchstrasse 19, tel. 040/444200. Jacket and tie. Reservations advised. Closed Sat. and Sun. lunch.*

Il Giardino. With its attractive courtyard-garden, Il Giardino is a pleasant setting for low-key summer dining. The menu offers a combination of Italian and nouvelle cuisine and an extensive wine list. *Ulmenstrasse 17–19, tel. 040/470147. Jacket and tie. Reservations advised. AE, MC, V. Closed lunchtime.*

Tre Fontane. At this fine Italian restaurant, the lady of the house prepares all the dishes herself, and she and her husband are happy to advise guests on the specials of the day. Be prepared for heaping portions. *Mundsburger Damm 45, tel. 040/223193. Dress: casual. Reservations advised. No credit cards. Closed Tues.*

Inexpensive   **At Nali.** This is one of Hamburg's oldest and most popular Turkish restaurants. It is friendly and comfortable and offers a very reasonable and extensive menu. It stays open late—until 2 AM. *Rutschbahn 11, tel. 040/4103810. Dress: casual. Reservations advised. AE, DC, MC, V.*

Avocado. This popular, modern restaurant offers excellent value and an imaginative menu. Try the salmon in Chablis. *Kanalstr. 9, tel. 040/2204599. Dress: casual. Reservations required. No credit cards. Closed Sun. and lunchtime.*

Lodging

For details and price category definitions, *see* Lodging in Essential Information.

Very Expensive   **Atlantic.** Since it first opened in 1909, the luxuriously appointed Atlantic has been a focal point of the Hamburg social scene. Two restaurants offer a choice between haute cuisine and traditional German fare. *An der Alster 72, tel. 040/28880. 265 rooms with bath. Facilities: rooftop pool, nightclub, bar, beer tavern, Lufthansa check-in desk. AE, DC, MC, V.*

Intercontinental. With its attractive lakeside setting, the Intercontinental offers superb city views. It is also known for its first-class service and amenities. A rooftop restaurant serves fine French cuisine. *Fotenay 10, tel. 040/414150. 600 rooms, all with bath. Facilities: pool, massage room, sauna, shops. DC, MC, V.*

Vier Jahreszeiten. This hotel, with its antique-style rooms, impeccable service, and excellent food, is rated among the world's best. It is currently being remodeled to increase the size of the rooms. Centrally located, it offers scenic views of the Binnenalster. An attractive, wood-paneled lounge provides a welcome haven for weary sightseers. *Neuer Jungfernstieg 9–14, tel. 040/34941. 150 rooms with bath. Facilities: two restaurants, nightclub, patisserie, farm. AE, DC, MC, V.*

Expensive **Abtei.** Located on a quiet, tree-lined street near the Alster lakeside park, the Abtei occupies an elegant period house with a tea salon and pretty garden. *Abteistr. 14, tel. 040/345-7565. 14 rooms with bath. AE, DC, MC, V.*

Aussen Alster. Only 7 minutes from the train station and 50 yards (46 meters) from the Alster Lake, the Aussen Alster is a small, tranquil hotel occupying a gracious 19th-century house. Many of the rooms have balconies with scenic views. Bicycles and sailboats stand ready for sporting guests, and the hotel will even provide tracksuits for joggers. *Schmilinskystr. 1, tel. 040/241557. 27 rooms with bath. Facilities: sauna, solarium. AE, DC, MC, V.*

Moderate **Baseler Hospiz.** Centrally located near the inner lake and the State Opera House, the Baseler Hospiz offers friendly and efficient service and neatly furnished rooms. There is no charge for children under 10 sharing a room with parents. *Esplanade 11, tel. 040/341921. 160 rooms, most with bath. Facilities: restaurant, meeting rooms. AE, DC, MC, V.*

Steen's. This is a small, intimate hotel decorated in a light, airy Scandinavian style. It is conveniently located, close to the main train station. Guests enjoy breakfast in a pleasant garden. *Holzdamm 43, tel. 040/244642. 11 rooms with bath. AE, MC.*

Wedina. This is a somewhat old-fashioned but comfortable hotel. It has a bar, pool, sauna, and garden but no restaurant. *Gurlittstr. 23, tel. 040/243011. 23 rooms, most with bath. AE, DC, MC, V. Closed Dec. 18–Jan. 1.*

Inexpensive **Alameda.** The Alameda offers guests good, basic accommodations. All rooms feature TV and radio. *Colonnaden 45, tel. 040/344290. 18 rooms with shower. AE, DC, MC, V.*

Metro Merkur. Centrally located near Hamburg's main train station, the recently renovated Metro Merkur is a convenient, functional hotel. There is no restaurant, but the bar offers a selection of evening snacks and warm dishes. *Bremer Reihe 12–14, tel. 040/247266. 109 rooms, most with bath. AE, DC, MC, V.*

Entertainment and Nightlife

Few visitors can resist taking a look at the Reeperbahn, if only by day. At night, however, from 10 onward, the place, really shakes itself into life, and *everything* is on sale. Among the Reeperbahn's even rougher side streets, the most notorious is the Grosse Freiheit, which means "a lot of freedom." A stroll through this small alley, where the attractions are on display behind plate glass, will either tempt you to stay or send you straight back to your hotel. Three of the leading clubs on the Grosse Freiheit are the **Colibri** (No. 34, tel. 040/313233), the **Safari** (No. 24, tel. 040/315400), and the **Salambo** (No. 11, tel. 040/315622).

A few tips for visiting the Reeperbahn: Avoid going alone; demand a price list whenever you drink, keep firm hold of it, and pay as soon as you're served; if you have trouble, threaten to call the cops. If that doesn't work—call the cops.

West Berlin

Arriving and Departing

By Plane Because of West Berlin's unique position in the heart of the foreign territory of the German Democratic Republic, the easiest way to arrive is by plane. Tegel Airport is centrally located, only four miles (seven kilometers) from downtown.

Between the Airport and Downtown An airport bus, city line No. 9, runs at 10-minute intervals between the airport and central Kurfürstendamm and Budapesterstrasse. The fare for the 40-minute trip is DM 2.20. The taxi fare runs between DM 15 and DM 20. If you've rented a car at the airport, the "Stadtautobahn" highway runs directly from the airport to the center.

By Train A transit visa is required for train travel to West Berlin; this is obtained on the train. The train service is run by the East German railways, called the Deutsche Reichsbahn, although half the rolling stock is West German. There are five rail crossing points from West Germany into East Germany, and the West Berlin terminus for all lines is the Bahnhof Zoologischer Garten (the Bahnhof Zoo), the main train station. The Bahnhof Zoo connects directly with the U-Bahn (subway) and S-Bahn (metropolitan railway) networks and the city bus system. For information or bookings in West Berlin, call the Deutsche Reichsbahn (030/313–3055 or 030/300–433).

By Bus Long-distance bus services connect West Berlin with all West German cities and, through the Europabus network, with the rest of Europe. A transit visa is issued at the border; have your passport ready. The city's bus station is at the corner of Masurenallee and Messedamm. For information, call 030/30882.

By Car The officially designated transit roads between West Germany and West Berlin must be strictly followed by drivers, and stops can be made only at clearly marked parking areas and service stations. There are four road-crossing points, and the necessary transit visa is obtained at the border before the driver from the west is allowed through. Western motorists must also produce a passport, driver's license, and car registration papers.

Getting Around

By Public Transportation West Berlin is surprisingly large, and only the center can comfortably be explored on foot. Fortunately, it is blessed with excellent public transportation, a combination of U-Bahn (subway) and S-Bahn (metropolitan train) lines, bus services, and even a ferry across the Wannsee lake. The eight U-Bahn lines alone have 116 stations. An all-night bus service (the buses are marked by the letter N next to their number) is also in operation. A ticket (DM 2.30, children DM 1.50) covers travel on the entire system. A multiple ticket, valid for five trips, costs DM 10.50 (children DM 6.50), but the best deal for visitors is the 24-hour inner-city ticket, costing DM 8 (children DM 5). A two-day ticket costs DM 16 (children DM 9.50) and a four-day ticket costs DM 32 (children DM 19). A 24-hour ticket covering the entire area of West Berlin (including lake travel) costs DM 14.50 (children DM 7.30). Information can be obtained from the office of the city transport authority, the Berliner Verkehrsbetriebe (BVG) at Hardenbergplatz, in front of the Bahnhof Zoo, or by calling 030/216–5088.

By Taxi Taxi meters start at DM 3.40 and the fare is DM 1.58 per kilometer (DM 1.69 after midnight). Taxi drivers charge 50 pfennigs for each piece of heavy luggage carried. A drive along the Kurfürstendamm will cost about DM 10. Taxis can be ordered by telephone: Call 030/6902, 030/216–060, 030/261–026, or 030/240–202.

Important Addresses and Numbers

Tourist Information The main tourist office is at the Europa Center, Budapesterstrasse, tel. 030/262–6031. It's open daily 7:30 AM–10:30 PM. There are other offices at the main hall of Tegel airport, tel. 030/410–1314, open daily 8 AM–11 PM; the Bahnhof Zoo, the main train station, tel. 030/313–9063, open daily 8 AM–11 PM; and at the border crossing point Dreilinden, tel. 030/803–9057, open daily 8 AM–11 PM. Accommodations can be reserved at all offices, which also issue a free English-language information brochure, "Berlin Turns On." Pretravel information on Berlin can be obtained by writing to the Verkehrsamt Berlin, Europa Center, D-1000 Berlin 30.

Consulates U.S. Clayallee 170, tel. 030/832–4087. U.K. Uhlandstrasse 7/8, tel. 030/309–5292.

Emergencies Police, tel. 030/110. **Ambulance and emergency medical attention,** tel. 030/310–031. **Dentist,** tel. 030/1141. **Pharmacies,** for emergency pharmaceutical assistance, tel. 030/1141.

English Bookstores **Marga Schoeller,** Knesebeckstrasse 33, tel. 030/881–1112; **Buchhandlung Kiepert,** Hardenbergstrasse 4–5, tel. 030/311–0090.

Guided Tours

By Bus Bus tours of West and East Berlin are offered by a number of West Berlin operators, the chief of which are **Severin & Kühn,** Kurfürstendamm 216, Charlottenburg, tel. 030/883–1015; **Berliner Bären Stadtrundfahrt,** Rankestrasse 35 (corner of Kurfürstendamm), tel. 030/213–4077; **Reisebüro Berolina,** Kurfürstendamm 220, tel. 030/883–3131; and **Bus Verkehr Berlin (BVB),** Kurfürstendamm 225, tel. 030/882–2063 or 030/882–6847). A two-hour tour of West Berlin costs about DM 20 and a combined tour of West and East Berlin about DM 50 (plus a fee of about DM 15 levied by the East Germans). There are also half-day tours to Potsdam and the Sanssoucis palace, favorite residence of Frederick the Great, now in East German territory. Lunch is included in the DM 99 cost of the tour. Passports and early booking are essential for tours to East Berlin and Potsdam.

By Boat West Berlin is a city of waterways, and boat trips can be made on the Spree and Havel rivers and on the city's canals. For details, contact the city tourist office at the Europa Center, Budapesterstrasse, tel. 030/262–6031.

Exploring West Berlin

Visiting West Berlin is a bittersweet experience, as so many of the triumphs and tragedies of the past are tied up with the bustling present. The result can be either dispiriting or exhilarating. And by European standards, Berlin isn't that old: Cologne was more than 1,000 years old when Berlin was born from the fusion of two tiny settlements on islands in the river Spree. Although already a royal residence in the 15th century, Berlin really came into its own three centuries later, under the rule of King Friedrich II—Frederick the Great—whose liberal reforms and artistic patronage led the way as the city developed into a major cultural capital.

The events of the 20th century would have crushed the spirit of most other cities. Hitler destroyed the city's reputation for tolerance and plunged Berlin headlong into the war that led to wholesale destruction of monuments and houses. And after World War II, Berlin was still to face the bitter division of the city and the construction of the infamous Wall.

Despite all this, West Berliners can revel and party as if there were no tomorrow—or perhaps as if there were no yesterday. The city has recovered much of the artistic energy and social whirl of better times. In its crowded bars, cafés, and nightclubs and in the lake-studded parks and woodland, you can recall that this was once the capital of a free Europe.

Bustling Kurfürstendamm, or Ku'damm as the Berliners call it, is one of Europe's greatest thoroughfares, throbbing with
1 activity day and night. At its eastern end is the **Kaiser Wilhelm Gedachtniskirche** (Kaiser Wilhelm Memorial Church Tower). This landmark has come to symbolize not only West Berlin, but the futile destructiveness of war. The shell of the tower is all that remains of the church that was built at the end of the 19th century and dedicated to the memory of Kaiser Wilhelm. Inside is a historical exhibition of the devastation of World War II. *Free. Open 10–6, Sun. 11–6, closed Mon.*

2 Cross Budapesterstrasse to enter the **Zoologischer Garten,** Berlin's zoo. It has the world's largest variety of individual types of fauna along with a fascinating aquarium. *Admission: DM 9 adults, DM 5 children. Open daily from 9 to dusk or 7 PM (whichever is later).*

The zoo is set in the 630-acre (2½ square kilometers) **Tiergarten Park,** which is recovering at last from the war, when it was not only ripped apart by bombs and artillery, but was stripped of its wood by desperate, freezing Berliners in the bitterly cold of
3 1945–46. In the northern section of the park is the **Englischer Garten** (English Garden), which borders the riverside **Bellevue Schloss,** a small palace built for Frederick the Great's brother: It is now the official West Berlin residence of the West German president.

West Berlin

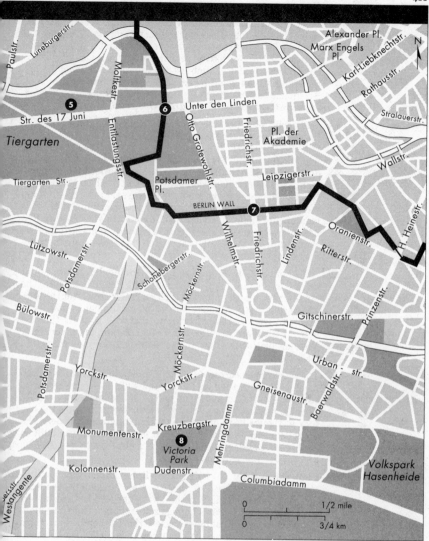

Paulstr. · Luneburgerstr. · Moltkestr. · Alexander Pl. · Marx Engels Pl. · Karl-Liebknechtstr. · Rathausstr. · N

⑤ · Str. des 17 Juni · ⑥ · Unter den Linden · Stralauerstr.

Tiergarten · Entlastungsstr. · Otto Grotewohlstr. · Friedrichstr. · Pl. der Akademie · Wallstr.

Tiergarten Str. · Leipzigerstr.

Potsdamer Pl. · BERLIN WALL · ⑦ · Oranienstr. · H. Heinestr.

Lützowstr. · Potsdamerstr. · Schöneberger str. · Möckernstr. · Wilhelmstr. · Friedrichstr. · Lindenstr. · Ritterstr.

Bülowstr. · Gitschinerstr. · Prinzenstr.

Potsdamerstr. · Yorckstr. · Möckernstr. · Urban str.

Yorckstr. · Gneisenaustr. · Baerwaldstr.

Monumentenstr. · Kreuzbergstr. · ⑧ · Victoria Park · Mehringdamm · Volkspark Hasenheide

Kolonnenstr. · Dudenstr. · Columbiadamm

Westangente · Gneisenstr.

0 · 1/2 mile
0 · 3/4 km

❹ The column in the center of a large traffic circle in the Tiergarten is the **Siegessaule** victory column, erected in 1873 to commemorate four Prussian military campaigns against the French. The granite and sandstone monument originally stood in front of the Reichstag (parliament), which was burned by Hitler's men in 1933. Climb the 285 steps to its 210-foot (64-meter) summit and you'll be rewarded with a fine view of West Berlin and, across the wall, East Berlin. *Admission: 50 pfennigs adults, 10 pfennigs children. Open 9–6, Mon. 1–6.*

❺ The Berlin Wall, ugly as it is, exerts a magnetic pull on any visitor to Berlin, so at the base of the Siegessaule, go east down the wide Strasse des 17 Juni, named in memory of the day, in 1953, when 50,000 East Germans staged an uprising that was put down by force. On the left, you'll pass the **Soviet Victory** monument, a semicircular colonnade topped with a statue of a Russian soldier and flanked by what are said to be the first Soviet tanks to have fought their way into Berlin in 1945. This monument is an important Soviet toehold in West Berlin: Red Army troops are permitted to guard it and the guard is changed every hour. (You can watch the goose-stepping ceremony from a discreet distance.)

❻ Ahead of you is **Brandenburger Tor** (Brandenburg Gate), built in 1788 as a victory arch for triumphant Prussian armies. The horse-drawn chariot atop the arch was reerected after the war, still facing west, although the great monument is now some way into East German territory. The wall is at its thickest here, more than three feet (1 meter) of tank-proof concrete. Viewing platforms allow you to peer over the ugly mass into East Berlin.

❼ The most famous crossing point, **Checkpoint Charlie,** is a half-hour walk south then east along the wall. It's much easier to save time and effort and go by taxi from Brandenburg Gate. At Checkpoint Charlie, you can go to a museum that tells the history of the wall and describes (with exhibits and models) the ingenious escapes that have been made since it was built in 1961. *Checkpoint Charlie Museum, Friedrichstr. 44, tel. 030/ 251–4569. Free. Open daily 9–8.*

❽ Find the nearby Kochstrasse U-Bahn station and go two stops south on the U-6 line to Mehringdamm. Head for Kreuzbergstrasse. Just on the left is the 200-foot (61-meter) **Kreuzberg,** West Berlin's highest natural hill. (There are higher hills made of the rubble gathered from the bombed-out ruins of the city when reconstruction began in 1945.) On the sheltered southern slopes of the Kreuzberg is a vineyard that produces some of Germany's rarest wines: They are served only at official Berlin functions.

❾ Bordering Kreuzberg to the west is the Schöneberg district, where you'll find the seat of the city and state government of West Berlin, the **Rathaus Schöneberg** (City Hall). In the belfry of the Rathaus is a replica of the Liberty Bell, donated to Berliners in 1950 by the United States and rung every day at noon. In a room at the base of the tower are stored 17 million American signatures expressing solidarity with West Berlin, some, no doubt, inspired by President Kennedy's famous "Ich bin ein Berliner" speech, which he made here in 1963.

Time Out While at the Rathaus, go downstairs to the **Ratskeller Schöneberg,** an inexpensive place to get a good, filling set-price lunch. The atmosphere is busy and friendly.

10 Take the U-Bahn north one stop from Rathaus Schöneberg station and change to the U-7 line for eight stops, to Richard-Wagner-Platz Station. From the station, walk left for about 500 yards (455 meters) to the handsome **Schloss Charlottenburg** (Charlottenburg Palace). Built at the end of the 17th century by King Frederick I for his wife, Queen Sophie Charlotte, the palace was progressively enlarged for later royal residents. Frederick the Great's suite of rooms can be visited; in one glass cupboard, you'll see the coronation crown he inherited from his father—stripped of jewels by the ascetic son, who gave the most valuable diamonds and pearls to his wife. *Schloss Charlottenburg, Luisenplatz, Charlottenburg. Admission: DM 4.50 adults, DM 2 children. Open 10–5, closed Mon.*

11 Opposite the palace is the **Ägyptisches Museum** (Egyptian Museum), home of perhaps the world's best-known portrait sculpture, the beautiful Nefertiti. The 3,300-year-old Egyptian queen is the centerpiece of a fascinating collection of Egyptology that includes one of the finest preserved mummies outside Cairo. *Ägyptisches Museum, Schlossstr. 70, Charlottenburg. Free. Open 9–5, closed Fri.*

12 If you like, you can take Nefertiti home with you. Behind Schloss Charlottenburg is the **Gipsformerei** (State Museum Plaster Foundry), which will turn out a copy of any of a dozen masterpieces in stock. They're not cheap (portrait busts cost between DM 700 and DM 900), but how can you put a price on having Nefertiti on the mantelpiece? *Gipsformerei, Sophie-Charlotten-Str. 17/18, Charlottenburg. Open weekdays 9–4.*

13 Take U-Bahn line U-7 back toward Schöneberg until Fehrbelliner Pl., where you change to line U-2 southwest for five stops to Dahlem-Dorf station. This is the stop for West-Berlin's leading art museum, the **Gemaldegalerie,** in the district of Dahlem. The collection includes many works by the great European masters, with 26 Rembrandts and 14 by Rubens. Or is it 25 Rembrandts? *The Man in the Golden Hat,* until recently attributed to Rembrandt, has now been ascribed to one of the great Dutch master's pupils. Does it really matter? Maybe not to the public, which still sees it as a masterpiece, but it could affect the value of the painting by a million or two. *Gemaldegalerie, Arnimallee 23/27, Dahlem. Free. Open 9–5, closed Mon.*

14 No visit to West Berlin is complete without an outing to the city's outdoor playground, the **Grunewald** park. Bordering the Dahlem district to the west, the park is a vast green space, with meadows, woodlands, and lakes. The city's total waterfront of 130 miles (208 kilometers) is longer than West Germany's Baltic Coast. There's even space for nudist beaches on the banks of the Wannsee lake, while in winter a downhill ski run and even a ski jump operate on the modest slopes of the Teufelsberg hill.

Dining

For details and price category definitions, *see* Dining in Essential Information.

Expensive **Alt-Luxembourg.** There are only nine tables at this popular restaurant in the Charlottenburg district, and the attentive service reflects this personal attention. Chef Kurt Wannebacher uses only fresh ingredients and announces his daily specials on the blackboard. If lobster lasagna is chalked up, look no further. *Pestalozzistr. 70, tel. 030/323–8730. Jacket and tie. Reservations essential. No credit cards. Closed Sun., Mon., two weeks in Jan., three weeks in July.*

★ **Bamberger Reiter.** Considered by Berliners to be the city's best restaurant, Bamberger Reiter is the pride of its chef, Franz Raneburger. He relies heavily on fresh market produce for his *Neue deutsche Küche* (new German cuisine), so the menu changes from day to day. Fresh flowers, too, abound in his attractive, oak-beamed restaurant. *Regensburgerstr. 7, tel. 030/24482. Jacket and tie. Reservations essential. No credit cards. Closed lunch, Sun., Mon., Aug. 1–20.*

Frühsammer's Restaurant an der Rehwiese. From your table, you can watch chef Peter Frühsammer at work in his open kitchen. He's ready with advice, too, on what's best on the daily menu: Salmon is always a treat here. The restaurant is located in the annex of a turn-of-the-century villa in the southern district of Zehlendorf (U-Bahn to Krumme Lanke and then bus No. 53 to Rehwiese). *Matterhornstr. 101, tel. 030/803–2720. Jacket and tie. Reservations essential. AE, DC, MC, V. Closed lunch, Sun., Mon.*

Moderate **Alt-Nürnberg.** Here is a corner of Bavaria in the center of Berlin. Step into the tavernlike interior and you could be in Füssen or Garmisch: The waitresses even wear dirndls. The Bavarian colors of blue and white are everywhere, and such Bavarian culinary delights as *Schweinshaxe* (knuckle of pork) are well represented on the menu. If you prefer to eat in the Prussian style, the calves' liver *Berliner Art* is recommended. *Europa Center, tel. 030/261–4397. Dress: casual. Reservations not needed. AE, DC, MC, V.*

★ **Blockhaus Nikolskoe.** Prussian King Wilhelm III built this Russian-style wooden lodge for his daughter Charlotte, wife of Russia's Czar Nicholas I. It's located in the south of the city, on the eastern edge of Glienicker Park. In summer, you can eat on the open terrace overlooking the Havel river. In character with its history and appearance, the Blockhaus features game dishes. *Nikolskoer Weg, tel. 030/805–2914. Dress: casual. Reservations not needed. AE, DC, MC, V.*

Forsthaus Paulsborn. Game is the specialty in this former woodsman's home deep in the Grunewald Forest. You dine here as the forester did—from an oak table in a great dining room and under the baleful eye of hunting trophies on the wall. Apart from game, the menu extends to various German and international dishes. *Am Grunewaldsee, tel. 030/813–8010. Dress: casual. Reservations advised on weekends. AE, DC, MC, V. Closed Mon., dinner in winter (Oct.–Mar.).*

Hecker's Deele. You could find yourself seated in one of the antique church pews that complete the oak-beamed interior of this restaurant that features Westphalian dishes. The *Westfälische Schlachtplatte* (a variety of meats) will set you up for a whole day's sightseeing—the Ku'damm is right outside. *Grolmannstr. 35, tel. 030/88901. Dress: casual. Reservations not needed. AE, DC, MC, V.*

Mundart Restaurant. Too many cooks don't spoil the broth (and certainly not the excellent fish soup) at this popular restaurant in the Kreuzberg district. Five chefs are at work in the spacious kitchen. Fortunately, they all agree on the day's specials, and you can follow their advice with impunity. *Muskauerstr. 33/34, tel. 030/612–2061. Dress: casual. Reservations not needed. No credit cards. Closed lunch, Mon., Tues.*

Inexpensive **Alt-Berliner Wiessbierstube.** A visit to the Berlin Museum (a permanent historical exhibition on Berlin) must include a stop at this pub-style restaurant in the museum building. There's a buffet packed with Berlin specialties, and a jazz band plays on Sunday morning. *Berlin Museum, Lindenstr. 14, tel. 030/251–0121. Dress: casual. No reservations. No credit cards. Closed Mon.*

Thürnagel. Also located in the Kreuzberg district, Thürnagel is a vegetarian restaurant where it's not only healthy to eat, but fun. The Seitan in sherry sauce or the Tempeh curry are good enough to convert a seasoned carnivore. *Gneisenaustr. 57, tel. 030/691–4800. Dress: casual. No reservations. No credit cards. Closed lunch.*

Lodging

For details and price category definitions, *see* Lodging in Essential Information.

Very Expensive **Bristol Hotel Kempinski.** Located on the Ku'damm in the heart of the city, this grand hotel not only has the best of Berlin's shopping on its doorstep, but it has some fine boutiques of its own. English-style furnishings give the "Kempi" an added touch of class. All the rooms and suites are luxuriously decorated and equipped, with marble bathrooms, air-conditioning, and cable TV. Children under 12 stay for free if they share their parents' room. *Kurfürstendamm 27, tel. 030/884340. 325 rooms with bath. Facilities: 2 restaurants, indoor pool, sauna, solarium, masseur, hairdresser, limousine service. AE, DC, MC, V.*

★ **Intercontinental Berlin.** The "Diplomaten Suite" is expensive, but it is in a class of its own: It's as large as a suburban house and furnished in the Oriental style. The other rooms and suites are not so exotically furnished but still show individuality and exquisite taste. The lobby is worth a visit even if you're not tempted to stay overnight: It's a quarter the size of a football field, opulently furnished, and just the place for afternoon tea and pastries. *Budapesterstr. 2, tel. 030/26020. 600 rooms with bath. Facilities: 3 restaurants (including a rooftop garden), indoor pool, sauna, 24-hour room service, boutiques, Pan-Am check-in service. AE, DC, MC, V.*

Steigenberger Berlin. A modern deluxe chain hotel, the Steigenberger puts the accent on impeccable accommodations, facilities, and service. All the rooms are identically furnished and are extremely comfortable. The hotel has a casino and is centrally located near the Ku'damm. *Los-Angeles-Platz 1, tel. 030/21080. 337 rooms with bath. Facilities: 3 restaurants, 2 bars, indoor pool, solarium, 24-hour room service. AE, DC, MC, V.*

Expensive **Berlin Excelsior Hotel.** Fixed rates that don't fluctuate with the seasons are offered by this modern, well-run establishment only 5 minutes from the Ku'damm. That means, however, that there are no special weekend offers (a usual feature of top German hotels). The comfortable rooms are furnished in dark teak, and the helpful front office staff will arrange sightseeing tours and try to obtain hard-to-get theater and concert tickets. *Hardenbergerstr. 14, tel. 030/31991. 320 rooms with bath. Facilities: garden terrace, winter garden. AE, DC, MC, V.*

★ **Palace.** The rooms here are comfortable and adequately furnished, but can't quite match the scale of the palatial lobby. Ask for a room on the Budapesterstrasse: The view is memorable. Or even take a suite with a whirlpool bath. The Palace is part of Berlin's Europa Center, and guests have free use of the center's pool and sauna. Work begins this year on an extension with 100 more rooms. The Palace is particularly popular with Americans, who account for more than a quarter of the rooms occupied. *Europa Center, tel. 030/269111. 160 rooms with bath. AE, DC, MC, V.*

Schweizerhof Berlin. There's a rustic, Swiss look about most of the rooms in this centrally located hotel, but they have a uniformly high standard of comfort and facilities, such as TV/video and minibar. Ask to be placed in the west wing, where rooms are larger. Children stay for free if they are in their parents' room. The indoor pool is the largest of any Berlin hotel, and the hotel is opposite Tiergarten Park. *Budapesterstr. 21–31, tel. 030/26960. 430 rooms with bath. Facilities: sauna, solarium, fitness room, hairdresser, beauty salon. AE, DC, MC, V.*

Moderate **Casino Hotel.** The owner of the Casino is Bavarian, so his restaurant serves south German specialties. The hotel itself is a former Prussian military barracks but bears little evidence of its former role: Rooms are large and comfortable and well equipped. The hotel is located in the Charlottenburg district. *Köningen-Elisabeth-Str. 47a, tel. 030/303090. 24 rooms with bath. AE, DC, MC, V.*

Riehmers Hofgarten. Located in the interesting Kreuzberg district, this hotel in a late 19th-century building is a short walk from the Kreuzberg hill and has fast connections to the center of town. The high-ceilinged rooms are elegantly furnished. *Yorckstr. 83, tel. 030/781011. 21 rooms with bath or shower. AE, DC, MC, V.*

Ravenna. This small, friendly hotel is located in the Steglitz district, close to the Botanical Garden and the Dahlen Museum. All the rooms are well equipped, but suite 111B is a bargain: It includes a large living room and kitchen for the rate of only DM 200. *Grunewaldstr. 8–9, tel. 030/792–8031. 45 rooms with bath or shower. AE, DC, MC, V.*

Inexpensive **Econtel.** Families are well cared for at this hotel that's situated within walking distance of Charlottenburg Palace. Lone travelers also appreciate the touches in the single rooms, which come with a trouser press and hair dryer. *Sommeringstr. 24, tel. 030/344001. 205 rooms with bath or shower. Facilities: snack bar. MC.*

The Arts and Entertainment

Today's Berlin has a tough task in trying to live up to the reputation it gained from the film *Cabaret*, but if nightlife is a little toned down since the '20s, the arts still flourish. Apart from the many hotels that book seats, there are three main ticket agencies: **Theaterkasse**, Kurfürstendamm 24; **Theaterkasse im Europa-Center**; and **Theaterkasse Centrum**, Mienekestrasse 25.

The Berlin Philharmonic, one of the world's leading orchestras, performs in the **Philharmonie**, Matthaikirchstrasse 1, tel.

030/254880. It plays a leading role in the annual festival months of August, September, and October. The **Deutsche Oper** (Opera House), by the U-Bahn stop of the same name, is the home of the opera and ballet companies. Tickets are hard to obtain, but call 030/341–4449 for information.

West Berlin is still Germany's drag show capital, as you'll see if you go to **Chez Nous**, Marburgerstrasse 14. Next door (No. 15) the girls are for real at the **Scotch Club 13**.

Dschungel at Nürnbergerstrasse 53, is the number-one disco, and is funky and fun. For an escape from the usual disco sounds, try the **Blue Note** (Courbierestr. 13), which mixes jazz, bebop and Latin American rhythms.

One of the best ways to feel the pulse of this exciting city is to visit one of the *kneippen*, bars with a relaxed feel where you might hear some music or just sit outside with a beer or coffee.

The Rhine

None of Europe's many rivers is so redolent of history and legend as the Rhine, known in German as the Rhein. For the Romans, who established forts and colonies along its western banks, the Rhine was the frontier between civilization and the barbaric German tribes. Roman artifacts can be seen in museums throughout the region. The Romans also introduced viticulture—a legacy that survives in the countless vineyards along the riverbanks—and later, Christianity. Throughout the Middle Ages, the river's importance as a trade artery made it the focus of sharp, often violent, conflict between princes, noblemen, and archbishops. Many of the picturesque castles that crown its banks were the homes of robber barons who held up passing ships and barges and exacted heavy tolls to finance even grander fortifications.

For poets and composers, the Rhine—or "Vater (Father) Rhine," as the Germans call it—has been an endless source of inspiration. As legend has it, the Lorelei, a treacherous, craggy mountain, was home to a beautiful and bewitching maiden who lured sailors to a watery grave. Wagner based four of his epic operas on the lives of the medieval Nibelungs, said to have inhabited the rocky banks. To travel the Rhine by boat, especially in autumn, when the rising mists enshroud the castles high above, is to understand the place the river occupies in the German imagination.

The Rhine does not belong to Germany alone. Its 820-mile (1,320-kilometer) journey takes it from deep within the Alps through Switzerland and Austria, Germany and France, into the Netherlands, and out into the North Sea. But it is in Germany—especially the stretch between Mainz and Bonn known as the Middle Rhine—that the riverside scenery is most spectacular. This is the "typical" Rhine: a land of steep and thickly wooded hills, terraced vineyards, tiny villages hugging the shore, and a succession of brooding castles.

A nine-hour steamer trip between Mainz and Bonn will give you a taste of this fabled region. But in order to really experience it, you will need to spend several days in the area. A town such as Koblenz provides a convenient base for excursions up and down the river and into the lovely Moselle Valley.

Getting Around

By Train One of the best ways to visit the Rhineland in very limited time is to take the scenic train journey from Mainz to Bonn along the western banks of the river. The views are spectacular, and the entire trip takes less than two hours. You can get on and off the train along the route. Most of the Rhine towns are also connected by bus services originating in Frankfurt and other major cities. For information about both train and bus services, contact German National Railways in Frankfurt, Reisedienst Friedrich-Ebert-Anlage 35, tel. 069/2651.

By Boat Passenger ships traveling up and down the Rhine and its tributaries offer a pleasant and relaxing way to see the region. Köln-Düsseldorfer Steamship Company (KD) operates a fleet of ships that travel between Düsseldorf and Mainz, daily from Easter to late October, and along the Mosel and Main rivers. They also offer cruises along the entire length of the Rhine. Passengers have a choice of buying an excursion ticket or a ticket to a single destination. For information about services, tel. 0221/20880. From March through November, Hebel-Line (tel. 06742/2420) offers a scenic cruise of the Lorelei Valley; night cruises feature music and dancing. For information about Neckar River excursions, contact Neckar Personen Schiffahrt in Stuttgart, tel. 0711/541073 or 0711/541074.

By Car If you prefer to drive, the Rhineland offers a comprehensive highway network that takes in some of the region's most spectacular scenery. Roads crisscross the entire province, from the historic vineyards of the Mosel Valley to the beautiful castle and wine-growing country of the Rhine's west bank. For information about routes available, contact the German Automobile Club, Lyoner Str. 16, Frankfurt-am-Main 71, tel. 069/66061.

By Bicycle Another enjoyable and inexpensive way to see the country is by bicycle. Tourist offices in all the larger towns will provide information and route maps. German Railways also provides bicycle rental facilities on some of its routes. For information, tel. 069/2651. You can also take advantage of the myriad "Wanderwegen" (walking paths) running throughout the region. These are marked with signs depicting red or green grapes. Contact local tourist offices for information.

Guided Tours

In addition to a number of special-interest cruises, KD (Köln-Düsseldorfer) operates a series of guided excursions covering the towns along its routes. The British-run European Yacht Cruises Ltd. conducts a variety of Rhine cruises, some with optional shore excursions (tel. in London 01/462–8843). The tourist offices in Mainz and Koblenz also offer tours (in English) of their respective cities.

Tourist Information

Bacharach. Fremdenverkehrsamt, Oberstr. 1, tel. 06743/2968.
Bad Godesberg. Moltkestr. 66, Bonn-Bad Godesberg, tel. 0228/356040.
Bonn. 2 Munsterstr. 20, tel. 0228/773466 and LVV Rheinland, Rheinallee 69, Bad Godesberg, Bonn, tel. 0228/362921.

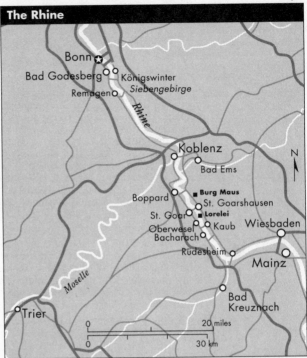

The Rhine

Boppard. Verkehrsamt, Karmeliterstr. 2, tel. 06742/5081.
Koblenz. Fremden Verkehrsamt, Verkehrspavillon, tel. 0261/31304 and Fremdenverkehrsverband Rheinland-Pfalz, Postfach 1420, tel. 0261/31079.
Königswinter. Verkehrsamt, Drachenfelsstr. 7, tel. 02223/21048.
Mainz. Verkehrsverein, Bahnhofstr. 15, tel. 06131/233741.
Rüdesheim. Verkehrsamt, Rheinstr. 16, tel. 06722/2962.

Exploring

Bonn Bonn, West Germany's capital city, marks the northern boundary of the Middle Rhine region. It offers a number of interesting historical sights and is a convenient spot from which to begin your tour of the Rhineland.

Like so many Rhine cities, Bonn began as a Roman settlement—called Castra Bonnensia—and this year celebrates its 2,000th anniversary. For 500 years—the 13th through the 18th centuries—it was the seat of power for the prince electors of Cologne. Its many Baroque monuments date from this later period. The most impressive Baroque building, the **Kurfürstliches,** houses the university. Other notable buildings include the **Rathaus** (City Hall), in the marketplace, the **Poppelsdorf Schloss** (Castle), and the **Kreuzberg Church.**

The center of Bonn is a maze of picturesque, winding streets and historic houses. Among them is Beethoven's birthplace.

This is now a museum brimming with objects, instruments, and documents associated with the great composer. Among the most poignant are the ear trumpets he used in his battle against deafness. *Bongasse 20, tel. 02221/635188. Admission: DM 1.50. Open Apr.–Sept. Mon.–Sat. 9–1, Sun. 9–1 and 3–6; Nov.–Mar., Mon.–Sat. 9:30–1 and 3–5, Sun. 10–1. Closed holidays.*

While you are in the Old Town center, stop in at the **Marketplatz,** the site of a colorful vegetable market. Nearby, on Munsterplace, is Bonn's oldest church, the **Münster of St. Martin.** Although it had to be heavily restored following severe bombing in World War II, it remains one of the Rhineland's best examples of Romanesque architecture. Bonn also offers a number of noteworthy museums. The **Rheinisches Landesmuseum** is a good place to get acquainted with the history and culture of the Rhine region. Exhibits include the famous Neanderthal skull. *Colmanstr. 16. Admission: DM 2. Open Tues.–Fri. 9–5 (9–8 Wed.); weekends and holidays 10–5.*

Just south of Bonn on the west side of the Rhine is **Bad Godesberg,** an ancient spa town and the center of Bonn's diplomatic community. The 105-foot (32-meter) **Godesburgwatch Tower** is one of the last remaining fortifications of a 13th-century castle that stood here. Most of the fortress was destroyed in the 16th century.

Across the river from Bad Godesberg—accessible by bridge or car ferry—is **Königswinter,** site of one of the most-visited castles on the Rhine. The ruins of **Drachenfels** crown the highest hill in the **Siebengebirge** (Seven Hills) area, commanding a spectacular view of the river. The castle was built in the 12th century by the archbishop of Köln. Its name—Drachenfels—commemorates a dragon said to have lived in a nearby cave. As legend has it, the dragon was slain by Siegfried, the Niebelunglied hero. While you are in the area, visit the **Kloster Heisterbach,** a Cistercian monastery about two miles (three kilometers) from Königswinter. This is a fine example of late Romanesque church architecture, characteristic of the ruins that fired the imagination of the Romantic poets and painters of the 19th century.

Continuing south along the west bank, you come to the ancient, half-timbered town of **Remagen.** Originally a Roman village built near the source of a mineral spring, where the Ayr River meets the Rhine, Remagen was an important bridgehead during World War II. Here, American forces were able to capture the bridge and speed their advance into Germany. The Ayr Valley, lined with picturesque, terraced vineyards, produces some of Germany's finest red wines.

Koblenz In the heart of the middle Rhine region, at the confluence of the Rhine and Moselle rivers, lies the city of **Koblenz,** the area's cultural and administrative center and the meeting place of the two great wine-producing districts. It is also one of the most important traffic points along the Rhine. Here you are ideally placed to sample and compare the light, fruity Moselle wines and the headier Rhine varieties. The city's **Weindorf** area, just south of the **Pfaffendorfer Bridge,** has a wide selection of taverns, where you can try the wines in traditional romer glasses, with their symbolic amber and green bowls.

The city of Koblenz began as a Roman camp—Confluentes—more than 2,000 years ago. The vaults beneath **St. Florin Church** contain an interesting assortment of Roman remains. In the 12th and 13th centuries, the city was controlled by the archbishop-electors of Trier, and a host of fine churches and castles were built.

A good place to begin your tour of Koblenz is the **Deutches Eck,** or "Corner of Germany," the tip of the sharp peninsula separating the Rhine and Moselle rivers. In the 12th century, the Knights of the Teutonic Order established their center here. The towering equestrian statue of Kaiser Wilhelm that once stood here was destroyed by Allied bombs during World War II, but the base remains as a monument to German unity. On summer evenings, concerts are held in the nearby **Blumenhof Garden.** Most of the city's historic churches are also within walking distance of the Deutsches Eck. The **Liebfrauenkirche** (Church of Our Lady), completed in the 13th century, incorporates Romanesque, late Gothic, and Baroque elements. **St. Florin,** a Romanesque church built around 1100, was remodeled in the Gothic style in the 14th century. Gothic windows and a vaulted ceiling were added in the 17th century. The city's most important church, **St. Kastor,** also combines Romanesque and Gothic elements and features some unusual altar tombs and rare Gothic wall paintings.

Although the city lost 85% of its buildings during wartime air raids, some of the old buildings survived and others have been built in complementary styles. Much of the **Old Town** of Koblenz is now a pedestrian district, and an attractive area for a leisurely stroll. Many of the ancient cellars beneath the houses have been rediscovered and now serve as wine bars and jazz clubs.

Koblenz also offers an assortment of castles and palaces. The former residence of the archbishop of Trier now houses the city administrative offices. The original 18th-century building was demolished during the war; today only the interior staircase remains. Across the river, on the Rhine's east bank, towers the city's most spectacular castle, the **Ehrenbreitstein,** now a youth hostel and a museum of ethnography and prehistory. The fortifications of this vast structure date back to the 1100s, although the bulk of it was built much later, in the 16th and 17th centuries. To reach the fortress, take the cable car *(sesslebahn)* or, if you're in shape, try walking up. The view alone is worth the trip. On the second Saturday in August, a magnificent fireworks display, "The Rhine Aflame," is presented here. Before you leave, visit the **Mittelrhein Museum** for a look at Rhenish art and artifacts from the Middle Ages to the present day. *15 Florinsmarkt. Free. Open Tues.–Sat. 10–1 and 2:30–5:30; Sun. 10–1.*

Rhine Gorge Between the cities of Koblenz and Mainz, the Rhine flows through the 40-mile (65-kilometer) stretch known as the **Rhine Gorge.** It is here that the Rhine lives up to its legends and lore and where the river, in places, narrows to a width of 200 yards. Once it was full of treacherous whirlpools, sudden shallows, and stark rock outcroppings that menaced passing ships. Today, vineyards occupy every inch of available soil on the steep, terraced slopes. High above, ancient castles crown the rocky shelves.

South of Koblenz, at a wide, western bend in the river, lies the quiet, old town of **Boppard,** once a bustling city of the Holy Roman Empire. Now the remains of its Roman fort and castle are used to house a museum of Roman artifacts and geological specimens. There are also several notable churches, including the **Carmelite Church,** with its fine Baroque altar, and the Romanesque Church of **St. Severus.** Boppard also offers a wonderful view across the Rhine to the ruined castles of **Liebenstein** and **Sterrenberg,** known as the "hostile brothers." As legend has it, the castles were built by two feuding brothers to protect their respective interests. The Boppard riverbanks also feature two miles of pleasure grounds and an extensive municipal forest.

Continuing south from Boppard, you come to the little town of **St. Goar,** crowded against the steep gorge cliff and shadowed by the imposing ruin of **Rheinfels Castle.** A steep, narrow road takes you up to the castle—a fine spot for scenic river vistas. Rheinfels was built in the mid-13th century by Count Dieter von Katzenelnbogen (whose name means "cat's elbow"). The count's enormous success in collecting river tolls provoked the other river barons to join together and lay siege to his castle. What transpired is unclear, but through the years Rheinfels survived numerous sieges. It was finally destroyed by the French in 1797. During the 19th century, the ruins served as a source of inspiration for a host of Romantic poets and artists. It is now in the process of restoration, and a luxury hotel has been built on the site *(see* Dining and Lodging). *Admission: DM 2.50. Open Apr. 1–Oct. 31, daily 9–5.*

On the east bank of the river, just across from the town of St. Goar, lies its sister village, **St. Goarshausen.** An hourly ferry service links the two. St. Goarshausen is dominated by **Burg Katz** (Cat Castle), a massive fortress built by a later Count von Katzenelnbogen. Today it is a government-run youth facility. Tourists are not permitted inside, but the top of the cliff offers a lovely view of the famous Lorelei rock. About two miles (three kilometers) north of St. Goarshausen is the **Burg Maus,** or Mouse Castle. Legend has it that an archbishop of Trier built the fortress to protect a strip of land he owned at the base of the cliff. The Count von Katzenbogen, annoyed at what he considered an intrusion into his territory, sent the archbishop a message explaining that his "Cat" (Burg Katz) was sufficient to protect the electoral "Mouse." Hence the nickname, Burg Maus.

Many tourists visit St. Goarshausen for its location—only a few miles from the legendary **Lorelei rock.** To get to Lorelei, follow the road marked with "Lorelei-Felsen" signs. Here the Rhine takes a sharp turn around a rocky, shrub-covered headland. This is the narrowest and shallowest part of the Middle Rhine, full of treacherous currents. According to legend, the beautiful maiden, Lore, sat on the rock here, combing her golden hair and singing a song so irresistible that passing sailors forgot the navigational hazards and were swept to their deaths.

Oberwesel, on the west bank, is a medieval wine town encircled by ancient walls and towers. Sixteen of the original 21 towers remain. Two churches deserve a visit: **St. Martin,** built in the 14th and 15th centuries, features a distinctive, brightly painted nave; the **Liebfrauen Kirche** (known as the "red church" because of its fiery facade) contains a magnificent choir screen, some fine sculpture, and an altarpiece depicting the magnanimous deeds of St. Nicholas.

One of the most photographed sites of the Middle Rhine region is the medieval village of **Kaub,** just south of Oberwesel on the east side of the river. Its unusual castles are well worth a visit. The **Pfalzgrafenstein,** situated on a tiny island in the middle of the Rhine, bristles with sharp-pointed towers and has the appearance of a small sailing ship. In the 14th century, the resident graf, or count, was said to have strung chains across the Rhine in order to stop riverboats and collect his tolls. A special boat takes visitors to the island. *Admission: DM 1.50. Open Tues.–Sun. 9–noon and 2–5:30.*

On a hillside above Kaub hovers another small castle: **Burg Gutenfels.** Built in the 13th century, Gutenfels was renovated completely at the end of the 18th century and is now an exquisite hotel *(see* Dining and Lodging).

The picturesque little village of **Bacharach,** encircled by 15th-century walls, is the best-preserved town of the Middle Rhine. It takes its name from the Roman "Baccaracum," or "altar of Bacchus"—a great stone that stood here until it was dynamited by river engineers during the last century. As its name implies, Bacharach is also a wine-trade center. Like many small towns of the Middle Rhine and Moselle valleys, the village holds a colorful wine festival each October. In addition to providing an excellent opportunity for liberal imbibing, Rhine wine festivals often feature lively displays of folk crafts and traditions.

Farther south, on the Rhine's east bank and at the center of the Rheingan region, lies another famous wine town. According to legend, **Rüdesheim's** first vines were planted by Charlemagne. More recent vintages can be enjoyed in the many taverns lining **Drosselgasse,** a narrow, colorful street in the heart of town. Rüdesheim is a tourist magnet—about the most popular destination on the Rhine—so if you plan to stay overnight, be sure to reserve well in advance. Besides its half-timbered houses, hidden courtyards, and medieval castles, Rüdesheim offers an interesting museum, **Rheinan und Weinmuseum,** devoted to the history of wine making and local lore. *Rheinstr. Admission: DM 2.50. Open Mar.–mid-Nov. 10–12:30 and 1:30–6.*

Mainz On the west side of the Rhine, at the mouth of the river Main, stands the city of **Mainz,** an old university town that's the capital of the Rhineland-Palatinate state. During Roman times, Mainz was a camp called Moguntiacum. Later it was the seat of the powerful archbishops of Mainz. But it is perhaps best known as the city in which, around 1450, printing pioneer Johannes Gutenberg established his first movable press. He is commemorated by a monument and square bearing his name and a museum containing his press and one of his Bibles. *Liebfrauenplatz 5. Free. Open Tues.–Sat. 10–6, Sun. and holidays 10–1. Closed Mon. and Jan.*

Today, Mainz is a bustling, modern city of nearly 200,000 inhabitants. Although it was heavily bombed during the war, many of the buildings have been faithfully reconstructed, and the city retains much of its historic charm. On **Gutenbergplatz** in the **Old Town** stand two fine Baroque churches, **Seminary Church** and **St. Ignatius.** The Gothic church of **St. Stephan** fea-

tures six windows by the French artist Marc Chagall. The
city's **cathedral** (Dom) is one of the finest Romanesque churches
in Germany. The Old Town also boasts the country's oldest
Renaissance fountain—**the Marktbrunnen**—and the **Dativius-
Victor-Bogen Arch**, dating back to Roman times. The **Romisch-
Germanisches Museum**, in the **Kurfurstliches Schloss**, contains
a notable collection of archaeological finds. *Rheinstr. Free.
Open 10–6, closed Mon.*

Dining and Lodging

When it comes to cuisine, the Rhineland offers a number of regional specialties. Be sure to sample the wide variety of
sausages available, the goose and duck dishes from the Ahr Valley, and Rhineland *Sauerbraten*—accepted by many as the
most succulent of pot roasts. Hotels in the Rhineland range
from simple little inns to magnificent castle hotels. Many smaller towns have only small hotels and guest houses, some of
which close during the winter months. During the peak summer season and in early autumn—wine festival time—
accommodations are scarce, so it is advisable to reserve well in
advance.

For details and price category definitions, *see* Dining and
Lodging in Essential Information.

Bacharach **Altkolnischer Hof.** The Altkolnischer Hof is a small guest house
Lodging with a rustic air. *Am Marktplatz, tel. 06743/1339. 20 rooms,
some with bath. No credit cards. Moderate.*

Bonn **Rheinterrassen.** Located near the city's diplomatic center, in
Dining Bad Godesberg, Rheinterrassen offers a lovely terrace and scenic views of the Rhine. *Ruengsdorf, Rheinstr. 82, tel. 0228/
332471. Dress: casual. Reservations advised. No credit cards.
Closed in winter. Expensive.*

★ **Schaarschmidt.** Situated on one of the Old Town's most charming streets, Schaarschmidt offers fine German cuisine and a
wide selection of Rhine wines. *Brudergasse 14, tel. 0228/
654407. Jacket and tie. Reservations advised. DC. Closed Sun.
Expensive.*

Zum Kapellchen. This is a colorful wine tavern featuring fine
German and French cuisine. *Brudergasse 12, tel. 0228/651052.
Dress: casual. Reservations advised. AE, DC, MC, V. Closed
Sun. Moderate.*

Lodging **Bristol.** This is a luxury hotel situated in a restored turn-of-the-
century building located in the city center and close to most
tourist sights. It features an elegant restaurant and conference
facilities. *Prinz-Albert-Str. 2, tel. 0228/26980, 117 rooms with
bath. Facilities: bar, coffee shop, pool, sauna, solarium, bowling. AE, DC, MC, V. Very Expensive.*

★ **Königshof.** The sleek, modern Königshof is a favorite hotel
among diplomatic visitors only partly for its convenient location near the Old Town and close to the Rhine. Patrons of the
fine terrace restaurant enjoy an excellent river view. There is
also a well-stocked wine cellar. *Adenauerallee 9, tel. 0228/
26010. 139 rooms, all with bath. AE, DC, MC, V. Expensive.*

Haus Daufenbach. Located on a narrow, winding road in the
heart of the Old Town, Haus Daufenbach has a friendly, hearty
atmosphere. *Brudergasse 6, tel. 0228/637444. 22 rooms, some
with shower. Facilities: wine bar and restaurant. No credit
cards. Moderate.*

Schlosspark. In a modern building close to the botanical gardens, the Schlosspark is a comfortably appointed, attractive hotel located only a short distance from the town center. *Venusbergweg 27–31, tel. 0228/217036. 67 rooms with bath. Facilities: restaurant, pool, sauna, solarium. AE, DC, MC, V. Moderate.*

Boppard   **Klostergut Jakobsberg.** This hotel is set in a handsome castle,
Lodging   formerly a monastery, overlooking the Rhine Valley. Horseback riding and a wedding chapel top the list of facilities. *Boppard, tel. 06742/3061. 110 rooms with bath. Facilities: restaurant, tennis court, pool, game park. AE, DC, MC, V. Closed in winter. Very Expensive.*

Kaub   **Burg Gutenfels.** The terrace of this luxurious castle hotel offers
Lodging   one of the finest views in the Rhine Valley. Guests can also en-
★   joy wine from the hotel's own vineyard. Be sure to reserve well in advance. *Kaub, tel. 06774/220. 12 rooms with bath. Facilities: restaurant, private chapel. AE, DC, MC. Very Expensive.*

Koblenz   **Weinhaus Hubertus.** This restaurant, named for the patron
Dining   saint of hunting, lives up to its sporting image. Its decor is 17th-century rustic, its specialty, fresh game in season. Guests enjoy generous portions and a congenial atmosphere. *Florinsmarkt 6, tel. 0261/31177. Dress: casual. Reservations advised. No credit cards. Moderate.*

Lodging   **Scandic Crown.** This elegant, modern hotel has a lovely garden and terrace overlooking the river. *Julius-Wegeler-Str., tel. 0261/1360. 170 rooms with bath. Facilities: 2 restaurants, bar, sauna, whirlpool. AE, DC, MC, V. Expensive.*
Hohenstaufen. Hohenstaufen is located in a modern building near the train station. Facilities include a restaurant and garage. *Emil-Schuller-Str. 41–43, tel. 0261/37081. 65 rooms with bath. AE, DC, MC, V. Moderate.*

Königswinter   **Zum Alten Brauhaus.** Located in a pleasant, shady garden in
Dining   the center of town, Zum Alten Brauhaus features hearty German fare, served with a selection of local wines and beers. *Hauptstr. 454, tel. 02223/22528. Dress: casual. No credit cards. Moderate.*

Lodging   **Günnewig Rheinhotel.** A modern hotel situated right on the banks of the Rhine, Gunnewig Rheinhotel offers pleasant river views. *Rheinallee 9, tel. 02223/24051. 110 rooms with bath. Facilities: restaurant, bar, pool, sauna, solarium. AE, DC, MC, V. Expensive.*

Mainz   **Drei Lilien.** This beautifully appointed restaurant offers an-
Dining   tique furnishings and excellent nouvelle cuisine. *Ballplatz 2,*
★   *tel. 06131/225068. Jacket and tie. Reservations advised. AE, DC, MC, V. Expensive.*
Rats und Zunftstuben Heilig Geist. Although the decor is predominantly modern, this popular restaurant also incorporates some Roman remains and offers a traditional atmosphere. The cuisine is hearty German fare. *Rentengasse 2, tel. 06131/225757. Reservations essential. AE, DC, MC, V. Moderate.*

Lodging   **Bristol.** Located near the city's picturesque Weisnaur Rhine Bridge, the Bristol is a new luxury hotel with comfortable rooms and good facilities. *Friedrich Eber-Str., tel. 06131/8060. 57 rooms with bath. Facilities: restaurant, bar, pool, sauna. AE, DC, MC, V. Expensive.*

Hilton International. This enormous, glossy hotel presents a number of attractive public rooms, including a rooftop restaurant and Roman wine cellar. The bedrooms are tastefully furnished. *Rheinstr. 68, tel. 06131/2450. 435 rooms with bath. Facilities: pool, sauna, health club, conference center. AE, DC, MC, V. Expensive.*

Rüdesheim
Lodging

Central. This is a friendly, family-run hotel. It also has a fine restaurant. *Kirchstr. 6, tel. 06722/2391. 53 rooms with bath. AE, DC, MC, V. Moderate.*

Hotel und Weinhaus Felfenkeller. Located just around the corner from Drosselgasse, Hotel and Weinhaus Felfenkeller is a traditional 18th-century establishment offering modern comforts. *Oberstr. 64, tel. 06722/2094. 64 rooms with bath. AE, MC, V. Inexpensive.*

St. Goar, St. Goarshausen
Dining

Roter Kopf. This is a historic wine restaurant brimming with rustic Rhineland atmosphere. *Burgstr. 5, St. Goarshausen, tel. 06771/2698. Dress: casual. No credit cards. Moderate.*

Lodging

Schlosshotel–Burg Rheinfels. Situated high above St. Goar, on a hill commanding spectacular river views, the Schlosshotel–Burg Rheinfels rises from the ruins of the adjacent castle *(see* Exploring). During the spring and fall, the hotel organizes medieval banquets. *Schlossberg 47, tel. 06741/2071. 48 rooms, all with bath. Facilities: restaurant, pool, sauna. AE, DC, MC, V. Very Expensive.*

Pohl's Rhein Hotel Adler. Perched right on the edge of the Rhine, this is a turn-of-the-century, family-run establishment. Facilities include an attractive garden and terrace. *St. Goarshausen, tel. 06771/2613. 73 rooms, all with bath. Facilities: restaurant, pool, solarium. AE, DC, MC, V. Closed Nov.– Feb. Moderate.*

The Black Forest

Only a century ago, the Black Forest (Schwarzwald) was one of the wildest stretches of countryside in Europe. It had earned its somber name because of the impenetrable stretches of dark forest that clothed the mountains and shielded small communities from the outside world. Today, it's a friendly, hospitable region, still extensively forested but with large, open valleys and stretches of verdant farmland. Among the trailblazing tourists of the adventurous 19th century was Mark Twain, who wrote enthusiastically about the natural beauty of the region. The deep hot springs first discovered by the Romans were rediscovered, and small forgotten villages became wealthy spas. Hikers treasured the lonely trails that cut through the forests and rolling uplands, skiers opened the world's first lift on the slopes of the region's highest mountain, and horseback riders cut bridle paths through the tangle of narrow river valleys.

The Black Forest is the southernmost German wine region and the custodian of some of the country's best traditional foods (Black Forest smoked ham and Black Forest cake are world-famous). It retains its vibrant clock-making tradition, and local wood-carvers haven't yet died out. Best of all, though, it's still possible to stay overnight in a Black Forest farmhouse and eat a breakfast hearty enough to last the day, all for the price of an indifferent meal at a restaurant in, say, Munich or Frankfurt.

Getting Around

Today the Black Forest is easily accessible from all parts of the country. The Rhine Valley autobahn, the A5, runs the entire length of the Black Forest and connects at Karlsruhe with the rest of the German expressway network. Well-paved, single-lane highways traverse the region. A main north–south train line follows the Rhine Valley, carrying Euro-City and Inter-City trains that call at hourly intervals at Freiburg and Baden-Baden, connecting those two centers directly with Frankfurt and many other German cities. Local lines connect most Black Forest towns, and two east–west services, the Black Forest Railway and the Höllental Railway, are spectacular scenic runs. The nearest airports are at Stuttgart and the Swiss border city of Basel, just 40 miles (64 kilometers) from Freiburg.

Guided Tours

Guided bus tours of the Black Forest begin in both Freiburg and Baden-Baden. In Freiburg, day tours are organized by the city tourist office *(see* Tourist Information) and include excursions into neighboring Switzerland (a day tour to the foot of the Eiger costs DM 40). In Baden-Baden, tours are offered by the Deutsches Reisebüro (Sofienstrasse 1b, tel. 07221/24666) and concentrate on the Black Forest, although one afternoon tour has the French border city of Strasbourg as its destination.

Tourist Information

Baden-Baden. Augustaplatz 8, tel. 07221/275200.
Freiburg. Rotteckring 14, tel. 07621/2163289.
Freudenstadt. Promenadenplatz 1, tel. 07441/8640.
Pforzheim. Marktplatz 1, tel. 07231/302314.

Exploring

The regional tourist authority has worked out a series of scenic routes covering virtually every attraction the visitor is likely to want to see (obtainable from the **Fremdenverkehrsverband,** Bertoldstrasse 45, 7800 Freiburg, tel. 0761/31317). Routes are basically intended for the motorist, but most points can be reached by train or bus. The following itinerary is accessible by all means of transportation and takes in parts of the Black Forest High Road, Low Road, Spa Road, Wine Road, and Clock Road.

The ancient Roman city of **Pforzheim** is the starting point here, accessible either from the Munich–Karlsruhe autobahn or by train from Karlsruhe/Frankfurt. Known even beyond Germany's borders as the Gold City because of its association with the jewelry trade, Pforzheim has the world's finest museum collection of jewelry in the **Reuchlinhaus,** spanning four centuries (Am Stadtgarten; closed Monday). Pforzheim was almost completely destroyed by wartime bombing and is a fine example of reconstruction work: Visit the centrally located parish church of **St. Michael** to see how faithfully the experts stuck to the original mixture of sturdy Romanesque and later, finer Gothic styles. For a contrast, take a look at Pforzheim's **St. Matthew's Church,** a tentlike construction erected in 1953 when the de-

The Black Forest

0   20 miles

0   30 km

FRANCE

Karlsruhe

Pforzheim

Bad
Liebenzell   Stuttgart

Baden-
Baden   Calw

Zavelstein   Talmühle

Kehl

Baiersbronn   Nagold

Offenburg   Freudenstadt

Zell   Neckar

B415   Alpirsbach

Lahr

Wolfach   Schiltach

Gutachtal
Valley

Rottweil

Kaiserstuhl   Triberg

Danube

Freiburg   Furtwangen

Himmelreich   Titisee   Tuttlingen

Staufen   Schluchsee

Radolfzell

Zell   Friedrichshafen

Rheinfelden   Bodensee

SWITZERLAND

signers of the similarly styled Olympic stadium in Munich were still at the drawing board.

On the way out of Pforzheim, toward B463, the Nagold Valley road, gardeners should make a detour to the **Alpine Garden** on the Tiefenbronn road. More than 100,000 varieties of plants, including the rarest Alpine flowers, are found here, and many are for sale. *Open daily Apr.–Sept.; closed Oct.–Mar.*

Bad Liebenzell, our first stop on B463, is one of the oldest spas of the Black Forest, with the remains of 15th-century installations. Visitors are welcome to take the waters at the **Paracelsus baths** on the Nagold riverbank. *Admission: DM 9.80 for 2 hours. Open Apr.–Oct., from 7:30; Nov.–Mar. from 8:30.*

Leave plenty of time to explore **Calw** (pronounced Calve), the next town on the road south. Its famous native son, the poet Hermann Hesse, called it the "most beautiful [town] of all I know." And Hesse, who died in Switzerland in 1962, had seen more than a few in his extensive travels. Pause on the town's 15th-century bridge over the rushing Nagold River—if you're lucky, you'll see a local tanner spreading hides over the river wall to dry, as his ancestors did for centuries past. Pause, too, in the town's market square and reflect on all the sights and sounds those 18th-century half-timbered houses, whose sharp gables stab the sky on all sides, must have been witness to in their time.

If you're traveling in spring, watch for a sign to **Zavelstein,** some three miles (five kilometers) out of Calw. Take the short detour up a side-valley to see the greatest natural display of wild crocuses Germany has to offer. Don't pick any of the flowers, however—the meadows are officially protected.

Back on the main road south, turn off at Talmühle for the **Neubulach silver mine.** Once the most productive workings of the Black Forest, the mine is now open to visitors—and is also home for an asthma therapy center thanks to its dry, dust-free interior. *Admission: DM 4 adults, DM 3 children (includes entry to mineral museum). Open Apr.–Oct., Mon.–Sat. 10–4, Sun. 9:30–5; closed Nov.–Mar.*

Time Out | In **Nagold,** the town that gave the river and the valley their name, drop in at the half-timbered **Alte Post** inn on the main street. Kings and queens have taken refreshment here on journeys through the Black Forest. Enjoy the local beer and a plate of Black Forest smoked ham or a pot of strong coffee and a slice of delectable Black Forest cake.

From Nagold, the road travels on through lush farmland to **Freudenstadt,** another war-flattened German city that has been painstakingly restored. It was originally built in the early 17th century as a model city to house not only workers in nearby silver mines but refugees from religious persecution in what is now Austrian Carinthia. The streets are still laid out in the grid pattern decreed by the original planners, while the vast central square continues to wait for the palace that was intended to stand here. It was to have been built for the city's founder, Prince Frederick I of Württemberg, but he died before work could begin. Don't miss Freudenstadt's **Protestant parish church,** just off the square. It's L-shaped, a rare architectural liberty in the early 17th century, when this imposing church was built.

A fine introduction to the history and traditions of the Black Forest can be obtained at the **Black Forest Museum** at Lossburg, five miles (eight kilometers) south of Freudenstadt. (In 1988, the museum was changing homes. Call the Lossburg tourist office, tel. 07446/2156, for its new address.)

Quench your thirst at nearby **Alpirsbach,** where the unusually soft water gives the local beer an especially smooth quality. South of Alpirsbach, stop at **Schiltach** to admire (and possibly giggle) at the frescoes on the 16th-century town hall that depict the history of this exceptionally pretty village. The devil figures prominently in the frescoes: He was blamed for burning Schiltach down on several occasions.

From here, take B294 to **Wolfach** to visit the last Black Forest factory, where glass is blown by centuries-old techniques once common throughout the region. *Die Wolfacher Glashutte, Glashuttenweg 4, tel. 07834/751. Admission: DM 2.50 adults, DM 1.50 children. Open Apr.–Oct., 9–3:30.*

Just outside Wolfach is the **Vogtsbauernhof Open-Air Museum** of Black Forest farmhouses, dismantled at their original sites and rebuilt here, complete with authentic interiors. *Admission: DM 4 adults, DM 2 children. Open Apr.–Oct., daily 8:30–6.*

The **Gutachtal Valley,** south of Wolfach, is famous for its traditional costumes, and if you're there at the right time (holidays and some Sundays), you'll see the married women sporting black pompoms on their hats to denote their matronly status (red pompoms are for the unmarried). At the head of the valley, at **Triberg,** are Germany's highest waterfalls, which reach a height of nearly 500 feet (152 meters). This is also cuckoo clock country. The Black Forest **Museum of Furtwangen,** south of Triberg, has lots of examples, plus one of the oldest wooden clocks in existence. It has just seven wheels and was carved (with a bread knife, no less!) in 1640. *Admission: DM 3 adults, DM 1 children. Open Apr.–Oct., daily 10–5.*

From Furtwangen, the road leads to the lakeland of the Black Forest. The two largest lakes, Titisee and Schluchsee, are beautifully set amid fir-clad mountains, but try to avoid them at the height of the summer holidays, when they are quite crowded. From here, it's a short run to Freiburg, capital of the Black Forest. The most direct route goes via the aptly named Höllental (Hell Valley). The first stop outside the narrow, gorgelike valley is called, appropriately enough, Himmelreich, meaning "Heaven." The village is said to have been given the name by railway engineers grateful finally to have run a line through Hell Valley. The Black Forest railway, more than 100 years old, still tackles the mountainous route, connecting Freiburg and the resort of Hinterzarten; details and tickets are available from the **Bundesbahn** (German Railways) in Freiburg (tel. 0761/36444).

Perched on the western slopes of the Black Forest, **Freiburg** was founded as a free market town in the 12th century, fought over by various rival armies throughout history, and badly bombed in World War II. Towering over the rebuilt, medieval streets of the city is its most famous landmark, the cathedral, or **Münster.** The cathedral took three centuries to build: Visitors can trace the progress of successive generations of builders through the changing architectural styles of the times, from the fat, 11th-century Romanesque columns and solid, rounded arches to the lofty 13th-century Gothic windows, interior, and 370-foot (113-meter) tower and delicately perforated spire, described by some art historians as the world's finest.

Try to visit Freiburg on a Friday, which is market day. The square in front of the cathedral then becomes a mass of color and movement, while a fitting backdrop is provided by **Kaufhaus,** the 16th-century market house.

Time Out Stroll up to the Oberlinden Square and call in at one of Germany's most ancient inns, **Zum Roten Bären** (the Red Bear). Order a "Viertel" of the local wine and perhaps a plate of locally smoked ham—and if you like the atmosphere, why not stay the night?

Having braved Hell Valley to get to Freiburg, a visit to the nearby town where Dr. Faustus is reputed to have made his deal with the devil should hold no horrors. **Staufen,** which claims the inquisitive doctor as one of its early burgers, is some 12 miles (19 kilometers) south of Freiburg. Local records show there really was an alchemist named Faustus who blew himself up in his laboratory. According to legend, the devil dragged him off to hell from the **Löwen** (Lion) tavern, which you can still visit on the market square.

Staufen is on the **Wine Road** and is the turning point of this tour. Now head north toward Baden-Baden, through the southernmost vineyards of Germany, source of the prized Baden wine. Some of the best vineyards are situated on a volcanic outcrop known as the Kaiserstuhl (Emperor's Chair). Sample a glass in the village of **Achkarren,** which has a fascinating **wine museum.** *Admission: DM 2 adults, DM 1 children. Open Apr.– Oct., weekdays 2–5, weekends 10:30–4.*

All the vineyards along the Wine Road offer tastings, so don't hesitate to drop in and try one or two. Leave the Wine Road at the town of Lahr and head inland, on B415, through the narrow Schuttertal valley to Zell, and from there to the Black Forest **High Road.** This is the land of fable and superstition, and if you're here during the mist-days of autumn, stop off at the mystery-shrouded **Mummelsee Lake,** immortalized by the poet Mörike in his ballad *The Spirits of the Mummelsee.* Legend has it that sprites and other spirits of the deep live in the cold waters of the small, round lake in its forest setting. It's true that no fish are found in the lake, but scientific sorts say this is a result of the high mineral content of the water.

From the Mummelsee, it's downhill all the way to fashionable **Baden-Baden,** idyllically set in a wooded valley of the northern Black Forest. The town sits on top of extensive underground hot springs that gave the city its name *(bad,* German for "spa"). The Romans first exploited the springs, which were then rediscovered by wealthy 19th-century travelers. By the end of the 19th century, there was scarcely a crowned head of Europe who had not dipped into the healing waters of Baden-Baden. The town became the unofficial summer residence of numerous royal and titled families, and they left their imprint in the form of palatial houses that grace its tree-lined avenues. Some are hotels: Brenner's Park-Hotel, in particular, is world-famous *(see* Dining and Lodging), though if the price of a room is too high, you can soak up the atmosphere over a cocktail in its piano bar.

One of the grand buildings of Baden-Baden's Belle Epoque is the pillared **Kurhaus,** home of Germany's first casino, which opened its doors to the world's gamblers in 1838. Entrance costs a modest DM 5, though visitors are required to sign a declaration that they enter with sufficient funds to settle subsequent debts! *Jacket and tie required. Passport necessary as proof of identity. Open Sun.–Fri. 2 PM–2 AM, Sat. 2 PM–3 AM. Daily tours (DM 2) from Apr.–Sept., daily 9:30–noon; Oct.–Mar., 10–noon.*

If jackets and ties are customary attire at the casino, no clothes at all are de rigueur at Baden-Baden's famous Roman baths, the **Friedrichsbad.** You "take the waters" here just as the Romans did nearly 2,000 years ago—nude. Römerplatz 1, tel. 07221/275940. *Admission: DM 25. Children under 16 not admitted. Open Mon., Wed.–Sat. 8 AM–10 PM, Tues. 8–4; Closed Sun.*

The remains of the Roman baths that lie beneath the Friedrichsbad can be visited in summer (April through October). *Admission: DM 2.*

Time Out Step into the warm elegance of the **Café König** in the nearby Lichtentalerstrasse pedestrian zone. Order a pot of coffee and a wedge of Black Forest cake and listen to the hum of contentment from the monied spa crowd who have made this quiet corner their haunt.

The attractions of the Friedrichsbad are rivaled by the neighboring **Caracalla baths,** opened in 1985. The huge, modern complex has five indoor pools, two outdoor ones, numerous whirlpools, a solarium, and what is described as a "sauna landscape"—you look out through windows at the countryside while steaming. Römerplatz 11, tel. 07221/275940. *Admission: DM 13 for 2 hours; no reduction for children. Open daily 8 AM– 10 PM.*

Dining and Lodging

For details and price category definitions, *see* Dining and Lodging in Essential Information.

Baden-Baden **Merkurius.** The owner-chef of the Merkurius is Czech born, and
Dining his menu features the best of Bohemian cooking. The comfort-
★ ably appointed restaurant, its homey atmosphere completed by an open fire, is part of a small country-house hotel 5 miles (8 kilometers) south of Baden-Baden; it's well worth the journey. Bohemian dumplings tussle with German potato pancakes for top honors. *Klosterberg 2, tel. 07223/5474. Jacket and tie. Reservations essential. AE, DC, MC. Closed all day Mon., Sun. and Tues. dinner. Expensive.*

Stahlbad. The Gallo-Germanic menu here is echoed by the restaurant's furnishings—19th century French oils adorn the walls, while French and German china are reflected in the mahogany gleam of antique tables and sideboards. An abundance of green velvet catches the tone of the parklike grounds of the stately house that accommodates this elegant restaurant. *Augustaplatz 2, tel. 07221/24569. Jacket and tie. Reservations advised. AE, DC, MC, V. Closed Sun. dinner and all day Mon. Expensive.*

Zum Alde Gott. A tiny rustic and comfortable (lots of wood, but cushions, too) restaurant in the Neuweier district, Zum Alde Gott specializes in traditional Baden dishes that are topped with imaginative touches. Try the lamb "pot au feu" and, as dessert, figs in beer pastry. *Weinstr. 10, Neuweier, tel. 07223/ 5513. Dress: casual. Reservations strongly advised. AE, DC, MC, V. Closed Thurs. and Fri. lunch. Moderate.*

Lodging **Brenner's Park Hotel.** This exceptional stately mansion, on Baden-Baden's leafy Lichtentaler Allee, is set in spacious private grounds. All rooms are luxuriously furnished and appointed—as they should be, since they cost up to DM 1,950 per day. *An der Lichtentaler Allee, tel. 07221/353353. 101 rooms with bath. Facilities: health club, pool, sauna. No credit cards. Very Expensive.*

★ **Der Kleine Prinz.** Each room of this beautifully modernized 19th-century mansion is decorated in a different style, from romantic Art Nouveau to Manhattan modern (owner Norbert Rademacher was director of New York's Waldorf Astoria for several years). Some rooms have whirlpool baths. The hotel's elegant restaurant offers "new German cuisine" with a French touch. *Lichtentalerstr. 36, tel. 07221/3464. 30 rooms with bath. Facilities: restaurant. AE, DC, MC, V. Restaurant closed Jan. Very Expensive.*

Laterne. Dating from the late 17th century, Laterne is one of Baden-Baden's oldest hotels. Public rooms, the restaurant, and some bedrooms have original beams and woodwork, as well as antique Black Forest furnishings. The hotel is central but quietly situated in a pedestrian zone, with a café-terrace at the front. *Gernsbacherstr. 10, tel. 07221/29999. 10 rooms with bath. Facilities: café, restaurant. AE, DC, MC, V. Moderate.*

Hotel am Markt. The Bogner family has run this historic, 250-year-old hotel for more than 30 years. It's friendly, popular, and right in the center of town. *Marktplatz 17–18, tel. 07221/22747. 27 rooms, 9 with bath. Facilities: restaurant and terrace. AE, DC, MC, V. Inexpensive.*

Baiersbronn
Dining
★

Bareiss. The mountain resort of Baiersbronn is blessed with 2 first-class restaurants that have become gastronomic shrines, pulling pilgrims from as far away as the French Alsace. The most famous of the two, the Bareiss, confines itself almost exclusively to French cuisine, although chef Manfred Schwarz is undeniably German (and has been voted one of Germany's top 10 cooks). *Kurhotel Mitteltal, Gärtnerbuhlweg 14, tel. 07442/471. Jacket and tie. Reservations essential. AE, DC. Closed end-Nov.–Christmas, and Mon. and Tues. Very Expensive.*

Traube Tonbach. French cuisine is also the specialty of the Traube Tonbach, where diners are settled at antique tables beneath a ceiling of gnarled beams and straw thatch. Try for a table by the large picture window overlooking the Tonbach valley. *Tonbachstr. 237, tel. 07442/4970. Jacket and tie. Reservations essential. AE, DC, MC, V. Closed Jan. 10–Feb. 10, Thurs. and Fri. lunch. Expensive.*

Freiburg
Dining

Falkenstube. A 10-course "gourmet menu" is one of the many attractions of the softly lit and oak-paneled Falkenstube restaurant in Freiburg's luxurious Colombi Hotel. The French influence is evident, from the snail and frog leg delicacies (including a delicately spiced snail soup) to a dish for 2 that dresses a whole veal fillet with pâté de foie gras and truffles. *Colombi Hotel, Rotteckring 16, tel. 0761/31415. Jacket and tie. Reservations essential. AE, DC, MC, V. Expensive.*

Kühler Krug. Venison is the staple dish here, though the restaurant's variety of fish dishes is large and imaginative. It makes its own pâté de foie gras. *Torplatz 1, tel. 0761/29103. Dress: casual. Reservations accepted. AE. Closed Thurs. and 3 weeks in June. Moderate.*

Ratskeller. In the shadow of the cathedral, the popular Ratskeller has a typical Black Forest ambience (lots of wood paneling and beams), which is matched by a menu of mostly traditional dishes (roasts and rich sauces). *Münsterplatz 11, tel. 0761/37530. Dress: casual. Reservations advised. AE, DC, MC, V. Closed Sun. dinner, Mon. Moderate.*

Zum Roten Baren. The Red Bear claims to be the oldest inn in Germany (it was first mentioned in official documents in 1311). True or not, it's the archetypal German history-book inn, with a traditional menu to match. Demand Swabian *Spätzle* (a delicious variety of noodle) with everything. *Oberlinden 12, tel. 0761/36913. Dress: informal. Reservations advised. AE, DC, MC, V. Moderate.*

Lodging

Panorama Hotel am Jägerhäusle. This hotel is situated high above Freiburg, although it's only a few minutes by car to the downtown area. All rooms have south-facing balconies, with fine views of the city and surrounding countryside. *Wintererstr. 89, tel. 0761/51030. 85 rooms with bath. Facilities: pool, sauna, solarium, tennis, ping-pong. AE, DC, MC, V. Very Expensive.*

Novotel. One of a European chain of modern hotels offering a high degree of comfort and conveniences at relatively modest rates, the Novotel is only a few minutes' walk from the old city. City tours and Black Forest excursions are willingly organized by the reception staff. *Am Karlsplatz 1, tel. 0761/31295. 112 rooms with bath. Facilities: garden terrace, conference room. AE, DC, MC, V. Expensive.*

★ **Romantik Hotel Stollen.** Run by the same family for the past 140 years, this half-timbered country house offers rooms decorated to a sophisticated standard; some have romantic detailing like canopied beds. The restaurant has won awards for its excellent concoctions. Located in Gutach im Elztal, 6 miles (9 kilometers) from Freiburg, the hotel is best reached from the Karlsrühe–Basle autobahn by taking the Freiburg north exit and following the Waldkirch road. *7809 Gutach im Elztal, tel. 07685/207. 10 rooms with bath. AE, DC, MC, V. Expensive.*

Rappen Hotel. You'll sleep like a pampered farmhouse guest here, in brightly painted rustic beds, beneath soft feather quilts. It's as quiet as a country village, too: The Rappen is in the center of the traffic-free old city. In the countrified but comfortable restaurant, patrons have the choice of more than 200 regional wines. *Am Münsterplatz 13, tel. 0761/31353. 20 rooms, most with bath. Facilities: bar-restaurant, terrace. AE, DC, MC, V. Moderate.*

Freudenstadt **Baren.** Fish is the Baren's strength (with local trout a special-
Dining ty), but simple, traditional Swabian dishes find a prominent place on the menu, too. If you like tripe, this is *the* place to indulge yourself. *Langestr. 33, tel. 07441/6585. Dress: casual. Reservations advised. AE, DC, MC, V. Closed Sun. dinner, Mon., and last 2 weeks in Jan. Moderate.*

Ratskeller. If it's cold outside, ask for a place near the Ratskeller's *Kachelofen*, a large, traditional, tiled heating stove. Swabian dishes and venison are prominent on the menu, but if the homemade trout roulade with crab sauce is featured, go for it. *Marktplatz 8, tel. 07441/2693. Dress: casual. Reservations accepted. AE, DC, MC, V. Closed Tues. and Feb. Moderate.*

Lodging **Golfhotel-Waldlust.** A spacious villa set in its own extensive grounds, the Waldlust is equipped with fine views of the Black Forest countryside. In its pillared lounge, tea dances are held most days and an orchestra plays in the evening. Its guest rooms are traditionally furnished and sport carefully selected antiques. *Lauterbachstr. 92, tel. 07441/4051. 110 rooms with bath. Facilities: bar, terrace. No credit cards. Expensive.*

Schwarzwaldhotel Birkenhof. This hotel describes itself as a sport hotel, although its old-fashioned comfort and woodland setting have appeal for the less active. The town center is, however, a 15-minute walk away. For the athletically inclined, the hotel provides a squash court, miniature golf course, outdoor ping-pong tables, a bowling alley, and an indoor swimming pool. The pool complex alone has a sauna, solarium, steam bath and whirlpool and offers massage and other beauty treatment. The hotel's 2 restaurants offer a choice of French or Black Forest cuisine. *Wildbaderstr. 95, tel. 07441/4074. 60 rooms with bath. AE, DC, MC, V. Expensive.*

Hotel Schwanen. The Schwanen has been efficiently managed by the capable Bukenberger family since 1900. Centrally situated, only 2 minutes' walk from the train station, it gives excellent value and above-average comfort. *Forststr. 6, tel. 07441/2267. 17 rooms with bath. No credit cards. Inexpensive.*

Landhaus Bukenberger. The Bukenbergers run this one, too.

Its country-lodge exterior is picked up by lots of wood inside: The paneled television and reading room is a particularly snug retreat. *Herrenfelderstr. 65, tel. 07441/2771. 14 rooms with bath. No credit cards. Inexpensive.*

Hinterzarten
Lodging
★

Park Hotel Adler. This hotel has been in the possession of the Riesterer family for more than five centuries: Since 1446, when an early ancestor gave 17 schillings for the original property, it has been developing into one of Germany's finest hotels. The hotel complex stands in nearly 2 acres (8,100 square meters) of grounds ringed by the Black Forest. Among the 7 rooms devoted to eating and drinking are a French restaurant and a paneled 17th-century dining room. An orchestra accompanies dinner and later moves to the bar for dancing. *Adlerplatz 3, tel. 07652/711. 75 rooms with bath. Facilities: pool, sauna, solarium, tennis (indoor and outdoor), Ping-Pong, golf. AE, DC, MC, V. Very Expensive.*

Nagold
Dining

Romantik Restaurant Alte Post. This centuries-old half-timbered inn has the kind of atmosphere lesser establishments believe can be built in with false beams. The menu ranges from Swabian traditional to pricey French, so stay with the local dishes (veal in a rich mushroom sauce or, in season, venison in the Baden-Baden style) and you won't be shocked by the bill. *Bahnhofstr. 2, tel. 07452/4221. Dress: casual. Reservations essential. AE, DC, MC, V. Closed for 2 weeks in Jan., and on Sat. morning. Moderate.*

Lodging

Hotel Post Gästehaus. Run by the former proprietors of the adjacent Alte Post restaurant, the Post Gästehaus is a modern, ivy-clad hotel offering a high degree of comfort—and home-made preserves for breakfast. *Bahnhofstr. 3, tel. 07452/4048. 24 rooms with bath. Facilities: English-language cable TV. AE, DC, MC, V. Expensive.*

Pforzheim
Dining

Rotisserie Le Canard. A little corner of France right in Pforzheim's Gute Hoffnung Hotel, this French country house-style restaurant doesn't restrict its menu solely to French cuisine but pays just as much attention to local Swabian fare. The home-made *Spätzle* (Swabian noodle) with fresh herbs is first-rate. *Dillsteinerstr. 9–11, tel. 07231/22011. Jacket and tie. Reservations advised. AE, DC, MC, V. Closed Sun. Expensive.*

Titisee
Lodging

Romantik Hotel Adler Post. This hotel is in the Neustadt district of Titisee, about 3 miles (5 kilometers) from the lake. The solid old building has been in the possession of the Ketterer family for nearly 140 years. Guest rooms are comfortably and traditionally furnished. The hotel's restaurant, the Rotisserie zum Postillon, has built up a good name locally. *Hauptstr. 16, tel. 07651/5066. 32 rooms with bath. Facilities: pool, sauna, solarium. AE, DC, MC, V. Expensive.*

14 Gibraltar

Introduction

Gibraltar is the tiny British colony that dominates the straits dividing Africa from Europe at the point where the Atlantic rushes past to become the Mediterranean. The outline of the great Rock is known to millions the world over, even if they have never seen it for themselves. This impressive promontory, 2¼ miles square and just under 1,400 feet high, was a well-known landmark in classical times. One of the fabled pillars of Hercules, Gibraltar acquired its present name in AD 711, when the Moorish chieftain Tarik captured it. The Rock became known as Gib el Tarik—the Rock of Tarik—later corrupted to Gibraltar.

Gibraltar was held briefly by Spain from 1309 to 1333, and again from 1462 until it was taken by an Anglo-Dutch force in 1704. It has been a British possession since the Treaty of Utrecht in 1713. Spain has been laying claim to Gibraltar for many years on geographical and historical grounds; for nearly 16 years, from 1969 to 1985, the frontier between Spain and Gibraltar was closed as a result of this dispute. In February 1985, after Spain had joined NATO and in readiness for her entry into the European Economic Community, the border was opened. As a result, elaborate plans are under way to develop the Rock's tourist potential, including building a modern tourist complex with a deluxe hotel, marina, casino, and shopping center.

Before You Go

When to Go The best times to visit Gibraltar are in May, early June, and from mid-September through October. July and August can be overpoweringly hot except when the strong levanter winds blow. It is very rainy in November and December and from mid-January through February. Frosts are practically unknown. The last time it snowed here was in 1954—for two minutes!

The following are the average daily maximum and minimum temperatures for Gibraltar.

Jan.	60F	16C	May	73F	23C	Sept.	79F	26C
	50	10		60	15		67	19
Feb.	62F	17C	June	78F	25C	Oct.	73F	23C
	51	11		64	18		62	17
Mar.	65F	18C	July	83F	28C	Nov.	66F	19C
	54	12		68	20		57	14
Apr.	68F	20C	Aug.	83F	29C	Dec.	62F	17C
	56	13		69	21		53	11

Currency Official currency is the British pound sterling (*see* Currency, in Great Britain). At press time (fall 1988), one pound was equal to $1.70. Most shops and restaurants will also accept payment in Spanish pesetas (ptas.), however.

What It Will Cost
Sample Prices A cup of coffee costs around 50 pence; a beer, 80 pence; Coca-Cola, 70 pence; a ham sandwich, £1.20, depending on where you buy it; a bus ride, 30 pence; and an average cab fare about £2.

Customs on Arrival Visitors 17 and over who have not been in Gibraltar within the previous 24 hours are allowed to bring in 200 cigarettes or 100

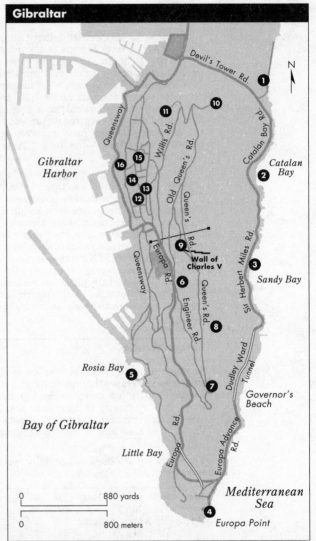

Gibraltar

cigarillos or 50 cigars or 250 grams of tobacco; 1 liter of liquor or 2 liters of fortified and sparkling wines and 2 liters of still wine; 50 grams of perfume and 0.25 liters of toilet water.

Language Gibraltarians are bilingual in English and Spanish. They speak mostly Spanish among themselves, but because English is the official language, you will have no problem communicating.

Arriving and Departing

By Plane **British Airways, G.B. Airways,** and **Air Europe** fly into Gibraltar's **North Front Airport** (tel. 53352) daily from London's Gatwick. Air Europe also operates from Manchester. The flight takes around 2½ hours, and some B.A. flights continue on to Casablanca in Morocco. Some charter flights operate in conjunction with package holidays, but most packages use scheduled flights. Further details are available from travel agencies or the **Gibraltar Government Tourist Office** (179 Strand, London WC2R 1EH, tel. 01/836–7777).

By Bus **Juliá Tours, Pullmantour,** and numerous cheaper small agencies operate one-day tours to Gibraltar from Spain's Costa del Sol resorts, daily except Sunday. Cost: 3,600 ptas. in 1988. A cheaper way to visit the Rock is to take the regular **Portillo** bus to La Linea, then walk across the border. Alternatively, Portillo buses run a Gibraltar trip daily in summer from Torremolinos bus station.

By Car If you're coming from Spain, leave the N340 coastal highway at San Roque, just east of Algeciras, and follow the signs to La Linea. You can either park your car in La Linea—but don't leave anything on view inside—and walk across the border, or take your car into Gibraltar, making sure you have a certificate of insurance, registration certificate or log book, a nationality plate ("E" for Spain), and a valid driver's license.

From Morocco In summer, **G.B. Airways** operates flights between Tetuan and Tangiers, though these are mostly in conjunction with one-day trips to Morocco. A sea service by fast catamaran operates between Tangiers and Gibraltar. The sea trip takes around an hour and runs daily in summer, less often in winter. There is no car ferry service at present.

Getting Around

By Car Driving is on the right, even though this is British territory. The crowds of Spanish, British, and American residents of the Costa del Sol who flock over the border daily cause a huge parking problem. Official parking lots are at Grand Parade (at the lower cable car station), Eastern Beach, Catalan Bay, and Casemates Square. Some street parking is allowed on Queensway, Line Wall Road, Devil's Tower Road, and Rosia Road. Most of the town center is for pedestrians only, so park outside the city walls.

By Taxi Taxi fares work out to around £1.50 a mile, or prearrange fares for longer trips. **Taxi Association,** tel. 70027.

By Bus There are half a dozen bus services that cover most parts of the Rock; a list of routes and schedules is available from the tourist information offices. The flat fare was 30 pence at press time.

By Cable Car The cable car to the summit of the Rock runs from Monday through Saturday. At the top is a bar and cafeteria, and there are breathtaking views of the Bay of Gibraltar, Andalusia, and Morocco. The cable car station is on Grand Parade at the southern end of Main Street, and there's a halfway station at the Apes' Den.

Essential Information

Telephones Pay phones are the same as those in Britain and take 10 pence and 50 pence coins; a few also work with peseta coins. To call a number in Spain, dial the code for the relevant province (e.g.,

952 for Malaga) followed by the number. Instructions for local and international calls are clearly posted in English.

Mail The central post office is on Main Street near Tuckey's Lane. It sells stamps and can advise on current mail rates.

Shopping Shopping has always been a big attraction in Gibraltar because goods are free of VAT (Value Added Tax). Duty-free facilities are available for visitors leaving by sea or air, and duty-free prices are among the lowest in Europe. The real bargains are in electrical and stereo goods, cameras, watches, and designer fashion accessories.

Opening and Closing Times **Banks.** Banks are usually open 9–3:30 Monday–Thursday, 9–3:30 and 4–6 on Friday.

Shops. Shops are usually open Monday–Saturday 9–1 and 3–7. Many shops close Saturday afternoon, especially in summer, and several stay open throughout the siesta.

National Holidays January 1; March 13 (Commonwealth Day); March 24 (Good Friday); March 27 (Easter Monday); May 1 (May Day Bank Holiday); May 29 (Spring Bank Holiday); June 13 (Queen's Birthday); August 28 (August Bank Holiday); December 25, 26.

Tipping Most restaurants include a 10% service charge on their bill, maybe 12% or 15% in some cases. If this charge is not included, then 10% is the norm if you are satisfied with the service. There is no need to tip for drinks in pubs. Taxi drivers get 10% of the fare as a tip.

Important Addresses and Numbers **Tourist offices** are on Cathedral Square, the Piazza, and John Mackintosh Square, tel. 76400. Open 8:45–5:30 daily.

Emergencies **St. Bernards Hospital,** tel. 79700; **Police,** tel. 190; **Fire and Ambulance,** tel. 199.

Guided Tours *Walking Tours* A town walking-tour leaflet is available from the tourist office, as is information on dolphin safaris, fishing, and boat cruises. A guided walking tour of places of worship leaves the Piazza Tourist Office on Wednesday at 10 AM; another walking tour of sea walls and defenses leaves from the Koehler Gun in Casemates Square on Friday at 10:30 AM. The Caleta Palace Hotel organizes a tour of World War II tunnels, including General Eisenhower's WW II headquarters inside the Rock.

Bus Tours Two good tours are run by **Bland Ltd.** (Cloister Bldg., Irish Town, tel. 79200), and **Calypso Tours** (21 Horse Barrack La., tel. 76520/28); cost is around £4. For a tour of the Rock by taxi, contact **Gibraltar Taxi Association** (12 Cannon La., tel. 956/70027). Cost: £4 with a minimum of four persons per taxi.

Exploring Gibraltar

This tour of Gibraltar follows a route around the Rock's circumference, starting on the eastern side, driving down to the southern tip, and back along the western slopes, ending in the town. As you enter the Rock, turn left down Devil's Tower Road, which will bring you to the eastern shores with the **Eastern Beach** and **Catalan Bay,** a small fishing village founded by Genoese settlers in the 18th century, now one of the Rock's most picturesque resorts. The road continues to another resort, **Sandy Bay,** then plunges through the Dudley Ward

Tunnel before bringing you out at the Rock's most southerly
④ tip, **Europa Point.** Stop here to admire the view across the
straits to the coast of Morocco, 14 miles away. You are standing
on what was known in ancient times as one of the two Pillars of
Hercules, which marked the known limits of the Western
world. Across the water, in Morocco, a mountain between the
cities of Ceuta and Tangiers was the second pillar. The lighthouse on Europa Point opened in 1841; its light can be seen from
a distance of 17 miles.

Europa Road winds its way high on the western slopes above
⑤ Little Bay, Camp Bay, and **Rosia Bay,** to which Admiral
Nelson's flagship, HMS *Victory*, was towed after the Battle of
Trafalgar in 1805. Aboard were the dead of the battle, who are
now buried in Trafalgar Cemetery on the southern edge of the
town. Nelson's body, until it was sent back to London for burial
in St. Paul's crypt, was preserved in a barrel of rum—a liquor
known ever since to the British navy as Nelson's blood.

⑥ Europa Road brings you to the **Casino** above the Alameda Gar-
⑦ dens. Make a sharp right here up Engineer Road to **Jews Gate,** a
lookout point with an unbeatable view over the docks and the
⑧ Bay of Gibraltar to Algeciras in Spain. Queens Road leads to **St.
Michael's Cave,** a series of underground chambers adorned
with stalactites and stalagmites, a subterranean lake, and a
mysterious breeze (perhaps blowing from Africa?). The cave
has been converted into an auditorium for concerts, ballet, and
drama. Sound and light shows are held in this magical setting
most days at 11 AM and 4 PM. *Tel. 76400. Admission: £1. Open
daily 10–7 (5:30 in winter).*

⑨ Old Queens Road brings you down to the **Apes' Den** near the
Wall of Charles V. The famous Barbary Apes are a breed of
cinnamon-colored, tailless monkeys, natives of the Atlas Mountains in Morocco. The legend is that as long as the apes remain,
the British will continue to hold the Rock. Winston Churchill, a
great believer in tradition, issued orders for the maintenance of
the ape colony when its numbers began to dwindle during
World War II. Today the apes are the responsibility of the British army, and a special officer in charge of apes is assigned to
look after them.

Passing beneath the cable car that runs to the Rock's summit,
⑩ drive up now to the **Upper Galleries** at the northern end of the
Rock. These huge galleries were carved out during the Great
Siege of 1779–83, when the French and Spanish made a great
effort to wrest Gibraltar from British control. The 18th-
century gallery leads to **St. Georges Hall,** where in 1878 the
Governor Lord Napier of Magdala entertained ex-President
Ulysses S. Grant and his wife at a banquet. From here, a dog-
leg tunnel, the **Holyland Tunnel,** leads out to the east side of the
Rock above Catalan Bay, enabling you to travel right through
the Rock, though you'll have to retrace your steps to leave by
the original entrance. *Upper Galleries, tel. 76400. Admission:
70 pence. Open daily 10–7 (5:30 in winter).*

The last stop before descending to the town is at the **Moorish
Castle** on Willis Road. Built originally by successors of the
⑪ Moorish invader Tarik-ibn-Zeyad, the present **Tower of Homage** was rebuilt by the Moors in 1333, after its destruction
during a seige by Spanish Christians. Admiral Rooke hoisted
the British flag from its top when he captured the Rock in 1704,

and it has flown here ever since. *Tel. 76400. Admission: 20 pence. Open daily 10–7 (5:30 in winter).*

Willis Road leads steeply down to the colorful, congested town of Gibraltar, an 18th-century British town built over the Spanish town of the 15th and 16th centuries (which, in its turn, was built on Moorish foundations from the Middle Ages). The dignified English Regency architecture blends well with the shutters, balconies, and patios of southern Spain. If you can tear yourself away from the attractions of the Main Street shops and restaurants, you'll want to visit some of the following: the **Governor's Residence,** a former Franciscan convent where the ceremonial Changing of the Guard takes place each Tuesday at 11 AM; the **Law Courts** on Main Street, where the famous case of the mysterious *Mary Celeste* sailing ship was heard in 1872 (both courts and residence can be seen from the outside only); the Anglican **Cathedral of the Holy Trinity,** head church of the Diocese of Gibraltar, which incorporates all Anglican churches in Europe from Portugal east to the Caspian Sea; the Catholic **Cathedral of St. Mary the Crowned,** a former mosque; and the most worthwhile sight of all, the **Gibraltar Museum,** whose 10 rooms recall the history of the Rock throughout the ages. Here you can see a Moorish 14th-century bathhouse, lighted by light from the star-shaped vents in its ceiling; and an 1865 model of the Rock. *Gibraltar Museum. Bomb House La., tel. 74289. Admission: 50 pence. Open Mon.–Sat. 10–6.*

Dining

Gibraltar has responded to its tourist tide by opening dozens of eateries, ranging from small select ones to fast-food outlets, with an English tearoom or two thrown in for good measure. Prices are higher than in Spain; service and cover charges are often added.

Ratings Our price categories are calculated per person for a three-course meal. Best bets are indicated by a star ★. At press time, one pound (£) was equal to $1.70.

Category	Cost
Expensive	over £14
Moderate	£8–£14
Inexpensive	under £8

Credit Cards The following credit card abbreviations are used: AE, American Express; DC, Diners Club; MC, MasterCard; V, Visa.

Expensive **La Bayuca.** This is one of the Rock's longest established restaurants. Prince Charles and Prince Andrew have dined here ★ when on naval service. It is especially renowned for its onion soup and Mediterranean dishes. *21 Turnbull's La., tel. 75119. Jacket and tie. Reservations advised. AE, DC, MC, V. Closed Tues. and Sun. lunch.*

Casino. Delicious barbecues are held in the Japanese Gardens here in the summer, and the Casino's main dining room offers panoramic views over the Bay and Straits of Gibraltar. *Europa Rd., tel. 76666. Jackets (ties required only in gambling rooms). Reservations advised. AE, DC, MC, V.*

Country Cottage. Opposite the Catholic Cathedral, this is the place to go for a taste of Old England. Enjoy steak and kidney pie, Angus steak, and roast beef by candlelight. *13 Giro's Passage, tel. 70084. Dress: informal. Reservations advised. AE, MC, V. Closed Sun.*

El Patio. This Basque-owned restaurant is ideal for anyone who likes Spanish food. It specializes in seafood and offers a good wine list. Try the *paella*—a sort of fishy stew—if it's on the menu. *54 Irish Town, tel. 70822. Dress: informal. Reservations not required. V. Closed Sat. lunch, Sun., and June.*

Moderate **Bacchus Bistro.** This informal bistro and wine bar right on the central piazza off Main Street offers dining on a pleasant outdoor terrace in the square. Specialties include crepes, pasta, kebabs, and T-bone steaks. *28 John Mackintosh Sq., tel. 71168. Dress: informal. Reservations not necessary. No credit cards.*

★ **Woods.** One of three good restaurants at the marina, Woods's menu includes crab roulade, noisettes of lamb, pork Dijonnaise, and beef Angus; fresh fish is available daily. *Marina Bay, tel. 79241. Dress: informal. Reservations advised but not required. AE, DC, MC, V. Closed Sat. and Sun. lunch.*

Inexpensive The budget-minded should try any of the pubs along Main Street or the streets just off it. They offer a tasty selection of "pub grub," ideal for a light lunch, and you won't face a service or cover charge.

Lodging

Prices are for two people in a double room; breakfast is usually extra. Best bets are indicated by a star ★. At press time, one pound (£) was equal to $1.70.

Category	Cost
Expensive	over £55
Moderate	£30–£55
Inexpensive	under £30

Credit Cards The following credit card abbreviations are used: AE, American Express; DC, Diners Club; MC, MasterCard; V, Visa.

Expensive **Holiday Inn.** This recently renovated member of the international chain is modern, comfortable, and right in the center of town. The ocean views are fantastic while you sun yourself by the side of the 10th-story rooftop pool or on the sun terrace. *Governor's Parade, tel. 70500. 112 rooms with bath. Facilities: restaurant, coffee shop, bar, health club, sauna, nightclub, pool. AE, DC, MC, V.*

★ **Rock.** Currently a £250,000 refurbishment program is under way, aimed at bolstering the Rock's reputation as Gibraltar's supreme luxury hotel. You'll find a comfortable, old-fashioned English atmosphere here, along with a pool and a sun terrace with its own gardens. Located on the Rock's western slopes, the hotel overlooks the town and harbor. *3 Europa Rd., tel. 73000. 160 rooms with bath. Facilities: restaurant, pool, bar, shops, nearby golf. AE, DC.*

Moderate **Bristol.** This colonial-style hotel is just off Gibraltar's main street, right in the heart of town. Rooms are unusually large and comfortable, and the tropical garden is a real haven for those guests who just want to relax in peaceful isolation. *10 Cathedral Sq., tel. 76800. 60 rooms with bath. Facilities: restaurant, garden bar, snack bar, sun terrace, pool. AE, DC, MC, V.*

★ **Caleta Palace.** Gibraltar's main package-tour hotel is situated on a cliff overhanging the picturesque village of Catalan Bay. Rooms at the front have sea views and are worth the extra charge. There's a pool on the terrace, which has steps leading down to the beach. This one is at the upper end of the Moderate range. *Catalan Bay, tel. 76501. 200 rooms with bath. Facilities: restaurant, coffee shop, 3 bars, game room, pool, private access to beach. AE, DC, MC, V.*

Inexpensive **Montarik.** Ten minutes away from the beach—but still with soul-stirring views of the sea—this mid-60s fabrication is not big on architectural beauty, and room decor is decidedly low-key. It's comfortable enough, though; the staff is friendly, and the glimpse of a Gibraltar sunset from the deck of the terrace bar should be enough to keep anyone happy. *Main St., tel. 77065. 64 rooms with bath. Facilities: restaurant, coffee shop, summer sunroof and bar. AE, V.*

Queen's. Located just outside the old city walls, the modern, hacienda-style Queen's is a fairly standard sort of hotel. Don't expect great luxury, but the price is right for what you get. *Boyd St., near the Southport Gate, tel. 74000. 62 rooms, some with bath. Facilities: restaurant, bar, TV room, game room. AE, DC, MC, V.*

15 Great Britain

Introduction

Great Britain is a small country with a long history spread out for all to see. Two factors have helped to ensure the preservation of so much of the nation's past. First is the absence of fighting on British soil. While for centuries Britain's armies crossed the channel to take part in European wars and during the 18th and 19th centuries it won for itself an extensive worldwide Empire, the physical fact of the English Channel has kept its shores from invasion for more than 900 years, thus avoiding the process of destruction and reconstruction seen in much of the rest of Europe. In addition, the nation's internal conflicts, though bloody, have generally been brief. The second factor is the innate sense of history (some would call it conservatism) of the British, who generally prefer the old to the new and are often reluctant to contemplate any kind of change, especially in their physical surroundings.

All this means that Great Britain is an ideal holiday destination for anyone with a feel for the past. Here are soaring medieval cathedrals, tributes to the faith of the churchmen and masons who built them; grand country mansions of the aristocracy filled with treasures—paintings, furniture, tapestries—and set in elegantly landscaped grounds; and grim fortified castles, their gray stone walls set fast against all challengers.

But Britain is not merely a historical theme park, and the visitor who concentrates solely on such traditional sights misses the essence of the land and the people. Many of the pleasures of exploration away from the main tourist routes derive from the constantly changing variety of the countryside. A day's drive from York, for example, will take you through long stretches of wild, heather-covered moorland, ablaze with color in the fall, or past the steep, sheep-covered mountainsides of the Dales, cut by deep valleys and scattered with isolated stone-built hamlets.

Wandering off the beaten track will also let you discover the distinctive character of Britain's many small country towns and villages. A medieval parish church, a high street of 18th-century buildings interrupted by occasional survivors from earlier centuries, and a grandiose Victorian town hall, all still in use today, help to convey a sense of a living past.

This direct continuity of past and present can be experienced in such a celebrated and tourist-filled place as Stratford-upon-Avon, but even more so in such communities as the little town of Chipping Campden, set in the rolling Cotswold Hills, or Bury St. Edmunds, in the gentle Suffolk countryside east of Cambridge. In such places, the visitor's understanding is often helped by small museums devoted to explaining local history, full of intriguing artifacts and information on trade, traditions, and social life. Such towns, too, are the places to look for specialty goods, such as knitwear, pottery, glass, and pictures, the product of a 1980s renaissance in craftsmanship.

In contrast is the hectic, at times aggressive, pace of life in London, still one of the world's great metropolises. This is a city that scarcely seems to sleep (never at all, for devotees of late-night clubs and dance spots), with a vibrant artistic, cultural, and commercial life. Yet here, too, the links with the past are numerous and plain for all to see. For instance, despite all the recent rebuilding, the basic street pattern of the City (the financial quarter between St. Paul's Cathedral and the Tower of London) is the one that evolved in the Middle Ages, more than 600 years ago; and still standing is much of the work of Christopher Wren, the master architect chiefly responsible for reconstruction after the disastrous fire of 1666. Most notable of these works is St. Paul's itself. Here again, exploration off the beaten track will reward you with the discovery of a London relatively untouched by tourists.

Finally, it is important to remember that Great Britain consists of two nations, England and Scotland, and that 400 miles (640 kilometers) north of London lies another capital city, Edinburgh, whose streets and monuments bear witness to the often turbulent and momentous history of the Scottish people.

Before You Go

When To Go   The main tourist season runs from mid-April to mid-October. In recent years, however, parts of the winter—especially December—have been almost as busy. Winter is also the height of London's theater, ballet, and opera season. Springtime reveals the countryside at its most verdant and beautiful, while fall offers soft vistas of muted, golden color. September and October are the months to visit the northern moorlands and Scottish highlands, while June is best for Wales and the Lake District. Most British people take their vacations during July and August, when costs and accommodations are at a premium.

Climate   On the whole, Britain's climate is a temperate one: Winters are rarely bitter and summers are unlikely to be scorchers. But wherever you are, and whatever the season, be prepared for sudden changes. What begins as a brilliant, sunny day often turns into a damp and dismal one by lunchtime. Take an umbrella and raincoat wherever you go, particularly in Scotland. In general, temperatures in the north are somewhat cooler.

The following are the average daily maximum and minimum temperatures for London.

Jan.	43F	6C	May	62F	17C	Sept.	65F	19C
	36	2		47	8		52	11
Feb.	44F	7C	June	69F	20C	Oct.	58F	14C
	36	2		53	12		46	8
Mar.	50F	10C	July	71F	22C	Nov.	50F	10C
	38	3		56	14		42	5
Apr.	56F	13C	Aug.	71F	21C	Dec.	45F	7C
	42	6		56	13		38	4

Currency   The British unit of currency is the pound sterling, divided into 100 pence (p). Bills are issued in denominations of 5, 10, 20, and 50 pounds (£). Coins are £1, 50p, 20p, 10p (the same as the old two-shilling piece, still in circulation), 5p (the old one-shilling piece), 2p, and 1p. Scottish banks issue their own currency, and all coins and notes—with the exception of the £1 notes—are accepted in England. At press time (fall 1988), the exchange rate was approximately $1.70 to the pound.

Credit cards and traveler's checks are widely accepted in Britain, and many banks, hotels, and shops offer currency-ex-

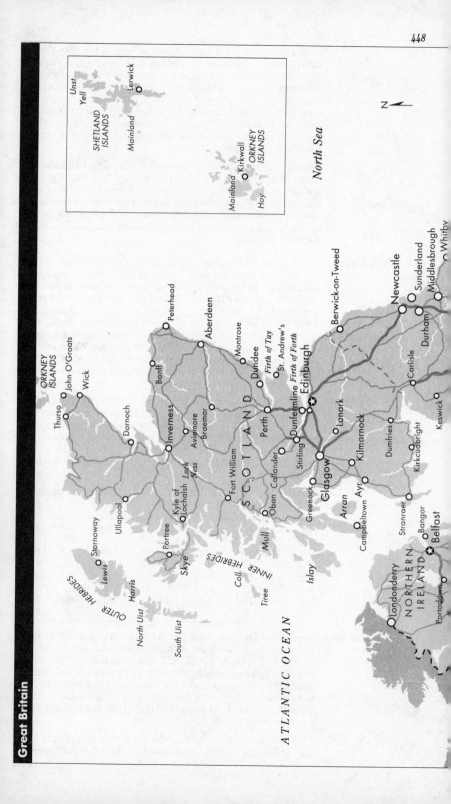

Great Britain

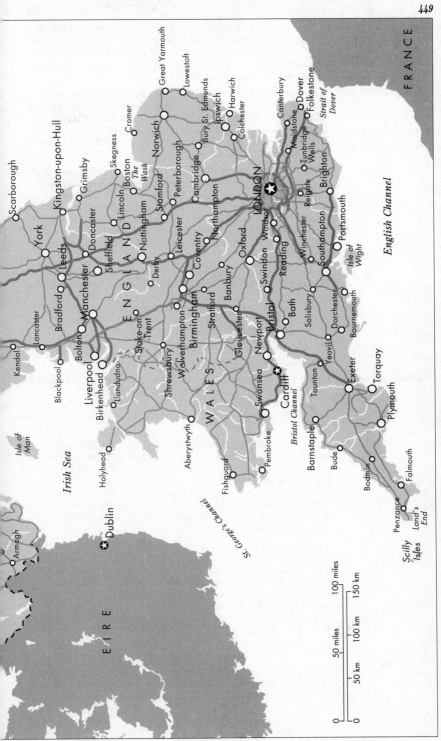

change facilities. You will probably lose from 1¢ to 4¢ on the dollar, however, depending on where you change them; banks offer the best rates. In London and other big cities, Bureaux de Change abound, but beware: They usually have a minimum charge of 50p, and often a great deal more.

What It Will Cost In general, transportation in Britain is expensive in comparison with other countries. You would be well advised to take advantage of the many reductions and special fares available on trains, buses, and subways. Always ask about these when buying your ticket. Gasoline prices are about the same as those on the Continent.

London now ranks with Tokyo as one of the world's most expensive hotel capitals. Finding budget accommodations—especially during July and August—can be difficult. Many London hotels offer special off-season (October–March) rates, however. Dining out, even in moderate restaurants, can be prohibitively expensive, though a large number of pubs offer excellent food at reasonable prices, and fast-food facilities are springing up all over.

Remember that the gulf between prices in the capital and outside is wide, so try to divide your time between London and the rest of the country. But take advantage of one ubiquitous bargain: All state-owned museums are free to visitors. Be prepared to pay 15% VAT (Value Added Tax) on almost everything you buy, however.

Sample Prices For London: Cup of coffee, 50p; pint of beer, £1.20; soda, 40p; one-mile taxi ride, £2.20; ham sandwich, £1.

Customs on Arrival There are two levels of duty-free allowance for people entering the United Kingdom; one, for goods bought outside the EEC or for goods bought in a duty-free shop within the EEC; two, for goods bought in an EEC country but not in a duty-free shop.

In the first category, you may import duty-free 200 cigarettes or 100 cigarillos or 50 cigars or 250 grams of tobacco *(Note:* If you live outside Europe, these allowances are doubled), plus one liter of alcoholic drinks over 22% volume or two liters of alcoholic drinks not over 22% volume or fortified or sparkling wine, plus two liters of still table wine, plus 50 grams of perfume, plus nine fluid ounces of toilet water, plus other goods to the value of £32.

In the second category, you may import duty-free 300 cigarettes or 150 cigarillos or 75 cigars or 400 grams of tobacco, plus 1.5 liters of alcoholic drinks over 22% volume or three liters of alcoholic drinks not over 22% volume or fortified or sparkling wine, plus four liters of still table wine, plus 75 grams of perfume, plus 13 fluid ounces of toilet water, plus other goods to the value of £250. *(Note:* Though it is not classified as an alcoholic drink by EEC countries for Customs' purposes and is thus considered part of the "other goods" allowance, you may not import more than 50 liters of beer.)

In addition, no animals or pets of any kind may be brought into the United Kingdom. The penalties for doing so are severe and are strictly enforced.

Getting Around

By Car
Road Conditions Britain has superhighways (called motorways) running almost the length of the country, with links connecting them in the South, Midlands, and North. Motorways, given the prefix M on maps and road signs, have two or three lanes in each direction and are designed for high-speed, rather than scenic, travel.

The main north–south road between London and Leeds is M1. Other principal routes are M5, running from the Midlands to the Southwest, and M6, from the Midlands north to Scotland. M4 covers the route from London to Wales via Bristol. Divided A roads are usually shown on maps as thick, red lines, and, except for occasional traffic lights, are similar to motorways. Most other major routes are the 19th-century coach and turnpike roads designed for horses and carriages. Although they—and the even narrower, winding village roads—will allow you to see much more of the real Britain, your journey could end up taking twice the time. In remote country areas, road travel can be slow, especially in icy winter. Good planning maps are available from the AA (Automobile Association) and the RAC (Royal Automobile Club); for in-depth exploring, try the Ordnance Survey 1:50,000-series maps. These show every road, track, and footpath in the country.

Rules of the Road You can use either your driver's license or an International Driving Permit in Britain. Drive on the left-hand side of the road and pay close attention to the varying—and abruptly changing—speed limits. Seat belts are obligatory for front-seat passengers. In general, speed limits are 30 mph in the center of cities and built-up areas, 40 mph in suburban areas, 70 mph on motorways and divided highways, and 60 mph on all other roads.

Parking Parking in London and other large cities can be a nightmare. On-street meters are hard to find, and lots, though available, can be very expensive. Cheaper pay-and-display lots are common in smaller towns and suburban areas. But wherever you are, in town or city, beware of yellow lines. A single yellow line denotes a loading zone—you may park for no longer than 20 minutes during daytime hours—and a double one means no parking anytime, day or night. In parts of London, as well as in some large northern cities, wheel clamping is on the rise as a parking penalty. Getting your car unclamped entails a hefty fine, so be sure to read street signs carefully before parking.

Gasoline In Britain, gas (called petrol) comes in three grades, though the price difference between them is negligible. Strangely enough, though most gas stations advertise prices by the gallon, pumps actually measure in liters. A British Imperial gallon is larger than its American equivalent—four of the former equal five of the latter. Most British people solve the dilemma by buying gas by the tankful, or several pounds' worth. At press time, the price of gasoline was about £1.80 per gallon.

By Train Despite severe financial restrictions and frequent complaints from commuters, Britain offers one of the fastest, safest, and most comfortable rail services in the world. All trains are run by the state-owned British Rail.

The country's principal—and most efficient—service is the InterCity network, linking London with every major city in the country. The most modern High Speed Trains travel up to 125 mph (200 kph) and offer comfortable, fully air-conditioned cars, both first- and second-class, with restaurant or buffet facilities. Local train services are not quite as reliable, particularly around congested city centers such as London. In general, seat reservations are not necessary except during peak vacation periods and on popular medium- and long-distance routes. Reserving a standard-class ticket costs £1.

Fares British Rail fares are high when compared with those in other countries. However, the network does offer a wide, and often bewildering, range of ticket reductions, and these can make a tremendous difference. The information office in each station is generally the most reliable source of information. Information and tickets can also be obtained from British Rail Travel Centers within the larger train stations and from selected travel agents displaying the double arrow British Rail logo.

One of the best bargains available to overseas visitors is the BritRail pass or the BritRail Youth Pass, the U.K. equivalent of the Eurail ticket. It provides unlimited travel over the entire British Rail network (and associated ferry and bus routes) for periods of seven, 14, or 21 days, or one month. The cost of a BritRail economy ticket for seven days is $166; for 14 days; $249; for 21 days, $319; and for a month, $369. The Youth Pass, for those aged 16 to 25, provides unlimited second-class travel, and costs $139 for seven days, $209 for 14 days, $269 for 21 days and $309 for one month. The Senior Citizen Pass entitles passengers over 65 to unlimited first-class travel. It costs $195 for seven days, $295 for 14 days, $375 for 21 days, and $445 for one month. These passes can be purchased only outside Britain, either in the United States, before you leave, or in one of 46 other countries. British Rail has its own information offices in New York, Los Angeles, Chicago, Dallas, Vancouver, and Toronto.

If you are planning to travel only short distances, be sure to buy inexpensive same-day return tickets. These cost only slightly more than ordinary one-way, standard-class tickets, but can be used only after 9:30 AM Mon.–Fri. Other special offers are regional Rover tickets, giving unlimited travel within local areas, and Saver returns, allowing greatly reduced round-trip travel during off-peak periods. For information about routes and fares, contact the British Travel Centre, 12 Regent Street, London SW1 (tel. 01/730–3400).

By Plane For a comparatively small country, Britain offers an extensive network of internal air routes. These are run by about a dozen different airlines. Hourly shuttle services operate every day between London and Glasgow, Edinburgh, Belfast, and Manchester. Seats are available on a no-reservations basis, and you can generally check in about half an hour before flight departure time. Keep in mind, however, that Britain's internal air services are not as competitive as those in the United States. And with modern, fast trains and relatively short distances, it is often much cheaper—and not much more time consuming—to travel by train.

By Bus Buses provide the most economical form of public transportation in Britain. Prices are invariably half that of train tickets, and the network is just as extensive. In recent years, both short- and long-distance buses have improved immeasurably in speed, comfort, and frequency. There is one important semantic difference to keep in mind when discussing bus travel in Britain. Buses (either double- or single-decker) are generally part of the local transportation system in towns and cities, and make frequent stops. Coaches, on the other hand, are comparable to American Greyhound buses and are used only for long-distance travel.

National Express offers the largest number of routes of any coach operator in Britain. It also offers a variety of discount tickets, including the BritExpress Card for overseas visitors, that covers all the National Express and Scottish Citylink services. This ticket entitles you to one-third off standard fares for any number of trips made during 30 consecutive days on services throughout England and Wales and selected services in Scotland. You can buy it from travel agents in the United States; in London, at the Victoria Coach Station, Buckingham Palace Road, SW1; or at main train stations in Edinburgh and Glasgow. Information about all services—including bargain fares and special Rover and Explorer tickets—can be obtained from the National Express Information Office at Victoria Coach Station or from Scottish Omnibuses, Buchanan Bus Station, Killermont Street, Glasgow G2 3NP.

By Boat Britain offers more than 1,500 miles (2,400 kilometers) of navigable inland waterways—rivers, lakes, canals, locks, and loughs—for leisure travel. Particular regions, such as the Norfolk Broads in East Anglia, the Severn Valley in the West Country, and the sea lochs and canals of Scotland, are especially popular among the nautically minded. Although there are no regularly scheduled waterborne services, hundreds of yachts, canal boats, and motor cruisers are available throughout the year. The British Tourist Authority's booklet, *UK Waterway Holidays*, is a good source of information. You can also contact the Inland Waterways Association, 114 Regents Park Road, London NW1 8UQ (tel. 01/586-2510).

By Bicycle Cycling provides an excellent way to see the countryside, and most towns—including London—offer bike rental facilities. Any bike shop or tourist information center should be able to direct you to the nearest rental firm. Rental fees generally run from £5 to £7.50 per day, plus deposit. If you're planning a tour and would like information on rental shops and special holidays for cyclists, contact a British Tourist Authority office in the United States before you leave home. An additional incentive: Except on InterCity 125 trains and selected London services, British Rail will carry bicycles free of charge.

On Foot Many organizations conduct group walking holidays during the summer months. These are especially popular in the Welsh mountains, the Lake District, Dartmoor, and Exmoor. Details are available from the British Tourist Authority.

Essential Information

Telephones For years, both foreign tourists and the British themselves have cursed the country's inefficient and antiquated phone system. The recent privatization of British Telecom has brought little improvement. Making a phone call in Britain—especially from a public booth—remains a frustrating experience at best.

Local Calls Public telephones are plentiful in British cities, especially London, although you will ordinarily find a high proportion out of order. Other than on the street, the best place to find a bank of pay phones is in a hotel or large post office. As part of Telecom's modernization efforts, the distinctive red boxes are gradually being replaced by generic glass and steel cubicles, but the red boxes still remain in more remote areas of the country. The workings of coin-operated telephones vary, but there are usually instructions in each unit. The oldest kind takes only 10p coins; the new ones take 10p, 20p, 50p, and £1 coins. But the newest innovation is the Phonecard, which comes in denominations of 10, 20, 40, and 100 units, and can be bought in a number of retail outlets. Cardphones are clearly marked with a special green insignia, and they will not accept coins.

A local call during the peak period (9 AM–1 PM) costs about 10p, or 1 unit. Each large city or region in Britain has its own numerical prefix, which is used only when you are dialing from outside the city. In provincial areas, the dialing codes for nearby towns are often posted in the booth, and some even list international codes.

International Calls The cheapest way to make an overseas call is to dial it yourself. But be sure to have plenty of coins or Phonecards close at hand. After you have inserted the coins or card, dial 010, the international code, then the country code—for the United States, it is 1—followed by the area code and local number. To make a collect or other operator-assisted call, dial 155.

Operators and Information For information anywhere in Britain, dial either 142 or 192. For the operator, dial 100.

Mail
Postal Rates Airmail letters to the United States and Canada cost 32p for the first 10 grams and 15p for each additional gram. Postcards and aerogrammes go for 27p. First-class letters within the United Kingdom cost 19p; second-class letters, 14p.

Receiving Mail If you're uncertain where you'll be staying, you can arrange to have your mail sent to American Express, 6 Haymarket, London SW1. The service is free to cardholders; all others pay a small fee. You can also collect letters at London's main post office. Ask to have them sent to Poste Restante, Main Post Office, London. The point of collection is King Edward Building, King Edward Street, London EC1A 1AA. Hours are Monday, Tuesday, Thursday, and Friday 8 AM–7 PM, Wednesday 8:30 AM–7 PM, and Saturday 9 AM–12:30 PM. You'll need your passport or other official form of identification.

Shopping Throughout Britain, souvenir and gift shops abound. And don't be surprised if you see many of the same items in very different corners of the country. Certain regions do offer particular specialties, however. Both Wales and Scotland are famous for woolen products. Many towns offer retail outlets selling sweaters, tartans, tweeds, scarves, skirts, and hats at very reasonable prices. Traditional Celtic jewelry is also popular. The Midlands offers world-renowned china and pottery, including Wedgwood, Royal Doulton, and Royal Worcester. The factory outlet shops are well worth a detour. The Southwest— especially Devon and Cornwall—is known for its scrumptious edibles—"scrumpy" (strong local cider), homemade toffees, rich fudge, and heavenly clotted cream. Museum and gallery shops all over the country offer high-quality posters, books, art prints, and crafts.

VAT Refunds   Foreign visitors can avoid Britain's crippling 15% Value Added Tax by taking advantage of a variety of special refund and export schemes. The easiest and most usual way of getting a refund is the Over the Counter method. To qualify for this, you must buy goods worth £75 or more. The shopkeeper will attach a special paper—Form VAT 407—to the invoice, and upon leaving the United Kingdom, you present the goods, form, and invoice to the customs officer. The form is then returned to the store, and the refund forwarded to you, minus a small service charge. The Direct Export method is another option. With this method, you are also issued Form VAT 407, but your purchases are sent home separately, and upon returning home, you must have the form certified by customs or a notary public. You then return the form to the store, and your money is refunded.

Opening and Closing Times   **Banks.** Banks are open weekdays 9:30–3:30. Some have extended hours on Thursday evenings, and a few are open on Saturday mornings.

Museums. Museum hours vary considerably from one part of the country to another. In large cities, most open weekdays 10–5; many are also open on Sunday afternoons. The majority close one day a week. Holiday closings vary, so be sure to check individual listings.

Shops. Usual business hours are Monday–Saturday 9–5:30. Outside the main centers, most shops observe an early closing day once a week, often Wednesday or Thursday; they close at 1 PM and do not reopen until the following morning. In small villages, many also close for lunch. In large cities—especially London—department stores stay open for late-night shopping (usually until 7:30 or 8) one day a week. Apart from some newsstands and small food stores, almost all shops are closed on Sunday.

National Holidays   *England and Wales:* January 1; April 1 (Good Friday); April 4 (Easter Monday); May 6 (May Day); May 30 (Spring Bank Holiday); August 29 (Summer Bank Holiday); December 25, 26, 27 (Christmas). *Scotland:* January 1; January 4; April 1; May 2; May 30; August 1; December 25, 26, and 27.

Dining   Until relatively recently, British food was condemned the world over for its plainness and mediocrity. But an influx of foreign restaurants and the birth of the New British Cuisine have had a noticeable effect on the quality of the nation's food. Nowadays, the problem is not so much bad food as expensive food. The best of traditional British cooking is solid and straightforward and dependent on top-quality, fresh materials, such as succulent spring beef and seasonal vegetables. The worst consists of heavy, starchy foods, overboiled and deep-fat fried.

Mealtimes   These vary somewhat, depending on the region of the country you are visiting. But in general, breakfast is served between 7:30 and 9, and lunch between 12 and 2. Tea—an essential and respected part of British tradition and often a meal in itself—is generally served between 4:30 and 5:30. Dinner or supper is served between 7:30 and 9:30, sometimes earlier, but rarely later. High tea, at about 6, replaces dinner in some areas, and in large cities, after-theater suppers are often available.

Ratings   Prices quoted here are per person and include a first course, main course, and dessert, but not wine or service. Best bets are indicated by a star ★ At press time, the pound was equal to $1.70.

Category	Cost
Very Expensive	over £35
Expensive	£20–£35
Moderate	£10–£20
Inexpensive	under £10

Credit Cards The following credit card abbreviations are used: AE, American Express; DC, Diners Club; MC, MasterCard; V, Visa.

Lodging Britain offers a wide variety of accommodations, ranging from enormous, top-quality, top-price hotels to simple, intimate farm and guest houses.

Hotels British hotels vary greatly, and there is no official system of classification. Most have rooms with private bathrooms, although there are still some—usually older hotels—that offer rooms with only wash basins; in this case, showers and bathtubs (and toilets) are usually just down the hall. Many also have "good" and "bad" wings. Be sure to check before you take the room. Generally, British hotel prices include breakfast, but beware: Many offer only a Continental breakfast—often little more than tea and toast. A hotel that includes a traditional English breakfast in its rates is usually a good bet. Hotel prices in London are significantly higher than in the rest of the country, and often the quality is not as good. Tourist information centers all over the country will reserve rooms for you, usually for a small fee. A great many hotels offer special weekend and off-season bargain packages.

Bed and Breakfasts These small, simple establishments are a special British tradition, and the backbone of budget travel. They offer modest, inexpensive accommodations, usually in a family home. Few have private bathrooms, and most offer only breakfast. Guest houses are a slightly larger, somewhat more luxurious version. Both provide the visitor with an excellent glimpse of everyday British life that's seldom seen in large city hotels.

Farmhouses Such accommodations have become increasingly popular in recent years. Farmhouses do not usually offer top hotel standards, but have a special appeal: the rustic, rural experience. Prices are generally very reasonable. Ask for the British Tourist Authority booklet *Farmhouse Vacations*.

Holiday Cottages Furnished apartments, houses, cottages, and trailers are available for weekly rental in all areas of the country. These vary from quaint, cleverly converted farmhouses to brand-new buildings set in scenic surroundings. For families and large groups, they offer the best value-for-money accommodations. Lists of rental properties are available free of charge from the British Tourist Authority. Discounts of up to 50% apply during the off-season (October to March).

Stately Homes It is possible to stay as a paying guest in a number of the famous stately homes scattered throughout the countryside. Styles range from Jacobean castles and manors to Regency houses. The equally stately prices usually include both meals and lodging. Reservations are essential. For details, contact the British Travel Centre (tel. 01/730–3400) or write to the

British Tourist Authority, Thames Tower, Blacks Road, London W6.

University Housing In larger cities and in some towns, certain universities offer their residence halls to paying vacationers. The facilities available are usually compact sleeping units, and they can be rented on a nightly basis. For information, contact the British Universities Accommodation Consortium, University Park, Nottingham.

Youth Hostels There are more than 350 youth hostels throughout England, Wales, and Scotland. They range from very basic to very good. Many are located in remote and beautiful areas; others can be found on the outskirts of large cities. Despite the name, there is no age restriction. The accommodations are inexpensive and generally reliable and usually include cooking facilities. For further information, contact the YHA Headquarters, Trevelyan House, 8 St. Stephens's Hill, St. Albans, Hertfordshire.

Camping Britain offers an abundance of campsites. Some are large and well equipped; others are merely small farmers' fields, offering primitive facilities. For information, contact the British Travel Authority in the United States, or the Camping and Caravan Club, Ltd., 11 Lower Grosvenor Place, London SW1 (tel. 01/828–1012).

Ratings Prices are for two people in a double room and include all taxes. Best bets are indicated by a star ★. At press time, the pound was equal to $1.70.

Category	Cost
Very Expensive	over £100
Expensive	£65–£100
Moderate	£30–£65
Inexpensive	under £30

Credit Cards The following credit card abbreviations are used: AE, American Express; DC, Diners Club; MC, MasterCard; V, Visa.

Tipping Some restaurants and most hotels add a service charge of 10–15% to the bill. In this case you are not expected to tip. If no service charge is indicated, add 10% to your total bill. Taxi drivers should also get 10%. You are not expected to tip theater or cinema ushers, elevator operators, or bartenders in pubs. Hairdressers and barbers should receive 10–15%.

London

Arriving and Departing

By Plane International flights to London arrive at either Heathrow Airport, 12 miles west of London, or at Gatwick Airport, 25 miles south of the capital. Most—but not all—flights from the United States go to Heathrow, while Gatwick mostly serves European destinations, often with charter flights.

Between the Airport and Downtown The Piccadilly Line serves **Heathrow** (all terminals) with a direct Underground (subway) link. The 40-minute ride costs £1.70. Two special buses also serve Heathrow: A1 leaves every

20 minutes for Victoria Station; A2 goes to Euston Station every 20 minutes and takes 80 minutes. The one-way cost for either is £3.

By Bus From Gatwick, the quickest way to London is the nonstop Gatwick Express, costing £5 one-way and taking 30 minutes. Regular bus services are provided by Greenline Coaches, including the Flightline 777 to Victoria Station. This takes about 70 minutes and costs £5 one-way.

Cars and taxis take M4 into London; the trip can take more than an hour, depending on traffic, and the taxi fare is about £18.

If you are driving, take M23 and then A23 to central London.

By Train London is served by no fewer than 15 train stations, so be absolutely certain of the station for your departure or arrival. All have Underground stations either in the train station or within a few minutes' walk from it, and most are served by several bus routes. British Rail controls all major services. The principal routes that connect London to other major towns and cities are on an InterCity network; unlike its European counterparts, British Rail makes no extra charge for the use of this express service network.

Seats cannot be reserved by phone. You should apply in person to any British Rail Travel Centre or directly to the station from which you depart. Below is a list of the major London rail stations and the areas they serve.

Charing Cross (tel. 01/928–5100) serves southeast England, including Canterbury, Margate, Dover/Folkestone.
Euston/St. Pancras (tel. 01/387–7070) serves East Anglia, Essex, the Northeast, the Northwest, and North Wales, including Coventry, Stratford-upon-Avon, Birmingham, Manchester, Liverpool, Windermere, Glasgow, and Inverness.
King's Cross (tel. 01/278–2477) serves the east Midlands; the northeast, including York, Leeds, and Newcastle; and north and east Scotland, including Edinburgh, and Aberdeen.
Liverpool Street (tel. 01/928–5100) serves Essex and East Anglia.
Paddington (tel. 01/262–6767) serves the south Midlands, west and south Wales, and the west country, including Reading, Bath, Bristol, Oxford, Cardiff, Swansea, Exeter, Plymouth, and Penzance.
Victoria (tel. 01/928–5100) serves southern England, including Gatwick Airport, Brighton, Dover/Folkestone (from May), and the south coast.
Waterloo (tel. 01/928–5100) serves the southwestern United Kingdom, including Salisbury, Bournemouth, Portsmouth, Southampton, Isle of Wight, Jersey, and Guernsey.

Fares There is a wide, bewildering range of "savers" and other ticket bargains. Unfortunately, ticket clerks cannot always be relied on to know which type best suits your needs, so be sure to ask at the information office first. **Cheap Day Returns** are best if you're returning to London the same day, and many family and other discount railcards are available. You can hear a recorded summary of timetable and fare information to many InterCity destinations by dialing the appropriate "dial and listen" numbers listed under British Rail in the telephone book.

By Bus "Bus" in Britain generally refers to part of the local transport system; "coach," meanwhile, is similar to a Greyhound and is used for longer, cross-country trips.

The **National Express** coach service has routes to over 1,000 major towns and cities in the United Kingdom. It's considerably cheaper than the train, although the trips will usually take longer. National Express offers two types of service: an ordinary service, which makes frequent stops for refreshment breaks, and a *Rapide* service, which has hostess and refreshment facilities on board. Day returns are available on both, but booking is advised on the *Rapide* service. National Express coaches leave Victoria Coach Station (Buckingham Palace Rd.) at regular intervals, depending on the destination. For travel information, dial 01/730–0202.

In addition to National Express, **Greenline** operates bus services within a 30–40 mile radius of London. A *Golden Rover* ticket, which allows unlimited travel, is available. Contact Greenline for more information, tel. 01/668–7261.

By Car London radiates with approach routes; the major ones are designated as either "motorways" (six-lane major highways; look for an "M" followed by a number), or "A" roads (the letter "A" followed by a number); the latter may be either "dual carriageways" (four lanes) or two-lane highways. The speed limit on motorways and dual carriageways is 70 mph, and on all other roads it is 60 mph.

Because of their greater number of lanes, motorways are usually a faster option for getting in or out of town than A roads, and many motorways merge back into A roads some distance out of London. That said, during peak hours on weekdays you can get caught in the commuter crush and easily spend half an hour or more stuck in traffic jams; stay tuned to radio stations for regular traffic updates.

The recently completed M25 encircles Greater London—ideal if you're staying in the suburbs and want a quick getaway or wish to connect with one of its many junctions.

Getting Around

By Underground Known colloquially as "the tube," London's extensive Underground system is by far the most widely used form of city transport. Trains run both beneath and above ground out into the suburbs, and all stations are clearly marked with the London Underground circular symbol. (A "subway" sign refers to an under-the-street crossing.) Trains are all one class; smoking is *not* allowed on board or in the stations.

There are nine basic lines—all named—plus the East London line, which runs from Shoreditch and Whitechapel across the Thames and south to New Cross. The Central, District, Northern, Metropolitan, and Piccadilly lines all have branches, so be sure to note which branch is needed for your particular destination. Electronic platform signs tell you the final stop and route of the next train, and some signs also indicate how many minutes you'll have to wait for the train to arrive.

From Monday to Saturday, trains begin running just after 5 AM; the last services leave central London between midnight and 12:30 AM. On Sundays, trains start two hours later and finish about an hour earlier. The frequency of trains depends on the route and the time of day, but normally you should not have to wait more than 10 minutes in central areas.

A pocket map of the entire tube network is available free from most Underground ticket counters. There should also be a large map on the wall of each platform—though often these are defaced beyond recognition.

Fares For both buses and tube fares, London is divided into five concentric zones; the fare goes up the farther afield you travel. Ask at Underground ticket counters for the London Regional Transport booklet "Tickets," which gives details of all the various ticket options and bargains for the tube; after some experimenting, you'll soon know which ticket best serves your particular needs. Till then, here is a brief summary of the major ticket categories, but note that these prices are subject to increase.

Singles and Returns. For one trip between any two stations, you can buy an ordinary single for travel anytime on the day of issue; if you're coming back on the same route the same day, then an ordinary return costs twice the single fare. Singles vary in price from 40p (50p in the central zone) to £1.70—not a good option for the sightseer who wants to make several journeys.

Cheap Day Return. Issued Monday–Friday after 9:30 AM and anytime on weekends. Basically good for a return journey from a station inside the zones to one outside—such as from Bond Street to Hampton Court.

One Day Off-Peak Travelcards. Allows unrestricted travel on both bus and tube; valid Monday–Friday after 9:30 AM, weekends, and all public holidays. Price £2.

One Day Capitalcard. Works the same way as a One Day Travelcard, but allows use of British Rail service within Greater London as well. Price £2.60. Both Travelcards and Capitalcards may be purchased for weekly or monthly use, as well as for one day; a photograph is required, and prices vary according to the number of zones traveled.

Visitor's Travelcard. May be bought in the United States and Canada as well as in London, for one, three, four, and seven days. The three- and four-day passes cannot be purchased in London. Apply to travel agents or to BritRail Travel International.

For more information, there are LRT Travel Information Centres at the following tube stations: **Oxford Circus,** open Monday–Saturday 8:30–6 and Thursday until 9:30; **Piccadilly Circus,** open Monday–Sunday 8:30–9:30; **Victoria,** upstairs open Monday–Sunday 8:30–9:30; **St. James's Park,** open Monday–Friday 8:30–6; and **Heathrow,** open daily. For information on all London bus and tube times, fares, etc., dial 01/222-1234; the line is operated 24 hours.

By Bus London's bus system now consists of the bright red double- and single-deckers, plus, in the outer zones, other buses of various colors. Destinations are displayed on the front and back, with the bus number on the front, back, and side. By no means do all buses run the full length of their route at all times, so always check the termination point before boarding, preferably with the conductor or driver. Many buses are still operated with a conductor whom you pay after finding a seat, but there is now a

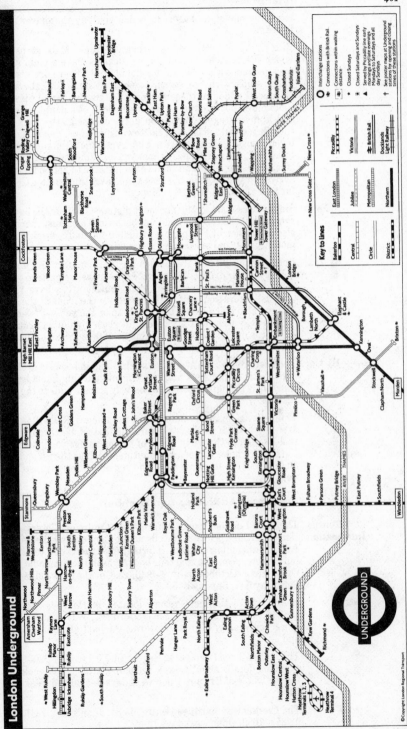

London Underground

move to "one-man" buses, in which you pay the driver upon boarding.

Buses stop only at clearly indicated stops. Main stops—at which the bus *should* stop automatically—have a plain white background with a red LRT symbol on it. There are also request stops with red signs, a white symbol, and the word "Request" added; at these you must hail the bus to make it stop. Smoking is not allowed on the lower deck of a double-decker, and is discouraged on the top deck, except at the back. Although you can see much of the town from a bus, *don't* take one if you want to get anywhere in a hurry; traffic often slows travel to a crawl, and during peak times you may find yourself waiting 20 minutes for a bus and then not being able to get on it once it arrives. If you do go by bus, ask at a Travel Information Centre for a free London Wide Bus Map.

Fares Single fares start at 35p for short distances (50p in the central zone). Travelcards are good for both tube and bus; there are also a number of bus passes available for daily, weekly, and monthly use, and prices vary according to zones.

By Taxi London's black taxis are famous for their comfort and for the ability of their drivers to remember the mazelike pattern of the capital's streets. Hotels and main tourist areas have ranks (stands) where you wait until you get to the front of the line. You can also hail a taxi if the flag is up or the yellow "for hire" sign is lit. Fares start at 80p and increase by units of 20p per 495 yards or 60 seconds. A surcharge of 60p or 80p is added in the evenings until midnight and on holidays.

By Car The best advice is to avoid driving in London because of the illogical street patterns and the chronic parking shortage. A constantly changing system of one-way streets adds to the confusion.

Things are a lot easier outside the rush hours (8AM–10AM and 4PM–6PM), and if you have the rare chance to drive through central London in the early hours of the morning, you'll see that the traffic-choked arteries of daytime (such as the Strand and Oxford Street) are convenient and sensible ways to cross London.

Important Addresses and Numbers

Tourist Information The main **London Tourist Information Centre** at Victoria Station Forecourt provides details about London and the rest of Britain, including general information; tickets for tube and bus; theater, concert, and tour bookings; and accommodations. Open April–October daily 9–8:30; rest of the year, Monday–Saturday 9–7, Sunday 9–5.

Other information centers are located in *Harrods* (Brompton Rd., SW3) and *Selfridges* (Oxford St., W1) and are open store hours only; also at *Heathrow Airport* (Terminals 1, 2, and 3).

The **British Travel Centre** (12 Regent St., W1, tel. 01/730–3400) provides details about travel, accommodations, and bookings for the whole of Britain. Open weekdays 9–6:30 and weekends 10–4.

The **Clerkenwell Heritage Centre,** 33 St. John's Sq., EC1, tel. 01/250–1039. Open weekdays 10–6.

Embassies and Consulates **American Embassy,** 24 Grosvenor Sq., W1A, 1AE, tel. 01/499–9000. Located inside the embassy is the American Aid Society, a charity set up to help Americans in distress. Dial the embassy number and ask for extension 570 or 571.

Canadian High Commission, Canada House, Trafalgar Sq., London SW1 Y 5BJ, tel. 01/629–9492.

Emergencies For police, fire brigade, or ambulance, dial 999.

The following hospitals have 24-hour emergency rooms: **Guys,** St. Thomas St., SE1, tel. 01/407–7600; **Royal Free,** Pond St., Hampstead, NW3, tel. 01/794–0500; **St. Bartholomew's,** West Smithfields, EC1, tel. 01/600–9000; **St. Thomas's,** Lambeth Palace Rd., SE1, tel. 01/928–9292; **University College,** Gower St., W1, tel. 01/387–9300; **Westminster,** Dean Ryle St., Horseferry Rd., SW1, tel. 01/828–9811.

Pharmacies Chemists (drugstores) with late opening hours include **Bliss Chemist,** 50–56 Willesden Lane, NW6, tel. 01/624–8000, open daily 9 AM–2 AM, also the branch at 5 Marble Arch, W1, tel. 01/723–6116, open daily 9 AM–midnight; **Boots,** 439 Oxford St., W1, tel. 01/409–2857, open Thursday 8:30–7; and **Underwoods,** 114 Queensway, W2, tel. 01/229–4819, open Monday–Saturday 9 AM–10 PM, Sunday 10–10.

Travel Agencies **American Express,** 6 Haymarket, SW1, tel. 01/930–4411, and at 89 Mount St., W1, tel. 01/499–4436; **Hogg Robinson Travel/Diners Club,** 176 Tottenham Court Rd., W1, tel. 01/580–0437; **Thomas Cook,** 45 Berkeley St., Piccadilly W1, tel. 01/499–4000.

Credit Cards Should your credit cards be lost or stolen, here are some numbers to dial for assistance: **Access (MasterCard),** tel. 0702/352255; **American Express,** tel. 0273/696933 for credit cards, tel. 0273/693555 for traveler's checks; **Barclaycard (Visa),** tel. 0604/21288; **Diners Club,** tel. 0252/516261.

Guided Tours

Orientation Tours
By Bus **London Regional Transport's** official guided sightseeing tours (tel. 01/222–1234) offer passengers a good introduction to the city from double-decker buses (seating capacity 64–72). Tours run daily every half hour 10–5, from Marble Arch (top of Park Lane near Speakers' Corner), Victoria Station, and Piccadilly Circus (Haymarket). The route covers roughly 18–20 miles and lasts 1½ hours; no stops are included. Tickets may be bought from the driver, or in advance from the London Tourist Information Centre at Victoria. Other agencies offering half- and full-day bus tours include **Evan Evans** (tel. 01/930–2377), **Frames Rickards** (tel. 01/837–3111), and **Travellers Check-In** (tel. 01/580–8284). These tours have a smaller seating capacity of approximately 53 passengers and include stops at places of special interest, such as St. Paul's Cathedral and Westminster Abbey. Prices and pick-up points vary according to the sights visited, but many pick-up points are at major hotels.

By River From April to October, boats cruise up and down the Thames, offering a different view of the London skyline. Most leave from Westminster Pier (tel. 01/930–4097), Charing Cross Pier (Victoria Embankment, tel. 01/839–3312), and Tower Pier (tel. 01/488–0344). Downstream routes go to the Tower of London, Greenwich, and Thames Barrier; upstream destinations include Kew, Richmond, and Hampton Court. Most of the launches seat between 100 and 250 passengers, have a public address system, and provide a running commentary on passing points of interest. Depending upon the destination, river trips may last from one to four hours. For more information, call **Catamaran Cruises**, tel. 01/839–2349, or **Travel Cruises**, tel. 01/928 –9009.

By Canal During summer, narrow boats and barges cruise London's two canals, the Grand Union and Regent's Canal; most vessels (seating about 62) operate on the latter, which runs between Little Venice in the west (the nearest tube is Warwick Ave. on the Bakerloo Line) and Camden Lock (about 200 yards north of Camden Town tube station). **Jason's Canal Cruises** (tel. 01/286–3428) operate one-way and round-trip narrow boat cruises on this route. During April, May, and September, there are two cruises per day; from June to August there are four. Trips last 1½ hours and cost £2.95 for adults, £1.50 for children and senior citizens.

Canal Cruises (tel. 01/485–4433) also offers cruises from March to October on the *Jenny Wren* (£2.10 adults, £1.10 children and senior citizens), and all year on the floating restaurant *My Fair Lady* (Tues.–Sat. dinner £16.95, Sun. lunch £12.75).

By Plane If land and water aren't enough, you may choose to see London by airship. The *Skyship 600* (tel. 01/995–7811) provides aerial tours of the city from a blimp during the summer months. Seating capacity is limited to 12, and the price is enormous: £125–£150 per person.

Walking Tours One of the best ways to get to know London is on foot, and there are many guided walking tours from which to choose. **London Walks** (tel. 01/882–2763), **Cockney Walks** (tel. 01/504–9159), **Streets of London** (tel. 01/882–3414), and **Discovering London** (tel. 0277/213704) are just a few of the better known firms, but your best bet is to peruse a variety of leaflets at the London Tourist Information Centre at Victoria Station. The duration of the walks varies (usually 1–3 hours), and you can generally find one to suit even the most specific of interests— Shakespeare's London, say, or a Jack the Ripper tour. Prices range around £2.25 for adults.

If you'd rather explore on your own, then the City of London Corporation has laid out a **Heritage Walk** that leads through Bank, Leadenhall, and Monument; follow the trail by the directional stars set into the sidewalks. A map of this walk may be found in *A Visitor's Guide to the City of London*, available from the City Information Centre across from St. Paul's Cathedral. Another option is to follow the **Silver Jubilee Walkway**, created in 1977 in honor of the 25th anniversary of the reign of the present Queen. The entire route covers 10 miles and is marked by a series of silver crowns set into the sidewalks; Parliament Square makes a good starting point. Several books are available from the British Travel Centre (12 Regent St., W1) that also list a number of different walks to follow.

Excursions **LRT, Evan Evans, Frames Rickards,** and **Travellers Check-In** (*see* Orientation Tours) all offer day excursions (some combine bus and boat) to places of interest within easy reach of London, such as Windsor, Hampton Court, Oxford, Stratford, and Bath. Prices vary and may include lunch and admission prices or admission only.

Personal Guides **Prestige Tours** (tel. 01/584–3118) operates a fleet of normal London taxis, each driven by a qualified guide. Tours are available all year, and a day's advance booking is usually enough to arrange an expert tour of the capital. There are three basic tours: full-day (around six hours) for £130; half-day (three hours) for £80; and the two-hour "Easy Rider" for £55. Alternatively, you can arrange an out-of-town trip, such as Stratford combined with Oxford. Rates may seem high, but are for up to four people.

Other personal guides operate their own service. **Heritage Services Jaguar Tour,** for instance, offers customized tours guided by the owner, Lord Dillon, who takes customers wherever they want, for however long they want, in his Jaguar. The price per hour is £20 in London, an extra £5 is added for out-of-the-city destinations. The Jaguar carries three passengers. For more information, tel. 01/994–9174 or 01/994–4319. Details of similar private operators may be found in brochures at the London Tourist Information Centre in Victoria Station or at the British Travel Centre.

Exploring London

Traditionally, London has been divided between the City, to the east, site of the original Roman settlement of Londinium, where its banking and commercial interests lie, and Westminster to the west, the seat of the royal court and of government. Today the distinction between the two holds good, and even the briefest exploration will demonstrate that each enjoys a quite distinct atmosphere. It is in these two areas also that you will find most of the grand buildings that have played a central role in British history: the Tower of London and St. Paul's Cathedral, Westminster Abbey and the Houses of Parliament, Buckingham Palace and the older royal palace of St. James's.

These sites are natural magnets for visitors to London, as the crowds of people and the ubiquitous tourist coaches demonstrate. But visitors who restrict their sightseeing to these well-known tourist traps miss much of the best the city has to offer. Within a few minutes' walk of Buckingham Palace, for instance, lie St. James's and Mayfair, two neighboring quarters of elegant town houses built for the nobility in the 17th and early 18th centuries, and now full of smart shops patronized by an international, jet-setting clientele. The same lesson applies to the City, where, tucked away in quiet corners, stand many of the churches Christopher Wren built to replace those destroyed during the Great Fire of 1666.

Other parts of London worth exploring include Covent Garden, where a former fruit and flower market has been converted into a bazaar where craftspeople sell their own wares. The atmosphere here is informal, and you can stroll for hours enjoying the friendly bustle of the streets. Hyde Park and Kensington Gardens, by contrast, offer a great swathe of green parkland across the city center, preserved by past kings and queens for their own hunting and relaxation. A walk across Hyde Park will bring you to the museum district of South Kensington, where are housed four major national collections: the Natural History Museum, the Science Museum, the Geological Museum, and the Victoria and Albert Museum, which specializes in costume and the fine and applied arts.

The key to London is thus a simple one. Explore for yourself off the beaten track. Use your feet, and when you are tired, take to the bus or the underground. And look around you, for London's centuries of history and its vibrant daily life are revealed as much in the individual streets and houses of the city as in its grand national monuments and galleries.

Westminster

Westminster is the royal backyard—the traditional center of the royal court and of government. Here, within a mile or so of each other, are virtually all London's most celebrated buildings (St. Paul's Cathedral and the Tower of London excepted), and there is a strong feeling of history all around you. Generations of kings and queens and their offspring have lived here since the end of the 11th century, in no less than four palaces, three of which (Buckingham, St. James's, and Westminster) still stand.

❶ Start at **Trafalgar Square,** which is on the site of the former Royal Mews. Both the square's name and its present appearance date from about 1830. A statue of Lord Nelson, victor over the French in 1805 at the Battle of Trafalgar, at which he lost his life, stands atop a 185-foot (56-meter) column. Lions guard the base of the column, which is decorated with four bronze panels depicting naval battles against France. The bronze equestrian statue on the south side of the square is of the unhappy Charles I; he is looking down Whitehall toward the spot where he was executed in 1649.

❷ In the **National Gallery,** which occupies the long classical building on the north side of the square, is a comprehensive collection of paintings, with works from virtually every famous artist and school from the 14th to the 19th centuries. The gallery is especially strong on Flemish and Dutch masters. Rubens and Rembrandt among them, and on Italian Renaissance works. *Trafalgar Sq., tel. 01/839–3321; 01/839–3526 (recorded information). Free. Open Mon.–Sat. 10–6, Sun. 2–6; July–Sept., Wed. until 8.*

❸ Around the corner, at the foot of Charing Cross Road, is a second major art collection, the **National Portrait Gallery,** which contains portraits of well-known (and not so well-known) Britons, including monarchs, statesmen, and writers. *2 St. Martin's Pl., tel. 01/930–1552. Free. Open Mon.–Fri. 10–5, Sat. 10–6, Sun. 2–6.*

❹ The Gallery's entrance is opposite the distinctive classical church of **St. Martin-in-the-Fields,** built in about 1730.

Time Out Both the **National Gallery Restaurant** and **Field's Restaurant** in the crypt of St. Martin's serve light lunches and a good selection of salads, sandwiches, and pastries.

❺ **Admiralty Arch** guards the entrance to **The Mall,** the great ceremonial way that leads alongside **St. James's Park** to Buckingham Palace. The Mall takes its name from a game called "pell mell," a version of croquet that society people, including Charles II and his courtiers, used to play here in the late 1600s. The park, one of central London's smallest and most attractive, with superbly maintained flowerbeds, was developed by successive monarchs, most recently by George IV in the 1820s, having originally been used for hunting by Henry VIII. Join office workers relaxing with a lunchtime sandwich, or stroll here on a summer's evening when the illuminated fountains play and Westminster Abbey and the Houses of Parliament beyond the trees are floodlit.

On the other side of the Mall, you pass along the foot of the imposing **Carlton House Terrace,** built in 1827–32 by John Nash. A right turn up Marlborough Road brings you to the complex of royal and government buildings known collectively as **St. James's Palace.** Although the earliest parts of this lovely brick building date from the 1530s, it had a relatively short career as the center of royal affairs, from the destruction of Whitehall Palace in 1698 until 1837, when Victoria became queen and moved the royal household down the road to Buckingham Palace. A number of royal functionaries have offices here, however, and various court functions are held in the state rooms.

At the end of Marlborough Road, beyond the open-sided **Friary Court,** turn left along **Cleveland Row,** and walk past **York House,** the London home of the Duke and Duchess of Kent. Another left turn into **Stable Yard Road** takes you to **Lancaster House,** built for the Duke of York by Nash in the 1820s and used today for government receptions and conferences. On the other side of Stable Yard is **Clarence House,** so called because it was designed and built by Nash in 1825 for the Duke of Clarence, who later became King William IV. It was restored in 1949 and is now the home of the Queen Mother. Inside the palace is the **Chapel Royal,** said to have been designed for Henry VIII by the painter Holbein; it was heavily redecorated in the mid-19th century. The ceiling still has the initials H and A, intertwined, standing for Henry VIII and his second wife, Anne Boleyn, the mother of Elizabeth I and the first of his wives to lose her head. The public can attend Sunday morning services here between the first week of October and Good Friday.

Buckingham Palace, at the end of the Mall, is the London home of the queen and the administrative hub of the entire royal family. When the queen is in residence (on weekdays except in January, August, September, and part of June), the royal standard flies over the east front. Inside, there are dozens of splendid state rooms used on such formal occasions as banquets for visiting heads of state. The private apartments of Queen Elizabeth and Prince Philip are in the north wing. Behind the palace lie some 40 acres (162,000 square meters) of private gardens, a haven for wildlife in the midst of the capital.

The ceremony of the **Changing of the Guard** takes place in front of the palace at 11:30 daily April through July and on alternate days during the rest of the year. It's advisable to arrive early; the Queen Victoria Memorial in the middle of the traffic roundabout provides a grandstand view.

Buckingham Palace is not open to the public. The former chapel, bombed during World War II and rebuilt in 1961, has been converted into the **Queen's Gallery,** however, where are held regular exhibitions drawn from the vast royal art collections. *Buckingham Palace Rd., tel. 01/930–4832. Admission: £1.20 adults, 60p children and senior citizens. Open Tues.–Sat. 10:30–5, Sun. 2–5; closed temporarily between exhibitions.*

London

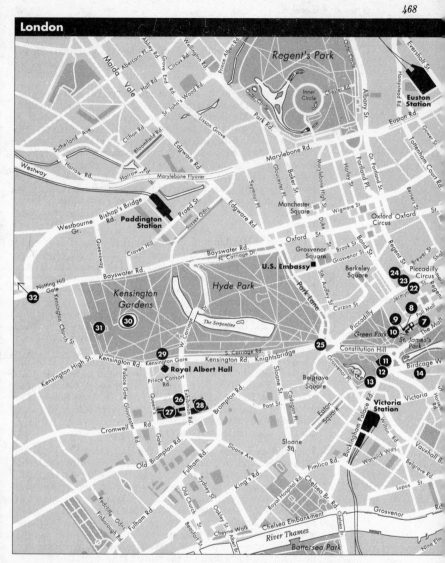

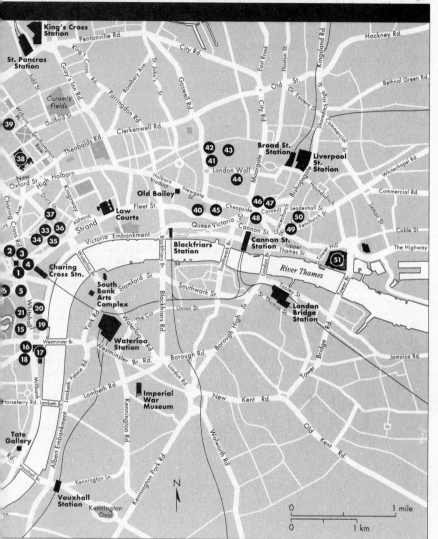

King's Cross Station

St. Pancras Station

Pentonville Rd.

City Rd.

Hackney Rd.

Bethnal Green Rd.

Coram's Fields

Old St.

Gt. Eastern St.

Kingsland Rd.

Shoreditch High St.

39

Guilford St.

Clerkenwell Rd.

London Wall

42 43

41

44

Broad St. Station

Liverpool St. Station

Whitechapel Rd.

38

New Oxford St.

High Holborn

Holborn Viaduct

Newgate

Old Bailey

Fleet St.

Cheapside

Cornhill

Commercial Rd.

37

Law Courts

40 45

46 47

48

50

49

Cable St.

33 36

34 35

Strand

Queen Victoria

Cannon St.

Cannon St. Station

Upper Thames St.

Tower Hill

The Highway

2

3

Charing Cross Stn.

Victoria Embankment

Blackfriars Station

London St.

51

4

1

South Bank Arts Complex

Stamford St.

Southwark St.

River Thames

Tooley St.

London Bridge Station

5

5

Waterloo Station

Union St.

Borough High St.

St. Thomas St.

Jamaica Rd.

21 20

19

15

Westminster Br.

Westminster Br. Rd.

London Rd.

Borough Rd.

Tower Bridge Rd.

16 17

18

Lambeth Rd.

Imperial War Museum

New   Kent   Rd.

Old Kent Rd.

Tate Gallery

Albert Embankment

Kennington Rd.

Walworth Rd.

Vauxhall Station

Kennington Ln.

Kennington Oval

N

0   1 mile

0   1 km

13 Just along Buckingham Palace Road from the Queen's Gallery
is the **Royal Mews,** where some of the queen's horses are stabled
and the elaborately gilded state coaches are on view. *Buckingham Palace Rd., tel. 01/930-4832. Admission: 60p adults, 30p
children. Open Wed. and Thurs. 2-4; occasionally closed
shortly before state occasions.*

Birdcage Walk, so called because it was once the site of the royal
aviaries, runs along the south side of St. James's Park, past the
14 **Wellington Barracks.** These are the regimental headquarters
of the Guards Division, the elite troops that traditionally guard
the sovereign and mount the guard at Buckingham Palace. The
Guards Museum relates the history of the Guards from the
1660s to the present day; paintings of battle scenes, uniforms,
and a cat o' nine tails are among the items on display. *Wellington Barracks, Birdcage Walk, tel. 01/930-4466, ext. 3271 or
3253. Admission: £2 adults, £1 children under 16 and senior
citizens. Open Sat.-Thurs. 10-4.*

15 The **Cabinet War Rooms,** between the Foreign Office and the
House Office, are the underground offices used by the British
High Command during World War II. Among the rooms on display are the Prime Minister's Room, where Winston Churchill
made many of his inspiring wartime broadcasts, and the Transatlantic Telephone Room, from which he spoke directly to
President Roosevelt in the White House. *Clive Steps, King
Charles St., tel. 01/930-6961 or 01/735-8922. Admission: £2.50
adults, £1.25 children under 16 and senior citizens. Open daily
10-5:50.*

16 **Parliament Square** is the large open space flanked, on the river
side, by the Palace of Westminster. Among the numerous statues of statesmen now long since dead are those of Churchill,
Abraham Lincoln, and Oliver Cromwell, the Lord Protector of
England during the country's sole, brief republican period
(1648-60).

17 The **Palace of Westminster** was the monarch's main residence
from the 11th century until 1512, when the court moved to the
newly built Whitehall Palace. The only part of the original
building to have survived, however, is **Westminster Hall,** which
has a fine hammer-beam roof. The rest was destroyed in a disastrous fire in 1834 and was rebuilt in the newly popular mock-
medieval Gothic style with ornate interior decorations. The architect, Augustus Pugin, provided many delightful touches,
such as Gothic umbrella stands. In addition to Westminster
Hall, which is used only on rare ceremonial occasions, the Palace contains the debating chambers and committee rooms of
the two Houses of Parliament—the Commons (whose members
are elected) and the Lords (whose members are appointed or
hereditary). There are no tours of the Palace, but the public is
admitted to the Public Gallery of each House; expect to wait in
line for several hours (the line for the Lords is generally much
shorter than that for the Commons).

The most famous features of the Palace are its towers. At the
south end is the 336-foot (102-meter) **Victoria Tower.** At the
other end is **St. Stephen's Tower,** better known, but inaccurate-
ly so, as Big Ben. That name properly belongs to the 13-ton bell
in the tower on which the hours are struck; Big Ben himself was
Sir Benjamin Hall, commissioner of works when the bell was

installed in the 1850s. A light shines from the top of the tower during a night sitting of Parliament.

⑱ Westminster Abbey is the most ancient of London's great churches and the most important, for it is here that Britain's monarchs are crowned. The abbey dates largely from the 13th and 14th centuries, although **Henry VII's Chapel,** an exquisite example of the heavily decorated late Gothic style, was not built until the early 1600s and the twin towers over the west entrance are an 18th-century addition. There is much to see inside, including the memorial to Winston Churchill; the tomb of the Unknown Warrior, a nameless World War I soldier buried in earth brought with his corpse from France; and Poets' Corner, where some of the country's finest writers are commemorated. Behind the high altar are the royal tombs, including those of Queen Elizabeth I, Mary Queen of Scots, and Henry V. In the Chapel of Edward the Confessor stands the Coronation Chair.

It is all too easy to forget, amid the crowds trying to see the abbey's sights, that this is a place of worship. Early morning is a good moment to catch something of the building's atmosphere. Better still, take time to attend a service. *Broad Sanctuary, tel. 01/222–5752. Admission to the nave is free, to Poet's Corner and Royal Chapels, £1.80 adults, 40p children (Royal Chapels, free Wed. 6–8 PM). Open Mon.–Fri. 9–4, Sat. 9–2, 3:45–5; Sun. all day for services only; closed weekdays to visitors during services.*

The Norman **Undercroft,** off the original monastic cloisters, houses a small museum with exhibits on the abbey's history. In the **Pyx Chamber** next door are fine examples of silver vessels and other treasures. The nearby **Chapter House** was where the English Parliament first met. *Tel. 01/222–5152. Joint admission: £1.20 adults, 60p children under 16 and senior citizens. Open daily 10:30–4.*

⑲ From Parliament Square, walk up **Parliament Street** and **Whitehall** (this is a single street—its name changes), past government offices, toward Trafalgar Square. The **Cenotaph** is the national memorial to the dead of both world wars. On the left is the entrance to **Downing Street,** an unassuming row of 18th-century houses. The prime minister's office is at No. 10 (she has a private apartment on the top floor). The chancellor of the exchequer, the finance minister, occupies No. 11.

⑳ On the right side of Whitehall is the **Banqueting House,** built by the architect Inigo Jones in 1625 for court entertainments. This is the only part of Whitehall Palace, the monarch's principal residence in the 16th and 17th centuries, that was not burned down in 1698. *Whitehall, tel. 01/930–4179. Admission: 70p adults, 35p children under 15 and senior citizens. Open Tues.–Sat. 10–5, Sun. 2–5.*

㉑ Opposite is the entrance to **Horse Guards Parade,** the former tilt yard of Whitehall Palace. This is the site of the annual ceremony of Trooping the Colour, when the queen takes the salute in the great military parade that marks her official birthday on the second Saturday in June (her real one is on April 21). There is also a daily guard-changing ceremony outside the guard house, at 11 AM, 10 on Sunday.

After such a concentrated dose of grand, historical buildings, it's time to explore two of London's elegant shopping areas, **St. James's** and **Mayfair.** Start by walking west from Piccadilly Circus along **Piccadilly,** which contains a mixture of airline offices, shops (including **Hatchards,** the booksellers, and **Fortnum and Mason,** the queen's grocer) and academic societies.

㉒ **St. James's Church** was designed by the 17th-century architect Christopher Wren and contains beautiful wood carvings by Grinling Gibbons.

Time Out   The Wren at St. James's is a friendly café in the church precincts. Coffee, pastries, and light lunches are served.

Jermyn Street, south of Piccadilly, is famous for upscale shops selling costly shirts, ties, and sweaters. **Paxton & Whitfield** sells an extraordinary variety of cheeses. Shops along **Duke Street** and **Bury Street** specialize in paintings, the former in Old Masters, the latter in early English watercolors. Don't be put off by the exclusive appearance of these establishments— anyone is free to enter, and there is no obligation to buy. **King Street** is home to **Christie's,** the fine art auctioneer, and to **Spink and Son,** renowned for Oriental art.

On the north side of Piccadilly, **Burlington House** contains the offices of many learned societies and the headquarters of the **㉓** **Royal Academy.** The RA, as it is generally known, stages major visiting art exhibitions. The best known is the Summer Exhibition, (May–Aug.) featuring works by living British artists.

Burlington Arcade is a covered walkway with tiny shops, selling primarily jewelry and craft goods such as woolens. Built in 1819, it was the first shopping precinct in the country, and it retains something of its original atmosphere.

㉔ The **Museum of Mankind** contains the British Museum's ethnographic collection. There are displays on the South Seas, the Arctic, and other regions of the world. *6 Burlington Gardens, tel. 01/437–2224. Free. Open Mon.–Sat. 10–5, Sun. 2:30–6.*

There are three special shopping streets in this section of Mayfair, each with its own specialties. **Savile Row** is the home of gentlemen's tailors. Nearby **Cork Street** has many dealers in modern art. **Bond Street** (divided into two parts, Old and New, though both are some 300 years old) is the smartest shopping street in London. This is *haute couture,* with famous names such as **Gucci, Hermès,** and **St. Laurent,** and costly jewelry, from shops such as **Asprey, Tiffany,** and **Cartier.**

Some of the original 18th-century houses survive on the west side of **Berkeley Square.** Farther along is **Curzon Street,** which runs along the northern edge of **Shepherd Market,** a maze of narrow streets full of antique shops and pubs that retain something of a village atmosphere.

Time Out   **L'Artiste Muscle** is a popular bistro serving French food; the *boeuf bourguignonne* is very tasty *(1 Shepherd Market).*

㉕ **Hyde Park Corner** is the start of a great expanse of green parkland that cuts right across the center of London. **Hyde Park,** which covers about 340 acres (1.38 square kilometers), was originally a royal hunting ground, while **Kensington Gardens,** which adjoins it to the west, started life as part of the royal Kensington Palace. These two parks contain many fine trees and are a haven for wildlife. **Rotten Row** is the sandy track that runs along the south edge of Hyde Park. There's nothing rotten about it; in fact, for several hundred years it has been one of the smartest places to go riding. The name derives from *route du roi* ("the King's Way")—the route William III and Queen Mary took from their home at Kensington Palace to the court at St. James's. There is boating and swimming in the **Serpentine,** the S-shaped lake formed by damming a river that used to flow here.

26 Leave the park at **Exhibition Road** and visit three of London's major museums. The **Science Museum** is the major national collection of science and technology, with extensive hands-on exhibits on outer space, astronomy, computers, transportation, and medicine. *Exhibition Rd., tel. 01/589-3456; 01/938-8123 (recorded information). Admission charges to be introduced in late 1988. Open Mon.–Sat. 10–6, Sun. 2:30–6.*

27 The **Natural History Museum** is housed in an ornate late-Victorian building with striking modern additions. As in the Science Museum, its displays on topics such as human biology and evolution are designed to challenge visitors to think for themselves. *Cromwell Rd., tel. 01/589-6323; 01/725-7866 (recorded information). Admission: £2 adults, £1 children under 15 and senior citizens. Open Mon.–Sat. 10–6, Sun. 2–6.*

28 The **Victoria and Albert Museum** (or V & A) originated in the 19th century as a museum of ornamental art and has extensive collections of costumes, paintings, jewelry, and crafts from every part of the globe. The collections from India, China, and the Islamic world are especially strong. *Cromwell Rd., tel. 01/938-8500; 01/938-8441 (recorded information). For admission, a donation is requested but is not essential. Open Mon.–Sat. 10–5:50, Sun. 2:30–5:50.*

Time Out The V & A restaurant is just the place to recuperate after visiting the museum. You can enjoy morning coffee, hot lunchtime dishes, or afternoon tea.

29 Back in Kensington Gardens, the **Albert Memorial** commemorates Queen Victoria's much-loved husband, Prince Albert, who died in 1861 at the age of 42. The monument, itself the epitome of high Victorian taste, commemorates the many socially uplifting projects of the prince, among them the Great Exhibition of 1851, whose catalog he is holding.

30 From the **Flower Walk,** behind the Albert Memorial, carefully planted so that flowers are in bloom virtually throughout the year, strike across Kensington Gardens to the **Round Pond,** a favorite place for children to sail toy boats.

31 **Kensington Palace,** across from the Round Pond, has been a royal home since the late 17th century—and is one still, for the Prince and Princess of Wales and Princess Margaret. From the outside, it looks less like a palace than a country house, which it was until William III bought it in 1689. Inside, however, are state rooms on a grand scale, mostly created in the early 18th century. Such distinguished architects as Wren, Hawksmoor, Vanbrugh, and William Kent were all employed here. Queen

Victoria lived at Kensington as a child, and several rooms are furnished as they were in her time. The public part of the palace also contains an exhibition of court dress. *Kensington Gardens, tel. 01/937–9561. Admission: £2.60 adults, £1.30 children under 16, £1.70 senior citizens. Open Mon.–Sat. 9–5, Sun. 1–5.*

North of Kensington Gardens are two lively districts, **Bayswater** and **Notting Hill,** both full of restaurants and cafés where young people gather. The best-known attraction in this area is ㉜ **Portobello Road,** where the celebrated antiques and bric-a-brac market is held each Saturday (arrive early in the morning for the best bargains). The street is also full of regular antiques shops that are open most weekdays.

Time Out **Geales** (2 Farmer St.) is a rather superior Notting Hill fish-and-chips establishment, popular with locals and the rich and famous alike. The fish really is fresh.

Covent Garden

You could easily spend a half-day exploring the block of streets ㉝ north of the Strand known as **Covent Garden.** The heart of the area is a former wholesale fruit and vegetable market, established in 1656. The market moved to more modern and accessible premises only in 1974. The Victorian **Market Building** is now an elegant and fashionable shopping center, with numerous boutiques, craft shops, and health-food bars. On the south side of the market building is the lively and much less formal **Jubilee open-air market,** where artists and craftspeople sell their wares at stalls.

The atmosphere in Covent Garden is friendly and informal. Look for the open-air entertainers performing under the portico ㉞ of **St. Paul's Church**—you can enjoy an excellent show for the price of a few coins thrown in the hat that's passed among the onlookers. The church, entered from Bedford Street, is known as the Actors' Church. The **Royal Opera House** and the **Theatre Royal Drury Lane,** two of London's oldest theaters, are close by, and inside are numerous memorials to theater people.

Time Out There's a good selection of eating places in and around the Market Building. **Crank's,** at No. 11, serves delicious quiches, salads, and cakes. The **Calabash,** in the basement of the Africa Center at 38 King Street, serves authentic African dishes at reasonable prices.

For interesting specialty shops, head north of the market building. Shops on **Long Acre** sell maps, art books, and glass; shops on **Neal Street** sell clothes, pottery, and jewelry, and goods from the East.

㉟ The collection of vehicles at the **London Transport Museum** includes a steam locomotive, a tram, and a subway car. Visitors are encouraged to operate many of the vehicles. *39 Wellington St., tel. 01/379–6344. Admission: £2.40 adults, £1.10 children under 16 and senior citizens. Open daily 10–6.*

㊱ The **Theatre Museum** contains a comprehensive collection of material on the history of the English theater—not merely the classics but also opera, music hall, pantomime, and musical comedy. Scripts, playbills, costumes, props are displayed;

there is even a re-creation of a dressing room filled with memorabilia of former stars. *Russell St., tel. 01/831-1227. Admission: £2.25 adults, £1.25 children under 16 and senior citizens. Open Tues.-Sun. 11-7.*

37 On **Bow Street** is the **Royal Opera House,** home of the Royal Ballet and the Royal Opera Company. The plush interior captures the richness of Victorian England.

Bloomsbury

Bloomsbury is a semiresidential district to the north of Covent Garden that contains some spacious and elegant 17th- and 18th-century squares. It's generally thought of as the intellectual center of London, since both the British Museum and the University of London are found here. The area also gave its name to the Bloomsbury Group, a clique of writers and painters that thrived here in the early 20th century.

38 The **British Museum** houses a vast and priceless collection of treasures, including Egyptian, Greek, and Roman antiquities; Renaissance jewelry; pottery; coins; glass; and drawings from virtually every European school since the 15th century. It's best to pick out one section that particularly interests you—to try to see everything would lead to an attack of cultural indigestion! Some of the highlights are the **Elgin Marbles,** sculptures that formerly decorated the Parthenon in Athens; the **Rosetta Stone,** which helped archaeologists to interpret Egyptian script; and the **Mildenhall treasure,** a cache of Roman silver found in East Anglia in 1842. *Great Russell St. tel. 01/636-1555; 01/580-1788 (recorded information). Free. Open Mon.-Sat. 10-5, Sun. 2:30-6.*

39 The **Courtauld Institute Galleries,** behind the British Museum, on Woburn Square, contain a small but outstanding collection of French Impressionist paintings from the late 19th century, including works by Cezanne, Manet, and Van Gogh. *Woburn Sq., tel. 01/580-1015. Free. Open Mon.-Sat. 10-5, Sun. 2-5.*

The City

The **City,** the traditional commercial center of London, is the most ancient part of the capital, having been the site of the great Roman city of Londinium. Since those days, the City has been built and rebuilt several times. The wooden buildings of the medieval City were destroyed in the Great Fire of 1666. There were further waves of reconstruction in the 19th century, and then again after World War II, to repair the devastation wrought by air attacks. The 1980s have seen the construction of many mammoth office developments, some undistinguished, others incorporating adventurous and exciting ideas.

Throughout all these changes, the City has retained its unique identity and character. The lord mayor and Corporation of London are still responsible for the government of the City, as they have been for many centuries. Commerce remains the lifeblood of the City, which is a world financial center rivaled only by New York, Tokyo, and Zurich. The biggest change has been in the City's population. Until the first half of the 19th century, many of the merchants and traders who worked in the City lived there, too. Today, despite its huge daytime population, scarcely 8,000 people live in the 677 acres (2.74 square kilometers) of the City. Try, therefore, to explore the City on a weekday morning or afternoon. On weekends, its streets are deserted, and many of the shops and restaurants, even some of the churches, are closed.

40 Following the Great Fire, **St. Paul's Cathedral** was rebuilt by Sir Christopher Wren, the architect who was also responsible for designing 50 City parish churches to replace those lost in the Fire. St. Paul's is Wren's greatest work. Fittingly, he is buried in the crypt, under the simple epitaph composed by his son: "Reader, if you seek his monument, look around you." The cathedral has been the site of many famous state occasions, including the funeral of Winston Churchill in 1965 and the marriage of the Prince and Princess of Wales in 1981. There is much fine painting and craftsmanship—the choir stalls are by the great 17th-century wood carver Grinling Gibbons—but overall the atmosphere is somewhat austere and remote. Perhaps this is because Wren produced a classical design based on the great churches of the Italian Renaissance, rather than following the more intricate English medieval tradition. The cathedral contains many monuments and tombs. Among those commemorated are George Washington; the essayist and lexicographer Samuel Johnson; and two military heroes—Nelson, victor over the French at Trafalgar in 1805, and Wellington, who defeated the French on land at Waterloo 10 years later. In the ambulatory (the area behind the high altar) is the American Chapel, a memorial to the 28,000 U.S. citizens stationed in Britain during World War II who lost their lives while on active service.

The greatest architectural glory of the cathedral is the dome. This consists of three distinct elements: an outer, timber-framed cone covered with lead; an interior dome built of brick and decorated with frescoes of the life of St. Paul by the 18th-century artist Sir James Thornhill; and, in between, a brick cone that supports and strengthens both. There is a good view of the church from the **Whispering Gallery**, high up in the inner dome. The gallery is so called because of its remarkable acoustics, whereby words whispered on one side can be clearly heard on the other, 112 feet (34 meters) away. Above this gallery are two others, both external, from where there are fine views over the City and beyond. *tel. 01/248-2705. Admission to Ambulatory (American Chapel): 60p adults, children free; to Crypt and Treasury: 80p adults, 40p children; to galleries: £1 adults, 50p children; Super Tours runs tours of the cathedral weekdays at 11, 11:30, 2, and 2:30, £3.50 adults, £2.50 children. Cathedral open Mon.–Sat. 7:30–6, Sun. 8–6; The Ambulatory, Crypt, and Galleries Mon.–Fri. 10–4:15, Sat. 11–4:15.*

Time Out **Balls Brothers Wine Bar** is a good place for a bite and a drink. Freshly made soup and grilled steak in a French bread sandwich are two specialties. Aim to arrive early to beat the crowds of lunchtime City workers. *2 Old Change Court, St. Paul's Churchyard. EC4.*

A short walk north of the cathedral, to **London Wall**, so called because it follows the line of the wall that surrounded the Roman settlement, brings you to the **Museum of London**. Its displays enable you to get a real sense of what it was like to live in London at different periods of history, from Roman times to the present day. Among the highlights are the Lord Mayor's Ceremonial Coach, an imaginative reconstruction of the Great Fire, and the Cheapside Hoard, jewelry hidden during an outbreak of plague in the 17th century and never recovered by its owner. The 20th-century exhibits include a Woolworth's counter and elevators from Selfridges; both stores were founded by Americans and had an immense impact on the life of Londoners. *London Wall, tel. 01/600–3699. Free. Open Tues.–Sat. 10–6, Sun. 2–6.*

42 **Royal Britain** is a newly opened exhibition using all the latest audiovisual techniques to re-create more than 1,000 years of royal history from semimythical figures, such as King Arthur, to the royal family of today. *Aldersgate St., tel. 01/588–0588. Admission: £5 adults, £3 children and senior citizens. Open daily 9–5:30.*

43 The **Barbican** is a vast residential complex and Arts Centre built by the City of London. It takes its name from the watchtower that stood here in the Middle Ages, just outside the City walls. The Arts Centre contains a concert hall, where the London Symphony Orchestra is based. It also has two theaters, an art gallery, a cinema, and several cafés and restaurants. The theaters are the London home of the Royal Shakespeare Company.

44 On the south side of London Wall stands the **Guildhall,** the much reconstructed home of the Corporation of London; the lord mayor of London is elected here each year amid much ceremony. *King St., tel. 01/606–3030. Free. Open Mon.–Fri. 9–5.*

Now walk south to **Cheapside.** This was the chief marketplace of medieval London (the word *ceap* meant market), as the street names hereabouts indicate: Milk Street, Ironmonger Lane, etc. Despite rebuilding, many of the streets still run on **45** the medieval pattern. The church of **St. Mary-le-Bow** in Cheapside was rebuilt by Christopher Wren after the Great Fire; it was built again after being bombed during World War II. It is said that to be a true Cockney, you must be born within the sound of Bow bells.

A short walk east along Cheapside brings you to a seven-way **46** intersection. The **Bank of England,** which regulates much of Britain's financial life, is the large windowless building on the left. At the eastern side of the intersection, at right angles to **47** the bank, is the **Royal Exchange,** originally built in the 1560s as a trading hall for merchants. The present building, opened in 1844 and the third on the site, is now occupied by the **London International Financial Futures Exchange.** You can watch the hectic trading from the Visitors' Gallery. *Royal Exchange, tel. 01/623–0444. Free. Visitors' Gallery open Mon.–Fri. 11:30–1:45.*

The third major building at this intersection, on its south side, **48** is the **Mansion House,** the official residence of the lord mayor of London.

Continue east along **Cornhill,** site of a Roman basilica and of a medieval grain market. Turn right into Gracechurch Street **49** and then left into **Leadenhall Market.** There has been a market here since the 14th century; the present building dates from 1881.

Just behind the market is one of the most striking pieces of contemporary City architecture: the headquarters of **Lloyd's of London,** built by the modernist architect Richard Rogers. Its main feature is a 200-foot (61-meter) high barrel vault made of sparkling glass. The underwriters of Lloyd's provide insurance for everything imaginable, from oil rigs to a pianist's fingers. An exhibit traces the history of Lloyd's from the 17th century. *1 Lime St., tel. 01/623-7100, ext. 6210 or 5786. Free. Open Mon.–Fri. 10–2:30.*

Time Out   Lloyd's was founded in a coffee house, and so **Lloyd's Coffee House,** at the foot of the modern building, is an apt place for coffee and pastries, a full lunch, or afternoon tea.

From here, it's a short walk east to the **Tower of London,** one of London's most famous sights and one of its most crowded, too. Come as early in the day as possible and head for the Crown Jewels, so you can see them before the crowds arrive.

The Tower served the monarchs of medieval England as both fortress and palace. Every British sovereign from William the Conqueror in the 11th century to Henry VIII in the 16th lived here, and it remains a Royal Palace. The **History Gallery,** south of the White Tower, is a walk-through display designed to answer questions about the inhabitants of the tower and its evolution over the centuries.

The **White Tower** is the oldest and also the most conspicuous building in the entire complex. When it was completed in about 1097, it dominated the surrounding buildings of London—a visual reminder of the might of England's new Norman overlords. Inside, the **Chapel of St. John** is one of the few unaltered parts. A structure of great simplicity, it is almost entirely lacking in ornamentation. The **Royal Armories,** England's national collection of arms and armor, occupies the rest of the White Tower. Armor of the 16th and 17th centuries forms the centerpiece of the displays, including pieces belonging to Henry VIII and Charles I.

Among other buildings worth seeing is the **Bloody Tower.** This name has been traced back only to 1571; it was originally known as the Garden Tower. Sir Walter Raleigh was held prisoner here, in relatively comfortable circumstances, between 1603 and 1616, during which time he wrote his *History of the World;* his rooms are furnished much as they were during his imprisonment. The little princes in the tower—the boy king Edward V and his brother Richard, Duke of York, supposedly murdered on the orders of Gloucester, later crowned Richard III— certainly lived in the Bloody Tower, and may well have died here, too. Another bloody death is alleged to have occurred in the **Wakefield Tower,** when Henry VI was murdered in 1471 during England's medieval civil war, the Wars of the Roses. It was a rare honor to be beheaded in private inside the tower; most people were executed outside, on **Tower Hill,** where the crowds could get a much better view. Important prisoners were held in the **Beauchamp Tower;** the walls are covered with graffiti and inscriptions carved by prisoners.

The **Crown Jewels,** housed in the **Jewel House,** are a breathtakingly beautiful collection of regalia, precious stones, gold, and silver. The Royal Scepter contains the largest cut diamond in the world. The Imperial State Crown contains some 3,000 precious stones, largely diamonds and pearls; it was made for the coronation of Queen Victoria in 1838. *Tower Hill, tel. 01/ 709–0765. Admission: £4.50 adults, £2 children under 16, £3 senior citizens; reduced admission charges apply during Feb. when the Jewel House is closed. Small additional admission charge to the Fusiliers Museum only. Open Mar.–Oct., Mon.–Sat. 9:30–5:45, Sun. 2–5:45; Nov.–Feb., Mon.–Sat. 9:30– 4:30.*

Yeoman Warder guides conduct tours daily from the Middle Tower, no charge, but a tip is always appreciated. Subject to weather and availability of guides, about every 30 minutes until 3:30 in summer, 2:30 in winter.

What To See and Do with Children

Make for the **Royal Mews,** where some of the Queen's horses can be seen close up. Try the **Whispering Gallery** in **St. Paul's Cathedral.** Gruesome instruments of torture are on display in the **Bowyer Tower** in the **Tower of London.** Climb the 311 steps to the top of the **Monument** or take the elevator to the high walkways of **Tower Bridge.**

Museums of special interest to children, where there are generally lots of hands-on activities, include the **London Transport Museum** in Covent Garden, the **Natural History Museum** and the **Science Museum** in South Kensington, and the **London Toy & Model Museum** north of Kensington Gardens. Another joy for children of all ages is brass-rubbing at the **Brass Rubbing Centre** in **Westminster Abbey** or at the **London Brass Rubbing Centre** at **St. Martin-in-the-Fields Church** on Trafalgar Square.

Hampstead Heath is a superb place for a walk; join the kite flyers on Parliament Hill Fields on the southern slopes. Hire a row boat on the **Serpentine** in **Hyde Park** or go for a swim; there's a designated swimming area with changing rooms.

Places where children might actually enjoy shopping are **Covent Garden** and **Hamley's,** the latter being a huge toy shop on Regent Street.

Take in a children's play at the **Unicorn Theatre** on Great Newport Street (box office tel. 01/836–3334; matinees only) or visit the tiny **Little Angel Marionette Theatre,** Dagmar Passage, off Upper Street in Islington; box office tel. 01/226–1787.

Off the Beaten Track

Visit **London Zoo** on the north side of **Regent's Park.** *Tel. 01/ 722–333. Admission: £3.90 adults, £2 children under 16 and senior citizens. Open Apr.–Sept., daily 9–6 (bank holidays 9–7), Oct.–Mar., 10–dusk.*

Walk along the bank of the **Regent's Park Canal** to **Camden Lock,** where there are lots of little shops selling gifts, secondhand clothes, and antiques. On weekends, there's an outdoor market as well.

You can extend the excursion in two different directions from Camden Lock. Either walk east along the canal towpath through the elegant streets of Islington and then through increasingly less prosperous areas until you reach the Thames at Limehouse or turn north to **Hampstead** and **Hampstead Heath.**

Hampstead is a village within the City, with a main shopping street and some rows of elegant 18th-century houses; the heath is one of London's largest and most attractive open spaces.

In **Keats Grove,** on the southern edge of the heath, is the house where the Romantic poet John Keats (1795–1821) lived. *Wentworth Place, Keats Grove, tel. 01/435–2062. Free. Open Mon.–Fri. 2–6, Sat. 10–5, Sun. 2–5.*

Standing alone in its own landscaped grounds on the north side of the Heath is **Kenwood House,** built in the 17th century and remodeled by Robert Adam, the talented exponent of classical decoration, at the end of the 18th. The house contains a collection of superb paintings by such masters as Rembrandt, Vermeer, Turner, Reynolds, Van Dyck, and Gainsborough, which gain enormously by being displayed in the grand country-house setting for which they were originally intended. *Hampstead Lane, tel. 01/348–1286. Free. Open Apr.–Sept., daily 10–6; Oct., daily 10–5; Nov.–Jan., daily 10–4; Feb. and Mar., daily 10–5.*

The historical and maritime attractions at **Greenwich,** on the Thames, some five miles (eight kilometers) east of central London, make it an ideal place for a day out. Visit the **National Maritime Museum,** a treasure house of paintings, maps, models, sextants, and, best of all, ships from all ages, including the ornate royal barges. *Romney Rd., tel. 01/858–4422. Joint admission with the Royal Observatory: £2.20 adults, £1.10 children and senior citizens. Open late Mar.–late Oct., Mon.–Sat. 10–6, Sun. 2–6; late Oct.–late Mar., Mon.–Sat. 10–5, Sun. 2–5.*

Two ships now in dry dock are the glorious 19th-century clipper ship *Cutty Sark* and the tiny *Gipsy Moth IV,* which Sir Francis Chichester sailed single-handed around the world in 1966. *Cutty Sark, King William Walk, tel. 01/858–3445. Admission: £1.30 adults, 70p children under 16 and senior citizens. Open late Mar.–late Oct., Mon.–Sat. 10–5:30, Sun. noon–5:30; late Oct.–late Mar., Mon.–Sat. 10–4:30, Sun. noon–4:30. Gipsy Moth IV, King William Walk, tel. 01/853–3589. Admission: 20p adults, 10p children and senior citizens. Open Apr.–Oct., Mon.–Sat. 10–6, Sun. noon–6.*

The **Royal Naval College** was built from 1694 as a home, or hospital, for old sailors: you can see the magnificent **Painted Hall,** where Nelson's body lay in state following the Battle of Trafalgar, and the College Chapel. *Open Fri.–Wed. 2:30–4:45.*

Behind the museum and the college is **Greenwich Park,** originally a royal hunting ground and today an attractive place to wander and relax. On top of the hill is the **Old Royal Observatory,** founded in 1675, where original telescopes and other astronomical instruments are on display. The prime meridian—zero degrees longitude—runs through the courtyard of the observatory. *Greenwich Park, tel. 01/858–4422. Joint admission with National Maritime Museum: £2.20 adults, £1.10 children and senior citizens. Open Apr.–Oct., Mon.–Sat. 10–6, Sun. 2–6; Nov.–Mar., Mon.–Sat. 10–5, Sun. 2–5.*

You can get to Greenwich by riverboat from Westminster and Tower Bridge Piers, by Thames Line's high-speed river buses, or by train from Charing Cross station. You can also take the Docklands Light Railway from Tower Gateway to Island Gardens and walk a short distance along a pedestrian tunnel under the river.

Shopping

Shopping is one of London's great pleasures. Different areas retain their traditional specialties, as described below, but part of the fun is to seek out the small craft, antiques, and gift stores that have sprung up all over the city during the past few years.

Chelsea is a mecca for those in search of up-to-the-minute fashions, antiques, and classy home furnishings. A Saturday stroll along the **King's Road** will reveal some of the weirder fashion trends among London's youngsters.

Covent Garden is the home of craft shops and trendy boutiques. Antiques are the main draw in **Kensington,** especially along **Kensington Church Street.** There are some good clothes stores on **Kensington High Street.**

The great Edwardian bulk of Harrods dominates **Knightsbridge,** but don't neglect the boutiques and art galleries on other shopping streets in the area, such as **Sloane Street, Beauchamp Place,** and **Walton Street.**

In **Mayfair,** the area between **Piccadilly** and **Oxford Street,** the emphasis is on traditional British clothing for men and women. **South Molton Street** adds a modern, raffish accent. Both quality and prices are tops here.

Noisy, crowded **Oxford Street** is to be endured rather than enjoyed. **Selfridges, Marks and Spencer,** and **John Lewis** are all good department stores here, and little **St. Christopher's Place,** almost opposite Bond Street tube, adds a chic touch.

There are still a number of classy stores along **Piccadilly,** including **Simpsons** (clothes), **Hatchards** (books), and **Fortnum and Mason** (foodstuffs, fashions). Side streets lead to several elegant shopping arcades, the best-known of which is the **Burlington Arcade.**

China, clothes, fabrics, and good department stores help to make **Regent Street** an appealing alternative to neighboring Oxford Street. The crowds are just as thick, but the presence of **Liberty's**—the city's most appealing department store, still with its original emphasis on Oriental goods—helps to compensate.

Though his suits may be made in Savile Row, the English gentleman comes to **St. James's** for the rest of his outfit, which includes shoes, shirts, silk ties, hats, and all manner of accessories. The prices mirror the quality.

Street markets are one aspect of London life not to be missed.

Here are some of the more interesting markets:

Bermondsey. Arrive as early as possible for the best treasure—or junk. *Tower Bridge Road, SE1. Open Fri. 4:30 AM–noon. Take the tube to London Bridge and walk or take the 15 or 25 bus to Aldgate and then a 42 bus over Tower Bridge to Bermondsey Square.*
Camden Lock (Dingwalls). This is just the place for an unusual and inexpensive gift; it's also a picturesque place to wander

around. There's an open-air antiques market on weekends, but it gets horribly crowded. *Chalk Farm Road. NW1. Tues.–Sun. 9:30–5:30. Take the tube or the 24 or 29 bus to Camden Town.*

Camden Passage. The rows of little antique shops are a good hunting ground for silverware and jewelry. Saturday is the day for stalls; shops are open during the rest of the week. *Islington, N1. Open Wed.–Sat. 8:30–3. Take the tube or 19 or 38 bus to the Angel.*

Petticoat Lane. Look for good-quality, budget-priced leather goods, dazzling knitwear, and bargain-price fashions, plus cameras, videos, and stereos at budget prices. *Middlesex Street. E1. Open Sun. 9–2. Take the tube to Liverpool Street, Aldgate, or Aldgate East.*

Portobello Market. Saturday is the best day to search the stalls for not-quite-bargain-priced silverware, curios, porcelain, and jewelry. Some of the clothes stalls offer excellent value, selling well-known labels at knock-down prices. It's always crowded, with an authentic hustle-and-bustle atmosphere, and firmly on the tourist route. *Portobello Road. W11. Open Fri. 5–3, Sat. 8–5. Take the tube or 52 bus to Notting Hill Gate or Ladbroke Grove.*

VAT Refunds Foreign visitors to Britain need not pay the 15% Value Added Tax added to every purchase if they take advantage of the Personal Export Scheme. Most main stores have export departments that will give you all the help you need.

Dining

Ratings Prices quoted here are per person and include a first course, main course, and dessert, but not wine or service. Best bets are indicated by a star ★. At press time, the pound was equal to $1.70.

Category	Cost
Very Expensive	over £35
Expensive	£20–£35
Moderate	£10–£20
Inexpensive	under £10

Credit Cards The following credit card abbreviations are used: AE, American Express; DC, Diners Club; MC, MasterCard; V, Visa.

Bloomsbury
Expensive **The White Tower.** The most upscale Greek restaurant in town has barely changed since it first opened in 1939. There are portraits on the walls, glass partitions between the tables, and an entertainingly rhapsodic menu. Dishes range from the traditional—*taramasalata*—to the more creative—roast duckling with crushed wheat. *1 Percy St., tel. 01/636–8141. Dress: casual chic. Reservations essential. AE, DC, MC, V. Closed weekends, 3 weeks in Aug., 1 week at Christmas, public holidays.*

Moderate **Auntie's.** Come to Auntie's for authentic English food—"the Colonel's curried egg mayonnaise," Barnsley lamb chop with plum and mint sauce, tipsy fruit trifle—served in an intimate Edwardian atmosphere of dark green walls hung with theater bills. *126 Cleveland St., tel. 01/387–1548. Dress: studied casu-*

al. Reservations advised. AE, DC, MC, V. Closed Sat. lunch, Sun., 2 weeks in mid-Aug., Dec. 25.

Inexpensive **The Agra.** An Indian restaurant, The Agra is popular with media folk for its good value and wide choice of meat and vegetarian curries. Overhead fans, low lighting, and attentive waiters add a touch of class. *135–137 Whitfield St., tel. 01/387–8833. Dress: casual. Reservations advised for dinner. AE, DC, MC, V. Closed Dec. 25.*

The North Sea Fish Restaurant. Only freshly caught fish is served in this popular haunt. Recommended are the seafood platter and Dover sole. You can eat in or take out. *7–8 Leigh St., tel. 01/387–5892. Dress: informal. Reservations advised. AE, DC, MC, V. Closed Sun., public holidays, Dec. 25.*

Chelsea **La Tante Claire.** Though cripplingly expensive, this spot is just-
Very Expensive ly famous for its superb haute cuisine: hot foie gras on shredded potatoes with a sweet wine and shallot sauce, and pig's trotter studded with mousse of white meat with sweetbreads and wild mushrooms. *68 Royal Hospital Rd., tel. 01/352–6045. Jacket and tie. Reservations 3–4 weeks in advance. AE, DC, MC, V. Closed weekends, Christmas and New Years Day, 10 days at Easter, 3 weeks in Aug.–Sept.*

Expensive **English House.** A charming private house decorated in chintz
★ with antiques and cream linen tablecloths. Authentic recipes include Holm Oak smoked pigeon breasts with rhubarb and ginger preserve and hot toffee and apple tart. *3 Milner St., tel. 01/584–3002. Dress: casual chic. Reservations essential for dinner. AE, DC, MC, V. Closed Dec. 25, Good Friday.*

Moderate **19.** This popular, informal Anglo-French bistro serves consistently high-standard mega-portions (fresh salmon and halibut terrine, venison casserole) in attractive country-cottage surroundings. *19 Mossop St., tel. 01/589–4971. Dress: informal. MC, V. Closed Sat. lunch, Christmas, Easter.*

Inexpensive **Henry J. Bean's.** Hamburgers and Tex-Mex food ("muchos nachos"—ground beef with sour cream, spicy sauce, melted cheese, and tortilla chips) are served to American oldies music. There's American-bar decor: the walls are covered with newspapers and other ephemera. *195–197 King's Rd., tel. 01/352–9255. Dress: casual. Closed Dec. 25, 26, 31.*

The City **Bill Bentley's.** Once a wine merchant's vaults with bare walls
Expensive and arched ceiling, this atmospheric spot is recommended for the seafood platters and Bill Bentley's special oysters. There are two other branches, at Beauchamp Place and Baker Street. *Swedeland Court, 202 Bishopsgate, tel. 01/283–1763. Dress: casual chic. Reservations essential. MC, V. Closed weekends, public holidays.*

Gallipoli. A 200-year-old Turkish bathhouse, with gleaming mosaics, has been transformed into a stylish restaurant with a live band from 9 PM to 2:30 AM. The clientele is a mix of City people and tourists, and the food has a marked Turkish flavor—try the yogurt kebab or the fillet of duck with honey, lime, and orange. *8 Bishopsgate Churchyard, tel. 01/588–1922. Dress: formal. Reservations advised. AE, DC, MC, V. Closed Sun., Dec. 25, 26, public holidays.*

★ **Le Poulbot.** This is one of the best fixed-price lunches in the entire City; it's also part of the Roux Brothers' empire. Top-class, well-balanced food is served in an intimate red-plush setting.

Specials include smoked salmon flan and lamb cutlets with cream of sweet pepper. *45 Cheapside, tel. 01/236-4379. Jacket and tie. Reservations 2-3 days in advance. AE, DC, MC, V. Open Mon.-Fri. for lunch only.*

Moderate **Rudland & Stubbs.** City gents stand in line to lunch at this tiny, basic Victorian restaurant close to a Roman temple. The service is Old World courteous; the fish, cheese, and puddings are comforting and well prepared. *39 Queen Victoria St., tel. 01/ 248-3062. Jacket and tie. Open Mon.-Fri. for lunch only; closed Christmas, public holidays.*

Covent Garden **Inigo Jones.** This is *the* place for beautifully presented French
Very Expensive nouvelle cuisine. You'll pay dearly for the supreme of duck with
★ black olive and mushroom puree and lavender honey sauce, but it is a gourmet's paradise—even though the bare brick and glass surroundings don't encourage you to linger. *14 Garrick St., tel. 01/836-6456. Jacket and tie. Reservations advised. AE, DC, MC, V. Closed Sat. lunch, Sun., Christmas through New Year, public holidays.*
The Savoy Grill. Continuing to attract more than its fair share of literary and artistic names, as well as the odd tycoon, this French-English place guarantees top-notch cooking. Order an omelet Arnold Bennett (seafood is the extra ingredient) or a fillet of pork with fresh cranberries. *Strand, tel. 01/836-4343. Jacket and tie. Reservations advised for lunch and for Thurs.-Sat. dinner. AE, DC, MC, V. Closed Sat. lunch, Sun.*

Expensive **Rules.** Although a London institution with a splendid Edwardian atmosphere, recent reports about the standard of the cooking have been mixed, but you can't go wrong if you stick to roast beef, lamb, or Dover sole. Try the homemade whiskey-and-ginger ice cream for dessert. *35 Maiden Lane, tel. 01/836-5314. Dress: casual to formal. Reservations at least 1 day in advance. AE, DC, MC, V. Closed Sun., Dec. 25.*

Moderate **Bertorelli's.** Opposite the stage door of the Royal Opera House, Bertovelli's is a favorite with opera goers. Chic, post-modern decor complements the traditional Italian food—try the hot mushroom and garlic salad and the *saltimbocca alla romana* (veal and ham in a butter and wine sauce). *44a Floral St., tel. 01/836-3969. Dress: casual chic. Reservations essential. AE, DC, MC, V. Closed Dec. 25.*
★ **The Café des Amis du Vin.** There's a choice of three venues here: a wine bar in the basement, the Café on the ground floor, and the Salon restaurant on the first. The Café is rather cramped, but the genuine French atmosphere and the eclectic mix of regional dishes and wines compensate. Experiment with calves' liver in onion sauce or roast guinea fowl with wild mushroom sauce. The Salon upstairs is considerably more expensive. *11-14 Hanover Pl., tel. 01/379-3444. Dress: informal. Reservations advised. AE, DC, MC, V. Closed Sun., Dec. 25.*
Orso. The staff is snappy and the clientele glitzy showbiz in this basement restaurant. The menu changes seasonally; a typical starter is warm scallops and asparagus salad, while for a main dish you could have grilled fillet of lamb. *27 Wellington St., tel. 01/240-5269. Dress: studied casual. Reservations essential. No credit cards. Closed Dec. 25, 26.*

Inexpensive **Food for Thought.** This is a simple downstairs vegetarian restaurant, with seats for only 50, so there's almost always a waiting line. The menu—stir fries, casseroles, salads and dessert—changes daily, and each dish is freshly made. There's no alcohol served here. *31 Neal St., tel. 01/836-0239. Dress: casual. No credit cards. Closed daily after 8 PM, 2 weeks at Christmas, public holidays.*

Porter's. Traditional but filling English fare is served here, with pies the specialty. Try the lamb and apricot or steak and mushroom, followed by bread-and-butter pudding or potted Stilton cheese. *17 Henrietta St., tel. 01/836-6466. Dress: casual. MC, V. Closed Dec. 25, 26.*

Kensington   **Drake's.** Watch the chefs preparing the best of traditional En-
Expensive   glish fare at this two-level, bare-brick basement restaurant. Spit-roast boar with mustard sauce, beef Wellington, or roast duck on a bed of mushrooms with calvados sauce are tempting specialties. *2a Pond Pl., tel. 01/584-4555. Dress: studied casual. Reservations advised. AE, DC, MC, V. Closed lunch (except Sun.), Dec. 25.*

Reads. This small Anglo-French restaurant with a country-house feel (lots of plants and wickerwork) is owned and operated by a husband and wife team who produce succulent roast beef and an excellent cheeseboard composed entirely of English cheeses. *152 Old Brompton Rd., tel. 01/373-2445. Dress: casual chic. Reservations advised. AE, DC, MC, V. Closed Sun. dinner, public holidays.*

Moderate   **Lou Pescadou.** Ring the bell for admission to this Provençal res-
★   taurant with a boating theme—there are pictures of boats, boats as lamps, and so on. Fish is the specialty: Try the petite bouillabaisse (fish soup) or red mullet poached in tarragon sauce. *241 Old Brompton Rd., tel: 01/370-1057. Dress: informal. AE, DC, MC, V. Reservations advised. Closed Aug., Dec. 25.*

Knightsbridge   **Waltons.** Formal and sumptuous, this Anglo-French restaurant
Very Expensive   with soft lighting and miles of mirrors has an imaginative menu. The seafood sausage and the roast duck are a must. *121 Walton St., tel. 01/584-0204. Jacket and tie. Reservations advised. AE, DC, MC, V. Closed Dec. 25, 26. Easter.*

Expensive   **Ménage à Trois.** Starters and desserts only are served at this
★   stylish pink-and-gray restaurant. Recommended are the terrine of leeks and duck confit served with grilled foie gras and, for a closer, the chocoholics anonymous—six chocolate puddings on one plate! *15 Beauchamp Pl., tel. 01/589-4252. Dress: casual chic. Reservations essential for dinner. AE, DC, MC, V. Closed Sat. and Sun. lunch, Dec. 25, 26, Good Friday.*

Moderate   **Luba's Bistro.** Long wooden tables, basic decor, and authentic Russian cooking—chicken Kiev, beef Stroganoff—give this spot a relaxed, informal atmosphere. Bring your own wine. *6 Yeoman's Row, tel. 01/589-2950. Dress: casual. Reservations advised. MC, V. Closed Sun., Dec. 25, public holidays.*

Stockpot. Speedy service is the mark of this large, jolly restaurant full of young people. The food is filling and wholesome; try the Lancashire hot pot or the apple crumble. *6 Basil St., tel. 01/589-8627. Dress: casual. Closed Dec. 25, public holidays.*

Mayfair   **Jam's.** "Colorful fresh food with a sense of humor" is served in
Very Expensive   this stylish split-level dining room (the parent restaurant is in New York). Try the deep-fried Missouri-style squid with chili mayonnaise or the rack of lamb on Chinese leaves with butter sauce and roasted pinenuts. *42 Albemarle St., tel. 01/493-3600. Dress: studied casual. Reservations essential for lunch, ad-*

vised for dinner. AE, MC, V. Closed Sat. lunch, Sun., public holidays.

★ **Le Gavroche.** Generally regarded as London's finest restaurant, Le Gavroche has excellent service, discreetly sumptuous decor, and lavish *haute cuisine*—duck with foie gras, lobster and champagne mousse. It's near the U.S. embassy. *43 Upper Brook St., tel. 01/408-0881. Jacket and tie. Reserve at least 1 week in advance. AE, DC, MC, V. Closed weekends, 10 days at Christmas, public holidays.*

Expensive **Langan's Brasserie.** Lately it's become rather exclusive, with wall-to-wall celebrities, but if you do manage to get in, you'll be impressed by the modern art on the walls, the vast menu, the frank service (the waiters sometimes advise against certain dishes), and the top-quality food. Try the spinach soufflé with anchovy sauce and the stuffed artichokes with hollandaise sauce. *Stratton St., tel. 01/491-8822. Dress: casual chic. Reservations necessary up to 6 weeks in advance. AE, DC, MC, V. Closed Sat. lunch, Sun., Dec. 25, public holidays.*

Moderate **Pizzeria Condotti.** Run by the cartoonist Enzo Apicella, the walls here are lined with cartoons and modern paintings. The pizzas are first-class, if calorific; the figure-conscious can choose salads instead, such as the *insalata Condotti* (mixed salad with mozzarella and avocado). *4 Mill St., tel. 01/499-1308. Dress: studied casual. Closed Sun., Dec. 25, 26.*

Smollensky's Balloon. This is an American-style bar-restaurant with fine food, good service, and air-conditioning. The menu changes weekly, but five types of steak and vegetarian dishes are standard. Calves' liver with couscous is recommended, as is the chewy nut cake. Sunday lunch is for families, often with live entertainment. *1 Dover St., tel. 01/491-1199. Dress: casual chic. Reservations advised Fri. through Sun. AE, DC, MC, V.*

Inexpensive **The Chicago Pizza Pie Factory.** Huge pizzas with salad and garlic bread are served at reasonable prices in this bright basement spot. The choice of toppings is a bit limited, but try the American sausage and mushroom version. There's also a cocktail bar, rock music, and videos. *17 Hanover Sq., tel. 01/629-2669. Dress: informal. Reservations advised for lunch. Closed Dec. 25, 26.*

Justin de Blank's. This attractive upscale self-service spot is ideal for a break from Oxford Street shopping. The food is all homemade. Favorites include the crab and cucumber mousse, fruit brûlé, and chocolate roulade. *54 Duke St., tel. 01/629-3174. Dress: casual. MC, V. Closed after 9 PM, Sat. dinner, Sun., Dec. 25, public holidays.*

Notting Hill Gate **Clarke's.** There's no choice of dishes here at all; chef Sally
Expensive Clarke plans the meal according to what is fresh in the market each day, using the freshest of herbs and the best of olive oils. *124 Kensington Church St., tel. 01/221-9225. Dress: studied casual. Reservations advised. MC, V. Closed weekends, 1 week at Christmas; Easter, 2 weeks in Aug.*

Moderate **L'Artiste Assoiffé.** The parrots Stanley and Sally will amuse
★ you in the bar of this eccentric Victorian house before you escape to eat in the can-can room or the merry-go-round room to the accompaniment of operatic music. Pop stars, actors, and royals come here for the unique atmosphere and the French food: fillet of steak caramelized with Dijon mustard and spinach

pancakes with nuts and cheese. *122 Kensington Park Rd., tel. 01/727–4714. Dress: studied casual. Reservations essential. AE, DC, MC, V.*

Inexpensive **Hung Toa.** So popular is this Cantonese restaurant that you should call ahead to reserve your dish. Specialties include roast duck, barbecued pork, and fried oysters. *54 Queensway, tel. 01/727–6017. Dress: informal. Reservations advised. Closed Dec. 25, 26.*

Wine Gallery. This is an art gallery where you have to eat or drink if you want to view the pictures. The food, too, is a lot more creative than that in the average wine bar (pastry parcels with duck, shallots, and garlic; blinis with sour cream, smoked salmon, and caviar), and the wine is reliable. *294 Westbourne Grove, tel. 01/229–1877. Dress: casual. MC, V. Closed public holidays.*

Soho **Alastair Little.** A favorite among media people, chef Alastair
Expensive serves Nouvelle British designer food, such as venison terrine with orange marmalade and mascarpone tart with figs. Drawbacks include the paper napkins, functional decor, and closely packed tables. *49 Frith St., tel. 01/734–5183. Dress: informal. Reservations advised. V. Closed weekends, Christmas, Easter, 3 weeks in Aug.*

Lindsay House. Inside this restored 16th-century town house, mouth-watering traditional English 17th-century recipes, such as "Brye favors" (brie in pastry with fresh tomato sauce), are served amid opulent decor, with hunting scenes and oil portraits on the walls. *21 Romilly St., W1, tel. 01/439–0450. Dress: studied casual. Reservations advisable. AE, DC, MC, V. Closed Christmas Day.*

Moderate **Chiang Mai.** The interior is modeled on a traditional Thai stilt
★ house. The food is delicious and spicy, all easy to order from an English menu. Try a *Tom Yum* (hot and sour soup) or a *Tad Tra Prou* (beef, pork, or chicken with fresh Thai basil and chili). *48 Frith St., tel. 01/437–7444. Dress: casual chic. Reservations advisable for dinner. AE, MC, V. Closed Sun. and public holidays.*

★ **The Gay Hussar.** Join politicians and journalists swallowing Magyar-size portions at what must be one of the best Hungarian restaurants outside Budapest. Solidly furnished in mock Tudor paneling, it also sports plush banquette seats. Try the cold cherry soup, the goulash, or the "heroic minced goose." *2 Greek St., tel. 01/437–0973. Dress: informal. Reservations required. No credit cards. Closed Sun. and public holidays.*

Manzi's. This is one of London's oldest and most traditional fish restaurants. The downstairs restaurant is the more lively and atmospheric; decor is kitsch Moulin Rouge murals and monstrous plastic lobsters. *1–2 Leicester St., tel. 01/734–0224. Dress: studied casual. Reservations advisable. AE, DC, MC, V. Closed Dec. 25, 26.*

Inexpensive **Crank's.** One restaurant of a popular vegetarian chain (other branches are at Covent Garden, Great Newport Street, Adelaide Street, Tottenham Street, and Barrett Street), Crank's has a nutritious and tasty menu. Lunch is self-service, dinner candle-lit waiter-service (many branches, though not this one, close at 8 PM). *8 Marshall St., tel. 01/437–9431. Dress: informal. Reservations advisable for dinner. AE, DC, MC, V. Closed Sun., Dec. 25.*

Poon's. A popular Chinese restaurant (there are long lines in the evening), Poon's specializes in wind-dried meats. There is a sister restaurant in Covent Garden, but this one is cheaper and more authentic. *4 Leicester St., tel. 01/437–1528. Dress: informal. Reservations essential. No credit cards. Closed Sun., Dec. 25, 26.*

St. James's
Very Expensive

Maxim's de Paris. A lavish replica of the Paris restaurant of the same name, the emphasis here is on luxury. Outstanding are the *terrine de foie gras* with salad and the lobster and fish cassoulet with asparagus tips in a white wine and cream sauce. After dinner, dance to a small band. *32 Panton St., tel. 01/839–4809. Jacket and tie. Reservations advised, especially on weekends. AE, DC, MC, V. Open Tues.–Sat. for dinner only.*

Expensive

Le Caprice. Furnished in sophisticated black-and-white decor, Le Caprice caters to equally stylish patrons. The menu should appeal to all tastes, from hamburgers to elaborate dishes such as salmon fishcakes with sorrel sauce. Finish with a mousse of dark and white chocolate. *Arlington House, Arlington St., tel. 01/629–2239. Dress: studied casual. Reservations required. AE, DC, MC, V. Closed public holidays for lunch.*

The Veeraswamy. London's oldest Indian restaurant, founded in 1927, has now shed its colonial trappings. The king prawn masala (medium hot prawn curry) and the lamb kadai ghost (curried lamb with capsicums) are both recommended. *99 Regent St., tel. 01/734–1401. Dress: casual but nice. Reservations advised. AE, DC, MC, V. Closed Dec. 25, 26.*

Wilton's. Traditional British fare—turtle soup, sausage and mashed potatoes, partridge, Stilton—is served here in Edwardian surroundings. The oysters are London's best—all the seafood arrives fresh up to four times a day. *55 Jermyn St., tel. 01/629–9955. Jacket and tie. Reservations advised 2 days in advance. AE, DC, MC, V. Closed Sat. lunch, Sun., last week in July and 1st 2 weeks in Aug., 10 days at Christmas.*

Lodging

Ratings

Prices are for two people in a double room and include all taxes. Best bets are indicated by a star ★. At press time, the pound was equal to $1.70.

Category	Cost
Very Expensive	over £100
Expensive	£65–£100
Moderate	£30–£65
Inexpensive	under £30

Credit Cards

The following credit card abbreviations are used: AE, American Express; DC, Diners Club; MC, MasterCard; V, Visa.

Bayswater
Very Expensive
★

Whites. This cream-faced Victorian "country mansion" has a wrought-iron portico and a view of Kensington Gardens, especially grand when floodlit at night. Thick carpets, gilded glass, marble balustrades, swagged silk draperies, and Louis XV-style furniture all help to give a sense of deep luxury. Some of the bedrooms have balconies, seating areas, and personal safes. Colors are muted: powder blue, old rose, and lemon yellow. *Lancaster Gate, W2 3NR, tel. 01/262–2711. 55 rooms with* *bath. Facilities: restaurant, lounge, free in-house movies. AE, DC, MC, V.*

Expensive **Abbey Court.** A short walk from Kensington Gardens brings you to this luxury bed-and-breakfast establishment in a historic 1850 building. Each bedroom is individually designed with 19th-century French furniture, Venetian mirrors, and oil portraits; some have four-posters. *20 Pembridge Gardens, W2, 4DU, tel. 01/221-7518. 22 rooms with bath. Facilities: Jacuzzis, drawing room. AE, DC, MC, V.*

Moderate **Camelot.** This affordable hotel has beautifully decorated
★ rooms. The breakfast room has a large open fireplace with wooden trestle tables and a polished wood floor. *45-47 Norfolk Sq., W2 1RX, tel. 01/723-9118. 34 rooms, 28 with bath. Facilities: lounge, free in-house videos. MC, V.*

Edward Lear. The former home of Edward Lear, the artist and writer of nonsense verse, this hotel has an imposing entrance leading to a black-and-white tiled floor. Ask for one of the quieter rooms to the rear. The breakfast room has huge French windows. *28-30 Seymour St., W1H 5WD, tel. 01/402-5401. 30 rooms, 15 with bath. V.*

Portobello. A faithful core of visitors returns again and again to this tiny hotel in a Victorian terrace near the Portobello Road antiques market. Some rooms are tiny, but the suites have sitting rooms attached, and the atmosphere is relaxed and informal. *22 Stanley Gardens, W11 2NG, tel. 01/727-2777. 25 rooms with bath. Facilities: bar, restaurant. AE, DC, MC, V. Closed 10 days at Christmas.*

Prince William. This is a handsome, mid-19th century building near Paddington Station. Most rooms have the original high ceilings, and some have balconies that catch the elusive London sun. *42-44 Gloucester Terrace, W2 3DA, tel. 01/724-7414. 42 rooms with bath. Facilities: bar, restaurant. AE, DC, MC, V.*

Inexpensive **Ashley.** The hotel consists of three handsome terraced houses in a slightly shabby neighborhood. Although some rooms are small and rather sparsely furnished, the very friendly and conscientious managers (two brothers) make this a decidedly good choice. *15 Norfolk Sq., W2 1RX, tel. 01/723-3375. 52 rooms, 18 with bath. Facilities: lounge. Closed Christmas.*

Norfolk. Though small, this is a modest, pleasant Regency hotel near Paddington Station. Some rooms have French windows and balconies overlooking the square. *20 Norfolk Sq., W2 1RS, tel. 01/723-4963. 28 rooms, none with bath.*

Bloomsbury **Grafton.** This hotel of great style features an Edwardian draw-
Expensive ing room with red-plush armchairs, classical columns, and an
★ open fireplace. The recently refurbished bedrooms are more modern. The Grafton's location makes it convenient for Euston and King's Cross stations. *130 Tottenham Court Rd., W1P 9HP. tel. 01/388-4131. 236 rooms with bath. Facilities: bar, lounge, restaurant, laundry, free in-house movies. AE, DC, MC, V.*

Moderate **White Hall.** Beyond the imposing entrance here, there's an elegant lobby with arched windows and a marble floor and a garden bar leading on to a patio and not-too-manicured garden. *2-5 Montague St., WC1B 5BU. tel. 01/580/5871. 80 rooms, 20 with bath. Facilities: bar, restaurant. AE, DC, MC, V.*

Inexpensive **Morgan.** This charming family-run hotel in an 18th-century terrace has rooms that are small and functionally furnished, but friendly and cheerful. The tiny paneled breakfast room is straight out of a doll's house. The back rooms overlook the British Museum. *24 Bloomsbury St., WC1B 3QU. tel. 01/636–3735. 17 rooms, 9 with bath. No credit cards.*

Ridgemount. The public rooms here have a friendly, cluttered feel, especially the family-style breakfast room. Some rooms overlook a leafy garden. *65 Gower St., WC1E 6HJ. tel. 01/636–1141. 15 rooms, none with bath. Facilities: lounge. No credit cards.*

Ruskin. Family-owned, pleasant and quiet, this popular hotel is immediately opposite the British Museum. All front windows are double-glazed. Bedrooms are clean though nondescript; back ones overlook a pretty garden. *23–24 Montague St., WC1B 5BN. tel. 01/636–7388. 35 rooms, 7 with shower. Facilities: lounge. AE, DC, MC, V.*

Chelsea and Kensington
Very Expensive
★

Blakes. Patronized by musicians and film stars, this hotel is one of the most exotic in town. Its Victorian exterior contrasts with the 1980s ultra-chic interior, with an arty mix of Biedermeier, leather, and bamboo furniture; rich fabrics; four-posters; and Oriental enameled screens. The bedrooms have individual designs, ranging from swaths of black moiré silk to a more severe plain gray. *33 Roland Gardens, SW7 3PF, tel. 01/370–6701. 50 rooms with bath. Facilities: restaurant, satellite TV. AE, DC, MC, V.*

Expensive **Chelsea.** The glittering glass atrium of this 1969 hotel, conveniently located near Harrods, immediately creates a striking effect. The lounge, with its portraits and period-style furniture, is old-fashioned and relaxing, while the spacious bedrooms have large beds and contemporary darkwood fitted units. *Sloane St., SW1X 9NU, tel. 01/235–4377. 228 rooms with bath. Facilities: cocktail bar, restaurant, lounge. AE, DC, MC, V.*

Eleven Cadogan Gardens. There's scarcely a sign of the 1980s in this aristocratic, late Victorian gabled town house hotel that's popular with international antiques dealers. There is fine period furniture, landscape paintings, and portraits throughout; the bedrooms have mahogany furniture, restful color schemes, and pretty bedspreads and draperies. The best rooms are in the rear. *11 Cadogan Gardens, Sloane Sq., SW3 2RJ, tel. 01/730–3426. 60 rooms with bath. Facilities: garden, chauffeur-driven car.*

Moderate **London Tara.** This vast, functional international hotel has a cordial atmosphere and light and colorful rooms. *Scarsdale Pl., W8 5SR, tel. 01/937–7211. 831 rooms with bath; 10 specially converted for the disabled. Facilities: 3 restaurants, lounge, bar. AE, MC, V.*

Prince. Unashamedly upscale, yet reasonably priced, with original cornices in the bathrooms and a high standard of furnishings, this hotel is a good accommodation for the money. The hall is papered in a pleasant mint-green Regency stripe. *6 Sumner Pl., SW7 3AB, tel. 01/589–6488. 20 rooms, 14 with bath. Facilities: garden, lounge. AE, MC, V.*

Inexpensive **Abbey House.** Standards are high and the rooms unusually spacious in this hotel in a fine residential block near Kensington Palace and Gardens. *11 Vicarage Gate, W8 4AG, tel. 01/727–2594. 15 rooms, none with bath. Facilities: orthopedic beds.*

Annadale. This comfortable hotel is efficiently run and a good "buy" for the money, as the many repeat visitors attest. Breakfast is traditional British: kippers, Welsh rarebit, cereal, and genuine Scottish porridge. *39 Sloane Gardens, SW1 8DG, tel. 01/730–5051. 12 rooms, 10 with bath.*

Oakley House. Impeccably Victorian outside and a bit dark inside—but not at all dreary—the rooms here are small yet pleasant, with attractive moldings and colorful Indian print bedspreads. The public showers are clean and gigantic. Breakfast is self-service. Located in the heart of Chelsea, the Oakley House is not near a tube station. *71–72 Oakley St., SW3 5HF, tel. 01/352–9362. 24 rooms, 1 with bath. No credit cards.*

Knightsbridge and Victoria
Very Expensive

Goring. Around the corner from Buckingham Palace and often used by visiting VIPs, this hotel was built by a Mr. Goring in 1910 and is now run by the third generation of Gorings. The atmosphere remains Edwardian: marble fittings in the bathrooms, with brass fittings and the original fitted closets in some of the bedrooms. *Beeston Pl., Grosvenor Gardens, SW1W 0JW. tel. 01/834–8211. 87 rooms, all with bath. Facilities: bar, restaurant, lounge. AE, DC, MC, V.*

Hyde Park Hotel. In the 1920s, this was the favored accommodation of Rudolph Valentino and of sultans and maharjahs, who would book whole floors. The decor is high Victorian, with sumptuous green-veined marble, gold-topped columns, potted palms, and sparkling chandeliers. The bedrooms are furnished in the best of English taste: Edwardian darkwood furniture and pretty arrangements of fresh flowers. It's well placed for shopping and Hyde Park, over which some rooms have good views. *66 Knightsbridge, SW1Y 7LA, tel. 01/235–2000. 186 rooms with bath. Facilities: bar, 2 restaurants, lounge, hairdresser. AE, DC, MC, V.*

St. James Court. This elegant 1900 apartment block has been converted into a stylish hotel with a stately courtyard adorned by a fountain and a brick frieze portraying Shakespearean scenes. The reception area is grand, all marble and wood and lots of greenery. The bedrooms are appealingly decorated in different color schemes; the bathrooms are glamorous. *Buckingham Gate, SW1E 6AF, tel. 01/834–6655. 390 rooms with bath. Facilities: 2 restaurants, coffee shop, fitness center with sauna, spa pools. AE, DC, MC, V.*

Expensive
★

Basil Street. Women guests here are granted automatic membership in the ladies' organization called "Parrot Club." Family-run for some 75 years, this is a gracious Edwardian hotel on a quiet street. The rooms are filled with antiques. The Gallery is a writing area, with desks in the window alcoves, unusual paintings on glass, polished wooden floors, and fine red and blue carpets. *Basil St., SW3 1AH. tel. 01/581–3311. 101 rooms, 90 with bath. Facilities: wine bar, lounge, ladies' club, restaurant. AE, DC, MC, V.*

Cadogan Thistle. A turreted Edwardian building with teak furniture and pretty fabrics in the bedrooms and boldly colored hand-painted tiles in the bathrooms. There's a fascinating collection of Edwardian photos in the cocktail bar. The front part of the hotel was once the home of Lily Langtry, the actress who was Edward VII's mistress while he was Prince of Wales. *75 Sloane St., SW1X 9SG, tel. 01/235–7141. 69 rooms with bath. Facilities: bar, lounge, restaurant. AE, DC, MC, V.*

Stakis St. Ermins. Convenient for Westminster Abbey, this is a Victorian hotel with high ceilings, a fine curved stairwell, and roomy bedrooms brightened by floral fabrics. Most of the guests are businesspeople. *Caxton St., SW1K 0QW, tel. 01/222–7888. 300 rooms with bath. Facilities: coffee lounge, 2 restaurants. AE, DC, MC, V.*

Moderate **Ebury Court.** This small, old-fashioned, country house-style hotel is near Victoria Station. The rooms are small and chintzy, with antique furniture to give them extra character. *26 Ebury St., SW1W 0LU, tel. 01/730–8147. 38 rooms, 15 with bath. Facilities: club with bar and lounge (membership fee payable), restaurant. MC, V.*

★ **Knightsbridge Green.** There are more suites than bedrooms at this recently refurbished 18th-century hotel just 2 minutes' walk from Harrods. The style of the second floor is French with white furniture; the third is English, in beech. Breakfast is served in your room—there's no restaurant. *159 Knightsbridge, SW1X 7PD, tel. 01/584–6274. 22 rooms/suites with bath. Facilities: club room. AE, MC, V. Closed 5 days at Christmas.*

West End **Berkshire.** Ideally situated for Oxford Street shopping, this un-
Very Expensive usual flatiron building was totally renovated in 1987–88. The
★ decor is in Chinese style throughout, with exquisite Oriental vases and lamp shades. The bedrooms have richly decorated cream walls and ceilings, red or blue carpets, and tasteful paintings. In the drawing room, you can doze peacefully in front of the open fire, browse along the bookshelves, or enjoy the afternoon with tempting cream cakes. *350 Oxford St., W1N 0BY, tel. 01/629–7474. 147 rooms with bath. Facilities: restaurant, free in-house videos. AE, DC, MC, V.*

Brown's. Close to Bond Street, Brown's is like a country house in the middle of town, with wood paneling, grandfather clocks, and large fireplaces. The elegant furnishings of the bedrooms include brass chandeliers and matching olive carpets, velour armchairs, and sweeping curtains. *34 Albemarle St., W1A 4SW, tel. 01/493–6020. 125 rooms with bath. Facilities: restaurant, lounge, writing room, cocktail bar. AE, DC, MC, V.*

Duke's. This small Edwardian hotel is situated in a cul-de-sac in St. James's and enjoys a distinct Old World character, helped by the portraits of dukes adorning the walls. The top-floor bedrooms are the most spacious. *5 St. James's Pl., SW1A 1NY, tel. 01/491–4840. 36 rooms with bath. Facilities: restaurant. AE, DC, MC, V.*

Inn on the Park. Said to be one of Howard Hughes's hideaways, this opulent hotel, with its polished marble entrance hall, is close to Hyde Park. The rooms are exquisitely furnished with gigantic beds and plenty of extras, such as guest bathrobes and phone extensions in the bathrooms. *Hamilton Pl., Park Lane, W1A 1AZ, tel. 01/499–0888. 228 rooms with bath. Facilities: restaurant, shopping arcade, free in-house movies, garden. AE, DC, MC, V.*

★ **Savoy.** This grand, historic late-Victorian hotel has long been the byword for luxury. The best rooms, with antiques and cream plasterwork, overlook the Thames; others are in 1920s style with the original splendid bathroom fittings. *Strand, WC2R 0EU, tel. 01/836–4343. 200 rooms with bath. Facilities: restaurant, grill room, hairdresser, florist, theater-ticket desk, free in-house movies. AE, DC, MC, V.*

Expensive **Clifton-Ford.** This is one of central London's most peaceful hotels, situated in an 18th-century street north of Oxford Street.

The public rooms have comfortable armchairs, chandeliers, and marble floors. Bedrooms are in light colors and have all the latest accessories. *47 Welbeck St., W1M 8DN, tel. 01/486–6600. 240 rooms with bath. Facilities: restaurant, bar, laundry, lounge with pianist, free in-house movies. AE, DC, MC, V.*

Pastoria. A recently refurbished hotel, the Pastoria stands on a quiet street only yards away from the restaurants and bright lights of Soho. The limed oak bedrooms have light pink walls and navy blue carpets. *3–6 St. Martin's St., WC2H 7HL, tel. 01/930–8641. 58 rooms with bath. Facilities: restaurant, bar. AE, DC, MC, V.*

Moderate **Bryanston Court.** Three 18th-century houses have been converted into a traditional English family-run hotel with open fires and comfortable armchairs; the bedrooms are more contemporary. *56–60 Great Cumberland Pl., W1H 7FD, tel. 01/262–3141. 56 rooms with bath. Facilities: bar, lounge, restaurant. AE, DC, MC, V.*

The Arts

For a list of events in the London arts scene, visit a newsstand or bookstore to pick up any of the weekly magazines: *Time Out, What's On,* or *City Limits* (the last is best for fringe events). The city's evening paper, the *Standard,* carries listings, as do the major Sunday papers, the daily *Independent* and *Guardian,* and, on Friday, *The Times.*

Theater London's theater life can broadly be divided into three categories: the national, subsidized, companies; the commercial, or "West End" theaters; and the fringe.

The main national companies are the *National Theatre* (NT) and the **Royal Shakespeare Company** (RSC). Each has its own custom-designed facilities, in the South Bank arts complex and in the Barbican Arts Centre, respectively. Each presents a variety of plays by writers of all nationalities, ranging from the classics of Shakespeare and his contemporaries to specially commissioned modern works. Box office information: N.T., tel. 01/928–2252; RSC, tel. 01/628–8795.

The West End theaters largely stage musicals, comedies, whodunits, and revivals of lighter plays of the 19th and 20th centuries, often starring television celebrities. Occasionally, there are more serious productions, and sometimes successful productions from the subsidized theaters, such as RSC's hugely successful musical *Les Misérables.*

The dozen or so established fringe theaters, scattered around central London and the immediate outskirts, frequently present some of London's most intriguing productions, if you're prepared to overlook occasional rough acting and uncomfortable seating.

Most theaters have an evening performance at 7:30 or 8 daily, except Sunday, and a matinee twice a week (Wednesday or Thursday and Saturday). Expect to pay from £5 for a seat in the upper balcony to £18.50 for a good seat in the stalls or dress circle (mezzanine). Tickets may be booked in person at the theater box office, over the phone by credit card, or through ticket agents such as **Keith Prowse** (tel. 01/749–9999, or look in the phone book under *Keith* for the nearest office). In addition, the ticket booth in Leicester Square sells half-price tickets on the day of performance for about 45 theaters; there is an 80p service charge. Fringe seats can also be bought at the **Fringe Box Office** at the Duke of York's Theatre (St. Martin's Lane, WC2E 7NA, tel. 01/379–6002; 50p service charge). Beware of unscrupulous ticket agents who sell tickets at four or five times their box office price (a small service charge is legitimate) and scalpers, who stand outside theaters offering tickets for the next performance; they've been known to charge £200 for a sought-after show.

Concerts Ticket prices for symphony orchestra concerts are still relatively moderate—between £2.50 and £12, although you can expect to pay more to hear big-name artists on tour. If you can't book in advance, arrive half an hour before the performance for a chance at returns.

The London Symphony Orchestra is in residence at the **Barbican Arts Centre** (tel. 01/628–8795), although other top symphony and chamber orchestras also perform here. The **South Bank arts complex** (tel. 01/928–3191), which includes the **Royal Festival Hall** and the **Queen Elizabeth Hall,** is another major venue for choral, symphony, and chamber concerts. For less expensive concert going, try the **Royal Albert Hall** (tel. 01/589–8212) during the summer Promenade season; special tickets for standing room are available at the hall on the night of performance. Inexpensive lunchtime concerts take place all over the city in smaller halls and churches, often featuring string quartets, singers, jazz ensembles, and gospel choirs. St. John's (tel. 01/222–1061) and St. Martin-in-the-Fields (tel. 01/839–1930) are two of the more popular sites.

Opera The **Royal Opera House** ranks alongside the New York Met in cost. Prices range from £2 (in the upper slips, from where only a tiny portion of the stage is visible) to £220 for a box in the Grand Tier. Bookings are best made at the box office (tel. 01/240–1066). The **Coliseum** (tel. 01/278–8916) is the home of the English National Opera Company; productions are staged in English and are often a good deal more exciting than those at the Royal Opera House. The prices, which start at £4, are generally lower, too.

Ballet The Royal Opera House is also the home of the **Royal Ballet.** The prices are slightly more reasonable than for the opera, but be sure to book well ahead. The **London Festival Ballet** and visiting companies perform at the Coliseum from time to time. **Sadler's Wells Theatre** (tel. 01/278–8916) hosts various ballet companies— including the Royal and the Rambert—as well as regional ballet and international modern dance troupes. Prices here are reasonable.

Cinema Most West End cinemas are in the Leicester Square-Piccadilly Circus area. Tickets average £3.50–4, but can run twice as high. Matinees and Monday evenings are cheaper. Cinema clubs screen a wide range of films: classics, continental, underground, rare, or underestimated masterpieces. The membership fee is usually about £1. One of the best-value clubs is the **National Film Theatre** (tel. 01/928–3232), part of the South Bank arts complex.

Nightlife

London's night spots are legion, and there is only space here to list a few of the best known.

Jazz **Bas Clef** (Coronet St., tel. 01/729–2440), situated in an out-of-the-way warehouse on the northern edge of the City, offers some of the best live jazz in town and a gourmet Anglo-French menu. **Ronnie Scott's** (Frith St., tel. 01/439–0747) is the legendary Soho jazz club where a host of American performers have played.

Nightclubs **Legends** (Old Burlington St., tel. 01/437–9933) has an impressive high-tech interior; a large choice of cocktails is served at the upstairs bar, while the downstairs area is graced with a large cool dance floor and central bar. Celebrity-packed **Stringfellows** (Upper St. Martins Lane, tel. 01/240–5534) has an Art Deco upstairs restaurant, mirrored walls, and a heady light show in the downstairs dance floor.

Disco Wednesday nights have made the **Café de Paris** (Coventry St., tel. 01/437–2036) one of London's hottest spots; dinner is served on the balcony overlooking the dance floor, where you can people-spot in comfort. There is a disco-dance on Friday and Saturday for the more mellow. **Xenon** (Piccadilly, tel. 01/734–9344) is a vast basement disco with three top international acts every night; the modern black-and-silver interior with a heady light show attracts a young and fashionable crowd.

Casinos By law, you must apply in person for membership in a gaming house; in many cases, clubs prefer an applicant's membership to be proposed by an existing member. Approval usually takes about two days.

Crockford's (Curzon St., tel. 01/493–7771) is a civilized and unflashy 150-year-old club with a large international clientele; American roulette, punto banco, and blackjack are played. **Sportsman Club** (Tottenham Court Road, tel. 01/637–5464) is one of the few gaming houses in London to have a dice table as well as punto banco, American roulette, and blackjack.

Rock **The Rock Garden** (The Piazza, Covent Garden, tel. 01/240–3961) is famous for encouraging younger talent; Talking Heads, U2, and The Smiths are among those who played here while still virtually unknown. Music is in the standing-room-only basement, so eat first in the American restaurant upstairs. The **Marquee** (Wardour St., tel. 01/437–6603) is Soho's original rock club; two live bands perform every night.

Cabaret The best comedy in town can be found in the small, crowded basement of the **Comedy Store** (Leicester Square, tel. 01/839–6665). There are two shows, 8 and midnight, with the famous improvised show *Comedy To Go* on Sunday. **Gaslight of St. James's** (Duke of York St., tel. 01/930–1648) is a basement night spot with attractive hostesses and three striptease cabarets each night.

Singles **The Limelight** (Shaftesbury Ave., tel. 01/434–1761) is one of London's most popular night spots, with lots of one-nighter shows and special events; it is owned by New Yorker Limelighter Peter Gatient. Just behind Harrods, **Wolfe's** (Basil St., tel. 01/589–8444) has recently become increasingly popular with

Americans; it is more expensive than the average American diner—but you get what you pay for.

Windsor, Oxford, the Cotswolds, Stratford-upon-Avon, and Bath

The Thames, England's second-longest river, winds its way toward London through an accessible and gracious stretch of countryside. An excursion west from the capital, roughly following the river toward its source in the Cotswold Hills, allows you to explore historic townships such as Windsor, where the castle is still regularly used by the royal family; Oxford, home of the nation's oldest university; and Shakespeare's birthplace at Stratford-upon-Avon. Traveling south, Bath's 18th-century streets recall an age more elegant than our own.

Getting Around

By Train Suburban services run from London (Waterloo and Paddington stations) to Windsor. Regular fast trains run from Paddington to Oxford and Bath, and less frequent and slower services requiring at least one change, to Stratford. For information, call 01/262–6767. An alternative route to Stratford is from London's Euston Station to Coventry, from where Guide Friday operates bus connections; not all trains are met—telephone 0789–294466 for details.

By Bus Regular long-distance services leave from Victoria Coach Station. For information, call 01/730–0202.

By Car The M4 and the M40 are the main highways out of London serving Oxford, the Cotswolds, and Bath. Once you're clear of London, take to the country roads and explore tiny villages and the countryside—your trip may take a bit longer, but you'll be rewarded by the best of the English countryside.

Tourist Information

Bath: Abbey Churchyard, tel. 0225/62831.
Oxford: St. Aldate's, opposite the Town Hall, tel. 0865/726871.
Stow-on-the-Wold: Public Library, St. Edwards Hall, tel. 0451/30352 (summer only).
Stratford: Judith Shakespeare's House, on the corner of High Street and Bridge Street, tel. 0789/293127/67522.
Windsor: Central Station, tel. 0753/852010.

Guided Tours

National Holidays operates five-day trips in the Cotswolds, some in Bath. **Wallace Arnold** offers a five-day tour of Shakespeare Country and the Cotswolds based in Coventry. Both companies have offices throughout the country. **Alder Valley** operates two-hour tours of the Thames Valley in open-top double-decker buses from Windsor Parish Church. Tel. 0628/21344. **White's of Oxford** runs daily coach tours of the Cots-

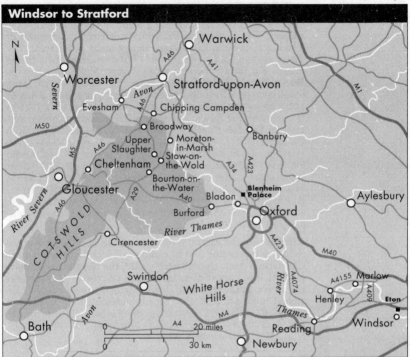

Windsor to Stratford

Map showing the region from Windsor to Stratford, including Warwick, Worcester, Stratford-upon-Avon, Evesham, Chipping Campden, Broadway, Upper Slaughter, Moreton-in-Marsh, Stow-on-the-Wold, Cheltenham, Bourton-on-the-Water, Bladon, Blenheim Palace, Banbury, Aylesbury, Gloucester, Burford, Oxford, Cirencester, River Thames, Cotswold Hills, Swindon, White Horse Hills, Marlow, Henley, Eton, Windsor, River, Bath, Reading, Newbury.

wolds from April through September and minibus and chauffeured car tours to a selection of stately homes. Tel. 0865/61295.

Exploring

Windsor **Windsor,** some 25 miles (40 kilometers) west of London, has been a royal citadel since the days of William the Conqueror in the 11th century. In the 14th century, Edward III revamped the old castle, building the Norman gateway, the great round tower, and new apartments. Almost every monarch since then has added new buildings or improved existing ones; over the centuries, the medieval fortification has been transformed into the lavish royal palace the visitor sees today. Windsor Castle remains a favorite spot of Queen Elizabeth and Prince Philip; they spend most weekends here, and there is a grand celebration with all the family at Christmas. Naturally, the royal family's private apartments are closed to the public, but you can see the State Apartments, where visiting heads of state are sometimes entertained.

The following are some of the highlights of the Castle: **St. George's Chapel,** more than 230 feet (70 meters) long with two tiers of great windows and hundreds of gargoyles, buttresses, and pinnacles, is one of the noblest buildings in England. Inside, above the choir stalls, hang the banners, swords, and helmets of the Knights of the Order of the Garter, the most senior Order of Chivalry. The many monarchs buried in the Chapel include Henry VIII and George VI, father of the present queen. The **State apartments** indicate the magnificence of the queen's art collection; here hang paintings by such masters as Rubens, Van Dyck, and Holbein; drawings by Leonardo da Vinci; and Gobelin tapestries, among many other treasures. There are splendid views across to Windsor Great Park, the remains of a former royal hunting forest. Make time to view **Queen Mary's Dolls' House,** a charming residence with every detail complete, including electricity, running water, and miniature books on the library shelves. It was designed in 1921 by the architect Sir Edwin Lutyens for the present queen's grandmother. *Windsor Castle, tel. 0753/868286. Precincts open daily 10–4:15 (till 7:15 mid-May–Aug.). St. George's Chapel. Admission: £1.50 adults, 60p children under 16 and senior citizens. Open Mon.–Sat. 10:45–3:45, Sun. 2–3:45. State Apartments. Admission: £1.80 adults, 80p children under 16 and senior citizens. Open Mon.–Sat. 10:30–5 (until 3, Nov.– Apr.), Sun. 1:30–5. Queen Mary's Dolls' House. Admission: 80p adults, 40p children under 16 and senior citizens. Open daily 10:30–5 (Oct.–Mar. until 3).*

After seeing the castle, stroll around the town and enjoy the shops; antiques are sold in cobbled Church Lane and Queen Charlotte Street. Opposite the castle, the **Royalty and Empire** exhibition in part of Central Station re-creates in waxworks the arrival at the station of Queen Victoria to celebrate her Diamond Jubilee in 1897; the scene is incredibly lifelike. *Thames St., tel. 0753/857837. Admission: £2.85 adults, £2 children under 16, £2.30 senior citizens. Open Apr.–Oct., daily 9:30–5:30, Nov.–Mar., daily 9:30–4:30.*

Time Out | The Adam and Eve pub opposite the walls of Windsor Castle serves hot snacks and plowmen's lunches, while the Chocolate House in Market Street is an inviting place for morning coffee, lunch, or a cream tea.

A short walk over the river brings you to **Eton,** Windsor Castle's equally historic neighbor and home of the famous public school. (In Britain, so-called "public" schools are private and charge fees.) Classes still take place in the distinctive red-brick Tudor-style buildings; the oldest buildings are grouped around a quadrangle called School Yard. The **Museum of Eton Life** has displays on the school's history, and a guided tour is also available. *Brewhouse Yard, tel. 0753/863593. Admission: £1.80 adults, £1.20 children under 16. Open daily during term 2–5, 10:30–5 on school holidays. Guided tours daily at 2:15 and 3:15; charge: £2.40 adults, £1.80 children under 16, including admission to museum.*

A relatively uncrowded route from Windsor to Oxford is along the river through Marlow and Henley on roads A409, then A4155, A4074, and A423. Both these riverside towns contain numerous historic buildings, many still in private residential use. In **Marlow,** there are some stylish 18th-century houses on Peter and West Streets, and several Princes of Wales have lived in Marlow Place on Station Road, which dates from 1721. Mary Shelley wrote her celebrated horror story *Frankenstein* in the town.

Henley has been famous since 1839 for the rowing regatta it holds each July. For the spectators, the social side of the regatta is as entertaining as the races themselves; elderly oarsmen wear brightly colored blazers and tiny caps, businessmen entertain wealthy clients, and everyone admires the ladies' fashions. The town is worth exploring for its small but good selection of specialty shops, such as Saffron on Bell Street (craft items) and Thames Gallery on Thameside (Georgian and Victorian silver). The Red Lion Hotel near the 200-year-old bridge has been visited by kings, dukes, and writers; the Duke of Marlborough stayed there while Blenheim Palace was being built. St. Mary's Church has a 16th-century "checkerboard" tower made of alternate squares of flint and stone, and the **Chantry House,** built in 1420 as a school for poor boys, is an unspoiled example of the rare overhanging timber-frame design. *Hart St. Free. Open Thurs. and Sat. 10–noon.*

Oxford Continue along A423 north to Oxford. The surest way to absorb **Oxford's** unique blend of history and scholarliness is to wander around the tiny alleys that link the honey-colored stone buildings topped by elegant "dreaming" spires, exploring the colleges where the undergraduates live and work. Oxford University, like Cambridge University, is not a single building but a collection of 35 independent colleges; many of their magnificent chapels and dining halls are open to visitors—times are displayed at the entrance lodges. **Magdalen College** is one of the most impressive, with 500-year-old cloisters and lawns leading down to the river Cherwell. **St. Edmund Hall,** the next college up the High Street, has one of the smallest and most picturesque quadrangles, with an old well in the center; **Christ Church,** on St. Aldate's, has the largest quadrangle, known as Tom Quad; in the medieval dining hall hang portraits of former pupils, including John Wesley, William Penn, and no less than 14 prime ministers. The doors between the inner and outer quadrangles of **Balliol College,** on Broad Street, still bear the scorch marks from the flames that burned Archbishop Cranmer and Bishops Latimer and Ridley at the stake in 1555 for their Protestant beliefs.

The **Oxford Story** on Broad Street is a brand-new multimedia presentation of the university's 800-year history, in which visitors travel through depictions of college life. *Broad St., tel. 0865/728822. Admission: £3 adults, £1.50 children. Open Apr.– Oct., daily 9–7, Nov.–Mar., daily 9–5:30.*

Also on Broad Street is the **Sheldonian Theatre,** which St. Paul's architect Christopher Wren designed to look like a semicircular Roman amphitheater: It's one of his earliest works. Graduation ceremonies are held here. *Sheldonian Theatre, Broad St. Small admission charge. Open Mon.–Sat. 10–12:45, 2–4:45; closes at 3:45 Dec.–Feb.*

The **Ashmolean Museum,** which you encounter by turning right out of Broad Street, into Magdalen Street then taking the first left, is Britain's oldest public museum, holding priceless collections of Egyptian, Greek, and Roman artifacts; Michelangelo drawings; and European silverware. *Beaumont St., tel. 08765/ 27800. Free. Open Tues.–Sat. 10–4, Sun. 2–4.*

For a relaxing walk, make for the banks of the river Cherwell, either through the University Parks area or through Magdalen College to Addison's Walk, and watch the undergraduates idly punting a summer's afternoon away. Or hire one of these narrow flat-bottomed boats yourself. But be warned: Navigating is more difficult than it looks!

Time Out The **Queen's Lane Coffee House** on High Street offers inexpensive snacks and is popular with undergraduates. The **Eagle and**

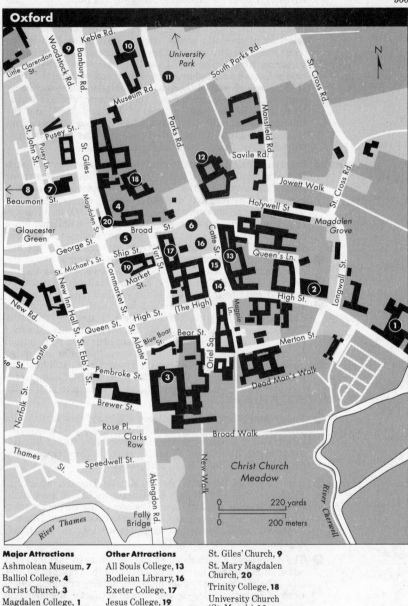

Oxford

Major Attractions

Ashmolean Museum, **7**
Balliol College, **4**
Christ Church, **3**
Magdalen College, **1**
Oxford Story, **5**
St. Edmund Hall, **2**
Sheldonian Theatre, **6**

Other Attractions

All Souls College, **13**
Bodleian Library, **16**
Exeter College, **17**
Jesus College, **19**
Keble College, **10**
Radcliffe Camera, **15**

St. Giles' Church, **9**
St. Mary Magdalen Church, **20**
Trinity College, **18**
University Church (St. Mary's), **14**
University Museum, **11**
Wadham College, **12**
Worcester College, **8**

Child is a historic pub in St. Giles. On the outskirts of the city are two excellent pubs, the **Perch** at Binsey and the **Trout** at Godstow. Connoisseurs go to the former at lunchtime to sit on the wide lawn, savour the exotic sandwiches, and listen to the cooing of white doves. In the evening, they visit the Trout for a meal or simply to enjoy a drink while watching the peacocks strutting by the tumbling weir.

Blenheim Palace, eight miles (13 kilometers) north of Oxford on the main A34 road, is a large and imposing mansion in classical style built in the early 18th century by the architect Sir John Vanbrugh; it stands in 2,500 acres (10 square kilometers) of beautiful gardens landscaped later in the 18th century by "Capability" Brown, perhaps the most famous of all English landscape gardeners. The house was built by the soldier and statesman John Churchill, 1st Duke of Marlborough, on land given to him by Queen Anne and with money voted him by Parliament on behalf of a "grateful nation" as a reward for his crushing defeat of the French at the Battle of Blenheim in 1704. The house is full of fine paintings, tapestries, and furniture. Winston Churchill, a descendant of Marlborough, was born in the palace; some of his paintings are on display, and there is an exhibition devoted to his life. *Woodstock, tel. 0933/811325. Admission: £4.25. Open mid-Mar.–end Oct., 10:30–6.*

Sir Winston Churchill (1874–1965) is buried in the nearby village of **Bladon.** His grave in the small tree-lined churchyard is all the more touching for its simplicity.

The Cotswolds   The A34 runs northwest from Oxford and Blenheim across the Cotswold Hills to Stratford-upon-Avon. The **Cotswolds** are high, bare hills patterned by stone walls that protect the sheep that have grazed here from the earliest times. In the Middle Ages, English wool commanded high prices, and the little towns and villages nestling in valleys and on hillsides grew in prosperity. Although the wool trade has now dwindled in importance, the legacy of those days remains in the solid, substantial churches, cottages, and manor houses built of the mellow, golden-gray local stone. Burford, Stow-on-the-Wold, Upper Slaughter, Bourton-on-the-Water, and Moreton-in-Marsh are just a few of the picturesque villages connected by pleasant country roads that are well worth the detour off the main road.

Stratford-upon-Avon   Even without its most famous son, **Stratford-upon-Avon** would be worth visiting. Its timbered buildings bear witness to its prosperity in the 16th century, when it was a thriving craft and trading center, and attractive 18th-century buildings are also of note.

❶ ❷ There are four main Shakespearean places of interest. The **Shakespeare Centre** and **Shakespeare's Birthplace,** on Henley Street, contain the costumes used in the BBC's dramatization of the plays and an exhibition of the playwright's life and work. *Henley St., tel. 0789/204016. Admission: £1.80 adults, 70p children. Open Apr.–Sept., Mon.–Sat. 9–6, Sun. 10–6; Oct., Mon.–Sat. 9–5, Sun. 10–5; Nov.–Mar., Mon.–Sat. 9–4:30, Sun. 1:30–4:30.*

Time Out   **Mistress Quickly** in Henley Street serves light refreshments and meals throughout the day; an unusual feature is the jigsaw

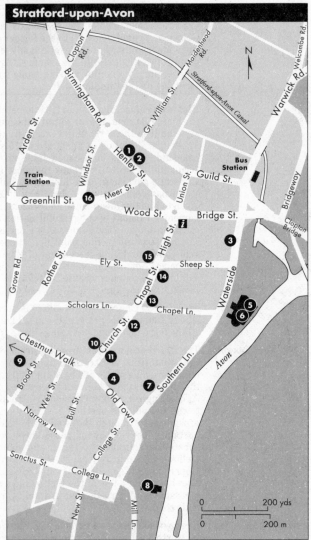

Major Attractions

Anne Hathaway's
Cottage, **9**

Hall's Croft, **4**

Holy Trinity Church, **8**

The Other Place, **7**

Royal Shakespeare
Theatre, **5**

Shakespeare's
Birthplace, **2**

Shakespeare Centre, **1**

The Swan, **6**

World of Shakespeare, **3**

Other Attractions

American
Foundation, **16**

Grammar School and
Guildhall, **11**

Harvard House, **15**

New Place, **13**

Shakespeare
Institute, **10**

Town Hall, **14**

---

tree sculpture. The **Black Swan**—better known locally as the Dirty Duck—is a riverside pub serving good ales and bar meals.

---

3 Two very different attractions reveal something of the times in which Shakespeare lived. **World of Shakespeare** is a lavish spectacle using modern multimedia techniques to describe Queen Elizabeth's royal progress from London to Kenilworth Castle in 1575. *13 Waterside, tel. 0789/69190. Admission: £2.50 adults, £2 children and senior citizens. Open daily 9:30–5:30.*

4 A complete contrast is **Hall's Croft,** a fine Tudor town house that was the home of Shakespeare's daughter Susanna and her doctor husband; it is furnished in the decor of the day, and the doctor's dispensary and consulting room can also be seen. *Old*

Town, tel. 0780/292107. Admission: £1.40 adults, 50p children. Opening times as for Shakespeare Centre.

⑤ The **Royal Shakespeare Theatre** occupies a perfect position on the banks of the Avon—try to see a performance if you can. The company (always referred to as the RSC) performs five Shakespeare plays each season, between March and January. It has
⑥ two other theaters in Stratford: The **Swan,** where plays by con-
⑦ temporaries of Shakespeare are staged, and **The Other Place,** where lesser-known Shakespeare plays are performed in repertory with new studio plays and fringe productions. It's best to book well in advance, but tickets for the day of performance are always available, and it is also worth asking if there are any returns. *Programs are available starting in February from the Royal Shakespeare Theatre, Stratford-upon-Avon, Warwickshire CV37 6BB, tel. 0789/205301.*

⑧ In **Holy Trinity Church,** close to the Royal Shakespeare Theatre, Shakespeare and his wife are buried.

⑨ **Anne Hathaway's Cottage,** in Shottery on the edge of the town, is the early home of the playwright's wife. *Times and admissions as for the Shakespeare Center.*

Warwick   **Warwick,** some eight miles (13 kilometers) north of Stratford along A46, is an unusual mixture of Georgian red-brick and Elizabethan half-timbered buildings, although some unattractive postwar developments have spoiled the town center. The **Castle** is one of the finest medieval structures of its kind in England, towering on a precipice above the river Avon. Most of the present buildings date from the 14th century; look for the remarkable gate house, which consists of a pair of towers above the doorway passage, and two massive towers, Guy's and Caesar's, both about 130 feet (40 meters) tall, the latter with a system of double battlements. The interior contains magnificent collections of armor, paintings, and furniture, while, outside, peacocks strut in the 60 acres (243,000 square meters) of landscaped riverside gardens. *Castle Hill, tel. 0926/495421. Admission: £4. Open Mar.–Oct., daily 10–5:30, Nov.–Feb., daily 10–4:30.*

Chipping Campden   From Stratford take A46, take an easy detour to Chipping Campden. If you have time to visit only one Cotswold town, make it this one. The broad High Street is lined with houses in an attractive disarray of styles, many dating from the 17th century. Look for the group of almshouses built in 1624 and raised above street level and for the gabled **Market Hall** built three years later for the sale of local produce.

One of the town's earliest buildings, dating from the 14th century, is the **Woolstaplers Hall,** which contains a museum of local history; besides material on the wool trade, there is a 1920s cinema and collections of medical equipment. *Admission: 80p. Open Apr.–Oct., daily 11–6.*

Three miles (five kilometers) outside Chipping Campden is **Hidcote Manor Garden,** a 20th-century garden created around a Cotswold manor house (not open to the public). The garden consists of a series of rooms divided by walls and hedges and each in a different style. *Hidcote Bartrim, tel. 038677/333. Admission: £2.70 (£3 Sun.) adults, £1.35 children. Open Apr.–Oct., Sat.–Mon., Wed., Thurs. 11–8.*

Major Attractions
Abbey, **2**
The Circus, **3**
Museum of Costume, **5**
Roman Baths
Museum, **1**
No. 1 Royal Crescent, **4**

Other Attractions
Camden Works
Museum, **6**
Carriage Museum, **7**
Octagon and National
Center of
Photography, **9**
Pulteney Bridge, **10**
Sally Lunn's, **11**
Theatre Royal, **8**

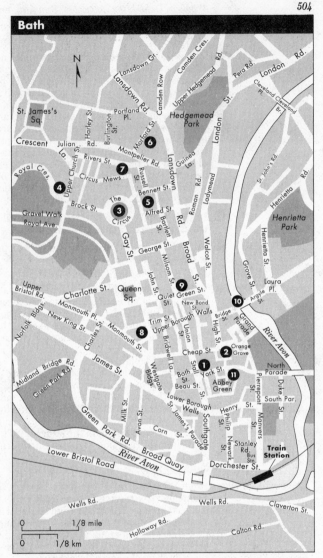

Bath

A46 runs along the western edge of the gently rolling Cotswold hills, through Cheltenham, once the rival of Bath in its Georgian elegance, now marred by modern developments. There are still unsurpassed examples of Regency style in its graceful secluded villas, lush gardens, and leafy crescents and squares.

Bath   Bath lies at the southern end of the Cotswolds (at the end of A46), some 70 miles (112 kilometers) from Stratford. A perfect 18th-century city, perhaps the best-preserved in all Britain, it is a compact place, easy to explore on foot; the museums and elegant shops and terraces of magnificent town houses are all close to each other.

It was the Romans who first took the waters at Bath, building a temple in honor of their goddess Minerva and a sophisticated series of baths to make full use of the curative hot springs. To this day, these springs gush from the earth at a constant temperature of 115.7°F (46.5°C). In the **Roman Baths Museum,** underneath the 18th-century Pump Room, you can see the excavated remains of almost the entire baths complex. *Abbey Churchyard. Admission: £2.50 adults, £1.25 children. Combined ticket with Museum of Costume £3 adults, £1.50 children. Open daily 10–5.*

Next to the Pump Room is the **Abbey,** built in the 15th century. There are superb fan-vaulted ceilings in the nave.

In the 18th century, Bath became the fashionable center for taking the waters. The architect John Wood created a harmonious city from the mellow local stone, building beautifully executed terraces, crescents, and villas. The heart of Georgian Bath is the perfectly proportioned **Circus** and the Royal Crescent. On the corner, **No. 1 Royal Crescent** is furnished as it might have been when Beau Nash, the master of ceremonies and arbiter of 18th-century Bath society, lived in the city. *Admission: £1.50 adults, 80p children and senior citizens. Open Mar.–Oct., Tues.–Sat. 10–5, Sun. 2–5.*

Also near the Circus are the Assembly Rooms, frequently mentioned by Jane Austen in her novels of early 19th-century life. This classical villa now houses a **Museum of Costume,** where some of the elegant fashions of Bath's heyday are featured. *Bennett St. Admission: £1.50 adults, 95p children. Combined ticket with Roman Baths Museum £3 adults, £1.50 children. Open daily 10–5.*

Time Out   Bath has a good selection of spots for coffee or lunch. Try the **Pump Room** (Abbey Churchyard) for morning coffee or afternoon tea in grand surroundings, perhaps listening to the music of a string quartet, or, in nearby North Parade Passage, **Sally Lunns,** where the famous Sally Lunn bun is still baked. The **Theatre Vaults** in Sawclose is a good place for a pre- or posttheater drink or meal; the theater itself is one of the finest surviving Georgian theaters in England.

Dining and Lodging

For details and price category definitions, *see* Dining and Lodging in Essential Information.

Windsor and Eton   **The Cockpit.** Cockfighting once took place in the courtyard of
Dining   this smart 500-year-old inn with oak beams in Eton's quiet main street. Specialties include guinea fowl and a casserole of bacon in mushroom sauce. *High Street, Eton, tel. 0753/860944. Jacket and tie. AE, DC, MC, V. Expensive.*
The House on the Bridge. Looking out across the river from Eton to Windsor Castle, this house was built as a boat house. Traditional English food is served here. *Windsor Bridge, Eton, tel. 0753/860914. Dress: casual. AE, DC, MC, V. Expensive.*
Bensons. Chicken in mushroom sauce and panfried sirloin with parsley butter are among the specialties at this oak-beamed restaurant in the oldest part of town. Downstairs there is a less formal champagne and wine bar. *Church Lane, Windsor, tel. 0753/858331. Dress: casual. MC, V. Moderate.*

Lodging **Oakley Court.** This Victorian mansion is set in leafy grounds beside the river, just outside Windsor. Some of the bedrooms are in a bright modern annex. *Windsor Rd., Water Oakley, tel. 0628/74141. 91 rooms with bath. AE, DC, MC, V. Expensive.*

Sir Christopher Wren's House. As the name suggests, this house was built by the famous architect, though modern additions have been made to turn it into a hotel. The restaurant overlooks the river, and the cream teas served on the terrace are renowned. *Thames St., Windsor, tel. 0753/861254. 41 rooms with bath. AE, DC, MC, V. Expensive.*

Ye Harte and Garter. Originally two Tudor taverns, this hotel was rebuilt during the last century. It is in a busy position immediately opposite the castle. *High Street, Windsor, tel. 0753/863426. 50 rooms, 43 with bath. AE, DC, MC, V. Moderate.*

Oxford **Elizabeth's.** These small, elegant dining rooms in a 16th-
Dining century bishop's palace overlook Christ Church and have the best views of any restaurant in Oxford. Salmon rolls and roast lamb are among the Spanish chef's specialties. *St. Aldates, tel. 0865/242230. Jacket and tie. MC, V. Expensive.*

Le Petit Blanc. The menus change with the seasons at this superb French restaurant, but you can be sure of finding exotic dishes, such as roast wild pigeon and leek terrine with monkfish. The setting is a Victorian conservatory. *Banbury Road, tel. 0865/53540. Jacket and tie. MC, V. Expensive.*

Fifteen North Parade. Just outside the city center, this is an intimate restaurant with cane furniture and plants. Dishes featuring stuffed quails and braised squid with black beans reflect the chef's whole-food background. *North Parade, tel. 0865/513773. Dress: casual. AE, DC, MC, V. Moderate.*

Munchy Munchy. A daily changing menu of spicy Malaysian dishes and a good selection of fresh fruit and vegetables makes this a refreshing and popular spot. The surroundings are unpretentious and the prices reasonable. *Park End St., tel. 0865/245710. Dress: informal. Inexpensive.*

Lodging **The Eastgate Hotel.** This welcoming hotel has the traditional style of an inn. Its bar is a favorite with undergraduates and is a good place for getting an insight into university life. *The High, tel. 0865/248244. 42 rooms with bath. AE, DC, MC, V. Expensive.*

The Randolph. Oxford's only large central hotel is particularly grand, with an elaborate Victorian Gothic interior. It's across from the Ashmolean Museum. *Beaumont St., tel. 0865/247481. 109 rooms with bath. AE, DC, MC, V. Expensive.*

Cotswold Lodge. This is a privately owned hotel about half a mile from the city center. There is a modern wing behind the original Victorian building. *Banbury Rd., tel. 0865/512121. 55 rooms with bath. AE, DC, MC, V. Moderate.*

Stratford **Box Tree Restaurant.** In the Royal Shakespeare Theatre, this
Dining elegant restaurant overlooks the river and is a favored spot for pre- and post-theater dining. Specialties include noisettes of lamb Box Tree and poached Scotch beef fillet. *Waterside. tel. 0789/293226. Dress: studied casual. AE, MC, V. Expensive.*

The Slug and Lettuce. Don't let the name put you off. This is a pine-paneled pub that serves excellent meals; the long-standing favorite is chicken breast baked in avocado and garlic. *38 Guild St., tel. 0789/299700. Dress: casual. MC, V. Moderate.*

The River Terrace. For less expensive fare at the theater, this spot provides informal meals and light refreshments. Hot dishes include lasagna and shepherd's pie, and there are also salads, cakes, and sandwiches. *Waterside, tel. 0789/293226. Dress: informal. Inexpensive.*

Lodging **The Shakespeare Hotel.** For a touch of typical Stratford, stay at this timbered Elizabethan town house in the heart of the town, close to the theater and to most of the attractions. It has been luxuriously modernized while still retaining its Elizabethan character. *Chapel St., tel. 0789/294771. 70 rooms with bath. Facilities: garden. AE, DC, MC, V. Very Expensive.*

The Falcon Hotel. Licensed as an ale house since 1640, its atmosphere is still that of a friendly inn. The heavily beamed rooms in the older part are small and quaint, those in the modern extension are in typical standard international style. *Chapel St., tel. 0789/205777. 78 rooms with bath. Facilities: garden. AE, DC, MC, V. Expensive.*

Arden Hotel. Across from the theater, these 18th-century town houses have been successfully converted into a comfortable Old World hotel with beamed bedrooms. *Waterside, tel. 0789/294949. 65 rooms with bath. Facilities: garden. AE, DC, MC, V. Moderate.*

Caterham House. Situated in the town center near the theater, Caterham House was built in 1830. Its pretty bedrooms are all decorated in period style and have brass beds and antique furniture. *Rother St., tel. 0789/67309/297070. 14 rooms, 2 with bath. Inexpensive.*

Bath **Popjoys Restaurant.** Beau Nash entertained the best of 18th-
Dining century society here, and Popjoys retains its air of elegance. *Sawclose, tel. 0225/460494. Jacket and tie. MC, V. Moderate.*

Peking. The excellent and well-presented Chinese food served here more than makes up for the waiters' rather brusque attitude. The sizzler dishes—served sizzling hot on an iron griddle —are exceptional. *New St., Kingsmead Sq., tel. 0225/66377/ 61750. Dress: casual. AE, DC, MC, V. Moderate.*

Pasta Galore. Fellow diners here may include actors from the nearby Theatre Royal after a performance. Best choices on the menu include tagliatle marinara and tagliatle with chili and bacon in tomato sauce. *Barton St., tel. 0225/63861. Dress: informal. AE, MC, V. Inexpensive.*

Lodging **Royal Crescent.** The ultimate in luxurious living is what the famous Royal Crescent is all about. Each bedroom has been individually designed to recapture the elegance of Bath's heyday. *Royal Crescent, tel. 0225/319090. 45 rooms, including 13 suites, all with bath. Facilities: whirlpool bath, garden, croquet. AE, DC, MC, V. Very expensive.*

Francis Hotel. Overlooking one of Bath's attractive Georgian squares, The Francis consists of six Georgian houses and a new wing. Bedrooms in the old building are decorated in period style. *Queen Sq., tel. 0225/24257. AE, DC, MC, V. Expensive.*

Royal York. The young Queen Victoria (whose room is still furnished as it was during her visit), the novelist Charles Dickens, and the statesman Benjamin Disraeli stayed here. The Royal York has been welcoming guests since 1759. *George St., tel. 0225/61541. 56 rooms, with bath. AE, DC, MC, V. Moderate.*

Cambridge

Cambridge, home of England's second-oldest university, is an ideal place to explore. Students began studying here in the late 13th century, and virtually every generation since then has produced fine buildings, often by the most distinguished architects of their day. The result is a compact gallery of the best of English architecture. There is also good shopping in the city, as well as relaxing riverside walks.

A short excursion outside Cambridge will introduce you to some characteristic East Anglian landscapes. To the north, on the edge of the Fens, is Ely, which boasts an impressive medieval cathedral. To the east is **Bury St. Edmunds,** a bustling market town rich with 17th- and 18th-century buildings and surrounded by cornfields, gentle hills, and tiny villages, each with its medieval church.

Getting Around

By Train Regular fast trains from London's Liverpool Street Station take an hour to Cambridge; there's somewhat slower service from London King's Cross Station. For information, call 01/928–5100. Local services connect Cambridge with both Ely and Bury St. Edmunds.

By Bus There's regular long-distance service from Victoria Coach Station that takes about two hours. Tel. 01/730–0202.

By Car The M11 is the main highway from London to Cambridge. This connects with the fast A45 road east to Bury St. Edmunds. Ely is reached along the A10 from Cambridge. The main car rental companies have offices in Cambridge.

Tourist Information

Cambridge. Wheeler Street, off King's Parade, tel. 0223/322640.
Ely. Public Library, Palace Green, tel. 0353/662062.
Bury St. Edmunds. Angel Hill, tel. 0284/763233.

Guided Tours

The **Cambridge Tourist Information Center** offers 1¼-hour walking tours of the city and longer tours of the colleges. It also runs excursions to Ely and the Fens.

Exploring Cambridge

The university is in the very heart of **Cambridge.** It consists of a number of colleges, each of which is a separate institution with its own distinct character and traditions. Undergraduates join an individual college and are taught by dons attached to the college, who are known as "fellows." Each college is built around a series of courts, or quadrangles; because students and fellows live in these courts, access is sometimes restricted, especially during examination weeks in early summer. Visitors are not normally allowed into college buildings other than chapels and halls.

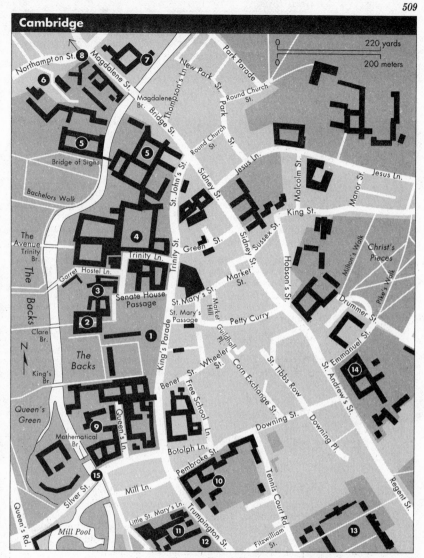

Cambridge

Clare College, **2**
Downing College, **13**
Emmanuel College, **14**
Fitzwilliam Museum, **12**
Kettle's Yard, **8**
King's College, **1**
Magdalene College, **7**
Merton Hall, **6**

Pembroke College, **10**
Peterhouse, **11**
Queen's College, **9**
St. John's, **5**
Silver Street Bridge, **15**
Trinity, **4**
Trinity Hall, **3**

① **King's College,** off King's Parade, is possibly the best known of all the colleges. Its chapel, started by Henry VI in the mid-1500s, is a masterpiece of late Gothic architecture, with a great fan-vaulted roof supported only by a tracery of soaring side columns. Behind the altar hangs Rubens's painting of the *Adoration of the Magi.* Every Christmas Eve the college choir sings the Festival of Nine Lessons and Carols, which is broadcast all over the world.

King's runs down to the famous "Backs," the tree-shaded grounds on the banks of the River Cam, onto which many of the colleges back. From King's make your way along the river and **②** **③** through the narrow lanes past **Clare College** and **Trinity Hall** to **④** **Trinity.** This is the largest college, established by Henry VIII in 1546. It has a handsome 17th-century Great Court around which are the Chapel, Hall, gates, and a library by Christopher Wren, who also designed St. Paul's Cathedral, London. In the massive gatehouse is Great Tom, a large clock that strikes each hour with high and low notes. Prince Charles was an undergraduate here in the late 1960s.

⑤ Beyond Trinity lies **St. John's,** the second-largest college. The white crenellations of the enormous mock-Gothic **New Building** of 1825 have earned it the nickname "the wedding cake." It is reached across a facsimile of the Bridge of Sighs in Venice. Behind St. John's is the oldest house in Cambridge, the 12th-**⑥** century **Merton Hall.**

Across **Magdalene Bridge** (pronounced maudlin) you come to **⑦** **Magdalene College** with its pretty red-brick courts. The **Pepysian Library** contains the 17th-century diarist's own books and desk. *Free. Open mid-Jan.–mid-Mar. and Oct.–Dec., Mon.–Fri. 2:30–3:30, mid-Apr.–Aug., Mon.–Fri. 11:30–12:30, 2:30–3:30.*

⑧ Beyond Magdalene is **Kettle's Yard.** This was originally the home of Jim Ede, a connoisseur of 20th-century art. Here, he displayed his collections to the public; a gallery extension now houses temporary exhibits. *Castle St., tel. 0223/352124. Free. House open daily 2–4; gallery open Tues.–Sat. 12:30–5:30, Sun. 2–5:30.*

Returning the way you've just come, along the Backs from **⑨** King's, you come to **Queen's College,** where Isaac Newton's **Mathematical Bridge** crosses the river. This arched wooden structure was originally held together by gravitational force; when it was taken apart to see how Newton did it, no one could reconstruct it without using nails.

⑩ Back from the river, on Trumpington Street, stand **Pembroke College,** which contains some 14th-century buildings and a **⑪** chapel by Wren, and **Peterhouse,** the oldest college, dating from **⑫** 1281. Next to Peterhouse is the **Fitzwilliam Museum,** which contains outstanding art collections (including paintings by Constable) and antiquities (especially from ancient Egypt). *Trumpington St., tel. 0223/332900. Free. Open Tues.–Sat. 10–5, Sun. 2:15–5.*

⑬ Other colleges worth visiting include **Downing College,** which has a unique collection of neoclassical buildings dating from **⑭** about 1800, and **Emmanuel College,** whose chapel and colonnade are by Christopher Wren. Emmanuel's spacious gardens have a pretty duck pond with several unusual breeds. Among the portraits of famous Emmanuel men hanging in the Hall is one of John Harvard, founder of Harvard University.

⑮ If you have time, hire a punt at **Silver Street Bridge** or at **Mill Lane** and navigate down past St. John's or upstream to **Grantchester,** the pretty village made famous by the Edwardian poet Rupert Brooke. On a sunny day, there's no better way to absorb Cambridge's unique atmosphere— somehow you will seem to have all the time in the world.

Time Out The coffee shop in the **Fitzwilliam Museum** is an excellent choice for a pastry or a light lunch. So is **Henry's** on Pembroke Street. **The Pickerel,** on Bridge Street beyond St. John's, is a pleasant pub with a small garden.

From Ely to Some 15 miles (24 kilometers) north of Cambridge, on A10, is
Bury St. Edmunds the small, compact town of Ely. Dominating the town is the **Cathedral,** whose commanding position atop one of the few Fenland ridges makes it visible from miles away; not for nothing is it nicknamed "the ship of the Fens." Within the cathedral, which was begun by the Normans in 1081, is one of the marvels of medieval construction: a vast stained-glass skylight that replaced the central tower when it collapsed in 1322. The **Lady Chapel,** restored during the 1970s with financial help from the United States, contains delicate decorative carving and a superb fan-vaulted ceiling. There is also a **Stained-Glass Museum.** *Chapter Office, The College, tel. 0353/67735. Cathedral admission: £1.60 adults, free on Sun. Up to 2 school-age children admitted free if accompanied by an adult. Open summer, daily 7–7; winter, weekdays 7–6:30, Sun. 7–5. Stained-Glass Museum admission: 80p adults, 40p children. Open May–Oct., daily 10:30–4.*

Around the cathedral are the well-preserved buildings of the cathedral close, where many of the clergy live, and of the King's School, which provides the cathedral with its choristers. To the north is the little market square and shopping streets leading down to the attractive riverside.

Time Out The **Steeplegate Café and Gallery** in the 16th-century Steeplegate is a convenient spot for lunch.

The route from Cambridge to Bury St., Edmunds, along A1303, passes by **Newmarket,** headquarters of British horse racing. The town is known both for its first-class race course and as a breeding and training center. The **National Horseracing Museum** traces the history of the sport and has a fine collection of paintings. *High St., tel. 0638/667333. Admission: £1.60 adults, 80p children and senior citizens. Open Apr.–Dec., Tues.–Sat. 10–5; Aug. Sun. 2–5.*

Tours can be made of the **National Stud,** one of Britain's principal racing stables, where you can see the stallions being trained. *Tours Mon.–Fri. 11:15 and 2:30 and also on some summer Sats. at 11:15. Admission: £2.50. Advance booking essential. Tel. 0638/663464.*

Bury St. Edmunds is a quintessential English country town with a picturesque gate tower and the ruins of a great 11th-century Norman abbey, **Angel Hill.** Medieval buildings along one side of the street face elegant 18th-century houses on the other; there are also some striking public buildings along **Abbeygate Street.**

The early 17th-century house on Angel Hill, known as **Angel Corner,** houses a fine collection of "time-measuring instruments." *Gershom-Parkington Memorial Collection of Clocks and Watches, 8 Angel Hill, tel. 0284/763233. Admission: free, but donations welcome. Open Mon.–Fri. 10–5, Sun. 2–5.*

The **Theatre Royal,** built in 1819, is a perfect example of a working Regency theater and a delightfully intimate place to watch a performance. If rehearsals are not taking place, you can look around during the day. *Westgate St., tel. 0284/755127. Open Mon.–Sat. 10–6.*

As if to remind visitors that Bury St. Edmunds remains a working town, not a museum piece, a livestock market is held every Wednesday and Saturday off **Risbygate.**

Time Out The **Harvest Café** on Abbeygate Street serves good-quality self-service lunches and snacks in a timbered building.

Dining and Lodging

For details and price category defintions, *see* Dining and Lodging in Essential Information.

Dining **Twenty-Two.** This intimate restaurant occupies a modest house a half-mile from the city center. The proprietor cooks the set dinner. Fish and game are the specialties. *Chesterton Rd., tel. 0223/351880. Dress: casual. Reservations advised. MC, V. Moderate.*

Upstairs. Moroccan furnishings provide the backdrop for such specialties as lamb couscous and *kala josh* (beef with cloves and yogurt). *Castle Hill, tel. 0223/312569. Dress: casual. MC, V. Moderate.*

Flames. The accent is on romantic, candlelit evenings in this renovated 18th-century building. Fondues of all kinds are the specialty—from fillet steak to chocolate. *53 Castle Hill, tel. 0223/60723. Dress: informal. Reservations advised. No credit cards. Inexpensive.*

Pentagon Restaurant. At the Arts Theatre, this spot has a suitably theatrical feel, with lots of signed photographs of actors who have played here. The menu changes daily according to the foods in season. *6 Edwards Passage, tel. 0223/359302. Dress: casual. Reservations essential. AE, DC, MC, V. Inexpensive.*

Lodging **The Garden House.** This fairly luxurious establishment is set among the colleges. The gardens back onto the river, and there is a large new extension. *Granta Pl, tel. 0223/63421. 117 rooms with bath. Facilities: restaurant, bar, garden. AE, DC, MC, V. Expensive.*

Arundel House. This hotel occupies an elegant Victorian house overlooking the river. The recently redecorated bedrooms are comfortably furnished with locally made mahogany furniture. *Chesterton Rd., tel. 0223/67701. 90 rooms, 73 with bath. Facilities: restaurant, bar, videos. AE, DC, MC, V. Moderate.*

Royal Cambridge. Seven renovated Victorian terraced town houses were renovated to form this hotel with spacious rooms decorated in period style. *Trumpington St., tel. 0223/351631.*

63 rooms, 48 with bath. Facilities: restaurant, bar. AE, DC, MC, V. Moderate.

York and Environs

Once England's second city, the ancient town of York has survived the ravages of time, war, and industrialization to remain one of the most perfectly preserved walled cities in Europe. It was King George VI, father of the present queen, who once remarked that the history of York is the history of England. Even in a brief visit to the city, you can see evidence of life from every era since the Romans, not only in museums, but in the very streets and houses.

York is surrounded by some of the grandest countryside England has to offer. A fertile plain dotted with ancient abbeys and grand aristocratic mansions leads both westward to the hidden valleys and jagged, windswept tops of the Yorkshire Dales and northward to the brooding mass of the North York Moors. This is a land quite different from the south of England—it's friendlier, emptier, and less aggressively materialistic. No visitor to Britain should overlook it.

Getting Around

By Train Regular fast trains run from London's King's Cross Station to York. The trip takes two hours. For information, call 01/278–2477.

By Bus Regular long-distance buses leave from Victoria Coach Station. The trip takes 4½ hours. For information, call 01/730–0202.

By Car Take A1, the historic main route from London to the north, which branches east onto the A64 near Tadcaster for the final 12 miles to York. Alternatively, take the M1, then the M18, and finally the A1. The drive from London takes a minimum of four hours. The main car rental companies have offices in York.

The best way to explore the area around York is by car—although it's inadvisable to take a car into the crowded city center. Coach tours (see below) visit most of the nearby attractions.

Tourist Information

De Grey Rooms, Exhibition Square, tel. 0904/621756.

Guided Tours

The **York Association of Voluntary Guides** arranges short walking tours around the city (free, but a gratuity is appreciated) each morning and afternoon, April through October, and in the evening from June through August; the departure point is Exhibition Square. Contact the Tourist Information Office for details.

Yorktour (12 Coney St., tel. 0904/645151) operates a SuperCity tour by open bus, by boat, and on foot. It departs each morning from major hotels. Excursions to attractions outside the city are also available.

Northern Rose (Rougier St., tel. 0904/611818) organizes a more conventional program of luxury coach trips to major attractions.

Exploring York

❶ York's greatest glory is the **Minster,** the largest Gothic church in England and one of the greatest in Europe. Take time to gaze at the soaring columns and intricate tracery of the 14th-century nave, the choir screen portraying the kings of England, and the rose window that commemorates the marriage of Henry VII and Elizabeth of York. Visit the exquisite 13th-century **Chapter House** and the Roman and Saxon remains in the **Undercroft Museum and Treasury.** Climb the 275 steps of the **Central Tower** for an unrivaled view of the city and the countryside beyond. *York Minster Undercroft Museum and Treasury, Chapter House, and Central Tower. Admission: Undercroft 80p adults, 60p children; Chapter House 40p adults, 30p children; Central Tower £1 adults, 50p children. Open Mon.–Sat. 10–6, Sun. 1–6.*

❷ At the **Jorvik Viking Centre,** south of the Minster through tiny medieval streets, you can take another journey into history—traveling in little "time cars" back to the sights, sounds, and even the smells of a Viking street, which archaeologists have re-created in astonishing detail. *Coppergate, tel. 0904/643211. Admission: £2.50 adults, £1.25 children. Open Apr.–Oct., daily 9–7, Nov.–Mar. 9–5:30.*

❸ Walk south down Castlegate and onto Tower Street, where you'll find the **Castle Museum,** housed in an 18th-century prison. It has a series of realistic period displays that bring the past to life. Highlights include a Victorian street scene, an 18th-century dining room, and a moorland farmer's cottage. Don't miss the Coppergate Helmet, one of only three Anglo-Saxon helmets ever found. *Clifford St., tel. 0904/653611. Admission: £2.25 adults, £1.15 children. Open Apr.–Oct., Mon.–Sat. 9:30–5:30, Sun. 10–5:30; Nov.–Mar., Mon.–Sat. 9:30–4, Sun. 10–4.*

Even more than the wealth of museums, it is the streets and city walls that bring the city's past to life. A walk along the **walls,** most of which date from the 13th century though with extensive restoration, provides delightful views across rooftops and gardens and the Minster itself. The narrow paved path winds between various fortified gates where the old roads ran out of the city.

❹ Within the walls, the narrow streets still follow the complex medieval pattern. **The Shambles,** in the heart of this walled city, is a perfectly preserved example; the half-timbered shops and houses have such large overhangs that you can practically **❺** reach from one second floor window to another. **Stonegate** is a narrow pedestrian street of 18th-century (and earlier) shops and courts. Along a narrow passage off Stonegate, you will find the remains of a 12th-century Norman stone house—one of the very few surviving in England.

❻ The **Merchant Adventurers' Hall** is a superb medieval building (1357-68) built and owned by one of the richest medieval guilds; it contains the largest timber-framed hall in York. *Fossgate, tel. 0904/654818. Admission: £2. Open May–Sept., daily 9:30–5.*

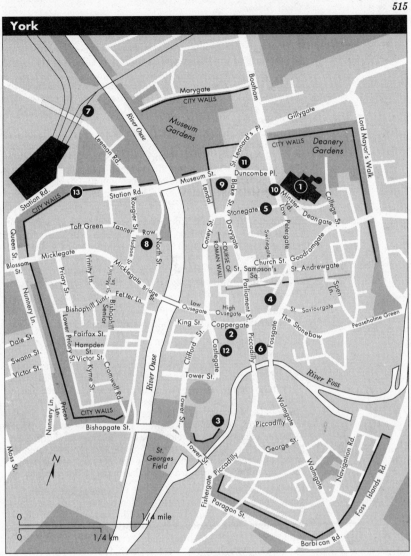

York

Major Attractions:

Castle Museum, **3**
Jorvik Viking Centre, **2**
Merchant Adventurers'
Hall, **6**
Minster, **1**
National Railway
Museum, **7**
The Shambles, **4**
Stonegate, **5**

Other Attractions:

All Saints, **8**
Assembly Rooms, **9**
Cholera Burial
Ground, **13**
St-Michael-le-Belfry, **10**
Theater Royal, **11**
York Story (Heritage
Center), **12**

❼ One very different attraction is the **National Railway Museum,** just outside the city walls, by the train station. This houses Britain's national collection of railway locomotives, including such giants of the steam era as *Mallard,* holder of the world speed record for a steam engine (126 mph, or 202 kph), early rolling stock, and pioneer diesel and electric locomotives. *Leeman Rd., tel. 0904/621261. Admission: £1.25 adults, 75p children and senior citizens, £4 family ticket. Open Mon.–Sat. 10–6, Sun. 11–6.*

Time Out   York's eating places tend to specialize in wholesome, traditional English cooking. Try **Hudson's Below Stairs** (60 Bootham) for morning coffee, lunch, and afternoon tea. The historic **Black Swan** pub on Peaseholme Green does genuine Yorkshire pudding, served, as it should be, with onion gravy.

Outside York   **Harrogate,** 20 miles (32 kilometers) west of York on A59, is an elegant early 19th-century spa town where countless mineral springs once brought high society to drink or bathe in the curative waters. You can still drink the evil-smelling spa waters at the newly restored **Royal Pump Room Museum.** *Tel. 0423/ 503340. Admission: 80p adults, 40p children and senior citizens, £2 family ticket. Open Mon.–Sat. 10–5, Sun. 2–5.*

Original Regency terraces, pleasant walkways, and extensive gardens make Harrogate an attractive place to visit.

Still traveling west on A59, you soon reach the **Yorkshire Dales,** made world-famous by the writings of a local veterinarian, James Herriot. The fertile river valleys of the Dales are separated from one another by areas of wild, high moorland that offer many opportunities for exhilarating walks and drives. At **Bolton Abbey,** about 16 miles (26 kilometers) west of Harrogate, the ruins of a 13th-century priory lie on a grassy embankment contained within a great curve of the River Wharfe. (There's unrestricted access during daylight.) Explore the ruins and walk through some of the most romantic woodland scenery in England, past the legendary **Strid,** where the river plunges through a rocky chasm only a few yards wide.

North from Bolton Abbey, on B6160, is **Grassington,** a village of stone houses with an ancient, cobbled marketplace—a convenient center to explore the wild landscapes of Upper Wharfedale. The **National Park Centre** has a wide choice of guidebooks, maps, and bus schedules to help you enjoy a day in the Dales. Organized tours depart from the Centre with qualified guides who explain the botanical and geological features of the area. *Colvend, Hebdon Rd., tel. 0756/752748. Open Apr.– Oct., daily 10–5.*

About 15 miles (24 kilometers) east from Grassington, along B6265, across the moors, is **Fountains Abbey and Studley Royal,** on the very edge of the hills. Here, the ruins of a 12th-century monastery are set in an 18th-century landscaped water garden and deer park, complete with lakes, half-moon ponds, statuary, and pseudo-Greek temples. *Tel. 076586/333. Admission: £1.90 adults, 90p children. Open Oct.–Mar., daily 10–4, Apr.– June and Sept., 10–7, July–Aug., 10–8.*

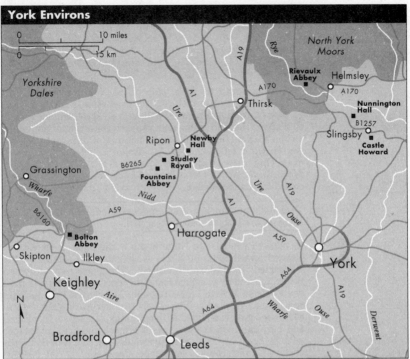

York Environs

Nearby **Newby Hall**—three miles (five kilometers) south of Ripon along a pleasant country road—has some celebrated interiors by the 18th-century master architect Robert Adam and some equally celebrated gardens with a collection of old breeds of roses and rare shrubs. Children will enjoy the adventure playground, steam railway, and river steamer. *Skelton-on-Ure, tel. 09012/2583. Admission: £2.50 adults, £1.25 children. Open Easter–Oct., daily, grounds 11–5:30, house 1–5:30.*

To the northeast, across the Vale of York, lie the **North York Moors,** dominated by a vast expanse of dense woodland and heather moorland that in late summer turns a rich blaze of crimson and purple. Nestled in deep valleys are charming villages built of brownstone—a contrast with the gray stone of the Dales.

Helmsley is a pleasant market town on the southern edge of the Moors, a good starting point for a more detailed exploration. It is not far, by road (B1257 north) or footpath, to the ruins of **Rievaulx Abbey,** a medieval seat of monastic learning whose graceful arches occupy a dramatic riverside setting. The ruins are best seen from the **Rievaulx Terraces,** a long grassy walkway on the hillside above, terminating in the remains of several classical temples. *Rievaulx Abbey, tel. 04396/228. Admission: £1.20 adults, 60p children. Open Mon.–Sat. 9:30–1 and 2–6:30 (closes at dusk in winter), Sun. 2–6:30. Rievaulx Terraces. Admission: £1.30 adults, 60p children. Open Easter–Oct., 10:30–6.*

Returning south to York, stop off at **Nunnington Hall** (off B1257), a largely late 17th-century manor house set on the river Rye containing a paneled hall with a carved chimneypiece, fine tapestries and china, and a superb collection of miniature rooms with intricate dollhouse furniture of different periods. *Nunnington, tel. 04395/283. Admission: £1.60 adults, 80p children. Open July, Aug., Tues.–Thurs. 2–6, Sat., Sun. noon–6; May, June, Sept., Oct., Tues.–Thurs., weekends 2–6, Apr. and Nov., weekends 2–6.*

Time Out	Teas (and light lunches on summer weekends) can be enjoyed at Nunnington Hall's excellent tearoom.

In marked contrast to Nunnington is the palatial majesty of **Castle Howard** (south off B1257 at Slingsby), the setting for the TV series "Brideshead Revisited." The great central domed tower, flanked by two huge and richly decorated wings, took 60 years—from 1699 to 1759—to build. The central hall, with its spectacular painted ceiling, leads to a series of grand staterooms and galleries, filled with paintings, sculpture, furniture, and porcelain. On the grounds is a mock classical landscape, with bridges, obelisks, even pyramids—more a conceit than a natural English country landscape. *Coneysthorpe, tel. 065384/333. Admission: £3.50 adults, £1.50 children, £2.80 senior citizens. Open late Mar.–Oct., daily, grounds 10–4:30, house 11–4:30.*

Dining and Lodging

For details and price category definitions, *see* Dining and Lodging in Essential Information.

Harrogate
Dining

Le Mange-Tout. This extremely popular French bistro does swift business in the evening. The food is excellent; staples, such as French onion soup, salmon, and chicken in a tarragon sauce, are carefully prepared and attractively presented. *7 Bower Rd., tel. 0423/66558. Dress: casual. Reservations advised. MC, V. Closed Sun. Moderate.*

Lodging

The Old Swan. Traditional English comfort, atmosphere, and service are offered at this hotel. This is where Dustin Hoffman found Agatha Christie after her mysterious disappearance in the film *Agatha.* It's on glorious grounds and the rooms are graciously decorated. *Swan Rd., tel. 0423/500055. 137 rooms with bath. Facilities: tennis courts, croquet, in-house movies, restaurant. AE, DC, MC, V. Expensive.*

York
Dining

Judges Lodging. This is a first-rate hotel restaurant. The fine 18th-century building, once a judge's house, is an ideal setting for a candlelit dinner of classic French cuisine. *9 Lendal, tel. 0904/38733. Jacket and tie. Reservations advised. AE, DC, V. Expensive.*
Freshneys. Fish is the name of the game here—salmon, lemon and Dover sole, local fresh trout and, when available, lobster.

Galtres Hotel, Petergate, tel. 0904/622478. Dress: casual. MC, V. Moderate.

Giovanni's Restaurant. Delicious pasta, veal, and beef dishes are served with Italian wine in this typical small Italian restaurant. It's close to the minster. *Goodramgate, tel. 0904/623529. Dress: casual. Reservations advised. AE, DC. Moderate.*

Oat Cuisine. Homemade soups, unusual salads, quiches, and sweets are served in a vegetarian restaurant with modern decor. The cashew nut slice and enchiladas with mozzarella are particularly worth trying. *High Ousegate, tel. 0904/627929. Dress: casual. Reservations advised. AE, MC, V. Moderate.*

Lodging **Middlethorpe Hall.** This handsome, superbly restored 18th-century mansion is located on the edge of the city. Rooms have antique furnishings, paintings, and flower arrangements, and you can eat by candlelight in the original dining room. The extensive gardens boast a lake and a 17th-century dovecote. *Bishopthorpe Rd., tel. 0904/641241. 31 rooms with bath. AE, DC, MC, V. Very Expensive.*

Mount Royale Hotel. Two elegant town houses, dating from the 1820s, are comfortably furnished in a traditional country-cottage style. It's about a 15-minute walk from the city center. *The Mount, tel. 0904/628856. 17 rooms with bath. Facilities: outdoor pool, garden. AE, DC, MC, V. Expensive.*

The Churchill. Rooms are in a large 18th-century house with many period features and lots of character. *Bootham, tel. 0904/644456. 10 rooms with bath. AE, DC, V. Moderate.*

Wheatlands Lodge Hotel. This small hotel-guest house occupies a handsome 19th-century bay-windowed house with a reputation for warm Yorkshire hospitality. The rooms are simple but of a high standard. *Scarcroft Rd., tel. 0904/654318/628601. 32 rooms, most with bath. MC, V. Inexpensive.*

Edinburgh

Scotland and England *are* different—and let no Englishman tell you otherwise. Although the two nations have been united in a single state since 1707, Scotland retains its own marked political and social character, with, for instance, legal and educational systems quite distinct from those of England. And by virtue of its commanding geographical position, on top of a long-dead volcano, and the survival of a large number of outstanding buildings carrying echoes of the nation's history, Edinburgh proudly ranks among the world's greatest capital cities.

Getting Around

By Train Regular fast trains run from London's King's Cross Station to Edinburgh Waverley; the fastest journey time is about 4½ hours. For information, call, in London, 01/278–2477; in Edinburgh, 031/557–3000.

By Plane British Airways operates a shuttle service from London's Heathrow Airport to Edinburgh; reservations are not necessary, and you are guaranteed a seat. Flying time from London is one hour 10 minutes. British Airways also runs bookable services from Gatwick. For information, call 01/897–4000 or 031/344–3152. British Midland (01/589–5599 or 031/344–3282) also flies from Heathrow. Transatlantic flights direct to Scotland use Prestwick Airport on the west coast.

By Bus Regular services are operated by Citylink Coaches (01/636–9373/9374 and 031/557–5717) and Cotters Coachline (01/930–5781 and 031/228–1106) between Victoria Coach Station, London, and St. Andrew Square bus station, Edinburgh. The journey takes approximately eight to nine hours.

By Car London and Edinburgh are 400 miles (640 kilometers) apart; allow a comfortable nine hours for the drive. The two principal routes to the Scottish border are the A1 (mostly a small but divided road) or the eight-lane M1 then M6. From there, the choice is between the dual-carriageway A74, which can be unpleasantly busy, followed by the A701 or A702, and the slower but much more scenic A7 through Hawick. All the main car rental agencies have offices in Edinburgh.

Tourist Information

City Information, 3 Princes Street, tel. 031/557-2727. The Scottish Travel Centre, South St. Andrew Street, tel. 031/332–2433 (individuals only), offers a travel service for those going beyond Edinburgh.

Guided Tours

Both **Lothian Regional Transport** (deep-red-and-white buses) and **Eastern Scottish** (green buses) operate tours in and around the city. For information, call 031/226–5087 or 031/554–4494 (Lothian), or 031/556–8464 (Eastern Scottish). Tickets allowing unlimited travel on city buses for various periods are also available.

The Cadies (Upper Bow, tel. 031/225–6745) offers historical and other special-interest tours. **Ghillie Personal Travel** (Silverknowes Rd., tel. 031/336–3120) provides personal tours by car and minibus.

Exploring Edinburgh

The key to understanding Edinburgh is to make the distinction between the Old and New Towns. Until the 18th century, the city was confined to the rocky crag on which its castle stands, straggling between the fortress at one end and the royal residence, the Palace of Holyroodhouse, at the other. In the 18th century, during a civilizing time of expansion known as the "Scottish Enlightenment," the city fathers fostered the construction of another Edinburgh, one a little to the north. This is the "New Town," whose elegant squares, classical facades, wide streets, and harmonious proportions remain largely intact and lived-in today.

❶ **Edinburgh Castle,** the brooding symbol of Scotland's capital and the nation's martial past, dominates the city center. The castle's attractions include the city's oldest building—the 11th-century **St. Margaret's Chapel**—the **Crown Room,** where the Regalia of Scotland are displayed, **Old Parliament Hall,** and **Queen Mary's Apartments,** where Mary, Queen of Scots gave birth to the future King James VI of Scotland (who later became James I of England). In addition, there are excellent views. *Tel. 031/225–9847. Admission: £2.20 adults, £1.10 chil-*

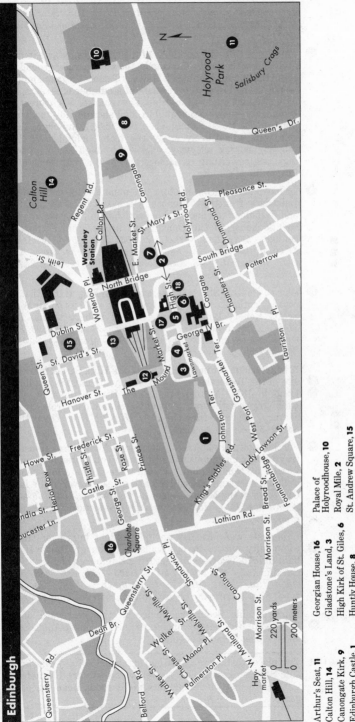

Edinburgh

Arthur's Seat, **11**
Calton Hill, **14**
Canongate Kirk, **9**
Edinburgh Castle, **1**
Festival Office, **17**
Fringe Office, **18**

Georgian House, **16**
Gladstone's Land, **3**
High Kirk of St. Giles, **6**
Huntly House, **8**
John Knox's House, **7**
Lady Stair's House, **4**
National Gallery of
Scotland, **12**

Palace of
Holyroodhouse, **10**
Royal Mile, **2**
St. Andrew Square, **15**
Scott Monument, **13**
Tolbooth, **5**

dren and senior citizens, £5 families. Open Apr.–Sept., Mon.–
Sat. 9:30–5:05, Sun. 11–5:05; Oct.–Mar., Mon.–Sat. 9:30–
4:20, Sun. 12:30–3:35.

② The **Royal Mile,** the backbone of the Old Town, starts immediately below the **Castle Esplanade,** the wide parade ground that
hosts the annual Edinburgh Military Tattoo—a grand military
display. The Royal Mile consists of a number of streets, running into each other—**Castlehill, Lawnmarket, High Street,** and
Canongate—leading downhill to the Palace of Holyroodhouse,
home to the Royal Family when they visit Edinburgh. Tackle
this walk in leisurely style; the many original Old Town
"closes," narrow alleyways enclosed by high tenement buildings, are rewarding to explore and give a real sense of the
former life of the city.

③ In Lawnmarket, the six-story tenement known as **Gladstone's
Land** dates from the 17th century. It has a typical arcaded front
and first-floor entrance and is furnished in the style of a merchant's house of the time; there are magnificent painted
ceilings. *483 Lawnmarket, tel. 031/226–5856. Admission:
£1.60 adults, 80p children and senior citizens. Open Apr.–
Oct., Mon.–Sat. 10–5, Sun. 2–5; Nov., Sat. 10–4:30, Sun. 2–
4:30.*

④ Close by is **Lady Stair's House,** a town dwelling of 1622 that now
recalls Scotland's literary heritage with exhibits on Sir Walter
Scott, Robert Louis Stevenson, and Robert Burns. *Lady
Stair's Close, Lawnmarket, tel. 031/225–2424, ext. 6593. Free.
Open Jun.–Sept., Mon.–Fri. 10–6; Oct.–May, 10–5, Sun. 2–5
during festival.*

**⑤
⑥**
A heart shape set in the cobbles of the High Street marks the
site of the **Tolbooth,** the center of city life until it was demolished in 1817. Nearby stands the **High Kirk of St. Giles,**
Edinburgh's cathedral; parts of the church date from the 12th
century, the choir from the 15th. *High St. Free. Open Mon.–
Sat. 9–5, Sun. for services.*

⑦ Farther down High Street you come to **John Knox's House.** Its
traditional connections with Scotland's celebrated religious reformer are tenuous, but it is said to be the only 15th-century
building surviving in Scotland and gives a flavor of life in the
Old Town in the Middle Ages. *45 High St., tel. 031/556–6961.
Admission: £1 adults, 60p children and senior citizens. Open
Mon.–Sat. 10–5.*

⑧
Canongate was formerly an independent burgh, or trading
community, outside the city walls of Edinburgh. **Huntly House,**
built in 1570, is a museum featuring Edinburgh history and social life. *142 Cannongate, tel. 031/225–2424, ext. 6689. Free.
Open Jun.–Sept., Mon.–Sat. 10–6; Oct.–May, Mon.–Sat.
10–5, Sun. 2–5 during the Edinburgh International Festival.*

⑨
Some notable Scots are buried in the graveyard of the
Canongate Kirk nearby, including the economist Adam Smith
and the poet Robert Fergusson.

Time Out Two places that serve a good cup of tea and a sticky cake (a notable Scottish indulgence) to weary walkers are **Clarinda's** in
Canongate and the **Abbey Strand Tearoom,** near the palace
gates.

⑩ The **Palace of Holyroodhouse,** still the Royal Family's official residence in Scotland, was founded by King James IV at the end of the 15th century and was extensively remodeled by Charles II in 1671. The state apartments, with their collections of tapestries and paintings, can be visited. *Tel. 031/556-7371. Admission: £1.50 adults, 70p children and senior citizens. Open Apr.-Oct., Mon.-Sat. 9:30-5:15, Sun. 10:30-4:30; Nov. -Mar., Mon.-Sat. 9:30-3:45; closed during royal and state visits.*

⑪ The open grounds of **Holyrood Park** enclose Edinburgh's distinctive originally volcanic mini-mountain, **Arthur's Seat,** with steep slopes and miniature crags.

In 1767, the competition to design the New Town was won by a young and unknown architect, James Craig. His plan was for a grid of three east-west streets, balanced at each end by a grand square. The plan survives today, despite all commercial pressures. Princes, George, and Queen Streets are the main thoroughfares, with St. Andrew Square at one end and Charlotte Square at the other.

⑫ The **National Gallery of Scotland,** on the Mound, the street that joins the Old and New Towns, contains works by the Old Masters and the French Impressionists and has a good selection of Scottish paintings. *The Mound, tel. 031/556-8921. Free. Open Mon.-Sat. 10-5, Sun. 2-5. Print Room, Mon.-Fri. 10-12:30, 2-4:30.*

⑬ To the east along Princes Street is the unmistakable soaring Gothic spire of the 200-foot (61-meter) high **Scott Monument,** built in the 1840s to commemorate the celebrated novelist of Scots history. There is a statue of Sir Walter and his dog within. The views from the top well are worth the 287-step climb. *Admission: 50p. Open Apr.-Sept., Mon.-Fri. 9-6; Oct.-Mar. Mon.-Fri. 9-3.*

⑭ There are more splendid views from **Calton Hill:** north across the Firth (or estuary) of Forth to the Lomond Hills of Fife and also to the Pentland Hills that enfold the city from the south. Among the various monuments on Calton Hill are a partial reproduction of the Parthenon in Athens begun in 1824 but left incomplete because the money ran out, the Nelson Monument, and the Royal Observatory.

⑮ Make your way to **St. Andrew Square,** then along **George Street,** where there is a wide choice of shops, and on to **Charlotte Square,** whose north side was designed by the great Scottish classical architect Robert Adam. The rooms of the elegant **⑯** **Georgian House** are furnished to show the domestic arrangements of a prosperous late 18th-century Edinburgh family. *7 Charlotte Sq., tel. 031/225-2160. Admission: £1.60 adults, 80p children and senior citizens. Open Apr.-Oct., Mon.-Sat. 10-5, Sun. 2-5; Nov. Sat. 10-4:30, Sun. 2-4:30.*

Time Out **La Lanterna,** at 9-11 Hope Street, offers no-nonsense, good-value Italian home cooking with self-service at lunchtime, waitress service at dinner. Bianco's, at 83 Hanover Street, close to the Georgian House, is good for coffee and croissants.

Finally, a word about the Edinburgh International Festival, the annual celebration of music, dance, and drama that the city stages each summer (the 1989 dates are Aug. 13-Sept. 2) fea-

turing international artists of the highest caliber. The Festival
Fringe, the unruly child of the official festival, spills out of halls
and theaters all over town, offering visitors a cornucopia of theatrical and musical events of all kinds—some so weird that they
defy description. While the official festival is the place to see
top-flight performances by established artists, at a Fringe
event you may catch a new star, or a new art form, or a controversial new play in the making. Or then again, you may not; it's
very much up to luck. Advance information, programs, and
ticket sales for the **official festival** are available at 21 Market
St. (tel. 031/226–4001); for the **Fringe**, from 170 High St. (Tel.
031/226–5257/5259).

Dining and Lodging

For details and price category definitions, *see* Dining and
Lodging in Essential Information.

Dining **The Pompadour.** The decor here is inspired by the France of
Louis XV, with ornate gilts and reds prevailing. A sophisticated French menu in the evening is balanced by a Scots flavor
at lunchtime. *Princes St., tel. 031/225–2433. Jacket and tie.
AE, DC, MC, V. Expensive.*

The Vintners Room. Away from the city center, the ornate
plasterwork here is a complete surprise. The atmosphere is one
of relaxed good taste, with such specialties as sautéed scallops
with smoked salmon and grilled oysters with bacon and hollandaise sauce. *Giles St., Leith, tel. 031/554–6767. Jacket and tie.
AE, DC, MC, V. Expensive.*

The Indian Cavalry Club. A cool and sophisticated atmosphere,
with a confident, up-to-date approach—almost Indian nouvelle
cuisine. Its specialties are mainly steam-cooked dishes. *Atholl
Pl., tel. 031/228–3282. Dress: studied casual. AE, DC, MC, V.
Moderate.*

Jackson's Restaurant. Intimate and candlelit in an historic Old
Town close, Jackson's offers good Scots fare. Aberdeen Angus
steaks and Border lamb. *Jackson Close, High St., tel. 031/225–
1793. Dress: casual. MC, V. Moderate.*

Ostlers. Enjoy an intimate meal in a traditional salmon-and-
white dining room. Salmon is a culinary theme as well; another
specialty is pheasant in cherry sauce. *Hill Street Lane North,
tel. 031/220–1796. Dress: casual. AE, DC, V. Moderate.*

Henderson's Salad Bowl. This friendly place claims to be the
city's original vegetarian restaurant, long before such places
became fashionable. Try the vegetarian haggis! *Hanover St.,
tel. 031/225–2131. Dress: informal. AE, DC, MC, V. Inexpensive.*

Ristorante Tinelli. A little away from the fashionable center,
Tinelli's has a chef who offers authentic Italian cooking in a relaxed atmosphere, amid pine and Hessian decor. *Easter Rd.
tel. 031/652–1932. Dress: informal. MC, V. Inexpensive.*

Lodging **The Caledonian Hotel.** Popularly known as "the Caley," this hotel echoes the days of the traditional great railway hotel,
though its neighbor station has long since closed. The imposing Victorian decor has been preserved in the recent total refurbishment. There's also an excellent restaurant. *Princes St.,
tel. 031/225–2433. 238 rooms with bath. Facilities: hairdresser,
in-house movies. Very expensive. AE, DC, MC, V.*

George Hotel. This extensively refurbished city-center hotel
has elegant 18th-century features in the public rooms and up-

to-date bedrooms. Though busy, the staff takes time to be helpful. *George St., tel. 031/225–1251. 195 rooms with bath. Facilities: restaurant. AE, DC, MC, V. Very Expensive.*

The Albany Hotel. Three fine 18th-century houses with many original features have been carefully converted into a comfortable city-center hotel. *Albany St., tel. 031/556–0397/0398. 22 rooms with bath. AE, DC, MC, V. Expensive.*

Bruntisfield. All the rooms have their own style and character, with the lavish use of floral patterns and antiques. *Bruntisfield Pl. tel. 031/229–1393. 52 rooms with bath. AE, DC, V. Expensive.*

Mount Royal Hotel. This modern hotel overlooks Edinburgh Castle. The public areas have recently been refurbished, while bedroom improvements were scheduled for 1988. A friendly staff makes up for the shortcomings in decor. *Princes St., 159 rooms with bath. AE, DC, MC, V. Expensive.*

Stewart House Hotel. This Victorian villa in a residential area has fully modernized rooms in a attractive pastel decor. *Merchiston Ave., tel. 031/229–5289. 8 rooms with shower. AE, DC, MC, V. Moderate.*

Dorstan Private Hotel. A Victorian villa in a quiet area, the fully modernized rooms are decorated in bright, country-cottage colors. *Priestfield Rd., tel. 031/667–6721. 14 rooms, 9 with bath. No credit cards. Inexpensive.*

Salisbury Hotel. Another successful 18th-century building conversion, this quiet hotel is situated in a pleasant area. It's a good value and a convenient location for city sightseeing. *Salisbury Rd. Tel. 031/667–1264. 14 rooms, 8 with bath. No credit cards. Inexpensive.*

16 Greece

Introduction

Natural beauty combined with archaeological treasures make Greece one of the world's most inviting countries. Sun, sea, and mountains; temples, fortresses, castles, monasteries, and churches; vestiges of Minoan, Mycenaean, Hellenistic, Roman, and Byzantine civilizations—Greece has them all, plus the heroes of Greek and Roman mythology, who still seem to haunt this ancient, sun-drenched land.

Unfortunately, the birthplace of Western culture has not escaped 20th century urban sprawl. The concrete high rises that disfigure so much of the Mediterranean landscape have sprouted in some of the loveliest parts of Greece, and unimaginative modern building is spreading along the 106,000 miles (169,600 kilometers) of coastline and onto many of the surrounding islands. The buildings house an influx of tourists, which in the summer, reaches numbers almost equal to the total Greek population. Despite the urban sprawl, however, there are still plenty of picturesque villages and small ports that haven't changed much in centuries, some with superb examples of classical architecture. Although the air and beaches of the cities and large towns are badly polluted, the more remote areas remain relatively unspoiled, ideal for sunbathing and swimming.

The Greeks invented many current forms of government, including democracy, and gave us many words that are part of our political vocabulary, such as monarchy, oligarchy, tyranny, and demagogy. Greece has tried all these forms of government and has had all types of foreign invaders with their own ideas of government, including Romans, Franks, Slavs, and Turks. The nearly 10 million present-day Greeks call themselves Hellenes and their country, *Elliniki Dimokratia* (the Hellenic democracy).

Greece's modern-day democracy came into being in 1974 after many years of dictatorship. Today, the country has a socialist government and is a member of the European Economic Community (EEC) and the North Atlantic Treaty Organization (NATO). Because the current government has loosened the country's traditional ties with the West, Greece is frequently at odds with its EEC and NATO partners.

Greece is 51,123 square miles in size (132,000 square kilometers), about the size of New York State. It is dotted with cypress groves, oleander, and olive trees and cut by rugged mountain chains that often plunge straight into the sea. The Pindus range runs north to south and includes the fabled peak of Mount Olympus, home of the Greek gods, and of Mount Parnassus, favorite haunt of Apollo, god of sunlight and prophecy, and the nine Muses, goddesses of poetry and science. From the quarries of Mount Penteli, on the outskirts of Athens, came the gleaming marble for the ancient temples on the Acropolis, and for the facing of the apartment buildings that today fill Athens.

Then there are the islands, waiting to offer visitors the vacation of a lifetime. There are 1,425 islands and islets scattered across the Aegean Sea in the east and the Ionian Sea in the west. Only about 130 have ever been inhabited. Fishermen, the early inhabitants of many of these islands, created distinctive

Greece

BULGARIA

YUGOSLAVIA

Stavroúpoli
Sidirókastro
Séres
Philippí
Eleftheroúpoli
Kilkis
Amfípoli
Kavala
Edessa
Gianitsa
Thessaloniki
ALBANIA
Florina
Alexandria
Thérmi
Nea
Appolonia
Vatopedia
Kastoria
Veria
Polygyros
Ormylia
Ivirion
Ptolemaïda
Katerini
Dafni
Kozani
Athos
Kónitsa
Siatista
Mount
Gulf of
Grevena
Olympus
Thermaikos
Gulf of Kassandra
Delvinákio
Elassóna
Kalithéa
Métsovo
Palioúri
Kerkyra
Kalambaka
Tirnavos
Corfu
Igoumenítsa
Ioanina
Agia
Paramythia
Trikala
Larissa
Parga
Karditsa
Volos
SPORADES
Arta
Stavros
Farsala
Aliki
Skiathos
Almiros
Preveza
Lamia
Skópelos
Lefkas
Karpenissi
Skyros
Vassiliki
Agrínio
Orhomenós
ÉVIA
Kymi
Kephalonia
Ithaki
Itea
Delphi
Livadia
Halkida
Nefpaktos
Galaxidi
Lixouri
Sami
Patras
Thiva
Messolongi
Gulf of Corinth
(Thebes)
Kárystos
Diakofto
Megara
Killini
Corinth
Athens
Loutra
Piraeus
Zákynthos
Amalias
Nemea
Egina
Lavrio
Kéa
Pyrgos
Olympia
Argos
Voula
Kaiafas
Trípoli
Náfplio
Poros
Sounio
Andritsena
Toló
Ermioni
Kythnos
Kyparissia
PELOPONNESE
Ydra
Serifos
Gargaliani
Messini
Sparta
Spetses
Ionian Sea
Pilos
Kalamata
Mystras
Leonidio
Methoni
Geraki
Koroni
Skala
Kyparíssi
Areopoli
Gythio
Monemvassía
Milos

Agía Pelagia

Kythira
Kythira

Haniá

CRETE

N

0   100 miles
0   300 km

civilizations that have fascinated the Western world. Ancient Greeks dominated the eastern Mediterranean, as both traders and pirates. Today, Greek tycoons dominate a large proportion of the world's shipping.

Although shipping continues to play an important role, tourism is the single most important element in the nation's economy. Exports are also important, thanks to the EEC, which has encouraged Greece to export olives, grapes, figs, currants, citrus fruit, and the best tobacco in Europe.

Before You Go

When to Go Greece is radiant with sunshine from May through October. June, July, and August are hot. The summer months are also humid on the west coast and the western islands. The best months for enjoying Greece are April, May, September, and October. The Aegean islands, on the other hand, are perfect for a seaside vacation in July and August because they are seldom hot and often breezy and there is usually more entertainment then than at other times of the year. The only problem is that the islands are packed with tourists in summer. In September, swimming is still pleasant and the beaches are almost deserted. Winters are mild near the sea but cold inland. Rain falls sporadically from October through May. If you don't mind a few spells of rainy or cold weather, winter is a good time to see the ruins.

The following are the average daily maximum and minimum temperatures for Athens.

Jan.	55F	13C	May	77F	25C	Sept.	84F	29C
	44	6		61	16		67	19
Feb.	57F	14C	June	86F	30C	Oct.	75F	24C
	44	7		68	20		60	15
Mar.	60F	16C	July	92F	33C	Nov.	66F	19C
	46	8		73	23		53	12
Apr.	68F	20C	Aug.	92F	33C	Dec.	58F	15C
	52	11		73	23		47	8

Currency The Greek monetary unit is the drachma (dr.). Bank notes are in denominations of 50, 100, 500, 1,000, and 5,000 dr.; coins, 1, 2, 5, 10, 20, and 50. At press time (fall 1988), there were 153 dr. to the U.S. dollar, 260 to the pound, and 124 to the Canadian dollar. Daily exchange rates are prominently displayed in banks. You'll get a better exchange rate at banks than from hotels or stores.

What It Will Cost Inflation is much higher in Greece than in most other European countries. Prices tend to rise between 15% and 20% a year, but since the drachma tends to lose its exchange value at about the same rate, the cost to the visitor remains about the same. However, there have been periods when prices have gone up more than the drachma has gone down, making Greece fairly expensive. On the whole, Greece offers good value compared with many other European countries. The values are especially good for modest hotels and restaurants, transportation, and entertainment.

There are few regional price differences for hotels and restaurants. Although hotel rates and restaurant prices are lower outside the cities, so are the standards. A modest hotel in a small town will charge the same rates as a modest hotel in Athens, with the same range of amenities. The same is true of restaurants. Rhodes, Corfu, and Crete are more expensive than other islands, but justifiably so. Car rentals are expensive in Greece, but taxis are inexpensive, even for long-distance runs.

Sample Prices At a central-city café, you can expect to pay about 200 dr. for a coffee or a beer, 140 dr. for a soft drink, and 240 dr. for a toasted cheese sandwich. A one-mile (1.6 kilometer) taxi ride will cost about 200 dr.

Customs on Arrival You may take in 200 cigarettes or 50 cigars or one-quarter pound smoking tobacco; one liter of alcohol, or two liters of wine; and gifts up to a total value of 5,000 dr. There's no duty on articles for personal use. Your car, camping and sport equipment, and items such as typewriters and cameras are registered in your passport upon entry to prevent their sale within the country. Foreign bank notes in excess of $500 (about £840) must be declared for re-export. There are no restrictions on traveler's checks. Only 3,000 dr. may be imported or exported.

Language English is widely spoken in hotels and at major tourist sites. Although waiters, taxi drivers, and sales clerks may speak little English, there will always be someone around who is delighted to help, even in relatively out-of-the-way places.

In this guide, names are given in the Roman alphabet according to the Greek pronunciation except when there is a familiar English form, such as "Athens."

Getting Around

By Car There are no first-class roads. Some sections of major routes
Road Conditions are turnpikes, but most are two-lane roads. Although most minor roads are poor, they are free of heavy traffic. The charge on turnpikes is 100 dr.

Rules of the Road Unless you are a citizen of an EEC country, you must have an International Driver's License. Driving is on the right, and although the vehicle on the right has the right of way, don't expect this or any other driving rule to be obeyed. The speed limit is 110 kph (68 mph) on the open road, 50 kph (31 mph) in town. The wearing of seat belts is compulsory.

Parking Parking spaces are difficult to find; thousands park illegally. In Athens or Thessaloniki, you can pay to use one of the many temporary parking lots set up in vacant lots, but you're better off leaving your car in the hotel garage and walking or taking a cab.

Gasoline At press time gas costs about 70 dr. a liter (about 300 dr. a gallon). Gas pumps and service stations are everywhere, and lead-free gas is widely available.

Breakdowns The Automobile and Touring Club of Greece (ELPA, Athens Tower, 2 Mesagoiu St., Athens, tel. 01/779–1615) assists tourists free of charge.

By Bicycle Mopeds and bikes can be rented on the islands, the only places where biking is safe.

By Train Few tourists use the trains because they are slow and railway networks are limited. The main line runs north from Athens to Yugoslavia. It divides into three lines at Thessaloniki. The main line continues on to Yugoslavia, a second line goes east to the Turkish border and Istanbul, and a third line heads northeast to Bulgaria. The Peloponnese in the south is served by a narrow-gauge line dividing at Corinth into the Mycenae–Argos section and the Patra–Olympic–Kalamata section. A "runabout" ticket, available only in Greece, gives unlimited second-class travel on trains and express buses operated by the railway (tel. 6/362–4402, for tickets and information).

By Plane **Olympic Airways** (6 Othonos, Syntagma, Athens, tel. 01/929–2247) has service between Athens and most towns and islands. Thessaloniki is also linked to the main islands, and there are many interisland connections.

By Bus Travel by bus is inexpensive, usually comfortable, and relatively fast. Buses operated by the Greek Railways are particularly good. Bus information and timetables are available at tourist information offices throughout Greece. Make reservations at least one day before your planned trip. Railway-operated buses leave from the main railway station in Athens. All other buses leave from one of two bus stations: 260 Liossiou—for central and eastern Greece and Evvia; 100 Kifissou—for the Peloponnese and northwestern Greece.

By Boat There are frequent car ferries from Piraeus, the port of Athens, to central and southern Aegean islands and Crete. Nearby islands also are served by hydrofoils from Rafina, east of Athens. Ships to other islands sail from ports nearer to them. Connections between the islands of a group, such as the Cyclades, are good. But between islands of different groups or areas, such as Rhodes and Crete, the service is less frequent. Travel agents and shipping offices in Athens and Piraeus have details. Buy your tickets two or three days in advance, especially if you are traveling in summer or taking a car. Reserve or confirm your return journey or continuation soon after you arrive.

Essential Information

Telephones Most curbside booths have red pay telephones for local calls
Local Calls only. They accept 50- or 10-dr. coins. You pay after the call.

International Calls The easiest way to make and pay for international and long-distance calls is to go to a Telecommunications Office (OTE), usually located in the center of towns and villages. There are several branches in Athens. There are also a few special telephone booths (distinguished by their orange band) for international and long-distance calls. Hotels tend to add a hefty service charge for long-distance calls.

Operators and There are English-speaking operators on the International Ex-
Information change. Ask your hotel reception desk or an employee at the OTE for help in reaching one.

Mail Letters or postcards within Greece cost 26 dr. for 20 grams;
Postal Rates within Europe, 50 dr.; and to the rest of the world, 60 dr.

Receiving Mail You can have your mail sent to Poste Restante, Aeolou 100, Athens (take your passport to pick up your mail), or to American Express (Syntagma Square 2, Athens). For holders of American Express cards or traveler's checks, there is no charge for the service. Others pay 250 dr. per item.

Shopping Greece isn't the best place to shop, but there are some things worth considering. Shoes (especially men's) and leather goods can be good buys. Jewelry, in materials other than gold, is less expensive than elsewhere. Some good handcrafted items are available, especially in the shops of the National Welfare Organization, but the quality of handicrafts, in general, has declined. Most so-called handicrafts are mass produced for the tourist trade. You can still find handwoven rugs and bags, objects carved in wood, pottery (especially from Skyros), enamel silverware, and occasionally some fine embroidery and lacework. One thing that is genuinely Greek, and a good value, is the *flokati*, a shaggy wool rug, often brightly colored. Fur coats, jackets, and stoles made from small scraps of pelts sewn together are attractive and inexpensive—the cost depends on the size of the scraps. Whatever Greece has to offer is as readily obtainable in Athens as it is in its place of origin.

VAT Refunds Prices quoted in shops include the Value-Added Tax (VAT). There are no VAT refunds.

Bargaining Prices in large stores are fixed. Bargaining may take place in small owner-managed souvenir and handicraft shops and in antique shops. In flea markets, bargaining is expected.

Opening and Closing Times The government is attempting to abolish the midday closing of businesses and shops, in an effort to cut down on the number of daily rush hours. It is also trying to stagger hours to alleviate the crush. Gradually, office, bank, and shopping hours are changing, but not all Greeks favor these changes. Check with your hotel for up-to-the-minute information on opening and closing times. Below is a rough guide:

Banks. Banks are open weekdays, 8 AM to 2:30 PM; closed weekends and public holidays.
Museums. Most major museums are open 8 AM to 6 PM; some smaller ones close earlier. Generally, museums are closed Tuesday and have shorter hours on Sunday and holidays. Archaeological sites are generally open from 8 AM to 6 PM (in midsummer they tend to open earlier and close at sunset). Hours vary according to the importance of the site and the time of year—everything closes earlier in winter. *See* Exploring for hours of individual museums and sites; also check hours with your hotel.
Shops. Most shops are open weekdays from 8 AM to 3 PM, but hours vary according to the type of shop. Some are open different hours on alternate days: Tuesday, Thursday, and Friday, 8 AM to 1:30 PM and 5 PM to 8 PM; Monday, Wednesday, and Saturday, 8 AM to 3 PM.

National Holidays January 1 (New Year's Day); January 6 (Epiphany); March 25 (Greek Revolution Memorial Day); April 28 (Greek Orthodox Good Friday); May 1 (Easter Monday, May Day); June 19 (Pentecost); August 15 (Feast of the Assumption); October 28 (Ohi Day); December 25–26 (Christmas).

Dining Visitors may choose between *tavernas, psistarias*, hotel dining rooms, restaurants, and snack bars. Tavernas range from modest and inexpensive to elaborate, with prices to match. They serve a good range of Greek dishes and appetizers, including some meat and fish items, to order. At psistarias, all dishes are cooked to order, over charcoal. Dishes include *souvlaki* (slices of pressed meat) and *donar kabab* (skewered lamb). Greek snack bars also serve souvlaki, as well as a pizzalike dish and such things as cheese pies and stuffed grape leaves. Most Greek restaurants and hotel dining rooms serve a bland version of international fare; few outside Athens and Thessaloniki meet high international standards. Set meals in hotel dining rooms, however, are reasonably priced. Seaside fish places may look ramshackle, but many serve excellent fish. Fresh fish is always expensive in Greece.

Mealtimes Most Greeks eat very late. Tavernas serve from about 9 PM to 1 AM; restaurants, from early evening until about midnight.

Precautions Tap water is safe to drink everywhere, but it is often heavily chlorinated. Excellent bottled mineral water, such as *Loutraki*, is available.

Ratings Prices are per person and include a first course, main course, and dessert (generally fruit and cheese). They do not include drinks or the 12%–15% service charge. Best bets are indicated by a star ★ . At press time, there were 153 drachma to the dollar.

Category	Cost: Athens/Thessaloniki	Cost: Other Areas
Very Expensive	over 5,000 dr.	over 4,000 dr.
Expensive	2,500 dr.–5,000 dr.	2,000 dr.–4,000 dr.
Moderate	1,200 dr.–2,500 dr.	1,200 dr.–2,000 dr.
Inexpensive	under 1,200 dr.	under 1,200 dr.

Credit Cards The following credit card abbreviations are used: AE, American Express; DC, Diners Club; MC, MasterCard; V, Visa.

Lodging Most accommodations are in standard hotels, sometimes called motels. There are a number of "cottage" complexes, especially at the beaches, and as part of some hotels. Some private houses, especially those on the islands, offer accommodations, usually a double room with shower. These are often better than accommodations at the local hotel. In a very few places, there are state-organized "traditional settlements"—fine old houses with guest accommodations.

Greek hotels are classified as Deluxe, A, B, C, etc. (a star system is about to be introduced). These classifications do not always indicate price. A Deluxe hotel, for example, may charge less than some B-classified hotels. In this guide, hotels are classified according to price: Very Expensive, Expensive, Moderate, and Inexpensive. All Very Expensive hotels and some Expensive and Moderate ones have air-conditioning. All have been built or completely renovated in the past 20 years, and all have private baths.

Prices quoted by hotels usually include service, local taxes, and VAT. Some may also include breakfast. Prices quoted are for double occupancy. Single occupancy is slightly less. The official price should be posted on the back of the door or inside a closet. Seaside hotels, especially those in the Very Expensive and Expensive categories, will frequently insist on guests taking half-board (lunch or dinner included in the price).

Ratings Prices quoted are for a double room in high season, including taxes and service, but not breakfast. Rates are the same throughout the country for each category. Best bets are indicated by a star ★ . At press time, there were 153 drachma to the dollar.

Category	Cost
Very Expensive	over 20,000 dr.
Expensive	8,000 dr.–16,000 dr.
Moderate	5,000 dr.–8,000 dr.
Inexpensive	under 5,000 dr.

Credit Cards The following credit card abbreviations are used: AE, American Express; DC, Diners Club; MC, MasterCard; V, Visa.

Tipping There are no absolute rules for tipping. In restaurants, cafés, and tavernas, in addition to the service charge, leave about 10% on a small check, less on a larger check, and about 50 drachmas for the bus boy. Try to see what the Greeks do in any particular place. In hotels, tip porters 50 dr. or 100 dr. per bag for carrying your luggage—more in a top hotel. Taxi drivers don't expect tips, but Greeks usually give something, especially to round off the fare or if the driver has been especially helpful. Hairdressers usually get 10% or slightly more. In legitimate theaters, tip ushers 20 dr. to 40 dr. if you are shown to your seat. In movie theaters, tip about the same if you receive a program from the usher. On cruises, cabin and dining-room stewards get about 250 dr. to 300 dr. per day.

Athens

Arriving and Departing

By Plane Most visitors arrive by air at Ellinikon Airport. All Olympic Airways flights, both international and domestic, use the Western terminal next to the ocean. All other flights arrive and depart from the Eastern terminal on the opposite side of the airport. From the Western terminal, buses run every 20 minutes to the Olympic Airways office at 45 Syngrou (fare: 80 dr.); from the Eastern terminal, they run every 20 minutes to 4 Amalia Avenue, near Syntagma Square (fare: 100 dr.). A taxi to the center of Athens costs about 600 dr.

By Train International trains from the north arrive and depart from the small central station (called Stathmos Larissis) not far from Omonia Square.

By Bus If you arrive in Athens from Italy by sea, you may dock at Igoumenitsa, on the mainland, across from the island of Corfu, or at Patra, and travel to Athens by bus or car. Greek buses arrive at the Athens bus station at 100 Kifissou. International buses drop their passengers on the street, usually in the Omonia Square area.

By Car Whether you approach Athens from the Peloponnese or from the north, you enter by the National Road and then follow signs for the center. Leaving Athens, routes to the National Road are well marked; signs usually name Lamia for the north and Corinth or Patras for the southwest.

By Ship Except for cruise ships, few passenger ships from other countries call at Piraeus, the port of Athens. If you do dock at Piraeus, you can take the metro or a bus to central Athens or take a taxi.

Getting Around

Many of the sights you'll want to see, and most of the hotels, cafés, and restaurants, are within a fairly small central area. It's easy to walk everywhere.

By Metro An electric (partially underground) railway is under construction. At present, it runs from Piraeus to Omonia Square and then on to Kifissia. It is not useful for getting around the central area. The standard fare is 50 dr. There are no special fares or day tickets for visitors, and there is, as yet, no public transport map.

By Bus The fare on blue buses and the roomier yellow trolley buses is 50 dr. You must have the exact change. Buses run from the center to all suburbs and suburban beaches until about midnight. For suburbs beyond central Kifissia, you have to change at Kifissia. Attica is well served by brown buses. Most buses, including those for Sounion, leave from Platia Aigyptou, at the corner of Patission and Alexandras Avenues.

By Taxi Taxis are plentiful except during rush hours and rain storms. But they are often on strike. Also, drivers seem to lead a maverick life—those without occupants often refuse to pick up passengers, while those with occupants often stop to pick up more. Many drivers are unfamiliar with the city; some automatically deposit every American at the Hilton Hotel. Fares are low, starting at 25 dr. and rising roughly 30 dr. per kilometer (0.6 mile). There is a 200-dr. minimum and a small surcharge for luggage and for travel after midnight. Some drivers overcharge foreigners, especially on trips from the airport or from Piraeus; insist that they use the meter.

Important Addresses and Numbers

Tourist Information There are **Greek National Tourist Offices** at Karageorgi Servias 2, in the bank (tel. 01/322-2545); at Ellinikon Airport (tel. 01/979-9500); and at Piraeus, Vasilissis Sofias 91 (tel. 01/412-1400).

Embassies **U.S.,** Vasilissis Sofias 91 (tel. 01/721-2951); **Canadian,** Gennadiou 4 (tel. 01/723-9511); and **U.K.,** Ploutarchou 1 (tel. 01/723-6211).

Emergencies **Police:** Tourist Police (tel. 171); Traffic Police (tel. 01/523-0111); and City Police (tel. 100). **Ambulance:** Tel. 166. **Doctors:** Top hotels usually have one on staff; any hotel will call one for you. You can also call your embassy. **Dentist:** Ask your hotel or embassy. **Pharmacies:** Most pharmacies in the central area have someone who speaks English and knows all the usual medical requirements. Try **Marinopoulois,** Kanari 23 (tel. 01/361-3051).

English Bookstore **Pantelides,** Amerikas 11 (tel. 01/364-5161).

Travel Agencies **American Express,** Ermou 2 (tel. 01/324-4975); **Wagons-Lits Travel,** Karageorgi Servias 2 (tel. 01/324-2281); and **CHAT Tours,** Stadiou 4 (tel. 01/322-2886).

Guided Tours

Orientation Tours All tour operators offer a four-hour morning bus tour of Athens. Make your reservations at your hotel or at a travel agency. The bus picks up passengers at some of the central hotels.

Special-Interest Tours For those interested in folk dancing, there is a four-hour evening tour (May–Sept.) that begins with a **Sound and Light Spectacle** at the Acropolis and then goes on to a performance of **Greek folk dances** in the open-air theater nearby. Another evening tour offers a **dinner show** at a taverna in the Plaka area.

Excursions A four-hour afternoon bus tour goes to Sounion to visit the **Temple of Poseidon.** A full-day cruise visits three nearby islands, **Aegina, Poros,** and **Ydra.**

Personal Guides All the major tourist agencies can provide English-speaking guides for personally organized tours.

Exploring Athens

Athens is essentially a modern city built around a steep-sided, flat-topped hill called the Acropolis, on which the holy places of the ancient city stood. All that remains of ancient Athens is on the Acropolis or around its base. It was at the Acropolis that the ancient Athenians laid the foundation for Western civilization, with their towering achievements in philosophy, literature, drama, art, and architecture.

Modern Athens, with its sprawl of suburbs, covers almost all the surrounding plain, from the sea to the three encircling mountains: Parnes (Parnitha), Pentell, and Hymettos. Except for some Byzantine churches, almost nothing here goes back much further than 1834, when Athens became the capital of the newly established Kingdom of Greece.

The central area of modern Athens is small, stretching from the Acropolis to Mount Lycabettos, with its small white church on top. The layout is simple—three parallel streets, Stadiou, Venizelou, and Academias, link two main squares, Syntagma and Omonia. A number of avenues and streets radiate out from these squares. Piraeus, Athens's port, is officially a separate town, but it is part of the metropolitan area. The Athens–Piraeus area has a population of about four million.

The Main Attractions

❶ At the center of modern Athens is **Syntagma (Constitution) Square.** It has several leading hotels, airline and travel offices, and numerous cafés. Along one side of the square stands the ❷ **Parliament Building,** completed in 1838 as the royal palace for the new monarchy. In front of the palace, you can watch the changing of the vividly costumed **Evzone** guard at the Tomb of the Unknown Soldier. Amalias Avenue, leading out of Syntagma will take you to the **National Gardens,** a large oasis in the vast sprawl of this largely concrete city.

Across the street, at the far end of the National Gardens, you ❸ will see the columns of the once huge **Temple of Olympian Zeus,** ❹ completed in AD 130. To the right stands **Hadrian's Arch,** built at the same time by the Roman emperor.

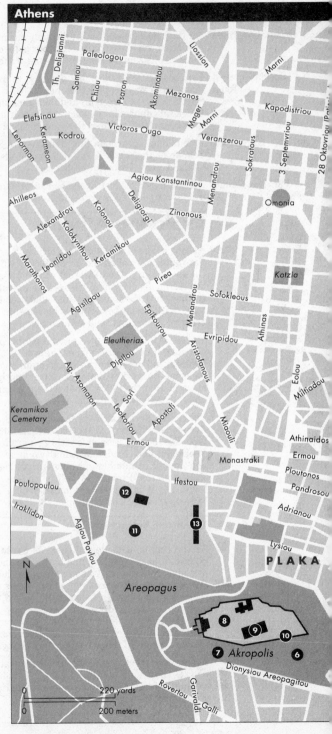

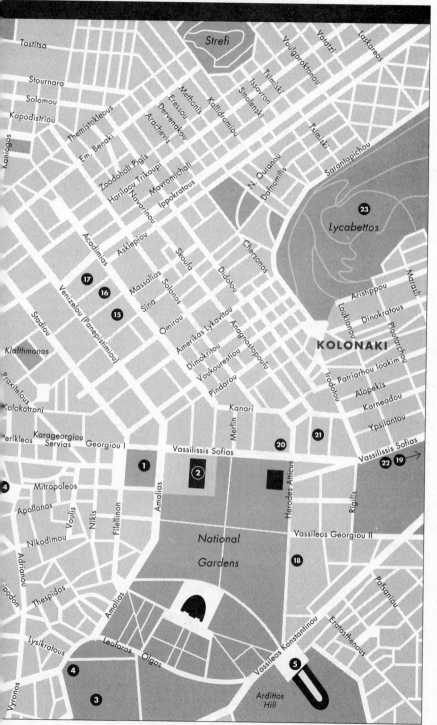

About a half mile to the left, down Leoforos Olgas Avenue, you come to the marble **stadium,** built for the first modern Olympic Games in 1896; it is a reproduction of the ancient Olympic stadium of Athens. Greece hopes to be chosen to host the games in the centennial year 1996.

After Hadrian's Arch, take the avenue to the right, Dionysiou Areopagitou, past the Acropolis to the **Theater of Dionysos,** built in the 6th century BC. Here, the famous ancient dramas and comedies were originally performed in conjunction with bacchanalian feasts. *Tel. 01/321-0219. Admission: 300 dr. Open Apr.–Oct., Mon.–Sat. 7:30 AM–7:30 PM; Sun. and public holidays, 9 AM–2 PM.*

A little higher up, on the right, you'll see the massive back wall of the much better preserved **Theater of Herodes Atticus,** built by the Romans in the 2nd century AD. Here, on pine-scented summer evenings, the **Athens Festival** takes place. It includes opera, ballet, drama, and concerts.

Beyond the theater, a paved path leads to the **Propylaea,** the monumental gates of the **Acropolis.** Above, to the right, stands the graceful **Temple of Wingless Victory,** commemorating the Athenians's victories over the Persians in the 5th century BC. The sly Athenians depicted the goddess of victory without wings so that she couldn't fly away. The elegant **Erechtheion** temple on the left underwent extensive repair work, sponsored by UNESCO, from 1979 to 1987. Copies of the Caryatids (six draped maidens) now support the roof of one of its three porticos. The **Acropolis Museum** houses five of the originals, their faces much damaged by acid rain. The sixth is in the British Museum in London.

The **Parthenon,** which dominates the Acropolis, is the temple dedicated to Athena, goddess of cities and wisdom. It was designed by Ictinus, and begun 447 BC. Pericles himself was the moving spirit behind the project. The great sculptor Phidias decorated it with 92 sculptured metopes, two superb pediments, and a frieze 523 feet (157 meters) long. The British Museum houses the largest part of what is left of the frieze ("The Elgin Marbles"). The Parthenon has 17 fluted columns along each side and eight at the ends. To counter balance natural optical distortion, the shafts of the columns lean slightly inward and bulge and the entablatures at the side and end rise slightly in the middle. *Admission: 400 dr. The Acropolis is open Apr.–Oct., 7:30–7:30; Nov.–Mar., 8–5. On nights when the moon is full, it is open 9–midnight.*

The **Acropolis Museum** contains a number of important sculptures, some dating to the 6th century BC. *Tel. 01/323-6665. Admission: 600 dr. Open Apr.–Oct., 7:30–7:30 and Sun. and public holidays, 8–6; Nov.–Mar., 8–5; Tues. 11–5.*

On the rocky outcrop facing the Acropolis, St. Paul preached to the Athenians; the road leading down between it and the hill of Pnyx is called Agiou Pavlou (St. Paul). To the right stands the **Agora,** which means marketplace in Greek. The Agora was the focal point of ancient Athens's community life—its market, civic center, and meeting place. The Agora is dominated by the best-preserved temple in Greece, the **Hephestaion** (or Thesion), built in the 5th century BC. Nearby, the impressive Stoa of Attalus, reconstructed by the American School of Classical Studies in Athens with the help of the Rockefeller

⑬ Foundation, houses the **Museum of the Agora Excavations.** *Tel. 01/321–0185. Admission: 400 dr. Open Mon., Wed.–Sat. 8:45–3 and Sun. and public holidays, 9:30–2:30. Closed Tues.*

Next to the Agora you'll find the **Plaka,** a bit of 19th-century Athens with narrow winding streets, many with steps leading to side streets; attractive old houses; and dozens of tavernas, restaurants, and bars. Below the Plaka, in **Cathedral Square,** stands a charming 12th-century Byzantine church known as the ⑭ **Cathedral.** From here, a short walk up Mitropoleos will take you back to Syntagma.

Leaving Syntagma along Venizelou Avenue (also known as Panepistimiou Ave.), you pass, on the right, three imposing ⑮ ⑯ buildings in classical style: the **Academy,** the **Senate House of** ⑰ **the University,** and the **National Library.** When you reach Omonia Square, you are in the heart of downtown Athens.

Returning to Syntagma, take Vassilissis Sofias Avenue along the edge of the National Gardens to reach the Evzone Guards' barracks. A street to the right, Herodes Atticus, leads ⑱ to the **Presidential Palace,** a neo-Renaissance building. Vas- ⑲ silissis Sofias will bring you to the Hilton Hotel and the **U.S. Embassy.**

Opposite the Evzone barracks, a fine mansion houses the ⑳ **Benaki Museum,** with a rich collection of Greek regional costumes, jewelry, and Byzantine and Moslem art objects, religious icons, and weapons. *Koumbari 1, tel. 01/361–1617. Admission: 200 dr. Open 8:30–2. Closed Tues.*

㉑ The new **Museum of Cycladic Art** is up the next street to the left. The ancient sculptures here seem strangely modern. *Neofytou Douka 4, tel. 01/321–3018. Admission: 200 dr. weekdays, free on Sat. Open weekdays 10–4, Sat. 10–3. Closed Tues. and Sun.*

㉒ A little farther along is the **Byzantine Museum,** with a unique collection of icons. *22 Vasilissis Sofias, tel. 01/721–1027. Admission: 300 dr. Open Tues.–Sat. 8:45–3; Sun. and public holidays, 9:30–2:30. Closed Mon.*

Kolonaki, a fashionable residential area, occupies the lower ㉓ slopes of **Mount Lycabettos.** Some way up, you can board the *teleferik* (cable car) for a ride to the top and a panoramic view of Athens.

What to See and Do with Children

Watch the **changing of the Evzone guard** in front of the Tomb of the Unknown Soldier. The best time is Sunday at 11 AM. The guards are tall men wearing traditional Greek costumes. Go into the nearby **National Gardens** to see swans in the pond, a small zoo, and a little cottage library for children. On the other side of the National Gardens, see more Evzone guards in front of the **Presidential Palace.** Walk past their barracks and through the Kolomaki residential area to the **teleferik station** and take a ride to the top of Mount Lycabettos. Visit the old battleship **Averoff,** anchored off Phaleron; it's now a naval museum.

Shopping

Gift Ideas   Better tourist shops sell copies of traditional Greek jewelry, silver filigree, enamel, Skyro pottery, onyx ashtrays and dishes, woven bags, attractive rugs (including flokates), good leather items, and furs. Furs made from scraps are inexpensive. Some museums sell replicas of small items that are in their collections. The best handicrafts are sold in **National Welfare Organization shops** (Voukourestiou 24a and Ypatias 6) near the cathedral. Other shops sell dried fruit, packaged pistachios, and canned olives. For books in English, go to **Pantelides** (Amerikas 11 or Eleftheroudakis, Nikis 4). Most large hotels also maintain good English-language book shops.

Antiques   Many shops, especially in **Pondrossou,** sell small antiques and icons. Keep in mind, however, that there are many fakes around and that you must have permission to export genuine objects from the Greek, Roman, or Byzantine periods.

Shopping Areas   The central shopping area lies between Syntagma and Omonia. The **Syntagma** area has good jewelers, shoe shops, and handicraft and souvenir shops, especially in Voukourestriou. **Stadiou** is the best bet for men's clothing. Try **Ermou** and the fascinating small streets that lead off it for fabrics and housewares. Go to **Mitropoleos** for rugs, inexpensive furs, and souvenirs. Ermou runs west to **Monastiraki,** a crowded market area popular with Athenians. Below the cathedral, **Pandrossou** has antiques, sandals (an especially good buy), and inexpensive souvenirs. The **flea market** area lies below Pandrossou. **Kolonaki,** just beyond central Athens, has the best shops for gifts and shoes. Its boutiques include branches of some of the top French fashion houses such as Dior, with prices lower than those in Paris.

Department Stores   The few that exist are neither large nor good. The best is **Lambropoulos** (Aeolou 99–101). **Marinopoulos** shops (Kanari 9, Kifissias 16, and elsewhere) specialize in toiletries and inexpensive casual clothing.

Flea Market   The flea market near Pandrossou operates on Sunday, but it is fascinating to explore at any time. There are shops selling souvenirs, antiques, metalwork, inexpensive shoes, furniture, and junk.

Dining

Restaurants in the luxury hotels serve excellent but expensive international cuisine. Less expensive restaurants fall short of top standards in both variety and taste. Greek food is a flavorful alternative.

Prices are per person and include a first course, main course, and dessert (generally fruit and cheese). They do not include drinks or the 12%–15% service charge. Best bets are indicated by a star ★. At press time, there were 153 drachma to the dollar.

Category	Cost
Very Expensive	over 5,000 dr.

Expensive	2,500 dr.–5,000 dr.
Moderate	1,200 dr.–2,500 dr.
Inexpensive	up to 1,200 dr.

Expensive **Blue Bayou.** Continental and Creole specialties are served in this restaurant, located across from the Holiday Inn. *Meandrou 15, Ilissia, tel. 01/724-8676. Dress: informal. Reservations recommended. AE, DC, MC, V.*

Dionysos. This beautifully landscaped restaurant has a marvelous view of the Acropolis. The menu is large and includes Greek and Continental food, but the quality varies. *Robertou Gali 43, tel. 01/923-3182. Jacket and tie. Reservations recommended. AE, DC, MC, V.*

G.B. Corner. High standards and good service are the trademark of this independently run restaurant in the Grande Bretagne Hotel. Cuisine is Greek and Continental. *Grande Bretagne Hotel, Platia Syntagma, tel. 01/323-0251. Jacket and tie. Reservations recommended. AE, DC, MC, V.*

★ **Gerfinikas.** This charming restaurant, tucked away on a street leading up to Kolonaki, has a loyal expense-account clientele. Go for Greek and Turkish specialties and seafood dishes. *Pinadrou 10, tel. 01/362-2719. Jacket and tie. Reservations recommended. AE, DC, MC, V.*

L'Abreuvois. Classic French cuisine is served on a garden terrace in Kolonaki. *Xenokratous 51, tel. 01/722-9061. Jacket and tie. Reservations recommended. AE, DC, MC, V. Closed Mon.*

Stage Coach. Located in the center of town, this restaurant is strong on steaks and has an evening piano bar. A good bet for lunch. *Voukourestiou 14, tel. 01/363-5145. Dress: informal. Reservations recommended. AE, DC. Closed Sun.*

Steak Room. The best of the steak houses, this restaurant is owned by a Greek-Canadian who knows what Americans look for in a charbroiled steak. Also try the genuine French snails. *Vas. Sofias and Aeginitou 6, tel. 01/721-7445. Dress: informal. Reservations recommended. AE, DC, MC, V. Closed Sun.*

Moderate **Aglamair.** Located in the small boat harbor of Mikrolimano (about 10 miles or 16 kilometers from Athens), this is one of the best seafood restaurants in the Athens area. Practically on the water's edge, it's recommended for lobster, which is as pricey here as elsewhere. *Akti Koumoundourou 54, tel. 01/411-5511. Dress: informal. Reservations recommended. AE, DC, MC, V.*

Dionyssos. Located on top of Mount Lycabettos, this restaurant has a sweeping view of Athens—and getting there is half the fun. Take the funicular railway starting on top of Ploutarhou. In addition to the restaurant, which serves Continental and Greek cuisine, there is a snack bar and café on the premises. *Mount Lycabettos, tel. 01/722-6374. Dress: informal. Reservations not necessary. Open breakfast, lunch, and dinner. AE, DC, V.*

Hermion. An English-language menu, a shady courtyard, and a location on a street below the cathedral make this restaurant very popular with visitors. It has two or three fixed-price menus, all offering excellent Greek and international fare. *Pandrossos 15, tel. 01/324-6725. Dress: informal. Reservations not necessary. AE, DC, MC, V.*

Ideal. This busy restaurant is filled with Athenians of all ages, as well as students from the nearby university. It has an extensive menu featuring Greek and Continental dishes. *Venizelou 46, tel. 01/361–4604. Dress: informal. Reservations not necessary. DC.*

★ **Kostoyannis.** Standing as it does in splendid isolation behind the Archaeological Museum, this taverna has lots of character. It serves fresh seafood, Greek dishes, and standard international cuisine. *Zaimi 37, tel. 01/822–0624. Dress: informal. Reservations not necessary. AE, DC, MC, V. Evenings only. Closed Sun.*

Othello. This small restaurant has a wide selection of international dishes at reasonable prices. *Mihalakoploulou 45, tel. 01/ 729–1481. Dress: informal. Reservations not necessary. AE, DC, MC, V.*

Xynus. A large, old-fashioned taverna, where a trio of musicians plays traditional Greek music as you dine, this is one of the friendliest places in Athens. It draws a local crowd year-round. The food is Greek and abundant. *Angelou Geronta 4, Plaka, tel. 01/322–1065. Dress: informal. Reservations recommended. AE, DC, MC, V. Evenings only. Closed Sun.*

Inexpensive **Delphi Restaurant.** Very popular and always crowded, this restaurant serves excellent Greek and international food. You may have to wait to be served, but you'll find it's worth the wait. *Nikis 13, tel. 01/323–4869. Dress: informal. No reservations. AE, DC. Closed Sun.*

Diros. Near Platia Syntagma, this small restaurant serves good Greek dishes and has warm, friendly service. *Xenofontos 10, tel. 01/323–2392. Dress: informal. Reservations not necessary. AE, V.*

O Platanos. Set in a picturesque corner of the Plaka, this is one of the oldest tavernas in the area. It has a shady garden for outdoor dining. There's no music, so prices are low. Although it's extremely friendly, not much English is spoken. *Diogenous 4, tel. 01/322–0666. Dress: informal. Reservations not necessary. AE, DC, MC, V.*

Syntrivani. Well established and reliable, Syntrivani offers a good range of traditional Greek dishes. It's near Syntagma and has a small garden for outdoor dining. *Filellinon 5, tel. 01/323– 8662. Dress: informal. Reservations not necessary. AE, DC, MC, V.*

Lodging

Most hotels are located in the central area; along the road southwest from the city, toward the sea; or along the seacoast. Each of these three areas has hotels in a range of price categories. Hotels in the central area are convenient but tend to be noisy. Taxis to outlying hotels are inexpensive but not always available.

Prices quoted are for a double room in high season, including taxes and service, but not breakfast. Best bets are indicated by a star ★. At press time, there were 153 drachma to the dollar.

Category	Cost
Very Expensive	over 20,000 dr.

Expensive	8,000 dr.–16,000 dr.
Moderate	5,000 dr.–8,000 dr.
Inexpensive	under 5,000 dr.

Very Expensive   **Aphrodite Astir Palace.** Located in a coastal area 16 miles (25.6 kilometers) from Athens, this is actually 3 hotels called Aphrodite, Arion, and Nafsika. The complex, on a pine-covered promontory, has its own beach and helicopter pad. This is Greece's top seaside hotel complex and is highly recommended. *Vouligmeni, tel. 01/896–210/9. 570 rooms with bath. Facilities: restaurants, 3 outdoor pools, miniature golf, nightclub, air-conditioning. AE, DC, MC, V.*

Athenaeum International. Athens's largest hotel, and one of its newest, is located on the way to the sea. Restaurants include La Rotisserie, featuring classical French cuisine; The Taverna, with typical Greek and Cypriot dishes; and the Café Pergola, which serves a good Sunday brunch. *Syngrou 89, tel. 01/902–3666. 605 rooms with bath. Facilities: 3 restaurants, roof garden, outdoor pool, disco, air-conditioning. AE, DC, MC, V.*

★ **Athens Hilton.** Set in a commanding position on a hill near the U.S. Embassy, the Hilton is about a 10-minute walk from Syntagma Square. All rooms and suites have fine views. There is a large pool with restaurant service and, on Monday evening in summer, a barbecue. Lunch can be enjoyed at the Galaxy on the roof (a piano bar by night), wines and appetizers at the new Kellari, and dinner at Ta Nissia, a Greek-style taverna. *Vasilissis Sofias 46, tel. 01/722–0201. 480 rooms with bath. Facilities: 2 restaurants, a lounge, nighttime piano bar; outdoor pool with food and beverage service; shops; air-conditioning. AE, CB, DC, MC, V.*

★ **Grande Bretagne.** G.B., as it is known, is centrally located on Syntagma Square. This distinguished hotel was modernized a few years ago but it maintains its traditions. Ask for an inside room to escape the noise of traffic. G.B. Corner is an excellent restaurant. *Syntagma Square, tel. 01/323–0251/9. 394 rooms with bath. Facilities: restaurant, rooftop garden, air-conditioning. AE, DC, MC, V.*

Ledra Marriott. Between Athens center and the sea, this is a popular chain hotel known for standard comfort and service. There's a Polynesian restaurant called Kona Kai, complete with waterfall, and the Zephyros Café, which serves an outstanding Sunday buffet brunch. *Syngrou 115, tel. 01/934–7711. 258 rooms with bath. Facilities: 4 restaurants, rooftop garden, outdoor pool, shops, air-conditioning. AE, DC, MC, V.*

Expensive   **Athens Chandris.** Located near the sea, the Athens Chandris
★ offers all the comfort, service, and facilities of a very expensive hotel, but at more reasonable prices. Visitors on combined flight-cruise tours stay here. The hotel runs a complimentary shuttle service to and from Syntagma. It has a fine Continental restaurant, the Four Seasons, a poolside snack bar, and a lounge. *Syngrou 385, tel. 01/941–4824. 386 rooms with bath. Facilities: restaurant, lounge, snack bar, rooftop garden, outdoor pool, air-conditioning. AE, DC, MC, V.*

Atrium. Near the airport and the sea, some 11 miles (17.5 kilometers) from Athens's Syntagma Square, this hotel is convenient for travelers arriving or leaving on flights or cruises. *Vasileos Georgiou 10, Glyfada, tel. 01/894–0971/5. 56* rooms with bath. Facilities: restaurant, roof garden, air-conditioning. AE, MC, V.

Divani-Zafolia Palace. On a small street near the Acropolis and other ancient sites, this hotel is an ideal base from which to stroll and explore. *Parthenos 19, tel. 01/922–2945. 193 rooms with bath. Facilities: restaurant, rooftop garden, outdoor pool, air-conditioning. AE, DC, MC, V.*

Holiday Inn. Centrally located, less than a mile from city center, this is a good base for sightseers. Its restaurant, the Bistro Greek, offers mainly French cuisine. *Mihalakopoulou 50, tel. 01/724–8322. 198 rooms with bath. Facilities: restaurant and lounge, bowling alley, disco, air-conditioning. AE, DC, MC, V.*

President Hotel. The largest hotel in the expensive category, it's a mile from the U.S. Embassy, on the other side of city center. *Kifissias 43, tel. 01/692–4600. 513 rooms with bath. Facilities: restaurant, nightclub, shops, rooftop pool, air-conditioning. AE, DC, MC, V.*

Riva Apartments. Ideal for families or those planning a longer stay, these furnished apartments are near the Hilton Hotel. One- and two-bedroom apartments are available. The Riva Grillroom is outstanding, one of the best restaurants in Athens. *Mihalakopoulou 114, tel. 01/770–6611/5. 57 apartments. Facilities: restaurant, air-conditioning. AE, DC, V.*

★ **St. George Lycabettos Hotel.** Situated on the wooded slopes of Mount Lycabettos, this hotel has a splendid view. Getting there, however, involves a steep short walk or a ride up (remember, taxis are inexpensive). It is friendly and has, as its trump card, Le Grand Balcon, rooftop restaurant with excellent food and a marvelous panorama. *Kleomenous 2, tel. 01/729–0710. 149 rooms with bath. Facilities: restaurant, nightclub, outdoor pool, roof garden, air-conditioning. AE, DC, MC, V.*

Moderate **Athens Gate Hotel.** This hotel looks across a busy street to the Arch of Hadrian. Front rooms have the view, but also the traffic noise; back rooms are quiet. The hotel is conveniently located between the center of town and the Acropolis. The restaurant is only mediocre, but it serves a good, American-style buffet breakfast. *Syngrou 10, tel. 01/923–8302/9. 106 rooms with bath. Facilities: restaurant, roof garden, air-conditioning. AE, DC, MC, V.*

Ilissia Hotel. This small, friendly hotel is located near the Hilton, in an area where there are many good restaurants and night spots. *Mihalakopoulou 25, tel. 01/724–4051. 60 rooms with bath. Facilities: restaurant, air-conditioning. AE, DC, MC, V.*

La Mirage. Conveniently located, this hotel overlooks busy Omonia Square. Rooms are comfortable, but ask for one that's soundproof. *Mirakis Kotopouli 3, tel. 01/523–4072/3. 208 rooms with bath. AE, DC, MC, V.*

Oscar Hotel. Young people appreciate this well-run hotel near the railroad station. *Samou and Filadelfias, tel. 01/883–4215/9. 124 rooms with bath. Facilities: roof garden, outdoor pool with bar, air-conditioning. AE, DC.*

Inexpensive **Alkistis Hotel.** The market area, where the Alkistis is located, is full of life and color by day, but deserted at night. The hotel is pleasant and well run and was recently redecorated. The roof garden has a fine view of the Acropolis. *Platia Theatrou 18, tel. 01/321–9811/9. 120 rooms with bath. Facilities: restaurant, roof garden, outdoor pool. AE, DC, MC, V.*

Aphrodite Hotel. This is near Syntagma and quite comfortable—don't be put off by its cold-looking entrance. *Apollonos 21, tel. 01/323-4354. 84 rooms with bath. Facilities: bar, roof garden. AE, DC, MC, V.*

★ **Austria.** This small, unpretentious hotel is on Filopappou Hill, opposite the Acropolis, ideal as a base for wandering around the heart of ancient Athens. It has no restaurant and is at the top of the inexpensive category, but is well worth considering. *Mouson 7, tel. 01/923-5151. 40 rooms with bath. AE, DC, MC, V.*

The Arts

The **Athens Festival** runs from late June through September and includes concerts, recitals, opera, ballet, folk dancing, and drama. Performances are in various locations, including the open-air theater of Herodes Atticus at the foot of the Acropolis, nearby Philopappou Hill, and Mount Lycabettos. Tickets are available a few days before the performance in the arcade at Stadiou 4 (tel. 01/322-1459). Admission ranges from 500 dr. to 3,000 dr.

In winter, cultural activities are much less frequent and rarely planned far in advance. Daily listings are published year-round in *The Athens News* and weekly listings, in *This Week in Athens*, both available in hotels.

Concerts Winter concerts are given at the Pallas, Voukourestiou, by the State Orchestra and the Radio/TV Orchestra. Tickets are available at the box office.

Opera The Lyriki Skini has a winter season and a small—not very good—ballet season at the Olympia Theater, Akademias 59 (tel. 01/361-2461). The top seat costs about 800 dr.

Films *The Athens News* lists films in English.

Entertainment and Nightlife

Athens has an active nightlife, with hundreds of places offering some sort of entertainment, much of it distinctly Greek. One way to get a taste is to take an "Athens by Night" guided tour. If you want to go on your own, try a *bouzoukia*, or a taverna with a floor show. Most are closed Sunday. Tavernas, with floor shows, are concentrated in the Plaka area. Be forewarned that you will have to pay for an overpriced, second-rate meal at most places with floor shows. The name, style, and quality of tavernas and bouzoukias change frequently. Ask your hotel for recommendations.

Tavernas **Palia Taverna Kritikou.** A fun taverna where there's room for you to indulge in Greek dances to the amusement of the few Greek customers. *Mniskleous 24, tel. 01/322-2809. Dress: informal. Reservations recommended. AE, DC, V. Expensive.*
Psarra. The specialty in this taverna is swordfish kabob. Customers are invited to play the guitar themselves and to join in the Greek dances. *Erehtheou 16, tel. 01/325-0285. Dress: informal. Reservations recommended. AE, DC, MC, V. Expensive.*

Bouzoukias **Athinaia.** Highly prized and priced, it's the real thing, where you'll find an orchestra, female vocalist, and lots of clanging of the *bouzouki*, an Oriental mandolin. *Leoforos Posidonos 63,* tel. 01/942–3089. Dress: informal. Reservations recommended. AE, DC, MC, V. Very Expensive.

Diogenes. Currently the "in" place with the Greek smart set, it's also the most expensive. *Leoforos Syngrou 255, tel. 01/942–4267. Dress: informal. Reservations necessary. AE. Very Expensive.*

The Peloponnese

Suspended from the mainland of Greece like a large leaf, with the isthmus of Corinth as its stem, the ancient land of Pelops offers beautiful scenery and a fascinating variety of ruins: temples, theaters, mosques, churches, palaces, and medieval castles built by crusaders. Four thousand years of history come to life more vividly here than anywhere else in Europe.

Legend and history meet in **Mycenae,** where Agamemnon, Elektra, and Orestes played out their grim family tragedy. This city dominated the entire area from the 16th to the 12th centuries BC, even conquering Minoan Crete. According to Greek mythology, Paris, son of the king of Troy, abducted the beautiful Helen, wife of Menelaus, the king of Sparta. Agamemnon, the king of Mycenae, was his brother. This led to the Trojan War in which Troy was defeated. The story of the war is told in Homer's *Iliad.*

Sparta, once a powerful city-state, contributed decisively to the defeat of the Persians who invaded Greece in the 5th century BC. Later, Athens and Sparta and their respective allies fought each other from 461 BC to 404 BC, in the two Peloponnesian Wars, for dominance of the Greek world. Sparta emerged the victor. In the 2nd century BC, both Sparta and Athens fell before the might of Macedon, whose king, Alexander the Great, was to take Hellenic civilization to the limits of the known world, from Europe to India.

Corinth was the largest, richest, and most pleasure-loving city of Greece in the 3rd century BC, a reputation it continued to enjoy after the Roman conquest. It gave St. Paul plenty to denounce when he came here in the 1st century AD.

In the middle ages, the Peloponnese was conquered by leaders of the Fourth Crusade and ruled as a feudal state by French and Italian nobles. It formed the cornerstone of the Latin (Christian) power in the eastern Mediterranean in the 13th and 14th centuries. In 1821, when the bishop of Patras raised the standard of revolt against Turkish domination, the Peloponnese played a key role in the Greek War of Independence. Nafplio was, for a short time in the 1800s, the capital of Greece. Among the region's many fine contributions to humanity are the Olympic Games, founded in 776 BC in Olympia.

Getting Around

A car is the best way to see all the important sights of the Peloponnese at your own pace. If you take the car ferry from Italy to Patras, capital of the Peloponnese, or if you rent a car in Patras, you can tour the area on the way to Athens. Otherwise, your tour will begin in Athens. Take the route suggested in the itinerary below. You could encounter a shortage of hotel rooms in summer, especially at Nafplio, so plan in advance.

The Peloponnese

Guided Tours

Major tour operators offer a variety of tours that include the Peloponnese. From the United States, **Globus Gateway/Cosmos Tours** (95–25 Queens Blvd., Rego Park, NY 11374, tel. 800/221–0090); and **American Express** (822 Lexington Ave., New York, NY 10021, tel. 212/758–6510). From the United Kingdom, **Swan Hellenic** (Canberra House, 47 Middlesex St., London E1 7AL, tel. 01/247–0401); and **Olympic Holidays** (17 Old Court Pl., London W8 4PL, tel. 01/727–8050). In Greece, **CHAT** (4 Stadiou, Athens, tel. 01/322–2886); and **Wagons-Lits/Cook** (Karageoi Servias 2, Athens, tel. 01/324–2281).

Tourist Information

In Patras, visit the **Greek National Tourist Organization** (Iroon Polytechniou, Glyfada, tel. 061/420–305); or **American Express**, inside the National Bank of Greece (Amalias St. 46, at corner of Othonos St., tel. 061/220–902).

Exploring

Shortly after you pass the last houses of the Athenian urban sprawl, you come to the 6th-century monastery of **Daphni**. It was rebuilt in the 12th century by Cistercian monks as the burial place for Athens's French rulers. It has superb mosaics. *Tel. 01/581–1558. Admission: 300 dr. Open Mon., Wed.–Sat. 8:45–3 and Sun. and public holidays 9:30–2:30. Closed Tues.*

Descending from Daphni to the sea, you face the narrow straits where the Persian fleet of Xerxes was defeated in 480 BC by Sparta. Shortly beyond are the ruins of **Eleusis,** site of antiquity's most important harvest celebrations, the Eleusinian Mysteries, where participants underwent rites commemorating the gift of corn cultivation given by Demeter, goddess of corn. Unfortunately, the area is badly polluted by surrounding factories.

When you cross the **Corinth Canal,** about 55 miles (88 kilometers) from Athens, you enter the **Peloponnese.** Modern Corinth lies by the sea; the ancient Greek city stood higher up. All that remains is the **Doric Temple of Apollo,** built in the 6th century BC and restored by Julius Caesar. In 51 AD, St. Paul fulminated against the sacred prostitutes who served Aphrodite on **Acro-Corinth,** the peak behind the ancient city. A museum beside the ruins contains finds from the excavations. Drive to a tourist pavilion below the imposing Franco-Turkish fortifications on the mountain and explore the citadel on foot. *Tel. 0741/312–07. Admission: 400 dr. Open Apr.–Oct., Mon., Wed.–Sat. 8–7 and Sun. and public holidays 8–6; Nov.–Mar., 8–5. Closed Tues.*

Mycenae, 80 miles (128 kilometers) from Athens, was the fabulous stronghold of the Achaean kings of the 13th century BC. Destroyed in 468 BC, it was forgotten until 1874 when German archaeologist Heinrich Schliemann, who discovered the ruins of ancient Troy, uncovered the remains of this ancient fortress city. Mycenae was the seat of the doomed House of Atreus—of King Agamemnon and his wife, Clytemnestra, sister of Helen of Troy, and of their tragic children, Orestes and Elektra. When Schliemann uncovered six shaft graves (so named because the kings were buried standing up) of the royal circle, he was certain that one was the tomb of Agamemnon. The gold masks and diadems, daggers, jewelry, and other treasures found in the graves are now in the Athens Archaeological Museum; the new local museum is dedicated to archaeological studies. Along with the graves, you'll find the astounding beehive tombs built into the hillsides outside the reconstructed wall, the **Lions Gate,** dating to 1250 BC, and the castle ruins crowning the bleak hill, all remnants of the first great civilization in Continental Europe. *Tel. 0752/275–02. Admission: 500 dr. Open Apr.–Oct., Mon.–Sat. 8–7 and Sun. and public holidays 8–6; Nov.–Mar. daily 8–5.*

Moving south, you pass Argos, Europe's oldest continuously inhabited town, and the Cyclopean ramparts (huge, irregular stones) of Tiryns. **Nafplio** is a picturesque town below the Venetian fortifications. Modern Greece's first king lived for a year or two within the walls of the higher fortress when Nafplio was capital of Greece. His courtiers had to climb 999 steps to reach him; you can still climb the long staircase or drive up to the fortress. The **Venetian naval arsenal** on the town square houses a museum crowded with Mycenaen finds. *Tel. 0752/275–02. Admission: 300 dr. Open weekdays 8:45–3 and Sun. and public holidays 9:30–2:30. Closed Tues.*

Epidauros, 18 miles (28.8 kilometers) east of Nafplio, was the sanctuary of Aesculapois, the Greek god of healing. You can visit the foundations of the temples and ancient hospitals. The most important site is the ancient open-air theater, which seats 16,000. In summer, during the **Epidavos Festival,** ancient Greek plays are staged here. The theater merits a visit any time of year. The acoustics are so good that you can sit in the top row and hear a whisper on stage. *Tel. 0753/220–09. Admission: 500 dr. Museum and theater open Apr.–Oct., weekdays 8–7 and Sun. and public holidays 8–6; Nov.–Mar. daily 8–5. Museum closed Tues.*

You can return from here to Athens along the coast, a lovely drive, or continue on to **Olympia** by way of the rugged mountains of Arcadia. The site of ancient Olympia lies a few miles from the sea, northeast of **Megalopolis**, once the largest town in ancient Greece. The first Olympic Games were held in Olympia in 776 BC and continued to be celebrated every four years until AD 393. Women were excluded from the games under penalty of death. Archaeologists are still uncovering statues and votive offerings among the olive groves and pine trees surrounding **Olympic Stadium** and the imposing **ruins of the temples of Zeus and Hera** within the sacred precinct. The **International Olympic Academy**, nearly four miles (6.4 kilometers) east, houses the **Museum of the Olympic Games**. *Tel. 0624/227–42. Admission: 400 dr. Open Apr.–Oct., Mon., Wed.–Sat. 8–7, Tues. noon–7 and Sun. and public holidays 8–6; Nov.–Mar., Wed.–Mon. 9–5 and Tues. 11–5.*

North of Olympia is **Patras**, third-largest city in Greece and its main western port. It has a Roman theater, a medieval castle, and streets covered by arcades. St. Andrew was crucified here and became the city's patron saint; the prominent new church on the waterfront has relics of the saint.

The shortest route back to Athens follows the National Road along the southern shore of the Gulf of Corinth, an exceptionally beautiful drive. You could choose instead to cross the entrance to the gulf and visit Delphi (*see* Exploring, in Mainland Greece) on your way back to Athens.

Dining and Lodging

Many of the towns in the Peloponnese have hotels with good dining rooms, as well as restaurants serving fresh seafood and Greek cuisine. For details and price category definitions, *see* Dining and Lodging in Essential Information.

Napflio
Dining

Savouras. Fresh seafood is served in this unpretentious taverna overlooking the bay. *Akti Miaouli, no telephone. Dress: informal. Reservations not necessary. No credit cards. Inexpensive.*

Lodging
★

Amalia. The hotel occupies a fine neoclassical building 2½ miles (4 kilometers) outside town, near ancient Tiryns. The public rooms are spacious and the service attentive. A beach is nearby. *Tel. 0752/244–01. 173 rooms with bath. Facilities: restaurant, outdoor pool, gardens, air-conditioning. AE, DC, V. Expensive.*

Park. Near the entrance to town, the Park is within easy walking distance of all the sights. Although it's not particularly distinctive, it provides good value. *Dervenakion 1, tel. 0752/274–28. 70 rooms with bath. Facilities: restaurant. DC, V. Inexpensive.*

Xenia's Palace. The hotel and cottages sit within the Venetian walls of the lower fortress of Acronafplia. The complex has superb views and a private beach. *Tel. 0752/289–81/3. 105 rooms* or cottages with bath. *Facilities: restaurant, outdoor pool, air-conditioning. DC. Expensive.*

Xenia. This hotel is also in the Acronafplia and has a private beach. Though all rooms have lovely views, they are not air-conditioned. *Tel. 0752/289–91/3. 58 rooms with bath. Facilities: restaurant. DC, MC. Moderate.*

Olympia
Dining

Taverna Pritannio. This is an unpretentious taverna serving abundant portions of basic Greek food. *Main St., no telephone. Dress: informal. Reservations not necessary. No credit cards. Inexpensive.*

Pete's Den. Owned by a Greek-German couple, this restaurant mixes traditional Greek and German cuisine, with sensational results. *Main St., tel. 0624/220–66. Dress: informal. Reservations not necessary. No credit cards. Inexpensive.*

Lodging
★

Amalia. Pleasantly situated a little outside the village near the museum, the Amalia is comfortable and well run. *Main St,. tel. 0624/221–90. 147 rooms with bath. Facilities: restaurant, swimming pool, air-conditioning. AE, DC, MC, V. Expensive.*

Apollon. There's a convenient self-service restaurant in this hotel; none of the rooms are air-conditioned. *Douma 13, tel. 0624/225–22. 110 rooms with bath. Facilities: restaurant, outdoor pool, roof garden. AE, DC. Closed Nov.–Mar. Moderate.*

Patras
Dining

Bieneza. A typical taverna, this one serves fish, noodles, and salad, along with Greek specialties. *Kolokotroni 18, tel. 061/221–209. Dress: informal. Reservations not necessary. No credit cards. Inexpensive.*

Evangelatos. This reliable Greek restaurant offers standard local fare. *Ag. Nikolaou 7, tel. 061/277–77/2. Dress: informal. Reservations not necessary. AE, DC, V. Moderate.*

Lodging

Astir. This large hotel enjoys an excellent location on the waterfront near the center of town. Spacious and pleasant, it looks out on the busy harbor and across to the mountains of Greece. *Ag. Andreou 16, tel. 061/277–502. 121 rooms with bath. Facilities: restaurant, roof garden, outdoor pool, air-conditioning. AE, DC, MC, V. Very Expensive.*

Galaxy Hotel. This small, air-conditioned hotel is conveniently located on the main street. Although it has no restaurant, it is near many restaurants and tavernas. *Ag. Nicolaou 9, tel. 061/278–815. 55 rooms with bath. AE, DC, MC, V. Moderate.*

★ **Porto Rio.** There's a large and varied selection of rooms and cottages with a wide range of prices at this hotel complex, on the sea at Rion, about 6 miles (9.6 kilometers) from Patras. It looks across the narrow entrance to the Gulf of Corinth. *Tel. 061/992–212. 267 rooms and cottages with bath. Facilities: restaurant, 2 outdoor pools, tennis, miniature golf, children's playground, nightclub, air-conditioning. AE, DC, MC, V. Closed Nov.–Mar. Moderate and Expensive.*

The Arts

The **Festival of Ancient Drama** in the theater at Epidauros takes place in July and August. There are also performances of Greek dramas in the ancient theater of Patras in August.

Mainland Greece

A rugged land of eagles and ancient gods, mainland Greece has many ranges of high, barren mountains enclosing narrow, wooded valleys. The massive Pindus range in the west and rocky Mount Olympus in the east have snowcapped peaks for much of the year. Mount Parnassus and nearby Elikon, sacred to Apollo and the Muses, rise in the south. Mount Pelion, near the eastern coast, looms over nearby Ossa.

The dramatic rocky heights of Greece provide an appropriate setting for man's attempt to approach divinity. The ancient Greeks placed their gods on Mount Olympus and chose the precipitous slopes of Parnassus, "the navel of the universe," as the site for Delphi, the most important religious center of the ancient world. Many centuries later, pious Christians built a great monastery (Ossios Loukas) in a remote mountain valley. Others settled on the rocky mountain peninsula of Athos, the Holy Mountain. Later, devout men escaping from Turkish persecution established themselves precariously on top of strange, towerlike rocks and built monasteries, such as the one at Meteora. In fact, all of mainland Greece's most memorable sights are closely connected with religion—including the remarkable Byzantine churches of Thessaloniki. Of course, there are remains of palaces and cities, but these do not have the impact of the great religious centers.

In this land of lonely mountain villages, narrow defiles, and dark woods, bands of *klephts* (a cross between brigands and guerrillas) earned their place in folk history and song during the long centuries of Turkish rule. The women of Souli, one of the mountain strongholds of the klephts, threw themselves dancing and singing over a cliff rather than be captured by the Turks. In these same mountains during the German occupation of Greece in World War II, guerrilla bands descended to the valleys and plains to assault the occupying army and drive it from their land.

Getting Around

This proposed itinerary begins in Athens. It can be done by public transport, by car, or by guided tour. A one-day tour of Delphi is rushed; two days will give you more leisure time. Your best bet is a three-day tour that includes Delphi and Meteora. A longer tour of the Peloponnese should include Ossios Lukas. Thessaloniki is usually included only in lengthy tours of northern Greece. If you don't have a car, you can leave the Delphi–Meteora tour at Trikala, take the train to Thessaloniki, and return to Athens by plane or train. You can also take a guided tour of northern Greece and leave the group at Thessaloniki. In September, during the Thessaloniki International Trade Fair, there are no hotel rooms to be had; make reservations well in advance. Travel agencies in Athens with tours of mainland Greece include **American Express** (Syntagma Square and in the Hilton Hotel) and **Wagons-Lits Travel** (Karageorgi Servias 2).

Exploring

To get from Athens to Delphi, take the National Road toward Thessaloniki and turn off to **Thebes** *(Thiva)*, the birthplace of the legendary **Oedipus,** who unwittingly fulfilled the prophesy of the Delphic Oracle by slaying his father and marrying his mother. Little now remains of the ancient city. Farther along the road, at **Livadia,** a medieval fortress towers above the springs of Lethe (Oblivion) and Mnemosyne (Remembrance). Halfway between Livadia and Delphi is the crossroads where, according to mythology, Oedipus killed his father.

The road to the left leads to a serene upland valley and the **Monastery of Ossios Loukas,** a fine example of Byzantine architecture and decoration. Built in the 11th century to replace the earlier shrine of a local saint, it has some of the world's finest Byzantine mosaics. *Tel. 0265/321–3571. Admission: 300 dr. Open Mon., Wed.–Sat. 8:45–3 and Sun. and public holidays 9:30–2:30. Closed Tues.*

Back on the road to Delphi, you climb a spur of Mount Parnassus to the village of **Arahova,** known for its brightly colored woolen handicrafts, especially rugs. From Arahova, a short, spectacular drive down to Delphi crosses the gorge of the Pleistos. You'll see a great cliff called Phaedriades and a deep narrow chasm at the bottom of which the **Castalian spring** gushes with cool, pure water. It was here that pilgrims to the Delphic Oracle came for purification.

The ancient Greeks believed that **Delphi** was the center of the universe because two eagles released by the gods at opposite ends of earth met here. For hundreds of years, the worship of Apollo and the pronouncements of the Oracle here made Delphi the most important religious center of the ancient world. As you walk up the Sacred Way to the **Temple of Apollo,** the **theater,** and the **stadium,** you have Mount Parnassus above, silver-green olive trees below, and, in the distance, the blue gulf. Most of the ruins date from the 5th to the 3rd centuries BC. They were first excavated in 1892.

Don't miss the famous bronze charioteer (early 5th century BC) in the **Delphi Museum.** Other interesting and beautiful works of art here include the column of the dancers (or Caryatids), 4th century BC; a statue of Antinous, Emperor Hadrian's lover; and the stone representing the navel of the earth. *Tel. 0265/82–313. Admission: 400 dr. Open Apr.–Oct., Mon., Wed.–Sat. 8–7 and Sun. and public holidays 8–6; Nov.–Mar., daily 8–5. Closed Tues.*

From Delphi, the road descends in sharp bends past groves of gnarled, ancient olive trees. Continue to Amphissa and over the Pourmaraki (Bralos) Pass to the small town of Lamia. Follow the road to Karditva and around the Thessalian plain to Trikala. You will then arrive at **Kalambaka,** the base for visits to the monasteries of **Meteora,** which sit atop gigantic rocks above the town. Monks and supplies once reached the top of the slopes by ladders or nets. Today steps are cut in the boulders, and some of the monasteries can be reached easily by car now. Not all of them are open to the public, however.

One of the more accessible monasteries, **Aghios Stephanon,** has a notable church. The fortresslike **Aghios Varlaam** monastery is also easy to reach. To get a better idea of what living in these monasteries was like 300 years ago, climb the steep rock steps to the **Great Meteoron,** the largest of the rocks. The monasteries are open mornings only. *Admission is free.*

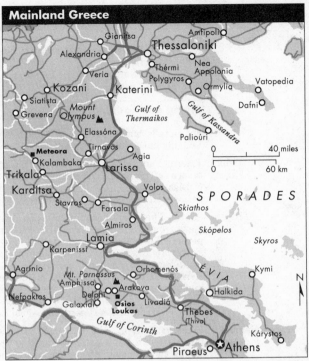

Mainland Greece

Leaving Kalambaka for Thessaloniki, you find the road crosses the plain of Thessaly, one of Europe's hottest places in summer, and joins the National Road at Larissa. Ahead you will see Mount Olympus, Greece's highest mountain. The road passes the valley of Tempe and then runs near the coast to **Thessaloniki**, birthplace of Aristotle as well as capital of modern Greece and its second-largest city. Although Thessaloniki still has some remains from the Roman period, the city is best known for its fine Byzantine churches. The city is compact enough for you to see the main sights on foot. Start at the 15th-century **White Tower,** symbol of Thessaloniki, and walk up Davlou Mela to the green-domed church of **Aghia Sophia,** which dates to the 8th century and has beautifully preserved mosaics. Enroute you will pass **Turkish tombs, bathhouses,** and **mosques.**

Walk up Egnatia, which traces the original Roman road leading from the Adriatic to the Bosporous. You will pass the **Roman Agora** (town center) and come to **Agios Dimitrios,** the principal church. Though it is only a replica of the original church that burned down in 1917, it is adorned with many 8th-century mosaics that were in the original building. Follow Aghiou Dimitriou to **Agios Georgios,** a rotunda built by Roman Emperor Galerius as his tomb in the 4th century AD. His successor, Constantine the Great, the first Christian emperor, turned it into a church. Particularly interesting are its 4th-century mosaics of Roman buildings.

Return to Egnatia and the **Arch of the Emperor Galerius,** built— shortly prior to the rotunda—to commemorate the Roman victories of Emperor Galerius over forces in Persia, Armenia, and

Asia Minor. A short walk downhill toward the sea will bring
you to the **Archaeological Museum.** Among its many beautiful
objects are a huge bronze vase from Deryeni and gold artifacts
from recent excavations of the royal tombs of Vergina. *Tel. 031/
830–583. Admission: 400 dr. Open Apr.–Oct., Mon., Wed.–
Sat. 8–7 and Sun. and public holidays 8–6; Nov.–Mar. daily
8–5. Closed Tues.*

Dining and Lodging

For details and price category definitions, *see* Dining and
Lodging in Essential Information.

Delphi **Taverna Pan.** Decorated with local folk art and weavings, this
Dining taverna offers fixed-price meals as well as à la carte Greek specialties. *Isaia St., tel. 0265/824–73. Dress: informal. Reservations not necessary. No credit cards. Inexpensive.*

Lodging **Vouzas.** The hotel sits on the edge of a gorge and has wonderful
★ views from every room. Friendly service may or may not compensate for the lack of air-conditioning. *Vas. Pavlou and
Friderikis 1, tel. 0265/822–324. 58 rooms with bath. Facilities:
restaurant. AE, DC, V. Expensive.*

Hermés. This small hotel on the main street is adequate for a
night's sleep. There is no restaurant or air-conditioning. *Vas.
Pavlou and Friderikis 29, tel. 0265/823–18. 24 rooms with
bath. No credit cards. Closed Nov.–Feb. Inexpensive.*

Kalambaka **Planotos Taverna.** A great place for people watching, this
Dining taverna has a large patio overlooking the main square and
serves simple meals of broiled meats and fresh vegetables.
*Central Square, no telephone. Dress: informal. Reservations
not necessary. No credit cards. Inexpensive.*

Lodging **Motel Divani.** Below the Meteora is a hotel (in spite of its name)
★ that is more comfortable than you might expect to find so far off
the beaten path. *Tel. 0432/225–83/4. 165 rooms with bath. Facilities: restaurant, outdoor pool, air-conditioning. AE, DC,
MC, V. Expensive.*

Xenia. Looking across to the great rocks, this is a small, pleasant hotel, adequate for an overnight stay. Half-board is
required. *Tel. 0432/223–27. 22 rooms with bath. Facilities: restaurant, air-conditioning. No credit cards. Closed Nov.–Mar.
Moderate.*

Thessaloniki **Stratis.** Continental and Greek cuisine are featured in this old,
Dining established restaurant. Snacks and light meals are also available. *Nikis 19, tel. 031/234–782. Dress: informal. Reservations
not necessary. AE, DC, MC, V. Moderate.*

Ta Nissia. The catch here is fresh seafood, especially mussels.
*Koromila 13, tel. 031/285–991. Dress: informal. Reservations
recommended. Evenings only. DC. Moderate.*

Lodging **Makedonia Palace.** This large, stylish hotel is beautifully situated at the edge of a bay in a new residential section on
reclaimed land. Ask for rooms overlooking the bay. *Megalou
Alexandrou, tel. 031/837–521/9. 287 rooms with bath. Facilities: several restaurants, roof garden, air-conditioning. AE,
DC, MC, V. Very Expensive.*

★ **Elektra Palace.** This is a comfortable hotel built in a neo-Byzantine style to match the other buildings on the square. It's conveniently located in the center of town. *Platia Aristotelous 5, tel. 031/232-21/30. 131 rooms with bath. Facilities: restaurant, air-conditioning. AE, DC, MC, V. Expensive.*

A.B.C. The International Trade Fair grounds and the Archaeological Museum are nearby. It has no restaurant. *Angelaki 41, Sindrivaniou, tel. 031/265-421. 107 rooms with bath. DC, MC, V. Moderate.*

Capsis. Near the railroad station, this is the largest hotel in Thessaloniki, popular with tour groups. *Monastiriou 28 and Prometheos, tel. 031/265-421. 428 rooms with bath. Facilities: restaurant, roof garden with pool, disco, air-conditioning. AE, DC, MC, V. Moderate.*

Vergina. This hotel, on a busy road near the railroad station, can be noisy, but it offers good value. *Monastiriou 19, tel. 031/527-400/8. 133 rooms with bath. Facilities: restaurant, roof garden. DC. Inexpensive.*

The Magic of the Isles

The islands of the Aegean have colorful legends of their own—the Minotaur in Crete; the lost continent of Atlantis, which some believe was Santorini; and the Colossus of Rhodes, to name a few. Each island has its own personality. **Mykonos** has windmills, dazzling whitewashed buildings, hundreds of tiny churches and chapels on golden hillsides, and small fishing harbors. Visitors to volcanic **Santorini** sail into what was once a vast volcanic crater and anchor near the island's forbidding cliffs. **Crete,** with its jagged mountain peaks, olive orchards, and vineyards, has the remains of the Minoan civilization. In **Rhodes,** a bustling modern town surrounds a walled town with a medieval castle.

Getting Around

The simplest way to visit the Aegean Islands is on a cruise, lasting from one to 10 days. Visitors should consider a three-day cruise, to the four most popular islands—Mykonos, Rhodes, Crete, and Santorini. Car ferries sail to these main destinations from Piraeus, the port of Athens. There is also frequent air service from Athens. In summer, it's important to book services well in advance.

Aegean Cruises From April through October there are many cruises to the Greek Islands from Piraeus: **Blue Aegean Sea Line, Cycladic Cruises, Epirotiki, Hellenic Cruises, Hellenic Mediterranean, K Lines, Oceanic Sun Line,** and **Saronic Cruises**—all offer one- to seven-day cruises. *Contact K Lines-Hellenic Cruises. In the U.S., Olympic Tower, 645 Fifth Ave., New York, NY 10022, tel. 212/751-2435; in the U.K., 50 Pall Mall, London, SW1, tel. 01/930-7610.*

Exploring

Cruise ships and car ferries to Mykonos leave from Piraeus, the port of Athens. As you sail to Mykonos, you will be able to see one of the great sights of Greece: the Temple of Poseidon looming on a hilltop at the edge of Cape Sounion, about two hours from shore.

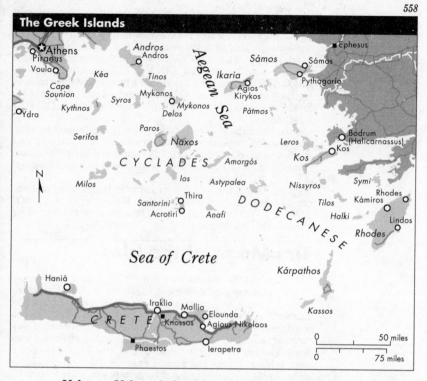

The Greek Islands

Mykonos

Mykonos is the name of the island and also of its chief village—a colorful place with narrow, paved streets lined with white-washed houses, many with bright blue doors and shutters. Every morning, women scrub the sidewalks and streets in front of their homes, undaunted by the many donkeys that pass by each day. Because Mykonos is windy in July and August, most of its restaurants, nightclubs, bars, and discos sit well back from the waterfront. Numerous shops sell excellent local handicrafts, much of it made by artists who have flocked to Mykonos from throughout the world and turned the island into an artists' colony. Mykonos is blessed with sandy beaches, tiny coves, and clear aqua waters, ideal for swimming and snorkeling.

Delos

A half-hour by boat from Mykonos and its 20th-century holiday pleasures is the ancient isle of **Delos,** the legendary sanctuary of Apollo. Its **Terrace of the Lions,** a remarkable group of five large sculptures from the 7th century BC, is a must. Worth seeing, too, are some of the houses of the Roman period, with their fine floor mosaics. The best of these mosaics are in a museum, the **House of Dionysos.** *Tel. 0289/222–59. Admission: 500 dr. Open Mon., Wed.–Sat. 8:45–3 and Sun. and public holidays 9:30–2:30. Closed Tues.*

Rhodes

The large island of **Rhodes,** southeast of Mykonos, is seven miles (11.2 kilometers) off the coast of Turkey. The northern end of the island is one of Greece's major vacation centers. The island as a whole is not particularly beautiful—most of the pine and cedar woods that covered its hilly center were destroyed by fire in 1987. But it has fine beaches and an excellent climate. The town of Rhodes has an attractive harbor with fortifications; the statue of the Colossus of Rhodes is supposed to have straddled the entrance. The old walled city, near the harbor, was built by crusaders, the Knights Hospitaller of St. John, who ruled the island from 1310 until they were defeated by the Turks in 1522. Within its fine medieval walls, on the Street of the Knights, stands the **Knights' Hospital,** now a museum. *Tel. 0241/276–57. Admission: 300 dr. Open Apr.–Oct., Mon., Wed.– Sat. 8–7 and Sun. and public holidays 8–6. Nov.–Mar., Mon., Wed.–Sun. 8–5. Closed Tues.*

Another museum that deserves your attention is the restored and moated medieval **Palace of the Grand Masters.** It is especially noted for its floor mosaics. *Tel. 0241/276–57. Admission: 300 dr. Open Apr.–Oct., Mon., Wed.–Sat. 8–7 and Sun. and public holidays 8–6. Nov.–Mar., Mon., Wed.–Sun. 8–5. Closed Tues.*

To get the best overall view of the walled city, including the surviving Turkish buildings, go to one of the flower-filled parks that surround it. Try to see the Son et Lumière (sound and light show)—English-language performances are held on Sunday evening.

Many attractive souvenir and handicraft shops in the old town sell decorative Rhodian pottery, local embroidery, and relatively inexpensive jewelry.

From the town of Rhodes, drive about 35 miles (56 kilometers) down the east coast to the enchanting village of **Lindos.** On a steep hill above the village, within a medieval castle, are the ruins of the ancient **Acropolis of Lindos.** The sight of its beautiful colonnade with the sea far below is unforgettable. *Tel. 0241/ 276–74. Admission: 400 dr. Open Apr.–Oct., Mon.–Sat. 8–7 and Sun. and public holidays 8–6; Nov.–Mar., daily 8–5.*

Rhodes is also a good base for visiting other islands of the Dodecanese—12 islands near the Turkish coast, with their mixture of Aegean and Turkish architecture.

Crete **Crete** was the center of Europe's earliest civilization, the Minoan, which flourished from about 2000 BC to 1200 BC. It was struck a mortal blow by a devastating volcanic eruption on the neighboring island of Santorini (Thera) in about 1450 BC.

The most important Minoan remains are to be seen in the **Archaeological Museum of Heraklion** near Iraklio, Crete's largest city. The museum houses many Minoan treasures, including some highly sophisticated frescoes and elegant ceramics depicting Minoan life. *Xanthoudidou St., tel. 081/226–092. Admission: 500 dr. Open Apr.–Oct., Tues.–Sat. 8–7 and Sun. and public holidays 8–6; Nov.–Mar., 8–5. Closed Mon.*

Not far from Iraklio is the partly reconstructed **Palace of Knossos,** which will also give you a feeling for the Minoan world. Note the simple throne room, which contains the oldest throne in Europe, and the bathrooms with their efficient plumbing. The palace was the setting for the legend of the Minotaur, a monstrous offspring of Queen Pasiphae and a bull confined to the **Labyrinth** under the palace. *Tel. 081/231–940. Admission: 500 dr. Open Apr.–Oct., Mon.–Sat. 8–7 and Sun. and public holidays 8–6; Nov.–Mar., daily 8–5.*

Crete belonged to Venice from 1210 to 1669, at which time it was conquered by the Turks. The island did not become part of Greece until early in this century. The **Venetian ramparts** that withstood a 24-year Turkish siege still surround Iraklio. In addition to archaeological treasures, Crete can boast beautiful mountain scenery and a large number of beach resorts along the north coast. The most attractive is **Mallia,** which contains the remains of another Minoan palace. Two other beach resorts, **Agios Nikolaos** and the nearby **Elounda,** are east of Iraklio. The south coast offers good beaches for getting away from it all.

Santorini The best way to approach **Santorini** is to sail into its harbor, once the vast crater of its volcano, and dock beneath its black and red cliffs. In some parts, the cliffs rise nearly 1,000 feet (300 meters) above the sea. The play of light across them can produce strange color effects. The white houses and churches of the main town cling to the rim in dazzling white contrast to the somber cliffs.

From the pier, you can reach the town by either bus, taxi, or cable car or by riding a donkey up a steep hill. Despite being packed with visitors in the summer, the tiny town is charming, with spectacular views. It has the usual souvenir and handicrafts shops and several reasonably priced jewelry shops. Be sure also to try the local white wine—the volcanic soil gives it a light, distinctive taste.

The island's volcano erupted in the 15th century BC, destroying its Minoan civilization. At **Acrotiri,** on the southern end of Santorini, the remains of a **Minoan city** buried by lava were recently excavated. The site, believed by some to be part of the legendary Atlantis, is open to the public. *Tel. 0286/813–66. Admission: 500 dr. Open Apr.–Oct., Mon.–Sat. 8–7 and Sun. and public holidays 9:30–2:30; Nov.–Mar., Mon.–Sat. 8:45–3 and Sun. and public holidays 9:30–2:30.*

For an enjoyable but slightly unnerving excursion, take the short boat trip to the island's still active small **offshore volcanoes.** You can descend into a small crater, hot and smelling of sulfur, and swim in the nearby water that has been warmed by the volcano.

Dining and Lodging

For details and price category definitions, *see* Dining and Lodging in Essential Information.

Crete Iraklio has many moderately priced open-air restaurants in the
Dining central area around Platia Venizelou and Platia Paedalou. The island is known for its fine local wine, fresh seafood, and fresh local produce, which is available year-round.
Minos Taverna. This is one of the many outdoor restaurants near the Venetian fountain. Lamb, fresh seafood, and yogurt dishes make this one of the island's most popular restaurants.

10 Daedelou St., tel. 081/281–263. Dress: informal. Reservations not necessary. No credit cards. Moderate.

Lodging **Minos Palace.** This north coast resort has a beautiful setting on a headland, near the village of Agios Nicolaos. *Tel. 0841/238–01/9. 151 rooms with bath. Facilities: restaurant, outdoor pool, tennis, miniature golf, beach, gardens, air-conditioning. AE, DC, MC, V. Closed Nov.–Feb. Very Expensive.*

Elounda Beach. Located 3 miles (5 kilometers) north of Agios Nicolaos, this is probably the best seaside resort complex on Crete. It's set on beautiful grounds and has a private beach. *Tel. 0841/414–12/3. 301 rooms with bath. Facilities: restaurants, outdoor pool, miniature golf, tennis, nightclub, air-conditioning. AE. Closed Nov.–Mar. Very Expensive.*

Astoria. In the center of Iraklio, near the Archaeological Museum, this hotel is situated on a large central square opening onto the park above the Venetian fortifications. *Pl. Eleftherias 5, tel. 081/229–002. 141 rooms with bath. Facilities: restaurant, nightclub, outdoor pool, tennis, air-conditioning. AE, DC, MC, V. Expensive.*

Irakos Village. This hotel complex, near Malia on Crete's north coast, was created by a German company and fits the image of a typical Greek village. It's on the beach, about 20 miles (32 kilometers) east of Iraklio, and near the ruins of a Minoan palace. *Malia Pediados, tel. 0897/312–67/9. 179 rooms with bath. Facilities: restaurant, outdoor pool, tennis, private beach. AE. Closed Nov.–Mar. Expensive.*

★ **Mediterranean.** This is another comfortable hotel in the center of Iraklio and 3 miles (5 kilometers) from the beach. It's priced at the top of its category. *Smyrnis 1, tel. 081/228–003. 55 rooms with bath. Facilities: restaurant, roof garden, air-conditioning. AE, MC, V. Moderate.*

Mykonos
Dining
Nikos Taverna. This large restaurant near the port offers a wide selection of Greek and international dishes. The food is usually good. *Harborfront, no telephone. Dress: informal. Reservations not necessary. AE, MC, V. Expensive.*

Philippi. A favorite with locals as well as tourists, this is where you can enjoy Continental cuisine and curries outdoors in a garden of olive trees or in the elegant dining room. *Kalogeras St., tel. 0289/222–94. Dress: informal. Reservations recommended. AE, MC, V. Dinner only. Expensive.*

Lodging
★ **Cavo Tagoo.** Within walking distance of the center of town, this small, charming hotel sits above a beach. It has an attractively designed saltwater pool in the garden and is well worth the high rates. *Tagoo Beach, tel. 0289/236–92/4. 24 rooms with bath. Facilities: restaurant, outdoor pool. AE, MC, V. Closed Nov.–Mar. Expensive.*

Mykonos Beach. This is a group of bungalows on the edge of town, overlooking a beach. *Kiklades St., tel. 0289/225–72/3. 27 bungalows. Facilities: nightclub. AE, MC, V. Closed Nov.–Mar. Moderate.*

Rhodes
Dining
Casa Castelana. Set in a 15th-century Inn of the Knights, this restaurant has a wonderful medieval atmosphere indoors; outdoors, there's a garden for dining. *Aristotelous 35, tel. 0241/288–03. Dress: informal. Reservations recommended. AE, DC, V. Expensive.*

The Plaka Taverna. The specialty here is fresh seafood, grilled or fried to order. *Ippocratous Square, tel. 0241/224–77. Dress: informal. Reservations not necessary. AE, DC. Expensive.*

Kabo n' Toro Taverna. You can't go wrong at this tiny restaurant, which is one of the best in the town of Rhodes and possibly on the entire island. *Omilou and Parado Sts., tel. 0241/361–82. Dress: informal. Reservations not necessary. No credit cards. Moderate.*

Lodging **Grand Hotel Astir Palace.** This beachfront establishment in Rhodes town has one of Greece's 3 casinos. Although the beach is ordinary, the hotel is definitely grand. *Vass. Konstantinou St., tel. 0241/262–84/9. 378 rooms with bath. Facilities: restaurants, 1 indoor and 2 outdoor pools, private beach, tennis, casino, air-conditioning. AE, DC, MC, V. Very Expensive.*

Golden Beach. This cottage resort complex is on Trianda beach at Ixia. *Acti Trianta, tel. 0241/924–11/5. 225 cottages. Facilities: restaurant, outdoor pool, miniature golf, beach, disco. AE, DC, MC, V. Closed Nov.–Mar. Expensive.*

Steps of Lindos. This hotel sits below the village of Lindos on an excellent beach. There is a playground for children. The service is friendly. *Vlyha Lindos, tel. 0244/422–49. 156 rooms with bath. Facilities: restaurant, outdoor pool, tennis, beach, air-conditioning. AE. Closed Nov.–Mar. Expensive.*

Spartalis. Many rooms have balconies overlooking the bay in this simple but lively hotel near the city's port. It does not have a restaurant. *Plastira 2, tel. 0241/243–71/2. 70 rooms with bath. AE, DC, MC. Moderate.*

Santorini **Camille Stefani.** This is one of the island's best restaurants, Dining where you can enjoy seafood, Greek and Continental cuisine, and the local wines. *Main St., tel. 0286/222–65. Dress: informal. Reservations recommended. AE, MC, V. Moderate.*

Lodging **Atlantis.** Located in the main village, this is the island's best hotel. It has a magnificent view. *Thera, tel. 0286/222–32. 27 rooms with bath. Facilities: restaurant. AE, DC, MC, V. Closed Nov.–Mar. Expensive.*

Kamari Hotel. This pleasant resort hotel is on a black-sand beach on the side away from the cliffs. *Tel. 0286/312–1243. 55 rooms with bath. Facilities: restaurant, roof garden, outdoor pool, tennis, disco. AE, MC, DC, V. Closed Nov.–Mar. Moderate.*

Corfu

The romantic island of Corfu doesn't easily fit into any itinerary, but it richly deserves to be included. It is one of the Ionian Islands, a chain that lies off the northwest coast of Greece. Corfu once belonged to Venice and is in many ways a bridge between Greece and Italy. The lovely countryside, attractive villages, and the quiet lanes bordered by olive trees, cypresses, and lush gardens all invite discovery. Corfu has excellent beaches in gorgeous settings, with pine woods running down to the sea.

Getting Around

There are several daily flights to Corfu from Athens, and in summer there are also flights from Thessaloniki. The island has frequent ferry service from Igoumenitsa, the closest port on

Corfu

the mainland. From Italy, car ferries from Brindisi, Bari, and Ancona call on Corfu en route to Patras. Other ships connect with Corfu through Yugoslav ports. Corfu also has an international airport. On the island, buses provide transportation.

Guided Tours

There are dozens of travel agencies in Corfu town as well as throughout the island that offer guided bus tours or licensed guides for individual tours. Your best bet is to visit the **National Tourist Office (EOT)** in Corfu town (Arseniou St. 1, tel. 0661/305–20; 0661/397–30; 0661/303–60) and ask for a list of registered agencies.

Exploring

The town of Corfu is filled with narrow, winding, cobbled streets lined with tall, green-shuttered Italian-style houses. Much of the great fortress that dominates the town is Venetian. There is a **Son et Lumière** (sound and light) performance at the fortress weekdays at 9:30 PM.

The French occupied the island at the beginning of the 19th century and left their mark in the *Liston,* a huge open space filled with arcades facing the *Spianada* (esplanade), at the upper end of town. The townspeople gather under them in cafés and restaurants to socialize and watch the world go by. Across the water, the rugged mountains of Albania provide a dramatic backdrop to the island's leisurely lifestyle.

From 1814 to 1864, Corfu was occupied by the British, who built the handsome **High Commissioner's Palace** on the Spianada. When George I became king of the Hellenes in 1864, Britain formally ceded the Ionian Islands to Greece.

The crowded little shops of the town may not offer anything unusual, but everything is tasteful and attractively displayed. The only local specialty is comquat liquor. The simple traditional costume, still worn by some of the village women, can also be purchased.

A short way from the town of Corfu is **Kanoni,** a resort area with several large hotels and a magnificent view of two small neighboring islands. South of Kanoni, near Gastouri, is the **Achilleion,** the palace built by order of the Empress Elizabeth of Austria in 1890. Although the palace itself is generally considered a monument to bad taste, it has attractive gardens sloping down toward the sea. The Achilleion is usually open to the public during the day; its casino is open at night.

Among the numerous scenic spots with fine beaches north and south of the town of Corfu, the most beautiful and unspoiled is **Paleokastritsa** on the west coast.

Dining

For details and price category definitions, *see* Dining in Essential Information.

Quattro Stagioni. This friendly new restaurant, in the old Campiello quarter of Corfu town, serves Italian and Continental cuisine. *Korkira, tel. 0661/42–956. Dress: informal. Reservations recommended. AE, DC, MC, V. Expensive.*
Xenichtis. A full range of Greek and Continental dishes is served in this restaurant in the suburb of Mandouki, next to the Platytera Monastery. *Tel. 0661/249–11. Dress: informal. Reservations recommended. AE, DC, MC, V. Expensive.*
Lucciola. This Italian-style inn in Sgombou, on the outskirts of Corfu town, has a simple, homey restaurant open year-round. *Paleokastritsa Rd., tel. 0661/914–19. Dress: informal. Reservations not necessary. No credit cards. Inexpensive.*

Lodging

Corfu has numerous hotels, especially in the more expensive categories. Reservations are essential in the summer. For details and price category definitions, *see* Lodging in Essential Information.

Hilton International. Three miles (5 kilometers) from the town of Kanoni, this Hilton has attractive, well-kept gardens sloping to the sea and the private beach. *Kanoni, tel. 0661/365–40/9. 274 rooms with bath. Facilities: restaurant, outdoor pool, tennis, air-conditioning. DC, MC, V. Closed Nov.–Mar. Very Expensive.*
Akrotiri Beach Hotel. This beautiful resort hotel is set among pine trees just above the lovely beaches of Paleokastritsa. It does not have air-conditioning. *Paleokastritsa, tel. 0663/412–75/6. 126 rooms with bath. Facilities: restaurant, outdoor pool, beach, tennis. AE, DC, MC. Closed Nov.–Mar. Expensive.*
Cavalieri. This hotel is conveniently located on the Spianada in

Corfu town. It has an aristocratic air, even though it's rather haphazardly run. *Kapodistria 4, tel. 0661/393–36. 48 rooms with bath. Facilities: restaurant, roof garden, tennis. AE, DC, MC, V. Closed Nov.–Feb. Expensive.*

Olympic. This pleasant, somewhat colorless hotel sits on a quiet tree-lined street in the newer part of Corfu town. *Doukissas Marias 4, tel. 0661/305–32/4. 50 rooms with bath. Facilities: restaurant, tennis. AE, DC, MC, V. Moderate.*

17 Holland

Introduction

The tourist posters of Holland feature windmills, tulips, canals, and girls wearing lacy caps and clogs. All these picturesque images are to be found, certainly, but there is more to this tiny country than just these clichés.

Holland, known widely and more correctly as The Netherlands, is one of Europe's smallest countries. It has a population of around 14 million, occupying a land area that is less than half the size of Maine—15,500 square miles (40,150 square kilometers), almost half of which has been reclaimed by the industrious Dutch from the North Sea. The nation's history has been dominated by continuous resistance to two forces of invasion—the sea and successive foreign armies. Over the centuries, the Romans, Franks, Burgundians, Austrians, Spanish, English, French, and Germans have all tried to win and hold Holland, but none has succeeded for long. These endless struggles against nature and enemies have made the Dutch into a determined and independent nation, yet a remarkably tolerant one, often at the forefront of many liberal social reforms and attitudes. Religious and political freedom are an essential part of Dutch life.

Holland's eventful history and the great cultural energy of its people have created an abundance of ancient towns and buildings and filled its many museums with great artwork. The Dutch revere their past and have gone to great lengths to preserve their heritage. They also have a progressive approach toward the creation of new design and architecture and to the development of efficient services, railroads, roads, and excellent amenities for the traveler.

Despite Holland's high population density, you certainly won't be conscious of any overcrowding as you travel through the spacious, flat countryside. This green rural world, with its tree-lined roads, its canals, its charming small farms, and its flowers everywhere, is so clean and neat that you may sometimes feel you're in a vast, lovingly maintained garden. In contrast, the huge port of Rotterdam and the industrial areas will remind you that this is a highly developed commercial nation whose prosperity is built on international trade.

Some visitors stay only briefly in Holland, concentrating on such major centers as Amsterdam, The Hague (Den Haag), Delft, and Rotterdam. This is a pity, since there are many smaller historic towns and villages to see, each with its own special attractions and individual character. The country is small; road, train, and bus systems are extremely efficient, making it simple to chart your own course.

The Dutch themselves reflect a number of contrasts. They are hospitable to visiting strangers, yet fiercely independent if their values are challenged by outsiders. They are dedicated to democracy, yet enjoy being one of the world's few remaining popular monarchies. Their ideals of social behavior are, perhaps, best described by their own two words *deftig* (dignified, respectable, and decorous) and *gezellig* (cozy, comfortable, and enjoying oneself).

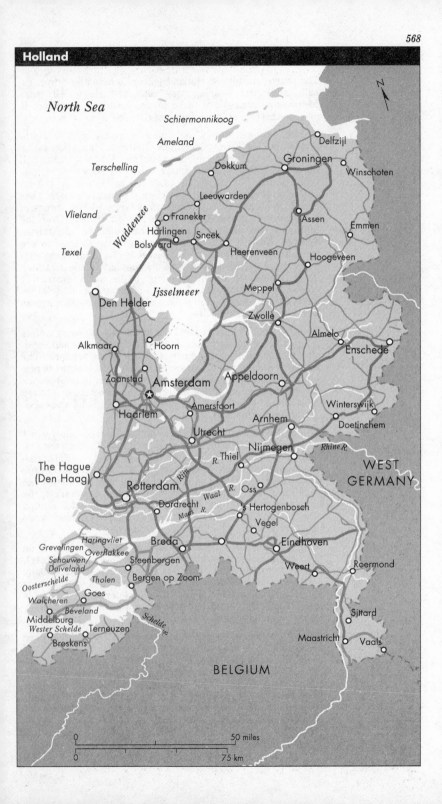

Holland

Finally, travel, shopping, dining, and lodging are made especially easy by the fact that virtually everyone in Holland speaks English.

Before You Go

When to Go The prime tourist season in Holland runs from mid-April through mid-October but peaks during school vacation periods (Easter, plus July and August) when hotels are likely to be full and may impose a high-season surcharge. Dutch bulb fields usually bloom from early April to mid-May, so hotels tend to fill up then, too. June is a good time to visit, since facilities are less busy and the weather is often excellent. Many hotels close during winter, but others offer enticing off-season discounts then.

Climate The weather is usually best during summer, when it is often warm and sunny, but beware of sudden rains and cold winds, especially by the sea. Winters are cold and wet with snow likely, but there are many bright, clear days.

The following are the average daily maximum and minimum temperatures for Amsterdam.

Jan.	40F	4C	May	61F	16C	Sept.	65F	18C
	34	1		50	10		56	13
Feb.	41F	5C	June	65F	18C	Oct.	56F	13C
	34	1		56	13		49	9
Mar.	47F	8C	July	70F	21C	Nov.	47F	8C
	38	3		59	15		41	5
Apr.	52F	11C	Aug.	68F	20C	Dec.	41F	5C
	43	6		59	15		36	2

Currency The unit of currency in Holland is the *guilden* (guilder or florin), written as Fl., which is divided into 100 cents. Bills are in denominations of 1,000, 250, 100, 50, 25, 10, and 5 guilders. Coins are 2.5 and 1 guilder and 25, 10, and 5 cents. Be careful not to confuse the 2.5 and 1 guilder coins. Bills have a code of raised dots that can be identified by touch; this is for the blind.

At press time (fall 1988), the exchange rate for the guilder was Fl. 1.8 to the U.S. dollar and Fl. 3.4 to the British pound.

Most major credit cards are accepted in hotels, restaurants, and shops, but check first; not all establishments accept all cards.

What It Will Cost Holland is a prosperous country with a high standard of living, so overall costs are similar to those in other northern European countries. Prices for hotels and other services in major cities are 10%–20% above those in rural areas. Amsterdam, The Hague, and Rotterdam are the most expensive. Hotel and restaurant service charges and the 20% value-added tax (VAT) are usually included in the prices quoted.

The cost of eating varies widely in Holland, from a snack in a bar or a restaurant "tourist menu" at around Fl. 19 to the considerable expense of gourmet cuisine. Breakfast, which is generally substantial, is usually included in the overnight hotel price.

One cost advantage of Holland over other European countries is that, because it is so small, traveling around is inexpensive, especially if you use the many price-saving transportation deals available.

Sample Prices Half a liter of wine, Fl. 10; bottle of beer, Fl. 2; cup of coffee, Fl. 2; ham sandwich, 4 Fl.; one-mile taxi ride, Fl. 10.

Museum Card The Museumkart, which can be bought either from local information offices (VVV) or from museums, is good for more than 250 museums throughout the country and will give you free or reduced admission.

Customs on Arrival There are three levels of duty-free allowance for visitors to Holland. For travelers arriving from outside Europe the allowances are (1) 400 cigarettes or 100 cigars or 500 grams of tobacco, (2) one liter of spirits more than 22% by volume or two liters of alcohol less than 22% by volume or two liters of liqueur wine and two liters of wine, (3) 50 grams of perfume, (4) other goods to the value of Fl. 500.

For travelers arriving from a non-EEC country or those coming from an EEC country who have bought goods in a duty-free shop, the allowances are (1) 200 cigarettes or 50 cigars or 100 cigarillos or 250 grams of tobacco, (2) one liter of alcohol more than 22% by volume or two liters of liqueur wine and two liters of wine, (3) 50 grams of perfume, (4) other goods to the value of Fl. 125.

For travelers arriving from an EEC country, the allowances for goods, provided they were not bought in a duty-free shop, are (1) 300 cigarettes or 75 cigars or 400 grams of tobacco; (2) 1½ liters of alcohol more than 22% by volume or three liters of alcohol less than 22% by volume or three liters of sparkling wine or three liters of liqueur wine and five liters of nonsparkling wine, (3) 75 grams of perfume and 37.5 centiliters of toilet water, (4) other goods to the value of Fl. 890.

All personal items are considered duty free, provided you take them with you when you leave Holland. Tobacco and alcohol allowances are for those 17 and older. There are no restrictions on the import and export of Dutch currency.

Language Dutch is a difficult language for foreigners, but luckily the Dutch are fine linguists, so almost everyone speaks at least some English, especially in larger cities and tourist centers. In any situation, you will be likely to find someone who is fluent, making this one of continental Europe's easiest destinations for the traveler who speaks English only.

Getting Around

By Car Holland has one of the best road systems in Europe, and even *Road Conditions* the longest trips between cities take only a few hours. Multilane expressways (toll-free) link major cities, but the smaller roads and country lanes provide more varied views of Holland. In towns, many of the streets are narrow, and there are complex one-way systems.

Rules of the Road The speed limit on expressways is 100 kph (62 mph); on major roads it is 80 kph (50 mph); on city streets and in residential areas it is 50 kph (30 mph) or less, according to the signs. Driving is on the right, as in the United States.

Parking   Parking in the larger towns is difficult and expensive, so consider parking on the outskirts of a town and using public transportation to get to the center.

Gasoline   Gas, *benzin* in Dutch, costs around Fl. 1.50 per liter.

Breakdowns   Experienced, uniformed mechanics of the *Wegenwacht* patrol the highways in yellow cars and will help if you have car trouble.

By Train   Fast, frequent, and comfortable trains operate throughout the country. All trains have first- and second-class compartments, and many have buffet or dining-car services. An express service operates from Amsterdam to Rotterdam over two routes, one via The Hague and one via Gouda, taking between an hour and an hour and a quarter. Often one train contains two separate sections that divide during the trip, so be sure you are in the correct section for your destination.

Fares   The best value in the Netherlands network (NS) is the **Rail Rover,** a ticket for unlimited train travel; You can buy one for one, three, or seven days, with no reductions for children. A second-class day pass costs Fl. 52.50; a three-day Rover costs Fl. 79.50; a seven-day Rover costs Fl. 115.50. If you buy a Rail Rover, for a small extra charge you can also get a Link Rover, which is good for unlimited travel on all public transportation within the major cities. Your passport may be needed when you purchase Rover tickets. There are also many special one-day excursion fares and sightseeing tours to major attractions. When families travel together, there can be reduced fares. Ask about these fares at railway information bureaus or local tourist offices (VVV). **The Netherlands Board of Tourism's** (NBT) offices abroad have information on train services, as do overseas offices of Netherlands Railways. **In the U.S.:** 355 Lexington Ave., New York, NY 10017, tel. 212/370–7367; **in the U.K.:** 25–28 Buckingham Gate, London SW1E 6LD, tel. 01/630–1735.

By Plane   **KLM** (Royal Dutch Airlines), under the banner of the NLM City Hopper, operates several domestic services connecting major cities. In this small country, however, it is probably as fast to travel by car or train.

By Bus   Holland has an excellent bus network between and within towns. Many bus companies offer excursions to various places of interest around the country. These trips can be booked on the spot and at local VVV offices. In major cities, the best buy is a *strippenkaart* ticket (Fl. 8.65), which can be used for all bus, tram, and metro services. Each card has 15 strips, which are canceled by the driver as you enter the vehicle. More than one person can travel on a strippenkaart, it just gets used up more quickly. You can buy a strippenkaart at train stations, post offices, and some VVV offices. A one-day *Dagkaart*, a travel-anywhere ticket, covers all urban bus/streetcar routes and costs Fl. 17.30. The NS train timetable also shows the areas served by the various bus companies. For details, write to **Streekvervoer ESO,** Postbus 19222, 3501 Utrecht.

By Bicycle   Cycling is one of the most delightful ways of getting around cities and enjoying the countryside when the weather is good. Bikes can be rented in most cities and towns, often near train stations. Rental costs around Fl. 6 per day or Fl. 25 or more per week, plus a deposit of Fl. 100–200. Local VVV offices can advise you on how and where to rent. The NBT produces a useful booklet on bike travel and tours. For a brochure detailing more than 60 cycling routes, write to **NRTU**, Postbus 326, 3900AH Veendaal. Organized, inclusive bike tours can be booked through **Ena's Bike Tours,** Box 2807, 2601CV Delft.

Essential Information

Telephones
Local Calls

The telephone system in Holland is excellent and reliable. All towns and cities have area codes that are to be used only when you are calling from outside the area. Pay phones take 25¢ and Fl. 2.50 coins. Local calls cost 25¢.

International Calls

Direct-dial international calls can be made from post offices and public booths (have plenty of coins ready). Read the instructions in the phone booth carefully, as there are several different systems. Lower rates are charged from 6 PM to 8 AM Mon. to Fri., and from 6 PM to 8 AM Fri. to Mon. Think twice before making calls, especially international calls, from your hotel room, because high service charges can double the cost.

Operators and Information

Dial 0010 for international operators, all of whom speak English (this service is not available through coin-operated booths).

Mail
Postal Rates

The Dutch post office is as efficient as the telephone network. Airmail letters to the United States cost Fl. 1.30 for the first 10 grams; postcards cost 75¢; aerograms cost Fl. 1. Airmail letters to the United Kingdom cost 75¢ for the first 20 grams; postcards cost 55¢; aerograms cost 60¢.

Receiving Mail

If you're uncertain where you'll be staying, have mail sent to Poste Restante, GPO, in major cities along your route, or to American Express offices, where a small charge will be made on collection.

Shopping

Pride of place among Dutch souvenirs must go to diamonds, for which Amsterdam is a world center. You can see diamonds being cut, polished, and set in the leading traders' factories, and, of course, you'll be encouraged to buy.

As Amsterdam is famous for diamonds, so Delft is famous for its blue and white ceramics, which may also be a little more within your price range. Lesser known, but just as attractive, is folk pottery, which is to be found in Makkum and Warkum. Edam and Gouda are famous for their cheeses, and the glassware of Maastricht and Leerdam is of a high standard. Typical souvenirs found throughout the country are wooden clogs, costumed dolls, Dutch cigars, gin, and, of course, tulip and other flower bulbs, but check your country's regulations to be certain you can bring them home.

Antiques shops and markets abound in Holland, offering a huge range of items, from silver to paintings, ceramics, and furniture. You will also find excellent pewter ware (old and new), clay pipes, liqueurs, chocolates, and candies.

VAT Refunds

Purchases of many goods leaving Holland qualify for a VAT refund of 20%, which can be claimed at the airport when you leave. Ask the salesperson for a VAT refund form when buying anything that may qualify.

Bargaining

Prices are fixed in most shops, but you can try to bargain for items in any of the open-air markets.

Opening and Closing Times

Banks. Banks are open weekdays from 9 to 4. You can also change money at **GWK bureaux de Change,** which are usually open daily 9–4 in major train and tourist centers.

Museums. Most major museums now close on Monday, but not all, so check with local VVV offices. In rural areas, some museums close or operate shorter hours during winter. Usual hours are 10–5.

Shops. In general, shops are open weekdays from 8:30 or 9 to 5:30 or 6, but some close for lunch. Department stores and most shops, especially in shopping plazas (The Hague, Amsterdam, Rotterdam) do not open until 1 PM on Monday, and many other shops close on Wednesday afternoon. Late-night shopping usually can be done until 9 PM Thursday or Friday.

National Holidays

January 1 (New Year's Day); March 26, 27 (Easter); April 30 (Queen's Day; shops open unless it falls on Sunday); May 5 (Liberation); May 4 (Ascension); May 15 (Pentecost Monday); December 25, 26 (Christmas).

Dining

Of the many earthly pleasures for the Dutch, eating probably heads the list. There is a wide variety of cuisines from traditional Dutch to Indonesian—the influence of the former Dutch colony.

Breakfasts tend to be hearty and substantial—several varieties of bread, butter, jam, ham, boiled eggs, and steaming coffee or tea. Dutch specialties for later meals include *Erwtensoep*, a rich, thick pea soup with pieces of tangy sausage or pigs' knuckles, and *Hutspot*, a meat, carrot, and potato stew; both are usually served in winter. *Haring* (herring) is particularly popular, especially the "new herring" caught between May and September and served in brine, garnished with onions. *Rodekool met Rolpens* is red cabbage and rolled spiced meat with sliced apple. If Dutch food begins to pall, try an Indonesian restaurant, where the chief dish is *rijstafel*, a huge bowl of steaming rice with 20 or more side dishes.

The indigenous Dutch liquor is potent and warming *jenever* (gin). Also popular are Dutch liqueurs and beers.

Eating places range from snack bars, fast-food outlets, and modest local cafés to gourmet restaurants of international repute. Of special note are the "brown cafés," traditional pub-style places of great character that normally offer substantial snack meals.

Mealtimes

The Dutch tend to eat dinner early, normally around 6 or 7 PM, so many restaurants close at about 10 PM and accept last orders earlier than this.

Ratings

Prices are per person including service and VAT but not drinks. For budget travelers, many restaurants offer a tourist menu at an officially controlled price, currently Fl. 18.75. Best bets are indicated by a star ★ . At press time, there were 1.8 guilders (Fl.) to the dollar.

Category	Cost: Amsterdam	Cost: Other Areas
Very Expensive	over Fl. 100	over Fl. 90
Expensive	Fl. 90–Fl. 100	Fl. 70–Fl. 90

Moderate	Fl. 50–Fl. 90	Fl. 30–Fl. 50
Inexpensive	under Fl. 40	under Fl. 30

Credit Cards The following credit card abbreviations are used: AE, American Express; DC, Diners Club; MC, MasterCard; V, Visa.

Lodging There is a wide range of accommodations in Holland. On one end are luxurious international chain hotels and traditional, though equally luxurious hotels and guest houses. At the other end are bed-and-breakfast establishments, hostels, and camping grounds.

Hotels Dutch hotels are generally spotless, no matter how modest their facilities, and service is normally courteous and efficient. There are many moderate and inexpensive hotels, most of which are relatively small. In the provinces, the range of accommodations is more limited, but there are pleasant, inexpensive family-run hotels that are usually centrally located and offer a friendly atmosphere. Most have good—if modest—dining facilities. English is spoken or understood by desk clerks almost everywhere. For a small charge, VVV offices can usually help you to find a hotel room.

Hotels usually quote room prices for double occupancy and include breakfast, service charges, and VAT. Standards of rooms do vary in older hotels, so if you do not like your room, ask to see another.

Ratings Prices are for two people sharing a double room. Best bets are indicated by a star ★. At press time, there were 1.8 guilders (Fl.) to the dollar.

Category	Cost: Amsterdam	Cost: Other Areas
Very Expensive	over Fl. 300	over Fl. 270
Expensive	Fl. 175–Fl. 300	Fl. 160–Fl. 270
Moderate	Fl. 120–Fl. 175	Fl. 100–Fl. 160
Inexpensive	under Fl. 120	under Fl. 100

Credit Cards The following credit card abbreviations are used: AE, American Express; DC, Diners Club; MC, MasterCard; V, Visa.

Tipping Hotels and restaurants almost always include 15% service and VAT in their charges. Give a doorman 50¢ to Fl. 1 for calling a cab. Bellhops in first-class hotels should be tipped Fl. 1 for each bag they carry. The official minimum for porters in train stations is Fl. 2.50 a bag; ushers in theaters and concert halls are given 25¢ for showing you to your seat, although this is not always expected. Hat-check attendants expect at least 25¢, and washroom attendants get 50¢. Hairdressers and barbers include service in their rates, but they also expect a small tip. Taxis in almost every town have a tip included in the meter charge, but you are expected to make up the fare to the nearest guilder.

Amsterdam

Arriving and Departing

By Plane Most international flights arrive at Amsterdam's Schiphol Airport, one of Europe's finest. Immigration and customs formalities on arrival are relaxed, with no forms to be completed.

Between the Airport and Downtown The best transportation between the airport and the city center is the direct rail link, with three stops en route to the Central Station, where you can get a taxi or streetcar to your hotel. The train runs every 10 to 15 minutes throughout the day and takes about half an hour. Second-class fare is Fl. 4.40.

Taxis are available at the airport, but they are expensive, about Fl. 40 to central hotels.

Getting Around

By Bus, Streetcar, and Metro A zonal fare system is used. Tickets (starting at Fl. 1.75) are bought from automatic dispensers on the metro or from the drivers on streetcars and buses; or buy a money-saving strippenkaart, *see* Getting Around By Bus. Route maps of the public transportation system are available from VVV offices.

By Taxi Taxis are expensive: The meter starts at anything from Fl. 3 to Fl. 4 and increases anywhere from Fl. 2 to Fl. 3 per kilometer. Taxis are not usually hailed on the street but are picked up at stands near stations and other key points. Alternatively, you can dial 777777.

By Bicycle Rental bikes are readily available for around Fl. 6 per day with a Fl. 100 to Fl. 200 deposit. Bikes are an excellent and inexpensive way to explore the city. Several rental companies are close to the Central Station, or ask at the VVV offices for details.

On Foot Amsterdam is a small, congested city of narrow streets, which makes it ideal for exploring on foot. The VVV issues leaflets detailing walking tours of the city center.

Important Addresses and Numbers

Tourist Information There are two VVV offices, one outside the Central Station in the Old Dutch Coffee House, Stationsplein 10, tel. 020/266444, and the other at Leidsestraat 106.

Consulates U.S., Museumsplein 19, tel. 020/790321. U.K., Koningslaan 44, tel. 020/764343.

Emergencies **Police,** tel. 020/2222; **Ambulance,** tel. 020/5555555; **Doctor, Academisch Medisch Centrum,** Meibergdreef 9, tel. 020/5669111. **Central Medical Service,** tel. 020/642111, will give you names of pharmacists and dentists as well as doctors.

English Bookstores **American Discount Book Center,** Kalverstrasse 158, 020/2555537. **Athenaeum Boekhandel,** Spui 14, tel. 020/233933, has a wide choice of English-language books.

Travel Agencies **American Express,** Damrak 66, tel. 020/262042; **Holland International,** Rokin 54, tel. 020/264466; **Key Tours** (Wagon Lits/Cooks), Dam 19, tel. 020/247310; **De Vries & Co.,** Damrak 6, tel. 020/248174.

Guided Tours

Boat Tours The most enjoyable way to get to know Amsterdam is by taking a boat trip along the canals. Several operators run trips, usually in glass-topped boats. There are frequent departures from points opposite the Central Station, by Smits Koffiehuis, beside the Damrak and along the Rokin and Stadhouderskade (near the Rijksmuseum). Most trips have multilingual guides and last from one to 1½ hours. Cost ranges from Fl. 7.50 to Fl. 12. A few have facilities for wheelchairs. Even more delightful are the nighttime trips that run in summer. They are more expensive (Fl. 29 to Fl. 35), but wine and cheese are usually included in the price.

Alternatively, you may want to rent a pedal-boat to make your own canal tour. Operated by **Canal-Bike,** the cost for one is Fl. 17.50 per hour; for details, tel. 020/265574.

Bus Tours Guided bus tours around the city are also available and provide an excellent introduction to Amsterdam. Most of these trips include brief visits to the Rijksmuseum and to a diamond-cutting factory. Bus tours on Sunday also include a canal trip.

Exploring Amsterdam

Amsterdam is a gem of a city for the tourist. Small and densely packed with fine buildings, many dating from the 17th century or earlier, it is easily explored on foot or by bike. The old heart of the city consists of canals, with narrow streets radiating out like spokes of a wheel. The hub of this wheel and the most convenient point to begin sightseeing is the Central Station. Across the street, in the Old Dutch Coffee House, is an office of VVV, offering helpful tourist information.

Amsterdam's key points of interest can be covered in two or three days, with each walking itinerary taking in one or two of the important museums and galleries. The following exploration of the city center can be broken up into several sessions.

Around the Dam

❶ Start at the **Central Station.** Just to the right, at Haalemmerstraat 75 (now an orphanage), a plaque commemorates the occasion in 1623 when the directors of the Dutch West India Company planned the founding of Nieuw Amsterdam on the southernmost tip of the island of Manhattan. In 1664, this colony was seized by the English and renamed New York.

The street directly across from the station is Prins Hendrik-
❷ kade. To the left is **St. Nicolaaskerk,** consecrated in 1306. The church is notable for its organ, stained-glass windows (dating from 1555 but extensively restored, 1761–63), and a lovely carillon. During the summer, organ concerts are held on Tuesday, Wednesday, Friday, and Saturday evenings. Beside the St.
❸ Nicolaaskerk is the **Tower of the Schreierstoren** (the Weeping or Criers' Tower), where seafarers used to say good-bye to their women before setting off to sea. The tower was erected in 1487, and a tablet marks the point from which Henrik Hudson set sail on the *Half Moon* on April 4, 1609, on a voyage that took him to what is now New York and the river that still bears his name.

Today the Weeping Tower is used as a combined reception and exposition center and Old World tavern. It also houses the world's first diamond museum. Farther left (east) at No. 131 is the house of Admiral De Ruyter, famous for his exploits against the British in the 1660s.

④ Close to the Schreierstoren, at Oudezijds Voorburgwal 40, is the **Amstelkring Museum,** whose facade carries the inscription "Ons Lieve Heer Op Solder," or "Our Dear Lord in the Attic." In 1578, Amsterdam embraced Protestantism and outlawed the church of Rome. So great was the tolerance of the municipal authorities, however, that secret Catholic chapels were allowed to exist; at one time there were 62 in Amsterdam alone. One such chapel was established in the attics of these three neighboring canalside houses, built around 1661. The lower floors were used as ordinary dwellings, while services were held in the attics regularly until 1887, the year when St. Nicolaaskerk was consecrated for Catholic worship. *Oude Zijds Voorburgwal 40, tel. 020/246604. Admission: Fl. 3. Open 10–5, Sun. 1–5.*

This is the heart of the *walletjes* or *rosse buurt*—the red-light district. If you decide to explore—and there are some noteworthy buildings in this area—take care, since purse snatching is quite common.

⑤ Return to the Damrak and continue up to the **Dam,** the broadest square in the old section of the town. It was here that the fishermen used to come to sell their catch; today it is busy with shops, people, and traffic. To the left, you will notice a simple monument to the Dutch victims of World War II. Eleven urns contain soil from the 11 provinces of Holland, while a 12th contains soil from the former Dutch East Indies, now Indonesia.

⑥ To the right of the square is the **Nieuwe Kerk** (New Church). It dates from around 1400 and is in the form of a late-Gothic cruciform basilica. It was gradually expanded until 1540, when it reached its present size. Gutted by fire in 1645, it was reconstructed in an imposing Renaissance style. The superb oak pulpit, the great organ (1645), the monumental tomb of Admiral de Ruyter, and several fine stained-glass windows are all worth noting. Today the church is used also for exhibitions and concerts.

Time Out   Just east of the Dam is **Wijnand Fockink,** a traditional tasting house for wines. Look for its doorway in a little alley: A naked Bacchus and the date 1679 on the door lead you to the small bar with a mind-boggling list of drinks. Don't walk too close to the canals if you've had the mysterious *half-en-halfje* in its special cone-shaped glass. *31 Pijlsteeg. Closes 8* PM.

⑦ The **Koninklijk Paleis** (Royal Palace) or **Dam Palace,** a vast, well-proportioned structure, was completed in 1655. It is built on 13,659 piles, sunk into the marshy soil. The great pedimental sculptures are an allegorical representation of Amsterdam surrounded by Neptune and mythological sea creatures. The seven archways at street level symbolize the then seven provinces of the Netherlands. In 1808, it was converted into a palace for Louis Bonaparte, Napoleon's brother, who abdicated two years later. *Dam, tel. 020/248698. Admission Fl. 1.50. Open summer, daily 12:30–4.*

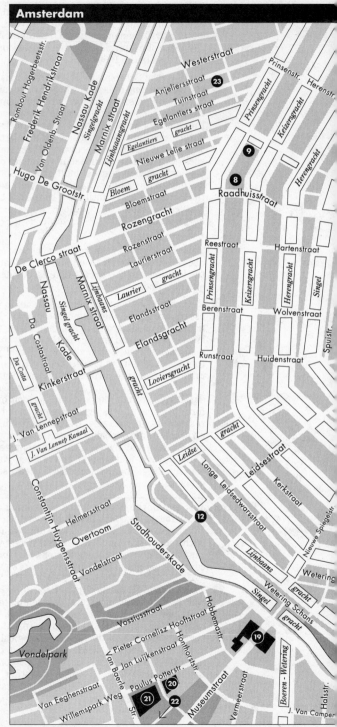

Amsterdam

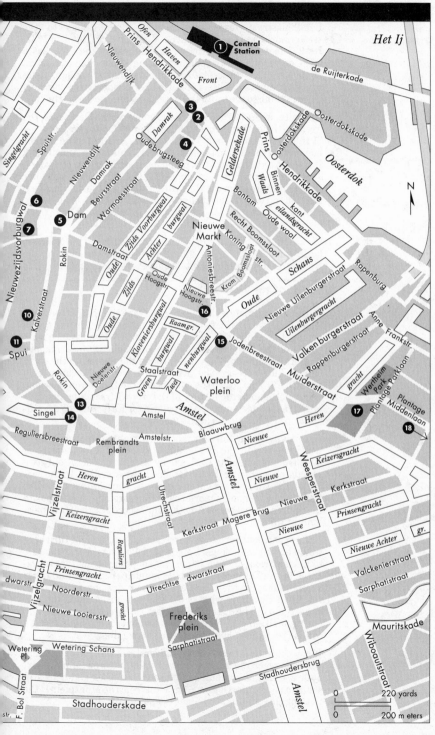

Directly behind the palace is the main post office. From here, Raadhuisstraat leads west across three canals to the **Westermarkt** and the **Westerkerk** (West Church), built in 1631. Its 275-foot (84-meter) tower, the highest in the city, has a large emperor's crown commemorating Maximilian of Austria at its summit. It also features an outstanding carillon. Rembrandt and his son Titus are buried here. During the summer, you can climb to the top of the tower for a fine view over the city.

Opposite, at Westermarkt 6, is the house where Descartes, the great 17th-century French philosopher (*"Cogito, ergo sum"*— "I think, therefore I am") lived in 1634. Another more famous house is farther down the same street. This is the **Anne Frank Huis,** immortalized by the poignant diary kept by the young Jewish girl Anne Frank, from 1942–1944, when as she and her family hid here from the German occupying forces. A small exhibition on the Holocaust can also be seen in the house. *Prinsengracht 263, tel. 020/264533. Admission: Fl. 5. Open 9–5, Sun. 10–5.*

Continuing right up the Prinsengracht, you reach the **Noorderkerk,** built 1623. In the square in front of the church, the Noorderplein, a bird market, is held every Saturday.

South of the Dam

Turning down Kalverstraat, an important shopping street that leads south from the left-hand side of the palace, you will notice among the shops and cafés the beautiful Renaissance gate (1581) of the **Burgerweeshuis** (city orphanage), once a monastery. It has an even older door around the corner, to the right on St. Luciensteeg. The attractive inner court dates from about 1670. This is also the entrance to the **Historisch Museum,** which documents the history of the city with striking displays of old maps, documents, and paintings. *Kalverstraat 92. Admission: Fl. 3.50. Open daily 9:30–5.*

Continuing down Kalverstraat, turn right into Begijnsteeg, which leads into the **Begijnhof,** a charming, quiet square of almshouses founded in 1346, among which is one of the only two remaining authentic Gothic facades in Amsterdam. In the center of the square is a church given to Amsterdam's English Reformed community more than 300 years ago, and opposite the church is another of Amsterdam's secret Catholic chapels, built in 1671.

The next street to cross Kalverstraat is **Spui.** A right turn here would bring you to Singel Canal and, following the tram tracks, to Leidsestraat, another important shopping street that terminates in the **Leidseplein,** with its municipal theater and other amusements. On the Singel's west bank, just past the lock at the Open Haven, is what is often erroneously called the narrowest house in Amsterdam. In fact, it is just a door opening onto a small alley. The real narrowest house is at Singel 166; it's called Den Gulden Fonteyn and houses a gallery.

If you continue straight along Kalverstraat instead of turning, you soon reach the **Muntplein,** with its **Munttoren** (Mint Tower, built in 1620), a graceful structure whose clock and bells still seem to mirror the Golden Age. West from the Muntplein is the floating **flower market** on Singel Canal.

Reguliersbreestraat leads east from this point to the **Rembrandtsplein,** where you will find De Gouden Hoffd, a complex of shops, cafés, and restaurants. To the right is the **Thorbeckerplein,** with its bandstand offering concerts every Sunday in the summer, in close proximity to many cafés and bars. From here, the Reguliersgracht Canal leads south across the ring canals, each of them crossed by attractive bridges.

Left (north) out of Muntplein, crossing Rokin, another shopping street, is the bridge that connects with Nieuwe Doelenstraat, home of some of Amsterdam's leading hotels. The bridge merges with Kloveniersburgwal, and on the left is the **university,** founded in 1632, and today attended by more than 10,000 students.

Cross the canal and follow the Raamgracht east to Zwanenburgwal, where the bridge to the left leads across to Jodenbreestraat. From 1639 to 1658, Rembrandt lived in the house at No. 4, now the **Museum Het Rembrandthuis.** The ground floor was used for over 20 years as living quarters; the upper floor was Rembrandt's studio. It is fascinating to visit, both as a record of life in 17th-century Amsterdam and of one of Holland's most illustrious artists. It contains a superb collection of his etchings. *Jodenbreestraat 4–6, tel. 020/249486. Admission: Fl. 2.50. Open 10–5, Sun. 1–5.*

The name Jodenbreestraat should give you a clue that Rembrandt's house was located in the midst of Amsterdam's Jewish quarter. Close by, at Waterlooplein 41, the philosopher Baruch Spinoza was born in 1632. The Dutch Israelite and Portuguese synagogues were built between 1671 and 1675, a few hundred yards east. Waterlooplein is also the site of the new **Stopera** building. The unusual name is derived from its role as Town Hall (Stadhuis) and Muzicktheater. The Waterlooplein **flea market** occupies the area around the Muzicktheater.

At the northern end of Jodenbreestraat is the **Zuiderkerk** (South Church). Built between 1603 and 1611, it was Amsterdam's first post-Reformation church. At the other end of Jodenbreestraat, on Jonas Daniel Meijerplein, is a recent addition to Amsterdam's museums. The **Joods Historisch Museum** is a complex of four synagogues, the oldest dating from 1670, with wide-ranging displays of the religious, ceremonial, and social history of the local Jewish community. *Jonas Daniel Meijerplein 204, tel. 020/269945. Admission: Fl. 5. Open Tues.– Sat. 10–5, Sun. 1–5.*

Jodenbreestraat continues east under different names to the **Hortus Botanicus** (the Botanical Gardens), **Natura Artis Magistra** (the zoo), and the **Aquarium,** which can be reached by following the streetcar line. Another half mile in the same easterly direction brings you to the **Tropenmuseum** (Tropical Museum). Its aim is to present the problems of the Third World, and there is a theater, the Soeterijn, showing movies and plays from developing nations. *Linnaeusstraat 2, tel. 020/924949. Admission: Fl. 5. Open weekdays 10–5, weekends noon–5.*

The Museum Quarter

On the southernmost edge of the outer Singelgracht Canal, a few minutes' walk from Leidseplein, you'll find three of the most distinguished museums in Holland—the Rijksmuseum,

the Stedelijk Museum, and the Rijksmuseum Vincent van
⑲ Gogh. Of the three, the **Rijksmuseum,** easily recognized by its
cluster of towers, is the most important, so be sure to allow it
adequate time. It was founded by Louis Bonaparte in 1808, but
the current rather lavish building dates from 1885. The museum contains significant collections of furniture, textiles,
ceramics, sculpture, and prints, as well as Italian, Flemish, and
Spanish paintings, many of the highest quality. But the great
pride of the Rijksmuseum is its collection of 16th- and 17th-
century Dutch paintings, a collection unmatched anywhere
else in the world. There are key works by Rembrandt (make a
point to see *The Night Watch*), Vermeer, Frans Hals, Ruysdael,
and many others. Allow at least two hours to savor these riches,
then relax in the pleasant restaurant before going on to see the
50-odd galleries containing the magnificent collections of furniture, glass, porcelain, gold, and silver. There is also a fascinating Asiatic department in the basement. *Stadhouderskade 42, tel. 020/732121. Admission: Fl. 6.50. Open Tues.–Sat.
10–5, Sun. 1–5.*

⑳ A few blocks down the road is the **Rijksmuseum Vincent van
Gogh.** This museum contains the world's largest collection of
the artist's works—200 paintings and 500 drawings—as well as
works by some 50 other painters of the period. *Paulus
Potterstraat 7, tel. 020/764881. Admission: Fl. 6.50. Open
Tues.–Sat. 10–5, Sun. 1–5.*

㉑ Next door is the **Stedelijk Museum** (Municipal Museum),
housed in a late-19th-century neoclassical building, with a
modern extension. The museum has a good collection of contemporary art, with many major artists represented—
Mondrian, Chagall, and Kandinsky, among them. It is also renowned for its stimulating temporary exhibitions. *Paulus
Potterstraat 13, tel. 020/5732911. Admission: Fl. 5. Open 11–5,
Sun. 1–5.*

Diagonally opposite the Stedelijk Museum, at the end of the
㉒ broad Museumplein, is the **Concertgebouw,** home of the two
major national orchestras, the Amsterdam Philharmonisch and
the Concertgebouworkest. Many visiting orchestras also perform here. The building has two auditoriums, the smaller of
which is used for chamber music and recitals. A block or two in
the opposite direction is **Vondelpark,** an elongated rectangle of
paths, lakes, and pleasant shady trees. A monument honors the
17th-century epic poet Joost van der Vondel, for whom the park
is named. From Wednesday to Sunday in summer, free concerts and plays are performed in the park.

Around the Jordaan

One old part of Amsterdam that must be mentioned and is cer-
㉓ tainly worth exploring is the **Jordaan,** the area between
Prinsengracht and Lijnbaansgracht. The canals and side
streets here are all named for flowers and plants. Indeed, at one
time, when this was the French quarter of the city, the area
was known as *le jardin,* a name that over the years has become
Jordaan. The best time to explore this area is on a Sunday
morning, when there are few cars and people about, or in the
evening. This part of the town has attracted many artists and
is sort of a "Bohemian" quarter, where run-down buildings are

being renovated and converted into restaurants, antiques shops, boutiques, and galleries.

Time Out   The Jordaan is the best part of Amsterdam for relaxing in a "brown café," so named because of the rich wood furnishings and—some say—because of the centuries-old pipe tobacco stains on the ceilings. Spend an hour over a beer or coffee at either **Doktorje** (Rozenboomsteeg 4) or **De Egelantier** (Egelantiersgracht 72).

What to See and Do with Children

For sightseeing, children will probably enjoy a canal boat trip in a glass-topped boat; there are many companies offering such trips. *(See* Guided Tours.)

Amsterdam's comprehensive zoo, the **Natura Artis Magistra** *(see* Exploring) has everything from ants to elephants.

With more than 40 museums, Amsterdam has plenty for children to take in. Try the **Electrische Museumtramlijn Amsterdam,** the streetcar museum, in the old Haarlemmermeer Station. There are old city streetcars on display with rides given on Saturday and Sunday. *Haarlemmermeer Station. Admission: Fl. 2.50. Open weekends 10–4.*

Children and adults alike will certainly be fascinated by the model ships and maritime exhibits at the **Scheepvaart Museum.** *Kattenburgerplein 1. Admission: Fl. 5. Open Tues.–Sat. 10–5, Sun. 1–5.*

Not to be missed is **Madame Tussaud's Waxworks Museum,** conveniently situated on one of the main shopping streets. *Kalverstraat 156, tel. 020/229949. Admission: Fl. 8. Open daily 10–6, summer 10–8.*

An unusual museum, which should appeal to most children, is the **Nationaal Spaarpotten Museum,** the money-box museum, with more than 300 piggy banks and other boxes on display. *Raadhuisstraat 20. Admission: Fl. 1. Open weekdays 1–4.*

Off the Beaten Track

An otherwise unremarkable building at **Singel 460** (near Herengracht) has a special significance for Americans. In this building—today used as an auction house—John Adams raised the first foreign loan ($2 million) for the United States from the banking house of Van Staphorst in 1782. Other loans from this and other banks soon followed, to a total of $30 million—a gesture of Dutch confidence in the future of America.

Beer lovers—or anyone with an interest in the production of a world-class product—will want to take time to visit the **Heineken Brewery.** There are two half-hour tours each morning (at 9 and 11), after which you may judge the product with some free samples. You even get a free beer stein if it's your birthday. *Van der Helstraat. Admission: Fl. 1.*

Shopping

Shopping Districts   Amsterdam's chief shopping streets, which have largely been turned into pedestrian-only areas, are the Leidsestraat;

Kalverstraat; de Nieuwendijk, on the other side of Dam Square; Rokin, somber and sedate, where the best antiques dealers are to be found; de Reulierdwasstraat, starting at Muntplein; the Nieuwe Spiegelstraat, where a series of old curiosity shops are clustered; P.C. Hoofstraat, strewn with small attractive boutiques favored by local residents; and Beethovenstraat, which converges with the Stadionweg.

Department Stores **De Bijenkorf** (Damrak) is the city's number-one department store and excellent for contemporary fashions and furnishings. Running a close second is **Vroom and Dreesman** (Kalverstraat 201) with well-stocked departments carrying all manner of goods. The restaurants and cafeterias in department stores are also worth trying.

Markets There's a lively open-air **flea market** on Waterlooplein around the Musicktheater (weekdays 10 to 4). The **flower market** is held on the Singel during weekdays and makes a lively and colorful diversion. There's a **bird market** held in the Noordmarkt every Saturday, while philatelists won't want to miss the **stamp market** at Nieuwwezijds Voorburgwal, Wednesday and Saturday afternoons. If you're interested in old books, head for the **book market** at Oudemanhuispoort, held Monday through Saturday. Go to **Nieuwe Markt** and the area around Nieuwe Spiegelstraat for small antiques shops, both specialized and general. You can also try the **Antiekmarkt de Looier,** Elandsgracht 109, open Monday to Thursday 11 to 5, Saturday 9 to 5. If you're interested in Dutch arts and crafts and watching traditional craftsmen at work try the center at Nieuwendijk 16, open Tuesday to Sunday 10 to 5.

Dining

Ratings Prices are per person including service and VAT but not drinks. For budget travelers, many restaurants offer a tourist menu at an officially controlled price, currently Fl. 18.75. Best bets are indicated by a star ★ . At press time, there were 1.8 guilders (Fl.) to the dollar.

Category	Cost
Very Expensive	over Fl. 100
Expensive	Fl. 90–Fl. 100
Moderate	Fl. 50–Fl. 90
Inexpensive	under Fl. 40

Very Expensive **Excelsior.** This restaurant, in the Hotel de l'Europe, is superb.
★ It has a varied menu of French cuisine that is based on local ingredients; try the seabass in curry sauce and the smoked eel. The service is discreet and impeccable. A special occasion deserves these elegant surroundings. *Nieuwe Doelenstraat 2–4, tel. 020/234836. Jacket and tie. Reservations required. AE, DC, MC, V. Closed Sat. lunch.*

La Rive. This is an excellent restaurant in one of the best hotels in the city. It serves superior international cuisine in the most sumptuous surroundings overlooking the Amstel River. Try its Sunday brunch of fresh salmon and champagne. *Professor Tulpplein 1, tel. 020/226060. Jacket and tie. Reservations required. AE, DC, MC, V. Closed lunch.*

Seven Seas. This restaurant is in 2 restored 17th-century mansions, close to the Holiday Inn Crowne Plaza Hotel. Its reputation is based on its excellent fish. Traditional Amsterdam recipes for herring and eel are worth trying, but the seafood also gets nouvelle and Oriental treatment. *Nieuwe Voorburgwal 5, tel. 020/200500. Jacket and tie. Reservations required. AE, DC, MC, V.*

Expensive **Dikker en Thijs.** One of the oldest good-quality restaurants in
★ town, it has typical Dutch decor and offers delightful canalside views to dine by. The cuisine is Dutch, but with unmistakable French influences evident in the sauces and some of the presentation. *Prinsengracht, tel. 020/267721. Jacket and tie. Reservations required. AE, DC, MC, V. Closed Sun.*

Edo. This restaurant is in the Grand Hotel Krasnapolsky. The cuisine is Japanese and the steaks are particularly good. But the real reason to come is to marvel at the way the freshest Dutch seafood and fish lend themselves to *sushi* preparation. *Dam 9, tel. 020/5549111. Jacket and tie. Reservations required. AE, DC, MC, V.*

De Kersentuin. This superb restaurant, in the Garden Hotel de Kersentuin, is known as one of the best in Holland. The dining room is elegant—you eat amid the greenery of a covered garden—and the menu has the flair of nouvelle cuisine originality. Try the salmon specialties. *Dijsselhofplantsoen 7, tel. 020/642121. Jacket and tie. Reservations required. AE, DC, MC, V. Closed Sun. lunch.*

Les Quatre Canetons. Pleasantly informal, this canalside restaurant is popular with local businesspeople. It serves mainly nouvelle cuisine and freshwater trout. *Prinsengracht 111, tel. 020/246307. Jacket and tie. Reservations required. AE, DC, MC, V. Closed Sat. lunch, Sun.*

't Swarte Schaep. This restaurant—the Black Sheep—dates from the 17th century and still has its narrow stairs and original wooden beams. It is particularly well known for its extensive wine list and wide-ranging menu du jour. *Korte Leidsewarsstraat, tel. 020/223021. Jacket and tie. Reservations required. AE, DC, MC, V.*

★ **d'Vijff Vlieghen.** Take a trip back into the 1600s at this restaurant that is located in 5 ancient houses with a warren of dining rooms furnished in traditional Dutch style. The menu has a touch of nouvelle cuisine, but seasonal game is a specialty. *Spuistraat 294, tel. 020/248369. Dress: casual. Reservations advised. AE, DC, MC, V. Closed lunch.*

Moderate **Bali.** Bali is one of Amsterdam's leading Indonesian restau-
★ rants. It's popular for its huge and diverse *Rijstafel* (soup, then rice accompanied by a vast range of side dishes). It's good advice to have beer or soft drinks here because the spicy sauces overshadow the taste of wine. Come with a massive appetite. *Leidsestraat 89, tel. 020/227878. Dress: casual. Reservations advised. AE, DC, MC, V. Closed Sun. lunch.*

Dorrius. This establishment has a typical Dutch-style decor and menu and is popular with businesspeople. It claims to serve the richest pea soup in Amsterdam. Among other specialties are sour meat rolls and fresh eel in season. *Nieuwe Zijds Voorburgwal 336, tel. 020/235245. Jacket and tie. Reservations required. AE, DC, MC, V. Closed Sun.*

Oesterbar. The Oesterbar's ground-floor bistro offers casual and relatively inexpensive dining, while upstairs things are a bit more concerned with style and presentation. The general theme—as the name implies—is fish and shellfish, and it is the sort of place where you can see your main course still swimming in a tank while you wait to be seated. The oysters themselves make a good, if slightly expensive, first course. *Leidseplein 10, tel. 020/362463. Dress: no jeans. Reservations advised. AE, DC.*

Sea Palace. The Sea Palace is an appropriate establishment for a city built on canals—it's a huge, floating Chinese restaurant. The Cantonese menu is only of modest quality, but the surroundings make up for it. *Oosterdokskade (near the Central Station), tel. 020/264777. Dress: casual. Reservations not usually necessary. No credit cards.*

Inexpensive
★
Keuken van 1870. Don't look for candlelit tables for two or discreet waiters hovering in anticipation of your slightest whim because the business here is eating plain, solid food in no-frills surroundings. This is the sort of place to visit when you are feeling guilty about the blowout the night before. At least it's clean and unusually good fun. *Spuistraat 4, tel. 020/248965. Dress: casual. No reservations. No credit cards. Closed weekends.*

Pancake Bakery. Here is a chance to try a traditionally Dutch way of keeping eating costs down. The name of the game is pancakes—for every course including dessert, for which the toppings can be ice cream, fruit, or liqueur. The Pancake Bakery is not far from Anne Frank Huis. *Prinsengracht 191, tel. 020/251333. Dress: casual. No reservations. No credit cards.*

Lodging

Ratings
Prices are for two people sharing a double room. Best bets are indicated by a star ★. At press time, there were 1.8 guilders (Fl.) to the dollar.

Category	Cost
Very Expensive	over Fl. 300
Expensive	Fl. 175–Fl. 300
Moderate	Fl. 120–Fl. 175
Inexpensive	under Fl. 120

Very Expensive
★
Amstel Intercontinental. The Amstel is generally considered to be the city's most exclusive hotel, with fine facilities and excellent service. It's located on the Amstel River, but if you want a room with a view of the river, be sure to say so. The views from the bar and terrace are particularly delightful. *Professor Tulpplein 1, tel. 020/226060. 111 rooms with bath. AE, DC, MC, V.*

Amsterdam Hilton. One of the first international chain hotels to open in Amsterdam, the Hilton is still one of the most gracious. In the southern part of the city, it overlooks the attractive Noorder Amstelkanal. There is a delightful glassed-in floral garden that is heated in winter. All the rooms are luxuriously appointed. *Apollolaan 138, tel. 020/780780. 274 rooms with bath. Facilities: casino. AE, DC, MC, V.*

Holiday Inn Crowne Plaza. Built behind an old facade, the Crowne Plaza is luxurious and very comfortable. All rooms have their own VCR and are lavishly equipped. The hotel is conveniently situated in the heart of the old city, near the Central Station. There are also several bars and an excellent restaurant, the Seven Seas (*see* Dining). *Nieuwe Voorburgwal, 5, tel. 020/200500. 270 rooms with bath. Facilities: swimming pool, sauna, fitness center. AE, DC, MC, V.*

Hotel de l'Europe. The Hotel de l'Europe hides its modern facilities behind a Victorian facade. It has larger than average rooms, all beautifully decorated and comfortably appointed. There's also an excellent restaurant, the Excelsior (*see* Dining). *Nieuwe Doelenstraat, 2–4, tel. 020/234836. 100 rooms with bath. Facilities: leisure complex with pool and sauna. AE, DC, MC, V.*

Expensive **Garden Hotel.** Near the Amstel Canal, this hotel is particularly striking—from its all-white lobby to the contemporary decor of its comfortable rooms. It also has one of Holland's finest restaurants, de Kersentuin (*see* Dining). *Dijsselhofplantsoen 7, tel. 020/642121. 98 rooms with bath. AE, DC, MC, V.*

Golden Tulip Pulitzer. This is one of Europe's most ambitious hotel restorations, using the shells of a row of 17th-century canalside houses. The rooms are comfortably appointed, each with its own TV/video. The patio garden is a pleasant place to relax. The hotel even has its own art gallery, with changing displays. There is also an excellent restaurant, de Goudsbloem. *Prinsengracht 315–331, tel. 020/228333. 250 rooms with bath. AE, DC, MC, V.*

★ **Grand Hotel Krasnapolsky.** This is one of the fine, Old World hotels in Amsterdam, dominated by its Winter Gardens, once a restaurant and now used for music recitals most Sundays. The cosmopolitan atmosphere carries through all the rooms, with decor ranging from Victorian to Art Deco. Each room is well equipped, and there is a choice of restaurants—Edo (*see* Dining) and the Reflet d'Or. *Dam 9, tel. 020/5549111. 370 rooms, all with bath. Facilities: garage. AE, DC, MC, V.*

Moderate **Ambassade.** With its beautiful canalside location, its Louis XV
★ (1750)-style decoration, and its Oriental carpets, the Ambassade seems more like a stately home than a hotel. Service is attentive; although there is no restaurant, the neighborhood has a good choice for eating out. *Herengracht 341, tel. 020/262333. 41 rooms with bath. AE, MC, V.*

Atlas Hotel. Renowned for its friendly atmosphere, this small hotel has moderate-size rooms, decorated in Art Nouveau style. The Atlas has a cozy bar and restaurant. It's also very handy for Museumsplein, whose major museums are within easy walking distance. Ask for a room facing Vondelpark. *Van Eegheerstraat 64, tel. 020/766336. 24 rooms with bath. AE, DC, MC, V.*

Het Canal House. This delightful hotel has been rebuilt from two canalside houses. Most rooms are spacious; larger rooms cost extra but are worth it. The American owner has recently refurbished the hotel, giving it a particularly welcoming and homey feel. *Keizersgracht 148, tel. 020/225182. 20 rooms with bath or shower. AE.*

Inexpensive **Hotel Rembrandt.** Very much a clean but basic hotel, the Rembrandt is ideal for those on a budget. Although the rooms are rather spartan, they are all quiet because of the hotel's location near the Botanical Garden and Zoo. *Plantage Middenlaan 17, tel. 020/272714. 90 rooms, some with shower. No credit cards.*

★ **Hotel Wiechman.** Both the decor and the warmth of the welcome at this affordable canalside hotel are traditional Dutch. There is good value, also, at the hotel's dining room and lounge bar. *Prinsengracht 328, tel. 020/263321. 35 rooms, 12 with bath or shower. No credit cards.*

The Arts

The arts flourish in tolerant and cosmopolitan Amsterdam. The best sources of information about performances are the monthly publication, *What's On* (in English), or the weekly *Amsterdam This Week;* both can be obtained free from the VVV office, which also can help in obtaining tickets for the more popular events.

Classical Music Classical music is featured at the **Concertgebouw,** on Van Baerlestraat 98. The Concertgebouw Orchestra ranks among the best in Europe. A smaller auditorium in the same building is used for chamber music, recitals, and even jam sessions.

Opera and Ballet The Dutch national companies are housed in the new Muzicktheater on Waterlooplein. Guest companies from foreign countries perform there during the three-week Holland Festival in June.

Movies The largest concentration of movie theaters is on Leidseplein and Reguliersbreestraat. Most foreign films are subtitled rather than dubbed, but to be sure—and to find out times—see *Amsterdam This Week.*

Entertainment and Nightlife

Amsterdam has a wide variety of nightclubs, bars, and cabarets, including some that surpass even the "hot spots" of cities such as Hamburg; none, however, has the elegance of Paris. Apart from the very expensive live shows around Rembrandtsplein, Leidseplein, and Thorbeckeplein, there are plenty of respectable, though earthy, nightclubs and near-honkytonk spots. Names and locations change from year to year, but most bars and clubs are open every night from 5 PM to 2 AM or 4 AM. It is wise to steer clear of the area around the Central Station at night. Except on weekends, very few of the nightclubs charge admission, though the more lively ones sometimes ask for a "club membership" fee of Fl. 15 or more. Drink prices are normally not exorbitant.

Cabaret If you are looking for a floor show, the **Carousel** (Thorbeckeplein 20) is popular with Amsterdam's socialites. It is an informal spot, with topless waitresses, and you'll be welcomed as a player if you bring your own instrument.

Bars The **Bamboo Bar** (Lange Leidsewarsstraat) is informal, expensive, relaxing, and typically international. It boasts the longest bar in Amsterdam.

Jazz Clubs For live music and singing, try **Cab Kaye's Jazz Piano Bar** (Beulingstraat 9). If you're longing for good Dixieland jazz, go to **Joseph Lam Jazz Club** (van Diemenstraat 8), which is only open Friday to Sunday.

Rock Clubs **Be-Bop** (Amstelstraat 24) caters to the slightly older-than-teenage crowd. A very trendy scene for teenagers and college-age music fans is **De Bios** (Leidseplein 12); it's open from 10 PM, and entrance is free.

Discos   **Disco Escape** (Rembrandtsplein 15) provides a lively pop scene; programs are recorded here for satellite TV. **Stip** (Lijnbaansgracht 161) offers live music.

Amsterdam Environs

This circular itinerary can be followed either clockwise or counterclockwise, but whichever way you decide to take it, you'll be sure to see some of Holland's most characteristic sights. There are the historic towns of Leiden and Utrecht and the major museums in Haarlem; in between these towns, you'll see the best of Holland's windmill-dotted landscape and pass through centers of tulip growing and cheese production.

Getting Around

The most convenient way to cover the following itinerary would be by rented car out of Amsterdam. If you want someone else to do the navigating, then all these destinations can be reached by train or bus as well. Check with the VVV office in Amsterdam for help in planning your trip.

Guided Tours

Alternatively, these towns are covered, in various permutations, by organized bus tours out of Amsterdam. Brochures for tour operators are available from the VVV offices in Amsterdam, either from Stationplein 10, tel. 020/266444, or from Leidsestraat 106.

Tourist Information

Amersfoort. Stationsplein 28, tel. 033/635151.
Apeldoorn. Stationsplein 6, tel. 055/788421.
Gouda. Markt 27, tel. 01820/13666.
Haarlem. Stationsplein 1, tel. 023/319059.
Leiden. Stationsplein 210, tel. 071/146846.
Utrecht. Vredenburg 90, tel. 030/314132.

Exploring

Apeldoorn   Traveling southeast from Amsterdam, 56 miles (90 kilometers) along highway A1, you will first visit **Apeldoorn,** but if you have time, stop off at **Amersfoort** en route. Although today it is a major industrial town, Amersfoort still manages to retain much of its medieval character and charm. Starting at the **Koppelport,** the imposing water gate across the Eem, dating from 1400, walk down Kleine Spui. On the right is **St. Pieters-en-Bloklands Gasthuis,** a hospice founded in 1390. Close by is the **Museum Flehite,** with its unusual medieval collections that give a fascinating insight into the history of the town. *Westsingel 50. Admission: Fl. 2. Open Tues.–Fri. 10–5, weekends 2–5.*

Continuing along Breestraat, you'll come to the graceful, 330-foot (100-meter-)high **Onze Lieve Vrouwetorn** (Tower of Our Lady). It's typically Gothic in style and has a delightful carillon that can be heard every Friday between 10 and 11 AM. Turning left down Langstraat, past the Gothic **St. Joriskerk,** you come to the **Kamperbinnenpoort,** the turreted land gate dating from the 15th century. Making your way left down Muurhuizen, you

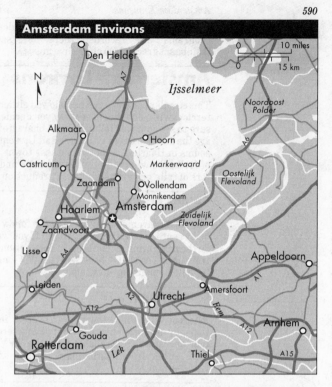

Amsterdam Environs

0 10 miles
0 15 km

N

Den Helder

Ijsselmeer

Noordoost
Polder

Alkmaar

Hoorn

Castricum

Markerwaard

Zaandam

Vollendam

*Oostelijk
Flevoland*

Monnikendam

Haarlem Amsterdam

*Zuidelijk
Flevoland*

Zaandvoort

Lisse

Appeldoorn

Leiden

Amersfoort

Utrecht

Arnhem

Rotterdam

Gouda

Lek

Thiel

come to a short canal, the **Hovik,** which was once the old harbor.
Just across from the Hovik you're back at the Museum Flehite.

The main attraction at **Apeldoorn** is the **Rijksmuseum Paleis
Het Loo.** This former royal palace was built in the late 17th century for Willem III and has been beautifully restored to
illustrate the domestic surroundings enjoyed by the House of
Orange for more than three centuries. The museum, which is
housed in the stables, has a fascinating collection of royal memorabilia, including cars and carriages, furniture and photographs, silver and ceramics. The formal gardens and the
surrounding parkland offer attractive walks. *Admission Fl.
2.50. Open Tues.–Sun. 10–5.*

Utrecht West from Apeldoorn (44 miles, 72 kilometers), is the city of
Utrecht, with so much to see that you may decide to spend a
couple of days here. The high gabled houses, the canals with
their water gates, the 13th century wharves and storage cellars, and the superb churches and museums are just some of the
key attractions, most of which are situated around the main cathedral square. The **Domkerk** (cathedral) was built between
1254 and 1517 on the site of a much earlier church, and it contains many monumental tombs and a series of fine modern
stained-glass windows. Across from the cathedral is its bell
tower, which was attached to the main body of the church until
the nave collapsed in 1674, separating the two. You can climb
the 456 steps to the top of the tower for a magnificent view of
the city. *Domplein. Admission: Fl. 1.50. Open May–mid-
Sept., 10:30–5.*

Close by the cathedral are two interesting museums, the **Nationaal Museum van Speelklok tot Pierement,** devoted to music machines—from music boxes to street organs (Achter de Dam 10. Admission: Fl. 3.50. Open Tues.–Sat. 11–5, Sun. 1–5), and the **Hedendaagse Kunst,** with its collection of modern art (Achter de Dam 14. Free. Open Tues.–Sun. 1–5).

Behind the museums is **Pieterskerk,** the country's oldest Romanesque church, built in 1048. Among the city's other Romanesque churches are Jacobikerk, Buurkerk, Nicolaikerk, and Janskerk.

Walk south out of Domplein, down Lange Nieuwstraat. Halfway down to your left is St. Catharijnekerk, on the left, which now houses the **Rijksmuseum Het Catharijneconvent.** This museum of Dutch religious history has interesting collections of paintings, sculpture, vestments, and religious relics. *Nieuwe Gracht 63. Admission: Fl. 3.50. Open Tues.–Fri. 10–5, weekends 11–5.*

Also in this area are some charming almshouses; the **Bruntenhofje,** on Lepelenburg, for women, and the **Bartholomei Gasthuis,** on Langesmee, for men. Continue walking down Lange Nieuwstraat past the **Butcher's Guildhall,** dating from 1673; the **Cracknel House** in Keistraat, with its extraordinary decorations; and the chained **"Devil's Stone"** on the Oude Gracht.

There are more museums to be explored on Agnientenstraat, which runs across Lange Nieuwstraat. The **Centraal Museum** houses the municipal collection of pictures and exhibits on the city. Particularly interesting is a ship unearthed in 1930 that is thought to date from the 9th century. *Agnietenstraat 1. Free. Open Tues.–Sat. 10–5, Sun. 2–5.*

Close by, following Tolstee Singel and Malie Singel, in the old train station, is the **Nederlands Spoorwegmuseum,** the Dutch Rail Museum. This is a must for train buffs. There are many steam engines, including a copy of one built in 1839, as well as smaller rail mementos. *Johan van Oldenbarneveltlaan 6. Admission: Fl. 1.50. Open Tues.–Sat. 10–5, Sun. 11–5.*

Gouda West of Utrecht, 22 miles (36 kilometers) along the A12, you come to **Gouda,** famous for its cheese. Try to be there on a Thursday morning in July or August, when the cheese market, centered around the **Waag** or Weigh House, is held. Brightly colored farm wagons are loaded high with orange cheeses. While the bargaining goes on, you can sample the cheese by stepping into the back of the **Stadhuis** (Town Hall), where a film explains how the cheese is made. Take a good look at the Stadhuis; it's one of Holland's quaintest, with parts dating back to 1449.

By the side of the market square is **Sint Janskerk;** what you see today was built in the 16th century. It has the longest nave in the country, 400 feet (122 meters) and 70 glorious stained-glass windows, the oldest of which dates from 1555. Around the corner from the cathedral is the Cathorina Gasthuis, now the **Stedelijk Museum Het Catharina Gasthuis,** the municipal museum that houses many unusual exhibits, including a fearsome collection of medieval surgical instruments. *Oosthaven 10. Admission: Fl. 2. Open Tues.–Sat. 10–5, Sun. noon–5.*

Leiden Heading due north on A4, you come to the ancient university city of **Leiden,** with its attractive streets and buildings. Make a start at the **Lakenhal,** built in 1639 for the city's cloth merchants and now an art gallery, cloth, and antiques museum. Pride of place in the collection goes to the 16th- and 17th-century Dutch paintings, with works by Steen, Dou, Rembrandt, and, above all, the triptych by Lucas van Leyden—the first great Dutch Renaissance painting. Other rooms are devoted to furniture, the history of the cloth guild, and the pilgrim fathers. *Oude Singel 28. Admission: Fl. 2.50. Open Tues.–Sat. 10–5, Sun. 1–5.*

Near the Lakenhal, there are other museums. The **Molenmuseum** (the Windmill Museum) is a small museum, actually in the windmill, and contains implements of the miller's craft. *Binnenvestgracht 2. Admission: Fl. 2.50. Open Tues.–Sat. 10–5, Sun. 1–5.*

The **Museum Boerhaave** (National Science Museum) is a splendid and fascinating place containing many important and historic Dutch scientific instruments, such as the two globes that belonged to the cartographer Blaeu, microscopes made by Van Leeuwenhoek, thermometers made by Farenheit, an early planetarium, and much more. *Steenstraat 1. Admission: Fl. 3.50. Open Tues.–Sat. 10–5, Sun. 1–5.*

Across from the science museum is the **Rijksmuseum voor Volkenkunde,** the Ethnographical Museum, which has a particularly rich collection of exhibits from the Far East, Africa, and the Americas. *Steenstraat 1. Admission: Fl. 3.50. Open Tues.–Sat. 10–5, Sun. 1–5.*

Crossing the canal and walking into narrow, bustling Breestraat, you'll come to the imposing **St. Pieterskerk,** with its memories of the pilgrim fathers who worshiped here and of their spiritual leader, John Robinson, who is buried here. A narrow street by the **Persijnhofje** almshouse, dating from 1683, takes you downhill, across the pretty Rapenburg Canal to the **university,** the **Hortus Botanicus** gardens, and the nearby **Museum van Oudheden,** containing prehistoric, Egyptian, Greek, and Roman antiquities. *Rapenburg 28. Admission: Fl. 3.50. Open Tues.–Sat. 10–5, Sun. 1–5.*

Follow Keiserstraat out of Rapenburg and turn left into Boisotkade. On your left is the **Pilgrim Fathers Documentatie Centrum.** This tiny museum contains photocopies of documents and maps related to the Pilgrims during their stay in Leiden, before going to Delftshaven on the first stage of their arduous voyage to the New World. *Vliet 45. Free. Open Mon.–Fri. 9:30–4:30.*

If you're interested in geology, walk northward across town via Steenschuur, Nieuwstraat, and Hooglandskerkgracht to the **Rijksmuseum van Geologie en Mineralogie** (the National Geological and Mineralogy Museum), which has excellent displays of minerals, jewels, and meteorites galore. *Hoolandsekerkgracht 17. Admission: Fl. 3. Open Mon.–Fri. 10–5, Sun. 2–5.*

Haarlem Continue north along the A12 for 20 miles (32 kilometers) to **Haarlem,** stopping off at **Lisse** if you have time, to visit the 70-acre (283,000 square kilometers) Keukenhof Gardens, a unique flower exhibition with amazing displays of tulips and other blooms (open late Mar.–late May, daily 8–7:30). Haarlem is one of Holland's earliest centers of art and was at its creative peak in the 16th and 17th centuries. The area around the large market square is surrounded by majestic architecture from the 15th to the 19th centuries. The **Stadhuis** (Town Hall) was once a hunting lodge, and the site dates from the 13th century, though there have been many changes since then. Nearby is the **Vleeshal,** or meat market, which has an especially fine gabled front. This dates from the early 1600s and is now used as an art gallery and museum of local history. *Lepelstraat. Free. Open Mon.–Sat. 10–5, Sun. 1–5.*

Across from the Vleeshal is the **Grote Kerk,** dedicated to St. Bavo. The church, built between 1400 and 1550, houses one of Europe's most famous organs. This massive instrument has 5,000 pipes and both Mozart and Handel played on it. It is still used for concerts, and an annual organ festival is held here in July. Make your way down Damstraat, behind the Grote Kerk, and turn left at the **Waag** (Weigh House). On the left is the **Teylers Museum,** which claims to be the oldest museum in the country. It was founded by a wealthy merchant in 1778 as a museum of science and the arts; it now houses a fine collection of the Hague school of painting as well as a collection of drawings and sketches by Michelangelo, Raphael, and other non-Dutch masters. *Spaarne 16. Admission: Fl. 2.50. Open Tues.–Sat. 11–5, Sun. 1–5.*

Follow the Binnen Spaarn and turn right into Kampervest and then Gasthuisvest. On your right, in Grootheligland, you'll find the **Frans Hals Museum.** This museum, in what used to be a hospice, contains a marvelous collection of the artist's work; his paintings of the guilds of Haarlem are particularly noteworthy. The museum also has works by Hals's contemporaries. *Grootheligland. Admission: Fl. 3. Open Mon.–Sat. 11–5, Sun. 1–5.*

Dining and Lodging

For details and price category definitions, *see* Dining and Lodging in Essential Information.

Amersfoort
Dining

De Witte. This excellent hotel restaurant offers specialty dishes such as fresh asparagus. Meals are served either in the cozy dining room or on the covered, heated terrace. Attentive service is guaranteed. *Utrechtseweg 2, tel. 033/14142. Jacket and tie. Reservations advised. AE, DC, MC, V. Closed Sat. lunch, Sun. Expensive.*

Lodging

Berghotel Amersfoort. The Berghotel is on the edge of town and commands fine views. All the rooms are comfortably furnished and the atmosphere is pleasantly relaxed. *Utrechtseweg 225, tel. 033/620444. 40 rooms, all with bath or shower. Facilities: tennis, miniature golf. AE, DC, MC, V. Moderate.*

Apeldoorn
Dining

De Echoput. This delightful restaurant is one of the best in town. There's a terrace, surrounded by greenery, for summer dining. De Echoput is out of the center of town but well worth the detour. *Amersfoortseweg 86, tel. 05769/248. Jacket and tie. Reservations essential. AE, DC, MC, V. Closed Sat. lunch, Mon. Expensive.*

★ **'t Koetshuis.** This restaurant is about 7 miles (10 kilometers) south of town beside the 14th-century Cannenburgh Castle.

Game and French cuisine are the specialties of this spot, all served in an intimate setting. *Maarken van Rossumsplein 1, tel. 05788/1501. Jacket and tie. Reservations essential. AE, DC, MC, V. Closed Mon. Expensive.*

Gouda **Mallemolen.** Mallemolen has a traditional Dutch interior with
Dining carved wood and Delft tiles much in evidence. The cuisine is traditional, too, with a choice of Dutch or French dishes. *Oosthaven 72, tel. 01820/15430. Jacket and tie. Reservations advised. AE, DC, MC, V. Closed Sun., Aug. Expensive.*

D'Ouwe Stee. If the weather permits, dine on the water's edge terrace; if not, the antique Dutch interior is just as charming. Though about 4 miles (6 kilometers) out of town, the trip is worth it for the fresh seafood. *'S-Gravenbroekseweg 80, tel. 01829/4008. Dress: studied casual. Reservations advised. AE, DC, MC, Closed Tues. Expensive.*

Rotisserie l'Etoile. This is a classic restaurant but with a modern style. Owner-chef R. Jorna has created a varied menu with both meat and fish specialties. He claims there are more than 100 different wines in his cellar. *Blekerssingel 1, tel. 01820/12253. Jacket and tie. Reservations advised. AE, DC, MC, V. Closed Sat. lunch, Sun. Expensive.*

Haarlem **Bokkedoorns.** This elegant French restaurant with a pleasant
Dining ambience is about 2 miles (3 kilometers) west of Haarlem, set amid the sand dunes at Bloemendaal. The house specialties are mainly seafood. *Zeeweg 53, tel. 023/263600. Dress: studied casual. Reservations recommended. AE, DC, MC, V. Expensive.*

★ **De Coninckshoek.** The restaurant is situated in a beautiful old wine house dating from the 1650s. You'll be offered a choice of classic or nouvelle cuisine or just an aperitif or snack if you prefer. *Koningsstraat 1–5, tel. 023/314001. Dress: studied casual. Reservations not necessary. AE, DC, MC, V. Closed Sun. Expensive.*

Kraantje Lek. This is another restaurant just out of town at Bloemendal. It is a simple rustic inn offering good wholesome Dutch cuisine. *Duinlustweg 22, tel. 023/241266. Dress: studied casual. Reservations not necessary. AE, DC, MC, V. Moderate.*

Leiden **Rotisserie Oudt Leyden.** This restaurant, near the Lakenhal,
Dining has a traditional Dutch interior and a good French and Dutch menu. An adjoining crêperie (moderate) serves typical Dutch *pannekocken,* (pancakes) on blue Delft plates. *Steenstraat 51, tel. 071/133144. Jacket and tie. Reservations recommended. AE, DC, MC, V. Closed Sun. Expensive.*

Lodging **Holiday Inn.** The rooms are well appointed and comfortable, and the restaurant, the Dutch Mill, is excellent. *Haagse Schouweg 10, tel. 071/355555. 220 rooms, all with bath. Facilities: tropical garden, swimming pool, solarium, sauna. AE, DC, MC, V. Expensive.*

Lisse **De Nachtegaal van Lisse.** This hotel, just outside town, is ideal
Lodging for visitors to the Keukenhof Gardens. The rooms are well equipped, and the restaurant serves international cuisine. *Heereweg 10, tel. 02521/14447. 148 rooms, all with bath. Facilities: swimming pool, tennis. AE, DC, MC, V. Expensive.*

Utrecht **Hoog Brabant.** The specialties here are the excellent meat and
Dining fish grills. It's right across from the train station. *Radboud-*

kwartier 23, tel. 030/331525. Jacket and tie. Reservations advised. AE, DC, MC, V. Closed Sun. Expensive.

Jean d'Hubert. In this small but modern restaurant, owner J. Bogaard will encourage you to order his 5-course menu—*Le Diner des Rois*—but there's an excellent à la carte menu, too. *Vleutenseweg 228, tel. 030/945952. Jacket and tie. Reservations advised. AE, DC, MC. Closed Sat. lunch, Sun., Mon. Expensive.*

Lodging **Holiday Inn.** This large hotel is close to the Exhibition and Conference Center. All the rooms are comfortable and equipped to the highest standards. It has several restaurants, of which the Utrecht House is the best. Go to the Rail Road Bar on the 21st floor for a magnificent view of the city. *Jaarbeursplein 24, tel. 030/910555. 280 rooms with bath. Facilities: swimming pool, sauna. AE, DC, MC, V. Expensive.*

Des Pays-Bas. This centrally located hotel is ideal for exploring the city. All the rooms are clean and comfortable, and the restaurant offers a wide international menu. *Janskerkhof 10, tel. 030/333321. 47 rooms with bath. AE, DC, MC, V. Expensive.*

The Hague, Scheveningen, and Delft

Within this itinerary you can visit The Netherlands's most dignified and spacious city, the royal, diplomatic, and governmental seat of Den Haag (in English, better known as The Hague); its close neighbor, the leading North-Sea beach resort of Scheveningen; and nearby Delft, a history-packed city with many canals and ancient buildings.

Getting Around

The Hague and Delft are on a main train line from Amsterdam with frequent service throughout the day; the trip takes about an hour. The hearts of both towns are compact enough to be explored on foot. Scheveningen is reached from The Hague's center by bus or tram. Travelers will find public transport more convenient than driving because of severe parking problems at the resort. If the weather is bad or walking becomes tiring, taxis are readily available.

Guided Tours

City sightseeing tours of The Hague can be arranged by or through the local VVV office, next to the Central Station in the Babylon Center. Scheveningen can easily be explored on foot: Get a map from the VVV office at the corner of Scheveningseslag and Gev. Deijnootweg. Walking and boat tours of Delft can be arranged through the VVV office in Delft at Markt 85.

Tourist Information

Delft. Markt 85, tel. 015/126100.
The Hague. Babylon Center, tel. 070/546200.
Scheveningen. Corner of Scheveningseslag and Gev. Deijnootweg, tel. 070/546200.

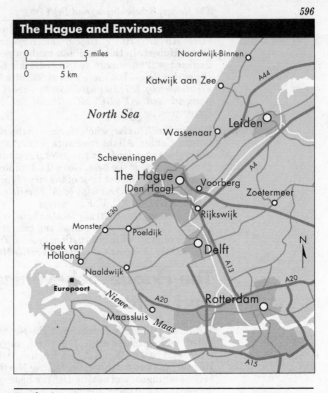

The Hague and Environs

0 — 5 miles
0 — 5 km

North Sea

Noordwijk-Binnen
Katwijk aan Zee
A44
Leiden
Wassenaar
Scheveningen
A4
The Hague (Den Haag)
Voorberg
Zoetermeer
Rijkswijk
E30
Monster
Poeldijk
Delft
A13
N
Hoek van Holland
Naaldwijk
Europoort
Nieuwe
A20
Rotterdam
A20
Maassluis
Maas
A15

Exploring

The Hague   The heart of **The Hague** is the **Ridderzaal** (Knight's Hall), the center of a government complex, by the charming Vijver lake. Inside are vast beams spanning a width of 59 feet (18 meters), flags, and stained-glass windows. A sense of history pervades this 13th-century great hall. It can be visited whenever it is not in use for official functions. The two chambers of Parliament sit separately in buildings on either side of the Ridderzaal.

Keeping the Ridderzaal on your right, pass through two narrow archways and emerge on the far side of the **Binnenhof,** the former Inner Court of the castle. The small, well-proportioned Dutch Renaissance building immediately on your left, its back bordering Vijver lake, is the **Mauritshuis,** one of the greatest art museums, for its size, in the world. This superb 17th-century palace, built originally for Count Johan Maurits van Nassau, contains a feast of the finest in Dutch 17th-century art, including 15 Rembrandts. *Korte Vijverberg 8. Admission: Fl. 5. Open Tues.–Sat. 10–5, Sun. 11–5.*

From the Mauritshuis, the Korte Vijverberg and Lange Vijverberg extend along the east and north sides of the Vijver lake: They are lined with houses whose facades reflect the stately aspect of The Hague during the 18th and 19th centuries. Parallel with Korte Vijverberg, Lange Houtstraat, with its cluster of nightclubs and jazz centers, leads north from the far side of the Plein to Toernooiveld. On the corner, across from the U.S. Embassy, is the **Koninklijke Schouwburg** (Royal Theater), which occupies a former palace of Nassau-Weilburg dating from 1770. This walk brings you to the L-shaped Lange Voorhout, a broad avenue lined with trees—an area of concert halls and some exclusive *couturiers* and fashionable hairdressers.

Along the Lange Voorhout's right-hand axis is the former **Koninklijke Bibliotheek** (Royal Library), which is being restored and redesigned as the Supreme Court. The **Royal Library,** which contains more than a million books, is now at Prins Willem Alexanderhofs, near the Central Station. The new building is striking, its modern design giving the impression of a huge ship.

With its skewed gable, Lange Voorhout 6, the remarkable building of the Dutch headquarters of the Red Cross, seems strangely out of place on this stately avenue. A few doors on, at the corner of Parkstraat, is The Hague's oldest church, the **Kloosterkerk,** built in 1400, and once used by the Black Friars.

On the far side of Plaats square, overlooking the lake, is the 14th-century **Gevangenpoort** (Prison Gate). For many centuries a prison, it is today a museum of instruments of torture *Buitenhof 33. Admission: Fl. 3.50. Open Mon.–Fri. 10–5; Apr.–Sept. only, also on Sun. 1–5.*

The Plaats, along with the Hoogstraat and Noordeinde running behind, is a pedestrians-only shopping center, bright with flowers, attractive shops, and coffee bars.

As you leave the Gevangenpoort, a right-hand turn brings you to the **Buitenhof** (Outer Court), opposite the entrance to the Binnenhof and Ridderzaal, where this tour began. Around its edges are several open-air restaurants and cafés.

Follow the streetcar line to the right into Gravenstraat to catch a glimpse of the 321-foot (98-meter) tower of the 15th-century **Grote or Sint Jacobs Kerk.** In between, facing the Groenmarkt, is The Hague's original Town Hall, the **Oude Stadhuis,** dating from 1565.

Return north across the center of The Hague to Zeestraat 65b, a building designed especially to display the **Panorama Mesdag,** a painting-in-the-round showing Scheveningen as it looked in 1880. Forty-five feet (14 meters) high, the canvas that encompasses you in its 400-foot (122-meter) circumference is amazingly lifelike. *Admission: Fl. 3. Open Mon.–Sat. 10–5, Sun. noon–4.*

Just around the corner in Laan van Meerdervoort is the house of painter Henrik Mesdag, now the Rijksmuseum H. W. Mesdag. Examples of his work are hung here beside those of Delacroix, Corot, Millet, and Rousseau. *Laan van Meerdervoort 7f. Admission: Fl. 3.50. Open Tues.–Sat. 10–5, Sun. 1–5.*

The **Vredespaleis** (Peace Palace), just behind Laan van Meerdervoort, is a monument to an ideal that still remains unrealized. Following the first peace conference at The Hague in 1899, the American millionaire Andrew Carnegie donated $1.5 million for the construction of a building to house the proposed Permanent Court of Arbitration. The Dutch government donated the grounds, and many other nations offered furnishings and decorations. The red-and-gray granite-and-brick building, built in Flemish style, was dedicated in 1913. Today, the **International Court of Justice**, consisting of jurists from 15 nations, has its seat here. There are guided tours daily when the court is not in session; tel. 070/469680 for details.

The adjacent **Haags Gemeentemuseum** (Municipal Art Museum) is the home of the largest collection of Mondrians in the world and a fascinating building in itself. It was built in 1935 and is an example of the International Movement in modern architecture. *Stadhouderslaan 41. Admission: Fl. 2. Open Tues.–Fri. 10–5, weekends noon–5.*

Between the Vredespaleis and the Haags Gemeentemuseum is the huge, modern **Congress Centre**. It contains three theaters and a concert hall that is the official home of the famous Residency Symphony Orchestra. The **Omniversum**, described as Europe's first space theater, is housed in a cylindrical building with a 75-foot (23-meter-)high dome that acts as a screen for the projection of striking presentations, not only of outer space but of other trips, such as oceanographic voyages. *President Kennedylaan 5, tel. 070/545454.*

One of The Hague's greatest attractions is **Madurodam**, a miniature city where everything is on a scale of 1/52 of lifesize. It occupies one acre on the left (south) side of one of the canals connecting The Hague with Scheveningen. Follow Prinsessegracht and Koniginnegracht to Haringkade. None of the details of a real city has been forgotten, from the harbor with its lighthouse, quayside cranes, and ferries to the airport with its bustle of planes. *Haringkade 175. Admission: Fl. 8. Open Apr.–July, daily 9:30 AM–10 PM; July–Sept., daily 9:30 AM–11 PM; Sept.–1st Sun. in Oct., daily 9:30–9:30; closed 2nd Mon. in Oct.–Apr.*

Scheveningen   **Scheveningen** is adjacent to The Hague, to the north. A fishing village since the 14th century, it became popular as a beach resort during the last century, when the Kurhaus Hotel was built. After years of decline, the resort has become popular again and has been revitalized, with a casino, shops, restaurants, bars, and discos.

The beach itself, protected from tidal erosion by stone jetties, slopes gently into the North Sea in front of a high promenade whose function is to protect the boulevard and everything behind it from the fury of the winter storms. The surface of the beach is fine sand, on which it is possible to bicycle or walk for miles to the north.

The Pier, completed in 1961, stretches 1,200 feet (366 meters) into the sea. Its four circular end buildings provide an attractive sun terrace and restaurant, a 141-foot (43-meter-)high observation tower, an amusement center with children's play area, and an underwater panorama. Part of the new design around the Kurhaus area includes the Golfbad, a "surf pool," complete with artificial waves.

Delft   Eight miles (13 kilometers) along the A13 from The Hague, you enter **Delft**. There is probably no spot in The Netherlands that is more intimate, more attractive, or more traditional than this little town, whose famous blue-and-white earthenware is so popular throughout the world. Compact and easy to explore, despite its web of canals, Delft is best discovered on foot, although water taxis are available in summer, when, on

Tuesday, Wednesday, Friday, and Saturday, you also can enjoy a ride on a horse-drawn bus that leaves from the market place. Every street is lined with attractive medieval Gothic and Renaissance houses.

In the marketplace, the only lively spot in this tranquil town, is the **Nieuwe Kerk** (New Church), built in the 14th century, with its piercing Gothic spire 300 feet (91 meters) high, magnificent carillon of 48 bells, and the tomb of Willem the Silent. Beneath this grandiose sarcophagus is a crypt containing the remains of members of the Orange-Nassau line, including all members of the royal family since King Willem I ascended the throne in the mid-16th century.

While in Delft, you will certainly want to see the famous local specialty—Delftware. Decorated porcelain was brought to Holland from China on East India Company ships and was so much in demand that Dutch potters of the time felt their livelihood was being threatened, so they set about the creation of pottery to rival Chinese porcelain. The most famous manufacturers are **De Porceleyne Fles**, Rotterdamseweg 196; **De Delftse Pauw**, Delftweg 133; and **Atelier de Candelaer**, Kerkstraat 13. On the other side of the marketplace is the **Town Hall**, with a collection of paintings by Delft artists.

Walk around the right side of the Nieuwe Kerk, then left at the back and along the Vrouwenregt canal for a few steps before another left turn into Voldergracht. To the left, the backs of the houses rise straight from the water as you stroll to the end of the street, which is marked by the sculptured animal heads and outdoor stairs of the old **Meat Market** on the right. Cross the Wijnhaven and turn left along its far side to the Koornmarkt, a stately canal spanned by a high arching bridge that is one of the hallmarks of Delft.

At 67 is the **Paul Tetar van Elven Museum,** an artist's house with 19th-century furnishings and an upstairs studio that seems to have been asleep since the time of Vermeer. *Koornmarkt 67. Admission: Fl. 2. Open mid-Apr.–mid.-Oct., Tues.–Sat. 11–5.*

Just before the end of the Koornmarkt is the **Wapenhuis van Holland** (arsenal), completed in 1692. Turn right to the **Oude Delft canal,** the city's oldest waterway. A few blocks farther along the canal, you will come upon the incredible Gothic facade of the **Gemeenlandshuis,** built as a private residence in 1520, with a flamboyant display of painted coats of arms from 1652. A few doors on is the **Prinsehof,** formerly the Convent of St. Agatha, founded in 1400. The chapel inside dates from 1471; its interior is remarkable for the wooden statues under the vaulting ribs. Today, the Prinsenhof is a museum that tells the story of the liberation of the Netherlands after 80 years of Spanish occupation (1568–1648). *Oude Delft 185. Admission: Fl. 3.50. Open Tues.–Sat. 10–5, Sun. 1–5.*

Across the Oude Delft canal is the **Oude Kerk** (Old Church), a vast Gothic monument of the 13th century. Its beautiful tower, surmounted by a brick spire, leans somewhat alarmingly. Beyond the Prinsenhof on the same side of the Oude Delft canal is the **Lambert van Meerten Museum,** a mansion whose timbered rooms are filled with the country's most complete collection of old Dutch tiles as well as Delft pottery. *Oude Delft 199. Admission: Fl. 3.50. Open Tues.–Sat. 10–5, Sun. 1–5.*

Dining and Lodging

For details and price category definitions, *see* Dining and Lodging in Essential Information.

The Hague
Dining
★

Chagall. This restaurant, set among the trees and lake of the Zijdepark in Leidschendam, 3 miles (5 kilometers) from The Hague, is in the most delightful surroundings. The interior is understated elegance, and the menu, with its fresh fish specialties alternating with traditional Dutch roasts is superb. *Weigelia 20, tel. 070/276910. Jacket and tie. Reservations essential. AE, DC, MC, V. Closed Sun. lunch, Mon. Very Expensive.*

Royal. The Royal certainly lives up to its name: It's the most luxurious and possibly the most expensive restaurant in The Hague. Situated in a 16th-century mansion, its elegant, antique furnishings seem to enhance the superb French haute cuisine. *Lange Voorhout 44, tel. 070/600772. Jacket and tie. Reservations essential. AE, DC, MC, V. Closed Sun. Very Expensive.*

Villa Rosenrust. The Villa Rosenrust is a converted 18th-century mansion, also in Leidschendam, with a terrace for outdoor dining in summer. Inside, there are masses of plants and flowers, and the ambience is elegant. There's a diverse menu of seasonal items—keep an eye peeled for truffles—and an excellent wine list. *Veursestraatweg 104, tel. 070/277460. Jacket and tie. Reservations essential. AE, DC, MC, V. Closed Sat. lunch, Sun. Very Expensive.*

Auberge de Kieviet. Northeast of The Hague, in Wassenaar, is the Auberge de Kieviet, a most delightful restaurant in a small hotel. There's a beautiful garden for summer dining. It offers a range of locally caught seafood, and the lobster is particularly good. *Stoeplaan 27, tel. 01751/19232. Jacket and tie. Reservations essential. AE, DC, MC, V. Closed Mon. Expensive.*

Lodging
★

Hotel des Indes. Located in the heart of the embassy area, with gracious public rooms, marble pillars, and crystal chandeliers, this popular and dignified hotel is popular with sophisticated travelers as well as diplomats. Over a century old, it features superbly equipped rooms, including such amenities as bathrobes and hair dryers. The fine Le Restaurant matches the hotel in the excellence of its service, cuisine, and atmosphere. *Lange Voorhout 54, tel. 070/469553. 77 rooms with bath. AE, DC, MC, V. Very Expensive.*

Promenadehotel. This is a modern and luxurious hotel; all the rooms are beautifully furnished and fully equipped. Its restaurant, Cigogne, is one of the finest in town, serving French cuisine in elegant surroundings. *Van Stolkweg 2, tel. 070/525161. 100 rooms with bath. AE, DC, MC, V. Very Expensive.*

Corona. Overlooking The Hague's central square, the Corona is an ideal base for sightseeing. It maintains a high level of service for its relatively small size. There's an old Dutch-style restaurant and a sidewalk terrace café. *Buitenhof 42, tel. 070/637930. 26 rooms with bath or shower. AE, DC, MC, V. Moderate.*

Scheveningen
Dining

Seinpost. Located near historic Seinpostdune, where Hendrik Mesdag painted his famous panorama, Seinpost has wonderful sea views from the Seinpost. The menu, which changes daily, is excellent; try the oysters, the new herring, or just about any of the seafood specialties. The owner-chef and his wife serve wonderful food in an attractive setting. *Zeekant 60, tel. 070/555250. Jacket and tie. Reservations essential. AE, DC, MC, V. Closed Sat. lunch, Sun., Mon., part of July. Expensive.*

Lodging **Steigenberger Kurhaus.** At the turn of the century, this was a
★ fashionable and aristocratic resort hotel. After a long time in decline, it was beautifully and tastefully restored and reopened, with a casino among its new attractions. Many of the rooms have balconies that overlook the sea, creating a comfortable, spacious effect. The restaurant, Kandinsky, is well known for its classic French cuisine as well as its decor, which includes signed Kandinsky prints. *Gevers Deijnootplein 30, tel. 070/ 520052. 250 rooms with bath. AE, DC, MC, V. Very Expensive.*
Carlton Beach Hotel. This is a modern and comfortable hotel, right on the beach. It has several restaurants, of which Le Homard is particularly recommended for its fresh seafood. *Gevers Deijnootweg 201, tel. 070/541414. 95 rooms with bath. AE, DC, MC, V. Expensive.*

Rotterdam and Dordrecht

These two cities offer a vivid contrast. Rotterdam, the largest port in the world, is lively, cosmopolitan, and essentially commercial. Almost totally destroyed by bombing in World War II, it now contains some of Holland's finest modern architecture and most memorable museums. The small port of Dordrecht, in contrast, claims to be the oldest town in Holland, and many of its buildings are original, reflecting its early importance and rich history.

Getting Around

The best—and cheapest—way of getting around Rotterdam is by bus or metro; ask at the VVV office for route maps. Dordrecht is small enough to be explored on foot, but the VVV map is also useful.

Guided Tours

The VVV organizes daily sightseeing tours of Rotterdam from April to October, by streetcar or by boat. Tours leave from in front of the Central Station and take in the major sights of the city and harbor. Harbor tours leave from Spido Pier by Willemsplein.

Tourist Information

Dordrecht. Stationsweg 1, tel. 078/132800.
Rotterdam. Stadhuisplein 19, tel. 010/4136000, and in the Central Station.

Exploring

Sightseeing in **Rotterdam** divides naturally into two tours, the first around the harbors and the second around the city. In addition to piers, dry docks, facilities for handling containers, wet and dry cargos, and the like, harbor tours take in the radar installations that enable ships to enter Rotterdam from the

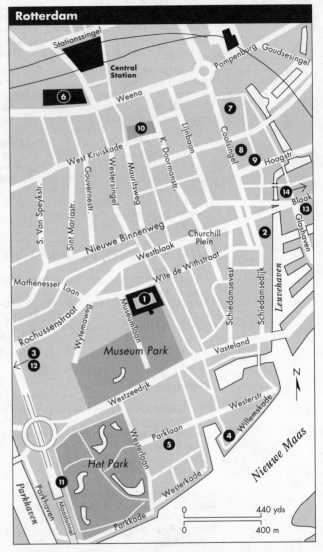

North Sea in complete safety even when visibility is reduced to
zero by fog.

❶ In the city, the **Museum Boymans-Van Beuningen** is the major
art museum, an impressive building ideally designed to house
the major collections of classical painting, sculpture, ceramics,
and furnishings. But it is not only the Old Masters that strike
the eye; a very fine collection of modern art is on display, with
works by Dali, Kandinsky, and Kokoschka. *Mathenesserlaan
20. Admission: Fl. 2.50. Open Tues.–Sat. 10–5, Sun. 11–5.*

❷ The **Museumschip de Buffel** at the Maritiem Museum Prins
Hendrik (Leuvehaven. Admission: Fl. 2.50. Open Tues.–Sat.
10–5, Sun. 11–5), is a former ironclad warship of the Royal
Dutch Navy and dates from 1868. It has been restored to its

❸ original condition. The **Museum de Dubbelde Palmboom** in Delfshaven (Voorhaven 12. Admission: Fl. 2.50. Open Tues.– Sat. 10–5, Sun. 11–5) offers insight into local history and has **❹** memorable collections of glass, silver, and Delft tiles. The **Museum voor Volkenkunde** (Willemskade 25. Admission: Fl. 2.50. Open Tues.–Sat. 10–5, Sun. 11–5) covers geography and ethnography, with an extensive collection of artifacts and an exhibition about developing nations and the problems they **❺** face. There is even a taxation museum, the **Belastingsmuseum Prof. Dr. van der Poel** (Parklaan 14. Open Mon.–Fri. 9–5), which explains taxation through the ages and has a cellar full of smugglers' equipment.

❻ The **Groothandelsgebouw** (Wholesale Center) is almost a city within a city, with more than 1.3 million square feet (360,000 square meters) of floor space, plus restaurants and shops. From the roof, there is a panoramic view of Rotterdam and its surroundings as far as Delft.

The main axis of Rotterdam's reconstructed center is **Coolsingel,** nearly all of whose buildings were built after the **❼** war. An exception is the **Stadhuis** (Town Hall), the largest in the country, which somehow withstood the catastrophic bombing. Erected in 1920, it has a handsome exterior and interesting murals in the civic reception room. A few blocks away from the **❽** Stadhuis is the **Schielandshuis,** the only 19th-century building to survive the destruction of 1940. It was built originally in 1665, but was destroyed by fire and rebuilt in 1864. The Schielandshuis contains the **Historisch Museum,** with wide-ranging coverage of the city's history. *Korte Hoogstraat 31. Admission: Fl. 2.50. Open Tues.–Sat. 10–5, Sun. 11–5.*

A strange beehive-walled building nearby dates from 1957. It was designed by U.S. architect Marcel Breuer to house the **❾** Rotterdam branch of a national department store called **De Bijenkorf** (beehive).

A block or two west of Coolsingel is the **Lijnbaan** pedestrian shopping center, a complex of 80 shops selling everything from **❿** pianos to pancakes. Close by is **De Doelen,** an imposing complex combining the functions of a theater, concert hall, and congress center. Near Leuvehaven is a statue called *Devastated City* by Ossip Zadkine. Here, too, is the Museumschip de Buffel and the Maritiem Museum Prins Hendrik.

Across the Museum Park, at the corner of Parkhaven and **⓫** Parkkade, stands the 600-foot (183-meter-)high **Euromast Tower,** with a glass-walled restaurant and memorable views.

⓬ In Rotterdam's western district is **Delfshaven,** once the harbor of Delft. Here, everything is on a smaller scale, with twisting waterways and tangled streets. In July 1620, the pilgrims set sail from here in the *Speedwell* for England and the New World. Most of the port areas have been reconstructed, and many of the district's 110 buildings now look as they did when originally built. The Pilgrim Fathers' Church, the **Zakkendragershuisje** (Sack Carriers' House), and the **Crane House** have been restored and are open to the public.

Those interested in modern architecture should explore the **⓭** **Blaak** district, where there are some unusual structures, including the "tree" houses, the "pencil" apartment block, and **⓮** the starkly modern city library. Around the **Oude Haven** (Old

Harbor) area there are ultramodern cube houses (Paal-woningen), and many cafés, pubs, restaurants, and shops.

Dordrecht was once among the most important towns and ports in Holland. Fortified in 1271, it retains many picturesque features. Today, the city is a major shipbuilding and yachting center with a mixture of new and old. The oldest section of Dordrecht lies along the riverfront—with the best view of the city from the north bank—and in the streets leading back inland to the Voorstraat. Dominating the scene is the imposing mass of the 15th-century **Grote Kerk.** A window depicts the 1421 flood disaster, and the huge 3,600-pipe organ has a 10-second echo. The interior is gleaming white. The carving on the choir stalls represents the history of the world from the Garden of Eden to Charles V (1542).

From the church, the Voorstraat (on the far side of the canal), with old houses at every turn, leads to the **Groenmarkt,** where you will find some of the city's most fascinating houses. No. 105 dates from 1562 and is called **De Sleutel** (the key). No. 43 has a late Gothic facade. From the Groenmarkt, Wijnstraat leads to the delightful early 17th-century **Groothoofdspoort Gate,** where the rivers Oude Maas, Noord, and Beneden Merwede merge.

Don't miss **de Hof** (the court), so-called because it was here that the representatives of Prince Willem the Silent met those of the largest towns, in 1572, to organize opposition to their Spanish overlords.

Dining and Lodging

For details and price category definitions, *see* Dining and Lodging in Essential Information.

Dordrecht
Dining

Camelot. This restaurant, in the center of town, is under the same management as the hotel Bellevue Groothoofdspoort. The Camelot has an 18th-century interior, made all the more attractive by the candlelit atmosphere. The cuisine is international—especially good are dishes using locally caught fish—and the wine list is good. *Singel 389, tel. 078/144929. Jacket and tie. Reservations essential. AE, DC, MC, V. Closed Sun., Mon. Expensive.*

Lodging
★

Bellevue Groothoofdspoort. This hotel is located in the old quarter of town and has remarkable views over the four-arm junction of the Maas River. The lounge is charming and the restaurant, Herberg de Hellebaard, serves traditional Dutch specialties, such as smoked eel. *Booursstraat 37, tel. 078/137900. 18 rooms with bath or shower. AE, DC, MC, V. Moderate.*

Rotterdam
Dining
★

Le Coq d'Or. Located in an old mansion that now graces the heart of the shopping area, near the harbor, this is one of Rotterdam's favorite meeting places. The second floor features an exclusive restaurant with rustic Dutch decor and old beams. Outside is a lovely garden, away from the city noise and very refreshing on a summer's day. The menu is excellent, mostly seasonal dishes—sample the duck or fish specialties. If you're short on time, try the snack bar on the ground floor. *Van Vollenhovenstraat 25, tel. 010/436405. Jacket and tie. Reservations advised. AE, DC, MC, V. Closed weekends. Expensive.*
Euromast. From the *Rotisserie Restaurant,* 302 feet (92 meters) above the ground, the views over the city and harbor are

magnificent. Though the quality of the food is, sadly, only average, this is still a worthwhile experience. *Parkhaven 20, tel. 010/4364811. Jacket and tie. Reservations advised. AE, DC, MC, V. Closed Sat. lunch, Sun. in winter. Expensive.*

★ **Het Kasteel van Rhoon.** Seven miles (11 kilometers) south of Rotterdam is Rhoon castle, with a romantic and stylish restaurant surrounded by parkland. During summer, meals are served on an outside terrace. Parts of the castle's interior date from 1199. The food is mainly international. *Dorpsdijk 63, tel. 01890/18896. Jacket and tie. Reservations advised. AE, DC, MC, V. Closed Sat. lunch. Expensive.*

The Old Dutch. Traditional and atmospheric, this is one of the best restaurants for Dutch decor and cuisine. Terrace dining in the summer is another attraction. *Rocherssenstraat, tel. 010/4360344. Jacket and tie. Reservations advised. AE, DC, MC, V. Closed Sat., Sun., Easter, Pentecost. Expensive.*

La Vilette. This restaurant is located in the city center and is popular with businesspeople. The owners, Carl and Yvonne Schuurs, have created a lively and elegant ambience. The menu is classic French and the service is excellent. *Westblaack 160, tel. 010/4148692. Jacket and tie. Reservations advised. AE, DC, MC, V. Closed Sat. lunch, Sun., and holidays. Expensive.*

Lodging **Hilton International Rotterdam.** The only true deluxe hotel in
★ the city, the Hilton has all you expect from its name. Every room is luxurious and excellently equipped. There are several restaurants, of which Le Restaurant is the best for elegance and cuisine. *Weena 10, tel. 010/4144044. 260 rooms with bath. AE, DC, MC, V. Very Expensive.*

Delta Crest Hotel. This recent addition to the city's hotel scene is another in which comfort is paramount. All the rooms are decorated to a high standard. There are also good views over the Maas River. *Maasboulevard 15, tel. 010/4345477. 78 rooms with bath. Facilities: indoor swimming pool. AE, DC, MC, V. Expensive.*

Golden Tulip Barbizon Capelle. Situated on the outskirts of town, 10 minutes from the city center and 10 minutes from the airport, this new hotel has all the latest comforts, but, like many hotels designed with the business traveler in mind, it lacks some atmosphere. For dining there is a brasserie, a spacious outdoor café, and a pub. *Barbizonlaan 2, tel. 010/4564455. 105 rooms with bath. AE, DC, MC, V. Expensive.*

Baan. This small hotel, set in a garden, lies en route to Delftshaven. It's modest but comfortable, ideal for those on a budget. *Rochussenstraat 345, tel. 010/4770555. 14 rooms, most with shower. No credit cards. Moderate.*

Van Walsum. This pleasant small hotel has its own garden and restaurant and is handy for the Museum Boymans van Beuningen. *Mathensserlaan 189, tel. 010/4363275. 28 rooms with shower or bath. AE, DC, MC, V. Closed Dec. 23–31. Moderate.*

---

18 Hungary

Introduction

Hungary—officially the Hungarian People's Republic—is a small country in the very heart of Europe whose special attractions are being more widely appreciated every year. With a better standard of living than their Eastern Bloc neighbors, Hungarians are now able to offer visitors all the grandeur, Old World charm, and high culture of Central Europe coupled with many of the modern comforts of the West.

Hungary is bisected by the Danube and bordered by the USSR, Romania, Czechoslovakia, Yugoslavia, and Austria. The clue to its survival may lie in its special talent for adapting to a sad history of repeated invasions and absorbing both eastern and western influences. Each brave but abortive uprising—against the Turks in the 17th century, the Hapsburgs in 1848, and the Soviet Union in 1956—has resulted in a period of readjustment, a return to politics as the art of the possible.

Since 1956, Hungary has evolved its own brand of socialism, which Khrushchev termed "goulash communism." These days thriving "private enterprises" are helping to ensure that shops are well stocked with consumer goods as well as with basic foodstuffs. Hungarians, many of whom hold down two jobs to maintain their present standard of living, complain with irony, wit, and some justification of the harsh effects of the present economic crisis, but will admit that they would not change places with any of their Eastern Bloc neighbors. Hungary manages to spare her visitors much of the bureaucratic unpleasantness encountered elsewhere in Eastern Europe and visitors may travel freely within the country. Budapest, the "pearl of the Danube," is lively and cosmopolitan, with spacious parks and rolling hills, medicinal springs, and a rich cultural life. Visitors who stroll along the riverbank promenade of 19th-century Pest, with its elegant hotels and impressive neo-Gothic Parliament building, enjoy memorable views across the river of the colorful churches and hilltop castle of Buda.

During the hot summer months, many of the capital's two million citizens decamp to *vikend* cottages on the crowded shores of Lake Balaton, Central Europe's largest lake, in the southwest of the country. Lined with pretty Baroque villages, its sunny northern hillsides thickly planted with vines, the lake offers good swimming and excellent water sports facilities. The Great Plain (Nagyföld) stretches across the eastern half of the country—a land of spicy food, strong wine, and horsemen. The provincial towns are also well worth visiting. Pécs, in the south, with its Mediterranean atmosphere; Eger, in the northeast, the home of Bull's Blood wine *(Egri bikavér);* the beautiful Baroque town of Sopron near the Austrian border; and the towns of the Danube Bend area north of Budapest—each give you a sense of the country's variety. Moderate distances, good roads, efficient public transport, and a wide choice of accommodations make travel within Hungary relaxing and pleasurable.

Hungarians are a hospitable people who welcome and take an interest in foreigners. (Many young people now speak some English.) You'll find them expansive and amusing on the subject of their country and its tumultuous history but also justly proud of their rich and varied cuisine and delicious wines. Par-

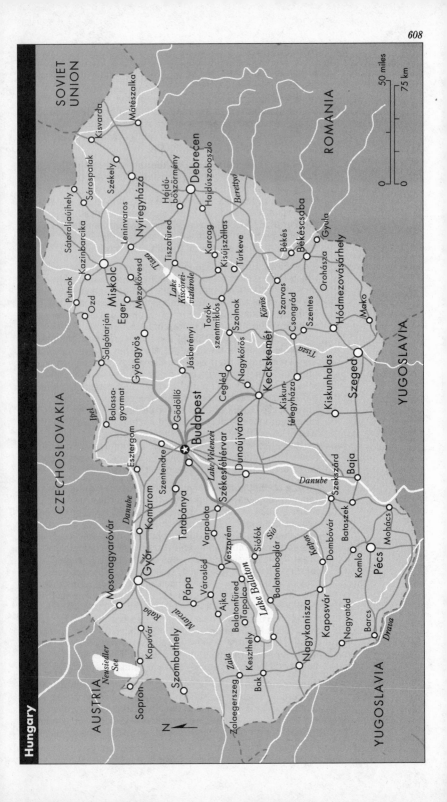

Hungary

ticularly attractive to music lovers, Hungary offers a feast of
musical events throughout the year, from Budapest's spring
and fall festivals to the lone violinist who accompanies your evening meal.

Before You Go

When to Go Many of Hungary's major fairs and festivals take place in the
spring and fall. During July and August, Budapest can be hot
and the resorts at Lake Balaton crowded, so May and September are perhaps the best months to visit.

Climate The following are average daily maximum and minimum temperatures for Budapest.

Jan.	34F	1C	May	72F	22C	Sept.	73F	23C
	25	−4		52	11		54	12
Feb.	39F	4C	June	78F	26C	Oct.	61F	16C
	28	−2		59	15		45	7
Mar.	50F	10C	July	82F	28C	Nov.	46F	8C
	36	2		61	16		37	3
Apr.	63F	17C	Aug.	81F	27C	Dec.	39F	4C
	45	7		61	16		30	−1

Currency The unit of currency is the forint (Ft.), divided into 100 fillérs
(f.). There are bills of 50, 100, 500, and 1,000; and coins of 10, 20,
and 50 fillérs and of 1,2,5,10, and 20 forints. The tourist exchange rate was 48 Ft. to the dollar and 80 Ft. to the pound
sterling at press time (fall 1988), but these rates are likely to
alter both before and during 1989.

Hungary, unlike other Eastern European countries, does not
require you to change a certain sum of money for each day of
your stay. Change money as you need it at banks, hotels, or
travel offices, but take care not to change too much because,
although in theory you can change back 50% (up to $100) of the
original sum when you leave, it may prove difficult in practice.

Most credit cards are accepted, though don't rely on them in
smaller towns or less expensive accommodations and restaurants.

There is a black market in currency but you will not gain much
and could lose a good deal by taking advantage of it. It is illegal
to give or sell hard currency to a Hungarian. While you may
bring in any amount of foreign currency, you may take out only
100 Ft. in Hungarian currency.

What It Will Cost Although first-class hotels in Budapest charge international
rates, prices generally are still modest by Western standards.
However, this may no longer be the case throughout 1989.
Faced with a serious economic crisis, the government is reaching for some stern capitalist remedies. In January 1988,
valued-added tax rates of up to 25% were introduced. This affected all the service industries, and the removal of price
controls in April 1988 has left the door open for substantial
price increases.

Sample Prices Cup of coffee, 15–40 Ft.; bottle of beer, 40–60 Ft.; soft drinks,
20–50 Ft.; ham sandwich, 100 Ft.; one-mile taxi ride, 30 Ft.

Visas American, Canadian, and British citizens need both a valid
passport and a visa to visit Hungary. If you arrive by plane or

car, you can obtain a visa on arrival, but it is advisable to arrange one in advance in order to avoid tiresome delays and an additional charge. If you are traveling by bus or train, you *must* get your visa in advance. Apply to the Hungarian consulate in your own country or to an accredited travel agent. For a 30-day visa, send your valid passport and two passport-size photos to: **Hungarian Consulate,** 8 E. 75th St., New York, NY 10021; **Hungarian Embassy,** 3910 Shoemaker St., NW, Washington, DC 20008; **Hungarian Embassy,** 7 Delaware Ave., Ottawa 4, Ontario, Canada; or **Hungarian Consulate,** 35b Eaton Place, London SW1. Visas are no longer required for groups staying less than 48 hours.

Visitors must register with the police within 48 hours of arrival —this is taken care of automatically if you are staying in a hotel or in private accommodations arranged for you through a tourist office. If you are staying with relatives or friends, a form, which costs 10 Ft., must be bought from the post office and taken with your passport to the local police station. Your visa can be extended for a further 30 days at a cost of 300 Ft. (in stamps available from the post office) on application to the local police station.

Customs on Arrival Objects for personal use may be imported freely. If you are over 16, you may also bring in 250 grams of tobacco, plus two liters of wine, one liter of stronger alcohol, and 250 grams of perfume. A 30% customs charge is made on gifts valued in Hungary at more than 10,000 Ft. Take care when you leave Hungary that you have the right documentation for exporting goods. Keep receipts of any items bought from Konsumtourist, Intertourist, or Kepcsarnok Vallalat. A special permit is needed for works of art valued at more than 1,000 Ft.

Language Hungarian, with its long words and variety of accents, is a very difficult language. You'll find that English is widely spoken by those Hungarians who come into contact with tourists. Many members of the older generation speak a little German, and more and more young people speak English.

Getting Around

By Car
Documentation To drive in Hungary, U.S. and Canadian visitors need an International Driver's License, and U.K. visitors need a domestic driving license.

Road Conditions There are three classes of road: highways (designated by the letter M and a single digit); secondary roads (designated by a two-digit number), and minor roads (three digits). Highways and secondary roads are generally excellent. The condition of minor roads varies considerably. There are no toll charges on highways.

Rules of the Road Hungarians drive on the right and observe the usual Continental rules of the road. The speed limit in developed areas is 60 kph (37 mph), on main roads 80 kph (50 mph) and on highways 120 kph (75 mph). Seat belts are compulsory and drinking strictly prohibited—the penalties are very severe.

Gasoline Gas stations are not as plentiful in Hungary as in Western Europe, so fill up whenever possible. A gallon of gasoline *(benzin)* costs about $2. Unleaded gasoline, available at some 12 stations in the provinces, five in Budapest, and on all the major routes out of the capital, is only a little more expensive. Interag Shell and Afor stations at busy traffic centers stay open all night; elsewhere, from 6 AM to 8 PM. Diesel oil can be bought only with coupons from IBUSZ travel offices at the border or from hotels. They are nonrefundable, so try to calculate how many you will need.

Breakdowns The Hungarian Automobile Club runs a 24-hour "Yellow Angels" breakdown service from Budapest XIV, Fráncia Út 38a, Tel. 1/691–831 or 1/693–714. There are repair stations in all the major towns and emergency telephones on the main highways.

By Train Travel by train is a cheap if rather slow option. Seat reservations, sold up to 60 days in advance, are generally compulsory for international express trains but also advisable for trains within Hungary. A *gyorsvonat* is a fast train, a *személyvonát* a very slow one.

Fares Cheap tickets, allowing unlimited travel for seven or 10 days, cost 700 Ft. and 1,200 Ft., respectively. Inter Rail cards are valid for those under 26, and the Rail Europe Senior Travel Pass entitles senior citizens to a 30% reduction on all trains.

By Bus Long-distance buses link Budapest with many main cities in Eastern and Western Europe. Services to the east of the country leave from **Népstadion Station** (tel. 1/187–315). Buses to the west and south, to Austria and Yugoslavia, leave from the main **VOLÁN** bus station at Engels Tér in the Inner City (tel. 1/182–122). Although cheap, they tend to be crowded, so reserve your seat.

By Bicycle A land of rolling hills and flat plains, Hungary recommends itself to the bicyclist. The larger train stations around Lake Balaton have bicycles for rent at about 50 Ft. a day. For information about renting bicycles in Budapest, contact **Tourinform** (Sütő Utca 2, tel. 1/179–800).

By Boat Hungary is well equipped with nautical transport, and Budapest is situated on a major international waterway—the Danube. Vienna (five hours away) and many Hungarian resorts are accessible by hydrofoil or boat. For information about excursions or pleasure cruises, contact **MAHART Landing Stage** (1 Vigadó Tér, V, Budapest, tel. 1/181–223).

Essential Information

Telephones **Local Calls.** Pay phones use 2 Ft. coins—the cost of a three-minute local call. Most towns in Hungary can be dialed directly. **International Calls.** Direct calls to foreign countries can be made from Budapest and all major provincial towns by dialing 00 and waiting for the international dialing tone. **Operators.** International calls can be made through the operator by dialing 01; for operator-assisted calls within Hungary, dial 06. **Information.** Dial 172–200 for information in English.

Mail Stamps may be bought from tobacco shops as well as post offices. The post offices at Keleti (East) and Nyugati (West) train stations are open 24 hours.

Postal Rates An airmail postcard to the USA costs 8 Ft., or 10 Ft., and an airmail letter costs from 12 Ft. Postcards to the United Kingdom and the rest of Western Europe cost 8 Ft., letters 10 Ft.

Receiving Mail	A poste restante service is available in Budapest. The address is Magyar Posta, H-1052 Budapest, 5 Petőfi Sándor Utca 13–15. Make sure the postal code number is written on all mail, on the right-hand side of the envelope, below the address.
Shopping	Peasant embroideries, cut glass, and Herend and Zsolnay porcelain are the best goods to buy, but quality classical records and Tokaj and Bull's Blood wine are also real bargains. Government tourist shops, called **Intertourist** or **Konsumtourist,** stock the widest choice and sell only against hard currencies. Be warned that many of the smaller shops still operate on the confusing three-line system—select, pay, then collect.
Opening and Closing Times	**Banks.** Banks are open weekdays 8–1. **Museums.** Most museums are open Tuesday through Sunday, 10–6. **Shops.** Shops are open weekdays 10–6, Saturday 10–1. Many shops stay open until 8 on Thursday.
National Holidays	January 1 (New Year's Day); March 27 (Easter Monday); April 4 (Liberation Day); May 1 (Labor Day); August 20 (St. Stephen's and Constitution Day); November 7 (Anniversary of Russian Revolution); December 25 and 26.
Dining	There is no shortage of excellent and moderately priced restaurants offering long and impressively varied menus. Meats, rich sauces, and creamy desserts are the dominant themes, but the more health- and figure-conscious will also find salads, even out of season. There are also self-service restaurants *(önkiszolgáló étterem)*, snack bars *(bistró* or *étel bár)*, buffets *(büfé)*, cafés *(eszpresszó)*, and bars *(drink-bár)*. The pastry shops *(cukrászda)* are also worth a try.
	There is often, even in high-class restaurants, an inexpensive fixed-price meal, called a *Menü*, for as little as 60 Ft.
Mealtimes	Hungarians eat early—you risk off-hand service and cold food after 9 PM. Lunch—for many the main meal—is 12–2.
Ratings	Prices are per person and include a first course, main course, and dessert, but no wine or tip. Best bets are indicated by a star ★. At press time, there were 48 forints to the dollar.

Category	Cost
Expensive	over 600 Ft.
Moderate	350–600 Ft.
Inexpensive	under 350 Ft.

Credit Cards	The following credit card abbreviations are used: AE, American Express; DC, Diners Club; MC, MasterCard; V, Visa.
Lodging *Hotels*	There are no Very Expensive and few Expensive hotels outside Budapest, but the Moderate hotels are generally comfortable and well-run, although single rooms with baths are scarce. Establishments in our Inexpensive category seldom have private baths, but plumbing is satisfactory almost everywhere. Reservations should be made as far in advance as possible, especially with the less expensive establishments, which are still in short supply.
Rentals	Apartments in Budapest and cottages at Lake Balaton are available. Rates and reservations can be obtained from tourist

offices in Hungary and abroad. A Budapest apartment might cost 4,000 Ft. a week, while a luxury cottage for two at Balaton costs around 3,000 Ft. a day.

Guest Houses Also called pensions, these offer simple accommodations in rooms with four beds. They are well suited to younger people on a budget, and, there are bathrooms for men and women on each floor. Some offer simple breakfast facilities. Arrangements can be made through local tourist offices or travel agents abroad.

In the provinces it is safe to accept rooms that you are offered directly. *Szoba kiadó* means room to rent. The rate per night for a double room in Budapest or at Lake Balaton is around 650 Ft., which includes the use of a bathroom but not breakfast. If you prefer, reservations can also be made through any tourist office.

Camping The 100 campsites in Hungary are open from May through September. Rates are 100–200 Ft. a day. There's a small charge for hot water and electricity plus an accommodations fee of 10–50 Ft. per person per night. Children get a 50% reduction. Camping is forbidden except in appointed areas. Reservations can be made through travel agencies or through the **Hungarian Camping and Caravanning Club** (Budapest VIII, Múzeum Utca 11, tel. 1/141–880).

Ratings The following price categories are for a double room with bath and breakfast during the peak season. For single rooms with bath, count on about 650–1,300 Ft. extra per person per night. Best bets are indicated by a star ★. At press time, there were 48 forints to the dollar.

Category	Budapest	Balaton	Provinces
Very Expensive	7,000–12,500	—	—
Expensive	5,000–7,000	4,000–6,000	2,250–3,250
Moderate	3,000–5,000	2,000–4,000	1,500–2,250
Inexpensive	1,000–3,000	600–2,000	500–1,500

Note: prices above are given in forints (Ft.)

During the peak season (June through August) full board may be compulsory at the Lake Balaton hotels. Rates are considerably lower than those given above during the off-season (in Budapest this is September through March; at Lake Balaton, May and September).

Credit Cards The following credit card abbreviations are used: AE, American Express; DC, Diners Club; MC, MasterCard; V, Visa.

Tipping Being a socialist state has not altered the Hungarian habit of tipping generously. Cloakroom and gas-pump attendants, hairdressers, waiters, and taxi drivers all expect a tip. Although hotel bills contain a service charge, you should also tip the lift boy, chambermaid, and head porter; together, they should get 10% of the bill. At least an extra 10% should be added to a restaurant bill or taxi fare. If a gypsy band plays for your table exclusively, you can leave 100 Ft. in a plate discreetly provided for that purpose.

Budapest

Arriving and Departing

By Plane Hungary's two international airports are about 22 kilometers (13 miles) southeast of the city. MALEV flights operate from the new **Ferihegy 2 Airport,** tel. 1/577–831; all other airlines from **Ferihegy 1,** tel. 1/572–122. The number to call for same-day flight information is 1/577–155.

Between the Airport and Downtown Buses to and from the Engels Tér station (metro: Deák Tér) leave every half-hour between about 5 AM and 9 PM. The 35-minute trip costs about 25 Ft. A taxi ride to the center of Budapest should cost no more than 250 Ft. Avoid taxi drivers who offer their services before you are out of the arrivals lounge.

By Train There are three main train stations in Budapest: **Keleti** (East), **Nyugati** (West) and **Déli** (South). Trains from Vienna usually operate from Keleti, those from Balaton and Yugoslavia from Déli.

By Bus Most buses to Budapest, including the one from Vienna, arrive at **Engels Tér** station.

By Car The main routes into Budapest are M1 from Győr and M7 from Székesfehervár.

Getting Around

Budapest is best explored on foot. The maps provided by tourist offices are not very detailed, so arm yourself with one from any of the bookshops in Váci Utca or from downtown stationery shops (Apisz) or card shops.

By Public Transportation The public transport system—a metro (subway), buses, streetcars, and trolley buses—is cheap, efficient, and simple to use but closes down at around 11:15 PM. A day ticket *(napjegy)* costs 24 Ft. and allows unlimited travel on all services within the city limits. You can also buy tickets for single rides—blue for buses, costing 3 Ft., and yellow for streetcars, metro, and trolley buses, costing 2 Ft. from metro stations or tobacco shops; you can travel any distance on these tickets but you can't change lines.

Bus, streetcar, and trolley bus tickets must be canceled on board—watch how other passengers do it. Don't get caught without a ticket: Spot checks are frequent, especially at the beginning of the month, and you can be fined 100 Ft.

By Taxi Taxis are plentiful and a good value, but make sure that they have a meter that is working. The initial charge is 10 Ft., plus 8 Ft. per kilometer plus 3 Ft. per minute of waiting time. You can order one by dialing 1/222–222 or 666–666.

By Boat In summer a regular boat service links the north and south of the city, stopping at points on both banks, including Margitsziget (Margaret Island). From May to September boats leave from the quay at Vigado Tér on 1½-hour cruises between the Árpád and Petőfi bridges. The trip, organized by IBUSZ, runs three times a day and costs around 60 Ft.

Important Addresses and Numbers

Tourist Information
Tourinform, Süto Utca 2 (Metro: Deák Tér), tel. 1/179–800. Open Mon.–Sat. 8–8, Sun. 8–1. **IBUSZ Accommodation Office,** Petolfi Tér 3, tel. 185/707. Open 24 hours. **Budapest Tourist,** Roosevelt Tér 5, tel. 1/173–555.

Embassies
American. Budapest V, Szabadság Tér 12, tel. 1/126–450. **Canadian.** Budapest II, Budakeszki Út 32, tel. 1/767–711. **British.** Budapest V, Harm-mincad Utca 6, tel. 1/182–888.

Emergencies
Police: tel. 07; **Ambulance:** tel. 04; **Doctor:** Ask your hotel or embassy to recommend one. U.S. and Canadian visitors are advised to take out full medical insurance. U.K. visitors are covered for emergencies and essential treatment.

English Bookstores
Foreign publications—including those in English—can be bought at the reception desks of major hotels and at newsstands at major traffic centers.

Guided Tours

Orientation Tours
Three-hour bus tours of the city operate all year and cost about 600 Ft. Starting from Engels Tér, they take in parts of both Buda and Pest and offer a good introduction for further exploring on foot. Contact IBUSZ (*see* Important Addresses and Numbers).

Special-Interest Tours and Excursions
IBUSZ and Budapest Tourist organize a number of unusual tours, featuring trips to the Buda Hills, goulash parties, tours around the spas and the Waxworks, as well as visits to the National Gallery and Parliament and some of the other more traditional sights. These tour companies will provide personal guides on request.

Excursions further afield include day-long trips to the Puszta (the Great Plain), the Danube Bend, and Lake Balaton.

Exploring Budapest

Budapest, attractively located on the banks of the Danube, retains much of the character and variety of a city that was once the three small towns of Buda, Óbuda, and Pest. On the southwest bank of the river, the cliffs of Buda rise steeply, while further north a decorative cluster of church domes, spires, patterned roofs, and colorful facades spills in artful disorder up and over the hills beyond. By contrast, Pest is a well-planned modern city born of the prosperity of the last century, much of it inspired by the wide boulevards of Baron Haussmann's Paris. The cultural, political, intellectual, and commercial heart of the nation beats here in Budapest; for the 20% of the nation's population who live in the capital, anywhere else is simply "the country."

So much of Budapest's real charm lies in unexpected glimpses into shadowy courtyards and in long vistas down sunlit cobbled streets. Although some 30,000 buildings were destroyed in the last war and in 1956, you'll find that a flavor of the past lingers on in the often crumbling architectural details of the structures, and in the memories and lifestyles of the citizens.

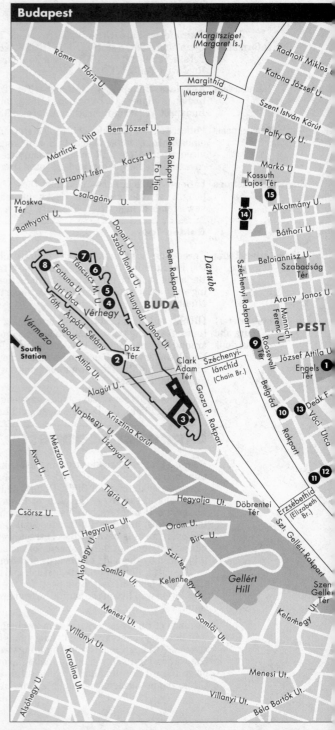

Budapest

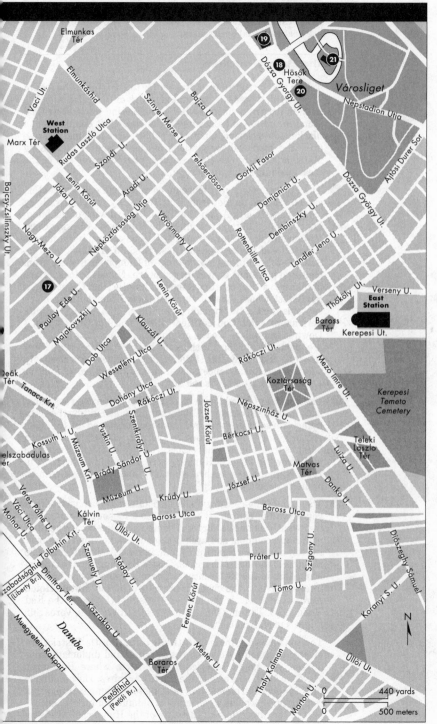

Elmunkas Tér

Elmunkáshíd

Váci Út.

West Station

Marx Tér

Rudas László Utca

Szondi U.

Szinyei Merse U.

Bajza U.

Dózsa György Út.

Hősök Tere

Városliget

Népstadion Utja

Ajtósi Dürer Sor

Lenin Körút

Jókai U.

Aradi U.

Felsőerdősor

Gorkij Fasor

Damjanich U.

Dembinszky U.

Dózsa György Út.

Bajcsy-Zsilinszky Út.

Nagy-Mező U.

Népköztársaság Útja

Vörösmarty U.

Rottenbiller Utca

Landler Jeno U.

Paulay Ede U.

Majakovszkij U.

Lenin Körút

Klauzál U.

Thököly Út.

Verseny U.

East Station

Baross Tér

Kerepesi Ut.

Dob Utca

Wesselény Utca

Rákóczi Ut.

Mező Imre Ut.

Deák Tér

Tanács Krt.

Dohány Utca

Rákóczi Ut.

Koztársaság Tér

Népszinház U.

Kerepesi Temeto Cemetery

Kossuth L. U.

Múzeum Krt.

Puskin U.

Szentkirályi U.

József Körút

Bérkocsi U.

Teleki László Tér

Luiza U.

elszabadulas ér

Veres Pálné U.

Váci Utca

Molnár U.

Bródy Sándor U.

Múzeum U.

Kálvin Tér

Krúdy U.

Baross Utca

József U.

Matvas Tér

Danko U.

Baross Utca

szabadsághíd (Liberty Br.)

Tolbuhin Krt.

Dimitrov Tér.

Szamuely U.

Ráday U.

Üllői Ut.

Ferenc Körút

Práter U.

Szigony U.

Diószeghy Sámuel

Muegyetem Rakpart

Danube

Köztárlar U.

Tömo U.

Koranyi S. U.

Boraros Tér

Mester U.

Thaly Kalman

Marton U.

Üllői Ut.

N

0   440 yards

0   500 meters

Petőfihíd (Petöfi Br.)

The principal sights of the city fall roughly into three areas,
which can be comfortably covered on foot. The hills of Budapest
are best explored by streetcar.

The Main Attractions

❶ ❷ Take a taxi or bus 16 from **Engels Tér** to **Dísz Tér** at the foot of
Castle Hill, where the painstaking work of reconstruction has
been in progress since the last war. Having made their final
stand in the Royal Palace itself, the Nazis left behind them a
blackened wasteland. Under the rubble, archaeologists discovered the medieval foundations of the palace of good King
Matthias who, in the 15th century, presided over one of the
most splendid courts in Europe.

❸ The **Palace,** now a vast museum complex and cultural center,
can be reached on foot from Dísz Tér, or by funicular railway
(Sikló) from Clark Adam Tér. The northern wing of the building is devoted to the **Museum of the Hungarian Working Class
Movement** (open Tues.–Sun. 10–6). The central block houses
the **National Gallery** (open Tues. 12–6, Wed. 12–8, Thurs.–
Sun. 10–6), exhibiting a wide range of Hungarian fine art, from
medieval paintings to modern sculpture. Names to look for are
Munkacsy, a 19th-century Romantic painter, and Csontváry, a
Surrealist whom Picasso much admired. The southern block
contains the **Castle Museum** (open Tues.–Sun. 10–6), with its
permanent exhibition entitled "1,000 Years of Our Capital."
Down in the cellars are the original medieval vaults of the palace, portraits of King Matthias and his second wife, Beatrice of
Aragon, and many late 14th-century statues that probably
adorned the Renaissance palace. *Palace Museums, 17 Dísz tér
1. Admission: 10 Ft., free on Sat.*

❹ The **Matthias Church,** with its distinctive patterned roof, dates
back to the 13th century. The former mosque built by the occupying Turks was destroyed and reconstructed in the 19th
century, only to be bombed in the last war. Only the south
porch is from the original structure. The Hapsburg emperors
were crowned kings of Hungary here, including Charles IV, in
1916. High mass is celebrated every Sunday at 10 AM with an
orchestra and choir.

❺ The turn-of-the-century **Fishermen's Bastion** is on your left as
you leave the church. It was built as a lookout tower to protect what was once a thriving fishing settlement. Its neo-Romanesque columns and arches provide frames for views over
the city and river. Near the church, in Hess Andras Tér, are the
remains of the oldest church on Castle Hill, built by the Dominican friars in the 13th century. These have now been brutally
integrated into the modern structure of the **Hilton Hotel.**
Across the street is the famous **Vörös Sün** (House of the Red
Hedgehog). The only inn in Budapest until 1785, the Vörös Sün
is now a private home.

The town houses lining the streets of the Castle District are
mostly occupied by offices, restaurants, and diplomatic residences, but no. 7 Táncsics Mihály Utca, where Beethoven
❻ stayed in 1800, now houses the **Bartók Archives.** The building is
full of papers and mementoes relating to the famous Hungarian
composer, as well as a collection of old musical instruments—
part of the Musicological Institute of the Hungarian Academy

of Sciences. *7 Táncsics Mihály Utca. Admission: 10 Ft., free on Sat. Open Tues.–Sun. 10–6.*

7 The remains of a **Medieval Synagogue** are also in the neighborhood and are open to the public. On show are a number of objects relating to the Jewish community including religious inscriptions, frescoes, and tombstones dating back to the 15th century. *26 Táncsics Mihály Utca. Admission: 10 Ft. Open Apr.–Oct., Tues.–Fri. 10–4; weekends 10–6.*

8 **The Hadtörténeti Múzeum** (War History Museum) is at the far end of Castle Hill. The collection includes uniforms and regalia, many belonging to the Hungarian generals who took part in the abortive uprising against Austrian rule in 1848. Other exhibits trace the military history of Hungary from the original Magyar conquest in the 9th century through the period of Ottoman rule and right to the middle of this century. *40 Tóth Árpád Sétány I. Admission: 10 Ft. Open Tues.–Sat. 9–5, Sun. 10–6.*

Nearby stands a monument to Abdurrahman, the last Pasha of Buda, commander of the Turkish troops in Hungary, who died, sword in hand in 1686. For a good view down to Vermezoliget (Blood Meadow Park) and over the Buda hills, stroll the length of Tóth Árpád Sétány, along the rampart that defended Castle Hill to the west.

9 Cross the **Széchenyilánchíd** (Chain Bridge) from Clark Adam Tér to reach **Roosevelt Tér** in Pest, with the 19th-century neo-Classical Academy of Sciences on your left. Pest fans out from the **Belváros** (Inner City), which is bounded by the **Kiskörút** (Little Boulevard). The **Nagykörút** (Grand Boulevard) describes a wider semicircle from the Margaret Bridge to Petőfi Bridge. To your right, an elegant promenade, the **Korzó,** runs south along the river.

Time Out The **Bécsi Kávéház** (Vienna Coffeehouse) in the Forum Hotel serves the best coffee and cream pastries in town. *12–14 Apaczai Csere Janos Utca V.*

---

10 A square called **Vigado Tér** is bordered by a Romantic-style concert hall, where Liszt, Brahms, and Bartók performed. Completely destroyed in World War II, it has been rebuilt in its **11** original style. Another square, **Március 15 Tér,** commemorates the 1848 struggle for independence from the Hapsburgs with a statue of the poet Petőfi Sandor, who died in the uprising. Every March 15, the square is thronged with patriotic Hun-**12** garians. Behind the square is the 12th-century **Belvárosi plébánia templon** (Inner City Parish Church), the oldest in Pest. The church has been redone in a variety of western architectural styles, but Turkish influences, such as the Muslim prayer niche, remain. Liszt, who lived only a few yards away, often played the organ here.

13 Parallel with the Korzó, in the Inner City, lies Budapest's most upscale shopping street, **Váci Utca. Vörösmarty Tér,** a pleasant and spacious square, is in the heart of the Inner City. Street musicians and sidewalk cafés make it one of the liveliest places in Budapest.

Time Out **Gerbeaud,** an elegant pastry shop in the old imperial style, is a fashionable meeting place. Try the chestnut purée with whipped cream while sitting on the terrace overlooking the square. *7 Vörösmarty Tér V.*

⑭ North of Vörösmarty Tér is the imposing neo-Gothic **Parliament** (open for tours only), the city's most famous landmark. To its left sits an expressive statue of Attila József (1905–37), Hungary's greatest poet of this century.

⑮ Across from the Parliament is the **Neprajzi Múzeum** (Museum of Ethnography), with exhibits relating to folk traditions and social customs including Hungarian costume and folklore. There is a particularly interesting collection from Oceania. *12 Kossuth Lajos Tér V. Admission: 10 Ft. Open Tues.–Sat. 10–6.*

⑯ Dark and massive, the 19th-century **St. Stephen's Basilica** is one of the chief landmarks of Pest. It was planned early in the 19th century as a neo-Classical building, but was in the neo-Renaissance style by the time it was completed more than 50 years later. During World War II, the most precious documents from the Municipal Archives were placed in the cellar of the Basilica—one of the few available bombproof sites.

Népköztársaság Útja (People's Republic Avenue) runs two miles from the Basilica to Hösök Tere (Heroes' Square). On the
⑰ left is the **State Opera House,** with its statues of the Muses in the second floor corner niches. Completed in 1884, it was the crowning achievement of architect Miklos Ybl. It has been restored to its original ornate glory—particularly inside—and has been fortunate enough to be spared any attempts to modernize it. In the center of Heroes' Square stands the 118-foot (36
⑱ meters) **Millennium Monument,** begun in 1896 to commemorate the 1,000th anniversary of the Magyar Conquest. Prince Arpad and six other founding Magyars occupy the base of the monument, while between the columns on either side are Hungary's greatest rulers and princes.

⑲ The **Szépművészeti Múzeum** (Fine Arts Museum) stands on one side of the square. Egyptian, Greek, and Roman artifacts dominate a whole section of the museum, with an emphasis on rare ceramics. The works by the greatest of European painters have been chosen with great care, and few artists of renown are unrepresented. *Hösok Tere XIV. Admission: 10 Ft. Open Tues.– Sun. 10–6.*

⑳ The **Műcsárnok** (Art Gallery), on the other side of the square, is the site of visiting exhibitions of fine arts, applied arts, and photography. *Hösok Tere XIV Admission: 10 Ft. Open Tues.– Sun. 10–6.*

The **City Park** extends beyond the square; on the left as you enter it are the zoo, state circus, amusement park, and outdoor swimming pool of the Széchenyi mineral baths. On the right is
㉑ the **Mezögazdasági Múzeum** (Agricultural Museum), housed in a number of buildings representing different styles of Hungarian architecture—again a part of the Millennium Exhibition of 1896. *Széchenyi Sziget, Varosliget XIV. Admission: 10 Ft. Open Tues.–Sun. 10–6.*

On the shores of the artificial lake stands the statue of **George Washington,** erected in 1906 from donations by Hungarians living in the United States. The recently renamed **Olaf Palme Walk** is a pleasant route through the park.

Off the Beaten Track

A chair lift *(libegő)* will take you to the highest point in Budapest, Janoshégy (Janos Hill), where you can climb a lookout tower for the best view of the city. *Take bus 158 from Moszkva Tér to the last stop, Zugligeti Ut.*

For a more strenuous route to another good view, climb the staircase up the steep cliff overlooking the Danube at the Buda end of the Szabadság Bridge. This will lead you to **Gellérthegy** (Gellert Hill), named for an 11th-century bishop who was hurled to his death here by some pagan Magyars. During the Middle Ages the hill was associated with witches; nowadays there is a memorial to the liberation of Budapest by the Red Army.

Shopping

You'll find plenty of folk art and souvenir shops, foreign-language bookshops, and classical record shops in or around **Váci Utca,** but a visit to some of the smaller, more typically Hungarian shops in **Lenin Körút,** and to the new **Skala** department store near Nyugati train station may prove more interesting.

The food market at **Dimitrov Tér** and the Flea Market *(Ecseri Piac)* some way out in **Nagykörösi Utca** (take bus No. 58 from Boráros Tér) are well worth a visit.

Dining

Eating out in Budapest can be a real treat and should provide you with some of the best value for money of any European capital. There is a good selection of restaurants, from the grander establishments that echo the imperial past of the Hapsburg era to the less expensive spots more favored by locals.

Prices below are per person and include a first course, main course, and dessert, but no wine or tip. Best bets are indicated by a star ★. At press time, there were 48 forints to the dollar.

Category	Cost
Expensive	over 600 Ft.
Moderate	350–600 Ft.
Inexpensive	under 150 Ft.

Expensive   **Alabardos.** Castle Hill is the setting for this small, intimate restaurant with a reputation for top-quality food and wine and outstanding service. The setting is medieval, and lute music helps to establish the Old World atmosphere. *12 Országház Utca I, tel. 1/160–828. Jacket and tie. Reservations essential. AE, DC, MC, V. Closed for lunch.*

Arany Hordó. True to its name (which means the Golden Barrel), this 14th-century building has a beer house on the ground floor. The cellar has a wine tavern, but the real attraction is the first-class restaurant on the second floor. The local specialty is *fogas,* a fish from Lake Balaton. *16 Tarnok Utca I, tel.*

1/566–765. Jacket and tie. Reservations advised for restaurant. AE, DC, MC, V.

★ **Fortuna.** Three medieval houses were reconstructed as a wood-furnished restaurant, nightclub, and café. The atmosphere, a key point, is matched by the range of food and the distinguished wine list. There is gypsy music in the evening. *4 Hess András Tér I, tel. 1/756–857. Jacket and tie. Reservations advised for dinner. AE, DC, MC, V.*

★ **Gundel.** Gundel is a famous restaurant in the City Park, where traditional meals are served with an almost stiff formality. *Gundel palacsinta* (pancakes, with chocolate, nuts, and cream) are the specialty. There are outdoor tables in the summer and gypsy music in the evenings. *2 Állatkerti Körút XIV, tel. 1/221–002. Jacket and tie. Reservations accepted. AE, DC, MC, V.*

Moderate **Kisbuda.** A small restaurant near the Buda end of the Margaret Bridge, Kisbuda serves meat and fish specialties and a delicious variety of salads. In warm weather there are tables outside in a courtyard. A piano and violin duet play in the evening. *34 Frankel L. Utca II, tel. 1/152–244. Dress: casual. Reservations advised in evenings. No credit cards. Closed Sun. dinner.*

Márvanyményasszony. Summer is the best time to appreciate this spacious restaurant in a back street near the Déli Train Station. It is popular with groups, probably because its long wooden tables and benches give way to space for dancing to gypsy music. *6 Márvany Utca I, tel. 1/756–165. Dress: casual. Reservations accepted. No credit cards. Closed lunch.*

Szeged. This is a traditional fish restaurant near the Szabadság Bridge and Gellert Hill. Folk art covers the walls, and there is gypsy music in the evening. The fish soup is fiery. *1 Bartók Béla Út XI, tel. 1/251–268. Dress: casual. Reservations accepted. No credit cards.*

Inexpensive **Halaszkert.** There is plenty of fun to be had in the noisy and live-★ ly Halaszkert, one of the most typical of the old-style Budapest fish restaurants. Virtuoso gypsy musicians will attempt any tune. *6 Lajos Utca II, tel. 1/686–480. Dress: informal. No reservations. No credit cards. Closed Sun.*

Tábani Kakas. Situated just below Castle Hill, Tábani Kakas is a popular restaurant with a friendly atmosphere. It specializes in large helpings of poultry dishes, particularly goose. A pianist plays and sings in the evening. *27 Attila Út. I, tel. 1/757–165. Dress: casual. No reservations. No credit cards.*

Lodging

If you arrive in Budapest without a reservation, go to the IBUSZ travel office (open 24 hours) at Petőfi Tér (tel. 1/185–707), or to one of the tourist offices at train stations and airports. Prices below are for a double room with bath and breakfast. Best bets are indicated by a star ★. At press time, there were 48 forints to the dollar.

Category	Cost
Very Expensive	over 7,000
Expensive	5,000–7,000 Ft.

Moderate	3,000–5,000 Ft.
Inexpensive	under 3,000 Ft.

Very Expensive **Atrium Hyatt.** The Atrium Hyatt is a large luxury hotel in
★ theInner City and has a good view over the Danube. Its range
of facilities has made it a popular stop for businesspeople and
those who don't mind being pampered. *2 Roosevelt Tér V, tel.
1/383–000. 356 rooms, all with bath. Facilities: 2 restaurants,
bar, indoor pool, sauna, gym, conference room, and ballroom.
AE, DC, MC, V.*

Duna Intercontinental. The Duna makes the best of its location
with a terrace café overlooking the river from the Danube
Quay. Ask for a room facing west, across the river toward
Gellert Hill in Buda. *4 Apáczai Csere János Utca V, tel. 1/175–
122. 340 rooms with bath. Facilities: 3 restaurants, penthouse
bar, nightclub, pool, squash. AE, DC, MC, V.*

Hilton. On Castle Hill in Buda, the Hilton has an excellent view
over the city. It incorporates the tower and other remains of a
13th-century church. Try your luck at the casino, where hard
currency is the language spoken. *1–3 Hess András Tér I, tel.
1/751–000. 323 rooms with bath. Facilities: 3 restaurants,
nightclub, casino. AE, DC, MC, V.*

Expensive **Béke.** This traditional hotel near Nyugati Train Station has undergone a face-lift to give it modern comforts and easy access.
Its nightclub Orfeus draws crowds. *97 Lenin Körút VI, tel. 1/
323–300. 246 rooms with bath. Facilities: 2 restaurants, 2 bars,
nightclub. AE, DC, MC, V.*

Buda-Penta. A new hotel, the Buda-Penta is located on a busy
street near Déli train station, close to Castle Hill and most of
the sights in Buda. Its Horoszkop nightclub is a fashionable
place in which to be seen. *41–43 Krisztina Körút I, tel. 1/566–
333. 399 rooms with bath. Facilities: indoor pool, sauna, gym.
AE, DC, MC, V.*

Gellért. This well-maintained old building overlooks the river
near the Buda end of Szabadsag Bridge. Rooms are all comfortable and many have a good view of the historic Gellért district.
*Szent Gellért Tér XI, tel. 1/852–200. 235 rooms with bath. Facil-
ities: thermal pools, outdoor terrace restaurant overlooking
the Danube. AE, DC, MC, V.*

Hotel Hungaria. Though Budapest's largest hotel is directly
across from Keleti Station and Metro, noise is kept firmly at
bay with the triple-glazed windows in all rooms. *90 Rákóczi Út
VII, tel. 1/229–050. 528 rooms with bath. Facilities: 3 restaurants, nightclub, sauna, gym. AE, DC, MC, V.*

Moderate **Astoria.** The Astoria, located at a busy Inner City crossroads,
has been soundproofed in a recent refurbishing. It makes a
good base for exploring Pest. *19 Kossuth Lajos Utca V, tel. 1/
173–411. 198 rooms with bath or shower. Facilities: nightclub,
café, sauna, gym. AE, DC, MC, V.*

Emke. Centrally located in Pest just off the busy Rákóczi Út,
Emke's nightclub, Maxim's, is one of the most popular in the
city. *3–5 Akácfa Utca VII, tel. 1/229–230. 70 rooms with bath.
Facilities: nightclub, café, restaurant. AE, DC, MC, V.*

Erzsebet. This well-known hotel with a long tradition of good
service has recently been refurbished and modernized. It is located in the center of the Inner City and has a popular beer hall
(Janos Pince) among its attractions. All rooms are equipped
with TV and minibar. *11–15 Károly Mihály Utca V, tel. 1/382–
111. 123 rooms, mostly doubles with shower. Facilities: restaurant, beerhall. AE, DC, MC, V.*

★ **Vörös Csillag.** Perched 1,000 feet (305 meters) above the Danube near the upper terminus of the cog-wheel railroad, Vörös Csillag resembles a hunting lodge. Unless you have vertigo, you will admire the view of the whole city from the terrace. *21 Rege Út VII, tel. 1/750–522. 40 rooms with bath. Facilities: restaurant, bar terrace, pool, sauna. AE, DC, MC, V.*

Inexpensive **Citadella.** Comparatively basic, with four beds in some rooms, and showers down the hall, the Citadella is nevertheless very popular, particularly with young people, who enjoy the lively communal atmosphere and the location—right inside the fortress. *Gellérthgy XI, tel. 1/665–794. 40 rooms, none with bath. No credit cards.*

Wien. The Wien is located in the southwestern outskirts of the city, near the junction of the highways to Vienna and Balaton, making it popular and convenient for drivers. *88 Budaörsi Út XI, tel. 1/665–400. 110 rooms, most with bath. Facilities: restaurant, café, gas station, car repairs. AE, DC, MC, V.*

The Arts

Hotels and tourist offices will provide you with a copy of the monthly publication *Programme,* which contains details of all cultural events in the city. Tickets are available from your hotel desk or from the **Central Booking Agency** (Vörösmarty Tér, tel. 1/176–222).

There are two **opera** houses, for which dress is casual. **Concerts** are given all year at the Academy of Music on Liszt F. Tér, the Vigado on Vigado Tér, and at the Old Academy of Music on Vörösmarty Út. Displays of Hungarian **folk dancing** are held at the Cultural Center on Corvin Tér.

Entertainment and Nightlife

By Eastern European standards, Budapest is a fun and lively city at night. Places stay open late and Western European-style *drink-bars* have sprung up all over the city.

Nightclubs Many of the nightclubs are attached to larger hotels. Admission starts at 100 Ft. Drinks cost from 200 Ft. to 500 Ft.

Casanova offers music and dancing in an attractive building a few yards from the river bank on the Buda side. *4 Batthyány Tér 11, tel. 1/338–320. Open 10 PM–4 AM.*

Dunabar Boat sails up and down the river with dancing and disco music on board. *Board at Quay 3, opposite the Forum Hotel, Tel. 1/170–803. Open 10 PM–3 AM.*

Pierrot is an elegant night spot in the Castle District with live piano music and good cocktails. *14 Fortuna Utca I, tel. 1/756–971. Open 5 PM–1 AM.*

Cabarets **Horoszkop,** in the Buda-Penta Hotel, is currently the favorite among Budapest's younger set. Floor shows begin at 11 PM. *41–43 Krisztina Körút, tel. 1/566–333. Open 10 PM–4 AM.*

Maxim Variete, in the Hotel EMKE, currently offers three variety shows daily plus a "Crazy Cabaret" show. *3 Akácfa Utca VII, tel. 1/227–858. Open 8 PM–3 AM.*

Fortuna, opposite the Matthias Church on Castle Hill, is one of the city's most elegant night spots. It is located in the medieval hall of a 14th-century building. The program starts at 12:30 AM. *Hess András Tér I, tel. 1/557–451. Open 10 PM–4 AM.*

Discos The University colleges organize the best discos in town. Try the **Eötvös Lorand Club** in the Inner City, on the corner of Károly Mihály Utca and Irányi Utca. Admission and the price of drinks are reasonable.

Casinos You are free to gamble, with hard currency only, at the *casino* in the Hotel Hilton, 1–3 Hess András Tér I, tel. 1/751–000.

The Danube Bend

About 25 miles (40 kilometers) north of Budapest, the Danube abandons its eastward course and turns abruptly south toward the capital, cutting through the Börzsöny and Visegrád hills. This area is called the Danube Bend and includes the Baroque town of Szentendre, the hilltop castle ruins and town of Visegrád, and the cathedral town of Esztergom. The attractive combination of hillside and river should dispel any notions of Hungary as being one vast, boring plain.

Here, in the heartland of Hungarian history, you can see traces of a frontier district of the Roman Empire, battlefields of the Middle Ages, and a center of the Hungarian Renaissance. Although the area can be covered by car in a day—the round-trip from Budapest is only 78 miles (126 kilometers)—two days, with a night in Visegrád or Esztergom, would be a better way to savor the charms of the area.

Getting Around

The most pleasant way to get around is by boat or hydrofoil on the Danube. The three main centers—Szentendre, Esztergom, and Visegrád—all have connections with each other and with Budapest. There is also regular bus service connecting all three with each other and with Budapest.

Guided Tours

IBUSZ organizes day trips to the Danube from May through September, costing about 2,000 Ft. with lunch. Boat trips run on Wednesdays and Saturdays; buses go on Tuesdays, Fridays, and Saturdays. There is also a special bus trip to Szentendre on Thursdays.

Tourist Information

Esztergom. IBUSZ Office, Széchenyi Tér, tel. 1/484.
Szentendre. Dunatours, 6 Bacsó Part, tel. 26/11–311.
Visegrád. Dunatours, 3/a Fö U., tel. 26/28–330.

Exploring

Heading north from Budapest toward Szentendre, either by car on Road 11, or by train, on your right look for the reconstructed remains of **Aquincum,** capital of the Roman province of Pannonia. Careful excavations have unearthed a varied selection of artifacts and mosaics, giving a tantalizing feel for what life was like on the northern fringes of the Roman Empire.

Szentendre, nowadays a flourishing artists' colony with a lively Mediterranean atmosphere, was first settled by Serbians and

The Danube Bend

Greeks fleeing from the advancing Turks in the 14th and 17th centuries. There is a Greek Orthodox church in the main square and a Serbian Orthodox cathedral on the hill. The narrow cobbled streets are lined with cheerfully painted houses. In summer, there are open-air theatrical performances in the main square. Part of the town's artistic reputation can be traced to the life and work of the ceramic artist Margit Kovács, whose work blended Hungarian folk art traditions with motifs from modern art. A museum devoted to her work is housed in a small 18th-century merchant's house with an attractive courtyard. *Margit Kovács Pottery Museum, 1 Vastagh Gyorgy Utca. Admission: 10 Ft. Open daily 9–7.*

A short drive up Szabadság Forras Út, or a bus ride from the train station, will take you to the **Open-Air Ethnographical Museum,** where a collection of buildings has been designed to convey the feel of daily life in 19th-century Hungary. Small houses and cottages typify the differences in needs and construction throughout the country. *Szabadtéri Néprajzi Múzeum. Admission: 10 Ft. Open Apr.–Oct., daily 10–5.*

Visegrád, 14 miles (23 kilometers) from Szentendre, was the seat of the kings of Hungary in the 14th century. Although the ruins of the Palace of King Matthias in the main street have been excavated and reconstructed and there are jousting tournaments in June, Visegrád is not the vibrant city it once was. Still, its historical resonances make up for the relative lack of prominence.

The Slovaks arrived in the 9th and 10th centuries and named the town after the **castle**—Visegrád means "high castle" in Slavonic—built by the Romans centuries before. You can still see the remains of this castle on present-day Sibrik Hill, where there is also an expansive view of the surrounding area and of the Danube Bend itself.

Esztergom, 13 miles (21 kilometers) farther upriver stands on the site of another Roman fortress. Stephen I, the first Christian king of Hungary, was crowned here in the year 1000. The kings are long gone, but Esztergom is still the home of the Archbishop of Esztergom, head of the Catholic Church in Hungary.

The **cathedral,** the largest in Hungary, is on a hill overlooking the town; it houses a valuable collection of ecclesiastical art. Below it are the streets of Vizíváros (Watertown), lined with Baroque buildings. The **Keresztény Múzeum** (Museum of Christian Art) is situated in the Primate's Palace. It is the finest art gallery in Hungary, with a large collection of early Hungarian and Italian paintings. The Italian collection of 14th- and 15th-century works is unusually large for a museum outside Italy. This collection, coupled with the extensive number of early Renaissance paintings from Flanders and the Lower Rhine, provide insights into the transition of European sensibilities from medieval Gothic to the humanistic Renaissance. *Primate's Palace, 2 Berenyi U. Admission: 10 Ft. Open Tues.– Sun. 10–6.*

To the north of the cathedral, on **Szent Tamás Hill,** is a small church dedicated to St. Thomas à Becket of Canterbury. From here you can look down on the town and see how the Danube temporarily divides, forming an island that locals use as a base for water skiing and swimming.

Dining and Lodging

For details and price category definitions, *see* Dining and Lodging in Essential Information.

Esztergom
Dining

Kispipa. Kispipa is on a busy thoroughfare a short distance from the town center, but it is locally popular and very lively. Its wine selection is memorable. *19 Kossuth Lajos Utca (no tel.). Dress: casual. No reservations. No credit cards. Moderate.*

Halászcsárda. Eating here gives you a good excuse for exploring the little island formed by the temporary branching of the Danube. The Halászcsárda is small, friendly, and informal, and reinforces its riverside atmosphere with a good selection of fish specialties. *14 Szabad Majus sétány (no tel.). Dress: casual. Reservations not needed. No credit cards. Inexpensive.*

Lodging

Furdo. This large hotel, near the center of town, has tennis courts and is attached to the local spa, which has an open-air swimming pool for those who like to work off some goulash calories. *14 Bajcsy-Zsilinszky Utca, tel. 1/292. 85 rooms with bath. Facilities: restaurant, bar. No credit cards. Moderate.*

Vadvirág. A small guest house on the outskirts of town, Vadvirág offers simple accommodations, a restaurant, and tennis courts. *Bánomi dulö, tel. 1/174. 28 rooms, some with bath. No credit cards. Closed Oct.–Apr. Inexpensive.*

Szentendre
Dining
★

Arany Sárkány. This popular restaurant in the old town center is a must for anyone visiting Szentendre. The cooking is of high quality, and the surroundings are pleasantly informal—long tables with checked tablecloths. *2 Vörös Hadsereg Utca. Dress: neat casual. Reservations essential. AE, DC, MC, V. Closed Feb. Moderate.*

Regi Modi. This attractive upstairs restaurant is approached through a courtyard across from the Kovács Margit Múzeum. The bright decor and wine and game specialties make up for the slow service. *3 Futo Utca, tel. 36/26–11–105. Dress: neat casual. Reservations recommended. No credit cards. Moderate.*

Lodging
Danubius. The quiet Danubius Hotel is to the north of town on the riverbank, and most rooms have good views of the river. Bicycles and other sports equipment can be rented by guests. *28 Ady Endre Utca, tel. 26/12–491. 50 rooms, mostly doubles with bath. No credit cards. Moderate.*

Visegrád
Lodging
Var. This is a good choice for those whose priorities include scenery and the great outdoors. Situated at the foot of a steep hill beside the Danube, there are excellent water sports facilities nearby, but the level of accommodations is very simple. *9–11 Fő Utca, tel. 26/28–264. 15 double rooms, all with hot water but no bath. No credit cards. Inexpensive.*

Lake Balaton

Lake Balaton, the largest lake in Central Europe, stretches for 50 miles (80 kilometers) across western Hungary. Sometimes known as the nation's playground, it goes some way toward making up for Hungary's much lamented lack of coastline. On its hilly northern shore, ideal for growing grapes, is Balatonfüred, the country's oldest and most famous spa town. The national park on the Tihany Peninsula is just to the south, and regular boat service links Tihany and Balatonfüred with Siófok on the southern shore.

This shore is not as attractive as the northern one—being flatter and more crowded—with resorts, cottages, and trade union rest houses. Still, it is worth visiting because of its shallower, warmer waters that make it a better choice for swimming.

A circular tour taking in Veszprem, Balatonfüred, and Tihany could be managed in a day, but two days, with a night in Tihany or Balatonfüred, would be more relaxed and allow for detours to Herend and its porcelain factory, or to the castle of Nagyvázsony.

Getting Around

Trains from Budapest serve all the resorts on the northern shore; a separate line links the resorts of the southern shore. Road 71 runs along the northern shore; M7 covers the southern. Bus services link most resorts. Regular ferries link the major resorts.

Guided Tours

IBUSZ has several tours to Balaton from Budapest; inquire at the head office in Budapest (*see* Important Addresses and

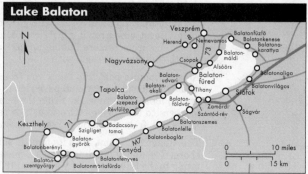

Lake Balaton

Numbers in Budapest). Other tours more easily organized from hotels in Balaton include boat trips to vineyards, folk music evenings, and overnight trips to local inns.

Tourist Information

Balatonfüred. Balatontourist Nord, 5 Blaha L. Utca, tel. 80/40–281.
Nagyvazsony. Balatontourist Nord, Kinizsi-var, tel. 80/31–015.
Tihany. Balatontourist, 20 Kossuth Utca, tel. 80/44–052.
Veszprém. Balatontourist, 3 Munnich F. Utca, tel. 80/13–750.

Exploring

Hilly **Veszprém** is the center of cultural life in the Balaton region. **Várhegy** (Castle Hill) is the most attractive part of town, north of Szabadság Tér. **Hősök Kapuja** (Heroes' Gate), at the entrance to the Castle, houses a small exhibit on Hungary's history (Admission: 10 Ft. Open May–Oct., Tues.–Sun. 10–6). Just past the gate and down a little alley to the left, is the **Tüztorony** (Fire Tower); note that the lower level is Medieval while the upper stories are Baroque. There is a good view of the town and surrounding area from the balcony.

Tolbuhin Út, the only street in the castle area, leads to a small square in front of the **Bishop's Palace** and **Cathedral;** outdoor concerts are held here in the summer. Tolbuhin Út continues past the square up to a terrace erected on the north staircase of the castle. Stand beside the modern statues of St. Stephen and his queen, Gizella, for a far-reaching view of the old quarter of town.

If you are traveling by car, go five kilometers (three miles) west to **Nemevamos,** where you can slake your thirst or conquer your hunger at **Vamosi Csárda** (Highwayman's Inn). This 18th-century Baroque building takes its name from the famous 19th-century highwayman Joska Savanyu, who claimed it as one of his bases. Go down to the cellar to see the tables and seats made from tree trunks—a local architectural feature.

Herend, 10 miles (16 kilometers) west of Veszprem on Road 8, is a little town known internationally for its porcelain factory, founded in 1839. The most valuable pieces are on display in the **Factory Museum.** *Admission: 10 Ft. Open Tues.–Sun. 10–6.*

Road 73 takes you the six miles (10 kilometers) or so to **Balatonfüred,** a spa and resort with good beaches as well as one of the finest vine-growing districts. Above the main square, where medicinal waters bubble up under a colonnaded pavilion, the hillsides are thick with vines.

A seven-minute boat trip takes you from Balatonfüred to the **Tihany Peninsula,** a national park rich in rare flora and fauna, and an ideal place to walk. From the ferry port, follow green markers to the springs (Oroszkút), or red ones to the top of **Csúcs Hill,** from which there is a good view of the lake.

The village of Tihany, with its famous **abbey,** is on the eastern shore. The abbey building houses a **museum** with exhibits relating to the Balaton area (Admission: 10 Ft. Open Tues.–Sun. 10–6). It is said locally that whoever looks down from the east windows along the second-floor corridor will have any wish come true. Also worth a look are the pink angels floating on the ceiling of the abbey church, and the abbey organ, on which recitals are given in summer. Consider a special detour to the **Rege pastry shop** at 38 Batthyány Út., not far from the abbey.

The castle of **Nagyvázsony,** about 12 miles (20 kilometers) northwest of Balatonfüred, dates to the early 15th century. The 92-foot-high keep is the oldest part, and its upper rooms now house the **Castle Museum** (Admission: 10 Ft. Open Tues.–Sun. 10–6). Try to get to the highest balcony in late afternoon for the best view. The surrounding buildings, preserved in their original style, date from the period when post horses were changed here.

Dining and Lodging

For details and price category definitions, *see* Dining and Lodging in Essential Information.

Balatonfüred
Dining

Baricska. A popular restaurant set among the vineyards on the outskirts of town, Baricska is conveniently located across from the hotels Marina and Margareta. A good selection of local wines helps keep the atmosphere informal, and the food is of high quality. *Baricska dülö. Dress: casual. Reservations not needed. No credit cards. Closed Nov.–Mar. Moderate.*

Lodging

Annabella. This is a large, modern hotel by the lakeside, offering excellent swimming and water sports facilities. It is just around the corner from the main square in town. *25 Beloiannisz Utca, tel. 86/42–222. 384 rooms; all double rooms have bath. No credit cards. Closed mid-Oct.–mid-Apr. Expensive.*

Hotel Margareta. The Margareta is right on the waterfront and is smaller and more intimate than some of its neighbors. Its restaurant is popular locally. *29 Szechenyi Utca, tel. 86/43–824. 52 rooms with bath. Facilities: restaurant, beach, fishing. No credit cards. Expensive.*

★ **Arany Csillag.** This is the choice if you've had enough of Hungary's more modern accommodations. The Arany Csillag is a simple and pleasantly old-fashioned hotel in the center of town, across from the park. *1 Zsigmond Utca, tel. 86/43–466. 79 rooms, none with bath. Facilities: restaurant. No credit cards. Inexpensive.*

Tihany
Dining

Fogas. Fogas is a type of perch native to Balaton, and the restaurant of the same name specializes in this and other fish dishes. It is right at the northern end of Tihany village. *1 Kossuth Utca (no tel.). Dress: casual. No reservations. No credit cards. Moderate.*

Halásztánya. The relaxed atmosphere and gypsy music in the evening help contribute to the popularity of the Halásztánya, which specializes in fish. *11 Visszhang Utca (no tel.). Dress: casual. No reservations. Closed Nov.–Mar. Moderate.*

Lodging
★

Club Tihany Complex. This complex, comprising the modern Tihany Hotel and Tihany Holiday Village, is near the landing stage where the ferries arrive from the south side of the lake. The top-quality facilities include cottages, restaurants, and sports of all sorts. *3 Rév Utca, 86/48–088. Facilities: restaurants, pools, squash, tennis, miniature golf. No credit cards. Closed Nov.–mid-Mar. Expensive.*

Veszprém
Dining

Bakony. An elegant restaurant in the center of town, Bakony specializes in fish dishes and has a wide-ranging menu. *2 Lenin Tér, tel. 80/12–215. Dress: casual. No reservations. No credit cards. Moderate.*

★

Vadasztánya. The Vadasztánya is just a little southwest of the town center, but worth the trip if you want to experience the old-fashioned charm of a small provincial Hungarian restaurant. The decor is what could be called "cozy traditional," and the fish and game specialties are perennial favorites. *22 József Attila Utca (no tel.). Dress: casual. No reservations. No credit cards. Moderate.*

19 Iceland

Introduction

Iceland is anything but icy. The country is actually 90% ice-free, with warm summer afternoon temperatures and a winter climate milder than New York's. The coastal farms lie in sweet green meadows, where cows, sheep, and ponies graze among raging streams. Wildflowers grow among the quaking grasses and the sheep-colored rocks. Distant waterfalls drop from heath-covered mountains with great spiked ridges and snow-capped peaks.

Iceland's name can be blamed on Hrafna-Floki, a 9th-century Norse settler who failed to plant enough crops to see his livestock through their first winter. Leaving in a huff, he passed a northern fjord filled with pack ice, and cursed the country with a name that's kept tourism in cold storage for 1,100 years.

Unfortunately, most visitors to Iceland see nothing more than the airport gift shop en route to Europe. What a shame. Even on a three-day stopover, you can go pony trekking, live on an Icelandic farm, cross the steaming lava fields on the Westmann Islands, and explore some of the most awesome scenery in the world.

The second largest island in Europe, Iceland is in the middle of the North Atlantic where the warm Gulf Stream from the south confronts the cold breezes from the north. Beneath some of the country's glaciers are burning fires that become visible during volcanic eruptions—fires that heat the hot springs and geysers that are all over the country. The springs, in turn, heat all the homes, hospitals, and public swimming pools in Reykjavik, keeping the nation's capital smokeless and smogless.

Nearly two-fifths of Iceland's 245,000 people live in Reykjavik and its suburbs. Although virtually everyone speaks English, the official language is Icelandic, a highly inflected Germanic tongue, brought to the country by early Norse settlers, that has changed little over the centuries.

The first permanent settlers arrived from Norway in 874, though some Irish monks had arrived a century earlier. The country came under Danish control in 1380 and did not win complete independence until 1944.

Today, Iceland tries to come to terms with being a neighbor of the USSR, yet having strong ties to Washington and Western Europe. Having played host to the memorable Fisher-Spassky chess match in 1972, Iceland moved onto the political chessboard in 1986, with the Reykjavik summit meeting of President Ronald Reagan and Soviet leader Mikhail Gorbachev.

Before You Go

When to Go The best time to visit is from May through November. The months of June and July are specially recommended because during that time there is perpetual daylight. In Reykjavik the sun disappears behind the mountains for only a couple of hours, and in the northern part of the island it barely sets at all. Although the weather is unpredictable, June through August is usually warm and sunny, mixed with a few short periods of rain showers.

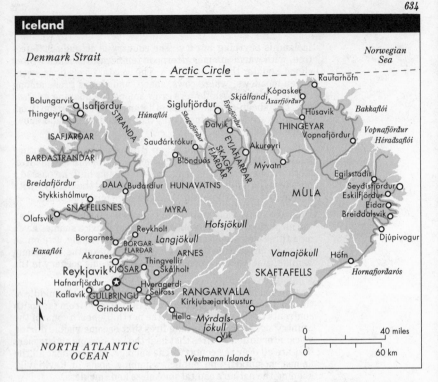

Climate Iceland enjoys a temperate ocean climate with cool summers
and surprisingly mild winters—the average temperature in
January is higher than New York's. In the northern part of the
country, the weather is more stable than in the south, with less
wind and rain. When there is rain and drizzle in the south, the
skies are usually clear in the north, and vice versa.

The following are the average daily maximum and minimum
temperatures for Reykjavik.

Jan.	35F	2C	May	50F	10C	Sept.	52F	11C
	28	−2		39	4		43	6
Feb.	37F	3C	June	54F	12C	Oct.	45F	7C
	28	−2		45	7		38	3
Mar.	39F	4C	July	57F	14C	Nov.	39F	4C
	30	−1		48	9		32	0
Apr.	43F	6C	Aug.	56F	14C	Dec.	36F	2C
	33	1		47	8		29	−2

Currency The Icelandic monetary unit is the krona (plural kronur), which
is equal to 100 aurar. Coins are the IKR 50 and 50 aurar. There
are kronur bills in denominations of 10 and 50 (both are rare)
and 500, 1,000, and 5,000. At press time (fall 1988), the rate of
exchange was IKR 39 to the dollar and IKR 72 to the pound
sterling. You are not permitted to bring more than IKR 8,000
into the country, but you may bring any amount of foreign currency, which is easily cashed into kronur at the Icelandic
banks. Major credit cards, especially MasterCard and Visa, are
widely accepted in the capital but to a far less extent in the
countryside.

What It Will Cost   Iceland is expensive. Since the late 1970s, it has had the greatest rate of inflation of any West European country. Hotels and restaurants cost about 20% more in Reykjavik than elsewhere in the country. The airport departure tax is about IKR 850.

Sample Prices   A cup of coffee, bottle of beer, or soft drink are about IKR 40 each; a sandwich, about IKR 60; and a 3.2 km (two-mile) taxi ride, about IKR 250.

Customs on Arrival   Tourists can bring in one liter of drinks with 21% alcohol content; six liters of imported beer; one liter of liquor with up to 47% alcohol content, and 200 cigarettes.

Language   The official language is Icelandic, a Nordic language with many similarities to Old English. English is widely understood and spoken, particularly by the younger people.

Getting Around

By Car   The Ring Road, which encircles the island, still has stretches that are unpaved, although improvements are made every year. Apart from this, there are asphalt roads connecting the major coastal towns and long stretches of paved highway from the capital to Keflavík and Selfoss. Except on these highways, driving can be a very bumpy experience, often along lava track or dirt and gravel surfaces. But the superb scenery more than makes up for it. Although service stations and garages are few and far between, the main roads are patrolled and fellow motorists are friendly and helpful. If you are traveling off the beaten path, you'll need a four-wheel-drive vehicle. An international driver's license is required—you can apply for one at the local police station if you are at least 20 years old and in possession of a valid driver's license from home.

By Plane   Icelandair and Arnarflug (Eagle Air) have domestic flights to some 50 towns and villages.

By Bus   A comprehensive network of buses compensates for the lack of any train network. A good buy, if you want to explore extensively, is the **Omnibus Passport,** a special ticket valid for unlimited travel by scheduled bus for one to four weeks and costing from about $170 to $310. Another is the **Full Circle Passport,** valid for a circular trip around Iceland without any time limit, which costs $145. An **Air/Bus Rover Ticket** entitles the bearer to special discounts on certain Central Highland tours, camping grounds, youth hostels, and ferries.

Essential Information

Telephones
Local Calls   Pay phones take IKR 5 and IKR 10 coins and are found in hotels, shops, bus stations, and post offices. There are not many outdoor telephone booths in the towns and villages.

International Calls   You can dial direct to almost anywhere in Europe and the United States. Hotels in Iceland, as elsewhere, add hefty service charges to international calls, so ask about the charges in advance before you place a call from your room.

Operators and Information   For collect calls and assistance on overseas calls, dial 09; for local calls, dial 02; for information, dial 03.

Mail
Postal Rates   Airmail letters to the United States cost IKR 32; letters to Europe, IKR 16.

Receiving Mail You can have your mail sent to the post office in any town or village in Iceland. In Reykjavik, have mail sent to the downtown post office (R/O Posthusstræti, 101 Reykjavik).

Shopping European goods—most often Scandinavian Modern—as a rule are more expensive in Iceland than in the United States. Best bets are locally made woolen goods and fine art. Prices at the airport shops are up to 35% higher than in Reykjavik. Hand-woven goods are more expensive than machine-made goods, which are often just as attractive. If you prefer the hand-woven goods, check carefully to be certain they are not machine-made, or you may end up paying the higher price.

Opening and Closing Times **Banks.** Banks are open weekdays 9:15 AM to 4 PM, and Thursdays, 5 PM to 6 PM.

Museums. Museums are usually open 1 PM to 4:30 PM, but some open as early as 10 AM and others stay open until 7 PM.

Shops. Shops are open weekdays from 9 to 6 PM and Saturdays from 9 AM to noon.

National Holidays January 1 (New Year's Day); March 23–27 (Easter); April 21 (first day of spring); May 1 (Labor Day); May 5 (Ascension Day); May 15–16 (Pentacost); June 17 (National Day); August 1 (public holiday); December 25–26 (Christmas).

Dining Seafood and lamb are the local specialties. There is a wide variety of eating establishments, including sophisticated, trendy restaurants, cafés, and cafeterias. Street vendors sell tasty hot dogs with fried onions.

Mealtimes Dinner, served between 6 and 9 PM, is the main meal; a light lunch is usually served between noon and 2. Most restaurants are open from midmorning until midnight.

Ratings The following ratings are for a three-course meal for one person. Prices include taxes and service charges but not wine or cocktails. Best bets are indicated by a star ★. At press time, there were 39 kronur (IKR) to the dollar.

Category	Cost
Expensive	over IKR 1,800
Moderate	IKR 1,000–IKR 1,800
Inexpensive	under IKR 1,000

Credit Cards The following credit card abbreviations are used: AE, American Express; DC, Diners Club; MC, MasterCard; V, Visa.

Lodging There is a wide range of accommodations in Iceland—hotels, hostels, rooms in private houses, guesthouses, and farmhouses. The **Iceland Tourist Board** (tel. 91/25855) offers information on where to stay. Most hotels in Reykjavik include breakfast in the price and have rooms with private baths.

Ratings Prices are for two people sharing a double room. Best bets are indicated by a star ★. At press time, there were 39 kronur (IKR) to the dollar.

Category	Reykjavik	Other Areas
Expensive	over IKR 4,000	over IKR 3,600
Moderate	IKR 3,600–IKR 4,000	IKR 2,200–IKR 3,600
Inexpensive	under IKR 3,600	under IKR 2,200

Credit Cards The following credit card abbreviations are used: AE, American Express; DC, Diners Club; MC, MasterCard; V, Visa.

Tipping There is no tipping in Iceland.

Reykjavik

Arriving and Departing

By Plane Flights from the United States and Europe arrive at Keflavík Airport, 30 miles (50 km) from Reykjavik. Flights from Greenland arrive at Reykjavik City Airport. For information on arrivals and departures at Keflavík Airport, call 91/690–100.

Between the Airport and Downtown Buses connect with all flights to and from Keflavík. The drive takes 45 minutes and costs IKR 250. Taxis are also available, but they are expensive.

By Boat During the summer, the North Atlantic ferry, **Norrona**, sails from the Faroe Islands, Shetland Islands, Denmark, and Norway to Seydisfjördur, magnificent fjords on the east side of Iceland, 450 miles (720 km) from Reykjavik. From Seydisfjördur, Reykjavik is a one-hour flight or a 10-hour drive. For information, contact **Smyril Line Passenger Department**, Box 370, 3800 Torshavn, Faroes, c/o Urval Travel, Posthusstræti 9, Reykjavik.

Getting Around

The best way to see Reykjavik is on foot. Most of the interesting sites are in the city center, within easy walking distance of one another. Sightseeing tours are also a good way to familiarize yourself with the city. There is no subway system.

By Bus Buses run from 6 AM to midnight. The fare is IKR 40 for adults, IKR 11 for children. A number of reduced-rate tickets are available at the main bus stations, including an exchange ticket that allows you to travel anywhere in the city within a 45-minute period.

By Taxi Rates start at about IKR 100. Because Reykjavik is small, most taxi rides do not exceed IKR 300.

Important Addresses and Numbers

Tourist Information The Tourist Information Center, Ingólfsstræti 5 (tel. 91/623045), is near Bankastræti/Lanfávegur, the main shopping district. It's open weekdays 10 AM—4 PM, weekends, 10 AM—2 PM.

Embassies U.S. Laufásvegur 21, tel. 91/21900. U.K. Laufásvegur 49, tel. 91/15883. **Canadian Consulate:** Laufásvegur 77, 91/13721.

Emergencies   **Police,** tel. 11166. **Ambulance,** tel. 11100. **Doctors and dentists,** weekdays 8 AM—5 PM, tel. 91/696600; weekdays 5 PM—8 AM and weekends, tel. 91/21230. **Pharmacies** operate on a rotating basis during nights and weekends. Those that are open overnight will post the information in their windows. At any given time, at least one of the following two will be open: **Ingolfs Apotek,** tel. 91/29300, and **Laugavegs Apotek,** tel. 91/24045.

English Bookstores   **Bókaverslun Snæbjarnar,** Hafnarstræti 4, tel. 91/14281. **Sigfús Eymudsson,** Austurstræti, tel. 91/27077. **Mál og menning,** Laugavegur 18, 91/24240.

Travel Agencies   **American Express,** Útsýn Travel, Austurstræti 17, tel. 91/26611. **Diners Club,** Atlantic Travel, Hallveigarstigur 2, tel. 91/28388. **Reykjavik Travel Bureau,** Adalstræti 16, tel. 91/621490. **Samvinn-Travel,** Austurstræti 12, tel. 91/27077. **Úrval Travel,** Pósthússtræti 9, tel. 91/13491. **Iceland Tourist Bureau,** Skógarhlid 6, tel. 91/25855.

Guided Tours

Tour operators use clean, comfortable buses that hold from 16 to 45 people. For information, call the **Tourist Information Center,** tel. 91/623045.

Orientation Tours   **Reykjavik Excursions** (tel. 91/621011/688922) offers **Reykjavik City-Sightseeing,** a daily tour that takes about two-and-a-half hours and includes commercial centers, folk museums, and art centers.

Special-Interest Tours   A popular tour with history buffs is to the island of **Videy,** once the cultural and trade center of Iceland. The island, across the harbor from Reykjavik (a 15-minute ferry ride), was the site of a monastery built in 1226 and boasts the country's oldest stone house, built in the 8th century. Guided tours are conducted daily and take about three hours. Tel. 91/623045.

Museums   Reykjavik has 13 major museums, including the **Maritime Museum,** the **Numismatic Collection Museum,** and the **Nature Study Centre.** A few of the most popular ones:

The **Arbær Open-Air Museum** has an exhibition of old buildings furnished in period style, including a farmhouse, turf-roofed church, and many buildings from early Reykjavik. *Arbaer, tel. 91/84412. Open July–Aug. Tues.–Sat. 10–6; in Sept. on weekends 10–6;* during the winter, call for hours.

National Museum (Pjoominjasafnio) has a wide-ranging exhibition of items illustrating Icelandic cultural history and works of art by both Icelandic and foreign artists. *Suourgata, tel. 91/28888. Open 11:30–4:30. Closed Mon.*

Museum of Natural History has geological, botanical, and zoological exhibitions. *Hlemmtorg, tel. 91/29822. Open 1:30–4:30. Closed Mon. and Wed.*

Excursions   **Reykjavik Excursions** (*see* Orientation Tours) has many different types of tours. Perhaps the most interesting are the daily **Gullfoss/Geysir** tour, an eight-hour visit to volcanic craters, geysers, and waterfalls; three-hour pony-trekking trips; and, during the whaling season, a four-hour trip to the only whaling station in the North Atlantic, just outside Reykjavik. For trout fishing excursions, contact **Úrval Travel** (tel. 91/28522).

Personal Guides   Many travel agencies offer English-speaking personal guides for tours of the city and outlying areas. For more extensive excursions, contact the **Touring Club of Iceland**, Öldugata 3, tel. 91/19533/11798, or **Outdoor Life Tours**, Grófin 1, 91/14606.

Exploring Reykjavik

Iceland has a population of just over 245,000, with nearly 100,000 living in the capital and its suburbs. Reykjavik is the political, business, and cultural center of the nation, and what "happens" there affects the entire country. It is a city with many restaurants, shops, cabarets, discos, museums, art galleries, and thermal-heated public swimming pools.

The Main Attractions

1 For most residents, the heart of Reykjavik is **Austurvöllur**, a small square in the center of the city. The square faces **Althing** (parliament building) and its statue of Jón Sigurdsson, the national hero who led Iceland's fight for independence. Next to **2** Althing is the **cathedral**, a small wooden church, and behind the cathedral is **Tjorrnin** (Pond), a beautiful lake close to the shopping center. Tjorrnin is fed by thermal springs that keep parts of it ice-free during the winter, making it an attraction for birds year-round and a popular area for bird lovers. Nearby, on Pósthússtræti, is a popular modern art gallery, **Galleri Borg** (tel. 91/24211).

Turn right onto Austuirstræto. On the facing corner is the main **post office**. This street, which has interesting shops and **3** cafés, leads onto a square, **Lækjartorg**. One of the two city bus centers is on the north side of the square. Leading out of the square is **Bankastræti**, the busiest shopping street in Reykjavik. To your right is a small hill with old houses. This is the **Bernhöftstorfa** district, virtually unchanged for the past century. The last building on the street was built in 1849 by a baker named Bernhoft. Today it houses a popular seafood restaurant, **Lækjarbrekka**. On the left side of Bankastræti is a former pris-**4** on building that now houses the **offices of Iceland's president and prime minister**. Walk left, toward Arnarhóll hill. On top of **5** the hill is a statue of the first settler in Iceland, **Ingólfur Arnarson**, a Viking who arrived in 874 and lived in Reykjavik. Nearby is the **Bank of Iceland**, a large black modern building in an architectural style that has created a great deal of controversy. Across the hill is a 19th-century building, which was **6** once the National Library but is now the **High Court**. Behind it **7** is the **National Theater**. Most of the other buildings in this area house government ministries.

8 Walk along Ingólfsstræti. To the right you'll see the **Icelandic Opera**, an old cinema. A bit farther up, across Bankastræti, is the **Tourist Information Center**. Turn left along Bankastræti and take your first right on Skólavördustígur. At the end of this **9** street towers **Hallgrimskirkja**, a church that dominates the city's skyline. Its namesake, **Hallgrimur Pétursson**, was an Icelandic medieval poet who wrote *Psalms of Passion*, theological poems that have been translated into more than 50 languages. During the day the church tower is open to the public, offering panoramic views of the city and surrounding areas.

10 Art lovers will want to visit the galleries of **Einar Jónsson** (next **11** to Eiriksgata; open weekends 1:30–4) and **Asmundur Sveinsson** (Kirkjumýrrarbletti 10, Sigtún; open weekdays 4–10, **12** weekends 2–10). The **Kjarvalsstradir** is the **Municipal Art Gal-**

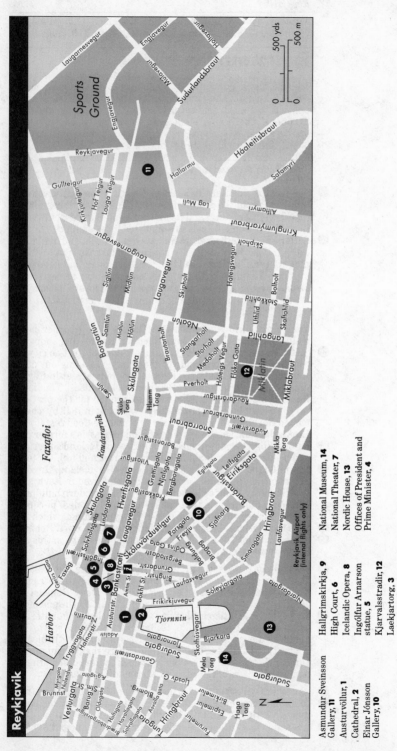

Reykjavik

500 yds
500 m

Asmundur Sveinsson
Gallery, **11**
Austurvöllur, **1**
Cathedral, **2**
Einar Jónsson
Gallery, **10**

Hallgrimskirkja, **9**
High Court, **6**
Icelandic Opera, **8**
Ingólfur Arnarson
statue, **5**
Kjarvalsstradir, **12**
Laekjartorg, **3**

National Museum, **14**
National Theater, **7**
Nordic House, **13**
Offices of President and
Prime Minister, **4**

lery, named in honor of Kjarval, the nation's best-loved painter (Miklatin; open daily 2–8).

Walk along the streets between the church and the lake, through a beautiful park, to **Nordic House,** a cultural center with exhibitions, lectures, and concerts (open daily 2–7). The **National Museum,** with its displays of Viking artifacts, national costumes, weaving, wood carving, and silver work, is also in this area (*see* Museums).

Shopping

The most attractive shops, selling Icelandic woolen goods, arts and crafts, are downtown on Adalstræti, Hafnarstræti, and Vesturgata streets. These include **Icelandic Handcrafts Centre** (Falcon House, Hafnarstræti 3, tel. 91/11784); the **Handknitting Association of Iceland,** a cooperative (Skolavoroustigur 19, tel. 91/21890/21912); and **Hilda Ltd.** (Borgartun 22, tel. 91/24590).

Dining

Most Reykjavik restaurants feature excellent seafood dishes, cooked in a wide variety of ways. Many serve European cuisine, as well as local fish and lamb specialties. Reservations are vital on weekends in the better restaurants. Jacket and tie are appreciated but rarely required. Most are open from noon to midnight, and most take major credit cards.

Ratings The following ratings are for a three-course meal for one person. Prices include taxes and service but not wine. Best bets are indicated by a star ★. At press time, there were 39 kronur (IKR) to the dollar.

Category	Cost
Expensive	over IKR 1,800
Moderate	IKR 1,000–IKR 1,800
Inexpensive	under IKR 1,000

Expensive **Alex.** A wide range of fish and meat dishes are served here in an atmosphere that is bright, modern, and relaxed. *Laugavegur 126, tel. 91/24631. Dress: casual. Reservations advised. AE, DC, MC, V.*

Arnarhóll. This formal restaurant is divided into small, intimate dining rooms and has exceptional service. Try the duck a l'orange. *Hverfisgata 8–10, tel. 91/18833. Jacket and tie. Reservations recommended. AE, DC, MC, V.*

Hótel Holt. This restaurant, in the hotel of the same name, has for many years enjoyed the reputation of having one of the best kitchens in Iceland. Paintings by some of the country's finest artists hang on the walls. *Bergstadastræti 37, tel. 91/25700. Jacket and tie. Reservations advised. AE, DC, MC, V.*

Vid Sjávarsíduna. This harbor-front restaurant features Continental seafood dishes. *Tryggvagötu, tel. 91/15520. Jacket and tie. Reservations advised. AE, DC, MC, V.*

★ **Vid Tjörnina.** This restaurant has a homey atmosphere, what the locals call a "grandmother ambience." The chef is a pioneer of Icelandic seafood cuisine; his marinated codgills are not to be missed. *Templarasund 3, tel. 91/18555. Dress: casual. Reservations advised. AE, MC, V.*

Moderate   **Gaukur á Stöng.** This is a lively, bar/restaurant near the harbor that attracts a young crowd. The menu is limited, but what's offered is well prepared. Don't come here if you want a quiet dinner for two, because it can get very noisy. *Tryggvagata 22, tel. 91/11556. Dress: casual. Reservations not necessary. AE, DC, MC, V.*

Hard Rock Café. This is similar to the others in the chain, though some say it's better than most. It has a large selection of burgers, desserts, and plenty of loud music. *Kringlan, tel. 91/ 689888. Dress: casual. Reservations not necessary. AE, DC, MC, V.*

Hornid Restaurant. Lamb dishes and French and Italian specialties are featured at this restaurant. *Hafnarstræti 15, tel. 91/20366. Dress: casual. Reservations advised. AE, MC, V.*

Potturinn og Pannan. This small restaurant on the edge of the downtown area has brisk and efficient service without being impersonal. Lamb and fish dishes and American-style salads are the specialties. *Brautarholt 22, tel. 91/11690. Dress: casual. Reservations advised. AE, MC, V.*

Torfan. This restaurant, in a 19th-century town house, is the best place for tasting authentic, traditional Icelandic cuisine. *Amtmannsstígur 1, tel. 91/13303. Dress: casual. Reservations advised. AE, DC, MC, V.*

Inexpensive   **Cafe Hressó.** This is the place for a quick snack and some local color; it's as close to a French café as you'll find in Iceland. Alcohol is not served. *Austurstræti 20, tel. 91/14353. Dress: casual. Reservations not necessary. MC, V.*

El Sombrero. Near the main square, this is another good spot for a snack and people watching. Spanish food and pizzas are served. *Lauggavegur 73, tel. 91/23866. Dress: casual. Reservations not necessary. AE, MC, V.*

Lauga-ás. If you've been for a dip in the nearby swimming pool, you'll be ready for the rich, wholesome meals served here. Don't let the lack of decor put you off; this is a very popular place. No alcohol. *Laugarásvegur 1, tel. 91/31620. Dress: casual. Reservations not necessary. MC, V.*

Múlakaffi. The fresh clean air of Reykjavik should give you the hearty appetite you'll need for this working-class café, especially popular for lunch. *Hallamúlli, tel. 91/37737. Dress: casual. Reservations not necessary. MC, V.*

Lodging

Ratings   Prices are for two people sharing a double room. Best bets are indicated by a star ★ . At press time, there were 39 kronur (IKR) to the dollar.

Category	Cost
Expensive	over IKR 4,400
Moderate	IKR 3,600–IKR 4,000
Inexpensive	under IKR 3,600

Expensive   **Esja.** This recently renovated hotel is a little way out of town, in the business area near the outdoor thermal swimming pool and sports hall. All rooms have been attractively decorated. There are fine views of the bay and Mount Esja from the Penthouse Cocktail Bar. *Sudurlandsbraut 2, tel. 91/82200. 134 rooms with* *bath or shower. Facilities: restaurant and lounge. AE, DC, MC, V.*

★ **Holt.** One of Reykjavik's finest hotels, the Holt is in a quiet residential suburb. Many of the rooms are furnished with Icelandic works of art. The restaurant (*see* Dining) is especially good. *Bergstadastræti 37, tel. 91/25700. 50 rooms with bath or shower. Facilities: restaurant and lounge. AE, DC, MC, V.*

Loftleider. The largest hotel in Iceland, the Loftleider accommodates both tourists and those attending meetings and conventions. Located near the airport, it's 15 minutes from the center of town. *Reykjavik Airport, tel. 91/22322. 218 rooms with bath. Facilities: indoor pool, sauna, solarium, restaurant, cafeteria, and several lounges. AE, DC, MC, V.*

★ **Saga.** In a class of its own, this hotel is very popular with American businesspeople. All rooms are above the fourth level and have spectacular views of the city and beyond. It's within walking distance of most museums, shops, and restaurants. *Hagatorg, tel. 91/29900. 162 rooms with bath. Facilities: restaurant with live music and dancing, rooftop grill, 6 bars, sauna, in-room video. AE, DC, MC, V.*

Moderate   **Borg.** Near the parliament and the cathedral, the Borg makes an ideal base for sightseeing. It's a traditional, comfortable hotel, with all rooms heated by water piped in from the hot springs. *Pósthússtræti 11, tel. 91/11440. 46 rooms, most with bath. Facilities: restaurant and lounge, rooftop terrace. AE, DC, MC, V.*

Inexpensive   **Gardur.** This establishment is owned by the university and is only open during the summer when the students are on vacation. It has basic but comfortable rooms, adequate for travelers on a tight budget. It's within easy reach of the National Museum and other attractions. *Hringbraut, tel. 91/15656. 44 rooms without private bath. No credit cards. Closed in winter.*

Guest house. *Brautarholt 22, tel. 91/20986. 24 rooms. Summer only. No credit cards.*

Guest house. *Snorrabraut 52, tel. 91/16522. 18 rooms. No credit cards.*

Royal Inn Guest house. *Laugavegur 11, tel. 91/24513. No credit cards.*

Salvation Army Guest house. *Kirkjustræti 2, tel. 91/13203. 24 rooms. No credit cards.*

Viking Guest house. *Ranargata 12, tel. 91/19367. 11 rooms. No credit cards.*

Away From Reykjavik

The real beauty of Iceland is in the countryside: The fjords of the east, the stark mountains of the north, the sands of the south, the rough coastline of the west, and the recently created lava fields of the interior. Spend at least an hour pouring over the literature at the Tourist Bureau in Reykjavik before deciding where to go first.

Getting Around

There are daily flights to most of the large towns. Although flights are expensive, special family fares and vacation tickets are available. The longest domestic flight takes just over an hour. Scheduled bus services cover most of the inhabited parts of the island and even stretch into the interior highlands. If you have the time, going by bus or private car is the best way to see the country, even though the roads are poor. There are car-rental agencies in Reykjavik and in many towns around the country. The ferries mainly go to the Westmann Islands in the south, and boat service is limited along the western coast.

Guided Tours and Exploring

Because of the remoteness of Iceland and the hassles of driving on roads that are often not in good condition, many people prefer an organized bus tour from Reykjavik. Those who do venture out on their own in rented cars will have the luxury of mapping out their own itinerary, touring at their own pace, and stopping at remote hot springs for skinny dipping whenever the mood strikes. If you go on your own, whether by public transportation or car, you can arrange to stay in **farmhouses** that have registered with the **Iceland Tourist Board** (tel. 91/ 27488). Its brochure, *Farm Holidays in Iceland,* lists 42 farms that take visitors. In addition, the **Icelandic Touring Club** operates a number of huts in the remote parts of the country that are clean, warm, and comfortable, but only available on a first-come, first-served basis.

Guided bus tours are excellent ways to relax and enjoy Iceland's spectacular scenery. Most tours operate between June and September and cost from $500 to $1,600 per person, including overnight accommodations and three meals a day. On some tours you'll stay in hotels; on others you'll camp out or sleep in tents. Tours are available for three days to 19 days and can be booked from the United States or the United Kingdom through **Icelandair** or travel agencies. Tours include:

Grand Safari. This 19-day trip along the coastlines and the interior includes camping at night (Úlvar Jacobsen Travel, Austurstræti 9, Reykjavik).
Birdwatchers' Paradise. This is a 12-day trip by both air and land to the great bird colonies. You'll stay in hotels or guest-houses. (Samvinn-Travel, Austurstræti 12, Reykjavik).
Riding in Landmannalauger. A six-day tour by Icelandic pony, mostly around the interior. You'll overnight in mountain huts. (Iceland Tourist Board, Laugavegur 3, Reykjavik, tel. 91/ 27488).
Meet the People. This is a six-day bus tour around the southwest of the country, visiting homes in the villages and on the farms. Lodging is in hotels (Utsýn Travel Agency, Austurstræti 17, Reykjavik).

Local Tours One-day tours are available in all the major towns in Iceland and can be arranged through agencies in Reykjavik (*see* Important Addresses and Numbers).

From Akureyri there are several excursions:

Tours to **Lake Myvatn** take about 10 hours and cost about $50 per person. On the **Midnight Sun Tour,** you drive along Eyjafjördur and watch the sun reach its lowest point and then rise again. This is a four-hour tour and costs about $35 per person. There's also a **Midnight Sun Flight** to **Grimsey,** which takes about one and a half hours and costs about $90. Tours around the **north of Iceland** are also available in Lake Myvatn and Husavik.

From **Egilsstadir** there's a tour to **Mjóifjödur** across the rough mountain passes—a strenuous eight-hour tour costing about $32 per person. From Höfn in Hornafjördur you can go by bus on a **Glacier Tour**. It's a 10-hour tour costing about $75 per person. One-day tours are also available from **Borgarnes** and **Flökalunder** in the western part of the country. There are also bus and boat tours available from **Vestmannæyjar**.

Dining and Lodging

Most restaurants outside of Reykjavik are in hotels. The following list is in alphabetical order within the four major regions of Iceland. Generally, lodging in the countryside is cheaper than in the capital, but meals cost about the same. Most exploring is done with tours that provide up to three meals a day as well as accommodations, but this list highlights some of the best-value and most interesting options in the outlying regions.

For details and price category definitions, *see* Dining and Lodging in Essential Information.

The South
Laugarvatn

Edda HSL. This hotel and restaurant combination benefits from its location by an attractive lake fed by warm springs. *Tel. 99/6154. 27 rooms with bath or shower. MC, V. Closed winter. Moderate.*

Edda ML. If money is a real consideration, then you might want to opt for this inexpensive neighbor of the Edda HSL; it, too, has a lakeside location, although conditions are just a little less plush. *Tel. 99/6118. 88 rooms with bath or shower. MC, V. Closed winter. Inexpensive.*

Skogar

Edda. There are memorable views—of the sea on one side and glaciers and mountains on the other—from this comfortable hotel near the Skogarfoss waterfall. *Tel. 99/8187. 34 rooms without bath. MC, V. Closed winter. Inexpensive.*

Thingvellir
★

Valholl. The Valholl has an excellent location, right by the lake where the world's oldest surviving parliament was founded. *Tel. 99/2622. 37 rooms with bath or shower. MC, V. Closed winter. Moderate.*

The West
Isafjordur

Isafjordur. You'll find more than the normal amount of creature comforts and pampering in this well-run, efficient hotel. *Silfurtorgi 2, tel. 94/4111. 31 rooms with bath. MC, V. Expensive.*

Reykholt

Edda. This comfortable hotel, in the town where the medieval saga writer Snorri Sturluson spent most of his life, has a peaceful location close to the cave, Surtshellir. *Tel. 93/51260. 64 rooms with bath. Facilities: swimming pool. MC, V. Closed winter. Moderate.*

Stykkisholmur

Stykkisholmur. This hotel makes a convenient stopping-off point for excursions to the islands of Breidafjordur. There is also a nearby ferry to Vestfirdir. *Vatnasi, tel. 93/81330. 26 rooms, some with bath or shower. MC, V. Moderate.*

The North
Akureyri

KEA. Prices are surprisingly modest in this first-class hotel with an excellent restaurant. *Hafnarstræti 89, tel. 96/2200. 51 rooms with bath or shower. MC, V. Expensive.*

Myvatn

Reykjahlid. Another good hotel with an excellent location (right on a lake), the Reykjahlid still manages to keep prices within check, at least by Icelandic standards. *Myvatnssveit, tel. 96/44142. 12 rooms without bath. MC, V. Closed winter. Moderate.*

Reynihlid. This comfortable hotel played host to U.S. astronauts when they were preparing for the moon voyages—the nearby terrain was as close to moon-surface conditions as anywhere on Earth. *Myvatnssveit, tel. 96/44170. 44 rooms, some with bath or shower. MC, V. Moderate.*

Saudarkrokur **Mælifell.** This small hotel hosts dances most weekends. *Adalgata 7, tel. 955265. 7 rooms with bath. MC, V. Moderate.*

The East **Valaskjalf.** The restaurant is recommended in this friendly ho-
Egilsstadir tel, but alcohol is not served. *v/Skogarstrond, tel. 97/11500. 24 rooms with bath or shower. MC, V. Moderate.*

Hallormsstadur **Edda.** The hotel has a good range of services and comforts, but
★ the main attraction is its peaceful location in a quiet wooded area. *Hallormsstad, tel. 97/1683. 22 rooms, none with bath. MC, V. Closed winter. Inexpensive.*

Seydisfjordur **Snæfell.** This new hotel is set in a 19th-century house; the good
★ restaurant is inside a greenhouse by a pretty pond. *Austurvegur 3, tel. 97/21460. 12 rooms, some with bath. MC, V. Moderate.*

20 Ireland

Introduction

Ireland, the most westerly country in Europe, is a small island on which you are never more than an hour's drive from the sea. It's actually two countries in one. The northeast corner of the island, Northern Ireland, remains a part of the United Kingdom, while the Republic, with a population of only 3½ million, has been independent since 1921.

The Republic of Ireland is virtually free from the "troubles" that dominate the news from Northern Ireland. Over the past few years, millions of pounds have been spent on upgrading tourist facilities, but the attractions of Ireland as a vacation destination remain the same as ever: those of a small, friendly country with a mild climate and a relaxed pace of life where simple pleasures are to be found in its scenery, its historical heritage, its sporting opportunities, and the informal hospitality of its loquacious inhabitants.

Dublin, the capital, is a thriving modern city, with the amenities of a leading European metropolis. It's a strikingly elegant city, too, a fact of which the Dubliners are well aware. Trinity College, Dublin Castle, and the magnificent public buildings and distinctive Georgian squares of the city have all been restored, allowing the elegance of 18th-century Dublin to emerge again after centuries of neglect. You will find, too, that the courtesy and charm of the Dubliners themselves make an important contribution to your visit, introducing you to a city with an atmosphere that belongs to an older, less frenetic age.

The Irish way of life is unpretentious and informal. Pubs play an important part in it. The Irish will be found at their most convivial when seated in front of a pint of their famous black beer, Guinness, consumed here in vast quantities. Even if you do not usually frequent bars, a visit to an Irish pub or two will add greatly to the enjoyment of your visit.

The pace of life outside Dublin is even more relaxed. When a local was asked for the Irish-language equivalent of *mañana*, the reply came that there is no word in Irish to convey quite the same sense of urgency. An exaggeration, of course, but the farther you travel from the metropolis, the more you will be inclined to linger. Apart from such sporting attractions as championship golf, horse racing, deep-sea fishing, and angling, the thing to do in Ireland is to take it easy, and look around you. The Lakes of Killarney—romantic, boulder-strewn mountains, strung with a chain of deep-blue lakes—are justifiably the country's most famous beauty spot. The Ring of Kerry provides the motorist with a day-long tour through lush coastal vegetation. By contrast, you will have to explore the eerie limestone desert called The Burren, in County Clare, on foot in order to find its rare Alpine and Mediterranean flowers. Likewise, if you want to stand on the summit of the Cliffs of Moher to watch the Atlantic breakers pounding on the rocks 700 feet (210 meters) below you, you'll have to walk a bit first. The blue hills of Connemara remain the inspiration for many paintings. The history buff will delight in the Shannon region, peppered with numerous castles, some of which have been meticulously restored. Throughout the country, there are prehistoric and early-Christian remains to be discovered. You can also seek out the places made famous by James Joyce, William Butler Yeats,

John Millington Synge, and other well-known writers and gain
a new insight into the land and the people that inspired them.

Before You Go

When to Go The main tourist season runs from June to mid-September.
The attractions of Ireland are not as dependent on the weather
as those in most other northern European countries, however,
and the scenery is just as attractive in the off-peak times of fall
and spring. Accommodations are more economical in winter,
although some of the smaller attractions are closed from October to March. In all seasons the visitor can expect to encounter
rain.

Climate Winters are mild though wet; summers can be warm and sunny,
but there's always the risk of a sudden shower. No one ever
came to Ireland for a suntan.

The following are the average daily maximum and minimum
temperatures for Dublin.

Jan.	46F	8C	May	60F	15C	Sept.	63F	17C
	34	1		43	6		48	9
Feb.	47F	8C	June	65F	18C	Oct.	57F	14C
	35	2		48	9		43	6
Mar.	51F	10C	July	67F	20C	Nov.	51F	10C
	37	3		52	11		39	4
Apr.	55F	13C	Aug.	67F	19C	Dec.	47F	8C
	39	4		51	11		37	3

Currency The unit of currency in Ireland is the pound, or punt (pronounced "poont"), written as IR£ to avoid confusion with the
pound sterling. The currency is divided into the same denominations as in Britain (although Ireland doesn't have pound
coins) with IR£1 divided into 100 pence (written *p*). There is
likely to be some variance in the rates of exchange between Ireland and the United Kingdom (which includes Northern
Ireland). This usually favors the visitor. Change U.K. pounds
at a bank when you get to Ireland (pound coins not accepted);
change Irish pounds before you leave.

Dollars and British currency are accepted only in large hotels
and shops licensed as "bureaux de change." In general, visitors
are expected to use Irish currency. Banks give the best rate of
exchange. The rate of exchange at press time (fall 1988) was .63
to the dollar and 1.15 to the pound sterling.

What It Will Cost Dublin is one of Europe's most expensive cities, an unfortunate
state of affairs that manifests itself most obviously in hotel and
restaurant rates. You can generally keep costs lower if you visit
Ireland on a package tour. Alternatively, consider staying in a
guest house or one of the multitude of bed-and-breakfasts; they
provide an economical and atmospheric alternative to staying
in a hotel (*see* Lodging in Essential Information). The rest of
the country—with the exception of the better-known hotels
and restaurants—is less expensive than Dublin. That the Irish
themselves complain bitterly about the high cost of living is
partly attributable to the high rate of VAT (Value-Added
Tax)—a stinging 25% on "luxury" goods and 10% on other
items. Some sample costs make the point. For instance, while a
double room in a moderate Dublin hotel will cost about IR£50,
with breakfast sometimes another IR£7 per person, the cur-

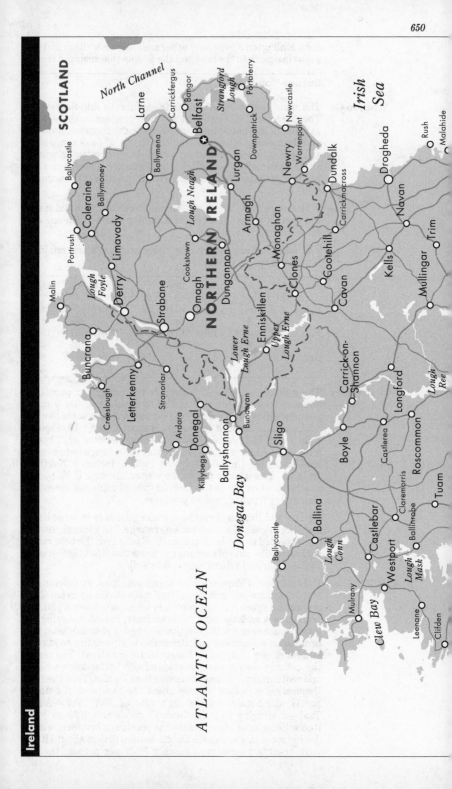

Ireland

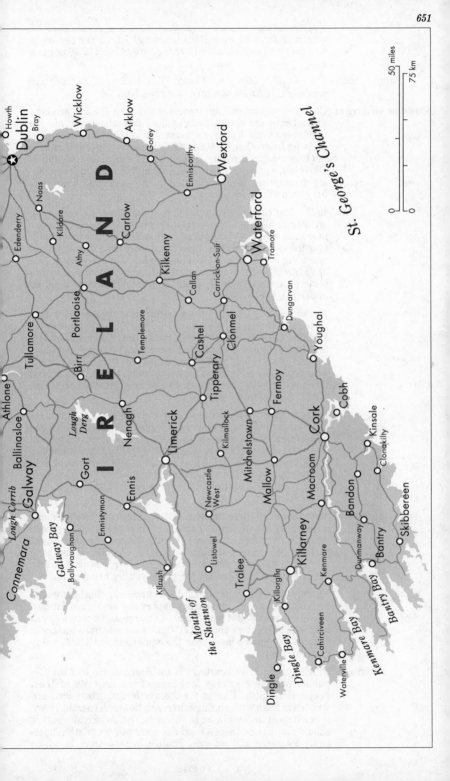

rent rate for a country B&B is around IR£10 per person. A modest small-town hotel will charge around IR£12.50 per person.

Sample Prices   Cup of coffee, 50p; pint of beer, IR£1.40; Coca-Cola, 60p; ham sandwich, IR£1.20; one-mile taxi ride, IR£2.50.

Customs on Arrival   Customs regulations for travelers entering Ireland are complex. There are three levels of duty-free allowance: one for residents of non-European countries; another for passengers arriving from other EEC countries bringing in goods that have *not* been bought in a duty-free shop; and a third for residents of European countries not in the EEC and for passengers arriving from other EEC countries with goods that *have* been bought in a duty-free shop.

In the first category you may import duty-free: 400 cigarettes or 200 cigarillos or 100 cigars or 500 grams of tobacco; plus one liter of alcoholic beverage of more than 22% volume or a total of two liters of alcoholic beverage of not more than 22% volume or sparkling or fortified wine, plus two liters of other wine; plus 50 grams of perfume and a quarter of a liter of toilet water; plus other goods to a value of IR£31 per person (IR£16 for children under 15).

In the second category you may import duty-free: 300 cigarettes or 400 grams of tobacco or 150 cigarillos or 75 cigars; plus 1½ liters of alcoholic beverage of more than 22% volume or a total of three liters of alcoholic beverage of not more than 22% volume or sparkling or fortified wines plus four liters of other wine; plus 75 grams of perfume and three-eighths of a liter of toilet water; plus, other goods to a value of IR£145 per person (IR£41 for children under 15).

In the third category you may import duty-free: 200 cigarettes or 100 cigarillos or 50 cigars or 250 grams of tobacco; plus one liter of alcoholic beverage of more than 22% volume or a total of two liters of alcoholic beverage of not more than 22% volume or sparkling or fortified wine plus two liters of other wine; plus 50 grams of perfume and a quarter of a liter of toilet water; plus, other goods to a value of IR£31 per person (IR£16 for children under 15).

Note that in all three categories the tobacco and alcohol allowances apply only to those 17 and older. If you have nothing more than the duty-free allowance when you arrive, walk straight through the green "nothing to declare" channel. If you have more than your duty-free allowance, however, you must go into the red channel and declare the goods you are bringing in.

Visitors may import any quantity of currency, whether foreign or Irish, and nonresidents may export any amount of foreign currency, provided it was declared on arrival. Otherwise, you may export no more than IR£100, in denominations no larger than IR£20, and no more than the equivalent of IR£500 in foreign currency.

Language   Officially, the Irish language is the first language of the Republic, but the everyday language of the majority of Irish people is English. Except for the northwest, most signs are written in Irish with an English translation underneath. There is one important exception to this rule, with which all visitors should familiarize themselves: *Fir* and *mna* translate respectively into *men* and *women*. The *Gaeltacht*—areas in which

Irish *is* the everyday language of most people—comprises only 6% of the land, and all its inhabitants are, in any case, bilingual.

Getting Around

By Car
Road Conditions

Ireland is one country where a car is more or less essential for successful travel. Despite improvements in public transportation, both the train and bus networks are limited, and many of the most intriguing areas are accessible only by car. Roads are reasonable, though the absence of turnpikes means that trip times can be long; on the other hand, you'll soon find that driving past an ever-changing and often dramatic series of unspoiled landscapes can be very much part of the fun. There's a bonus in the fact that traffic is normally light, though you can easily find yourself crawling down country lanes behind an ancient tractor or a flock of sheep. This is not a country for those with a taste for life in the fast lane.

All principal roads are designated by the letter N, meaning National Primary Road. Thus, the main highway north from Dublin is N1, the main highway northwest is N2, and so on. Road signs are normally in both Irish and English; in the northwest, most are in Irish only, so make sure you have a good road map. Distances on the new green signposts are in kilometers; the old white signposts give distances in miles.

Rules of the Road

Driving is on the left. There is a general speed limit of 55 mph (88 kph) on most roads; in towns, the limit is 30 mph (48 kph). In some areas, the limit is 40 mph (64 kph); this will always be clearly posted. At junctions, traffic from the right takes priority.

Seat belts must be worn by the driver and front-seat passengers. Children under 12 must ride in the back. Drunk-driving laws are strict.

Parking

Despite the relative lack of traffic, parking in towns is a real problem. Signs with the letter P indicate parking lots, but if there's a stroke through the P, keep away or you'll collect a stiff fine, normally around IR£20. After 6 PM, restrictions are lifted. Give attendants in lots about 20p when you leave.

Frontier Posts

There are 20 approved routes for crossing the border between the Republic of Ireland and Northern Ireland. If you plan to drive into Northern Ireland in a rented car, be sure the rental company furnishes the necessary papers. Formalities of crossing the border are minimal, though you may find additional checks just north of the border. *Don't* drive on roads near the border marked "Unapproved Road."

By Train

Trains and buses are owned and operated by the state-owned Coras Iompair Eireann (**CIE**). The rail network, although much cut back in the past 25 years, is still extensive, with main routes radiating from Dublin to Cork, Galway, Limerick, Tralee, Killarney, Westport, and Sligo; there is also a line for the north and Belfast. All trains are diesel; cars on principal expresses have air-conditioning. There are two classes on many trains—Super Standard (first class), and Standard (second class). Dining cars are carried on main expresses. There are no sleeping cars.

Speeds are not high in comparison with those of other European trains. Dublin, however, now has a modern commuter train—

the DART—running south from the suburb of Howth through the city to Bray on the Wicklow coast, with various stops along the way.

Fares For the strictly independent traveler, the 15-day "Rambler" ticket gives unlimited travel by train and bus and is an excellent value at IR£95. It can be purchased from any city bus terminal or train station ticket office. A "train only" ticket is available for about IR£83. One- and four-day round-trip train tickets are also available at discounted rates.

In addition, CIE offers excellent vacations, lasting from one to 10 days, touring by train or bus, or both. These include accommodations and main meals. Costs range from around IR£230 for a four-day tour, to IR£410 for a 10-day tour in July and August.

By Plane Distances are not great in Ireland, so air travel plays only a small role in internal travel. **Aer Lingus** has flights from Dublin to Shannon and Cork, with flying time around 30 minutes. There is frequent service to the Aran Islands, off Galway Bay, from Carnmore Airport, Galway. The flight takes between 15 and 25 minutes.

By Bus The bus system, operated by CIE, is widespread—more so than the train system—even if the frequency of services in the more remote areas is not great. But the routes cover the whole country and are often linked to the train services; *see* By Train for details of combined train and bus discount tickets and vacations.

By Boat Exploring Ireland's lakes, rivers, and canals is a delightful offbeat way to get to know the country. Motor cruisers can be chartered on the Shannon, the longest river in the British Isles. The Irish Tourist Board has details of the wide choice of trips and operators.

For drifting through the historic Midlands on the Grand Canal and river Barrow, contact **Celtic Canal Cruisers,** Tullamore, County Offaly, tel. 353506/21861.

By Bicycle Biking can be a great way to get around Ireland. Details of bicycle rentals are available from the Irish Tourist Board. Rates average IR£3.50 per day or IR£20 per week. You must pay a IR£30 deposit. Be sure to make reservations, especially in July and August. If you rent a bike in the Republic, you may *not* take it into Northern Ireland; nor may you take a bike rented in Northern Ireland into the Republic.

Essential Information

Telephones
Local Calls There are pay phones in all post offices and most hotels and bars, as well as in street booths. Local calls cost 20p for three minutes, calls within Ireland cost about 50p for three minutes, and calls to Britain cost about IR£1.75 for three minutes. Rates go down by about a third after 6 PM and all day Saturday and Sunday.

International Calls For calls to the USA and Canada, dial 161 followed by the area code. For calls to the United Kingdom, dial 031 for London followed by the number, and 03 for the rest of the country. Don't make international calls from your hotel room unless absolutely necessary. Most hotels add 200–300% to calls.

Mail *Postal Rates*	Airmail rates to USA, Canada, and the Commonwealth are 46p for the first 10 grams, air letters 40p, and postcards 30p. Letters to Britain and continental Europe cost 28p, postcards 24p.
Receiving Mail	A general delivery service is operated free of charge from Dublin's **General Post Office** (O'Connell St., Dublin 1, tel. 01/728888).

Shopping   There is an abundance of home-produced Irish goods to suit all tastes and budgets, from Waterford crystal to tweed, lace, linen, chunky handknits, blackthorn walking sticks, and the modest tin whistle.

Irish silver is a prized gift and investment. Jewelry, inset with Connemara marble and other semiprecious stones, is available in both modern designs influenced by abstract Celtic motifs and in exact reproductions of Celtic originals. Look, too, for Irish pewter and handcrafted Irish ceramics. Many visitors are tempted by Waterford crystal (prices can be as much as 40% below the U.S. equivalent). Waterford crystal may be the most famous Irish glass, but it is by no means the only sort. Many of the larger stores carry a selection of Dublin and Galway crystal and less formal uncut hand-blown glass. The musically inclined will find *bodhrans* (animal-hide hand drums) if they persist. Handmade whole Irish cheeses—Milleens, Durrus, and Cashel Blue, among others—are popular and unusual gourmet gifts.

The specialist shops—for antiques, ready-to-wear tweeds, high fashion, sporting goods, silver, and linen—are concentrated in Dublin and Cork. Almost every town visited by tourists has its craft shop, offering traditional goods at competitive prices; most will arrange to ship goods back home. Most of these shops stock a similar range of durable, handwoven tweed, traditional cotton crochet, and fine linen shirts and blouses. The Aran sweater is a perennially popular buy, but look out also for "picture" sweaters, fashionable variations on the traditional Aran, and mohair handknits. Handmade goods are one of a kind; when you see what you like, buy it; you may never run across the same style or size again.

VAT Refunds   Visitors from outside Europe can take advantage of the "cashback" system if their purchases total more than IR£50. A cashback voucher must be filled out by the retailer at the point of sale. The visitor pays the total gross price, including VAT, and receives green and yellow copies of the invoice; both must be retained. These are presented to—and stamped by—customs, as you leave the country. Take the stamped form along to the cashier and you will be refunded the VAT.

Opening and Closing Times   **Banks.** Banks are open weekdays 10–12:30 and 1:30–3, and to 5 on selected days.

Museums. Museums are usually open Monday–Friday 10–5, Saturday 10–1, Sunday 2–5. Always make a point of checking, however, as hours can change unexpectedly.

Shops. Shops are open Monday–Saturday 9–5:30, closing earlier on Wednesday, Thursday, or Saturday, depending on the locality.

National Holidays   January 1; March 17 (St. Patrick's Day); March 24 (Good Friday); March 27 (Easter Monday); June 5; August 7; October 30; December 25, 26 (Christmas). If you're planning a visit at Easter, remember that theaters and cinemas are closed for the last three days of the preceding week.

Dining When it comes to food, Ireland has some of the best raw materials in the world: prime beef, locally raised lamb and pork, free-range poultry, game in season, abundant fresh seafood, and locally grown seasonal vegetables. Despite the near legendary awfulness of much Irish cooking in the recent past, times are definitely changing, and a new generation of chefs is beginning to take greater advantage of this abundance of magnificent produce. In almost all corners of the country, you'll find a substantial choice of restaurants, many in hotels, serving fresh local food imaginatively prepared and served.

If your tastes run to traditional Irish dishes, there are still a few old-fashioned restaurants serving substantial portions of excellent, if plain, home cooking. Look for boiled bacon and cabbage; Irish stew; and *colcannon:* cooked potatoes diced and fried in butter with onions and either cabbage or leeks and covered in thick cream just before serving. The best bet for daytime meals is "pub grub"—a choice of soup and soda bread, two or three hot dishes of the day, salad platters, or sandwiches. Most bars serve food, and a growing number offer coffee and tea as an alternative to alcohol. Guinness, a dark beer or "stout," brewed with malt, is the Irish national drink, consumed in vast quantities. Even if you never go out for a drink at home, you should visit at least one or two pubs in Ireland. The pub is one of the pillars of Irish society, worth visiting as much for entertainment and conversation as for drinking.

Mealtimes Breakfast is served between 8 and 10—earlier by special request only—and is a substantial meal of cereal, bacon, eggs, sausage, and toast. Lunch is eaten between 12:30 and 2. Having enjoyed a hearty breakfast, however, most visitors tend to take a light lunch and to eat their main meal in the evening. The old tradition of "high tea" taken around 5, followed by a light snack before bed, is still encountered in many Irish homes, including many bed-and-breakfasts. Elsewhere, however, it is generally assumed that you'll be eating between 7 and 9:30, and that this will be your main meal of the day.

Ratings Prices are per person and include a first course, main course, and dessert, but no wine or tip. VAT at 10% is included in all Irish restaurant bills. Some places, usually the more expensive establishments, add a 12% or 15% service charge, in which case no tip is necessary; elsewhere a tip of 10% is adequate. The most highly recommended restaurants are indicated by a star ★. At press time, there were .63 Irish pounds to the dollar.

Category	Cost
Expensive	over IR£20
Moderate	IR£12–IR£20
Inexpensive	under IR£12

Credit Cards The following abbreviations are used: AE, American Express; DC, Diners Club; MC, MasterCard; V, Visa.

Lodging Accommodations in Ireland range all the way from deluxe castles and renovated stately homes to thatched cottages and farmhouses to humble B&Bs. Standards everywhere are high and are continuing to rise all the time. Pressure on hotel space reaches a peak between June and September, but it's a good idea to make reservations in advance at any time of year, particularly at the more expensive spots. Rooms can be reserved directly from the USA; ask your travel agent for details. The **Irish Tourist Board's (ITB) Central Reservations Service** (14 Upper O'Connell St., Dublin 1, tel. 01/747733) can make reservations, as can local tourist board offices.

The Irish Tourist Board has an official grading system and publishes a detailed price list of all approved accommodations, including hotels, guest houses, farmhouses, B&Bs, and hostels. No hotel may exceed this price without special authorization from the ITB; prices must also be displayed in every room. Don't hesitate to complain either to the manager or the ITB, or both, if prices exceed this maximum.

In general, hotels charge per person. In most cases (but not all, especially in more expensive places), the price includes a full breakfast. VAT is included, but some hotels—again, usually the more expensive ones—add a 10–15% service charge. This should be mentioned in their price list. In moderate and inexpensive hotels, be sure to specify if you want a private bath or shower; the latter is cheaper. Off-season (October–May) prices are reduced by as much as 25%.

Guest Houses Some smaller hotels are graded as guest houses. To qualify, they must have at least five bedrooms. A few may have restaurants; those that do not will often provide evening meals by arrangement. Few will have a bar. Otherwise, their rooms can be as comfortable as those of a regular hotel, and in major cities they offer very good value for money compared with the inexpensive hotels.

Bed-and-Breakfast Bed-and-breakfast means just that. The bed can vary from a four-poster in the wing of a castle to a feather bed in a white-washed farmhouse or the spare bedroom of a modern cottage. Rates are generally around IR£10 per person, though these can vary significantly. Although many larger B&Bs offer rooms with bath or shower, in the majority you'll have to use the bathroom in the hall and, in many cases, to pay 50p–IR£1 extra for the privilege.

Rentals In nearly 30 locations around Ireland, there are clusters of cottages for rent. The majority are built in traditional styles but have central heating and all other conveniences. The average rent for a three-bedroom cottage equipped for six adults is around IR£220 in mid-season; be sure to make reservations well in advance. The Irish Tourist Board's booklet "Self Catering" (IR£2) has full details.

Camping There are a variety of beautifully sited campgrounds and trailer parks, but be prepared for wet weather! The Irish Tourist Board publishes a useful booklet "Caravan and Camping Parks" (IR£1.50).

Ratings Prices are for two people in a double room, based on high season (June to September) rates. Best bets are indicated by a star ★. At press time, there were .63 Irish pounds to the dollar.

Category	Cost: Dublin	Outside Dublin
Very Expensive	IR£90 and up	IR£90 and up
Expensive	IR£70–IR£90	IR£60–IR£90
Moderate	IR£50–IR£70	IR£40–IR£60
Inexpensive	under IR£50	under IR£40

Credit Cards The following credit card abbreviations are used: AE, American Express; DC, Diners Club; MC, MasterCard; V, Visa.

Tipping Other than in upscale hotels and restaurants, the Irish are not really used to being tipped. Some hotels and restaurants will add a service charge of about 12% to your bill, so tipping is not necessary unless you have received particularly good service.

Tip taxi drivers about 10% of the fare if the taxi has been using its meter. For longer journeys, where the fare is agreed in advance, a tip will not be expected, unless some kind of commentary (solicited or not) has been provided. In luxury hotels, porters and bellhops will expect IR£1; elsewhere, 50p is adequate. Hairdressers normally expect a tip of about IR£1. You don't tip in pubs, but if there is waiter service in a bar or hotel lounge, leave about 20p.

Dublin

Arriving and Departing

By Plane All flights arrive at Dublin's **Collinstown Airport,** six miles (10 kilometers) north of town. For information on arrival and departure times, call individual airlines.

Between the Airport and Downtown Buses leave every 20 minutes from outside the Arrivals door for the central bus station in downtown Dublin. The ride takes about 30 minutes, depending on the traffic, and the fare is IR£2.50. A taxi ride into town will cost from IR£5 to IR£10, depending on the location of your hotel.

By Train There are three main stations. **Heuston Station** at Kingsbridge is the departure point for the south and southwest; **Connolly Station** at Amiens Street, for Belfast, the east coast, and the west; **Pearse Station,** on Westland Row, for Bray and connections via Dun Laoghaire to the Liverpool/Holyhead ferries. Phone 01/771871 for information.

By Bus The central bus station, **Busaras,** is at Store Street near the Custom House. Some buses terminate near Connolly Bridge. Phone 01/771871 for information.

By Car The main access route from the north is N1; from the west, N4; from the south and southwest, N7; from the east coast, N11. On all routes there are clearly marked signs indicating the center of the city: An Lar.

Getting Around

Dublin is small as capital cities go—the downtown area is positively compact—and the best way to see the city and soak in the full flavor is on foot.

By Train An electric train commuter service, DART (Dublin Area Rapid Transport), serves the suburbs out to Howth, on the north side of the city, and to Bray, County Wicklow, on the south. Fares are about the same as for buses. Street direction signs to DART stations read Staisiun/Station.

By Bus Most city buses originate in or pass through the area of O'Connell Street and O'Connell Bridge. If the destination board indicates An Lar, that means that the bus is going to the city's central area. Timetables (45p) are available from the CIE Office, 59 Upper O'Connell St., and give details of all routes, times of operation, and price codes. The minimum fare is 45p.

By Taxi Taxis do not cruise, but are located beside the Central Bus Station, at train stations, at O'Connell Bridge, at St. Stephen's Green, and near major hotels. They are not of uniform type or color. Make sure the meter is on. The initial charge is IR£1.80; the fare is displayed in the cab. A one-mile trip in city traffic costs about IR£2.50.

Important Addresses and Numbers

Tourist Information There is a tourist information office in the entrance hall of the **Irish Tourist Board** headquarters, Baggot Street Bridge, tel. 01/765871; open weekdays 9–5. More conveniently located is the office at 14 Upper O'Connell St., tel. 01/747744; open weekdays 9–5, Saturday 9–1. There is also an office at the **Airport**, tel. 01/376387. From mid-June to September, there is an office at the **Ferryport**, Dun Laoghaire.

Embassies **U.S.** 42 Elgin Rd., Ballsbridge, tel. 01/688777. **Canadian.** 65 St. Stephen's Green, tel. 01/781988. **U.K.** 33 Merrion Rd., tel. 01/695211.

Emergencies **Police,** tel. 999; **Ambulance,** tel. 999; **Doctor,** tel. 01/537951 or 01/767273; **Dentist,** tel. 01/978435; **Pharmacy,** Hamilton Long, 5 Upper O'Connell St., tel. 01/748456.

Travel Agencies **American Express,** 116 Grafton St., tel. 01/772874. **Thomas Cook,** 118 Grafton St., tel. 01/771721.

Guided Tours

Orientation Tours Both **CIE** (tel. 01/302222) and **Gray Line Sightseeing** (tel. 01/744466) offer bus tours of Dublin and its surrounding areas. **Gogan Tours** (tel. 01/796022) has a series of afternoon and evening bus tours, with author and historian Eamonn MacThomais as guide, which guarantee a real taste of Dublin wit.

Special-Interest Tours **CIE** has a *Traditional Irish Music Night* tour. **Elegant Ireland** (tel. 01/751665) organizes tours for groups interested in architecture and the fine arts; these include visits with the owners of some of Ireland's stately homes and castles.

Walking Tours **Tour Guides Ireland** (tel. 01/794291) offers a selection of walking tours, including *Literary Dublin, Georgian Dublin,* and *Pub Tours.* The **Irish Tourist Board** has a *Tourist Trail* walk, which takes in the main sites of central Dublin and can be completed in about three hours. An accompanying booklet (75p) can be obtained from the office at 14 Upper O'Connell Street. Guided walking tours of Old Dublin, conducted by native Dubliners, leave from Christ Church Cathedral; for information, phone 01/556970 or 01/553423.

Excursions **CIE/Bus Eireann** (tel. 01/302222) and **Gray Line Sightseeing** (tel. 01/744466) offer day-long tours into the surrounding countryside, and longer tours elsewhere; price includes accommodations, breakfast, and admission fees.

Exploring Dublin

Dublin is a small city with a population of just over one million. For all that, it has a distinctly cosmopolitan air, one that complements happily the individuality of the city and the courtesy and friendliness of its inhabitants. Originally a Viking settlement, Dublin is situated on the banks of the river Liffey. The Liffey divides the city north and south, with the more lively and fashionable spots, like the Grafton Street shopping area, to be found on the "southside." Most of the city's historically interesting buildings date from the 18th century and, although many of its finer Georgian buildings disappeared in the overenthusiastic redevelopment of the '70s, enough remain, mainly south of the river, to recall the elegant Dublin of the past. The slums romanticized by writers Sean O'Casey and Brendan Behan have virtually been eradicated, but literary Dublin can still be recaptured by those who want to follow the footsteps of Leopold Bloom's progress, as described in James Joyce's *Ulysses.* And Trinity College, alma mater of Oliver Goldsmith, Jonathan Swift, and Samuel Beckett, among others, still provides a haven of tranquility.

Dubliners are talkative, self-confident people, eager to have visitors enjoy the pleasures of their city. You can meet a lively cross section of people in the city's numerous bars, still probably the best places to sample the famous wit of the only city to have produced three winners of the Nobel Prize for Literature: William Butler Yeats, George Bernard Shaw, and Samuel Beckett.

O'Connell Street

1 Begin your tour of Dublin at **O'Connell Bridge,** the city's most central landmark. Look closely and you will notice a strange feature: The bridge is wider than it is long. The north side of O'Connell Bridge is dominated by an elaborate memorial to Daniel O'Connell, "The Liberator," erected as a tribute to the great 19th-century orator's achievement in securing Catholic Emancipation in 1829. Today, **O'Connell Street** is the city's main shopping area, though it seems decidedly parochial to anyone accustomed to a Fifth Avenue or a Rodeo Drive. Turn left just before the General Post Office and take a look at Henry Street. This pedestrians-only shopping area leads to the colorful **Moore Street Market,** where street vendors recall their most famous ancestor, Molly Malone, by singing their wares—mainly flowers—in the traditional Dublin style.

2 The **General Post Office,** known as the GPO, occupies a special place in Irish history. It was from the portico of its handsome classical facade that Padraig Pearse read the Proclamation of the Republic on Easter Monday, 1916. You can still see the scars of bullets on its pillars from the fighting that ensued. The GPO remains the focal point for political rallies and demonstrations even today and is used as a viewing stand for VIPs during the annual St. Patrick's Day Parade.

3 The **Gresham Hotel,** opposite the GPO, has played a part in Dublin's history since 1817; it, along with the whole O'Connell

Street area, though, is less fashionable now than in the last century. Just below the Gresham is the **Irish Tourist Board Information Office;** drop in for a free street map, shopping guides, and information on all aspects of Dublin tourism; 14 Upper O'Connell St., tel. 01/747733. Open weekdays 9–5, Saturday 9–1. Opposite is the main office of **CIE,** which can supply bus timetables and information on excursions. *59 Upper O'Connell St., tel. 01/30222. Open weekdays 9–5, Sat. 9–1.*

④ At the top of O'Connell Street is the **Rotunda,** the first maternity hospital in Europe, opened in 1755. Not much remains of the once-elegant Rotunda Assembly Rooms, a famous haunt of fashionable Dubliners until the middle of the last century. The **Gate Theater,** housed in an extension of the Rotunda Assembly Rooms, however, continues to attract crowds to its fine repertoire of classic Irish and European drama. The theater was founded by the late Micheál MacLiammoir in 1928.

⑤ Beyond the Rotunda, you will have a fine vista of **Parnell Square,** one of Dublin's earliest Georgian squares. You will notice immediately that the first-floor windows of these elegant brick-face buildings are much larger than the others and that it is easy to look in from street level. This is more than simply the result of the architect's desire to achieve perfect proportions on the facades: These rooms were designed as reception rooms, and fashionable hostesses liked passersby to be able to peer in and admire the distinguished guests at their luxurious, candle-lit receptions.

⑥ Charlemont House, whose impressive Palladian facade dominates the top of Parnell Square, now houses the **Hugh Lane Municipal Gallery of Modern Art.** Sir Hugh Lane, a nephew of Lady Gregory, who was Yeats's curious, high-minded aristocratic patron, was a keen collector of Impressionist paintings. The gallery also contains some interesting works by Irish artists, including Yeats's brother Jack. *Parnell Sq. Free. Open Tues.–Sat. 10–6, Sun. 11–2.*

The area surrounding Parnell Square is rich in literary associations and features in the work of Sean O'Casey, James Joyce, and Brendan Behan. Only devout literary pilgrims will care for the detour to Mountjoy Square, since this badly run-down area is in the middle of a rebuilding program.

⑦ Return back down to O'Connell Street where a sign on the left will lead you to **St. Mary's Pro Cathedral,** the main Catholic church of Dublin. Try to catch the famous Palestrina Choir on Sunday at 11 AM. John McCormack is one of many famous voices ⑧ to have sung with this exquisite ensemble. The **Abbey Theatre,** a new brick building dating from 1966, is a boxy disappointment from the outside but has some noteworthy portraits and mementoes in the foyer. Seats are usually available at about IR£7.50, and with luck you may just have a wonderful evening. The luck element, unfortunately, must be stressed, since the Abbey has had both financial and artistic problems lately.

Time Out On Westmoreland Street is **Bewley's Coffee House** (there's another one nearby on Grafton Street), an institution that has been supplying Dubliners with coffee and buns since 1842. The aroma of coffee is irresistible, and the dark interior, with marble-topped tables, original wood fittings, and stained-glass

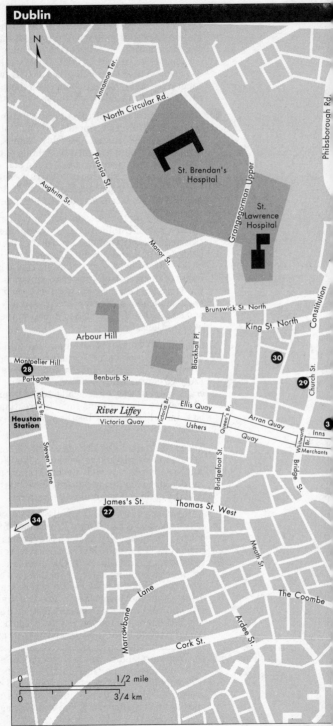

Dublin

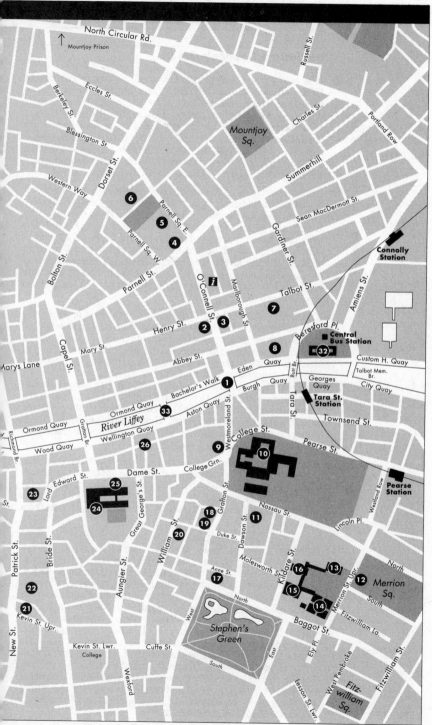

windows, evokes a more leisurely Dublin of the past. *12 West-moreland St. and 78 Grafton St. Open Mon.–Sat. 9–5:30.*

Trinity and Stephen's Green

⑨ It is only a short walk across O'Connell Bridge to **Parliament House.** Today, this stately early 18th-century building is no more than a branch of the Bank of Ireland; originally, however, it housed the Irish Parliament. The original House of Lords, with its fine coffered ceiling and 1,233-piece Waterford glass chandelier, is open to the public during banking hours (week-days 10–12:30 and 1:30–3). It's worth taking a look at the main banking hall, too, whose judicial character—it was previously the Court of Requests—has been sensitively maintained.

⑩ Across the road is the facade of **Trinity College,** whose memora-bly atmospheric campus is a must for every visitor. Trinity College, Dublin (familiarly known as TCD) was founded by Elizabeth I in 1591 and offered a free education to Catholics—provided that they accepted the Protestant faith. As a legacy of this condition, right up until 1966, Catholics who wished to study at Trinity had to obtain a dispensation from their bishop or face excommunication. Today more than 70% of Trinity's students are Catholics, a clear indication of how far away those days seem to today's generation.

The facade, built between 1755 and 1759, consists of a magnifi-cent portico with Corinthian columns. The design is repeated on the interior, so the view from outside the gates and from the quadrangle inside is the same. On the sweeping lawn in front of the facade are statues of two of the university's illustrious alumni—statesman Edward Burke and poet Oliver Goldsmith. Other famous students include the philosopher George Berke-ley, who gave his name to the San Francisco area campus of the University of California; Jonathan Swift; Thomas Moore; Oscar Wilde; John Millington Synge; Henry Grattan; Wolfe Tone; Robert Emmet; Bram Stoker; Edward Carson; Douglas Hyde; and Samuel Beckett.

The 18th-century building on the left, just inside the entrance, is the chapel. There's an identical building opposite, the Exam-ination Hall. The oldest buildings are the library in the far right-hand corner and a row of red-brick buildings known as the Rubrics, which contain student apartments; both date from 1712.

Ireland's largest collection of books and manuscripts is housed in **Trinity College Library.** There are more than 2½ million vol-umes gathering dust here; about half a mile of new shelving has to be added every year to keep pace with acquisitions. The li-brary is entered through the library shop. Its principal treas-ure is the **Book of Kells,** a beautifully illuminated manuscript of the Gospels dating from the 8th century. Because of the beauty and the fame of the Book of Kells, at peak hours you may have to wait in line to enter the library; it's less busy early in the day. Quite apart from the many treasures it contains, the aptly named Long Room is impressive in itself, stretching as it does for 209 feet (64 meters). Originally it had a flat plaster ceiling, but the perennial need for more shelving resulted in a decision to raise the level of the roof and add the barrel-vaulted ceiling and the gallery bookcases. *Admission: IR£1.50. Open week-days 9:30–4:45, Sat. 9:30–12:45.*

A breath of fresh air will be welcome after the library, so, when you're done admiring the award-winning modern architecture of the New Library and the Arts Building, pass through the gate to the sports grounds—rugby fields on your left, cricket on your right. Leave Trinity by the Lincoln Place Gate—a handy "back door."

(11) Shoppers will find a detour along **Nassau Street** in order here. As well as being well-endowed with bookstores, it contains the **Kilkenny Design Workshops,** which, besides selling the best in contemporary Irish design for the home, also holds regular exhibits of exciting new work by Irish craftsmen. *Open Mon.–Sat. 9–5.*

Time Out The **Kilkenny Kitchen,** a self-service restaurant on the first floor of the Kilkenny Design Workshops, overlooking the playing fields of Trinity, is an excellent spot for a quick, inexpensive lunch in modern, design-conscious surroundings. The emphasis is on natural fresh foods and home baking. *Nassau St. Open Mon.–Sat. 9–5.*

(12) Nassau Street will lead you into **Merrion Square,** past a distinctive corner house that was the home of Oscar Wilde's parents. Merrion Square is one of the most pleasant in Dublin. Its flower gardens are well worth a visit in the summer months. Note the brightly colored front doors and the intricate fan lights above them—a distinctive feature of Dublin's domestic architecture.

(13) The **National Gallery** is the first of a series of important buildings on the west side of the square. It is one of Europe's most agreeable and compact galleries, with more than 2,000 works on view, including a major collection of Irish landscape painting, 17th-century French works, paintings from the Italian and Spanish schools, and a collection of Dutch masters. *Merrion Sq. Free. Open weekdays 10–5, Sat. 10–1, Sun. 2–5.*

(14) Next door is **Leinster House,** seat of the Irish parliament. This imposing, 18th-century building has two facades: Its Merrion Square facade is designed in the style of a country house, while the other facade, in Kildare Street, is in the style of a town house. Visitors may be shown the house when the Dail (pronounced "Doyle"), the Irish parliament, is not in session.

Time Out A half-block detour to your left, between Merrion Square and Stephen's Green, will bring you to the door of **Doheny & Nesbitt's,** an old Victorian-style bar whose traditional "snugs"—individual, wood-paneled booths—are a popular place for that "quick drink after work," or indeed at any time outside the "holy hour." Usually noisy and smoky, but always friendly, it is one of the few authentic pubs left in the city.

Stephen's Green, as it is always called by the Dubliners, suffered more from the planning blight of the philistine '60s than did its neighbor, Merrion Square. An exception is the magnificent **Shelbourne Hotel,** which dominates the north side of the green. It is still as fashionable—and as expensive—as ever.

Time Out Budget-conscious visitors should put on their finery and try afternoon tea in the elegant splendor of the **Shelbourne's Lord Mayor's Room.** You can experience its old-fashioned luxury for around IR£5 (including sandwiches and cakes) per head.

Around the corner on Kildare Street, the "town house" facade
⑮ of Leinster House is flanked by the **National Museum** and the
⑯ **National Library**, each featuring a massive colonnaded rotunda
entrance built in 1890. The museum (open Tues.–Sat. 10–5,
Sun. 2–5) houses a remarkable collection of Irish treasures
from 6000 BC to the present day, including the Tara Brooch, the
Ardagh Chalice, and the Cross of Cong. Every major figure in
modern Irish literature, from James Joyce onward, studied in
the National Library at some point. In addition to a comprehensive collection of Irish authors, it contains extensive newspaper
archives. It is also the headquarters of the Genealogical Office.
Kildare St. Open Mon.–Thurs. 10–10, Fri. 10–5, Sat. 10–1.

⑰ The **Royal Irish Academy,** on Dawson Street, is the country's
leading learned society and has many important manuscripts in
its unmodernized 18th-century library (open Mon.–Fri. 9:30–
5:15). Just below the academy is **Mansion House,** the official
residence of the Lord Mayor of Dublin. Its Round Room was
the location of the first assembly of the Dail Eireann—the Irish
parliament—in January 1919. It is now used mainly for exhibitions.

Grafton Street, which runs between Stephen's Green and Trini-
⑱ ty College, is a magnet for shoppers. Check out **Brown Thomas,**
Ireland's most elegant and old-fashioned department store; it
has an extremely good selection of sporting goods and Waterford crystal—an odd combination. Many of the more stylish
boutiques are just off the main pedestrians-only areas, so be
⑲ sure to poke around likely corners. Don't miss the **Powerscourt
Town House,** an imaginative shopping arcade installed in and
around the covered courtyard of an impressive 18th-century
⑳ building. Nearby is the **Civic Museum** containing drawings,
models, maps of Dublin, and other civic memorabilia. *58 S. William St. Free. Open Tues.–Sat. 10–6, Sun. 11–4.*

㉑ A short walk from Stephen's Green will bring you to one of the
smaller and more unusual gems of old Dublin, **Archbishop
Marsh's Library**. It was built in 1701, and access is through a
tiny but charming cottage garden. Its interior has been unchanged for more than 300 years and still contains "cages" into
which scholars who wanted to peruse rare books were locked.
(The cages were to discourage students who, often impecuni-
ous, may have been tempted to make the books their own.) *St.
Patrick's Close. Open Wed.–Fri. 10:30–12:30 and 2–4, Mon.
2–4, Sat. 10:30–12:30; closed Tues. and Sun.*

㉒ Opposite, on Patrick Street, is **St. Patrick's Cathedral.** Legend
has it that St. Patrick baptized many converts at a well on the
site of the cathedral in the 5th century. The building dates from
1190 and is mainly early English in style. At 300 feet (91 meters), it is the longest church in the country. Its history has not
always been happy. In the 17th century, Oliver Cromwell, dour
ruler of England and no friend of the Irish, had his troops stable their horses in the cathedral. It wasn't until the 19th
century that restoration work to repair the damage was put in
hand. St. Patrick's is the national cathedral of the Protestant
Church of Ireland and has had many illustrious deans. The
most famous was Jonathan Swift, author of *Gulliver's Travels,*
who held office from 1713 to 1745. Swift's tomb is in the south
aisle, and Dean Swift's corner at the top of the north transept
contains his pulpit, his writing table and chair, his portrait,

and his death mask. Memorials to many other celebrated figures from Ireland's past line the walls of St. Patrick's.

(23) St. Patrick's originally stood outside the walls of Dublin. Its close neighbor, **Christ Church Cathedral** (Christ Church Rd.), on the other hand, stood just within the walls and belonged to the See of Dublin. It is for this reason that the city has two cathedrals so close to one another. Christ Church was founded by Strongbow, a Norman baron and conqueror of Dublin for the English crown, in 1172, and it took 50 years to build. Strongbow himself is buried in the cathedral beneath an impressive effigy. The vast and sturdy **crypt** is Dublin's oldest surviving structure, and should not be missed.

(24) Signs in the Christ Church area will lead you to **Dublin Castle.** Guided tours of the lavishly furnished state apartments are offered every half hour and provide one of the most enjoyable sightseeing experiences in town. Only fragments of the original 13th-century building survive; the elegant castle you see today is essentially an 18th-century building. The state apartments were formerly the residence of the English viceroys—the monarch's representative in Ireland—and are now used by the president of Ireland to entertain visiting heads of state. The state apartments are closed when in official use, so phone first to check. *Off Lord Edward St., tel. 01/777129. Admission: IR£2.50. Open weekdays 10–12:15 and 2–5, weekends 2–5.*

(25) Step into the **City Hall** on Dame Street to admire the combination of grand classical ornament and understated Georgian simplicity in its circular main hall. It also contains a good example of the kind of gently curving Georgian staircase that is a typical feature of most large town houses in Dublin.

Time Out A mosaic stag's head in the pavement of Dame Street marks the entrance to a narrow alley and a beautiful pub, **The Stag's Head,** (1 Dame Court), dating from the early 19th century. Amid tall mirrors, stained-glass skylights, and mounted stags' heads, of course, you can enjoy a typical selection of lunchtime "pub grub"—smoked salmon sandwiches, hot meat dishes—and a pint of anything.

(26) Between Dame Street and the river Liffey is a new pedestrians-only area known as **Temple Bar,** which should interest anyone wanting to discover "young Dublin." The area is chockfull of small, imaginative shops, innovative art galleries, and inexpensive restaurants.

(27) The **Guinness Brewery,** founded by Arthur Guinness in 1759, dominates the area to the west of Christ Church, covering 60 acres. Guinness is proud of its brewery and invites visitors to attend a 30-minute film shown in a converted hops store next door to the brewery itself. After the film, you can sample the famous black beverage. *Guinness Museum and Visitors' Center, James's St. Free. Open weekdays 10–3.*

Phoenix Park and the Liffey

(28) Across the Liffey is **Phoenix Park,** 1,760 acres (seven square kilometers) of green open space. Though the park is open to all, it has only two residents: the president of Ireland and the American ambassador. The park is dominated by a 205-foot-high (62 meters) obelisk, a tribute to the first duke of Wellington. Sun-

day is the best time to visit: A large open-air market is held from noon on the racecourse, while elsewhere games of cricket, soccer, polo, baseball, hurling—a combination of lacrosse, baseball, and field hockey—or Irish football will be in progress.

Returning to the city's central area along the north bank of the Liffey, you pass through a fairly run-down section that's scheduled for major redevelopment. A diversion up Church Street to **St. Michan's** will be relished by those with a macabre turn of mind. Open coffins in the vaults beneath the church reveal mummified bodies, some more than 900 years old. The sexton, who can be found at the church gate on weekdays, will guide you around the church and crypt.

Irish Whiskey Corner is just behind St. Michan's. A 90-year-old warehouse has been converted into a museum to introduce visitors to the pleasures of Irish whiskey. There's an audiovisual show and free tasting. Reservations are necessary. *Bow St., tel. 01/725566. Admission: IR£2.*

The Liffey has two of Dublin's most famous landmarks, both of them the work of 18th-century architect James Gandon and both among the city's finest buildings. The first is the **Four Courts,** surmounted by a massive copper-covered dome, giving it a distinctive profile. It is the seat of the High Court of Justice of Ireland. The building was completed between 1786 and 1802, then gutted in the Civil War of the '20s; it has since been painstakingly restored. You will recognize the same architect's hand in the **Custom House,** farther down the Liffey. Its graceful dome rises above a central portico, itself linked by arcades to the pavilions at either end. Behind this useful and elegant landmark is an altogether more workaday structure, the **Central Bus Station,** known as Busaras (pronounced Boo-SAR-us).

Midway between Gandon's two masterpieces is the Metal Bridge, otherwise known as the **Halfpenny Bridge,** so-called because, until early in this century, a toll of a half-penny was charged to cross it. The poet W. B. Yeats was one among many Dubliners who found this too high a price to pay—more a matter of principle than of finance—and so made the detour via O'Connell Bridge. No such high-minded concern need prevent you today from marching out to the middle of the bridge to admire the view up and down the Liffey as it wends its way through the city.

The **Royal Hospital Kilmainham** is a short ride by taxi or bus from the center; it's well worth the trip. The hospital is considered the most important 17th-century building in Ireland and has recently been renovated. It was completed in 1684 as a hospice—the original meaning of the term "hospital"—for veteran soldiers. Note especially the chapel with its magnificent Baroque ceiling. Although open year-round, it is also used as a cultural center for conferences, concerts, and state functions, and certain parts are sometimes closed to the general public. *District of Kilmainham, tel. 01/718666. Open weekends and holidays 11–6.*

Devotees of James Joyce may wish to take the DART train south to Sandycove, about five miles (eight kilometers) out of the center. It was here, in a Martello tower (a circular fortification built by the British as a defense against possible invasion by Napoleon at the beginning of the 19th century), that the maverick Irish genius lived for some months in 1904. It now houses the **Joyce Museum** in his honor. *Sandycove Coast. Admission: IR£1.10. Open Apr.–Oct., Mon.–Sat. 10–1 and 2–5, Sun. 2:30–6.*

What to See and Do with Children

Visit the **Irish Life Viking Adventure Center** in the crypt of St. Audeon's Church near Christ Church Cathedral, where a real-life Viking will introduce you to the everyday life of the Dublin of a thousand years ago. Let off steam in **Phoenix Park** and visit the large collection of animals and birds in the famous **Zoological Gardens** (admission IR£3, children IR£1.50). Discover the toys of yesterday in the charming **Museum of Childhood** (20 Palmerston Park, Rathmines, tel. 01/973223). Feed the ducks on **Stephen's Green** and hunt for the tiny but fragrant **Garden for the Blind**. Book a show at the **Lambert Puppet Theater** (Clifton Lane, Monkstown, tel. 01/800974). If the weather is hot and sunny, take a DART train along the coast and try the seawater swimming pool at **Blackrock**.

Off the Beaten Track

It is all too easy for the visitor to forget how close Dublin is to the sea: Take advantage of fine weather and visit the fishing village of **Howth**—it's easily reached on the DART train—and watch the fishermen mending their nets on the pier. Or take the DART in the opposite direction to **Sandycove**, where intrepid all-weather swimmers brave the waves at the men-only **Forty Foot** bathing beach.

Everyone has heard of Waterford glass, but what about Dublin crystal? The **Dublin Crystal Glass Co.** is open year-round, and visitors are welcome to watch skilled crystal cutters at work and to purchase crystal—seconds are available, too—at a discount. Phone for an appointment. *Carysfort Ave., Blackrock, tel. 01/887932.*

The **Irish Jewish Museum** was opened in 1985 by Chaim Herzog, the president of Israel and an ex-Dubliner himself, and displays memorabilia of the Irish-Jewish community covering approximately 120 years of history. *3–4 Walworth Rd., tel. 01/832703.*

Shopping

Although the rest of the country is well-supplied with craft shops, Dublin is the place to seek out more specialized items—antiques, traditional sportswear, haute couture, designer ceramics, books and prints, silverware and jewelry, and designer handknits.

Gift Ideas The most sophisticated shopping area is around **Grafton Street:** Its delis stock Irish whiskey marmalade, Irish lakeside whole-grain mustard, whole handmade cheeses, and sides of smoked salmon or trout. **Molesworth** and **Dawson Streets** are the places to browse for antiques; **Nassau** and **Dawson Streets,** for books; the smaller cross side streets for jewelry, art galleries, and old prints.

Department Stores The shops north of the river tend to be less expensive and less design conscious; chain stores and lackluster department stores make up the bulk of them. The **ILAC Shopping Center,** on

Henry Street, is worth a look, however. **Switzers** and **Brown Thomas** are Grafton Street's main department stores; the latter is an old-fashioned establishment noted for traditional sporting clothes and accessories and its food department. **Arnotts**, on Henry Street, is Dublin's largest department store and has a good range of cut crystal. Visit **Kilkenny Design Workshops** on Nassau Street for the best selection of Irish designs for the home. Nearby, the **House of Ireland** has an abundance of traditional gifts and souvenirs.

Tweeds and Woolens
Ready-made tweeds for men can be found at **Kevin and Howlin,** on Nassau Street, and at **Cleo Ltd.,** on Kildare Street. **Westbury Designs,** at the Westbury Center, has an interesting range of high-fashion tweed and linen clothing for women. The **Woolen Mills,** at Halfpenny Bridge, has a good selection of handknits and other woolen sweaters at competitive prices.

Dining

The restaurant scene in Dublin has improved beyond recognition in recent years. Though no one is ever likely to confuse the place with, say, Paris, the days of chewy boiled meats and soggy, tasteless vegetables are long gone. Food still tends to be substantial rather than subtle (which, if it means avoiding the minuscule portions common in nouvelle cuisine, is not altogether to be scoffed at), but more and more restaurants are at last taking advantage of the magnificent livestock and fish that Ireland has in such abundance.

Ratings
Prices quoted here are per person and include a first course, main course, and dessert, but not wine or tip. Best bets are indicated by a star ★. At press time, there were .63 Irish pounds to the dollar.

Category	Cost
Expensive	over IR£20
Moderate	IR£12–IR£20
Inexpensive	under IR£12

Expensive
Ernie's. This luxurious place is built around a small floodlit courtyard shaded by an imposing mulberry tree. The luxuriously rustic interior's granite walls and wood beams are adorned by paintings of Kerry, where, for generations, owner-chef Ernie Evans's family ran the famous Glenbeigh Hotel. Ernie serves generous portions of the very best seafood—try scallops Mornay or prawns in garlic butter—and steaks. *Mulberry Gardens, Donnybrook, tel. 01/693300. Dress: casual chic. Reservations advised. AE, DC, MC, V. Dinner only. Closed Sun., Mon.*

Gallery 22. In a small basement room, with an open fire, modish pink-and-gray decor, and delicate bentwood chairs, Gallery 22 is *the* place to see and be seen for the style conscious. The restaurant is noted for rack of lamb with fresh rosemary and port-wine sauce, or try one of the imaginative seasonal combinations of meat and fruit: lamb with strawberries, for example, or chicken with lemon sauce. *22 St. Stephen's Green, tel. 01/616669. Dress: upscale casual. Reservations advised, especially at lunch. AE, DC, MC, V. Closed Sun., Mon. dinner.*

★ **King Sitric.** This quayside restaurant in the fishing village-cum-suburb of Howth is a 20-minute ride north of Dublin by DART or cab. It's worth the journey to taste the succulent selection of locally caught seafood; try wild Irish salmon steaks with Hollandaise sauce, or *goujons* of turbot with saffron. You eat in the quietly elegant Georgian dining room of the former harbormaster's house under the supervision of owner-chef Aidan MacManus. *East Pier, Howth, tel. 01/325235. Dress: jacket preferred. Reservations advised. AE, DC, MC, V. Closed Sun., Sat. lunch, holidays, Dec. 24–Jan. 1, and the week preceding Easter.*

★ **Le Coq Hardi.** Award-winning owner-chef John Howard is noted for his wine cellar and specialties like Coq Hardi smokies—smoked haddock baked in tomato, cream, and cheese—and (in season) roast loin of venison with fresh cranberries and port wine. The seriousness of the cooking is complemented by the polished wood and brass and the gleaming mirrors of the sumptuous interior. *35 Pembroke Rd., Ballsbridge, tel. 01/689070. Jacket and tie. Reservations essential. AE, DC, MC, V. Closed Sun., Sat. lunch.*

Patrick Guilbaud. This is an authentic, rather formal, French restaurant with a consistently good reputation, decked out in a refreshing combination of pink, white, and green with hanging plants. The emphasis is firmly on traditional *bourgeois* cuisine; the Gallic connection is reinforced by the all-French staff. *46 James Pl., tel. 01/764192. Dress: elegant attire. Reservations advised. AE, DC, MC, V. Closed Sun.*

Whites on the Green. A sophisticated spot with soothing cream-and-white decor, this place will appeal to those who appreciate delicate and subtle nouvelle cuisine. Typical dishes include medallions of veal gratiné with a parsley mousse and roast mallard with honey and juniper berries. *119 St. Stephen's Green, tel. 01/751975. Dress: formal. Reservations essential. AE, DC, MC, V. Closed Sun., Sat. lunch.*

Moderate ★ **Beefeaters.** The clientele here has long been loyal to this restaurant's type of hearty meat dishes. Specialties are fillets, sirloins, and T-bones of prime Irish beef, prepared in 15 different ways. Try Gaelic steak, with a sauce of Irish whiskey, onions, mushrooms, and cream, or Surf 'n' Turf, an eight-ounce fillet accompanied by Dublin Bay prawns. The restaurant is located in the labyrinthine basement of two Georgian town houses and is furnished with wood-top tables and burgundy drapes and carpets. *99–100 Lower Baggot St., tel. 01/760784. Dress: casually chic. Reservations advised. AE, DC, MC, V. Closed Sun., Sat. lunch.*

Dobbin's Wine Bistro. Though Dobbin's aims at a French identity, with its red-and-white gingham tablecloths and sawdust-strewn slate floor, the cooking here is international and imaginative, with an emphasis on fresh Irish produce. Specialties are phyllo pastry with pepper and seafood filling, paupiettes of salmon and sole with spinach and dill sauce, and Szechuan boned crispy duckling with fresh peaches. *Stephen's La., tel. 01/764670. Dress: jacket preferred. Reservations advised. AE, DC, MC, V. Closed Sun.*

Rudyard's. The three small floors that make up Rudyard's have an austere air: much dark unpolished wood, simple wooden tables with bentwood chairs, paper napkins, and a hint of art nouveau elegance in the mirrors and framed posters. The food, by contrast, is light; typical dishes include smoked-salmon eclairs, and canneloni with spinach and cream cheese stuffing.

There's a quiet wine bar on the top floor. *15–16 Crown Alley, tel. 01/710846. Dress: informal. Reservations for parties over 6 only. AE, DC, MC, V. Closed Sun.*

Inexpensive **Captain America.** The collection of outrageous Americana strewn throughout is dominated by a replica of the Statue of Liberty that visibly shudders at the loud rock music. A wide selection of specialty hamburgers graces the menu, plus beef tacos, burritos, enchiladas, and chili. *Grafton Court, Grafton St., tel. 01/715266. Dress: casual. Reservations not accepted. AE, DC, MC, V.*

★ **Casper & Giumbini's Food Emporium.** This is a combination pub-restaurant near Trinity College where live piano music keeps the joint jumping, especially at weekend brunch. Charcoal-grilled steak, seafood, burgers, and pizza are served either at the bar or at your own table, with a choice of more than a dozen imported beers. *Wicklow St., tel. 01/794347. Dress: casual. Reservations advised, especially weekends. AE, DC, MC, V.*

Flanagan's. Flanagan's, located half a block north of the General Post Office, is two restaurants in one: a reliable steak house on the ground floor, divided by velour-covered banquettes, and an excellent pizzeria in the basement, much patronized by Dublin's Italian community. *61 Upper O'Connell St., tel. 01/731388. Dress: informal. Reservations advised on weekends. MC, V. Closed Sun.*

Pasta Pasta. This small, bright, and unpretentiously pretty Italian eatery serves combinations of pasta shapes and sauces plus a few Italian specials—medallions of pork *à la funghi, escalope milanesa*—against a background of muted jazz-rock. It's an excellent value. *27 Exchequer St., tel. 01/792565. Dress: informal. Reservations advised for groups over 6 and on weekends. MC, V. Closed Sun.*

Pub Food All the pubs listed here serve food at lunchtime; some also have food in the early evening. They form an important part of the dining scene in Dublin and make a pleasant and informal alternative to a restaurant meal. In general, a one-course meal should not cost much more than IR£4–IR£5, but a full meal will put you in the lower range of the Moderate category. In general, credit cards are not accepted.

Barry Fitzgerald's. Salads and a freshly cooked "house special" are available in the upstairs bar at lunch on weekdays. Pretheater dinners are served in the early evening. *90 Marlboro St.*

Davy Byrne's. James Joyce immortalized Davy Byrne's in his sprawling novel *Ulysses*. Nowadays it's more akin to a cocktail bar than a Dublin pub, but it's good for fresh and smoked salmon, salads, and a hot daily special. Food is available at lunchtime and in the early evening. *21 Duke St.*

Kitty O'Shea's. Kitty O'Shea's cleverly, if a little artificially, re--creates the atmosphere of old Dublin. *23–25 Grand Canal St., tel. 01/609965. Reservations for lunch and Sun. brunch (with music) accepted.*

Lord Edward Bar. With its Old World ambience, the Lord Edward Bar serves a wide range of salads and a hot dish of the day at lunchtime only. *23 Christ Church Pl.*

Old Stand. Located conveniently close to Grafton Street, the Old Stand offers grilled food, including steaks. *37 Exchequer St.*

Lodging

Although no major hotels have opened in Dublin in the past few years, considerable investment in redevelopment, updating of facilities, and refurbishing of some of the older establishments is taking place. As in most major cities, there is a shortage of mid-range accommodations. For value-for-money, try one of the registered guest houses; in most respects they are indistinguishable from small hotels. Most economical of all is the bed-and-breakfast. Both guest houses and B&Bs tend to be located in suburban areas—generally a 10-minute bus ride from the center of the city. This is not in itself a great drawback, and savings can be significant.

The Irish Tourist Board (14 Upper O'Connell St.) publishes a comprehensive booklet "Guest Accommodation" (IR£2), which covers all approved possibilities in Dublin and the rest of the country, from the grandest hotel to the humblest B&B. The office can usually help if you find yourself without reservations.

There is a VAT of 10% on hotel charges, which should be included in the quoted price. A service charge of 12–15% is also included and listed separately in the bills of top-grade hotels; elsewhere, check to see if the service is included. If it's not, a tip of between 10% and 15% is usual—if you think the service is worth it.

Ratings Prices quoted here are for two people in a double room. Best bets are indicated by a star ★. At press time, there were .63 Irish pounds to the dollar.

Category	Cost
Very Expensive	over IR£90
Expensive	IR£70–IR£90
Moderate	IR£50–IR£70
Inexpensive	under IR£50

Very Expensive **Berkeley Court.** The most quietly elegant of Dublin's large modern hotels, Berkeley Court is located in Ballsbridge—a leafy suburb about a 10-minute cab ride from the center of town. Its new conservatory gives freshness and spaciousness to the atmosphere of the public rooms; among the other new features are five luxury suites, each with its own Jacuzzi. *Lansdowne Rd., Ballsbridge, Dublin 4, tel. 01/601711. 220 rooms with bath. Facilities: underground parking. AE, DC, MC, V.*

Jury's. This lively and fashionable spot has more atmosphere than most comparable modern hotels. It's a short (10 minutes) cab ride from the center of town. Bedrooms are relatively spacious, standard modern plush, and each comes with a picture-window view of town. Head for the Dubliner Bar—all polished mahogany and brass fittings—between 5 and 7 PM to observe the stylish media set. *Ballsbridge, Dublin 4, tel. 01/605000. 300 rooms with bath. Facilities: indoor/outdoor pool, Jacuzzi, 2 bars, 3 restaurants, cabaret May–Oct. AE, DC, MC, V.*

★ **Shelbourne.** The Shelbourne is one of Europe's grand old hotels whose guestbook contains names ranging from the Dalai Lama and Princess Grace to Laurel and Hardy, Richard Burton, and

Peter O'Toole. The blazing open fire in its bustling marble lobby, flanked by two huge rose brocade sofas, is proof that the Shelbourne has not lost the sense of grandeur of its past. Between 1986 and 1988, IR£7 million was lavished on major refurbishment, which included restoring many original Georgian features and emphasizing them with luxurious drapes and a prominently displayed collection of fine antiques and heirlooms. A supplement is charged for rooms overlooking the leafy but busy green; the back bedrooms without views are far quieter, however. *27 Stephen's Green, tel. 01/766471. 170 rooms with bath. Facilities: bar, restaurant, coffee shop, sporting facilities available by arrangement. AE, DC, MC, V.*

Westbury. The Westbury overlooks the shopper's mecca of the Grafton Street area. The hotel is a relative newcomer, having opened only in 1984, and is still regarded with suspicion by some for its ostentatious display of pastel-and-gilt luxury; others praise its restful atmosphere and central location. *Grafton St., tel. 01/791122. 150 rooms with bath. Facilities: gourmet restaurants, seafood bar, parking. AE, DC, MC, V.*

Expensive **Ashling.** This family-run hotel sits on the edge of the river Liffey, close to Heuston Station. Some may find that the Ashling's relentlessly bright modern decor verges on the garish. It has a faithful following, however, not least because of its proximity to the 1,760-acre (seven square kilometers) Phoenix Park (practically next door, and ideal for joggers) and its friendly staff. The center of town is a brisk 10–15-minute walk away, taking in many famed landmarks en route. *Parkgate St., Kingsbridge, tel. 01/772324. 56 rooms with bath. AE, DC, MC, V.*

Burlington. Dublin's largest hotel is popular with American tour groups and Irish and European business travelers. It is about five minutes by car from the city's central area. Its bars and restaurants are busy in the day with a mainly local clientele; at night its disco and Irish cabaret turn the Burlington into a lively spot for overseas visitors. Bedrooms are the usual modern plush in neutral tones. *Upper Leeson St., tel. 01/605222. 500 rooms with bath. AE, DC, MC, V.*

Buswell's. You'll either love or hate Buswell's. The hotel is located just across the street from the Dail—Ireland's parliament—and its bars and conference rooms are dominated by the frantic bustle of politicians and lobbyists. Curiously, Buswell's also has a loyal provincial clientele, who seem blissfully blind to the clashing patterns of carpets, drapes, and wallpaper; the smallness of the bedrooms; and the grim food. Perhaps the reason is that staying at Buswell's when "in town" is so ingrained a part of their family traditions that they simply don't notice the hotel's more eccentric features. The combination of a central location (between Stephen's Green and Grafton Street), a charming Georgian facade, and the buzz of politicians proves a potent attraction for many independent American travelers, too. *Molesworth St., tel. 01/764013. 67 rooms with bath. AE, DC, MC, V.*

★ **Gresham.** With a prime central location opposite the historic General Post Office, this place has played a part in Dublin's history since 1817. The interior has a predominantly '30s character, with an emphasis on comfort rather than upscale chic. Bedrooms are reached via long windowless corridors, and the monumentally solid plumbing arrangements give character to the bland modern-repro style of the newly decorated rooms.

The hotel feels much bigger than it actually is, and the lobby, decked out with "Gresham (royal) Blue" carpet and gold brocade armchairs, exudes a sense of history. *Higher O'Connell St., tel. 01/746881. 179 rooms with bath. AE, DC, MC, V.*

Moderate **Ariel Guest House.** This red-brick Victorian town house lies only 50 paces from Lansdowne Train Station, a 5-minute ride from the center of Dublin. The lobby, lounge, and restaurant are cozied-up with Victoriana and lace curtains, "Irish style." The bedrooms, by contrast, are standard hotel-modern, most in a new extension at the back. *52 Lansdowne Rd., tel. 01/685512. 15 rooms with bath. AE, MC, V. Closed Dec. 21–Jan. 31.*

Clarence. You'll find the Clarence either charmingly old-fashioned or just plain dowdy; it's all a matter of taste. Most of its Edwardian interior is dominated by oak-paneled walls and solid leather sofas and chairs. The restaurant and lobby have been prettified by fake art deco drapes and cane chairs. Bedrooms are small and functional: no frills here. Its central Liffey-side location is relentlessly urban. Beware of early-morning traffic noise in the front bedrooms. It remains an excellent place to meet a cross section of "real" Dubliners and mildly eccentric provincials. *6–7 Wellington Quay, tel. 01/776178. 70 rooms, 53 with bath. AE, DC, MC, V.*

Montrose. This well-designed modern hotel is located in Donnybrook—nowadays a staid suburb 10 minutes by car from central Dublin. It is next door to the Irish TV and radio studios (RTE), and across the road from University College's Belfield campus. Bedrooms are relatively spacious, if impersonal. *Stillorgan Rd., Donnybrook, tel. 01/693311. 190 rooms with bath. Facilities: health center. AE, DC, MC, V.*

Inexpensive **Abrae Court Guest House.** This is a typical, large early-Victorian house in the highly respectable suburb of Rathgar. It's a 10-minute bus ride to the center of Dublin. There are 6 bedrooms in the main house; the rest are in a carefully designed period-style annex with ornate stucco ceilings. All are furnished with Irish carpets and handcrafted Irish furniture. The restaurant is open for evening meals but cannot serve alcohol. *9 Zion Rd., Rathgar, tel. 01/979944. 20 rooms with bath. AE, DC, MC, V.*

Egan's Guest House. A large Edwardian house, Egan's is just a 10-minute drive from the city's central area, 6 minutes from the car ferry, and 15 minutes from the airport. John and Betty Egan estimate that about half their guests are American and pride themselves on the friendly, helpful atmosphere of their family-run establishment. Bedrooms are small but well-equipped, each with a direct-dial phone, color TV, and hair dryer. The guest house is located in a leafy, if unexciting, suburb close to the Botanic Gardens, with good bus service (7 routes) to central Dublin. *7–10 Iona Park, Glasnevin, tel. 01/303611. 25 rooms with bath. Closed Dec. 20–Jan. 1.*

★ **Maples House.** According to the Irish Tourist Board's complex grading system, Maples House is a guest house; to the rest of the world, however, it is quite definitely a small hotel. The lobby of this Edwardian house is decked out with oil paintings, Waterford crystal chandeliers, and a discreetly modern carpet and is dominated by a vast mirror-topped Victorian rococo sideboard that sets the tone for the ornate decor of the public rooms. There is a grill restaurant and a bar. The bedrooms are small but adequate, lacking the rococo splendor of the rest of the building. *Iona Rd., Glasnevin, tel. 01/303049. 21 rooms with bath. AE, DC, MC, V. Closed Dec. 25, 26.*

Mount Herbert Guest House. Located close to the swank luxury hotels in the tree-lined inner suburb of Ballsbridge, a 10-minute bus ride from Dublin's center of town, the Mount Herbert is popular with budget-minded American visitors in the high season. Bedrooms are small, but all have 10-channel TV and hair dryers. The restaurant has a wine license; there is no bar on the premises, but there are plenty to choose from nearby. *7 Herbert Rd., Ballsbridge, tel. 01/684321. 88 rooms, 77 with bath. AE, DC, MC, V.*

The Arts

The fortnightly magazine *In Dublin* contains comprehensive details of upcoming events, including ticket availability. In peak season, consult the free ITB leaflet "Events of the Week."

Theaters Ireland has a rich theatrical tradition. The **Abbey Theatre,** Marlborough Street, is the home of Ireland's national theater company, its name forever associated with J. M. Synge, W. B. Yeats, and Sean O'Casey. The **Peacock Theatre** is the Abbey's more experimental small stage. The **Gate Theatre,** Parnell Square, is an intimate spot for modern drama and plays by Irish writers. The **Gaiety Theatre,** South King Street, features musical comedy, opera, drama, and revues. The **Olympia Theatre,** Dame Street, has seasons of comedy, vaudeville, and ballet. The **Project Arts Centre,** East Essex Street, is an established fringe place. The new **National Concert Hall,** in Earlsfort Terrace, just off Stephen's Green, is where to go for classical concerts.

Entertainment and Nightlife

Dublin does not have sophisticated nightclubs in the international sense. Instead, there is a choice of discos (often billed as nightclubs) and cabarets, catering mainly to visitors. There is also a very animated bar-pub scene—some places with live music and folksinging. No visit to this genial city will be complete without spending at least one evening exploring them.

Discos **New Annabels** (Mespil Rd., tel. 01/605222) is a popular late-evening spot; so is **Raffles** (Morehampton Rd., tel. 01/680995).

Cabarets The following all offer "Irish cabaret," designed to give visitors a taste of Irish entertainment: **Braemor Rooms** (Churchtown, tel. 01/988664); **Burlington Hotel** (Upper Leeson St., tel. 01/605222, closed Nov.–Mar.); **Jury's Hotel** (Ballsbridge, tel. 01/605000, closed mid-Oct.–Mar.).

Pubs Check advertisements in evening papers for "sessions" of folk, ballad, Irish traditional, or jazz music. The **Brazen Head** (20 Lower Bridge St., tel. 01/779549)—Dublin's oldest pub, dating from 1688—and **O'Donoghue's** (15 Merrion Row, tel. 01/607194) feature some form of musical entertainment on most nights. Several of Dublin's centrally located pubs are noted for their character and ambience; they're usually at their liveliest from 5 to 7 PM and again from 10. The **Bailey** (2 Duke St.) is mentioned in *Ulysses* (under its original name, Burton's) and retains something of its Edwardian character, while **William Ryan's** (28 Parkgate St.) is a beautifully preserved Victorian gem. **Henry Grattan** (47–48 Lower Baggot St.) is popular with the business and sporting crowd; **O'Neill's Lounge Bar** (37 Pearse St.) is always busy with students and faculty from nearby Trinity College; and the **Palace Bar** (21 Fleet St.) is a journalists' haunt. You can eavesdrop on Dublin's social elite and their hangers-on at the expensive **Horseshoe Bar** in the Shelbourne Hotel or bask in the theatrical atmosphere of **Neary's** (Chatham St.)

For details on pubs serving food, *see* Dining.

Dublin to Cork

Ireland can be covered in three itineraries that, taken together, form a clockwise tour of the country, starting and ending in Dublin. Distances in Ireland seem small—the total mileage of the three itineraries combined is less than 600 miles (970 kilometers)—but roads are small and often twisty and hilly, and side attractions are numerous, so you should aim for a daily mileage of no more than 150 miles (240 kilometers). The consistently dazzling scenery, intriguing ruins, and beguiling small villages will lead to many impromptu stops and explorations along the way. (We have tried to state full addresses for hotels, restaurants, and sights, though many of Ireland's villages and towns are so tiny they barely have street names, much less numbers. If in any doubt, just ask for directions.)

The first tour takes you southwest from Dublin to hilly Cork, the Republic's second largest city. On the way, you'll see the lush green fields of Ireland's famous stud farms and imposing Cashel, where Ireland built its reputation as the "Land of Saints and Scholars" while most of Europe was slipping into the Dark Ages.

Getting Around

By Train The terminus at Cork is Kent Station. There are direct services from Dublin and Tralee and a suburban line to Cobh. Phone 021/504422 for information.

By Bus The main bus terminus in Cork is at Parnell Place, tel. 021/504422.

By Car All the main car rental firms have desks at Cork Airport. Be sure to get a map of Cork's complicated one-way system.

By Bicycle Bicycles can be rented from **D.M.D. Cycles**, 18 Grafton St., Cork, tel. 021/21529.

Guided Tours

CIE operates a number of trips from Parnell Place in Cork; phone 021/503399 for details.

Tourist Information

Tourist House, Grand Parade, Cork, tel. 021/273251.

Exploring: Dublin to Cork

Leaving Dublin by N7 for Naas (pronounced "Nace"), you will pass through the area known as "The Pale"—that part of Ire-

Dublin to Cork

land in which English law was formally acknowledged up to Elizabethan times. Beyond Naas, the road takes you to the center of the Irish racing world. **Goff's Kildare Paddocks** at Kill sells more than 50% of all Irish-bred horses. Naas has its own racecourse and lies just three miles (five kilometers) from Punchestown, famous for its steeplechases. The **Curragh** begins just after Newbridge and is the biggest area of common land in Ireland, containing about 12 square miles (31 square kilometers). You will see the **Curragh Racecourse,** home of the Irish Derby, on your right-hand side; to the left is the training depot of the Irish army.

If you are interested in horses, Kildare, the traditional home of St. Brigid, is not to be missed. The main attraction is the **National Stud and Horse Museum** and its **Japanese Gardens.** *Tel. 045/261617. Open Easter–Oct., Mon.–Fri. 10:30–5, Sat. 10:30–5:30, Sun. 2–5:30. Guided tours on request.*

Also in Kildare is a 6th-century round tower, next to the cathedral. It is open to the public.

At Portlaoise (pronounced "Portleash")—the location of Ireland's top-security prison—follow N8 to Cashel. Your first glimpse of the famous **Rock of Cashel** should be an unforgettably majestic sight: It rises imposingly to a height of 200 feet (61 meters) above the plains and is crowned with a magnificent group of gray stone ruins. The kings of Munster held it as their seat for about seven centuries, and it is here that St. Patrick reputedly plucked a shamrock from the ground, using it as a symbol to explain the mystery of the Trinity, giving Ireland, in the process, its universally recognized symbol. The central building among the ruins is a 13th-century Gothic cathedral; next to it is the Romanesque Cormac's chapel. There is also a round tower and an impressive 12th-century cross. *Open Apr.–Sept., daily 9–7:30; Oct.–Mar., Mon.–Sat., 10–5, Sun. 2–5.*

Cashel and the next town, Cahir (pronounced "Care"), are both popular stopping places to break the Dublin–Cork journey. In the center of Cahir, you will discover a formidable **medieval fortress** with a working portcullis, the gruesome barred gate that was lowered to keep out attackers. An audiovisual display can be seen in the castle complex. *Open mid-June–mid-Sept., daily 10–7:30; mid-Apr.–mid-June and mid-Sept.–Oct., Tues.–Sat. 10–5, Sun. 2–5; Nov.–Mar., Tues.–Sat. 10–1 and 2–5.*

The road continues through Mitchelstown and Fermoy, both of them busy market towns serving Cork's dairy farmers. A short detour at Mitchelstown will allow you to visit President Reagan's ancestral home, **Ballyporeen,** a pretty little village with wide streets built to accommodate the open-air cattle markets held there until the '60s.

The road to **Cork City** passes through the beautiful wooded glen of Glanmire and along the banks of the river Lee. In the center of Cork, the Lee divides in two, giving the city a profusion of picturesque quays and bridges. The name Cork derives from the Irish *corcaigh,* meaning a marshy place. The city received its first charter in 1185 and grew rapidly in the 17th and 18th centuries with the expansion of its butter trade. It is the major metropolis of the south, and, with a population of about 135,000, the second-largest city in Ireland.

The main business and shopping center of Cork lies on the island created by the two diverging channels of the Lee, and most places of interest are within walking distance of the center. **❶ ❷ Patrick Street** is the focal point of Cork. Here, you will find the city's most famous statue, that of **Father Theobald Mathew** (1790–1861), who led a nationwide temperance crusade, no small feat in a country as fond of a drink (or two) as this one. In the hilly area to the north of Patrick Street is the famous 120-foot (36 meters) **Shandon Steeple,** the bell tower of **St. Anne's ❸ Church.** It is shaped like a pepper pot and houses the bells immortalized in the song "The Bells of Shandon." Visitors can climb the tower, read the inscriptions on the bells, and, on request, have them rung over Cork.

Patrick Street is the main shopping area of Cork, and here you will find the city's two major department stores, **Roches** and **Cash's.** Cash's has a good selection of Waterford crystal. The liveliest place in town to shop is just off Patrick Street, to the west, near the City Center Parking Lot, in the pedestrians-❹ only **Paul Street** area. The **Stephen Pearce Shop** stocks the best in modern Irish design, including tableware, ceramics, knitwear, hand-woven tweeds, and high fashion. The **Donegal Shop** next-door specializes in made-to-order tweed suits and rain wear. At the top of Paul Street is the **Crawford Art Gallery,** which has an excellent collection of 18th- and 19th-century views of Cork and mounts adventurous exhibitions by modern artists. *Open Mon.–Fri. 10–5, Sat. 9–1.*

One of Cork's most famous sons was William Penn (1644–1718), founder of the Pennsylvania colony. He is only one of thousands

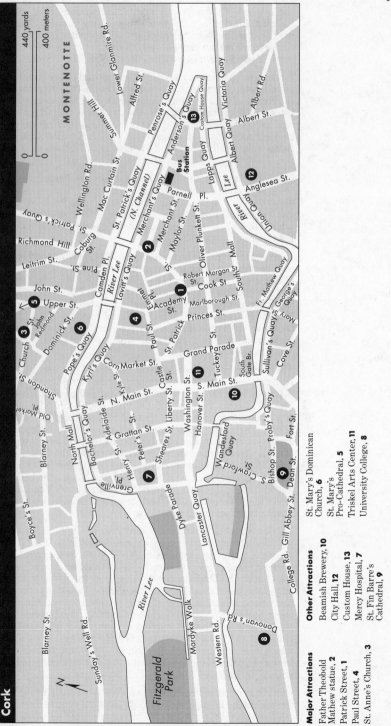

Cork

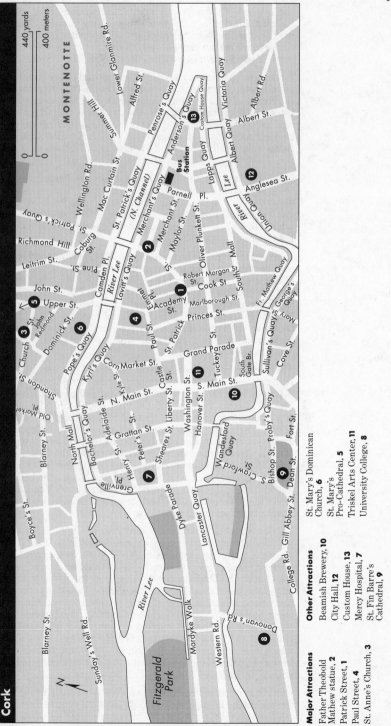

440 yards

400 meters

N

MONTENOTTE

Lower Glanmire Rd.

Summerhill

Alfred St.

Penrose's Quay

Anderson's Quay

Custom House Quay

13

Victoria Quay

Albert Rd.

Albert St.

Lapps Quay

Albert Quay

Lee

12

Anglesea St.

Bus Station

Parnell Pl.

Union Quay

River Lee

Mac Curtain St.

Wellington Rd.

St. Patrick's Quay

St. Patrick's Quay

Richmond Hill

Coburg St.

Leitrim St.

Pine St.

Camden Pl.

Merchant's Quay (N. Channel)

Merchant's Quay

St. Patrick's St.

Maylor St.

Oliver Plunkett St.

South Mall

River Lee

Lavitt's Quay

2

Robert Morgan St.

Cook St.

Emmet Pl.

Academy St.

Marlborough St.

Princes St.

F.F. Mathew Quay

George's Quay

John St.

5

Upper St.

John Redmond

3

Church St.

Dominick St.

6

1

4

Paul St.

St. Patrick St.

Grand Parade

Mary St.

Cove St.

Shandon St.

Pope's Quay

Kyrl's Quay

Corn Market St.

Castle St.

Kyle St.

Washington St.

Tuckey St.

S. Main St.

11

10

Sullivan's Quay

South Gate Br.

Old Market Pl.

Blarney St.

North Mall

Bachelor's Quay

Adelaide St.

N. Main St.

Liberty St.

Hanover St.

Proby's Quay

Fort St.

Boyce's St.

Grenville Pl.

Henry St.

Peter's St.

Grattan St.

Sheares St.

Wandesford Quay

S. Crawford St.

Bishop St.

Dean St.

9

Sunday's Well Rd.

River Lee

Dyke Parade

Lancaster Quay

College Rd.

Gill Abbey St.

Fitzgerald Park

Mardyke Walk

Western Rd.

Donovan's Rd.

8

Major Attractions

Father Theobold Mathew statue, **2**

Patrick Street, **1**

Paul Street, **4**

St. Anne's Church, **3**

Other Attractions

Beamish Brewery, **10**

City Hall, **12**

Custom House, **13**

Mercy Hospital, **7**

St. Fin Barre's Cathedral, **9**

St. Mary's Dominican Church, **6**

St. Mary's Pro-Cathedral, **5**

Triskel Arts Center, **11**

University College, **8**

680

who sailed from Cork's port, the Cove of Cork on Great Island, 15 miles (24 kilometers) down the harbor. **Cobh,** as it is known nowadays, can be reached by train from Kent Station, and the trip provides excellent views of the magnificent harbor. Cobh is an attractive hilly town dominated by its 19th-century **cathedral.** It was the first and last European port of call for transatlantic liners, one of which was the ill-fated *Titanic.* Cobh has other associations with shipwrecks: It was from here that destroyers were sent out in May 1915 to search for survivors of the *Lusitania*, torpedoed by a German submarine with the loss of 1,198 lives. The tragedy is commemorated by a memorial on the quay. Many of the victims are buried at Cobh, and the **museum** has a display of contemporary photographs and reports of the disaster.

Fota Island, midway between Cork and Cobh, is a recent and very welcome addition to Cork's tourist attractions. The Royal Zoological Society has created a 70-acre (280,000 square meters) wildlife park here, and an enterprising Cork businessman has restored its 18th-century hunting lodge, which is a splendid example of Irish Regency (early 19th-century) architecture, and has furnished its neoclassical interior in such a way as to give the impression that it is still lived in. *Open mid-Mar.– Sept., Tues.–Sat. 11–6, Sun. 1–6.*

Most visitors to Cork want to kiss the famous **Blarney Stone** in the hope of acquiring the "gift of gab." Blarney itself, five miles (eight kilometers) from Cork City, should not, however, be taken too seriously as an excursion. All that is left of **Blarney Castle** is its ruined central keep containing the celebrated stone. This is set in the battlements and to kiss it, you must lie on the walk within the walls, lean your head back and touch the stone with your lips. Nobody knows how the tradition originated, but Elizabeth I is credited with giving the word *blarney* to the language when, commenting on the unfulfilled promises of Cormac MacCarthy, Lord Blarney of the time, she remarked, "This is all Blarney; what he says, he never means." Adjoining the castle is a first-rate craft shop, and the outing provides a good opportunity to shop around for traditional Irish goods at competitive prices. *Open daily 10–5.*

Dining and Lodging

For details and price category definitions, *see* Dining and Lodging in Essential Information.

Cahir
Lodging
Kilcoran Lodge Hotel. Set in its own grounds on the main road, Kilcoran Lodge Hotel is an ideal place to break the journey with coffee or a plainly cooked lunch. It occupies a bucolic country setting on the southern slope of the Galtees. *Just off N8, tel. 052/41288. 25 rooms, most with bath. AE, MC, V. Closed Dec. 26–30, Jan. 2–15. Moderate.*

Cashel
Lodging
Cashel Palace. This elegant Palladian mansion was once a bishop's palace. It has luxurious rooms and a beautiful garden. *Main St., tel. 062/61411. 20 rooms with bath. AE, MC, V. Closed Dec. 25–26. Expensive.*

Cork
Dining
★
Arbutus Lodge. One of Ireland's most highly acclaimed restaurants, the Arbutus Lodge is run by the Ryan family and is famous for its excellent wine list. There are 20 rooms as well. *Middle Glanmire Rd., Montenotte, tel. 021/501237. Jacket and*

tie. Reservations essential. AE, DC, MC, V. Closed Sun. and 1 week at Christmas. Expensive.

★ **Ballymaloe House.** This country-house hotel is half an hour's drive from the city, but it's well worth the effort because the restaurant—run by Myrtle Allen, a world expert on Irish cookery—is outstanding. *Shanagarry, near Ballycotton, tel. 021/652531. Jacket and tie. Reservations recommended. AE, DC, MC, V. Expensive.*

Glassialley's. Graced with marble-top tables and better-than-average food, this is a small, informal wine bar and restaurant near the Opera House. *17 Drawbridge St., tel. 021/272305. Dress: casual. Reservations accepted. MC, V. Moderate.*

Oyster Tavern. This delightfully old-fashioned bar-restaurant has changed little in the past 30 years. *Market Lane, off Patrick St., tel. 021/272716. Dress: casual. MC, V. Moderate.*

Bully's. This popular and busy wine bar does an excellent business serving pizza and pasta to visitors and locals. *Paul St. No credit cards. Inexpensive.*

Halpin's. This is a popular self-service restaurant at lunchtime; at night, the atmosphere is more intimate. It serves generous salads, curries, and pizzas. *Cook St., MC, V. Inexpensive.*

Lodging **Arbutus Lodge.** This exceptionally comfortable hotel has an
★ outstanding restaurant and panoramic views of the city and the river. *Montenotte. Middle Glanmire Rd., tel. 021/501237. 20 rooms with bath. AE, DC, MC, V. Closed 1 week at Christmas. Expensive.*

Jury's. This modern two-story hotel has a lively bar and occupies a riverside location just five minutes' walk from the downtown area. *Western Rd., tel. 021/966377. 140 rooms with bath. Facilities: restaurant, indoor and outdoor pools, health club, sauna. AE, DC, MC, V. Closed Dec. 25, 26. Expensive.*

Metropole. The Metropole is a well-established central hotel; Rooms in front can be noisy. *MacCurtain St., tel. 021/508122. 91 rooms with bath. AE, DC, MC, V. Moderate.*

Moore's. Good for its central location on a quiet part of the river bank, the hotel has a fine reputation for friendliness and personal attention. *Morrison's Island, tel. 021/271291. 39 rooms, most with bath. MC, V. Moderate.*

Glenvera House. A Victorian town house, the Glenvera is just 3 minutes from the bus and train stations. *Wellington Rd., tel. 021/502030. No credit cards. Inexpensive.*

★ **John Barleycorn Inn.** This converted 19th-century coaching inn retains much rustic charm. It's situated in its own grounds with a river and trees, 4 miles (6½ kilometers) from Cork, off the main Dublin–Cork road. *Riverstown, Glanmire, tel. 021/821499. 16 rooms with bath. AE, DC, MC, V. Inexpensive.*

Newbridge **Red House Inn.** The Red House Inn is a cozy restaurant with
Dining open turf fires. Home-grown vegetables are a house specialty. *Tel. 045/31516. AE, DC, MC, V. Moderate.*

Cork to Galway

The trip from Cork to Galway is about 188 miles (300 kilometers) and includes stops in Killarney and Limerick. Killarney and the mysterious regions of the Burren are two very different areas of outstanding natural beauty. The Shannon region around Limerick is littered with castles, both ruined and restored.

Getting Around

By Train Trains run from Cork to Tralee, via Killarney, and from Cork to Limerick, changing at Limerick Junction.

By Bus Buses offer a more flexible service than trains; details are available from local tourist information offices.

By Car All major rental companies have facilities at Shannon Airport. **Killarney Autos Ltd.**, Park Rd., tel. 064/31355, is the major firm in Killarney. Taxis do not operate on meters; agree on the fare beforehand.

By Bicycle You can rent bicycles from: **O'Callaghan Bros.**, College St., Killarney, tel. 064/31465; **D. O'Neill**, Plunkett St., Killarney, tel. 064/315900; **Limerick Sports Store**, 10 William St., Limerick, tel. 061/45647.

Guided Tours

CIE offers day tours by bus from Killarney and Tralee train stations. **Shannon Castle Tours** (tel. 061/61788), and **Gray Line** (tel. 01/744466) also operate tours.

Tourist Information

All tourist information offices are open weekdays 9–6, Sat. 9–1.
Killarney: Town Hall, tel. 064/31633.
Limerick: The Granary, Michael St., tel. 061/317522.
Shannon Airport: tel. 061/67664.
Tralee: Godrey Pl., tel. 066/21288.

Exploring: Cork to Galway

Beyond Macroom, the main Cork–Killarney road passes through the west-Cork **Gaelteacht**—a predominantly Irish-speaking region—and begins its climb into the Derrynasaggart mountains. A detour to the left at Ballyvourney will take you to the lake of **Gougane Barra,** source of the river Lee and now a national park. The 6th-century monk St. Finbar, founder of Cork, had his cell on an island in the lake; this island can now be reached by causeway.

Killarney itself is an undistinguished market town, well-developed to handle the tourist trade that flourishes here in the peak season. To find the famous scenery, you must head out of town toward the lakes that lie in a valley running south between the mountains. Part of Killarney's lake district is within **Killarney National Park.** At the heart of the park is the 10,000-acre (40-square-kilometer) **Muckross Estate.** (Open Easter–May and Sept.–Oct., daily 8 AM–7 PM; June–Aug., daily 9–5). Cars are not allowed in the estate, so if you don't want to walk, rent a bicycle in town or take a trip in a jaunting car—a small two-wheeled horse-drawn cart. At the center of the estate is **Muckross House,** a 19th-century manor that contains a folk museum and visitors' center. *Open Sept.–Oct., daily 10–7; Nov.– mid-Mar., Tues.–Sun. 11–5; July–Aug., daily 9–9.*

To get an idea of the splendor of the lakes and streams—of the massive glacial sandstone and limestone rocks and lush vegeta-

Cork to Galway

tion that characterize the Killarney district—take one of the day-long tours of the **Gap of Dunloe, the Upper Lake, Long Range, Middle and Lower Lakes,** and **Ross Castle.** The central section, the Gap of Dunloe, is not suitable for cars, but horses and jaunting cars are available at **Kate Kearney's Cottage,** which marks the entrance to the gap.

The **Ring of Kerry** will add about 110 miles (176 kilometers) to your trip, but in good weather it provides a pleasant experience. Leave Killarney by the Kenmare road. Kenmare is a small market town 21 miles (34 kilometers) from Killarney at the head of Kenmare Bay. Across the water, as you drive out along the Iveragh Peninsula, will be views of the gray-blue mountain ranges of the Beara Peninsula. **Sneem,** on the estuary of the river Ardsheelaun, is one of the prettiest villages in Ireland, although its English-style central green makes it an exception among Irish villages. Beyond the next village, Caherdaniel, is **Derrynane House,** home of the 19th-century politician and patriot Daniel O'Connell, "The Liberator," and completed by him in 1825. It still contains much of its original furniture. *Open mid-June–Sept., daily 10–1 and 2–7; Oct.–mid-June, Tues.–Sat. 10–1, Sun. 2–5.*

The village of **Waterville** is famous as an angling center; it also has a fine sandy beach and a championship golf course. Offshore, protruding in conical shapes from the Atlantic, are the **Skellig Rocks,** which contain the cells of early-Christian monks. Beyond Cahirciveen, you are on the "other side" of the Ring, with views across Dingle Bay to the rugged peaks of the Dingle Peninsula. At the head of the bay is Killorglin, which has a three-day stint of unbridled merrymaking the first weekend in August, known as Puck Fair.

If time and the weather are on your side, turn off the main Killorglin–Tralee road and make a tour of the Dingle Peninsula, one of the wildest and least spoiled regions of Ireland, taking in the Connor Pass, Mount Brandon, the Gallarus Oratory, and stopping at Dunquin to hear some of Ireland's best traditional musicians. For an adventure off the beaten path, arrange for a boat ride to the Blasket Islands and spend a few blissful hours wandering along the cliffs. Tralee is the commercial center of Kerry but has little to recommend it unless you happen to be visiting in September when the "Rose of Tralee" is selected from an international lineup of young women of Irish descent. Listowel is similarly transformed during its race week in October. From Tarbert (where a ferry provides a handy shortcut direct to County Clare and the Burren), the road skirts the estuary of the river Shannon. Limerick is the third-largest city in the Republic, with a population of 60,000; it's also arguably the least attractive city in Ireland. Its Newtown area, however, is dominated by pleasant Georgian buildings, one of which, the Granary, has been converted into the main tourist office.

Bunratty Castle is a famous landmark midway between Limerick and Shannon Airport. It is one of four castles in the area that offer nightly "medieval" banquets, which, though as fake as they come, at least offer some fairly uninhibited fun. The castle was the stronghold of the princes of Thomond and is the most complete and—despite its ye-olde-world banquets—authentic medieval castle in Ireland, restored in such a way as to give an idea of the 15th- and 16th-century way of life. The **Folk Park** on its grounds has farm buildings and craft shops typical of the 19th-century. *Open daily 9:30–5.*

Time Out Drop in to **Durty Nelly's,** beside Bunratty Castle—it's one of Ireland's most popular old-time bars.

There is an incredible number of castles—almost 900—in the Shannon area, ranging from fully restored ones like **Knappogue** at Quin, nine miles (14 kilometers) from Bunratty, to the multitude of crumbling ruins that loom up all over the area.

Beyond Shannon Airport, you reach County Clare and its principal town, Ennis, the campaigning base of Eamon de Valera, the fearsome New York-born politician and demagogue whose character and views dominated the Republic in its early years. Just beyond Ennis, a detour to Corofin will take you to the **Clare Heritage Center,** which explains the traumatic story of Ireland in the 19th century, a story of famines and untold misery that resulted in the mass emigrations of the Irish to England and the U.S.A.

Ennistymon or Lisdoonvarna, both quiet villages with an old-fashioned charm, make excellent bases for touring the Burren. Lisdoonvarna has developed something of a reputation over the years as a matchmaking center, with bachelor farmers and single women converging here each year around harvest time in order to get to know each other better. This strange, rocky, limestone district is a superb nature reserve, with a profusion of unique wildflowers that are at their best in late May. Huge colonies of puffins, kittiwakes, shags, guillemots, and razorbills nest along its coast. The **Burren Display Center** at Kilfenora explains the extraordinary geology and wildlife of the area in an audiovisual display. (Open mid-Mar.–Oct., daily 10–5:45 except May–Aug. 10–6:45.) The dramatic **Cliffs of Moher** are a must: They rise vertically out of the sea in a five-mile (eight-kilometer) wall that varies in height from 440 to 700 feet (135–215 meters) with **O'Brien's Tower** at their highest point. This contains a visitors' center. (Open Mar.–Oct. 10–6). On a clear day, the Aran Islands are visible from the cliffs, and in the summer there are regular day trips to them from Doolin, a small village popular with young travelers and noted for its spontaneous traditional music sessions.

At **Ailwee Cave** near Ballyvaughan, you can take a guided tour into the underworld of the Burren, where 1,120 yards (1,025 meters) of cave formed millions of years ago can be explored. *Open mid-Mar.–Sept., Sat. 10–5, Sun. 2–5; Oct.–mid-Mar. weekends and public holidays 10–3.*

The coast road continues into County Galway, through the pretty fishing village of Kinvara. Galway City itself is approached through Clarinbridge, the village that hosts Galway's annual Oyster Festival in September, featuring the superlative products of the village's oyster beds.

Dining and Lodging

For details and price category definitions, *see* Dining and Lodging in Essential Information.

Ennis
Dining

Brogan's. Situated in the center of town, Brogan's offers a cheerful fire and cozy surroundings. *24 O'Connell St., tel. 065/29859. Dress: casual. AE, DC, MC, V. Moderate.*
The Cloister. There is an Old World bar here, as well as a patio garden. *Abbey St., tel. 065/29521. DC, MC, V. Moderate.*

Lodging
★

Old Ground. A gracious, creeper-clad old building, Old Ground is carefully updated. *O'Connell St., tel. 065/28127. 60 rooms with bath. AE, DC, MC, V. Expensive.*
Queen's. This is a busy, unpretentious place in the center of town. *Tel. 065/28963. 36 rooms, some with bath. AE, DC, MC, V. Moderate.*

Ennistymon
Lodging
★

Falls Hotel. A Georgian manor house set in its own grounds just outside the village, close to two 18-hole golf courses. *Tel. 065/71004. 30 rooms with bath. AE, DC, MC, V. Inexpensive.*

Kenmare
Dining

Anchorage. Head here to enjoy the pleasant nautical atmosphere of the aptly named Anchorage. *Killaha E., tel. 064/41024. MC, V, Moderate.*
Jug's. This place specializes in seafood. *Gortamullen, tel. 064/41099. AE, DC, MC, V. Moderate.*

Lodging

Park. A guest feels truly pampered at this antique-laden hotel, widely considered one of Ireland's best. The French restaurant is superb. *Tel. 064/41200. 50 rooms with bath. Facilities: tennis, park land, garden. DC, MC, V. Closed mid-Nov.–Easter, except Christmas–New Years Day. Very Expensive.*

Killarney
Dining
★

Foley's. This popular eatery specializes in seafood, steaks, and Kerry mountain lamb. *23 High St., tel. 064/31217. AE, DC, MC, V. Moderate.*
Gaby's. For simple and fresh seafood, Gaby's can't be beat. *17*

High St., tel. 064/32519. AE, DC, MC, V. Closed Mon. lunch
and all day Sun. except for dinner in July and Aug.; closed
Dec.–mid-Mar. Moderate.

Lodging **Great Southern.** The Great Southern is housed in a vast 19th-
century red-brick building set in large gardens. *Tel. 064/31262.
180 rooms with bath. Facilities: heated indoor pool. AE, DC,
MC, V. Closed Jan.–mid-Mar. Expensive.*
Arbutus. Newly refurbished and centrally located, the Arbutus
benefits from a lively bar and an Old World atmosphere. *College St., tel. 064/31037. 35 rooms with bath. No credit cards.
Moderate.*
Cahernane. This is a manor house-turned-hotel in a pretty setting. *Muckross Rd., tel. 064/31895. 36 rooms with bath.
Facilities: 9-hole golf course. AE, DC, MC, V. Closed Nov.–
Easter except Christmas–New Year's Day. Moderate.*

Lisdoonvarna **Bruach na Haille.** This prettily converted cottage, 2 miles (3 kilometers) from town, serves imaginative, country-style Irish
Dining meals. *V. Moderate.*

Lodging **Hydro.** The Hydro is an old-fashioned spa-hotel that has undergone a recent facelift to make it perfectly adequate for the
price. *Tel. 065/74027. 70 rooms with bath. V. Inexpensive.*
Sheedy's Spa View. A friendly, family-run establishment with
open turf fires. *Sulphir Hill, tel. 065/74026. 11 rooms with
bath. Facilities: restaurant, tennis. DC, MC, V. Closed Nov.–
Mar. Inexpensive.*

The Wild West

This route from Galway to Sligo and then back to Dublin, via
Kells, takes you through the rugged landscape of Connemara
to the fabled Yeats country in the northwest and then skirts the
borders of Northern Ireland before returning to Dublin. The
whole trip is about 250 miles (400 kilometers) and passes
through some of the wildest and loneliest parts of Ireland.

Getting Around

By Train Trains to Galway, Westport, and Sligo operate from Dublin's
Heuston or Connolly (Sligo) stations. There is no train service
north of Sligo.

By Bus Travel within the area is more flexible by bus; details are available from local tourist information offices.

By Car In Galway, cars can be rented from **Avis**, tel. 091/68901; **Hertz**,
tel. 091/66674; or **Murray's**, tel. 091/62222. Taxis do not operate
on meters; agree on the fare beforehand.

By Bicycle You can rent bikes from **Salthill Rentals**, Galway City, tel. 091/
22085; **John Mannion**, Railway View, Clifden, tel. 095/21160;
Gerry Conway, Wine St., Sligo, tel. 071/61240.

Guided Tours

CIE operates day tours of Connemara out of Galway City and
bus tours into the Donegal highlands from Sligo train station;
details are available from local tourist offices. **CIE** (tel. 01/
302222 Bus Eireann) and Gray Line (tel. 01/744466) offer tours
of the Boyne Valley and County Meath out of Dublin.

Tourist Information

All are open weekdays 9–6, Sat. 9–1.
Galway: Victoria Pl., off Eyre Sq., tel. 091/63081.
Sligo: Temple St., tel. 071/61201.
Westport: The Mall, tel. 098/2711.

Exploring: The Wild West

Galway City is the gateway to the ancient province of Connacht, the most westerly seaboard in Europe. Galway City was well established even before the Normans arrived in the 13th-century, rebuilding the city walls and turning the little town into a flourishing port. Later, its waterfront was frequented by Spanish grandees and traders. The salmon fishing in the river Corrib, which flows through the lower part of the town, is unsurpassed. In early summer, you can stand on the **Weir Bridge** beside the town's cathedral and watch thousands of salmon as they leap and twist through the narrow access to the inner lakes. **Lynch's Castle** in Shop Street, now a bank, is a good example of a 16th-century fortified house—fortified because the neighboring Irish tribes persistently raided Galway City, from whose commercial life they were excluded. Nowadays, the liveliest part of town is around the area between **Eyre Square** (the town's center) and **Spanish Arch.** Galway is a compact city, best explored on foot. Drop in at **Noctan's** pub on the corner of Abbeygate Street for food at lunchtime and the latest news of what's on in town. Galway has a lively and informal arts scene, particularly in mid-August during its annual Arts Festival. It is the home base of the **Druid Theatre;** if the group is performing, a visit to the tiny auditorium is highly recommended.

On the west bank of the Corrib estuary is the **Claddagh,** said to be the oldest fishing village in Ireland. **Salthill Promenade,** with its lively seaside amenities, is the traditional place "to sit and watch the moon rise over Claddagh, and see the sun go down on Galway Bay"—in the words of the city's most famous song.

Connemara is a land of romantic, underpopulated landscapes, and rugged craggy coastlines, where the Irish language is still used by many people. Rossaveale, a port on the coast road beyond Spiddal, is the handiest port for a trip to the Aran Islands, 30 miles (48 kilometers) off the coast, where J. M. Synge drew the inspiration for his play *Riders to the Sea*. The islands are still 100% Irish speaking and retain an atmosphere distinct from that of the mainland, which will be appreciated by those in search of the peace and quiet of a past century. Inishmaan, the middle island, is considered the most unspoiled of the three and will delight botanists, ornithologists, and walkers. *Sailings daily from Rossaveale and less frequently from Galway; round-trip about IR£12. Details from Galway Tourist Information Office. Also accessible by air from Galway City: daily flights, round-trip about IR£35.*

Oughterard is an important angling center on Lough Corrib. Boats can be rented for excursions to the lake's many wooded islands. The road to Clifden runs between the Maamturk and the Cloosh mountains beside a string of small lakes. Clifden,

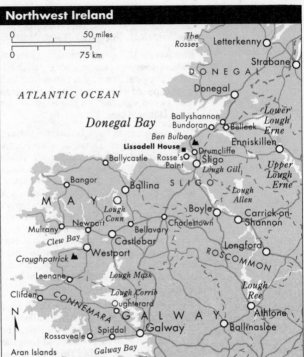

Northwest Ireland

the principal town of Connemara, has an almost Alpine setting, nestling on the edge of the Atlantic with a spectacular mountain backdrop. Just beyond Clifden is the **Connemara National Park,** with its many nature trails offering views of sea, mountain, and lake. Its Visitor Centre features an audiovisual presentation and has a collection of farm furniture. *Open Easter–Sept., daily 10–1 and 2–6.*

Westport is a quiet, mainly 18th-century town overlooking Clew Bay—a wide expanse of water studded with nearly 400 islands. The distinctive silhouette of **Croagpatrick,** a 2,500-foot (760 meters) mountain, dominates the town. Today some 25,000 pilgrims climb it on the last Sunday in July in honor of St. Patrick, who is believed to have spent 40 days fasting on its summit in AD 441. Whether he did or not, the climb is an exhilarating experience and can be completed in about three hours; it should be attempted only in good weather, however.

County Sligo is noted for its seaside resorts, the famous golf course at Rosse's Point (just outside Sligo Town), and its links with Ireland's most famous 20th-century poet, William Butler Yeats, who is buried just north of Sligo Town at Drumcliffe. An important collection of paintings by the poet's brother, Jack B. Yeats, can be seen in the **Sligo Museum** (Stephen St., tel. 071/2212), which also has displays on the folk life of the area. Take a boat from Sligo up to Lough Gill and see the Lake Isle of Innishfree and other places immortalized in the poetry of W. B. Yeats. His grave is found beneath the slopes of Ben Bulben, just north of the town. Nearby is **Lissadell House,** a substantial mansion dating from 1830 that features prominently in his writings. It was the home of Constance Gore-Booth, later Countess Markeviecz, who took part in the 1916 uprising. (Admission: IR£1. Open May–Sept. Mon.–Sat. 2:25–5:15.)

Bundoran, the southernmost town of Donegal, is one of Ireland's major seaside resorts, with excellent sandy beaches. From Donegal Town, you can set off to tour the ever-changing landscape of Donegal's rugged coastline and highlands, visiting the "tweed villages" on the coast at the Rosses where the famous Donegal tweed is woven.

This route heads back to Dublin through **Belleek,** on the borders of Counties Donegal and Fermanagh, known for its fragile, lustrous china; a factory visit can be arranged (tel. 036565/501). Belleek is a frontier post on an approved road that passes through Enniskillen in Northern Ireland and Newtown Butler, re-emerging in Clones, County Monaghan. (Tourists in private cars can cross the borders here with a minimum of formality.) At Cootehill (reached via Newbliss) is **Bellamont Forest,** a compact Palladian villa in its own park between two lakes, with fine plasterwork and statuary in the interior. (Open Mon.–Fri. 2:30–5 and by appointment, tel. 049/32227.) This is one of many fine Irish country homes available for rent and overnight stays to small groups and individuals; details may be obtained from Elegant Ireland (tel. 01/751665).

The main N3 returns you to Dublin by way of Kells, in whose 8th-century abbey the Book of Kells was completed; a facsimile can be seen in **St. Columba's Church.** Among the remains of the abbey is a well-preserved round tower and a rare example of a stone-roof church dating from the 9th century. There are five richly sculptured stone crosses in Kells. Just south of Navan is the **Hill of Tara,** the religious and cultural capital of Ireland in ancient times. Its importance waned with the arrival of Christianity in the 5th century, and today its crest is, appropriately enough, crowned with a statue of the man who brought Christianity to Ireland—St. Patrick.

Dining and Lodging

For details and price category definitions, *see* Dining and Lodging in Essential Information.

Cashel Bay
Dining and Lodging

Zetland. This hotel and restaurant offers excellent sea trout and salmon fishing amid the grandeur of Connemara. *Tel. 095/31011. 19 rooms with bath. AE, MC, V. Closed mid-Oct.–mid-Apr. Expensive.*

Castlebar
Lodging

Breaffy House. This sturdy stone mansion is charmingly set in its own parkland. *Located 3 mi (5 km) southeast of town, on the N6, tel. 094/22033. 40 rooms with bath. Facilities: 18-hole golf course. AE, DC, MC, V. Moderate.*

Clifden
Lodging

Abbeyglen Castle. This comfortable hotel is quietly set a half-mile west of town, featuring panoramic views over the rolling green hillsides. The secluded garden is a haven for travel-weary souls. *Sky Rd., tel. 095/21070. 40 rooms with bath. Facilities: heated pool, tennis. AE, DC, MC, V. Closed Jan. 10–Feb. 1. Moderate.*

Rock Glen Country House. Dating from 1815, this converted hunting lodge is one mile (1½ kilometers) south of town in exceptionally peaceful surroundings. *l102, tel. 095/21035. 30 rooms with bath. AE, DC, MC, V. Moderate.*

Cong
Lodging
★
Ashford Castle. This imposing castle is set in its own park on the edge of Lough Corrib and has a superb restaurant, the Connaught Room. President Reagan stayed here in 1984. *Tel. 092/ 46003. 84 rooms with bath. Facilities: 9-hole golf course, tennis, fishing, garden. AE, DC, MC, V. Very Expensive.*

Galway City
Dining
Eyre House. Irish cuisine is served with a French accent. *Eyre Sq., tel. 091/62396. AE, MC, V. Moderate.*

Rabbitt's Bar and Restaurant. A well-established, family-run eating place. *Forster St., tel. 091/66490. DC, MC, V. Moderate.*

Lodging
Great Southern. Recently refurbished, this old-style town hotel enjoys a conveniently central location. *Eyre Sq., tel. 091/64041. 120 rooms with bath. Facilities: roof-top heated pool, sauna, health complex. AE, DC, MC, V. Closed Dec. 24–26. Expensive.*

Ardilaun House. This hotel is set in pleasant grounds midway between Galway City and the seaside suburb of Salthill. *Taylors Hill, tel. 091/21433. 95 rooms with bath. AE, DC, MC, V. Moderate.*

Moycullen
Dining
Drimcong House. The chef-owner prepares his award-winning meals in a 300-year-old lakeside house, 8 miles (13 kilometers) from Galway City. *One mi (1½ km) northwest on N59, tel. 091/ 85115. AE, MC, V. Closed Sun. dinner, Mon., and Jan.–Feb. Moderate.*

Sligo Town
Dining
Knockmuldowney. This fine country-house inn is just outside town, near Strandhill. It has 6 rooms, as well. *Culleenamore, tel. 071/68122. AE, DC, MC, V. Closed Nov.–Feb. Expensive.*

Reflections. Located in the center of town, Reflections is a modern restaurant. *Gratten St., tel. 071/43828. MC, V. Moderate.*

Lodging
Sligo Park. This is a modern 2-story building, set in spacious grounds. *Pearse Rd., tel. 071/60291. 60 rooms with bath. AE, DC, MC, V. Expensive.*

Ballincar House. Just outside of town, this converted country house with gardens serves excellent food. *Rosses Point Rd., tel. 071/45361. 20 rooms with bath. Facilities: squash, tennis, sauna, solarium. AE, DC, MC, V. Closed Dec. 23–Jan. 12. Moderate.*

Southern. This solid, 4-story, 19th-century hotel is set in its own pretty gardens. *Lord Edward St., tel. 071/62101. 52 rooms, most with bath. AE, DC, MC, V. Inexpensive.*

Westport
Dining
Asgard. The Asgard is a pub with award-winning food in both its bar and second-floor restaurant. *The Quay, tel. 098/25319. AE. Moderate.*

Lodging
Westport Ryan. Woodlands surround this smart modern hotel beside a lake. *Louisburgh Rd., tel. 098/25811. 56 rooms with bath. AE, DC, MC, V. Dinner only. Expensive.*

Hotel Westport. Set in its own parkland, the Hotel Westport is 5 minutes from town. *The Demesne, tel. 098/25122. 49 rooms with bath. AE, DC, MC, V. Moderate.*

21 Italy

Introduction

Where else in Europe can you find the blend of great art, delicious food and wines, and sheer verve that awaits you in Italy? This Mediterranean country has profoundly contributed to the Western way of life, and has produced some of the world's greatest thinkers, writers, politicians, saints, and artists. Impressive traces of their lives and works can still be seen in the great buildings and lovely countryside.

The whole of Italy is one vast attraction, but the triangle of its most-visited cities—Rome, Florence, and Venice—gives a good idea of the great variety to be found here. In Rome and Florence, especially, you can feel the uninterrupted flow of the ages, from the Classical era of the ancient Romans to the bustle and throb of contemporary life carried on in centuries-old settings. Venice, by contrast, seems suspended in time, the same today as when it held sway over the eastern Mediterranean and the Orient. Each of these cities presents a different aspect of the Italian character: the Baroque exuberance of Rome, Florence's serene stylishness, and the dreamy sensuality of Venice.

The uninhibited Italian lifestyle can be entertaining or irritating, depending on how you look at it. Rarely do things run like clockwork here; it's more likely you will encounter unexplained delays and incomprehensible complications. Relax and try to see the bright side: There's usually something you can smile about even in the darkest circumstances.

For us as tourists, one of the current problems with visiting Italy is the country's rich artistic heritage. It draws hordes of visitors, all wanting to see the same thing at the same time. Especially from June, even May, through the middle of September, the Sistine Chapel, Michelangelo's *David*, St. Mark's Square, and other key sights are more often than not swamped by mobs of fellow tourists. Try to organize seeing the highlights at off-peak times in the day. If they are open during lunch—and many are not—that is often a good time. Special attractions for 1989 include the sight of Michelangelo's vibrant original colors on the half of the Sistine Chapel that has been cleaned so far, and the restored Masaccio frescoes in the Church of the Carmine in Florence. In Rome, the imposing Arch of Constantine and several other classical monuments are due to emerge from the shrouds that covered them during a recent and extended restoration.

Best of all, recent regulations barring most automobile traffic from the centers of Rome and Florence (Firenze) have made those cities much pleasanter to visit, and a lot less noisy.

Even in the major tourist cities, Italians generally take a friendly interest in their visitors. Only the most blasé waiters and salespeople will be less than courteous and helpful. However, the persistent attention Italian males pay to foreign females can be oppressive and annoying. If you're not interested, the best tactic is to ignore them. Security is important in Italy: Always be on guard against pickpockets and purse snatchers.

Making the most of your time in Italy doesn't mean rushing through it. To gain a rich appreciation for Italy, don't try to see everything all at once. Do what you really want to do, and if

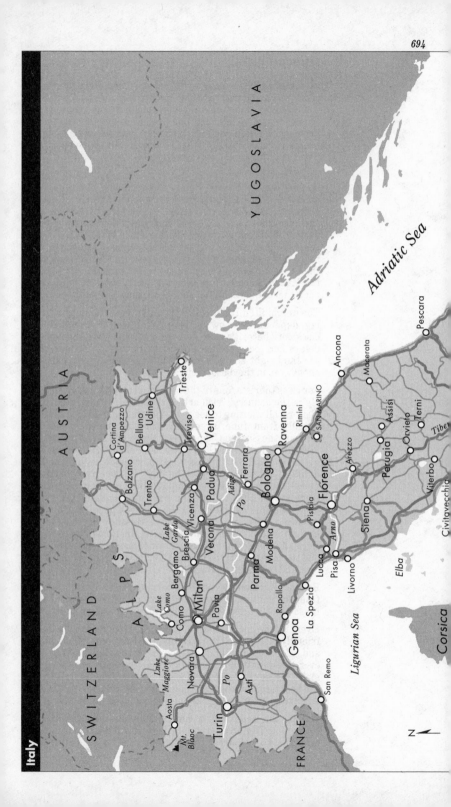

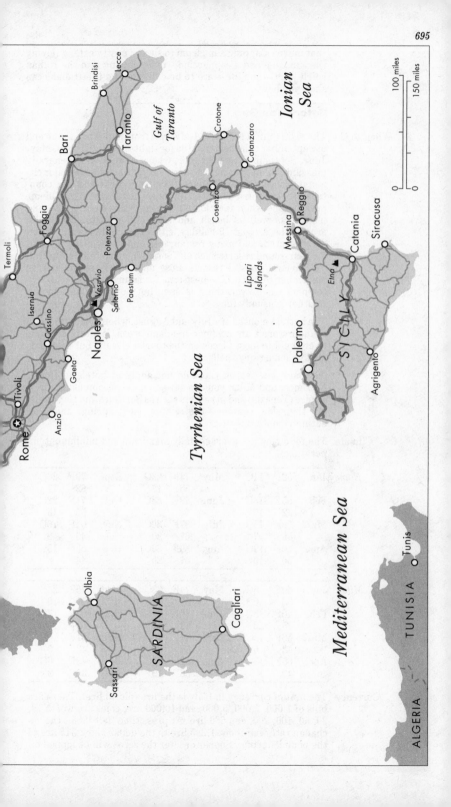

that means skipping a museum to sit at a pretty café, enjoying the sunshine and a cappuccino, you're getting into the Italian spirit. Art—and life—are to be enjoyed, and the Italians can show you how.

Before You Go

When to Go The main tourist season in Italy runs from mid-April to the end of September. The best months for sightseeing are April, May, June, September, and October, when the weather is generally pleasant and not too hot. Foreign tourists crowd the major cities at Easter, when Italians flock to resorts and the countryside. Avoid traveling in August, when the heat can be oppressive and when vacationing Italians cram roads, trains, and planes, as well as beach and mountain resorts. Especially around the August 15 holiday, cities such as Rome and Milan are deserted, and many restaurants and shops close. Except for year-round resorts such as Taormina, and a few on the Italian Riviera, coastal resorts close up tight from October or November to April. The best time for resorts is June and September, when everything is open but not crowded and the weather is usually fine.

The hottest months are July and August, when brief afternoon thunderstorms are common in inland areas. Winters are relatively mild in most places on the tourist circuit, but there are always some rainy spells.

Although low-season rates do not apply at hotels in Rome, Florence, and Milan you can save on hotel accommodations in Venice (Venezia) and in resorts such as Sorrento and Capri during their low seasons—the winter, early-spring, and late-autumn months.

Climate The following are average daily maximum and minimum temperatures.

Rome								
Jan.	52F	11C	**May**	74F	23C	**Sept.**	79F	26C
	40	5		56	13		62	17
Feb.	55F	13C	**June**	82F	28C	**Oct.**	71F	22C
	42	15		63	17		55	13
Mar.	59F	15C	**July**	87F	30C	**Nov.**	61F	16C
	45	7		67	20		49	9
Apr.	66F	19C	**Aug.**	86F	30C	**Dec.**	55F	13C
	50	10		67	20		44	6

Milan								
Jan.	40F	5C	**May**	74F	23C	**Sept.**	75F	24C
	32	0		57	14		61	16
Feb.	46F	8C	**June**	80F	27C	**Oct.**	63F	17C
	35	2		63	17		52	11
Mar.	56F	13C	**July**	84F	29C	**Nov.**	51F	10C
	43	6		67	20		43	6
Apr.	65F	18C	**Aug.**	82F	28C	**Dec.**	43F	6C
	49	10		66	19		35	2

Currency The unit of currency in Italy is the lira (plural lire). There are bills of 1,000, 2,000, 5,000, and 10,000 lire; coins are worth 10, 20, 50, 100, 200, and 500 lire. At press time (fall 1988), the exchange rate was about 1,245 lire to the dollar and 2,315 lire to the pound sterling. Sooner or later the zeros will be lopped off the lire in order to simplify money dealings and life in general. The long-heralded move has not yet been made, but seems imminent. If it does come to pass, 5,000 lire would become 5 lire, 50 lire would become 50 centesimi. When it does happen, both old and new values will be in effect until people become accustomed to the new system.

While the present system continues, and especially when your purchases run into hundreds of thousands of lire, beware of being short-changed, a dodge that is practiced at ticket windows and cashiers' desks as well as in shops and even banks. *Always count your change before you leave the counter.*

Always carry some smaller-denomination bills for sundry purchases; you're less likely to be short-changed, and you won't have to face the eye-rolling dismay of cashiers chronically short of change.

Credit cards are generally accepted in shops and hotels but may not be welcome in restaurants, so always look for those little signs in the window or ask, when you enter, to avoid embarrassing situations. When you wish to leave an extra tip beyond the 15% that is usually included with your bill, leave it in cash rather than add it to the credit card slip.

What It Will Cost Rome and Florence, and, especially, Milan and Venice, are the more expensive cities to visit. Taxes are usually included in hotel bills; a cover charge appears as a separate item in restaurant checks, as does the service charge, usually about 15%, if added. There is an 18% tax on car rentals.

Sample Prices A cup of espresso consumed while standing at a bar costs from 700 to 1,000 lire, triple that for table service. A bottle of beer costs from 1,600 to 3,000 lire, a Coca-Cola costs 1,500 lire. A small sandwich *(tramezzino)* costs about 1,200 lire, a more substantial one about 2,000. You will pay about 5,000 lire for a short taxi ride in Rome, less in Florence, more in Milan. Admission to a major museum is about 5,000 lire; a three-hour sightseeing tour, about 25,000 lire.

Customs on Arrival Two still cameras and one movie camera can be brought in duty-free. Travelers arriving in Italy from an EEC country are allowed, duty-free, a total of 300 cigarettes (*or* 150 cigarillos *or* 75 cigars), 1½ liters plus 3 liters of still wine, and 99 milliliters of perfume if duty and taxes have been paid on them at the time of purchase. Visitors traveling directly from non-European countries are allowed 400 cigarettes and cigars or tobacco not exceeding 500 grams, 0.75 liter of spirits, 2 liters of still wine. Not more than 400,000 lire in Italian bank notes may be taken into or out of the country.

Language Italy is accustomed to English-speaking tourists, and in major cities you will find that many people speak at least a little English. In smaller hotels and restaurants, a smattering of Italian comes in handy.

Getting Around

By Car The extensive network of *autostrade* (toll motorways) connect-
Road Conditions ing all major towns is complemented by equally well-maintained but nonpaying *superstrade* (highways), *strade di grande communicazione* (main trunk roads), *strade di interesse regionale* (regional highways), *strade importanti* (main roads),

and *altre strade* (other roads). All are clearly signposted and numbered. The ticket issued on entering an *autostrada* must be returned on leaving, along with the toll. On some shorter *autostrade*, mainly connections, the toll is payable on entering.

The *Autostrada del Sole*, A1, A2, and A3, crosses the country from north to south, connecting Milan to Reggio Calabria. A4 from west to east connects Turin to Trieste.

Rules of the Road Driving is on the right. At press time, the speed limit on an autostrada on weekdays is 130 kph (81 mph) and 110 kph (68 mph) weekends. The limit is 90 kph (56 mph) on other roads. Other regulations are largely as in the USA except that police have power to levy on-the-spot fines—even as high as $500!

Parking Check with your hotel as to the best place to park. Parking is greatly restricted in the center of most major Italian cities. Parking in *Zona Disco* is for limited periods.

Gasoline Gas costs about 1,300 lire per liter (more than $4 a gallon). Vouchers with tourist discounts of about 15%, together with five 2,000-lire autostrada vouchers and free breakdown service, are available as a package from the AA or RAC. Except on the autostrade, most gas stations are closed Sunday; they also close from 1 to 3 PM and at 7 PM for the night. Self-service pumps can be found in most cities and towns.

Breakdowns Dial 116 for towing and repairs, also for ambulance and highway police.

By Train The fastest trains on the FS (Ferrovia dello State), the state-owned railroad, are the *Intercity* and *Rapido*, for which you pay a supplement and for which seat reservations may be required (and are always advisable). *Espresso* trains usually make more stops and are a little slower. *Diretto* and *Locale* are slowest of all. You can buy tickets and make seat reservations at travel agencies displaying the FS symbol, avoiding long lines at station ticket windows. There is refreshment service on all long-distance trains. Tap water on trains is not potable. Carry compact bags for easy overhead storage. Trains are very crowded at holiday times; always reserve.

By Plane **Alitalia** and domestic affiliates **ATI** and **Aermed,** plus several privately owned companies, provide service throughout Italy. Alitalia offers several discount fares; inquire at travel agencies or at Alitalia agencies in major cities.

By Bus An extensive network of bus routes provides service throughout Italy. A timetable of routes of interest to tourists is published by **ANAC** (Piazza Esquilino 29, Rome, tel. 06/463383).

By Boat Ferries connect the mainland with all the major islands. Car ferries operate to Sicily, Sardinia, Elba, Ponza, Capri (though cars are not advised), and Ischia, among others. Lake ferries connect the towns on the shores of the Italian lakes: Como, Maggiore, and Garda.

Essential Information

Telephones Pay phones take either 200-lire coins, two 100-lire coins, or a
Local Calls token *(gettone)*. Some older phones take only tokens, which you insert in the slot before picking up the receiver; dial, and, when

your party answers, push the little knob on the slot to release the token and complete the connection. Tokens can be purchased from the token machine or from the nearest cashier. Local calls cost 200 lire for nine minutes. For *teleselezione* (long-distance direct dialing), have a handful of coins ready and place several in the slot; unused coins are returned when you push the large yellow knob.

International Calls Since hotels tend to add exorbitant service charges for long-distance and international calls, it's best to go to the *Telefoni* telephone exchange, where the operator assigns you a booth, can help place your call, and will collect payment when you have finished. Telefoni exchanges (usually marked *SIP)* are found in all cities.

Operators and Information For Europe and the Mediterranean area, dial 15; for intercontinental service, dial 170.

Mail The Italian mail system is notoriously erratic and often excruciatingly slow. Allow up to 21 days for mail to and from the USA and Canada, almost as much to and from the United Kingdom, and much more for postcards.

Postal Rates Airmail letters to the USA cost 1,000 lire for up to 20 grams; postcards with a short greeting and signature cost 750 lire but cost letter rate if the message is lengthy. Airmail letters to the United Kingdom cost 700 lire, postcards 550 lire.

Receiving Mail You can have mail sent to American Express offices or to Italian post offices, marked *Fermo Posta* and addressed to you c/o Palazzo delle Poste, with the name of the city in which you will pick it up. In either case you must show your passport and pay a small fee.

Shopping Rome, Florence, and Milan are known for good buys in quality leather goods, silk scarves and ties, and fashion, especially knitwear. In Florence, Siena, and throughout Tuscany you can find ceramics and straw goods. In addition, Florence and Venice offer gold jewelry and embroidered linens. Venice's glassware is famous; authentic Venetian lace is an expensive rarity.

VAT Refunds At Rome airport citizens of a non-Common Market country can avail themselves of a VAT (IVA in Italy) refund of the tax paid on articles worth between 525,000 and 10,000,000 lire purchased in shops displaying a Tax-Free System sign. The procedure: at time of purchase, ask for an invoice describing the article and price, and have the relevant data from your passport included on that invoice. At Fiumicino airport upon departure, show the article to the customs officer, who will put an exit stamp on the invoice. A teller at the exchange window in the transit area will refund the amount of the tax in cash. For refunds of smaller amounts, inquire at shops displaying VAT refund signs.

Bargaining Most shops now have fixed prices *(prezzi fissi)*, but you may be able to get a discount on a large purchase. Always bargain with a street vendor or at a market (except for food).

Opening and Closing Times **Banks.** Banks are open weekdays 8:30–1:30 and 3 or 3:30 to 4 or 4:30.
Churches. Churches are usually open from early morning to noon or 12:30, when they close for about two hours or more, opening again in the afternoon until about 7 PM.

Museums. National museums are usually open until 2 PM and close on Monday, but there are many exceptions. Other museums have entirely different hours, which may vary according to season. Archaeological sites are usually closed Monday. At all museums and sites, ticket offices close an hour or so before official closing time. Always check with the local tourist office for current hours.

Shops. Shops are open, with individual variations, from 9 to 1, and 3:30 or 4 to 7 or 7:30. They are open from Monday through Saturday, but close a half-day during the week; for example, in Rome most shops (except food shops) close Monday morning, or Saturday afternoon in July and August. Some tourist-oriented shops are open all day, every day, as in Venice.

National Holidays New Year's Day, January 6 (Epiphany), March 26 and 27 (Easter Sunday and Monday), April 25 (Liberation Day), May 1, June 2, August 15 (the religious feast of the Assumption, known as *Ferragosto*, when cities are literally deserted and most restaurants and shops are closed), November 1, December 8, December 25 and 26.

Dining Generally speaking, a *ristorante* pays more attention to decor, service, and menu than does a *trattoria*, which is simpler and often family-run. An *osteria* used to be a lowly tavern, though now the term may be used to designate a chic and expensive eatery. A *tavola calda* offers hot dishes and snacks, with seating. A *rosticceria* has the same, to take out.

The menu is always posted in the window or just inside the door of an eating establishment. Check to see what is offered, and note the charges for *coperto* (cover) and *servizio* (service), which will increase your check. A *menu turistico* includes taxes and service, but beverages are extra.

Mealtimes Lunch hour in Rome lasts from 1 to 3, dinner from 8 to 10. Service begins and ends a half-hour earlier in Florence and Venice, later in the south. Practically all restaurants close one day a week; some close for winter or summer vacation.

Precautions Tap water is safe in large cities and almost everywhere else unless noted "Non Potabile." Bottled mineral water is available everywhere, *gassata* (with bubbles) or *non gassata* (without). If you prefer tap water, ask for *acqua semplice*.

Ratings Prices are per person and include first course, main course, dessert or fruit, and house wine, where available. Best bets are indicated by a star ★. At press time, there were 1,245 lire to the dollar. Note that restaurant prices in Venice are slightly higher than those shown here.

Category	Cost: Rome	Cost: Other Areas
Very Expensive	over 100,000 lire	over 85,000 lire
Expensive	65,000–100,000 lire	60,000–85,000 lire
Moderate	30,000–65,000 lire	25,000–60,000 lire
Inexpensive	under 30,000 lire	under 25,000 lire

Credit Cards The following credit card abbreviations are used: AE, American Express; DC, Diners Club; MC, MasterCard; V, Visa.

Lodging Italy, and especially the main tourist capitals of Rome, Florence, and Venice, offers a good choice of accommodations.

Room rates are on a par with other European capitals, and services such as porters, room service, and in-house cleaning and laundering are disappearing in Moderate and Inexpensive hotels. Taxes and service are included in the room rate. Breakfast is an extra charge, and you can decline to take breakfast in the hotel, though the desk may not be happy about it; make this clear when booking or checking in. Air-conditioning also may be an extra charge. In older hotels, room quality may be uneven; if you don't like the room you're given, ask for another. This applies to noise, too; some front rooms are bigger and have views but get street noise. Specify if you care about having either a bath or shower, as not all rooms have both. In Moderate and Inexpensive places, showers may be the drain-in-the-floor type guaranteed to flood the bathroom. Major cities have hotel reservation service booths in the rail stations.

Hotels Italian hotels are officially classified from five-star (deluxe) to one-star (guest houses and small inns). Prices are established officially and a rate card on the back of the door of your room or inside the closet door tells you exactly what you will pay for that particular room. Any variations should be cause for complaint and should be reported to the local tourist office. **CIGA, Jolly, Space, Atahotels,** and **Italhotels** are among the reliable chains or groups operating in Italy, with CIGA among the most luxurious. There are a few Relais et Châteaux member hotels which are noted for individual atmosphere, personal service, and luxury; they are also expensive. The **AGIP** chain is found mostly on main highways.

Pensions Good-value accommodations can be found at *pensione* and *locande* (inns), often found in the streets nearest train stations. Rooms are usually spotlessly clean but basic, with shower and toilets down the hall.

Rentals More and more people are discovering the attractions of renting a house, cottage, or apartment in the Italian countryside. These are ideal for families or for groups of up to eight people looking for a bargain—or just independence. Availability is subject to change, so it is best to ask your travel agent or the nearest branch of ENIT, the Italian tourist board, about rentals.

Camping Italy has a wide selection of campgrounds, and the Italians themselves are taking to camping by the thousands, which means that beach or mountain sites will be crammed in July and August. It's best to avoid these peak months and to send for the (necessary) camping license from **Federazione Italiana del Campeggio,** Casella Postale 649, 50100 Firenze.

Ratings The following price categories are determined by the cost of two people in a double room. Best bets are indicated by a ★. At press time, there were 1,245 lire to the dollar. As with restaurant prices, the cost of hotels in Venice is slightly more than those shown here.

Category	Cost: Rome	Cost: Other Areas
Very Expensive	over 330,000 lire	over 300,000 lire
Expensive	150,000–330,000 lire	140,000–300,000 lire

Moderate	90,000–150,000 lire	80,000–140,000 lire
Inexpensive	under 90,000 lire	under 80,000 lire

Credit Cards The following credit card abbreviations are used: AE, American Express; DC, Diners Club; MC, MasterCard; V, Visa.

Tipping In restaurants, a 15% service charge is usually added to the total, but it doesn't all go to the waiter. In large cities and resorts it is customary to give the waiter a 5% tip in addition to the service charge made on the check.

Charges for service are included in all hotel bills, but smaller tips to staff members are appreciated. In general, chambermaids should be given about 1,000 lire per day, 3,000–4,000 per week; bellhops, 1,000–2,000 lire; doormen, about 500 lire. Give the concierge about 15% of his bill for services. Tip a minimum of 1,000 lire for room service and valet service.

Taxi drivers expect 10%. Porters at railroad stations and airports charge a fixed rate per suitcase; tip an additional 500 lire per person, more if the porter is very helpful. Service station attendants are tipped a few hundred lire if they are especially helpful. Tip guides about 1,000 lire per person for a half-day tour, more if very good.

Rome

Arriving and Departing

By Plane Rome's principal airport is at **Fiumicino,** 18 miles (29 kilometers) from the city. Though its official name is Leonardo da Vinci Airport, everybody calls it Fiumicino. For flight information, phone 06/60121. The smaller military airport of **Ciampino** is on the edge of Rome and is used as an alternative by international and domestic lines, especially for charter flights.

Between the Airport and Downtown ACOTRAL buses connect Leonardo da Vinci Airport with the air terminal on Via Giolitti, on one side of the Termini railway station. They leave every 20 minutes or so, and the trip takes about 40 minutes, more if there's traffic at the city end. Fare is 5,000 lire; before boarding the bus, buy your ticket at booths inside the terminals. There's a taxi stand on Via Giolitti near the bus stop.

A taxi to or from the airport at Fiumicino costs about 50,000 lire, including supplements. At a booth inside the terminal you can hire a car with driver for about the same amount. If you decide to take a taxi, use only yellow cabs, which must wait outside the terminal; make sure the meter is running. Gypsy drivers solicit your trade as you come out of customs; they're not reliable, and their rates may be rip-offs.

Ciampino is connected with the Subaugusta station of the Metro Line A by bus. A taxi to or from Ciampino costs about 30,000 lire.

Train service between Leonardo da Vinci Airport and Ostiense Station, with connections at the Piramide stop of Metro Line B, is due to start toward the end of 1989. Centrally located hotels are a fairly short taxi ride from Ostiense Station.

By Train **Termini Station** is Rome's main train terminal, while **Tiburtina** and **Ostiense** stations are used principally by commuters. For train information, try the English-speaking personnel at the Information Office in Termini, or at any travel agency. Tickets and seats can be reserved and purchased at travel agencies bearing the FS (Ferrovia dello Stato) emblem.

By Bus There is no central bus station in Rome; long-distance and suburban buses terminate either near Termini Station or near strategically located Metro stops.

By Car The main access routes from the north are the Autostrada del Sole (A1) from Milan and Florence, or the Aurelia highway (SS 1) from Genoa. The principal route to or from points south, such as Naples, is the southern leg of the Autostrada del Sole (A2). All highways connect with the GRA (Grande Raccordo Anulare), a beltway that encircles Rome and funnels traffic into the city. Markings on the GRA are confusing; take time in advance to study which route into the center best suits you.

Getting Around

The best way to see Rome is to choose an area or a sight that you particularly want to see, reach it by bus or Metro (subway), then explore the area on foot, following one of our itineraries or improvising one to suit your mood and interests. Wear comfortable, sturdy shoes, preferably with bouncy crepe soles to cushion you against the cobblestones. Heed our advice on security, and try to avoid the noise and polluted air of heavily trafficked streets, taking parallel byways wherever possible.

You can buy transportation route maps at newsstands and at ATAC information and ticket booths.

By Metro The subway, or Metro, provides the easiest and fastest way to get around. The Metro opens at 5:30 AM, and the last train leaves each terminal at 11:30 PM. The newer Line A runs from the eastern part of the city, with a stop at San Giovanni Laterano on the way, to Termini Station and past Piazza di Spagna and Piazzale Flaminio to Ottaviano, near St. Peter's and the Vatican Museums. Fare is 700 lire. As elsewhere, there are change booths and complicated ticket machines at major stations; it's best to buy single tickets or books of five or 10 (latter only 6,000 lire) ahead of time at newsstands and tobacco shops. A daily tourist ticket known as a BIG is good on buses as well, costs 2,800 lire, and is sold at ATAC ticket booths.

By Bus Orange city buses (and two streetcar lines) run from about 6 AM to midnight, with skeleton (*notturno*) services on main lines throughout the night. The fare is 700 lire; you must buy your ticket before boarding. They are sold singly or in books of five or 10 (latter only 6,000 lire) at tobacco shops and newsstands. A Biglietto Orario, valid on all lines for a half-day (either 6 AM–2 PM or 2 PM–midnight), costs 1,000 lire. Weekly tourist tickets cost 10,000 lire and are sold at ATAC booths. When entering a bus, remember to board at the rear, exit at the middle.

By Taxi Taxis wait at stands and, for a small extra charge, can also be called by phone. The meter starts at 2,800 lire; there are supplements for service after 10 PM, on Sundays and holidays, and for each piece of baggage. Use yellow cabs (with meters) only, and be very sure to check the meter. To call a cab, phone 3570, 3875, 4994, or 8433.

By Bicycle Bikes provide a pleasant means of getting around when traffic isn't heavy. There are bike rental shops at Via del Pellegrino

89, near Campo dei Fiori, and at Piazza Navona 69, next to Bar Navona. Rental concessions are at the Metro stop of Piazza di Spagna, Piazza del Popolo, Largo San Silvestro, and Largo Argentina. There are also two in Villa Borghese, at Viale della Pineta and Viale del Bambino on the Pincio.

By Moped You can rent a moped or scooter and mandatory helmet at **Scoot-a-Long** (Via Cavour 302, tel. 06/6780206) or **Scooters For Rent** (Via della Purificazione 66, tel. 06/465485).

Important Addresses and Numbers

Tourist Information The main **EPT** (Rome Provincial Tourist) office is at Via Parigi 5 (tel. 06/463748, open Mon.–Sat. 9–1:30 and 2–7). There also are EPT booths at Termini Station and Leonardo da Vinci Airport. A booth on the main floor of the **ENIT** (National Tourist Board) building at Via Marghera 2 (tel. 06/4971222, open weekdays 9–1, Wed. also 4–6) can provide information on destinations in Italy outside Rome.

Consulates **U.S.** Via Veneto 121, tel. 06/46741. **Canadian.** Via Zara 30, tel. 06/8441841. **U.K.** Via Venti Settembre 80a, tel. 06/4755441.

Emergencies **Police:** tel. 06/4686; **Carabinieri:** tel. 06/112; **Ambulance:** tel. 06/5100 (Red Cross). **Doctor:** Call your consulate or the private **Salvator Mundi Hospital** (tel. 06/586041), which has an English-speaking staff, for a recommendation. **Pharmacies:** You will find American and British medicines, or their equivalents, and English-speaking personnel at **Farmacia Internazionale Capranica** (Piazza Capranica 96, tel. 06/6794680), **Farmacia Internazionale Barberini** (Piazza Barberini 49, tel. 06/462996), and **Farmacia Doricchi** (Via Venti Settembre 47, tel. 06/474–1471), among others. Open 8:30–1, 4–8; some open all night.

English Bookstores You'll find English-language books and magazines at newsstands in the center of Rome, especially on Via Veneto. Also try the **Economy Book and Video Center** (Via Torino 136, tel. 06/4746877); the **Anglo-American Bookstore** (Via della Vite 57, tel. 06/6795222), or the **Lion Bookshop** (Via del Babuino 181, tel. 06/3605837).

Travel Agencies **American Express**, Piazza di Spagna 35, tel. 06/6796108. **CIT**, Piazza Repubblica 64, tel. 06/47941. **Wagons-Lits Travel**, Via Buoncompagni 25, tel. 06/4817545.

Guided Tours

Orientation Tours **American Express** (tel. 06/67641), **CIT** (tel. 06/4794372), and **Appian Line** (tel. 06/464151) offer three-hour tours in air-conditioned buses with English-speaking guides, covering Rome with four separate itineraries: "Ancient Rome" (including the Roman Forum and Colosseum), "Classic Rome" (including St. Peter's Basilica, Trevi Fountain, and the Janiculum Hill, with its panorama of the city), "Christian Rome" (some major churches and the Catacombs), and the "Vatican Museums and Sistine Chapel." Most tours cost about 25,000 lire, though the Vatican Museums tour is about 33,000 lire. American Express tours depart from Piazza di Spagna, CIT from Piazza della Repubblica, and Appian Line picks sightseers up at their hotel.

American Express can provide a car for up to three persons, limousine for up to seven, and minibus for up to nine, all with English-speaking driver. Guide service is extra. A minibus costs about 250,000 lire for three hours. Almost all operators offer "Rome by Night" tours, with or without dinner and entertainment. Reservations can be made through travel agents.

Special-Interest Tours You can arrange to attend a public papal audience in the Vatican or at the Pope's summer residence at Castelgandolfo through **CIT** (tel. 06/4794372), **Appian Line** (tel. 06/464151), or **Carrani** (tel. 06/460510).

Excursions Most operators offer half-day excursions to Tivoli to see Villa D'Este's fountains and gardens; Appian Line's morning tour to Tivoli also includes Hadrian's Villa and its impressive ancient ruins. Most operators have all-day excursions to Assisi, to Pompei and/or Capri, and to Florence. CIT also offers excursions to Anzio and Nettuno; its Etruscan Tour takes in some fascinating old towns and lovely countryside northwest of Rome.

Personal Guides Visitors can arrange for a personal guide through **American Express** (tel. 06/67641), **CIT**, or the main **EPT** tourist office (tel. 06/463748).

Exploring Rome

Antiquity is taken for granted in Rome, where successive ages have piled the present on top of the past—building, layering, and overlapping their own particular segments of Rome's 2,500 years of history to form a remarkably varied urban complex. Most of the city's major sights are located in a fairly small area known as the *centro*. At its heart lies ancient Rome, where the Forum and Colosseum stand. It was around this core that the other sections of the city grew up through the ages: medieval Rome, which covered the horn of land that pushes the Tiber toward the Vatican and which extended across the river into Trastevere; and Renaissance Rome, which was erected upon medieval foundations and extended as far as the Vatican, creating beautiful villas on what was then the outskirts of the city.

The layout of the *centro* is highly irregular, but several landmarks serve as orientation points to identify the areas that visitors will most likely want to see: the Colosseum, the Pantheon and Piazza Navona, St. Peter's, the Spanish Steps, and Villa Borghese. You'll need a good map to find your way around; newsstands offer a wide choice. Energetic sightseers will walk a lot, a much more pleasant way to see the city now that most traffic has been barred from the centro during the day; others might choose to take taxis, buses, or the Metro. The important thing is to relax and enjoy Rome. Don't try to see everything, but do take time to savor its pleasures. If you are in Rome during a hot spell, do as the Romans do: Start out early in the morning, have a light lunch and a long siesta in the hottest hours, then resume sightseeing in the late afternoon and end your evening with a leisurely meal outdoors, refreshed by cold Frascati wine and the *ponentino*, the cool evening breeze.

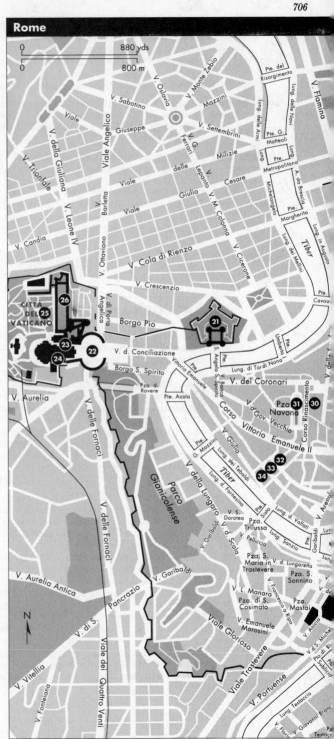

Campidoglio, the Forum, and the Colosseum

1 Your first tour could very well start at the city's center, in **Piaz-za Venezia.** Behind the enormous marble monument honoring the first king of unified Italy, Victor Emmanuel II, stands the
2 **Campidoglio** (Capitol Square) on the Capitoline Hill. The majestic ramp and beautifully proportioned piazza are Michelangelo's handiwork, as are the three palaces. **Palazzo Senatorio** at the center is still the ceremonial seat of Rome's city hall; it was built over the Tabularium, where ancient Rome's state archives were kept.

The palaces flanking Palazzo Senatorio contain the **Capitoline**
3 **Museums.** On the left, the **Museo Capitolino** holds some fine classical sculptures, including the *Dying Gaul*, the *Capitoline Venus*, and a fascinating series of portrait busts of ancient phi-
4 losophers and emperors. In the courtyard of the **Palazzo dei Conservatori** on the right of the piazza, you can use the mammoth fragments of a colossal statue of the emperor Constantine as amusing props for snapshots. Inside you will find splendidly frescoed salons, as well as sculptures and paintings. *Piazza del Campidoglio, tel. 06/6782862. Admission: 4,000 lire (ticket valid for both museums). Open Tues. and Sat., 9–1:30 and 5–8, Wed.–Fri., 9–1:30, Sun. 9–1; closed Mon.*

The Campidoglio is also the site of the very old church of the
5 **Aracoeli,** which you can reach by way of the stairs on the far side of the Museo Capitolino. Stop in to see the medieval pavement; the Renaissance gilded ceiling that commemorates the victory of Lepanto; some Pinturicchio frescoes; and a much-revered wooden statue of the Holy Child. The Campidoglio gardens offer some good views of the heart of ancient Rome, the Imperial Fora, built when the original Roman Forum became too small for the city's burgeoning needs.

6 In the valley below the Campidoglio, the **Roman Forum,** once only a marshy hollow, became the political, commercial, and social center of Rome, studded with public meeting halls, shops, and temples. As Rome declined, these monuments lost their importance and eventually were destroyed by fire or the invasions of barbarians. Rubble accumulated, much of it was carted off by medieval home-builders as construction material, and the site reverted to marshy pastureland; sporadic excavations began at the end of the 19th century.

You don't really have to try to make sense of the mass of marble fragments scattered over the area of the Roman Forum. Just consider that 2,000 years ago this was the center of the then-known world, and that much of the history you studied at school happened right here. Wander down the Via Sacra and climb the Palatine Hill, where the emperors had their palaces and where 16th-century cardinals strolled in elaborate Italian gardens. From the belvedere you have a good view of the Circus Maximus. *Entrances on Via dei Fori Imperiali, Piazza Santa Maria Nova and Via di San Gregorio, tel. 06/6790333. Admission: 5,000 lire. Open Apr.–Sept., Wed.–Mon. 9–6; Oct.–Mar., Wed.–Mon. 9–3; closed Tues.*

Leave the Forum from the exit at Piazza Santa Maria Nova,
7 near the Arch of Titus, and head for the **Colosseum,** inaugurated in AD 80 with a program of games and shows that lasted 100 days. On opening day alone 5,000 wild animals perished in the arena. The Colosseum could hold more than 50,000 spectators; it was faced with marble, decorated with stuccoes, and

had an ingenious system of awnings to provide shade. Try to see it both in daytime and at night, when yellow floodlights make it a magical sight. The Colosseum, by the way, takes its name from a colossal, 115-foot (35-meter) statue of Nero that stood nearby. You must pay a fee to explore the upper levels, where you can also see a dusty scale model of the arena as it was in its heyday. *Piazza del Colosseo, tel. 06/735227. Admission: 3,000 lire to upper levels. Open daily 9–one hour before sunset.*

Time Out   Facing the Colosseum, **Il Gladiatore** is a handy place for a good, moderately priced lunch. *Piazza del Colosseo 15. Closed Wed.* For delicious ice cream try **Ristoro della Salute,** one of Rome's best *gelaterie. Piazza del Colosseo 2a.*

8 Stroll past the **Arch of Constantine,** still shrouded by scaffolding and netting as we go to press, but due to be unveiled soon; the reliefs depict Constantine's victory over Maxentius at the Milvian Bridge. Just before this battle in AD 312 Constantine had a vision of a cross in the heavens and heard the words, "In this sign thou shalt conquer." The victory led not only to the construction of this majestic marble arch but, more importantly, was a turning point in the history of Christianity: Soon afterward a grateful Constantine decreed that it was a lawful religion and should be tolerated throughout the empire.

9 A fairly long but pleasant walk takes you to the **Baths of Caracalla,** which numbered among ancient Rome's most beautiful and luxurious, inaugurated by Caracalla in 217 and used up until the 6th century. An ancient version of a swanky athletic club, the baths were open to the public; citizens could bathe, socialize, and exercise in huge pools and richly decorated halls and libraries, now towering ruins. An open-air opera performance here can be an exciting experience, especially if the opera is *Aïda,* but dress warmly as the night air is very cool and damp. *Via delle Terme di Caracalla. Admission: 3,000 lire. Open Apr.–Sept., Tues.–Sat. 9–6, Sun. and Mon. 9–1; Oct.– Mar., Tues.–Sat. 9–3, Sun.–Mon. 9–1.*

Pretty Piazzas and Splashing Fountains

10 **Piazza del Popolo** is one of Rome's most vast and airy squares, but for many years it was just an exceptionally beautiful parking lot with a 3,000-year-old obelisk in the middle. Now most traffic and all parking has been barred, and the piazza is open to **11** strollers. The church of **Santa Maria del Popolo** over in the corner of the piazza near the arch is unobtrusive but rich in art, including two stunning Caravaggios in the chapel to the left of the main altar.

Time Out   **Rosati** is a café that has never gone out of style, forever a rendezvous of literati, artists, and actors. Its sidewalk tables, tearoom, and new upstairs dining room can revive you with an espresso, snack, lunch, or dinner—all with a hefty price tag, of course! *Piazza del Popolo 4. Closed Tues.*

12 If you're interested in antiques, stroll along **Via del Babuino.** If trendy fashion and accessories suit your fancy, take Via del **13** Corso and turn into **Via Condotti,** Rome's most elegant and expensive shopping street. Here you can ogle fabulous jewelry and designer fashions and accessories in the windows of Buccellati, Ferragamo, Valentino, Gucci, and Bulgari.

Time Out The **Antico Caffè Greco** is a 200-year-old institution, haunt of writers, artists, and well-groomed ladies toting Gucci shopping bags. With its tiny, marble-topped tables and velour settees, it's a nostalgic sort of place—Goethe, Byron, and Liszt were regulars here, and even Buffalo Bill stopped in when his road show came to town. Table service is expensive. *Via Condotti 86. Closed Sun.*

Via Condotti gives you a head-on view of the Spanish Steps in **Piazza di Spagna,** and of the church of **Trinità dei Monti.** In the center of the piazza is Bernini's **Fountain of the Barcaccia** (the Old Boat) around which Romans and tourists cool themselves on hot summer nights. The 200-year-old **Spanish Steps,** named for the Spanish Embassy to the Holy See, opposite the American Express office, is a popular rendezvous, especially for the young people who throng this area. On weekend afternoons, Via del Corso is packed with wall-to-wall teenagers, and McDonald's, tucked away in a corner of Piazza di Spagna beyond the American Express office, is a mob scene. In contrast, **Babington's Tea Room,** to the left of the Spanish Steps, is a stylish institution catering to an upscale clientele.

Opposite, on the right of the steps, is the **Keats and Shelley Memorial House,** in which these Romantic poets lived; it's now a quaint museum. *Piazza di Spagna 26, tel. 06/6784235. Open Apr.–Sept., weekdays 9–1 and 3:30–6:30; Oct.–Mar., weekdays 9–1 and 2:30–5:30.*

Time Out In a corner of Piazza Mignanelli behind the American Express office, **La Rampa** is one of the best restaurants in this area. It's usually crowded, however, and you may have to wait for a table. *Piazza Mignanelli 18. Closed Sun.*

Head for Via Tritone and cross this heavily trafficked shopping street into narrow Via della Stamperia, which leads to the **Fountain of Trevi,** a spectacular fantasy of mythical sea creatures and cascades of splashing water. Legend has it that visitors must toss a coin into the fountain to ensure their return to Rome, but you'll have to force your way past crowds of tourists and aggressive souvenir vendors to do so. The fountain as you see it was completed in the mid-1700s, but there had been a drinking fountain on the site for centuries. Pope Urban VIII almost sparked a revolt when he slapped a tax on wine to cover the expenses of having the fountain repaired.

At the top of Via del Tritone, **Piazza Barberini** boasts two fountains by Bernini: the jaunty **Triton** in the middle of the square, and the **Fountain of the Bees** at the corner of Via Veneto. Decorated with the heraldic Barberini bees, this shell-shaped fountain bears an inscription that was immediately regarded as an unlucky omen by the superstitious Romans, for it erroneously stated that the fountain had been erected in the 22nd year of the reign of Pope Urban VIII, who had commissioned it, while in fact the 21st anniversary of his election was still some weeks away. The wrong numeral was hurriedly erased, but to no avail: Urban died eight days before the beginning of his 22nd year as pontiff.

A few steps up Via Quattro Fontane is **Palazzo Barberini,** Rome's most splendid 17th-century palace, now surrounded by rather unkempt gardens and occupied in part by the **Galleria Nazionale di Arte Antica.** Visit the latter to see Raphael's *Fornarina*, many other good paintings, some lavishly frescoed ceilings, and a charming suite of rooms decorated in 1782 on the occasion of the marriage of a Barberini heiress. *Via Quattro Fontane 13, tel. 06/4754591. Admission: 3,000 lire. Open Sun.– Tues. 9–1, Wed.–Sat. 9–7.*

19 One of Rome's oddest sights is the **crypt** of the **Church of Santa Maria della Concezione** on Via Veneto, just above the Fountain of the Bees. In four chapels under the main church, the skeletons and scattered bones of some 4,000 dead Capuchin monks are arranged in decorative motifs, a macabre practice peculiar to the bizarre Baroque Age. *Via Veneto 27, tel. 06/462850. Free, but a donation is encouraged. Open daily 9–noon and 3–6.*

The lower reaches of Via Veneto are quiet and sedate, but at the intersection with Via Bissolati, otherwise known as "Airline Row," the avenue comes to life. The big white palace on the right is the U.S. Embassy, and the even bigger white palace beyond it is the luxurious **Hotel Excelsior.** Together with Doney's next door and the Café de Paris across the street, the Excelsior was a landmark of La Dolce Vita, that effervescent period during the 1950s when movie stars, playboys, and exiled royalty played hide-and-seek with press agents and *paparazzi*, ducking in and out of nightclubs and hotel rooms along the Via Veneto. The atmosphere of Via Veneto is considerably more sober now, and its cafés cater more to tourists and expensive pickups than to barefoot cinema *contessas.*

Via Veneto ends at **Porta Pinciana,** a gate in the 12-mile (19-kilometer) stretch of defensive walls built by Emperor Aurelian in the 3rd century; 400 years later when the Goths got too close for comfort, Belisarius reinforced the gate with two massive towers. Beyond is **Villa Borghese,** most famous of Rome's parks, studded with tall pines that are gradually dying off as pollution and age take their toll. Inside the park, strike off to

20 the right toward the **Galleria Borghese,** a pleasure palace created by Cardinal Scipione Borghese in 1613 as a showcase for his fabulous sculpture collection. In the throes of structural repairs for several years, the now-public gallery is, at press time, only partially open to visitors. It's still worth a visit to see the seductive reclining statue of Pauline Borghese by Canova, and some extraordinary works by Bernini, among them the unforgettable *Apollo and Daphne* in which marble is transformed into flesh and foliage. If restorations have been completed, go upstairs to the picture gallery to see Titian's *Sacred and Profane Love* and a number of other fine works. *Via Pinciana (Piazzale Museo Borghese-Villa Borghese), tel. 06/858577. Free for duration of renovations. Open Tues.–Sat. 9–7, Sun. 9–1, Mon. 9–2.*

Castel Sant'Angelo–St. Peter's–Vatican Museums

Ponte Sant'Angelo, the ancient bridge across the Tiber in front of Castel Sant'Angelo, is decorated with lovely Baroque angels designed by Bernini and offers fine views of the castle and of

21 St. Peter's in the distance. **Castel Sant'Angelo,** a formidable fortress, was originally built as the tomb of Emperor Hadrian in the 2nd century AD. It looked much like the **Augusteo,** or

Tomb of Augustus, which still stands more or less in its original form across the river. Hadrian's Tomb was incorporated into the town walls and served as a military stronghold during the barbarian invasions. According to legend it got its present name in the 6th century, when Pope Gregory the Great, passing by in a religious procession, saw an angel with a sword appear above the ramparts to signal the end of the plague that was raging. Enlarged and fortified, the castle became a refuge for the popes, who fled to it along the **Passetto**, an arcaded passageway that links it with the Vatican. Inside the castle you see ancient corridors, medieval cells and Renaissance salons, a museum of antique weapons, courtyards piled with stone cannonballs, and terraces with great views of the city. There's a pleasant bar with outdoor tables on one level. The highest terrace of all, under the newly restored bronze statue of the legendary angel, is the one from which Puccini's heroine, Tosca, threw herself. *Lungotevere Castello 50, tel. 06/6875036. Admission: 3,000 lire. Open Apr.–Sept., Mon. 3–8, Tues., Wed., Fri. 9–2, Thurs., Sat. 9–7, Sun. 9–1; Oct.–Mar., Tues.– Sat. 9–1, Sun. 9–noon, closed Mon.*

Via della Conciliazione, the broad avenue leading to St. Peter's Basilica, was created by Mussolini's architects by razing blocks of old houses. This opened up a vista of the basilica, giving the eye time to adjust to its mammoth dimensions, and thereby spoiling the effect Bernini sought when he enclosed his vast square (which is really oval) in the embrace of huge quadruple **❷²** colonnades. In **Piazza San Pietro** (St. Peter's Square), which has held up to 400,000 at one time, look for the stone disks in the pavement halfway between the fountains and the obelisk. From this point the colonnades seem to be formed of a single row of columns all the way around.

When you enter Piazza San Pietro (completed in 1667) you are entering Vatican territory. Since the Lateran Treaty of 1929, **Vatican City** has been an independent and sovereign state, which covers about 108 acres (437,000 square meters) and is surrounded by thick, high walls. Its gates are minded by the Swiss Guards, who still wear the colorful dress uniforms designed by Michelangelo. Sovereign of this little state is John Paul II, 264th Pope of the Roman Catholic Church. At noon on Sunday, the Pope appears at his third floor study window in the **❷³** **Vatican Palace,** to the right of the basilica, to bless the crowd in the square. *Entry to St. Peter's and the Vatican Museums is barred to those wearing shorts, miniskirts, sleeveless T-shirts, and otherwise revealing clothing. Women should carry scarves to cover bare shoulders and upper arms or wear blouses that come to the elbow. Men should dress modestly, in slacks and shirts.*

❷⁴ **St. Peter's Basilica** is one of Rome's most impressive sights. It takes a while to absorb the sheer magnificence of it, however, and its rich decoration may not be to everyone's taste. Its size alone is overwhelming, and the basilica is best appreciated when providing the lustrous background for ecclesiastical ceremonies thronged with the faithful. (It is important to note that the Sistine Chapel is part of the Vatican Museums–not St. Peter's.) The original basilica was built in the early 4th century AD by the Emperor Constantine, over an earlier shrine that supposedly marked the burial place of St. Peter. After more than a thousand years, the old basilica was so decrepit it had to be torn down. The task of building a new, much larger one took almost 200 years and employed the architectural genius of Alberti, Bramante, Raphael, Peruzzi, Antonio Sangallo the Younger, and Michelangelo, who died before the dome he had planned had been completed. Finally, in 1626, St. Peter's Basilica was finished.

The basilica is full of extraordinary works of art. Among the most famous is Michelangelo's *Pietà* (1498), seen in the first chapel on the right just as you enter from the square. Michelangelo has four *Pietàs* to his credit. The most famous is entitled simply *Pietà*, and can be seen here. Two others—*Pietà (Deposition From the Cross)* and *Palestrina Pietà (Entombment)*—are in Florence, and the fourth, the *Rondanini Pietà*, is in Milan.

At the end of the central aisle is the bronze statue of **St. Peter,** its foot worn by centuries of reverent kisses. The bronze throne above the altar in the apse was created by Bernini to contain a simple wood and ivory chair once believed to have belonged to St. Peter. Bernini's bronze *baldacchino* (canopy) over the papal altar was made with metal stripped from the portico of the Pantheon at the order of Pope Urban VIII, one of the powerful Roman Barberini family. His practice of plundering ancient monuments for material to implement his grandiose schemes inspired the famous quip, *"Quod non fecerunt barbari, fecerunt Barberini"* (What the barbarians didn't do, the Barberini did).

As you stroll up and down the aisles and transepts, observe the fine mosaic copies of famous paintings above the altars, the monumental tombs and statues, and the fine stucco work. Stop at the **Treasury** (Historical Museum), which contains some priceless liturgical objects, and take the elevator up to the roof of the basilica. From here you can climb a short interior staircase to the base of the dome for an overhead view of the interior of the basilica. Only if you are in good shape should you attempt the strenuous climb up the narrow, one-way stairs to the balcony of the lantern atop the dome, where the view embraces the Vatican Gardens as well as all of Rome.

The entrance to the **Crypt of St. Peter's** is in one of the huge piers at the crossing. It's best to leave this visit for last, as the crypt's only exit takes you outside the church. The crypt contains chapels and the tombs of many popes. It occupies the area of the original basilica, over the **grottoes,** where evidence of what may be St. Peter's burial place has been found. (Special permission is required to visit the grottoes.) *St. Peter's Basilica, tel. 06/6982. Open daily 7–7. Treasury (Museo Storico-Artistico): entrance in Sacristy. Admission: 2,000 lire. Open daily 9–1:30. Roof and Dome: entrance between Gregorian Chapel and right transept. Admission: 3,000 lire, including use of elevator to roof, 2,000 lire if you climb the spiral ramp on foot. Open daily 8–4:30. Crypt (Tombs of the Popes): Entrance alternates among the piers at the crossing. Admission: Free. Open daily 7–6. Grottoes: Apply several days in advance to Ufficio Scavi, left beyond the Arco delle Campane entrance to the Vatican, left of the basilica, tel. 06/6985318. Admission: 5,000 lire for 2-hour guided visit, 3,000 lire with tape cassette. Ufficio Scavi office hours: Mon.–Sat. 9–noon and 2–5; closed Sun. and religious holidays.*

For many visitors, a **papal audience** is the highlight of a trip to Rome. The Pope holds mass audiences on Wednesday morning; during the winter they take place in a modern audience hall (capacity 7,000) off the left-hand colonnade. From March to October they are held in **St. Peter's Square,** and sometimes at the papal residence at **Castel Gandolfo.** Since you have to apply for tickets in advance, you may find it easier to arrange for them through a travel agency. *For tickets, apply to the Papal Prefecture (Prefettura) which you reach through the Bronze Door in the right-hand colonnade, tel. 06/6982. Open Tues. 9–1, Wed. 9–shortly before audience commences. Or arrange for tickets through a travel agent: Carrani Tours, Via V.E. Orlando 95, tel. 06/460510; Appian Line, Via Barberini 109, tel. 06/464151. Admission: about 25,000 lire if booked through an agent or hotel concierge.*

25 Guided minibus tours through the **Vatican Gardens** show you some attractive landscaping, a few historical monuments, and the Vatican mosaic school, which produced the mosaics decorating St. Peter's. These tours give you a different perspective on the basilica itself. From March through October, you can choose a garden tour that includes the Sistine Chapel, which you would otherwise see as part of a tour of the Vatican Museums. *Vatican Gardens. Tickets at Information Office, on the left side of St. Peter's Square, tel. 06/6984466. Open Mar.–Oct., Tues. and Sat., gardens and basilica. Admission: 10,000 lire; Mon. and Thurs., gardens and Sistine Chapel. Admission: 18,000 lire; Fri., gardens only. Admission: 9,000 lire. Nov.– Feb., Tues., Thurs., Sat., gardens only. Admission: 8,000 lire. All tours begin at 10 AM.*

From St. Peter's Square Information Office you can take a shuttle bus (Cost: 1,000 lire) direct to the Vatican Museums. This operates every morning, except Wednesday and Sunday, and saves you the 15-minute walk that goes left from the square and continues along the Vatican walls.

26 The collections in the **Vatican Museums** cover nearly five miles (eight kilometers) of displays. If you have time, allow at least half a day for Castel Sant'Angelo and St. Peter's, and another half-day for the museums. Posters at the museum entrance plot out a choice of four color-coded itineraries; the shortest takes about 90 minutes, the longest more than four hours, depending on your rate of progress. All include the **Sistine Chapel.**

In 1508, Pope Julius II commissioned Michelangelo to fresco the more than 10,000 square feet (930 square meters) of the chapel's ceiling. For four years Michelangelo dedicated himself to painting over fresh plaster, and the result was his masterpiece. The cleaning operations, still under way, are revealing its original and surprisingly brilliant colors.

You can try to avoid the tour groups by going early or late, allowing yourself enough time before the closing hour. In peak season, the crowds definitely detract from your appreciation of this outstanding artistic achievement. Buy an illustrated guide or rent a taped commentary in order to make sense of the figures on the ceiling. A pair of binoculars helps.

The Vatican collections are so rich that unless you are an expert in art history, you will probably want only to skim the surface, concentrating on a few pieces that strike your fancy. If you really want to see the museums thoroughly, you will have to come back again and again. Some of the highlights that might be of interest on your first tour include the *Laocoön*, the *Belvedere Torso*, and the *Apollo Belvedere*, which inspired Michelangelo. The Raphael Rooms are decorated with masterful frescoes, and there are more Raphaels in the Picture Gallery *(Pianoteca)*. At the Quattro Cancelli, near the entrance to the Picture Gallery, a rather spartan cafeteria provides basic nonalcoholic refreshments. *Viale Vaticano, tel. 06/698–3333. Admission: 7,000 lire, free on last Sun. of the month. Open Easter period and July–Sept., Mon.–Sat. 9–5 (no admission after 4); Oct.– June, Mon.–Sat. 9–2 (no admission after 1). Closed Sun., except last Sun. of the month, and on religious holidays.*

Old Rome

㉗ Take Via del Plebiscito from Piazza Venezia to the huge **Church of the Gesù.** This paragon of Baroque style is the tangible symbol of the power of the Jesuits, who were a major force in the Counter-Reformation in Europe. Encrusted with gold and precious marbles, the Gesù has a fantastically painted ceiling that flows down over the pillars, merging with painted stucco figures to complete the three-dimensional illusion.

㉘ On your way to the Pantheon you will pass **Santa Maria Sopra Minerva,** a Gothic church built over a Roman temple. Inside there are some beautiful frescoes by Filippo Lippi; outside, a charming elephant by Bernini with an obelisk on its back.

㉙ Originally built in 27 B.C. by Augustus's general Agrippa and rebuilt by Hadrian in the 2nd century AD, the **Pantheon** is one of Rome's most perfect, best-preserved, and perhaps least appreciated ancient monuments. Romans and tourists alike pay little attention to it, and on summer evenings it serves mainly as a backdrop for all the action in the square in front. It represents a fantastic feat of construction, however. The huge columns of the portico and the original bronze doors form the entrance to a majestic hall covered by the largest dome of its kind ever built, wider even than that of St. Peter's. In ancient times the entire interior was encrusted with rich decorations of gilt bronze and marble, plundered by later emperors and popes. *Piazza della Rotonda. Open Mon.–Sat. 9–2, Sun. 9–1.*

Time Out There are two sidewalk cafés on the square in front of the Pantheon, both good places to nurse a cappuccino while you observe the scene. The **Bar Sant'Eustachio** (Piazza Sant'Eustachio 82) is famous for its coffee (which is served with plenty of sugar in it; if you prefer, tell the counter man you want it without *(senza)* or with only a little *(poco)* sugar *(zucchero)*. Serious coffee drinkers also like **Tazza d'Oro** (Via degli Orfani 84), just off Piazza della Rotonda. And for a huge variety of ice cream in natural flavors, **Giolitti** (Via Uffizi del Vicario 40; closed Mon.) is generally considered by *gelati* addicts as the best in Rome. It also has good snacks and a quick-lunch counter.

㉚ Stop in at the church of **San Luigi dei Francesi** on Via della Dogana Vecchia to see the three paintings by Caravaggio in the last chapel on the left; have a few hundred-lire coins handy for the light machine. The clergy of San Luigi considered the artist's roistering and unruly lifestyle scandalous enough, but his realistic treatment of sacred subjects was just too much for them. They rejected his first version of the altarpiece and weren't particularly happy with the other two works either. Thanks to the intercession of Caravaggio's patron, an influential cardinal, they were persuaded to keep them—a lucky thing, since they are now recognized to be among the artist's finest paintings.

③① Just beyond San Luigi, **Piazza Navona** is an elongated 17th-century piazza that traces the oval form of the underlying Circus of Diocletian. At the center, Bernini's lively **Fountain of the Four Rivers** is a showpiece. The four statues represent rivers in the four corners of the world: the Nile, with its face covered in allusion to its then unknown source; the Ganges; the Danube; and the River Plate, with its hand raised. And here we have to give the lie to the legend that this was Bernini's mischievous dig at Borromini's design of the facade of the church of **Sant'Agnese in Agone,** from which the statue seems to be shrinking in horror. The fountain was created in 1651; work on the church's facade began some time later. The piazza dozes in the morning, when little groups of pensioners sun themselves on the stone benches and children pedal tricycles around the big fountain. In the late afternoon the sidewalk cafés fill up for the aperitif hour, and in the evening, especially in good weather, the piazza comes to life with a throng of street artists, vendors, tourists, and Romans out for their evening *passeggiata* (promenade).

Time Out The sidewalk tables of the **Tre Scalini** café (Piazza Navona 30; closed Wed.) offer a grandstand view of this gorgeous piazza. Treat yourself to a *tartufo*, the chocolate ice cream specialty invented here. The restaurant is a pleasant place for a moderately priced lunch. For a more lavish meal, try **Mastrostefano** (Piazza Navona 94, tel. 06/6541669; closed Mon.), a popular restaurant with a view of the piazza. Prices are at the top of the moderate range. There are a few café tables for those who want just coffee.

③② Across Corso Vittorio, **Campo dei Fiori** (Field of Flowers) is the site of a crowded and colorful daily morning market. The hooded bronze figure brooding over the piazza is philosopher Giordano Bruno, who was burned at the stake here for heresy.
③③ The adjacent **Piazza Farnese**, with fountains made of Egyptian granite basins from the Baths of Caracalla, is an airy setting for
③④ **Palazzo Farnese**, now the French Embassy, one of the most beautiful of Rome's many Renaissance palaces. There are several others in the immediate area: **Palazzo Spada,** a Wedgwood kind of palace encrusted with stuccoes and statues; **Palazzo della Cancelleria,** a massive building that is now the Papal Chancellery, one of the many Vatican-owned buildings in Rome that enjoy extraterritorial privileges; and the fine old palaces along Via Giulia.

This is a section to wander through, getting the feel of daily life carried on in a centuries-old setting, and looking into the dozens of antique shops. Stroll along Via Arenula into a rather gloomy part of Rome bounded by Piazza Campitelli and Lungotevere Cenci, the ancient Jewish ghetto. Among the most interesting sights here are the pretty **Fountain of the Tartarughe** (Turtles) on Piazza Mattei, the **Via Portico d'Ottavia,** with medieval inscriptions and friezes on the old buildings, and the **Teatro di Marcello,** a theater built by Julius Caesar to hold 20,000 spectators.

㉟ A pleasant place to end your walk is on **Tiberina Island.** To get
㊱ there, walk across the ancient **Fabricio Bridge,** built in 62 BC,
the oldest bridge in the city.

What to See and Do with Children

Explore the nooks and crannies of **Castel Sant'Angelo,** the **Roman Forum,** and the **Colosseum** *(see* Exploring); have a picnic
lunch in **Villa Borghese,** where you can also row a boat around
the little lake in the Botanical Garden; go to **Lunaeur,** a well-
kept permanent amusement park in the EUR district (a 25-
minute taxi ride from Piazza Venezia, or 30 minutes by bus 97
from Piazza di Monte Savello, behind the Teatro di Marcello). If
your children like scary sights, visit the **Crypt of Santa Maria
della Concezione** on Via Veneto just above the Fountain of the
Bees *(see* Exploring).

Off the Beaten Track

If the sky promises a gorgeous sunset, head for the **terrace of
the Pincio** above Piazza del Popolo, a vantage point prized by
Romans.

For a look at a real patrician palace, see the **Galleria Doria
Pamphili,** still the residence of a princely family. You can visit
the gallery housing the family's art collection and part of the
magnificently furnished private apartments, as well. *Piazza
del Collegio Romano 1/a, near Piazza Venezia, tel. 06/6794365.
Admission: 2,000 lire; additional 2,000 lire for guided visit
of private rooms. Open Tues., Wed., Sat., Sun. 10–1; closed
Mon., Thurs., and Fri.*

Make an excursion to **Ostia Antica,** the well-preserved Roman
port city near the sea, as rewarding as an excursion to Pompeii, and much easier to get to from Rome. There's a regular
train service from the Ostiense Station (Piramide Metro stop).
*Via dei Romagnoli, Ostia Antica, tel. 06/5651405. Admission:
4,000 lire. Open daily 9–4.*

Delve into the world of the Etruscans, who inhabited Italy even
in pre-Roman times and have left fascinating evidence of their
relaxed, sensual lifestyle. Visit the **Museo Nazionale di Villa
Giulia,** in a gorgeous Renaissance mansion with a full-scale
Etruscan temple in the garden. You'll see a smile as enigmatic
as that of the Mona Lisa on deities and other figures in terra
cotta, bronze, and gold. Ask especially to see the **Castellani collection of ancient jewelry** hidden away on the upper floor.
*Piazza di Villa Giulia 9, tel. 06/3601951. Admission: 4,000 lire.
Open Tues.–Sat. 9–7, Sun. 9–1; closed Mon.*

Shopping

Gift Ideas Shopping in Rome is part of the fun, no matter what your budget. The best buys are leather goods of all kinds, from gloves to
handbags and wallets to jackets, silk goods, and quality knitwear. Shops are closed on Sunday and on Monday morning; in
July and August, they close Saturday afternoon as well.

Antiques A well-trained eye will spot some worthy old prints and minor
antiques in the city's fascinating little shops. For prints,
browse among the stalls at **Piazza Fontanella Borghese;** at

Casali, Piazza della Rotonda 81a, at the Pantheon; and **Tanca,** Salita de'Crescenzi 10, also near the Pantheon. For minor antiques, **Via dei Coronari** and other streets in the **Piazza Navona** area are good. The most prestigious antiques dealers are situated in **Via del Babuino** and its environs.

Boutiques Via Condotti, directly across from the Piazza di Spagna, and the streets running parallel to Via Condotti as well as its cross streets, form the most elegant and expensive shopping area in Rome. Lower-price fashions may be found on display at shops on Via Frattina and Via del Corso.

Shopping Districts In addition to those mentioned, Romans themselves do much of their shopping along **Via Cola di Rienzo** and **Via Nazionale.**

Religious Articles These abound in the shops around St. Peter's, on **Viale di Porta Angelica** and **Via della Conciliazione,** and in the souvenir shops tucked away on the roof and at the crypt exit in St. Peter's itself.

Department Stores You'll find a fairly broad selection of women's, men's, and children's fashions and accessories at the **Rinascente** stores on Piazza Colonna and at Piazza Fiume (the latter with a good housewares department in the basement), and at the **Coin** department store on Piazzale Appio near San Giovanni Laterano. The **UPIM** and **Standa** chains have shops all over the city that offer medium-quality, low-price goods.

Food and Flea Markets The open-air markets at **Piazza Vittorio** and **Campo dei Fiori** are colorful sights. The flea market held at **Porta Portese** on Sunday morning is stocked mainly with new or second-hand clothing. If you go, beware of pickpockets and purse snatchers.

Dining

There are plenty of fine restaurants in Rome serving various Italian regional cuisines and international specialties with a flourish of linen and silver, as well as a whopping *conto* (check) at the end. If you want family-style cooking and prices, try the *trattorias*, usually smallish and unassuming, often family-run places. Fast-food places and Chinese restaurants are proliferating in Rome; very few can be recommended. Fixed-price tourist menus can be scanty and unimaginative. The lunch hour in Rome lasts from about 1 to 3 PM, dinner from 8 or 8:30 to about 10:30, though some restaurants stay open much later. During August many restaurants close for vacation.

Ratings Prices are per person and include first course, main course, dessert or fruit, and house wine, where available. Best bets are indicated by a star ★. At press time, there were 1,245 lire to the dollar.

Category	Cost
Very Expensive	over 100,000 lire
Expensive	65,000–100,000 lire
Moderate	30,000–65,000 lire
Inexpensive	under 30,000 lire

Very Expensive **Eden Panoramico Roof Garden.** The Eden Hotel's rooftop restaurant is a favorite haunt of Italian politicians and other powerbrokers drawn by the classic regional Italian cooking and breathtaking views. The decor—pink and green with gilt moldings and banks of flowers—is more than a little overblown but reflects the elegant garden ambience and sense of airy space. Try the deceptively simple *spaghetti alla carrettiera* (spaghetti tossed in hot olive oil, with grated pecorino cheese and black pepper). Regulars also love *piccata di vitello ai carciofi* (veal with artichokes). *Eden Hotel, Via Ludovisi 49, tel. 06/4743551, ext. 437. Jacket and tie preferred. Reservations advised for dinner. AE.*

★ **Le Restaurant.** The resplendent dining room of the Grand Hotel's restaurant is a model of 19th-century opulence, lavish with fine damasks and velvets, crystal chandeliers, and oil paintings. The menu varies with the seasons; there is always a daily recommended menu. Among the specialties are *carpaccio tiepido di pescatrice* (brill with thin slices of raw beef) and *medaglioni di vitello al marsala con tartufo* (veal medallions with marsala wine and truffles). The wine list offers some majestic vintages. *Via Vittorio Emanuele Orlando 3, tel. 06/4709. Jacket and tie. Reservations advised. DC, MC, V. Closed Aug.*

★ **El Toulà.** On a little byway off Piazza Nicosia in Old Rome, El Toulà has the warm, welcoming atmosphere of a 19th-century country house, with white walls, antique furniture in dark wood, heavy silver serving dishes, and spectacular arrangements of fruits and flowers. There's a cozy little bar off the entrance where you can sip a *prosecco*, the aperitif best suited to the chef's Venetian specialties, among them the classic *pasta e fagioli* (bean soup), risotto with radicchio, and *fegato alla veneziana* (liver with onions). *Via della Lupa 29/b, tel. 06/6873750. Jacket and tie. Reservations required. AE, DC, MC, V. Closed Sat. lunch, Sun., Aug., and Dec. 24–26.*

Expensive **Andrea.** Ernest Hemingway and King Farouk used to eat here;
★ FIAT motors supremo Gianni Agnelli and other Italian powerbrokers still do. A half-block off Via Veneto, Andrea offers classic Italian cooking in an intimate, clubby ambience in which snowy table linens gleam against a discreet background of dark green paneling. The menu features delicacies such as homemade *tagliolini* (thin noodles) with shrimp and spinach sauce, spaghetti with seafood and truffles, and mouth-watering *carciofi all'Andrea* (artichokes simmered in olive oil). *Via Sardegna 26, tel. 06/493707. Dress: Informal. Reservations advised. AE, DC, MC, V. Closed Sun. and most of Aug.*

★ **Alberto Ciarla.** Located on a large square in Trastevere, scene of a busy morning food market, Alberto Ciarla is one of Rome's best seafood restaurants. In contrast with its workaday location, the ambience is upscale, with red-and-black decor. Bubbling aquariums, a sure sign that the food is super-fresh, are set around the wall. Seafood salads are a specialty. Meat eaters will find succor in the house pâté and the lamb. *Piazza San Cosimato 40, tel. 06/5818668. Jacket and tie. Reservations required. AE, DC, MC, V. Closed lunch, all day Sun., Aug. 5–25, and Christmas.*

Coriolano. The only tourists who find their way to this classic restaurant near Porta Pia are likely to be gourmets looking for quintessential Italian food—that means light homemade pastas, choice olive oil, and market-fresh ingredients, especially seafood. Although seafood dishes vary, *tagliolini all'aragosta* (thin noodles with lobster sauce) is usually on the menu, as are *porcini* mushrooms (in season) cooked to a secret recipe. The wine list is predominantly Italian but includes some French and California wines, too. *Via Ancona 14, tel. 06/861122. Jacket and tie preferred. Reservations advised. No credit cards. Closed Sun. and Aug. 1–25.*

Piperno. Located in the old Jewish ghetto next to historic Palazzo Cenci, Piperno has been in business for more than a century. It is *the* place to go for Rome's extraordinary *carciofi alla giudia*, crispy-fried artichokes, Jewish-style. You eat in three small, wood-paneled dining rooms or, in fair weather, at one of a handful of tables outdoors. Try *filetti di baccala* (cod fillet fried in batter), *pasta e ceci* (a thick soup of pasta tubes and chickpeas), and *fiori di zucca* (stuffed zucchini flowers)—but don't miss the *carciofi*. *Monte dei Cenci 9, tel. 06/654-2772. Dress: informal. Reservations advised. No credit cards. Closed Sun. dinner, Mon., Christmas, Easter, and Aug.*

★ **Ranieri.** On a quiet street off fashionable Via Condotti near the Spanish Steps, this historic restaurant was founded by a one-time chef of Queen Victoria. It remains a favorite with tourists for its traditional atmosphere and decor, with damask-covered walls, velvet banquettes, crystal chandeliers, and old paintings. Among the many specialties on the vast menu are *gnocchi alla parigina* (souffléed gnocchi with tomato and cheese sauce) and *mignonettes alla Regina Vittoria* (veal with pâté and cream). *Via Mario de' Fiori 26, tel. 06/6791592. Dress: Informal. Reservations advised. AE, DC, MC, V. Closed Sun.*

Il Veliero. The attractive sailing ship decor of this top fish restaurant near Piazza Farnese sets the scene for seafood feasts accompanied by fresh-baked bread from a wood-burning oven. There are many types of pasta and risotto, with shellfish or squid to follow the splendid choice of seafood *antipasti*. For your main course, try grilled or baked fish, or succulent Mediterranean crayfish, scampi, or shrimp. Have the bluefish if it's on the menu. *Via Monserrato 32, tel. 06/6542636. Jacket and tie preferred. Reservations advised. AE, DC, V. Closed Mon.*

Moderate **Colline Emiliane.** Located near Piazza Barberini, the Colline Emiliane is an unassuming trattoria offering exceptionally good food. Behind an opaque glass facade, there are a couple of plain little dining rooms where you are served light homemade pastas, a very special chicken broth, and meats ranging from pot roast to *giambonetto di vitella* (roast veal) and *cotoletta alla bolognese* (veal cutlet with cheese and tomato sauce). *Via degli Avignonesi 22, tel. 06/4757538. Dress: informal. Reservations advised. No credit cards. Closed Fri.*

Pierluigi. Pierluigi, in the heart of Old Rome, is a longtime favorite: On busy evenings it's almost impossible to find a table, so make sure you reserve well in advance. Seafood predominates—if you fancy a splurge, try the lobster—but traditional Roman dishes are offered, too, such as *orecchiette con broccoli* (disk-shaped pasta with greens) or just simple spaghetti. In summer eat in the pretty piazza. *Piazza dei Ricci 144, tel. 06/6861302. Dress: informal. Reservations advised. AE. Closed Mon. and 2 weeks in Aug.*

★ **Quattro Mori.** Quattro Mori is probably the best Sardinian restaurant in town. The menu includes a tempting *antipasto* selection, then a choice between such Sardinian pastas as *malloreddus* (small shells made of semola), *culingiones* (vegetarian ravioli), or *spaghetti all'aragosta* (with lobster sauce). Second courses offer either meat or fish, including the Sardinian *maialino* (roast piglet) and the Roman *pajata* (baby lamb innards). For dessert, try *sebadas* (fried cheese-filled ravioli doused with honey). *Via Santa Maria delle Fornaci 8/a (near the Vatican), tel. 06/632609. Dress: informal. Reservations advised. No credit cards. Closed Mon. and Aug. 10–Sept. 4.*

★ **Romolo.** Generations of Romans have enjoyed the romantic garden courtyard and historic dining room of this charming Trastevere haunt, the Fornarina, reputedly once home of Raphael's ladylove. In the evening, strolling musicians serenade diners. The cuisine is appropriately Roman; specialties include *mozzarella alla fornarina* (deep-fried mozzarella with ham and anchovies) and *braciolette d'abbacchio scottadito* (grilled baby lamb chops). Alternatively, try one of the new vegetarian pastas featuring *carciofi* (artichokes) or *radicchio* (the fashionable reddish leaf). *Via di Porta Settimiana 8, tel. 06/5818284. Dress: informal. Reservations advised. AE, DC, V. Closed Mon. and Aug. 2–23.*

★ **Vecchia Roma.** The frescoed walls of this historic restaurant located in a onetime palace in Old Rome, and the specialties— among them *fettucine verdi* (spinach-flavored pasta with cream sauce) and *petti pollo con gamberi di fiume* (chicken breasts with freshwater shrimp)—have long made this a classic choice of resident foreigners and sophisticated travelers. In summer you dine under white umbrellas. *Piazza Campitelli 18, tel. 06/6564604. Dress: informal. Reservations advised. No credit cards. Closed Wed. and Aug.*

Inexpensive **Baffetto.** Rome's best-known inexpensive pizza restaurant is
★ plainly decorated and *very* popular: You'll probably have to wait in line outside on the *sampietrini*—the cobblestones. The interior is mostly given over to the ovens, the tiny cash desk, and the simple paper-covered tables. *Bruschetta* (toast) and *crostini* (mozzarella toast) are the only variations on the pizza theme. Expect to share a table. *Via del Governo Vecchio 114, tel. 06/6861617. Dress: informal. Reservations not accepted. No credit cards. Closed lunch, Sun., and all of Aug.*

★ **L'Eau Vive.** This is an offbeat choice for an inexpensive lunch, but be aware that prices rise sharply in the evening. The restaurant is run by trainee Catholic missionaries, many from developing countries. The food is predominantly French. Order one of the fixed-price menus; they are among Rome's best-kept gastronomic secrets. You may have to hunt for the inconspicuous entrance, a little door hard by the entrance to Palazza Lante, just off Piazza Sant'Eustachio near the Pantheon. *Via Monterone 85, tel. 06/6541095. Dress: informal (for lunch). Reservations advised. AE, DC, V. Closed Sun. and 2 weeks in Aug.*

Hostaria Farnese. This is a tiny trattoria between Campo dei Fiori and Piazza Farnese, in the heart of Old Rome. Papa serves, Mamma cooks and, depending on what they've picked up at the Campo dei Fiori market, you may find *rigatoni* with tuna and basil, spaghetti with vegetable sauce, *spezzatino* (stew), and other homey specialties. *Via dei Baullari 109, tel. 06/6541595. Dress: informal. Reservations advised. AE, V. Closed Thurs.*

Reali. This family-run enterprise, located on a main thoroughfare near the Vatican Museums, is short on decor but offers good-value pastas, thick soups, and vegetable dishes. Roman specialties include *abbacchio* (lamb chops) and *pollo con peperoni* (chicken with peppers). Try the house wine, a very dry white. *Via Leone IV 91, tel. 06/386744. Dress: informal. Reservations advised for groups. AE. Closed Wed. and Aug.*

Lodging

The list below covers only those hotels that are within walking distance of at least some sights, and which are handy to public transportation. Those in the Moderate and Inexpensive categories do not have restaurants but serve Continental breakfast. Rooms on street level can get traffic noise throughout the night, and few hotels in the lower categories have double glazing. Ask for a quiet room, or bring earplugs!

We strongly recommend that you always make reservations in advance. Should you find yourself in the city without reservations, however, contact one of the following EPT offices: at Fiumicino Airport (tel. 06/6011255); Termini train station (tel. 06/4750078); on the A1 autostrada at the Feronia service area (tel. 06/0765/255465); and on the A2 autostrada at the Roma-Sud Frascati service area (tel. 06/9420058).

Ratings The following price categories are determined by the cost of two people in a double room. Best bets are indicated by a star ★. At press time, there were 1,245 lire to the dollar.

Category	Cost
Very Expensive	over 330,000 lire
Expensive	150,000–330,000 lire
Moderate	90,000–150,000 lire
Inexpensive	under 90,000 lire

Very Expensive **Cavalieri Hilton.** Though it is outside the main part of Rome and a taxi ride to wherever you are going, this is a large elegant resort hotel set in its own park and with an excellent restaurant. *Via Cadiolo 101, tel. 06/3151. 387 rooms with bath. Facilities: restaurant, pool, terrace. AE, DC, V.*

D'Inghilterra. On a side street off Via Condotti, the main shopping street, the D'Inghilterra is conveniently located. Ask for a room with a full bath, as some have not much more than a cramped shower stall, and make sure not to be on the street side, as it can be very noisy. *Via Bocca di Leone 14, tel. 06/ 672161. 102 rooms with bath or shower. Facilities: bar. AE, DC, V.*

Lord Byron. The most elegant and civilized hotel in Rome is the Lord Byron. Located in the diplomatic residential section of Rome away from its bustling center, the small villa has neat, fresh, and cheerful bedrooms that do, however, tend to be small. The staff offers the best service in any Rome hotel, and its dining room has extremely creative Italian cooking that has earned it two Michelin stars. *Via de Notaris 5, tel. 06/3609541. 55 rooms with bath. Facilities: bar, restaurant, garden. AE, DC, V.*

Expensive **Forum.** A centuries-old palace converted into a fine hotel, the Forum is on a quiet street within hailing distance of the Roman Forum and Piazza Venezia. The wood-paneled lobby and street-level bar are warm and welcoming, as are the smallish, pink-and-beige bedrooms. The view of the Colosseum from the rooftop restaurant is superb: Breakfast here—or a nightcap at the roof bar—can be memorable. *Via Tor dei Conti 25, tel. 06/6792446. 80 rooms with bath. Facilities: bar, restaurant. AE, DC, MC, V.*

Eden. Just off the Via Veneto, the Eden celebrates its centenary in 1989, and has prepared for it by renovating three of its four floors. The uncluttered decor is a fun mix of antiques, Art Deco, and streamlined modern, augmented by mirrors and marbles. Rooms on the upper floors have terrific views (the best is from the penthouse bar and restaurant). *Via Ludovisi 49, tel. 06/4743551. 93 rooms with bath. Facilities: bar and restaurant. AE.*

Grand. This 100-year-old establishment located between Termini Station and Via Veneto caters to an elite international clientele. The spacious guest rooms are decorated in Empire style, with smooth fabrics and thick carpets in blue and pale gold tones. Crystal chandeliers and marble baths add luxurious notes. Afternoon tea is served daily in the split-level main bar. One of Italy's most beautiful dining rooms, Le Restaurant, is here as well *(see* Dining). *Via Vittorio Emanuele Orlando 3, tel. 06/4709. 170 rooms with bath. Facilities: 2 bars, 2 restaurants. AE, DC, MC, V.*

★ **Hassler-Villa Medici.** Guests can expect a warmly cordial atmosphere and magnificent service at this hotel, just at the top of the Spanish Steps. The public rooms are memorable, especially the first-floor bar (a chic city rendezvous), and the glass-roof lounge, with gold marble walls and hand-painted tile floor. The elegant bedrooms are decorated in a variety of classic styles; some feature frescoed walls. *Piazza Trinità dei Monti 6, tel. 06/6792651. 101 rooms with bath. Facilities: bar, restaurant. AE.*

★ **Valadier.** Once famous as an elite bordello, the Valadier will appeal to guests with a taste for understated luxury. Bedrooms feature textured fabrics in light blue and beige with black accents, while mirrored walls, indirect lighting, and sleek bathrooms heighten the effect. Suite 308 and room 201 are among the larger rooms in what is bound to become one of Rome's classiest little hotels. The 300-year-old building is a short walk from the Spanish Steps. *Via della Fontanella 15, tel. 06/3610592. 46 rooms with bath. Facilities: bar, restaurant. AE, DC, MC, V.*

Victoria. Oriental rugs, oil paintings, welcoming armchairs, and fresh flowers add charm to the public rooms of this hotel, a favorite of American businessmen who prize the personalized service and restful atmosphere. Some upper rooms and the roof terrace overlook the Villa Borghese. *Via Campania 41, tel. 06/473931. 150 rooms with bath. Facilities: bar, restaurant. AE, DC, MC, V.*

Moderate **Gregoriana.** Bedroom decor at this former convent near the Spanish Steps is low-key enough, but the owners have gone wild in the public rooms: Two floors have leopard-skin wallpaper; the third has a splashy floral print; and the lobby is decked out in rattan. Reserve well in advance: The Gregoriana is popular with the high-fashion crowd. *Via Gregoriana 18, tel. 06/6994269. 19 rooms with bath or shower. No credit cards.*

★ **Internazionale.** Within easy walking distance of many downtown sights, this has long been one of Rome's best midsize hotels. Decor throughout is in soothing pastel tones, with some antique pieces, mirrors, and chandeliers heightening the English country-house look. Guests relax in small, homey lounges downstairs and begin the day in the pretty breakfast room. *Via Sistina 79, tel. 06/6793047. 40 rooms with bath. AE, DC, MC, V.*

Inexpensive **Ausonia.** This small pension has big advantages in its location
★ on Piazza di Spagna and in its helpful management and family atmosphere. Six rooms face the famous square (quieter now that most through traffic has been banished); all others face the inner courtyard. Furnishings are simple, but standards of cleanliness are high, and rates are low. The hotel has many American guests; make sure you make reservations well in advance. *Piazza di Spagna 35, tel. 06/6795745. 10 rooms, none with bath. No credit cards.*

Suisse. The mood in the Suisse's public rooms may be old-fashioned—the check-in desk is distinctly drab—but bedrooms, while small, are cheerful enough, with bright bedspreads, framed prints, and some charming old furniture. Some rooms face the (fairly) quiet courtyard. There's an upstairs breakfast room, but no restaurant. *Via Gregoriana 56, tel. 06/6783649. 28 rooms, half with bath or shower. No credit cards.*

The Arts

Pick up a copy of the "Carnet di Roma" at EPT tourist offices; issued monthly, it's free and has an exhaustive listing of scheduled events and shows. The bi-weekly booklet "Un Ospite a Roma," free from your hotel concierge, is another source of information. If you want to go to the opera, ballet, or to a concert, it's best to ask your concierge to get tickets for you. They are on sale at box offices only, just a few days before performances.

Opera The **Teatro dell'Opera** is on Via del Viminale (tel. 06/463641); the summer season at the **Baths of Caracalla** in July and August is famous for spectacular performances amid the Roman ruins. Tickets are on sale at the opera box office or at the box office at Caracalla (*see* Exploring).

Concerts The main concert hall is the **Accademia di Santa Cecilia** (Via della Conciliazione 4, tel. 06/6541044). The Santa Cecilia Symphony Orchestra has a summer season of concerts in the splendid setting of **Piazza del Campidoglio.**

Film The only English-language movie theater in Rome is the **Pasquino** (Vicolo del Piede, just off Piazza Santa Maria in Trastevere, tel. 06/5803622). The program is listed in Rome daily newspapers.

Entertainment and Nightlife

Rome's "in" nightspots change like the flavor of the month, and many fade into oblivion after a brief moment of glory. The best source for an up-to-date list is the weekly entertainment guide, "Trovaroma," published each Saturday in the Italian daily *La Repubblica.*

Bars Jacket and tie are in order in the elegant **Blue Bar** of the Hostaria dell'Orso (Via dei Soldati 25, tel. 06/6564221), and in **Le Bar** of the Grand Hotel (Via Vittorio Emanuele Orlando 3, tel. 06/4709). **Harry's Bar** (Via Veneto 150, tel. 06/4745832) is popular with American businessmen and journalists residing in Rome.

Young Romans favor **Calisé** (Piazza Mastai 7, tel. 06/5809404) in Trastevere, where sandwiches and salads, as well as drinks, are available until 3 AM. Current favorites around the Pantheon, a hub of after-dark activity, include **Le Cornacchie** (Piazza Rondanini 53, tel. 06/654485), where Roman yuppies hang out, and **Hemingway** (Piazza delle Coppelle 10, tel. 06/6544135), which attracts a crowd from the movie, TV, and fashion world. Both are open evenings only, but until very late.

Discos and Nightclubs There's deafening disco music for an under-30s crowd at the **Acropolis** (entrance at Via Luciani 52, tel. 06/870504). Special events such as beauty pageants or theme parties are a feature, and there's a restaurant on the premises. **Jackie-O** (Via Boncompagni 11, tel. 06/461401) has long been a favorite of the wealthy, who party to disco music, dine in La Graticola restaurant, or sip drinks in the cocktail lounge. Sports personalities and other celebrities are attracted to **Veleno** (Via Sardegna 27, tel. 06/493583), one of the few places in Rome to offer black dance music, including disco, rap, funk, and soul.

Singles Scene Locals and foreigners of all nations and ages gather at Rome's cafés on **Piazza della Rotonda** in front of the Pantheon, at **Piazza Navona**; and **Piazza Santa Maria** in Trastevere. The cafés on **Via Veneto** and the bars of the big hotels draw tourists mainly and are good places to meet other travelers in the over-30 age group. In fair weather, under-30s will find crowds of contemporaries on the **Spanish Steps**, where it's easy to strike up a conversation.

Florence

Arriving and Departing

By Plane The nearest, medium-size airport is the **Galileo Galilei Airport** at Pisa (tel. 050/28088), connected with Florence by train direct from the airport to the Santa Maria Novella Station. Service is hourly through the day and takes about 60 minutes. Some domestic and a few European flights use Florence's **Peretola Airport** (tel. 055/317123), connected by bus to the downtown area.

By Train The main train station is **Santa Maria Novella Station**, abbreviated SMN on signs. There is an Azienda Transporti Autolinee Fiorentina (ATAF) city bus information booth in the station, as well as an Informazione Turistiche Alberghiere (ITA) hotel association booth, where you can get hotel information and bookings.

By Bus The bus terminal is near Santa Maria Novella train station.

By Car The north–south access route to Florence is the Autostrada del Sole (A1) from Milan or Rome. The Florence–Mare autostrada (A11) links Florence with the Tyrrhenian coast, Pisa, and the A12 coastal autostrada.

Getting Around

On Foot You can see most of Florence's major sights on foot, as they are packed into a relatively small area in the city center. It's best not to plan to use a car in Florence; most of the center is off-limits and ATAF buses will take you where you want to go.

Wear comfortable shoes and wander to your heart's content. It is easy to find your way around in Florence. There are so many landmarks that you cannot get lost for long. The system of street numbers is unusual, with commercial addresses written with a red "r" and residential addresses in blue (32/r might be next to or even a block away from 32 blue).

By Bus ATAF city buses run from about 5:15 AM to 1 AM. Buy tickets before you board the bus; they are on sale singly or in books of five at many tobacco shops and newsstands. Cost is 600 lire for one ride, 700 lire for a ticket good for 70 minutes on all lines. An all-day ticket *(giornaliero)* costs 2,500 lire.

By Taxi Taxis wait at stands. Use only authorized cabs, which are white with a yellow stripe or rectangle on the door. The meter starts at 2,000 lire. To call a taxi, tel. 055/4798 or 055/4390.

By Bicycle You can rent a bicycle on Via Alamanni on the stairway side of the train station; at **Ciao & Basta,** Via Costa dei Magnoli 24 (tel. 055/263985), near Ponte Vecchio; and at Piazza Pitti and Fortezza da Basso.

By Moped For a moped, go to **Program,** Borgo Ognissanti 96, tel. 055/282916.

Important Addresses and Numbers

Tourist Information The municipal tourist office has a booth outside the railway station. The Azienda Autonoma Turismo (AAT) tourist board is at Via Tornabuoni 15 (tel. 055/217459; open Mon.–Sat. 9–1). The Ente Provinciale per il Turismo (EPT) provincial tourist board has an information office at Via Manzoni 16 (tel. 055/2478141; open Mon.–Sat. 8:30–1:30).

Consulates U.S. Lungarno Vespucci 38, tel. 055/298276. U.K. Lungarno Corsini 2, tel. 055/284133.

Emergencies **Police:** tel. 113. **Ambulance:** (Red Cross) tel. 055/215381. **Doctor:** Call your consulate for recommendations, or call the **Tourist Medical Service** (tel. 055/475411), associated with IAMAT, for English-speaking medical assistance 24 hours a day. **Pharmacies:** There are 24-hour pharmacies at Via Calzaiuoli 7/r (tel. 055/263490); Piazza San Giovanni 20/r (tel. 055/284013); and at the train station (tel. 055/263435).

English Bookstores You'll find English-language magazines and paperbacks on the newsstands in Piazza della Repubblica. **The Paperback Exchange** (Via Fiesolana 31/r, tel. 055/2478154), in the Santa Croce area, has new and used paperbacks for sale. **The BM Bookshop** (Borgognissanti 4/r, tel. 055/294575) has a good selection of English-language books.

Travel Agencies **American Express,** Via Guicciardini 49/r, tel. 055/278751. **CIT,** Via Cavour 56, tel. 055/294306. **Wagons-Lits,** Via del Giglio 27/r, tel. 055/218851.

Guided Tours

Orientation Tours **American Express** (tel. 055/278751), **CIT** (tel. 055/294306), and **SITA** (tel. 055/214721) offer three-hour tours in air-conditioned buses. Two tours cover most of the important sights: the morning itinerary gives you a look at the outside of the cathedral, baptistry, and bell tower, takes you to the Accademia to see Michelangelo's *David*, to Piazzale Michelangelo for the view, and then to the Pitti Palace to visit the Palatine Gallery; the afternoon tour includes Piazza della Signoria, a visit to the Uffizi Gallery and to Santa Croce, and an excursion to Fiesole. Cost is about 30,000 lire for a three-hour tour, including entrance fees, and can be booked through travel agents.

The 45-minute "Florence Experience" program is a fine way to get oriented, at the **Edison Cinema** (Piazza della Repubblica). Admission is 8,000 lire and it is shown every hour on the hour, weekdays 9–5, weekends 9–3. During July and August it's shown daily 9 AM–10 PM.

Personal Guides **American Express** (tel. 055/278751) can arrange for limousine or minitours and personal guide services. **Europedrive** (Via Tartini 7, tel. 055/351025) will provide cars with English-speaking drivers.

Special-Interest Tours Inquire at travel agents or at **Agriturist** (Piazza San Firenze 3, tel. 055/287838) for visits to villa gardens around Florence from April to June, or for visits to farm estates during September and October.

Excursions Operators offer a half-day excursion to Pisa, usually in the afternoon, and a full-day excursion to Siena and San Gimignano, costing about 26,000 lire and 38,000 lire, respectively. Pick up a timetable at ATAF information offices in the train station, at Piazza Duomo 57/r (tel. 055/580528), or at the AAT Tourist Office (*see* Tourist Information in Important Addresses and Numbers).

Exploring Florence

Founded by Julius Caesar, Florence has the familiar grid pattern common to all Roman colonies. Except for the major monuments, which are appropriately imposing, the buildings are low and unpretentious. It is a small, compact city of ocher stone and pale plaster; its narrow streets open unexpectedly into spacious squares populated by strollers and pigeons. At its best, it has a gracious and elegant air, though it can at times be a nightmare of mass tourism. Plan, if you can, to visit Florence in late fall, early spring, or even in winter, to avoid the crowds.

A visit to Florence is a visit to the living museum of Italian Renaissance. The Renaissance began right here in Florence, and the city bears witness to the proud spirit and unparalleled genius of its artists and artisans. In fact, there is so much to see that it is best to savor a small part rather than attempt to absorb it all in a muddled vision.

Piazza del Duomo and the Piazza della Signoria

The best place to begin a tour of Florence is **Piazza del Duomo**, where the cathedral, bell tower and baptistery stand in the rather cramped square. The lofty **cathedral of Santa Maria del Fiore** is one of the longest in the world. Begun by master sculptor and architect Arnolfo di Cambio in 1296, its construction took 140 years to complete. Gothic architecture predominates; the facade was added in the 1870s but is based on Tuscan Gothic models. Inside, the church is cool and austere, a fine example of the architecture of the period. Among the sparse decorations, you should take a good look at the frescoes of equestrian monuments on the left wall; that on the left is by Paolo Uccello, the

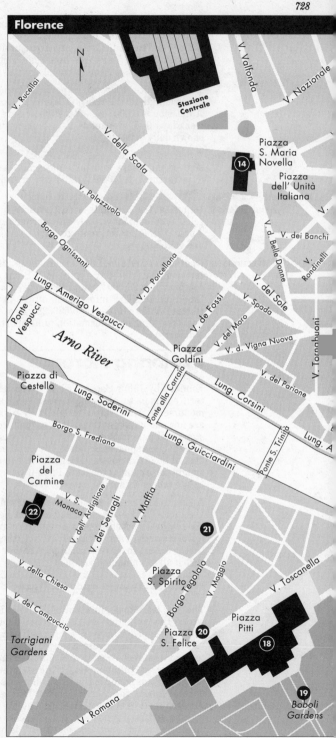

Florence

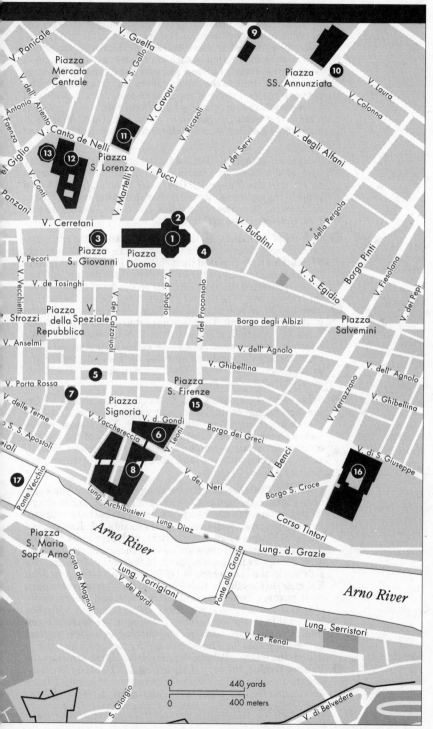

V. Panicale

Piazza
Mercato
Centrale

V. Guelfa

V. S. Gallo

9

Piazza
SS. Annunziata

10

V. Laura

V. Colonna

V. del' Ariento

Antonio

Faenza

V. Canto de Nelli

el Giglio

13

12

11

Piazza
S. Lorenzo

V. Cavour

V. Ricasoli

V. dei Servi

V. degli Alfani

V. Conti

Panzani

V. Cerretani

V. Martelli

V. Pucci

V. Bufalini

V. della Pergola

Borgo Pinti

V. Fiesolana

V. dei Pepi

2

1

3

Piazza
S. Giovanni

Piazza
Duomo

4

V. S. Egidio

V. Pecori

V. de Tosinghi

V. d. Studio

V. del Proconsolo

Borgo degli Albizi

Piazza
Salvemini

V. Vecchietti

V. dei Calzaiuoli

. Strozzi

Piazza
della
Repubblica

V.
Speziale

V. dell' Agnolo

V. dell' Agnolo

V. Anselmi

V. Ghibellina

V. Ghibellina

5

Piazza
S. Firenze

15

V. Verrazzano

V. Porta Rossa

7

Piazza
Signoria

Borgo dei Greci

V. delle Terme

V. Vaccchereccia

V. d. Gondi

6

V. Leoni

V. di S. Giuseppe

S. S. Apostoli

ioli

8

V. dei Neri

V. Benci

Borgo S. Croce

16

17

Ponte Vecchio

Lung. Archibusieri

Lung. Diaz

Corso Tintori

Piazza
S. Maria
Sopr' Arno

Arno River

Lung. d. Grazie

Arno River

Costa de Magnoli

Lung. Torrigiani

V. dei Bardi

Ponte alla Grazia

Lung. Serristori

V. de' Renai

S. Giorgio

0   440 yards
0   400 meters

V. di Belvedere

one on the right is by Andrea del Castagno. The dome frescoes by Vasari have been hidden by the scaffolding put up years ago in order to study a plan for restoring the **dome** itself, Brunelleschi's greatest architectural and technical achievement. It was also the inspiration of such later domes as Michelangelo's dome for St. Peter's in Rome and even the Capitol in Washington. You can climb to the cupola gallery, 463 fatiguing steps up between the two skins of the double dome for a fine view of Florence and the surrounding hills. *Dome entrance is in the left aisle of cathedral. Admission: 3,000 lire. Open Mon.–Sat. 8:30–12:30 and 2:30–5:30. Cathedral open daily 7–noon and 2:30–6.*

2 Next to the cathedral, Giotto's 14th-century **bell tower** is richly decorated with colored marble and fine sculptures (the originals are in the Museo dell'Opera del Duomo). The 414-step climb to the top is less strenuous than that to the cupola. *Piazza del Duomo. Admission: 3,000 lire. Open Apr.–Sept., daily 9– 7:30; Oct.–Mar. 9–5:30.*

3 In front of the cathedral, the **baptistery** is one of the city's oldest and most beloved edifices, where, since the 11th century, Florentines have baptized their children. Pollution is threatening the bronze reliefs on the baptistery's three portals, and had so badly affected those by Ghiberti on the doors facing the cathedral (dubbed "The Gate of Paradise" by Michelangelo), they
4 have had to be relocated to the **Museo dell'Opera del Duomo** (Cathedral Museum). The museum contains some superb sculptures by Donatello and Luca della Robbia—especially their *cantorie*, or choir decorations—as well as an unfinished *Pietà* by Michelangelo, which he intended for his own tomb. *Piazza del Duomo 9, tel. 055/213229. Admission: 3,000 lire. Open Mon.–Sat. 9–6, Sun. 9–1.*

5 Stroll down fashionable Via Calzaioli to the church of **Orsanmichele,** for centuries an odd combination of first-floor church and second-floor wheat granary. The statues in the niches on the exterior constitute an anthology of the work of eminent Renaissance sculptors, including Donatello, Ghiberti, and Verrocchio, while the tabernacle inside is an extraordinary piece by Andrea Orcagna.

Continuing another two blocks along Via Calzaioli you come upon **Piazza della Signoria,** the heart of Florence, and the city's largest square. It's now being torn up in patches to be repaved. In the process, well-preserved remnants of Roman and medieval Florence have come to light, and there's talk of creating an underground museum so that these can still be seen after the square has been repaved. In the center of the square a slab marks the spot where in 1497 Savonarola—the Ayatollah Khomeini of the Middle Ages—induced the Florentines to burn their pictures, books, musical instruments, and other worldly objects—and where a year later he was hanged and then burned at the stake as a heretic. The square, the **Neptune Fountain** by Ammanati, and the surrounding cafés are popular gathering places for Florentines and for tourists who come to admire the massive **Palazzo della Signoria,** better known as the
6 **Palazzo Vecchio,** the copy of Michelangelo's *David* on its steps, and the frescoes and art works in its impressive salons. *Piazza della Signoria, tel. 055/27681. Admission: 4,000 lire; Sun. free. Open weekdays 9–7, Sun. 8–1; closed Sat.*

Time Out Stop in at **Riviore**, a Florentine institution, for some of its delectable ice cream and/or chocolate goodies. *Piazza della Signoria 5/r.*

7 If you'd like to do a little shopping, make a brief detour off Piazza della Signoria to the **Loggia del Mercato Nuovo** on Via Calimala. It's crammed with souvenirs and straw and leather goods at reasonable prices; bargaining is acceptable here. *Open Mon.–Sat. 8–7 (closed Mon. AM).*

8 If time is limited, this is your chance to visit the **Uffizi Gallery**, which houses Italy's most important collection of paintings. (Try to see it at a more leisurely pace, though—it's too good to rush through!) The Uffizi Palace was built to house the administrative offices of the Medicis, one-time rulers of the city. Later, their fabulous art collection was arranged in the Uffizi Gallery on the top floor, which was opened to the public in the 17th century—making this the world's first public gallery of modern times. The emphasis is on Italian, especially Italian Gothic or Renaissance art. Make sure you see the works by Giotto, and look for the Botticellis in Rooms X–XIV, Michelangelo's *Holy Family* in Room XXV, and the works by Raphael next door. In addition to its art treasures, the gallery offers a magnificent close-up view of Palazzo Vecchio's tower from the little coffee bar at the end of the corridor. *Loggiato Uffizi 6, tel. 055/218341. Admission: 5,000 lire. Open Tues.–Sat. 9–7, Sun. 9–1; closed Mon.*

Accademia, San Marco, San Lorenzo, Santa Maria Novella

9 Start at the **Accademia Gallery**, and try to be first in line at opening time so you can get the full impact of Michelangelo's *David* without having to fight your way through the crowds. Skip the works in the exhibition halls leading to the *David;* they are of minor importance and you'll gain a length on the tour groups. Michelangelo's statue is a tour de force of artistic conception and technical ability, for he was using a piece of stone that had already been worked on by a lesser sculptor. Take time to see the forceful *Slaves*, also by Michelangelo; the roughhewn, unfinished surfaces contrast dramatically with the highly polished, meticulously carved *David*. Michelangelo left the *Slaves* "unfinished" for the aesthetic power that accentuates their trying to escape the bondage of stone. *Via Ricasoli 60, tel. 055/214375. Admission: 4,000 lire. Open Tues.–Sat. 9–2, Sun. 9–1; closed Mon.*

10 You can make a detour down Via Cesare Battisti to Piazza Santissima Annunziata to see the arcade of the **Ospedale degli Innocenti** (Hospital of the Innocents) by Brunelleschi, with charming roundels by Andrea della Robbia, and the **Museo Archeologico** (Archaeological Museum) on Via della Colonna, under the arch. It has some fine Etruscan and Roman antiquities, and a pretty garden. *Via della Colonna 36, tel. 055/ 2478641. Admission: 3,000 lire. Open Tues.–Sat. 9–2, Sun. 9–1; closed Mon.*

Retrace your steps to Piazza San Marco and the **Museo di San Marco**, housed in a 15th-century Dominican monastery. The unfortunate Savonarola meditated on the sins of the Florentines here, and Fra Angelico decorated many of the austere cells and corridors with his brilliantly colored frescoes of religious subjects. (Look for his masterpiece, *The Annunciation*.) Together with many of his paintings arranged on the ground floor, just off the little cloister, they form an interesting collection. *Piazza San Marco 1, tel. 055/210741. Admission: 3,000 lire. Open Tues.–Sat. 9–2, Sun. 9–1; closed Mon.*

⑪ Lined with shops, Via Cavour leads to **Palazzo Medici Riccardi,** a massive Renaissance mansion (*see* Off the Beaten Track).

⑫ Turn left here to the elegant **Church of San Lorenzo,** with its Old Sacristy designed by Brunelleschi, and two pulpits by Donatello. Rounding the left flank of the church, you'll find yourself in the midst of the sprawling **San Lorenzo Market,** dealing in everything and anything, including some interesting leather items. *Piazza San Lorenzo, Via dell'Ariento. Open Tues.–Sat. 8–7.*

Time Out On Via Sant'Antonino near the big covered food market, **Palla d'Oro** is a favorite with market workers for a quick sandwich or plate of pasta, which they usually eat standing at the counter. You can sit at the tables in the back for an extra charge. It's impossibly crowded between 1 and 1:30. *Via Sant'Antonino 45/r. Closed Sun.*

⑬ Enter the **Medici Chapels** from Piazza Madonna degli Aldobrandini, behind San Lorenzo. These remarkable chapels contain the tombs of practically every member of the Medici family, and there were a lot of them, for they guided Florence's destiny from the 15th century to 1737. Cosimo I, a Medici whose acumen made him the richest man in Europe, is buried in the crypt of the Chapel of the Princes, and Donatello's tomb is next to that of his patron. The chapel upstairs is decorated in an eye-dazzling array of colored marble. In Michelangelo's New Sacristy, his tombs of Giuliano and Lorenzo Medici bear the justly famed statues of *Dawn* and *Dusk*, and *Night* and *Day*. *Piazza Madonna degli Aldobrandini, tel. 055/213206. Admission: 4,350 lire. Open Tues.–Sat. 9–2, Sun. 9–1; closed Mon.*

Time Out **Baldini** is an unpretentious trattoria, low on atmosphere but offering a good range of antipasti and delicious *fazzoletti*, pasta filled with ricotta and spinach. *Via Panzani 57. Closed Wed.*

You can take either Via Panzani or Via del Melarancio to the
⑭ large square next to the massive church of **Santa Maria Novella,** a handsome building in the Tuscan version of Gothic style. See it from the other end of Piazza Santa Maria Novella for the best view of its facade. Inside are some famous paintings, especially Masaccio's *Trinity*, a Giotto crucifix in the sacristy, and Ghirlandaio's frescoes in the apse. *Piazza Santa Maria Novella, tel. 055/210113. Open daily 7–noon and 3–7.*

Next door to the church is the entrance to the **cloisters,** worth a visit for their serene atmosphere and the restored Paolo Uccello frescoes. *Piazza Santa Maria Novella 19, tel. 055/282187. Admission: 3,000 lire. Open Mon.–Thurs., Sat. 9–2, Sun. 8–1; closed Fri.*

Only a few blocks behind Piazza della Signoria, the **Bargello** is a fortresslike palace that served as residence of Florence's chief magistrate in medieval times, and later as a prison. Don't be

⑮ put off by its grim look, for it now houses Florence's **Museo Nazionale** (National Museum), a treasure house of Italian Renaissance sculpture. In a historically and visually interesting setting, it displays masterpieces by Donatello, Verrochio, and Michelangelo, and many other major sculptors. This museum is on a par with the Uffizi, so don't shortchange yourself on time. *Via del Proconsolo 4, tel. 055/210801. Admission: 3,000 lire. Open Tues.–Sat. 9–2, Sun. 9–1; closed Mon.*

Time Out From Piazza San Firenze follow Via degli Anguillara or Borgo dei Greci toward Piazza Santa Croce. Don't miss the chance to taste what's held by many to be the best ice cream in Florence at **Vivoli,** on a little side street, the second left off Via degli Anguillara as you head toward Santa Croce. *Via Isole delle Stinche 7/r.*

⑯ The mighty church of **Santa Croce** was begun in 1294; inside, Giotto's frescoes brighten two chapels and monumental tombs of Michelangelo, Galileo, Machiavelli, and other Renaissance luminaries line the walls. In the adjacent museum, you can see what remains of a **Giotto crucifix,** irreparably damaged by a flood in 1966, when water rose to 16 feet (five meters) in parts of the church. The **Pazzi Chapel** in the cloister is an architectural gem by Brunelleschi. *Piazza Santa Croce, tel. 055/244619. Church open daily 7–12:30 and 3–6:30. Opera di Santa Croce (Museum and Pazzi Chapel), tel. 055/244619. Admission: 2,000 lire. Open Thurs.–Tues. 9–12:30 and 3–5; closed Wed.*

The monastery of Santa Croce harbors a leather-working school and showroom, with entrances at Via San Giuseppe 5/r and Piazza Santa Croce 16. The entire Santa Croce area is known for its leather factories and inconspicuous shops selling gold and silver jewelry at prices much lower than those of the elegant jewelers near Ponte Vecchio.

Time Out You have several eating options here. For ice cream, the **bar** on Piazza Santa Croce has a tempting selection. If it's a snack you're after, the **Fiaschetteria** (Via dei Neri 17/r) makes sandwiches to order and has a choice of antipasti and a hot dish or two. **Da Marco,** between Santa Croce and the Arno, is a typical trattoria, where you can either eat downstairs or outdoors. (Via dei Benci 13/r. Closed Mon.)

⑰ Now head for **Ponte Vecchio,** Florence's oldest bridge. It seems to be just another street lined with goldsmiths' shops until you get to the middle and catch a glimpse of the Arno flowing below. Spared during World War II by the retreating Germans (who blew up every other bridge in the city), it also survived the 1966 flood. It leads into the **Oltrarno district,** which has its own charm and still preserves much of the atmosphere of old-time Florence, full of fascinating craft workshops.

⑱ But for the moment you should head straight down Via Guicciardini to **Palazzo Pitti,** a 15th-century extravaganza that the Medicis acquired from the Pitti family shortly after the latter had gone deeply into debt to build it. Its long facade on the immense piazza was designed by Brunelleschi: Solid and severe, it looks like a Roman aqueduct turned into a palace. The palace houses several museums: One displays the fabulous Medici collection of objects in silver and gold; another is the

Gallery of Modern Art. The most famous museum, though, is the **Palatine Gallery,** with an extraordinary collection of paintings, many hung frame-to-frame in a clear case of artistic overkill. Some are high up in dark corners, so try to go on a bright day. *Piazza Pitti, tel. 055/216673. Admission: 4,000 lire. Open Tues.–Sat. 9–2, Sun. 9–1; closed Mon. Same hours, separate 4,000-lire admission fees for Silver Museum, State Apartments, Modern Art Gallery, and Historical Costume Gallery.*

⑲ Take time for a refreshing stroll in the **Boboli Gardens** behind Palazzo Pitti, a typical Italian garden laid out in 1550 for Cosimo Medici's wife, Eleanor of Toledo. *Piazza dei Pitti, tel. 213440. Free. Open May–Aug., daily 9–6:30; Sept.–Oct. and Mar.–Apr., 9–5:30; Nov.–Feb., 9–4:30.*

In the far corner of Piazza dei Pitti, poets Elizabeth Barrett ⑳ and Robert Browning lived at No. 9 **Casa Guidi,** facing the smaller Piazza San Felice.

Time Out From Piazza San Felice it's not far to the **Caffè Notte,** a wine and sandwich shop featuring a different salad every day (corner of Via della Caldaia and Via della Chiesa). For more substantial sustenance, go to the **Cantinone del Gallo Nero,** an atmospheric wine cellar where Chianti is king and locals lunch on soups, pastas, and salads (Via Santo Spirito 6/r. Closed Mon.). The street directly opposite Palazzo Pitti's main entrance leads into Via Michelozzi, where **La Casalinga** is a favorite neighborhood trattoria (Via Michelozzi 9/r. Closed Sun.).

㉑ The church of **Santo Spirito** is important as one of Brunelleschi's finest architectural creations, and it contains some superb paintings, including a Filippino Lippi *Madonna.* Santo Spirito is the hub of a colorful neighborhood of artisans and intellectuals. An **outdoor market** enlivens the square every morning except Sunday; in the afternoon, pigeons, pet owners, and pensioners take over. The area is definitely on an upward trend, with new cafés, restaurants, and upscale shops opening every day.

Walk down Via Sant'Agostino and Via Santa Monaca to the ㉒ church of **Santa Maria del Carmine,** of no architectural interest but of immense significance in the history of Renaissance art. It contains the celebrated frescoes painted by Masaccio in the **Brancacci Chapel,** unveiled not long ago after a lengthy and meticulous restoration. The chapel was a classroom for such artistic giants as Botticelli, Leonardo da Vinci, Michelangelo, and Raphael, since they all came to study Masaccio's realistic use of light and perspective, and his creation of space and depth. *Piazza del Carmine.*

Time Out The small trattoria on the square has a friendly atmosphere and is a delightful spot where you can eat outdoors and enjoy the view. *Piazza del Carmine 18/r. Closed Sat. evening and Sun.*

What to See and Do with Children

Children are fascinated by the bizarre **Stibbert Museum,** with its fully armed unit of 16th-century horsemen, among other oddities. *Via Stibbert 26, tel. 055/475520. Admission: 2,000 lire. Open Mon.–Wed., Fri.–Sat. 9–2, Sun. 9–12:30; closed Thurs.*

Take bus No. 7 to **Fiesole** and explore the Roman amphitheater. *Via Portigiani 1, tel. 055/59477. Admission: 2,500 lire. Open daily in summer 9–7; winter 10–4, closed Mon.*

Roam over the ramparts and picnic on the lawns of Forte Belvedere. *Costa San Giorgio, tel. 055/287055. Free. Open daily 9–7 (grounds only).*

Visit the **History of Science Museum,** next to the Uffizi; it has a large collection of prototypes and antique scientific instruments, as interesting for adults as it is for children. *Piazza dei Giudici 1, tel. 055/293493. Admission: 5,000 lire. Open weekdays 9:30–1, also Mon., Wed., Fri. 2–5.*

Rent bicycles and ride through the **Cascine** park, where there's a playground, or feed the swans at the **Fortezza da Basso.**

Off the Beaten Track

Few tourists get to see one of Florence's most precious works of art, Benozzo Gozzoli's glorious frescoes in the tiny chapel on the second floor of **Palazzo Medici Riccardi,** representing the Journey of the Magi as a spectacular cavalcade with Lorenzo the Magnificent on a charger. *Via Cavour 1, tel. 055/2760. Free. Open Mon.–Tues., Thurs.–Sat. 9–noon and 3–5, Sun. 9 –noon; closed Wed.*

One of Europe's oldest **botanical gardens,** founded in 1545, is a pleasant place for a pause; gardening hobbyists will enjoy the **Botanical Museum** next door. *Via Micheli 3, tel. 055/284696. Free. Open Mon., Wed., Fri. 9–noon.*

The **English Cemetery** is on a cypress-studded knoll in the middle of heavily trafficked Piazza Donatello, not far from the botanical garden. Here you can walk with the shades of Elizabeth Barrett Browning, Algernon Swinburne, and other poets. You will need to ask the custodian to let you into the cemetery. It is kept locked. *Piazza Donatello. Ring bell at entrance for admission.*

Take afternoon tea with the Florentines at **Giacosa,** an elegant café at Via Tornabuoni 83/r, or in the plush salon of the **Hotel Excelsior** on Piazza Ognissanti.

Take the No. 13 bus from the train station or cathedral up to Piazzale Michelangelo, then walk along Viale dei Colli and climb to **San Miniato al Monte,** a charming green-and-white marble Romanesque church full of artistic riches.

Visit the **synagogue** on Via Farini and the **Jewish Museum** next door, which contains antique scrolls and ritual objects. *Via Farini 3, tel. 055/245252. Free. Open May–Sept., Sun., Mon., Wed. 9–6, Tues. and Thurs. 9–1; Oct.–Apr., Sun. and Thurs. 9–1.*

Shopping

Gift Ideas Florence offers top quality for your money in leather goods, linens and upholstery fabrics, gold and silver jewelry, and cameos. Straw goods, gilded wooden trays and frames, hand-printed paper desk accessories, and ceramic objects make good inexpensive gifts. Many shops offer fine old prints.

Shopping Districts The most fashionable streets in Florence are **Via Tornabuoni** and **Via della Vigna Nuova.** Goldsmiths and jewelry shops can be found on and around **Ponte Vecchio** and in the **Santa Croce area,** where there is also a high concentration of leather shops.

Antiques Most of Florence's many antiques dealers are located in **Borgo San Jacopo** and **Borgo Ognissanti,** but you'll find plenty of small shops throughout the center of town.

Department Stores **Principe,** in Piazza Strozzi, is a quality apparel store incorporating several designer boutiques. At the other end of the price range, **UPIM,** in Piazza della Repubblica and various other locations, has inexpensive goods of all types.

Markets The big food market at **Piazza del Mercato Centrale** is open in the morning (Mon.–Sat.) and is worth a visit. The **San Lorenzo market** on Piazza San Lorenzo and Via dell'Ariento is a fine place to browse for buys in leather goods and souvenirs (open Tues. and Sat. 8–7; also Sun. in summer). The **Mercato del Porcellino,** Piazza del Mercato Nuovo, takes its name from the famous bronze statue of a boar at one side, and is packed with stalls selling souvenirs and straw goods (open Tues.–Sat. 8–7; closed Sun. and Mon. morning in winter). There's a colorful neighborhood market at **Sant'Ambrogio,** Piazza Ghiberti (open Mon.–Sat. morning).

Dining

Mealtimes in Florence are 12:30–2 and 7:30–9 or later. Many Moderate and Inexpensive places are small and you may have to share a table. Reservations are always advisable; to find a table at inexpensive places, get there early.

For details and price category definitions, *see* Dining in Essential Information.

Very Expensive **Cestello.** The restaurant of the Hotel Excelsior has a lovely setting, whether you dine on the rooftop terrace overlooking the Arno in the summer, or in a ritzy salon with coffered ceiling, pink linen tablecloths, and antique paintings in the winter. The menu features such deliciously visual delights as *linguine con rughetta e scampi* (flat spaghetti with chicory and shrimps) and *tagliata di manzo con mosaico di insalatine* (sliced beef on a bed of salad greens arranged in a mosaic pattern). *Piazza Ognissanti 3, tel. 055/294301. Dress: formal. Reservations advised in summer. AE, DC, MC, V.*

★ **Enoteca Pinchiorri.** In the beautiful Renaissance palace and its charming garden courtyard that was home to Giovanni da Verrazzano (a 15th-century Florentine navigator), husband-and-wife team Giorgio Pinchiorri and Annie Feolde have created an exceptional restaurant that ranks as one of Italy's best. Guests can enjoy Annie's rediscoveries of traditional Tuscan dishes, or her own brand of imaginatively creative nouvelle cuisine, while Giorgio oversees the extraordinary wine cellar. There is a moderately priced luncheon menu. *Via Ghibellina 87, tel. 055/242777. Dress: informal. Reservations well in advance are advised at all times. AE, DC, V. Closed Sun., Mon. lunch, Aug.*

★ **Terrazza Brunelleschi.** The rooftop restaurant of the Hotel Baglioni has the best view in town. The dining room, in creamy tones and with a floral carpet, has big picture windows; the summer dining terrace is charming, with tables under arbors, and turrets for guests to climb to get an even better view. The menu offers traditional Tuscan dishes such as *minestra di fagioli* (bean soup), and other more innovative choices, such as a pâté of peppers and tomato. *Hotel Baglioni, Piazza Unità Italiana 6, tel. 055/215642. Jacket and tie in winter. Reservations advised, especially in summer. AE, DC, MC, V.*

Expensive **Cammillo.** This is a classic Florentine eating place, with terracotta tiles on the floor and several brick-vaulted rooms where guests enjoy regional and international specialties such as chicken livers with sage and beans, or curried scampi. The menu usually features truffled dishes as well. The excellent house wine and olive oil are made by the owners. *Borgo San Jacopo 57/r, tel. 055/212427. Dress: informal. Reservations advisable; required for dinner between Easter and Oct. AE, DC, MC, V. Closed Wed., Thurs.; 3 weeks in Aug.; 3 weeks in Dec.–Jan.*

★ **Da Noi.** Located near Santa Croce, Da Noi has a reputation as one of Florence's best for creative cuisine and a relaxed atmosphere. It's small, seating only 28 in a dining room whose dark antique sideboards contrast with rustic white walls. The cooking reflects French influences; among the specialties are crêpes with a sauce of peppers, and warm squab salad. *Via Fiesolana 46/r, tel. 055/242917. Dress: informal. Reservations required; call 3 days ahead. No credit cards. Closed Sun., Mon., Aug.*

★ **Sabatini.** One of Florence's finest for many years, Sabatini upholds the tradition very well. Classic Florentine decor, with dark wood-paneled walls, terra-cotta floors, and white linen tablecloths, is brightened by the paintings on the walls and by a cordial welcome. Specialties on the menu, which offers both Tuscan and international cuisine, are *panzerotti alla Sabatini* (creamy, cheese-filled crêpes) and baked spinach with a chicken liver sauce. *Via Panzani 9/a, tel. 055/211559. Dress: informal. Reservations advised. AE, DC, MC, V. Closed Mon.*

Moderate **Buca Mario.** Visitors can expect to share a table at this characteristically unadorned *buca* (downstairs trattoria), whose menu includes such hearty down-to-earth Tuscan food as homemade *pappardelle* (noodles) and *stracotto* (beef stew with beans). It's near Santa Maria Novella Station. *Piazza Ottaviani 16/r, tel. 055/214179. Dress: informal. Reservations not accepted. AE, V. Closed, Wed., Thurs. lunch, and all of Aug.*

Il Fagioli. This typical Florentine trattoria near Santa Croce has a simple decor and a menu in which local dishes such as *ribollita* (a sort of minestrone) and *arista* (roast pork) predominate. The antipasti are always tempting here. *Corso Tintori 47/r, tel. 055/244285. Dress: informal. Reservations advised. No credit cards. Closed Sun., also Sat. in summer, Aug.*

Leo. Located in the Santa Croce area, Leo is decorated in tune with the medieval building that it occupies, with vaulted ceilings and dark Tuscan-style wooden chairs. Order the daily specials here and the *crostini* (toast with a creamy chicken liver, anchovy and caper spread) and fried chicken. *Via Torta 7/r, tel. 055/210829. Dress: informal. Dinner reservations advised. AE, DC, MC, V. Closed Mon. and mid-July–mid-Aug.*

Mario da Ganino. Highly informal, rustic, and cheerful, this trattoria greets you with a taste of mortadella, and offers

homemade pastas and *gnudoni* (ravioli without pasta), plus a
heavenly cheesecake for dessert. There are plenty of other
taste-tempters on the menu. It's tiny, seating only 35, double
that in summer at outdoor tables. *Piazza dei Cimatori 4/r, tel.
055/214125. Dress: informal. Reservations advised. AE, DC.
Closed Sun. and Aug. 15–25.*

Inexpensive **Angiolino.** You won't regret taking a meal at this bustling little
★ trattoria, which has a real charcoal grill and an old wood-
burning stove to keep its customers warm on nippy days. Glowing with authentic atmosphere, Angiolino offers Tuscan specialties such as *ribollita* (minestrone) and juicy *bistecca alla
fiorentina* (T-bone steak basted in olive oil and black pepper).
The bistecca will push the bill up into the Moderate range. *Via
Santo Spirito 36/r, tel. 055/298976. Dress: informal. Reservations advised in the evening. No credit cards. Closed Sun.
dinner, Mon., and last 3 weeks in July.*

Caminetto. Try the *maccheroni alla Maremmana* (pasta with
sausages, tomato, and black olive) or *pappa al pomodoro* (tomato and bread soup) in the typically rustic setting of Caminetto. It's very handy for a quick lunch before or after visiting
the cathedral. *Via dello Studio 34/r, tel. 055/296274. Dress: informal. Dinner reservations advised. No credit cards. Closed
Tues., Wed., and July.*

Lodging

What with mass tourism and trade fairs, rooms are at a premium in Florence for most of the year. Make reservations well in
advance. If you arrive without a reservation, the ITA office in
the railway station (open 9–8:30) can help you, but there may
be a long line. Now that most traffic is banned in the downtown
area, hotel rooms are quieter. Local traffic and motorcycles can
still be bothersome, however, so check the decibel level before
you settle in.

For details and price category definitions, *see* Lodging in Essential Information.

Very Expensive **Excelsior.** One of the flagships of the CIGA chain, the Excelsior
★ provides consistently superlative service and is lavishly ap-
pointed with old prints, bouquets of flowers, pink marble, and
carpets so deep you could lose a shoe in them. The hotel occupies a former patrician palace on the Arno, and many rooms
have river views (some with Tuscan antiques scattered around
as well). The Cestello restaurant (*see* Dining) is excellent.
*Piazza Ognissanti 3, tel. 055/264201. 205 rooms with bath. Fa-
cilities: garage. AE, DC, MC, V.*

Regency. One of the Ottaviani family's small, select hotels, the
Regency has the intimate and highly refined atmosphere of a
private villa, luxuriously furnished with antiques and decorated with great style. Just outside the historic center of the
city, it has a charming garden and the pleasant Le Jardin restaurant. *Piazza Massimo d'Azeglio 3, tel. 055/245247. 31 rooms
with bath. Facilities: garage. AE, DC, MC, V.*

Villa Cora. Located in a residential area on a hill overlooking
the Oltrano section of Florence and across the Arno to the
Duomo and Bell Tower, the Villa Cora is a converted private
villa. Furnishings are exquisite and the atmosphere is quietly
elegant. There are gardens in which to stroll, a pool in which to
wallow, and a formal but charming restaurant in which to dine.

There is a Mercedes shuttle service between the hotel and the center of Florence. *Viale Machiavelli 18, tel. 055/229–8451. 48 rooms with bath. AE, DC, V.*

Expensive ★ **Baglioni.** Spacious, elegant, and very grand, Baglioni has well-proportioned rooms tastefully decorated in antique Florentine style. Many rooms have leaded glass windows, and some have views of Santa Maria Novella. The hotel also has a charming roof terrace, and the splendid Terrazza Brunelleschi restaurant (*see* Dining), which has the best view in all Florence (the food is memorable, too). *Piazza Unità d'Italia 6, tel. 055/218441. 195 rooms with bath. Facilities: garage. AE, DC, MC, V.*

Bernini Palace. The atmosphere here is one of austere yet elegant simplicity: Rooms are unostentatious but well-furnished in pastel fabrics and mahogany furniture. Entirely air-conditioned and double-glazed, the Bernini has a quiet, tranquil feel, yet is only a few steps from the frenetically busy Piazza della Signoria. There is no restaurant, but breakfast is served in a historic salon. *Piazza San Firenze 29, tel. 055/278621. 86 rooms with bath. AE, DC, MC, V.*

Grand Hotel Minerva. A modern building just around the corner from the train station, the Minerva will suit travelers who care more for efficiency than atmosphere. The nicest rooms overlook the garden, and the rooftop pool provides a refreshing diversion. *Piazza Santa Maria Novella 16, tel. 055/284555. 111 rooms with bath. Facilities: pool. AE, DC, MC, V.*

★ **Monna Lisa.** This place is the closest you may come to living in an aristocratic palace in the heart of Florence. American visitors in particular are fond of its smallish but homey bedrooms, and sumptuously comfortable sitting rooms. Ask for a room on the quiet 17th-century courtyard, especially the one with a delightful balcony. A lavish buffet breakfast is included in the price. Make reservations months in advance to be assured of a room at this very special pension. *Borgo Pinti 27, tel. 055/ 2479751. 20 rooms with bath. Facilities: garden bar. AE, DC, MC, V.*

Moderate **Calzaiuoli.** While there's an elegant entrance on the pedestrians-only shopping street connecting the cathedral with Piazza della Signoria, don't expect distinctive decor once you're inside (it's actually anemic modern). Still, you couldn't ask for anything more central. *Via dei Calzaiuoli 6, tel. 055/212456. 37 rooms with bath. Facilities: bar. AE, DC.*

★ **Loggiato dei Serviti.** You'll find the Loggiato dei Serviti tucked under an arcade in one of the city's quietest and most attractive squares. Vaulted ceilings and tasteful furnishings (some of them antiques) go far to make this hotel a real find for those who want to get the genuine Florentine feel and who will appreciate the 19th-century town house surroundings while enjoying modern creature comforts. There is no restaurant. *Piazza Santissima Annunziata 3, tel. 055/219165. 20 rooms with bath. No credit cards.*

Porta Rossa. This period piece is only a few steps from the Porcellino straw market and the city's major sights. The authentic Art Nouveau lobby gives a clue to the age of this establishment, as do the worn carpets and creaky plumbing. But it exudes atmosphere; most of the rooms are spacious and comfortable in an old-fashioned way, and a lot of discerning people love it. There is no restaurant. *Via di Porta Rossa 19, tel. 055/287551. 71 rooms, half with bath. AE, DC, MC, V.*

Inexpensive   **Byron.** This pleasant, old-fashioned hotel is near the train station and is close to most of the city's major sights. The newly tiled bathrooms are a real plus, much nicer than you'd expect of a Florentine hotel in this category. *Via della Scala 49, tel. 055/216700. 46 rooms, most with bath. Facilities: restaurant. No credit cards.*

Palazzo Vecchio. The Vecchio presents a fine example of minimal decor in an otherwise attractive 19th-century building. It's close to the train station, and the proprietor owns a restaurant a block or two away. *Via Cennini 4, tel. 055/212182. 18 rooms, 16 with bath or shower. Facilities: parking lot. AE, DC, MC, V.*

The Arts

For a list of events, pick up a *Florence Concierge Information* booklet from your hotel desk, or the monthly information bulletin published by the **Comune Aperto** city information office (available at the booth in front of the train station).

Music and Ballet   Most major musical events are staged at the **Teatro Comunale** (Corso Italia 16, tel. 055/2779236). The box office is open daily except Monday, from 9 to 1, and a half-hour before performances. It's best to order your tickets by mail, however, as they're difficult to come by at the last minute. You can also order concert and ballet tickets through **Universalturismo** (Via degli Speziali 7/r, tel. 055/217241). **Amici della Musica** (Friends of Music) puts on a series of concerts at the **Teatro della Pergola** (box office, Via della pergola 10a/r, tel. 055/242361). For program information, contact the Amici della Musica directly at Via Sirtori 49 (tel. 055/608420).

Film   English-language films are shown at the **Cinema Astro,** on Piazza San Simone near Santa Croce. There are two shows every evening, Tuesday through Sunday. It closes in July.

Entertainment and Nightlife

Piano Bars   Many of the top hotels have piano bars; that of the **Plaza Lucchesi** (Lungarno della Zecca Vecchia 38, tel. 055/264141) is particularly spacious and pleasant. The terrace of the **Hotel Baglioni** (*see* Lodging) has no music but has one of the best views in Florence, candlelit tables, and a wonderful atmosphere. **Loggia Tornaquinci** (Via Tornabuoni 6, tel. 055/219148) is a sophisticated cocktail lounge with yet another soul-stirring view.

Nightclubs   **The River Club** (Lungarno Corsini 8, tel. 055/282465) has winter-garden decor and a large dance floor (closed Sunday). **Central Park** (Via Fosso Macinante 13, tel. 055/356723), in the Cascine park, is the sophisticated summer premises of the Yab Yum disco (*see* below), open from May to September.

Discos   **Jackie O** (Via dell'Erta Canina 24a, tel. 055/2342443) is a glittering Art Deco disco with cream leather upholstery, lots of mirrors and marble, and a trendy clientele (closed Wed.). **Space Electronic** (Via Palazzuolo 37, tel. 055/293082) is exactly what its name implies: ultramodern and psychedelic (closed Mon.). **Yab Yum** (Via Sassetti 5/r, tel. 055/282018) is another *Star Wars*-style disco popular with the young international set. It's closed Monday and May through September, when it moves to the Cascine (*see* above).

Tuscany

Tuscany is a blend of rugged hills, fertile valleys, and long stretches of sandy beaches that curve along the west coast of central Italy and fringe the pine-forested coastal plain of the Maremma. The gentle, cypress-studded green hills may seem familiar: Leonardo and Raphael often painted them in the backgrounds of their masterpieces. The cities and towns of Tuscany house the centuries-old heritage of culture and art that produced magnificent medieval cathedrals and the marvels of the Renaissance. Come to Tuscany to enjoy its unchanged and gracious atmosphere of good living, and, above all, its unparalleled artistic treasures, many still in their original settings in tiny old churches and patrician palaces.

Getting Around

By Train The main train network connects Florence with Arezzo and Prato. Another main line runs to Pisa, while a secondary line goes via Lucca.

By Bus The entire region is crisscrossed by bus lines, good alternatives to trains, especially for reaching Siena. Use local buses to tour the many pretty hill towns around Siena such as San Gimignano, and then take a SITA bus from Siena to Arezzo, from where you can get back onto the main Rome–Florence train line.

By Car The main autostrade run parallel to the train routes. Roads throughout Tuscany are in good condition, though often narrow.

Guided Tours

American Express (Via Guicciardini 49/r, tel. 055/278751) operates one-day excursions to Siena and San Gimignano out of Florence, and can arrange for cars, drivers, and guides for special-interest tours in Tuscany. **CIT** (Via Cavour 56, tel. 055/294306) has a three-day Carosello bus tour from Rome to Florence, Siena, and San Gimignano, as well as a five-day tour that also takes in Venice.

Tourist Information

Arezzo. Piazza Risorgimento 116, tel. 0575/20839.
Cortona. Via Nazionale 72, tel. 0575/603056.
Lucca. Via Vittorio Veneto 40, tel. 0583/43639.
Pisa. Piazza del Duomo, tel. 050/501761.
Pistoia. Piazza del Duomo, tel. 0573/21622.
Prato. Via Cairoli 48, tel. 0574/24112.
Siena. Via di Città 5, tel. 0577/47051; Piazza del Campo 56, tel. 0577/280551.

Exploring Tuscany

Prato Since the Middle Ages, **Prato** has been Italy's major textile-producing center: It now supplies the country's knitwear and fashion industries. Ignore the drab industrial outskirts and devote some time to the fine old buildings in the downtown area,

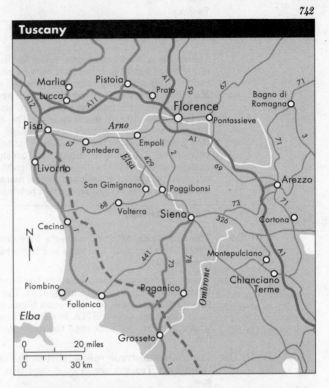

Tuscany

Marlia · Pistoia · Prato · Florence · Pontassieve · Bagno di Romagna · Lucca · A11 · A1 · 65 · 67 · 71 · Pisa · Arno · Empoli · A12 · Pontedera · 67 · Elsa · 429 · 2 · A1 · 69 · 71 · 3 · Livorno · San Gimignano · Poggibonsi · Arezzo · Cecina · 68 · Volterra · Siena · 73 · 326 · Cortona · 71 · A1 · Montepulciano · 441 · 73 · 78 · Ombrone · Chianciano Terme · Piombino · Paganico · Follonica · Elba · Grosseto

N

0 — 20 miles
0 — 30 km

crammed with artworks commissioned by Prato's wealthy merchants during the Renaissance. The **Duomo** (cathedral), erected in the Middle Ages, was decorated with paintings and sculptures by some of the most illustrious figures of Tuscan art, among them Fra Filippo Lippi, who took 12 years to complete the frescoes in the apse (perhaps because in the meantime he was being tried for fraud, as well as wooing the nun with whom he then eloped). Look in particular for his passionate portrayals of *Herod's Feast* and *Salome's Dance*. *Piazza del Duomo.*

In the former bishop's palace, now the **Museo dell'Opera del Duomo,** you can see the original reliefs by Donatello for the Pulpit of the Holy Girdle (Mary's belt, supposedly given to Doubting Thomas as evidence of her assumption; the relic is kept in a chapel of the cathedral). *Piazza del Duomo 49, tel. 0574/26234. Free. Open Tues.–Sat. 9–noon and 3–6, Sun. 9–noon; closed Mon.*

Architects and architecture buffs rhapsodize over the church of **Santa Maria delle Carceri,** off Via Cairoli. Built by Giuliano Sangallo in the 1490s, it was a landmark of Renaissance architecture. Next to it, the formidable **castle** built for Frederick II of Hohenstaufen is another impressive sight, the only castle of its type to be seen outside southern Italy. *Piazza Santa Maria dell Carceri. Free. Open Tues.–Sat. 9–noon and 3–6, Sun. 9–noon; closed Mon.*

Pistoia　Pistoia lies about 10 miles (14 kilometers) northwest of Prato. A floricultural capital of Europe, it's surrounded by greenhouses and plant nurseries. Flowers aside, Pistoia's main sights are all in the downtown area, so you can easily see them on the way to Lucca. The Romanesque **Duomo** (cathedral) is flanked by a 13th-century bell tower, while in a side chapel dedicated to San Jacopo (St. James) there's a massive **silver altar** that alone is worth the stopover in Pistoia. Two hundred years in the making, it's an incredible piece of workmanship, begun in 1287. *Piazza del Duomo.*

Follow Via delle Pappe to the church of **Sant'Andrea** (Via Sant'Andrea) to see Pistoia's greatest art treasure, Giovanni Pisano's powerfully sculpted 13th-century **pulpit,** before heading back toward the train station and bus terminal, stopping on the way to take in the green and white marble church of **San Giovanni Fuorcivitas** (Via Francesco Crispi, off Via Cavour). Highlights here include a *Visitation* by Luca della Robbia, a painting by Taddeo Gaddi, and a holy water font by Giovanni Pisano.

Lucca Your next destination is **Lucca,** Puccini's hometown and a city well-loved by sightseers who appreciate the careful upkeep of its medieval look. Though it hasn't the number of hotels and other tourist trappings that, say, Pisa does, for that very reason it's a pleasant alternative. (And you can easily make an excursion to Pisa from here—it's only 14 miles (22 kilometers) away. Enjoy first the views of the city and countryside from the tree-planted 16th-century **ramparts** that encircle Lucca. Then explore the city's marvelously elaborate Romanesque churches, fronted with tiers and rows of columns, and looking suspiciously like oversize marble wedding cakes.

From vast **Piazza Napoleone,** a swing around the old town will take you past the 11th-century **Duomo** (cathedral, Piazza San Martino), with its 15th-century tomb of Ilaria del Carretto by Jacopo della Quercia. Don't neglect a ramble through the **Piazza del Mercato,** which preserves the oval form of the Roman amphitheater over which it was built, or the three surrounding streets that are filled with atmosphere: **Via Battisti, Via Fillungo,** and **Via Guinigi.** In addition to the Duomo, Lucca has two other fine churches. **San Frediano** (Piazza San Frediano) is graced with an austere facade ornamented by 13th-century mosaic decoration. Inside, check out the exquisite reliefs by Jacopo della Quercia in the last chapel on the left. **San Michele in Foro** (Piazza San Michele) is an exceptional example of the Pisan Romanesque style and decorative flair peculiar to Lucca: Note its facade, a marriage of arches and columns crowned by a statue of St. Michael.

Five miles (eight kilometers) outside town is the **Villa Reale,** at Marlia. Gardening buffs, especially, will appreciate this handsome villa, surrounded by attractive parkland and gardens laid out in the 17th century. *Marlia, tel. 0583/30108. Admission: July–Oct. 3,000 lire, Nov.–June 2,500 lire. Guided visits on the hour, July–Sept., Tues.–Sun. 10, 11, 4, 5, and 6; Oct.–June, Tues.–Sun. 10, 11, 3, 4, and 5; closed Mon.*

Pisa Now looping southwest, the next Tuscan town of note you'll come to is **Pisa,** a dull, overcommercialized place, though even skeptics have to admit the **Torre Pendente** (Leaning Tower) really is one of the world's more amazing sights. Theories vary as to whether the now famous list is due to shifting foundations or an amazing architectural feat by Bonanno Pisano (the first of three architects to work on the tower). A 294-step staircase spirals its way up the tower, providing a marvelous view from the top; a visit to Pisa wouldn't be the same without a trip up those worn steps. If you want a two-foot marble imitation of the Leaning Tower, perhaps even illuminated from within, this is your chance to grab one! *Campo dei Miracoli. Admission: 4,000 lire. Open daily from 9 to an hour before sunset.*

Pisa has two other fine buildings, and, conveniently enough, they're near the Leaning Tower. The **Baptistery** was begun in 1153 but not completed until 1400, the Pisano family doing most of its decoration. Test out the excellent acoustics (occasionally the guard will slam shut the great doors and then sing a few notes—the resulting echo is very impressive, and costly, too, since he'll expect a tip). *Piazza del Duomo, in the Campo dei Miracoli. Open daily 9–1 and 3–7.*

Pisa's **Duomo** (cathedral) is elegantly simple, its facade decorated with geometric and animal shapes. The cavernous interior is supported by a series of 68 columns, while the pulpit is a fine example of Giovanni Pisano's work. Be sure to note the suspended lamp that hangs across from the pulpit; known as Galileo's Lamp, it's said to have inspired his theories on pendular motion. *Piazza del Duomo. Open daily 9–1 and 3–7.*

Visitors may find it more convenient to take a train back to Florence and get a SITA bus there for the 85-minute journey to Siena, but for a more leisurely look at the Tuscan countryside, investigate the possibility of taking a local bus directly from Pisa to Siena, passing through **Certaldo,** a pretty hill town that's the birthplace of Giovanni Boccaccio, 14th-century author of the *Decameron.*

Siena **Siena** is one of Italy's best-preserved medieval towns, rich both in works of art and in expensive antique shops. The famous **Palio** is held here, a breakneck, two-day horse race that takes place each year in the Piazza del Campo on July 2 and August 16. Built on three hills, Siena is not an easy town to explore, for everything you'll want to see is either up or down a steep hill or stairway. But it is worth every ounce of effort. Siena really gives you the chance of seeing and feeling what the Middle Ages must have been like: dark stone palaces, low dwellings, and narrow streets opening out into airy squares.

Siena was a center of learning and art in the Middle Ages, and almost all the public buildings and churches in the town have enough artistic or historical merit to be worth visiting. Unlike most churches, Siena's **Duomo** has a mixture of religious and civic symbols ornamenting both its interior and exterior. The cathedral museum in the unfinished transept contains some fine works of art, notably a celebrated *Maestà* by Duccio di Buoninsegna. The animated frescoes of papal history in the Piccolomini Library (with an entrance off the left aisle of the cathedral) are credited to Pinturicchio, and are worth seeking out. *Piazza del Duomo. Admission: 1,000-lire ticket covers both Museum and Library. Cathedral Museum and Library open May–Oct., daily 9–7:30, Nov.–Apr. 9–2.*

Nearby, the fan-shaped **Piazza del Campo** is Siena's main center of activity, with 11 streets leading into it. Farsighted planning has preserved it as a medieval showpiece, containing the 13th-century **Palazzo Pubblico** (City Hall) and the Torre del

Mangia (Bell Tower). Try to visit both these buildings, the former for Lorenzetti's frescoes on the effects of good and bad government, the latter for the wonderful view (you'll have to climb 503 steps to reach it, however). *Piazza del Campo, tel. 0577/292111. Admission: 4,000 lire. Open Apr.–Oct., Mon.–Sat. 9–6:30; Nov.–Mar. 9:30–1:30; Sun. 9:30–1.*

Time Out **Al Mangia** is a good outdoor café-cum-restaurant where you can enjoy a Tartufo ice cream and a cup of coffee, imagining the noise and excitement generated by the Palio riders careening around the corners of the piazza during the 90-second race.

From Siena make an excursion to **San Gimignano,** perhaps the most delightful of the Tuscan medieval hill towns with their timeless charm. There were once 79 tall towers here, symbols of power for the wealthy families of the Middle Ages. Thirteen are still standing, giving the town its unique skyline. The bus stops just outside the town gates, from which you can stroll down the main street to the picturesque Piazza della Cisterna.

Just around the corner is the church of the **Collegiata.** Its walls, and those of its chapel dedicated to Santa Fina, are decorated with radiant frescoes. From the steps of the church you can observe the town's countless crows as they circle the tall towers. In the pretty courtyard on the right as you descend the church stairs, there's a shop selling **Tuscan and Deruta ceramics,** which you'll also find in other shops along the Via San Giovanni. The excellent San Gimignano wine could be another souvenir of your visit; it's sold in gift cartons from just about every shop in town.

Arezzo A local bus or train takes you from Siena to **Arezzo** (about 30 miles, or 48 kilometers, east), over thickly wooded hills, past vineyards and wheat fields, and the broad ribbon of the Autostrada del Sole in the fertile Chiana valley, known for its pale beef cattle that provide the classic *bistecca Fiorentina.* Arezzo is not a beautiful town, nor is it quaint. What makes Arezzo worth a visit, however, is its fine array of Tuscan art treasures, including frescoes, stained glass, and ancient Etruscan statues.

The **Museo Archeologico** (Archaeological Museum) is near the train station, next to what's left of an ancient **Roman amphitheater.** The museum has a rich collection of Etruscan art, artifacts, and pottery, copied by Arezzo's contemporary artisans and sold in the local ceramic shops of the town. *Via Margaritone 10, tel. 0575/20882. Admission: 3,000 lire. Open Tues.–Sat. 9–2, Sun. 9–1; closed Mon.*

Via Guido Monaco, named after the 11th-century originator of the musical scale, leads to the church of **San Francesco,** where one of the town's main attractions, the **frescoes by Piero delle Francesca,** are currently due for restoration and will probably be at least partially hidden through 1989. Faded as they are, they still rank among the outstanding examples of Italian painting, and art lovers are looking forward to seeing them in renewed splendor. *Via Cavour.*

Now you enter the old part of Arezzo, where the poet Petrarch (1304–74), the artist Vasari (1511–74), and the satirical author Pietro Aretino (1492–1556) all lived. Climb Via Cesalpino uphill to the fine Gothic **cathedral** (Piazza del Duomo), then stroll past **Petrarch's House** to **Piazza Grande,** an attractive, sloping square where an extensive open-air fair of antiques and old bric-a-brac is held the first weekend of every month. The shops around the piazza also specialize in antiques, with prices lower than those you will encounter in Florence. The colonnaded apse and bell tower of the Romanesque church of **Santa Maria della Pieve** grace one end of this pleasant piazza.

Cortona A full day may be enough for you to get the feel of Arezzo, but you may wish to stay overnight, especially during the antique fair, or if you want to use the town as a base for an excursion to **Cortona,** about 18 miles (30 kilometers) south. This medieval town is known for its excellent small art gallery and a number of fine antiques shops, as well as for its colony of foreign residents. Cortona has the advantage of being on the main train network, though you will have to take a local bus from the station up into the town, passing the Renaissance church of **Santa Maria del Calcinaio** on the way.

The heart of Cortona is formed by **Piazza della Repubblica** and the adjacent **Piazza Signorelli.** Wander into the courtyard of the picturesque **Palazzo Pretorio,** and, if you want to see a representative collection of Etruscan bronzes, climb its centuries-old stone staircase to the **Museo dell'Accademia Etrusca** (Gallery of Etruscan Art). *Piazza Signorelli 9, tel. 0575/62534. Admission: 2,000 lire. Open June–Sept., Tues.–Sun. 10–1 and 4–7; Oct.–May 9–1 and 3–5; closed Mon.*

The nearby **Museo Diocesana** (Diocesan Museum) houses an impressive number of large and splendid paintings by native son Luca Signorelli, as well as a beautiful *Annunciation* by Fra Angelico, a delightful surprise to find in this small, eclectic town. *Piazza del Duomo 1, tel. 0575/62830. Admission: 2,000 lire. Open June–Sept., Tues.–Sun. 9–1 and 3–6; Oct.–May 9–1 and 3–5; closed Mon.*

Dining and Lodging

For details and price category definitions, *see* Dining and Lodging in Essential Information.

Arezzo **Buca di San Francesco.** Travelers and passing celebrities come
Dining to this rustic and historic cellar restaurant for the 13th-century
★ cantina atmosphere, but locals love it for the food, especially *ribollita* (minestrone) and *sformato di spinaci con cibreo* (spinach with giblet sauce). *Piazza San Francesco 1, tel. 0575/ 23271. Dress: informal. Dinner reservations advised. AE, DC, MC, V. Closed Mon. dinner, Tues., and July. Moderate.*

Tastevin. Arezzo's purveyor of creative *nuova cucina* serves traditional Tuscan dishes as well, in three attractive, elegantly rustic rooms, with a Belle Epoque café doubling as a piano bar. Specialties are *risotto Tastevin,* with cream of truffles, and seafood or meat *carpaccio* (sliced raw). *Via de'Cenci 9, tel. 0575/ 28304. Dress: informal. Dinner reservations advised. AE, MC, V. Closed Mon. (Sun. in summer). Moderate.*

Spiedo d'Oro. Cheery red-and-white tablecloths add a colorful touch to this large, reliable trattoria near the Archaeological Museum. The menu offers Tuscan home-style specialties like *zuppa di pane* (bread soup), *pappardelle oll'ocio* (noodles with duck sauce), and *ossobuco aretina* (sautéed veal shank). *Via Crispi 12, tel. 0575/22873. Dress: informal. Reservations not* *needed. No credit cards. Closed Thurs. and first 2 weeks in July. Inexpensive.*

Lodging **Minerva.** This six-story 1960s construction is on a main road in the newer part of town (you'll have to take a taxi or bus to the downtown area). The expanses of plate glass and dull brown furnishings may leave you cold, but it's the best in Arezzo, and it has a good restaurant. *Via Fiorentina 6, tel. 0575/27891. 118 rooms with bath. AE, DC, V. Moderate.*

Continental. The circa-1950 Continental has fairly spacious, though functionally decorated, rooms, and the advantage of a central location within walking distance of all major sights. *Piazza Guido Monaco 7, tel. 0575/20251. 74 rooms with bath. Facilities: restaurant. AE, DC, MC, V. Inexpensive.*

Cortona
Dining
★
Tonino. This is the place to eat in Cortona, known for its delicious *antipastissimo*, and for succulent steaks of Chiana valley beef. It's best on weekdays, for the big dining room with a window-wall overlooking the valley. The restaurant is crowded and noisy on weekends. *Piazza Garibaldi, tel. 0575/603100. Dress: informal. Weekend reservations advised. AE, DC, MC, V. Closed Mon. dinner and Tues. Moderate.*

Lucca
Dining
★
Buca di Sant'Antonio. Near the church of San Michele, Buca di Sant'Antonio was around more than a century ago, and it has retained something of its rustic look. It specializes in traditional local dishes, some unfamiliar but well worth trying, among them *tacconi al sugo* (fresh pasta in rabbit or mushroom sauce), and kid or lamb roasted with herbs. *Via della Cervia 1, tel. 0583/55881. Dress: informal. Dinner reservations advised. AE, DC, MC, V. Closed Sun. dinner, Mon., and July 10–31. Moderate.*

Il Giglio. Off vast Piazza Napoleone, Il Giglio has a quiet, turn-of-the-century charm and a dignified atmosphere. In the summer the tables outdoors have a less formal air. The menu is classic: *crostini* (savory Tuscan chicken liver, anchovy and caper paste on small pieces of toast), *stracotto* (braised beef with mushrooms), and seafood, as well. *Piazza del Giglio 2, tel. 0583/44058. Dress: informal. Dinner reservations advised. AE, DC, MC, V. Closed Tues. dinner and Wed. Moderate.*

★ **La Mora.** You'll need a car or a taxi to take you to this charming old way station six miles (10 kilometers) outside Lucca, but its authentic local cooking is worth every effort. It is widely considered to be one of the best regional restaurants in Italy. *Via Sesto di Moriano 104, Ponte a Moriano, tel. 0583/57109. Dress: informal. Reservations advised. AE, DC, MC, V. Closed Wed. dinner, Thurs., and July 1–12. Moderate.*

Lodging
★
Villa La Principessa. Two miles (three kilometers) outside Lucca, this pretty 19th-century country mansion is an exclusive hotel whose rooms feature original beamed ceilings. All rooms are individually, and tastefully, decorated. Antique floors, furniture, and portraits set the tone, and the restaurant is known for its fine Tuscan dishes. *Massa Pisana, tel. 0583/ 370087. 44 rooms with bath. Facilities: park, pool, restaurant. AE, DC, MC, V. Closed Mid-Nov.–Feb. Expensive.*

★ **Universo.** There's plenty of genteel, Old World charm here to please those looking for the atmosphere of times past. In the spacious, high-ceilinged rooms, even huge 1920s wardrobes look small, and you have to climb two steps to open the tall windows. Bathrooms are on the same scale. Furnishings are old

but comfortable, and the plumbing works! *Piazza del Giglio 1,
tel. 0583/49046. 60 rooms, half with bath. AE, DC, MC, V.
Moderate.*

Ilaria. This small, family-run hotel sits in a pretty location on a
minuscule canal within easy walking distance of the main
sights. Renovated in 1987, rooms are smallish but fresh and
functional. *Via del Fosso 20, tel. 0583/47558. 17 rooms, most
with bath. AE, DC, MC, V. Inexpensive.*

Pisa
Dining

Bruno. Checked curtains, wood paneling, and soft lights make
Bruno a pleasant place to lunch on classic Tuscan dishes, from
crostini—toast topped with a creamy mixture of chicken
livers, capers, and anchovy—to *coniglio* (rabbit). It's just outside the old city walls and only a short walk from the bell tower
and cathedral. *Via Luigi Bianchi 12, tel. 050/550964.
Dress: informal. Dinner reservations advised. AE, DC, MC, V.
Closed Mon. dinner, Tues., Aug. 1–20. Moderate.*

Spartaco. Centrally located on the station square, Spartaco has
the solid look of the well-established trattoria that it is, with
contemporary white chairs contrasting with terra-cotta-tiled
walls and some fine antique pieces. It's large, and seating doubles in the summer when tables are set out on the square.
Specialties include a cocktail of ravioli in different colors, and
grilled fish, along with the usual Tuscan dishes. *Piazza Vittorio Emanuele 22, tel. 050/23335. Dress: informal. Reservations not required. AE, DC, MC, V. Closed Sun. Moderate.*

Pistoia
Dining

Cucciolo della Montagna. Just a block or two from the cathedral
and the church of San Giovanni Fuorcivitas, Cucciolo della
Montagna is popular with businesspeople and does a big lunch
trade, so get there early or reserve ahead. The specialties are
Tuscan in flavor: pasta with duck sauce, and grilled duck. *Via
Panciatichi 4, tel. 0573/29733. Dress: informal. Reservations
advised. AE, DC, MC, V. Closed Mon. and Aug. 1–25. Moderate.*

Il Duomo. This unpretentious trattoria is practically on Piazza
del Duomo, and locals as well as tourists enjoy its typical Tuscan *ribollita* (minestrone) and *carne in umido* (stewed meats)
at very reasonable prices. *Via Bracciolini 5, tel. 0573/31948.
Dress: informal. Reservations not required. No credit cards.
Closed Sun. Moderate.*

Prato
Dining

Da Bruno. Decor at this upscale little restaurant near the castle is simple, with wood-paneled walls and yellow and white
accents. The menu offers traditional dishes with creative
touches, such as *farinata*, made of cornmeal, red cabbage and
tomato, or the duck breast in a sauce of balsamic vinegar and
sweet peppers. *Via Verdi 12, tel. 0574/23810. Dress: informal.
Reservations advised. AE, DC, MC, V. Closed Thurs. dinner,
Sun., and Aug. Moderate.*

Stefano. At the lower end of the moderate price range, this
trattoria is popular with the locals. A simple place, it serves
regional dishes such as *ribollita* (minestrone), *fagioli* (beans)
laced with local olive oil, and grilled meat. *Via Pomeria 23, tel.
0574/34665. Dress: informal. Reservations not accepted. No
credit cards. Closed Sun. Moderate.*

San Gimignano
Dining
★

Le Terrazze. You'll find this one tucked under the eaves of
the Hotel Cisterna on the town's prettiest square. Under
low, beamed ceilings, windows give you a panoramic view of
red-tiled rooftops and the surrounding countryside. Cooking

is appropriately Tuscan, from *ribollita* (minestrone) that's heated in the oven to make it even thicker, to *fritto misto* (fried meats and vegetables). *Piazza della Cisterna, tel. 0577/ 940328. Dress: informal. Reservations advised. AE, DC, MC, V. Closed Tues., Wed. lunch, mid-Nov.–mid Mar. Moderate.*

Bel Soggiorno. A slightly simpler version of Le Terrazze, Bel Soggiorno, too, is attached to a small hotel. It has a homey, familiar atmosphere and slightly lower prices. Specialties are *morsello di San Gimignano* (a hearty vegetable soup) and a spicy fillet of pork. *Via San Giovanni 89, tel. 0577/ 940375. Dress:informal. Reservations advised. AE,DC,MC,V. Closed Mon. Moderate.*

Siena Dining
★
Ai Marsili. Located in a medieval palace near the Duomo, Ai Marsili is a spacious, brick-vaulted wine cellar with refectory tables and excellent Tuscan cuisine; it's a place for a leisurely meal accompanied by classic Chianti wines. Specialties include *ceci* (chick-peas with garlic and rosemary) and *faraona* (guinea hen). *Via del Castoro 3, tel. 0577/47154. Dress: informal. Reservations advised. AE, DC, MC, V. Closed Mon. Moderate.*

Osteria Le Logge. Just off Piazza del Campo, this is a fine choice for an informal but memorable meal. Get there early to claim a table. Among the specialties are *pennette all'Osteria* (spicy pasta) and *terra di Siena*, a piquant roast beef. *Via del Porrione 33, tel. 0577/48013. Dress: informal. Reservations advised. No credit cards. Closed Sun., and mid-Nov.–mid-Dec. Moderate.*

Le Tre Campane. Between Piazza del Campo and the Duomo, this small trattoria expands into the little square in fair weather. Popular with the locals, it specializes in seafood, as well as the standard Tuscan *crostini*. *Piazzetta Bonelli, tel.0577/286091. Dress: informal. Reservations advised. No credit cards. Closed Tues., and Jan.–Feb. Moderate.*

Lodging
Certosa di Maggiano. Less than a mile from the city, this old Carthusian monastery has been converted into a sophisticated oasis furnished in impeccable style. The bedrooms have every comfort, though regulations forbid installation of an elevator. *Strada di Certosa 82, tel. 0577/288180. 14 rooms with bath. Facilities: pool, tennis. AE, DC, MC, V. Closed Dec.–Feb. Expensive.*

★
Park Hotel. Just outside the walls of the old city, Park Hotel is a handsome 15th-century villa on its own grounds. Furnished in classic Tuscan style, with antiques and luxuriant plants in gleaming copper planters on highly polished terra-cotta floors, it has a simple but sophisticated ambience, in which you can pretend you're a house guest of the Medicis. There's a fine restaurant and garden terrace. *Via di Marciano 18, tel. 0577/44803. 69 rooms with bath. Facilities: pool, tennis. AE, DC, MC, V. Expensive.*

Palazzo Ravizza. Set just within the town walls, these accommodations are not far from the cathedral (though it's an uphill walk). The hotel is a converted 17th-century building with garden, and it's furnished as a private residence, with comfortable bedrooms, some small. *Piano del Mantellini 34, tel. 0577/280462. 28 rooms, most with bath. AE, DC, MC, V. Moderate.*

★
Santa Caterina. This newcomer to the Siena hotel scene opened in 1986 in a totally renovated and air-conditioned town house, a few steps from Porta Romana and a 10-minute walk from the cathedral. It's decorated in classic Tuscan style, with light

walls and dark wood furniture. Bedrooms are cheery, with floral prints, and two have the original frescoed ceilings. The hotel has a pretty garden and a small parking area. *Via Piccolomini 7, tel. 0577/221105. 19 rooms with bath. AE, DC, MC, V. Closed mid-Nov.–Feb. Moderate.*

Milan

Arriving and Departing

As Lombardy's capital and the most important financial and commercial center in northern Italy, Milan is well connected with Rome and Florence by fast and frequent rail and air service, though the latter is often delayed in winter by heavy fog.

By Plane **Linate Airport,** seven miles (11 kilometers) outside Milan, handles mainly domestic and European flights (tel. 02/74852200). **Malpensa,** 30 miles (50 kilometers) from the city, handles intercontinental flights (tel. 02/868028).

Between the Airport and Downtown Buses connect both airports with Milan, stopping at the Central Station and at the Porta Garibaldi Station. Fare from Linate is 700 lire, from Malpensa 6,000 lire. A taxi from Linate to the center of Milan costs about 25,000 lire, from Malpensa about 90,000 lire.

By Train The main train terminal is the **Central Station** in Piazzale Duca d'Aosta (tel. 02/67500). Several smaller stations handle commuter trains. There are several fast Intercity trains between Rome and Milan, stopping in Florence. A nonstop Intercity leaves from Rome or Milan morning and evening, taking less than five hours to go between the two cities.

By Car From Rome and Florence, take the A1 Autostrada. From Venice, take the A4. With bans on parking throughout the center of Milan, it's easier to park on the outskirts and use public transportation.

Getting Around

By Subway Milan's subway network, the **Metropolitana,** is modern, fast, and easy to use. "MM" signs mark Metropolitana stations. There are at present two lines, with another scheduled to open soon. The ATM (city transport authority) has an information office on the mezzanine of the Duomo Metro station (tel. 02/875495). Tickets are sold at newsstands at every stop, and in ticket machines *for exact change only.* The fare is 700 lire, and the subway runs from 6:20 AM to midnight.

By Bus and Streetcar There is an extensive network. Buy tickets at newsstands, tobacco shops, and bars. Fare is 700 lire. One ticket is valid for 75 minutes on all surface lines, and one subway trip. Daily tickets valid for 24 hours on all public transport lines are on sale at EPT offices at Via Marconi 1 and in the Central Station, at the Duomo Metro station ATM Information Office, and at the ATM office, Via Ricasoli 2.

By Taxi Use yellow cabs only. They wait at stands or can be telephoned in advance (tel. 6767, 8585, or 8388).

Guided Tours

City Tours The **EPT Information Office** (Via Marconi 1, tel. 02/809662) sells tickets to morning or afternoon sightseeing tours departing from Piazza del Duomo; cost is about 31,000 lire. You can arrange for pickup at a main hotel.

Excursions **CIT** (Galleria Vittorio Emanuele, tel. 02/866661, or Central Station, tel. 02/220224) offers an all-day tour of Lake Maggiore, including a boat trip to the Borromean Islands and lunch. There is a brief stop at Lake Como. Cost is about 80,000 lire.

Personalized Tours Arrange for guide service and interpreters through the **Centro Guide Turistiche** (Via Marconi 1, tel. 02/863210).

Tourist Information

EPT information offices are located at the following addresses: Via Marconi 1, tel. 02/809662; Central Station, tel. 02/6690432; Linate Airport, tel. 02/744065. There's a **Municipal Information Office** at Galleria Vittorio Emanuele at the corner of Piazza della Scala, tel. 02/870545.

Exploring Milan

The center of Milan is the Piazza del Duomo. The massive ❶ **Duomo** (cathedral) is one of the largest churches in the world, a mountain of marble fretted with statues, spires, and flying buttresses. The interior is a more solemn Italian Gothic. Take the elevator or walk up 158 steps to the roof, from where—if it's a clear day—you can see over the city to the Lombard plain and the Alps beyond, all through an amazing array of spires and statues. The **Madonnina,** a gleaming gilt statue on the highest spire, is a Milan landmark. *Entrance to elevator and stairway outside the cathedral, to the right. Admission: 3,500 lire. Open Mar.–Oct., daily 9–5:45; Nov.–Feb., 9–4:15.*

Outside the cathedral to the right is the elegant, glass-roofed ❷ **Galleria,** where the Milanesi and visitors stroll, window-shop, and sip pricey cappuccinos at trendy cafés. At the other end of ❸ the Galleria is **Piazza della Scala,** with Milan's city hall on one ❹ side and the world-famous **Teatro alla Scala** opposite. Obtaining tickets to an opera or major concert at La Scala is no easy task, and it's best to ask your hotel for help. You can also book tickets at CIT travel agencies elsewhere in Italy and in foreign countries, but no more than ten days before the performance. *Box Office, Teatro alla Scala, Piazza della Scala, tel. 02/809126. Open Tues.–Sun. 10–1 and 3:30–5:30; closed Mon. Tickets for the same evening's performance are on sale from 5:30 PM.*

Via Verdi, flanking the opera house, leads to Via Brera, where ❺ the **Pinacoteca di Brera** houses one of Italy's great collections of paintings. Most are of a religious nature, confiscated in the 19th century when many religious orders were suppressed and their churches closed. *Via Brera 28, tel. 02/808387. Admission: 4,000 lire. Open Tues., Wed., Thurs. 9–6:30, Fri.–Sat. 9–2, Sun. 9–1; closed Mon.*

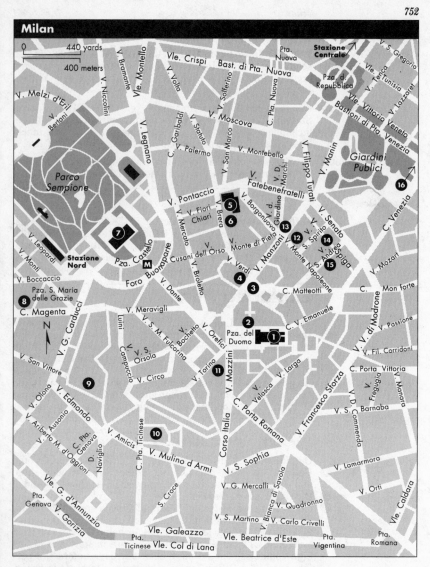

Milan

0 ——— 440 yards
400 meters

- V. Melzi d'Eril
- V. Berlani
- V. Bramante
- V. Niccolini
- V. Montello
- Vle. Crispi
- Bast. di Pta. Nuova
- Pta. Nuova
- Stazione Centrale
- V. S. Gregorio
- V. Tenca
- V. Tunisia
- V. Lazzaretto
- Pza. d. Repubblica
- Vle. Tunisia
- V. Volta
- V. Solferino
- C. Pta. Nuova
- Vle. Vittoria Veneto
- V. Moscova
- Bastioni di Pta. Venezia
- Parco Sempione
- C. Garibaldi
- V. Statuto
- V. Palermo
- V. San Marco
- V. Montebello
- V. Filippo Turati
- V. Manin
- Giardini Publici
- V. Fatebenefratelli
- V. D. Marchi
- V. Pontaccio
- V. Fiori Chiari
- Brera
- V. Borgonuovo
- V. Giardino
- V. Senato
- C. Venezia
- 16
- Stazione Nord
- V. Leopardi
- Pza. Castello
- Foro Buonaparte
- Cusani dell'Orso
- Mercato
- V. Broletto
- V. Monte di Pietà
- V. Manzoni
- Monte Napoleone
- S. Spirito
- V. Andrea
- Spiga
- V. Mozart
- C.
- Mon forte
- V. Leopardi
- V. Monti
- V. Boccaccio
- Pza. S. Maria delle Grazie
- C. Magenta
- N
- V. G. Carducci
- V. Meravigli
- V. Dante
- V. Verdi
- C. Matteotti
- V. d. Modrone
- V. Passione
- V. San Vittore
- Luini
- V. S. M. Fulcorina
- V. Bocchetto
- V. Orefici
- Pza. del Duomo
- C. V. Emanuele
- V. Fil. Corridoni
- V. S. Orsola
- Campuccio
- V. Circo
- V. Torino
- V. Mazzini
- V. Velasca
- V. Larga
- C. Porta Vittoria
- V. Freguglia
- V. Manara
- V. Olona
- V. Edmondo
- C. Pta. Genova
- V. Amicis
- C. Pta. Ticinese
- C. Porta Romana
- V. Francesco Sforza
- V. S. Barnaba
- V. D. Commenda
- V. Ariberto
- Ausonio
- M. d'Oggioni
- D. Naviglio
- V. Mulino d'Armi
- S. Croce
- V. S. Sophia
- V. Lamarmora
- Pta. Genova
- Vle. G. d'Annunzio
- V. Gorizia
- Pta. Ticinese
- Vle. Galeazzo
- Vle. Col di Lana
- Corso Italia
- V. G. Mercalli
- V. Bianca di Savoia
- V. Quadronno
- V. S. Martino
- V. Carlo Crivelli
- Vle. Beatrice d'Este
- Pta. Vigentina
- Pta. Romana
- V. Orti
- Vle. Caldara

Time Out A pleasant café with tables outdoors in fair weather is open to Brera visitors, just inside the entrance to the gallery.

After an eyeful of artworks by Mantegna, Raphael, and many other Italian masters, explore the Brera neighborhood, dotted with art galleries, chic little restaurants, and offbeat cafés such as the **Jamaica** (Via Brera 26), once a bohemian hangout. Take Via dei Fiori Chiari in front of the Brera and keep going in the same direction to the moated **Castello Sforzesco,** a somewhat sinister 19th-century reconstruction of the imposing 15th-century fortress built by the Sforzas, who succeeded the Viscontis as lords of Milan in the 15th century. It now houses wide-ranging collections of sculptures, antiques, and ceramics, including Michelangelo's *Rondanini Pietà*, his last work, left unfinished at his death. *Piazza Castello, tel. 02/6236 ext. 3947. Free. Open Tues.–Sun. 9:30–12:15 and 2:30–5:15; closed Mon.*

From the vast residence of the Sforzas it's not far to the church of **Santa Maria delle Grazie.** Although portions of the church were designed by Bramante, it plays second fiddle to the **Refectory** next door, where, over a three-year period, Leonardo da Vinci painted his mega-famous fresco, *The Last Supper*. The fresco has suffered more than its share of disaster, beginning with the experiments of the artist, who used untested pigments that soon began to deteriorate. *The Last Supper* is now a mere shadow of its former self, despite meticulous restoration that proceeds at a snail's pace. To save what is left, visitors are limited in time and number, and you may have to wait in line to get a glimpse of this world-famous work. *Piazza Santa Maria delle Grazie 2, tel. 02/4987588. Admission: 4,000 lire. Open Tues.–Sat. 9–1:30 and 2–6:30, Sun.–Mon. 9–1.*

If you are interested in medieval architecture, go to see the medieval church of **Sant'Ambrogio** (Piazza Sant'Ambrogio). Consecrated by St. Ambrose in AD 387, it's the model for all Lombard Romanesque churches, and contains some ancient works of art, including a remarkable 9th-century altar in precious metals and enamels, and some 5th-century mosaics. On December 7, the feast day of St. Ambrose, the streets around the church are the scene of a lively flea market. Another noteworthy church is **San Lorenzo Maggiore** (Corso di Porta Ticinese), with 16 archaic Roman columns in front and some 4th-century mosaics in the Chapel of St. Aquilinus. Closer to Piazza del Duomo on Via Torino, the church of **San Satiro** is another architectural gem in which Bramante's perfect command of proportion and perspective, a characteristic of the Renaissance, made a small interior seem extraordinarily spacious and airy.

Time Out Stop in at the **Peck** shops a few steps from San Satiro. One is a gourmet delicatessen, the other has a tempting array of snacks to eat on the premises. *Via Spadari 9; Via Cantù 3.*

Now head for Milan's most elegant shopping streets: **Via Monte Napoleone, Via Manzoni, Via Spiga,** and **Via Sant'Andrea.** The **Café Cova** (Monte Napoleone 8) is famous for its pastries; Hemingway loved them. And the **Sant'Ambroeus,** not far away, is the epitome of a genteel tearoom (Corso Matteotti 7). If the chic goods of this area are a shock to your purse, make your way to **Corso Buenos Aires,** near the Central Station, which has hundreds more shops and accessible prices, too.

Dining

For details and price category definitions, *see* Dining in Essential Information.

Expensive **Biffi Scala.** The elegant Biffi Scala caters mainly to the after-opera crowd that pours in around midnight. Built in 1861, it features a high ceiling and polished wood walls. Specialties include *crespelle alle erbette* (pancakes stuffed with wild mushrooms and other vegetables) and *carpaccio alla biffi scala* (thin slices of cured raw beef with a tangy sauce). *Piazza della Scala, tel. 02/876332. Jacket and tie. Dinner reservations required, especially after the opera. AE, DC, MC, V. Closed Sun., Aug.*

★ **Boeucc.** Milan's oldest restaurant is situated not far from La Scala, and is subly lit, with fluted columns, chandeliers, thick carpet, and a garden for warm-weather dining. In addition to the typical Milanese foods, it also serves such exotica as *penne al branzino e zucchine* (pasta with sea bass and zucchini sauce) and *gelato di castagne con zabaglione caldo* (chestnut ice cream with hot zabaglione). *Piazza Belgioioso 2, tel. 02/790224. Jacket and tie. Reservations required. AE. Closed Sat., Sun. lunch, and all of Aug.*

Don Lisander. This 17th-century chapel has been drastically redecorated, and now features designer lighting, abstract prints, and a modern terra-cotta tile floor, creating an uncompromisingly contemporary effect. Try the *terrina di brasato alle verdure* (terrine of braised beef with vegetables), or else go for the *branzino al timo* (sea bass with thyme). *Via Manzoni 12A, tel. 02/90130. Jacket and tie. Reservations required. AE, DC, MC, V. Closed Sat. dinner, Sun., 2 weeks in mid-Aug., and 2 weeks at Christmas.*

Giannino's. You'll find great character and style at this roomy, old-fashioned restaurant, with oak beams, stained-glass windows, and a huge lobster aquarium. If it's on the menu, be daring and try the *dadolata di capriolo* (venison in cream sauce) or *quaglie con risotto* (quails with rice). *Via A. Sciesa 8, tel. 02/5452948. Jacket and tie. Dinner reservations required. AE, DC, MC, V. Closed Sun., Aug.*

★ **Gualtiero Marchesi.** Owner Gualtiero Marchesi has written several books on nuova cuccina. Your eye, as well as your taste buds, should relish his *raviolo aperto* (pasta, scallops, and a ginger sauce) or the *costata di manzo bollita alle piccole verdure* (thinly sliced boiled pork with steamed vegetables). *Via Bonvesin de la Riva 9, tel. 02/741246. Dress: casual. Reservations advised. AE, DC, MC, V. Closed Sun., Mon. lunch, and all of Aug.*

Savini. Red carpets and cut-glass chandeliers characterize the classy Savini, a typical, Old World Milanese restaurant whose dining rooms spread over three floors. There's also a "winter garden" from which patrons can people-watch shoppers in the Galleria. The *rissotto al salto* (rice cooked as a pancake, tossed in the pan, a Milanese specialty) is excellent here, as is the *costoletta di vitello* (fried veal cutlets). *Galleria Vittorio Emanuele, tel. 02/8058343. Jacket and tie. Dinner reservations advised. AE, DC, MC, V. Closed Mon., 3 weeks in Aug.*

Moderate **Antica Brasera Meneghina.** A huge fireplace, ornate mirrors, ★ black-and-white tiled floor, and bentwood chairs lend this restaurant a 17th-century air, while the long garden, shaded by a 450-year-old wisteria and featuring fig trees, fountains, and frescoes, make it absolutely delightful in the summer. The menu features typical Milanese dishes such as *rustin negàa* (veal cooked in white wine with ham, bacon, sage, and rosemary) and *cassoeula* (casserole of pork, sausage, and cabbage). *Via Circo 10, tel. 02/808108. Dress: casual. Winter reservations advisable. No credit cards. Closed Mon. and all of Aug.*

Al Buon Convento. The granite columns and oak beams here date back to the 15th century, when a bevy of nuns occupied the premises. Expect genuine, home-style cooking served up in an intimate, candlelit ambience. Don't miss the *spaghetti alla lucans* (spaghetti with a tomato and chili sauce). *Corso Italia 26, tel. 02/8050623. Jacket and tie. Reservations advised. V. Closed Sun., Aug.*

Opera Prima. If you've always imagined yourself dining by candlelight, from silver plates, and with strains of classical music lilting in the background—well, then, Opera Prima is the place you've been searching for. The *crespelle alla vaniglia e al cioccolate* (vanilla and chocolate pancakes) are sinfully good, the *tagliolini opera prima* (pasta with chicken, vegetables, and a cream and chile sauce) is a good way to start off your meal. *Via Rovello 3, tel. 02/865235. Dress: casual. Reservations advised. AE, DC, MC, V. Closed Sun., middle 2 weeks in Aug.*

★ **Tencitt.** This chic, ultra-1980s restaurant is decorated in stark black and white, with suffused wall lighting and a striped tent effect on the ceiling. Dishes that sit well with the professional/academic clientele (it's near the university) are the *risotto con zucche e scampi* (rice with squash and scampi) and the *storione all'erba e cipolline* (sturgeon with herbs and spring onions). *Via Laghetto 2, tel. 02/795560. Dress: casual chic. Reservations required. AE, DC, MC, V. Closed Sat. lunch, Sun., Aug.*

Inexpensive **Al Cantinone.** Opera goers still come to the Cantinone bar for a drink after the final curtain, just as they did a century ago. Decor is basic, the atmosphere lively, the service fast, and the food reliable. The proprietor stocks 240 different wines. Try the *costolette al Cantinone* (veal cutlets with mushrooms, olives, and a cream and tomato sauce). *Via Agnello 19, tel. 02/807666. Dress: casual. Reservations advised. AE, MC, V. Closed Sat. lunch, Sun., 3 weeks in Aug.*

La Bruschetta. A winning partnership of Tuscans and Neapolitans run this tiny, busy, and first-class pizzeria near the Duomo. It features the obligatory wood-burning stove, so you can watch your pizza being cooked, though there are plenty of other dishes to choose from as well—try the *spaghetti alle cozze e vongole* (spaghetti with clams and mussels). *Piazza Beccaria 12, tel. 02/802494. Dress: casual. Reservations are handy, but service is so fast you don't have to wait long. No credit cards. Closed Mon., 3 weeks in Aug.*

13 (Tredici) Giugno. Gino Sant'Ercole, the proprietor, is an ex-pop star, and his restaurant features live music in the evenings. Enjoy *lasagne con le noci e prosciutto di prage* (lasagne with walnuts and ham sauce) in the garden in summer, or in the Art Deco dining room in winter. *Via Giulio Uberto 5 (corner of Via Goldoni), tel. 02/719654. Dress: casual chic. Dinner reservations advised. AE, MC, V. Closed Sat. lunch, Sun., Aug.*

Lodging

Make reservations well in advance, particularly when trade fairs are on, which can be most of the year except for August (when many hotels close) and mid-December to mid-January. March and October are months with the highest concentration of fairs, and it's virtually impossible to find a room at this time. Should you arrive without reservations, there's a booking service at the Stazione Centrale, and at the EPT office on Via Marconi, off Piazza Duomo.

For details and price category definitions, *see* Lodging in Essential Information.

Very Expensive **Duomo.** Just 20 yards (18 meters) from the cathedral, this hotel's first-, third-, and fourth-floor rooms all look out onto the church's Gothic gargoyles and pinnacles. Rooms are spacious, snappily furnished in gold, cream, and brown. *Via San Raffaele 1, tel. 02/8833. 160 rooms with bath. Facilities: restaurant, bar. MC, V. Closed Aug.*

Galileo. In spite of its location on busy Corso Europa, this hotel is surprisingly quiet. Rooms have chic designer lighting, tartan carpets, and original modern prints on the walls. Bathrooms are particularly grand, with two basins each. *Corso Europa 9, tel. 02/7743. 76 rooms with bath. Facilities: piano bar, restaurant. AE, DC, MC, V.*

★ **Pierre.** No expense was spared to furnish each room of Milan's newest luxury hotel in a different style, using the most elegant fabrics and an assortment of modern and antique furniture. Electronic gadgetry is rife: you can open the curtains, turn off the lights, and who knows what else, merely by pressing buttons on a remote-control dial. The Pierre is located near the medieval church of Sant'Ambrogio. *Via De Amicis 32, tel. 02/8056220. 47 rooms with bath. Facilities: restaurant, bar. AE, DC, MC, V.*

Principe e Savoia. The most fashionable and glitzy hotel in Milan is the Principe e Savoia. This is where fashion buyers and expense account businesspeople stay and, if you want all the amenities of an international hotel, you may want to stay here. *Piazza della Repubblica 17, tel. 02/6240. 280 rooms with bath. Facilities: restaurant, bar. AE, DC, V.*

Expensive **Carlton-Senato.** Visitors who intend to spend lots of time shopping in nearby high-fashion streets (Via della Spiga, Via Sant'Andrea, and Via Monte Napoleone) will find this place ideally located. The atmosphere is very light and airy, and there are lots of little touches (such as complimentary chocolates and liqueurs in the rooms) to make up for the rather functional room furnishings. *Via Senato 5, tel. 02/798583. 79 rooms with bath. Facilities: restaurant, bar, private parking. AE, MC, V. Closed Aug.*

Excelsior Gallia. This vast, circa-1930 mock-Victorian hotel is located near the Central Station. Rooms are opulently decorated in a variety of 1930s, '40s, and '80s styles, and bathrooms are big enough to hold a party in. Rooms overlooking the station are more attractive, but noisier. *Piazza Duca d'Aosta 9, tel. 02/6277. 266 rooms with bath. Facilities: sauna, Turkish bath, health club, restaurant. AE, DC, MC, V.*

★ **Grand Hotel et de Milan.** With its marble fireplace, bronze statues, and palms in the lobby, and antique furniture and tapestry curtain pelmets in the bedrooms, the Grand is definitely Milan's most atmospheric hotel, even if the parquet floors do creak and some of the curtains are faded. It's just down from La Scala. *Via Manzoni 29, tel. 02/870757. 89 rooms with bath. Facilities: bar. AE, DC, MC, V.*

Moderate **Centro.** The fragments of a Roman column and bust in the entrance lead you to expect something more old-fashioned and classier than is the case: Rooms are decorated in 1960s modern, with floral wallpaper and bare wood floors. Avoid rooms on the Via Broletto side—cars rumbling over cobblestones sound like thunder. *Via Broletto 46, tel. 02/875232. Facilities: bar, coffee shop. AE, DC, MC, V.*

Gritti. This bright, clean hotel has a cheerful atmosphere. Rooms are adequate, with picturesque views from the upper floors over the tiled roofs to the gilt Madonnina on top of the Duomo, only a few hundred yards away. *Piazza Santa Maria Beltrade (north end of Via Torino), tel. 02/801056. 48 rooms with bath. AE, DC, MC, V.*

King. Within easy walking distance of Leonardo's *Last Supper* at Santa Maria delle Grazie, the King has high ceilings and an imposing mock Louis XV lobby. Built in 1966, it was restored in 1986 in pseudo-antique style, with aptly regal red rugs, armchairs, and bedsteads. *Corso Magenta 19, tel. 02/874432. 48 rooms, 44 with bath. AE, MC, V.*

Inexpensive **Antica Locanda Solferino.** Make reservations well in advance for this one: Rooms are few, and provide excellent value. The building is 19th-century, but rooms were all recently redecorated with delightful peasant-print bedspreads, low bedside lights draped with lace-edge cloths, attractive dried-flower arrangements on the tables, and 19th-century prints on the walls. *Via Castelfidardo 2, tel. 02/6570129. 11 rooms with bath. No credit cards (will possibly accept AE and V in 1989). Closed 10 days mid-Aug., and another 10 at Christmas.*

Pensione Rovello. Accommodations here are simple and spanking clean, with warm terra-cotta tile floors and plain white walls. It's a favorite with younger travelers and American fashion models. Expect to pay in advance. *Via Rovello 18A, tel. 02/873956. 12 rooms, 3 with bath. No credit cards.*

The Arts

The most famous spectacle in Milan is **La Scala Opera,** which presents some of the world's most impressive operatic productions. The house is invariably sold out in advance; ask at your hotel if tickets can be found for you. The opera season begins early in December and ends in May. The concert season runs from May to the end of June and from September through November. There is a brief ballet season in September. Programs are available at principal travel agencies and tourist information offices in Italy and abroad.

Venice

Arriving and Departing

By Plane **Marco Polo International Airport** is situated about six miles (10 kilometers) northeast of the city on the mainland. For flight information, tel. 041/661262.

Between the Airport and Downtown ATVO and ACTV (Venice City Transit) buses make the 25-minute trip in to Piazzale Roma, going through the city's unappealing outlying regions; cost is around 4,000 lire. From Piazzale Roma visitors will most likely have to take a *vaporetto* (water bus) to their hotel. The Cooperative San Marco motor launch is only slightly more costly (11,000 lire), and presents a far more attractive introduction to the city; it drops passengers directly across the lagoon at Piazza San Marco. (It works on a limited schedule in winter.) Land taxis are available, running the same route as do the buses; cost is about 40,000 lire. Water taxis (slick high-power motorboats) are a real rip-off: Negotiate the fare in advance, usually upward of 100,000 lire.

By Train Make sure your train goes all the way to **Santa Lucia** train station in Venice's northeast corner; some trains leave passengers at the Mestre station on the mainland, from where you must connect with a local to Santa Lucia. The EPT-AAST information booth/hotel booking service (open daily 8 AM–8 PM) and the baggage depot in the station are usually festooned with long lines of tourists. Vaporetto landing stages are directly outside the station. *Make sure you know how to get to your hotel before you arrive.* Don't take water taxis, as they are expensive and probably can't take you right to the door of your hotel. By water taxi or vaporetto you'll have to walk some distance anyway. For this reason, try to obtain a map of Venice before you arrive —and take a luggage cart, as porters are hard to find.

By Car You will have to leave your car in the Piazzale Roma garage, on the Tronchetto parking island, or even on the mainland. Some visitors park in Padua or Mestre and then take the train into Venice. From Tronchetto take ACTV bus 17 to Piazzale Roma, where you can get a vaporetto or take Line 34 water bus direct to St. Mark's.

Getting Around

First-time visitors find that getting around Venice presents some unusual problems: the complexity of its layout (the city is made up of more than 100 islands, all linked by bridges); the bewildering unfamiliarity of waterborne transportation; the illogical house numbering system and duplication of street names in its six districts; and the necessity of walking whether you enjoy it or not. It's essential you have a good map showing all street names and water bus routes; buy one at any newsstand.

By Vaporetto ACTV (Venice public transport) water buses run the length of the Grand Canal and circle the city. There are several lines, some of which connect Venice with the major and minor islands in the lagoon; Line 1 is the Grand Canal local. Timetables are posted on all landing stages, where ticket booths are located (open early morning–9 PM). Buy single tickets or books of ten, and count your change carefully; shortchanging is a nasty habit in these parts. Fare is 1,500 lire on most lines, 2,000 lire for the Line 2 express between the railway station, Rialto, San Marco, and the Lido. Stamp your ticket in the machine on the landing stage. A daily tourist ticket costs 8,000 lire. *Vaporetti* run every ten minutes or so during the day; Lines 1, 2, and 5 run every hour between midnight and dawn. Landing stages are clearly marked with name and line number and serve boats going in both directions.

By Water Taxi Known as *motoscafi*, or *taxi*, these are excessively expensive, and the fare system is as complex as Venice's layout. A minimum fare of about 35,000 lire gets you nowhere, and you'll pay three times as much to get from one end of the Grand Canal to the other. *Always agree on the fare before starting out.* To avoid arguments, overcharging, and rip-offs, avoid them altogether.

By Traghetto Few tourists know about the two-man gondolas that ferry people across the Grand Canal at various fixed points. It's the cheapest and shortest gondola ride in Venice, and can save a lot of walking. Fare is 300 lire, which you hand to one of the gondoliers when you get on. Look for "Traghetto" signs.

By Gondola Don't leave Venice without treating yourself to a gondola ride, preferably in the quiet of the evening, when the churning traffic on the canals has died down, the palace windows are illuminated, and the only sounds are the muted splashes of the gondolier's oar. Make sure he understands you want to see the *rii*, or smaller canals, as well as the Grand Canal. They're supposed to charge a fixed minimum rate of about 50,000 lire for 50 minutes, but in practice they ask for 80,000–100,000 lire for a 30- to 40-minute ride. Come to terms with your gondolier *before* stepping into his boat.

On Foot This is the only way of reaching many parts of Venice, so wear comfortable shoes. Invest in a good map naming all streets, and count on getting lost more than once.

Important Addresses and Numbers

Tourist Information The main Venice **AAST Tourist Office** (tel. 041/5226356) is at Calle Ascensione 71C, just off Piazza San Marco, under the arcade in the far left corner opposite the basilica. Open Mon.–Sat., Nov.–Mar., 8:30–1:30; Apr.–Oct., 8:30–7:30. There are EPT-AAST information booths at the Santa Lucia Station (tel. 041/715016); in the bus terminal at Piazzale Roma (tel. 041/5227402), open summer only; at Marco Polo airport; and at Tronchetto parking lot.

Consulates U.K. Campo Santa Maria della Carità 1051, Dorsoduro, tel. 041/5227207. U.S. The nearest U.S. Consulate is in Milan, at Largo Donegani 1, tel. 02/652841.

Emergencies Police: tel. 113. **Ambulance:** tel. 041/5230000. **Doctor:** Try the emergency room at Venice's hospital (tel. 041/5230000), or call the British Consulate (*see* above) and ask for recommendations. **Pharmacies:** *Farmacia Italo-Inglese*, Calle della Mandola (tel. 041/5224837). *International Pharmacy*, Calle Lunga San Marco (tel. 041/5222311). Pharmacies are open weekdays 9–12:30 and 4–7:45; Saturday 9–12:45; Sunday and night service by turns.

Travel Agencies **American Express,** San Moise 1471, tel. 041/5200844. **CIT,** Piazza San Marco 4850, tel. 041/5285480. **Wagons-Lits/Travel,** Piazzetta dei Leoncini 289, tel. 041/5223405.

Guided Tours

Orientation Tours **American Express** (tel. 041/5200844) and **CIT** (tel. 041/5285480) offer two-hour walking tours of the San Marco area, taking in the basilica and the Doge's Palace. Cost is about 25,000 lire.

American Express also has an afternoon walking tour from April to October that ends with a gondola ride and glass-blowing demonstration. Cost is about 30,000 lire. "The Venice Experience" is a 45-minute multivision show about the history of the city, shown daily at **Cinema Centrale** (Piscina di Frezzeria, tel. 041/5228201). Admission 8,000 lire.

Special-Interest Tours American Express, CIT, and other operators offer group gondola rides with serenade. Cost is about 21,000 lire. During July and August free guided tours of St. Mark's basilica are offered by the Patriarchate of Venice; information is available at a desk in the atrium of the church (tel. 041/5200333). Some tours are in English, and there are several daily, except Sunday.

Excursions Don't take organized tours to the islands of Murano, Burano, and/or Torcello. These towns are annoyingly commercial and emphasize glass factory showrooms, pressuring you to buy. You can easily do these islands on your own. American Express offers a bus trip to the Venetian Villas and Padua. Cost is about 50,000 lire, and they run from April to October on Tuesday, Thursday, and weekends. CIT runs an excursion on the Burchiello motor launch along the Brenta Canal, with return by bus.

Personal Guides American Express and CIT can provide guides for walking or gondola tours of Venice, or cars with driver and guide for excursions on the mainland. Pick up a list of licensed guides and their rates from the AAST Information Office in Piazza San Marco (tel. 041/5226356).

Exploring Venice

Venice—La Serenissima, the Most Serene—is disorienting in its complexity, an extraordinary labyrinth of narrow streets and waterways, opening now and again onto some airy square or broad canal. The majority of its magnificent palazzos are slowly crumbling; though this sounds like a recipe for a down-at-the-heels slum, somehow in Venice the shabby, derelict effect is magically transformed into one of supreme beauty and charm rather than horrible urban decay. The place reeks with atmosphere, especially at night when the lights from the vaporetti and the overhead stars pick out the gargoyles and eastern-inspired arches of the centuries-old facades. For hundreds of years Venice was the unrivaled mistress of trade between Europe and the Orient, and the staunch bulwark of Christendom against the tide of Turkish expansion. Though the power and glory of its days as a wealthy city-republic are gone, the art and exotic aura remain.

To really enjoy the city, you will have to come to terms with the crowds, which take over from May through September. Hot and sultry in the summer, Venice is much more welcoming in early spring and late fall. Romantics like it in the winter when prices are much lower, the streets are deserted (well, nearly), and the sea mists impart a haunting melancholy to the *campi* (squares) and canals. Piazza San Marco (St. Mark's Square) is the pulse of Venice, crowded with people and pigeons no matter what time of year. But after joining with the crowds to visit the Basilica di San Marco and the Doge's Palace, strike out on your own and just follow where your feet take you—you won't be disappointed.

Piazza San Marco and the Accademia District

❶ Even the pigeons have to fight for space on **Piazza San Marco,** and pedestrian traffic jams clog the surrounding byways. Despite the crowds and because it is the most famous piazza in Venice, San Marco is the logical starting place of each of our various itineraries. Pick up pamphlets and a copy of *A Guest in Venice,* a free information booklet, at the **AAST Information Office** at Ascensione 71c in the far left corner of Piazza San Marco, opposite the basilica. (Open Nov.–Mar., Mon.–Sat. 8:30–1:30; Apr.–Oct., 8:30–7:30.) The information office is in the wing built by order of Napoleon to complete the much earlier palaces on either side of the square, enclosing it to form what he called "the most beautiful drawing room in all of Europe."

❷ Upstairs is the **Museo Correr,** with eclectic collections of historical objects and a picture gallery of fine 15th-century paintings. *Piazza San Marco, Ala Napoleonica, tel. 041/5225625. Admission: 3,000 lire. Open Mon., Wed., Thurs. 10–4; Fri.–Sat. 10–9 PM; Sun. 9–9; closed Tues.*

❸ The **Basilica di San Marco** (St. Mark's Cathedral) was begun in the 11th century to hold the relics of St. Mark the Evangelist, the city's patron saint, and its richly decorated facade is surmounted by copies of the four famous gilded bronze horses (the originals are in the basilica's upstairs museum). Inside, golden mosaics sheathe walls and domes, lending an extraordinarily exotic aura, half Christian church, half Middle Eastern *souk.* Be sure to see the **Pala d'Oro,** an eye-filling 10th-century altarpiece in gold and silver, studded with precious gems and enamels. From the atrium, climb the steep stairway to the museum: The bronze horses alone are worth the effort. *The Basilica is open from early morning, but tourist visits are allowed Mon.–Sat. 9:30–5:30, Sun. 2:30–5:30. No admission to those wearing shorts or otherwise revealing clothing. Pala d'Oro: Admission: 500 lire. Visible Mon.–Sat. 10–5, Sun. 2–5. Gallery and Museum: Admission: 500 lire. Open daily 10–5.*

❹ Next to St. Mark's is the **Palazzo Ducale** (Doge's Palace), which, during Venice's prime, was the epicenter of the Serene Republic's great empire. More than just a palace, it was a combination White House, Senate, Supreme Court, torture chamber, and prison rolled into one. The exterior is striking: The lower stories consist of two rows of fragile-seeming, almost flimsy, arches, while above rests a massive pink-and-white marble wall, whose solidity is barely interrupted by its six great Gothic windows. The interior is a maze of vast halls, monumental staircases, secret corridors, state apartments, and the sinister prison cells and torture chamber. The palace is filled with frescoes, paintings, carvings, and statuary by some of the Renaissance's greatest artists. Don't miss the famous view from the balcony, overlooking the piazza and St. Mark's Basin, and the church of San Giorgio Maggiore across the lagoon. *Piazzetta San Marco, tel. 041/5224951. Admission: 5,000 lire. Open daily 8:30–7.*

❺ For a pigeon's-eye view of Venice take the elevator up to the top of the **Campanile di San Marco** (St. Mark's bell tower) in Piazza San Marco, a reconstruction of the 1,000-year-old tower that collapsed one morning in 1912, practically without warning. Fifteenth-century clerics found guilty of immoral acts were

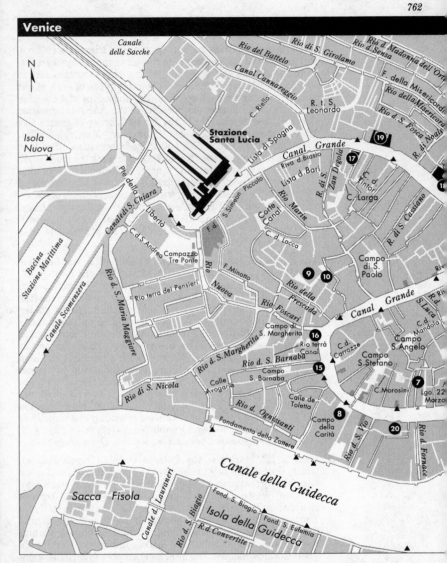

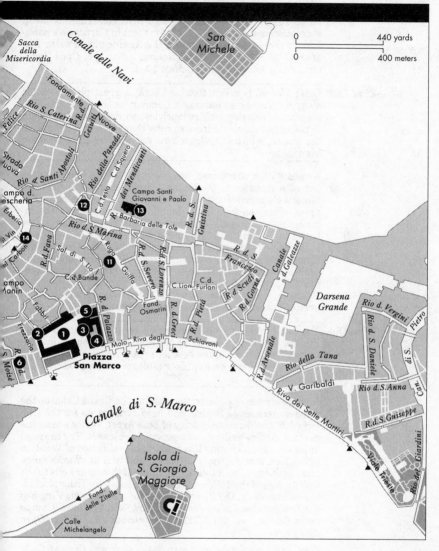

suspended in wooden cages from the tower, sometimes to live on bread and water for as long as a year, sometimes to die of starvation and exposure. (Look for them in Carpaccio's paintings of the square that hang in the Accademia.) *Piazza San Marco, tel. 041/5224064. Admission: 1,500 lire. Open Apr.– Oct., daily 9:30–7:30, Nov.–Mar. 10–4.*

Time Out **Caffè Florian** is a Venetian landmark, a great place to while away an hour or so nursing a Campari or a cappuccino. The pleasure of relaxing amid so much history does not come cheap. A pot of hot chocolate indoors runs about $10, and outside on the piazza, which is really where you want to sit, prices are even higher.

⑥ Armed with a street map, head west out of San Marco (in the opposite direction to the basilica), making your way past **San Moisè's** elaborate Baroque facade and by the American Express office, on into Calle Lunga 22 Marzo, where the inconspicuous **Caravella** restaurant of the Hotel Saturnia (*see* both Dining and Lodging) is one of the city's best. Continue on ⑦ to the church of **Santa Maria del Giglio,** behind the **Gritti Palace Hotel** (also considered tops). Across the bridge behind the church, **Piazzesi** on Campiello Feltrina is famous for its hand-printed paper and desk accessories. In the next little square, **Norelene** (Campo San Maurizio 2606) has stunning hand-printed fabrics in opulent Fortuny designs.

Time Out You must cross yet another bridge to get to Campo Santa Stefano, also known as Campo Morosini, where you can indulge yourself with some of the best ice cream you've ever eaten, at **Paolin,** a tiny bar whose outdoor tables occupy a good chunk of the vast campo.

⑧ Join the stream of pedestrians crossing the Grand Canal on the wooden **Accademia Bridge,** and head straight on for the **Galleria dell'Accademia** (Academy of Fine Arts), Venice's most important picture gallery and a must for art lovers. Try to spend at least an hour viewing this remarkable collection of Venetian art, which is attractively displayed and well lit. Works range from 14th-century Gothic and Bellini's 15th-century oils to the Golden Age of the 16th century, represented by Titian, including his last work, the *Pieta;* Tintoretto, including his *Virgin of the Treasures* and *Miracles of St. Mark;* and Veronese. *Campo della Carità, tel. 041/5222247. Admission: 4,000 lire. Open daily 9–2.*

Once again consulting your map, make your way through Calle Contarini, Calle Toeletta, and Campo San Barnaba to Rio Terra canal, where **Mondonovo** ranks as one of the city's most interesting mask shops (Venetians love masks of all kinds, from gilded lions to painted sun faces and sinister death's heads). Just around the corner, Campo Santa Margherita has a homey feel.

Time Out **Antico Capon** is a good, simple trattoria whose tables spill out onto the square in fair weather. Stop in for a pizza, or just relax outside with a glass of beer. *Campo Santa Margherita.*

⑨ Continue past Campo San Pantalon to Campo San Rocco, just beside the immense church of the Frari. The **Scuoli di San**

Rocco was embellished with more than 50 canvases by Tintoretto in the 1500s; they are an impressive sight, dark paintings aglow with figures hurtling dramatically through space amid flashes of light and color. *The Crucifixion* in the Albergo (the room just off the great hall) is held to be his masterpiece. *Campo di San Rocco. Admission: 5,000 lire. Open daily 9–1 and 3:30–6:30.*

The church of Santa Maria Gloriosa dei Frari (known simply as the **Frari**) is one of Venice's most important churches, a vast soaring Gothic building of brick. As the principal church of the Franciscans, its design is suitably austere to reflect that order's vows of poverty, though paradoxically it contains a number of the most sumptuous pictures in any Venetian church. Chief among these are the magnificent Titian altarpieces, notably the immense *Assumption of the Virgin* over the main altar. Titian was buried here at the ripe old age of 88, the only one of 70,000 plague victims to be given a personal church burial. *Campo dei Frari. Admission: 500-lire donation "for lighting expenses."*

San Zanipolo and the Rialto

Backtracking once again to the Piazza San Marco, go to the arch under the Torre dell'Orologio (Clock Tower) and head off northeast into the **Merceria,** one of Venice's busiest streets and, with the **Frezzeria** and **Calle Fabbri,** part of the shopping area that extends across the Grand Canal into the **Rialto district.** At Campo San Zulian, turn right into Calle Guerra and Calle delle Bande to the graceful white marble church of **Santa Maria Formosa;** it's situated right on a lively square (of the same name) with a few sidewalk cafés and a small vegetable market on weekday mornings.

Use your map to follow Calle Borgoloco into Campo San Marina, where you turn right, crossing the little canal, and take Calle Castelli to **Santa Maria dei Miracoli.** Perfectly proportioned and sheathed in marble, this late-15th-century building embodies all the Classical serenity of the early Renaissance. The interior is decorated with marble reliefs by the church's architect, Pietro Lombardo, and his son Tullio. *Calle Castelli.*

Retrace your steps along Calle Castelli and cross the bridge into Calle delle Erbe, following signs for "SS. Giovanni e Paolo." The massive Dominican church of Santi Giovanni e Paolo—**San Zanipolo,** as it's known in the slurred Venetian dialect—is the twin (and rival) of the Franciscan Frari. The church is a kind of pantheon of the doges (25 are buried here), and contains a wealth of artworks. Outside in the campo stands Verrocchio's equestrian statue of Colleoni, who fought for the Venetian cause in the mid-1400s. *Campo Santi Giovanni e Paolo.*

Cross the canal in front of the church (keeping an eye out to the left for the pop-eyed, tongue-lolling gargoyle at head height), and continue along Calle Larga, crossing a pair of bridges to Campiello Santa Maria Nova. Take Salita San Canciano to Salita San Giovanni Crisostomo to find yourself once again in the mainstream of pedestrians winding their way to the **Rialto Bridge.** Street stalls hung with scarves and gondolier's hats signal that you are entering the heart of Venice's shopping district. Cross over the bridge, and you'll find yourself in the market district. Try to visit the Rialto market when it's in full swing, with fruit and vegetable vendors hawking their wares in a colorful and noisy jumble of sights and sounds. Not far beyond is the fish market, where you'll probably find sea creatures you've never seen before (and possibly won't want to see again). A left turn into Ruga San Giovanni and Ruga del Ravano will bring you face to face with scores of shops: At **La Scialuppa** you'll find hand-carved wooden models of gondolas and their graceful oar locks known as *forcole. Calle Saoneri 2695.*

The Grand Canal

Just off the Piazzetta di San Marco (the little square that abuts St. Mark's) you can catch Vaporetto Line 1 at either the San Marco or San Zaccaria landing stages (on Riva degli Schiavoni), to set off on a boat tour along the **Grand Canal.** Serving as Venice's main thoroughfare, the canal winds in the shape of an "S" for more than two miles (three kilometers) through the heart of the city, past some 200 Gothic-Renaissance palaces. This is the route taken by vaporetti, gondolas, water taxis, mail boats, police boats, fire boats, ambulance boats, barges carrying provisions and building materials, bridal boats, and funeral boats. See it both when traffic is at a peak (preferably from a vantage point such as the Rialto Bridge), and again when it's calm and quiet. Your vaporetto tour will give you an idea of the opulent beauty of its palaces, and a peek into the side streets and tiny canals where the Venetians go about their daily business. *Vaporetto Line 1. Fare: 1,500 lire.*

Here are some of the key buildings that this tour passes. The **Gallerie dell'Accademia,** with its fine collection of 14th- to 18th-century Venetian paintings, that were visited earlier. The **Ca' Rezzonico** was built in 1680 and is now a museum with Venetian paintings and furniture. **Ca' Foscari** is a 15th-century Gothic building that was once the home of Doge Foscari, who was unwillingly deposed and died the following day! The **Fondaco dei Turchi** was an original Byzantium "house-warehouse" of a rich Venetian merchant, but the building has suffered some remodeling in the last 100 years. **Ca' d'Oro** is the most flowery palace on the canal; it now houses the Galleria Francheti. The **Palazzo Vendramin Calergi** is a Renaissance building where Wagner died in 1883. And last but not least, there is the **Peggy Guggenheim Museum,** which usually has excellent exhibitions, but charges an exorbitant entrance fee.

What to See and Do with Children

Take little ones to the **Naval Museum** at the Arsenale to see the ships' models and full-scale boats of all kinds. *Riva San Biagio, tel. 041/5200276. Admission: 1,000 lire. Open weekdays 9–1, Sat. 9–noon.*

Off the Beaten Track

Explore the **Ghetto,** where Venice's Jewish community lived in cramped quarters for many centuries, and visit the **Museo Ebraico** (Jewish Museum, Campo del Ghetto, tel. 041/715359) and the Ghetto's several synagogues. In the same area, go to view the Tintorettos in the Gothic church of the **Madonna dell'Orto** (just off the Strada Nuova).

Visit late heiress Peggy Guggenheim's house and collection of modern art, **Palazzo Venier dei Leoni** on the Grand Canal. *Entrance: Calle San Cristo, tel. 041/5206288. Admission: 5,000 lire, free on Sat. Open Apr.–Oct., Sun., Mon., Wed– Fri.noon–6 PM. Sat. 6–9 PM. Closed Tues.*

Have an ice cream at one of the cafés on the Zattere and watch the big ships steam slowly down the Giudecca Canal.

Explore the island of San Pietro di Castello, at the end of Via Garibaldi. The Renaissance church of **San Pietro** and its tipsy bell tower stand on a grassy square surrounded by workaday canals and boatyards. San Pietro was Venice's cathedral for centuries (St. Mark's was the Doges' ceremonial chapel).

Take Vaporetto Line 20 from Riva degli Schiavoni to visit the Armenian monastery on the island of San Lazzaro degli Armeni, near the Lido. *Tel. 041/5260104. Donation welcome. Open Thurs.–Tues. 3:30–5:10 PM. Closed Wed.*

Shopping

Glass Venetian glass is as famous as the city's gondolas, and almost every shop window displays it. There's a lot of cheap glass for sale; if you want something better, among the top showrooms are **Venini** (Piazzetta dei Leoncini 314), **Pauly** (Calle dell' Ascensione 72, opposite the AAST information office), **Salviati** (Piazza San Marco 78 and 110), **Cenedese** (Piazza San Marco 139), and **Isola** (Campo San Moisè and Mercerie 723). On the island of Murano, where prices are generally no lower than in Venice, **Domus** (Fondamenta dei Vetrai) has a good selection.

Shopping District The main shopping area extends from the Piazza San Marco through the Mercerie and Calle Fabbri toward the Rialto.

Department Stores The **Coin** store (Campo San Bartolomeo) specializes in fashion and accessories. **Standa** has stores on Campo San Luca and Strada Nuova, where you can pick up medium-price goods of all kinds.

Dining

Venetian restaurants are more expensive than those in Florence or Rome; figure on spending about 15,000 to 20,000 lire more for the same sort of meal. Beware of the tourist traps around the Piazza San Marco: prices here are higher than most, and the food isn't up to par. City specialties include *pasta e fagioli*, a thick bean soup; risotto and all kinds of seafood; and the delicious *fegato alla veneziana*, thin strips of liver cooked with onions, served with grilled *polenta*, cornmeal cakes.

For details and price category definitions, *see* Dining in Essential Information.

Very Expensive **Danieli Terrace.** Seafood is the star here: Try the *branzino al* ★ *forno* (baked sea bass) if it's on the menu, otherwise the scampi is almost as good as that at the Gritti. Desserts such as *zabaglione* (a fluffy confection combining egg yolk, sugar, and dry marsala) are fabulous—it's worth bearing this in mind as you order the main meal. Fair weather sees patrons dining on the candlelit terrace, otherwise you'll be seated in the opulent pastel-toned dining room—either way you'll be treated to a view of San Giorgio and the lagoon. *Hotel Danieli, Riva degli Schiavoni 4196, tel. 041/5226480. Jacket and tie. Reservations advised. AE, DC, MC, V.*

Gritti. The dining room of the Gritti Palace hotel is one of Venice's most elegant eating spots. Its flower-filled terrace overlooking the Grand Canal is magical in the evening when the traffic dies down and the white dome of Santa Maria della Salute gleams in the distance. The *risotto con scampi* is delicious as prepared by the Gritti's talented chef, and the sole is well worth trying, too. *Hotel Gritti, Campo Santa Maria del Giglio 2467, tel. 041/5226044. Jacket and tie. Reservations advised. AE, DC, MC, V.*

Expensive **Antico Martini.** This Venetian institution is both chic and discreet, and its menu is made up mostly of Venetian specialties, though there are a few concessions to international palates. The seafood cocktail is first-class, the creamy *tiramesù* (a coffee-flavored sponge cake with soured cream cheese) an admirable end to any meal. There are outdoor tables in the summer, and a softly lit wood-paneled winter dining room. *Campo San Fantin 1983, tel. 041/5224121. Dress: informal. Reservations advised. AE, DC, MC, V. Closed Tues., Wed. lunch, Dec., and Feb.*

★ **La Caravella.** Tiny and intimate, La Caravella is decorated like the dining saloon of an old Venetian sailing ship, with lots of authentic touches. The menu is huge and slightly intimidating, though the highly competent maître d' will advise you well. The *granseola* (crab) is marvelous in any of several versions. *Calle Larga XXII Marzo 2397, tel. 041/5208901. Dress: casual. Reservations essential. AE, DC, MC, V. Closed Wed. from Nov.–Apr.*

Moderate **Da Arturo.** The tiny Da Arturo makes a refreshing change from the numerous seafood restaurants Venetians are so fond of. The cordial proprietor prefers, instead, to offer spaghetti with seasonal vegetables, and meat dishes like the excellent *braciolona di maiale* (pork chop in vinegar). *Calle degli Assassini, tel. 041/5286974. Dress: casual. Reservations essential. No credit cards. Closed Sun., Aug., and the week after Christmas.*

★ **Fiaschetteria Toscana.** This is one of the city's best Moderate restaurants, which is why you'll see so many Venetians in the pleasant upstairs dining room or under the arbor in the square out front. Courteous, cheerful waiters serve such specialties as *rombo* (turbot) with capers, and an exceptionally good *spaghetti con frutti di mare* (pasta with shellfish). *Campo San Giovanni Crisostomo, tel. 041/5285281. Dress: informal. Reservations advised. DC, MC, V. Closed Tues. and first 2 weeks in July.*

Locanda Montin. Though unlikely to win any gastronomic awards, Montin is friendly and fun, and enjoys a considerable reputation. You'll find all sorts of patrons sharing white linen-clothed tables, from the neighborhood locals to Viscount Linley, nephew of England's Queen Elizabeth. The garden out back is used as a flower-filled extension during summer months. At any time of year, try the *fegato alla veneziana* (liver and onions) or the delicious veal escalope. *Fondamenta Eremite 1147, tel. 041/5227151. Dress: informal. Reservations advised. No credit cards. Closed Tues. eve. and Wed.*

Inexpensive **Ai Coristi.** This family-run restaurant near the Teatro La Fen-
★ ice has a wood-beamed indoor dining room and an attractive
summer terrace across the narrow street, candlelit on summer
evenings. Among the specialties are *papardelle alla buranea*
(noodles with scallops), and grilled meat or fish. The salads are
excellent. *Calle della Chiesa, tel. 041/522677. Dress: informal.
Reservations advised. No credit cards. Closed Wed.*

Da Ignazio. A smiling waiter will welcome you to this attractive
little trattoria in the Rialto district, where you'll find a tempting display of fruits and vegetables fresh from the nearby
market. Specialties include *pasta e fagioli* (bean soup) and
seppie (squid) Venetian-style. *Calle dei Saoneri, near San
Polo, tel. 041/5234852. Dress: informal. Dinner reservations
advised. No credit cards. Closed Sat.*

Osteria ai Schiavoni. If it's authentic Venetian atmosphere and
cooking you're after, this is the place. A few steps off Riva degli
Schiavoni near Campo Bandiera e Moro, the Schiavoni has a
few tables outdoors and a dark-paneled dining room. Seafood is
the specialty; try *sardine in saor* (marinated sardines) or fish
risotto, but don't expect large portions. *Calle del Dose 3743,
tel. 041/5226763. Dress: informal. Dinner reservations advised. AE, DC, MC, V. Closed Wed. and last week in Nov.*

Lodging

Venice is made up almost entirely of time-worn buildings, so it
stands to reason that the majority of hotels are in renovated
palaces. Top hotels may still contain palatial trappings, though
some Cinderella-type rooms may be small and dowdy. Rooms in
Moderate and Inexpensive hotels are often cramped and spartanly decorated, with thin walls, and little or no lounging
space. Air-conditioning is essential for survival in summer
heat; many hotels charge a hefty supplement for it. The main
tourist season runs from mid-March through October, December 20 to New Year's Day, and the two-week Carnival period in
mid-February. Make reservations well in advance at all times,
but especially so for these periods.

Hotel rates are higher than those in Rome or Florence, but you
can save considerably on low-season rates. For details and price
category definitions, *see* Lodging in Essential Information.

Very Expensive **Cipriani.** A sybaritic oasis of stunningly decorated rooms and
suites, the Cipriani is located across St. Mark's Basin on the island of Giudecca (pronounced jew-dekka), offering a panorama
of romantic views of San Giorgio Maggiore and the entire lagoon. The hotel launch whisks guests back and forth to the
Piazza San Marco at any hour of day or night. Cooking courses
and fitness programs are offered as special programs to occupy
the guests. Then, for sheer dining pleasure, there is the excellent Cipriani restaurant. Some rooms have pretty garden
patios. *Guidecca 10, tel. 041/5207744. 98 rooms with bath. Facilities: pool, gardens, tennis, health club. AE, DC, MC, V.
Closed Nov. 11–Feb. 26.*

Danieli. A 15th-century palazzo is the hub of this exceptionally
gracious and opulent hotel, surrounded by a cluster of modern,
balconied wings. Sumptuous Venetian decor and atmosphere
predominates, though some lower-price rooms can be drab. Celebrities love the Danieli, and it's an especial favorite of
English-speaking visitors. The restaurant (*see* Dining) and bar

are swank personified, and the terrace has a fantastic view of St. Mark's Basin. *Riva degli Schiavoni 4196, tel. 041/5226480. 230 rooms with bath. AE, DC, MC, V.*

★ **Gritti Palace.** The atmosphere of an aristocratic private home is what the management is after here, and they succeed beautifully. Fresh-cut flowers, fine antiques, sumptuous appointments, and Old World service make this a terrific choice for anyone who wants to be totally pampered. The dining terrace overlooking the Grand Canal is best in the evening when boat traffic dies down. *Campo Santa Maria del Giglio 2467, tel. 041/ 794611. 98 rooms with bath. AE, DC, MC, V.*

Expensive **Londra Palace.** You get the obligatory view of San Giorgio and St. Mark's Basin at this distinguished hotel whose rooms are decorated in dark paisley prints, with sophisticated touches such as canopied beds. Do Leoni restaurant serves creative cuisine (try the avocado with scampi), the piano bar is open late, and a jogging map thoughtfully provided by the management will help you work off the previous night's excesses. *Riva degli Schiavoni 4171, tel. 041/5200533. 69 rooms with bath. Facilities: terrace solarium. AE, DC, MC, V.*

★ **Metropole.** With a wonderful decadence, guests can step from their water taxi or gondola nearly into the lobby of this small hotel just five minutes from the Piazza San Marco. Many rooms have a view of the lagoon, but some are very small. Ask for one of the quiet spacious rooms on the garden (room 141 is the nicest). *Riva degli Schiavoni 4149, tel. 041/5205044. 65 rooms with bath. Facilities: grill room. AE, DC, MC, V.*

Saturnia Internazionale. Beamed ceilings, damask-hung walls, and authentic Venetian decor impart real character and charm to the solid comfort of the Saturnia's rooms and salons. Many rooms, among them 80, 82, and 84, have been redecorated in chic style and endowed with glamorous bathrooms. The historic palace-hotel is centrally located near Piazza San Marco. *Calle Larga XXII Marzo 2398, tel. 041/5208377. 97 rooms with bath. Facilities: 2 restaurants, bar. AE, DC, MC, V.*

Moderate **Flora.** Quietly located near San Moisè, the Flora is unusual for ★ a Moderate hotel in that it has plenty of sitting rooms and a pretty garden scattered about with wrought-iron café tables. Rooms have Venetian period decor and some are very elegant; most bathrooms are tiny. The Art Deco staircase is a work of art. *Calle Bergamaschi 2283 (off Calle Larga XXII Marzo), tel. 041/5205844. 44 rooms with bath. AE, DC, MC, V. Closed mid-Nov.–Jan.*

La Residenza. A Gothic palace makes a delightful setting for this charming hotel, conveniently close to both San Marco and the San Zaccaria landing stage. The comfortable breakfast room is furnished with some antique touches, and rooms on the lower floor are especially good. Make reservations well in advance. *Campo Bandiera e Moro 3608, tel. 041/5285315. 19 rooms, some with bath. AE, DC, MC, V. Closed 2nd week Jan– mid-Feb, mid-Nov.–2nd week Dec.*

Scandinavia. Despite its curiously un-Italian name, this hotel indulges heavily in traditional—and somewhat overpowering —Venetian decor, with cut-glass chandeliers and dizzying combinations of damask patterns on walls, floor, sofas, and chairs. The entrance is at the top of a very steep staircase, just off the lively Campo Santa Maria Formosa (near the San Zaccaria landing stage). *Campo Santa Maria Formosa 5240, tel. 041/ 5223507. 27 rooms, 17 with bath. AE, V.*

Inexpensive **Accademia.** There's plenty of atmosphere and a touch of the ro-
★ mantic in this delightful pension in a 17th-century villa. Rooms
are comfortable and nicely furnished, as are the sitting rooms
on the ground floor. Many rooms overlook the pretty gardens,
where you can sit in warm weather. Lots of regulars come back
year after year. *Fondamenta Bollani 1058, Dorsoduro, tel.
041/710188. 26 rooms, some with bath. DC, MC, V.*

Galleria. Guests won't find much in the way of luxury here, but
low prices, friendly staff (definitely no English spoken, but lots
of smiles and nods), and a fine location hard by the Accademia
Bridge make this a strong favorite. Ask for a room overlooking
the Grand Canal—the view is one of the best in Venice. *Accademia 878–A, Dorsoduro, tel. 041/704172. 10 rooms, most
with bath. No credit cards.*

San Stefano. This is a hotel in miniature, from the tiny reception area to the minuscule courtyard and breakfast room; even
the elevator is skinny. Rooms are well-furnished in Venetian
style, with optional air-conditioning and TV. All in all, it's an
excellent value, and centrally located, too. *Campo San Stefano
2957, tel. 041/5200166. 14 rooms, most with bath. No credit
cards.*

The Arts

For a program of events, pick up the free *Guest in Venice* booklet at the AAST tourist office in Piazza San Marco, or at most
hotel desks. Your hotel may also be able to get you tickets for
some events.

Concerts A **Vivaldi Festival** is held in September, and concerts are held
year-round in the city's churches; contact the **Kele e Teo Agency**
(Piazza San Marco 4930, tel. 041/5208722), which supplies tickets for many of the city's musical events.

Opera The opera season at **Teatro La Fenice** (Campo San Fantin, tel.
041/5210161) runs from December to May. The box office is
open September to July, daily 9:30–noon and 4–6.

Entertainment and Nightlife

You won't find much in the way of organized nightlife in this
city, though there is one nightclub, **Martini** (tel. 041/5224121),
near Teatro La Fenice. The bars of the top hotels stay open as
long as their customers keep on drinking, and there's an
attractive bar, **Al Cherubim** (Calle Sant'Antonin, just off
Salizzada San Luca), where young Venetians and tourists socialize over drinks.

Campania

Campania (made up of Naples and its environs) is where most
people's preconceived ideas of Italy become a reality. You'll
find lots of sun, good food that relies heavily on tomatoes and
mozzarella, acres of classical ruins, and gorgeous scenery. The
exuberance of the locals doesn't leave much room for efficient
organization, however, and you may have to revise your concept of real time; here minutes dilate into hours at the drop of a
hat.

Once a city that rivaled Paris as a brilliant and refined cultural capital, Naples is afflicted by acute urban decay and chronic delinquency. You need patience, stamina, and a healthy dose of caution to visit Naples on your own, but it's worth it for those who have a sense of adventure and the capacity to discern the enormous riches the city has accumulated in its 2,000-year existence.

On the other hand, if you want the fun without the hassle, head for Sorrento, Capri, and the Amalfi coast, legendary haunts of the sirens who tried to lure Odysseus off course. Sorrento is touristy but has some fine old hotels and beautiful views; it's a good base for a leisurely excursion to Pompeii. Capri is a pint-size paradise, though sometimes too crowded for comfort, while the Amalfi coast has some enchanting towns and spectacular scenery.

Getting Around

By Plane There are several daily flights between Rome and Naples's **Capodichino Airport** (tel. 081/7803042), four miles (seven kilometers) north of the downtown area. During the summer months there's a direct helicopter service between Capodichino and Capri; for information, phone 081/8370644.

By Train A great number of trains run between Rome and Naples every day; Intercity and Rapido trains make the journey in less than two hours. There are several stations in Naples, and a network of suburban trains connects the city with several points of interest in Campania. The **Central Station** is at Piazza Garibaldi (tel. 081/264644). Naples has a **Metropolitana** (subway), but it's old, and trains are infrequent; fare is 600 lire.

By Bus For bus information, call **SITA** (tel. 081/5522176) or the **Naples Transport Board** (tel. 081/5540507).

By Car The Naples–Pompeii–Salerno toll road has exits at Ercolano (Herculaneum) and Pompeii, and connects with the tortuous coastal road to Sorrento and the Amalfi coast at the Castellamare exit. Driving within Naples is not recommended: Window smashing and robbery are not uncommon.

By Boat Boats and hydrofoils for the islands, the Sorrento peninsula, and the Amalfi coast leave from the Molo Beverello, in Naples's Piazza Municipio. **Caremar** (tel. 081/5513882) has frequent passenger and car ferry service, and operates hydrofoils as well. **Alilauro** (tel. 081/684288) and **SNAV** (tel. 081/660444) provide hydrofoil service.

Guided Tours

Aside from the one-, two-, or three-day guided tours of the area departing from Rome, offered by **American Express** (tel. 06/67641), **CIT** (tel. 06/47941), **Appian Line** (tel. 06/464151) and other operators, **CIT** in Naples (Piazza Municipio 70, tel. 081/325426) has a wide range of half-day and all-day tours on the mainland and to the islands. Similar tours are offered by **Cima Tours** (Piazza Garibaldi 114, tel. 081/220646), **Tourcar** (Piazza Matteotti 1, tel. 081/323310), and **Aritur** (Piazza Trieste e Trento 7, tel. 081/400487).

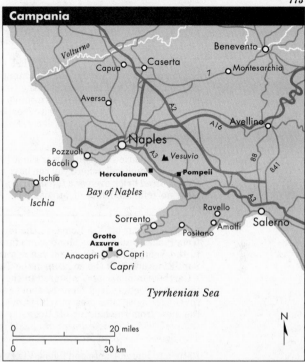

Campania

Benevento
Montesarchia
Capua
Caserta
Volturno
Aversa
Avellino
Naples
Pozzuoli
Vesuvio
Bácoli
Herculaneum
Pompeii
Ischia
Bay of Naples
Ischia
Ravello
Sorrento
Amalfi
Salerno
Positano
Grotto
Azzurra
Anacapri
Capri
Capri
Tyrrhenian Sea
N
0   20 miles
0   30 km

Tourist Information

Capri. Piazza Umberto I 19, tel. 081/8370686.
Naples. EPT Information Offices at Via Partenope 10, tel. 081/
406289; Central Station, tel. 081/268779; Mergellina Station,
tel. 081/7612102; and Capodichino Airport, tel. 081/7805761.
AAST Information Office, Piazza del Gesù, tel. 081/5523328.
Sorrento. Via De Maio 35, tel. 081/8782104.

Exploring

Naples Founded by the Greeks, **Naples** became a playground of the Romans, and was ruled thereafter by a succession of foreign
dynasties, all of which left traces of their cultures in the city
and its environs. The most splendid of these rulers were the
Bourbons, who were responsible for much of what you will
want to see in Naples, starting with the 17th-century **Palazzo
Reale** (Royal Palace), still furnished in the lavish Baroque style
that suited them so well. *Piazza Plebiscito, tel. 081/413888. Admission: 3,000 lire. Open Mon.–Sat. 9–2, Sun. 9–1.*

Across the way, the massive stone **Castel Nuovo** was built by
the city's Aragon rulers in the 13th century; it's not open to the
public. Walk up Via Toledo, keeping an eye on the antics of the
Neapolitans, whose daily lives are fraught with theatrical ges-
tures and fiery speeches: They all seem to be unselfconscious
actors in their Human Comedy.

Time Out Stop in at **Caflish,** a historic café that has recently added a good fast-food counter, and try a *sfogliatella*, a delicious, clam-shaped Neapolitan pastry. *Via Toledo 253.*

Turn right onto the huge and busy Via Roma and make a detour to the right to see the oddly faceted stone facade and elaborate Baroque interior of the church of the **Gesù** and, directly opposite, the church of **Santa Chiara,** built in the early 1300s in Provençal Gothic style. A favorite Neapolitan song celebrates the quiet beauty of its cloister, decorated in delicate floral tiles. *Via Benedetto Croce.*

Time Out For an authentic Neapolitan pizza in a 100% genuine pizzeria, stop in at **Lombardi,** where you can have a classic pizza made in a wood-fired brick oven or a full meal in a tiny, crowded setting with no frills and lots of atmosphere. *Via Benedetto Croce 59.*

Another detour off Via Roma, to the left this time, takes you from **Piazza Dante** to the Montesanto funicular, which ascends to the Vomero hill, where you can see the bastions of **Castel Sant'Elmo** and visit the museum in the **Certosa di San Martino,** a Carthusian monastery restored in the 17th century. It contains an eclectic collection of Neapolitan landscape paintings, royal carriages, and *presepi* (Christmas crèches). Check out the view from the balcony off Room 25. *Certosa di San Martino, tel. 081/377005. Admission: 3,000 lire. Open Tues.–Sat. 9–2, Sun. 9–1; closed Mon.*

Return to Piazza Dante and follow Via Pessina to (an extension of Via Roma) the **Museo Archeologico Nazionale.** Dusty and unkempt, the museum undergoes perpetual renovations, but it holds one of the world's great collections of antiquities. Greek and Roman sculptures, vividly colored mosaics, countless objects from Pompeii and Herculaneum, and an equestrian statue of Nerva are all worth seeing. *Piazza Museo, tel. 081/440166. Admission: 4,000 lire. Open Tues.–Sat. 9–2, Sun. 9–1; closed Mon.*

About a mile north on the same road (take a bus or a taxi), you'll come to the **Museo di Capodimonte,** housed in an 18th-century palace built by Bourbon king Charles III, and surrounded by a vast park that must have been lovely when it was better cared for. In the picture gallery are some fine Renaissance paintings; climb the stairs to the terrace for a magnificent view of Naples and the bay. Downstairs you can visit the State Apartments and see the extensive collection of porcelain, much of it produced in the Bourbons' own factory right here on the grounds. *Parco di Capodimonte, tel. 081/7410881. Admission: 4,000 lire. Tues.–Sat. 9–2, Sun. 9–1; closed Mon.*

Herculaneum **Herculaneum** (Ercolano) lies nine miles (14 kilometers) southeast of Naples. Reputed to have been founded by the legendary Hercules, the elite Roman resort was devastated by the same volcanic eruption that deluged Pompeii in AD 79. Remarkably, the eruption claimed few lives at Herculaneum, but the slow-moving mud slide embalmed the entire town by covering it with a 35-foot (11-meter) deep blanket of volcanic ash and ooze. While that may have been unfortunate for Herculaneum's home owners, it was fortunate for us. Herculaneum has been marvellously preserved for nearly two milleniums! *Orso Er-*

colano, tel. 081/7390963. Admission: 4,000 lire. Open Tues.–
Sun. from 9 to an hour before sunset; closed Mon.

Pompeii   The people of **Pompeii,** a larger community five miles (eight kilometers) farther to the east, did not fare so well. An estimated 2,000 of them perished on that fateful August day. The ancient city of Pompeii was much larger than Herculaneum, and excavations have progressed to a much greater extent (though the remains are not as well preserved, due to some 18th-century scavenging for museum-quality artworks, most of which you are able to see at Naples's Museo Archeologico Nazionale). This prosperous Roman city had an extensive forum, lavish baths and temples, and patrician villas richly decorated with frescoes. It's worth buying a detailed guide of the site in order to give meaning and understanding to the ruins and their importance. Be sure to see the **Villa dei Misteri,** whose frescoes are in mint condition. Perhaps that is a slight exaggeration, but the paintings are so rich with detail and depth of color that one finds it difficult to believe that they are 1,900 years old. Look at how the women in the frescoes impose sensuality, how the depictions of sacrifices give spirit, how the scenes of flagellation give torment, how the wedding of Dionysus and Ariadne gives ribald joy, and how the dressing of the bride inspires anticipation. Have lots of small change handy to tip the guards at the more important houses so they will unlock the gates for you. *Pompeii Scavi, tel. 081/8621181. Admission: 5,000 lire. Open Tues.–Sun. from 9 to an hour before sunset; closed Mon.*

Sorrento   Continuing south, another seven miles (10 kilometers) or so brings you to **Sorrento,** in the not-too-distant past a small, genteel resort for a fashionable elite. Now the town has spread out along the crest of its fabled cliffs. Once this was an area full of secret haunts for the few tourists who came for the beauty of this coastline. Now, it has been "discovered" and the secret haunts are the playground for package tours. In Sorrento's case, however, the change is not as grim as it sounds, since nothing can dim the delights of the marvelous climate and view of the Bay of Naples. For the best views go to the **Villa Comunale,** near the old church of **San Francesco** (in itself worth a visit), or to the terrace behind the **Museo Correale.** The museum, an attractive 18th-century villa, houses an interesting collection of decorative arts (furniture, china, and so on), and paintings of the Neapolitan school. *Via Capasso, tel. 081/8780000. Open Oct.–Jan. and Mar., Mon., Wed.–Sat. 9:30–12:30 and 3–5, Sun. 9:30–12:30; Apr.–Sept., Mon., Wed.–Sat. 9:30–12:30 and 4–7, Sun. 9:30–12:30; closed Tues. and Feb.*

Capri   Sorrento makes a convenient jumping-off spot for a boat trip to **Capri.** No matter how many day-trippers crowd onto the island, no matter how touristy certain sections have become, Capri remains one of Italy's loveliest places. Incoming visitors disembark at Marina Grande, from where you can take some time out for an excursion to the **Grotta Azzurra** (Blue Grotto). Be warned that this must rank as one of the country's all-time great rip-offs: Motorboat, rowboat, and grotto admissions are charged separately, and if there's a line of boats waiting, you'll have little time to enjoy the grotto's marvelous colors. At Marina Grande you can also embark on an excursion boat around the island.

A cog railway or bus service takes you up to the town of Capri, where you can stroll through the **Piazzetta,** a choice place to watch the action and window-shop expensive boutiques on your way to the **Gardens of Augustus,** which have gorgeous views. The town of Capri is deliberately commercial and self-consciously picturesque. To get away from the crowds, hike to **Villa Jovis,** one of the many villas that Roman emperor Tiberius built on the island, at the end of a lane that climbs steeply up-hill. The walk takes about 45 minutes, with pretty views all the way and a final spectacular vista of the entire Bay of Naples and part of the Gulf of Salerno. *Via Tiberio. Admission: 2,000 lire. Open Tues.–Sun. from 9 to one hour before sunset; closed Mon.*

Or take the bus or a jaunty open taxi to **Anacapri** and look for the little church of **San Michele,** where a magnificent hand-painted majolica tile floor shows you an 18th-century vision of the Garden of Eden. *Off Via Orlandi.*

From Piazza della Vittoria, picturesque Via Capodimonte leads to **Villa San Michele,** charming former home of Swedish scientist-author Axel Munthe, now open to the public. *Via Axel Munthe. Admission: 2,000 lire. Open daily Apr.–Sept. 9–6; Oct.–Mar., 10–3.*

Amalfi and Positano From Sorrento, the coastal drive down to the resort town of **Amalfi** provides some of the most dramatic and beautiful scenery you'll find in all Italy. Midway along, **Positano's** jumble of pastel houses, topped by whitewashed cupolas, cling to the mountainside above the sea. The town—the prettiest along this stretch of coast—attracts a sophisticated group of visitors and summer residents who find that its relaxed and friendly at-mosphere more than compensates for the sheer effort of moving about this exhaustingly vertical town, most of whose streets are stairways. This former fishing village has now opted for the more regular and lucrative rewards of tourism and commercialized fashion. Practically every other shop is a boutique displaying locally made casual wear. The beach is the town's main focal point, with a little promenade and a multi-tude of café-restaurants.

Amalfi itself is a charming maze of covered alleys and narrow byways straggling up the steep mountainside. The piazza just below the cathedral forms the town's heart—a colorful assort-ment of pottery stalls, cafés, and postcard shops grouped around a venerable old fountain.

Ravello Do not miss **Ravello,** ten miles (16 kilometers) north of Amalfi. Ravello is not actually on the coast, but on a high mountain bluff overlooking the sea. The road up to the village is a series of switchbacks, and the village itself clings precariously on the mountain spur. The village flourished in the 13th century and then fell into tranquility, unchanging for the past six centuries. The center of the town is piazza **Vescovada** with its cathedral, founded in 1087 but renovated in the 18th century. Note its fine bronze 12th-century door, and, just inside on the left, the pul-pit with mosaics telling the story of Jonah and the whale. Look to the right as well and you will see another pulpit with fantas-tic carved animals.

To the right of the cathedral is the entrance to the 11th-century **Villa Rufolo.** Using the fact that Wagner once stayed in Ravello, there is a Wagner festival every summer on the villa's garden terrace. There is a moorish cloister with interlacing pointed arches, beautiful gardens, an 11th-century tower, and a belvedere with a fine view of the coast.

Across the square from the cathedral is a lovely walk leading to the Villa Cimbrone. At the entrance to the villa complex is a small cloister, looking medieval but actually built in 1917, with two bas-reliefs: one representing nine Norman warriors, the other illustrating the seven deadly sins. Then, the long avenue leads through peaceful gardens scattered with grottoes, small temples and statues emphasizing a contemplative silence, to a belvedere and the infinite terrace where, on a clear day, the view stretches beyond the horizon resting on the Mediterranean Sea.

Dining and Lodging

For details and price category definitions, *see* Dining and Lodging in Essential Information.

Amalfi **La Caravella.** Tucked away under some arches lining the coast
Dining road, the Caravella has a nondescript entrance but pleasant interior decorated in a medley of colors and paintings of old Amalfi. It's small and intimate, and proprietor Antonio describes the cuisine as *"sfiziosa"* (taste-tempting). Specialties include *scialatelli* (homemade pasta with shellfish sauce) and *pesce al limone* (fresh fish with lemon sauce). *Via M. Camera 12, tel. 089/871029. Dress: informal. Reservations advised. AE, MC, V. Closed Tues. and Feb. 11–28. Moderate.*

Lodging **Santa Caterina.** A large mansion perched above terraced and
★ flowered hillsides on the coast road just outside Amalfi proper, the Santa Caterina is one of the best hotels on the entire coast. Rooms are tastefully decorated, and most have small terraces or balconies with great views. There are lounges and terraces for relaxing, and an elevator whisks guests down to the seaside saltwater pool, bar, and swimming area. Amid lemon and orange groves, there are two romantic villa annexes. Some rooms and suites are in the Very Expensive category. *Strada Amalfitana, tel. 089/871012. 54 rooms with bath. Facilities: restaurant, bar, pool, swimming area, and beach bar. AE, DC, MC, V. Expensive.*

Capri **La Capannina.** Only a few steps away from Capri's social cen-
Dining ter, the Piazzetta, La Capannina has a delightful vine-hung courtyard for summer dining, and a reputation as one of the island's best eating places. Antipasto features fried ravioli and eggplant stuffed with ricotta, and house specialties include chicken, scaloppine, and a refreshing, homemade lemon liqueur. *Via Botteghe 14, tel. 081/8370732. Dress: informal. Reservations advised. AE, V. Closed Wed. (except during Aug.), and Nov.–mid-Mar. Moderate.*

Da Gemma. One of Capri's favorite places for a homey atmosphere and a good meal, Da Gemma features spaghetti *con cozze* or *vongole* (with mussels or clams) and *fritto misto* (mixed fish fry). If you're budgeting, don't order fish that you pay for by weight; it's always expensive. You can have pizza as a starter in the evening. *Via Madre Serafina 6, tel. 081/8370461. Dress: casual. Reservations advised. AE, DC, MC, V. Closed Mon. and Nov.–Dec. 10. Moderate.*

★ **Pizzeria Aurora.** This lively, central spot is popular with the island's younger set. There is a tempting selection of *antipasti,* and the *pizza cosacca* is a tasty combination of parmesan cheese, tomato, and basil. *Via Fuorlovado 18, tel. 081/8370181. Dress: casual. Reservations not accepted. No credit cards. Closed Nov.–Apr. Moderate.*

Lodging **Quisisana.** One of Italy's poshest hotels is sited right in the center of the town of Capri. Rooms are spacious, and many have arcaded balconies with views of the sea; decor is traditional or contemporary, with some antique accents. From the small terrace at the entrance you can watch all of Capri go by, but the enclosed garden and pool in the back are perfect for getting away from it all. The bar and restaurant are casual in a terribly elegant way. *Via Camerelle 2, tel. 081/8370788. 143 rooms with bath. Facilities: Restaurant, pool. AE, DC, MC, V. Closed Nov.–Feb. Very Expensive.*

★ **Scalinatella.** *Scalinatella* means little stairway, and that's how this hotel is built, on terraces overlooking its own gardens and pool, the Certosa's pretty little domes, and the sea. Bedrooms are intimate, with alcoves and fresh, bright colors. This small hotel has an ambience of sophisticated luxury at rates that are not astronomical. *Via Tragara 8, tel. 081/8370633. 28 rooms with bath. Facilities: pool, bar. No credit cards. Closed Nov.–mid-Mar. Expensive.*

Flora. This one has the look of a genteel resort hotel, with pretty garden furniture, potted plants, and terraces. It's decorated in the sparse but sparkling local style. *Via Serena 26, tel. 081/8370211. 25 rooms with bath. AE, DC, MC, V. Closed Nov.–Mar. Moderate.*

Naples **La Sacrestia.** This lovely restaurant is in an elevated position,
Dining above Mergellina, with a fine view and a delightful summer terrace. The menu offers traditional Neapolitan cuisine; among the specialties are *vermicelli al sughetto di gamberi* (pasta with shrimp sauce) and *spigola* (sea bass), either steamed or baked. *Via Orazio 116, tel. 081/664186. Jacket and tie. Reservations required. AE, V. Sept.–June closed Wed; July closed Sun.; closed all of Aug. Expensive.*

★ **Ciro a Santa Brigida.** Centrally located off Via Toledo near the Castel Nuovo, this no-frills place is a favorite with businessmen, artists, and journalists. Tables are arranged on two levels, and the decor is classic trattoria. This is the place to try traditional Neapolitan *sartù di riso* (a rich rice dish with meat and peas) and *melanzane* (eggplant) *alla parmigiana* or *scaloppe alla Ciro*, with prosciutto and mozzarella. There's pizza, too. *Via Santa Brigida 71, tel. 081/324072. Dress: informal. Reservations advised. No credit cards. Closed Sun., Aug. Moderate.*

La Bersagliera. This restaurant has been making tourists happy for years, with a great location on the Santa Lucia waterfront, cheerful waiters, mandolin music, and good spaghetti *alla disgraziata* (with tomatoes, capers, and black olives) and *mozzarella in carrozza* (cheese fried in batter). *Borgo Marinaro 10, tel. 081/415692. Dress: informal. Reservations advised. No credit cards. Closed Tues. Moderate.*

Lodging **Excelsior.** Splendidly located on the shore drive, the Excelsior has views of the bay from its front rooms. The spacious bedrooms are well-furnished in informal floral prints and Oriental carpets, and have a comfortable, traditional air. The salons are more formal, with chandeliers and wall paintings, and the excellent Casanova restaurant is elegant. *Via Partenope 48, tel.*

081/417111. 138 rooms with bath. Facilities: restaurant, bar, sauna. AE, DC, MC, V. Very Expensive.

★ **Jolly Ambassador.** This hotel is the only skyscraper on the downtown skyline, and its rooms and roof restaurant have wonderful views of Naples and the bay. It's furnished in dark brown, beige, and white in the functional, modern style typical of this reliable chain, which promises comfort and efficiency in a city where these are scarce commodities. *Via Medina 70, tel. 081/416000. 251 rooms with bath. Facilities: restaurant. AE, DC, MC, V. Expensive.*

Palace. The Palace is an older hotel on the Central Station square, handy to all types of transportation and overlooking a lively crossroads of Neapolitan life—rooms can be noisy. It's best considered an adequate overnight in a very convenient location. *Piazza Garibaldi 9, tel. 081/267044. 100 rooms, half with bath or shower. Facilities: bar, restaurant. AE, DC, MC, V. Moderate.*

Positano

Dining

Capurale. Among all the popular restaurants on the beach promenade, Capurale (just around the corner) has the best food and lowest prices. Tables are set under vines on a breezy sidewalk in the summer, upstairs and indoors in winter. *Spaghetti con melanzane* (with eggplant) and *crèpes al formaggio* (cheese-filled crèpes) are good choices here. *Via Marina, tel. 089/875374. Dress: informal. Reservations advised for outdoor tables. No credit cards. Closed mid-Dec.–Mar. Moderate.*

Lodging

Palazzo Murat. The location is perfect, in the heart of town, near the beachside promenade, but set within a walled garden. The old wing is a historic palazzo, with tall windows and wrought-iron balconies; the newer wing is a whitewashed Mediterranean building with arches and terraces. Guests can relax in antique-strewn lounges, or on the charming vine-draped patio. *Via dei Mulini, tel. 089/875177. 28 rooms with bath. Facilities: bar, garden. No credit cards. Closed mid-Oct.–Mar. Moderate.*

Il San Pietro di Positano. This is quite possibly one of the world's most attractive hotels. Situated on the side of a cliff, the views over the Mediterranean are magnificent. The decor of the hotel is eclectic with unusual antiques and, everywhere, hanging bougainvillea. The furnishings are perfectly arranged to give an openness and to create an easy elegance. The guest rooms are decorated with an eye to detail, and even the smallest rooms are a delight. Strewn with flowers, the light open dining room offers some of the best Italian cuisine on the Amalfi coast. The only limitation to San Pietro is its small, pebbly beach. *Via Laurito 2, tel. 089/875454. 55 rooms with bath. Facilities: restaurant, pool, tennis. AE, DC, V. Very Expensive.*

Le Sireneuse. The most conservative, fashionable hotel in Positano is this converted 18th-century villa that has been in the same family for eight generations. The hotel rambles alongside the hill about 200 feet above Positano's harbor. Most of the bedrooms face the sea—these are the best. Because of the hotel's location, the dining room is like a long, closed-in terrace overlooking the village of Positano—a magnificent view. The cuisine, however, is best described as acceptable, rather than exceptional. *Via C. Columbo 30, tel. 089/875454. 65 rooms with bath. Facilities: restaurant, pool, sauna, whirlpool. AE, DC, V. Very Expensive.*

Ravello
Lodging

Hotel Palumbo. Of all the hotels on the Amalfi coast, the Hotel Palumbo is the most genteel—a refined 12th-century retreat for the Renaissance man. Some of the bedrooms do tend to be small, but they are beautifully furnished and full of character. Also, the rooms in the main house facing the sea are the choice ones—and the more expensive. The lounge area is filled with the owner's antiques and, with the greatest of ease, guests quickly come to view the Hotel Palumbo as their private palazzo. Unfortunately, the food in the dining room tends to be bland, prepared more for English than Italian taste buds. *Via Toro 28, tel. 089/857244. 25 rooms with bath. Facilities: restaurant, bar, garden. AE, DC, MC, V. Very Expensive.*

Sorrento
Dining

Kursaal. Occupying a 19th-century villa perched on the edge of the vine-covered gorge of the Mulini, Kursaal is an elegant veranda restaurant. Try the *spaghetti del vallone* (with a tangy sauce) or the *pesce al cartoccio* (fish baked in parchment). *Via Fuorimura 7, tel. 081/8781216. Dress: informal. Reservations advised. AE, DC, MC, V. Closed Mon. Moderate.*

★ **Parrucchiano.** One of the town's best and oldest, Parrucchiano features greenhouse-type dining rooms dripping with vines and dotted with plants. Among the antipasti, try the *panzarotti* (pastry crust filled with mozzarella and tomato); as a main course, a good choice would be *scalloppe alla sorrentina*, again with mozzarella and tomato. *Corso Italia 71, tel. 081/8781321. Dress: informal. Reservations advised. AE, V. Closed Wed. from Nov.–May. Moderate.*

Zi'Ntonio. Zi'Ntonio is a cheerful sort of place, with a fresh, country-inn look. The specialties of the house are a classic *spaghetti al pomodoro* (with fresh tomato sauce and basil), fish (which can be pricey), and *melanzane* (eggplant) *alla parmigiana. Via de Maio 11, tel. 081/8781623. Dress: informal. Reservations advised. AE, DC, MC, V. Closed Thurs. Moderate.*

Lodging

Cocumella. In a lovely cliffside garden in a quiet residential area just outside Sorrento, this historic old villa (it features a 17th-century chapel) has been totally renovated for comfort. Furnishings are a tasteful blend of antique and modern: There are vaulted ceilings and archways, a dining veranda, and stunning tiled floors. Cocumella has an exclusive, elegant atmosphere, without being stuffy. *Via Cocumella 7, tel. 081/8782933. 60 rooms with bath. Facilities: pool, tennis, restaurant. AE, DC, MC. Expensive.*

Excelsior Vittoria. In the heart of Sorrento, but removed from the main square by an arbored walk, the Excelsior Vittoria is right on the cliff and has old-fashioned, Art Nouveau furnishings, some very grand, though faded. Tenor Enrico Caruso's bedroom is preserved as a relic; guest bedrooms are spacious and elegant in a turn-of-the-century way. It overlooks the bay, and is recommended for those who like a lot of atmosphere with their views. *Piazza Tasso 34, tel. 081/8781900. 125 rooms with bath. Facilities: pool. AE, DC, MC, V. Expensive.*

★ **Bellevue Syrene.** A palatial villa in a garden overlooking the sea, the Syrene features solid, old-fashioned comforts and plenty of charm, with nooks and crannies and antique paintings. *Piazza della Vittoria 5, tel. 081/8781024. 50 rooms, most with bath. AE, DC, MC, V. Moderate.*

Eden. Eden occupies a fairly quiet but central location, with a garden. Bedrooms are bright but undistinguished; the lounge and lobby have more character. It's an unpretentious but friendly hotel, with some smaller rooms in the Inexpensive category. *Via Correale 25, tel. 081/8781909. 60 rooms with bath. Facilities: pool. AE, V. Closed Nov.–Feb. Moderate.*

Introduction

Nestled between Switzerland and Austria is tiny Liechtenstein, a territory of 61 square miles (158 square kilometers) with a population of less than 30,000. It takes the international express trains only 16 minutes to cross the country; they don't bother to stop.

Liechtenstein, which is united with Switzerland in a customs union and represented by Switzerland abroad, became an independent nation in 1719, when a wealthy Austrian prince, Johann Adam von Liechtenstein, bought out two bankrupt counts in the Rhine Valley, united their lands, and obtained an imperial deed, creating the Principality of Liechtenstein.

While cherishing its past, Liechtenstein lives very much in the present. Its flourishing economy is proof that low taxation and high prosperity can coexist, as the monarchy and democracy do here.

Liechtenstein's main attractions include Prince Franz Josef's stunning art collection, part of which is on view daily in Vaduz; its unique postage stamps; its dramatic mountain scenery; and its mostly mild climate.

Before You Go

When to Go Liechtenstein claims that its vacation season lasts all year. Winter sports begin before Christmas and last until late March or early April. Spring comes swiftly, and by early May the orchards of the Rhine Valley are in full bloom. Summer days are delightful, but the nights can be chilly. The brisk fall is perfect for exploring.

Climate The following are the average daily maximum and minimum temperatures for Liechtenstein.

Jan.	36F	2C	May	67F	19C	Sept.	69F	20C
	26	−3		47	8		51	11
Feb.	41F	5C	June	73F	23C	Oct.	57F	14C
	28	−2		53	12		43	6
Mar.	51F	10C	July	76F	25C	Nov.	45F	7C
	34	1		56	14		35	2
Apr.	59F	15C	Aug.	75F	24C	Dec.	37F	3C
	40	4		56	13		29	−2

Currency The Swiss franc is Liechtenstein's unit of currency. At press time (fall 1988), the rate was 1.39 Fr. to the dollar, 2.42 Fr. to the pound. Swiss currency regulations apply. Major credit cards are widely accepted.

What It Will Cost Liechtenstein shares Switzerland's prosperity, so prices are high. But, as in Switzerland, quality and value for your money are guaranteed.

Sample Prices Cup of coffee, 2.20 Fr.; bottle of beer 2.50 Fr.; Coca-Cola 2 Fr.; a large ham sandwich, 7 Fr.

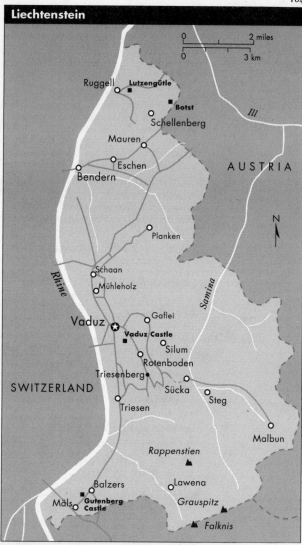

Customs on Arrival If you arrive in Liechtenstein from Switzerland, there are no formalities; coming from Austria, Swiss customs regulations apply (*see* Customs on Arrival, in Switzerland).

Language The official language is German, but Liechtensteiners have a dialect that varies from place to place: Don't worry, though, English is spoken almost everywhere.

Essential Information

Telephones Calls to Europe and most of the rest of the world can be dialed direct. For rates and useful numbers, *see* Essential Information, in Switzerland.

Mail All mail goes by air. The rates are the same as in Switzerland (*see* Essential Information in Switzerland), but remember that you must use Liechtenstein stamps. This country is famous for its finely engraved stamps and frequent new issues; if you have philatelist friends, they'll certainly want to hear from you.

Shopping Watches and other goods that you find in Switzerland can be bought in Liechtenstein for about the same price, but your choice will be rather limited. The unique postage stamps are a popular souvenir. In 1989, new stamps will be issued in March, June, September, and December. Other specialties include beautifully costumed dolls, hand-painted pottery, and wood carvings.

Opening and **Banks.** Banks are open weekdays 8–noon, 1:30–4:30.
Closing Times **Museums.** Most museums are open daily, though some close Monday in winter. Check locally.
Shops. Shops are open weekdays 8–noon and 2–6:30, Sat. 8–4.

National Holidays January 1, 2 (New Year); January 6 (Epiphany); February 2 (Candlemas); February 7 (Shrove Tuesday); March 19 (St. Joseph's Day); March 24, 27 (Easter); May 4 (Ascension); May 15 (Pentecost); May 25 (Corpus Christi); August 15 (Assumption, National Day); September 8 (Nativity); November 1 (All Saints Day); December 8 (Immaculate Conception); December 25, 26 (Christmas).

Dining Contrary to popular belief, there is a distinct Liechtenstein cuisine. It's best described as Swiss with Austrian influences. Recently, there has been a revival of interest in Liechtenstein cooking, and more restaurants are adding national dishes, such as *Hafaläb* and *Kasknöpfle* (cheese dumplings) to their menus.

Ratings Prices are for a three-course meal for one, not including wine or tip. Best bets are indicated by a star ★. At press time, there were 1.39 Swiss francs to the dollar.

Category	Cost
Expensive	over 50 Fr.
Moderate	20 Fr.–50 Fr.
Inexpensive	under 20 Fr.

Credit Cards The following credit card abbreviations are used: AE, American Express; DC, Diners Club; MC, MasterCard; V, Visa.

Lodging Considering its size, Liechtenstein is well stocked with hotels. The best are in Vaduz and the Rhine Valley. Some are small, family-run concerns; others are simple mountain inns at altitudes of 4,000 feet (1,220 meters) or more, providing peace and clean, fresh air. You can also rent a châlet or stay with a family; contact the local tourist information office for details.

Ratings Prices are for two people sharing a double room. Best bets are indicated by a star ★. At press time, there were 1.39 Swiss francs to the dollar.

Category	Cost
Expensive	over 150 Fr.
Moderate	70 Fr.–150 Fr.
Inexpensive	under 70 Fr.

Credit Cards The following credit card abbreviations are used: AE, American Express; DC, Diners Club; MC, MasterCard; V, Visa.

Tipping As in Switzerland, the general rule is not to tip; service charges amounting to 15% are included in hotel and restaurant bills. If someone does something special or particularly helpful, a tip is appropriate; otherwise one will not be expected.

Arriving and Departing

By Train and Bus No international express trains stop in Liechtenstein. The best way to get there is to take a train to the station at Buchs in St. Gallen, Switzerland, or to Sargans, a little farther away, and then take the excellent connecting post bus into Vaduz. The bus from Buchs takes 15 minutes; the one from Sargans, about 45 minutes. If you're coming from Austria, there is good train service to Feldkirch on the border. From Feldkirch, there is similarly good post bus service. A weekly bus ticket is available, allowing holders to make an unlimited number of trips on all post bus routes in the country as well as to neighboring places across the border. The ticket can be bought at any Liechtenstein post office, at the Swiss post offices in Buchs and Sargans, or at the train station in Sargans.

Getting Around

By Car Roads in Liechtenstein are well maintained and clearly marked. Driving regulations are the same as those for Switzerland (*see* Getting Around, By Car, in Switzerland).

By Bus The post buses, which run throughout most of the country, are a real bargain: In 1988 the government decided that travel within Liechtenstein by bus would be free.

By Bicycle Though much of Liechtenstein is mountainous, it has marked bicycle routes along the Rhine and around Schellenberg. Bikes can be rented at **Hans Melliger,** Velos Motos, Kirchstrasse 10, Vaduz, tel. 075/21606; or **Rad-Zenter Hermann,** Feldkircherstrasse 74, Schaan, tel. 075/24699.

Important Addresses and Numbers

Tourist The principal tourist office in Liechtenstein is at Städtle 38,
Information Box 139, FL 9490, Vaduz, tel. 075/21443. Open weekdays 8–noon, 1:30–5. There are local offices at **Vaduz,** Städtle 37, tel. 075/21443. Open weekdays 8–noon, 1:30–5:30; Sat. 9–noon, 1–4. **Malbun,** FL 9497, tel. 075/26577. Open 9–noon, 1:30–5; closed Sun., Thur. **Schaan,** Landstrasse, 9, tel. 075/26565. Open Mon.–Thurs. 8:30–noon, 1:30–6, Fri. 8:30–noon, 1:30–7, Sat. 9–noon. **Triesenberg,** Dorfzentrum, tel. 075/21926. Open Tues.–Sat. 1:30–4:30, also open Sun., June–Aug., 2–5.

Emergencies Police, tel. 117; **Ambulance,** tel. 144.

Guided Tours

Orientation Tours Guided bus tours of the principality can be arranged for groups and last between two and four hours. The cost is 50 Fr. for the first hour, 25 Fr. for each extra hour. Reservations are necessary; inquire at the tourist office in Vaduz (*see* Important Addresses and Numbers).

Walking Tours There are guided tours in the Malbun area taking in the Galinakopf; Schönberg, with its wonderful views; Rappenstein, famous for its wildlife; Pfälzer-Hütte; and Naafkopf, where the frontiers of Liechtenstein, Switzerland, and Austria meet. Most hikes take about six hours. Inquire at the Malbun tourist office.

Excursions Excursions by horse-drawn carriages are available from the town hall in Vaduz; routes are designed to your specifications. Get more information from **Franz Beck,** Zollstrasse, 71, Schaan, tel. 075/21753, or from local tourist offices.

Bus excursions can be arranged to the castles of Switzerland, the Rhine Valley, the Appenzell region, the Rhine Falls, and St. Moritz. Take your passport if you plan excursions to Bregenz, the Vorarlberg, Lindau, and Mainau island.

Personal Guides The local tourist offices will be able to recommend a personal guide.

Exploring Liechtenstein

Outside the tiny capital of Vaduz (population 5,000), exploring is best done by car, but leave plenty of time for stops to admire the views or to walk along the many miles of clearly marked paths. If you don't have a car, you won't be stuck—use the free postal bus service.

The Main Attractions

In the capital, make the guarded fairy-tale **Vaduz Castle** your first stop. It was originally built in the 12th century in its dominating position perched high on a cliff. The castle was burned down by the troops of the Swiss confederacy in 1499. It was gradually rebuilt and altered over the centuries until it took its present form after a massive restoration at the beginning of this century. In places, the walls are more than 12 feet (3½ meters) thick. This is the home of the ruling Prince Franz Josef II and his family, so unless you're a very honored guest, you won't get to see inside, but you can admire the glorious views from its aerielike terraces.

Back in the center of town, head for the tourist information office. The main museums are in this street, two of them in the same building as the tourist office. When you've collected your maps and brochures, go upstairs to the **Prince's Art Gallery and the State Art Collection** and to the **Postage Stamp Museum.** The art collection is one of the finest private collections in the world, and since the prince insisted that it should be made available to all his subjects, visitors can also view it. The collection includes works by Flemish masters—Rubens and Pieter and Jan Brueghel. A recent acquisition is Van Dyck's portrait of the first Duke of Hamilton, bought by the prince from the present duke for nearly $2 million. *Städtle 37, tel. 075/22341. Admission: 3 Fr. adults, 1.5 Fr. children. Open Apr.–Oct. daily 10:30–noon, 1:30–5:30. Nov.–Mar. daily 10–noon, 2–5:30.*

The one-room **Postage Stamp Museum** attracts philatelists from all over the world. There are 300 frames of Liechtenstein's beautifully designed stamps on view. You can place subscriptions here for future first-day covers. *Städtle 37, tel. 075/66259. Free. Open daily 10–noon, 2–6.*

Next, move on to the **Liechtenstein National Museum,** which houses historical artifacts, church carvings, ancient coins, and items from the prince's private arms collection. If you collect stamps for your passport, have it stamped here with Liechtenstein's distinctive crown insignia. *Städtle 43, tel. 075/ 22310. Admission: 2 Fr. Open May–Oct., daily 10–noon, 1:30– 5:30; Nov.–Mar., Tues.–Sun. 2–5:30.*

Take an afternoon trip to **Schaan,** north of Vaduz, to see the Roman excavations and the parish church built on the foundations of a Roman fort.

Back in Vaduz, leave the town by the winding road that takes you past the castle, south toward Triesenberg. From this road, you'll get spectacular views of the Rhine Valley. **Triesenberg** is memorable for its characteristic Valaisan-style houses. A mile out, a left turn leads to Gaflei, where begins the **Fürstensteig,** or Prince's Climb, a path leading along the ridge of the Rhine Valley.

The road continues upward through a tunnel to **Steg,** a hamlet in a high Alpine valley and another stepping-out point for summer walks. An excellent new road takes you to **Malbun,** an expanding village nestled on the floor of a huge mountain bowl. Malbun is fast becoming an important winter sports center and is an ideal base for walking and enjoying the countryside before returning to the capital.

Dining and Lodging

For details and price category definitions, *see* Dining and Lodging in Essential Information.

Malbun
Dining

Montana. The chef at the hotel-restaurant Montana has a magical way with his regional dishes and international cuisine. Save room to sample the calories-loaded Viennese desserts. *Tel. 075/ 27333. Dress: casual. Reservations advised. AE, DC. Moderate.*

Alpenhotel. Despite the modest surroundings of the hotel itself, the food here is very good. There's an ample choice of local specialties or Continental cuisine, both with an emphasis on fresh, locally produced ingredients. *Tel. 075/21881. Dress: casual. Reservations advised. No credit cards. Inexpensive.*

★ **Galina.** The Galina Hotel has a well-respected restaurant that's popular with the locals, which is recommendation enough. It specializes in a variety of fondues and *raclette. Tel. 075/23424. Dress: casual. Reservations advised. No credit cards. Inexpensive.*

Scesaplana. Dine in a relaxed, convivial atmosphere on an amazing array of fondues or the imaginative cooking of the region. *Tel. 075/24544. Dress: casual. Reservations advised. No credit cards. Inexpensive.*

Lodging
★

Gorifon. This is a very attractive châlet-style hotel. Some of the rooms have balconies and glorious views of the mountains. All the rooms are tastefully decorated and comfortable. The extensive facilities will keep you busy most of the day, but be sure to relax with a good meal on the terrace. *Tel. 075/24307. 37 rooms with bath. Facilities: pool, tennis courts, downhill and cross-country skiing, disco. AE, DC, V. Closed Nov.–mid-Dec. Expensive.*

★ **Malbunerhof.** A short drive from the station at Buchs will bring you to this homey, typical Alpine hotel. It's a medium-size establishment, comfortable and welcoming. There's a good terrace restaurant and a well-stocked bar; the inviting open-fire lounge is an ideal place to relax in the evening. *Tel. 075/22944. 30 rooms with bath. Facilities: indoor pool, sauna, solarium, tennis courts, skiing, fishing, bowling. AE, DC, V. Expensive.*

Montana. For the convenience of a central location, try the Montana. It's small but comfortable, with a welcoming and helpful staff. There's a good restaurant (*see* Dining) and a cozy bar. This is an ideal sightseeing base. *Tel. 075/27333. 15 rooms with bath. Facilities: sauna. AE, DC. Moderate.*

Alpenhotel Malbun. Bring the family to the Alpenhotel, it's geared to deal with the needs of the whole family. It has an ideal central location and pleasant comfortable rooms. *Tel. 075/21181. 25 rooms with bath. Facilities: indoor pool. AE, DC. Inexpensive.*

Walserhof. You'll get good value for your money at this modest but comfortable hotel in the center of town. There's also a restaurant. *Tel. 075/23396. 6 rooms, none with bath. AE, DC. Inexpensive.*

Schaan
Dining
★ **Schaanerhof.** In the pleasant surroundings of the Schaanerhof Hotel, this restaurant serves well-prepared and imaginatively presented traditional cuisine. The chef here has his own distinctive way of dealing with the traditional Swiss *emince foié de veau* and *rösti. Tel. 075/21877. Jacket and tie. Reservations advised. AE. Moderate.*

Dux. If you're not staying at the Dux, be sure to try the fine regional and international dishes served in any of its three restaurants. *Tel. 075/21727. Jacket and tie. Reservations advised. AE, DC, V. Inexpensive.*

Gassner. This is a pleasant, modest café-restaurant serving wholesome regional dishes. It's well known for its sweet, light pastries. *Tel. 075/21710. Dress: casual. Reservations not necessary. AE, DC. Inexpensive.*

Lodging
★ **Schaanerhof.** For peace and an idyllic setting, stay at the Schaanerhof. Most of the well-decorated rooms have balconies; the views of the Rhine Valley and the mountains are exceptional. The public rooms are cozily rustic; relax with a drink in the bar or by the open-fire lounge. *Tel. 075/21877. 39 rooms, most with bath. Facilities: indoor pool, sauna, solarium, tennis courts. AE. Moderate.*

★ **Dux.** Another of Liechtenstein's value-for-your-money hotels, the Dux has a glorious setting with views of the mountains and extensive views of the Rhine Valley. It's a cozy, country house-style place, where you'll be cared for by helpful, friendly staff. There are facilities for disabled guests, too. Try all three of its restaurants. *Tel. 075/21727. 11 rooms with bath. Facilities: solarium; tennis courts, playground. AE, DC, MC, V. Inexpensive.*

Triesenberg
Lodging
Kulm. Comfortable, tastefully decorated rooms in this modern hotel make it a popular, good-value place to stay. Most rooms

have attractive views across the Rhine Valley. Dine in the pleasant restaurant or relax in the bar with a drink. *Dorfzentrum, tel. 075/28777. 20 rooms with bath. AE, MC, V. Inexpensive.*

Vaduz
Dining

Torkel. Dine in a restaurant owned by Prince Franz Josef, set in the pleasant surroundings of his vineyards. Try the potent local red wine, Vaduzer. The menu offers a choice of international and local dishes. *Hintergass 9, tel. 075/24410. Jacket and tie. Reservations advised. AE, DC, V. Expensive.*

★ **Engel.** The restaurant at the Engel Hotel has earned itself an excellent reputation. Dishes of international cuisine are served with Liechtenstein imagination. Dine to music on the terrace. *Städtle 13, tel. 075/21057. Jacket and tie. Reservations advised. AE, DC, V. Moderate.*

Real. An extensive wine cellar complements the excellent French dishes that are this restaurant's specialty. The *truite sauvage au Riesling* is worth a try. *Städtle 21, tel. 075/22222. Jacket and tie. Reservations advised. AE, DC, V. Moderate.*

Café Wolfe. If you don't need a full meal, drop into Café Wolfe for a quick snack. Coffee and pastries are a real treat here. *Städtle 29, tel. 075/22818. Dress: casual. Reservations not necessary. AE. Inexpensive.*

The Old Castle Inn. This is an atmospheric, old-style country inn. The food has a distinctly international flavor but is filling and wholesome. Open till 1 AM, it's an ideal spot for late-night dinners. *Aeulstr. 22, tel. 075/21065. Dress: casual. Reservations advised. AE, DC, V. Inexpensive.*

Lodging
★

Park-Hotel Sonnenhof. Arguably the best hotel in town, the Park-Hotel Sonnenhof commands superb views overlooking the town. It's in an idyllic setting with glorious gardens. All the rooms are attractively decorated in country-garden style. The restaurant is exclusive to hotel guests. *Mareestr. 29, tel. 075/21192. 29 rooms with bath. Facilities: indoor pool, sauna. AE, DC, MC, V. Expensive.*

Schlössle. On the road to the Vaduz Castle, the Schössle is a comfortable, well-appointed hotel. It's popular with business travelers, but a warm welcome is guaranteed to all guests. The decor has a distinctive regional touch, as does the food served in the small restaurant. *Schloss Str. 68, tel. 075/25621. 22 rooms with bath. AE, MC, V. Expensive.*

Real. The centrally located Real is an ideal sightseeing base. It's quite a small hotel, but all the rooms are elegantly decorated and furnished. The restaurant (*see* Dining) has a fine reputation. *Städtle 21, tel. 075/22222. 11 rooms with bath. Moderate.*

Engel. With its good restaurant, this is a delightful place to stay. The rooms are simply but adequately furnished, and the public rooms, particularly the bar, have an authentic rustic ambience. It's in the center of town and offers music for dancing most nights. *Städtle 13, tel. 075/21057. 19 rooms with bath. AE, MC, V. Inexpensive.*

23 Luxembourg

Introduction

Luxembourg, one of the smallest countries in the United Nations, measures only 999 square miles (2,600 square kilometers)—less than the size of Rhode Island. Nestled in the heart of Europe between Belgium, Germany, and France, it was fought over and occupied for centuries until 1868, when it declared its independence. Now, the Grand Duchy of Luxembourg is the working center of the European Community.

In the north of the country is a hilly, wooded region known as La Petite Suisse (little Switzerland). There are valleys in the center, and along the western boundary lies the fertile Moselle Valley, renowned for its crisp white wines. The capital city, also called Luxembourg, is located in the south. Throughout the country, castles and chateaux abound, and many of the towns and cities have a magic, fairy-tale air.

Although the entire country is small enough to be seen in three or four days and all parts of the land are accessible via an excellent system of railroads, highways, and footpaths, for the purposes of this guide, we have concentrated on the city of Luxembourg itself.

Before You Go

When to Go The main tourist season in Luxembourg is the same as in Belgium—early May to late September. But temperatures in Luxembourg tend to be cooler than those in Belgium, particularly in the hilly north, where there is frequent snow in winter.

Climate In general, temperatures in Luxembourg are moderate. It does drizzle frequently, however, so be sure to bring a raincoat.

The following are the average daily maximum and minimum temperatures for Luxembourg.

Jan.	37F	3C	May	65F	18C	Sept.	66F	19C
	29	−1		46	8		50	10
Feb.	40F	4C	June	70F	21C	Oct.	56F	13C
	31	−1		52	11		43	6
Mar.	49F	10C	July	73F	23C	Nov.	44F	7C
	35	1		55	13		37	3
Apr.	57F	14C	Aug.	71F	22C	Dec.	39F	4C
	40	4		54	12		33	0

Currency In Luxembourg, as in Belgium, the unit of currency is the franc, although Luxembourg issues its own money. Belgium issues bills in denominations of 50, 100, 500, 1,000, and 5,000 francs, Luxembourg, in denominations of 50 and 100 francs. Coins come in denominations of 1, 5, 10, and 20 francs and 50 centimes. Belgian money can be used freely in Luxembourg, but not the reverse—you will have to change your Luxembourgish money if you are traveling on to Belgium. At press time (fall 1988), the exchange rate was 35 fr.L. to the dollar and 56 fr.L. to the pound.

What It Will Cost The cost of living in Luxembourg is generally high. Hotel and restaurant rates are about the same as in London. But certain items, such as cigarettes, alcohol, and gasoline, are significantly cheaper in Luxembourg.

Luxembourg

Sample Prices   Cup of coffee, 35 fr. L.; glass of beer, 35 fr. L.; movie ticket, 150 fr. L.

Customs on Arrival   For information on customs regulations, *see* Customs on Arrival in Belgium.

Language   Native Luxembourgers speak three languages fluently: Luxembourgish (best described as a dialect of German), German, and French. Most also speak English.

Essential Information

Telephones   You can find public phones both on the street and in city post offices. A local call costs about 5 fr. L. (slightly more from restaurants and gas stations). The cheapest way to make an international call is to dial direct from a public phone. For operator-assisted calls, dial 0010.

Mail   Airmail postcards and letters weighing less than 20 grams cost
Postal Rates   18 fr. L. to the United States. Letters to the United Kingdom cost 12 fr. L., postcards 10 fr. L.

Receiving Mail   If you are uncertain of where you'll be staying, have your mail sent care of American Express, 52 avenue de la Liberté, 1930 Luxembourg.

Shopping   Luxembourg is famous for its white wines and its Villeroy and Boch porcelain. The Fonderie de Mersch also produces distinctive cast-iron miniature firebacks (called "TAK"), made in the shape of castles, arms, and other heraldic figures.

Opening and Closing Times	**Banks.** Banks generally are open weekdays 9–noon and 2–4:30. **Museums.** Opening hours vary, so check individual listings. Many close on Monday, and most also close for lunch between 12 and 2. **Shops.** Large city department stores and shops are generally open weekdays and Saturday 9–6. Many stay open one evening a week. Small family businesses are open Sunday morning from 8 to noon.

National Holidays January 1; March 27 (Easter Monday); May 1 (May Day); May 4 (Ascension); May 15 (Pentecost Monday); June 23 (National Day); August 15 (Assumption); November 1 (All Saints Day); December 25 and 26. *In Luxembourg City:* February 6 (Carnival Monday); November 2 (All Souls Day).

Dining Restaurants in Luxembourg are generally excellent. The cuisine is a combination of French and German styles. Local dishes—they tend to be fairly heavy—include black pudding *(treipen)* and sausages with mashed potatoes; smoked pork with broad beans; Ardennes ham; jellied suckling pig; and calf's liver dumplings *(quenelles)* with sauerkraut and boiled potatoes. You can also find excellent fresh fish from the country's many rivers.

Mealtimes Most hotels serve breakfast until 10 AM. Lunch hours are 12 to 2, sometimes extending until 3. Luxembourgers eat their main meal in the evening between 7 and 10.

Lodging
Hotels Luxembourg boasts a generous selection of reasonably priced hotels, many offering greatly reduced prices off-season and most featuring first-rate restaurants. Contact the National Tourist Office in Luxembourg for details of year-round special offers.

Youth Hostels Inexpensive youth hostels are plentiful in Luxembourg. They are often set in ancient fortresses and castles. For information, contact Centrale des Auberges de Jeunesse, Place d'Armes 18, Luxembourg.

Camping The Grand Duchy is probably the best organized country in Europe for camping. It offers some 120 sites, all with full amenities and most with scenic views. Information is available from the Fédération Luxembourgeoise de Camping et de Caravaning, 174 rue de Soleuvre, Belvaux. You can also get a list at the National Tourist Office.

Tipping In Luxembourg hotels and restaurants, taxes and service charges are included in the overall bill. Only taxi drivers expect a tip; add about 15% to the amount on the meter.

Luxembourg City

Arriving and Departing

By Plane All international flights arrive at Luxembourg's Findel Airport, about five miles (eight kilometers) from the city.

Between the Airport and Downtown Bus No. 9 leaves the airport at regular intervals for Luxembourg's main bus depot, located just beside the train station. Buses 2, 4, 11, and 12 go to the city center. Individual tickets cost 25 fr.L. A taxi will cost you about 800 fr.L. If you are driving, follow the signs for the city center *(Centre Ville)*.

Getting Around

One of the best transportation options in Luxembourg is the 5-Day Travel Card, good for unlimited transportation on trains and buses throughout the country. Cards are on sale, for 658 fr.L, at the Main Train Station in Luxembourg City.

By Bus Luxembourg City has a highly efficient bus service. The blue-and-yellow buses outside the city train station will take you all around the city and also to some of the outlying areas. Get details about services at the information counter in the station arrivals hall. Fares are low, but the best bet is to buy a 10-ride ticket, available from banks or from the bus station in the Aldringen Center. Other buses, connecting Luxembourg City with towns throughout the country, leave from the Luxembourg Train Station.

By Train Luxembourg is served by frequent direct trains from both Liège and Brussels. From Liège, travel time is about 2½ hours; from Brussels, just under three hours. Outside Luxembourg City, three major train routes extend north, south, and west into the Moselle Valley. For all train information, phone 492424. All service is from the Main Train Station in place de la Gare.

By Car You can easily see most of the country in a day or two, and you might want to rent a car for this purpose. Both major highways and smaller roads are excellent, and they are usually fairly uncrowded. Speed limits are 120 kph (70 mph) on highways, 90 kph (55 mph) on major roads, and 60 kph (35 mph) in built-up areas.

Although there are a number of parking lots available, parking in Luxembourg City is extremely difficult. It is best to get into the city very early—before 8 AM, when many businesses begin their day—or to park at the train station or fairground and take a bus from there into the center of town.

By Bicycle Bicycling is a popular sport in Luxembourg, and it is an excellent way to see the city and outlying regions. In Luxembourg City, you can rent bikes from Velo Francis Hansen, 16 rue Beaumont, tel. 29654. To rent a bike for about half the price, travel 30 miles (48 kilometers) outside the city to Syndicat D'Initiative, Station, Reisdorf, tel. 86778 or 86698. Maps are available from the tourist office.

By Taxi Taxis in Luxembourg are expensive and difficult to find. It is almost impossible to stop one in the streets, and there are few taxi stands available. To call a taxi, phone 480058 or 482223.

Important Addresses and Numbers

Tourist Information The main Office de Nationale du Tourisme (ONT) in Luxembourg City is located at the Air Terminal, place de la Gare, tel. 481199, open daily 9–12 and 2–6:30 (July 1–mid-Sept., 9–7:30).

Embassies U.S. 22 blvd. Emmanuel Servais, tel. 460123. U.K. 14 blvd. F. D. Roosevelt, tel. 026791.

Emergencies Police, Ambulance, Doctor, Dentist, tel. 012. Pharmacies in Luxembourg stay open nights on a rotation system. Signs listing late-night facilities are posted outside each pharmacy.

English Bookstores Magasin Anglais, 13 allée Scheffer, tel. 024925.

Travel Agencies **American Express,** 52 avenue de la Liberté, tel. 482111 or 489966.

Wagons Lits, 80 place de la Gare, tel. 481919.

Guided Tours

Orientation Tours **H. Sales** (tel. 501050) offers year-round tours of Luxembourg City. During the peak tourist season, both half-day and full-day tours are available.

Walking Tours Information on weekend walking tours can be obtained from the tourist office or from the **Federation Luxembourgeoise des Marches Populaires,** 176 rue de Rollingergrund.

Excursions Pick up the booklet "Circuits Auto-Pedestres," available at newsstands and bookstores, for information on combination driving-walking tours outside the city.

Exploring Luxembourg City

1 You should begin your tour of Luxembourg City at the **Train Station,** located in the southern—and most modern—section of the city. As you head from the station toward the city center, you will pass through a bustling shopping district. Take the **2** **Passerelle Viaduct** across the **Valley of the Petrusse.** Then, for a splendid view of the valley and city center, take a stroll along **3** the **Boulevard Roosevelt.** The war monument at the **place de la Constitution** is the starting point for tours of the impressive Petrusse fortifications.

4 Just north of the Place de la Constitution is the **Cathedral Notre Dame,** with its interesting Baroque organ gallery and crypt. The latter now houses a permanent exhibition of modern art. The building itself dates from the 17th century. *Open daily 8–12 and 2–7; crypt open 9–12 and 2–6.*

Opposite the cathedral lies the **place Guillaume,** with its regal equestrian statue of William II (1792–1849), former grand duke of Luxembourg. On the south side of the square stands **5** the **Town Hall,** built in the 1830s. On market days, the square is filled with noise and bright color, and in summer, open-air concerts are held here.

Time Out The place de Guillaume is an excellent spot to sit in an outdoor café and enjoy the passing scene. Or walk one block north to the **place d'Armes** and have lunch at the traditional, and very reasonable, **l'Academie,** 11 place d'Armes, tel. 27131.

Northeast of the Place Guillaume and the Place d'Armes is the **6** 16th-century **Grand Ducal Palace.** You can see the changing of the guards here each day at 10, 12, 2, 4, or 6. Tours of the palace can be arranged through the National Tourist Office. Continuing north, you come to the **Grand Rue,** Luxembourg City's main shopping street. If you walk west along the Grand Rue, you will **7** arrive at the **Municipal Park.** At the northern end of the park **8** are the **New Theatre** building and the **Grand Duchess Charlotte Bridge,** which leads across the valley to the **Kirchberg Plateau** and the 23-story **Centre Européen** (European Community

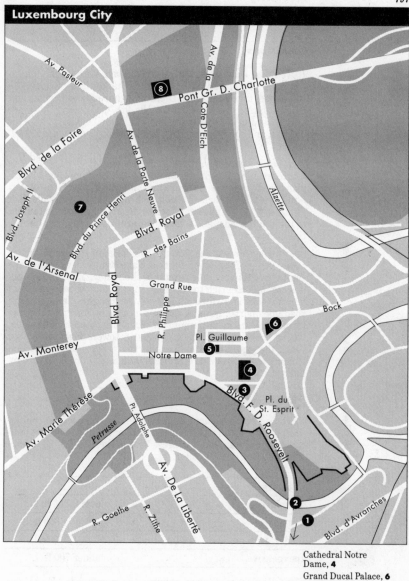

Luxembourg City

Cathedral Notre
Dame, **4**
Grand Ducal Palace, **6**
Municipal Park, **7**
New Theatre, **8**
Passerelle Viaduct, **2**
Place de la
Consitution, **3**
Train Station, **1**
Town Hall, **5**

buildings). The European Council meets here three times a
year.

Excursions

It would be a shame to leave Luxembourg without having explored some of the areas around the capital. To see the
Ardennes, take Route 7 to **Diekirch,** where there is an ancient
church dating from the 7th to the 9th centuries. There are
traces here of older occupation: The "Devil's Altar," a Celtic
dolmen, and some 4th-century Roman mosaics from nearby villas.

Another rewarding drive is northeast on Route E27 to
Echternach, where St. Willibrord, a 7th-century English mis-
sionary, founded a Benedictine abbey. Many of the abbey
buildings are now schools, but each year on the Tuesday after
Pentecost, 15,000 pilgrims flock to the basilica, built on the site
of the original chapel. In the crypt are frescoes dating back to
the 11th century.

Another scenic route is through the **Valley of the Eisch,** known
as the Valley of the Seven Castles. Take Route E9 west from the
capital to Steinfort, the capital of the valley. The road continues through Koerich to Septfontaines, situated below the cliff
where there is a ruined Castle of the Knights Templar. The
road goes north, passing the two castles of Ansembourg, the
former monastic settlement of Marienthal, and Hollenfells,
where there is a 9th-century castle tower. Eventually you
reach the castle town of Mersch, the geographical center of
Luxembourg: From here, you can take Route 7 back to Luxembourg City.

Dining

Prices quoted here are per person and include a first course,
main course, and dessert, but no wine or tip. Best bets are indicated by a star ★. At press time, there were 35 francs
(Luxembourg) to the dollar.

Category	Cost
Very Expensive	over 3,000 fr.L.
Expensive	1,200–3,000 fr.L.
Moderate	700–1,200 fr.L.
Inexpensive	under 700 fr.L.

Credit Cards The following credit card abbreviations are used: AE, American Express; DC, Diners Club; MC, MasterCard; V, Visa.

Expensive **Au Gourmet.** Located in the city center close to the place
★ d'Armes, Au Gourmet is a popular restaurant offering fine regional dishes in a lovely, old town-house setting. *8 rue Chimay,
tel. 25561. Jacket and tie. Reservations required. AE, V.
Closed Sun. evening, Mon., and July 23–Aug. 15.*
St. Michel. A charming first-floor restaurant located in the city
center, St. Michel offers a wide variety of seafood specialties
and an exhaustive wine list. Try the *blanc de turbot au borgeuil*
and, for dessert, *désir de la reine. 32 rue Eau, tel. 23215. Jack-*

*et and tie. Reservations recommended. AE, DC, V. Closed
Sat., Sun., all of Aug., and Dec. 23–Jan. 5.*

Moderate **Club 5.** In summer, Club 5 offers pleasant terrace dining and a
choice of tasty salads. *5 rue Chimay, tel. 461763 Dress: casual.
Reservations recommended. MC, V.*

★ **Osteria del Téatro.** Conveniently located just beside the Foire
(fairground), Osteria del Téatro specializes in authentic Italian
cuisine. It also offers an attractive bar and terrace. *21–25 allée
Scheffer, tel. 28811. Dress: casual. Reservations recommended. AE, DC, MC, V. Closed Thurs.*

Inexpensive **Mister Grill.** This is the place for good, inexpensive grills and
salads. *15 place d'Armes, tel. 27537. Dress: casual. Reserva-
tions not required. AE, DC, MC, V.*

Lodging

Price categories are determined by the cost of a double room.
Best bets are indicated by a star ★. At press time, there were
35 francs (Luxembourg) to the dollar.

Category	Cost
Very Expensive	over 3,300 fr.L.
Expensive	2,200–3,300 fr.L.
Moderate	1,200–2,200 fr.L.
Inexpensive	under 1,200 fr.L.

Credit Cards The following credit card abbreviations are used: AE, American Express; DC, Diners Club; MC, MasterCard; V, Visa.

Very Expensive **Aerogolf-Sheraton.** Located in a pleasant, wooded setting close
★ to the airport and directly across from the city golf course, the
Aerogolf-Sheraton is billed as one of the nicest—and one of the
most expensive—hotels in the country. It is also near the European Parliament. All rooms feature soundproofing and air-
conditioning. *Rte. de Trèves, tel. 34571. 150 rooms with bath.
Facilities: 2 restaurants, meeting rooms, garden terrace,
horseback riding. AE, DC, MC, V.*

Royal. The city's newest and probably most expensive hotel, le
Royal is located on Luxembourg's "Wall Street," close to parks
and tourist sites. It offers 2 restaurants, a nightclub, and a piano bar. *12 boulevard Royal, tel. 41616. 170 rooms, all with
bath. Facilities: indoor pool, sauna, solarium, terrace. AE,
DC, MC, V.*

Expensive **Kons.** A popular hotel located directly across from the train station, the Kons is a convenient, comfortable establishment.
Built in 1930, it was renovated in 1983. The decor combines traditional and modern styles. *24 place de la Gare, tel. 486021. 141
rooms, most with bath. Facilities: restaurant, bar, cocktail
lounge, meeting rooms. AE, DC, MC, V.*

★ **International.** The International is a comfortable, centrally located hotel offering guests a fine French restaurant and easy
access to all downtown sights. *20–22 place de la Gare, tel.
485911. 60 rooms, most with bath. Facilities: meeting rooms,
sidewalk café, bar. AE, DC, MC, V.*

Moderate **Dauphin.** Centrally located, yet only 3 miles (5 kilometers) from the airport, the Dauphin is a small, modest hotel, particularly suited to youth groups. It offers simple, modern furnishings. Only breakfast is served. *42 avenue de la Gare, tel. 485252. 37 rooms, most with bath. AE, MC, V.*

24 Malta

Introduction

The Mediterranean island of Malta, and its two sister islands of Gozo and Comino, enjoy a mild sunny climate and attractive bays and beaches—a felicitous setting for such a festive and hospitable people.

For those interested in history and archaeology, there are the remains of a long and eventful history. Among the most fascinating ruins are Neolithic temples and huge stone megaliths left by prehistoric inhabitants. In AD 60, St. Paul, shipwrecked here, converted the people to Christianity. Other, less welcome visitors, attracted by Malta's strategic position, conquered and ruled. These included the Phoenicians, Carthaginians, and Romans. The Knights of the Order of St. John of Jerusalem arrived here in 1530 after they had been driven from their stronghold on the island of Rhodes by the Ottoman emperor Suleiman the Magnificent. In 1656, with only a handful of men, the Knights held Malta against the Ottoman Turks in one of the most famous sieges of all time. They ruled the islands until Napoleon arrived on the scene in 1798 and left massive fortifications, rich architecture, and the city of Valletta, Malta's capital. The British drove the French out in 1800 and gave the island the distinctive British feel that it retains to this day. In 1942, during World War II, King George VI awarded the Maltese people the George Medal for their courage in withstanding repeated German and Italian attacks, especially from the air. Malta gained independence from Britain in 1964.

For an excellent introduction to the island, take in *Malta Experience*, a multimedia presentation tracing the history of the island. It is shown in the beautifully restored "hospital" (inn) of the Order of St. John in Valletta.

Before You Go

When to Go The archipelago is a year-round delight, but May through October is the time of the main tourist season. April and May are the months for spring freshness; the summer months can be very hot, though tempered by sea breezes. If you visit in the winter, you'll find the climate pleasant and mild, but you may encounter sudden rainstorms.

Climate The following are the average daily maximum and minimum temperatures for Valletta.

Jan.	58F	14C	May	71F	22C	Sept.	81F	27C
	50	10		61	16		71	22
Feb.	59F	15C	June	79F	26C	Oct.	75F	24C
	51	10		67	19		66	19
Mar.	61F	16C	July	84F	29C	Nov.	67F	20C
	52	11		72	22		60	16
Apr.	65F	18C	Aug.	85F	29C	Dec.	61F	16C
	56	13		73	23		54	12

Currency The unit of currency is the Maltese lira (LM), also sometimes referred to as the pound. It's divided into 100 cents, and the cents are divided into 10 mils. There are 10 LM, 5 LM, and 1 LM bills; coins are bronze and silver. At press time (fall 1988), the exchange rate was .31 LM to the dollar and .57 LM to the pound.

Malta

What It Will Cost With Malta's rapid tourist development, prices are inevitably rising, though less so than in most other European countries. Prices tend to be uniform across the island, except in Valletta, the capital, where they are slightly higher.

Sample Prices Cup of coffee, 40 (Maltese) cents; bottle of beer, 15 (Maltese) cents; Coca-Cola, 25 (Maltese) cents.

Customs on Arrival You may bring into Malta, duty-free, 200 cigarettes, one bottle of liquor, one bottle of wine, and perfume not exceeding 2 LM in value. You may bring in up to 50 LM.

Language Don't let the bewildering spelling of many Maltese words put you off. Both English and Maltese are the official languages on the island, so you shouldn't experience any problems.

Getting Around

By Car The roads around Valletta can get busy at times, but road conditions are generally good, and driving around the island is pleasant. Driving is on the left-hand side of the road. Speed limits are 40 kph (25 mph) in towns, 80 kph (50 mph) elsewhere. International and British driving licenses are acceptable.

By Bus Most routes begin and end at Valletta, which facilitates travel out of the capital, but makes cross-country trips difficult, though not impossible. Buses are remarkably inexpensive; you can cover the whole island for about 12c. The old green buses sometimes have difficulty keeping to the timetable, however, and are often filled to capacity.

By Boat Daily ferries operate year-round from Marfa to Mġarr on Gozo and Comino. Telephone 33011 for details.

By Taxi There are plenty of metered taxis available and fares are reasonable compared with those in other European countries. Be sure the meter is switched on when your trip starts.

Essential Information

Telephones There is direct dialing to most parts of the world from Malta. The best place to make calls is either from your hotel or from the Overseas Telephone Division of Telemalta at St. George's, Qawra, Buggiba, and Valletta. Calls from hotels generally are much more expensive.

Mail Airmail letters to the United States cost 14 cents, postcards cost 10 cents. Airmail letters to the United Kingdom cost 9 cents, postcards 8 cents.

Shopping Traditional Maltese handcrafted goods include intricate gold and silver filigree jewelry. The handmade lace, though not as fine as Belgian lace, is very attractive and makes an easily packed gift. Mdina glass comes in all colors and designs. Locally woven fabrics, hand-painted pottery, and brass door knockers are all reasonably priced and make distinctive gifts. Watches and French perfumes cost less than elsewhere in Europe, and the excellent local wine, boxed for easy transportation, is a bargain.

A visit to the **Crafts' Village** at Ta' Qali is a must. Here, in this converted World War II aerodrome, you can see filigree silver, gold jewelry, and hand-blown Mdina glass being made by age-old methods. There are also leather workshops and pottery shops selling gaily colored items. And, of course, you'll be invited to buy. Some of the seconds in the glass workshops are good buys; the faults are often noticeable only to those with a trained eye.

Opening and Closing Times **Banks.** Banks are open Monday–Friday 8:30–noon, Saturday 8:30–11:30.

Museums. Most museums run by the Museums Department are open mid-June through September daily 8–2; closed public holidays; October through mid-June daily 8:30–5. Other museums' hours may vary slightly, so check locally.

Shops. Shops are open Monday–Friday 9–7, Saturday 9–1, 4–8.

National Holidays January 1 (New Year's Day); February 10 (St. Paul's shipwreck); March 31 (National Freedom Day); March 24, 27 (Easter); May 1 (Workers' Day); August 15 (Assumption); December 13 (Republic Day); December 25.

Dining There is a good choice of restaurants, ranging from expensive hotel restaurants to fast-food hamburger joints. Fish is a staple on the Maltese menu. Local specialties include *lampuki* (fish pie), *dentici* (sea bream), tuna, and lobster. *Minestra* is the local variant of minestrone soup, and the *timpana* (baked macaroni and meat) is filling. Rabbit and chicken also appear on the menu quite often. Accompany your meal with the locally produced wine: *marsonvin* comes in red, white, or rosé; *lachryma vitis*, in red or white. Maltese beers are good, too.

Precautions | The water on Malta is safe to drink, with the only drawback being its bitter salty taste: You've probably never tasted water quite like it. You may prefer bottled mineral water.

Ratings | Prices are for a three-course meal, not including wine or tip. Best bets are indicated by a star ★. At press time, there were .31 Maltese lire (LM) to the dollar.

Category	Cost
Expensive	over 6 LM
Moderate	2 LM–6 LM
Inexpensive	under 2 LM

Credit Cards | The following credit card abbreviations are used: AE, American Express; DC, Diners Club; MC, MasterCard; V, Visa.

Lodging | Malta has a variety of lodgings, from deluxe modern hotels to modest guest houses. Since Malta is primarily a coastal resort, most accommodations are to be found along the beaches. There are also self-contained complexes geared mainly to package tours. You will undoubtedly pay according to the degree of comfort and facilities offered by your hotel, but generally, most places will be clean and comfortable. Breakfast is usually included in the price of your room.

Ratings | Prices are for two people sharing a double room. At press time, there were .31 Maltese lire (LM) to the dollar.

Category	Cost
Very Expensive	over 35 LM
Expensive	20 LM–25 LM
Moderate	12 LM–20 LM
Inexpensive	8 LM–12 LM

Credit Cards | The following credit card abbreviations are used: AE, American Express; DC, Diners Card; MC, MasterCard; V, Visa.

Tipping | A tip of 10% is expected when a service charge is not included.

Valletta

Arriving and Departing

By Plane | There are no direct flights from the United States, but several airlines, including Air Malta, fly from London, Paris, Frankfurt, Milan, and Rome to Luqa Airport, four miles (six kilometers) south of Valletta.

Between the Airport and Downtown | There is a local bus service from the airport to Valletta. It operates every 20 minutes from 6 AM to 11 PM, and the trip takes about 20 minutes.

Taxis are also available and prices are reasonable.

By Boat | The **Gozo Channel Co.** (tel. 603964) operates weekly car and passenger ferries from Syracuse, Sicily, during the summer. The **Tirrenia Line** (agents in the United Kingdom Serena Holi-

days, 40–42 Kenway Rd., London SW5 ORA, tel. 01/248–
8422), operates ferries year-round, three times a week from
Syracuse, Catania, and Reggio Calabria, and a weekly ferry
service from Naples.

Important Addresses and Numbers

Tourist Information 1 City Gate Arcade, Valletta, tel. 227747. Luqa Airport, tel.
229915. Bisazza St., Sliema, tel. 313409.

Embassies **American.** Development House, St. Anne St., Floriana, tel.
620424. **British High Commission.** 7 St. Anne St., Floriana, tel.
233134.

Emergencies **Hospital,** St. Luke's, Gwardamanga, Valletta, tel. 621251. **Police,** 991. **Ambulance,** 996. **Fire Brigade,** 999.

Travel Agencies Thomas Cook, 20 Republic St., Valletta, tel. 620538.

Guided Tours

Orientation Sightseeing tours are arranged by local travel agents and the
large hotels.

Two-hour boat trips of the harbor of Valletta leave regularly
from Sliema jetty. Prices vary; you pay on board.

Personal Guides Licensed guides can be hired through the tourist information
office at the City Gate Arcade in Valletta.

Exploring Valletta

The mini-city of Valletta, with ornate palaces and museums
protected by massive honey-colored walls, was built by the
Knights of the Order of St. John after they broke the Turkish
siege in 1565.

The main entrance to the city is through the arched **City Gate**
(where all bus routes end), which leads onto Republic Street,
the spine of the city and the main shopping street. From Republic Street, other streets are laid out on a grid pattern, many
sloping precipitously to the harbors on either side. Some
streets are stepped. Houses along the narrow streets have
overhanging wooden balconies so close to each other they nearly touch.

Valletta's small size makes it ideal to explore on foot. Before
setting out along Republic Street, with all its shops and banks,
stop at the **Tourist Information Office** for maps, brochures, and
a copy of *What's On*. On your left is the Auberge de Provence
(the hostel of the knights from Provence), which now houses
the **National Museum of Archaeology.** Its collection includes
finds from Malta's many prehistoric sites—Taxien, Hagar
Qim, and the Hypogeum of Hal Saflini. You'll see pottery, statuettes, temple carvings, and, on the upper floor, finds from
Punic and Roman tombs. *Republic St., tel. 225577. Admission:
15c. Open mid-June–Sept. daily 8–2, Oct.–mid-June daily
8:30–5; closed public holidays.*

From Republic Street, turn right to St. John's Square. Dominating the square (where an open-air market is held) is **St.
John's Co-Cathedral.** This was the Order of St. John's own
church, completed in 1578. It became a co-cathedral with that
of Mdina in 1822 when it was placed under the authority of the

Bishops of Mdina for the first time. A side chapel was given
to each national group of knights, who decorated it in their
own distinctive way. The cathedral **museum** is in the oratory
in which hangs *The Beheading of St. John*, the masterpiece
painted by Caravaggio when he was staying on Malta in 1608.
In the museum, you'll find a rich collection of Flemish tapestries based on drawings by Poussin and Rubens, a ceremonial
church plate, and illuminated manuscripts. Keep your ticket,
since you can use it to get into the cathedral at Mdina.
*St. John's Sq. Admission: 50c. Open weekdays 9:30–noon,
3–5:30.*

While in St. John's Square, visit the **Government Craft Center,**
which has a wide range of traditional, handmade goods. *Open
Mon.–Fri. 9–7, Sat. 9–1, 4–8.*

Continue along Republic Street to the **Magisterial Palace,**
where Malta's parliament sits. Inside, friezes in the sumptuously decorated state apartments depict scenes from the history of the Knights. There is also a gallery with Gobelin tapestries. At the back of the building is the **Armoury of the Knights,**
with displays of arms and armor down through the ages. *Republic St. Admission: 15c. Open mid-June–Sept. daily 8–2,
Oct.–mid-June 8:30–5; closed public holidays.*

Another building from the days of the Knights of Malta is the
Order's **Library,** now the Royal Malta Library, which stands on
Republic Square. There are some outdoor cafés here, where
you can dine beneath a statue of Queen Victoria. On Old Theatre Street, you can see the elegant **Manoel Theatre.** Built in
1731, it is said to be Europe's oldest theater still in operation.

Return to Republic Street and continue to Fort St. Elmo and
the War Museum. **Fort St. Elmo** was built by the Knights to defend the harbor. Though completely destroyed during the siege
of 1565, it was rebuilt by succeeding military leaders. Today,
part of the fort houses the **War Museum,** with its collection of
armamants largely related to Malta's role in World War II.
Here you can see an Italian E-boat and the Gladiator "Faith"
aircraft that defended the island. *St. Elmo. Admission: 15c.
Open mid-June–Sept. daily 8–2, Oct.–mid-June daily 8:30–5;
closed public holidays.*

Continue along the seawall to the **Hospital of the Order.** This
gracious building has been sensitively converted into the
Mediterranean Conference Center. It's here you'll see *Malta
Experience,* the multimedia presentation on the history of Malta that is given six times a day.

Continue along the seawall and climb up to the **Upper Barracca
Gardens.** Once part of the city's defenses, they're now a pleas-
ant area from which to watch the comings and goings in the
Grand Harbour.

Next, cut along South Street, across Republic Street, to the
National Museum of Fine Art. The former 18th-century palace
has paintings from the 16th century to the present day, including works by Tintoretto, Preti, and Tiepolo, as well as local
artists. *South St., tel. 225769. Admission: 15c. Open mid-
June–Sept. daily 8–2, Oct.–mid-June 8:30–5; closed public
holidays.*

Dining

Prices are per person for a three-course meal, not including wine or tip. Best bets are indicated by a star ★. At press time, there were .31 Maltese lire (LM) to the dollar.

Category	Cost
Expensive	over 6 LM
Moderate	2 LM–6 LM
Inexpensive	under 2 LM

Credit Cards The following credit card abbreviations are used: AE, American Express; DC, Diners Club; MC, MasterCard; V, Visa.

Expensive **Bologna.** On the main shopping street in Valletta, this is an excellent place for typical Maltese food or well-cooked international cuisine, both presented with imagination and flair. *59 Republic St., tel. 626149. Jacket and tie. Reservations advised. AE, MC, DC, V.*

Moderate **Barrakka.** For a meal with a genuine Maltese touch, try Barrakka. All the Maltese favorites are served here, along with a good selection of locally produced wines and beers. *Castille Pl., tel. 226257. Dress: casual. Reservations advised. AE, DC, MC, V.*

★ **Pappagallo.** This is the new "in" place in Valletta, and it's popular with locals and visitors alike. Traditional Maltese food is featured, and the bustling atmosphere is warm and friendly. *Melitte St., tel. 226195. Dress: casual. Reservations advised. AE, DC, MC, V.*

Inexpensive **The Midland.** Come here for good, filling Maltese fare at excellent prices. The fish dishes are all worth a try. This is a good place for a quick lunch during a busy sightseeing day. *25 St. Ursula St. (no phone). Reservations not necessary. No credit cards.*

Lodging

Prices are for two people sharing a double room. At press time, there were .31 Maltese lire (LM) to the dollar.

Category	Cost
Very Expensive	over 35 LM
Expensive	20 LM–25 LM
Moderate	12 LM–20 LM
Inexpensive	8 LM–12 LM

Credit Cards The following credit card abbreviations are used: AE, American Express; DC, Diners Club; MC, MasterCard; V, Visa.

Very Expensive **Grand Hotel Excelsior.** Admire the view of Ta' Xbiex Marina and Lazaretto Creek from this elegantly modern hotel. The rooms are beautifully and comfortably furnished, all with balconies. There's an excellent restaurant as well as a poolside bar-restaurant. *Great Siege Rd., Floriana, tel. 623661. 188* rooms with bath. *Facilities: air-conditioning, pool, children's pool, water sports, tennis courts. AE, DC, MC, V.*

Phoenicia. The best-known hotel in Valletta is a typically grand hotel, with comfort and service second to none. The rooms are large and elegantly classical; the ambience is just right for a truly luxurious vacation. There is a choice of restaurants and bars. The Phoenicia has an idyllic setting in 8 acres (32,500 square meters) of landscaped gardens and is only a few minutes from the center of Valletta. *The Mall, tel. 22541. 110 rooms with bath. Facilities: air-conditioning, pool, children's pool, shops, hairdresser, music and dancing every evening. AE, DC, MC, V.*

Expensive **Fortina Hotel.** At Sliema seafront, the Fortina has excellent views of Valletta's dramatic fortifications. The atmosphere here is relaxed and informal; the service, attentive. *Tigne Seafront, tel. 30449. 98 rooms with bath. Facilities: air-conditioning, game room, waterfront lido with pool and snack bar, sunroof, regular entertainment. AE, DC, MC, V.*

Moderate **British.** If you want to be at the center of things, stay at the British, within Valletta's city walls. The garden is a lovely spot for a drink. There are pleasant views across the harbor. *267 St. Ursula St., tel. 226019. 42 rooms with bath. Facilities: restaurant, bar. MC, V.*

Castille. For a touch of old Malta, stay at the Castille in what used to be a 16th-century palazzo. This is a gracious, comfortable, Old World hotel with a friendly, relaxed ambience. It has an ideal central location, close to the museums and the bus terminus. There's a good restaurant with stunning views across the Grand Harbour. *St. Paul's St., tel. 623677. 26 rooms with bath. Facilities: air-conditioning, coffee shop-bar, sun terrace. AE.*

Inexpensive **Regina.** This is one of many inexpensive hotels that line the Sliema seafront. Offering excellent value, the Regina has its own restaurant and a pleasant garden. The rooms, though modest, are clean and comfortable, and the staff is helpful and friendly. *Tower Rd., tel. 330721. 14 rooms, most with bath. AE, DC, MC, V.*

Beyond Valletta

The rest of Malta has much to offer, ranging from strange prehistoric sites to richly decorated churches. Leaving Valletta, head first for the **Hypogeum of Hal Saflieni** at Paola, 3½ miles (six kilometers) south of the capital. This massive area of underground chambers was used for burials more than 4,000 years ago. Built on three levels, the chambers extend up to 40 feet (12 meters) beneath the ground, and there are examples of fine carving to be seen. *Admission: 15c. Open mid-June–Sept. daily 8–2, Oct.–mid-June daily 8:30–5; closed public holidays.*

Nearby is Tarxien, an ordinary suburban town with extraordinary megalithic monuments. The **Tarxien Temples** are three interconnecting temples with curious carvings, oracular chambers, and altars, all dating from about 2000 BC. *Admission: 15c. Open mid-June–Sept. daily 8–2, Oct.–mid-June daily 8:30–5; closed public holidays.*

Now make your way south to **Ghar Dalam.** A cave here, dating from the late stone age, was found to contain the semifossilized remains of now long-extinct species of dwarf elephants and hippopotomuses that roamed the island. You can visit the cave in which they were found and see the fossils on display in the small museum. *Admission: 15c. Open mid-June–Sept. daily 8–2, Oct.–mid-June, daily 8:30–5; closed public holidays.*

Follow the coast northwest to the **Blue Grotto,** near Wiedzi-Zurrieq. This is part of a group of water-filled caves made vivid by the phosphorescent marine life that color the water a distinctive and magical blue. You can reach the grotto only by sea. Local fishermen will take you there for about 4 LM.

Continue northwest to Rabat and Mdina via the colorful **Buskett Gardens,** best in the spring when the orange and lemon trees are in blossom. In **Rabat,** visit the beautiful **St. Paul's Church,** built next to a grotto where St. Paul is said to have taken refuge when he was shipwrecked on Malta in AD 60. Also of interest are the 4th century **catacombs** of St. Paul and St. Agatha, unusual for their rock "agape" tables where mourners would hold celebratory meals for the dead. *Admission: 15c. Open mid-June–Sept. daily 8–2, Oct.–mid-June daily 8:30–5; closed public holidays.*

Adjoining Rabat is **Mdina,** Malta's ancient walled capital. Also called the Silent City, it certainly lives up to its sobriquet: There's no traffic here, and the noise of the busy world outside somehow doesn't penetrate the thick, golden walls. Wandering through the peaceful streets is like entering an earlier age. Visit the serene Baroque cathedral of **St. Peter and St. Paul** for a look at Preti's fresco *The Shipwreck of St. Paul.* In the museum (you can use the ticket from the cathedral museum of St. John in Valletta), see the Dürer woodcuts and illuminated manuscripts. *Admission: 50c. Open Mon.–Sat. 9–1, 2–5.*

You have two choices. The first is to make your way back to Valletta by way of **Mosta** to see the **Church of St. Mary.** The Rotunda, as it is also known, has the third largest unsupported dome in Europe, after the Pantheon and St. Peter's, both in Rome. You can also see the bomb (now rendered harmless) that crashed through the dome during a service in 1942 and fell to the ground without exploding—a miraculous escape for those in the crowded church.

The second choice is to head for the northwest tip of the island and take a ferry to **Gozo,** Malta's lusher, quieter sister island. The capital, Victoria, has a charming old town with attractive cafés and bars, around the main square, and a hilltop citadel with an impressive **Roman-Baroque cathedral.** The museum here offers displays of ceremonial silver and manuscripts. *Admission: 15c. Open mid-June–Sept. daily 8–2, Oct.–mid-June daily 8:30–5; closed public holidays.*

The town also has a recent **Folklore Museum** (Milite Bernardo St.) and an impressive archaeological collection in the **Gozo Museum** (Cathedral Square). *Admission to each: 15c. Open mid-June–Sept. daily 8–2, Oct.–mid-June daily 8:30–5; closed public holidays.*

On Xaghra Plateau stand the extraordinary pair of **Ggantija Prehistoric Temples.** *Admission: 15c. Open mid-June–Sept.*

daily 8–2, Oct.–mid-June daily 8:30–5; closed public holidays.

In the town of **Xaghra** itself, there are two underground alabaster caves with delicately colored stalagmites and stalactites. In the cliffs nearby is the cave where the sea nymph Calypso, mentioned in Homer's *Odyssey*, is said to have lived; with such stunning views, it's easy to imagine that the myth might be true.

Dining and Lodging

For details and price category definitions, *see* Dining and Lodging in Essential Information.

Gozo **Calypso.** There's so much to do at this modern hotel that you
Lodging don't even need to relax. The choice of dining spots includes a Chinese restaurant. Rooms are comfortably furnished and have balconies, most with sea views. *Marsalforn, tel. 556131. 92 rooms with bath. Facilities: nightclub, squash courts, lighted tennis courts, game room, rooftop splash pool, boutique, bank. AE, DC, MC, V. Moderate.*

Cornucopia. For pleasant, personal service and a restful vacation, try this lovingly restored farmhouse near the village of Xaghra—it's an ideal base for exploring the island, and the sea is just a short drive away. There's a good restaurant and barbecues in the summer. *10 Grien Imrik St., Xaghra, tel. 556486. 16 rooms with bath. Facilities: pool. AE, DC, MC, V. Moderate.*

Mdina **Mdina Restaurant.** There's a tempting choice of Maltese dishes
Dining or well-presented international cuisine. The decor is attractive and restful, and the service, attentive and professional. *Holy Cross St., tel. 774004. Jacket and tie. Reservations advised. AE, DC, MC, V. Expensive.*

Lodging **Xara Palace.** Staying at the romantic Xara Palace is rather like taking a step back in time. It's situated in the 16th-century palace of one of Malta's old noble families, and it retains much of a dusty, aristocratic feel, with high-ceiling rooms, antique furnishings, and grand oil paintings. There isn't much in the way of modern-day facilities, but this is more than made up for by the charm and character of the place. *St. Paul's Sq., tel. 674002. 19 rooms with bath. V. Inexpensive.*

Tarxien **Il Kastell.** If you're into healthy eating, try this restaurant at-
Dining tached to the Malta Health Farm. Dishes are imaginative and specialties wholesome, particularly the flambé specialties. *62 Main St., tel. 823581. Jacket and tie. Reservations advised. AE, DC, MC, V. Moderate.*

Lodging **Malta Health Farm.** Your stay in this converted hunting lodge will include an individually planned diet, supervised gym sessions, and a daily steam bath and massage. Then relax in the garden in the glorious Maltese sunshine. *62 Main St., tel. 786477. Facilities: tennis courts, health and fitness center, pool, disco. AE, DC, MC, V. Moderate.*

25 Monaco

Introduction

The tiny horseshoe-shaped principality of Monaco lies toward the eastern edge of the French Riviera and does more than its fair share to live up to that region's glittering sybaritic image. Its entire land area measures just under one square mile, squeezed between the Alpes-Maritimes and the Mediterranean; as far as sovereign states go, only the Vatican City is smaller.

The country divides neatly into four quarters. Monaco Town, the picturesque old quarter where the palace stands, is built on a rocky promontory. To the eastern side of the Port de Monaco lies the resort of Monte Carlo, still synonymous with gambling and glamour. Between Monte Carlo and Monaco Town is the commercial and residential area of La Condamine, which includes the harbor. Tucked behind the old quarter is Fontvieille, where industry flourishes discreetly on reclaimed land.

Though Monaco is a self-governed state, with its own tiny army and police force, its language, food, and way of life are French. To the casual eye, it may seem like any other small French town, but Monaco has its own distinct atmosphere. Its luxurious Hôtel de Paris, its famous casino, its highly visible royal Grimaldi family, its wealth of jet-setters, its chic fashions, and its opulent yachts all ensure that it maintains its reputation as a "golden ghetto"—one of the last enclaves in the world to which the rich, the titled, and the merely curious flock in droves to breathe in the aura of money.

Before You Go

When to Go
Climate
Monaco's climate is roughly similar to that of San Diego, with a great deal of sunshine and an average daily temperature of 68°. The principality is crowded year-round with visitors, but like the very wealthy, you should try to avoid the summer onslaught and visit instead in the spring or fall.

The following are the average daily maximum and minimum temperatures for Monte Carlo.

Jan.	54F	12C	May	66F	19C	Sept.	74F	24C
	47	8		59	15		67	20
Feb.	55F	13C	June	73F	23C	Oct.	68F	20C
	47	8		66	19		61	16
Mar.	57F	14C	July	78F	26C	Nov.	61F	16C
	50	10		71	22		54	12
Apr.	61F	16C	Aug.	78F	26C	Dec.	56F	14C
	54	12		71	22		49	10

Currency
The French franc is legal currency in Monaco; for a breakdown of the coinage system *see* Currency, in France.

What It Will Cost
Prices in Monaco are comparable to those in Paris. Here are a few samples of what to expect: open-face sandwich, 12–15 francs; one-mile (.62 kilometers) taxi ride, 20–25 francs; Coca-Cola, 6–10 francs; beer, 8.50 francs; foreign newspaper, 8 francs.

Visas
The same requirements apply as for visiting France; *see* Visas, in France.

Customs on Arrival None if you enter from France; otherwise (if you arrive by boat), the same as for France (*see* Customs and Duties, in France).

Language Although French is the major language, English is usually spoken in shops and hotels.

Arriving in Monaco

By Plane The nearest airport is **Nice–Riviera International,** some 14 miles (22 kilometers) away.

Between the Airport and Downtown. Take a taxi (40 minutes), minibus (50 minutes), rental car, or helicopter (six minutes).

By Train The Monaco–Monte Carlo train station is at avenue Prince Pierre, tel. 93–87–50–50.

By Car Monaco is reached via the A8. Some sample distances: Paris, 600 miles (958 kilometers); Cannes, 30 miles (50 kilometers); Nice, 11 miles (17 kilometers); Italian border, 8 miles (12 kilometers); Rome, 425 miles (678 kilometers).

Getting Around

By Bus There are five bus routes that travel the major arteries; see the tourist office's pamphlet *Getting About the Principality* for details. There's a 50% discount on a book of eight tickets.

By Taxi Two taxi ranks are in service 24 hours a day: at the train station (tel. 93–50–92–27), and near the Casino on allée des Boulingrins (tel. 93–50–56–28). Taxis can be hailed on the street.

On Foot Monaco is truly hilly, and walking even short distances can be exhausting. For this reason, the powers-that-be have installed elevators in strategic locations on the most demanding inclines.

Essential Information

Telephones The cost of a local call is .74 francs, with no time limit. Information and inquiries, tel. 12.

Mail French postal rates apply (*see* Mail, in France), though Monaco stamps must be used.

Opening and Closing Times **Banks.** Banks are open weekdays, usually 9:30–noon and 2:30–4:30.
Museums. Most museums are open daily year-round, with varying schedules depending upon the season.
Shops. Shops are generally open Monday–Saturday 9–noon and 3–7; a few close on Saturday afternoon or Monday morning.

National Holidays January 1 (New Year's Day); March 27 (Easter Monday); May 1 (Labor Day); May 8 (VE Day); May 4 (Ascension); May 14 (Whit Monday); August 15 (Assumption); November 1 (All Saints); November 11 (Armistice); November 19 (National Day); December 25.

Tipping Hotels, restaurants, and cafés will always include a service charge on the bill, so don't feel obliged to tip.

Important Addresses and Numbers

Tourist Information: *La Direction du Tourisme et des Congrès,* 2-A blvd. des Moulins, tel. 93–30–87–01.

Consulates: *American.* 31 rue Maréchal Joffre, Nice, tel. 93–88–89–55. *British.* 11 rue Paradis, Nice, tel. 93–82–32–04. *Canadian.* "Le Continental," pl. des Moulins, Monte Carlo, tel. 93–25–58–22.

Emergencies: Police, tel. 93–30–42–46; **Ambulance,** tel. 93–30–04–85; **Doctor,** tel. 141; **Dentist,** *see* Monaco yellow pages under *Dentistes;* **Pharmacies,** tel. 141; **Fire,** tel. 18.

English Bookstore: *Scruples,* 9 rue Princesse Caroline, tel. 93–50–43–52.

Travel Agency: *American Express,* 35 blvd. Princesse Charlotte, tel. 93–25–74–45.

Guided Tours: *Contact Welcome Travel Team SAM,* "Le Panorama," Bloc C/D, 57 rue Grimaldi, tel. 93–50–19–19.

Exploring Monaco

For more than a century Monaco's livelihood was centered ❶ around it's splendid copper-roof **casino.** The oldest section dates from 1878 and was conceived by Charles Garnier, architect of the Paris opera house. It's as elaborately ornate as anyone could wish, bristling with turrets and gold filigree, and masses of interior frescoes and bas-reliefs. There are lovely sea views from the **terrace,** and the **gardens** out front are meticulously tended. The main activity is in the American Room, where beneath the gilt-edged ceiling busloads of tourists feed the one-armed bandits. *Pl. du Casino, tel. 93–50–69–31. Persons under 21 not admitted. Admission for American Room free. Open daily 10 AM–4 AM; closed May 1.*

❷ The **Musée National des Automates et Poupées d'Autrefois** (Museum of Dolls and Automatons) has a compelling collection of 18th- and 19th-century dolls and mechanical figures, the latter shamelessly showing off their complex inner workings. It's magically set in a 19th-century seaside villa (designed by Garnier). *17 av. Princesse Grace, tel. 93–30–91–26. Admission: 30 francs. Open daily 10–12:15, 2:30–6:30.*

Monaco Town, the principality's old quarter, has many vaulted passageways and exudes an almost tangible medieval feel. The ❸ magnificent **Palais du Prince** (Prince's Palace), a grandiose Italianate structure with a Moorish tower, was largely rebuilt in the last century. Here, since 1297, the Grimaldi dynasty has lived and ruled. The spectacle of the **Changing of the Guard** occurs each morning at 11:55; inside, guided tours take visitors through the state apartments and a wing containing the **Palace Archives** and **Musée Napoléon** (Napoleonic Museum). *Pl. du Palais, tel. 93–25–18–31. Admission: 30 francs. Palace open daily July–Sept., 9:30–12:30, 2–6:30; closed Oct.–June. Musée Napoléon and Palace Archives open year-round, Tues.–Sun.*

❹ Monaco's **cathedral** (4 rue Colonel Bellando de Castro) is a late 19th-century neo-Romanesque confection where Philadelphia-born Princess Grace lies in splendor along with past members

Monaco

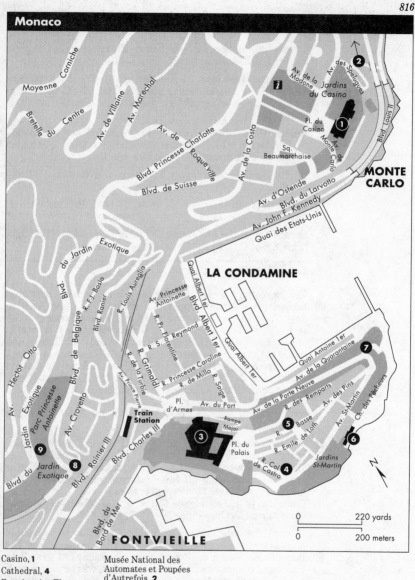

Casino, **1**

Cathedral, **4**

Fort Antoine Theater, **7**

Jardin Exotique, **8**

Musée Historial des
Princes de Monaco, **5**

Musée National des
Automates et Poupées
d'Autrefois, **2**

Musée
Océanographique, **6**

Museum of Prehistoric
Anthropology, **9**

Palais du Prince, **3**

⑤ of the Grimaldi dynasty. Nearby is the **Musée Historial des Princes de Monaco** (Waxworks Museum, 27 rue Basse, tel. 93–30–39–05), a Monégasque Madame Tussauds, with none-too-realistic wax figures stiffly portraying various episodes in the Grimaldi history. The waxworks may not convince, but the **rue Basse** is wonderfully atmospheric.

Next to the **St-Martin Gardens**—which contains an evocative bronze monument in memory of **Prince Albert I** (Prince Ranier's great-grandfather, the one in the sou'wester and flying oil skins, benignly guiding a ship's wheel)—is the **Musée** **⑥** **Océanographique** (Oceanography Museum and Aquarium). As well as being a fascinating museum, it is also an internationally renowned research institute founded by the very Prince Albert who is remembered outside for being an eminent marine biologist in his day; the well-known underwater explorer Jacques Cousteau is the present director. The aquarium is the undisputed highlight, however, where a collection of the world's fish and crustacea live out their lives in public, some colorful, some drab, some the stuff nightmares are made of. *Av. St-Martin, tel. 93–30–15–14. Admission: 40 francs. Open Sept.–June, daily 9:30–7; July and Aug. 9–9.*

Time Out Take the elevator to the aquarium's roof terrace for a fine view of the sea—which may look a little different now that you know what's lurking down there—and have a restorative drink at the bar.

Before heading back inland, take a short stroll to the eastern **⑦** tip of the rock, to the **Fort Antoine Theater,** a converted 18th-century fortress that certainly looks a lot prettier now than it would have in more warlike times, covered as it is in ivies and flowering myrtle and thyme. In the summer, this is an open-air theater seating 350. *Av. de la Quarantaine, tel. 93–30–19–21.*

⑧ The Moneghetti area is the setting for the **Jardin Exotique** (Tropical Gardens), where 600 varieties of cacti and succulents cling to the rock face, their improbable shapes and sometimes violent coloring a further testimony to the fact that Mother Nature will try anything once. Your ticket also allows you to **⑨** explore the **caves,** adjacent to the gardens, and to visit the **Museum of Prehistoric Anthropology,** adjacent. *Blvd. du Jardin Exotique, tel. 93–30–33–65. Admission: 20 francs. Open Oct.–May, daily 9–5:30; June–Sept. 9–7.*

Shopping

Monte Carlo is the perfect place for shopping in the grand style, but don't look for bargains. All the big names are here, from **Cartier** to **Vuitton;** all the sales assistants speak English; and all the cashiers are happy to accept dollars, pounds, yen, and, of course, plastic. Most boutiques are on streets surrounding the casino: place du Casino, ave. des Beaux-Arts, blvd. de Moulins, and ave. Princess Grace. Somewhat younger, friendlier boutiques are in the Park Palace complex at the head of the casino gardens.

Dining

Monaco has more than 100 places to dine, from pizzerias to restaurants in the top hotels, but serious *gourmands* should be warned that the ambience and the clientele often take precedence over the quality of the meals. The cuisine is decidedly French, with light breakfasts the norm (coffee and croissants), and lunches and multicourse dinners awash with wine, by the carafe or bottle.

Ratings Prices are per person for a three-course meal, with a half-bottle or carafe of house wine. Best bets are indicated by a star ★. At press time, there were 5.7 francs to the dollar.

Category	Cost
Very Expensive	over 400 francs
Expensive	250–400 francs
Moderate	150–250 francs
Inexpensive	under 150 francs

Credit Cards The following credit card abbreviations are used: AE, American Express; DC, Diners Club; MC, MasterCard; V, Visa.

Very Expensive **Louis XV.** A strong contender for the best-in-Monaco award, Louis XV is more formally geared than its main opposition, Dominique le Stanc (see below), with a heavily opulent decor and chef Alain Ducasse's beautifully conceived dishes, such as ravioli with foie gras and truffles. The wine cellar is exceptional. *Hotel de Paris, pl. du Casino, tel. 93–50–80–80. Jacket and tie required. Reservations advised. AE, DC, MC, V.*

Expensive **Bec Rouge.** This is where all the best Monégasques can be observed tucking into their *gratin de langoustes* at dinnertime, linen napkins billowing. Food is classic French, decor *le plus* chic. *11 av. de Grande Bretagne, tel. 93–30–74–91. Jacket and tie required. Reservations essential. AE, DC. Closed Jan. and mid-June.*

★ **Dominique le Stanc.** This restaurant is cited by some authorities as Monaco's top dining experience, and its young owner-chef certainly has the basic qualifications to back it up. The inventive cuisine doesn't rely on the obvious foie gras, caviar, and lobster to justify the high prices. The delightful decor features a collection of toys, both antique and modern. *18 blvd. des Moulins, tel. 93–50–63–37. Dress: elegantly casual. Reservations recommended, essential in summer. AE, DC, V. Closed Sun. and Mon.*

Rampoldi. The epitome of chic and very popular with the blue blazer-and-white cap yachting set. The emphasis here is on Italian fare. *Av Spélugues, tel. 93–30–70–65. Jacket required (cap optional). Reservations advised. AE, DC, V. Closed Nov.*

Moderate **Café de Paris.** This café, brasserie, drugstore, and bar is an institution, an unpretentious spot to meet people or to grab a great hamburger and glass of wine. *Pl. du Casino, tel. 93–50–57–75. Casually chic dress. No reservations. AE, DC, MC, V.*

★ **Restaurant du Port.** Top-notch Italian cuisine is the specialty here; the fish dishes are particularly memorable. The terrace provides a terrific view of the harbor, dotted with those small liners tycoons like to call yachts. *Quai Albert ler, tel. 93–50–67–94. Dress: casual. Reservations advised. AE, DC, MC, V. Closed Mon. and Nov.*

Inexpensive **Popletta.** This popular trattoria is close enough to the Italian
★ border to pass as the real thing. It's an excellent value for the

money, with delicious home cooking to boot. *Rue Paradis, tel. 93–50–67–84. Dress: casual. Reservations essential in high season. V. Closed Thurs.–Sun. and Feb.*

Lodging

Monaco's top five-star hotels are the last word in luxurious trappings and correspondingly expensive. There are more economical places, of course, but, on the whole, vacationers on a budget might do better to stay in Menton or Nice and visit by bus or train.

Ratings   Prices are given per double room. Best bets are indicated with a star ★. At press time, there were 5.7 francs to the dollar.

Category	Cost
Very Expensive	over 1,000 francs
Expensive	525–1,000 francs
Moderate	260–525 francs
Inexpensive	under 260 francs

Credit Cards   The following credit card abbreviations are used: AE, American Express; DC, Diners Club; MC, MasterCard; V, Visa.

Very Expensive   **Hermitage.** One of Monaco's big three, the Hermitage was built at the end of the last century and is as sumptuous a place as you could hope for. The recently reappointed rooms are huge, with deep carpets, but disappointing in comparison with the lavish public areas. *Sq. Beaumarchais, tel. 93–50–67–31. 236 rooms with bath. Facilities: pool, restaurant, conference room. AE, DC, MC, V.*

★ **Hôtel de Paris.** A really exceptional establishment, where elegance, luxury, dignity, and Old World charm are the watchwords. Built in 1864, it still exudes the gold-plated splendor of an era when kings and grand dukes stayed here. *Pl. du Casino, tel. 93–50–80–80. 271 rooms with bath. Facilities: 2 restaurants, bar, pool, health club, shops, tennis. AE, DC, MC, V.*

★ **Loews.** This complex is an offspring of the modern travel world of adventure and gambling junkets. Though there are those who mutter about brash vulgarity, many love it. Its casino has already surpassed Monaco's famous original in terms of gambling turnovers, if not in taste. *12 av. des Spélugues, tel. 93–50–65–00. 636 rooms with bath. Facilities: rooftop freshwater pool, health club, casino, 5 restaurants, shopping mall, Jacuzzi. AE, DC, MC, V.*

Expensive   **Beach Plaza.** Rooms at this Trust House Forte hotel can be as highly priced as at the top spots, but less expensive space is available, too. An enticing feature is the private beach. Don't expect great architectural charm: This is a modern high rise. *22 av. Princesse Grace, tel. 93–30–98–80. 316 rooms with bath. Facilities: 2 restaurants, 3 freshwater pools, beach. AE, DC, MC, V.*

Mirabeau. This five-star high rise benefits from comfortablly proportioned rooms and terraces overlooking the sea. It's just moments from the beach, and a find for those who revel in sun and sand. *1 av. Princesse Grace, tel. 93–25–45–45. 100 rooms* *with bath or shower. Facilities: restaurant, pool, tennis, casino. AE, DC, MC, V.*

Moderate   **Alexandra.** One of Monaco's few moderately priced hotels, this one lies close to the casino. Its exterior magnificence doesn't extend to its internal workings, but the place is clean and friendly nonetheless. Some rooms are inexpensive. *35 blvd. Princesse Charlotte, tel. 93–50–63–13. 55 rooms, 46 with bath or shower. Facilities: restaurant. AE, DC, V.*

Balmoral. Despite the name, there's nothing even vaguely Scottish about this somewhat old-fashioned hotel overlooking the harbor. Rooms are a reasonable size if blandly decorated; many have balconies. *12 av. de la Costa, tel. 93–50–62–37. 68 rooms with bath or shower. Facilities: restaurant. AE, DC, MC, V. Restaurant closed Nov.*

Inexpensive   **France.** The modest hotel France, near the train station, can't begin to compete with the opulence of some of the others on our list, but it's one of the cheapest around and worth a look if you are on a tight budget. *6 rue de la Turbie, tel. 93–30–24–64. 26 rooms, 18 with bath or shower. DC, MC, V.*

The Arts

Ballet, opera, concert, and theater tickets can be obtained from the **Atrium du Casino de Monte Carlo** (pl. du Casino, tel. 93–50–76–54; open Tues.–Sun. 10–12:30, 2–5). Information on all cultural events is available from the **Direction des Affaires Culturelles** (4 rue des Iris, tel. 93–30–19–21).

Nightlife

As you'd expect, Monaco has a sophisticated range of night spots, some the talk of the Riviera. Here are a few of the best discos and cabarets: **Jimmy'z,** pl. du Casino (moves in summer to Monte Carlo Sporting Club, av. Princesse Grace, tel. 93–30–71–71); **Living Room,** 7 av. des Spélugues (tel. 93–50–58–31); Navy Club, plage du Lavrotto; **Tiffany's,** 3 av. des Spélugues (tel. 93–50–53–13); **Cabaret du Casino,** pl. du Casino (tel. 93–50–80–90); **La Folie Russe;** Loews Hotel (tel. 93–50–65–00); and **Parady'z, Chez Regine,** and **La Salle des Etoiles,** all at the Monte Carlo Sporting Club.

26 Norway

Introduction

Norway has some of the remotest and most dramatic scenery in
Europe, with deep fjords cutting sometimes more than a hundred miles into the heart of steep, coastal mountain ranges.
Cobbled streets wind past wooden houses down to docks where
Viking ships and, later, whaling vessels once set sail. Inland,
miles of cross-country ski trails pass by frozen trout streams,
and downhill runs career through forests that in summer are
full of wildflowers and berries.

So why isn't the place overrun with weary tourists eager to get
away from it all? The main answer is cost. There is no avoiding
the fact that Norway is at least as expensive as the rest of
Scandinavia. On the positive side, Norwegians prefer entertainment of the outdoor variety; so, inexpensive or free
activities—such as cross-country skiing or fishing—are widely
available.

Keep an eye out, too, for special reductions in accommodations;
there are both seasonal and group discounts. Other ways of
beating the cost of living include sampling the famous
smørgasbord, which can make a substantial, good-value lunch,
and investing in the cost-cutting Oslo Card, which offers reductions in travel and sightseeing in the capital and environs.

After even a brief visit to Norway, you'll encounter an important feature of the national character—pride. The Norwegians
are proud not only of their mountainous land but also of their
distinguished history. Their fiercely independent spirit has
been evident from the Viking era right up to the present century, when daring Resistance fighters changed the course of
World War II by crippling Nazi efforts to develop atomic weapons. Their winter raids across seemingly impassable Telemark
trails would have been impossible without the confidence
gained from centuries of struggle against a harsh and unforgiv-
ing land.

A similar sense of struggle has been the source of inspiration
for Norway's creative geniuses, which you'll discover in the music of Edvard Grieg (1843–1907), the plays of Henrik Ibsen
(1828–1906), and the paintings of Edvard Munch (1863–1944).

Before You Go

When to Go Cross-country skiing was born in Norway, and the country remains an important winter sports center. Cold winters, with
little risk of thaw, give way to the brighter, longer days of February and early March. This is the best time for skiing, and
many hotels have more space then (prior to the peak time at
Easter). The rest of March and April presents a frustrating
succession of thaws and freezes, with slush and scudding gray
clouds.

This weather is gradually replaced by generally pleasant summer weather and the famous midnight sun, when even in the
"southern" city of Oslo there is a sort of twilight around midnight, and dawn comes by 2 AM. The weather can be fickle,
however, and rainwear and sturdy waterproof shoes are recommended even in summer.

Norway

0 — 200 miles
0 — 300 km

North Cape

Vardø
Vadsø
Kirkenes
Hammerfest
Alta
Masi
Tromsø

FINLAND

Bardu
Narvik

ATLANTIC
OCEAN

Vestfjorden

Bodø Fauske
Saltdal

Arctic Circle

Mo-i-Rana Umbukta
Sandnessjøen
Mosjøen
Brønnøysund

SWEDEN

Gulf of Bothnia

Vikna
Namsos

Steinkjer

Trondheim Meraker
Støren
Kristiansund
Oppdal Røros
Ålesund Tynset
Dombås
Nord fjord Otta
Florø Jostedalsbreen Koppang
Sognafjord Rena
Voss Hamar
Bergen
Hardangerfjord Hønefoss Oslo
Kongsberg Sarpsborg
Haugesund Drammen Fredrikstad
Larvik
Porsgrunn
Stavanger Oslofjord
Sandnes Arendal
Evje
Grimstad Skagerrak Kattegat
Mandal Kristiansand

Baltic Sea

N

The best times to avoid crowds in museums and on ferries are May and September; Norwegians themselves are on vacation in July and August. Bear in mind that the country virtually closes down for the five-day Easter holidays, when Norwegians make their annual migration to the mountains. Hotels are more crowded and expensive during this period, but some offer discounts in the two weeks before Easter—which is a good time for skiing.

Climate The following are the average daily maximum and minimum temperatures for Oslo.

Jan.	28F	−2C	May	61F	16C	Sept.	60F	16C
	19	−7		43	6		46	8
Feb.	30F	−1C	June	68F	20C	Oct.	48F	9C
	19	−7		50	10		38	3
Mar.	39F	4C	July	72F	22C	Nov.	38F	3C
	25	−4		55	13		31	−1
Apr.	50F	10C	Aug.	70F	21C	Dec.	32F	0C
	34	1		53	12		25	−4

Currency The unit of currency in Norway is the krone, written as kr., but known internationally as NOK. It is divided into 100 øre. Bills of 10, 50, 100, 500, and 1,000 NOK are in general use. Coins are 1, 5, 10, 50, and 100 øre. Credit cards are accepted in most hotels, stores, restaurants, and many gas stations and garages, but generally not in smaller shops and inns in rural areas. Bank charges are per transaction, so it is more economical to change larger amounts of money or traveler's checks. The exchange rate at press time (fall 1988) was NOK 6.2 to the dollar and NOK 10.7 to the pound.

What It Will Cost Norway has a high standard—and cost—of living, but there are ways of saving money by taking advantage of some special offers for accommodations and travel during the tourist season and on weekends throughout the year.

The **Oslo Card**—valid for one, two, or three days—entitles you to free admission to all museums and galleries and unlimited travel on transportation operated by the Oslo Transport system and the Norwegian Railways commuter trains within the city limits. It also gives a 50% discount for trains to and from Oslo, free parking, and discounts in restaurants, shops, and sports facilities. You can get the Oslo Card at the main tourist information office in Oslo (*see* Oslo Important Addresses and Numbers). *Cost: adults, one day NOK 75, two days NOK 100, three days NOK 140; children, one day NOK 35, two days NOK 50, three days NOK 65.*

Urban hotels have special weekend and summer rates from late June to early August. Even during the peak season, you can get discounts in rural hotels by staying several days and having meals included in your rate. Alcohol is expensive and difficult to obtain, and meals are on the high side, too, although portions are large. Do as the Norwegians do, and have a large breakfast (included in room prices) so that lunch can be little more than a light snack.

Sample Prices Cup of coffee, NOK 8–NOK 10; bottle of beer, NOK 35; Coca-Cola, NOK 15; ham sandwich, NOK 35; one-mile taxi ride, NOK 40.

Customs on Arrival Residents of non-European countries may import duty-free into Norway 400 cigarettes or 50 grams of cigars or tobacco, two liters of alcohol (not stronger than 60% content) or two liters of wine and two liters of beer, 50 grams of perfume and 0.5 liter of eau-de-cologne, plus other goods to the value of NOK 3,500.

Residents of European countries may import 200 cigarettes or 250 grams of tobacco or cigars, one liter of liquor and one liter of fortified wine or two liters of fortified wine or two liters of table wine and two liters of beer, a small amount of perfume or eau-de-cologne, and goods to the value of NOK 700.

Language In larger cities, most hotels, restaurants, and shops, and on public transport, there will be no difficulty in finding people who speak English. Most Norwegians under the age of 45 can speak it fairly well; it is the main foreign language taught at schools, and the movies and cable TV have brought English-language telecasts into thousands of Norwegian homes.

Norwegian has many regional dialects, and there are two forms of the official language, so even if you pick up a few words, don't be disheartened if you can't understand them when spoken by a native. The Norwegian alphabet has three extra letters—all vowels—which come at the end of the normal alphabet. Remember this if you are looking up anything in a phone book. The three extras are Æ, Ø, and Å.

Getting Around

By Car
Road Conditions Roads are narrow and winding, so never expect to cover more than 150 miles (250 kilometers) in a day. The climate plays havoc with the roads: Even the best suffer from frost, and the Telemark is the only Bergen–Oslo route to remain open all year. Make sure you have snow tires or chains; if renting, choose a smaller model with front-wheel drive.

Rules of the Road Driving is on the right. The speed limit is 90 kph (55 mph) on highways, 80 kph (50 mph) on main roads, 50 kph (30 mph) in towns, and 30–40 kph (20–25 mph) in residential areas. Passing areas on narrow roads are marked with a white M (for Møtepas) on a blue background. Do not drink and drive: There are spot checks, and you can face a jail sentence, the loss of your license, and a heavy fine.

Parking Parking in cities and towns is clearly marked on streets, and there are municipal parking lots, as well. You cannot park on main roads or on bends. Exact details on Oslo streets, including specific parking restrictions, can be found in the leaflet "Parking in Oslo," available free from tourist offices and gas stations.

Gasoline Gas costs about NOK 5.30 per liter.

Breakdowns The Norwegian Automobile Association (NAF) has patrols on main roads and a network of emergency telephones on mountain roads. For NAF 24-hour service, dial 02/429400.

By Train Norwegian trains are comfortable and punctual, and the scenery makes any trip memorable. Unfortunately, the network is limited, with most routes fanning out from Oslo, leaving the coasts—except in the south—with no service. Some express trains have observation cars, and all have dining or buffet cars.

Reservations are required on all express *(Ekspresstog)* and some fast *(Huritog)* services.

Fares Apart from the Europe-wide passes (Eurailpass, Inter-Rail), a special Scandinavian pass called **Nordturist** allows unlimited travel in Norway, Sweden, Denmark, and Finland for 21 days. Cost is NOK 1,433, and the ticket is available through the **Norwegian State Railway** (21–24 Lockspur St., London SW1Y 5DA, tel. 01/930–6666); there is no U.S. branch, so U.S. tourists should write or call the London office. Credit card payments are accepted. A 21-day **Youth Pass** is also available for 12–26 year olds, at a cost of NOK 1,075.

By Plane The remoteness of so much of Norway means that air travel is a necessity for many inhabitants. The main Scandinavian airline, **SAS**, operates a network, along with **Braathens SAFE** and **Wideroe's**. Fares are high, but the time saved makes it attractive if you are in a hurry.

By Bus The Norwegian bus network makes up for some of the limitations of the country's train system, and several of the routes are particularly scenic. For example, the north Norway bus service, starting at Fauske (on the train line to Bodø), goes right up to Kirkenes on the Russian-Norwegian border, covering the 625 miles (1,000 kilometers) in four days. Long-distance bus routes also connect Norway with all its Scandinavian neighbors.

By Ferry Norway's long, fjord-indented coastline is served by an intricate network of ferries and larger passenger ships, in many places providing an essential means of transport and communication. A wide choice of services is available, from simple hops across fjords (saving many miles of traveling) and excursions among the thousands of islands, to luxury cruises and long journeys the entire length of the coast. Reservations are required on ferry journeys of more than one day but are not needed for simple fjord crossings. Fares and exact times of departures depend on the season and the availability of ships, but the main Norwegian tourist office (*see* Important Addresses and Numbers) has the most accurate information.

One of the world's great sea voyages is a mail and passenger service called the **Hurtigrute** (*see* Ten Great Itineraries, at the front of this book), which runs up the Norwegian coast from Bergen to Kirkenes, well above the Arctic Circle.

Essential Information

Telephones Norway's phone system is one of the world's most expensive, so try to make calls when rates are reduced (5 PM–8 AM weekdays, or all day weekends). Also, avoid using room phones in hotels unless you're willing to pay a hefty service charge. In public booths, place coins in the phone before dialing. Unused coins are returned. The largest coins accepted are NOK 5, so make sure you have enough small change.

Local Calls Costs of calls within Norway vary according to distance: Within Oslo, the cost goes up according to the amount of time used after the three-minute flat fee. Pages 1–9 of the Oslo phone book have full details on charges.

International Calls To call the USA, dial 095–1, then the area code and number. For the United Kingdom, dial 095–44, then the area code (minus the first 0) and number.

Operators and Information Dial 093 for an English-speaking operator. For local information, dial 0180. For international information, dial 0181.

Mail *Postal Rates* Letters and postcards to the USA cost NOK 4.80 for the first 20 grams. For the United Kingdom, the rate is NOK 3.80 for the first 50 grams.

Receiving Mail Have letters marked "poste restante" after the name of the town, with your surname underlined. The service is free, and letters are directed to the nearest main post office.

Shopping The high cost of living in Norway makes it difficult to find bargains of the sort you could find in, say, southern Europe. Norwegians specialize in pewter, ceramics, and glass, as do all Scandinavians. Norwegian ceramic designs have a heavier, more traditional feel to them, with peasant motifs given emphasis. Sweaters and knitwear also incorporate traditional designs; most department stores have a good selection.

VAT Refunds Most of the 20% Norwegian VAT will be refunded to any visitor who spends more than NOK 300 in any one store. Ask for a special tax-free check and show your passport. All items must be presented together with the tax-free check at the tax-free counter at ports, airports, and border posts. The VAT will be refunded, minus a 4.5% service charge.

Opening and Closing Times **Banks.** Banks are open weekdays 8:30–3:30.
Museums. Museums are usually open 10–6 and are either closed or have shorter hours on Sunday.
Shops. Though times vary enormously, most shops are open Monday to Friday from 8:30 to 4:30 or 5, and Saturday from 8:30 to 1. Many stay open one day a week until 7.

National Holidays January 1; March 23–27 (Easter); May 1 (Labor Day); May 4 (Ascension Day); May 14, 15 (Pentecost); May 17 (Constitution Day); December 25, 26 (Christmas).

Dining The Norwegians need a lot of protein and carbohydrates to outlast the fierce winters, and their cuisine reflects this. Breakfast is usually a large buffet of smoked fish, cheeses, sausage, cold meats, and cereal, washed down with tea, good coffee, or milk. Lunch, as a result, is never very expansive—usually a similar cold table, or those same ingredients combined to make the famous *smörbröd* open sandwich. Dinners are wholesome preparations of three or four courses, starting with cold hors d'oeuvres and soup and often ending with delicious fresh fruit and berries. The main course is often salmon, summer trout, or other fish; alternatives can include lamb or pork, reindeer, or even ptarmigan.

The most expensive part of eating is—drinking. Alcohol is taxed severely and is not served on Sunday in most areas. One consolation is the quality of the water, which is among the purest in the world.

Mealtimes Lunch is usually served from noon to 3. Dinner has traditionally been early, but in hotels and major restaurants it is now more often from 6 to 10. Some rural places still serve dinner from 4 to 7.

Ratings Prices are per person and include a first course, main course, and dessert, without wine or tip. Best bets are indicated by a star ★. At press time, there were 6.2 krones (NOK) to the dollar.

Category	Cost
Very Expensive	over NOK 300
Expensive	NOK 200–NOK 300
Moderate	NOK 100–NOK 200
Inexpensive	under NOK 100

Credit Cards The following credit card abbreviations are used: AE, American Express; DC, Diners Club; MC, MasterCard; V, Visa.

Lodging
Hotels Accommodations in Norway are always spotless, of manageable scale, and often family run. In keeping with the national character, they are pleasant and modest—neither extravagantly expensive nor rock-bottom inexpensive. Service is thoughtful and considerate, right down to the dark curtains and nightshades to block out the midnight sun. Passes are available for discounts in hotels. The **Scandinavia Bonus Pass,** costing approximately $20 and also valid in Denmark, Sweden, and Finland, gives average discounts of 25% in many hotels in summer. In addition, children under age 15 stay in their parents' room at no extra charge. For full details, write to Inter Nor Hotels, Kronsprinsensgt 5, Oslo 2, Norway. **Nordturist** passes (*see* Getting Around, By Train) also offer discounts of about 40% in nearly 100 top hotels.

Camping Camping is a popular way of keeping down the cost of a stay in Norway. There are more than 1,400 authorized campsites in the country, many set in spectactular surroundings. Prices vary according to the facilities provided: A family with a car and tent can expect to pay about NOK 100 per night. Some campsites have log cabins available for about NOK 200 per night.

Youth Hostels There are about 80 youth hostels in Norway; some are schools or farms doing extra summer duty. You must be a member of the Youth Hostel Association to stay in the hostels. For a full list, write to Norske Ungdom-Sherberger (NUH), Dronningens-gata 2b, N Oslo 1.

Rentals Norwegians escape to mountain chalets whenever they have a chance. Stay in one for a week or two and you'll see why—magnificent scenery, pure air, fresh fruits and berries, and the chance to hike, fish, or cross-country ski. For full details of this most popular of Norwegian vacations, write to Norske Hytte formidlingen, Kierschowsgt 7, 0405 Oslo 4 (tel. 02/356710).

Ratings Prices are for two people in a double room with bath and include breakfast, service, and all taxes. Best bets are indicated by a star ★. At press time, there were 6.2 krones (NOK) to the dollar.

Category	Cost: Oslo	Cost: Other Areas
Very Expensive	over NOK 850	over NOK 650

Expensive	NOK 600–NOK 850	NOK 400–NOK 650
Moderate	NOK 400–NOK 600	NOK 200–NOK 400
Inexpensive	under NOK 400	under NOK 200

Credit Cards The following credit card abbreviations are used: AE, American Express; DC, Diners Club; MC, MasterCard; V, Visa.

Tipping In Norway, a 10% service charge is generally added to bills at hotels and restaurants. If you have had exceptional service, then give an additional tip. It is not the custom to tip taxi drivers unless they act as tourist guides; tip porters at airports NOK 5 per bag. If a doorman hails a taxi for you, you can give NOK 5. If 10% has not been added to the check at a restaurant or café (ask if in doubt), then leave this amount and round it off to the nearest krone. On sightseeing tours, tip the guide if you are satisfied; NOK 5 is the usual tip for all services.

Oslo

Arriving and Departing

By Plane Most international flights go to **Fornebu Airport** on the edge of the fjord, about 20 minutes west of Oslo. Charter flights usually go to **Gardemoen Airport,** about 50 minutes north of Oslo.

Between the Airport and Downtown Buses from Fornebu to **Oslo Central Station** leave every 15 minutes (7:30 AM–11:30 PM) and run every half hour on weekends; the fare is NOK 20. Buses meet flights to Gardemoen and take passengers to the Central Station; the fare is NOK 50. Taxis from either airport to downtown cost between NOK 80 and NOK 100.

By Train Trains from all international routes arrive at **Central Station.** **West Station** is used by trains from the south of Norway.

Getting Around

By Public Transportation Far and away the best way to get around Oslo is by using the **Oslo Card** (*see* What It Will Cost), which offers unlimited travel for one, two, or three days on all Oslo's public transportation—bus, subway, streetcar, and even local ferries. You can buy the Oslo Card at the Tourist Office, City Hall, Oslo 1 (tel. 02/427170), or from hotels, travel agents in Oslo, larger stores, and downtown branches of ABC Bank.

If you are using public transportation only occasionally, you can get tickets (NOK 10—flat fare) at bus and subway stops.

By Taxi Taxis are expensive but always available. Hail one if its roof light is on; go to a taxi stand at Central or West Station; or call 02/388090, but be prepared to wait for up to an hour.

Important Addresses and Numbers

Tourist Information Ground floor of City Hall (harbor side), tel. 02/427170. Open May–Sept., Mon.–Sat. 8–7, Sun. 9–5; Oct.–Apr., Mon.–Fri. 8–4, Sat. 8–3, closed Sun.

Embassies U.S. Drammensvn 18, tel. 02/448550. **Canadian.** Oscarsgate 20, tel. 02/466955. U.K. Thos. Heftyesgate 8, tel. 02/563890.

Emergencies **Police,** Gronlandsleiret 44, tel. 02/669050 (24-hour service–02/669966). **Ambulance,** 24-hour service, tel. 02/201090. **Dentist** (emergencies), Oslo Kommunal Tannlegevakt, Toyen Center, Kolstadsgate 18, Oslo 6, tel. 02/674846. Emergency treatment, weekdays 8 PM–11 PM, weekends and holidays 11 AM–2 PM. **24-hour Pharmacy,** Jernbanetorgets Apotek, Jernbanetorget 4B, tel. 02/412482.

English Bookstores **Tanum,** Karl Johansgate 43, tel. 02/429310. **Ovist,** Drammensvn 16, tel. 02/440326 (beside the U.S. Embassy).

Travel Agencies **Winge** (agent for American Express), Karl Johansgate 33–35, tel. 02/429150; **Bennett,** Karl Johansgate 3, tel. 02/209090; **Berg-Hansen** (agent for Thomas Cook), Arbiensgate 3, tel. 02/391901.

Guided Tours

Orientation Tours **H. M. Kristiansen** provides three tours, all lasting three hours, and all starting from the City Hall harbor side. Tickets are available on the bus or from the Oslo Tourist Information Office (*see* Important Addresses and Numbers). The "Oslo Highlights" morning tour goes to the Vigeland Sculpture Park, Holmenkollen Ski Jump, the Viking Ship Museum, and the *Kon-Tiki. May–Sept., daily at 10 AM. Admission: NOK 100, children NOK 50.*
The "Morning Sightseeing" tour visits Akerhus Castle, Vigeland Sculpture Park, the Munch Museum, and Holmenkollen Ski Jump. *Apr.–Oct., daily at 10 AM. Admission: NOK 100, children NOK 50.*
The "Afternoon Tour" goes to the Norwegian Folk Museum, Viking Ships, *Kon-Tiki,* and the Polar Ship *Fram. Apr.–Oct., daily at 2:30. Admission: NOK 120.*

Walking Tours The "Oslo Guide" brochure (free from the tourist office) has several walking tours on its map. Some go farther afield and link up with public transportation.

Personal Guides Taxis also give sightseeing tours in English for a fee of NOK 190 per hour. Call 02/388090 to reserve a personal tour.

Exploring Oslo

Oslo is a small capital city, with a population of just under half a million. The downtown area is compact, and all the main sights are no more than 20 minutes on foot from most central hotels. But the special quality of this attractive city is its setting, with fjords, forests, and mountains on its doorstep. When you've explored the downtown on foot, you may want to venture outside the city by bus or train.

The Main Attractions

Oslo's main street, an avenue called **Karl Johansgate** (Karl Johan's Gate), runs right through the center of town, from Central Station uphill to the Royal Palace. Half its length is closed to traffic, and it is in this section that you will find most of the city's shops, outdoor cafés, and markets.

 Start at the **Slottet** (Royal Palace), the King's residence (there is no visiting inside). The Palace was built in the early 19th-

century Classical style and is as sober, sturdy, and unpretentious as the Norwegian character. The surrounding park is
open to the public. Time your visit to coincide with the changing of the guard (daily at 1:40), when there is often a band
concert.

2 Walk down Karl Johansgate to the **universitet** (university) on
your left. A small park in front of the building, which is open
except on official occasions, has a collection of **runic stones,**
some dating back to the 5th century. The main hall of the university is decorated with murals by Edvard Munch, Norway's
most famous artist; this is where the Nobel Peace Prize is presented each year on December 10.

3 Behind the University is the **Nasjonalgalleriet** (National Gallery), Norway's largest public gallery. It has a small but high-
quality selection of paintings by European masters of the period from Rembrandt to Picasso. Of particular interest is the
collection of works by Norwegian artists, including Harriet
Backer, Per Krohg, and Jakob Weidemann. Edvard Munch is
represented here, but most of his work is in the Munch Museum
(see below) east of the center. *Universitetgaten 13. Free. Open
Mon.–Fri. 10–4, Sat. 10–3, Sun. noon–3.*

4 The **Historisk Museum** (The Historical Museum) is just across
from the National Gallery. It features displays of daily life and
art from the Viking period, including treasures recovered from
Viking ships. The Ethnographic Section houses a collection related to the great polar explorer Roald Amundsen. *Frederiks-
gate 2. Free. Open 11–3, closed Mon.*

Return to Karl Johansgate and cross the road to look at the
5 **National Theater,** which is surrounded by attractive gardens
and an open-air restaurant. Gardens continue to line this side of
the road as you go down Karl Johansgate.

Time Out If the weather is good, stop for a snack or a drink at one of the
open-air café-stands in the gardens surrounding **Studenter-
lunden** pond, which is the setting for band concerts, election
rallies, and other special events.

---

6 At the far (eastern) end of the gardens is the **Storting** (Parliament), a bow-windowed, yellow-brick building stretched
across the block. It is open to visitors when Parliament is not in
session (mid-June through August): A guided tour takes visitors around the frescoed interior and into the debating
chamber. *Karl Johansgate, tel. 02/313050. Free. Open mid-
June–Aug., Mon.–Sat. Guided tours noon–2.*

7 Karl Johansgate closes to traffic as it approaches the **Dom
Kirken** (Cathedral). The cathedral, consecrated in 1697, is
modest by the standards of some European capital cities, but
the interior is rich with treasures, such as the Baroque carved
wooden altarpiece and pulpit. The ceiling frescoes by Hugo
Lous Mohr were done after World War II.

You can wander behind the cathedral, through an area of arcades, small restaurants, and street musicians. Or, facing away
from the cathedral, you can turn left and walk along Storgata,
8 past the flower market, to **Youngstorvet,** the fruit and vegetable market. This is the best place to buy the makings of a picnic
lunch.

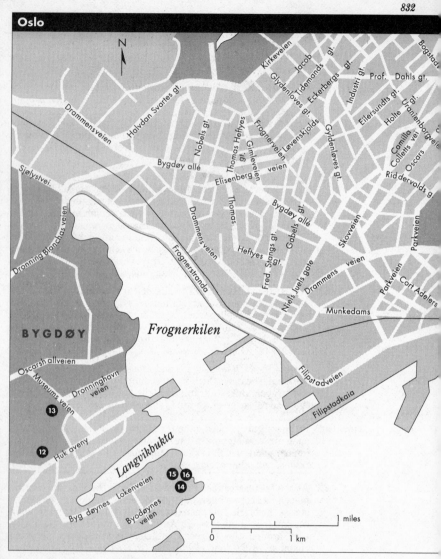

Oslo

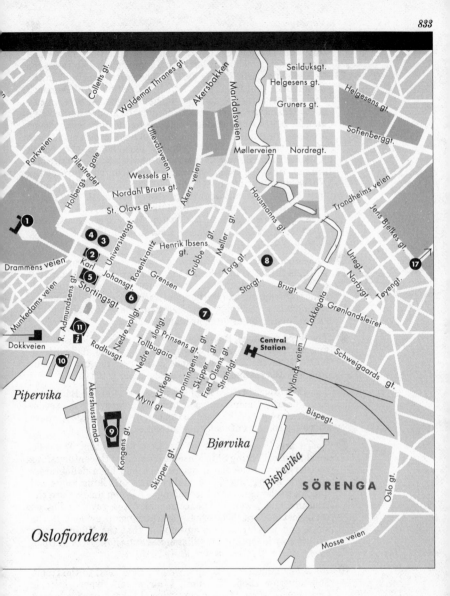

Seildukgt.

Helgesens gt.

Gruners gt.

Helgesens gt.

Sofienberggt.

Collets gt.

Waldemar Thranes gt.

Akersbakken

Maridalsveien

Møllerveien   Nordregt.

Parkveien

Pilestredet

Holbergs gate

Ullevålsveien

Akers veien

Hausmanns gt.

Trondheims veien

Jens Bjelkes gt.

Wessels gt.

Nordahl Bruns gt.

St. Olavs gt.

Universitetsgt.

Rosenkrantz

Henrik Ibsens gt.

Møller gt.

Grubbe

Torg gt.

Urtegt.

Norbgt.

Tøyengt.

Drammens veien

Karl

Johansgt.

Grensen

Storgt.

Brugt.

Lakkegaia

Grønlandsleiret

Munkedams veien

R. Admundsens gt.

Stortingsgt.

Nedre vollgt.

Prinsens gt.

Storgt.

Schweigaards gt.

Dokkveien

Radhusgt.

Nedre slottgt.

Tollbugaia

Dronningens gt.

Skipper gt.

Fred Olsens gt.

Strandgt.

Central
Station

Nylands veien

Bispegt.

Pipervika

Akershusstranda

Kongens gt.

Mynt gt.

Kirkegt.

Skipper gt.

Bjørvika

Bispevika

SÖRENGA

Oslo gt.

Oslofjorden

Mosse veien

Head back toward the cathedral until you reach Kirkegate and turn left. Three blocks down, turn right onto Radhusgate and then almost immediately left onto Kongensgate. This takes you to **Akershus Castle** on the harbor. The castle was built in the Middle Ages but restored in 1527 by Christian IV of Denmark and Norway after fire damage; he then laid out the present city of Oslo (naming it Christiana after himself) around his new residence. Oslo's street plan still follows his design. Some rooms are open for guided tours, and the grounds form a sort of park around the castle. The grounds also house the **Norsk Hjemmefrontsmuseum (Norwegian Defense and Resistance Museums)**. Between them, you can get a clearer picture of the Norwegian fighting spirit from the time of the Vikings to the time of the German occupation. *Akershus Castle and Museums. Entrance from Festingpl., tel. 02/412521. Admission: NOK 5. Guided tours of the castle, May–Sept., 11–4, Sun. 12:30–4. Museums open Tues., Thurs. 10–8, Wed., Fri. 10–3, Sat. 10–4, Sun. 11–4.*

Continue along the waterfront toward the central **harbor,** which is the heart of Oslo and the head of the fjord. Shops and cafés stay open later here, and you can buy some shrimp, sit amid the fountains and statues, and watch the colorful activity— fishing boats returning, sightseeing vessels setting off, the idle rich returning home on their luxury yachts.

The large red-brick **Rådhuset** (City Hall) is here: Go inside (admission free) and enjoy the murals depicting daily life in Norway, myths, and Resistance activities. You can set your watch by the astronomical clock in the inner courtyard.

The **Oslo Tourist Office** is on the harbor side of the Rådhuset. From nearby Pipervika, you can board a ferry for the seven-minute crossing of the fjord to the peninsula of **Bygdøy,** where there is a complex of seafaring museums.

There are two museums at the first ferry stop. The **Vikingskiphuset** (Viking Ship Museum) contains 9th-century ships recovered from the fjord, where they had been deliberately sunk while carrying the mortal remains of Viking kings and queens to the next world in Valhalla. Also on display are the treasure and jewelry that accompanied the royal bodies on their last voyage. The ornate craftsmanship evident in the ships and jewelry dispels any notion that the Vikings were skilled only in looting and pillaging. *Admission: NOK 5. Open summer, daily 10–8; winter, daily 10:30–4.*

It's a few minutes' walk up a well-marked road to the **Norsk Folkemuseum** (Folk Museum), a large park where historic farmhouses, some of them centuries old, have been collected from all over the country and reassembled intact. A whole section of 19th-century Oslo was moved here, as was a 12th-century wood stave church. There are displays of weaving and sheepshearing on Sunday, and throughout the park there are guides in period costume. *Admission: NOK 15. Open 10–6, Sun. 11–6.*

Reboard the ferry or follow signs for the 10-minute walk to the **Kon-Tiki Museum,** where the *Kon-Tiki* raft and the reed boat *RA II* are on view. Thor Heyerdahl made no concessions to the modern world when he used these boats to cross the Pacific (*Kon-Tiki*) and the Atlantic (*RA II*). *Admission: NOK 10. Open summer, 10–6, Sun. 11–6; winter daily 10:30–5.*

⑮ Directly across from the Kon-Tiki Museum is a large triangular building, the **Framhuset.** This museum is devoted to the polar ship *Fram*, the sturdy wooden vessel that has sailed farther north into the Arctic and south into the Antarctic than any other ship. You can board the ship and imagine yourself in one of the tiny berths, while outside a force-nine gale is blowing and the temperature is dozens of degrees below freezing. *Admission: NOK 7. Open summer, 10–6; closed winter.*

⑯ The **Maritime Museum** next door focuses not on an individual ship but on the entire history of Norwegian seamanship. Attractions include a slide show, demonstrations, and a fascinating model of a Norwegian shipyard. *Admission: NOK 7. Open summer, daily 10–8; winter, daily 10:30–4.*

Time Out Before catching the ferry back to the center of Oslo, consider a meal or snack at the **Najaden** restaurant and cafeteria on the top floor of the Maritime Museum. In summer, you can sit on the terrace, which commands a view of the whole harbor.

⑰ Back at City Hall, board the 29 bus to **Toyen,** the area northeast of Oslo that contains the **Munch-Museet** (Munch Museum). In 1940, four years before his death, Munch bequeathed much of his work to the city of Oslo; the museum opened in 1963, the centennial of his birth. Although only a fraction of its 22,000 items—books, paintings, drawings, prints, sculptures, and letters—are on display, you can still get a sense of the tortured expressionism that was to have such an effect on European painting. *Toyengaten 53. Admission: NOK 10 (free mid-Sept.– mid-May). Open 10–8, Sun. noon–8; closed Mon.*

What to See and Do with Children

The swimming pools in **Frogner Park** (*see* Off the Beaten Track) are very popular with children; older children will like the spiral water slide.

The **Norsk Teknisk Museum** (Science and Industry Museum) is a hands-on museum where children can operate models and exhibits showing the evolution of technology through the Space Age. Among the attractions are model cars and a miniature railroad. The museum is next to **Frysja Park,** which has a swimming pool and picnic area. From downtown, take bus 18, 22, or 25. *Kjelsaavn 141. Admission: NOK 10. Open 10–8; closed Mon.*

The **Viking Ship Museum** (*see* Exploring Oslo) is always a popular choice with children, and the ferry ride to get there is a treat, too.

Off the Beaten Track

The jury is still out on the question of the artistic merit of Gustav Vigeland's magnum opus *The Wheel of Life*, but few would deny the perseverance involved in its creation. More than 50 feet (15 meters) high and covered with more than 100 linked human forms, this sculpture is the focal point of Frogner Park, which is north of the Bygdø Peninsula. The park includes some 100 pieces of sculpture, which have a powerful cumulative effect. Frogner Park is well equipped with open-air restaurants, tennis courts, and swimming pools. To get there, take a

No. 2 streetcar; look for the word "Frogner" on the front. *Free. Park open 24 hours.*

Vertigo sufferers will want to avoid the **Holmenkollen Ski Jump,** one of the world's highest, at 200 feet (61 meters) above ground level. Visitors can go down the same elevator that took them up, but competitors at the Holmenkollen International Ski-Jumping Contest each March know they face a more heart-stopping descent. At the base of the jump is a museum carved into the rock face and a cafeteria. To reach Holmenkollen, take a suburban train from the National Theater terminus (make sure the train has "Frognerseter/Holmenkollen" on its front) and get off at Holmenkollen station. The half-hour ride itself is memorable, starting underground in Oslo, and ending up 1,300 feet (396 meters) above sea level.

Shopping

Gift Ideas Oslo is the best place to buy typical Norwegian gifts because the sale of handicrafts is strictly controlled and prices are more or less the same throughout the country. Popular gifts are silver, pewter, enamelware, and knitted sweaters and jackets.

Shopping Districts Many of the larger stores are located in the area **between the Storting and the cathedral;** much of this area is for pedestrians only. Oslo's newest shopping area is **Aker Brygge** (meaning quayside). Right on the waterfront, it is a complex of stalls, offices, and gardens. Shops stay open until 8, compared with the city's normal shopping hours of 9–5 (Thurs. to 7).

Department Stores Oslo's best department stores, **Steen & Strøm** and **Glasmagasin,** are both in the shopping district near the cathedral.

Food and Flea Markets **Youngstorvet,** on Storgata near the cathedral, is the best place for fresh fruit and vegetables.

Dining

The following prices are per person and include a first course, main course, and dessert, without wine but including the 10% service charge. Best bets are indicated by a star ★. At press time, there were 6.2 krones (NOK) to the dollar.

Category	Cost
Very Expensive	over NOK 300
Expensive	NOK 200–NOK 300
Moderate	NOK 100–NOK 200
Inexpensive	under NOK 100

Very Expensive ★ **Annen Etage.** Top-quality food is prepared with an international flavor at this restaurant in the Continental Hotel. Inside it's all elegant rococo decor with red damask and gilt-edged furnishings. Annen Etage is a favorite with visiting celebrities, and its kitchen provides the food for state banquets in Akerhus Castle. *Continental Hotel, Stortingsgate 24/26, tel. 02/419060. Jacket and tie. Reservations essential. AE, DC, MC, V.*

De Fem Stuer. The tab is high, but you're still getting good value in this 19th-century building next to the famous ski jump in Holmenkollen. Gourmet entrées include a wide variety of game. *Holmenkollen Park Hotel, Kongevn. 26, tel. 02/146090. Jacket and tie. Reservations essential. AE, DC, MC, V.*

Expensive ★ **Blom.** The coats of arms and mottoes lining Blom's paneled walls belong to the many artists who have dined here in nearly a century. A lunch buffet helps keep prices within reason, as does the Fru Blom wine and food bar next door, serving pâté and quiche. *Karl Johansgate 41, tel. 02/427300. Jacket and tie. Reservations essential. MC, V.*

Etoile. Fresh Norwegian fish and shellfish are given classic and nouvelle treatment in this restaurant on the roof of the Grand Hotel, with panoramic views of the city. *Grand Hotel, Karl Johansgate 31, tel. 02/429390. Jacket and tie. Reservations essential. AE, DC, MC, V.*

Frognerseteren. Located next to the Holmenkollen ski jump, this restaurant looks down on the whole city. Come for the view, for the Norwegian specialties, or for a decor dominated by traditional old timbers and an open hearth. *Voksenkollen, tel. 02/143736. Jacket and tie. Reservations essential. DC, MC, V.*

★ **Mølla.** This charmingly renovated spinning mill on the Aker River has a unique atmosphere enhanced by candle-lit vaults, live music, cabaret, and dancing. The menu features fresh fish and game. *Sagvn 21, tel. 02/375450. Jacket and tie. Reservations advised. AE, DC, V.*

Moderate **La Brochette.** Choose your own steak in this intimate French-style, Italian-run restaurant next door the Concert Hall. The atmosphere is subdued, and there's much attention to detail. *Dronning Maudsgate 1–3, tel. 02/416733. Jacket and tie. Reservations advised. AE, MC, V.*

Gamle Rådhus. The "old city hall," Oslo's oldest restaurant, is located in a building dating from 1640. Specialties include mussels and fresh shrimp. *Nedre Slottsgate 1, tel. 02/420107. Jacket and tie. Reservations advised. No credit cards. Closed Sun.*

Mamma Rosa. Under the same management as La Brochette, this Italian restaurant is located on the second floor of a building looking down on Karl Johansgate. The atmosphere is informal, with guitar music in the evening. Pasta and pizza are at the lower end of a menu featuring mainly Italian specialties. *Øvre Slotsgate 12, tel. 02/420130. Dress: casual. Reservations advised. AE, MC, V.*

Peking House. Crisp white damask table linen, dark mahogany furniture, and friendly service create an attractive atmosphere for this Chinese restaurant near the center of town. *St. Olavsgate, tel. 02/114878. Dress: casual. Reservations accepted. AE, DC, MC, V.*

Inexpensive ★ **Albin Upp.** A real find for people who like the unusual, this intimate wine and snack bar is in a renovated farmer's cottage, right in the heart of town. It's directly behind a stop for Streetcar 1. Contemporary Norwegian arts and crafts are on display inside. *Briskebyvn. 42, tel. 02/564448. Dress: casual. No reservations. No credit cards.*

Café Frohlich. Oslo's only café with music is furnished in Old Viennese style. Entertainment—jazz, classical, and even rock—is provided by music students or any guest competent enough to play the instruments, one of which is a grand piano. The menu features light meals and ice-cream specials. *Drammensvn. 20, tel. 02/443737. Dress: casual. No reservations. No credit cards.*

Vegeta. Next to the bus and streetcar National Theater station, this is a popular spot for hot and cold vegetarian meals and salads. The all-you-can-eat specials offer top value. *Munkedamsvn. 36, tel. 02/428557. Dress: casual. No reservations. No credit cards.*

Lodging

The tourist office's accommodations bureaus (open 7 AM–11 PM) in Central Station can help you find rooms in hotels, pensions, and private homes. You must apply in person and pay a fee of NOK 10 (children NOK 5) plus 10% of the room rate, which will be refunded when you check in.

Prices are for two people sharing a room and include all taxes and service. Best bets are indicated by a star ★. At press time, there were 6.2 krones (NOK) to the dollar.

Category	Cost
Very Expensive	over NOK 850
Expensive	NOK 600–NOK 850
Moderate	NOK 400–NOK 600
Inexpensive	under NOK 400

Very Expensive **Bristol.** Quietly located on a side street, the Bristol offers plush comfort and tranquility as well as a central location. Rooms are spacious and airy, and the hotel features two good restaurants: the excellent international-style Bristol Grill and El Toro, a Spanish restaurant with dancing and floor shows. *Kristian IV Gate, tel. 02/415840. 220 rooms with bath. Facilities: 2 bars, nightclub, disco. AE, DC, MC, V.*

★ **Grand.** It's hard to beat the Grand's location on Oslo's main street, opposite the Parliament and city park. The hotel has all the comforts and history to match its name: Ibsen had a permanent table in its Grand Café, a famous Oslo rendezvous. It has four other restaurants, ranging from the Palmen, a sandwich bar, to the gourmet French Etoile and the exclusive Speilen. *Karl Johansgate 31, tel. 02/429390. 350 rooms with bath or shower. Facilities: indoor pool, sauna, solarium. AE, DC, MC, V.*

Holmenkollen Park. Located near the ski jump, this hotel is an imposing Norse-style building with a luxurious annex dating to 1981. Rooms are bright, and most have balconies with excellent views of the city below. The hotel runs a shuttle bus for its guests. It's probably the best place for anyone hoping to do some skiing. *Kongeveien 26, tel. 02/146090. 200 rooms with bath. Facilities: ski trails, bar, nightclub, whirlpool, sauna, squash, indoor pool, curling rink. AE, DC, MC, V.*

SAS Hotel Scandinavia. Norway's largest hotel and tallest building is more like a small town under one roof. The hotel is comfortable and has impeccable service, while its gourmet grill, the Café Royal, offers a spectacular *smørgasbord* for lunch. Summit 21 is the rooftop lunch bar, with commanding views of the whole city. Downstairs you'll find a shopping center and the city air terminal. *Holbersgate 30, tel. 02/113000. 476 rooms with bath. Facilities: 2 bars, indoor pool, tennis, disco. AE, DC, MC, V.*

Expensive **Gabelshus Hotel.** Only 5 minutes from the center of town, the Gabelshus is a moderate-sized hotel on an attractive side street. Rooms are spacious and airy, and the hotel has more of the feel of a large country house. Its restaurant is recommended. *Gabelsgate 16, tel. 02/552260. 45 rooms with bath. No credit cards.*

KNA. The Royal Norwegian Auto Club runs this comfortable hotel in a quiet street just west of the downtown area, so you can capitalize on some expert advice on touring options and road conditions. All rooms are clean and comfortable, and there is an intimate restaurant and bar as well as a lively bistro. *Parkvein 68, tel. 02/562690. 226 rooms with bath or shower. AE, DC, MC, V.*

SAS Park Royal Hotel. Ten minutes from the center of Oslo, this hotel is clean, efficient, and convenient for Fornebu airport. Rooms are large, and the top-class facilities are well suited for business stays. *Fornebu Park, Lysaker, tel. 02/120220. 350 rooms and 10 suites with bath. Facilities: 23-seat restaurant, sauna, fitness room, tennis, direct airport check-in, executive office space. AE, DC, MC, V.*

Moderate **Europa.** This centrally located modern hotel is a more moderately priced alternative to its next-door neighbor, the SAS Hotel Scandinavia. Rooms are comfortable (all have color TV), and there are special reductions for children. *St. Olavsgate 31, tel. 02/209990. 150 rooms with bath. DC, MC, V.*

Stefan. Service is cheerful and accommodating in this hotel in the center of Oslo. One of its main attractions is the popular restaurant Eighth Floor (no alcohol is served); the excellent buffet includes *rommegrot*, a traditional sour cream porridge eaten with smoked meats. *Rosenkrantzgate 1, tel. 02/336290. 140 rooms with bath or shower. AE, MC, V.*

Inexpensive **Anker Stiftelsen Yrkesskolens Hybelhus.** These centrally located accommodations are rather basic student residences open during the summer vacation (May to September), but they do have cooking facilities, a supermarket, cafeteria, and restaurant. Some rooms are like dormitories, with four beds to the room, but it's clean and friendly. *Storgate 55, tel. 02/114005. 426 beds, a few rooms with shower. AE, MC, V.*

Ritz. A little less grand than some of its namesakes, the Ritz still is an attractive place on a quiet street, about 7 minutes from downtown by streetcar. It also has a restaurant. *Fr. Stansgate, tel. 02/443960. 42 rooms, some with bath. AE, DC, MC, V.*

The Arts

For a small city, Oslo has a surprising amount of artistic life. Consult the "Oslo Guide" or "Oslo This Week" for details. Winter is the cultural season, with the **National Theater** featuring modern plays, classics, and usually a good sampling of Ibsen. Its experimental stage, called the **Amphitheater,** is more intimate and goes in for avant-garde productions. The **Dukketeatret** in the City Museum (Frognerveien 67) is a puppet theater that is popular with families.

Oslo's modern **Konserthuset** (Concert Hall), at Ruseløkkveien, is the home of the Oslo Philharmonic, famous for its recordings of Tchaikovsky's symphonies. A smaller hall in the same building is the setting for performances of chamber music and—in summer only—folk dancing. There are also musical performances at the **Henie-Onstad Art Center** at Høvikodden. This center specializes in 20th-century art and was a gift from the Olympic Norwegian skater Sonje Henie.

Nightlife

The deadly combination of prices and puritanism used to put a damper on spirits in Oslo, but now, with the influx of free-spending oil men and the generally high standard of living, things have begun to loosen. For those who like discos, the best are in the luxury hotels (*see* Lodging). Jazz is a bit more established, with a few of the recommended spots listed below.

Amalienborg Jazzhouse. This place is unpretentious but frequently erupts with a furious jam session. *Arbeidergate 2, tel. 02/423024.*

Ben Joseph (La Petite Cuisine). Come here for a meal at the grill/restaurant and then stay for the nightclub. *Solligate 2, tel. 02/444575.*

Jazz Alive. Live bands perform every night, making this a popular choice with visitors. *Observatoriegate 2, tel. 02/440745.*

Stortovets Gjaestiveri. There are Saturday lunchtime sessions in this 18th-century building beside the cathedral. The sandwich bar has courtyard service in good weather. *Grensel 1, tel. 02/428863.*

The Coast Road to Stavanger

This tour follows the Sørland coast south of Oslo toward the busy port of Kristiansand and then west to Stavanger. This is an area where whaling has given way to lumber and more modern industries, such as paper production and even petrochemicals. But the scenery remains virtually unspoiled, and the air is as fresh and bracing as ever.

The 380-mile (630-kilometer) route winds through forests and rocky headlands, with some commanding views of nature. The road closely follows the coast, but you can also take an inland route—the one followed by the train—and detour at Kongsberg for Telemark, the region famous for skiing and the heroic exploits of its Resistance fighters in World War II.

Getting Around

By Car Driving is recommended because it gives visitors the chance to stop at coastal villages that are either not served by trains or have only sporadic service. The route is simple: E18 as far as Flekkefjord, and then E44 to Stavanger. When driving in even this relatively populated part of Norway, make sure to keep your tank full because gas stations can be a rarity on some rural roads.

By Train The best train service is the Sørland line, which leaves West Station in Oslo and goes all the way to Stavanger. The Oslo–Drammen stretch is an engineering feat and features Norway's longest tunnel, a seven-mile (11-kilometer) connection through sheer rock.

By Bus Local buses cover the entire route. For details on fares and schedules, check with the tourist offices listed below or the main one in Oslo (*see* Important Addresses and Numbers).

Guided Tours

In summer, there is a daily boat excursion from Oslo to the coastal resorts of Kragerø, Jomfruland, and Risør. Sightseers return the same day, and refreshments are served on board. The excursion is organized by the Oslo Tourist Information Office (*see* Important Addresses and Numbers).

Tourist Information

Arendal: Box 344, tel. 041/22193.
Drammen: Rådhuset, tel. 03/834094.
Flekkefjord: tel. 043/24254.
Kristiansand: Henrik Wergelandsgate. 17, tel. 042/26065.
Larvik: Storgaten 20, tel. 034/82623.
Stavanger: Tourist Pavilion, tel. 04/528437.
Tønsberg: Storgate 55, tel. 033/14819.

Exploring

From Oslo, take highway E18 west for about 25 miles (40 kilometers) to the bustling port of **Drammen.** Located at the mouth of a large timber-floating river, Drammen operates as a processing and shipping center for lumber and paper products. Take a short detour west of town on E76, turn right on Kongsgate, and climb the mile-long **"Corkscrew Road,"** a series of spiraling tunnels leading to the top of **Bragernes Hill.** In the '50s, locals decided against any further quarrying of building stone and turned instead to tunneling for it. The result is this scenic and dramatic road with panoramic views of **Drammensfjord** and the larger **Oslo Fjord** beyond.

Return to E18 and continue to the coastal town of **Åsgårdstrand,** an unspoiled summer resort where Edvard Munch painted many of his best works. His small white frame house is open to visitors during the summer (admission: NOK 10). Farther along is **Tønsberg,** which inhabitants claim is Norway's oldest town, founded in AD 870. The steep hill beside the train station leads to the ruins of **Tønsberghus,** an extensive fortress and abbey. The outlook tower, built in 1870 to commemorate the town's millenium, has a good view of the coast. The rise of Oslo as Norway's capital led to the decline of Tønsberg, although it developed as a whaling port in the 18th century.

Attractive **Sandefjord,** nine miles (15 kilometers) down E18, is a whaling port that served as the base for the Norwegian whaling fleet until after World War II, when large-scale competition from the Soviet Union and Japan made the operation uneconomical. The port remains busy as a depot for timber shipping.

Just beyond Sandefjord, E18 crosses the important lumbering river Lågen and then follows it to the port of **Larvik,** which is the terminus for ferries to Frederikshavn in Denmark. Like Tønsberg and Sandefjord, Larvik once looked to whaling for its livelihood, but it, too, has turned to lumber and ferrying for employment.

The Coast Road to Stavanger

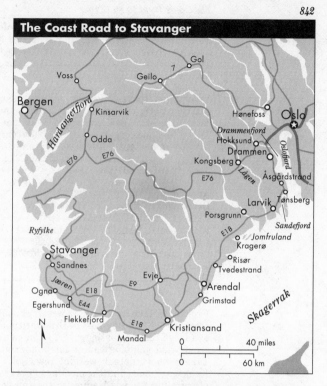

Bergen
Voss
Geilo
Gol
7
Kinsarvik
Hardangerfjord
Odda
E76
E76
Hønefoss
Oslo
Drammenfjord
Hokksund
Drammen
Kongsberg
E76
Lågen
Åsgårdstrand
Tønsberg
Larvik
Porsgrunn
Sandefjord
Jomfruland
Kragerø
Risør
Tvedestrand
Ryfylke
Stavanger
Sandnes
Evje
E9
Arendal
Grimstad
Jæren
Ogna
E18
Egershund
E44
Flekkefjord
E18
Kristiansand
Skagerrak
N
Mandal
0   40 miles
0   60 km

Larvik is the birthplace of Thor Heyerdahl, so it is fitting that pride of place should go to the **Maritime Museum** (admission and opening times vary; check with the tourist office). Located in the former customs house, it chronicles Larvik's seafaring history and gives special emphasis to Heyerdahl's voyages, with models of *Kon-Tiki* and *RA II*.

After Larvik, you begin to progress down the coast more quickly, as E18 cuts across some of the narrower peninsulas on its way south. Side roads offer the chance to explore the smaller coastal village of **Kragerø** and its neighboring islands, **Risør,** with its patrician 19th-century harbor-front homes, and the winding streets of **Tvedestrand. Arendal,** 70 miles (120 kilometers) beyond Larvik, was once called Little Venice, but its canals have now been turned into wide streets. The atmosphere of bygone whaling prosperity in this and other Sørland ports is like that of Nantucket, and tidy cottages and more imposing captains' houses are all within shouting distance of the docks. Explore Arendal's **Tyholmen quarter** for a glimpse into this 19th-century world.

Kristiansand is another 30 miles (50 kilometers) along the coast from Arendal. With a population of 60,000, it's the largest town in Sørland and has important air, sea, road, and rail links. It was laid out in the 17th century in a grid pattern, with the imposing **Christiansholm Fort** guarding the eastern harbor approach. (Exhibitions are sometimes held inside the fort in summer.) Just to the northeast of Kristiansand is the open-air **Agder County Museum,** with 28 old buildings and farms rebuilt in the local style of the 18th and 19th centuries. There are also displays of folklore and costumes. *Admission: NOK 15. Open 10–6, Sun. noon–6.*

Continue along E18 for another 20 miles (30 kilometers) to **Mandal,** Norway's most southerly town, famous for its beach, its salmon, and its narrow streets lined with 18th- and 19th-century houses. For the next 20 miles, the road climbs and weaves its way through steep, wooded valleys and then descends to the fishing port of **Flekkefjord,** with its charming **Hollenderbyen,** or Dutch Quarter.

E18 heads inland here to Stavanger, but it is more rewarding to follow the coast road (E44) past the fishing port of **Egershund,** 25 miles (40 kilometers) ahead, and a little farther to **Ogna,** with its good, sandy beach. For the last hour or so as you approach Stavanger, you will be in the region known as the **Jaeren.** Flat and stony, it is the largest expanse of level terrain in this mountainous country. The mild climate and the absence of good harbors meant that the population here turned to agriculture, and the miles of stone walls are a testament to their labor.

Stavanger, at the end of the tour, is a former trading town that, in the past 15 years, has become a champion (some environmentalists say victim) of the oil boom. The population has gone from 10,000 to nearly 100,000, and drilling platforms and oil tankers take the place of fishing boats in the harbor. Fortunately, the old quarter still exists, with narrow cobbled lanes and clapboard houses at odd angles. The town itself was founded in 1100, and its Anglo-Norman **St. Svithens Cathedral,** next to the central market, was established in 1125 by the Bishop of Winchester in England. (Trading and ecclesiastical links between Norway and England were strong throughout the Middle Ages.)

The **Ryfylke fjords** north and east of Stavanger form the southern end of the Fjord Country. The city is a good base for exploring this region, since its "white fleet" of low-slung seabuses makes daily excursions into even the most distant fjords of Ryfylke.

Dining and Lodging

For details and price category definitions, *see* Dining and Lodging in Essential Information.

Arendal **Grand Restaurant.** Norwegian seafood specialties are featured
Dining in this traditional restaurant in attractive Arendal. *Langbryggen 19, tel. 041/25160. Jacket and tie. Reservations advised. AE, DC, MC, V. Moderate.*

Lodging **Phønix.** Despite being the hub of Arendal's nightlife—with its restaurant, bar, and disco—the Phønix has rooms that are quiet and comfortable. *Tyholmen, tel. 041/25160. 80 rooms with bath or shower. DC, MC, V. Expensive.*

Drammen **Skansen.** At the top of the spiraling "Corkscrew Road" that
Dining tunnels its way up from town, the Skansen offers excellent views as well as freshly prepared fish and game specialties. *Bragernessen (no tel.). Dress: casual. No reservations. No credit cards. Moderate.*

Lodging **Park.** This comfortable and centrally located hotel has well-equipped rooms and a good restaurant. *Gamle Kirkeplass 3,* *tel. 03/838280. 120 rooms with bath or shower. MC, V. Moderate.*

Kristiansand **Bowlers Steakhouse.** Good portions of steaks and roasts are
Dining served here with fresh salads. Try the fruit desserts in summer. *Kirkegate 7, tel. 042/29009. Jacket and tie. No reservations. No credit cards. Expensive.*
Bølgen Grill. Local soups and game are featured in this attractive waterfront restaurant in the eastern part of central Kristiansand. *Elvegate 1, tel. 042/25838. Jacket and tie. Reservations advised. No credit cards. Moderate.*

Lodging **Rica Fregatten.** You're right in the center of town in this medium-size hotel, a stone's throw from the Town Hall and Cathedral. Rooms are comfortable and well appointed, and there is a good restaurant. *Droningensgate 66, tel. 042/21500. 70 rooms, most with bath. AE, DC, MC, V. Moderate.*
Savoy. The clean and comfortable rooms in this pension and inn are quite adequate for an inexpensive overnight stay. *Kr. Ivsgate 1, tel. 042/24175. 14 rooms, none with bath. No credit cards. Inexpensive.*

Larvik **Grand.** The rooms are spotless and service is attentive in this
Lodging large hotel overlooking the fjord. There is a choice of restaurants to sample the local fish soup and smoked meat platters, which are particularly good at lunchtime. *Storgaten 38–40, tel. 034/83800. 117 rooms, most with bath. AE, MC, V. Moderate.*

Sandefjord **Park.** Overlooking Sandefjord's attractive harbor, the impos-
Lodging ing Grand is considered one of the best hotels in Norway. The
★ rooms are large and comfortable, with excellent views over the water. Service is flawless. *Strandprom 9, tel. 034/65550. 160 rooms with bath or shower. Facilities: restaurant, bar, pool, saunas. AE, DC, MC, V. Expensive.*

Stavanger **La Gondola.** Freshly caught local seafood in spicy fish soups
Dining with risotto add some variety to the palates of oilmen jaded from a surfeit of cafeteria meals. La Gondola is located right by the market. *Nytorget 8, tel. 04/534235. Jacket and tie. Reservations advised. No credit cards. Moderate.*
Viking. Don't be put off by a name that suggests a tourist come-on. Game and seafood are served here in healthy portions and with no gimmicks. *Jernbaven 15, tel. 04/588747. Dress: casual. Reservations advised. No credit cards. Moderate.*

Lodging **SAS Royal.** Like its counterparts in Oslo (Park Hotel and Scandinavia), the Royal is modern, clean, and efficient, but still has a pleasant, informal atmosphere. The rooms are large and comfortable, and the hotel is capable of dealing, with equal ease, with a gathering of business tycoons demanding conference space or with a party of fly fishermen. *Løkkevn. 26. 210 rooms with bath. Facilities: pool, sauna, airport check-in, business service center. AE, DC, MC, V. Very Expensive.*
Commandør. The Commandør is much smaller and considerably more basic than the Royal, but it offers clean and comfortable accommodations. *Valbergsgate 9, tel. 04/528000. 48 rooms with bath. AE, DC, MC, V. Moderate.*

Through Telemark to Bergen

Telemark is the region located between Oslo and Norway's second city, Bergen. It is an area of steep valleys, pine forests, lakes, and fast-flowing rivers full of trout. The following itinerary takes you through Telemark on a westward course toward Bergen. The last leg goes from Telemark to Hardanger Fjord, the source of inspiration for Grieg and other Norwegian artists.

This whole area is a source of pride for Norwegians: You'll pass Morgedal, birthplace of Sondre Nordheim, pioneer of modern skiing. Another proud chapter is the story of the exploits of the Norwegian Resistance, which sabotaged Nazi efforts to develop heavy water for use in the atomic bomb. Things are much more peaceful these days: Many of the wooden houses you will pass have grass and even flowers growing from their turf roofs.

Guided Tours

Bergen is the center for many excursions, covering most of the last half of this tour as well as the fjords farther north. Contact the Tourist Information Office (see below) for details of these constantly changing tours.

Tourist Information

Bergen: Slottsgate 1, tel. 05/313680.
Drammen: Rådhuset, tel. 03/834094.
Kinsarvik: tel. 054/63450.
Kongsberg: tel. 03/731526.
Røldal: tel. 054/47289.

Exploring

Take E18 west from Oslo to **Drammen** (*see* The Coast Road to Stavanger). Following E76 west out of town, you pass Kongsgate Street on the right. This leads to the "Corkscrew Road" up to the top of Bragernes Hill. The brief detour pays dividends, with a good view back toward Oslo Fjord.

Return to E76 and continue west for about 25 miles (40 kilometers) to **Kongsberg,** on the fast-flowing Lager river. Kongsberg was founded in 1624 as a silver-mining town. Although there is no more mining, the town is still the seat of the Royal Norwegian Mint. In the center of town is an 18th-century Rococo church that's the size of some cathedrals. Its size alone reflects the town's former wealth from silver.

Kongsberg is one of the gateways to Telemark, and you'll know you've reached it once the road climbs past Meheia on the county border. Forests give way to rocky peaks and desolate spaces farther into the plateau. **Heddal** is the first town you encounter in Telemark. Norway's largest stave church is here. Stave churches, found almost exclusively in southern Norway, were in some ways the medieval forerunners of modern high-rise buildings. Steep wooden roofs are piled one above the other so that the height of the church is more than twice the width. The Heddal church is typical in having richly carved ornamentation on the doors and around the aisle.

E76 climbs up from Heddal and skirts the large Telemark plateau. You'll see its highest peak, **Lifjell** (4,200 feet, 1,280 meters), on the left before descending toward **Seljord,** on the lake of the same name. The countryside down by the lake is richer than up on the plateau; meadows and pastureland run down to the lakefront. The attractive village of Seljord has richly ornamented wooden houses and a medieval church.

Continue south from Seljord, making sure to stay right (on E76) at the Brunkeberg crossroads, while the other road continues south to Kristiansand. You are now entering the steep valley of **Morgedal,** famed as the cradle of modern ski technique. It was here in the last century that Sondre Nordheim developed the slalom method of skiing, and you can see how it all started and where it all has led in **Olav Bjaland's Museum.** *Admission: NOK 10. Open July–Aug. 20, 10–3; closed Mon.*

Many visitors find it worth the 18-mile (30-kilometer) detour to turn left at Hoydalsmo and visit **Dalen,** which has harnessed the power of mountain waters to create **Tokke I,** one of Europe's largest hydroelectric power stations. From here, it's an five-mile (eight-kilometer) drive to **Eidsborg,** where there is a stave church and a dramatic view back down to the Dalen Valley.

From Dalen, you can also drive up to one of Telemark's wonders, the **Ravnejuvet ravine,** a 1,000-foot (305-meter) sheer drop into the Tokke Valley. Throw paper into the ravine and a peculiar updraft returns it to you. But experiment with waste paper rather than money!

Take E38 from Dalen along the Tokke Valley to **Åmot.** The 300-foot (91-meter) Hyllandfoss Falls were destroyed by the hydroelectric project, but the drive through the valley is still spectacular.

Rejoin E76 at Åmot. At the next crossroads (Haukeigrend), E76 begins really to climb, and you'll see why the Norwegians are so proud of keeping this Telemark route open all year. Before leaving Telemark, you'll pass through the 3½-mile (six-kilometer) Haukeli Tunnel and then begin a long descent to **Røldal,** another lakefront town with a hydroelectric plant.

Turn north on Route 47 a few miles after Røldal, and drive to the **Sør Fjord** at Odda. Continue along the fjord to the attractive town of **Kinsarvik.** For the best view of the junction of the Sør and mighty Hardanger fjords, take the ferry across the Sør to Utne. On the dramatic 30-minute ferry crossing from Utne to

Kyvanndal, you will understand how this area was such a rich source of inspiration for Grieg.

At Kyvanndal, turn left on E68. The road follows the fjord west, then veers right to **Nordheimsund.** After climbing over another coastal mountain spur, it winds through the wild **Tokagjel Gorge** and across the mountains of **Kramskogen,** and then descends in a series of twists and tunnels into Bergen, capital of the fjords.

Bergen is Norway's second largest city, with a population of 200,000. It is the most international of Norway's cities, having been an important trading and military center when Oslo was an obscure village. Bergen was a member of the medieval Hanseatic League, benefiting from its ice-free harbor and convenient trading location on the west coast. Natives of Bergen still think of Oslo as a dour provincial town in the grip of a dreary climate.

Despite a series of devastating fires over the years, much of medieval Bergen remains intact, nestled beneath the seven mountains that surround it. Old wooden houses still crowd onto steep cobbled streets, and the old Hanseatic warehouses still stand along the **Bryggen** (quayside). When SAS built its modern hotel in the center, the architect was charged with the task of designing the new building to match the existing warehouses and their steep roofs.

The original town was founded on the **Vågen** (harbor) in 1070 by Olav Kyrre; the present-day **Torget** (fish market) stands on this site. The best way to get a feel for Bergen's medieval trading heyday is to visit the **Hanseatic Museum** on the Bryggen. One of the oldest and best-preserved of Bergen's wooden buildings, it is furnished in 16th-century style. *Admission: NOK 5, children NOK 3. Open June–Aug., daily 10–4; May, Sept., daily 10–2; Oct.–Apr., 11–2, closed Tues., Thurs., Sat.*

On the western end of the Vågen is the Rosenkrantz Tower, part of the **Bergenhus,** the 13th-century fortress guarding the harbor entrance. The tower and fortress were destroyed in World War II but restored meticulously in the '60s, and are now rich with furnishings and household items from the 16th century. *Admission: NOK 10. Open mid-May–mid-Sept., daily 10–4.*

Across the Vågen is the Nordness Peninsula, where you can look back toward the city and the mountainous backdrop. Save time to meander through the winding back streets, intersected by broad *almenninger* (wide avenues built as protection against fires). For the best view of Bergen and its surroundings, take the funicular from the corner of Lille Øvregate and Vetrlidsalmenning. It climbs 1,000 feet (305 meters) to the top of Fløyen, one of the seven mountains guarding this ancient port.

Dining and Lodging

For details and price category definitions, *see* Dining and Lodging in Essential Information.

Bergen
Dining

Bellevue. It's hard to imagine a more imposing or dramatic setting for a restaurant than the Bellevue's, high up on a hillside looking down on Bergen and the Hardanger Fjord. The restaurant itself is a 17th-century manor house, with the crystal and silverware you'd expect from such a grand residence. The food is excellent and has an unsurprising emphasis on fresh seafood. Service is attentive and polished. *Bellevuebakken 9, tel. 05/ 310240. Jacket and tie. Reservations essential. AE, DC, MC, V. Expensive.*

Bryggen Tracteursted. Set among the medieval Hanseatic warehouses, this is the place to try the freshest ingredients from the adjacent fish market. *Bryggestredet, tel. 05/314046. Dress: casual. Reservations not necessary. DC. Moderate.*

Wesselstuen. In some respects, you'll find this more of a café than a restaurant: Notice particularly how Bergeners wander in and out throughout the day, seeming to sense when the latest catch of fresh fish has arrived. The atmosphere is bustling and friendly. *Engen 14, tel. 05/322900. Dress: casual. No reservations. No credit cards. Moderate.*

Lodging   **SAS Royal.** Located right at the harbor, the SAS Royal was opened in 1982 on the site of old warehouses ravaged by a series of nine fires since 1170. The houses were rebuilt each time in the same style, which SAS has incorporated into this well-equipped hotel. *Bryggen, tel. 05/318000. 265 rooms with bath. Facilities: pool, sauna, Hanseatic exhibition. AE, DC, MC, V. Very Expensive.*

Scandic. Located just outside town near Bergen's Flesland airport, Scandic is comfortable and well equipped, making it a convenient stop if you are driving or flying into Bergen. *Kokstadflaten 2, Kokstad, tel. 05/227150. 175 rooms with bath. Facilities: taverna, restaurant, indoor pool, sauna. DC, MC, V. Moderate.*

Strand. Facing the harbor in the center of Bergen, the Strand is a moderate-size, efficient hotel. Most rooms have a view of the harbor. *Strandkaien 2–4, tel. 05/310815. 60 rooms, most with bath. AE, DC, MC, V. Moderate.*

Kinsarvik   **Kinsarvik Fjord Hotel.** There are good views of Hardanger
Lodging   Fjord and the glacier above it from this attractive hotel near the busy ferry port. Rooms are bright and spacious. *Kinsarvik, tel. 054/63100. 70 rooms with bath or shower. AE, MC, V. Moderate.*

Kongsberg   **Ernst's Kafeteria.** Good, fresh food is well presented in this in-
Dining   expensive cafeteria in the center of town. *Drammensvn. 87, tel. 03/733530. Dress: casual. No reservations. No credit cards. Inexpensive.*

Utne   **Utne Hotel.** The white frame house dates from 1722 and the ho-
Dining and Lodging   tel, the oldest in Norway, has been run by the same family since 1787. The Utne has all the cared-for atmosphere of an old home. The dining room is wood paneled and hand painted, decorated with copper pans, old china, and paintings. Old furniture also fills the rooms, many of which have good views of the ferry port and Hardanger Fjord. The Utne makes a good base for hiking or cycling in the region. *Utne, tel. 054/66983. 28 rooms with bath or shower. AE, DC, MC. Moderate.*

27 Poland

Introduction

A country about the size of the British Isles or New Mexico, Poland is a land rich in natural beauty and contrasts. Its landscape varies from rolling plains with slow-moving rivers, broad fields, and scattered villages to lakes, forests, and marshes in the north and jagged mountains in the south. This makes for a wide variety of outdoor activities, from hunting to hiking, sailing, and skiing.

Every one of the major cities, with the exception of Cracow, had to be rebuilt after the destruction of World War II. Particularly fine restoration work has been done on Warsaw's Old Town and in Gdańsk on the Baltic coast.

Poland does not fit into preconceptions of a Communist country. After 40 years of Communist rule, a majority of the people remain devoutly Catholic. In the countryside especially, the people are religious and conservative. Both rural and urban life remain centered on the home and family, where old traditions are diligently upheld. Four-fifths of the country's farmland is privately owned, while in the towns, the number of private boutiques and restaurants is increasing.

Being situated geographically between Germany and Russia has determined Poland's history of almost continual war and struggle for independence since the late 18th century. After "liberation" by the Red Army in 1945, a Communist government was imposed. Although the country recovered economically and experienced rapid industrialization, 40 years of such government have today left Poland in prolonged economic crisis. The hopes and aspirations of the postwar generations, promised for so long, have failed to be satisfied.

Social discontent erupted in 1980 with strikes and the formation of Solidarity, the first free trade union in the Communist bloc. After a year, martial law was imposed and Solidarity was banned. Though martial law has since been lifted, life for the average Pole remains hard, and no one has simple answers to the country's complicated political and economic problems. In spite of all this, the Polish people continue to be resilient, resourceful, and not without hope.

Poles openly welcome visitors; their uninhibited sense of hospitality makes them generally eager to please their guests. It is easy to make friends here and to exchange views with strangers on trains and buses. Poles have a passionate interest in all things Western, from current affairs to the arts, clothes, and music. Though nurtured on Western culture, Poles still regard themselves as a link between East and West. Their bond with the Western Church has been strengthened immeasurably by the election of the first Polish pope in history.

Before You Go

When to Go The official tourist season runs from May through September. The best times for sightseeing are in late spring and early fall. Major cultural events usually take place in the cities during the fall. The early spring is often wet and windy.

Poland

The following are the average daily maximum and minimum temperatures for Warsaw.

Jan.	32F	0C	May	67F	20C	Sept.	66F	19C
	22	−6		48	9		49	10
Feb.	32F	0C	June	73F	23C	Oct.	55F	13C
	21	−6		54	12		41	5
Mar.	42F	6C	July	75F	24C	Nov.	42F	6C
	28	−2		58	16		33	1
Apr.	53F	12C	Aug.	73F	23C	Dec.	35F	2C
	37	3		56	14		28	−3

Currency The monetary unit in Poland is the złoty (Zł), which is divided into 100 groszy (rarely seen). There are notes of 10, 20, 50, 100, 200, 500, 1,000, 2,000, and 5,000 złoty and coins of 1, 2, 5, 10, and 20 złoty. At press time (fall 1988), the exchange rate for the złoty was 400 to the U.S. dollar and 720 to the pound sterling. There is a black market rate that offers at least four times the official rate, but this is illegal. You will find that Polish taxi drivers, waitresses, and porters are only too happy to be paid in dollars or any other Western currency. Money exchanged into złoty can be reconverted upon presentation of official exchange receipts when leaving the country.

Credit Cards American Express, Diners Club, MasterCard, and Visa are accepted in all Orbis hotels, in the better restaurants and nightclubs, and for other Orbis services. In small cafés and shops, credit cards may not be accepted.

What It Will Cost All visitors must exchange foreign currency to the value of $15 a day. Exceptions are persons under 21 years of age, students, and persons whose Polish descent has been recognized by the appropriate Polish consular office: They must exchange $7 daily (including arrival day but excluding day of departure). Exempt altogether from obligatory currency exchange are children under 16, visitors in transit to neighboring countries, and visitors who have prepaid their stay through vouchers or package bookings. Vouchers may be used toward hotel costs and must be paid at the official exchange rate.

Poland is one of the least expensive countries of Eastern Europe. Although inflation is high—about 20–30%—the złoty is devalued against Western currencies about three times a year. This offsets rising costs and keeps expenses down. Don't buy more złoty than you need or you will have to go to the trouble of changing them back at the end of your trip. Prices are highest in the big cities, especially in Warsaw. The more you stray off the tourist track, the cheaper your vacation becomes. The cost difference can sometimes be enormous. What you save in money, however, you may lose in quality of service.

Sample Prices A cup of coffee, 200–400 Zł; a bottle of beer, 300–500 Zł; a soft drink, 400–800 Zł; a ham sandwich, 700 Zł; one-mile taxi ride, 1,200 Zł.

Visas Visas are required and cost $18 or £15. Apply at any Orbis office, an affiliated travel agent, or from the Polish Consulate General in any country (see below). Each visitor must complete three visa application forms and provide two photographs. Allow about two weeks for processing. Visas are issued for a specific length of time but can be extended in Poland, if necessary, either through the local county police headquarters or through Orbis.

Polish Consulate General, United States: 233 Madison Ave., New York, NY 10016 (tel. 212/391–0844); 1530 North Lake Shore Dr., Chicago, IL 60610 (tel. 312/337–8166); 2224 Wyoming Ave., Washington DC 20008 (tel. 202/234–2501).

Polish Consulate General, Canada: 1500 Pine Ave., Montreal, Quebec H3G (tel. 514/937–9481); 2603 Lakeshore Blvd. W., Toronto, Ont. M8V 1G5 (tel. 416/252–5471).

Polish Consulate General, United Kingdom: 73 New Cavendish St., London W.1 (tel. 01/636–4533).

Customs on Arrival Persons over 17 may bring in duty-free: personal belongings, up to 250 cigarettes or 50 cigars, musical instruments, typewriter, radio, two cameras with 24 rolls of film, one liter each of wine and spirits, and goods to the value of 10,000 Zł. Any amount of foreign currency may be brought in but must be declared on arrival.

Language German is spoken by older people, and English by younger. In the big cities, you will find people who speak English, especially in hotels, but you may have difficulties in the provinces and countryside.

Getting Around

By Car
Road Conditions Despite the extensive road network, driving conditions, even on main roads, have deteriorated in the past few years. Minor roads tend to be narrow and cluttered with horse-drawn carts and farm animals. Drivers in a hurry should stick to roads marked E or T.

Rules of the Road Driving is on the right, as in the United States. The speed limit on highways is 110 kph (68 mph) and on roads in built-up areas, 60 kph (37 mph). A built-up area is marked by a white rectangular sign with the name of the town on it.

Gasoline Foreigners can obtain gas only by presenting prepurchased coupons at gas stations. Coupons can be bought prior to departure at Orbis travel agencies, at the Polish frontier, or at Orbis offices in Poland. The price of gas is about $5.50 for 10 liters of high octane. Filling stations are located every 20 miles (30 kilometers) or so and are usually open 6 AM–10 PM; there are some 24-hour stations.

Breakdowns Poland's **Motoring Association** (BTM PZMot) offers breakdown, repair, and towing services to members of various international insurance organizations. For names of affiliated organizations, check with Orbis before you leave home. Carry a spare parts kit. For emergency road help, call 981 or 954.

Car Rentals Cars are available for rent from Avis or Hertz at international airports or through Orbis offices. Rates vary according to season, car model, and mileage. Fly/drive vacations are also available through Orbis.

By Train Poland's PKP railway network is extensive and cheap. Most trains have first- and second-class accommodations, but most foreign visitors prefer to travel first class. Arrive at the station at least one hour before departure time. The fastest trains are intercity and express trains, which require reservations. Some Orbis offices furnish information, reservations, and tickets. Overnight trains have first- and second-class sleeping cars and second-class couchettes. All long-distance trains carry buffets, but the quality of the food is variable and you may want to bring your own.

Fares Highly recommended is a **Polrailpass,** which offers unlimited first-class travel for one ($72), two ($84), three ($96), or four ($108) weeks.

By Plane LOT, Poland's national airline, operates daily flights linking 11 main cities. Fares begin at about $100 round-trip. Tickets and information are available from LOT or Orbis offices. All flights booked through Orbis in the United Kingdom cost £30. In Poland, flights must be paid for in foreign currency. Be sure to book well in advance, especially for the summer season.

By Bus Express bus services link all main cities as well as smaller towns and villages off the rail network. Buses are inexpensive but crowded. PKS bus stations are usually located near railway stations. Tickets and information are best obtained from Orbis. A two-week unlimited travel ticket costs 1,200 Zł. from Warsaw's central bus terminal on al. Jerozolimskie.

Essential Information

Telephones Public phone booths (for local as well as long-distance calls)
Local Calls take 5, 10, and 20 Zł coins. Place a 5 Zł coin in the groove on the side or top of the phone, lift the receiver, and dial the number. Push the coin into the machine when the call is answered.

International Calls Post offices and first-class hotels have assigned booths, at which you pay after the completion of your call. To place an international call, dial 901; for domestic long-distance calls, dial 900. There's a heavy surcharge on calls made from hotel rooms.

Information General information (including international codes), 913.

Mail Airmail letters to the United States cost 50 Zł, postcards, 35 Zł.
Postal Rates Letters to the United Kingdom or Europe cost 45 Zł, postcards, 30 Zł. Post offices are open 8 AM–8 PM (except weekends). At least one post office is open 24 hours in every major city. In Warsaw, it is located on ul. Swietokrzyska 31.

Shopping Shopping in Poland is relatively inexpensive but, because of shortages of certain goods, not necessarily easy. Glassware, ceramics, wood carving, silverware, amber, and embroideries make ideal gifts. Illustrated books, sports equipment, and vodka are also good buys.

Some of the best souvenirs can be bought from **Cepelia** (Folk Arts and Crafts Cooperative), which has stores throughout the country. **Desa** stores stock tapestries, paintings, sculptures and porcelain, while **Orno** shops specialize in handmade silverwork. Local as well as foreign currency is accepted. Other shopping in Poland can be divided into three categories: State-owned department stores, which sell standardized goods of mediocre quality; private boutiques, specializing in clothes and leatherwear of higher quality and cost; and so-called hard-currency stores such as **Pewex** and **Baltona,** where you can buy a variety of Western goods with Western currency only. The hard-currency stores often give excellent value, especially in electrical appliances, liquor, and chocolates. All goods purchased at Pewex and Baltona may be taken out of Poland duty-free on presentation of sales receipts.

Opening and **Banks.** Banks are open weekdays 8 AM–1 PM.
Closing Times **Museums.** Museums are open Tuesday–Sunday 9–5.
Shops. Food shops are open 7 AM–7 PM; other stores are open 11–7.

National Holidays January 1 (New Year's Day); March 26, 27 (Easter); May 1 (Labor Day); June 2 (Corpus Christi); July 22 (National Day); November 1 (Remembrance); December 25, 26.

Dining Polish food and drink are basically Slavic with Baltic overtones. There is a heavy emphasis on soups and meat (especially pork) as well as fresh-water fish. Much use is made of cream, and pastries are rich and often delectable.

The most popular soup is *barszcz* (known to many Americans as borscht), a clear beet soup often served with such Polish favorites as sausage, cabbage, potatoes, sour cream, coarse rye bread, and beer. Other dishes: *pierogi* (a kind of ravioli), which may be stuffed with savory or sweet fillings; *golabki*, cabbage leaves stuffed with minced meat; *bigos*, sauerkraut with meat and mushrooms; *flaki*, a select dish of tripe, served boiled or fried. Polish beer is good; vodka is a specialty and is often downed before, with, and after meals.

There is a wide selection of eating places, but as a result of continuing food shortages, the quality of the cuisine may vary from one day to the next. The more expensive hotels and restaurants offer the most consistently high-quality dining.

Roadside inns (*Zajazdy*), which are less expensive than regular restaurants, serve more traditional food. More economical yet, and ideal for snacks, are the milk bars *(Bary Mleczne)* selling dairy and vegetable dishes. As elsewhere in central Europe, cafés are a way of life in Poland and are often stocked with delicious pastries and ice creams.

Mealtimes At home, Poles eat late lunches and late suppers; the latter is their main meal. Many restaurants, however, close around 9 PM. Most hotel restaurants serve the evening meal until 10:30 PM.

Precautions Tap water is unsafe, so ask for mineral water. Beware of meat dishes served in cheap snack bars. Avoid the food on trains.

Ratings Prices are for one person and include three courses and service but no drinks. Best bets are indicated by a star ★. At press time, there were 400 złoty to the dollar.

Category	Cost: Warsaw	Cost: Other Areas
Very Expensive	over 3,000 Zł	over 2,500 Zł
Expensive	2,000–3,000 Zł	1,500–2,500 Zł
Moderate	1,000–2,000 Zł	750–1,500 Zł
Inexpensive	under 1,000 Zł	under 750 Zł

Credit Cards The following credit card abbreviations are used: AE, American Express; DC, Diners Club; MC, MasterCard; V, Visa.

Lodging The government rates hotel accommodations on the basis of one
Hotels to five stars. **Orbis** hotels are the only ones that can guarantee a reasonable standard of cleanliness and service, and you are strongly advised to stick to them in order to avoid unpleasant surprises. Almost all Orbis hotels are of four- or five-star quality. Orbis hotels include a number of foreign-built luxury hotels such as Intercontinental and Holiday Inn. Prices range from Moderate to Very Expensive.

Municipal Hotels and **Dom Turysty** hotels are run by local authorities or the Polish Tourist Association. They are frequently rather old and limited in bath and shower facilities. Prices are inexpensive.

Hostels The Polish Youth Hostels Association operates hostels at a very inexpensive 100–300 Zł per night; in addition, hostels are open to people of all ages. Information is available from your local branch of the International Youth Hostel Association.

Roadside Inns	A number of roadside inns *(Zajazdy)*, often very attractive, offer inexpensive food and a few guest rooms at moderate rates.
Private Accommodations	Rooms can be arranged either in advance through Orbis or on the spot at the local tourist information office. Villas, lodges, or houses are more personal than hotels, and the prices are often negotiable. Rates vary from Inexpensive to Very Expensive.
Ratings	Guests are charged per person, with breakfast usually included. The following chart is based on a per-person rate in a double room, with bath or shower and breakfast. Best bets are indicated by a star ★. At press time, there were 400 złoty to the dollar.

Category	Cost: Warsaw	Cost: Other Areas
Very Expensive	over 35,000 Zł	over 32,000 Zł
Expensive	27,000–35,000 Zł	19,500–32,000 Zł
Moderate	19,500–27,000 Zł	14,000–19,500 Zł
Inexpensive	under 19,500 Zł	under 10,000 Zł

Credit Cards	The following credit card abbreviations are used: AE, American Express; DC, Diners Club; MC, MasterCard; V, Visa.
Tipping	Waiters get a standard 10% of the bill. Hotel porters and doormen should get about 100–200 Zł. In Warsaw and other big towns frequented by foreign tourists, waiters also often expect a tip to help find you a table. If you choose to tip in foreign currency (readily accepted), remember that on the black market $1 is worth an average day's wage.

Warsaw

Arriving and Departing

By Plane	All international flights arrive at Warsaw's Okęcie Airport just southwest of the city. Another airport nearby, also called Okęcie, serves all domestic flights. For flight information, contact the airlines, or call the airport at tel. 46–96–70 or 46–11–43.
Between the Airport and Downtown	LOT operates a regular bus service into Warsaw. Orbis cars or minivans also transport visitors to their hotels. Otherwise, the 175 bus leaves every 10 minutes from the international terminal. The trip takes about 15 minutes. Getting a taxi may be difficult.
By Train	Trains to and from Western Europe arrive at Dworzec Centralny on al. Jerozolimskie in the center of town. For tickets and information, contact Orbis.
By Car	There are seven main access routes to Warsaw, all leading to the city center. Drivers heading to or from the West will use the E8 or E12 highways.

Getting Around

By Tram and Bus	These are often crowded, but they are the cheapest ways of getting around. Trams and buses cost 15 Zł; express buses cost 27 Zł. The bus fare goes up to 50 Zł between 11 PM and 5:30 AM.

Tickets must be bought in advance from Ruch newsstands. You must cancel your own ticket in a machine on the tram or bus when you get on; watch others do it.

By Taxi Consider yourself lucky if you catch a taxi in less than 15 minutes. Taxis are a relatively cheap ride, and you can either hail them or line up at a stand. The best places to find one are in front of the Victoria Hotel or the Forum Hotel.

By Buggy Horse-drawn carriages can be hired at a negotiated price from the Old Town Market Square.

Important Addresses and Numbers

Tourist Information. Center for Tourist Information (open 24 hours), ul. Krucza 16, tel. 27–00–00. **Orbis**, ul. Bracka 16, tel. 26–02–71; ul. Marszałkowska 142.
Embassies. U.S. al. Ujazdowskie 29–31, tel. 28–30–40; **Canadian** ul. Matejki 1/5, tel. 29–80–51; **U.K.** al. Róż 1, tel. 25–80–31.
Emergencies. Police, tel. 997; **Ambulance**, tel. 998; **Doctor**, tel. 998 or call your embassy.
Travel Agencies. Polish Motoring Association (PZMot), al. Jerozolimskie 63, tel. 29–45–30.

Guided Tours

Bus tours of the city depart in the morning and afternoon from the major hotels. Orbis also has half-day excursions into the surrounding countryside. These usually include a meal and some form of traditional entertainment. Check for details with your hotel receptionist, Orbis office, or tourist information office.

Exploring Warsaw

At the end of World War II, Warsaw lay in ruin, a victim of systematic Nazi destruction. Only one-third of its prewar population survived the horrors of German occupation. The experience has left its mark on the city and is visible everywhere in the memorial plaques describing mass executions of civilians and in the bullet holes on the facades of buildings.

Against all the odds, Warsaw's survivors have rebuilt their historic city. The old districts have been painstakingly reconstructed according to old prints and paintings, including those of Belotto and Canaletto from the 18th century. The result, a city of warm pastel colors, is remarkable.

Surrounding the old districts, however, is the modern Warsaw, built since the war in functionalist Socialist-Realist style. Whether you like it or not is your business, but it is worth noting as testimony to one approach to urban life. The sights of Warsaw are all relatively close to each other, making most attractions accessible by foot.

The Old Town

A walking tour of the old historic district takes about two hours. Begin in the heart of the city at **Plac Zamkowy,** where you will see a slender column supporting the statue of Zygmund III Vasa, the king who made Warsaw his capital in

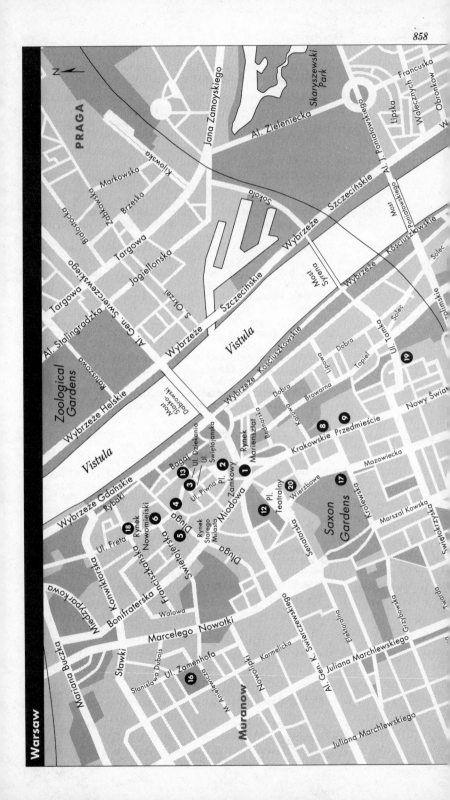

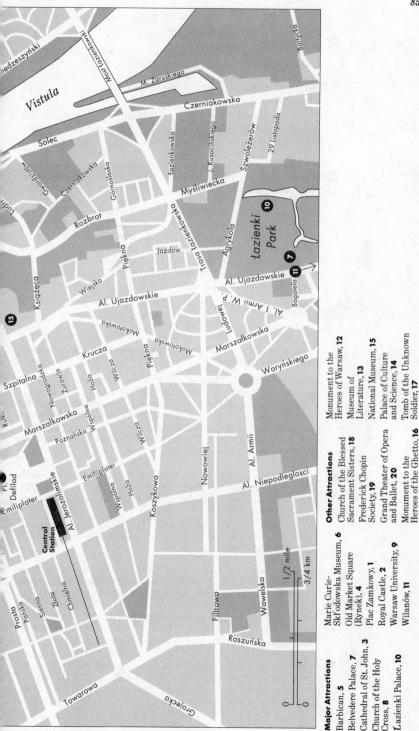

859

Major Attractions
Barbican, **5**
Belvedere Palace, **7**
Cathedral of St. John, **3**
Church of the Holy Cross, **8**
Łazienki Palace, **10**

Marie Curie-Skłodowska Museum, **6**
Old Market Square (Rynek), **4**
Plac Zamkowy, **1**
Royal Castle, **2**
Warsaw University, **9**
Wilanów, **11**

Other Attractions
Church of the Blessed Sacrament Sisters, **18**
Frederick Chopin Society, **19**
Grand Theater of Opera and Ballet, **20**
Monument to the Heroes of the Ghetto, **16**

Monument to the Heroes of Warsaw, **12**
Museum of Literature, **13**
National Museum, **15**
Palace of Culture and Science, **14**
Tomb of the Unknown Soldier, **17**

1586. It is the city's oldest monument and, symbolically, the first to be rebuilt after the wartime devastation. Dominating ② the square is the **Royal Castle.** Restoring the interior was a herculean task, requiring workers to relearn traditional skills, match ancient woods and fabrics, even reopen abandoned quarries to find just the right kind of stone. A visit is worthwhile, despite the crowds. *Royal Castle, Plac Zamkowy. Open Tues., Thurs. 10–2:45; Wed., Fri., Sat. 12–5:30; Sun. 10–6.*

Enter the narrow streets of the Old Town, with its colorful medieval houses, cobblestone alleys, uneven roofs, and wrought-iron grillwork. On your right as you proceed along Swięto-③ janska Street is the **Cathedral of St. John,** the oldest church in Warsaw, dating back to the 14th century. Several Pol-④ ish kings were crowned here. Soon you will reach the **Old Market Square,** the charming and intimate center of the old town. The old Town Hall, which once stood in the middle, was pulled down in the 19th century. It was not replaced, and today the square is full of open-air cafés, tubs of flowering plants, and the inevitable artists displaying their talents for the tourists. At night, the brightly lighted Rynek (marketplace) is the place to go if you want good food and atmosphere. You may feel like stopping for a coffee now; remember the location if you want to return in the evening.

Continue along Nowomiejska Street until you get to the im-⑤ posing red brick **Barbican,** a fine example of a 16th-century defensive fortification. From here, you can see the partially restored town wall that was built to enclose the Old Town; enjoy a splendid view of the Vistula River, with the district of Praga on its east bank.

Follow ul. Freta to Warsaw's **New Town,** which was founded at the turn of the 15th century. Rebuilt after the war in 18th-century style, this district has a more elegant and spacious ⑥ feeling about it. Of interest here is the **Marie Curie-Skłodowska Museum,** ul. Freta 16, where the Polish discoverer of radium and polonium was born. *Marie Curie-Skłodowska Museum, ul. Freta 16, Open Tues.–Sun. 10–5.*

Time Out Before retracing your steps, stop for refreshments at the **Cafe Bombonierka,** *Rynek Starego Miasta 13*—good for ice cream, pastries, and people watching both inside the café and out on the square.

The Royal Way

All towns with kings had their "Royal Routes"; the one in Warsaw stretched south from Castle Square down Krakowskie Przedmieście, curving through Nowy Świat and on along al. ⑦ Ujazdowskie to the **Belvedere Palace** and Łazienki Park. Some of Warsaw's finest churches and palaces are found along this ⑧ route, as well as the names of famous Poles. The **Church of the Holy Cross** contains a pillar in which the heart of the great Polish composer Frédéric Chopin is entombed. Farther down, on ⑨ your left, is **Warsaw University,** founded in 1818. As you pass the statue of Nicolaus Copernicus, Poland's most famous astronomer, you enter the busy Nowy Świat thoroughfare. Crossing al. Jerozolimskie, on your left is the Polish Communist Party headquarters, a large solid gray building typical of the Socialist-Realist architectural style.

Aleje Ujazdowskie is considered by many locals to be Warsaw's finest street. It is lined with some magnificent buildings and has something of a French flavor to it. A hundred years ago, this fashionable Corso (avenue) was thronged with smart carriages and riders eager to see and be seen. It is now a favorite with Sunday strollers. Down at its southern end, before the name inexplicably changes to Belwederska, the French-style landscaped **Łazienki Park,** with pavilions and a royal palace, stands in refreshing contrast to the bustling streets. The

⑩ **Łazienki Palace,** a gem of Polish neoclassicism, was the private residence of Stanisław August Poniatowski, last king of Poland. It stands on a lake filled with huge carp. At the impressionistic Chopin monument nearby, you can stop for a well-deserved rest and, on summer Sundays, listen to an open-air concert.

⑪ The Royal Route extends along al. Belwederskie to **Wilanów,** six miles (10 kilometers) from the town center. This charming Baroque palace was the summer residence of King Jan III Sobierski, who, in 1683, stopped the Ottoman advance on Europe at the Battle of Vienna. The palace interior is open and houses antique furniture and a fine poster museum. *Wilanów Palace, al. Belwederskie. Open Mon., Wed., Fri.–Sun. 10–2:30.*

What to See and Do with Children

Take a **horse-drawn carriage** through the Old Town from the Old Market Square.

Visit the **Puppet Theater** in the Palace of Culture and Science (*see* Off the Beaten Track below).

Go to the **Zoo** on al. Gen. Swierczewskiego on the east bank of the Vistula.

There is a town **beach** with recreational facilities at Wał Miedzeszyński on the east bank between the Poniatowski and Łazienkowski bridges.

Off the Beaten Track

The Jewish contribution to Polish culture, tradition, and achievement cannot be overstated. Some three million Polish Jews were put to death by the Nazis during World War II. A simple monument to the **Heroes of the Warsaw Ghetto,** a slab of dark granite with a bronze bas relief, stands on ul. Zamhofa in the Muranow district, the historic heart of the old prewar Warsaw ghetto. The armed revolt that broke out in April 1943 was put down with unbelievable ferocity, and the Muranow district was flattened. Now there are only bleak gray apartment blocks here.

With ironic humor, Warsaw locals tell you that the best vantage point from which to admire their city is atop the 37-story **Palace of Culture and Science.** Why? Because it is the only point from which you can't see the Palace of Culture and Science. This wedding cake-style skyscraper was a personal gift from Stalin. Although it is disliked by Poles as a symbol of Soviet domination, it does afford a panoramic view and is the best ex-

ample of 1950s "Socialist Gothic" architecture. *Plac Défilad.
Open daily 9–5.*

Shopping

Nowy Świat, Krakowskie Przedmieście, and ul. Rutkowskiego
are lined with boutiques selling good-quality leather goods,
clothing, and trinkets. Try **Cepelia** stores, Marszałkowska 99
and Nowy Świat 35, for a wide range of handcrafts, such as
glass, enamelware, amber, and handwoven woolen rugs. **Orno**
shops, Marszałkowska 83 and Nowy Świat 52, offer handmade
jewelry and silverware. **Desa** stores, Marszałkowska 34, specialize in ornaments and objets d'art. Foreign currency shops
called **Pewex** and **Baltona** can be found all over the city (try the
Victoria hotel). These sell imported items, especially spirits,
clothing, and chocolates, at competitive prices. Film and cigarettes are carried here, also. State-owned department stores,
Junior and **Dom Centralny**, which sell standardized goods of
questionable quality, are on ul. Marszałkowska opposite the
Palace of Culture and Science.

For the more adventurous, there is a flea market, **Bazar
Różyckiego**, on ul. Targowa 55, where you can find almost anything. Another market is open at the Skra Warszawa sports
stadium on Sunday.

Dining

Current difficulties with food supplies mean that only hotels
and the very best restaurants can guarantee a full menu and
quality meals. If you want to avoid eating at hotels, your best
bet is the Old Town and its atmospheric Market Square. The
area is brightly lighted at night and makes for a pleasant walk
before or after dinner. Reservations for dinner can be made by
telephone (by your hotel receptionist if you don't speak Polish),
but if you decide to go to a restaurant on the spur of the moment, a table (for Westerners) will always be found.

Ratings Prices are for one person and include three courses and service,
but no drinks. Best bets are indicated by a star ★. At press
time, there were 400 złoty to the dollar.

Category	Cost
Very Expensive	over 3,000 Zł
Expensive	2,000–3,000 Zł
Moderate	1,000–2,000 Zł
Inexpensive	under 1,000 Zł

Credit Cards The following credit card abbreviations are used: AE, American Express; DC, Diners Club; MC, MasterCard; V, Visa.

Expensive **Bazyliszek.** Dimly lit and elegant, the Bazyliszek excels in such
game as boar, venison, and duck. A good café and snack bar are
located downstairs. *Rynek Starego Miasta 7/9. Dress: formal
or casual elegant. No reservations. AE, DC, MC, V.*
Canaletto. Located in the Victoria Intercontinental hotel, this
is probably the best restaurant in town and serves Polish specialties with a good selection of European wines. The two
paintings of old Warsaw on the walls are by Canaletto himself.

Plac Zwycięstwa, tel. 22/27–92–91. Dress: formal. Reservations advised. AE, DC, MC, V.

Forum. Another good hotel restaurant, the Forum's menu is traditional Polish mixed with conventional central European (meat dishes). Like Canaletto, it is frequented by Western businesspeople and tourists. *ul. Nowogrodzka 24, tel. 22/21–01–19. Dress: formal. Reservations advised. AE, D, MC, V.*

Moderate **Kamienne Schodki.** This intimate, candlelit restaurant is located in one of the Market Square's medieval houses. Try the duck and the pastries. *Rynek Starego Miasta 26. Dress: casual. No reservations. No credit cards.*

Pod Sansonem. This small restaurant, decorated in wood, has a smoke-filled Warsaw atmosphere and friendly waitresses. The fish and pierogi are good, when available. *ul. Freta 4. Dress: casual. No reservations. No credit cards.*

Staropolska. Fish dishes and old-fashioned Polish cuisine are the specialties. Portions are on the small side. *Krakowskie Przedmieście 8. Dress: informal. No reservations. Open until 11 PM. No credit cards.*

Lodging

Orbis hotels are recommended for convenience and high standards. Rooms are comfortable though standardized, with functional, nondescript carpeting and furniture. Since no new hotels have been built in Warsaw since 1980, some are beginning to show signs of wear. Private accommodations are available through Orbis or through the Center for Tourist Information. There is no off-season for tourism.

Ratings Guests are charged per person, with breakfast usually included. The following prices are based on a per-person rate in a double room, with bath or shower and breakfast. Best bets are indicated by a star ★. At press time, there were 400 złoty to the dollar.

Category	Cost
Very Expensive	over 35,000 Zł
Expensive	27,000–35,000 Zł
Moderate	19,500–27,000 Zł
Inexpensive	under 19,500 Zł

Credit Cards The following credit card abbreviations are used: AE, American Express; DC, Diners Club; MC, MasterCard; V, Visa.

Very Expensive **Victoria Intercontinental.** Frequented by Western businesspeople, this is a large 1970s hotel in an ideal location in the center of town. It has a variety of facilities ranging from a fine restaurant and nightclub to sauna and indoor pool. Try to get a room facing Victory Square. *ul. Królewska 11, tel. 22/27–92–91. 370 rooms, most with bath or shower. AE, DC, MC, V.*

Expensive **Hotel Europejski.** Warsaw's finest old hotel is located in the heart of the city. It was built in the 19th century in neo-Renaissance style, and its decor is elegant and refined. Rooms are spacious and attractive; some have hosted kings, presidents, and diplomats. The hotel takes pride in its restaurant.

ul. Krakowskie Przedmieście 13, tel. 22/25–50–51. 279 rooms, most with bath or shower. AE, DC, MC, V.

Hotel Forum. The Swedes built this Intercontinental Hotel Corporation chain hotel in the '70s. Frequented by businesspeople and the Arab community, it has a good restaurant, hairdresser, and nightclub. A room higher up will give you a view of the city. *ul. Nowogródzka 24, tel. 22/21–01–19. 750 rooms, some with bath or shower. AE, DC, MC, V.*

Moderate **Hotel Solec.** This comfortable, modest, '70s hotel is down by the river in a residential area of the central town. Food and service are good, but the hotel tends to be inundated with group tours. *ul. Zagórna 1, tel. 22/25–92–41. 150 rooms, all with bath. AE, DC, MC, V.*

Novotel. This small member of the French Novotel chain is ideal for visitors with a car. Well situated near Warsaw's airport, the hotel offers a café, restaurant, and outdoor swimming pool. *ul. 1 Sierpnia 1, tel. 22/46–40–51. AE, DC, MC, V.*

Orbis Grand. Conveniently located in the center of the city, this large hotel was built in the 1950s and is a prime example of the Socialist-Realist architecture of the period. It houses a rooftop restaurant-café and offers live jazz, dancing, or cabaret in the evening. Facilities include a Pewex shop, indoor pool, and hairdresser. *ul. Krucza 28, tel. 22/29–40–51. 415 rooms, some with shower. AE, DC, MC, V.*

Zajazd Karczma Napoleonska. This small, privately owned inn has an excellent restaurant and deluxe facilities. Napoleon reputedly stayed here when his Grand Army passed through Warsaw on its way to Russia. Book well in advance. Situated about 8 miles (13 kilometers) outside of town on *ul. Plowiecka 83, no tel. AE, DC, MC, V.*

Inexpensive **Hotel Vera.** All the modern conveniences are available at this medium-size functionalist-style hotel, but it lacks character. Built in 1980, it is situated in the western part of town. *ul. Wery Kostrzewy 16, tel. 22–74–21. AE, DC, MC, V.*

The Arts

For information, buy the newspaper *Życie Warszawy* or the weekly *Stolica* at *Ruch* newsstands. Tickets can be ordered by your Orbis hotel receptionist, through the Tourist Information Center (ul. Kurcza 16, tel. 22/27–00–00), or at al. Marszałkowska 104.

Theaters There are 17 theaters in Warsaw, attesting to the popularity of this art form, but none offers English performances. **Teatr Narodowy,** opened in 1764 and the oldest in Poland, is on Plaza Teatralny. **Teatr Polski** (Foksal 16) has a small stage and is thus more intimate. **Współczesny** (Mokotowska 13) shows contemporary works.

Concerts **The National Philharmonic** puts on the best concerts. The hall is on ul. Sienkiewicza 12. In the summer, free Chopin concerts take place both at the Chopin monument in **Lazienki Park** and, each Sunday, at **Żelazowa Wola,** the composer's birthplace, 36 miles (58 kilometers) outside Warsaw.

Opera **Teatr Wielki** (Plaza Teatralny) hosts the Grand Theater of Opera and Ballet. It has a superb operatic stage—one of the largest in Europe.

Film Non-Polish films are nearly always dubbed. Of interest on a rainy day, however, is the nonstop cinema of short films on ul. Rutkowskiego 33.

Entertainment and Nightlife

Cabaret The Victoria, Forum, Grand, and Europejski hotels all have nightclubs that are popular with Westerners. The acts vary, so check listings in the weekly *Stolica*. These clubs also present striptease and jazz. The most famous cabaret is **Pod Egida** on Nowy Świat, renowned for its risqué political satire.

Bars **Fukier** (Rynek Starego Miasta 27) is a crowded, noisy wine bar-café in medieval style. **Gwiazdeczka** (Piwna 42) is a noisy, hip, upscale joint, popular with chic young Warsovians.

Jazz Clubs **Akwarium** (ul. Emilii Platter) and **Wanda Warska's Modern Music Club** (Stare Miasto) are popular jazz clubs. Jazz musicians are booked frequently at the major hotels, too.

Discos Apart from the hotels, the most popular discos are **Hybrydy** (ul. Koniewskiego 7) and **Stodola** (ul. Batorego 2).

Cafés Warsaw is filled with cafés *(kawiarnie)*, which move outdoors in the summer. They are popular meeting places and usually serve delicious coffee and pastries in the best central European style.

Antyczna is an elegant 19th-century-style café with a fine assortment of cakes. *Plaza Trzech Krzyży 10.*
Bombonierka is in the New Town Square. It is elegant, spacious, and tranquil. *Rynek Nowego Miasta 1.*
Le Petit Trianon is a tiny, intimate 18th-century French-style restaurant and café. It is difficult to find a seat, but worth it once you do. *ul. Piwna 40.*
Telimena is a small corner café with outdoor tables in summer. *Krakowskie Przedmiéscie 27.*
Trou Madame has a secluded setting in Lazienki Park.
Ujazdowska is elegant and spacious in a 19th-century French-style house. *al. Ujazdowska 47.*

Cracow and its Environs

Cracow, seat of Poland's oldest university and once the capital of the country (before losing the honor to Warsaw in 1611), is the only major Polish city to escape devastation in the last war. Hitler's armies were driven out before they had a chance to destroy it. Today its fine ramparts, towers, facades, and churches, illustrating seven centuries of Polish architecture, make Cracow a major attraction for visitors. Its location—about 160 miles (270 kilometers) south of Warsaw—also makes it a good base for hiking and skiing trips in the mountainous south of Poland.

Also within exploring range from Cracow are the famous Polish shrine to the Virgin Mary at Częstochowa, and, at Auschwitz, the grim reminder of man's capacity for inhumanity.

Getting Around

Cracow is reached by major highways—E7 direct from Warsaw and E82 from Częstochowa. Trains link Cracow with most major destinations in Poland; the station is in the central city on ul. Pawia. The bus station is nearby.

Guided Tours

Bus or walking tours of Cracow and its environs are provided by Orbis. Horse-drawn carriages may be hired at the main market for a negotiated price.

Tourist Information

Cracow. ul. Pawia 8, tel. 12/204–71.
Częstochowa. II al., tel. 12/40–42.

Exploring Cracow

① Cracow's old city is ringed by a park called the **Planty.** The park replaced the old walls of the town, which were torn down in the mid-19th century. Begin your tour at **St. Florian's Gate,** which leads to the old town. The gate is guarded by an imposing 15th-century fortress called the Barbican. Enter the city, passing along Florianska Street, the beginning of the "Royal Route" through the town.

Time Out Don't pass up the chance to stop for refreshments at Cracow's most famous café, **Jama Michalikowa.** *Ul. Florianska 8.*

② Ul. Florianska leads to the **Main Market,** one of the largest and finest Renaissance squares in Europe. The calm of this spacious square, with its pigeons and flower stalls, is interrupted every hour by four short bugle calls drifting down from the spire of the Church of the Virgin Mary. The plaintive notes recall a centuries-old tradition in memory of a trumpeter whose throat was pierced by a well-aimed enemy arrow as he was warning his fellow citizens of an impending Tartar attack. The square Goth-**③** ic **Church of the Virgin Mary** contains a 15th-century wooden altarpiece—the largest in the world—carved by Wit Stwosz. The faces of the saints are reputedly those of Cracovian burghers. In the center of the square stands a covered market called **④** **Sukiennice** (Cloth Hall), built in the 14th century but remodeled during the Renaissance. The ground floor is still in business, selling trinkets and folk art souvenirs.

From the Main Market, turn down ul. Sw. Anny to No. 8, the **⑤** **Collegium Maius,** the oldest building of the famous **Jagiellonian University** (founded 1364). Its pride is the Italian-style arcaded courtyard. Inside is a museum where you can see the Copernicus globe, the first on which the American continent was shown, as well as astronomy instruments belonging to Cracow's most famous graduate.

⑥ Backtracking on ul. Grodzka will lead you to the **Wawel Castle and Cathedral.** This impressive complex of Gothic and Renaissance buildings stands on fortifications dating as far back as the 8th century. Inside the castle is a museum with an exotic collection of Oriental tents that were captured from the Turks at the battle of Vienna in 1683 and rare 16th-century Flemish tapestries. Wawel Cathedral is where, until the 18th century, Polish kings were crowned and buried. Up to 1978, the cathedral was the see of Archbishop Carol Wojtyla, now known as Pope John Paul II. *Wawel Castle and Cathedral. ul. Grodzka. Open 9–5.*

Cracow

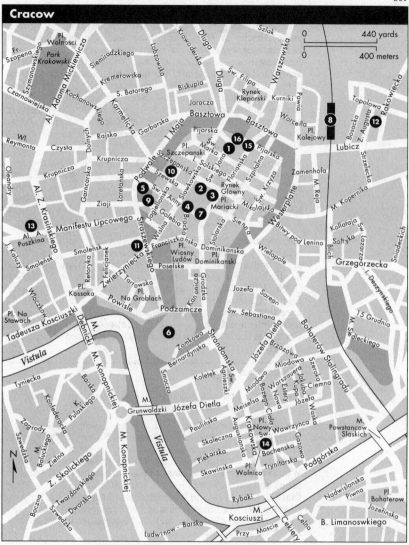

Major Attractions:

Church of the Virgin Mary, **3**

Jagiellonian University, **5**

Main Market, **2**

St. Florian's Gate, **1**

Sukiennice, **4**

Wawel Castle and Cathedral, **6**

Other Attractions:

Barbican, **15**

Central Station, **8**

Czartoryski Museum, **16**

Ethnographic Museum, **14**

Helena Modrzejewska Stary Theater, **10**

Jagiellonian University Museum, **9**

K. Szymanowski State Philharmonic Hall, **11**

Lenin Museum, **12**

National Museum, **13**

St. Adalbert Romanesque Church, **7**

About 30 miles (50 kilometers) west of Cracow is the Nazi concentration camp of Oswięcim, better known by its German name, **Auschwitz.** Here four million victims (mostly Jews) from 29 countries were executed by the Nazis during World War II. The camp has been left just as it was found in 1945 by the Soviet army, and crematoria and barracks now house dramatic displays of Nazi atrocities. Oswięcim itself is an industrial town with good connections from Cracow; buses and trains leave Cracow approximately every hour, and signs in Oswięcim direct visitors to the camp. *Free. Open Mar. and Nov. Tues.–Sun. 8–4; Apr. and Oct. Tues.–Sun. 8–5; May–Sept. 8–6; June–Aug. 8–7; Dec.–Feb., Tues.–Sun. 8–3.*

Wieliczka, about five miles (eight kilometers) southeast of Cracow, is the oldest salt mine in Europe, in operation since the end of the 13th century. It is famous for its magnificent underground chapel hewn in crystal rock, the **Chapel of the Blessed Kings.** *Wieliczka Mines. Admission: 250 Zł.Open Apr.–Oct. 8–6; Nov.–Mar. 8–4. Guided tours only.*

Czestochowa, 70 miles (120 kilometers) from Cracow and reached by regular trains and buses from Cracow, is the home of the holiest shrine in a country that is more than 90% Catholic. Inside the 14th-century Pauline monastery on Jasna Gora (Light Hill) is the famous **Black Madonna,** a painting of Our Lady of Czestochowa attributed by legend to St. Luke. It was here that an invading Swedish army was halted in 1655 and finally driven out of the country. Between Czestochowa and Cracow is the little town of **Wadowice,** birthplace of Pope John Paul II.

Dining and Lodging

For details and price category definitions, *see* Dining and Lodging in Essential Information.

Cracow Dining

Staropolska. Traditional Polish cuisine is served in a medieval setting. Try the pork, duck, or veal. *ul. Sienna 4. Dress: casual. No reservations. AE, DC, MC, V. Expensive.*

Wierzynek. One of the best restaurants in the country, Wierzynek serves traditional Polish specialties and excels in soups and game. It was here in 1364, after a historic meeting, that the king of Poland wined and dined the German Emperor Charles IV, five kings, and a score of princes. *Rynek Główny 15, tel. 12/210–25. Dress: formal. Reservations advised. AE, DC, MC, V. Expensive.*

Lodging

Cracovia. This large, Orbis-run five-story hotel boasts one of the best restaurants in town. There is also a lively night club where Western tourists like to meet. *al. Puszkina 1, tel. 12/22–86–66. 427 rooms, all with bath. AE, DC, MC, V. Expensive.*

Holiday Inn. This was the first Holiday Inn in Eastern Europe. Rather bland but comfortable with a fine restaurant, solarium, sauna, and indoor swimming pool, this high-rise establishment is pleasantly located near Cracow's "Green Meadows." *ul. Koniewa 7, tel. 12/37–50–44. 310 rooms, all with bath. AE, DC, MC, V. Expensive.*

Europejski. This small, older hotel overlooking the Planty park has seen better days, so make sure you see your room before you accept it. *ul. Lubicz 5, tel. 12/209–11. 55 rooms, some with bath. No credit cards. Moderate.*

Francuski. This small hotel is just inside the old town's walls, within walking distance of all the main sites. Built at the turn of the century, it offers an intimate atmosphere and friendly service. Rooms are elegant but a little tacky in a homey, East European way. The excellent restaurant is tranquil and plush and has a café with dancing. *ul. Pijarska 13, tel. 12/22–51–22. 59 rooms, most with bath or shower. No credit cards. Moderate.*

Czestochowa   **Centralny.** The Centralny makes a good base for exploring
Lodging   Poland's holiest shrine, and since most of the other guests are pilgrims, the atmosphere is an interesting mixture of piety and good fun. *ul. Swierczewkiego, tel. 12/440–67. 62 rooms, most with bath or shower. No credit cards. Moderate.*

Gdańsk and the North

In contrast to Cracow and the south, Poland north of Warsaw is the land of medieval castles and chateaux, dense forests and lakes, and sandswept beaches along the Baltic coast. If you haven't a car, consider going straight to Gdańsk and making excursions from there. The alternative is to travel by car along the course of the Vistula River through majestic countryside.

Getting Around

Gdańsk is a major transportation hub, with an airport just outside town (and good bus connections to downtown) and major road and rail connections with the rest of the country.

Guided Tours

Orbis arranges an eight-day tour of Warsaw, Toruń, Gdańsk, and Poznań. It also handles group and individual tours of Toruń, Gdańsk, and the surrounding areas.

Tourist Information

Elblag. ul. Maja 1, tel. 222–75; Orbis, ul. Hetmańska 23, tel. 223–64. Ostróda. Orbis, ul. Czdrnieckiego 10, tel. 35–57.
Gdańsk. ul. Heweliusza 8, tel. 31–03–38; Orbis, pl. Górskiego 1, tel. 31–49–44.
Płock. ul. Tuńska 4, tel. 226–00; Orbis, al. Jachowa 47, tel. 229–89.
Toruń. ul. Kopernika 27, tel. 272–99; Orbis, ul. Zeglarska 31, tel. 261–30.

Exploring

From Warsaw, follow routes E81 and 107 through **Płock.** Once you get through Płock's industrial area, you'll find a lovely medieval city that was, for a short time, capital of Poland. Worth seeing are the 12th-century cathedral, where two Polish kings are buried, and the dramatic 14th-century Teutonic castle. Continue through Włocławek to **Toruń,** where an overnight stay is recommended.

Toruń, birthplace of Nicolaus Copernicus, is an interesting medieval city that made its fortune from its location on the north-south trading route along the Vistula. Its old town district is a remarkably successful blend of Gothic buildings—

Gdansk and the North

N

Slupsk · Lebork · Gdyńia · Sopot · Gdańsk · Nowy Dwar Gdańsk · Braniewo · Elbląg · Tczew · Starogard · Malbork · Szczecinek · Chojnice · Kwidzyń · Ostróda · Swiecie · Chelmno · Grudziadz · Piła · Wyrzysk · Chelmża · Bydgoszcz · Toruń · Brodnica · Vistula · Inowrocław · Sierpc · Poznań · Gniezno · Wrzesznia · Włocławek · Płock · Koło

0 ___ 40 miles
0 ___ 60 km

churches, town hall, and burghers' homes—with Renaissance and Baroque patricians' houses. The **Town Hall's Tower** (1274) is the oldest in Poland. Don't leave without trying some of Toruń's famous gingerbread and honey cakes.

The route leading north from Toruń to Gdańsk passes through some of the oldest towns in Poland. Along the way are many medieval castles, chateaux, and churches that testify to the wealth and strategic importance of the area. Two short detours are a must: one is to **Kwidzyń** to see the original 14th-century castle and cathedral complex. The other is to **Malbork.** This huge castle, 36 miles (58 kilometers) from Gdańsk, was one of the most powerful strongholds in medieval Europe. From 1308 to 1457, it was the residence of the Grand Masters of the Teutonic Order. The Teutonic Knights were a thorn in Poland's side until their defeat at the battle of Grunwald in 1410. Inside Malbork castle is a museum with beautiful examples of amber—including lumps as large as melons and pieces containing perfect specimens of prehistoric insects.

Gdańsk, formerly the free city of Danzig, is another of Poland's beautifully restored towns, displaying a rich heritage of Gothic, Renaissance, and Mannerist architecture. This is where the first shots of World War II were fired and where the free trade union Solidarity was born after strikes in 1980. The city's old town has a wonderful collection of historic town houses and narrow streets. The splendid Długa and Długi Targ streets (best for shopping) form the axis of the town and are a good starting point for walks into other parts of the city. The evocative **Solidarity Monument** stands outside the Lenin shipyards—erected in honor of workers killed by the regime during strikes in 1970. The nearby town of *Sopot* is Poland's most popular seaside resort.

Dining and Lodging

For details and price category definitions, *see* Dining and Lodging in Essential Information on Poland.

Elbląg   **Karczma Słupska.** This is the best restaurant in town. It's usu-
Dining   ally crowded and specializes in fresh fish. *ul. Krotka 1. No reservations. No credit cards. Moderate.*

Gdańsk   The best restaurants—here as elsewhere in Poland—are in the
Dining   more expensive Orbis hotels. Other good places, however, can be recommended.

Pod Lososiem. The name of this restaurant refers to salmon, which, if available on the day you visit, is highly recommended. You can't go wrong with any fish dishes, however. *ul. Szeroka 51 (no tel.). No reservations. AE, DC, MC, V. Expensive.*

Pod Wieza. This restaurant has a reputation for good meat dishes and generous portions. *Piwna 51 (no tel.). No reservations. AE, DC, MC, V. Expensive.*

Kashubska. The specialties here come from Kahubia, a hilly and wooded lakeland region near the coast. Smoked fish dishes are highly recommended. *ul. Kartuska 1 (no tel.). No reservations. AE, DC, MC, V. Moderate.*

Lodging   **Hewelius.** This large, modern, high-rise hotel is situated in the center of the city, within walking distance of the old town. Rooms are standard, spacious, blandly furnished, with all the modern conveniences. The hotel has a good restaurant and one of the best nightclub-discos in town. *ul. Heweliusza 22, tel. 31–56–31. 250 rooms, most with bath. AE, DC, MC, V. Expensive.*

Marina. Built in 1982, this large high rise, popular with Western businesspeople, is one of the newest hotels in Poland and probably the best in town. Upper floors have splendid views. Facilities include a popular restaurant, a night club, an indoor swimming pool, tennis courts, and a bowling alley. *ul. Jelitkowska 20, tel. 53–12–46. 193 rooms, all with bath or shower. AE, DC, MC, V. Expensive.*

Posejdon. Though modern, functional hotel is a bit out of town, it is well equipped with leisure facilities, including solarium, sauna, indoor swimming pool, and disco. *ul. Kapliczna 30, tel. 53–02–27. 140 rooms, most with bath or shower. AE, DC, MC, V. Moderate.*

Ostróda   This town is not visited by many foreign tourists and is lacking
Lodging   in good-quality facilities. The undistinguished *Panorama Hotel* is the best, unless Orbis can find you private lodging. *ul. Krasickiego 23, tel. 22–27.*

Toruń   The best restaurants are in the expensive Orbis hotels. Others
Dining   are listed below.

Pod Kurantem. Regional cuisine is featured in this attractive old wine cellar. Slow service is the penalty for popularity. *Rynek Staromiejski 28 (no tel.). No reservations. No credit cards. Expensive.*

Polonia. Try the Polonia for the excellent meat dishes and soups such as *barszcz. pl. Armii Czerwonej 5 (no tel.). No reservations. No credit cards. Moderate.*

Wodnik. This large café along the banks of the Vistula is very popular with locals. *Blvd. Filadelfijski (no tel.). No credit cards. Inexpensive.*

Lodging **Helios.** This friendly, medium-size, hotel is situated in the city center and offers a good restaurant (albeit with slow service), sauna, nightclub, and beauty parlor. *ul. Kraszewskiego 1, tel. 250–33. 140 rooms, most with bath or shower. AE, DC, MC, V. Moderate.*

Kosmos. A functional 1960s hotel, Kosmos is beginning to show signs of wear and tear. It is situated near the river, in the city center. *ul. Portowa 2, tel. 298–00. 180 rooms, most with bath or shower. AE, DC, MC, V. Moderate.*

28 Portugal

Introduction

Given its long Atlantic coastline, it is not surprising that Portugal has been a maritime nation for most of its history. The valor of Portuguese seamen culminated in the great era of discoveries masterminded by Prince Henry the Navigator in the 15th century. But despite its sailors' worldly adventures, Portugal has remained relatively undiscovered.

Although it shares the Iberian Peninsula with Spain, it attracts far fewer foreign visitors than does its neighbor to the east. Yet Portugal has much to recommend it to tourists: fine beaches and splendid sports facilities along the coast, beautiful castles and palaces, picturesque fishing villages, well-maintained hotels and *pousadas* (government-owned inns), excellent restaurants, and colorful folk traditions.

Portugal, about the size of the state of Maine, is small enough that its main attractions can be seen in a short time. It lies in a long, narrow coastal strip that has more geographic and climatic variations than virtually any other country in Western Europe. But at Portugal's widest point, the distance between the Atlantic coast and Spain is a mere 150 miles (240 kilometers). There are good air, rail, and bus systems throughout the country. However, while distances between places of interest are short, visitors may find driving a challenge: There are few turnpikes, traffic is fast, and the Portuguese are reckoned to be among the world's rashest drivers.

Observant visitors are likely to notice a distinct difference between the north, which is more Celtic in character, and the south, where Moorish antecedents are apparent. But the Portuguese people are welcoming wherever you meet them.

For the purposes of this guide, we have concentrated on the southern part of the country—the section most frequented by foreign visitors—including Portugal's sophisticated capital, Lisbon; and the Algarve.

Before You Go

When to Go The tourist season runs from spring through autumn, but some parts of the country, especially the Algarve, which boasts some 3,000 hours of sunshine annually, are balmy even in winter. Hotel prices are greatly reduced between November and February.

Climate Since Portugal's entire coast is on the Atlantic Ocean, the country's climate is temperate year-round. Portugal rarely suffers the extremes of heat that Mediterranean countries do. Even in August, the hottest month, the Algarve is the only region where the midday heat may be uncomfortable, and most travelers go there to bathe and soak up the sun anyway. What rain there is falls from November to March; December and January can be chilly outside the Algarve, but there is no snow except in the mountains of the Serra da Estrela in the northeast. Almond blossoms and vivid wildflowers that cover the countryside start to bloom early in February. The dry months of June, July, August, and September can turn much of the landscape the color of a lion's tawny hide, but there is always a

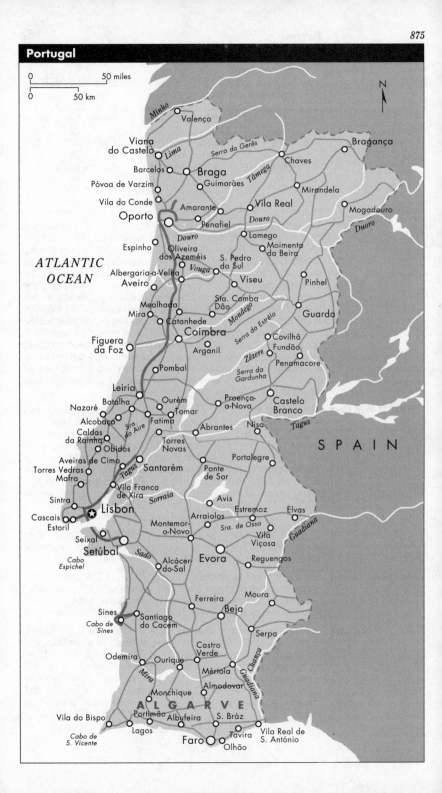

875

Portugal

50 miles

50 km

N

Minho

Valença

Viana do Castelo

Lima

Serra do Gerês

Chaves

Bragança

Barcelos

Braga

Guimarães

Tâmega

Mirandela

Póvoa de Varzim

Vila do Conde

Amarante

Vila Real

Mogadouro

Oporto

Penafiel

Douro

Duoro

Douro

Lamego

Espinho

Oliveira dos Azeméis

Moimenta da Beira

ATLANTIC OCEAN

Albergaria-a-Velha

S. Pedro do Sul

Vouga

Viseu

Pinhel

Aveiro

Mealhada

Sta. Comba Dão

Mondego

Guarda

Mira

Catanhede

Serra da Estrela

Covilhã

Figuera da Foz

Coimbra

Arganil

Fundão

Penamacore

Zêzere

Pombal

Serra da Gardunha

Leiria

Ourém

Proença-a-Nova

Castelo Branco

Nazaré

Batalha

Tomar

Alcobaça

Fatima

Abrantes

Nisa

Tagus

SPAIN

Caldas da Rainha

Sra. do Aire

Torres Novas

Obidos

Aveiras de Cima

Santarém

Portalegre

Torres Vedras

Tagus

Ponte de Sor

Mafra

Vila Franca de Xira

Sorraia

Avis

Sintra

Lisbon

Arraiolos

Estremoz

Elvas

Cascais

Estoril

Montemor-o-Novo

Sra. de Ossa

Guadiana

Seixal

Setúbal

Vila Viçosa

Cabo Espichel

Sado

Evora

Reguengos

Alcácer-do-Sal

Ferreira

Moura

Beja

Sines

Cabo de Sines

Santiago do Cacem

Serpa

Odemira

Castro Verde

Ourique

Chança

Mértola

Guadiana

Almodovar

Mira

Monchique

ALGARVE

Vila do Bispo

Portimão

Albufeira

S. Bráz

Lagos

Tavira

Vila Real de S. António

Cabo de S. Vicente

Faro

Olhão

breeze in the evening in Lisbon, as well as along the Estoril coast west of the capital.

The following are the average daily maximum and minimum temperatures for Lisbon.

Jan.	57F	14C	May	71F	21C	Sept.	79F	26C
	46	8		55	13		62	17
Feb.	59F	15C	June	77F	25C	Oct.	72F	22C
	47	8		60	15		58	14
Mar.	63F	17C	July	81F	27C	Nov.	63F	17C
	50	10		63	17		52	11
Apr.	67F	20C	Aug.	82F	28C	Dec.	58F	15C
	53	12		63	17		47	9

Currency The unit of currency in Portugal is the *escudo* (Esc.), which can be divided into 100 centavos. Escudos come in bills of 100$00, 500$00, 1,000$00 and 5,000$00. (In Portugal the dollar sign stands between the escudo and the centavo.) Coins are 1 escudo, 2.50, 5, 10, 20, 25, 50, and 100. At press time (fall 1988), the exchange rate was 140$00 to the U.S. dollar and 240$00 to the pound sterling. Owing to the complications of dealing in millions of escudos, 1,000$00 is always called a *conto*, so 10,000$00 is referred to as 10 contos. Credit cards are accepted in all the larger shops and restaurants, as well as in hotels; however, better exchange rates are obtained in banks and exchange offices *(cambios)* than in hotels. Short-changing is rare but, as in every country, restaurant bills should be checked. Change in post offices and railway booking offices should also be counted. Shops are usually honest.

What It Will Cost The cost of hotels and restaurants in Portugal is about half what it is in the rest of Europe. Produce is fresh, and few luxury foodstuffs are imported, so dining is generally inexpensive, except in the very top restaurants. The most expensive areas are Lisbon, the Algarve, and the tourist resort areas along the Tagus estuary. The least expensive areas are country towns, which all have reasonably priced hotels and *pensão*, or pensions, as well as numerous café-type restaurants. A sales tax (VAT) of 17% is imposed on hotel, restaurant, and car rental bills, as well as for services such as car repairs.

Sample Prices Cup of coffee, 60$00; bottle of beer, 80$00; Coca-Cola, 80$00; bottle of house wine (vinho da casa), 200$00; a ham sandwich, 120$00; one-mile taxi ride, 150$00.

Customs on Arrival You are allowed to bring in 200 cigarettes or 250 grams of tobacco, one liter of liquor over 22% volume, and a "reasonable" amount of perfume. (The general impression is that customs officials here are not too strict; but don't try anything stupid.)

Language Portuguese is easy to read by anyone with even slight knowledge of a Latin language, but it is difficult to pronounce and understand, (most people speak quickly and eliptically). However, you will find that in the larger cities and major resorts many people, especially the young, speak English. In the countryside, the people are so friendly and eager to be helpful that visitors can usually make themselves understood in sign language.

Getting Around

By Car
Road Conditions
Apart from the few turnpikes (moderate tolls) and the major highways between Lisbon and the Algarve, Oporto, and Guincho beyond Cascais alongside the river Tagus, road conditions in Portugal are poor. The roads are winding and surfaces unpredictable.

Motorists going north from Lisbon will find the recently built autoroute from Leiria up to Oporto well designed and fast driving easy. From Lisbon to Leiria, there is a turnpike through Vila Franca de Xira up to Aveiras de Cima that will be extended sometime in the future. The current road from Aveiras de Cima to Leiria is often congested.

Driving to the Algarve from Lisbon is a pleasure; except for the section between Setúbal and Alcacer do Sal, the entire route is via motorway. South of Alcacer all the towns are bypassed by a new motorway built down to Messines, inland from Albufeira. At Messines, the old roads, now widened, go west to Portimão, Lagos, and Sagres, south for Albufeira, and east for Faro and the frontier with Spain at Vila Real de Sto. Antonio.

There are no motorways from Lisbon to the nearest frontier post with Spain at Caia, outside Elvas, but the route through Setúbal (turnpike from Lisbon), over the Tagus bridge to Montemor-o-Novo, Arraiolos, and Estremoz, is good and fast.

Rules of the Road
Driving is on the right. At the junction of two roads of equal size, traffic coming from the right has priority. At traffic circles, vehicles on the inside have priority. Traffic in the country is light, but local people are apt to walk in the road and occasional horse- or donkey-drawn carts may hold things up. Seat belts are obligatory. Horns should not be used in built-up areas, and a red warning triangle, for use in a breakdown, must be carried. The speed limit on turnpikes is 120 kph (72 mph); on other roads it is 90 kph (54 mph), and in built-up areas, 50–60 kph (30–36 mph). Speed bumps are sometimes placed across the road entering a village. Side roads usually have stop signs at the intersections.

Parking
Parking lots are available in Lisbon, Oporto, and major cities at a comparatively small hourly fee. Parking at the side of city streets is limited. Parking in the country is unlimited, but on narrow roads it is wise to draw in as much as possible and avoid curves.

Gasoline
Gas prices are among the highest in Europe: Esc. 119 per liter for super and Esc. 115 per liter for regular. Many gas stations throughout the country are self-service.

Breakdowns
All large garages in and around towns have breakdown services. Special emergency (SOS) telephones are located at intervals on turnpikes and motorways. Motorists in Portugal are very helpful; if your car breaks down, aid from a passing driver is usually forthcoming within a short time. There is no danger in accepting such help, though some caution is advisable.

By Train
The Portuguese railway system is surprisingly extensive for so small a country. Trains are clean and leave on time, but there are few express runs except between Lisbon and Oporto. These

take under 3 hours for the 210-mile (350 kilometer) journey.
Several of the Oporto/Lisbon trains take cars, as does one train
a day between Lisbon–Castelo Branco–Regua–Guarda and
some Lisbon–Algarve trains during the summer. Cars must be
at the station an hour before departure. Prices are reasonable,
and tickets can be bought then or in advance. Most trains have
first- and second-class compartments; suburban lines around
Lisbon have a single class. Tickets should be bought, and seats
reserved if desired, at the stations or through travel agents,
two or three days in advance. Timetables are the same on Saturday and Sunday as on weekdays, except on suburban lines.
Wasteels-Expresso, Avenida Antonio Augusto de Aguiar 88,
1000 Lisbon, tel. 01/579180, is reliable for all local and international train tickets and reservations.

International trains to Madrid, Paris, and other parts of Europe depart from the Apolonia Station in Lisbon and Cam-
panhã in Oporto.

By Plane The internal air services of Air Portugal (TAP) are good. Lisbon is linked at least four times daily with Oporto and Faro;
daily with Funchal (Madeira), more at peak periods; weekly
with Porto Santo, an island some way off Madeira; and several
times a week with the archipelago of the Azores. Flights to
Viseu, Vila Real, and Bragança are all run by TAP, Praça
Marques Pombal 3, 1200 Lisbon, tel. 01/575020.

By Bus The nationalized bus company, **Rodoviaria Nacional,** has passenger terminals in Lisbon at 18, Avenida Casal Ribeiro, tel.
01/577715, and Avenida Santos Dumont, 57, tel. 01/775245,
with regular bus services throughout Portugal. Most long-
distance buses have toilet facilities, and the fares are cheaper
than for trains, which usually are faster and more restful.

By Boat Ferries across the river Tagus leave from Praça do Comerçio,
Cais do Sodré, and Belém. From April to October, a two-hour
boat excursion leaves the ferry station at Praça do Comerçio in
Lisbon daily at 2:30 PM for Paço d'Arcos. The price is 1,500$00.

Boat trips on the river Douro (Oporto) are organized from May
to October by **Porto Ferreira,** Rua da Cavalhosa, 19, Vila Nova
de Gaia, Oporto. They leave every day on the hour, except Saturday afternoon and Sunday.

By Bicycle **Tip Tours,** Avenida Costa Pinto 91-A, 2750 Cascais, tel. 01/
283821 rents out bicycles by the day, or half day. **Cycle Portugal,** Box 877, San Antonio, FL 34266, tel. USA 800/2828932, or
in Portugal, tel. 01/2471032, offers bicycle tours throughout the
country with accommodations in first–class hotels. Each tour
is accompanied by a guide, a mechanic, and a van for luggage.

Essential Information

Telephones Pay phones work with 2$50, 5$00 and 25$00 coins; 7$50 is the
minimum for short local calls. Long-distance calls cost less
from 8 PM to 8 AM. All telephone calls are more expensive when
made from a hotel, so it is wise to make international phone
calls from a post office, where you are assigned a private booth.
Collect calls can also be made from post offices. Some call boxes
accept international calls.

Mail Postal rates, both domestic and foreign, increase twice a year.
Country post offices close for lunch and at 6 PM weekdays; they

are not open on weekends. Main post offices in towns are open all day until 6:30 PM. In Lisbon, the post office in the Restauradores is open 24 hours.

Receiving Mail Mail can be sent in care of **American Express Star,** Avenida Sidonio Pais 4, 1000 Lisbon; there is no service charge. Main post offices also accept *poste restante* letters.

Shopping Portugal is a rewarding country in which to shop, for a large proportion of goods are still handmade, and crafts flourish. Wonderful pottery and fascinating basketwork are to be found throughout Portugal, which is also renowned for its *azulejos* (highly glazed tiles). Embroidered carpets are a specialty of Arraiolos, and embroidered table and bed linens, blouses, and dresses vary in style, depending on the district in which they are made. Fine shoes and other leather goods made in Portugal are exported all over the world. Gold and silver filigree jewelry is another speciality.

The Centro de Turismo Artesanato, Rua Castilho 61, 1200 Lisbon will ship goods abroad even if they are not bought there.

VAT Refunds VAT is included in the price of goods and can be reclaimed at a special department at the airports on presentation of a receipt.

Weekly country markets are good hunting grounds for local crafts such as sheepskin slippers, tinsmith's work, pottery, rag carpets, woven materials, cork buckets, and woolen blankets.

Bargaining is not usual in city stores or shops, but is possible in flea markets, antiques shops, and outdoor markets that sell fruit, vegetables, and household goods.

Opening and **Banks.** Banks are open weekdays 8:30–11:45 and 1–2:45.
Closing Times **Museums.** Museums are usually open 10–5; some close for lunch and on Monday. At palaces closing days vary.
Shops. Shops are open weekdays 9–1 and 3–7; Saturday, 9–1. Shopping malls in Lisbon and other cities remain open until 10 or midnight and often are open on Sunday.

National Holidays January 1 (New Year's Day); February 16 (Carnival, Shrove Tuesday); April 1 (Good Friday); April 25 (Anniversary of the Revolution); May 1 (Labor Day); June 2 (Corpus Christi); June 10 (National Day); August 15 (Assumption); October 5 (Day of the Republic); November 1 (All Saints); December 1 (Independence Day); December 8 (Immaculate Conception); December 25 (Christmas Day).

Dining Eating is taken quite seriously in Portugal, and, not surprisingly, seafood is a staple. Freshly caught lobster, crab, prawns, tuna, sole, and squid are prepared innumerable ways, but if you want to sample a little bit of everything, try *Caldeirada*, a piquant stew made with whatever is freshest from the sea. The Portuguese also like pork and go so far as to combine it with clams in a dish called *carne de porco á alentejana*. There are some excellent local wines, and even in modest restaurants the house wine *(vinho da casa)* is usually very good. Water is generally safe, but visitors may want to drink bottled water—"sem gas" for still, "com gas" for fizzy—from one of the many excellent Portuguese spas.

Mealtimes Lunch usually begins around 1–1:30 PM; dinner is served at about 8 PM. Note that these times are earlier than those in Spain.

Ratings Taxes and service are usually included, but a tip of 5–10% is always appreciated. All restaurants must post a Bill of Fare with prices in a window facing the street. Best bets are indicated by a star ★. At press time, there were 140 escudos (140$00) to the dollar.

Category	Cost
Very Expensive	over 6,000$00
Expensive	4,000$00–6,000$00
Moderate	2,000$00–4,000$00
Inexpensive	under 2,000$00

Credit Cards The following credit card abbreviations are used: AE, American Express; DC, Diners Club; MC, MasterCard; V, Visa.

Lodging Visitors have a wide choice of lodgings in Portugal, which offers the lowest rates in Europe for accommodations. Hotels are graded from one up to five stars, as are the smaller inns called *estalagems*, which usually provide breakfast only. *Pensions* go up to four stars and often include meals. The state-subsidized *pousadas*, most of which are situated in castles, old monasteries, or have been built where there is a particularly fine view, are five-star luxury properties. Most rooms in *residencias*, located in every town and large village, have private baths or showers, and breakfast is usually included in the charge. They are extremely good value, under Esc. 2,000 a night.

A recent innovation is **Turismo de Habitacão** (Country House Tourism), in which private homeowners all over the country, but mostly in the north, offer visitors a room and breakfast (and sometimes provide dinner on request). This is an excellent way to experience life on a country estate. Particulars are available from Rua Alexandre Herculano 51, 3°D, 1000 Lisbon, tel. 01/681713.

Tourist offices can help visitors with hotel or other reservations, and will provide lists of the local hostelries without charge. Few international chains have hotels in Portugal, which makes for an interesting variety. Almost all bathrooms have showers over the tubs.

Aparthotels, with double rooms, bath, and kitchenette, are to be found in the main resorts and are good value. Villas can be hired by the week or longer in the Algarve from various agents. One of the best-run complexes is Luz Bay Club, at Praia da Luz near Lagos, where all the well-designed villas have daily maid service.

Camping Camping has become increasing popular in Portugal in recent years, and there are now more than 100 campsites throughout the country offering a wide range of facilities. The best-equipped have markets, swimming pools, and tennis courts. For further information, contact: Federacão Portuguesa de Campsimo, Rua Voz de Operario 1, 1100 Lisbon, tel. 01/852350.

Ratings Prices are for two people in a double room, based on high-season rates. Best bets are indicated by a star ★. At press time, there were 140 escudos (140$00) to the dollar.

Category	Cost
Very Expensive	over 17,000$00
Expensive	12,000$00–17,000$00
Moderate	7,500$00–12,000$00
Inexpensive	under 7,500$00

Credit Cards The following credit card abbreviations are used: AE, American Express; DC, Diners Club; MC, MasterCard; V, Visa.

Tipping In Portugal those who render services accept gratuities with dignity and are not disagreeable if they aren't tipped. Service is included in bills at hotels and most restaurants. In luxury hotels, give the porter who carries your luggage 200$00, in less expensive establishments, 100$00. If the maid brings your breakfast, give her 100$00 a day or 500$00 for a stay of a week or two. If you regularly dine in the hotel, give between 500$00 and 1,000$00 to your waiter at the end of your stay, somewhat less to the wine waiter if you order wine with every meal. Otherwise, tip 5–10% on restaurant bills, except at inexpensive establishments where you may just leave any coins given in change. Taxi drivers get 10–15%; cinema and theater ushers who seat you, 20$00 to 50$00; train and airport porters, 100$00 per bag; service station attendants, 5$00–10$00 for gas, 20$00–25$00 for checking tires and cleaning windshields; hairdressers, around 10–20%.

Lisbon

Arriving and Departing

By Plane Lisbon airport is only about 20 minutes from the city by car or taxi. The airport is small, and the people who work there are friendly and helpful to tourists. Information: tel. 01/802060.

Between the Airport and Downtown There are buses from the airport into the city center—Nos. 44 and 45 and Green Line—but taxis are so much cheaper than in other European capitals that visitors would be wise to take a taxi straight to their destination. The cost into Lisbon is about 500$00, and to Estoril or Sintra, 3,000$00. There are no trains or subways between the airport and the city. There is a good tourist center at the airport that will provide free maps, as will the car-rental firms with offices there.

By Train International trains from Paris and Madrid arrive at Sta. Apolonia station, tel. 01/876025, in the center of the city. There is a tourist office at the station and plenty of taxis and porters; but car-rental firms do not have offices there.

Getting Around

Lisbon is a hilly city, and the sidewalks are paved with small stones, so walking can be tiring, even when wearing comfortable shoes. Fortunately, Lisbon's tram service is one of the best in Europe and buses go all over the city. A Tourist Pass for unlimited rides on the tram or bus costs Esc. 1,175 for a week or Esc. 850 for four days; it can be purchased at the Cais do Sodré station and other terminals. Books of 20 half-price tickets also are available.

By Tram and Bus Buses and trams operate from 4 AM to 2 AM. Try tram routes 13, 24, 28, 29, and 30 for an inexpensive tour of the city; buses No. 52, 53, and 54 cross the Tagus bridge. Many of the buses are double-deckers, affording an exceptional view of the city's architecture, which includes a remarkable number of art nouveau buildings.

By Subway Avoid the subway, called the Metropolitano, which operates from 6:30 AM to 1 AM; it isn't extensive and has become a favorite haunt of pickpockets.

By Taxi Taxis are easily recognizable by a lighted sign on green roofs. There are ranks in the main squares, but it is easy to hail a cruising vehicle. Taxis take up to four passengers at no extra charge. Rates start at 70$00.

Important Addresses and Numbers

Tourist Information The main Lisbon tourist office, tel. 01/363314, is in the Palacio Foz, Praça dos Restauradores, at the bottom of the Avenida da Liberdade, the main artery of the city. Open Monday–Saturday 9–8, Sunday 10–6. The tourist office at Lisbon airport, tel. 01/885974 or 01/893689, is open daily 9 AM–midnight, and the office at Avenida Antonio Augusto de Aguiar 86, tel. 01/575091 is open 9–6.

Embassies U.S.; Avenida Forças Armadas, tel. 01/726600. **Canadian;** Rua Rosa Araujo é, tel. 01/563821. **U.K.;** Rua S. Domingos à Lapa 37, tel. 01/661191.

Emergencies SOS Emergencies: tel. 115. **Police:** tel. 01/849716. **Ambulance:** tel. 01/617777. **Fire Brigade:** tel. 01/322222. **Doctor:** British Hospital, Rua Saraiva de Carvalho 49, tel. 01/602020; night: 01/603785. **Pharmacies:** open 9–1, 3–7, Saturday 9–1; consult notice on door for nearest one open on weekends or after hours.

Travel Agencies **American Express Star,** Avenida Sidonio Pais 4, tel. 01/539871. **Wagons-Lits/Thomas Cook,** Avenida da Liberdade 103, tel. 01/361521.

Guided Tours

Orientation Tours **Capristanos** (Ave. Duque de Loulé 47, tel. 01/542973) offers organized bus tours of Lisbon and environs, as does **Citirama** (Ave. Praia da Vitoria, 12-B, tel. 01/575564). Tourist offices and hotels have lists of tours. Reservations can be made through travel agencies or hotels.

Excursions **Rodoviaria Nacional** (Ave. Casal Ribeiro 18, 1000 Lisbon, tel. 01/577715) and **Tip Tours** (Ave. Costa Pinto 91-A, 2750 Cascais, tel. 01/283821) operate day and half-day tours of Lisbon including Alcobaça, Batalha, Fátima, Nazaré, and Tomar. Certain tours pick up at hotels.

Personal Guides You can arrange to have the services of a personal guide by contacting the main Lisbon Tourist Office (*see* Important Addresses and Numbers). Beware of unauthorized guides who will approach you at some of the most popular attractions. These people usually are more concerned with "guiding" you to a particular shop or restaurant.

Lisbon's major sights can be seen in several days, but if you have more time, there are numerous small pleasures to be discovered at a more leisurely pace.

Exploring Lisbon

Spread out over a series of hills on the north back of the River Tagus, Portugal's capital seems to present unending treats for the eye. Its wide boulevards are bordered by black-and-white mosaic sidewalks. Pastel-colored modern apartment buildings vie for attention with art nouveau houses and buildings faced with decorative tiles. And the hills are dotted with natural lookout points called *miradouros* from which there are lively views of the Tagus estuary.

Lisbon is not a city easily explored on foot, however. Some of its streets are quite steep, and others are paved with cobblestones that make walking difficult. Although Lisbon is small compared with many European capital cities, visitors are often surprised to find that, because of the hills, places that appear to be close to one another on a map are actually on different levels. Fortunately, there are elevators and cable cars to transport you up and down the steepest hills, in addition to a very efficient tram system and numerous, reasonably priced taxis.

The center of Lisbon stretches from Rossio Square to Praça do Comércio, one of the largest riverside squares in Europe. This district, known as Baixa, is one of the earliest examples of town planning on a large square. This geometrical alignment of perfectly proportioned buildings was built after an earthquake destroyed most of the city in 1775. The old Moorish quarter, Alfama, which survived that catastrophe, lies to the east of Baixa, while the Belém section, with its many museums, is to the west.

St. George's Castle and the Alfama

The Moors who imposed their rule on most of the southern Iberian Peninsula in the 8th century left their mark on Lisbon in many subtle ways, but the most concrete reminders of the invaders today are the huge **St. George's Castle** on one of the city's highest hills and the **Alfama,** a district of narrow, twisting streets and houses on the slopes leading up to it. Much of the Alfama quarter remains as it was in the 12th century when the Moors finally were driven from the city. This jumble of buildings, with their flower-bedecked balconies and red-tiled roofs, managed to survive devastating earthquakes because they rest on dense bedrock. You can stroll up to the castle grounds through these colorful streets or take bus No. 37, which starts at **Rossio Square,** or take a taxi up and walk down. Within the walls of the castle is an Arabic palace that was a residence for kings of Portugal until the 16th century; a formal, plane tree-shaded square, the Largo de Santa Cruz do Castelo; a Medieval village of narrow lanes and houses now occupied by artisans, and a grassy terrace with tables and benches where you can enjoy a picnic and watch ducks, swans, turkeys, and other birds strut about the grounds. *Free. Open daily.*

Edward VII Park and the Gulbenkian Foundation

At the top of **Avenida da Liberdade,** Lisbon's "Champs-Elysées," is the cool, green **Parque Eduardo VII (Edward VII Park)** with its Estufa Fria (Cool House) and Estufa Quente

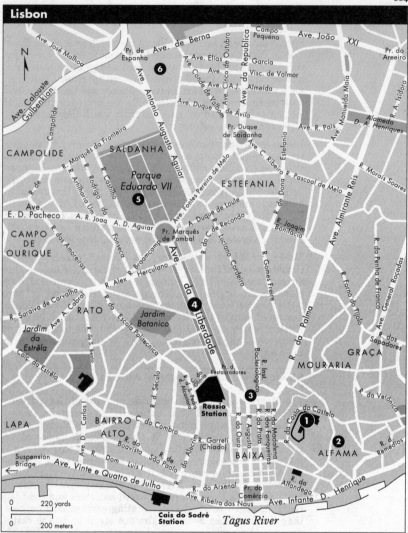

Alfama, **2**
Avenida da Liberdade, **4**
Gulbenkian
Foundation, **6**
Parque Eduardo VII, **5**
Rossio Square, **3**
St. George's Castle, **1**

(Hot House), where rare flowering shrubs, plants, and even trees thrive. *Admission: $100$00.*

Slightly northwest of the park, just off Praça de Espanha, is ⑥ the world-famous **Gulbenkian Foundation,** whose Art Center houses treasures collected by Calouste Gulbenkian, an Armenian oil magnate, and donated to the people of Lisbon. These range from superb examples of Greek and Roman coins and Persian carpets to Chinese porcelain and paintings by Rembrandt, Rubens, and other masters. (Admission: 50$00. Open Tues., Thurs., Fri., and Sun. 10–5; Wed. and Sat. 2–7:30). The complex also has two concert halls where music and ballet festivals are held in winter and spring. Tickets available at the box office, tel. 01/774167, are modestly priced, thanks to subsidies from the Gulbenkian Foundation.

Belém

To see the best examples of that uniquely Portuguese, late Gothic architecture known as Manueline, you should head for the Belém section at the far western edge of the city. The ⑦ **Mosteiro dos Jerónimos** (Hieronymite Monastery), in the Praça do Império, was conceived and planned by King Manuel II to honor the discoveries of Vasco da Gama (whose tomb is here) and other Portuguese explorers. The slender columns and a double cloister are heavily sculpted in marine motifs. *Open Oct. to Apr. 10–5 and May to Oct. 10–6:30.*

⑧ Beside the church is a **Naval Museum** with handsomely displayed ship models, as well as state barges and other large craft that can be viewed from catwalks. *Admission: 200$00. Open 10–1, 2:30–5.*

⑨ Another masterpiece of Manueline architecture is the **Tower of Belém,** off the Avenida Marginal, with its openwork balconies, loggia, and dome-topped turrets. Although it was built in the 16th century on an island in the middle of the Tagus, it now stands near the north bank because, over the centuries, the river's course has changed. *Admission: 200$00. Open Tues.–Sun. 9–8, 9–6 in winter.*

⑩ Nearby, the **Monument to the Discoveries,** built some 40 years ago, depicts Henry the Navigator leading his men toward the Tagus under the billowing sails of their tiny craft.

⑪ Also in the Belém District is the **Coach Museum,** Praça de Albuquerque, which has one of the largest collections of coaches in the world. The oldest vehicle on display was made in the late 16th century for Philip II of Spain, but the most stunning are three golden Baroque coaches, made in Rome in 1716 for King John V. *Admission: 200$00. Open 10–5 (summer until 6:30).*

What to See and Do with Children

More than 3,500 animals live at the 65-acre **Lisbon Zoo,** where children can ride on an elephant, ponies, or a small train, or skate at a roller rink when not being entertained by puppets or clowns in the children's playground. *Between Parque das Laranjeiras an and Estrada de Benifca, 01/782041. Admission: 200$00. Open 9–8, 9–6 in winter.*

The newly opened **Marionette Museum,** Largo Rodrigues de Freitas 19-A, not far from the Ricardo Espirito Santo Founda-

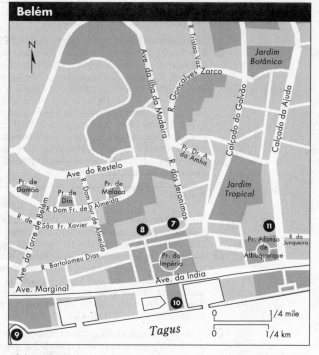

tion by St. George's castle, has an amusing collection, both old and new. *Admission: 200$00. Open 11–5.*

In the winter, various **circus** companies have short seasons in the Coliseu, Rua das Portas de S. Antão, just off the Rossio, tel. 01/361997. This huge circular hall, which holds 7,000 spectators, was built a hundred years ago. In addition to the circus, there are also operas, ballets, and concerts at very moderate prices.

Campo Grande, a long narrow park toward the airport, is particularly pleasant in warm weather, with tall, shady trees, tennis courts, and a lake on which boats can be hired.

A little to the north, the **Costume Museum,** Largo Julio Castilho, and the **Theater Museum,** Estrada do Lumiar, are well arranged in adjoining 18th-century country houses set in formal gardens. There is an excellent, though expensive, restaurant attached to the Costume Museum. *Admission: 200$00. Both open 10–1, 2:30–5.*

The **Feira Popular,** open in the summer, set between the Campo Pequeno and the Campo Grande on the way to the airport, features side shows and amusements for children of all ages.

The **planetarium** next to the Naval Museum at Belém posts its hours, which differ from week to week, on a board outside. A tram from here to Dafundo passes the Vasco da Gama **Aquarium,** Avenida Marginal, which features exotic fish, sea lions, and other marine creatures. *Admission: 200$00. Open noon–6, closed Mon.*

Off the Beaten Track

North of the city in the suburb of São Domingos de Benfica is one of the most beautiful private houses in the capital. The **Palacio da Fronteira** was built in the late 17th century and contains splendid reception rooms with 18th-century figurative tiles, contemporary furniture, and paintings, but it is the gardens that are unique. A long rectangular water tank is backed by 17th-century tiled panels of heroic-size knights on prancing horses. Stone steps at either side lead to a terraced walk above, between pyramid pavilions roofed with copper-colored tiles. Surrounding this beautiful conceit is a topiary garden, statuary, fountains, and terraces. *Admission: 1,000$00. Open Sat. 1–5; Mon. 10–12 and 2:30–5; first Sunday of every month 2:30–5.*

Shopping

Gift Ideas The best things to buy in Portugal are leather goods (shoes, handbags, etc.) and handcrafted items such as embroidered linens, wickerwork, copperware, pottery, and decorative tiles. Because it has hundreds of specialty shops, Lisbon offers the widest selection of these and other items.

Shopping Districts A tragic fire destroyed much of Lisbon's smartest shopping street in August 1988, and it was not known immediately when, or if, many of the affected stores in and around Rua Garrett, or the **Chiado**, as it is always called, would reopen. The other important shopping area is in the Baixa quarter between Rossio Square and the Tagus. Stores are generally open 9–1 and 3–7 weekdays; some open 9–1 on Saturday, but all are closed on Sunday.

Flea Markets A **Feira da Ladra** (flea market) is held on Tuesday and Saturday in the Largo de Santa Clara behind the Church of São Vicente, near the Alfama district.

Leather Goods Fine leather handbags and luggage are sold at **Galeão**, Rua Agusto 190, and at **Casa Canada,** 232 Rua Agusto. Shoe stores abound in Lisbon, but they may have a limited selection of large sizes (the Portuguese have relatively small feet); however, the better shops can make shoes to measure on short notice. Leather gloves can be purchased at a variety of specialty shops on Rua do Carmo and Rua do Ouro.

Handcrafts **Vivuva Lamego,** Largo do Intendente 25, has the largest selection of tiles and pottery, while **Fabrica Sant'Anna,** Rua da Misericordia 37, sells wonderful tiles based on antique patterns. For embroidered goods and baskets, try **Casa Regional da Ilha Verde,** Rua Paiva de Andrade 4, or **Tito Cunha** at Rua do Ouro, 179 and 246. Hand-embroidered rugs are the specialty at **Casa Quintão,** Rua Ivens 30.

Jewelry and Antiques **Antonio da Silva,** Praça Luis de Camoes 40, at the top of the Chiado, specializes in antique silver jewelry. The best costume jewelry in the city can be found at **Casa Batalha,** Rua Nova de Almada 75, at the bottom of the Chiado. Most of the antiques shops are along the Rua Escola Politecnica, the Rua de Sao Bento, and the Rua de Santa Marta.

Look for characteristic Portuguese gold- and silver-filigree work at **Sarmento,** Rua do Ouro 251.

Dining

Prices quoted here are per person, and include three courses, tax, and service but not wine. Best bets are indicated by a star ★. At press time, there were 140 escudos (140$00) to the dollar.

Category	Cost
Expensive	over 6,000$00
Moderate	4,000$00–6,000$00
Inexpensive	under 4,000$00

Expensive **António Clara.** Housed in an attractive art nouveau building where the Businessmen's Club meets, this restaurant serves French and international dishes with a flourish in an elegant room with heavy draperies, decorated ceiling, and huge chandelier. *Ave. Republica 38, tel. 01/766380. Dress: formal. Reservations required. AE, DC, MC, V.*

★ **Aviz.** One of the best and smartest restaurants in Lisbon, Aviz has a Belle Époque decor—even the washrooms are impressive —and an excellent French and international menu. *Serpa Pinto 12, tel. 01/328991. Dress: formal. Reservations required. AE, DC, MC, V. Closed Sat. lunch and Sun.*

Casa da Comida. Imaginative French and Portuguese fare is served in a former private house surrounding a flower filled patio. *Travessa das Amoreiras 1, tel. 01/685376. Dress: formal. Reservations advised. AE, DC, MC, V. Closed Sat. lunch and Sun.*

Gambrinus. One of Lisbon's older restaurants, Gambrinus is noted for its fish and shellfish. Entered through an inconspicuous door on a busy street, the restaurant has numerous small dining rooms. *Rua Portas S. Antão 23, tel. 01/321466. Dress: formal. Reservations recommended. AE, DC, MC, V.*

Gondola. In good weather, delicious Italian food can be enjoyed out-of-doors under a pergola at this pleasant establishment opposite the Gulbenkian Foundation. *Ave. Berna 64, tel. 01/770426. Dress: informal. MC, V.*

Michel's. French cooking is served in an appealing setting St. George's Castle.: a tree-lined square just inside the walls of *Largo S. Cruz do Castelo 5, tel. 01/867763. Dress: informal. AE, DC.*

★ **Tavares.** Superb food, an excellent wine list, and a handsome Edwardian dining room have made this one of Lisbon's most famous restaurants. *Rua Misericordia 35, tel. 01/321112. Dress: formal. AE, DC, MC, V. Closed Sat. and Sun. lunch.*

Moderate **Anarquistas.** One of the oldest restaurants in Lisbon, this place
★ is full of atmosphere and serves traditional Portuguese food, such as calf's liver and potatoes. *Largo de Trinidade 14, tel. 01/323510. Dress: informal. No credit cards. Closed Sun. in summer.*

Caravela. Well-heeled Portuguese women take tea—and scones, waffles, or homemade cakes—here in late afternoon, but light lunches are also served. There's a cozy fireplace to enjoy in winter. *Rua Paiva Andrade 8, tel. 01/328811. Dress: informal. AE, DC, MC. Closed Sat. and Sun.*

Forno da Brites. The food is practical, the red and white decor is cheery, and the staff is helpful to tourists. *Rua Tomas Ribeiro 73, tel. 01/542724. Dress: casual. No credit cards.*

O Paco. Good steaks and regional food and folkloric decor attract a literary crowd to this restaurant opposite the Gulbenkian Museum. *Ave. Berna 44, tel. 01/770642. Dress: informal. No credit cards.*

Petit Folie. French and Portuguese dishes are the specialties at this pleasant restaurant near Eduardo VII Park. In summer, you can dine on a garden terrace. *Ave. Antonio Augusto Aquiar 74, tel. 01/521948. Dress: informal. AE, DC, V.*

A Quinta. A menu of Portuguese, Russian, and Hungarian dishes is available at this country-style restaurant overlooking the Baixa and the Tagus from next to the top of the elevator from the Rua do Ouro to the Carmo square. *Top of Elevador de Santa Justa, tel. 01/265588. Dress: informal. AE, MC. Closed Sat. and Sun. dinner.*

Solmar. This restaurant near Rossio, Lisbon's main square, is best known for its seafood and shellfish, but try the wild boar or venison in season. *Rua Portas de Santo Antão 106, tel. 01/323371. Dress: informal. AE, DC, MC.*

Inexpensive **Atinel Bar.** The only Lisbon restaurant right on the Tagus, the Atinel is just off the Praça do Comercio and serves good, unpretentious food. You can watch seagulls wheeling about from behind a large picture window, or dine at one of the tables outside. *Cais dos Cacilheiros, tel. 01/372419. Dress: informal. No credit cards.*

Bonjardim. Good barbecued suckling pig and spit-roasted chicken are specialties at this restaurant just off the Restauradoes. It gets very crowded at peak hours. *Travesssa Santo Antão 11, tel. 01/324389. Dress: informal. AE, DC, MC, V.*

Cervejaria Trindade. You get good value for your money at this large restaurant which has a garden and a cave-style wine cellar. *Rua Nova da Trindade 20, tel. 01/323506. Dress: informal. No credit cards.*

Lodging

Lisbon has a good array of hotels in all price categories, from major international chain hotels to charming little family-run establishments. During peak season, however, reservations should be made well in advance.

Ratings Prices quoted here are for two people in a double room. Best bets are indicated by a star ★. At press time, there were 140 escudos (140$00) to the dollar.

Category	Cost
Very Expensive	over 20,000$00
Expensive	15,000$00–20,000$00
Moderate	10,000$00–15,000$00
Inexpensive	under 10,000$00

Very Expensive **Meridian Lisboa.** The rooms in Lisbon's newest luxury hotel are a bit on the small side, but they are soundproofed and attractively decorated; the front ones overlook the park. *Rua*

Castilho 149. tel. 01/690900. 331 rooms with bath. Facilities: sauna, shops, garage. AE, DC, MC, V.

★ **Ritz Lisboa.** One of the finest hotels in Europe, this Intercontinental is renowned for its excellent service. The large, handsomely decorated guest rooms all have terraces, and the elegantly appointed public rooms feature tapestries, antique reproductions, and fine paintings. The best rooms are in the front overlooking Eduardo VII Park. *Rua Rodrigo da Fonseca 88, tel. 01/692020. 304 rooms with bath. Facilities: nightclub, shops, garage. AE, DC, V.*

Expensive **Lisboa Sheraton.** This is a typical Sheraton hotel with a huge reception area and medium-size rooms. The deluxe rooms in the Towers section, which has a separate reception desk in the lobby and a private lounge, are about the same size but are more luxuriously appointed. The hotel is centrally located and is just across the street from a large shopping center. *Rua Latino Coelho 1, tel. 01/575757. 388 rooms with bath. AE, DC, MC, V. Facilities: outdoor pool, health club and sauna, disco. AE, DC, MC, V.*

Tivoli Lisboa. Located on a main thoroughfare, this comfortable, well-run establishment has a large public area furnished with inviting armchairs and sofas. The guest rooms are all pleasant, but the ones in the rear are quieter. There's also a good restaurant, and the grill on the top floor has wonderful views of the city and the Tagus. *Ave. da Liberdade 185, tel. 013/530181. 344 rooms with bath. Facilities: shops, garage. AE, DC, V.*

Moderate **Lisboa Penta.** The city's largest hotel, the Penta is located about midway between the airport and the city center, next to the U.S. Embassy and close to the Gulbenkian Museum (shuttle-bus service to the center of the city is available). The rooms are rather small, but each one has a terrace. *Ave. dos Combatantes, tel. 01/7264054. 592 rooms with bath. Facilities: outdoor pool, health club and solarium, shops, garage. AE, DC, MC, V.*

★ **Novotel Lisboa.** There's an attentive staff and a quiet, welcoming atmosphere at this pleasant, modern hotel near the U.S. Embassy. The public rooms are spacious and the guest rooms attractive. *Ave. Jose Malhoa, tel. 01/7266022. 246 rooms with bath. Facilities: pool, garage. AE, MC, V.*

Inexpensive **Eduardo VII.** An elegant old hotel, the Eduardo is well-located
★ in the center of the city. The best rooms are in the front overlooking Eduardo VII Park, but the ones in the rear are quieter. The top-floor restaurant has a marvelous view of the city and the Tagus. *Ave. Fontes Pereira de Melo 5, tel. 01/530141. 110 rooms with bath. AE, DC, MC, V.*

Fenix. Located at the top of Avenida de Liberdade, this hotel has largish guest rooms and a pleasant first-floor lounge. Its restaurant serves good Spanish food. *Praça Marques de Pombal 8, tel. 01/535121. 114 rooms with bath. AE, DC, MC, V.*

Flamingo. Another good value near the top of the Avenue de Liberdade, this hotel has a friendly staff and pleasant guest rooms, though the ones in the front tend to be noisy. There's a pay parking lot right next door, which is a bonus in this busy area. *Rua Castilho 41, tel. 01/532191. 39 rooms with bath. AE, DC, MC, V.*

Florida. This centrally located hotel has a pleasant atmosphere and is very popular with Americans. *Rua Duque de Palmela 32, tel. 01/576245. 112 rooms with bath. AE, DC, MC, V.*

★ **Senhora do Monte.** The rooms in this unpretentious little hotel, located in the oldest part of town near St. George's Castle, have terraces that offer some of the loveliest views of Lisbon, especially at night when the castle and Carmo ruins in the middle distance are softly illuminated. The top-floor grill has a picture window. The surrounding neighborhood is quiet, and parking is available. *Calcada do Monte 39, tel. 01/862846. 27 rooms with bath. AE, DC, MC, V.*

York House. A former convent, this pension is set in a shady garden, up a long flight of steps, near the Ancient Art Museum. It has a good restaurant, and full or half-board is available. But book well in advance; this atmospheric place is small and has a loyal following among repeat visitors to Lisbon. *Rua das Janelas Verdes 32, tel. 01/662544. 46 rooms, plus 12 in an annex at No. 47 on the same street, with bath. AE, MC, V.*

The Arts

Plays are performed in Portuguese at the **Teatro Nacional de D. Maria II**, Praça Dom Pedro IV, year-round except in July, and there are revues at small theaters in the Parque Mayer. Classical music, opera, and ballet are presented in the beautiful **São Carlos Opera House;** the season is from mid-December to May.

Nightlife

Adegas tipicas, where you listen to the **fado,** those haunting songs unique to Portugal, dine on Portuguese specialties, and drink wine are the most popular night spots. Most of these establishments are scattered throughout the Alfama and Bairro Alto districts. Try the **Cota d'Armas,** Beco São Miguel 7, tel. 01/868682 (closed Sun.); **Lisboa à Noite,** Rua das Gaveas 69, tel. 01/368557 (closed Sun.); or **Machado,** Rua do Norte 91, tel. 01/360095 (closed Mon.). The singing never stops before 11 PM.

Discos   New discos open and close with frequency in Lisbon, and many have high cover charges. Among the more respectable ones are **Ad Lib,** Rua Barata Salgueiro 28–7, tel. 01/561717; **Banana Power,** Rua Cascais 51, tel. 01/631815; and **Stones,** Rua do Olival 1, tel. 01/664545.

The Algarve

The Algarve, which encompasses some 150 miles (240 kilometers) of sun-drenched coast below the Monchique Mountains and the Caldeirão hills, is the top destination for foreign visitors to Portugal. During the past two decades, this area, indelibly marked by centuries of Arab occupation, has been heavily developed in an effort to create a playground for international sun worshipers. Well-known by Europeans as a holiday center of clean, sandy beaches, championship golf courses, and local color, this most southerly section of Portugal is only now being discovered by Americans. Although some parts of the coastline have been seriously overbuilt, there are still plenty of picturesque fishing villages and secluded beaches to leaven the concentration of hotels, casinos, disco nightclubs, and sports facilities that provide visitors with all the latest distractions.

This itinerary takes you to some of the most interesting and typical towns and villages in the Algarve, starting near the Portuguese border with Spain in the east and ending at the most southwesterly point of the European continent.

Getting Around

Faro, the capital of the Algarve, is only 45 minutes from Lisbon by air. TAP Air Portugal has daily service from Lisbon, and there are frequent international flights to Faro from London, Frankfurt, and Brussels. There is also daily bus and rail service between Lisbon and several towns in the Algarve. The drive from Lisbon to Faro or Portimão takes about 5 to 5½ hours.

The main east-west highway in the Algarve is the two-lane N125, which extends 100 miles (165 kilometers) from Vila Real de Santo António, on the Spanish border, to a point above Cabo de São Vicente, the southwesternmost point of the European continent. This road does not run right along the coast, but turnoffs to beachside destinations mentioned here are posted along the route. Local rail and bus services link most of the villages and towns in the Algarve, and organized guided bus tours of some of the more noteworthy villages and towns depart from Faro, Quarteira, Vilamoura, and Albufeira.

Tourist Information

Albufeira. Rua 5 de Outubro, tel. 089/52144 or /55428.
Armação de Pêrá. Ave. Marginal, tel. 082/32145.
Faro. Airport, tel. /22582; Rua da Misericorida 8/12, tel. 089/25404 or Rua Afaide de Oliveira 100, tel. 089/24067.
Lagos. Largo Marquês de Pombal, tel. 082/63031.
Loulé. Ave. do República, tel. 089/62538.
Olhão. Largo da Lagoa, tel. 089/73936.
Portimão. Largo 1° de Dezembro, tel. 082/22065 or 23695.
Praia da Rocha. Ave. Tomás Cabreira, tel. 082/22290.
Quarteira. Ave. Infante de Sagres, tel. 082/32217.
Sagres. Promontory, tel. 082/64125.
Silves. Rua 25 de Abril, tel. 082/42256.
Tavira. Praça da República, tel. 081/22511.
Vila Real de Santo António. Praça Marquês de Pombal, tel. 081/44495; Frontier Tourist Post, tel. 081/43272.

Exploring the Algarve

Visitors coming to the Algarve from Spain by car can take a ferry from Ayamonte, the Spanish frontier town, across the River Guadiana to **Vila Real de Santo António.** This showcase of 18th-century Portuguese town planning is set out on a grid pattern, similar to the Baixa section of Lisbon. A few miles west of this border town, pine woods and orchards break up the flat landscape around **Praia de Monte Gordo,** a town of brightly colored houses and extensive tourist facilities, including hotels, a casino, nightclubs, and discos. The long, flat stretch of beach here is steeply sloped, and swimmers quickly find themselves in deep water.

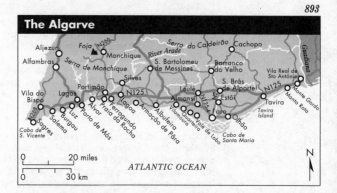

The Algarve

Aljezur · Foja · N266 · Monchique · Serra do Caldeirão · Cachopo
Alfambras · Serra de Monchique · River Arade · S. Bartolomeu de Messines · Barranco do Velho · Vila Real de Sto António
Silves · S. Brás de Alportel · Monte Gordo
Vila do Bispo · Lagos · Portimão · N125 · Loulé · Estôi · N125 · Manta Rota
Almansil · Faro · Olhão · Tavira Island
Vila do Bispo · Ferragundo · Lagoa · Praia da Rocha · Alvor · Porto de Mós · Armação de Pêra · Albufeira · Vilamoura · Quarteira · Vale de Lobo · Tavira
Sagres · Solema · Burgau · Luz
Cabo de S. Vicente · Cabo de Santa Maria

0   20 miles
0   30 km
ATLANTIC OCEAN   N

Continuing west past the excellent **Manta Rota** beach, you come to **Tavira,** which many people call the prettiest town in the Algarve. Situated at the mouth of the River Gilão, it is famous for its figs, arcaded streets, a seven-arched Roman bridge, old Moorish defense walls, and interesting churches. There are good sand beaches on nearby Tavira Island. Another 14 miles (22 kilometers) west, you arrive at the fishing port and market town of **Olhão.** Founded in the 18th century, Olhão is most notable for its North African-style architecture—cube-shaped whitewashed buildings, many with outside staircases.

From Olhão, it's just six miles (nine kilometers) to **Faro,** the provincial capital at roughly the center of the coast. When this city was finally taken by Afonso III in 1249, it ended the Arab domination of Portugal, and remnants of the Medieval walls and gates that surrounded the city then can still be seen in the older district. One of the gates, the **Arco da Vila,** with a white marble statue of St. Thomas Aquinas in a niche at the top, leads to the Largo de Sé. The **Gothic cathedral** here has a stunning interior decorated with 17th-century tiles. There are also several fascinating museums in Faro, notably the **Algarve Ethnographic Museum,** with good historical and folkloric displays, and the **Maritime Museum,** near the yacht basin. There's a large sand beach on Faro Island, which is connected to land by road.

About six miles (nine kilometers) north of Faro, a road branches east from N2 to the village of Estôi, which has an 18th-century palace with a formal park and fountains, and to the 1st-century Roman ruins at Milréu. Another worthwhile excursion from Faro is to **Loulé.** Take N1245-4 northwest from N125 about five miles (eight kilometers) west of Faro. This little market town in the hills was once a Moorish stronghold and is now best known for its crafts—you can usually see coppersmiths, and leather craftsmen toiling in their workshops along the narrow streets—and the highly decorative white chimney stacks on its houses. You can also visit the ruins of a Medieval Saracen castle and a 12th-century church decorated with handsome tiles and wood carvings that features an unusual wrought-iron pulpit.

Back on N125, in the town of **Almansil** stop at the 18th-century Baroque chapel of **São Lourenco,** with its blue-and-white tile panels and intricate gilt work. As you continue west, look for turnoffs to the south for the beach resort areas of Vale de Lobo,

Quarteira, and Vilamoura. The tennis center at **Vale de Lobo,** one of the Algarve's earliest resort developments, is among the best in Europe. **Quarteira,** once a quiet fishing village, now has a casino, golf courses, and tennis courts as well as an excellent beach. **Vilamoura** is one of the most highly developed resort centers in the Algarve: There's a large yacht marina, several golf courses, a major tennis center, one of Europe's largest shooting centers, and other sports facilities, as well as modern luxury hotels.

Continuing on N125, you arrive at **Albufeira,** the largest resort center in the Algarve. With its steep, narrow streets and hundreds of whitewashed houses snuggled on the slopes of nearby hills, the town has a distinctly Moorish flavor. Its attractions include the lively fish market held daily; interesting rock formations, caves, and grottos along the beach; and plenty of night life. Just west of Albufeira is the fishing village of Amarção de Pêra, which has the largest beach in the Algarve and local boats that take sightseers on cruises to the caves and grottos along the shore.

At **Lagoa,** a market town known for its wine, turn north to **Silves,** the old Moorish capital on the south slopes of Serra de Monchique. Its 12th-century, red sandstone **fortress-castle,** restored in 1835, has impressive parapets. Other sights include the Gothic **Santa Maria Cathedral,** built in the 12th and 13th centuries, and the **Cruze de Portugal,** a 16th-century limestone cross.

Return to N125 and continue to **Portimão,** the most important fishing port in the Algarve and the center of the canning industry. There was a settlement here at the mouth of the river Arade even before the Romans arrived. This is the main terminal point for trains from Lisbon and a good center for shopping. In the morning you can watch fishermen unload the day's catch from their colorful boats in the dock area; the open-air wood shacks here are a good place to sample the local specialty, grilled sardines. Across the bridge, in the fishing hamlet of **Ferragudo,** are the ruins of a 16th-century castle, and less than a mile south of town is **Praia da Rocha.** This was the first resort area developed in the Algarve; it has an excellent beach, made all the more interesting by a series of huge, colored rocks that have been worn by sea and wind into strange shapes.

For an entirely different aspect of the Algarve, you can drive north from Portimão on routes 2 and 266 about 15 miles (24 kilometers) into the hills of the Serra de Monchique to the spa town of **Monchique.** Besides its attractive 17th-century buildings, in a shady wood there's a theraputic spa that dates from Roman times. The cool breezes here can provide a welcome respite from the heat of the coast during the height of summer.

Return to N125 to continue your route west through **Lagos,** a busy fishing port with an attractive harbor. The 18th-century Baroque church of Santo António, off the Rua Henrique C. Silva, is renowned for its gilt, carved wood, and exuberant decoration. Lagos is the western terminus of the coastal railway that runs from Vila Real de Santo António.

After Lagos, the terrain becomes more rugged as you approach the windy headland at **Sagres,** where Prince Henry established his famous school of navigation in the 15th century. Take N268 south from N125 at Vila do Bispo to the promontory hundreds of feet above the sea. From here, a small road leads through the tunnel-like entrance to the **Sagres Fortress,** which was rebuilt in the 17th century. The **Compass Rose** of stone and earth in the courtyard was uncovered in this century, but is believed to have been used by Prince Henry in his calculations. There are spectacular views from here and from Cape São Vincente to the west. This point, where the tip of the continent juts into the rough waters of the Atlantic, is sometimes called *O Fim do Mundo,* the end of the world. Admiral Nelson defeated the French off this cape in 1797. The lighthouse at Cape São Vincente is said to have the strongest reflectors in Europe, casting a beam 60 miles (96 meters) out to sea; it is open to the public.

From this breathtaking spot, where Christopher Columbus, Vasco da Gama, Ferdinand Magellan, and other great explorers learned their craft 500 years ago, you can return to the sybaritic diversions of the modern Algarve along the N125.

Dining and Lodging

For details and price category definitions, *see* Dining and Lodging in Essential Information.

Albufeira
Dining

Vila Jova. One of the most luxurious places in the area, the Jova serves excellent French food. It also has 14 rooms. *Praia da Cale, tel. 089/54795. Dress: formal. AE, DC. Expensive.*

A Ruina. A big, rustic restaurant on the beach, built on several levels, this is the place for charcoal-grilled seafood. *Off Praca da Republica, tel. 089/52094. Dress: informal. DC, MC. Moderate.*

Lodging

Hotel du Balaia. This modern clifftop hotel 2 miles (3 kilometers) east of Albufeira is a Club Mediterranée property. *Praia Maria Luisa, tel. 089/52681. 193 rooms with bath. Facilities: two pools, water sports, tennis courts. AE, DC, MC. Expensive.*

Hotel-Apartamento Auramar. This complex offers well-appointed self-service apartments. *Just outside of town at Areias de S. João, tel. 089/53337. 282 units. Closed Nov.–Mar. DC, MC. Moderate.*

Vila Recife. This big old house right in the center of town has a pleasant atmosphere and good service. *Rua Miguel Bombarda 6, tel. 089/52047. 29 rooms with bath. AE, DC, MC, V. Moderate.*

Alvor
Lodging

Penina Golf. This impressive golf hotel, on 360 well-maintained acres off the main road between Portimão and Lagos, has spacious, elegant public rooms, pleasant guest rooms, and offers attentive service. Most of the guest rooms have balconies, with the best views from those in the back of the hotel. There's a special bus to the beach. *Montes de Alver, tel. 082/22051. 202 rooms with bath. Facilities: 18-hole championship golf course plus two 9- hole courses, tennis, pool, small private airport, shops. AE, DC, MC, V. Expensive.*

Apartamentos Torralta. This large complex offering good-size rooms, fully equipped kitchens, and daily maid service is a very good value and has exceptionally low winter rates. *Praia de Alvor, tel. 082/20211. 644 units. Facilities: pools, horseback riding, restaurants, discos, tennis, shop. AE, DC, MC, V. Moderate.*

Faro   **Cidade Velha.** Small, smart, and cheerful, this restaurant serves
Dining   excellent international cuisine. *Larguarda Se 19, tel. 089/
*27145. Dress: informal for lunch, formal at dinner. AE, DC,
MC. Expensive.*
Alfagher. Portuguese dishes are served in this attractive former private home with a terrace. *Rua Tenente Valadim 30, tel.
089/23740. Dress: casual. DC, MC. Moderate.*

Lodging   **Hotel Eva.** This well-appointed, well-managed property is located on the main square overlooking the yacht basin. The best
rooms overlook the sea. There's a courtesy bus to the beach.
*Ave. da República, tel. 089/24054. 146 rooms. Facilities: pool,
restaurant, disco. AE, DC, MC, V. Expensive.*
Casa de Lumena. Pleasant rooms are available in this fine old
Portuguese ducal residence. *Praça Alexandre Herculaho 27,
tel. 089/22028. 11 rooms with bath. Facilities: restaurant. DC,
MC. Moderate.*

Lagos   **Alpendre.** This famous establishment specializes in flambés.
Dining   *Rua António Barbosa Viana 17, tel. 082/62705. Dress: informal. No credit cards. Expensive.*
Dom Sebastião. Portuguese cooking and charcoal-grilled specials and fish are the main attractions at this cheerful restaurant. *Rua 25 de Abril 20, tel. 082/62795. Dress: informal.
AE, DC, MC. Closed Sun. in winter. Expensive.*

Lodging   **Golfinho.** Good-size rooms are offered at this large, rather impersonal hotel overlooking the beach, which is reached by a
long flight of steps. *Praia Dona Ana, tel. 082/62081. 262 rooms
with bath. Facilities: pool. AE, DC, MC, V. Expensive.*
Hotel de Lagos. This modern hotel is right in town and has spacious rooms and a good restaurant. There's a courtesy bus to
the beach. *Rua Nova Aldria, tel. 082/62011. 273 rooms with
bath. Facilities: pool. AE, DC, MC, V. Expensive.*

Monchique   **Estralagem Abrigo da Montanha.** This pleasant inn, noted for
Dining   its garden of magnolias and camelias, serves excellent regional
dishes. It also has six bedrooms. *Estrada da Foia, tel. 0882/
92131. Dress: casual. AE, DC, MC, V. Moderate.*
Restaurant Terezinha. Country decor and country cooking are
the hallmarks of this pleasant restaurant. The terrace overlooks a lovely valley and the coastline. *Estrada da Foia, no
phone. Dress: casual. Closed Mon. Inexpensive.*

Monte Gordo   **Mota.** This popular restaurant with an esplanade on the beach
Dining   is noted for its seafood and regional cuisine. *Tel. 081/42650.
Dress: informal. No credit cards. Inexpensive.*

Lodging   **Alcazar.** This attractive hotel near the beach has good service.
*Rua de Ceuta, tel. 081/42184. 95 rooms with bath. Facilities:
pool. AE, DC, MC, V. Expensive.*
Vasco da Gama. The best rooms in this large, modern,
beachfront hotel face the sea. *Ave. Infante Dom Henrique, tel.
081/42321. 165 rooms with bath. Facilities: pool, tennis, bowling, disco, water sports. AE, DC, MC, V. Moderate.*

Portimão   **Alfredo's.** Smart and exclusive, Alfredo's serves dinner only.
Dining   The fish dishes are exceptional. *Rua Pé da Cruz 10, tel. 082/
22954. Dress: formal. AE, DC, MC. Closed Tues. Expensive.*
Belle Epoque. This elegant restaurant with well-spaced tables
serves French nouvelle cuisine. *Rua Nova 1, tel. 082/26688.
Dress: semiformal. Reservations suggested. AE, DC, MC.
Closed Sun. Expensive.*

Laterna. Located just over the bridge at Ferragudo, this restaurant serves exceptionally good duck and fish soup. *Tel. 082/ 23948. Dress: informal. MC. Closed Sun. Moderate.*

Praia da Luz
Lodging

Luz Bay Club. You can rent well-appointed, self-service villas (with daily maid service) here for short or long stays. One of the best villa complexes in the Algarve, the Luz Bay is located near the beach. *Rua da Praia, tel. 089/69640. Facilities: 3 pools, 3 restaurants, various sports. AE, DC, MC, V. Expensive.*

Praia da Rocha
Dining

Titanic. The kitchen is in full view of diners at this smartly decorated restaurant specializing in shellfish. *Edificio Columbia, tel. 082/22371. Dress: informal. AE, DC, MC. Expensive.*

Lodging

Algarve. All the rooms in this modern luxury property are of good size and have balconies facing the sea. *Ave. Tomás Cabraira, tel. 082/24001. 219 rooms with bath. Facilities: pool, disco, AE, DC, MC, V. Expensive.*

Solar Penguin. English-owned and run, this charming old house has a terrace and steps leading down to the beach. Winter rates are particularly reasonable. *Ave. António Féu, tel. 082/24308. 14 rooms with bath. No credit cards. Inexpensive.*

Vale do Lobo
Dining

Caprice. A small elegant restaurant, the Caprice has a high reputation for its international cuisine. *8100 Loule, tel. 089/ 94848. Dress: informal for lunch, formal for dinner. AE, DC, MC. Closed Thurs. Expensive.*

Olimpia. Charcoal-grilled fish is the specialty here. *Quarteira-Villa do Lobo turnoff, tel. 089/94397. Dress: informal. AE, DC, MC. Closed Wed. Moderate.*

Lodging

Dona Filipa. One of the best hotels in the Algarve, the Dona Filipa has beautifully landscaped grounds, pleasant rooms, and first-rate service. All the rooms face the sea. *Vale do Lobo/ Almansil, tel. 089/94141. 135 rooms with bath. Facilities: golf, pool, tennis center. AE, DC, MC, V. Expensive.*

Vilamoura
Dining

Casino de Vilamoura. The food is okay, but the big attraction in this opulently decorated dining room is the live music for dancing and a floor show. *8125 Quarteira, tel. 089/32919. Dress: formal. AE, DC, MC. Expensive.*

Au Petit Port. This smart restaurant, specializing in Oriental cuisine, serves dinner only. *Aldeia do Mar, tel. 089/234414 089/ 34393. Dress: formal. Reservations recommended. AE, DC, MC, V. Expensive.*

Lodging

Hotel Vilamoura. This is a large, luxurious hotel with good, if a bit impersonal, service. *Tel. 0989/34414. 399 rooms with bath. Facilities: pool. AE, DC, MC, V. Expensive.*

Vila Real de Santo Antonio
Dining

Caves do Guadiana. Located in a large, old-fashioned building facing the fishing docks, this restaurant is well known for its seafood and Portuguese specialties. *Ave. Republica 90, tel. 081/44498. Dress: informal. Closed Thurs. DC, MC. Inexpensive.*

29 Romania

Introduction

Romania, the least visited but perhaps the most beautiful of the countries of Eastern Europe, welcomes many visitors from the West each year, principally to the summer resorts on the Black Sea coast, to the excellent ski resorts in the Carpathian mountains, and to its numerous spas and health resorts.

Comparable in size to the state of Oregon, Romania is made up of the provinces of Wallachia, Moldavia, and Transylvania and borders the Soviet Union, Bulgaria, Yugoslavia, and Hungary. With a population of 22 million, Romania is a "Latin Island" in a sea of Slavs and Magyars. Her people are the descendants of the Dacian tribe and of the Roman soldiers who garrisoned this easternmost province of the Roman Empire. Romanians speak a language more closely related to vernacular Latin than any other, have the dark, romantic looks of a Mediterranean race, and boast a tradition and temperament to match. Barbaric invasions, struggles against the Turks, the Austro-Hungarian domination of Transylvania, and a strong French cultural influence have endowed them with a rich heritage to add to a folk culture that survives to this day.

Bucharest, with its wide, tree-lined avenues, Arc de Triomph, and lively café life was once known as the Paris of the East. Transylvania, a region wrapped in myth, is home to a sizable minority of Hungarians, with their own folk traditions and distinctive building styles. This area has long been a favorite with tourists because of the real and fictional sites associated with Dracula. Many enchanting Orthodox monasteries, including some of medieval origin that sport colorful frescoes on their outside walls, characterize the remote and mountainous region of Moldavia. To the south of Bucharest lies the Danube Delta, a watery wilderness populated by fishermen (many of Ukrainian origin) and visited by hundreds of rare bird species, including pelicans. The Carpathian mountain ranges, which form a crown in the center of the country, offer the double pleasure of skiing in winter and hiking in summer. Unattractive effects of industrialization are generally confined to the cities; life in the countryside remains picturesquely simple. Horse and cart is a popular means of transportation, horse-drawn ploughs a common sight, and folk costume everyday wear.

The state imposes no tiresome restrictions on the independent traveler's freedom of movement within Romania, but it must be stressed that the individual is at a serious disadvantage when compared with the package tourist. The independent traveler will encounter varying standards of service, a scarcity of tourist amenities, overpriced hotels, and undersupplied restaurants. Visas, obligatory money exchange, accommodations, and meals work out to be a great deal more expensive than the very reasonably priced seaside, skiing, and spa holidays or the quite flexible fly-and-drive arrangements with vouchers for accommodations.

Romania enjoyed a period of comparative prosperity in the 1970s but is currently the poorest country in Europe after Albania. The present leadership, under Mr. Ceaușescu, has decided to repay quickly a substantial foreign debt incurred by his country's development from a mainly agricultural economy

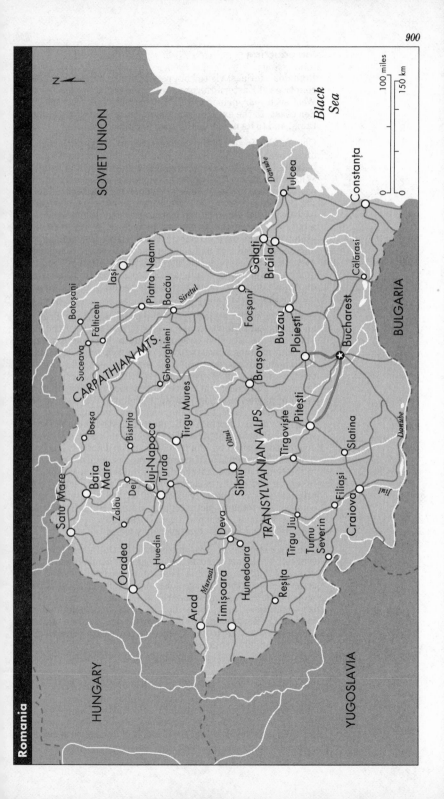

Romania

into an industrial one. Most of Romania's farm produce is now being exported for hard currency, while imports are kept to a minimum. As an important source of foreign currency, tourists are given priority, but, outside the main resorts, it is difficult to escape or ignore the effects of nationwide food and fuel shortages. Many of the most basic commodities are scarce, waiting lines are long, and street lighting is inadequate. Inevitably, there is a thriving black market in practically everything—from lipstick and toothpaste to food and gasoline.

Romania is likely to remain underexplored until these serious economic difficulties are resolved, but, in the meantime, the package tourist is still assured a good bargain, while the intrepid independent traveler will experience that rare sensation of having stepped back in time to a world that, for the most part, exists only in the memories of another generation.

Before You Go

When to Go Bucharest, like Paris, is at its best in the spring. The Black Sea resorts open in mid-to-late May and close at the end of September. Winter ski resorts in the Carpathians are now well developed and increasingly popular, while the best time for touring the interior is late spring to fall.

Climate The Romanian climate is temperate and generally free of extremes, but snow as late as April is not unknown, and the interior can be very hot in midsummer.

The following are the average daily maximum and minimum temperatures for Bucharest.

Jan.	34F	1C	May	74F	23C	Sept.	78F	25C
	19	−7		51	10		52	11
Feb.	38F	4C	June	81F	27C	Oct.	65F	18C
	23	−5		57	14		43	6
Mar.	50F	10C	July	86F	30C	Nov.	49F	10C
	30	−1		60	16		35	2
Apr.	64F	18C	Aug.	85F	30C	Dec.	39F	4C
	41	5		59	15		26	−3

Currency Unless you have booked on a prepaid tour, you must exchange $10 or its equivalent per day in any hard currency for the number of days for which you have requested your visa. Children under 14 are exempt from this requirement. It is possible to change surplus *lei* back into hard currency at the end of your stay, but be sure to keep all exchange receipts. The import and export of Romanian currency is not allowed, but you may bring in any amount of hard currency and exchange it at currency desks in hotels, banks, and border stations.

The unit of currency is the *leu* (plural *lei*), divided into 100 *bani*. There are coins of 15 and 25 bani, and 1, 3, and 5 lei. Banknotes come in denominations of 10, 25, 50, and 100 lei. The tourist exchange rate was about 8 lei to the dollar and 14.50 lei to the pound sterling at press time (fall 1988). Despite the disadvantageous exchange rates, tourists are advised to follow currency regulations, since dabbling in the extensive currency black market is illegal. That said, however, packs of Kent cigarettes are practically an alternative currency and work wonders in speeding up service and generally achieving the impossible; they are also useful barter in more remote areas of the country. The lack of consumer goods also means that people appreciate such items as coffee and pocket calculators.

Credit Cards Major credit cards are welcome in the major hotels and their restaurants but are not accepted in shops and independent restaurants.

What It Will Cost Prices of hotels and restaurants are at least comparable with those in Western Europe as far as the independent traveler is concerned. Those with prepaid arrangements enjoy reductions of up to 30% and more.

Sample Prices A room in a four-star hotel in Bucharest will come to around 900 lei a night; a bottle of beer in a restaurant around 25 lei; a bottle of good wine in a top restaurant around 150 lei. A one-mile taxi ride will cost around 10 lei.

Visas All visitors to Romania must have a visa, obtainable from Romanian embassies abroad or on arrival at any entry point by whatever means of transport. Long delays may be avoided by getting a visa in advance, but only visitors born in Romania are obliged to do so. For those with prepaid arrangements, the cost of the visa (USA, $16; Canada, $16; UK, £20) is included and substantially reduced. Send the price of the visa, a letter explaining your reasons for wanting to go to Romania, a stamped, self-addressed envelope, and your passport to the relevant consulate: in the **United States,** Romanian Consulate, 1067 23rd Street NW, Washington DC 20008; in **Canada,** Romanian Consulate, 655 Rideau Street, Ottawa, Ontario; in the **United Kingdom,** Consular Section of the Romanian Embassy, 4 Palace Green, London W8.

Customs on Arrival Personal belongings: two cameras, 20 rolls of film, one small movie camera, two rolls of movie film, a typewriter, binoculars, a radio/tape recorder, 200 cigarettes, two liters of liquor and four of wine, as well as gifts up to the value of 2,000 lei are permitted; camping and sports equipment may be imported freely.

Language Romanian sounds appealingly familiar to anyone with a smattering of French, Italian, or Spanish. French is widely spoken and understood. Romanians involved with the tourist industry, in all hotels and major resorts, speak English.

Getting Around

By Car A good network of main roads covers the country, though the
Road Conditions great majority are still a single lane wide in each direction. Progress may be impeded by convoys of farm machinery on the move, by horses and carts, or herds of animals. Night driving can be dangerous: Roads and vehicles are lighted either poorly or not at all.

Rules of the Road Driving is on the right, as in the United States. Speed limits are 60 kph (37 mph) in built-up areas and 80–100 kph (50–62 mph) on all other roads. Driving under the influence of alcohol is prohibited. Police are empowered to levy on-the-spot fines of 250 lei for speeding. Radar checks are very frequent; keep an eye out for the police force's black cables stretched across the road.

Gasoline Gas must be purchased with coupons paid for in hard currency; these are obtainable from hotel reception desks, border crossing points, and tourist offices. Gas is expensive (around 36 lei a gallon) and gas stations scarce, usually cropping up on the outskirts of towns. The Automobil Club Roman *(see* Breakdowns) and tourist offices can provide visitors with a useful Tourist and Motor Car Map, pinpointing the location of each gas station. Stations should have two pumps marked *Comturist*, reserved for foreign tourists. Keep your tank filled and be sure to carry a spare-parts kit.

Breakdowns **Automobil Club Roman** (ACR, Strada Cihoschi 2, Bucharest 1, tel. 40/123456 in Bucharest and tel. 12345 elsewhere) offers mechanical assistance in case of breakdown and medical and legal assistance at fixed rates in case of accident.

By Train Romanian Railways (CPR), operates *accelerat, rapide,* and *personal* trains; avoid, if possible, the *personal* trains because they are very slow. Trains are inexpensive but can be crowded. It is always advisable to make reservations in advance (up to six hours before departure). If you're in Bucharest, go to the Advance Reserve Office, Strada Brezoianu 10, tel. 40/132644, just behind the Bucureşti Hotel. Allow plenty of time, since lines are usually long. For a commission fee, ONT offices will make reservations for you. Tickets may be bought from the station itself two hours before departure.

By Plane *Tarom* operates daily flights to 15 major cities from Bucharest's Baneasa Airport. In summer, additional flights link Constanţa with major cities, including Cluj and Iaşi. Fares are low, but be prepared for delays.

By Bus Bus stations, or *autogara*, are usually located near train stations. Buses are generally crowded and far from luxurious. Tickets are sold at the stations up to two hours before departure.

By Boat Regular passenger services operate on various sections of the Danube; tickets are available at the ports. Often included in package tours to the Black Sea coast is a trip by pleasure boat via the middle or southern arms of the Danube Delta.

Essential Information

Telephones The Romanian telephone system is erratic, but calls can be made from hotels or post offices. Be warned that international calls are outrageously expensive—three minutes to Western Europe cost 98 lei. Calls to the United States are even more costly—nearly $100 (payable in hard currency) for three minutes.

Try to use phone books instead of searching in vain for the number for Information—it is different at each exchange.

Mail The Central Post Office is at Calea Victoriei 37 and is open Monday through Saturday from 7 AM to 8 PM.

Postal Rates A letter to the United States costs 16 lei, a postcard 13 lei. Letters to Western Europe, including the United Kingdom, cost 11 lei, postcards 8 lei.

Shopping Romanian folk art is varied and can be highly attractive—it never is cheap, however. Worth looking for are hand-painted icons on glass. There are also embroidered textiles from many regions, wood carvings from Maramureş, and pottery from Bukovina. Comturist shops in hotels accept payment in hard currency only. Clothes, furs, liqueurs, and glassware are sold in these shops, as well as some items in short supply, such as chocolate, toothpaste, and soap.

Opening and Closing Times
Banks. Open weekdays 9 to noon and 1 to 3, Saturday 9 to noon.
Museums. Museums and art galleries are usually open from 10 to 6, but it's best to check with local tourist offices. Most museums are closed on Monday.
Shops. Shops are generally open from 9 or 10 AM to 6 or 8 PM, though some food shops open earlier.

National Holidays
January 1 (New Year's Day); January 2; May 1 (Labor Day); May 2; August 23 (Liberation); August 24.

Spas
Romania's many spas enjoy an excellent reputation abroad. Treatments are available for ailments ranging from obesity and secondary sterility to neuroses and other more conventional complaints. Fifteen out of the 160 spas offer first-class accommodations to foreign visitors. Romania has developed such anti-aging compounds as Gerovital and Aslavital, the Pell-Amar mud-packings, and Boicil rheumatism treatments—all of which are immensely successful and priced reasonably. Two full weeks, including round-trip airfare from the United States, board, and treatment at the Deluxe Flora Hotel in Bucharest, cost only $1,759.

Dining
Chronic food shortages and problems of distribution mean that the range and quality of food, even in the deluxe hotels in Bucharest, remain low by international standards. Traditional Romanian cuisine is not easy to come by; instead, french fries and meat coated in thick sauces predominate. Outside the capital your choice may be limited to one dish. Where no menu is provided, you should check the price in advance. In most resorts, package tour guests are given a choice of dishes from which to make their selection for the following day's meals.

Mealtimes
Plan to dine early. Outside the Black Sea and Carpathian resorts, restaurants close at 10 PM, when the lights are turned off, and you'll find it difficult to get served anywhere after 9 PM (though a packet of Kent cigarettes will sometimes do the trick!).

Precautions
The far less expensive *bufet expres, lacto vegetarian* snack bars, and *autoservire* cannot be recommended, but excellent creamy cakes are available at the better cafeterias. If you cannot survive without a heavy intake of coffee, you should bring your own.

Ratings
Prices are per person and include first course, main course, and dessert, plus wine and tip. Best bets are indicated by a star ★. At press time, there were 8 lei to the dollar.

Category	Cost
Very Expensive	over 200 lei
Expensive	150–200 lei
Moderate	80–150 lei
Inexpensive	under 80 lei

Credit Cards
The following credit card abbreviations are used: AE, American Express; DC, Diners Club; MC, MasterCard; V, Visa.

Lodging Prepaid arrangements with reductions and advance reservations are highly recommended, but it is possible to book hotels, campsites, and self-contained cottages through the local national tourist office (ONT) or directly with a hotel. In each case you must have proof of official money exchange if you want to pay in lei. Inexpensive accommodations outside the capital, in the form of pensions and hostels, are almost nonexistent.

Hotels The star system of hotel classification does not operate in Romania. Instead, you will encounter Deluxe categories A and B, First-class categories A and B, and so on. Deluxe A is equivalent to five-star or Very Expensive, Deluxe B to four-star or Expensive, first-class A to three-star or Moderate, and first-class B to two-star or Inexpensive. Plumbing may be erratic in the Moderate and Inexpensive categories, and cost-cutting measures have meant that in some areas hot water is available only at certain hours of the day; these hours will always be clearly posted in the reception area. In principle, at least, all hotels leave a certain quota of rooms unoccupied until 8 PM, for unexpected foreign visitors.

Rentals A few delightfully rustic cottages may be rented at such skiing resorts as Sinaia and Predeal. Details are available from Romanian tourist offices abroad *(see* Important Addresses and Numbers).

Private Accommodations Foreigners are forbidden to stay with Romanians in their homes.

Hostels There are a number of student hostels in major towns, though open only in July and August. Bookings can be made through the ONT office on arrival in Bucharest, but availability is limited.

Camping There are more than 100 campsites in Romania; they provide an inexpensive way of exploring the country, though overcrowding has been reported. Rates start at around 90 lei a day. A few offer bungalow accommodations at around 145 lei a day. Details are available from Romanian tourist offices abroad.

Ratings The following hotel price categories are for two people in a double room. Supplements for single rooms range from 90 to 180 lei per night. Best bets are indicated by a star ★. At press time, there were 8 lei to the dollar.

Category	Bucharest	Black Sea Coast
Very Expensive	over 900 lei	over 540 lei
Expensive	675–900 lei	400–540 lei
Moderate	360–675 lei	270–400 lei
Inexpensive	under 360 lei	under 270 lei

Credit Cards The following credit card abbreviations are used: AE, American Express; DC, Diners Club; MC, MasterCard; V, Visa.

Tipping A 12% service charge is added to meals at most restaurants. Elsewhere, tipping is discouraged; the practice persists, however, though nowhere is it obligatory. You may want to leave about 10% if service is exceptional. Give porters and taxi drivers about 5–10 lei.

Bucharest

Arriving and Departing

By Plane All international flights to Romania operate from Bucharest's **Otopeni Airport** (tel. 40/333137), nine miles (16 kilometers) north of the city.

Between the Airport and Downtown Buses leave every one to two hours from outside the airport and stop outside the ONT office on Boulevard General Magheru; tickets cost 15 lei. Your hotel can arrange transport by car from the airport for around 90 lei. Taxis are in short supply.

By Train There are five main stations in Bucharest, though international lines operate from **Gara de Nord** (tel. 052). For tickets and information, go to the Advance Reserve Office (Str. Brezoianu 10, (tel. 40/132644).

By Car There are two main access routes into the city—E70 west from the Hungarian border and E60 north via Braşov.

Getting Around

Bucharest is spacious and sprawling. Though the old heart of the city and the two main arteries running the length of it are best explored on foot, long, wide avenues and vast squares make some form of transport necessary. Hotels and the ONT office will supply maps of the downtown area, but no map is absolutely up to date because of the city's rapid rate of change.

Public transportation is efficient but best avoided during rush hours. Tickets can be bought at ITB kiosks and tobacconists. Note that the system shuts up at 11:30 PM.

By subway. Thirty kilometers (18 miles) of the city's projected 56 kilometers (34 miles) are now in operation. Tickets cost 2 lei for any distance.

Trolley, Bus, and Trolleybus. Trams cost 1 leu (pay as you enter), buses 1.75 lei, and trolley buses 1.50 lei.

By Taxi and Maxi-taxi. Inexpensive but in short supply, taxis can be ordered by phoning 053. All have meters, but some drivers will not use them. Prices should start at around 6 lei, plus 6 lei per kilometer; around 20 lei should take you anywhere in the city. Maxi-taxis are blue-and-white minibuses that stop as requested along a given route; tickets cost 5 lei.

Important Addresses and Numbers

Tourist Information The main Romanian National Tourist Office (ONT) is located at 7 Boulevard General Magheru, tel. 40/145160, and deals with all inquiries related to tourism (open weekdays 8–4). There are ONT offices at Otopeni Airport, open 24 hours, and at the Gara de Nord, open 7:30 AM–3:30 PM. ONT offices in major hotels close at 3:30 PM. There are also county offices, known as UJT, in most Romanian towns and resorts. For information before your trip, write or call **in the United States**—573 Third Avenue, New York, NY 10016, tel. 212/697–6971; **in the United Kingdom**—29 Thurloe Place, London, SW7 2HP, tel. 01/584–8090.

Guided Tours

For detailed information on guided tours, contact the ONT office *(see* Tourist Information).

Orientation Tours ONT offices organize sightseeing tours of the city by car, bus, or minibus, depending on the size of the group. A four-hour tour by car will cost 135 lei.

Special-Interest Tours The ONT office arranges tours of Romanian folk art, museums, and the city's churches.

Excursions Day and weekend excursions outside Bucharest cover the ski resorts, the Danube Delta, and the monasteries of Bukovina. A half-day tour by car to monasteries nearer Bucharest costs 270 lei.

Exploring Bucharest

The old story goes that a simple peasant named Bucur settled on the site upon which the city now stands. True or not, the name Bucurest was officially used first only in 1459, by none other than Vlad Ţepeş, the real-life Dracula (sometimes known as Vlad the Impaler for his bloodthirsty habit of impaling unfortunate victims on wooden stakes). Two centuries later, this "citadel on the Dimboviţa (the river that flows through Bucharest) became the capital of Wallachia, and after another 200 years, it was named the capital of Romania. The city developed along the old trading route, now Boulevard 1848, Boulevard North Bălcescu, Boulevard General Magheru, and Boulevard Ana Ipătescu. The first Princely Court was built just west of the lower stretch of these boulevards. The bustling trading area near by, known as the Lipscani District, links the old trading route with another main street, Calea Victoriei, where many of the city's historical buildings, elegant shops, and hotels are found.

Like Paris, Bucharest is at its best in the spring. However, though once a gracious city characterized by pretty villas set in leafy courtyards and elegant neo-Classical 19th-century buildings, Bucharest is rapidly being transformed into a modern capital of high-rise buildings. Even the course of the Dimboviţa River has been altered, and the speed of the transformation has been such that no up-to-date map yet exists for the Romanians, much less for tourists. Parts of the city look like they have undergone a blitz: The bewildered inhabitants seem to be waiting patiently for this man-made earthquake to stop, which it is scheduled to do in 1990. The replanning of Bucharest and the completion of the new Metro system appear to be just as urgent as the repayment of the foreign debt. For a preview of the Bucharest of the 21st century, don't miss the impressive and almost completed civic center to the southeast of the Piaţa Unirii.

Against a backdrop of such dramatic upheaval, Bucharest has acquired a new and peculiarly subtle aura, unlike that of anywhere else in Europe. Though the population looks well nourished enough, grocery stores are stocked with little else but champagne and canned tomatoes; there are many more flowers than there is food in the markets. The roads seem far wider and grander than is warranted by the number of cars

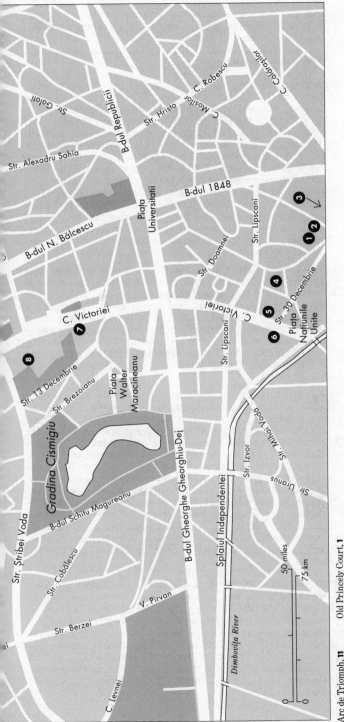

Arc de Triomph, **11**
Cretulescu Church, **7**
Curtea Veche Church, **2**
Hanul Manuc, **3**
National Art Museum, **8**
Natural History
Museum, **10**

Old Princely Court, **1**
Orthodox Church
(Stavreopolos), **4**
Romanian Athenaeum
Concert Hall, **9**
Romanian History
Museum, **5**
Trajan's Column, **6**
Village Museum, **12**

that use them. In even the most expensive restaurants, supplies of food often run out by 9 PM, and, as if recalling those days at summer camp, it's lights out at 10 PM.

The Main Attractions

1 A tour of this city should start at its core, the **old Princely Court** and the Lipscani District. The Princely Court now houses a **museum** exhibiting the remains of the palace built by Vlad Țepeș in the 15th century. One section of the cellar wall presents the palace's history from the 15th century onward. You can see the rounded river stones used in the early construction, later alternating with red brick, and later still in plain brick. Prisoners were once kept in these cellars, which extend far into the surrounding city; a pair of ancient skulls belonging to two young *boyars* (aristocrats), decapitated at the end of the 17th century, will interest some. In the 18th century, the palace was auctioned off in sections, and during the last century, the lower levels of the complex were used as the cellars of merchants' premises and craftsmen's workshops. *Str. 30 Decembrie 31. Admission: 5 lei. Open Tues.–Sun. 10–6.*

2 The **Curtea Veche Church,** beside the Princely Court, was founded in the 16th century and remains an important center of
3 worship in the city. **Hanul Manuc,** a renovated 19th-century inn arranged in the traditional Romanian fashion around a courtyard, now houses a hotel and restaurant. Manuc was a wealthy Armenian merchant who died in Russia by poisoning— at the hand of a famous French fortune-teller who, having forecast Manuc's death on a certain day, could not risk ruining her reputation. The 1812 Russian-Turkish Peace Treaty was signed here.

Nearby, Lipscani is a bustling area of narrow streets, open stalls, and small artisans' shops, which combine to create the atmosphere of a bazaar. At Strada Selari 11–13, you'll find glassblowers hard at work; glassware is sold next-door. On
4 Strada Stavreopolos, a small but exquisite circa 1724 **Orthodox church** combines late Renaissance and Byzantine styles with elements of the Romanian folk-art style. Go inside to look at the superb wood and stone carving and a richly ornate iconostasis, the painted screen that partitions off the altar. Boxes on either side of the entrance contain votive candles—for the living on the left, for the "sleeping" on the right.

Time Out Down the road, at Strada Stavreopolos 3, is the **Carul cu Bere,** serving half-liter tankards of beer, appetizers, and Turkish coffee.

5 At the end of the street is the **Romanian History Museum,** which contains a vast collection of exhibits from neolithic to modern times. The Treasury, which can be visited and paid for separately, has a startling collection of objects in gold and precious stones—royal crowns, weapons, plates, and jewelry— dating from the 4th millenium BC through the 20th century. Op-
6 posite the Treasury is a full-size replica of **Trajan's Column** (the original is in Rome), commemorating a Roman victory over Dacia in AD 2. *Calea Victoriei 12. Admission: 5 lei. Open Tues.–Sun. 10–6.*

(7) Turning north along the Calea Victoriei, you pass a military club and academy before reaching the pretty little **Creţulescu Church** on your left. Built in 1722, the church and some of its original frescoes were restored during the 1930s. Immediately north is a massive building, once the royal palace and

(8) now the Palace of the Republic. The **National Art Museum** is housed here, with its fine collection of Romanian art, including works by the world-famous sculptor Brâncuşi. The foreign section has many fine examples of European, Eastern, and Far Eastern art. *Str. Stribei Voda 1. Open Tues.–Sun. 10–6.*

Opposite the palace, in Piaţa Gheorghiu-Dej, is the **headquarters of the Romanian Communist Party;** you are forbidden to walk in front of it, and God forbid you should try to photo-

(9) graph it. **The Romanian Athenaeum Concert Hall** is impressive, with its Baroque dome and Greek columns. Built in 1888, the building has an ornate art nouveau entrance hall that is well worth a look. The George Enescu Philharmonic Orchestra is based here.

Time Out The **cafeteria of the Athenée Palace Hotel,** opposite the concert hall, has excellent cream cakes and a terrace.

---

(10) Follow Calea Victoriei as far as the Piaţa Victoriei. Opposite is the Grigore Antipe **Natural History Museum** (Şoseaua Kiseleff 1. Open Tues.–Sun. 10–6) with its exceptional butterfly collection and the skeleton of *Dinotherium gigantissimum.* Şoseaua

(11) Kiseleff, a pleasant tree-lined avenue, brings you to the **Arc de Triomph,** built in 1922 to commemorate the Allied victory in World War I. Originally constructed of wood and stucco, it was rebuilt in the 1930s and carved by some of Romania's most talented sculptors.

(12) Still farther north lies Herăstrău Park, accommodating the fascinating **Village Museum** as well as Herăstrău Lake itself. The museum is really outstanding, with more than 300 authentic, fully furnished peasant houses, with folk styles taken from all over Romania. *Şoseaua Kiseleff 28–30. Open daily 10–5.*

What to See and Do with Children

Children and adults alike enjoy the swimming and boating facilities at **Herăstrău Lake,** in the park of the same name. Both will also enjoy a few sunny hours in the green oasis of **Cişmigiu Gardens** in the downtown area, just west of Piaţa West Maracineanu.

Shopping

Gifts and Souvenirs There are Comturist branches in all the main hotels, but stroll down Calea Victoriei and you'll find glassware at **Stirex,** handicrafts at **Arta Populara,** woolens at **Electa,** records and musical instruments at **Muzica,** and jewelry at **Bijuteria. Horizont,** almost directly opposite the Intercontinental on Boulevard North Balcescu, specializes in high-quality arts and crafts.

Antiques **Bazarul Hanul cu tei,** a picturesque, restored inn in the old district, is now a complex of small, specialized shops. **Consignaţia,** on the second floor, is a vast warehouse of antique and second-hand items, with a particularly fine selection of carpets.

Market The main food market is in Piaţa Unirii, open seven days a week and best visited in the morning.

Dining

The restaurants of the Athenée Palace, Minerva, Bucureşti and Intercontinental hotels are all recommended for a reasonable meal in pleasant surroundings. Depending on your choice of menu, you can eat moderately in most expensive restaurants and inexpensively in most moderate restaurants. Generally low standards of cuisine, owing to food shortages, are often combined with loud live music, to make eating out in Bucharest an interesting but frequently disappointing experience.

Ratings Prices are per person and include first course, main course, and dessert, plus wine and tip. Best bets are indicated by a star ★. At press time, there were 8 lei to the dollar.

Category	Cost
Very Expensive	over 200 lei
Expensive	150–200 lei
Moderate	80–150 lei
Inexpensive	under 80 lei

Expensive **Capşa.** Elegant in the *belle epoque* style, Capşa was founded in 1842 and has a tradition of haute cuisine that it is struggling to maintain. Recommendations from the headwaiter are useful. The restaurant also has some excellent vintage wines, and the creamy desserts are delicious. *Calea Victoriei 34, tel. 40/134482. Dress: formal. Reservations required for lunch. No credit cards.*

Hanul Manuc. Downtown opposite the Princely Court, this renovated 19th-century inn now houses the city's most appealing hotel and restaurant. Courtyard and gallery tables make for a lively atmosphere and the "pastrame" ham and sweet pastries are good bets. *Str. 30 Decembrie 62, tel. 40/131415. Jacket and tie. Weekend reservations advised. No credit cards.*

Pescarus. This modern, wooden hunting lodge-style restaurant on the edge of Herăstrău Park by the lake, offers an evening folklore show on the terrace. A relaxed and convivial atmosphere make Pescarus one of the city's most popular restaurants. Try the *frigarui*—meat and onion on a skewer. *Herăstrău Park, tel. 40/794640. Dress: casual. Evening reservations advised. No credit cards.*

Moderate **Cina.** Alongside the Athenaeum and centrally located with its garden café, Cina is popular with the locals. Stained-glass windows, neoclassical decor, dim lighting, and soulful live music lend a pleasantly romantic atmosphere. The house specialty is *cotelet Valdostana*, a hearty veal dish. Service may be slow. *Str. C. A. Rossetti 1, tel. 40/130217. Dress: casual. Reservations advised. No credit cards.*

Carul cu Bere. This beautifully restored old beer house is situated near the Museum of Romanian History. Once a meeting place for artists and writers, it retains an Old World feel. Guests are served with tankards of delicious cold beer to wash down *cîrnati*, a tasty spiced sausage. *Str. Stavreopolos 3, tel. 40/163793. Dress: casual. No credit cards.*

La Doi Cocosi. "The Two Cockerels" specializes in chicken; supplies are unreliable, though, so you may want to check beforehand. Located about nine miles (14 kilometers) out of town, it is an excellent choice for large parties, with its informal and pleasant outdoor terrace. *Şoseaua Strauteşti 6, tel. 40/671998. Dress: no jeans. Reservations required. No credit cards.*

Doina. Located on one of the main boulevards heading out of town, Doina was once much frequented by elegant promenaders. It has a pretty garden terrace and an attractive wine cellar; make it a point to sample wines from the vineyards inscribed over the door. There's music and dancing in the evenings. *Şoseaua Kiseleff 4, tel. 40/176715. Jacket and tie. Reservations required. No credit cards.*

Inexpensive
★ **Beijin.** This is an exceptionally good restaurant in its own right, as well as being Bucharest's one and only Chinese eatery. It's located in the Hotel Minerva and gives excellent value for the money. *Str. Lt. Lemnea 2–4, tel. 40/506010. Dress: casual. Reservations advised. AE, DC, MC, V.*

Lodging

Hotels in Bucharest are often heavily booked during the tourist season. If you don't have reservations, the ONT office will be of help in suggesting available alternatives.

Ratings The following price categories are for two people in a double room. Supplements for single rooms range from 90 to 180 lei per night. Best bets are indicated by a star ★. At press time, there were 8 lei to the dollar.

Category	Cost
Very Expensive	over 900 lei
Expensive	675–900 lei
Moderate	360–675 lei
Inexpensive	under 360 lei

Very Expensive
★ **Athenée Palace.** The old-fashioned Athenée Palace is one of the city's most famous hotels, still comfortable despite ongoing renovation. The restaurant is the most elegant the city can offer, and there is also a popular nightclub with a floor show. *Str. Episcopiei 1–3, tel. 40/140899. 300 rooms with bath. Facilities: pool, health club, sauna. AE, DC, MC, V.*

Bucureşti. The city's largest hotel has an excellent central location and spacious, pleasantly furnished rooms. Its modern ambience is complemented by the vast range of facilities. *Calea Victoriei 63–81, tel. 40/154580. 442 rooms with bath. Facilities: 2 pools, health club, sauna, cafeteria, restaurant. AE, DC, MC, V.*

Flora. The modern Flora, situated on the outskirts of the city near Herăstrău Park, offers its cosmopolitan clientele top facilities for geriatric (anti-aging) treatment. The sun terraces are havens of relaxation. Most guests stay in this quiet, restful hotel for at least two weeks. *Blvd. Poligrafiei 1, tel. 40/184640. 155 rooms with bath. Facilities: pool, spa care unit, health club, sauna, restaurant. AE, DC, MC, V.*

★ **Intercontinental.** The Intercontinental is a good landmark to set your bearings by, since it's the city's tallest building. Every room is air-conditioned, and all come complete with balcony.

Facilities include a fitness center, sun terrace, mini casino, and a choice of no less than seven bars and restaurants. *Blvd. N. Bălcescu, tel. 40/140400/137040. 423 rooms with bath. AE, DC, MC, V.*

Expensive

Ambassador. The 13-story Ambassador was built in 1937 and enjoys a fine central location. Its rooms are comfortably furnished if somewhat spartan in decoration. *Blvd. General Magheru 6–8, tel. 40/110440. 233 rooms with bath. Facilities: Restaurant, pool, health club. AE, DC, MC, V.*

Bulevard. This old-style hotel is conveniently situated near the main tourist attractions. Small and intimate and benefiting from attractive *fin de siècle* furnishings, it exudes a charming Old World feel. Category B rooms are less expensive since their windows don't look out onto the busy Boulevard Georghiu-Dej (this means they can be quieter, however). *Blvd. Georghiu-Dej 1, tel. 40/153300. 89 rooms with bath. AE, DC, MC, V.*

Dorobanţi. The modern and busy Dorobanţi has 18 floors of colorfully—one could say garishly—furnished rooms; they will not appeal to everyone! On the bright side, however, the restaurant offers dancing in the evenings, and the Video Discotheque Club is open until 1 AM. *Calea Dorobanţi 1, tel. 40/110860. 298 rooms with bath. AE, DC, MC, V.*

★ **Hanul Manuc.** This restored 19th-century inn near the busy Lipscani District houses a fine hotel as well as a good restaurant *(see* Dining, above). Rooms are comfortable, whether decorated with pale Biedermeier furniture or in folk-art style. The only drawback is that some rooms are noisy. *Str. 30 Decembrie 62, tel. 40/131415. 30 rooms with bath. No credit cards.*

Moderate

Capitol. The circa 1907 Capitol is situated in a lively part of town near the Cişmigiu Gardens. In days gone by, it was the stamping ground of Bucharest's mainstream artists and writers. Today the Capitol is fully modernized and offers comfortable rooms and a large restaurant—though the literati have long since moved on. *Calea Victoriei 29, tel. 40/140926. 70 rooms with bath. No credit cards.*

Parc. Located near the Herăstrău Park and the Flora Hotel, the Parc is modern and within easy reach of the airport; many guests stay here before moving on to the Black Sea resorts. There's a good restaurant that provides music each evening. *Blvd. Poligrafiei 3, tel. 40/506081. 314 rooms with bath. Facilities: pool, sauna, tennis. AE, DC, MC, V.*

The Arts

Bucharest's lively theater and music life can be enjoyed at prices way below those in the West. Tickets can be obtained directly from the theater or hall, or from your hotel (for a commission fee). Performances usually begin at 7 PM. The **Opera House** (Blvd. Georghiu-Dej 70) and the **Operetta House** (Piaţa Natiunile 1) regularly present excellent productions. Theater performances range from serious drama at the **Caragiale National Theater** (Blvd. N. Bălcescu 2) to lighter entertainment at the **Comedy Theater** (Str. Mandinesti); despite the language barrier, there is often enough spectacle to ensure a very good evening's entertainment. The **Tandarica Puppet Theater** (Calea Victoriei 50) has an international reputation, and the **State Jewish Theater** (Str. Barasch 15) stages Yiddish-language performances. Don't miss the fine folkloric show at the **Rapsodia Romana Artistic Ensemble** (Str. Lipscani 53). Bucharest has many movie theaters; some run old, undubbed American and English films.

Entertainment and Nightlife

Strict economy measures, such as unlit restaurants after 10 PM and dark streets, mean that the city's nightlife is very limited.

Nightclubs The Athenée Palace and Intercontinental hotels have nightclubs with floor shows. Several other hotels in the Expensive category run video shows.

Cafés Cafés with outdoor terraces remain a feature of the city. The Gradinița, Casata, and Turist on Boulevard General Magheru are all lively in summer.

The Black Sea Coast and Danube Delta

The southeastern Dobruja region, only 45 minutes by air from Bucharest, is one of the major focal points of Romania's rich history. Within a clearly defined area are the historic port of Constanța; the Romanian Riviera pleasure coast; the renowned Murfatlar vineyards; Roman, Greek, and earlier ruins; and the Danube Delta, one of Europe's leading wildlife sanctuaries. The rapid development of the Black Sea resorts and increasing interest in the delta region mean that tourist amenities (such as hotels and restaurants) and train, bus, and plane connections are good.

Getting Around

By Bus Bus trips from the Black Sea resorts and Constanța to the Danube Delta, the Murfatlar vineyards, Istria, and Adamclisi are arranged by ONT offices *(see* Tourist Information).

By Car Rental cars can be arranged through local ONT offices.

By Boat Regular passenger and sight-seeing boats operate along the middle and southern arms of the delta. If money is no object, there are motorboats for rent in the Danube Delta—or rent one of the more restful fishermen's boats.

Guided Tours

ONT Litoral offers trips to the Danube Delta; the two-day trip is a particularly good value at 450 lei a head. Transport to Tulcea by bus is followed by a visit to the Danube Delta museum and a hydrobus ride down the center channel of the delta to Crișan, with accommodation at the Lebeda Hotel. A boat tour of the delta's channels, topped off by a meal of locally caught fish, completes the trip. Daily bus trips from Mamaia and Constanța connect in Tulcea, with pleasure boats plying the middle arm of the river.

Tourist Information

ONT Litoral, Hotel București, Mamaia, tel. 31780. UJT Strada Garii Faleza 2, Tulcea.

The Black Sea Coast

N

Durankulak

Tolbuhin

Balčik
Šabla

Novi Pazar
Albena
Kavarna

Vetrino
Zlatni Pjasâci
(Golden Sands)

Družba

Varna

Goljama

Staro Orjahovo

Kamčija

Bjala

Kamčija

Obzor

Orizare

Black Sea

Slânčev Brjag
(Sunny Beach)

Ajtos

Nesebâr

Pomorie

Burgas

Sredecka

Sozopol

Djuni

Primorsko

Mičurin

Ahtopol

0   40 miles

0   60 km

TURKEY

Exploring

Tulcea, the main town of the Danube Delta, is the gateway to
the splendors of the region. Built, like Rome, on seven hills,
this former Oriental-style market town is now an important sea
and river port and the center of the Romanian fish industry.
The **Danube Delta Museum** provides a good introduction to the
flora, fauna, and way of life of the communities in the area.
Str. Progresului 32. Open 10–6.

The **Danube Delta** is Europe's largest nature reserve, covering
1,676 square miles (4,340 square kilometers), with a sprawling,
watery wilderness that stretches from the Soviet border to a
series of lakes north of the Black Sea resorts. It is Europe's
youngest land; more than 47 square yards (40 square kilometers) are added each year by normal silting action. As it
approaches the delta, the great Danube divides into three. The
northernmost branch forms the border with the Soviet Union,
the middle arm leads to the busy port of Sulina, and the southernmost arm meanders gently toward the little port of Sfîntu
Gheorghe. From these channels, countless canals widen into
tree-fringed lakes, reed islands, and pools covered with water
lilies; there are sand dunes and pockets of lush forest. More
than 80% of the delta area is water. Over 300 bird species visit
the area; 70 of them come from as far away as China and India.
The delta is a natural stopover for migratory birds, but the
most characteristic bird is the common pelican, the featured
star of this bird-watchers' paradise. Fishing provides most of

the area's inhabitants, many of whom are of Ukrainian origin, with a livelihood. Common sights are the long lines of fishing boats strung together to be towed by motorboats to remote fishing grounds. Smaller communities, such as Independența on the southern arm and Crişan on the middle arm, rent out the services of a fisherman and his boat to foreigners. The waters here are particularly rich in caviar-bearing sturgeon, catfish, perch, and carp.

There are good roads to the Black Sea resorts from Tulcea, which take you via the strange, eroded Macin hills to **Babadag**. It was here, according to local legend, that Jason and his Argonauts cast anchor in their search for the mythical golden fleece. Farther south is **Istria,** an impressive archeological site founded in 6 BC by Greek merchants from Miletus. Its name derives from *Istros*, the Greek word for the Danube; these early merchants mistakenly thought they had reached one of the mouths of the great river. Once sited on a sea bay, over the centuries it has become closed off by the vast quantities of silt carried down the Danube. The Romans and Byzantines followed the Greeks, and the town thrived until AD 6, defending itself successfully from barbarian attacks. Defensive walls, hastily constructed in any material found near at hand, are still visible today. Early settlers overcame the problem of a freshwater supply by constructing sophisticated pipelines to transport it from the hills over nine miles (15 kilometers) away; sections of these pipes survive, too. There are traces of early Christian churches and baths and even residential, commercial, and industrial districts. A useful English-language booklet, available on the spot, will help make sense of the remains of a number of cultures.

Istria is a popular excursion from the Black Sea resorts and lies only 37 miles (60 kilometers) from **Mamaia,** the largest. The resort is four miles (seven kilometers) long—a strip of land bordered by the Black Sea and fine beaches on one side, and the fresh waters of the Mamaia lake on the other. Like all the resorts along this stretch of the coast, facilities include high-rise modern apartments, villas, restaurants, nightclubs, and discos. Now that all the hotels have been built, all resources are being channeled into improving the quality of services and expanding the range of entertainment, sports facilities, and excursions. There are cruises down the coast to Mangalia and along the new channel now linking the Danube with the Black Sea near Constanța. Sea-fishing expeditions can also be arranged for early risers, with all equipment provided. These resorts are completely self-contained communities, offering everything necessary for a vacation by the sea.

Constanța is Romania's second-largest city, only a short ride by trolley bus from Mamaia. With the polyglot flavor characteristic of so many seaports, Constanța is also steeped in history. Founded by Greeks in the 6th century BC, Constanța was known as Tomis until AD 4, when it was renamed after Constantine the Great. The famous Roman poet Ovid was exiled here from Rome in AD 8, probably for his part in court scandals and for the amorality of his poem *Ars Amandis (The Art of Making Love)*. He became desperately homesick and appears to have spent much of his time writing letters of complaint back to Rome. A city square has been named in his honor and provides a fine backdrop for a statue of him by sculptor Ettore

Ferrari. Behind the statue, in the former town hall, is one of the best museums in Europe, the **National History and Geographical Museum.** Of special interest here are the unique *Glykon Serpent* and the *Goddess of Fortune,* protector of the city of Tomis, both surviving from the 2nd and 3rd centuries AD. Two other items not to be missed are the statuettes of the *The Thinker* and *The Seated Woman,* from the neolithic Hamangian culture (4000 to 3000 BC). Collections from the Greek, Roman, and Daco-Roman cultures are generally outstanding. *Piata Ovidiu 12. Open Tues.–Sun. 10–6.*

Near the museum is a **Roman complex of warehouses and shops** from the 4th century AD, including a magnificent mosaic floor measuring over 21,000 square feet (2,000 square meters). Not far away are the remains of the Roman Thermae from the same period. **The Archaeology Park** (Blvd. Republicii), contains items dating from the 3rd and 4th centuries AD and from a tower erected by the butchers' guild in the 6th century. Modern-day attractions include an **aquarium** (Str. Februarie 16) and **Dolphinarium** (Blvd. Lenin 265), which offers aquatic displays by trained dolphins.

A whole string of seaside resorts lie just south of Constanța. **Eforie Nord** is an up-to-date thermal treatment center. A series of resorts built in the 1960s are named for the coast's Greco-Roman past—**Neptune, Jupiter, Venus,** and **Saturn.** Not in any way typically Romanian, these resorts offer good amenities for relaxed, seaside vacations. The old port of **Mangalia** is the southernmost resort.

Most of the old Greek city of **Callatis** lies under water now, but a section of the walls and the remains of a Roman villa are still visible.

ONT offices organize regular excursions from the seaside resorts to the **replica of Trajan's Column,** the **Murfatlar vineyards** for wine tastings, and the ruins of the Roman town at **Tropaeum Trajani.**

Dining and Lodging

For details and price category definitions, *see* Dining and Lodging in Essential Information on Romania.

Constanța
Dining

Casino. A turn-of-the-century former casino situated close to the aquarium, the Casino is decorated in an ornate 20th-century style; there's an adjoining bar by the sea. Seafood dishes are the house specialties. *Str. Februarie 16 (no tel.). Dress: informal. No credit cards. Moderate.*

Lodging

Palas. Located near the city's historic center, the large and gracious old Palas has been renovated recently. It has a good restaurant and a terrace overlooking the sea and the tourist port of Tomis. *Str. Opreanu 5–7, tel. 916/14696. 132 rooms. Expensive.*

Continental. Older, slightly less luxurious, but larger than the Palas, the Continental is conveniently situated near the open-air archaeological museum in the downtown area. *Blvd. Republicii 20, tel. 916/15660. 140 rooms. Moderate.*

Crişan
Lodging

Lebeda. This is a comfortable hotel from which to make fishing trips into the more remote parts of the delta. *Tel. 915/14720. 74 rooms. Facilities: restaurant, currency exchange. Moderate.*

Mamaia
Dining

Insula Ovidiu. This is a reed-thatched complex of rustic-style buildings with lively music every evening. A relaxed, informal atmosphere provides a good setting for delicious seafood dishes. *Lake Siurghiol (no tel.). Moderate.*

Satul de Vacanţa. This holiday village is an attractive complex of traditional Romanian buildings, built in styles from all over Romania and featuring many small restaurants serving local specialties.

Lodging

International. One of King Carol's former residences, this is the largest and grandest of all the hotels in Mamaia. An outdoor swimming pool, an excellent restaurant, a bar, and a cafeteria are among its facilities. *Tel. 918/31592 or 31520. 102 rooms. Very Expensive.*

Ambassador, Lido, and **Savoy.** Among the many modern hotels, these three are all newly built and moderately priced. They are grouped in a horseshoe around open-air pools near the beach at the north of the resort. All *Moderate.*

Tulcea
Lodging

Delta. A large, modern hotel on the banks of the Danube, the Delta currently enjoys a mixed reputation. Amenities include a restaurant, bar, and cafeteria. *Str. Isaacei 2, tel. 915/14720. 117 rooms. Moderate.*

30 Spain

Introduction

Spain has long had a rather schizophrenic reputation as a vacation destination among English-speaking tourists. On the one hand, as Europe's premier package-vacation destination, the country is almost instinctively associated in many minds with the worst excesses of the cheap-holiday-in-the-sun, an image conjured up by the vast numbers of faceless hotels along the Mediterranean coasts. The other half of the equation is infinitely more appealing. For Spain is also the land of the fountain-singing courtyards of Moorish Granada and Cordoba, dusty plains where Don Quixote fought imaginary enemies, and of timeless hill-top towns.

Still, if it's beaches you're after, there is the jet-set Costa del Sol in the south, or San Sebastián in the Basque country, formerly the summer capital of Spain. Farther west is the resort city of Sandandor and La Coruña, a long-standing favorite of British visitors. In the east is the Costa Brava, while to the south, around Alicante, is the Costa Blanca, with its most popular tourist center at Benidorm. When you tire of roasting in the sun, rent a car and head for one of the thousands of castles, ruins, or museums. Perhaps the number-one tourist attraction is the Alhambra, in Granada. Following close behind it come the Mosque of Cordoba, and the Alcazar and cathedral of Seville. Avila is a historic walled town and Segovia boasts a Roman aqueduct and proud Alcazar. Madrid, the capital, contains some of the greatest art collections in the world, while Toledo, home of El Greco, and boasting a cathedral, synagogues, and startling views, is one of Spain's greatest treasures. Finally, Barcelona, capital of Catalun, has a charm and vitality quite its own.

Before You Go

When to Go The tourist season runs from Easter to mid-October. The best months for sightseeing are May, June, September, and early October, when the weather is usually pleasant and sunny without being unbearably hot. During July and August try to avoid Madrid or the inland cities of Andalusia, where the heat can be stifling and many places close down at 1 PM. If you visit Spain in high summer, the best bet is to head for the coastal resorts or to mountain regions such as the Pyrenees or Picos de Europa. The one exception to Spain's high summer temperatures is the north coast, where the climate is similar to that of northern Europe.

As for crowds, Easter is always a busy time, especially in Madrid, Barcelona, and the main Andalusian cities of Seville, Córdoba, Granada, Málaga, and the Costa del Sol resorts. July and August, when most Spaniards and other Europeans take their annual vacation, see the heaviest crowds, particularly in coastal resorts. Holiday weekends are naturally busy, and major fiestas such as Seville's April Fair or Pamplona's bull runnings make advance booking essential and cause prices to soar. Off-season travel offers fewer crowds and lower rates in many hotels.

Climate The following are the average daily maximum and minimum temperatures for Madrid.

Jan.	47F	9C	May	70F	21C	Sept.	77F	25C
	35	2		50	10		57	14
Feb.	52F	11C	June	80F	27C	Oct.	65F	19C
	36	2		58	15		49	10
Mar.	59F	15C	July	87F	31C	Nov.	55F	13C
	41	5		63	17		42	5
Apr.	65F	18C	Aug.	85F	30C	Dec.	48F	9C
	45	7		63	17		36	2

Currency The unit of currency in Spain is the peseta. There are bills of 500, 1,000, 2,000, 5,000, and 10,000 ptas. Coins are 1 pta., 5, 25, 50, 100, 200, and 500 ptas. The 2- and 10-ptas. coins and the old 100-ptas. bills are rare but still legal tender. At press time (fall 1988), the exchange rate was about 110 ptas. to the U.S. dollar and 200 ptas. to the pound sterling.

Credit Cards Most hotels, restaurants, and stores (though not gas stations) accept payment by credit card. Visa is the most widely accepted piece of plastic, followed by MasterCard (called EuroCard in Spain). More expensive establishments may also take American Express and Diners Card.

Changing Money The word to look for is *Cambio* (Exchange). Most Spanish banks take a 1½% commission, though some less scrupulous places charge more; always check, as rates can vary greatly. To change money in a bank, you need your passport and a lot of patience, because filling out the forms takes time. Hotels offer rates lower than banks, but they rarely make a commission, so you may well break even. Restaurants and stores, other than those catering to the tour bus trade, usually will not accept payment by dollars or traveler's checks.

Currency Regulations Visitors may take any amount of foreign currency in bills or traveler's checks into Spain as well as any amount of pesetas. When leaving Spain you may take out only 100,000 ptas. per person in Spanish bank notes and foreign currency up to the equivalent of 500,000 ptas. unless you can prove you declared the excess at customs on entering the country.

What It Will Cost Prices rose fast in the first decade of Spain's democracy, and Spain's inflation rate was one of the highest in Europe. By the end of 1987, however, inflation had been curbed and was running at just under 5%. Generally speaking, the cost of living in Spain is now on a par with that of most other European countries, and the days of Spain being the bargain basement of Europe are truly over. Hotel rates compare favorably with those of France or Britain, restaurants are fairly expensive but offer value-for-money, snacks in cafés and bars are expensive by American or British standards, and alcohol is generally cheap, except for cocktails in hotel bars. Trains and long-distance buses are inexpensive, and car rental rates are lower than in many other countries. City buses and subways are good value, and cab fares are bargains compared with rates in the United States.

Taxes A value-added tax known as IVA was introduced in 1986 when Spain joined the European Economic Community (EEC). IVA is levied at 6% on most goods and services, but a luxury rate of 12% applies to five-star hotels and to car rental. IVA is always included in the purchase price of goods in stores, but for hotels and car rentals, the tax will be added to your bill. Most restaurants now include IVA in their menu prices, but some do not. Large stores such as the *Corte Inglés* and *Galerías Preciados* department stores operate a tax refund plan for foreign visitors who are not EEC nationals; but to qualify for this refund, you need to spend at least 48,000 ptas. in any one store. There is no airport tax in Spain.

Sample Prices   A cup of coffee will cost around 100 ptas., a Coca-Cola 120 ptas., bottled beer 140 ptas., a small draught beer 90 ptas., a glass of wine in a bar 60–80 ptas., an American-style cocktail 300–400 ptas., a ham sandwich 200 ptas., an ice cream cone about 90 ptas., a local bus or subway ride 60–80 ptas., and a one-mile taxi ride about 350 ptas.

Language   In major cities and coastal resorts you should have no trouble finding people who speak English. In such places, reception staff in hotels of three stars and up are required to speak English. Don't expect the man in the street or the bus driver to speak English, although you may be pleasantly surprised.

Getting Around

By Car
Road Conditions   Roads marked A *(autopista)* are toll roads. N stands for national or main roads, and C for country roads. A huge road improvement scheme is currently under way, but many N roads are still single lane and the going can be slow. Tolls vary but are high; for example, Bilbao–Zaragoza 2,930 ptas., Salou–Valencia 2,065 ptas., Sevilla–Jemez 585 ptas.

Rules of the Road   Driving is on the right, and horns and high-beam headlights may not be used in cities. The wearing of front seat belts is compulsory on the highway but not in cities (except the M30 Madrid ring road). Children may not ride in front seats. At traffic circles give way to traffic coming from the right unless your road has priority. Your home driving license is essential and must be carried with you at all times, along with your car insurance. Non-EEC nationals also need an International Driving License and a Green Card if bringing their own car into Spain. Speed limits are 120 kph (74 mph) on autopistas, 100 kph (62 mph) on N roads, 90 kph (56 mph) on C roads and 60 kph (37 mph) in cities unless otherwise signed.

Parking   Parking restrictions should be checked locally. A red-and-white-striped line on the curb means no parking. Never leave *anything* on view inside a parked car. Thefts are common and it is safer to leave your car in one of the many paying parking lots; charges are reasonable.

Gasoline   At press time, gas cost 78 ptas. a liter for super and 72 ptas. a liter for regular. Unleaded gas *(sin plombo)* is now available at a few pumps. Outside cities, gas stations are few and far between, so don't run low on gas. There is attendant service at most pumps, but there's no need to tip for just a fill-up. Few gas stations accept payment by credit card.

By Train   The Spanish railroad system, known usually by its initials RENFE, has greatly improved in recent years. Air-conditioned trains are now widespread but by no means universal. Most overnight trains have first- and second-class sleeping cars and second-class *literas* (couchettes). Dining, buffet, and refreshment services are available on most long-distance trains. There are various types of trains—*Talgo*, ELT (electric unit expresses), TER (diesel rail cars) and ordinary *expresos* and *rápidos*. Fares are determined by the kind of train you travel on and not just by the distance traveled. Talgos are by far the quickest and most comfortable and expensive train; *expresos* and *rápidos* are the slowest and cheapest of the long-distance services. A few lines, such as the FEVE routes along the north coast from San Sebastián to El Ferrol and on the Costa Blanca around Alicante, do not belong to the national RENFE network, and international rail passes are not valid on these lines.

Ticket Purchase and Seat Reservation Tickets can be bought from any station (whether or not it is your point of departure), and from downtown RENFE offices and travel agents displaying the blue and yellow RENFE sign. The latter are often best in the busy holiday season. At stations, buy your advance tickets from the window marked "Largo Recorrido, Venta Anticipada" (Long Distance, Advance Sales). Seat reservation can be made up to 60 days in advance and is obligatory on all the better long-distance services.

Fare Savers The RENFE Tourist Card is an unlimited-kilometers pass, valid for eight, 15, or 22 days' travel and can be bought by anyone who lives outside Spain. It is available for first- or second-class travel and can be purchased from RENFE's General Representative in Europe, 3 Ave Marceau, 75116 Paris, France; from selected travel agencies and main railroad stations abroad; and within Spain, at RENFE travel offices and the stations of Madrid, Barcelona, Port Bou, and Irún. At press time the second-class pass cost 9,000 ptas. for eight days, 15,000 ptas. for 15 days, and 19,000 ptas. for 22 days. RENFE has no representative in the United States or Great Britain.

Blue Days *(Días Azules)* leaflets are available from RENFE offices and stations and show those days of the year (approximately 270) when you can travel at reduced rates. Be warned, though, that some of these bargains may apply only to Spaniards or to foreigners officially resident in Spain.

By Plane **Iberia** and its subsidiary **Aviaco** operate a wide network of domestic flights, linking all the main cities and the Balearic Islands. Distances are great and internal airfares are low by European standards, so plane travel around Spain is well worth considering. Flights from the mainland to the Balearics are heavily booked in summer, and the Madrid–Málaga route is frequently overbooked at Easter and in high season. A frequent shuttle service operates between Madrid and Barcelona. Iberia has its own offices in most major Spanish cities and acts as agent for Aviaco. In Madrid, Iberia headquarters are at Velázquez 130 (tel. 91/4112011 reservations). Flights can also be booked at most travel agencies.

By Bus Spain has an excellent bus network, but there is no national or nationwide bus company. The network simply consists of numerous private regional bus companies *(empresas)* and there are therefore no comprehensive bus passes. Some of the buses on major routes are now quite luxurious, although this is not always the case in some of the more rural areas. Buses tend to be more frequent than trains, they are sometimes cheaper, and often let you see more of the countryside. On major routes and at holiday times it is advisable to buy your ticket a day or two in advance. Some cities have central bus stations but in many, including Madrid and Barcelona, buses leave from various boarding points. Always check with the local tourist office. Bus stations, unlike train stations, usually provide luggage storage facilities.

Essential Information

Telephones
Local Calls

Pay phones work with coins of 5, 25, 50, and 100 ptas. Ten ptas. is the minimum for short local calls. Place several coins in the slot, or in the groove on top of the phone, lift the receiver, and dial the number. Coins then fall into the machine as needed. Area codes always begin with a 9 and are different for each province. In Madrid province, the code is 91; in Málaga province, it's 952.

International Calls

Calling abroad can be done from any pay phone marked *Teléfono Internacional*. Though good for short European calls, pay phones are not really feasible for transatlantic calls. Use 50 ptas. (or 100 if the phone takes them) coins initially, then coins of any denomination to prolong your call. Dial 07 for international, wait for the tone to change, then 1 for the USA, or 44 for England, followed by the area code and number. For calls to England, omit the initial 0 from the area code. For lengthy international calls, go to the *telefónica*, a telephone office found in all sizable towns, where an operator assigns you a private booth and collects payment at the end of the call; this is the least expensive way of phoning abroad. The cost of calls made from your hotel room includes a service charge, even for collect calls.

Operators and Information

For the operator and information for the city you are in, dial 003; for information for the rest of Spain, 009. If you're in Madrid, dial 008 for Europe; 005 for the rest of the world. From anywhere else in Spain, dial 9198 for Europe, and 9191 for the rest of the world.

Mail
Postal Rates

To the United States, airmail letters up to 15 grams cost 68 ptas., postcards 58 ptas., to the United Kingdom and the rest of Europe, letters up to 20 grams cost 48 ptas., postcards 40 ptas. Within Spain, letters cost 19 ptas., postcards 14 ptas. Rates may well change by 1989. Mailboxes are yellow with red stripes, and the slot marked "Extranjero" is the one for mail going abroad. Buy your stamps *(sellos)* at a post office *(correos)* or in a tobacco shop *(estanco)*.

Receiving Mail

If you're uncertain where you'll be staying, have mail sent to American Express or to the *poste restante* of the local post office. To claim your mail, you'll need to show your passport. American Express has a $2 service charge per letter, for noncardholders. The Spanish mail is notoriously slow and not always very efficient.

Shopping

Prices are similar to those in the United States or Britain, although clothes and good-quality shoes are often a little more expensive. Typical souvenirs include fans, castanets, bullfight posters, *botas* (wine-skin bottles), ceramics, carved wooden figures of Don Quixote and Sancho Panza, and Lladró porcelain. Lladró is made in the Manises factory near Valencia and, although expensive, it is much cheaper than in the United States. In Córdoba, look for filigree silver and embossed leather; in Seville, for flamenco costumes, leather hats, embroidered shawls and tablecloths, lace mantillas and decorative pottery; in Granada, for brass and copperware, marquetry goods such as chess sets and boxes inlaid with mother-of-pearl, woven goods from the Alpujarras and the green and blue Fajaluaza pottery. Alicante is famous for *turrones*, a kind of nougat candy, and Toledo for its Talavera pottery, embroidery from the village of Lagartera, and its Damascene ware, in which intricate patterns of filigree gold are inlaid on blackened steel; look especially for swords, knives, and jewelry.

IVA Refunds If you purchase goods up to a value of 48,000 ptas. or more in any one store, you are entitled to a refund of the IVA tax paid (usually 6% but more in the case of certain luxury goods), provided you leave Spain within three months. You will be given two copies of the sales invoice, which you must present at customs together with the goods as you leave Spain. Once the invoice has been stamped by customs, mail the blue copy back to the store, which will then mail your tax refund to you. If you are leaving via the airports of Madrid, Barcelona, Málaga or Palma de Mallorca, you can get your tax refund immediately from the Banco Exterior de España in the airport. The above does not apply to residents of EEC countries, who must claim their IVA refund through customs in their own country. The Corte Inglés and Galerías Preciados department stores operate the above system, but don't be surprised if other stores are unfamiliar with the tax refund procedure and do not have the necessary forms.

Bargaining Prices in city stores and produce markets are fixed; bargaining is possible only in flea markets, some antiques stores, and with gypsy vendors, with whom it is *essential*, though you'd do best to turn them down flat as their goods are almost always fake and grossly overpriced.

Opening and Closing Times **Banks.** Banks are open weekdays 9–2, Saturday 9–1, though many close earlier in summer.

Museums and churches. Opening times vary. Most are open in the morning, and most close one day a week, often Monday.

Post offices. These are usually open weekdays 9–2, but this can vary; check locally.

Stores. Stores are open weekdays from 9 or 10 until 1:30 or 2, then again in the afternoon from around 4–7 in winter, and 5–8 in summer. In some cities, especially in summer, stores close on Saturday afternoon. The Corte Inglés and Galerías Preciados department stores in major cities are open continuously from 10–8, and some stores in tourist resorts also stay open through the siesta.

National Holidays January (New Year's Day); January 6 (Three Kings); March 19 (St. Joseph); March 23 (Holy Thursday); March 24 (Good Friday); May 1 (May Day); May 25 (Corpus Christi); July 25 (St. James); August 15 (Assumption); October 12 (National Day); November 1 (All Saints); December 6 (Constitution); December 8 (Immaculate Conception); December 25 (Christmas Day). Other holidays include May 2 (in the province of Madrid) and June 24 (St. John).

Dining Visitors have a choice of restaurants, tapas bars, and cafés. Restaurants are strictly for lunch and dinner; they do not serve breakfast. Tapas bars are ideal for a glass of wine or beer accompanied by an array of savory tidbits *(tapas)*. Cafés, called *cafeterías*, are basically coffee houses serving snacks, light meals, tapas, pastries, and coffee, tea, and alcoholic drinks. They also serve breakfast, and are perfect for afternoon tea.

Mealtimes Mealtimes in Spain are much later than in any other European country. Lunch begins between 1 and 3:30, with 2 being the usual time, and 3 more normal on Sunday. Dinner is usually available from 8:30 onward, but 10 PM is the usual time. An important point to remember is that lunch is the main meal, not dinner. Tapas bars are busiest between noon and 2 and from 8 PM on. Cafés are usually open from around 8 AM to midnight.

Precautions Tap water is said to be safe to drink in all but the remotest villages. However, most Spaniards drink bottled mineral water; ask for either *agua sin gas* (without bubbles) or *agua con gas* (with). A good paella should be served only at lunchtime and should be prepared to order (usually 30 minutes); beware the all-too-cheap version.

Typical Dishes Paella—a mixture of saffron-flavored rice with seafood, chicken, and vegetables—is Spain's national dish. Gazpacho, a cold soup made of crushed garlic, tomatoes, and olive oil and garnished with diced vegetables, is a traditional Andalusian dish and is served mainly in summer. The Basque Country and Galicia are the gourmet regions of Spain, and both serve outstanding fish and seafood. Asturias is famous for its *fabadas* (bean stews), cider, and dairy products; Extremadura for its hams and sausages, and Castile for its roasts, especially *coehinillo* (suckling pig), *cordero asado* (roast lamb), and *perdiz* (partridge). The best wines are those from the Rioja and Penedés regions. Valdepeñas is a pleasant table wine, and most places serve a perfectly acceptable house wine called *vino de la casa*. Sherries from Jerez de la Frontera make fine aperitifs; ask for a *fino* or a *manzanilla;* both are dry. In summer you can try *horchata*, a sweet white drink made from ground nuts, or *granizados de limón* or *de café*, lemon juice or coffee served over crushed ice. *Un café solo* is a small, black, strong coffee, and *café con leche* is coffee with cream, cappuccino-style; weak black American-style coffee is hard to come by.

Ratings Spanish restaurants are officially classified from five forks down to one fork, with most places falling into the two- or three-fork category. In our rating system, prices are per person and include a first course, main course, and dessert, but not wine or tip. In most places the IVA tax is included in the menu price; check the menu for *IVA incluido* or *IVA non incluido.* When it's not included, a further 6% will be added to your bill. Most restaurants offer a fixed price set menu called a *menu del día.* This is usually the cheapest way of eating; *à la carte* dining is more expensive. Service charges are never added to your bill; leave around 10%, less in inexpensive restaurants and bars. Major centers such as Madrid, Barcelona, Marbella, and to a lesser extent, Seville, tend to be a bit more expensive. Best bets are indicated by a star ★. At press time, there were 110 pesetas to the dollar.

Category	Cost
Very Expensive	over 6,000 ptas.
Expensive	3,600–5,900 ptas.
Moderate	1,500–3,500 ptas.
Inexpensive	under 1,400 ptas.

Credit Cards The following credit card abbreviations are used: AE, American Express; DC, Diners Club; MC, MasterCard; V, Visa.

Lodging Spain has a wide range of accommodations, including luxury palaces, medieval monasteries, converted 19th-century houses, modern hotels, high rises on the coasts, and inexpensive hostels in family homes. All hotels and hostels are listed with their rates in the annual *Guía de Hoteles* available from bookstores for around 500 ptas., or you can see a copy in local tourist offices. Rates are always quoted per room, and not per person. Single occupancy of a double room costs 80% of the normal price. Breakfast is rarely included in the quoted room rate; always check. The quality of rooms, particularly in older properties, can be uneven; always ask to see your room *before* you sign the acceptance slip. If you want a private bathroom, state your preference for shower or bathtub; the latter always costs more. Local tourist offices will provide you with a list of accommodations in their region, but they are not allowed to make reservations for you. In Madrid and Barcelona, hotel booking agencies are found at the airports and railroad stations.

Villas Villas are plentiful all along the Mediterranean coast, but elsewhere they are few and far between. Several agencies in both the United States and United Kingdom specialize in renting property; check with the Spanish National Tourist Office.

Hotels and Hostels Hotels are officially classified from five stars (the highest) to one star, hostels from three stars to one star. Hostels are usually a family home converted to provide accommodations that often occupy only part of a building. If an R appears on the blue hotel or hostel plaque, the hotel is classified as a *Residencia*, and full dining services are not provided, though breakfast and cafeteria facilities may be available. A three-star hostel usually equates with a two-star hotel; two- and one-star hostels offer simple, basic accommodations. The main hotel chains are Hesperia, Husa, Iberotel, Meliá, and Sol, and the state-run paradores. Some half dozen hotels belong to the luxury *Château et Relais* chain; only these and the paradores have any special character. Of the others, Meliá hotels tend to be large, faceless, and the most expensive. The others provide clean, comfortable accommodation in the two- to four-star range.

Paradores There are about 80 state-owned-and-run parador hotels, many of which are located in magnificent medieval castles or convents or in places of great natural beauty. Most of these fall into the four-star category and are priced accordingly. All have restaurants that specialize in local regional cuisine and serve a full breakfast. The most popular paradores (Granada's San Francisco parador, for example) are booked far in advance, and many close for a month or two in winter (January or February) for renovations.

Camping There are approximately 530 campsites in Spain, with the highest concentration along the Mediterranean coast. The season runs from April to October, though some sites are open all year-round. Sites are listed in the annual publication *Guía de Campings* available from bookstores or local tourist offices, and further details are available from the Spanish National Tourist Office. Reservations for the most popular seaside sites can be made either directly with the site or through camping reservations at: Federación Española de Empresarios de Campings, Gran Vía 88, Grupo 3–10°–8, Madrid (tel. 91/242–3168).

Ratings   Prices are for two people sharing a double room and do not include breakfast. Best bets are indicated by a star ★. At press time, there were 110 pesetas to the dollar.

Category	Cost: Madrid	Cost: Other Areas
Very Expensive	over 14,000 ptas.	over 12,000 ptas.
Expensive	9,000–13,950 ptas.	7,000–11,950 ptas.
Moderate	5,500–8,950 ptas.	4,500–6,950 ptas.
Inexpensive	under 5,450 ptas.	under 4,450 ptas.

Credit Cards   The following credit card abbreviations are used: AE, American Express; DC, Diners Club; MC, MasterCard; V, Visa.

In many hotels rates vary according to the time of year. The hotel year is divided into *estación alta, media,* and *baja* (high, mid, and low season); high season covers the summer and usually Easter and Christmas periods, plus the major fiestas. IVA is never included in the quoted room rates, so be prepared for a further 6%, or, in the case of a luxury five-star hotel, 12%, to be added to your bill. Service charges are never included.

Tipping   Spaniards appreciate being tipped, though the practice is becoming less widespread, especially for smaller services. Restaurants and hotels are by law not allowed to add a service charge to your bill, though confusingly your bill in both will most likely say *servicios y impuestos incluidos* (service and tax included). Ignore this unhelpful piece of advice, and leave 10% in most restaurants where you have had a full meal; in humbler eating places, bars, and cafés, 5% is often enough, or you can round out the bill to the nearest 100 ptas. A cocktail waiter in a hotel will expect at least 25 ptas. a drink, maybe 50 ptas. in a luxury establishment. Tip taxi drivers 10% when they use the meter, otherwise *nothing*—they'll have seen to it themselves. Movie and theater ushers sometimes get 10 ptas., though this is dying out—look to see what the locals do. Gas station attendants get no tip for pumping gas, and about 50 ptas. for checking tires and oil and cleaning windshields. Train and airport porters usually operate on a fixed rate of about 40 ptas. a bag. Coat-check attendants get 25 ptas., and rest room attendants 5 ptas., or 10 ptas. in smarter establishments. In top hotels doormen get 100 ptas. for carrying bags to the check-in counter or for hailing taxis, and bellhops get 50 ptas. for room service or for each bag they carry to your room. In moderate hotels 35–50 ptas. is adequate for the same services. Leave your chambermaid about 300 ptas. for a week's stay. There's no need to tip for just a couple of nights. The waiter in your hotel dining room will appreciate 500 ptas. a week.

Madrid

Arriving and Departing

By Plane All international and domestic flights arrive at Madrid's Barajas Airport (tel. 91/205–4372), 10 miles (16 kilometers) northeast of town just off the N-II Barcelona highway. For information on arrival and departure times, call **Inforiberia** (tel. 91/411–2545) or the airline concerned.

Between the Airport and Downtown Buses leave the national and international terminals every 15 minutes from 5:15 AM to 12:45 AM for the downtown terminal at Plaza Colón just off the Castellana. The ride takes about 20 minutes and the fare at press time was 175 ptas. Most city hotels are then only a short ride away. The fastest and most expensive way to go (about 1,200 ptas. plus tip) is by taxi. Pay what is on the meter plus 150 ptas. surcharge. By car, take the N-II into town, which becomes Avda. de América, then head straight into María de Molina, and left on either Serrano or the Castellana.

By Train Madrid has three main railroad stations. **Chamartín,** in the northern suburbs beyond the Plaza Castilla, is the main station, with trains to France, the north and northeast (including Barcelona). Many trains to Valencia, Alicante, and Andalusia now leave from here, too. **Atocha,** on the Glorieta del Emperador Carlos V, at the southern end of Paseo del Prado, has trains for Toledo, Andalusia, Extremadura and Lisbon; also some services to Valencia and Alicante. **Norte** (or **Príncipe Pío**), on Paseo de la Florida, in the west of town below the Plaza de España, is the departure point for Salamanca, Santiago, La Coruña and all destinations in Galicia.

Trains to nearby places like Alcalá, Avila, Segovia, and El Escorial, but *not* Toledo, leave from the suburban stations of **Atocha Apeadero** and **Chamartín Cercanías;** you can board at either station.

For all train information, call 91/733–3000 or 91/733–2200, or go to the RENFE office on Alcalá 44, open Monday to Friday 8:30–2:30 and 4–5; Saturday 8:30–1:30. There's another RENFE office at Barajas Airport in the International Arrivals Hall, or you can purchase tickets at any of the three main stations, or from travel agents displaying the blue and yellow RENFE sign.

By Bus Madrid has no central bus station. The two main bus stations are the **Estación del Sur,** Canarias 17 (tel. 91/468–4200), nearest metro Palos de la Frontera, for buses to Toledo, La Mancha, Alicante, and Andalusia; and **Auto Res,** Plaza Conde de Casal 6 (tel. 91/251–6644), nearest metro Conde de Casal, for buses to Extremadura, Cuenca, Salamanca, Valladolid, Valencia, and Zamora. **Auto Res** has a central ticket and information office at Salud 19 near the Hotel Arosa, just off Gran Vía. Buses to other destinations leave from various points, so check with the tourist office. For Avila, Segovia, and La Granja, **Empresa La Sepulvedana** (tel. 91/247–5261) leaves from Paseo de la Florida 11, metro Norte; and to El Escorial and Valley of the Fallen, **Empresa Herranz** (tel. 91/243–8167) leaves from Isaac Peral 10, metro Moncloa.

By Car The main roads are north–south, the Paseo de la Castellana and Paseo del Prado; and east–west, Calle de Alcalá, Gran Vía, and Princesa. The M30 ring road circles Madrid to the east and south. For Burgos and France, drive north up the Castellana and follow the signs for the N-I. For Barcelona, head up the Castellana to Plaza Dr. Marañón, then right onto María de Molina and the N-II; for Andalusia and Toledo, head south down Paseo del Prado, then follow the signs to the N-IV and N401, respectively. For Segovia, Avila, and the Escorial, head west along Princesa to Avenida. Puerta de Hierro and onto the N-VI La Coruña road.

Getting Around

Madrid is a fairly compact city and most of the main sights are close enough together to be visited on foot. But if you're staying in one of the modern hotels in the north of town off the Castellana, you may well need to use the bus or subway (metro). As a rough guide, the walk from the Prado to the Royal Palace at a comfortable sightseeing pace but without stopping, takes around 30 minutes; from Plaza Callao on Gran Vía to the Plaza Mayor takes about 15 minutes.

By Metro The subway offers the simplest and quickest means of transport and is open from 6 AM to 1:30 AM. Metro maps are available from ticket offices, hotels, and tourist offices. Fares are 60 ptas. a ride. Savings can be made by buying a *taco* of 10 tickets, or a tourist card called *Metrotour* that is good for unlimited travel for three or five days. Keep some change (5, 25, and 50 ptas.) handy for the ticket machines, especially after 10 PM.

By Bus City buses are red and run from 6 AM to midnight (though check, as some stop earlier). Again there is a flat fare system, 60 ptas., or 70 ptas. with a transfer *(correspondencia)*. Yellow microbuses cost 70 ptas. and are faster. Route plans are displayed at bus stops *(paradas)*, and a map of the entire system is available from EMT *(Empresa Municipal de Transportes)* booths on Cibeles, Callao, or Puerta del Sol. Savings can be made by buying a *Bonobus*, good for 10 rides on red buses, from EMT booths or any branch of the Caja de Ahorros de Madrid. Books of 20 tickets valid for yellow microbuses are available from EMT booths.

By Taxi Madrid has more than 15,500 taxis, and fares are low by New York or London standards. The average city ride costs 300–400 ptas. Cabs available for hire display a "Libre" sign during the day and a green light at night. They hold four passengers. Make sure the driver puts his meter on when you start your ride, and tip 10% of the fare.

Important Addresses and Numbers

Tourist Information The main Madrid Tourist Office (tel. 91/241–2325) is on the ground floor of the Torre de Madrid in Plaza de España, near the beginning of Calle Princesa and is open Monday to Friday 9–7, Saturday 10–2. The Municipal Tourist Office is at Señores de Luzón 10 (tel. 91/248–7426), just off Calle Mayor near the City Hall and is open Monday to Saturday 9–2; also 3:30–5:30 on Tuesday. A third office is in the International Arrivals Hall of Barajas Airport (tel. 91/205–8656) and is open Monday to Friday 8–8; Saturday 8–1.

Embassies	**U.S.,** Serrano 75 (tel. 91/276–3600); **Canadian,** Nuñéz de Balboa 35 (tel. 91/431–4300); **U.K.,** Fernando el Santo 16 (tel. 91/419–1528).
Emergencies	**Police:** Emergency 091; Municipal Police 092; Main Police (National) Station, Puerta del Sol 7 (tel. 91/221–6516). To report lost passports, go to Los Madrazo 9 (tel. 91/221–9350) just off the top of Paseo del Prado. **Ambulance:** Municipal Ambulance Service (tel. 91/230–7145); Red Cross (tel. 91/734–4794). **Doctor:** Your hotel reception will contact the nearest doctor for you. Emergency clinics: *Clínico San Carlos,* Ciudad Universitaria (tel. 91/244–1500); *La Paz Ciudad Sanitaria,* Paseo de la Castellana 261 (tel. 91/734–2600). *Bel-San,* Princesa 10, 4th floor (tel. 91/542–6068/6301) is a small clinic with English-speaking doctors and dentists. **Pharmacies:** A list of pharmacies open 24 hours *(farmacias de guardia)* is published daily in *El País.* Hotel receptions usually have a copy. *Company,* Puerta del Sol 14, has English-speaking pharmacists. It does not stock American medicines but will recognize many American brand names.
English Bookstores	**Booksellers S.A.,** José Abascal 48 (tel. 91/442–7959); **Turner's English Bookshop,** Genova 3 (tel. 91/410–2915); **Librería Franco Española,** Gran Vía 54, is good for maps and guidebooks in English.
Travel Agencies	**American Express,** Plaza de las Cortes 2 (tel. 91/429–7943); **Marsans,** Gran Vía 59 (tel. 91/241–5584); **Wagons-Lits/Cook,** Alcalá 23 (tel. 91/231–5940).
Airlines	**Iberia,** Plaza Cánovas del Castillo 5 (tel. 91/429–7443); **British Airways,** Serrano 60 (tel. 91/431–7575); **Pan Am,** Gran Vía 88 (tel. 91/241–4200); **TWA,** Gran Vía 66 (tel. 91/247–4200).

Guided Tours

Orientation Tours	City sightseeing tours are run by **Juliá Tours,** Gran Vía 68 (tel. 91/270–4600), **Pullmantur,** Plaza de Oriente 8 (tel. 91/241–1805), and **Trapsatur,** San Bernardo 23 (tel. 91/266–9900). All three run the same tours, mostly in 48-seat buses and conducted in Spanish and English. Book tours directly with the offices above, through any travel agent, or through your hotel. Departure points are from the addresses above, though in many cases you can be picked up at your hotel. "Madrid Artístico" is a morning tour of the city with visits to the Royal Palace and Prado Museum, entrances included. The "Madrid Panorámico" tour includes the University City, Casa del Campo park, and the northern reaches of the Castellana. This is a half-day tour, usually in the afternoon, and makes an ideal orientation for the first-time visitor. Also offered are "Madrid de Noche," a night tour combining a drive round the illuminations, dinner in a restaurant, flamenco show, and cabaret at La Scala nightclub; and "Panorámica y Toros," on bullfight days only (usually Sunday), a panoramic drive and visit to a bullfight.
Walking and Special-Interest Tours	Spanish-speaking people can take advantage of a hugely popular selection of tours recently launched by the *Ayuntamiento* (City Hall) under the title "Conozcamos Madrid." Walking tours are held most mornings and afternoons in spring and summer, and visit many of the capital's hidden corners, as well as the major sights. Special-interest tours include "Madrid's

Railroads," "Medicine in Madrid," "Goya's Madrid," and "Commerce and Finance in Madrid." Some tours are by bus, others on foot. Schedules are listed in the "Conozcamos Madrid" leaflet available from the Municipal Tourist Office at Sres. de Luján 10.

Excursions Juliá Tours, Pullmantur, and Trapsatur run full- or half-day trips to the Escorial, Avila, Segovia, Toledo, and Aranjuez, and in summer to Cuenca and Salamanca; for further details, see Ring Around Madrid. The "Tren de la Fresa" (Strawberry Train) is a popular excursion on summer weekends; a 19th-century train carries passengers from the old Delicias Station to Aranjuez and back. Tickets can be obtained from RENFE offices, travel agents, and the Delicias Station, Paseo de las Delicias 61.

Personal Guides Contact any of the tourist offices, or the Association of Madrid Guides, Duque de Medinacelli 2 (tel. 91/429–4951). A most knowledgeable English-speaking guide is Conchita de los Reyes, Alcalde Sainz de Baranda 63-8°-B (tel. 91/273–7620). She can arrange private transport and is qualified to take tours of Madrid and all surrounding cities.

Exploring Madrid

You can walk the following route in a day, or even half a day if you stop only to visit the Prado and Royal Palace. Two days should give you time for browsing. Begin in the Plaza Atocha, more properly known as the Glorieta del Emperador Carlos V, at the bottom of the Paseo del Prado, and check out what's showing in the exciting new **Reina Sofía Arts Center** opened by Queen Sofía in 1986. This converted hospital, home of art and sculpture exhibitions and symbol of Madrid's new cultural pride, aims to become one of Europe's most dynamic venues—a Madrileño rival to Paris's Pompidou Center. *Open daily except Tues. 10 AM–9 PM.*

Walk up Paseo del Prado to Madrid's number-one sight, the famous **Prado Museum,** one of the world's most important art galleries. Plan on spending at least 1½ hours here, though to view its treasures properly will take at least two full days. Brace yourself for the crowds. The greatest treasures—the Velázquez, Murillo, Zurbarán, El Greco, and Goya galleries—are all on the upstairs floor. Two of the best works are Velázquez's *Surrender of Breda* and his most famous work, *Las Meninas,* which occupies a privileged position in a room of its own. The Goya galleries contain the artist's none-too-flattering royal portraits—Goya believed in painting the truth—his exquisitely beautiful *Marquesa de Santa Cruz,* and his famous *Naked Maja* and *Clothed Maja,* for which the 13th Duchess of Alba was said to have posed. Goya's most moving works, the *2nd of May* and the *Fusillade of Moncloa* or *3rd of May,* vividly depict the sufferings of Madrid patriots at the hands of Napoleon's invading troops in 1808. Before you leave, feast your eyes on the fantastic flights of fancy of Hieronymous Bosch's *Garden of Earthly Delights* and his triptych *The Hay Wagon,* both downstairs on the ground floor. *Admission: 400 ptas. Open Tues.– Sat. 9–7, Sun. 9–2; closed Mon.*

Time Out Downstairs is a pleasant cafeteria, ideal for a light lunch.

Major Attractions

Other Attractions

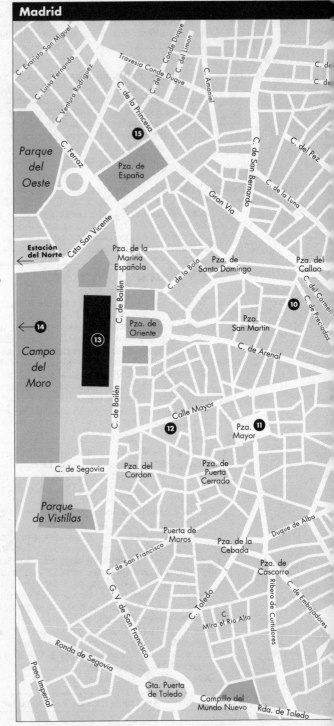

Madrid

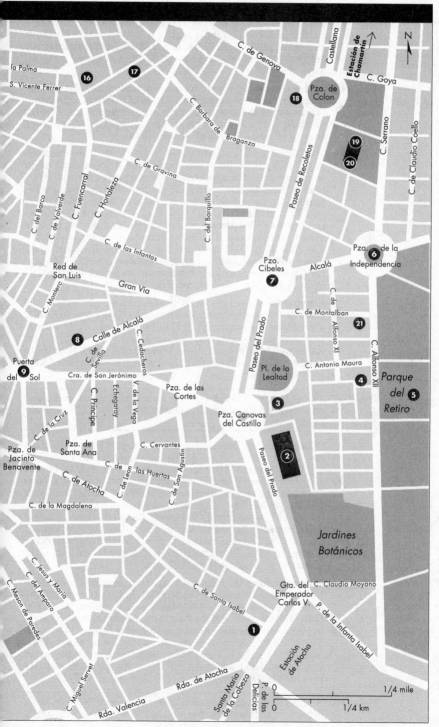

❸ Across the street is the **Ritz,** the grand old lady of Madrid's hotels, built in 1910 by Alfonso XIII when he realized that his capital had no hotels elegant enough to accommodate the guests at his wedding to English Queen Ena in 1906. The Ritz garden is a delightfully aristocratic place to lunch in summer—men always need ties.

❹ In the **Casón del Buen Retiro,** entrance on Alfonso XII, Picasso's *Guernica* hangs behind bulletproof glass, a haunting expression of the artist's anguish and outrage at the German bombing of this small Basque town in April 1937. *Open same hours as Prado and visited on same ticket.*

❺ The **Retiro,** once a royal retreat, is today Madrid's prettiest park. Visit the beautiful rose garden, **La Rosaleda,** and enjoy the many statues and fountains. You can hire a carriage, row a boat on **El Estanque,** gaze up at the monumental **statue to Alfonso XII,** one of Spain's least notable kings though you wouldn't think so to judge by its size, or wonder at the **Monument to the Fallen Angel**—Madrid claims the dubious privilege of being the only capital to have a statue dedicated to the Devil. The **Palacio de Velázquez** and the beautiful steel and glass **Palacio de Cristal,** built as a tropical plant house in the 19th century, now serve as major exhibition houses for art or sculpture. *Open Tues.–Sun. 10–6; closed Mon.*

❻ Leaving the Retiro via its northwest corner, you come to the Plaza de la Independencia, dominated by the **Puerta de Alcalá,** a grandiose gateway built in 1779 for Charles III. A customs post once stood beside the gate, as did the old bullring until it was moved to its present site at Ventas in the 1920s. It's hard to realize now that at the turn of the century, the **Puerta de Alcalá** more or less marked the eastern limits of Madrid.

Time Out The **Café Lyon,** Alcalá 57, with its marble-topped tables and charming Old World air, is an ideal place for some light refreshment.

❼ Continue to the **Plaza Cibeles,** one of the great landmarks of the city, at the intersection of its two main arteries, the Castellana and Calle Alacalá. If you can see it through the roar and fumes of the thundering traffic, the square's center is the **Cibeles Fountain,** the unofficial emblem of Madrid. Cybele, the Greek goddess of fertility, languidly rides her lion-drawn chariot, overlooked by the mighty **Palacio de Comunicaciones,** a splendidly pompous cathedrallike building often jokingly dubbed Our Lady of Communications. In fact, it's the main post office, erected in 1918. The famous goddess looks her best at night when she's illuminated by floodlights.

❽ Now head down the long and busy Calle de Alcalá toward the Puerta del Sol, resisting the temptation to turn right up the Gran Vía, which beckons temptingly with its mile of stores and cafés. Before you reach the Puerta del Sol, art lovers may want to step inside the **Real Academia de Bellas Artes** at Alcalá 13. This recently refurbished fine arts gallery boasts an art collection second only to the Prado's and features all the great Spanish masters: Velázquez, El Greco, Murillo, Zurbarán, Ribera, and Goya. *Open Tues.–Sat. 9–7, Sun., Mon. 9–2.*

Time Out A small detour down Sevilla, then right down San Jerónimo, brings you to two atmospheric places for a drink or light lunch.

Lhardy, San Jerónimo 8 (tel. 91/222–2207), is a veritable old Madrid institution that opened as a pastry shop in 1839. Today it combines the roles of expensive restaurant and delicatessen. *Closed Sun. evenings and in Aug.*

Next door, at no. 6, on the corner of Espoz y Mina, is the more moderately priced **Museo de Jamón,** a relative newcomer on the Madrid scene, with hundreds of hams hanging from its ceilings. It's ideal for a beer or glass of wine and a generous plate of cheese or ham.

⑨ The **Puerta del Sol** is at the very heart of Madrid. Its name means Gate of the Sun, though the old gate disappeared long ago. It's easy to feel you're at the heart of things here—indeed, of all of Spain—for the kilometer distances for the whole nation are measured from the zero marker in front of the Police Headquarters. The square was expertly revamped in 1986 and now accommodates both a copy of **La Mariblanca** (a statue that 250 years ago adorned a fountain here) and, at the bottom of Calle Carmen, the much loved statue of the **bear and *madroño*** (strawberry tree). The Puerta del Sol is inextricably linked with the history of Madrid and of the nation. Here, half a century ago, a generation of literati gathered in the long-gone cafés to thrash out the burning issues of the day; and if you can cast your thoughts back almost 200 years, you can conjure up the heroic deeds of the patriots' uprising immortalized by Goya in the *2nd of May*.

This is a good place to break the tour if you've had enough sightseeing for one day. Head north up Preciados or Montera for some of the busiest and best shopping streets in the city, or southeast toward Plaza Santa Ana, for tavern-hopping in the **tascas** of Old Madrid.

Time Out If it's teatime (6–7 PM), don't miss **La Mallorquina,** an old pastry shop between Calle Mayor and Arenal. Delicious pastries are sold at the downstairs counter; the old-fashioned upstairs tea salon offers an age-old tea ritual and unbeatable views over the Puerta del Sol.

---

⑩ Art lovers will want to make a detour to the **Convento de las Descalzas Reales** on Plaza Descalzas Reales just above Arenal. It was founded by Juana de Austria, daughter of Charles V, and is still inhabited by nuns. Over the centuries the nuns, daughters of the royal and noble, endowed the convent with an enormous wealth of jewels, religious ornaments, superb Flemish tapestries, and the works of great masters like Titian and Rubens. A bit off the main tourist track, it's one of Madrid's better kept secrets. *Guided tours only. Open Tues.–Thurs., Sat. 10:30–12:30 and 4–5:15; Fri. 10:30–12:30; Sun. 11–1:15; closed Mon. The 200 ptas. ticket includes admission to the nearby but less interesting,* **Convento de la Encarnación.**

Walk up **Calle Mayor,** the Main Street of Old Madrid, past the shops full of religious statues and satins for bishops' robes, to **⑪** the **Plaza Mayor,** the capital's greatest architectural showpiece. It was built in 1617–19 for Philip III—that's Philip on the horse in the middle. The plaza has witnessed the canonization of saints, burning of heretics, fireworks and bullfights, and is still one of the great gathering places of Madrid.

Time Out In summer you can relax over a drink in any of the delightful sidewalk cafés that adorn the square; in winter, head for the **Mesón del Corregidor** at no. 8, near the Cuchilleros arch. This colorful tavern restaurant has typical dishes and tapas.

⑫ If you're here in the morning, take a look inside the 19th-century steel and glass San Miguel market, a colorful provisions market, before continuing down Calle Mayor to the **Plaza de la Villa.** The square's notable cluster of buildings includes some of the oldest houses in Madrid. The **Casa de la Villa,** the Madrid City Hall, was built in 1644 by the same architect as the Plaza Mayor and has also served as the city prison and the mayor's home. Its sumptuous salons are now open to the public on Monday at 5 PM. The free guided visits are usually in Spanish, but English tours can be arranged with advance notice. An archway joins the Casa de la Villa to the **Casa Cisneros,** a palace built in 1537 for the nephew of Cardinal Cisneros, primate of Spain and infamous inquisitor general. Across the square, the **Torre de Lujanes** is one of the oldest buildings in Madrid. It once imprisoned Francis I of France, archenemy of the Emperor Charles V.

Time Out If it's lunchtime, close by are two excellent choices, both moderately priced and long-standing Madrid traditions: **Casa Ciriaco** on Calle Mayor 48, and **La Quinta del Sordo,** Sacramento 10, just behind the City Hall.

⑬ The last stop on the tour, but Madrid's second most important sight, is the **Royal Palace.** This magnificent granite and limestone residence was begun by Philip V, the first Bourbon king of Spain, who was always homesick for his beloved Versailles, the opulence and splendor of which he did his best to emulate. His efforts were successful, to judge by the 2,800 rooms with their lavish Rococo decorations, precious carpets, porcelain, time pieces, mirrors, and chandeliers. From 1764, when Charles III first moved in, till the coming of the Second Republic and the abdication of Alfonso XIII in 1931, the Royal Palace proved a very stylish abode for Spanish monarchs. Today King Juan Carlos, who lives in the far less ostentatious Zarzuela Palace outside Madrid, uses it only for official state functions.

⑭ The Palace can be visited only on guided tours, available in English. The **Royal Carriage Museum,** which belongs to the palace but has a separate entrance on Paseo Vírgen del Puerto, can be visited on an all-inclusive or separate ticket. One of its highlights is the wedding carriage of Alfonso XIII and his English bride, Victoria Eugenia, daughter of Queen Victoria, which was damaged by a bomb thrown at it in the Calle Mayor during their wedding procession in 1906; another is the chair that carried the gout-stricken old Emperor Charles V to his retirement at the remote monastery of Yuste. The 90–120-minute Palace tours (in English) cost 400 ptas. Most visitors opt for the shorter Salones Oficiales tour at 300 ptas. *The Palace and Carriage Museum are open Mon.–Sat. 9:30–12:45 and 4–6 (3:30–5:15 in winter), Sun. 9:30–1 only. Closed to visitors when in use for official functions.*

What to See and Do with Children

Visit the **Retiro Park** on a Sunday, when there are often puppet shows and band concerts. You can rent paddleboats on the lake, known as El Estanque, or a horse carriage from the kiosk near the Puerta de España entrance on Alfonso XII. Children will also enjoy a trip to the **Casa de Campo,** where there is a small **amusement park** (tel. 91/463–2900) and a **zoo** (open 10–9:30 in summer, tel. 91/711–9950) with performing dolphins. The zoo is best reached by cable car from Paseo de Rosales (runs Mon.–Sat. 11:45–7, Sun. 10:45–8). Visit the **Wax Museum,** Paseo de Recoletos 41, on the Plaza Colón (open daily 10:30–2 and 4–9); the **Bullfighting Museum** at Ventas Bullring at the end of Calle Alcalá (open Tues.–Sun. 9–3); or the **Train Museum,** Paseo de las Delicias 61 (open Tues.–Sat. 10–5, Sun. 10–2). In summer you can take a trip on the **Manzanares River** or hire a rowboat from the Polideportivo Virgen del Puerto, Paseo Bajo de la Virgen del Puerto, below the Royal Palace (tel. 91/266–4120, open daily 10–8). Teenagers will enjoy a trip to the fashionable **La Vaguada** shopping center in the Barrio del Pilar (metro Barrio del Pilar).

Off the Beaten Track

Stroll around the narrow streets of the **Chueca** between Hortaleza and Paseo de Recoletos. Look for the architectural features of the old houses, the dark, atmospheric bars and restaurants well known to discerning Madrileños, the small stores with their wooden counters and brass fittings, many of which have been run by the same family for generations. Calle Infantas has some real gems: the *Bolsa de los Licores* at no. 13 selling wines and liqueurs from every corner of Europe; the splendid silver shop at no. 25; the Old World grocery store **Casa Jerez** at no. 32. And don't miss the *Tienda de Vinos* restaurant in Augusto Figueroa, affectionately nicknamed *El Comunista* and long famed for its rock-bottom prices. The whole quarter seems to come straight from the pages of a 19th-century novel.

The old **Lavapiés quarter,** between Calle Atocha and Embajadores, is another area with plenty of atmosphere. Traditionally one of the poorest parts of Old Madrid, it is now the home of artists and actors, writers and musicians. Health-food restaurants—a novelty in Spain generally—have flourished. You can get a good cheap lunch at *La Biótica*, Amor de Diós 3, or *El Granero de Lavapiés*, Argumosa 10. In summer you can eat in the courtyard of the old tenement building *La Corrala*, Meson de Paredes 32, and watch a *zarzuela* performance on its ancient balconies.

Casa Mingo, Paseo de la Florida 2 (tel. 91/247–7918), is a tiny Asturian tavern behind Norte Station. A real Madrid institution, it's long been famous for its Astorian cider, goat cheese, and succulent chicken at amazingly low prices.

Shopping

Gift Ideas There are no special regional crafts associated with Madrid itself, but traditional Spanish goods are on sale in many stores. The *Corte Inglés* and *Galerías Preciados* department stores both stock good displays of Lladró porcelain, as do several specialist shops on the Gran Vía and behind the Plaza hotel on Plaza de España. Department stores stock good displays of fans, but for really superb examples, try the long-established *Casa Diego* in Puerta del Sol. Two stores opposite the Prado on Plaza Cánovas del Castillo, *Artesanía Toledana* and *El Escudo* *de Toledo*, have a wide selection of souvenirs, especially Toledo swords, inlaid marquetry ware, and pottery.

Antiques The main areas to see are the Plaza de las Cortes, the Carrera San Jerónimo, and the Rastro flea market, along the Ribera de Curtidores and the courtyards just off it.

Boutiques Calle Serrano has the largest collection of smart boutiques and designer fashions. Another up-and-coming area is around Calle Argensola, just south of Calle Génova. **Loewe,** Spain's most prestigious leather store, has boutiques on Serrano 26 and Gran Vía 8. Adolfo Domínguez, one of Spain's top designers, has several boutiques in Salamanca, and another on Calle Orense in the north of town.

Shopping Districts The main shopping area in the heart of Madrid is around the pedestrian streets of **Preciados** and **Montera,** between Puerta del Sol and Plaza Callao on Gran Vía. The smartest and most expensive district is the **Barrio de Salamanca** northeast of Cibeles, centered around Serrano, Velázquez, and Goya. **Calle Mayor** and the streets to the **east of Plaza Mayor** are lined with fascinating old-fashioned stores straight out of the 19th century.

Department Stores *El Corte Inglés* is the biggest, brightest, and most successful Spanish chain store. Its main branch is on Preciados, just off the Puerta del Sol. *Galerías Preciados* is its main rival, with branches on Plaza Callao right off Gran Vía, Calle Arapiles, Goya corner of Conde de Peñalver, Serrano and Ortega y Gasset, and its newest branch at La Vaguada. Both stores are open Monday–Saturday 10–8, and neither closes for the siesta.

Food and Flea Markets **The Rastro,** Madrid's most famous flea market, operates on Sunday from 9 to 2 around the Plaza del Cascorro and the Ribera de Curtidores. A **Stamp and Coin** market is held on Sunday morning in the Plaza Mayor, and there's a **Secondhand Book** market most days on the Cuesta Claudio Moyano near Atocha Station.

Bullfighting

The Madrid bullfighting season runs from March to October. Fights are held on Sunday, and sometimes also on Thursday; starting times vary between 4:30 and 7 PM. There are two bullrings: The main one is Ventas, Alcalá 237 (metro Ventas); the other is Vista Alegre, Avenida Plaza de Toros in Carabanchel, south of the Manzanares River. Buy your tickets at the rings or from the official *Despacho* (ticket office) on Calle Victoria 9 (tel. 91/221–4870), just off Carrera San Jerónimo and Puerta del Sol. The best fights are held during the San Isidro festivals in mid-May.

Dining

Ratings Prices are for two people sharing a double room and do not include breakfast. Best bets are indicated by a star ★. At press time, there were 110 pesetas to the dollar.

Category	Cost
Very Expensive	over 14,000 ptas.
Expensive	9,000–13,950 ptas.

Moderate	5,500–8,950 ptas.
Inexpensive	under 5,450 ptas.

Credit Cards The following credit card abbreviations are used: AE, American Express; DC, Diners Club; MC, MasterCard; V, Visa.

Very Expensive **Irízar Jatetxea.** Owned by the famous Basque restaurateur Luis Irízar, this is one of Madrid's most luxurious and renowned restaurants. It's opposite the Teatro Zarzuela (next to Armstrong's) and the cuisine is Basque, but much influenced by nouvelle cuisine from France and Navarre. Definitely a place for a treat. *Jovellanos 3, tel. 91/231–4569. Jacket and tie. Reservations essential. AE, DC, V. Closed Sat. lunch, Sun. dinner.*

Zalacaín. This private villa with elegant decor, top-notch cuisine, and personalized service is the highest-rated restaurant in Spain. Located just off the Castellana and María de Molina, it is the only Spanish restaurant awarded three Michelin rosettes. *Alvarez de Baena 4, tel. 91/261–4840. Jacket and tie. Reservations essential. AE, DC. Closed Sat. lunch, Sun., Holy Week, Aug.*

Expensive **El Cenador del Prado.** This elegant and stylish restaurant just
★ off Plaza Santa Ana offers beautiful decor and an imaginative menu with more than a hint of nouvelle cuisine. The chef learned his trade in New York, and specialties include *caracoles con setas en hojaldre* (snails and mushrooms en croute) and *salmón marinado a la pimienta verde* (salmon marinated in green peppers). *Calle del Prado 4, tel. 91/429–1549). Jacket and tie. Reservations advised. AE, DC, MC, V. Closed Sat. lunch, Sun., two weeks in Aug.*

La Dorada. One of Madrid's most outstanding fish restaurants, the seafood here is flown in daily in the owner's private plane from the Costa del Sol. Its sister restaurants in Barcelona and Seville are equally esteemed. It's located in the modern north of town, near the Azca Center and Holiday Inn. *Orense 64, tel. 91/270–2004. Jacket and tie. Reservations essential. AE, DC, V. Closed Sun., Aug.*

New Yorker. This fashionable restaurant, popular with businesspeople, opened in 1985. The ambience is elegant, and contemporary Spanish paintings adorn the walls. The menu offers international specialties and service that's highly professional. *Amador de los Rios 1, to the west of the Castellana just above the Plaza Colón, tel. 91/410–1522. Jacket and tie. Reservations essential. AE, V. Closed Sat. lunch, Sun.*

Solchaga. Here you can choose between several dining rooms, each with its own distinctive character. Pot-bellied stoves and ornate gilt mirrors help convey the atmosphere of an old-fashioned private house rather than a restaurant; a charming find. *Plaza de Alonso Martínez 2, tel. 91/447–1496. Dress: Smart, but jacket and tie not required. Reservations advised. AE, DC, MC, V. Closed Sat. lunch, Sun.*

Moderate **Armstrong's.** This charming English-owned restaurant opposite the Teatro Zarzuela is bright and modern with refreshing pink decor and is quite a change from the usual Madrid scene. Its imaginative menu mixes French and Spanish nouvelle cuisine with English and American favorites, and there's a good choice of salads, brunch on weekends, and a special teatime menu. It even opens for dinner at 6 PM! *Jovellanos 5, tel.*

91/522–4230. Dress: informal. Reservations advised but not essential. AE, DC, MC, V. Closed Sun. PM and Mon.

★ **La Barraca.** A Valencian restaurant with cheerful blue and white decor, colorful windowboxes, and ceramic tiles, this is the place to go for a wonderful choice of paellas. Located just off Gran Vía (Alcalá end), behind Loewe, it's popular with businesspeople and foreign visitors. Try the *paella reina* or the *paella de mariscos. Reina 29, tel. 91/232–7154. Dress: informal. Reservations advisable. AE, DC, MC, V.*

Botín. Madrid's oldest and most famous, restaurant, just off the Plaza Mayor, has been catering to diners since 1725. Its decor and food are traditionally Castilian. *Cochinillo* (suckling pig) and *cordero asado* (roast lamb) are its specialties. It was a favorite with Hemingway; today it's very touristy and a bit overrated, but fun. Insist on the *cueva* or upstairs dining room. *Cuchilleros 17, tel. 91/266–4217. Dress: informal. Reservations advisable, especially at night. AE, DC, MC, V. Two sittings for dinner, at 8 and 10:30.*

★ **Carmencita.** Dating back to 1850, this charming restaurant is small and intimate, with ceramic wall tiles, brass hat racks, and photos of bullfighters. The menu recounts the famous who have dined here and their life stories. The cuisine is part traditional, part nouvelle with an emphasis on *pasteles* (a kind of mousse) both savory and sweet. *Libertad 16, on the corner of San Marcos in the Chueca area above Gran Vía; tel. 91/231–6612. Dress: informal. Reservations not essential. V. Closed Sun.*

Casa Ciriaco. In this atmospheric old standby only a few paces from the Plaza Mayor and City Hall, the Madrid of 50 years ago lives on. You won't find many foreigners here—just businesspeople and locals, enjoying traditional Spanish cooking and delicious *fresones* (strawberries) for dessert. *Mayor 84, tel. 91/248–0620. Dress: informal. Reservations usually unnecessary. No credit cards. Closed Wed., and Aug.*

Inexpensive **Fuente Real.** Dining here is like eating in a 19th-century home.
★ Tucked away between Arenal and Mayor, it's full of antique furniture and mirrors. The cuisine is French and Spanish with an emphasis on quality meats and crêpes. Try the *pastel de espinacas* (spinach mousse) or *crêpes de puerros* (leaks). *Fuentes 1, tel. 91/248–6613. Dress: informal. Reservations not needed. AE, MC, V. Closed Sun. PM and Mon.*

El Luarqués. One of many budget restaurants on this street, El Luarqués is decorated with photos of the port of Luarca on Spain's north coast, and it's always packed with Madrileños who recognize its good value. *Fabada asturiana* (bean and meat stew) and *arroz con leche* (rice pudding) are two of its Asturian specialties. *Ventura de la Vega 16, tel. 91/429–6174). Dress: informal. Reservations not accepted. No credit cards. Closed Sun. PM, Mon., and Aug.*

La Quinta del Sordo. Named after Goya's house, which stood across the river, this long-standing favorite just behind the Ayuntamiento is famous for its soup, its baked chicken, and its choice of Castilian roasts, all at reasonable prices. *Sacramento 10, tel. 91/248–1852. Dress: informal. Reservations unnecessary. AE, DC.*

Lodging

Hotels around the center in the midst of all the sights and shops are mostly located in old 19th-century houses; many of these are currently undergoing restoration to bring them up to standard. Most of the newer hotels that conform to American standards of comfort are located in the northern part of town on either side of the Castellana and are a short metro or bus ride to the center. There are hotel reservation desks in the national and international terminals of the airport, and at Chamartín and Atocha stations. Or you can contact *La Brújula* (tel. 91/248 –9705) on the sixth floor of the Torre de Madrid in Plaza de España, which is open 9–9. It has English-speaking staff and can book hotels all over Spain.

Ratings   Prices are for two people sharing a double room and do not include breakfast. Best bets are indicatd by a star ★. At press time, there were 110 pesetas to the dollar.

Category	Cost
Very Expensive	over 6,000 ptas.
Expensive	3,600–5,900 ptas.
Moderate	1,500–3,500 ptas.
Inexpensive	under 1,400 ptas.

Credit Cards   The following credit card abbreviations are used: AE, American Express; DC, Diners Club; MC, MasterCard; V, Visa.

Very Expensive   **Fenix.** Located just off the Castellana near the Plaza Colón and convenient for the Salamanca shopping district, this is fast becoming Madrid's leading four-star hotel. It's a favorite with influential businesspeople and conveys a feeling of style and luxury. Its bar and cafeteria are popular meeting places. *Hermosilla 2, tel. 91/431–6700. 216 rooms. 6% IVA. AE, DC, MC, V.*

Palace. This dignified turn-of-the-century hotel opposite parliament and the Prado is a slightly less dazzling step-sister of the nearby Ritz. Long a favorite of politicians and journalists, its *belle époque* decor—especially the glass dome over the lounge—is superb, if just a little faded in parts. *Plaza de las Cortes 7, tel. 91/429–7551. 518 rooms. IVA. AE, V.*

★ **Ritz.** Spain's most exclusive hotel is elegant and aristocratic with beautiful rooms, spacious suites, and sumptuous public salons furnished with antiques and handwoven carpets. Its palatial restaurant is justly famous and its garden terrace is the perfect setting for summer dining. Features are brunches with harp music on weekends and tea or supper chamber concerts from February through May. Close to the Retiro Park and overlooking the famous Prado Museum, it offers pure unadulterated luxury. *Plaza Lealtad 5, tel. 91/521–2857. 156 rooms. AE, DC, MC, V.*

Villa Magna. Second in luxury only to the Ritz, a modern facade belies a palatial interior exquisitely furnished with 18th-century antiques. Set in a delightful garden, it offers all the facilities one would expect in a hotel of international repute. *Paseo de la Castellana 22, tel. 91/261–4900. 194 rooms. AE, DC.*

Expensive   **Emperador.** This older hotel on the corner of San Bernardo has been renovated throughout, and storm windows now help to shut out the roar of Gran Vía traffic. All the rooms have TV and VCR, and a special feature is the rooftop pool and terrace with superb views. *Gran Vía 53, tel. 91/247–2800. 231 rooms. AE, DC, MC, V.*

★ **Plaza.** This elegant hotel at the bottom of Gran Vía has long been a favorite with American visitors. New storm windows cut down the traffic noise, security safes have been installed in each room, and the mattresses have all been changed for harder ones more suited to American tastes. The view from its legendary rooftop pool is a favorite with Spanish and foreign photographers. *Plaza de España, tel. 91/247–1200. 306 rooms. AE, DC, MC, V.*

Sanvy. Backing onto the Fenix, the Sanvy, located just off the Plaza Colón on the edge of the Salamanca district, is a comfortable, well-renovated hotel with a swimming pool on the top floor. Its **Belagua Restaurant** is gaining prestige. *Goya 3, tel. 91/276–0800. 141 rooms. AE, DC, MC, V.*

Moderate **Alcalá.** Close to the Retiro Park and Goya shopping area, this
★ comfortable hotel has long been recognized for high standards. The rooms are well furnished, each with TV and minibar, and the cafeteria serves a good lunch menu for around 900 ptas. The hotel restaurant, **Le Basque** (closed Sun. and Mon. lunch) is owned by Luis Irízar of the famous Irízar restaurant, and its Basque culinary delights are well known to Madrileños. *Alealá 66, tel. 91/435–1060. 153 rooms. AE, DC, MC, V.*

Capitol. If you like being right in the center of things, then this hotel on the Plaza Callao is for you. It's an older hotel, of which four floors have been renovated, and these rooms are comfortable indeed. There's a well-decorated reception area and a pleasant cafeteria for breakfast. *Gran Vía 41, tel. 91/521–8391. 145 rooms. AE, DC, V.*

Mayorazgo. An older hotel that has yet to be renovated, but comfortable as long as you're not seeking all the conveniences of home. Advantages are its friendly old-fashioned service and its prime location right in the heart of town, yet it's tucked away in a quiet back street off Gran Vía leading down to Plaza de España. *Flor Baja 3, tel. 91/247–2600. AE, DC, MC, V.*

Rex. This is a sister hotel to the Capitol next door, and both belong to the Tryp chain. It's located on the corner of Silva just down from Callao, and the lobby, bar, restaurant, and two floors have so far been completely refurbished. The unrenovated rooms are considerably cheaper, but you'll be much more comfortable in one of the newer ones. *Gran Vía 43, tel. 91/247–4800. 147 rooms. AE, DC, V.*

Inexpensive **Asturias.** An older hotel on the corner of Canalejas, Asturias
★ has a certain period charm and has been partly refurbished. The renovated rooms are far more spacious and comfortable and well worth the extra money. The location is convenient, if busy; you're a few paces from the Puerta del Sol one way, and from the Prado the other; and hundreds of inexpensive restaurants are across the road in Echegaray and Ventura de la Vega. *Sevilla 2, tel. 91/429–6676. 144 rooms. AE, V.*

Cliper. This simple hotel offers good value for the cost-conscious traveler. It's tucked away in a side street off the central part of Gran Vía between Callao and Red San Luis. *Chinchilla 6, tel. 91/231–1700. 52 rooms. AE, MC, V.*

Paris. Overlooking the Puerta del Sol, the Paris is a stylish hotel full of old-fashioned appeal. It has an impressive turn-of-the-century lobby and a restaurant where you can dine for around 1500 ptas. Currently being refurbished, it's to be hoped that the renovations do nothing to detract from the charm. *Alcalá 2, tel. 91/521-6496). 114 rooms. MC, V.*

Bars and Cafés

Bars   **The Mesones.** The most traditional and colorful taverns are on Cuchilleros and Cava San Miguel just west of Plaza Mayor, where you'll find a whole array of mesones with names like *Tortilla, Champiñón* and *Huevo.*

Old Madrid. Wander the narrow streets between Puerta del Sol and Plaza Santa Ana, which are packed with traditional tapas bars. Favorites here are the **Cervecería Alemana,** Plaza Santa Ana 6, a beer hall founded more than 100 years ago by Germans and patronized, inevitably, by Hemingway; **Los Gabrieles,** Echegaray 17, with magnificent ceramic decor; **La Trucha,** M. Fernández y González 3, with loads of atmosphere; and **Viva Madrid,** Fernández y González 7, a lovely old bar.

Calle Huertas. Fashionable wine bars with turn-of-the-century decor and chamber or guitar music, often live, line this street. **La Fídula** at no. 57 and **El Elhecho** at no. 56 are two of the best.

Plaza Santa Barbara. This area just off Alonso Martínez is packed with fashionable bars and beer halls. Stroll along Santa Teresa, Orellana, Campoamor or Fernando VI and take your pick. The **Cervecería Santa Barbara** in the plaza itself is one of the most colorful, a popular beer hall with a good range of tapas.

Cafés   If you like cafés with old-fashioned atmosphere, dark wooden counters, brass pumps and marble-topped tables, try any of the following: **Café Comercial,** Glorieta de Bilbao 7; **Café Gijón,** Paseo de Recoletos 21, a former literary hangout and the most famous of the cafés of old, now one of the many café-terraces that line the Castellana; **Café Lyon,** Alcalá 57, just up from Cibeles; and **Café Roma** on C. Serrano. And don't forget **La Mallorquina** tearooms on Puerta del Sol (*see* Exploring).

The Arts

Details of all cultural events are listed in the daily newspaper *El País* or in the weekly *Guía del Ocio.*

Concerts and   The main concert hall and opera house is the **Teatro Real,** Car-
Opera   los III, tel. 91/248-1405, at the end of Arenal opposite the Royal Palace. The main concert season runs from October to March, and opera from February to July. The ticket office is open Monday 5–7, Tuesday–Friday 10–5, Saturday 11–1, Sunday 10:30–12, and one hour before performances.

Zarzuela and   Zarzuela, a combination of light opera and dance ideal for non-
Dance   Spanish speakers, is held at the **Teatro Nacional Lírico de la Zarzuela,** Jovellanos 4, tel. 91/429-8216. The season runs from October to July.

Nightlife and Entertainment

Cabaret   **Florida Park** (tel. 91/273-7804), in the Retiro Park, offers dinner and a show that often features ballet, Spanish dance, or flamenco and is open Monday to Saturday from 9:30 PM with shows at 11 PM. **Lola** (Costanilla de San Pedro 11, tel. 91/265–8801) opens at 9:30 PM for a dinner that is good by most cabaret standards, followed by a show and dancing until 4 AM. **La Scala** (Rosario Pino 7, tel. 91/450–4500), in the Meliá Castilla hotel, is Madrid's top nightclub, with dinner, dancing, and cabaret at 8:30, and a second, less expensive show around midnight. This is the one visited by most night tours.

Flamenco Madrid offers the widest choice of flamenco shows in Spain; some are good, but many are aimed at the tourist trade. Dinner tends to be mediocre and overpriced, but it ensures the best seats; otherwise, opt for the show and a drink *(consumición)* only, usually starting around 11 PM and costing 2,000–2,500 ptas. **Arco de Cuchilleros** (Cuchilleros 7, tel. 91/266–5867), behind the Plaza Mayor, is one of the better of the cheaper ones. **Café de Chinitas** (Torija 7, tel. 91/248–5135) and **Corral de la Morería** (Morería 17, tel. 91/265–8446) are two of the more authentic places where well-known troupes perform. **Venta del Gato** (Avda de Burgos 214, tel. 91/202–3427) is authentic, too, but it's 11 miles (7 kilometers) to the north. **Zambra** (Velázquez 8, tel. 91/435–5164), in the Hotel Wellington, is one of the smartest (jacket and tie essential), with a good show and dinner served into the small hours.

Jazz **Whisky Jazz Club** (Diego de León, tel. 91/261–1165) is the leading old-timer. Other venues with live jazz are **Café Berlín** (Jacometrezo 4, tel. 91/231–0810) just off Callao; **Clamores** (Albuquerque 14, tel. 91/445–7938); **El Despertar** (Torrecilla del Leal 18, tel. 230–8095) in Lavapiés, open Thursday to Sunday 8:30–11; and **Hamilton Jazz Club** (Alberto Aguilera 54, tel. 91/241–1695), open Tuesday to Saturday 11 PM–3 AM.

Casino **Madrid's Casino** (tel. 91/859–0312) is 45 miles (28 kilometers) out at Torrelodones on the N-VI road to La Coruña. *Open 5 PM–4 AM. Free transport service from Plaza de España 6.*

Ring Around Madrid

The beauty of the historic cities surrounding Madrid and the role they have played in their country's history rank them among Spain's most worthwhile sights. Ancient Toledo, the great palace-monastery of the Escorial, the sturdy medieval walls of Avila, Segovia's Roman aqueduct and fairy-tale Alcazar, and the magnificent Plaza Mayor of the old university town of Salamanca, all lie within an hour or so from the capital.

All the towns below except Salamanca can easily be visited on day-trips from the capital. But if you've had your fill of the hustle and bustle of Spain's booming capital, you'll find it far more rewarding to tour from one place to another, spending a day or two in one or more of these fascinating locales. Then, long after the day-trippers have gone home, you can enjoy the real charm of these small provincial towns and wander at leisure through their mazes of medieval streets.

Getting There from Madrid

Trains to Toledo leave from Madrid's Atocha Station; to Salamanca, from Norte Station; and to El Escorial, Avila, and

Segovia, from either Atocha Apeadero or Chamartín Cercanías.

Getting Around

There's a direct train line between El Escorial, Avila, and Salamanca; otherwise, train connections are poor and you'll do better to go by bus. All places are linked by bus services and the local tourist offices will advise on schedules. Toledo has a brand-new bus station on the *Circunvalación* (ring road) just off the road from Madrid. Avila's bus station is on Avda de Madrid (tel. 220154); Segovia's is on Paseo Ezequiel González (tel. 427725); and Salamanca's is on Filiberto Villalobos 73 (tel. 236717).

By Car The N403 from Toledo to Avila passes through spectacular scenery in the Sierra de Gredos mountains, as does the C505 Avila–Escorial route. From the Escorial to Segovia, both the Puerto de León and Puerto de Navacerrada mountain passes offer magnificent views. The N501 from Avila to Salamanca will take you across the tawny plain of Castile.

Guided Tours

Juliá Tours, Pullmantur, and Trapsatur run day tours from Madrid. Details are available from any travel agent.

Tourist Information

Avila. Plaza de la Catedral 4, tel. 211387; open Monday to Friday 9–2 and 4–6 (5–7 in summer), Saturday 9–2 only.
El Escorial. Floridablanca 10, tel. 890–1554); open Monday to Friday 9:45–2:15 and 3–6, Saturday 9:45–1:15.
Salamanca. Gran Vía (C. España) 39, tel. 243730; open Monday to Friday 9:30–2 and 4:30–8, Sat. 9:30–2. There's also an information booth on the Plaza Mayor (market side).
Segovia. Plaza Mayor 10, tel. 430328; open Monday to Friday 9–2 and 4–6, Saturday 9–2.
Toledo. Puerta Nueva de Bisagra tel. 220843; open Monday to Friday 9–2 and 4–6, Saturday 9:30–1:30.

Exploring

The following tour goes from Toledo to El Escorial, the Valley of the Fallen, La Granja, Segovia, Riofrio, Avila, Alba de Tormes, and Salamanca.

Toledo Head south from Madrid on the road to Toledo. About 20 minutes from the capital look left for a prominent rounded hill topped by a statue of Christ. This is the **Hill of the Angels**, which marks the geographical center of the Iberian Peninsula. After 90 minutes of drab, industrial scenery, the unforgettable silhouette of Toledo suddenly rises before you, the imposing bulk of the Alcázar and the slender spire of the cathedral dominating the skyline. This former capital, where Moors, Jews, and Christians once lived in harmony, is now a living national monument, depicting all the elements of Spanish civilization in hand-carved, sun-mellowed stone. For a stunning view and to capture the beauty of Toledo as El Greco knew it, begin with a

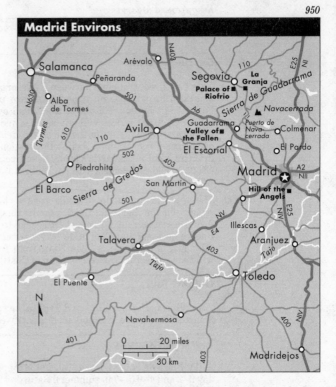

Madrid Environs

Salamanca
Arévalo
Peñaranda
Alba de Tormes
Segovia
La Granja
Palace of Riofrio
Sierra de Guadarrama
Navacerrada
Avila
Guadarrama
Valley of the Fallen
Puerto de Nava-cerrada
Colmenar
El Escorial
El Pardo
Piedrahita
Sierra de Gredos
Madrid
El Barco
San Martín
Hill of the Angels
Talavera
Illescas
Aranjuez
Tajo
El Puente
Tajo
Toledo
N
Navahermosa
0   20 miles
0   30 km
Madridejos

panoramic drive around the Carretera de Circunvalación, crossing over the Alcántara bridge and returning by way of the bridge of San Martín. As you gaze at the city rising like an island in its own bend of the Tagus, reflect how little the city skyline has changed in the four centuries since El Greco painted *Storm Over Toledo.*

Toledo is a small city steeped in history and full of magnificent buildings. It was the capital of Spain under both Moors and Christians until some whim caused Philip II to move his capital to Madrid in 1561. Begin your visit with a drink in one of the many terrace cafés on the central **Plaza Zocodover,** study a map, and try to get your bearings, for a veritable labyrinth confronts you as you try to find your way to Toledo's great treasures. While here, search the square's pastry shops for the typical marzipan candies *(mazapanes)* of Toledo.

Begin your tour with a visit to the 13th-century **cathedral,** seat of the Cardinal Primate of Spain, and one of the great cathedrals of Spain. Somber but elaborate, it blazes with jeweled chalices, gorgeous ecclesiastical vestments, historic tapestries, some 750 stained-glass windows, and paintings by Tintoretto, Titian, Murillo, El Greco, Velázquez, and Goya.

En route to the real jewel of Toledo, the **Chapel of Santo Tomé,** you'll pass a host of souvenir shops on Calle Santo Tomé, bursting with damascene knives and swords, blue and yellow pottery from nearby Talavera, and El Greco reproductions. In the tiny chapel that houses El Greco's masterpiece, *Burial of the Count* *of Orgaz*, you can capture the true spirit of the Greek painter who adopted Spain, and in particular Toledo, as his homeland. Do you recognize the sixth man from the left among the painting's earthly contingent? Or the young boy in the left-hand corner? The first is El Greco himself, the second his son Jorge Manuel—see 1578, the year of his birth, embroidered on his handkerchief. *Admission: 75 ptas. Open 10–1:45 and 3:30–5:45 (6:45 in summer).*

Not far away is **El Greco's house,** a replica containing copies of his works. *Admission: 200 ptas. Open 10–1:45 and 3:30–5:45; Sun. AM only; closed Mon.*

The splendid **Sinagoga del Tránsito** is on the corner of Samuel Levi and Reyes Católicos. Commissioned in 1366 by Samuel Levi, chancellor to Pedro the Cruel, the synagogue shows Christian and Moorish as well as Jewish influences in its architecture and decoration—look at the stars of David interspersed with the arms of Castile and León. There's also a small **Sephardic Museum** chronicling the life of Toledo's former Jewish community. *Admission: 200 ptas. Open 10–2 and 3:30–6 (4–7 in summer); closed Sun. PM and Mon.*

Another synagogue, the incongruously named **Santa María la Blanca** (it was given as a church to the Knights of Calatrava in 1405), is just along the street. Its history may have been Jewish and Christian, but its architecture is definitely Moorish, for it resembles a mosque with five naves, horseshoe arches, and capitals decorated with texts from the Koran. *Admission: 50 ptas. Open 10–2 and 3:30–6 (7 in summer).*

Across the road is **San Juan de los Reyes,** a beautiful Gothic church begun by Ferdinand and Isabella in 1476. Wander around its fine cloisters and don't miss the iron manacles on the outer walls; they were placed there by Christians freed by the Moors. The Catholic kings originally intended to be buried here, but then their great triumph at Granada in 1492 changed their plans. *Admission: 60 ptas. Open 10–2 and 3:30–6 (7 in summer).*

Walk down the hill through the ancient **Cambrón Gate** and your visit of Toledo is over. Should you have more time, however, head for the **Museum of Santa Cruz,** just off the Zocodover, with its splendid El Grecos. *Admission: 200 ptas. Open Tues.–Sat. 10–6:30, Sun. 10–2.*

Also consider a visit to the **Hospital de Tavera,** outside the walls, where you can see Ribera's amazing *Bearded Woman. Admission: 150 ptas. Open 10:30–1:30 and 3:30–6.*

El Escorial In the foothills of the Guadarrama Mountains, 31 miles (50 kilometers) from Madrid, and 74 miles (120 kilometers) from Toledo, lies **San Lorenze de El Escorial,** burial place of Spanish kings and queens. The **monastery,** built by the religious fanatic Philip II as a memorial to his father, Charles V, is a vast rectangular edifice, conceived and executed with a monotonous magnificence worthy of the Spanish royal necropolis. It was designed by Juan de Herrera, Spain's greatest Renaissance architect. The **Royal Pantheon** contains the tombs of monarchs from Charles V to Alfonso XIII, grandfather of Juan Carlos, and those of their consorts. Only two kings are missing, Philip

V, who chose to be buried in his beloved La Granja, and Ferdinand VI in Madrid. In the **Pantheon of the Infantes** rest the 60 royal children who died in infancy, and those queens who bore no heirs. The lavishly bejewelled tomb here belongs to Don Juan, bastard son of Charles V and half-brother of Philip II, dashing hero and victor of the Battle of Lepanto. The monastery's other highlights are the magnificent **library** of Philip II with 40,000 rare volumes and 2,700 illuminated manuscripts, including the diary of Santa Teresa; and the **Royal Apartments.** Contrast the spartan private apartment of Philip II and the bare cell in which he chose to die, in 1598, with the beautiful carpets, porcelain, and tapestries with which his less austere successors embellished the rest of his somber monastery-palace. *Admission: 175 ptas. Open Tues.–Sun. 10–1 and 3:30–6:30 (3–6 in winter). Last entry is 45 mins. before closing time.*

The Valley of the Fallen Thirteen miles (8 kilometers) along the road to Segovia, the mighty cross of the **Valley of the Fallen** looms up on your left. This vast basilica hewn out of sheer granite was built by General Franco between 1940 and 1959 as a monument to the dead of Spain's Civil War of 1936–39. Buried here are 43,000 war dead, José Antonio Primo de Rivera, founder of the Falangists and early martyr of the war, and Franco himself, who died in 1975. *Admission for two: 200 ptas. Open daily 10–7 (6 in winter).*

A spectacular drive lies ahead, from the resort of Navacerrada 6,000 feet (1,830 meters) up through the Guadarrama Mountains by way of the **Navacerrada** pass. The steep descent through fragrant pine forests via the hairpin bends of the *Siete Revueltas* (Seven Curves) brings you straight into La Granja.

La Granja The **Palace of La Granja,** with its splendid formal gardens and fountains, was built 1719–39 by the homesick Philip V, first Bourbon king of Spain and grandson of France's Louis XIV, to remind him of his beloved Versailles. The whole place is like an exquisite piece of France in a Spanish wood, and it's small wonder that Philip chose to be buried here in the splendor of his own creation rather than in the austerity of the Escorial. The splendid gardens are open until dusk. *Admission: 300 ptas. Palace open Tues.–Sat. 10–1:30 and 3–5:30, Sun. 10–2:30; closed Mon. Fountains play on Thurs., weekend afternoons in summer (but check).*

Segovia A ten-minute drive and you arrive in the small golden-stone market town of **Segovia,** with its mighty, 2,000-year-old **Roman aqueduct,** held together without mortar. At its foot is a small bronze statue of Romulus and the wolf, presented by Rome in 1974 to commemorate the 2,000-year history of this Roman monument.

Drive or walk around the base of the rock on which Segovia stands. The Ronda de Santa Lucía leads to the most romantic view of the Alcázar, perched high on its rock like the prow of a mighty ship. Return via the Ctra de los Hoyos for yet another magical view, this time of the venerable cathedral rising from the ramparts. Climb the main shopping street, the **Calle Real,** and pass the Romanesque church of **San Martín,** with its porticoed outer gallery. Continue to the picturesque **Plaza Mayor** with its colorful ceramic stalls (good bargains) and pleasant cafés set against the backdrop of ancient arcaded houses and one of the loveliest (externally, at least) Gothic cathedrals in Spain. For refreshment, head down the nearby Calle Infanta Isabel, lined with numerous tapas bars and inexpensive cafés. It was on the steps of the church of **San Miguel**, in 1474, that Isabella was proclaimed Queen of Castile. The **cathedral** was the last Gothic cathedral to be built in Spain (the one in Avila was the first). Begun in 1525 by order of Charles V, its interior is sadly disappointing, as many of its treasures were carried off by Napoleon's troops in the Peninsular War of the early 1800s. Its museum has the first book printed in Spain (1472), and the tomb of Don Pedro, two-year-old son of Henry IV who slipped from his nurse's arms and tumbled to his death over the battlements of the Alcázar (his distraught nurse cast herself over after him). *Admission: 100 ptas. Open daily in summer, 9–7; in winter weekdays 9:30–1 and 3–6, weekends 9:30–6.*

The turreted **Alcázar** with its *esgrafiado* facade—an architectural peculiarity of Segovia whereby houses were embellished with small pieces of coke—is largely a fanciful re-creation of the 1880s, the original 13th-century castle having been destroyed by fire in 1862. The view from its ramparts—and, even better, from its tower if you can manage the 156 steps—is breathtaking. The Alcázar served as a major residence of the Catholic kings. Here Isabella met Ferdinand, and from here she set out to be crowned Queen of Castile. The interior successfully re-creates the time of this dual monarchy that established Spain's Golden Age. *Admission: 125 ptas. Open 10–6 in winter, 10–7 in summer.*

The **Palace of Riofrio,** 13 miles (8 kilometers) south of Segovia, off the road to San Rafael, was bought by Isabel Farnese, widow of Philip V, with the idea of turning it into a splendid dwelling along the lines of Madrid's Royal Palace. Her dream was never fulfilled and the palace, which houses a small **Hunting Museum,** is now of minor importance. Far more attractive is its surrounding parkland, where deer will come right up to your car. *Admission: 200 ptas. Palace open 10–1:30 and 3–5:30, Sun. 10–2:30; closed Tues.*

Avila   **Avila,** almost 4,000 feet (1,220 meters) above sea level, is the highest provincial capital in Spain. Alfonso VI and his son-in-law, Count Raimundo de Borgoña, rebuilt the town and **walls** in 1090, bringing it permanently under Christian control. It is these walls, the most complete military installations of their kind in Spain, that give Avila its special medieval quality. Thick and solid, with 88 towers, they stretch for 4 miles (2.5 kilometers) around the entire city, and make an ideal focus for the start of your visit.

The personality of Santa Teresa the Mystic, to whom the city is dedicated, lives today as vividly as it did in the 16th century. Several religious institutions associated with the life of the saint are open to visitors, the most popular of which is the **Convent of Santa Teresa,** which stands on the site of her birthplace. There's an ornate Baroque chapel, a small gift shop, and a museum with some of her relics: her rosary, books, walking stick, a sole of her sandal, and her finger wearing her wedding ring. *Free. Located at Plaza de la Santa, just inside the southern gate. Open 9–1:30 and 3:30–7.*

Avila's other ecclesiastical monuments are far older and more rewarding than those that commemorate the saint. The impregnable hulk of the **cathedral** is in many ways more akin to a fortress than a house of God. Though of Romanesque origin— the Romanesque sections are recognizable by their red and white brickwork—it is usually claimed as Spain's first Gothic cathedral. Inside, the ornate alabaster tomb of Cardinal Alonso de Madrigal, a 15th-century bishop whose swarthy complexion earned him the nickname of El Tostado ("toasted one"), is thought to be the work of Domenico Fancelli, who also sculpted the sepulchers of the Catholic kings in Granada's Royal Chapel. *Admission: 75 ptas. Open 10–1:30 and 3–6 (5 in winter), Sun. 11–5.*

The **Basilica of San Vicente,** just outside the walls, is one of Avila's finest Romanesque churches, standing on the spot where St. Vincent and his sisters Sabina and Cristeta were martyred in AD 306. Here, too, Santa Teresa is said to have experienced the vision that told her to reform the Carmelite order. *Admission: 35 ptas. Open 10–1 and 4–6; Sun. 10:30–2.*

Before continuing to the **Monastery of Santo Tomás,** our final stop, relax in the pleasant **Plaza de Santa Teresa** with its outdoor cafés and statue of the saint erected for Pope John Paul's visit in 1982. Built 1482–93 by Ferdinand and Isabella, who used it as a summer palace, it houses the tomb of their only son, Prince Juan—who died at the age of 19 while a student at Salamanca—as well as the tomb of that far less lovable character, the notorious Inquisitor General Tomás de Torquemada. *Admission: 50 ptas. for the cloisters that house the Museum of Oriental Art. Monastery free. Open 10:30–1 and 4–7.*

Salamanca   From Avila it's straight sailing all the way to Salamanca unless you're a devotee of Santa Teresa and choose to take a small detour to the old ducal town of **Alba de Tormes** to visit the **Carmelite Convent** (open 9–2 and 4–8) where the saint is buried. **Salamanca** is an ancient city, and your first glimpse of it is bound to be unforgettable. Beside the road flows the Tormes River and beyond it rise the old houses of the city, then the golden walls, turrets, and domes of the Plateresque cathedrals. Plateresque comes from *plata* (silver) and implies that the stone is chiseled and engraved as intricately as that delicate metal. A superb example of this style is the facade of the Dominican **Monastery of San Esteban** (50 ptas.; open 9–1 and 4–7), which you'll pass on your way to the cathedrals. The **old cathedral** far outshines its younger sister, the **new cathedral,** in beauty. (The new cathedral's funds ran out during construction—1513–1733—leaving a rather bare interior.) Inside the sturdy Romanesque walls of the old cathedral, built 1102–60, your attention will be drawn to Nicolás Florentino's stunning altarpiece with 53 brightly painted panels. Don't miss the splendid **cloisters** of the **Degree Chapel,** where anxious students sought inspiration on the night before their final exams. They now house a worthwhile collection of religious art. *New*

*cathedral free; old cathedral and cloisters 50 ptas. Open 10–1
and 3:30–6 in summer; 9:30–1:15 and 3:30–5:45 in winter.*

Founded by Alfonso IX in 1218, **Salamanca University** is to
Spain what Oxford is to England. On its famous Plateresque
doorway in the Patio de las Escuelas are carvings of Ferdinand
and Isabella and Charles V. The frog on Charles's skull was
said to bring good luck to students in their examinations. The
famous **Library** boasts some 50,000 parchment and leather-
bound volumes. *Admission: 100 ptas. Open 9–1:30 and 4–6,
Sat. 9:30–1:30 only, Sun. 11–1.*

Now make for Salamanca's greatest jewel, the elegant 18th-
century **Plaza Mayor.** Here you can browse in stores offering
typical *charro* jewelry (silver and black flowerheads), head
down the steps to the market in search of colorful tapas bars, or
simply relax in an outdoor café. In this, the city's crowning glory, and the most exquisite square in Spain, you've found the
perfect place to end your tour of Salamanca and Castile.

Dining and Lodging

For details and price category definitions, *see* Dining and
Lodging in Essential Information.

Note that for all restaurants listed below, dress is informal and
reservations unnecessary unless otherwise stated.

Avila
Dining
★
El Rastro. This ancient inn tucked into the city walls is Avila's
most atmospheric place to dine. Local specialties include
Avila's famous veal *(ternera)* and *yemas de Santa Teresa*, a
rather sickly dessert made from candied egg yolks. *Plaza del
Rastro 1, tel. 211219. AE, DC, MC, V. Moderate.*
El Torreón. Castilian specialties are served in this typical me-
són situated in the basement of the old Velada Palace, opposite
the cathedral. *Tostado 1, tel. 213171. AE, MC, V. Moderate.*

Lodging
Palacio de Valderrábanos. Avila's best hotel is located in a 15th-
century mansion opposite the cathedral. It was once the residence of the first bishop of Avila. Plaza *Catedral 9, tel. 211023.
73 rooms. AE, DC, MC, V. Expensive.*
Parador Raimundo de Borgoña. The location of this parador in a
15th-century palace just inside the northern walls of the city is
superb, but the service is not always equal to the setting. Its
dining room is atmospheric and serves local Avilan dishes, including the inevitable *yemas*, and the parador garden offers
the only access to the walls. *Marqués de Canales y Chozas 16,
tel. 211340. 62 rooms. AE, DC, MC, V. Expensive.*
Don Carmelo. This functional, modern, and comfortable hotel
close to the station is Avila's best moderate bet. *Paseo Don
Carmelo 30, tel. 228050. 60 rooms. V. Moderate.*

El Escorial
Dining
★
Charolés. This elegant restaurant has a terrace above the
street for summer dining. Its meat dishes are famous through-
out the region. Try the *Charolés a la pimienta* (pepper steak).
Fresh fish is brought in daily from Spain's north coast.
*Floridablanca 24, tel. 890–5975. Jacket and tie in winter. Res-
ervations essential most weekends. AE, DC, MC, V.
Expensive.*
Mesón de la Cueva. Founded in 1768, this atmospheric mesón

has several small, rustic dining rooms. The food is okay, but the place is a must for ambience. *San Antón 4, tel. 890–1516. Jacket and tie. Reservations advised on weekends. AE, DC, MC, V. Expensive to Moderate.*

El Candil. One of the best of the many middle-range restaurants in El Escorial, El Candil is situated above a bar on the corner of Plaza San Lorenzo on the village's main street. In summer you can dine outdoors in the square, a delightful spot. *Reina Victoria 12, tel. 896–0111. AE, DC, MC, V. Moderate.*

Lodging **Victoria Palace.** The rooms at the back of this grand Old World hotel close to the monastery have balconies and a splendid view toward Madrid; there's a garden and pool, too. *Juan de Toledo 4, tel. 890–1511. 89 rooms. AE, DC, MC, V. Expensive.*

Miranda Suizo. Rooms are comfortable in this charming old hotel on the main street, and the hotel café, with its dark wood fittings and marble tables, is right out of the 19th century. *Floridablanca 20, tel. 890–4711. 47 rooms. AE, DC, MC, V. Moderate.*

Salamanca **Chez Victor.** Salamanca's best restaurant ranks among the top
Dining in Spain. There's a distinctly French touch to the cuisine. *Espoz y Mina 26, tel. 213123. Dress: smart/casual. Reservations advised. Closed Sun. PM, Mon., and Aug. AE, V. Expensive.*

Nuevo Candil. The two Candil restaurants are a long-standing tradition in Salamanca, offering high standards of cuisine. This, the more formal of the two, is a restaurant only; its twin on Ruíz Aguilera 10 is also a colorful tapas bar. *Plaza de la Reina 2, tel. 215058. Dress: smart/casual. AE, DC, MC, V. Expensive but with a moderate set menu.*

El Mesón. There's plenty of colorful atmosphere and good traditional Castilian food in this typical mesón just off the Plaza Mayor, beside the Gran Hotel. *Plaza Poeta Iglesias 10, tel. 217222. AE, MC, V. Moderate.*

Río de la Plata. This small, atmospheric restaurant close to El Mesón and the Gran Hotel, serves superb *farinato* sausage; it's a great find. *Plaza del Peso 1, tel. 219005. No credit cards. Closed Mon., July. Moderate.*

Lodging **Monterrey.** A pleasant older hotel that offers the best accom-
★ modation in the center of town, the Monterrey was renovated a few years ago, and its El Fogón restaurant has a good reputation. *Azafranal 21, tel. 214400. 89 rooms. AE, DC, MC, V. Expensive.*

Parador. One of Spain's newest paradors stands across the river with superb views of the city's skyline. Its rooms are spacious and comfortable and there's a pool, but it's a bit far from the center. *Teso de la Feria 2, tel. 228700. 110 rooms. AE, DC, MC, V. Expensive.*

Castellano III. Overlooking the Alamedilla Park just a few minutes' walk from the center, this comfortable, modern hotel is considered the best medium-price hotel in town. *San Francisco Javier 2, tel. 251611. 73 rooms. MC, V. Moderate.*

Condal. A functional but comfortable hotel in a central location just off Calle Azafranal, two minutes from the Plaza Mayor. *Santa Eulalia 2, tel. 218400. 70 rooms. AE, DC, MC, V. Inexpensive.*

Segovia **Casa Duque.** Located at the end of the main shopping street,
Dining this restaurant has several floors of beautifully decorated traditional dining rooms and is the main rival to the famous

Cándido. There's plenty of local atmosphere, and the food is pure Castilian—try the *ponche segoviano* for dessert. *Cervantes 12, tel. 430537. Reservations advisable on weekends. AE, DC, V. Expensive to Moderate.*

★ **Mesón de Candido.** Segovia's most prestigious restaurant has seven dining rooms pulsating with atmosphere and decorated with bullfighting memorabilia and photos of the dignitaries who have dined here over the years. Specialties are *cochinillo* (suckling pig) and *cordero asado* (roast lamb). *Plaza Azoguejo 5, tel. 428102. Reservations advised for Sun. lunch. AE, DC, MC, V. Expensive to Moderate.*

César. This agreeable restaurant near the aqueduct specializes in fish dishes and fresh vegetables—a refreshing change in this mecca of traditional Castilian roasts. *Ruíz de Alda 10, tel. 428101. AE, DC. Closed Wed., Nov. Moderate.*

La Oficina. Traditional Castilian dishes are served in two delightful dining rooms that date back to 1893. It's just off Plaza Mayor. *Cronista Lecea 10, tel. 431643. AE, DC, MC, V. Moderate.*

Lodging **Los Linajes.** The advantages of this pleasant, modern hotel, built in Castilian style, are its central location and its superb views. *Dr. Velasco 9, tel. 431201. 55 rooms. AE, DC, MC, V. Expensive.*

★ **Parador.** To the north of town is this modern parador offering comfortable, spacious rooms and a pool. The views of the city, especially when illuminated, are magnificent. *Off the N601 toward Valladolid, tel. 430362. 80 rooms. AE, DC, MC, V. Expensive.*

Acueducto. Ask for a room at the front in this comfortable older hotel with balconies overlooking the famous aqueduct. Well renovated, it's Segovia's best medium-range bet. *Padre Claret 10, tel. 424800. 73 rooms. AE, DC, MC, V. Moderate.*

Toledo **Hostal del Cardenal.** Toledo's best restaurant is set in the 17th-
Dining century palace of Cardinal Lorenzana, up against the city ram-
★ parts, and boasts five dining rooms and a delightful garden for summer dining. Both food and service are excellent (try the roast suckling pig). *Paseo Recaredo 24, tel. 220862. Dress: casually smart. Reservations advised in high season. AE, DC, V. Expensive to Moderate.*

Asador Adolfo. This restaurant is situated near the cathedral and is well known for its good food (try the superb roast meat) and service. *La Granada 6, tel. 227321. AE, DC, MC, V. Moderate.*

La Bótica. Enjoy your aperitif in a café on the main square, then make for this stylish French restaurant nearby. *Plaza Zocodover 13, tel. 225557. AE, DC, V. Moderate.*

Casa Aurelio. There are two branches of this popular restaurant, both around the corner from the cathedral. Try the partridge or quail. *Sinagoga 6, tel. 222097, and Sinagoga 1, tel. 221392. AE, DC, MC, V. Closed Wed. Moderate.*

Los Cuatro Tiempos. The picturesque downstairs bar, decorated with ceramic tiles, is an ideal place for a *fino* and tapas before you head upstairs for a traditional Toledo meal. *Sixto Ramon Parro 7, tel. 223782. MC, V. Moderate to Inexpensive.*

Los Arcos. Located off Toledo de Ohio, this attractive modern restaurant offers good value *menus del día* as well as inexpensive main courses such as roast partridge, and is fast gaining in popularity. *Cordonerías 11, tel. 210051. AE, DC, MC, V. Inexpensive.*

Lodging
★

Parador Conde de Orgaz. This is one of Spain's most popular paradors, and the best and most expensive hotel in Toledo (a 15-minute drive from city center). It's a modern parador built in traditional Toledo style and stands on a hill across the river, commanding magnificent views of the city. Book far ahead. *Paseo de los Cigarrales, tel. 221850. 57 rooms, pool. AE, DC, MC, V. Expensive.*

María Cristina. You'll pass this comfortable new hotel on your way from Madrid. Located beside the bullring, it opened in 1986 and provides excellent facilities. Its El Abside restaurant is fast gaining in prestige. *Marqués de Mendigorría 1, tel. 213204. 43 rooms. AE, V. Expensive to Moderate.*

Alfonso VI. This pleasant modern hotel has Castilian-style decor and is conveniently located in the center of town by the Alcázar. *Gen. Moscardó 2, tel. 222600. 80 rooms. AE, DC, MC, V. Moderate.*

Maravilla. This simple but charming Old World hotel just off Plaza Zocodover has a good, old-fashioned restaurant. *Barrio Rey 7, tel. 223304. 18 rooms. AE, DC, MC, V. Inexpensive.*

Barcelona

Barcelona, capital of Catalonia, and Spain's second-largest city, thrives on its business acumen and industrial muscle. Its fashion industry is fast rivaling those of Paris and Milan. Its hardworking citizens are enormously proud of their Generalitat, their home-rule parliament, and almost militant in their use of their own language—with street names, museum displays, newspapers, radio programs, and movies all in Catalan. Their latest cause for rejoicing is the achievement of their long-cherished goal to host the Olympic Games, and the city is currently in the throes of a massive building program in eager anticipation of the big event of 1992.

Barcelona also boasts an active cultural life. This is, after all, the city of Gaudí and Miró, and the place where Pablo Picasso spent his formative years.

This thriving metropolis also has a rich history and an abundance of sights. Few places can rival the narrow alleys of its Gothic Quarter for medieval atmosphere, or the elegance and distinction of its Modernista Eixample. The fantasies of Gaudí's whimsical imagination have a lure that is unique, and the museums of Montjuïc and the Picasso collection are irresistible attractions.

Arriving and Departing

By Plane
All international and domestic flights arrive at El Prat de Llobregat airport, 8½ miles (14 kilometers) south of Barcelona just off the main highway to Castelldefels and Sitges. For information on arrival and departure times, call the Iberia airport (tel. 370–1011) or Iberia information (tel. 325–4304).

Between the Airport and Downtown
The airport-city train leaves every 20 minutes between 6:30 AM and 11:10 PM and reaches the Barcelona Central (Sants) Station in 15 minutes. Taxis will then take you to your hotel. RENFE provides a bus service to the Central Station during the night hours. A cab from the airport to your hotel, including airport and luggage surcharges, will cost about 1,500 ptas.

By Train The main railroad station is **Barcelona Central** (or Sants) on the Plaça Països Catalans (tel. 322–4141). Almost all long-distance trains arrive and depart from here. **Terminal Station** (tel. 319–3200), on Avenida Marquès d'Argentera, near the port, at present is the arrival point for trains from France, but it is due to be demolished to make way for the 1992 Olympic Village and may well be closed by 1989.

An underground train runs across the city from Terminal to Central. For information, call RENFE at 310–7200.

By Bus Barcelona has no central bus station, but most buses to Spanish destinations operate from the old **Estació Vilanova** (or Norte) at the end of Avenida Vilanova.

Getting Around

Modern Barcelona above the Plaça de Catalunya is mostly built on a grid system, though there's no helpful numbering system as in the USA. The Old Town from the Plaça de Catalunya to the port is a warren of narrow streets, however, and you'll need a good street map to get around. Most sightseeing can be done on foot—you won't have any other choice in the Gothic Quarter—but you'll need to use the metro or buses to link sightseeing areas. If you're using an old map, you'll find that all the street names are now written in Catalan.

By Metro The subway is the fastest and cheapest way of getting around, as well as the easiest to use. You pay a flat fare of about 60 ptas., no matter how far you travel, or purchase a *targeta multiviatge*, good for 10 rides.

By Bus City buses run from about 5:30 or 6 AM to 10:30 PM, though some stop earlier. Fares are about 70 ptas. Plans of the routes followed are displayed at bus stops. A reduced-rate *targeta multiviatge* is good for 10 rides.

By Taxi Taxis are black and yellow, and when available for hire show a "Libre" sign in the daytime and a green light at night. The meter starts at about 90 ptas., and there are small supplements for luggage, night travel (10 PM–6 AM), Sundays and fiestas, rides from a station or the port, and for going to or from the bullring or a soccer match. The supplement to the airport is about 200 ptas. There are cab stands all over town; cabs may also be flagged down on the street. Make sure the driver puts on his meter.

By Cable Car and Funicular Montjuïc Funicular is a cog railroad that runs from the junction of Avenida Paral-lel and Nou de la Rambla to the Miramar Amusement Park on Montjuïc. It is open daily from 9:30 AM to 9:30 PM. A cable car *(teleferic)* then runs from the amusement park up to Montjuïc Castle; same hours.

A *Transbordador Aeri* Harbor Cable Car runs from Miramar on Montjuïc across the harbor to the Torre de Jaume I on Barcelona *moll* (jetty), and on to the Torre de Sant Sebastià at the end of Passeig Nacional in Barceloneta. You can board at either stage. The cable car runs from 11:30 AM to 9:30 PM in summer, and only on Sunday in winter.

To reach Tibidabo summit, take the metro to Avenida Tibidabo, then the *tramvía blau* (blue tram) to Peu del Funicular, and the Tibidabo Funicular from there to the Tibidabo

Fairground. It runs from 6:50 AM to 8:40 PM, shorter hours in winter.

By Boat **Golondrinas** harbor boats operate short harbor trips from the Porta de la Pau near the Columbus Monument between 9 AM and 9:30 PM in summer, and on Sundays in winter.

Important Addresses and Numbers

Tourist Information Tourist offices are located at the **airport; Central Station**, tel. 250–2594; **Terminal Station**, tel. 319–2791, **Gran Vía Corts Catalanes 658**, tel. 301–7443; the **Columbus Monument** in Plaça Porta de la Pau at the bottom of Ramblas, tel. 302–5234; and in the **Ajuntament** in Plaça Sant Jaume, tel. 318–2525.

American Visitors' Bureau, Gran Vía 591 between Rambla de Catalunya and Balmes, 3rd floor; tel. 301–0150/0032.

Consulates U.S.: Vía Laietana 33, tel. 319–9550; **Canadian:** Vía Augusta 125, tel. 209–0634; U.K.: Diagonal 477, tel. 322–2151.

Emergencies **Police:** National police, tel. 091; municipal police, tel. 092; main police station, Vía Laietana 43, tel. 301–6666. **Ambulance:** tel. 300–0422. **Doctor:** Hospital Clínic, Casanova 143, tel. 323–1414; Hospital Evangélico, Alegre de Dalt 87, tel. 219–7100.

English Bookstores The **Corte Inglés** (Plaça Catalunya) sells a few English guidebooks and novels. Also try **Laie** (Pau Claris 85, tel. 318–1739) or **Librería Francesa** (Passeig de Gràcia 91).

Travel Agencies **American Express,** Rosselló 257, on the corner of Passeig de Gràcia, tel. 218–6664; **Wagons-Lits/Cooks,** Passeig de Gràcia 8, tel. 317–5500.

Guided Tours

Orientation Tours City sightseeing tours are run by **Juliá Tours,** Ronda Universitat 5 (tel. 317–6454) and **Pullmantur,** Gran Vía Corts Catalanes 635 (tel. 318–0241). Tours leave from the above terminals, though it may be possible to be picked up at your hotel. Both operators run similar tours at the same price, and there's little to help you choose between them. Other tours offered are "Panorámica y Toros," a visit to a bullfight and a panoramic city drive; and "Night Tours," which may include city illuminations, flamenco shows, dinner, and cabaret.

Special-Interest and Walking Tours Consult any tourist office for details. Serious Gaudí enthusiasts should contact **Friends of Gaudí,** (Avenida Pedralbes 7, tel. 204–5250 well ahead of their visit.

Excursions These are run by **Juliá Tours** and **Pullmantur** and are booked as above. Principal trips are either a full- or half-day tour to **Montserrat** to visit the monastery and shrine of the famous Black Virgin; a full-day trip to the **Costa Brava** resorts, including a boat cruise to Lloret de Mar; and a full-day trip to **Andorra** for tax-free shopping. In high season excursions may also run to the seaside resort of **Sitges,** to **Tarragona** to see the famous Roman aqueduct, and, at grape harvest time, to the wine towns of the **Penedés** region.

Personal Guides Ask at any tourist office, or contact the Barcelona Tourist Guide Association (tel. 255–1355).

Exploring Barcelona

It should take you two full days of sightseeing to complete the following tour. The first part covers the Gothic Quarter, the Picasso Museum, and the Ramblas. The second part takes you to Passeig de Gràcia, the Sagrada Familia, and Montjuïc.

1 Start on Plaça de la Seu, where on Sunday morning the citizens of Barcelona gather to dance the *Sardana*, a symbol of Catalan pride. Step inside the magnificent Gothic **Cathedral** built 1298–1450 (the spire and neo-Gothic facade were added in 1892). Highlights are the beautifully carved choir stalls, Santa Eulalia's tomb in the crypt, the battle-scarred crucifix in the Lepanto Chapel, and the **cloisters**. *Open 7:30–1:30 and 4–7:30.*

2 Around the corner at Comtes de Barcelona 10 is the **Museo Frederic Marès**, where you can browse for hours among the miscellany of sculptor-collector Frederic Marès. On display is everything from polychrome crucifixes to hat pins, pipes, and walking sticks. *Admission: 85 ptas. Open Tues.–Sat. 9–2 and 4–7, Sun. 9–2; closed Mon.*

3 The neighboring **Plaça del Rei** embodies the very essence of the Gothic Quarter. Legend has it that after Columbus's first voyage to America, the Catholic kings received him in the **Saló de Tinell,** a magnificent banqueting hall built in 1362. Other ancient buildings around the square are the **Lieutenant's Palace;** the 14th-century **Chapel** of St. **Agatha** built right into the Roman city wall; and the **Padellás Palace,** which houses the City History Museum.

4 Cross Vía Laietana, walk down Princesa, and turn right into Montcada, where you come to one of Barcelona's most popular attractions, the **Picasso Museum.** Two 15th-century palaces provide a lovely setting for the collections donated in 1963 and 1970, first by Picasso's secretary, then by the artist himself. The collection ranges from early childhood sketches done in Málaga to exhibition posters done in Paris shortly before his death. Of particular interest are pictures from his Blue Period. *Admission: 190 ptas. Open Tues.–Sat. 9:30–1:30 and 4–8:30, Sun. 9:30–1:30, Mon. 4–8:30.*

Time Out At the bottom of Montcada, on the left, is **La Pizza Nostra** (Arc de Sant Vicens 2, tel. 319–9058), an ideal spot for a cup of coffee, a slice of cheesecake, or a pizza and a glass of wine.

5 **Santa María del Mar** is one of the loveliest Gothic churches in Barcelona. It was built 1329–83 in fulfillment of a vow made a century earlier by Jaume I to build a church for the Virgin of the Sailors. Its simple beauty is enhanced by a lovely rose window and magnificent soaring columns. *Open 8–1 and 4–7:30.*

6 **Plaça Sant Jaume** is a lovely square built in the 1840s in the heart of the Gothic Quarter. The two imposing buildings facing each other across the square are very much older. The 15th-century **Ajuntament,** or City Hall, has an impressive black and gold mural (1928) by Josep María Sert (who also painted the murals for New York's Waldorf Astoria), and the famous **Saló de Cent** from where the Council of One Hundred ruled the city from 1372 to 1714. The **Palau de la Generalitat,** seat of the Catalan Regional Government, is a 15th-century palace open to the public on Sunday morning.

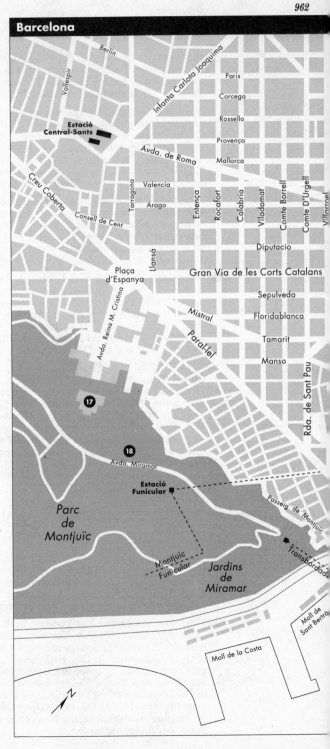

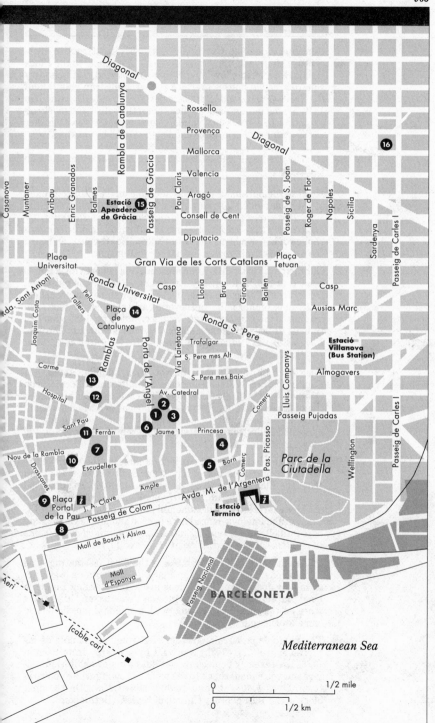

Diagonal

Rossello

Provença

Diagonal

Mallorca

Valencia

Pau Claris

Aragó

Consell de Cent

Diputacio

Rambla de Catalunya

Passeig de Gràcia

Estació Apeadero de Gràcia **15**

Casanova

Muntaner

Aribau

Enric Granados

Balmes

Passeig de S. Joan

Roger de Flor

Napoles

Sicilia

Sardenya

Passeig de Carles I

16

Plaça Universitat

Gran Via de les Corts Catalans

Plaça Tetuan

Ronda Universitat

Casp

Lloria

Bruc

Girona

Bailen

Casp

Ausias Marc

Rda. Sant Antoni

Joaquim Costa

Pelai

Tallers

Plaça de Catalunya **14**

Porta de l'Angel

Ramblas

Ronda S. Pere

Trafalgar

Via Laietana

S. Pere mes Alt

S. Pere mes Baix

Lluis Companys

Estació Villanova (Bus Station)

Almogavers

Carme

Hospital

Sant Pau

13

12

Av. Catedral

2

1 **3**

6 Jaume 1

Comerç

Passeig Pujadas

Passeig de Carles I

Ferràn **11**

7

Princesa

4

Pas. Picasso

Parc de la Ciutadella

Wellington

Nou de la Rambla

10

Escudellers

5 Born

Comerç

Drassanes

Ample

9 Plaça Portal de la Pau

i

J. A. Clavé

Avda. M. de l'Argentera

Estació Termino

i

Passeig de Colom

8

Moll de Bosch i Alsina

Aeri

(cable car)

Moll d'Espanya

Passeig Nacional

BARCELONETA

Mediterranean Sea

0   1/2 mile

0   1/2 km

Time Out Among the best lunch spots in this area are **Agut d'Avignon, La Cuineta,** and **Tinell.**

7 Continue along the Carrer Ferrán, with its attractive 19th-century shops and numerous Modernista touches, to the **Plaça Reial.** Here in this lovely, if rather dilapidated, 19th-century square arcaded houses overlook the wrought-iron **Fountain of the Three Graces,** and lampposts designed by a young Gaudí in 1879. Watch out for drug pushers here; the safest and most colorful time to come is on a Sunday morning when crowds gather at the stamp and coin stalls and listen to soap box orators.

Time Out Nearby are two excellent restaurants, **Los Caracoles** and **Can Culleretes.**

8 Head to the bottom of Ramblas and take an elevator to the top of the **Columbus Monument** for a breathtaking view over the city. *The monument is open Mon.–Sat. 9:30–1:30 and 4:30–8:30, Sun. 11:30–7:30.* Columbus faces out to sea, overlooking a replica of his own boat, the **Santa María.** Nearby you can board the cable car that crosses the harbor to Montjuïc.

9 Our next stop is the **Maritime Museum** (Plaça Porta de la Pau 1) housed in the 13th-century Atarazanas Reales, the old Royal Dockyards. The museum is packed with ships, figureheads, nautical paraphernalia, and several early navigation charts, including a map by Amerigo Vespucci, and the 1439 chart of Gabriel de Valseca from Mallorca, the oldest chart in Europe. *Admission: 150 ptas. Open Tues.–Sat. 10–2 and 5–7, Sun. 10–1; closed Mon.*

10 Turn back up the Ramblas to Nou de la Rambla. At no. 3 is Gaudí's **Palau Güell,** which houses the **Museum of Scenic Arts.** Gaudí built this mansion between 1885 and 1890 for his patron Count Eusebi de Güell, and it's the only one of his houses readily open to the public. It makes an intriguing setting for the museum's collection of theatrical memorabilia. *Admission: 100 ptas. Open Mon.–Sat. 11–1 and 5–8.*

11 Back to the Ramblas and our next landmark, the **Gran Teatre del Liceu,** on the corner of Sant Pau. Built between 1845 and 1847, the Liceu claims to be the world's oldest opera house and is the only one in Spain. A fairly mundane facade conceals an exquisite interior with ornamental gilt and plush red velvet fittings. Anna Pavlova danced here in 1930 and Maria Callas sang here in 1959. *Admission: 100 ptas. Open for guided visits (some in English) Mon., Wed., Fri. at 11:30 and 12:15.*

12 This next stretch of the **Ramblas** is the most fascinating. The colorful paving stones on the Plaça de la Boquería were designed by Joan Miró. Take a look inside the bustling **Boquería Food Market** and at the **Casa Antigua Figueras,** an old grocery store on the corner of Petxina, with a splendid mosaic facade and exquisite old fittings.

13 The **Palau de la Virreina** (corner of Carme and Rambla de las Flores 99, tel. 301–7775) was built by a viceroy from Peru in 1778. It's recently been converted into a major exhibition center, and you should check to see what's showing while you're in town. *Open 9:30–1:30 and 4:30–9; closed Mon.* On the next block is the 18th-century **Church of Betlem** (Bethlehem).

The final stretch of the Ramblas brings us out onto the busy **Plaça de Catalunya,** the frantic business center and transport hub of the modern city. The first stage of the tour ends here. You may want to head for the *Corte Inglés* department store across the square or for any of the stores on the nearby **Porta de l'Angel.** Alternatively, you can relax on the terrace of the ancient **Café Zurich** on the corner of Pelai, or stop at the colorful beer hall, the **Cervecería,** opposite the Hostal Continental.

Above the Plaça de Catalunya you come into modern Barcelona and an elegant area known as the **Eixample,** which was laid out in the late 19th century as part of the city's expansion scheme. Much of the building here was done at the height of the **Modernista** movement, a Spanish and mainly Barcelonian offshoot of Art Nouveau, whose leading exponents were the architects Antoní Gaudí, Domènech i Montaner, and Puig i Cadafalch. The principal thoroughfares of the Eixample are the Rambla de Catalunya and the Passeig de Gràcia, where some of the city's most elegant shops and cafés are found. Modernista houses are one of Barcelona's special drawing cards, so walk up **Passeig de Gràcia** until you come to the **Manzana de la Discordía,** or Block of Discord, between Consell de Cent and Aragó. Its name is a pun on the word *manzana,* which means both *block* and *apple.* The houses here are quite fantastic: The floral **Casa Lleó Morera** at no. 35 is by Domènech i Montaner. The pseudo-Gothic **Casa Amatller** at no. 41 is by Puig i Cadafalch. At no. 43 is Gaudí's **Casa Batlló.** Farther along the street on the right, on the corner of Provença, is Gaudí's **Casa Milà,** more often known as **La Pedrera.** Its remarkable curving stone facade with ornamental balconies actually ripples its way around the corner of the block.

Time Out You can ponder the vagaries of Gaudí's work over a drink in **Amarcord,** a terrace café in the Pedrera building. If you're feeling a bit homesick, sip a cocktail or munch a deep-pan pizza in the **Chicago Pizza Pie Factory** at Provença 300. For a more sedate, Old World tearoom, head for the **Salón de Te Mauri** on the corner of Rambla de Catalunya and Provença.

Now take the metro at Diagonal directly to Barcelona's most eccentric landmark, Gaudí's **Church of the Sagrada Familia** (Holy Family). Unfinished at his untimely death—the absent-minded Gaudí was run over by a tram and died in a pauper's hospital in 1926—this striking creation will cause consternation or wonder, shrieks of protest or cries of rapture. During the Civil War in 1936 the citizens of Barcelona loved their crazy temple enough to spare it from the flames that engulfed all their other churches (except the cathedral). An elevator takes visitors to the top of one of the towers for a magnificent view of the city. Gaudí is buried in the crypt. *Admission: 200 ptas. Open 9–6 in winter, 8–8 in summer.*

Montjuïc, a hill to the south of town, was named for the Jewish community that once lived on its slopes. The hill is home to a castle, an amusement park, several delightful gardens, a model Spanish village, the recently rebuilt Mies van der Rohe Pavilion, and a cluster of museums—all of which could keep you busy for a day or more.

One of the leading attractions here is the **Museum of Catalan**

Art in the Palau Nacional atop a long flight of steps. The collection of Romanesque and Gothic art treasures—medieval frescoes and altarpieces, mostly from small churches and chapels in the Pyrenees—is simply staggering. *Admission: 200 ptas; free on Sun. Open 9–2; closed Mon.* The **Ceramics Museum** is in the same building (same hours and ticket).

⑱ Nearby is the **Miró Foundation,** a gift from the artist Joan Miró to his native city. One of Barcelona's most exciting contemporary galleries, it has several exhibition areas, many of them devoted to Miró's works. Miró himself now rests in the cemetery on the southern slopes of *Montjuïc. Admission: 250 ptas. Open Tues.–Sat. 11–8, Sun. 11–2:30; closed Mon.*

It's time now to sail across the harbor on the cable car and indulge in a hearty meal in one of the many restaurants on the Passeig Nacional, in the old fishermen's quarter of Barceloneta.

What to See and Do with Children

Take the children to the **Zoo** (open 9:30–7:30) to visit the world's only captive albino gorilla. They'll also enjoy exploring the replica of Columbus's flagship, the **Santa María,** or going for a trip across the harbor in one of the Golondrinas boats. Ride the **Cable Car** across the harbor to the **Amusement Park** on Montjuïc. Visit the **Poble Espanyol** (the model village), also on Montjuïc. Take them to see the **Illuminated Fountains** at Montjuïc's Avenida Reina María Cristina on weekend evenings (also Thurs. in summer). They'll enjoy riding the old *tramvía blau* (tram) and then the **funicular** up to the **Fun Fair** atop Mount Tibidabo. Above all, don't miss the fairy-tale extravaganza of the **Parc Güell;** it's a popular playground for Barcelona's children, especially on Sunday afternoon.

Off the Beaten Track

If you're hooked on **Modernista** architecture, you can follow a walking trail around the **Dreta de l'Eixample.** Ask at a tourist office for a Gaudí or Modernismo trail brochure for the Eixample. Attend a concert at Domènech i Montaner's fantastic **Palau de la Música.** Make a trip to the **Parc Güell,** Gaudí's magical but uncompleted attempt at creating a garden city. *Open daily 8:30–7:30. Metro: Lesseps. Buses: 10, 24, or 31.*

Explore the **Major de Gràcia** area, above the Diagonal. It's a small, almost independent village within a large city, a warren of narrow streets, changing name at every corner, and filled with tiny shops where you'll find everything from old-fashioned tin lanterns to feather dusters.

Take a stroll around **Barceloneta,** the old fishermen's quarter built in 1755 below Terminal Station and the Ciutadela Park. Along its narrow streets are atmospheric taverns (try C. Maquinista). There are no-frills fish restaurants on the Passeig Nacional and beach restaurants along the Passeig Marítim that are well known to locals and worth experiencing.

Hunt out the tiny **Shoe Museum** in Plaça Sant Felip Neri, in a hidden corner of the Gothic Quarter, between the cathedral and Bishop's Palace. The collection includes clowns' shoes and a pair worn by Pablo Casals. *Admission: 10 ptas. Open weekends 11–4.*

Shopping

Gift Ideas There are no special handicrafts associated with Barcelona, but you'll have no trouble finding typical Spanish goods anywhere in town. If you're into fashion and jewelry, then you've come to the right place, as Barcelona makes all the headlines on Spain's booming fashion front. Silver *Xavier Roca i Coll*, Sant Pere mes Baix 24, just off Laietana, specializes in silver models of Barcelona's buildings.

Antiques Carrer de la Palla and Banys Nous in the Gothic Quarter are lined with antiques shops where you'll find old maps, books, paintings, and furniture. An antiques market is held every Thursday morning in Plaça Nova in front of the cathedral. The **Centre d'Antiquaris,** Passeig de Gràcia 57, has some 75 antiques stores. **Gothsland,** Consell de Cent 331, specializes in Modernista designs.

Boutiques The most fashionable boutiques are in the *Gallerías* on Passeig de Gràcia and Rambla de Catalunya. Others are on Gran Vía between Balmes and Pau Claris; and on the Diagonal between Ganduxer and Passeig de Gràcia. **Adolfo Domínguez,** Spain's top designer, is at Passeig de Gràcia 89 and Valencia 245; *Loewe,* Spain's top leather store, is at Passeig de Gràcia 35 and Diagonal 570; *Joaquín Berao,* a top jewelry designer, is at Roselló 277.

Shopping Districts Elegant shopping districts are the Passeig de Gràcia, Rambla de Catalunya, and the Diagonal. For more affordable, more old-fashioned and typically Spanish-style shops, explore the area between Ramblas and Vía Laietana, especially around C. Ferran. The area around Plaça del Pi from Boquería to Portaferrisa and Canuda is recommended for young fashion stores and imaginative gift shops.

Department Stores **El Corte Inglés** is on the Plaça de Catalunya 14 (tel. 302–1212). **Diagonal 617** (tel. 259–1449) is near María Cristina metro. Both are open Monday to Saturday 10–8.

Food and Flea Markets The **Boquería** or **Sant Josep Market** on the Ramblas between Carme and Hospital is a superb, colorful food market, held every day except Sunday. **Els Encants,** Barcelona's fascinating Flea Market, is held every Monday, Wednesday, Friday, and Saturday at the end of Dos de Maig on the Plaça Glòries Catalanes. **Sant Antoní Market,** at the end of Ronda Sant Antoní, is an old-fashioned food and clothes market, best on Sunday when there's a secondhand **Book Market** with old postcards, press cuttings, lithographs, and prints. There's a **Stamp and Coin Market** in the Plaça Reial on Sunday morning, and an **Artists' Market** in the Placeta del Pi just off Ramblas and Boquería on Saturday morning.

Bullfighting

Barcelona has two bullrings, the **Arènes Monumental** on Gran Vía and Carles I, and the smaller **Arènes las Arenas** on the Plaça d'Espanya. Bullfights are held on Sunday between March and October; check the newspaper for details. The official ticket office, where there is no markup on tickets, is at Muntaner 24 (tel. 253–3821) near Gran Vía. There's a **Bullfighting Museum** at the Monumental ring, open daily 10–1 and 5:30–7.

Bars and Cafés

Cafés and Tearooms **Zurich,** Plaça Catalunya 35, on the corner of Pelai, is one of the oldest and most traditional cafés, perfect for watching the world go by. **The Croissant Show,** Santa Anna 10 just off Ramblas, is a small coffee and pastry shop, ideal for a quick mid-morning or afternoon break. **Salon de Te Mauri,** on the corner of Rambla de Catalunya and Provença, and **Salon de Te Llibre i Serra,** Ronda Sant Pere 3, are both traditional tearooms with a good selection of pastries.

Tapas Bars You'll find these all over town, but two of the most colorful are **Alt Heidelberg,** Ronda Universitat 5, with German beer on tap and German sausages; and the **Cervecería** at the top of Ramblas, opposite the Hostal Continental.

Cocktail Bars These places are both popular and plentiful everywhere, but the two best areas are the **Passeig del Born,** which is near the Picasso Museum and very fashionable with the affluent young; and the **Eixample,** near Passeig de Gràcia. A bar called **Dry Martini,** at Aribau 162, has more than 80 different gins; **Ideal Cocktail Bar,** on Aribau 89, has some good malt whiskeys. **El Paraigua,** on Plaça Sant Miquel, in the Gothic Quarter behind the city hall, serves cocktails in a stylish setting with classical music.

Champagne Bars *Xampanyerías,* serving sparkling Catalan *cava,* are popular all over town and are something of a Barcelona specialty. Try **Brut,** Trompetas 3, in the Picasso Museum area; **La Cava del Palau,** Verdaguer i Callis 10, near the Palau de la Música; **La Folie,** Bailen 169, one of the best; or **La Xampanyería,** Provença 236, on the corner of Enric Granados.

Special Cafés **Els Quatre Gats,** Montsió 5, off Porta de l'Angel, is a reconstruction of the original café that opened in 1897, and a real Barcelona institution. Literary discussions, jazz, and classical music recitals take place in this café where Picasso held his first show, Albéniz and Granados played their piano compositions, and Ramón Casas painted two of its original murals. **Pastis,** Santa Mónica 4, just off Ramblas, above the Columbus Monument, is a nostalgic turn-of-the-century café with French ambience.

Dining

For details and price category definitions, *see* Dining in Essential Information.

Very Expensive **El Dorado Petit.** In 1984 Luis Cruañas moved to Barcelona from
★ the Costa Brava and opened this restaurant, which rapidly became known as the best in Barcelona and one of the top restaurants in Spain. The setting—a private villa with a delightful garden for summer dining—is simply beautiful, and so is the cuisine. *Dolors Monserdá 51, tel. 204–5153. Jacket and tie. Reservations essential. AE, MC, V. Closed Sun. and two weeks in Aug.*

Expensive **Agut d'Avignon.** This venerable Barcelona institution takes a bit of finding; ask for directions in the Gothic Quarter. The ambience is rustic and it's a favorite with businesspeople and politicians from over the road in the Generalitat. The cuisine is traditional Catalan and game specialties are recommended in season. *Trinidad 3, tel. 302–6034. Dress: formal. Reservations essential. AE, DC, MC, V. Closed Sun., Holy Week.*

Azulete. This is one of Barcelona's most beautiful restaurants —its dining room an old conservatory filled with flowers and plants. The highly imaginative cuisine is a mixture of Catalan, French, and Italian with an interesting blend of traditional and new dishes. *Vía Augusta 281, tel. 203–5943. Jacket and tie. Reservations essential. AE, DC, MC, V. Closed Sat. lunch, Sun., and first two weeks of Aug.*

La Cuineta. This small intimate restaurant in a 17th-century house just off Plaça Sant Jaume specializes in Catalan *nouvelle cuisine.* The decor is smart but charming, the service professional; and it's popular with businesspeople at lunchtime. *Paradis 4, tel. 315–0111. Dress: stylishly casual. Reservations not essential. AE, DC, MC, V. Closed Mon.*

Quo Vadis. Located just off the Ramblas, near the Boquería Market and Betlem Church, is an unimpressive facade camouflaging one of Barcelona's most respected restaurants. Its much-praised cuisine includes delicacies like *pot pourri de setas* (mushrooms), *lubina al hinojo* (sea bass in fennel) and *hígado de ganso con ciruelas* (goose liver with cherries). *Carme 7, tel. 317–7447. Dress: stylishly casual. Reservations advised. AE, DC, MC, V. Closed Sun.*

Moderate **Can Culleretes.** This picturesque old restaurant began life as a pastry shop in 1786, and it is one of the most atmospheric and reasonable finds in Barcelona. Located on an alleyway between Ferran and Boquería, its three dining rooms are decorated with photos of visiting celebrities. It serves real Catalan cooking and is very much a family concern; don't be put off by the prostitutes outside! *Quintana 5, tel. 317–6485. Dress: informal. Reservations not necessary. No credit cards. Closed Sun. PM and Mon.*

★ **Los Caracoles.** Just below the Plaça Reial is Barcelona's most famous restaurant, which caters to tourists but has real atmosphere. Its walls are hung thick with photos of bullfighters and visiting celebrities; its specialties are mussels, paella and, of course, snails *(caracoles).* Don't miss it, it's fun. *Escudellers 14, tel. 301–2041. Dress: informal. Reservations not essential. AE, DC, MC, V.*

Sete Portes. With plenty of Old World charm, this delightful restaurant near the waterfront has been going strong since 1836. The cooking is Catalan, the portions enormous, and specialties are *paella de pescado* and *zarzuela sete portes* (seafood casserole). *Passeig Isabel II 14, tel. 319–3033. Dress: informal. Reservations advisable at weekends. AE, DC, MC, V. Open 1 PM–1 AM.*

★ **Sopeta Una.** Dining in this delightful small restaurant with old-fashioned decor and intimate atmosphere is more like eating in a private home. The menu is in Catalan, all the dishes are Catalan, and the atmosphere is very genteel and middle class. For dessert, try the traditional Catalan *música*—a plate of raisins, almonds, and dried fruit served with a glass of muscatel. It's near the Palau de la Música; don't be put off by the narrow street. *Verdaguer i Callis 6, tel. 319–6131. Dress: informal. Reservations not essential. V. Closed Sun., and Mon. AM.*

Inexpensive **Agut.** Simple, hearty Catalan fare awaits you in this unpreten-
★ tious restaurant in the lower reaches of the Gothic Quarter.
Founded in 1924, its popularity has never waned. There's plenty of wine to wash down the traditional home cooking, but you
won't find frills like coffee or liqueurs. *Gignàs 16, tel. 315–*
1709. Dress: informal. Reservations not necessary. No credit
cards. Closed Sun. PM, Mon., and July.

★ **Egipte.** This small, friendly restaurant hidden away in a very
convenient location behind the Boquería Market—though it's
far better known to locals than to visitors—is a real find. Its
traditional Catalan home cooking, huge desserts, and swift
personable service all contribute to its popularity and good value. *Jerusalem 12, tel. 317–7480. Dress: informal. No*
reservations. No credit cards.

Lodging

For a city of its size and importance, Barcelona has long been
underendowed with hotels, but with the coming of the Olympics in 1992, the city's hotel industry is having to think afresh.
New hotels are going up fast, international chains are vying for
business, and existing hotels are undergoing extensive renovations. Hotels in the Ramblas and Gothic Quarter have plenty of
Old World charm, but are less strong on creature comforts;
those in the Eixample are mostly '50s or '60s buildings, often
recently renovated; and the newest hotels are found out along
the Diagonal or beyond, in the residential district of Sarriá.
There are hotel reservation desks at the airport and Central
Station.

For details and price category definitions, *see* Lodging in Essential Information.

Very Expensive **Avenida Palace.** Right in the center of town, between the
Rambla de Catalunya and Passeig de Gràcia, this hotel dates
from 1952 but conveys a feeling of elegance and Old World
style. Some rooms are rather plain, but most have been recently renovated and there's a superbly ornate lobby. *Gran Vía*
605, tel. 301–9600. 211 rooms. AE, DC, MC, V.

★ **Ritz.** Founded in 1919 by Caesar Ritz, this is still the grand old
lady of Barcelona hotels. Extensive refurbishment has now restored it to its former splendor. The entrance lobby is awe-
inspiring, the rooms spacious, and the service impeccable.
Gran Vía 668, tel. 318–5200. 314 rooms. AE, DC, MC, V.

Sarriá Gran Hotel. This is a bit far out off the Diagonal, but if
you like modern, luxurious hotels, this is the one for you. It's
been dramatically refurbished with a spectacular waterfall and
special executive floor ideal for businesspeople. *Avda Sarriá*
50, tel. 239–1109. 314 rooms. AE, DC, V.

Expensive **Colón.** This cozy, older hotel has a unique charm and intimacy
★ reminiscent of an English country hotel. It's in an ideal location
right in the heart of the Gothic Quarter, and the rooms on the
front overlook the cathedral. It was a great favorite of Joan
Miró. *Avda Catedral 7, tel. 301–1404. 161 rooms. AE, DC,*
MC, V.

Condes de Barcelona. Situated in the Old Batlló House with
plenty of Modernista character, this is one of Barcelona's most
popular hotels, and rooms need to be booked well in advance.
The decor is stunning, with marble floors and columns, an im-

pressive staircase, and an outstanding bar area. *Passeig de Gràcia 75, tel. 215–0616. 100 rooms. AE, DC, MC, V.*

Regente. This smallish hotel on the corner of Valencia has a rooftop pool, plenty of style and charm, and a wonderful Modernista lobby. *Rambla de Catalunya 76, tel. 215–2570. 78 rooms. AE, DC, MC, V.*

Moderate **Gran Vía.** Architectural features are the special charm of this 19th-century mansion, close to the main tourist office. The original chapel has been preserved, you can have breakfast in a hall of mirrors, climb its Modernista staircase, and call from elaborate Belle Epoque phone booths. *Gran Vía 642, tel. 318–1900. 48 rooms. AE, DC, MC, V.*

★ **Oriente.** Barcelona's oldest hotel has retained all its style and charm, with ornate public rooms and glowing chandeliers. It's been refurbished, is popular with businesspeople, and is located just below the Liceu. At night, for safety, head up the Ramblas, rather than down. *Ramblas 45, tel. 302–2558. 142 rooms. AE, DC, MC, V.*

Rialto. In the heart of the Gothic Quarter, just two paces down from the Plaça Sant Jaume, this old 19th-century house has been renovated to high standards of comfort while preserving its charm. Here you're surrounded by sights, shops, and some of Barcelona's best restaurants. *Ferran 40, tel. 318–5212. 112 rooms. AE, DC, MC, V.*

Inexpensive **Continental.** Something of a legend among cost-conscious travelers, this comfortable hostel with canopied balconies stands at the top of Ramblas, just below Plaça Catalunya. The rooms are homey and comfortable, the staff is friendly, and the location's ideal. *Ramblas 136, tel. 301–2508. 30 rooms. V.*

★ **Urbis.** This beautifully decorated house on Barcelona's central parade is well known to businesspeople and Spanish visitors. It's family-run, with a colorful lobby, and its location and standards make it a bargain for its price. *Passeig de Gràcia 23, tel. 317–2766. 61 rooms. AE, DC, MC, V.*

The Arts

To find out what's on in town, look in the daily papers or in the weekly *Guía del Ocio,* available from newsstands all over town. *Actes a la Ciutat* is a weekly list of cultural events published by the Ajuntament and available from its information office on Plaça Sant Jaume.

Concerts Catalans are great music lovers, and their main concert hall is **Palau de la Música** (Amadeo Vives 1, tel. 301–1104). The ticket office is open Monday to Friday 11–1 and 5–8; and Saturday 5–8 only. Its Sunday morning concerts are a popular tradition. Tickets are reasonable and can usually be purchased just before the concert.

Opera The **Gran Teatre del Liceu** is one of the world's finest opera houses, considered by some second only to Milan's La Scala. The box office for advance bookings is on Sant Pau 1 (tel. 318–9277), open Monday to Friday 8–3, Saturday 9–1. Tickets for same-day performances are on sale in the Ramblas entrance (tel. 301–6787) 11–2 and 4:30 onward. Tickets are inexpensive by New York or London standards.

Dance You can watch the traditional Catalan Sardana danced in front of the cathedral on Sunday morning and often on Wednesday evening, too.

Theater Most theater performances are in Catalan but look out for mime shows, especially if Els Joglars or La Claca, two famous Catalan troupes, are appearing.

Film Most foreign movies are dubbed into Spanish. Try the **Filmoteca** on Travessera de Gràcia 63, on the corner of Tusset, for original English-language films.

Nightlife

Cabaret **Arnau** (Paral·lel 60, tel. 242–2408) and **El Molino** (Vilà i Vilà 93, tel. 241–6383) are both traditional old-time music halls that have retained their popularity. **Belle Epoque** (Muntaner 246, tel. 209–7385) is a beautifully decorated music hall with the most sophisticated shows. **Scala Barcelona** (Passeig Sant Joan 47, tel. 232–6363) is the city's leading nightclub, with two shows nightly, the first with dinner.

Jazz Clubs Try **Abraxas Jazz Auditorium**, Gelabert 26; **La Cova del Drac,** Tuset 30, just off the Diagonal; and **Zeleste,** Argentería 65, near Santa María del Mar.

Rock Check out **Zeleste,** Argentería 65. Major concerts are usually held in sports stadiums; keep an eye out for posters.

Flamenco The best place is **El Patio Andaluz** (Aribau 242, tel. 209–3378). Also check out **La Venta Andaluza** (Obradors 11, in the heart of the Gothic Quarter) but after dark take a cab there and back. **El Cordobés** (Ramblas 35, tel. 317–6653) is aimed at tour groups but can be fun.

Casino The **Gran Casino de Barcelona** (tel. 893–3866), 26 miles (42 kilometers) south in Sant Pere de Ribes, near Sitges, also has a dance hall and some excellent international shows in a 19th-century atmosphere.

Moorish Spain

Stretching from the dark mountains of the Sierra Morena in the north, west to the plains of the Guadalquivir valley, and south to the mighty snowcapped Sierra Nevada, Andalusia rings with echoes of the Moors. In the kingdom they called Al-Andalus, these Muslim invaders from North Africa dwelt for almost 800 years, from their first conquest of Spanish soil (Gibraltar) in 711 to their expulsion from Granada in 1492. And to this day the cities and landscapes of Andalusia are rich in their legacy. The great Mosque of Córdoba, the magical Alhambra Palace in Granada, and the Giralda tower, landmark of Seville, were the inspired creations of Moorish architects and craftsmen working at the behest of Al-Andalus's Arab emirs. The brilliant white villages with narrow shady streets and sturdy-walled houses clustered round cool inner patios, the white-washed facades with heavily grilled windows, and the deep wailing song of Andalusia's flamenco, so reminiscent of the muezzin's call to prayer, all stem from centuries of Moorish occupation.

Moorish Spain

Getting There from Madrid

Seville, Córdoba, and Granada all lie on direct train routes
from Madrid, and Seville and Córdoba are on the same line.
Two fast *talgos* (express trains) leave Atocha Station during
the day and take 4½ hours to reach Córdoba, and 5½–6 hours to
reach Seville. Or you can opt for a slower (8¼-hour) overnight
sleeper to Seville that arrives at 7 AM. To Granada you have the
choice of a talgo that leaves Atocha at 3 PM and arrives Granada
at 9 PM, or an overnight sleeper leaving Atocha at 11:30 PM and
arriving in Granada at 8 AM. These services may have been
transferred to Chamartín Station by 1989. Major bus services
also run from Madrid (usually Estación del Sur) to all three cities. Check details at tourist offices. By car, it's plain sailing
down the N-IV by way of La Mancha (shades of Don Quixote)
and the Despeña-perros Pass into Andalusia. Then the N-IV
follows the course of the Guadalquivir to Córdoba, and on to Seville. For Granada, you leave the N-IV at Bailén and head down
the N323 through endless olive groves to Jaén and Granada.
Both routes offer dramatic scenery.

Getting Around

From Seville to Córdoba, there's a direct train line or bus services by way of Carmona and Ecija. If you're driving, head out
of Seville by way of Avenida de Kansas, or Carretera de
Carmona, past the airport and onto the N-IV; this will take you
through Carmona and Ecija, too. Elsewhere in this area, it's

best to travel by bus or car as train services between Córdoba and Granada tend to be slow and tortuous and often involve changing trains at Andalusia's infamous Bobadilla junction. Buses to Granada go by way of Jaén or Baena. If you're driving, it's faster via Jaén, but even more picturesque by way of the N432 to Baena. Seville's Bus Station (tel. 417111) is on José María Osborne and Manuel Vázquez Sagastizabal not far from the San Bernardo train station (trains from Madrid usually arrive at Plaza de Armas Station). Córdoba has no central bus depot, so check at the tourist office for departure points. Granada's main bus station is *Alsina Graells* (Camino de Ronda 97, tel. 251358).

Guided Tours

Guided tours of Seville, Córdoba, Granada, and Ronda are run by **Juliá Tours, Pullmantur,** and **Trapsatur,** both from Madrid, and resorts of the Costa del Sol; check with travel agents. Local excursions are available from Seville to the sherry bodegas and equestrian museum of Jerez de la Frontera. From Granada, there's a once-weekly day trip to the villages of the Alpujarras; check details with tourist offices. In Córdoba, ask about trips to the ruins of Medina Azahara, a fabulous 10th-century Moorish palace about seven miles (12 kilometers) northwest of town.

Tourist Information

Córdoba. Palacio de Congresos y Exposiciones, Torrijos 10, tel. 471235, right beside the mosque. Municipal Tourist Office, Plaza Judas Levi, tel. 290740.
Granada. Casa de los Tiros, Pavaneras 19, tel. 221022, a short walk from Plaza Isabel la Católica.
Seville. Avenida Constitución 24, tel. 225653 or 221094), not far from the cathedral and Archives of the Indies.

Exploring

Our tour begins in Seville and continues to Carmona, Ecija, Córdoba, Baena, Granada, Sierra Nevada, Lanjarón, Orgiva and Alpujarras.

Seville Lying on the banks of the Guadalquivir, Seville—Spain's fourth-largest city and capital of Andalusia—is one of the most beautiful and romantic cities in Europe. Here in this city of the sensuous Carmen and the amorous Don Juan, famed for the spectacle of its Holy Week processions and April Fair, you'll come close to the spiritual heart of Moorish Andalusia. Begin your visit in the **Cathedral,** begun in 1402, a century and a half after St. Ferdinand delivered Seville from the Moors. This great Gothic edifice, which took just over a century to build, is traditionally described in superlatives. It's the biggest and highest cathedral in Spain, the largest Gothic building in the world, and the world's third-largest church after St. Peter's in Rome and St. Paul's in London. And it boasts the world's largest carved wooden altarpiece. Despite such impressive statistics, the inside can be dark and gloomy with too many

Seville

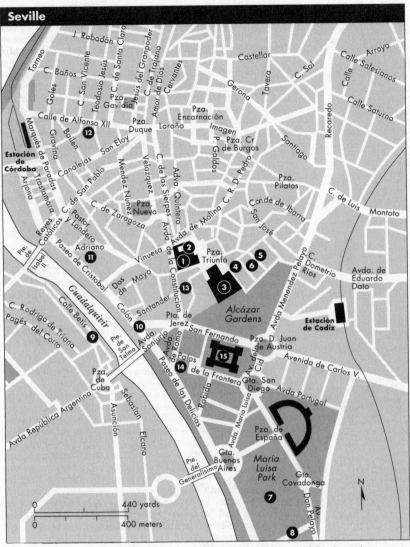

J. Rabadán · Torneo · C. Baños · Goles · Gravina · Bailén · C. San Vicente · Teodosio Jesús · C. de Santa Clara · Pza. Gavidia · Jesús del Granpoder · C. de Trajano · Amor de Dios · Cervantes · Castellar · C. Sol · Gerona · Tavera · Calle Arroyo · Calle Salesianos · Calle · Calle Saturno · Recaredo

Marqués de Paradas · Trastámara · Ariona · Calle de Alfonso XII · Pza. Duque · Laraña · Pza. Encarnación · Imagen · C. Galdos · Pza. Cr de Burgos · Santiago

Estación de Córdoba · Canalejas · San Eloy · Mendez Nuñez · C. de San Pablo · C. de las Sierpes · Velazquez · Adva. Quintero · Avda. de Molina · C. R. D. Pedro · San José · Pza. Pilatos · C. de Luis · Montoto

Reyes Católicos · C. Pastor Y Landero · Adriano · Pza. Nueva · C. de Zaragoza · Vinuesa · Avda. de la Constitución · Pza. Triunfo · Conde de Ibarra · C. de Eduardo Dato

Pte. de Isabel II · Paseo de Cristobal · Dos de Mayo · Santander · Colón · Avda. · Pta. de Jerez · Pza. Triunfo · Alcázar Gardens · Avda. Menendez Pelayo · C. Dometrio Rios · Estación de Cadiz

Guadalquivir · C. Rodrigo de Triana · Calle Betis · Pagés del Corro · Pte. de San Telmo · Santurio · Avda. Paloma · de Palos · San Fernando · Pza. D. Juan de Austria · Av. del Cid · Avenida de Carlos V.

Pza. de Cuba · Asunción · Sebastián Elcano · Rabida · de la Frontera · Gta. San Diego · Avda Portugal · Avda. Maria Luisa · Av. Don Pelayo

Avda República Argentina · Pte. del Generalísimo · Gta. Buenos Aires · Pza. de España · María Luisa Park · Gta. Covadonga

Pza. de América

N

0 — 440 yards
0 — 400 meters

Major Attractions

Alcázar, **3**
Barrio Santa Cruz, **5**
Calle Betis, **9**
Cathedral, **1**
Giralda, **2**
Golden Tower, **10**
Maestranza Bullring, **11**
María Luisa Park, **7**
Patio de las Banderas, **4**
Plaza de América, **8**
Plaza Doña Elvira, **6**

Other Attractions

Museo de Arte
Contemporaneo, **13**
Museo de Bellas
Artes, **12**
San Telmo Palace, **14**
Tobacco Factory
(University), **15**

overly ornate Baroque trappings. But seek out the beautiful Virgins by Murillo and Zurbarán, and reflect on the history enshrined in these walls. In a silver urn before the high altar rest the precious relics of Seville's liberator, St. Ferdinand, said to have died from excessive fasting, and down in the crypt are the tombs of his descendants Pedro the Cruel, founder of the Alcazar, and his mistress María de Padilla. But above all, you'll want to pay your respects to Christopher Columbus, whose mortal vestiges are enshrined in a flamboyant mausoleum in the south aisle. Borne aloft by statues representing the four medieval kingdoms of Spain, it's to be hoped the great voyageur has found peace at last after the transatlantic quarrels that carried his body from Valladolid to Santo Domingo, and from Havana to Seville. *Admission: 125 ptas. Open in summer 10:30–1:30 and 4:30–6:30; in winter 10:30–1 and 4–6.*

Every day the bell that summons the faithful to prayer rings out from a Moorish minaret, relic of the Arab mosque whose admirable tower of Abu Yakoub the Sevillians could not bring themselves to destroy. Topped in 1565–68 by a bell tower and weather vane and called the **Giralda**, this splendid example of Moorish art is one of the marvels of Seville. In place of steps, a gently sloping ramp climbs to the viewing platform 230 feet (70 meters) above Seville's rooftops. St. Ferdinand is said to have ridden his horse to the top to admire the view of the city he had conquered. Seven centuries later your view of the Golden Tower and shimmering Guadalquivir will be equally breathtaking. Try, too, to see the Giralda at night when the floodlights cast a new magic on this gem of Islamic art. *Open same hours as cathedral and visited on same ticket.*

The high fortified walls of the **Alcázar** belie the exquisite delicacy of the palace's interior. It was built by Pedro the Cruel—so known because he murdered his stepmother and four of his half-brothers—who lived here with his mistress María de Padilla from 1350 to 1369. Don't mistake this for a genuine Moorish palace as it was built more than 100 years after the reconquest of Seville; rather its style is Mudéjar—built by Moorish craftsmen working under orders of a Christian king. The Catholic kings (Ferdinand and Isabella), whose only son, Prince Juan, was born in the Alcázar in 1478, added a wing to serve as administration center for their New World empire, and Charles V enlarged it further for his marriage celebrations in 1526. Pedro's Mudéjar palace centers around the beautiful **Patio de las Doncellas** (Court of the Damsels) whose name pays tribute to the annual gift of 100 virgins to the Moorish sultans whose palace once stood on the site. Resplendent with the most delicate of lacelike stucco and gleaming azulejo decorations, it is immediately reminiscent of Granada's Alhambra, and is in fact the work of Granada craftsmen. Opening off this are the apartments of María de Padilla whose hold over her lover, and seemingly her courtiers, too, was so great that they apparently vied with one another to drink her bath water! The **Alcázar Gardens** are fragrant with jasmine and myrtle, an orange tree said to have been planted by Pedro the Cruel, and a lily pond well stocked with fat, contented goldfish. The end of your visit brings you to the **Patio de las Banderas** for an unrivaled view of the Giralda. *Admission: 150 ptas., free on Sat. Open daily 9–12:45 and 3–5:45.*

⑤ The **Barrio Santa Cruz,** with its twisting alleyways, cobbled squares, and whitewashed houses, is a perfect setting for an operetta. Once the home of Seville's Jews, it was much favored by 17th-century noblemen and today boasts some of the most expensive properties in Seville. All the romantic images you've ever had of Spain will come to life here: Every house gleams white or deep ochre yellow; wrought-iron grilles adorn the windows, and every balcony and patio is bedecked with geraniums and petunias. You'll find the most beautiful patio at Callejón del Agua 12. Ancient bars nestle side by side with antiques shops and tasteful souvenir stores. Don't miss the famous *Casa Román* bar in Plaza de los Venerables Sacerdotes with its ceilings hung thick with some of the best hams in Seville, or the *Hostería del Laurel* next door, where in summer you can dine in one of the loveliest squares in the city. Souvenir and excellent **⑥** ceramic shops surround the **Plaza Doña Elvira,** where the young of Seville gather to play guitars around the fountain and azulejo benches. And in the **Plaza Alianza,** with its well-stocked antiques shops and **John Fulton gallery** (Fulton is the only American ever to qualify as a full-fledged bullfighter), stop a moment and admire the simplicity of the crucifix on the wall, framed in a profusion of bougainvillea.

⑦ Take a cab, or better still, hire a horse carriage from the Plaza Virgen de los Reyes, below the Giralda, and visit **María Luisa park,** whose gardens are a delightful blend of formal design and wild vegetation, shady walkways, and sequestered nooks. In the 1920s the park was redesigned to form the site of the 1929 Hispanic-American exhibition, and the impressive villas you see here today are the fair's remaining pavilions. Feed the hundreds of white doves that gather round the fountains of the **⑧** lovely **Plaza de América;** it's a magical spot to while away the sleepy hours of the siesta.

⑨ An early evening stroll along the **Calle Betis** on the far side of the Guadalquivir is a delight few foreigners know about. Between the San Telmo and Isabel II bridges, the vista of the sparkling water, the palm-lined banks, and the silhouette of **⑩ ⑪** the **Golden Tower** (built 1220) and the **Maestranza bullring** (built 1760–63), one of Spain's oldest, is simply stunning.

Carmona Nineteen miles (30 kilometers) from Seville, the N-IV brings you to **Carmona.** This unspoiled Andalusian town of Roman and Moorish origin is worth a visit, either to stay at the parador or to enjoy its wealth of Mudéjar and Renaissance churches, and its streets of whitewashed houses of clear Moorish influence. Most worthwhile is the **Church of San Pedro** begun in 1466, whose extraordinary interior is an unbroken mass of sculptures and gilded surfaces, and whose tower, erected in 1704, is an unabashed imitation of Seville's famous Giralda. Carmona's most moving monument is its splendid **Roman Necropolis,** where in huge underground chambers some 900 family tombs dating from the 2nd–4th centuries AD have been chiseled out of the rock. *Open Tues.–Sat. 10–2 and 4–6; closed Sun., Mon.*

Ecija A little farther along the N-IV brings you to **Ecija,** a dazzling white cluster reputed to be the hottest town in Spain–its nickname is *sarten de Andalucía,* "Andalusia's frying pan." With its history going back to Greek and Roman times, you'll find plenty of Renaissance and Baroque palaces here and a bewildering array of churches whose towers and turrets rise before you as you approach along the main road.

Córdoba Ancient **Córdoba,** city of the caliphs, is one of Spain's oldest cities and the greatest embodiment of Moorish heritage in all Andalusia. From the 8th to the 11th centuries, the Moorish emirs and caliphs of the West held court here and it became one of the Western world's greatest centers of art, culture, and learning. Moors, Christians, and Jews lived together in harmony within its walls. Two of Córdoba's most famous native sons were Averröes, the great Arab scientist, and Maimónides, the notable Jewish doctor and philosopher. But above all it is for its ❶ famous **Mosque** (or Mezquita), one of the finest mosques ever built by the Moors, that Córdoba is known first and foremost. Its founder was Abd ar-Rahman I (756–788), and it was completed by Al Mansur (976–1002) around the year 987. As you step inside you'll come face to face with a forest of gleaming pillars of precious marble, jasper, and onyx, rising to a roof of red and white horseshoe arches, one of the most characteristic traits of Moorish architecture. Not even the heavy Baroque cathedral that Charles V so mistakenly built in its midst—and later regretted—can detract from the overpowering impact and mystery wrought by the art of these Moorish craftsmen of a thousand years ago. It was indeed a fitting setting for the original copy of the Koran and a bone from the arm of the Prophet Mohammed, holy relics that the Mezquita is said to have once possessed and which brought thousands of pilgrims to its doors in the great years before St. Ferdinand reconquered Córdoba for the Christians in 1236. In Moorish times, the mosque opened onto the Orange Tree Courtyard, where the faithful performed their ablutions before worshiping, and the bell tower, which you can climb for a magnificent view of the city, served as the mosque's minaret. *Admission: 200 ptas. Open daily 10–1:30 and 3:30–6 (4–7 in summer).*

Near the mosque, the streets of Torrijos, Cardenal Herrero, and Deanes are lined with tempting souvenir shops specializing in local handicrafts, especially the filigree silver and embossed leather for which Córdoba is famous. In her niche on Cardenal ❷ Herrero, the **Virgin of Lanterns** stands demurely behind a lantern-hung grille, rather like a lovely lady awaiting a serenade. In a narrow alleyway off to your left is the Callejón de las Flores, its houses decked with hanging flower baskets. Now ❸ make your way westward to the old **Judería,** or Jewish quar-❹ ter. On the **Plaza Judás Levi** you'll find the Municipal Tourist Office. A few paces down, on C. Manriquez, is another outstanding patio open to visitors.

❺ Overlooking the Plaza Maimónides (or Bulas) is the **Museum of Bullfighting,** housed in two delightful mansions built around a patio. You'll see a well-displayed collection of memorabilia, paintings, and posters by early 20th-century Córdoban artists —even the hide of the bull that killed the legendary Manolete in 1947. *Admission: 50 ptas. Open Tues.–Sat. 9:30–1:30 and 5–8 (4–7 in winter); closed Sun. PM and Mon.*

❻ A moving statue of the great Jewish philosopher **Maimónides** stands in the Plaza Tiberiades. A few paces along Judíos, you

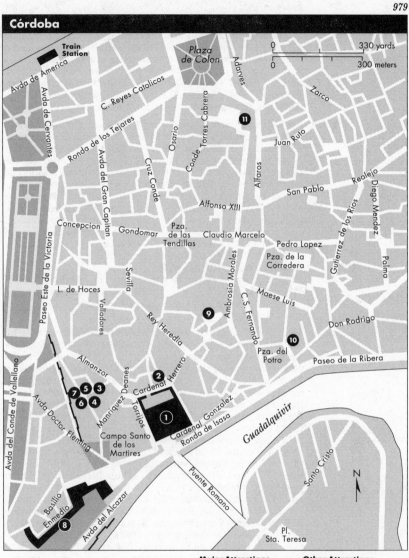

Córdoba

Train Station

Plaza de Colon

330 yards
300 meters

Avda de America

Avda de Cervantes

C. Reyes Catolicos

Ronda de los Tejares

Avda del Gran Capitan

Cruz Conde

Osorio

Conde Torres Cabrera

Adarves

Zarco

Juan Ruto

Alfaros

San Pablo

Realejo

Diego Mendez

Gutierrez de los Rios

Palma

Alfonso XIII

Concepcion

Gondomar

Pza. de las Tendillas

Claudio Marcelo

Pedro Lopez

Pza. de la Corredera

Paseo Este de la Victoria

L. de Hoces

Sevilla

Valladares

Ambrosia Morales

Maese Luis

C.S. Fernando

Don Rodrigo

Rey Heredia

9

10

Pza. del Potro

Paseo de la Ribera

Almanzor

Manriquez Deanes

Torrijos

Cardenal Herrero

2

5 **3**

7 **6** **4**

1

Cardenal Gonzalez

Ronda de Isasa

Guadalquivir

Avda del Conde de Vallellano

Avda Doctor Fleming

Campo Santo de los Martires

Puente Romano

Santo Cristo

N

Basilio Enmedia

8

Avda del Alcazar

Pl. Sta. Teresa

11

Major Attractions

Judería, **3**
Maimónides Statue, **6**
Mosque, **1**
Museum of Bullfighting, **5**
Plaza Judás Levi, **4**
Synagogue, **7**
Virgin of Lanterns, **2**

Other Attractions

Alcázar, **8**
Cristo de los Faroles, **11**
Museo Arqueologico, **9**
Museo de Bellas Artes, **10**

❼ come to the only **synagogue** in Andalusia to have survived the expulsion of the Jews in 1492. It's one of only three remaining synagogues in Spain—the other two you saw in Toledo—and it boasts some fine Hebrew and Mudéjar stucco tracery and a women's gallery. *Admission: 50 ptas. Open Tues.–Sat. 10–2 and 5–7; closed Sun. PM and Mon.* Across the way is the court-yard of El Zoco, a former Arab souk, with some pleasant shops and stalls, and sometimes a bar open in summer.

Baena As you leave Córdoba and head for Granada, the N432 climbs from the Guadalquivir valley up into the mountains of central Andalusia. It is 39 miles (63 kilometers) to **Baena,** a pictur-esque Andalusian town of white houses clustered on the hillside, where you may want to stop for a drink and wander the narrow streets and squares as yet largely untouched by tour-ism. Mountain views line the route as the road twists toward its highest point, the 3,000-foot (914-meter) **Puerto del Castillo,** before dropping down onto the *vega* (fertile plain) of Granada. Just beyond Atarfe, you can take a short detour to the village of **Fuentevaqueros** where Federico García Lorca was born on June 5, 1898. In 1986, to commemorate the 50th anniversary of his assassination in Granada at the outbreak of the Civil War, his birthplace was restored as a museum. The nearby village of Valderrubio inspired his *Libro de Poemas* and *La Casa de Bernarda Alba. Museo de Lorca, open 10–1 and 6–8 with tours every hour on the hour.*

Granada The city of **Granada** rises majestically on three hills dwarfed by the mighty snowcapped peaks of the Sierra Nevada, Europe's highest mountain range. Atop one of these distant hills the pink-gold palace of the Alhambra, at once splendidly imposing yet infinitely delicate, gazes out across the rooftops and gypsy caves of the Sacromonte to the fertile *vega* rich in orchards, to-bacco fields, and poplar groves. Granada, the last stronghold of the Moors and the most treasured of all their cities, fell finally to the Catholic kings in January 1492. For Ferdinand and Isa-bella their conquest of Granada was the fulfillment of a long cherished dream to rid Spain of the Infidel, and here they built **❶** the flamboyant **Royal Chapel** where they have lain side by side since 1521, later joined by their daughter Juana la Loca. Begin your tour in the nearby Plaza de Bib-Rambla, a pleasant square with flower stalls and outdoor cafés in summer, then pay a **❷** quick visit to the huge Renaissance **Cathedral** commissioned in 1521 by Charles V who thought the Royal Chapel "too small for so much glory" and determined to house his illustrious grand-parents somewhere more worthy. But his ambitions came to little, for Granada Cathedral is a grandiose and gloomy monu-ment, not completed until 1714, and is far surpassed in beauty and historic value by the neighboring Royal Chapel, which, de-spite the great emperor's plans, still houses the tombs of his grandparents and less fortunate mother. *Admission to both: 75 ptas., Sun. AM free. Cathedral and Royal Chapel open 11–1 and 3–6 in winter (4–7 in summer).*

❸ The adjacent streets of the **Alcaicería,** the old Arab silk ex-change, will prove a haven for souvenir hunters. Here you can find any number of local handicrafts inspired by Granada's Moorish heritage: brass and copperware, green and blue Fajalauza pottery, wooden boxes, tables and chess sets inlaid with mother of pearl, and woven goods from the villages of the Alpujarras in which the colors green, red, and black predomi-

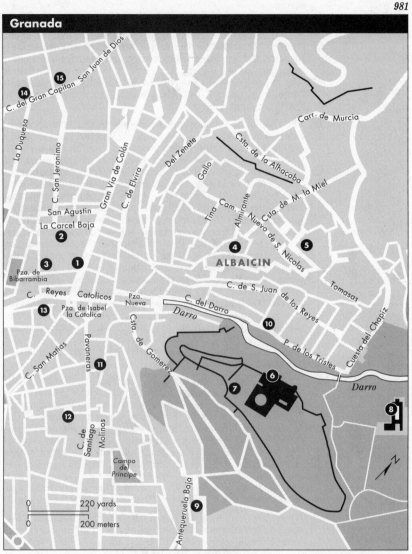

Granada

Major Attractions

Albaicín, **4**
Alcaicería, **3**
Alhambra, **6**
Cathedral, **2**
Puerta de la Justicía, **7**
Generalife, **8**
San Nicolás Church, **5**
Royal Chapel, **1**

Other Attractions

Casa de los Tiros, **11**
Casa Museo de Falla, **9**
Corral del Carbón, **13**
Museo Arqueológico, **10**
San Jerónimo, **14**
San Juan de Diós, **15**
Santo Domingo, **12**

nate. Across the Gran Vía de Colón, Granada's main shopping street, the narrow streets begin to wind up the slopes of the

4 **Albaicín,** the old Moorish quarter, which is now a fascinating mixture of dilapidated white houses and beautiful *cármenes,* luxurious villas with fragrant gardens. Few visitors find their

5 way to the balcony of **San Nicolás church,** which affords an unforgettable view of the Alhambra, particularly when it is floodlit at night.

6 The Cuesta de Gomerez climbs steeply to the **Alhambra** precincts where the British Duke of Wellington planted shady elms, and Washington Irving tarried among the gypsies from whom he learned the Moorish legends so evocatively recounted

7 in his *Tales of the Alhambra.* Above the **Puerta de la Justicia** the hand of Fatima, her fingers evoking the five laws of the Koran, beckons you inside the mystical Alhambra, the most imposing and infinitely beautiful of all Andalusia's Moorish monuments. The history of the Alhambra is woven through the centuries. Once inside its famous courts the legends of the Patio of the Lions, the Hall of the Two Sisters, and the murder of the Abencerrajes spring to life in a profusion of lacy walls, frothy stucco, gleaming tiles, and ornate domed ceilings. Here in this realm of myrtles and fountains, festooned arches and mysterious inscriptions, every corner holds its secret. Here the emirs installed their harems, accorded their favorites the most lavish of courts and bathed in marble baths. In the midst of so much that is delicate the Baroque palace of Charles V seems an intrusion, heavy and incongruous, were it not for the splendid acoustics that make it a perfect setting for Granada's summer music festival.

8 Wysteria, jasmine, and roses line your route to the **Generalife,** the nearby summer palace of the caliphs, where crystal drops shower from slender fountains against a background of stately cypresses. The view of the white, clustered houses of the Albaicín, the Sacromonte riddled with gypsy caves, and the imposing bulk of the Alhambra towering above the tiled roofs of the city will etch on your memory an indelible image of this most beautiful of settings and greatest of Moorish legacies. *Admission: 350 ptas. Free Sun. after 3 PM. Alhambra and Generalife open daily 9:30–6 (ticket office closes 5:15), and Sat. 8–10 PM.*

If you have a day to spare, you can drive to the mountains of the nearby **Sierra Nevada.** The ski resort itself, where you can ski from December to May, is truly unmemorable, but the surrounding scenery viewed from the highest mountain route in Europe makes for a memorable day out. A bus leaves Granada daily from the Hotel Zaida on the Acera de Darro and returns at around 6 PM. Above the resort the road climbs to the Pico de Veleta, Spain's second-highest mountain (10,000 feet/ 3,048 meters), and the view across the Alpujarra range to the sea at Motril is simply stunning.

If you opt instead for a trip to the villages of the high **Alpujarras,** leave Granada on the N323 toward Motril, then branch east to **Lanjarón,** a delightful old spa town with an air of faded gentility. From **Orgiva,** the main town of the Alpujarras, the highest road in Europe ascends to picturesque villages like **Bubión, Capileira** beneath the summit of the Veleta, and **Trevélez,** Europe's highest village, on the slopes of the Mulhacén. These ancient villages, only recently brushed by modern tourism, became the final refuge of the Moors as they fled the Conquest of Granada, and here they remained until their expulsion from Spain in 1609. With their squat, square houses and flat roofs so reminiscent of the land across the Straits of Gibraltar, they are the last vestige of Andalusia's great Moorish past.

Dining and Lodging and Other Information

For details and price category definitions, *see* Dining and Lodging in Essential Information.

Carmona
Lodging
★
Parador del Rey Don Pedro. The beauty of this modern parador is its splendid, peaceful setting in the ruins of the old Moorish alcázar on top of the hill above Carmona, and its magnificent views across the vast fertile plain below. *Tel. 954–14 1010. 59 rooms. Facilities: pool. AE, DC, MC, V.*

Córdoba
Dining
★
El Caballo Rojo. The Red Horse, located close to the mosque, is Córdoba's most outstanding restaurant, famous throughout Andalusia and all of Spain. The decor resembles a cool Andalusian patio, and the menu features traditional specialties such as *rabo de toro* (bull's tail); *salmorejo*, a local version of gazpacho with chunks of ham and egg; and other exotic creations inspired by Córdoba's Moorish heritage. *Cardenal Herrero 28, tel. 475375. Dress: casual but smart. Reservations advisable. AE, DC, MC, V. Expensive.*

La Almudaina. This attractive restaurant is located in a 15th-century house and former school that overlooks the Alcázar at the entrance to the Judería. It has an Andalusian patio, and the decor and cooking are both typical of Córdoba. *Campo Santo de los Mártires 1, tel. 474342. AE, DC, MC, V. Closed Sun. evening. Moderate.*

★
El Churrasco. Ranking second only to El Caballo Rojo, this atmospheric restaurant with a patio is famous for its grilled meat dishes. Specialties are, of course, *churrasco*, a pork dish in pepper sauce, and an excellent *salmorejo*. *Romero 16, tel. 290819. AE, DC, MC, V. Closed Thurs. and Aug. Moderate.*

El Gallo Dorao. Close to the mosque, beside the Marisa hotel, the Golden Cock is popular with locals and tourists alike. You'll find the dining room one floor up, pleasantly decorated with ceramic plates. The menu offers a wide choice of dishes and some economical *menus turísticas*. *Cardenal Herrero 14, tel. 480108. AE, DC, MC, V. Closed Sun. evenings. Moderate.*

Café Judas Levi. This inexpensive café in the heart of the Judería offers several set menus in a picturesque Córdoban patio, and is ideal for a light lunch or quick snack. *Plaza Judas Levi, no phone. Dress: casual. V. Inexpensive.*

Lodging
★
Adarve. This delightful contemporary hotel on the east side of the mosque is built in Andalusian Moorish style with a charming patio and ceramic decor. The hotel itself has no restaurant, but guests can dine in the attractive **Mesón del Bandolero** in Calle Torrijos on the opposite side of the mosque. *Magistral González Francés 15, tel. 481102. 103 rooms, pool. AE, DC, MC, V. Expensive.*

El Califa. This is a small, modern hotel in a reasonably quiet, central location in the heart of the old city. It accepts no tour groups, only individual guests, and is a comfortable place to stay, with the sights and shops close at hand. *Lope de Hoces 14, tel. 299400. 46 rooms. V. Moderate.*

Maimónides. Its location is convenient, right beside the mosque, with restaurants and souvenir shops outside the door. The lobby is impressive; rooms are functional but comfortable. *Torrijos 4, tel. 471500. 61 rooms. AE, DC, MC, V. Moderate.*

Marisa. A charming old Andalusian house whose location in the heart of the old town overlooking the mosque's Patio de los Naranjos is its prime virtue. You'll find the decor quaint and charming, and the rates reasonable. *Cardenal Herrero 6, tel. 473142. 28 rooms. AE, DC, V. Inexpensive.*

Granada Dining

Cunini. Located in the center of town, close to the cathedral, Cunini has long been famous for the quality of its seafood. *Pescadería 9 or Capuchina 14, tel. 263701. Dress: smart. Reservations advised. AE, DC, MC, V. Closed Sun. night. Expensive.*

★ **Baroca.** Located one block above the Camino de Ronda, the locals consider this Granada's best restaurant. The menu favors international cuisine; desserts are especially good. Service is professional and the ambience agreeable. *Pedro Antonio de Alarcón 34, tel. 265051. Dress: formal. Reservations advised. AE, DC, MC, V. Closed Sun. and Aug. Expensive.*

Carmen de San Miguel. This is a restaurant to visit for its superb setting in a villa with an outdoor terrace and magnificent views over Granada. Located on the Alhambra hill beside the Alhambra Palace hotel, the setting is unbeatable, the food rather more average. *Paseo Torres Bermejas 3, tel. 226723. V. Closed Sun. Moderate.*

Sevilla. This is a very atmospheric, colorful restaurant located in the Alcaicería beside the cathedral. There's a superb tapas bar at the entrance, and the dining room is picturesque but rather small and crowded. The menu can be rather tourist-oriented. *Oficios 12, tel. 221223. AE, DC, MC, V. Closed Sun. night. Moderate.*

Los Manueles. This old inn dating back to 1917 is one of Granada's long-standing traditions. The walls are decorated with ceramic tiles, and the ceiling is hung with hams. There's lots of atmosphere, good old-fashioned service, and plenty of traditional Granada cooking. *Zaragoza 2, tel. 223415. No credit cards. Inexpensive.*

Lodging

Parador de San Francisco. Magnificently located in an old convent right within the Alhambra precincts, the parador was where Queen Isabella was entombed before the completion of the Royal Chapel. It's one of Spain's most popular hotels, and you need to book at least six months in advance. *Alhambra, tel. 221440. 39 rooms. AE, DC, MC, V. Very expensive.*

★ **Alhambra Palace.** This flamboyant ochre-red Moorish-style palace was built about 1910, and sits halfway up the hill to the Alhambra. The mood is more harried than at the more isolated parador. Though recently renovated, it remains a conversation piece with rich carpets, tapestries, and Moorish tiles. Front rooms facing the town are preferable. The terrace is the perfect place for an early evening drink as the sun sets over the Sierra Nevada mountains. *Peña Partida 2, tel. 221468. 121 rooms. AE, DC, MC, V. Expensive.*

América. A simple but charming hostel in a magnificent location not far from the Alhambra, this is very popular, and you should book months ahead. *Real de la Alhambra 53, tel.*

227471. 14 rooms. No credit cards. Open March–Oct. only. Moderate.

Generalife. This is the most modern hotel near the Alhambra. Rooms are clean and comfortable but small, with little character. The drawing card is the pool. *Avenida de los Alixares, tel. 958/225506. AE, MC, V. Moderate.*

Juan Miguel. This comfortable, modern hotel right in the center of town opened in 1987. The rooms are well equipped, service is professional, and there's a good restaurant. *Acera del Darro 24, tel. 258912. 66 rooms. AE, DC, MC, V. Moderate.*

Inglaterra. Set in a period house just two blocks above the Gran Vía de Colón in the heart of town, this is a hotel that will appeal to those who prefer Old World charm to creature comforts, though accommodations are perfectly adequate for the reasonable rates. *Cetti Meriem 6, tel. 221559. 40 rooms. V. Inexpensive.*

★ **Kenia.** A distinctive hotel set in a personalized villa in a quiet residential section of town. Service is attentive, and there's a large leafy garden, a blessing in summer. Accommodations are simple, but the Kenia has a charm not found in functional business hotels. *Molinos 65, tel. 227506. 16 rooms. No credit cards. Inexpensive.*

Shopping Granada's main shopping streets are around the Puerta Real—along Reyes Católicos, Zacatín, Angel Ganivet, and the Gran Vía de Colón. The **Galerías Preciados** department store is on Carrera del Genil. The **Corte Inglés** is halfway down Recogidas. The narrow streets of the Alcaicería are ideal for souvenir hunters, as is the Cuesta Gomérez leading up to the Alhambra.

Flamenco There are several "impromptu" flamenco shows in the caves of the Sacromonte, but these can be dismally bad and little more than tourist rip-offs. Go only if accompanied by a Spanish friend who knows his way around. There are also two regular flamenco clubs that cater largely to tourists and tour groups: **Jardines Neptuno** and **Reina Mora.** Both can be booked through your hotel.

Seville **La Albahaca.** Set in an attractive old house in the heart of the
Dining Barrio Santa Cruz, the Albahaca offers plenty of style and atmosphere and original, imaginative cuisine. Specialties of the chef, who was formerly in the Hotel Alfonso XIII, are *ajo blanco con pasas de Corinto* (garlic with raisins) and *filetitos de ciervo con ciruelas* (venison and cherries). *Plaza Santa Cruz 12, tel. 220714. Dress: casual. Reservations advised. AE, DC, MC, V. Closed Sun. Expensive.*

★ **Egaña Oriza.** This is currently one of Seville's most fashionable restaurants. Basque specialties include *merluza con almejas en salsa verde* (white fish in clam sauce) and *solomillo con foie en salsa de trufas* (steak with goose liver pâté in truffle sauce). It's opposite the old tobacco factory, now Seville University. *San Fernando 41, tel. 227211. Dress: informal. Reservations essential. AE, DC, MC, V. Closed Sun. and Aug. Expensive.*

Enrique Becerra. This small intimate restaurant in an old Andalusian house just off the Plaza Nueva is well known for its Andalusian cuisine. *Gamazo 2, tel. 213049. Dress: informal. Reservations advised. AE, V. Closed Sun. Expensive to Moderate.*

El Bacalao. This popular fish restaurant, opposite the church of Santa Catalina, is in an Andalusian house decorated with ceramic tiles. As its name suggests, the house specialty is *bacalao* (cod); try the *bacalao con arroz* or the *bacalao al pilpil. Plaza Ponce de León 15, tel. 216670. Dress: informal. Reservations advised. AE, DC, V. Closed Sun. and Aug. Moderate.*

La Isla. Located in the center of town between the cathedral and the Convent of La Caridad, La Isla has long been famous for its superb seafood and paella. *Arfe 25, tel. 215376. AE, DC, MC, V. Closed Aug. Moderate.*

★ **La Judería.** This bright, modern restaurant near the Hotel Fernando III is fast gaining recognition for the quality of its Andalusian and international cuisine and reasonable prices. Fish dishes from the north of Spain, and meat from Avila are specialties. Try *cordero lechal* (roast baby lamb) or *urta a la roteña* (a fish dish unique to Rota). *Cano y Cueto 13, tel. 412052. Dress: smart. Reservations essential. AE, DC, MC, V. Closed Tues. Moderate.*

★ **Mesón Don Raimundo.** Located in an old convent close to the cathedral, the atmosphere and decor are "deliberately" Sevillian. Its bar is the perfect place to sample a *fino* and some splendid tapas, and the restaurant, when not catering to tour groups, is one of Seville's most delightful. *Argote de Molina 26, tel. 223355. Reservations advised. AE, DC, MC, V. Closed Sun. night. Moderate.*

La Rayuela. This is a charming and intimate restaurant with a short imaginative menu, just a few minutes' walk from the cathedral. Try the chicken salad with kiwi fruit, or the *entrecot a la pimienta verde* (pepper steak). *Don Remondo 1, tel. 217952. Reservations advised. AE, DC, MC, V. Closed Sat. lunch and Sun. evening. Moderate.*

Mesón Castellano. This old Sevillian house opposite the church of San José is an ideal place for lunch after a morning's shopping on Calle Sierpes. Specialties are Castilian meat dishes, at reasonable prices. *Jovellanos 6, tel. 214128. Open for lunch only. AE, DC, V. Closed Sun. Inexpensive.*

Lodging **Alfonso XIII.** This ornate Mudejar-style palace was built for Alfonso XIII's visit to the 1929 exhibition. It is worth a visit for its splendid Moorish decor, despite the fact that parts of the hotel are faded and fall short of five-star expectations. Rooms are spacious. The restaurant is elegant but falls short of expectations, too. *San Fernando 2, tel. 222850. 128 rooms and 21 suites, pool. AE, DC, MC, V. Very expensive.*

★ **Doña María.** Close to the cathedral, this is one of Seville's most charming hotels. Some rooms are small and plain; others are tastefully furnished with antiques. Room 310 has a four-poster double bed, and 305 two single four-posters; both have spacious bathrooms. There's no restaurant, but there's a rooftop pool with a good view of the Giralda. *Don Remondo 19, tel. 224990. 61 rooms. AE, DC, MC, V. Expensive.*

Inglaterra. A modern, comfortable hotel right on the main square, it was renovated throughout in 1988. Rooms on the fifth floor have the best view, and the restaurant is well known for its good food and professional service. *Plaza Nueva 7, tel. 224970. 120 rooms. AE, DC, MC, V. Expensive.*

★ **Sevilla Sol.** This new hotel behind the Plaza de España opened in 1988. Rooms are comfortable and spacious, with views over the city, wide beds, and large bathrooms. The best rooms are on the eighth and ninth floors. *Avenida de la Borbolla 3, tel. 422611. AE, DC, MC, V. Expensive.*

Bécquer. This functional, modern hotel with attentive service is convenient for the shopping center and offers comfortable if unexciting accommodations. It's one of the best moderate bets. *Reyes Católicos 4, tel. 228900. 126 rooms. AE, DC, MC, V. Moderate.*

Fernando III. Located on the edge of the Barrio Santa Cruz, close to the Murillo gardens, this is a functional, modern hotel that has recently been renovated throughout. Rooms are comfortable but somber, and there's a rooftop pool open from June to September *San José 21, tel. 217307. 156 rooms. AE, DC, MC, V. Moderate.*

Giralda. Recently modernized and extensively renovated, this is a comfortable, functional hotel with spacious, light rooms decorated in typical Castilian style. Located in a cul-de-sac off Avenida Menéndez Pelayo, it lies on the edge of the old city; rooms on the fifth floor are best. *Sierra Nevada 3, tel. 416661. 107 rooms, garage. AE, DC, MC, V. Moderate.*

Internacional. Well maintained and charming, this Old World hotel lies in the narrow streets of the old town near Casa Pilatos. *Aguilas 17, tel. 213207. 26 rooms. Inexpensive.*

Murillo. This picturesque hotel in the heart of the Barrio Santa Cruz was redecorated in 1987. Rooms are simple and small, but the setting is a virtue. You can't reach the hotel by car, but porters with trolleys will fetch your luggage from your taxi. *Lope de Rueda 7, tel. 216095. 61 rooms, 30 with bath, 31 with shower. AE, DC, MC, V. Inexpensive.*

La Rábida. With lots of delightful 19th-century touches, this is a charming old-fashioned hotel in the center of town. *87 rooms and a restaurant. Castelar 24, tel. 954/220960. Inexpensive.*

Shopping Seville's main shopping streets are the **Calle de Sierpes, Tetuan,** and **Velázquez.** Around the Plaza del Duque is the **Corté Inglés** department store, which stays open during the siesta. A newer Corté Inglés is opposite the Hotel Los Lebreros, on Luis Montoto, in an area fast becoming the new commercial center of Seville. Dozens of souvenir shops surround the cathedral; try Calle Alemanes and the delightful streets of the Barrio Santa Cruz.

Flamenco Regular flamenco clubs cater largely to tourists, but their shows are colorful and offer a good introduction for the uninitiated. Try any of the following: **El Arenal** (Rodo 7, tel. 216492); **Los Gallos** (Plaza Santa Cruz 11, tel. 216981), a small intimate club in the heart of the Barrio Santa Cruz offering fairly pure flamenco; and **El Patio Sevillano** (Paseo de Colón, tel. 214120), which caters largely to tour groups.

Bullfights Corridas take place at the Maestranza bullring on Paseo de Colón, usually on Sunday from Easter to October. The best are during the April Fair. Tickets can be bought in advance from the windows at the ring (one of the oldest and most picturesque in Spain) or from the kiosks in Calle Sierpes (these charge a commission).

Costa del Sol

What were impoverished fishing villages in the 1950s are now retirement villages and package tour meccas for northern Europeans and Americans. Despite the abuses of this naturally lovely area during the boom years of the 1960s and '70s, and the continuing brashness of the resorts that cater to the package tour trade, the Costa del Sol has managed to preserve at least some semblance of charm. Behind the hideous concrete monsters—some of which are now being demolished—you'll come across old cottages and villas set in gardens that blossom with jasmine and bougainvillea. The sun still sets over miles of sandy beaches and the lights of small fishing craft still twinkle in the distance. Most of your time should be devoted to indolence—swimming in the ocean, sunbathing on sandy beaches or by the hotel pool. When you need something to do, you can head inland to the historic town of Ronda and the perched white villages of Andalusia. You can also make a day trip to Gibraltar or Tangier.

Getting There

Daily flights on Iberia or Aviaco from Madrid to Málaga take about one hour; from Barcelona, 1½ hours. Iberia has direct flights from New York or London to Málaga. Málaga Airport (tel. 952–322000) is seven miles (12 kilometers) west of Málaga. There's bus and train service from the airport to Torremolinos. A fast train runs from Madrid to Málaga; there's also a comfortable overnight sleeper that arrives in Málaga around 7:30 AM. The best way to reach Málaga from Seville or Granada is by bus. Córdoba has good train and bus connections to Málaga.

Getting Around

Buses are the main means of transport on the Costa del Sol. Contact **Portillo** (Córdoba 7, Málaga, tel. 227300) or Portillo bus stations in Torremolinos, Fuengirola, Marbella, Mijas, Ronda, and Gibraltar. For bus service to Granada, Córdoba, Seville, and Nerja contact *Alsina Graells* (Plaza de Toros Vieja, Málaga, tel. 310400. There's also a useful suburban train service among Málaga, the airport, Torremolinos, and Fuengirola and all intermittent resorts. It runs every half hour between 6:30 A.M. and 10:30 P.M., and its terminus is Málaga's Guadalmedina station just over the river opposite the Corté Inglés. In Fuengirola the train terminus is close to the bus station, where you can make connections for Mijas, Ronda, and Marbella.

Guided Tours

Organized one- and two-day excursions are run by **Juliá Tours** and **Pullmantur** and numerous smaller companies from all the Costa del Sol resorts and can be booked through your hotel desk or any travel agent.

Tourist Information

Estepona. Paseo Marítimo Pedro Manrique, tel. 800913.
Fuengirola. Plaza de España, in the park, tel. 476166.
Málaga. Larios 5, tel. 213445, and at the airport in both national and international terminals.

Marbella. Miguel Cano 1, tel. 771442. **Nerja.** Puerta del Mar 4, tel. 521531.
Ronda. Plaza de España 1, tel. 871272.
Torremolinos. La Nogalera 517, tel. 381578.

Exploring the Costa del Sol

Nerja Our tour of the Costa del Sol begins in Nerja, some 30 miles (50 kilometers) to the east of Málaga, and takes us along the coast as far west as Estepona, then inland to the picturesque town of Ronda set high in the mountains. Nerja is a small but expanding resort that so far has escaped the worst excesses of the property developers. Its growth so far has been largely confined to villages such as El Capistrano, one of the showpieces of the Costa del Sol. There's pleasant bathing here, though the sand is gray and gritty. The **Balcón de Europa** is a fantastic lookout, high above the sea. The famous **Cuevas de Nerja** (a series of stalactite caves) are off the road to Almuñecar and Almería. A kind of vast underground cathedral, they contain the world's largest known stalactite (200 feet/61 meters). *Admission: 175 ptas. Open May–Sept., daily 9:30–9; Oct.–Apr., 10–1:30 and 4–7.*

Málaga Málaga is a busy port city with ancient streets and lovely villas set among exotic foliage, but it has little to commend itself to the overnight visitor. The central **Plaza de la Marina,** overlooking the port, is a pleasant place for a drink. The main shops are along the **Calle Marqués de Larios.**

The **Alcazaba** is a fortress begun in the 8th century when Málaga was the most important port of the Moorish kingdom. The ruins of the Roman amphitheater at its entrance were uncovered when the fort was restored. The inner palace dates from the 11th century when, for a short period after the breakup of the Caliphate of the West in Córdoba, it became the residence of the Moorish emirs. Today you'll find the **Archaeological Museum** here and a good collection of Moorish art. *Admission: 50 ptas. Open Mon.–Sat. 10–1 and 4–7 (5–8 in summer); closed Sun.*

Energetic souls can climb through the Alcazaba gardens to the summit of **Gibralfaro.** Others can drive by way of Calle Victoria or take the parador minibus that leaves roughly every 1½ hours from near the cathedral on Molina Lario. The Gibralfaro fortifications were built for Yusuf I in the 14th century. The Moors called it Jebelfaro meaning "rock of the lighthouse" after the beacon that stood here to guide ships into the harbor and warn of invasions by pirates. Today the beacon has gone, but there's a small parador that makes a delightful place for a drink or a meal, and some stunning views.

Torremolinos As you approach Torremolinos through an ocean of concrete blocks, it's hard to grasp that only 30 years ago this was an inconsequential fishing village. Today, this grossly overdeveloped resort is a prime example of 20th-century tourism run riot. The town center, with its brash Nogalera Plaza, is full of overpriced bars and restaurants. Much more attractive is the district of La Carihuela, further west, below the Avenida Carlota Alexandra. You'll find some old fishermen's cottages here, a few excellent seafood restaurants, and a traffic-free esplanade for an enjoyable stroll on a summer evening.

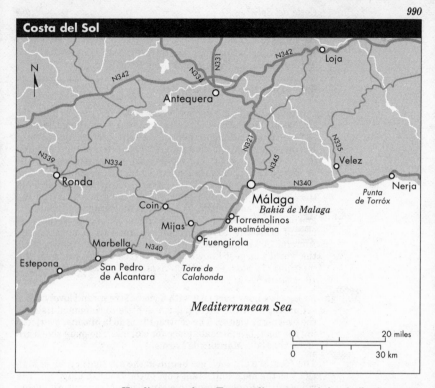

Costa del Sol

Heading west from Torremolinos, toward the similar but more staid resorts of **Benalmádena** and **Fuengirola,** both retirement havens for British and American senior citizens, you'll pass the **Atlantis Aquapark** (tel. 388888, on the Torremolinos bypass). This huge aquatic playground is very popular with vacationers. *Admission: 1,000 ptas. Open Apr.–Oct., 10 AM–10 PM.*

On the same route, just outside Benalmádena, is **Tivoli World** (tel. 441896), the Costa del Sol's leading amusement park. *Open Mar.–Oct. evenings only.*

Mijas It's a short drive from Fuengirola up into the mountains to the picturesque village of Mijas. Though the vast tourist-oriented main square may seem like an extension of the Costa's tawdry bazaar, there are hillside streets of whitewashed houses where you'll discover an authentic village atmosphere that has changed little since the days before the tourist boom of the 1960s. Visit the bullring and the chapel of Mijas's patroness, the Virgen de la Peña (to the side of the main square), and enjoy shopping for quality gifts and souvenirs.

Marbella Marbella is the most fashionable and sedate resort area along the coast. It does have a certain Florida land boom feel to it, but development has been controlled, and Marbella will, let's hope, never turn into another Torremolinos. There is a town with both a charming old Moorish quarter and a modern, T-shirt-and-fudge section along the main drag; but when people speak of Marbella they refer both to the town and to the resorts—some more exclusive than others—stretching 10 miles (16 kilometers) or so on either side of town, between the highway and the beach. If you're vacationing in southern Spain, this is the place to stay. There's championship golf and tennis, fashionable waterfront cafés, and trendy boutiques in the charming, medieval quarter of town.

Ronda Ronda, our last stop on this tour, is reached via a spectacular mountain road from San Pedro de Alcantara. One of the oldest towns in Spain, and last stronghold of the legendary Andalusian bandits, Ronda's most dramatic feature is its ravine, known as **El Tajo,** which is 900 feet (275 meters) across and divides the old Moorish town from the "new town" of El Mercadilla. Spanning the gorge is the *Puerte Nuevo,* an amazing architectural feat built between 1755 and 1793, whose parapet offers dizzying views of the River Guadalevin way below. Countless people have plunged to their deaths from this bridge, including its own architect, who accidentally fell over while inspecting his work, and numerous victims of the Civil War of 1936–39 who were hurled into the ravine—an episode recounted in Hemingway's *For Whom the Bell Tolls.* Ronda is visited more for its setting, breathtaking views, and ancient houses than for any particular monument. Stroll the old streets of **La Ciudad;** drop in at the historic **Reira Victoria** hotel, built by the English from Gibraltar as a fashionable resting place on their Algeciras to Bobadilla railroad line; and visit the **bullring,** one of the earliest rings in Spain. Here Ronda's most famous native son, Pedro Romero (1754–1839), father of modern bullfighting, is said to have killed 5,600 bulls during his 30-year career; and in the **Bullfighting Museum** you can see posters dating back to the very first fights held in the ring in May 1785. Above all, don't miss the cliff-top walk and the lovely gardens of the **Alameda del Tajo,** where you can contemplate one of the most dramatic views in all of Andalusia—a perfect place to end our tour of southern Spain.

Dining and Lodging

For details and price category definitions, *see* Dining and Lodging in Essential Information.

Estepona **El Libro Amarillo.** In English, this restaurant's name means
Dining the Yellow Book. Located three miles (five kilometers) out on
★ the road to Málaga, this is one of the Costa del Sol's most outstanding restaurants. The menu changes frequently. The service is excellent, and the decor is tasteful with attractive potted plants. Meat dishes are a specialty; try the *cordero asado* (roast lamb) or *pintado a la crema* (guinea fowl in cream sauce). *Rte. N340, km. 161, tel. 800484. Open for dinner only, 8 PM–midnight. Closed Sun. and Jan. Jacket and tie. Reservations essential; book well ahead. AE, MC, V. Expensive.*

El Molino. Situated in an old windmill, seven miles (12 kilometers) out on the road to Málaga, this restaurant has gained an excellent reputation over the last 20 years for its professional service and classic French cuisine. *Rte. N340, km. 166, tel. 782337. Dress: smart/casual. Reservations advised. AE, DC, MC, V. Open for dinner only. Closed Tues., Sun., and Jan. Expensive.*

★ **La Pulga que Tose.** Don't let the name (the Coughing Flea) put you off! This charming Belgian-owned restaurant is located in a beautiful old Andalusian house right in the center of town. The food is delicious, offering nouvelle cuisine specialties alongside classic dishes, and the atmosphere is delightful. *Pozo Pila 25, tel. 802749. Dress: informal. Reservations strongly advised. MC, V. Open for dinner only. Closed Sun. Expensive to Moderate.*

Lodging **Atalaya Park.** Closer to San Pedro de Alcantara than to Estepona itself, this resort hotel has its own private beach, pool, sports facilities (including an 18-hole golf course), and nightclub. Rooms facing the sea are more expensive than those overlooking the mountains. *Rte. N340, km. 168, tel. 781300. 239 rooms. AE, DC, MC, V. Expensive.*

Santa Marta. This is a small, quiet hotel with just 37 rooms in chalet bungalows set in a large, peaceful garden. Some rooms are a little faded after 30 years, but the tranquil setting is a plus. Good lunches are served by the pool. *Rte. N340, km. 173, tel. 780716. AE, MC, V. Open Apr.–Sept. only. Moderate.*

Málaga **Café de Paris.** The owner of this stylish restaurant in the Paseo
Dining Marítimo area is a former chef of Maxim's in Paris, and La Hacienda in Marbella. The *menu degustacion* lets you try a little of everything. Specialties include *rodaballo con espinacas* (sea bass and spinach). *Vélez Málaga, tel. 225043. Dress: casual/ smart. Reservations advised. AE, DC, MC, V. Closed Tues. and last 2 weeks of Sept. Expensive.*

★ **La Alegria.** This old-fashioned restaurant in the heart of town has long been famous for its fresh seafood dishes, though meat entrées are served, too. It's one of the classic restaurants of Málaga. *Marin Garcia 18, tel. 224143. Dress: informal. Reservations not essential. AE, DC, MC, V. Closed Sat. Expensive to Moderate.*

Antonio Martin. This is another old Málaga standby, with a splendid terrace overlooking the ocean, at the beginning of the Paseo Marítimo. It's long been famous for its fresh seafood and paella. Try the local *fritura malagueña. Paseo Marítimo 4, tel. 222113. Dress: informal. Reservations advised. AE, DC, MC, V. Closed Sun. night. Moderate.*

Guerola. This is one of the best of the many restaurants in the pedestrian shopping streets between Calle Larios and Calle Nueva. Its menu is more original than most. In summer, there are tables outside on the sidewalk. *Esparteros 8, tel. 223121. Dress: informal. Reservations not needed. V. Moderate.*

La Cancela. This is a colorful restaurant in the center of town, just off Calle Granada. Dine indoors or alfresco. *Denis Belgrano 3, tel. 223125. Dress: informal. Reservations not necessary. V. Inexpensive.*

Lodging **Los Naranjos.** This small hotel owned by the Luz chain is situated on a pleasant avenue in a residential district a little to the east of the city center. There's a small garden in front, but rooms overlooking the street can be noisy. *Paseo de Sancha 35, tel. 224317. 41 rooms. AE, DC, V. Expensive.*

★ **Parador de Gibralfaro.** Located in a small wood on top of Gibralfaro mountain two miles (three kilometers) above the city, this tiny parador has recently been renovated and offers spectacular views over the city and bay. Its accommodations are the best in Málaga, and it's a good place to dine even if you're not staying here. A bus service runs between the parador and cathedral. *Gibralfaro, tel. 221902. 12 rooms. Res-*

ervations essential, long in advance. AE, DC, MC, V. Expensive.

Las Vegas. In a pleasant part of town, just east of the center, this hotel has a dining room overlooking the Paseo Marítimo, an outdoor pool, and a large leafy garden. Rooms at the back enjoy a good view of the ocean. *Paseo de Sancha 22, tel. 217712. 73 rooms. AE, DC, V. Moderate.*

Victoria. This small, recently renovated hostel in an old house just off Calle Larios, offers excellent budget accommodations in a convenient central location. *Sancha de Lara 3, tel. 224223. 13 rooms. Inexpensive.*

Marbella
Dining
★

La Fonda. In a beautiful 18th-century house with antique furniture located in one of the loveliest old squares in Marbella, La Fonda is owned by one of Madrid's leading restaurateurs. Its cuisine combines the best of Spanish, French, and Austrian influences, and it has been awarded the National Gastronomic Prize. A delightful garden-patio filled with potted plants makes a perfect setting for summer dining. *Plaza del Santo Cristo 9, tel. 772512. Jacket and tie. Reservations essential. AE, DC, V. Open for dinner only, 8 PM–midnight. Closed Sun. Very expensive.*

★ **La Hacienda.** This restaurant, owned by Belgian chef-proprietor Paul Schiff, belongs to the Relais Gourmand group, and is one of the highest rated in Spain. The menu reflects the influence of both Paul Schiff's native Belgium and his adopted Andalusia. The *menu degustacion* at around 5,500 ptas. will enable you to sample the very best creations of this famous European chef. *Las Chapas, Rte. N340, km. 193, seven miles (12 km) east on the road to Málaga; tel. 831267. Jacket and tie. Reservations essential. AE, DC, V. Closed Mon. lunch in Aug.; also, mid-Nov.–mid-Dec. Very expensive.*

La Meridiana. Another of Marbella's most outstanding restaurants and a favorite with the local jet set, La Meridiana is located just west of town, toward Puerto Banus, and is famous for its original Bauhaus-type architecture and the superb quality and freshness of the ingredients. *Carmine de la Cruz, tel. 776190. Jacket and tie. Reservations essential. Closed Thurs. lunch, and mid-Jan.–mid-Feb. Open for dinner only from July 1–mid-Sept. AE, DC, MC. Very Expensive.*

Mena. One of the best of the many colorful restaurants in the delightful main square of Marbella, Mena offers indoor dining in beautifully decorated dining rooms or on a terrace. Food and service are good, and the atmosphere, charming. *Plaza de los Naranjos 10, tel. 771597. Dress: informal. Reservations not essential. AE, V. Expensive to Moderate.*

El Refugio. Located 2 miles (3 kilometers) from Marbella on the road to Ojén, El Refugio is in a charming Andalusian house with a garden and a terrace offering splendid views of the coast. Food and service are both outstanding. *Rte. de Ojén, km. 3, tel. 771848. Dress: informal. Reservations advised. AE, V. Closed Sun., Mon., and Feb.–mid-Mar. Expensive to Moderate.*

You'll find a whole cluster of expensive and moderately priced restaurants in the marina of Puerto Banus. Some of the best are **Don Leone** (Expensive; tel. 811716); **Taberna de Alabadero** (Expensive; tel. 782794); and **Taberna del Puerto Repito** (Moderate; tel. 785344).

Lodging The only reason to stay in town is if you're on a tight budget and have no car. Students can stay in small, family-run hotels in the old quarter of Marbella for as little as $15 a night. There are a few reasonably priced, package-tour-type high-rise hotels only a block from the busy town beach. For most visitors, air-conditioning in summer is a must. The ocean is uninviting at times, thanks to improper pollution controls, so a hotel pool is a plus. Most visitors prefer to stay at one of the sparkling white resorts strung along the beach on either side of town. Finding the right one is critical.

★ **Los Monteros.** Situated 1½ miles (2½ kilometers) east of Marbella, on the road to Málaga, this deluxe hotel offers all the facilities of a top hotel, including an 18-hole golf course, seven tennis courts, three pools, horseback riding, and gourmet dining in its famous El Corzo Grill restaurant. This is the third most expensive hotel in Spain, after the Ritz and Villa Magna in Madrid. Eighty percent of the guests are British, which may explain the somewhat starched formality of the rooms. *Urb. Los Monteros, tel. 771700. 171 rooms. AE, DC, MC, V. Very Expensive.*

Marbella Club. The grande dame of Marbella is smaller, older, more aristocratic, and also more worn than Puente Romano. It tends to attract an older, more established clientele, who request the same room year after year. Because the local patricians all belong to the club and come down from their villas for drinks and dinner, the club has a color and class that the more international Puente Romano lacks. Some, of course, will prefer the greater anonymity and the greater number of American guests at Puente Romano. The bungalow-style rooms at the Marbella Club run from cramped to spacious, and the decor varies from Beach Modern to regional; specify what you want, but ask for a room that's been recently renovated. Facilities include a beach and pool. The grounds are exquisite. Breakfast is served on a patio where songbirds flit through the lush, subtropical vegetation. *Rte. N340, tel. 952–771300.*

Puente Romano. A spectacular, modern hotel and apartment complex of low, white stucco buildings located two miles (three kilometers) west of Marbella on the road to Puerto Banus. The "village" has a Roman bridge in its beautifully landscaped grounds as well as two pools, a tennis club, and a disco run by Regine. *Rte. N340, km. 184, tel. 770100. 171 rooms. AE, DC, V. Very Expensive.*

El Fuerte. This is the best of the only hotels in the center of Marbella, with simple, adequate rooms. It's located in a 1950s-type building in the midst of a large garden with an outdoor pool. *Avenida El Fuerte, tel. 771500. 146 rooms. AE, DC, V. Moderate.*

Alfil. If you're looking for inexpensive accommodations right in the heart of town, then this recently renovated hotel on the main street will meet your needs. Rooms at the back are quieter. *Avenida Ricardo Soriano 19, tel. 772350. 41 rooms. V. Inexpensive.*

Mijas
Dining **Valparaíso.** *Pato a la naranja* (duck in an orange sauce) is one of the specialties served in a pleasant villa with garden and terrace on the road leading from Fuengirola to Mijas. And it's all set to live piano music. *Tel. 952/485996. AE, DC, MC, V. Dinner only. Closed Sun. Expensive.*

Mirlo Blanco. Here in the "White Blackbird," set in an old village house just below the bullring, you can sample Basque specialties such as *txangurro* (crab) and *merluza a la vasca* (hake with asparagus, eggs, and clam sauce). *Plaza Constitución 13, tel. 485700. Dress: informal. Reservations not essential. AE, DC, V. Moderate.*

La Reja. This charming restaurant has two dining rooms overlooking the main square of Plaza Virgen de la Peria. There's an atmospheric bar and an inexpensive pizzeria, too. *Caños 9, tel. 485068. Dress: informal. Reservations not needed. AE, DC, V. Closed Mon. Moderate.*

Lodging   **Byblos Andaluz.** In this new, luxury hotel set in a huge garden
  ★   of palms, cypresses, and fountains, you'll find every comfort for a pampered vacation. Facilities include pools, saunas, tennis, and an 18-hole golf course. The hotel is known for its water cures. Its Le Nailhac restaurant is famous for its French cuisine; special low-calorie meals are also available. *Urbano Mijas-Golf, tel. 473050. 135 rooms. AE, DC, MC, V. Very Expensive.*

Hotel Mijas. You'll find this beautifully situated hotel at the entrance to Mijas village. The hotel is modern and peaceful, with a delightful rose garden, terrace, and afternoon tea. *Urbano Tamisa, tel. 485800. 106 rooms, pool. AE, DC, MC, V. Expensive.*

Nerja   **Casa Luque.** This is one of the most authentically Spanish of
Dining   Nerja's restaurants, located in a charming old Andalusian house behind the Balon de Europa church. The menu is small and often includes pasta dishes. *Plaza Cavana 2, tel. 520032. Dress: informal. Reservations not essential. AE, DC, MC, V. Closed Wed. Moderate.*

Cortijo. This small, family-run restaurant in a 200-year-old house is owned by a father and his two sons, who act as host, chef, and waiter. Andalusian dishes share the menu with international favorites. *Varrio 26, no phone. DC, MC, V. Inexpensive.*

Lodging   **Monica.** Nerja's newest beach hotel opened in 1986. It's spacious and luxurious, with Moorish-style architecture. Facilities include tennis, pool, nightclub and disco. *Playa Terrecilla, tel. 521100. 234 rooms. AE, DC, MC, V. Expensive.*
  ★   **Parador.** All the rooms in this small parador a little to the east of the center of Nerja have balconies overlooking the sea. There's a pleasant leafy garden and outdoor pool, and an elevator takes you down to the beach. The restaurant is well known for its fish dishes. *El Tablazo, tel. 520050. 73 rooms. AE, DC, MC, V. Expensive.*

Ronda   **Don Miguel.** Located by the bridge over the Tajo gorge, the res-
Dining   taurant's terrace offers spectacular views of the ravine. Lamb
  ★   is a specialty; try *piema de cordero lechal Don Miguel* (leg of baby lamb). *Villanneva 4, tel. 871090. Dress: informal but smart. Reservations advised. Closed Tues. night and all day Sun. June–Sept.; closed Tues. night and all day Wed. Oct.–May. AE, DC, MC, V. Expensive.*

Pedro Romero. Located opposite the bullring, with the inevitable bullring decor. Try the *sopa de mesón*—the soup of the house. *Virgen de la Paz 18, tel. 871061. AE, DC, MC, V. Moderate.*

Mesón Santiago. This typical Andalusian mesón with colorful decor opens for lunch only and has a pleasant outdoor patio. It

serves hearty portions of home-cooked food—but be prepared
for long waits. *Marina 3, tel. 871559. Dress: informal. MC, V.
Open 1–4 PM only. Inexpensive.*

Lodging **Reina Victoria.** A spectacularly situated Old World hotel with a
distinctly British air, the Reina Victoria sits atop the very rim
of the gorge. Views and style are tops but, unfortunately, it's
very much patronized by tour groups. *Jerez 25, tel. 871240. 89
rooms. AE, DC, MC, V. Moderate to Expensive.*

Polo. A cozy, old-fashioned hotel in the center of town, Polo
sports a reasonably priced restaurant. The staff is friendly and
the rooms simple but comfortable. *Mariano Soubiron 8, tel.
872447. 33 rooms. AE, DC, V. Moderate.*

Torremolinos **El Atrio.** This small, stylish restaurant is located in the Pueblo
Dining Blanco. Its cuisine is predominantly French. In summer, you
can dine on the Terrace. *Off Calle Casablanca, no phone. AE,
V. Open 8 PM–midnight. Closed Sun. and Dec. Moderate.*

El Cangrejo. This is one of several classic seafood restaurants in
La Carihuela. You can succumb to a full dinner in the restaurant or enjoy succulent seafood tapas in the entrance bar. *Bulto
25, tel. 380479. Dress: informal. Reservations not needed. MC,
V. Moderate.*

La Primavera. Set in one of the old Torremolinos villas just below Calle Casablanca, its patio offers delightful outdoor dining
amid foliage, and its indoor restaurant is attractively decorated
with paintings and ceramic plates. Service is good, food attractively presented, but the cuisine only average—go for the
setting rather than the food. *Guetaria, tel. 380909. Dress: informal. Reservations not needed. AE, DC, MC, V. Moderate.*

El Roqueo. Owned by a former fisherman, this is one of the locals' favorite Carihuela fish restaurants. Ingredients are
always fresh and the prices, very reasonable. *Carmen 35, tel.
384946. Dress: informal. No credit cards. Closed Tues. and
Nov. Moderate.*

Lodging **Cervantes.** This busy cosmopolitan hotel in the heart of town
has comfortable rooms, good service, and a well-known dining
room on its top floor; this is one of Torremolinos's consistently
good hotels. *Las Mercedes, tel. 384033. 393 rooms. AE, DC,
MC, V. Expensive.*

Melia Torremolinos. Torremolinos's only five-star hotel is located west of town, off the main highway toward Benalmádena.
It overlooks the sea and offers all the facilities of a luxury hotel,
but standards are not always up to par. *Arda Carlota
Alessandri 109, tel. 380500. 282 rooms. AE, DC, MC, V. Expensive.*

Tropicana. Located on the beach at the far end of the Carihuela
in one of the pleasantest areas of Torremolinos, this is a comfortable, relaxing resort hotel with several good restaurants
nearby. *Tropico 6, tel. 386600. 86 rooms. Facilities: pool. AE,
DC, MC, V. Moderate.*

★ **Miami.** Set in an old Andalusian villa in a shady garden to the
west of the Carihuela, this is something of a find amid the ocean
of concrete blocks. It's small, friendly, and intimate, and very
popular with Spaniards, so book ahead. *Aladino 14, tel.
385255. 26 rooms. Inexpensive.*

31 Sweden

Introduction

Sweden's 173,730 square miles (444,750 square kilometers) contain only 8.4 million people, so its population density ranks among Europe's lowest, and its vast open spaces and good, uncrowded roads make it a country where you can easily escape the frantic pace of modern life. But the long, narrow shape of the country means that on a typical visit it is possible to explore only a relatively small area, and it is unwise to be overly ambitious when planning your trip. The distances are considerable, especially by European standards—almost 1,000 miles (1,600 kilometers), as the crow flies, from north to south. The 1,330-mile (2,130-kilometer) train journey from Trelleborg, in the far south, through endless birch forests to Riksgränsen, in the Arctic north, is claimed to be the world's longest stretch of continuously electrified railroad.

For the purposes of this guide, we have concentrated on the more densely populated southern part of the country—essentially the area dominated by the two largest cities, Stockholm and Gothenburg—although we have suggested an itinerary through the celebrated Folklore District, where the most distinctly Swedish cultural traditions are faithfully maintained.

The Swedish Tourist Board would be the first to admit that it faces something of an uphill task in marketing the country to the overseas visitor, if only because it does not have such a long-established tourist industry as neighboring Norway or traditional favorites such as France, Italy, and Switzerland. But those who do visit Sweden usually return home raving about its exceptionally high standards of lodging and dining. Even the most modest establishment is always spotlessly clean, and you will be given a warm welcome (almost certainly in excellent English, too).

Sweden still needs to do a lot more to encourage visitors from abroad by extending its tourist season, however. It's disappointing to note how many visitor attractions and excursions do not start operating until mid-June and then suddenly close down in mid-August, when the Swede's own vacation season ends and the children return to school. The weather can be magnificent in the spring and fall, and there must be plenty of foreign visitors—and Swedes, too, for that matter—who would like to do some sightseeing when there are fewer people around.

Sweden may not have scenic attractions as spectacular as the Norwegian fjords across the border, but it offers a more varied landscape, with more than 96,000 lakes and a jagged coastline with countless archipelagoes, forests, mountains, and rushing rivers. And there is a fascinating contrast in lifestyles between the bustling, sophisticated cities and the isolated, rural communities where the leisurely pace of life has changed little with the passing centuries.

Each of Sweden's major cities has its own special atmosphere. Stockholm, with its spectacular lakeside setting, has an exhilarating quality. Gothenburg, on the other hand, is a comfortable city of wide avenues and verdant parks. Malmö, 45 minutes by hovercraft from Denmark, combines a cosmopolitan flavor with small-town friendliness.

Before You Go

When to Go The main tourist season runs from June through August, although a more enterprising attitude toward tourism could extend it to include April, May, and September. Because of the relatively short summer, the Swedes themselves tend to think of the season as running only from mid-June to the middle of August, when the schools reopen. As a result, some visitor attractions restrict their opening times outside these periods or even close down altogether. Sweden virtually shuts up shop for the entire month of July, so avoid planning a business trip at that time. The concentrated nature of the Swedes's own vacation period can make it difficult to get hotel reservations during July and early August. On the other hand, the big city hotels, which cater mainly to business travelers, reduce their rates drastically in the summer, when their ordinary clients are on vacation. Ask your travel agent about special discount schemes offered by the major hotel groups.

Climate As in the rest of northern Europe, Sweden's summer weather is unpredictable but, as a general rule, it is more likely to be rainy on the west coast than in the east. When the sun shines, the climate is usually agreeable; it is rarely unbearably hot. In Stockholm, it never really gets dark in mid-summer, while in the far north, above the Arctic Circle, the sun doesn't set between the end of May and the middle of July.

The following are the average daily maximum and minimum temperatures for Stockholm.

Jan.	30F	−1C	May	58F	14C	Sept.	60F	15C
	23	−5		43	6		49	9
Feb.	30F	−1C	June	67F	19C	Oct.	49F	9C
	22	−5		51	11		41	5
Mar.	37F	3C	July	71F	22C	Nov.	40F	5C
	26	−4		57	14		34	1
Apr.	47F	8C	Aug.	68F	20C	Dec.	35F	2C
	34	1		56	13		29	−2

Currency The unit of currency in Sweden is the krona (plural kronor), which is divided into 100 öre and is written as SEK or kr. Coins come in values of 10 or 50 öre and 1 or 5 kronor, while bills come in denominations of 10, 50, 100, 500, 1,000, and 10,000 SEK. Traveler's checks and foreign currency can be exchanged at banks all over Sweden and at post offices bearing the "PK Exchange" sign. At press time (fall 1988), the exchange rate was 5.87 kronor to the dollar and 10.58 kronor to the pound.

What It Will Cost Sweden has a not-altogether-justified reputation as an expensive country. Hotel prices are marginally above the European average, probably about the same as in the United Kingdom, but higher than in France. As in most countries, the most expensive hotels are found in major cities such as Stockholm and Gothenburg. Restaurant prices are generally fairly high, but there are plenty of bargains to be had: Look for the *dagens ratt* (dish of the day) in many city restaurants. This costs about SEK 40 and includes a main dish, salad, soft drink, bread and butter, and coffee.

Sweden

N

Norwegian Sea

Kiruna

Luleälven Jokkmokk

Arjeplog

Tärnaby

Kalix

Tornio

Arvidsjaur

Sorsele

Luleå

Storuman

Piteå

Lycksele

Skellefteå

Strömsund

Åsele

Umeälven

Umeå

Åre

Östersund

FINLAND

Tännäs

Sundsvall

Ljungan

Gulf of Bothnia

NORWAY

Hudiksvall

Idre

Bollnäs

Söderhamn

Mora

Klarälven

Falun

Borlänge

Avesta

Fagersta

Uppsala

Karlstad

Västerås

Mellerud

Lake Mälaren

Stockholm

Strömstad

Lake Vänern

Örebro

Gulf of Finland

Uddevalla

Trollhättan

Norrköping

Gotska Sandön

Lake Vättern

Linköping

Gothenburg

Jönköping

Baltic Sea

Falkenberg

Borås

Nässjö

Visby

Gulf of Riga

Värnamo

Gotland

Halmstad

Växjö

Oskarshamn

SOVIET UNION

Helsingborg

Kalmar

Karlskrona

Oland

Malmö

Kristianstad

0   50 miles

DEN.

Trelleborg

Ystad

0   75 km

Many hotels have special low summer rates and cut costs during weekends in winter. But because of heavy taxes and excise duties, liquor prices are among the highest in Europe. It pays to take in your maximum duty-free allowance. Value-added tax (known as *Moms* in Swedish) is imposed on all goods and services at a flat rate of 19% and is included in all prices. You can avoid most of this tax if you take advantage of the Tax-free Shopping Service offered at some 10,000 stores throughout the country (*see* Shopping).

Sample Prices   Cup of coffee, SEK 10; bottle of beer, SEK 10–40; Coca-Cola, SEK 10–12; ham sandwich, SEK 10–15; one-mile taxi ride, SEK 50.

Customs on Arrival   You may bring duty-free into Sweden 400 cigarettes or 200 cigarillos or 100 cigars or 500 grams of tobacco. You may also import one liter of spirits and one liter of wine *or* two liters of beer, plus a reasonable amount of perfume and other goods to the value of SEK 600. Residents over the age of 15 of other European countries may bring duty-free into Sweden 200 cigarettes or 100 cigarillos, or 50 cigars or 250 grams of tobacco; visitors aged 20 or more may import one liter of spirits, one liter of wine, and two liters of beer, plus a reasonable amount of perfume, and other goods to the value of SEK 600. You can take up to SEK 6,000 in and out of Sweden, and there is no limit on the amount of foreign currency that can be imported.

Language   Virtually all Swedes you are likely to meet will speak English, for it is a mandatory subject in all schools and is the main foreign language that Swedish children learn. Some of the older people you meet in the rural areas may not be quite so familiar with English, but you'll soon find someone who can help out. Swedish is one of the Germanic languages and is similar to Danish and Norwegian. Grammatically it is easier than German, although pronunciation can pose some problems. Also, the letters Å, Ä, and Ö, rank as separate letters in the Swedish alphabet and come at the end after Z. So if you're looking up a Mr. Ängelholm in a Swedish telephone book, you'll find him near the end. Few Swedish place-names have anglicized spellings, with the notable exception of Göteborg (Gothenburg).

Getting Around

By Car   Sweden has an excellent highway network of more than 50,000
Road Conditions   miles (80,000 kilometers). The fastest routes are those with numbers prefixed with an E (for "European"), some of which are the equivalent of American superhighways or British motorways—for part of the way, at least. Road E4, for instance, covers the whole of the distance from Malmö, in the south, to Stockholm, and on to Sundsvall and Umeå, in the north, finishing at Haparanda, on the frontier with Finland. All main and secondary roads are well surfaced, but some minor roads, particularly in the north, are graveled. No tolls are levied on Swedish highways.

Rules of the Road   You drive on the right and must always yield to traffic coming from the right, unless signs indicate otherwise. You must also yield to traffic already in a traffic circle. No matter where you sit in a car, you must wear a seat belt, and cars must have low-beam headlights on at all times. Signs indicate five basic speed limits, ranging from 30 kph (18 mph) in school or playground areas to 110 kph (68 mph) on E roads. For vehicles towing a trailer, the limit is 70 kph (43 mph) if the towed unit has brakes; otherwise, 40 kph (25 mph). Drunk-driving laws are strictly enforced.

Parking Vehicles must always be parked on the right-hand side of the road, but if you want to park overnight, particularly in suburban areas, be sure not to do so on the night the street is being cleaned; signs should indicate when this occurs. Parking meters are available for use in larger towns, usually between 8 AM and 6 PM. The fee varies from about SEK 6 to SEK 15 per hour. A circular sign with a red cross on a blue background with a red border means parking is prohibited. A yellow plate with a red border below it means restricted parking.

Gasoline Gas costs the equivalent of about $2.70 per U.S. gallon, depending on grade. Lead-free gasoline is readily available. Most gas stations are self-service places, indicated by the sign "Tanka Själv." Many have automatic pumps, which accept SEK 10 or SEK 100 bills, and where you can fill up at any time, night or day.

Breakdowns The **Larmtjänst** organization, run by a confederation of Swedish insurance companies, provides a 24-hour breakdown service. Its phone numbers are listed in all telephone books. A toll-free emergency number, tel. 90000, is also available.

By Train Sweden's rail network, mostly electrified, is highly efficient, and trains operate frequently, particularly on the main routes linking Stockholm with Gothenburg and Malmö, on which there is an hourly service. First- and second-class cars are provided on all main routes, and sleeping cars are available in both classes on overnight trains. On virtually all long-distance trains, there is a buffet or dining car. Seat reservations are always advisable, and on some trains—indicated with R, IC, or V in the timetable—they are compulsory. Reservations can be made right up to departure time at a cost of SEK 15 per seat.

Fares The full second-class fare applies only on Friday and Sunday trains; the price is reduced by about 25% on all other days. A price ceiling applies on all journeys of 560 miles (900 kilometers) or more. For groups of two to five passengers traveling second class, the first adult pays the normal fare applicable on the day of travel, and additional adults receive a discount of 30%.

By Plane Sweden's domestic air network is highly developed. Most major cities are served by **SAS** (Scandinavian Airlines) or its domestic partner **LIN** (Linjeflyg). From Stockholm, there are services to about 30 points around the country. SAS and LIN offer cut-rate round-trip "mini-fares" every day of the week on selected flights, and these fares are available on most services during the peak tourist season, from late June to mid-August. Special fares for families, students, and senior citizens are also available.

By Bus Sweden has an excellent network of express bus services that provides an inexpensive and relatively speedy way of getting around the country. **GDG** offers daily express services from Gothenburg to many parts of Sweden; **SJ** (Swedish State Railroads) is another major bus operator. A number of other private companies operate weekend-only services on additional routes. In the far north of Sweden, Post Buses delivering mail to remote areas also carry passengers, and provide an offbeat and inexpensive way of seeing the countryside.

By Boat The classic boat trip in Sweden is the four-day journey along the Göta Canal between Gothenburg, and Stockholm, operated by **Göta Kanal,** Gothenburg, tel. 031/177615. A new tourist route is the 300-mile (500-kilometer) coastal cruise between Öregrund, northeast of Stockholm, and Byxelkrok, on the island of Öland. It's operated by **KustLinjen,** tel. 08/240970.

By Bicycle Cycling is a popular activity in Sweden, and the country's uncongested roads make it ideal for extended bike tours. Bicycles can be rented throughout the country; inquire at the local tourist information office. Rental costs average around SEK 30 per day or SEK 150 per week. The **Swedish Touring Club** (STF) in Stockholm (tel. 08/227200) can give you information about cycling packages that include bike rental, overnight accommodation, and meals. **Cykelfrämjandet** (tel. 08/7516204) has an English-language guide to cycling trips.

Essential Information

Telephones Sweden has plenty of pay phones, although they are not found
Local Calls (as in many other European countries) in post offices. There are, however, special offices marked "Tele" or "Telebutik" from which you can make calls. There are two types of pay phones in Sweden: One accepts only SEK 1 coins, while the other takes 50 öre, SEK 1, and SEK 5 coins. For a local call, you need a SEK 1 coin.

International Calls These can be made from any pay phone. For calls to the USA and Canada, dial 009, then 1 (the country code), then wait for a second dial tone before dialing the area code and number. When dialing the United Kingdom, omit the initial zero on area codes (for London you would dial 009 followed by 44, then 1 and the local number). Making calls from your hotel room is convenient, but can be expensive, so check with the front desk about rates first. You pay the normal rate at Telebutik offices.

Operators and There is no single number to dial for an English-speaking oper-
Information ator. Check the telephone book for the service you require.

Mail Airmail letters to the USA and Canada weighing less than 20
Postal Rates grams cost SEK 3.40; airmail postcards, SEK 2.90. Postcards and letters within Europe cost SEK 2.30 and 3.00, respectively.

Receiving Mail If you're uncertain where you will be staying, have your mail sent to Poste Restante, S-101 10 Stockholm. The address for collection is Vasagatan 28–32. A Poste Restante service is also offered by **American Express** (*see* Important Addresses and Numbers in Stockholm).

Shopping Swedish goods have earned an international reputation for elegance and quality, and any visitor to the country should spend some time exploring the many impressive shops and department stores. The midsummer tourist season is as good a time as any to go shopping, for that is when many stores have their annual sales. The best buys are to be found in glassware, stainless steel, pottery and ceramics, leather goods, and textiles. You will find a wide selection of goods available in major stores such as NK, Athléns, Tempo, and Domus, which have branches all over the country.

High-quality furniture is a Swedish specialty, and it is worthwhile visiting one of the many branches of IKEA, a shop usually located on the outskirts of major towns. IKEA's prices are extremely competitive, and the company also operates an export service. For glassware at bargain prices, head for the "Kingdom of Glass" (*see* The West Coast, and The Glass Country). All the major glassworks, including Orrefors and Kosta Boda, have large factory outlets where you can pick up "seconds" (normally indistinguishable from the perfect product) at only a fraction of the normal retail price. For clothing, the best center is Boras, not far from Gothenburg. Here you can find bargains from the leading mail-order companies. In country areas, look for the local "Hemslöjd" craft centers, featuring high-quality clothing and needlework items at low prices.

VAT Refunds   About 10,000 Swedish shops—1,000 in Stockholm alone—participate in the Tax-free Shopping Service for visitors, enabling you to claim a refund on most of the value-added tax (*Moms*) that you have paid. Shops taking part in the scheme display a distinctive black, blue, and yellow sticker in the window. (Some stores offer the service only on purchases worth more than SEK 200.) Whenever you make a purchase in a participating store, you are given a "Tax-free Shopping Check" equivalent to the tax paid, less a handling charge. This check can be cashed when you leave Sweden, either at the airport or aboard ferries. Goods that you have bought using the Tax-free Shopping Service will be sealed, and the seal must not be broken until you have left the country. You should have your passport with you when you make your purchase and when you claim your refund.

Opening and   **Banks.** Banks are open weekdays 9:30–3, and in some larger
Closing Times   cities remain open until 5:30, except on Friday.

Museums. Hours vary widely, but museums are typically open weekdays 10–4 or 10–5. Many are also open weekends, but may close Monday.

Shops. Shops are generally open weekdays 9 or 9:30 to 6 and Saturday 9–1 or 9–4. Some large department stores stay open until 8 or 10 on certain evenings, and some also open on Sunday.

National Holidays   January 1 (New Year's Day); January 6 (Epiphany); March 24 (Good Friday); March 27 (Easter Monday); May 1 (Labour Day); May 4 (Ascension Day); May 15 (Pentecost Monday); June 24 (Midsummer's Day); November 4 (All Saints' Day); December 25 (Christmas); December 26 (St. Stephen's Day).

Dining   Swedish cuisine used to be considered somewhat uninteresting, but lately it has become much more cosmopolitan. The inevitable fast-food outlets, such as McDonald's and Wimpy, have come on the scene, as well as Clock, the homegrown version. But there is also a good range of more conventional restaurants, ranging from the usual top-class establishments to inexpensive places where you can pick up a bargain-price lunch or snack.

High-class cafés and cafeterias are increasingly popular, and in larger cities some stay open during the night, serving open-face sandwiches, salads, and snacks. Many restaurants all over the country specialize in *Husmanskost*—literally "home cooking"—which is based on traditional Swedish recipes.

Sweden is best known for its *smörgåsbord*, a word whose correct pronunciation defeats non-Swedes. It consists of a tempting buffet of hot and cold dishes, with usually a strong emphasis on seafood, notably herring, prepared in a wide variety of ways. Authentic smörgåsbord can be enjoyed all over the country, but the best is found in the many inns in Skåne, where you can eat as much as you want for about SEK 140. Virtually all Swedish hotels now serve a lavish smörgåsbord-style breakfast, often included in the room price. Do justice to your breakfast and you'll probably want to skip lunch!

Mealtimes The Swedes tend to eat early. Restaurants start serving lunch at about 11 AM, and outside the main cities you may find that they close quite early in the evening (often by 9) or may not even open at all. Don't wait too late to look for someplace to have a meal.

Ratings Prices are per person and include a first course, main course (Swedes tend to skip desserts), and service charge, but no drinks. A service charge of 13–15% is added to meal prices, so there is no need to tip. If you want to leave something extra, round the total to the nearest SEK 5 or so. Best bets are indicated by a star ★. At press time, there were 5.87 kronor (SEK) to the dollar.

Category	Cost
Very Expensive	over SEK 300
Expensive	SEK 175–300
Moderate	SEK 90–175
Inexpensive	under SEK 90

Credit Cards The following credit card abbreviations are used: AE, American Express; DC, Diners Club; MC, MasterCard; V, Visa.

Lodging Sweden offers a wide range of accommodations, from simple village rooms and campsites to top-class hotels of the highest international standard. Except at the major hotels in the larger cities, catering mainly to business clientele, rates are fairly reasonable. Prices are normally on a per-room basis and include all taxes and service and usually breakfast. Apart from the more modest inns and the cheapest budget establishments, private baths and showers are now standard features, although it is just as well to double-check when making your reservation. Whatever their size, virtually all Swedish hotels provide scrupulously clean accommodations and courteous service. In Stockholm, there is a hotel reservation office—**Hotellcentralen**—at the Central Train Station. In other areas, local tourist offices will help you with hotel reservations.

Hotels There is no official star-rating system in Sweden, but you can get a good idea of the facilities and prices at a particular hotel by consulting the official annual guide, *Hotels in Sweden*, obtainable free of charge from the Swedish National Tourist Office. There is a good selection of hotels in all price categories in every town and city, though major international chains such as Sheraton have made only small inroads in Sweden thus far.

The main homegrown chains are SARA, Scandic, and RESO. The Sweden Hotels group has about 90 independently owned hotels and offers a central reservation office. The group also has its own classification scheme—A, B, or C—based on the facilities available at each establishment. Chain hotels in Sweden, as elsewhere, tend to be rather standardized, but there are many attractive, privately owned country hotels, some of which are modernized farmhouses and manors dating back many centuries.

House-Rental Vacations In Sweden, these are popular among other Europeans, particularly the British and Germans. There are about 250 chalet villages with amenities, such as grocery stores, restaurants, saunas, and tennis courts. You can often arrange such accommodations on the spot at local tourist information offices. An alternative is a package, such as the one offered by **Longship Holidays** (run by DFDS Seaways), which combines a ferry trip from Britain across the North Sea with a stay in a chalet village. Longship is based in the United Kingdom at Parkeston Quay, Harwich, Essex (tel. 0255/554681).

Camping Camping is also popular in Sweden. There are more than 700 officially approved sites throughout the country, most located next to the sea or a lake and offering activities such as windsurfing, riding, and tennis. They are generally open between June 1 and September 1, though some are available year round. The Swedish Tourist Board publishes, in English, an abbreviated list of sites.

Ratings Prices are for two people in a double room, based on high-season rates. Best bets are indicated by a star ★. At press time, there were 5.87 kronor (SEK) to the dollar.

Category	Cost
Very Expensive	over SEK 950
Expensive	SEK 750–950
Moderate	SEK 550–750
Inexpensive	under SEK 550

Credit Cards The following credit card abbreviations are used: AE, American Express; DC, Diners Club; MC, MasterCard; V, Visa.

Tipping Unlike some countries, Sweden cannot be described as "the land of the outstretched palm"—probably because earnings are relatively high anyway, and hotel and restaurant staffs do not depend on their tips for their existence. In hotels, the only extra tip you need to give is to the porter who carries your bags (say SEK 5 per case). Taxi drivers expect a tip of about 10%, and it is quite safe to ask them to add this on themselves. Checkroom attendants should receive about SEK 6 per coat.

Stockholm

Arriving and Departing

By Plane All international flights arrive at Arlanda Airport, 25 miles (about 40 kilometers) north of the city. The airport is linked to

Stockholm by a fast freeway. For information on arrival and departure times, call the individual airlines.

Between the Airport and Downtown Buses leave every 10–15 minutes from 7:10 AM to 10:30 PM, stopping at the Haga Terminal to the north of the city and terminating at Vasagatan, adjoining the Central Train Station and opposite the Sheraton Hotel. In addition, a minibus service from Vasagatan operates at 15–20-minute intervals between 7:45 AM and 8 PM and calls at seven Stockholm hotels: the Sergel Plaza, Birger Jarl, Stockholm Plaza, Karelia, Kung Carl, Anglais, and Eden Terrace. A taxi from the airport will cost at least SEK 350, but a useful alternative is the SAS (Scandinavian Airlines) limousine service to any point in Greater Stockholm. It operates as a shared taxi at between SEK 165 and SEK 210, depending on the distance. If two or three people travel together in a limousine to the same address, only one pays the full rate; all others pay half price.

By Train All major domestic and international services arrive at Stockholm Central Station on Vasagatan, in the heart of the city. This is also the terminus for local commuter services. For 24-hour train information, tel. 08/225060. At the station, there is a ticket and information office, where you can make seat or sleeping-car reservations. An automatic ticket-issuing machine is also available. If you buy your ticket from the conductor on the train, you must pay a surcharge of SEK 12, plus a seat reservation fee of SEK 15, if applicable.

By Bus Long-distance buses, from such places as Härnosand and Sundsvall, arrive at Norra Bantorget, a few blocks north of the Central Station, and all others at Klarabeergsviadukten, just beside it. Bus tickets can also be bought at the railroad reservations office.

By Car There are two main access routes from the west and south: the E3 main highway from Gothenburg and E4 from Malmö, which continues as the main route to Sundsvall, the far north, and Finland. All routes to the city center are well marked.

Getting Around

The most cost-effective way of getting around Stockholm is to use a *Stockholmskortet* (Key to Stockholm) card. Besides giving unlimited transportation on city subway, bus, and rail services, it offers free admission to 50 museums and several sightseeing trips. The card, valid for up to four days, costs from SEK 70 to SEK 240, depending on the time allotted. It is available from the **Tourist Center** at Sweden House, at Kungsträdgården, and the Hotellcentralen accommodations bureau at the Central Station.

Maps and timetables for all city transportation networks are available from the SL information desks at Norrmalmstorg or Sergels Torg. You can also obtain information by phone (tel. 08/ 236000).

By Bus and Subway The Stockholm Transit Authority (SL) operates both the bus and subway systems. Tickets for the two networks are interchangeable.

The subway system, known as "T-banan" (the *T* stands for "tunnel"), is the easiest and fastest way of getting around the city. Some of the stations offer permanent art exhibitions. Station entrances are marked with a blue T on a white background. The T-banan has about 100 stations and covers more than 60 route-miles (100 route-kilometers). Trains run frequently between 5 AM and 2 AM, although some services cease at midnight.

Although individual tickets are available at ticket counters, it is cheaper to buy 18-coupon booklets, available at Pressbyrån newsstands. A one-day ticket for the city center alone, valid on both bus and subway, costs SEK 22. A ticket covering the entire Greater Stockholm area costs SEK 40 for 24 hours or SEK 76 for 72 hours.

The Stockholm bus network is one of the world's largest. Services run not only within the central area but also to out-of-town points of interest, such as **Waxholm,** with its historic fortress, and **Gustavsberg,** with its well-known porcelain factory. Within Greater Stockholm, buses run throughout the night.

By Train SL operates conventional train services from Stockholm's Central Station to a number of nearby points, including **Nynäshamn,** a departure point for ferries to the island of Gotland. Trains also run from the Slussen station to the fashionable beach resort of **Saltsjobaden.**

By Taxi Taxis are difficult to come by on the street (although you may find one at an official taxi stand), so they usually have to be ordered. Telephone 08/150000 or 08/150400 if you need to reserve one well in advance. It costs between SEK 10 and SEK 20 just for the taxi to get to you. You will then pay from SEK 30 to SEK 40 for a trip of up to six miles (10 kilometers), depending on the number of people in the taxi and the time of day.

Important Addresses and Numbers

Tourist Information The main Tourist Center is at **Sweden House,** Kungsträdgarden, tel. 08/7892000; weekends, 08/7892417. During the peak tourist season (mid-June to mid-August), it is open weekdays 8:30–6; weekends 8–5. Off-season the hours are 9–5 and 9–2, respectively. Besides providing information, it is the main ticket center for sightseeing excursions. There are also information centers at the Central Station, in the City Hall (summer only), and in the Kaknäs TV tower.

Embassies U.S. Strandvägen 101, tel. 08/783–5300. **Canadian.** Tegelbacken 4, tel. 08/237920. **U.K.** Skarpögatan 6–8, tel. 08/670140.

Emergencies Police, tel. 08/769–3000 (emergencies only: 08/90000); **Ambulance,** tel. 08/90000; **Doctor** (Medical Care Information), tel. 08/449200—tourists can get hospital attention in the district where they are staying or can contact the private clinic, **City Akuten,** tel. 08/117177; **Dentist,** tel. 08/235845; **Pharmacy,** C. W. Scheele, tel. 08/248280 (all are indicated by the sign "Apotek").

English Bookstores Most bookstores have a good selection of English books. **Hedengrens Bokhandel,** Kungsgatan 4 (tel. 08/212107) offers dictionaries and maps in all languages.

Travel Agencies **American Express,** Birger Jarlsgatan 1, tel. 08/235330. **Wagon Lits/Thomas Cook,** Vasagatan 22, tel. 08/762–5827.

Guided Tours

Orientation Tours A guided sightseeing tour lasting 2½ hours departs from Karl XII Torg every morning. Multilingual commentary is provided. The tour covers the central city area, the Old Town (Gamla Stan), the Cathedral, and the Royal Palace. An afternoon tour leaving at 2 takes in the Djurgarden leisure area and the Wasa Museum, as well as the City Hall. A convenient budget-price tour by boat and/or bus is SL's **Tourist Route** (Turistlinjen). The tour departs every 15 minutes during peak vacation periods and every half hour at other times; you can get on and off at any one of the 14 stops.

Boat Tours You'll find a bewildering variety of tours available at Stockholm's quaysides. The **Waxholm Steamship Company** (tel. 08/1408300) operates scheduled services to many of the islands in the archipelago on its famous white steamers. Trips range from one to three hours each way. Popular one-day excursions include Waxholm, Utö, Sandhamn, and Möja. Conventional sightseeing tours include a one-hour circular city tour operated by the **Strömma Canal Company** (tel. 08/233375). It leaves from the Nybroplan quay every hour between 10 and 5 during the summer.

Special-Interest Tours A new "Stimulating Stockholm" program offers a range of unusual and offbeat excursions. These include free trips to the Gustavsberg Ceramics Center, the Stockholm auction chambers, and the Association of Friends of Textile Art (Handarbetets Vänner). Information on the full range of excursions is available at the "Stimulating Stockholm" desk at the Tourist Center.

Excursions Not to be missed is the boat trip to the Palace of Drottningholm, the 17th-century private residence of the Royal Family and a smaller version of Versailles. It departs from the City Hall Bridge (Stadshusbron) every half hour between 9:30 and 4:30 during the summer. Another popular trip goes from Stadshusbron to the ancient towns of Sigtuna and Skokloster, and then to Uppsala, where you can catch a train back to Stockholm. Information is available from the **Stromma Canal Company** (tel. 08/233375) or the Tourist Center at Sweden House.

Personal Guides Contact the **Guide Center** at **Stockholm Information Service,** tel. 08/789–2000.

Exploring Stockholm

Because Stockholm's main attractions are concentrated in a relatively small area, the city itself can be explored in several days. But if you want to take advantage of some of the full-day excursions offered, it is worthwhile to devote a full week to your visit.

The city of Stockholm, built on 14 small islands among open bays and narrow channels, has been dubbed the "Venice of the North" by advertising copywriters. It is a handsome, civilized city, full of parks, squares, and airy boulevards, and a bustling, modern metropolis. Glass-and-steel skyscrapers abound, yet you are never more than five minutes' walk from twisting, medieval streets and waterside walks.

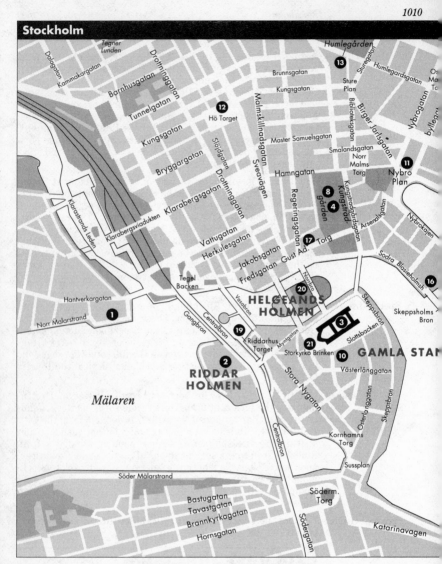

Stockholm

Major Attractions
City Hall, **1**
Gröna Lund Tivoli, **6**
Kungsträdgården, **4**
Museum of National
Antiquities, **9**
Nordic Museum, **8**
Riddarholm Church, **2**
Royal Palace, **3**
Skansen, **7**
Wasa, **5**

Other Attractions
Cathedral, **21**
Concert Hall, **12**
Kaknäs Tower, **15**
Museum of Far Eastern
Antiquities, **18**
Museum of Modern
Art, **14**
National Museum, **16**

Parliament, **20**
Royal Dramatic
Theater, **11**
Royal Library, **13**
Royal Opera House, **17**
Supreme Court, **19**
Stock Exchange, **10**

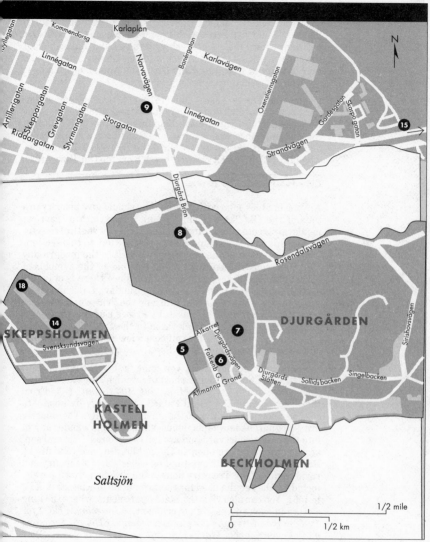

The first written mention of Stockholm dates from 1252, when a powerful regent named Birger Jarl is said to have built a fortified castle and city here. And it must have been this strategic position, where the calm, fresh waters of Lake Mälaren meet the salty Baltic Sea, that prompted King Gustav Vasa to take over the city in 1523, and King Gustavus Adolphus to make it the heart of an empire a century later.

During the Thirty Years' War (1618–48), Sweden gained importance as a Baltic trading state, and Stockholm grew commensurately. But by the beginning of the 18th century, Swedish influence was waning, and Stockholm's development had slowed. It did not revive until the Industrial Revolution, when the hub of the city moved north from the Old Town area.

City Hall and Old Town

Anyone in Stockholm with limited time should give priority to a tour of the **Old Town** (Gamla Stan), a labyrinth of narrow, medieval streets, alleys, and quiet squares just south of the city center. Ideally, you should devote a whole day to this section. But before crossing the bridge, pay a visit to the modern-day **City Hall,** constructed in 1923 and now one of the symbols of Stockholm. You'll need an early start, since there is only one guided tour per day at 10 AM, 12 on Sunday. Lavish mosaics grace the walls of the **Golden Hall,** and the **Prince's Gallery** features a collection of large murals by Prince Eugene, brother of King Gustav V. Take the elevator to the top of the 348-foot (106-meter) tower for a magnificent view of the city. *Admission: SEK 5. Tower open May–Sept., daily 11–3.*

Crossing into the Old Town, you come first to the magnificent **Riddarholm Church,** where a host of Swedish kings are buried. *Admission: SEK 5. Open Mon.–Sat. 10–3, Sun. 1–5.* From there, proceed to the **Royal Palace**—preferably by noon—to see the colorful changing-of-the-guard ceremony. The smartly dressed guards seem superfluous, since tourists wander at will into the castle courtyard and around the grounds. Several separate attractions are open to the public. Be sure to visit the **Royal Armory,** with its outstanding collection of weaponry and royal regalia. The **Treasury** houses the Swedish crown jewels, including the regalia used for the coronation of King Erik XIV in 1561. You can also visit the **State Apartments,** where the king swears in each successive government. *Admission: SEK 7 for Treasury and Armory; State Apartments: SEK 10. Treasury and Armory open Mon.–Fri. 10–4, weekends 11–4. State Apartments open Tues.–Fri. 10–3, Sun. 12–3.*

From the palace, stroll down **Västerlånggatan,** one of two main shopping streets in the Old Town. This is a popular shopping area, brimming with boutiques and antique shops. Walk down to the Skeppsbron waterfront, then head back toward the center over the Strömbridge, where anglers cast for salmon. If you feel like a rest, stop off at **Kungsträdgården** and watch the world go by. Originally built as a royal kitchen garden, the property was turned into a public park in 1562. During the summer, entertainments and activities abound, and you can catch a glimpse of local people playing open-air chess with giant chessmen.

Djurgården

Be sure to spend at least a day visiting the many attractions on the large island of **Djurgården.** Although it's only a short walk from the city center, the pleasantest way to approach it is by ferry from Skeppsbron, in the Old Town. The ferries drop you off beside two of Stockholm's best-known attractions, the Wasa Museum and Gröna Lund Tivoli. The *Wasa,* a restored 17th-century warship, is the oldest preserved war vessel in the world, and has become Sweden's most popular tourist sight. She sank ignominiously in Stockholm harbor on her maiden voyage in 1628, reportedly because she was not carrying sufficient ballast. Recovered in 1961, she has now been restored to her original appearance. *Admission: SEK 8. Open daily 9:30–7 in summer, 10–5 off-season.*

⑥ **Gröna Lund Tivoli,** Stockholm's version of the famous Copenhagen amusement park, is only a few minutes from the *Wasa's* berth. This is a favorite family attraction, featuring hair-raising roller coasters as well as tamer delights. *Admission: SEK 20. Summer hours: 1 PM–midnight.*

⑦ Just across the road is **Skansen,** a large, open-air folk museum consisting of 150 reconstructed traditional buildings from Sweden's different regions. Here you can see a variety of handcraft displays and demonstrations. There is also an attractive open-air zoo—with many native Scandinavian species, such as lynxes, wolves, and brown bears—as well as an excellent aquarium. *Admission: SEK 17. Open June–Aug. 8 AM–11:30 PM; check off-season hours.*

⑧ From the zoo, head back toward the city center. Just before the Djurgård bridge, you come to the **Nordic Museum,** which, like Skansen, provides an insight into the ways Swedish people have lived over the past 500 years. The collection includes displays of peasant costumes, folk art, and Lapp culture. *Admission: SEK 10. Open Mon.–Sat. 10–4, Sun. noon–5.*

⑨ Once you're back on the "mainland," drop into the **Museum of National Antiquities.** Though its name is uninspiring, it houses some remarkable Viking gold and silver treasures. **The Royal Cabinet of Coin,** located in the same building, boasts the world's largest coin. *Narvavagen 13–17. Admission: SEK 20. Open Tues.–Sun. 11–4; closed Mon.*

Time Out For a snack with a view, try the **Solliden Restaurant** at Skansen. Skansen also offers a selection of open-air snack bars and cafés; Gröna Lund itself has four different restaurants.

Outside Stockholm

The region surrounding Stockholm offers many attractions that can easily be seen on day trips out of the capital.

One "must" is certainly the trip to the majestic 16th-century **Gripsholm Castle,** at Mariefred, on the southern side of Lake Mälaren and about 40 miles (64 kilometers) from Stockholm. Gripsholm, with its drawbridge and four massively built round towers, is one of Sweden's most romantic castles. There had been a castle on the site as far back as the 1380s, but this was

Stockholm Environs

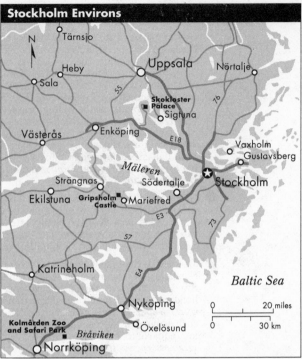

N

Tärnsjö

Heby

Sala

Uppsala

Nörtalje

55

Skokloster
Palace

Sigtuna

Enköping

Västerås

E18

Vaxholm

Gustavsberg

Mälaren

Strängnas

Ekilstuna

Gripsholm
Castle

Södertalje

Mariefred

Stockholm

70

73

E3

57

Katrineholm

E4

Baltic Sea

Nyköping

Kolmården Zoo
and Safari Park

Bråviken

Öxelösund

0   20 miles

0   30 km

Norrköping

destroyed, and King Gustav Vasa had the present building erected in 1577. The castle is known best today for housing the Swedish state collection of portraits and is one of the largest portrait galleries in the world, with some 3,400 paintings.

The pleasantest way of traveling to Gripsholm from Stockholm is on the vintage steamer *Mariefred*, the last coal-fired ship on Lake Mälaren. Departures, between mid-June and late August, are from Klara Mälarstrand, near the City Hall, daily except Monday at 10 AM, returning from Mariefred at 4:30. The journey takes 3½ hours each way, and there is a restaurant on board. *Round-trip fare: SEK 90. Tel. 08/698850. Admission to castle: SEK 10. Open daily 10–4.*

Another popular boat trip goes to **Skokloster Palace,** about 43 miles (70 kilometers) from Stockholm. Departures are from the City Hall Bridge (Stadshusbron) daily, except Monday and Friday, between early June and mid-August. The route follows the narrow inlets of Lake Mälaren along the "Royal Waterway" and calls at Sigtuna, the ancient capital of Sweden. You can get off the boat here, visit the town, which has medieval ruins and an 18th-century town hall, and catch the boat again on the return journey. But it is worthwhile, too, to stay on board and continue to Skokloster, an impressive palace dating from the 1650s. Built by the Swedish Field Marshal Carl Gustav Wrangel, it contains many of his trophies from the Thirty Years' War. Other attractions include what is reckoned to be the largest private collection of arms in the world, as well as some magnificent Gobelin tapestries. Next door to the palace is a motor museum that houses Sweden's largest collection of vintage cars and motorcycles. The round-trip boat fare is SEK 90, and there is a restaurant and cafeteria on board. *Admission to Skokloster Palace: SEK 12 (free with Key to Stockholm card). Open daily 11–4. Admission to motor museum: SEK 15 (free with Key to Stockholm card). Open May–Sept., daily 10–5; Oct.–Apr., daily 11–4.*

A popular day excursion by tour bus from Stockholm takes you to **Kolmården Zoo** and **Safari Park,** on the shores of Bråviken, a large bay in the Baltic near Norrköping. It is claimed to be one of Europe's largest zoos in terms of area, and one of the most popular attractions is the dolphinarium, where the dolphins can be seen performing daily. The bus takes you through the safari park, where lions, zebras, wolves, and other animals roam freely. *Departures from Sweden House, late June–mid-Aug., every Saturday at 9 AM, arriving back at about 6:15. Fare: SEK 200, includes admission to the zoo. Information and reservations are available at the Tourist Center.*

Lovers of the sea could easily spend a whole week cruising among the 24,000 islands in the **Stockholm archipelago.** The Inter-Islands Card (Båtluffarkortet), available from early June to mid-August, gives you 16 days' unlimited travel on the Waxholm Steamship Company boats, which operate scheduled services throughout the archipelago. The card is on sale in the Excursion Shop at the Sweden House Tourist Center and at the Waxholm Steamship Company terminal at Strömkajen. If your time is more limited, the "Sandhamn Package" is a good idea for an offbeat trip. Sandhamn is Stockholm's main marine outpost and pilot station, but today it is best known as a sailing center. *Cost of Inter-Islands card: SEK 125.*

The Sandhamn Package price includes the round-trip boat fare plus one night's lodging and breakfast at the comfortable Sandhamns Hotel, where most of the rooms overlook the water. The package price is SEK 245 per person, plus SEK 160 for an additional night. The Sandhamn Package should be booked in advance at the Excursion Shop in the Tourist Center.

What to See and Do with Children

The prime target for most youngsters is the **Gröna Lund Tivoli** amusement park across the road from Skansen. It's full of exciting rides and offers a choice of stage shows and restaurants (*see* Djurgården for price and opening times). The **Toy Museum** (Mariatorget 1, tel. 08/416100), a major attraction for tourists of all ages, has a collection of more than 10,000 toys and two large model railroads (Admission: SEK 12, children SEK 6).

Off the Beaten Track

Just over 500 feet (155 meters) tall, the **Kaknäs TV Tower** at Djurgården is the highest structure in Scandinavia. From the top you can catch a magnificent view of the city and surrounding archipelago. Facilities include a cafeteria, restaurant, and souvenir shop. *Djurgården, tel. 08/678030.*

You can see the world's largest variety of water lily at the **Bergius Botanical Garden,** just north of the city center. Its leaves are more than seven feet (two meters) in diameter. *Frescati, tel. 08/153912.*

Fjäderholmarna (the Feather Islets), the collective name for a group of four secluded islands in the Stockholm archipelago, have only recently been opened to the public after 50 years as a military zone. An archipelago museum and fish farm are under construction. Boats leave from Slussen and Stromkajen, in downtown Stockholm.

Shopping

Gift Ideas Stockholm is an ideal place to find items that reflect the best in Swedish design and elegance, particularly glass, porcelain, furs, handcrafts, home furnishings, and leather goods. The quality is uniformly high, and you can take advantage of the Tax-free Shopping Service in most stores (*see* Essential Information). Film, cameras, and hi-fi equipment are generally cheaper here than in most other European countries.

Department Stores The largest is **NK**, on Hamngatan, where you can find just about anything. Other major stores are **PUB**, on Hötorget, and **Ahlens City**, on Klarabergsgatan. All three are open on Sunday.

Shopping Districts The center of Stockholm's shopping activity has shifted from Kungsgatan to **Hamngatan**, a wide boulevard along which a huge, covered shopping complex, or Gallerian, has been built. The **Old Town** area is best for handcrafts, antiquarian bookshops, and art shops.

Food and Flea Markets The biggest flea market in northern Europe is located in **Skärholmen** shopping center, a 20-minute subway ride from the downtown area. Market hours are Mon.–Fri. 11–6, Sat. 9–3, Sun. 10–3. Superior food markets selling such Swedish specialties as marinated salmon and reindeer can be found on **Ostermalmstorg** and **Hötorget**.

Glassware For the best buys, try **Nordiska Kristall**, on Kungsgatan, or **Rosenthal Studio-Haus**, on Birger Jarlsgatan. The latter operates its own shipping service. The **Crystal Showrooms**, on Drottninggatan and Norrmalmstorg, cater mainly to American visitors, and all prices—claimed to be 30–50% lower than their advertised U.S. prices—are in U.S. dollars. Shipping and insurance are included, and these shops even send a limousine to pick you up at your hotel!

Handcrafts A good center for all kinds of Swedish handcrafts in wood and metal is **Svensk Hemslojd**, on Sveavägen. It also sells embroidery kits and many types of weaving and knitting yarn. For reindeer purses and wooden craft items, try **Brinkens Konsthantverk** on Storkyrkobrinken, in the Old Town. **Länshemslojden,** on Drottninggatan, has a wide selection of Swedish folk costumes and handcraft souvenirs from different parts of Sweden.

Dining

Prices quoted here are per person and include a first course, main course, tax, and service, but not wine. Best bets are indicated by a star ★. At press time, there were 5.87 kronor (SEK) to the dollar.

Category	Cost
Very Expensive	over SEK 300
Expensive	SEK 175–300
Moderate	SEK 90–175
Inexpensive	under SEK 90

Very Expensive **Erik's.** The authentic marine atmosphere owes much to its location: a restored barge moored in Stockholm harbor. The cuisine is principally French, with an accent on seafood—especially salmon. During the summer, guests enjoy deck-side dining and a pleasant harbor view. *Strandvägskajen 17, tel. 08/660–6060. Dress: casual. Reservations advised. AE, DC, MC, V. Closed Sun., Christmas, New Years, and Midsummer Night (June 23).*

★ **Operakällaren.** Located in part of the elegant Opera House building, this is one of Stockholm's best-known traditional restaurants. Royal chef Werner Vogli prepares both Scandinavian and Continental cuisine; the specialty is Turbot Karl XII. The restaurant faces Kungstradgarden, the waterfront, and the Royal Palace. *Operahuset, tel. 08/111125. Jacket and tie. Reservations advised. AE, DC, MC, V. Closed July.*

Teatergrillen. Small, friendly, and centrally located, Teatergrillen is a favorite among local businesspeople. The cuisine is international, but steaks are a specialty. *Nybrogatan 3, tel. 08/107044. Dress: casual chic. Reservations advised. AE, DC, MC, V. Dinner only weekends. Closed Christmas and Midsummer.*

Expensive **Aurora.** Located in a 300-year-old building complete with authentic cellar vaults, Aurora is one of the best-known restaurants in the Old Town. The cuisine is both Swedish and international. Try the house specialty, the 3-course "Queen's Menu". *Munkbron 11, tel. 08/219359. Dress: casual. Reservations advised. AE, DC, MC, V. Closed lunch, Sun.*

Clas på Hörnet. Located just outside the city center, Clas på Hörnet is a small, intimate establishment occupying the ground floor of a restored 200-year-old town house, now a hotel (*see* Lodging). It offers a choice of international or Swedish cuisine. *Surbrunnsgatan 20, tel. 08/155130. Dress: casual. Reservations advised. AE, DC, MC, V. Closed Christmas.*

Fem Små Hus. "Five small houses" is a well-known Old Town restaurant. The menu features both Swedish and French dishes. The chef's specialty is fillet of veal "Anna Lindberg." *Nygrand 10, tel. 08/100482. Dress: casual chic. Reservations advised. AE, DC, MC, V.*

Gourmet. The accent is on French cuisine, but Swiss and Swedish specialties are also available. Seafood figures prominently. Try the house specialty, Sea Crayfish in Love. *Tegnérgatan 10, tel. 08/314398. Dress: casual. Reservations advised. AE, DC, MC, V. Closed weekends for lunch, July.*

La Brochette. This popular, French-style restaurant specializes in charcoal-broiled steak served on skewers. *Storgatan 27, tel. 08/622000. Dress: casual. Reservations advised. AE, DC, MC, V. Closed Sat. lunch, Sun.*

Quarter Deck. Located on the Old Town waterfront near the Royal Palace, the Quarter Deck, part of the Hotel Reisen, offers a superb harbor view. The cuisine is both Swedish and French, and a moderate fixed-price weekend menu is available.

Skeppsbron 12–14, tel. 08/223260. Jacket and tie. Reservations advised. AE, DC, MC, V.

★ **Stallmästaregården.** An historic old inn with an attractive courtyard and garden, Stallmästaregården is near the Haga Air Terminal, some distance from the city center. But the fine French and Swedish cuisine is well worth the journey. After-dinner coffee is served in the courtyard overlooking Brunnsviken Lake. During the weekends and throughout the summer, a lower, fixed-price menu is available. *Norrtull, near Haga, tel. 08/243910. Jacket and tie. Reservations advised. AE, DC, MC, V.*

Moderate **Glada Laxen.** Since the name means "Happy Salmon," it is not
★ surprising that salmon in various guises, from smoked to mousse, is the star attraction here. Centrally located in the Gallerian shopping center near the Sweden House Tourist Center, this is a popular spot. *Regeringsgatan 23, tel. 08/211290. Dress: casual. Reservations advised, especially for lunch. AE, DC, MC, V. Closed Sun. Dinner finishes at 8 PM.*

Gondolen. Suspended under the gangway of the *Katarina* elevator at Slussen, Gondolen offers a magnificent view over the harbor, Lake Mälaren, and the Baltic Sea. The cuisine is international, and a range of fixed-price menus is available. *Slussen, tel. 08/402021. Dress: casual. Reservations advised. AE, DC, MC, V.*

Markurell's. The two separate restaurants, the Wärdshuset and the Bistro, are conveniently located opposite the Central Station. It's a busy establishment serving international cuisine. *Mäster Samuelsgatan 73, tel. 08/211012. Dress: casual. Reservations advised. AE, DC, MC, V.*

Sturehof. Centrally located, with an unpretentious, nautical ambience, Sturehof's specialty is its seafood. It also boasts an English-style pub. *Stureplan 2, tel. 08/142750. Dress: casual. Reservations advised. AE, DC, MC, V. Closed Sat. lunch, Sun., Christmas, New Years, and Midsummer Night.*

Inexpensive **Annorlunda.** This is a small, self-service restaurant specializing in light meals and salads. The daily "Annorlunda Special" features a main course, dessert, and coffee for SEK 95. *Malmskillnadsgatan 50, tel. 08/219569. Dress: casual. AE, DC, MC, V. Closed Sun.*

Cassi. This centrally located restaurant specializes in French cuisine at reasonable prices. *Narvavägen 30, tel. 08/617461. Dress: casual. Reservations advised. MC. Closed Sat.*

★ **Open Gate Yet.** Located near the Slussen locks, on the south side of Stockholm harbor, this is a popular, trendy Art Deco Italian-style trattoria. Pasta dishes are the house specialty. *Högbergsgatan 38, tel. 08/439776. Dress: casual. No reservations. AE, DC, MC, V. Closed lunch.*

Lodging

Stockholm has plenty of hotels in most price brackets, although relatively few are in the Inexpensive category. Many hotels cut their rates in high season, however, when business travelers are on vacation, so that during the summer even a hotel classified as Very Expensive can become affordable. The major hotel chains also have a number of bargain schemes available on weekends throughout the year and daily during the summer.

More than 40 hotels offer the **"Stockholm Package,"** providing accommodations for one night, costing between SEK 200 and

SEK 400 per person, including breakfast and a Key to Stockholm card *(see* Getting Around). Details of the Stockholm Package can be obtained from the **Stockholm Information Service,** Excursion Shop, Box 7542, S-103 93 Stockholm. Also, you can call **The Hotel Center** (tel. 08/240880) or reserve the package through travel agents.

If you arrive in Stockholm without a hotel reservation, the **Hotellcentralen** in the Central Station will arrange accommodations for you. The office is open daily, 8 AM–9 PM, June through Sept.; Monday to Friday 8:30 to 5 the rest of the year. There's a small fee for each reservation. Or phone one of the central reservations offices run by the major hotel groups: RESO (tel. 08/5700); SARA (tel. 08/7535350); or Sweden Hotels (tel. 08/151950).

Ratings   Prices quoted here are for two people in a double room. Best bets are indicated by a star ★. At press time, there were 5.87 kronor (SEK) to the dollar.

Category	Cost
Very Expensive	over SEK 950
Expensive	SEK 750–950
Moderate	SEK 550–750
Inexpensive	under SEK 550

Very Expensive   **Amaranten.** Only 5 minutes' walk from the Central Station, Amaranten is a large, modern hotel, built in 1969 and refurbished in 1988. The "executive tower" offers a roof garden and 52 rooms. Guests enjoy a gourmet restaurant and brasserie, nightclub and piano bar. *Kungsholmsgatan 31, tel. 08/541060. 415 rooms with bath. Facilities: sauna, pool, and solarium. AE, DC, MC, V.*

★ **Continental.** Located in the city center across from the Central Station, the Continental is popular with American guests. It was first opened about 25 years ago and is now undergoing renovation that's scheduled for completion in 1992. It offers 3 restaurants in different price brackets—an international gourmet restaurant, a French-style bistro, and a café that's popular for lunch and quick meals. *Klara Vattugränd 4, tel. 08/244020. 250 rooms, 42 without bath. AE, DC, MC, V.*

★ **Diplomat.** This is an elegant hotel located within easy walking distance of Djurgården Park and Skansen, and offers magnificent views over Stockholm harbor. The building itself is a 1900-era town house that was converted into a hotel in 1966. The teahouse is a popular spot for light meals. *Strandvagen 7C, tel. 08/635800. 132 rooms, all but one with bath. AE, DC, MC, V. Closed Christmas and New Years.*

Grand. Located on the waterfront in the center of town, the Grand is a large, gracious, Old World-style hotel dating back to 1874. It faces the Royal Palace. The two restaurants—French and Swedish—offer harbor views; there is also a café for light snacks. *S. Blasieholmen 8, tel. 08/221020. 330 rooms with bath, all but 60 with waterfront views. Facilities: sauna, beauty salon. AE, DC, MC, V. Closed Christmas and New Years.*

★ **Lady Hamilton.** The Lady Hamilton, in the Old Town. Considered one of Stockholm's most desirable hotels, was built as a private home in 1470 and has been a hotel only since 1980. It houses an extensive collection of antiques, including one of

George Romney's portraits of Lady Hamilton. *Storkyr-kobrinken 5, tel. 08/234680. 34 rooms with bath. Facilities: sauna, pool, cafeteria. AE, DC, MC, V. Closed Christmas and New Years.*

Reisen. The building dates from 1819, although it was refurbished several years ago. It's situated in a waterfront sector of the Old Town and offers a fine restaurant, a grill, and what is reputed to be the best piano bar in town. The swimming pool is built under medieval arches. *Skeppsbron 12–14, tel. 08/223260. 113 rooms with bath. Facilities: sauna, pool, library. AE, DC, MC, V. Closed Christmas and New Years.*

Royal Viking. This is a large, modern, somewhat impersonal hotel adjoining the Central Station. Rooms are on the small side for a hotel in this price category. *Vasagatan 1, tel. 08/141000. 340 rooms with bath. Facilities: sauna, pool, rooms for disabled guests. AE, DC, MC, V.*

SAS Strand. Acquired only recently by the SAS group, this is a gracious, Old World hotel. It was built in 1912 but fully modernized in 1982–83. No two rooms are the same; many are furnished with antiques. An SAS check-in counter adjoins the main reception area. The principal restaurant specializes in seafood dishes and offers a superb selection of wines. Lighter meals are served in the Piazza. *Nybrokajen 9, tel. 08/222900. 137 rooms with bath. Facilities: sauna, cafeteria, function rooms. AE, DC, MC, V.*

Sergel Plaza. Opened in 1984, the modern Sergel Plaza incorporates part of an older building located in the city center. Its distinctive feature is its glass-roof lobby, complete with trees and waterfall. The young staff provides attentive service. *Brunkebergstorg 91, tel. 08/226600. 407 rooms with bath. Facilities: restaurant, café, sauna, health club. AE, DC, MC, V.*

Expensive **Birger Jarl.** A short subway ride from the city center, Birger Jarl is a modern, characteristically Scandinavian hotel that opened in 1974. There is no full-service restaurant. *Tulegatan 8, tel. 08/151020. 252 rooms with bath. Facilities: sauna, pool, coffee shop. AE, DC, MC, V. Closed Christmas and New Years.*

★ **Clas på Hörnet.** An 18th-century inn converted into a small hotel in 1982, Clas på Hörnet is just outside the city center. Its rooms, furnished with antiques of the period, go quickly. If you can't manage to reserve one, at least have a meal in the gourmet restaurant *(see* Dining). *Surbrunnsgatan 20, tel. 08/165130. 10 rooms with bath. AE, DC, MC, V.*

Karelia. A modern, medium-size hotel built in the early 1980s, Karelia has a family atmosphere, and, with its sauna and Finnish bands, a somewhat Finnish flavor. The restaurant specializes in Russian cooking. *Birger Jarlsgatan 35, tel. 08/247660. 103 rooms with bath. AE, DC, MC, V. Closed Christmas and New Years.*

Lord Nelson. This companion hotel to the Lady Hamilton was built in much the same style. Its location on a busy pedestrian street in the Old Town makes it rather noisy at night. The atmosphere throughout is distinctly nautical—even down to the cabin-size rooms. There is no restaurant, but light snacks are available. *Västerlаångatan 22, tel. 08/232390. 31 rooms with bath. AE, DC, MC, V. Closed Christmas and New Years.*

Mornington. Although it is not particularly imposing from the outside, Mornington is a comfortable, quiet hotel, situated near the indoor market at Ostermalmstorg and within walking distance of the city center. It has an excellent fish restaurant.

Nybrogatan 53, tel. 08/631240. 139 rooms with bath. AE, DC, MC, V. Closed Christmas and New Years.

Moderate **Alfa.** About 20 minutes from the city center, Alfa is a medium-size, medium-class hotel. Opened in 1972, it has recently been refurbished. *Marknadsvägen 6, tel. 08/810600. 104 rooms with bath. Facilities: sauna, restaurant. AE, DC, MC, V. Closed Christmas and New Years.*

City. A large, modern-style hotel built in the 1940s but modernized in 1982–83, City is located near the city center and the Hötorget market. It is owned by the Salvation Army, so alcohol is not served in either the restaurant or café. *Slöjdgatan 7, tel. 08/222240. 300 rooms with bath. Facilities: rooms for disabled guests. AE, DC, MC, V.*

Stockholm. This hotel has an unusual location—the upper floors of a downtown office building. The mainly modern decor is offset by traditional Swedish furnishings that help create its family atmosphere. Breakfast is the only meal served. *Norrmalmstorg 1, tel. 08/221320. 92 rooms with bath. AE, DC, MC, V. Closed Christmas and New Years.*

Inexpensive **Alexandra.** Although it is in the Södermalm area, to the south of the Old Town, the Alexandra is only 5 minutes by subway from the city center. It is a small, modern hotel, opened 13 years ago and renovated in 1988. Only breakfast is served. *Magnus Ladulåsgatan 42, tel. 08/840320. 80 rooms with bath. Facilities: sauna, solarium. AE, DC, MC, V. Closed Christmas and New Years.*

Gustav af Klint. A "hotel ship" moored at Stadsgaården quay, near Slussen subway station, the Gustav af Klint is better described as a youth hostel—albeit with its own sauna. *Stadsgaårdskajen 153, tel. 08/404077. 28 cabins, none with bath. No credit cards. Closed Christmas and New Years.*

Zinken. The Zinken complex consists of a number of pavilions near Zinkensdam subway station, 5 minutes from the city center. It is a popular spot for travelers on a budget. There is an adjacent youth hostel. *Pipmakargränd 2, tel. 08/585011. 28 rooms, none with bath. Facilities: sauna, solarium, Jacuzzi, garden, children's play area, access to washing machine and kitchen. AE, DC, MC, V. Closed Christmas and New Years.*

The Arts

Stockholm's main theater and concert season runs from September through May or June, so there are not many major performances during the height of the tourist season. But for a list of events, pick up the free booklet "Stockholm This Week," available from hotels and tourist information offices. You can get last-minute tickets to theaters and shows at the cut-price ticket booth on **Norrmalmstorg Square.** Tickets sold here are priced 25% below box office rates. The booth is open Monday noon–5 and Tuesday to Saturday noon–7. There is also a central reservation office for regular-price tickets (tel. 08/108800).

Concerts The city's main concert hall is the **Concert House** (Konserthuset) at Hötorget 8, home of the Stockholm Philharmonic Orchestra. The main season runs from mid-September to mid-May. In addition to full-scale evening concerts, there are "coffee break" or lunchtime concerts some days. During the summer, free concerts are given in many city parks. For information, phone 08/221800.

Opera The season at the **Royal Opera House,** just across the bridge from the Royal Palace, runs from mid-August to early June and offers performances at top-class international standards (tel. 08/248240). And from early June to early September, there are performances of opera, ballet, and orchestral music at the exquisite **Drottningholm Court Theater,** which was the setting for Ingmar Bergman's film *The Magic Flute.* The original 18th-century stage machinery is still used in these productions. You can get to Drottningholm by subway or special theater-bus (leaving from the Grand Hotel or Vasagatan, opposite the Central Station) or by boat *(see* Getting Around Stockholm). For tickets, tel. 08/660–8285 or 08/660–8281.

Theater Stockholm has about 20 top-rank theaters, but dramatic productions are unlikely to interest those who don't understand Swedish. A better option is to go to a musical; several city theaters hold regular performances. Plays in English are featured at the **Regina Theater,** Drottninggatan 71A (tel. 08/207000).

Film English and American films predominate, and they are screened with the original soundtrack and Swedish subtitles. Programs are listed in the local evening newspapers, which usually give titles in both Swedish and English. Movie buffs should visit **Filmstaden** (Film City), Mäster Samuelsgatan 25 (tel. 08/225420), where 11 cinemas under one roof show a variety of films from noon until midnight.

Entertainment and Nightlife

Cabaret Stockholm's biggest nightclub, **Borsen** (Jakobsgatan 6, tel. 08/249210), offers high-quality international cabaret shows. Another popular spot is the **Cabaret Club,** Barnhusgatan 12 (tel. 08/110608). Although it can accommodate 450 guests, reservations are advised.

Bars and Nightclubs **Alexandra** (Birger Jarlsgatan 29, tel. 08/104646) is one of Stockholm's most famous night spots. Reservations are advised. Piano bars are also an important part of the Stockholm scene. Try the **Anglais Bar** at the Hotel Anglais (tel. 08/249900) or the **Clipper Club** at the Hotel Reisen, Skeppsbron (tel. 08/223260).

Jazz Clubs **Fasching,** (Kungsgatan 63, tel. 08/219365) is Stockholm's largest, but another popular spot is **Stampen** (Gramunkegränd 7, tel. 08/205793). Get here in good time if you want a seat, and phone first to be sure the establishment hasn't been reserved for a private party.

Discos **Café Opera** (tel. 08/110026), adjoining the Opera House, is one of the most popular night spots for the younger generation. Others are **Downtown** (Norrlandsgatan 5A, tel. 08/119488) and **Karlsson** (Kungsgatan 65, tel. 08/119298).

Uppsala and the Folklore District

The area of Sweden referred to as the "Folklore District"—essentially the provinces of Dalarna and Värmland—has the merit of being both easily accessible from Stockholm and the best region in which to see something of the country's enduring folk traditions. This itinerary takes you to Dalarna through the ancient city of Uppsala and returns to Stockholm through the Bergslagen region, the heart of the centuries-old Swedish iron industry.

Getting Around

The route can be covered entirely by train. The ride from Stockholm to Uppsala takes only 45 minutes, and the service is fairly frequent. A car, however, will give you the flexibility to explore some of the attractions that are not so accessible by public transportation.

Guided Tours

While Uppsala is compact enough to explore on foot, guided sightseeing tours are available each day. Check with the **Tourist Information Office.**

Tourist Information

Falun. Stora Torget, tel. 023/83637.
Ludvika. Sporthallen, tel. 0240/86050.
Mora. Ångbåtskajen, tel. 0250/26550.
Örebro. Drottninggatan 9, tel. 019/130760.
Rättvik. Torget, tel. 0248/10910.
Uppsala. Smedsgränd 7, tel. 018/117500.

Exploring

Uppsala is really the cradle of Swedish civilization, so it is well worth spending a day or two exploring it. If you opt for a guided tour, you'll be taken first to **Old Uppsala** (Gamla Uppsala), the site of an ancient pagan temple just outside of town. The temple consists of three huge burial mounds, sometimes called the **Pyramids of Scandinavia.** During the fifth century AD, Aun, Egil, and Edils, the first Swedish kings, were buried here. Adjoining the burial mounds is the **Odinsborg** restaurant, where you can sample local mead, brewed from a 14th-century recipe.

Back in Uppsala itself, your first stop should be the enormous **cathedral,** with its twin towers dominating the city skyline. The cathedral has been the seat of the archbishop of the Swedish church for 700 years, although its present appearance owes much to major restoration work completed in the late 19th century. Make a point of visiting the **Cathedral Museum** in the north tower, which boasts one of Europe's finest collections of ecclesiastical textiles. *Free. Open weekdays 8–8, weekends 8–6.*

Nearby, in a strategic position atop a hill, is **Uppsala Castle.** This prepossessing structure was built in the 1540s by King Gustav Vasa. Having broken his ties with the Vatican, the king was eager to show who was actually running the country. He arranged to have the cannons aimed directly at the archbishop's palace. *Admission: SEK 5 for main hall, SEK 10 for museum and ruins. Open mid-May–Sept. Check times with the local tourist office.*

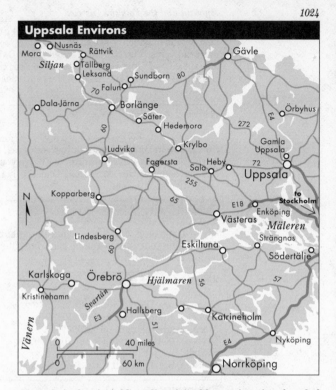

Uppsala Environs

Uppsala is the site of Scandinavia's oldest university, founded in 1477. Be sure to visit one of its most venerable, old buildings, the **Gustavianum,** located near the cathedral. Just below the cupola is the anatomical theater, where public dissections of executed convicts were a popular 17th-century tourist attraction. *Admission: SEK 3. Open daily noon–3.* Also, try to fit in a visit to the university library, called **Carolina Rediviva,** for a look at the **Codex Argenteus** (Silver Bible), a priceless relic dating from the 6th century. *Admission: SEK 2 on weekends, free weekdays. Open Mon.–Fri. 9–7, Sat. 9–6, Sun. 1–3:30.*

One of Uppsala's most famous sons was **Carl von Linné,** known as Linnaeus. A professor of botany at the university during the 1740s, he developed a system of plant and animal classification that is still used today. You can visit the gardens he designed, as well as his former residence, now a museum. *Admission: SEK 5. Open 1–4; closed Mon.*

From Uppsala, the route heads northwest through a pleasant agricultural landscape into the province of **Dalarna,** passing through **Säter,** one of the best-preserved wooden villages in Sweden. This is a pleasant spot just to wander around. For an overnight stop it is best to head for **Falun,** Dalarna's provincial capital.

Falun is best known for a huge hole in the ground, referred to as the **"Great Pit."** The hole has been there since 1687, when an abandoned copper mine collapsed. Other mines on the site are still working today. You can take a guided tour down into some of the old shafts and hear the gruesome story of 17th-century miner Fat Mats, whose body was perfectly preserved in brine for 40 years following a cave-in. There is also a museum that tells the story of this important local industry. *Admission: SEK 20. Open May–mid-June, daily 10–4:30; mid-June– Aug., daily 9–7; Sept.–mid-Nov., weekends only 10–4:30.*

Just outside Falun, at **Sundborn,** is the former home of Swedish artist Carl Larsson. Here, in an idyllic, lakeside setting, you can see a selection of his paintings, which owe much to local folk-art traditions. His grandchildren and great-grandchildren are on hand to show you around. *Admission: SEK 25. Open May–Sept., Mon.–Sat. 10–5, Sun. 1–5.*

But the real center of Dalarna folklore is the area around **Lake Siljan,** by far the largest of the 6,000 lakes in the province. A good base from which to begin your tour is the attractive lake-side village of **Tällberg,** or **Mora,** toward the north end of the lake. In the neighboring village of **Rättvik,** hundreds of people wearing traditional costumes arrive in longboats to attend Midsummer church services. Mora itself is best known as the home of the artist **Anders Zorn.** His house and studio are open to the public. *Admission: SEK 10. Open Mon.–Sat. 9–5, Sun. 11–5; closed Mon. in winter.*

Near Mora is the village of **Nusnäs.** This is the village where the famous, brightly colored **Dalarna wooden horses** are produced. You can visit either of the two workshops where they are made.

Heading south again you come to **Ludvika,** an important center of the old Bergslagen mining region. This region stretches from the forests of Värmland in the west to the coastal forges in the east. Ludvika has a notable open-air mining museum, **Gammelgarden.** *Admission: SEK 7. Open May 15–Aug., daily 11–5.*

Another local attraction is **Luosa Cottage.** The poet **Dan Andersson** lived here during the early part of the century so he could experience for himself the rigorous life of the local char-coal burners. *Admission: SEK 10. Open daily 11–4.*

"Safaris" from Ludvika into the local outback can be arranged for visitors eager to try their hands at gold panning, canoeing, fishing, shooting, and wildlife watching. Information about these trips is available from the local tourist office.

Continuing south from Ludvika, you come to **Örebro,** a sizable town at the western edge of **Lake Hjälmaren,** which is connected to Lake Mälaren and the sea by the Hjalmäre Canal. Örebro received its charter in the 13th century and developed as a trading center for the farmers and miners of the Bergslagen region. Rising from a small island in the Svartån River, right in the center of town, is an imposing castle, parts of which date back to the 13th century. The castle is now the residence of the regional governor. Guided tours run from mid-June to mid-August at 11, 12, 1, and 3 each day. Check with the **Örebro Tourist Office** for further information. An added attraction is the excellent restaurant in the castle tower.

To get a feel for the Örebro of bygone days, wander around the **Wadköping** district, where a number of old houses and craftsmen's workshops have been painstakingly preserved. At the north end of town is **"Svampen"** (The Mushroom), a water tower rising 190 feet (58 meters) into the air. If you climb to the

top, you can catch a magnificent view of the surrounding countryside. There is also a cafeteria and tourist office there. *The
tower is open daily from May through Sept.*

Direct train service from Örebro back to Stockholm operates at
two-hour intervals, and the journey takes just under three
hours. You can also take the hourly train to Hallsberg and
change there to the frequent Gothenburg–Stockholm service.

Dining and Lodging

For details and price category definitions, *see* Dining and
Lodging in Essential Information.

Falun
Dining and Lodging

Bergmästaren Falun. Situated in the town center, Bergmästaren Falun is a small, cozy hotel built in traditional
Dalarna style and filled with antique furnishings. It was completely refurbished in 1985. The restaurant serves breakfast
only. *Bergskolegränd 7, tel. 023/63600. 88 rooms, most with
bath. Facilities: sauna, solarium. AE, DC, MC, V. Closed
Christmas. Expensive.*

Sara Hotel Grand. Centrally located and close to the train station, the Sara Hotel Grand is a large, modern hotel. Part of the
building dates from the turn of the century, though it underwent a complete modernization in 1987. The restaurant serves
international cuisine. *Trotzgatan 9–11, tel. 023/18700. 183
rooms with bath. Facilities: disco, swimming pool, solarium.
AE, DC, MC, V. Expensive.*

Ludvika
Lodging

Grand. A medium-size, modern-style hotel, the Grand is located in the town center. It was built 11 years ago and
refurbished in 1986. *Eriksgatan 6, tel. 0240/18220. 103 rooms
with bath. Facilities: sauna, disco, 2 restaurants. AE, DC,
MC, V. Moderate.*

Rex. The Rex is a fairly basic but modern hotel conveniently located near the city center. It was built in 1960. Its restaurant
serves breakfast only. *Engelbrektsgatan 9, tel. 0240/13690. 27
rooms with bath. AE, DC, MC, V. Closed Christmas and one
week in summer. Inexpensive.*

Mora
Lodging
★

Siljan. Taking its name from the nearby lake, the largest in
Dalarna, the Siljan is a popular small but modern-style hotel.
Opened 65 years ago, it was renovated in 1983. *Moragatan 6,
tel. 0250/13000. 44 rooms with bath. Facilities: sauna, disco,
restaurant. AE, DC, MC, V. Moderate.*

Örebro
Dining and Lodging

Grand. Located in the heart of town, the Grand is the city's
largest hotel. Though it was built 85 years ago, it has been refurbished periodically and offers all the modern comforts.
*Fabriksgatan 23, 700 08 Örebro, tel. 019/150200. 227 rooms
with bath. Facilities: sauna, Jacuzzi, à la carte restaurant,
VIP rooms. AE, DC, MC, V. Expensive.*

City. Opened only within the past several years, City is a modern, centrally located hotel. It offers special facilities for
disabled guests and those suffering from allergies. The restaurant serves "home cooking" at lunchtime and more elaborate, à
la carte fare in the evening. *Kungsgatan 24, tel. 019/100200.
113 rooms with bath. AE, DC, MC, V. Moderate.*

Tällberg
Lodging
★

Åkerblads. Located near the shores of Lake Siljan, Åkerblads
is a real rural Swedish experience. The hotel occupies a typical
Dalarna farmstead, parts of which date back to the 16th century. It is run by the 14th and 15th generations of the Åkerblad

family. A hotel since 1910, it was modernized in 1987. The restaurant serves table d'hôte meals only. *793 03 Tällberg, tel. 0247/50800. 62 rooms with bath. Facilities: sauna, Jacuzzi, pub-style bar. AE, DC, MC, V. Closed Christmas. Moderate.*

Uppsala **Domtrappkällaren.** One of the city's most popular restaurants,
Dining Domtrappkällaren is located in a 14th-century cellar near the
★ cathedral. The cuisine is a mixture of French and Swedish. *St. Eriksgränd 15, tel. 018/130955. Dress: casual. Reservations essential. AE, DC, MC, V. Moderate.*

Lodging **Sara Gillet.** A centrally located, medium-size, modern hotel, the Sara Gillet was opened 18 years ago and has been modernized recently. *Dragarbrunnsgatan 23, tel. 018/155360. 169 rooms with bath. AE, DC, MC, V. Closed Christmas. Expensive.*

Grand Hotel Hornan. An Old World, medium-size hotel, the Grand Hotel Hornan is in the city center near the train station. Opened in 1906, it has been refurbished during the past several years. The restaurant serves breakfast only. *Bangårdsgatan 1, tel. 018/139380. 37 rooms with bath. AE, MC, Closed Jul. 15–31. Moderate.*

The West Coast and the Glass Country

For many visitors traveling to Sweden by ferry, Gothenburg (or Göteborg) is the port of arrival. But those who arrive in Stockholm should not miss making a side trip to this great shipping city and Sweden's scenic western coast. This itinerary combines a western trip with a route through the Glass Country to the medieval fortress town of Kalmar, on the east coast.

Getting Around

As with the previous itinerary, the route can be followed by both train and car. Trains for Gothenburg depart from Stockholm's Central Station about every hour, and normal travel time is about 4½ hours. There are also four daily "City Express" trains that make faster time, but these require a supplementary fare of SEK 100 in first class (this includes breakfast on morning trains) or SEK 30 in second class. Seat reservations are compulsory on most trains to Gothenburg. There are also hourly flights to Gothenburg from Stockholm's Arlanda Airport between 7 AM and 9 PM on weekdays, slightly less frequently on weekends. The trip by air takes 55 minutes.

For getting around the city of Gothenburg itself, the best transportation option for the visitor is the Key to Gothenburg card (Göteborgskortet), similar to the Key to Stockholm card. This entitles the user to free travel on all public transportation, free parking, and free admission to the Liseberg amusement park and all city museums. Prices for the card range from SEK 70 for one day to SEK 200 for four days.

Guided Tours

Free 50-minute sightseeing tours of Gothenburg leave regularly from **Kungsportsplatsen,** just beside the city tourist office. They must be reserved at the office in advance.

The West Coast and the Glass Country

Tourist Information

Gothenburg. Basargartan 10, tel. 031/100740.
Jönköping. Kyrkogatan 6, tel. 036/169050.
Kalmar. Ölandshomnen, tel. 0480/15350.
Växjö. Kronobergsgatan 8, tel. 0470/22325.

Exploring

Gothenburg   Visitors arriving in Gothenburg by car often drive straight through the city in their haste to reach their coastal vacation spots, but it is well worth spending a day or two exploring this attractive harbor city. A quayside jungle of cranes and warehouses attests to the city's industrial might, yet within 10 minutes' walk of the waterfront is an elegant, modern city of broad avenues, green parks, and gardens. It is an easy city to explore: Most of the major attractions are within walking distance of each other, and there is an excellent streetcar network. In the summer, you can even take a sightseeing trip on a vintage open-air streetcar.

Gothenburg's development was pioneered mainly by British merchants in the 19th century, when it acquired the nickname "Little London." But a more accurate name would have been "Little Amsterdam," for the city was designed in the 17th century by Dutch architects, who gave it its extensive network of straight streets divided by canals. There is only one major canal today, but you can explore it on one of the popular "Paddan"

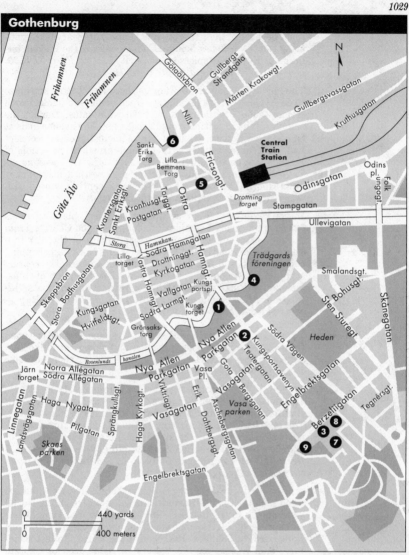

Gothenburg

Major Attractions
Götaplatsen Square, **3**
Kungsportsavenyn, **2**
Maritime Center, **6**
Nordstan, **5**
Paddan Terminal, **1**
Trädgårdföreningen, **4**

Other Attractions
Art Gallery, **7**
City Theater, **8**
Concert Hall, **9**

sightseeing boats. The boats got their nickname, Swedish for toad, because of their short, squat shape, necessary for negotiating the city's 20 low bridges. You embark at the **Paddan terminal** at Kungsportsplatsen in the city center. *Fare: SEK 30. Departures: May 1–mid-Sept., daily 10–5.*

❷ The hub of Gothenburg is **Kungsportsavenyn,** better known as "The Avenue." It is a broad, tree-lined boulevard flanked with elegant shops, restaurants, and sidewalk cafés. During the summer, it has a distinctively Parisian air. The avenue ends at ❸ **Götaplatsen Square,** home of the municipal theater, concert hall, and library (where there's an excellent selection of English-language newspapers). Just off the avenue is ❹ **Trädgårdsföreningen,** an attractive park with a magnificent Palm House that was built in 1878 and recently restored. *Admission: SEK 2. Open summer, daily 7 AM–9 PM.*

If you're interested in shopping, the best place to go is ❺ **Nordstan,** a covered complex of shops near the Central Train Station. Many of its businesses participate in the Tax-free Shopping Service. In the harbor near the Nordstan shopping ❻ complex, you will find the new **Maritime Center.** The center, still under development, houses a historic collection of ships, including a destroyer, a lightship, a trawler, and tugboats. *Admission: SEK 45. Open June 5–Aug. 28, daily 10–6; May 1–June 4 and Aug. 29–Sept. 25 weekends only.*

Jönköping To reach Jönköping, the next stop on the journey, take the train from Gothenburg's Central Station and change at **Falköping.** Jönköping is an attractive town on the southern shores of **Lake Vättern,** Sweden's largest lake.

Jönköping, which celebrated its 700th anniversary in 1984, is known as the "matchstick town." For it was here, in the 19th century, that the match-manufacturing industry got its start. The **Matchstick Museum,** built on the site of the first factory, has an exhibition on the development and manufacture of matches. *Admission: SEK 5. Open May 19–Sept. 12, Mon.– Fri. 9–7, Sat. 10–noon, and Sun. 3–5. Limited opening times the rest of the year.*

A few miles from Jönköping is **Riddersberg,** home of the famous wood sculptor **Calle Örnemark.** You can get here on the No. 30 bus from the Jönköping Train Station. Örnemark's home boasts an impressive selection of his works, among them *The Indian Rope-trick,* at 338 feet (103 meters) the world's tallest sculpture, and *Mutiny on the Bounty,* a re-creation of Captain Bligh's famous vessel. If you are lucky, the artist himself may show you around. *Free. Open daily.*

Växjö To the southeast of Jönköping lies Växjö, Kronoberg County's main town and the best center for exploring Sweden's **Glass Country.** It is also an important sightseeing destination for hundreds of American visitors each year, for it was from this area that their Swedish ancestors set sail in the 19th century. The **Emigrants' House,** located in the town center, tells the story of the migration, during which close to a million Swedes— one quarter of the entire population—departed for the promised land. The museum exhibits provide a vivid sense of the rigorous journey, and an archive room and research center allow American visitors to trace their ancestry. On the second

Sunday in August, Växjö celebrates "Minnesota Day." Swedes and Swedish-Americans come together to commemorate their common heritage with fun and festivities.

Many of Sweden's most famous glassworks are within easy reach of Växjö, and it is usually possible to take an organized sightseeing tour of the facilities. Inquire at the **tourist office** for information. The manufacture of Swedish glass dates back to 1556, when Venetian glassblowers were first invited to the Swedish court. But it was another 200 years before glass manufacturing became a real Swedish industry. The area between Växjö and Kalmar was chosen for its dense forest—offering limitless wood supplies for heating the furnaces. All the major Swedish glass companies, including **Orrefors** and **Kosta Boda,** still have their works in this area, and most of them are open to the public. Most also have factory outlets where you can pick up near-perfect "seconds" at bargain prices. *Open Mon.–Sat. 8–3, Sun. 11–4.*

Kalmar An attractive coastal town, Kalmar is dominated by its imposing seaside castle. The town was once known as the "lock and key" of Sweden, for it is situated on the southern frontier of the kingdom, and thus open to constant enemy invasion. The castle's history goes back 800 years, although the present building dates only from the 16th century, when it was rebuilt by King Gustav Vasa. Among other treasures, its museum contains a selection of relics from the royal battleship *Kronan,* which sank off the nearby island of Oland in 1676 during a battle with a combined Danish and Dutch fleet. The wreck, unearthed in 1980, has already yielded some rich archaeological finds, including a cask of 300-year-old brandy. *Admission: SEK 10. Open May–Sept., Mon.–Sat. 10–4, Sun. 1–4. Tours begin once an hour, mid-June–mid-Aug.*

To return to Stockholm from Kalmar, catch the train to **Alvesta** (the service runs every two hours) and change there for the Stockholm service. Two trains–one day service and one night service–run to Stockholm each day. The journey takes about 6½ hours. **Linjeflyg** operates several flights a day to Stockholm from the **Kalmar airport,** located three miles (five kilometers) from the town center. The trip takes about 50 minutes. For information, phone 0480/58800 or 0480/58811.

Dining and Lodging

For details and price category definitions, *see* Dining and Lodging in Essential Information.

Gothenburg **Johanna.** This must rate among Sweden's most celebrated res-
Dining taurants. It is presided over by its distinguished owner-chef,
★ Crister Svanteson, trained at the famous Paris Tour d'Argent. The entrance is unpretentious, but the interior suggests a London club. It features nouvelle cuisine, with an accent on seafood. *Södra Hamngatan 47, tel. 031/112250. Dress: casual. Reservations advised. AE, DC, MC, V. Closed lunchtime, Sun., July, Christmas, and New Years. Expensive.*

★ **Räkan.** An informal and popular restaurant, Räkan makes the most of an unusual gimmick. The tables are arranged around a long tank, and if you order shrimp, the house specialty, they arrive at your table in radio-controlled boats you navigate yourself. *Lorensbergsgatan 16, tel. 031/169839. Dress: casual. Reservations essential. AE, DC, MC, V. Closed lunchtime on* *weekends, Christmas, New Years, and Midsummer. Expensive (with moderate fixed-price menus also available).*

Bräutigams. Near the tourist office, Bräutigams is an elegant café, ideal for a snack or light meal in a turn-of-the-century atmosphere. The restaurant specializes in homemade cakes and coffee, but light lunches—open-faced sandwiches and salads—are also available. *Östra Hamngatan 50B, tel. 031/136046. Dress: casual. AE, DC, MC, V. Closed Christmas Eve. Moderate.*

Lodging **Sheraton Hotel and Towers.** Opened in 1986, the Sheraton Hotel
★ and Towers is Gothenburg's most modern and spectacular international-style hotel. It features an American atrium-style lobby. There are several restaurants with varying prices, including a popular Italian-style café, open at lunchtime, and a gourmet restaurant. *Södra Hamngatan 59–65, tel. 031/101600. 342 rooms with bath. Facilities: health club, nightclub, 16 rooms especially equipped for handicapped guests. AE, DC, MC, V. Closed Christmas. Very Expensive.*

★ **Eggers.** Dating back to 1859, Eggers has probably more Old World character than any other hotel in the city. It is located near the train station and was probably the last port of call in Sweden for many emigrants to the United States. The rooms feature antique furnishings, and there is a popular brasserie-style restaurant. *Drottningtorget, tel. 031/171570. 76 rooms with bath. AE, DC, MC, V. Closed Christmas. Expensive.*

Liseberg Heden. Not far from the famous Liseberg amusement park, Liseberg Heden is a popular, modern family hotel. It offers a sauna and gourmet restaurant. *Sten Sturegatan, tel. 031/ 200280. 160 rooms with bath. AE, DC, MC, V. Closed Christmas and New Years. Moderate.*

Royal. Located in the city center near the train station, the Royal is a small and fairly basic traditional-style hotel. It was built in 1854 and refurbished in the mid-1980s. Only breakfast is served. *Drottninggatan 67, tel. 031/170100. 80 rooms, 55 with shower. AE, DC, MC, V. Closed Christmas and New Years. Inexpensive.*

Jönköping **City.** City is a medium-size hotel located in the city center.
Lodging Rooms offer a view of Lake Vaettern. Built in the late 1960s, the hotel was recently renovated. *Västra Storgatan 23–25, tel. 036/119280. 70 rooms with bath. Facilities: sauna, car rental, restaurant. AE, DC, MC, V. Closed Christmas. Moderate.*

Stora Hotellet. Translated to mean "The Big Hotel," Stora Hotellet is an old-fashioned establishment opened in 1861 but recently modernized. It is centrally located, only 100 yards (90 meters) from the train station. Its restaurant serves international cuisine. *Hotellplan, tel. 036/119300. 110 rooms with shower. Facilities: sauna, tennis courts. AE, DC, MC, V. Moderate.*

Dining **Mäster Gudmunds Källare.** Nestled in cozy, 16th-century cellar
★ vaults and only 2 minutes from the train station, Mäster Gudmunds Källare is a particularly inviting restaurant. Though the cuisine is international, there is one typically Swedish specialty: "plank steak." *Kapellgatan 2, tel. 036/ 112633. Dress: casual. Reservations advised. AE, DC, MC, V. Closed Sun. dinner, Christmas, New Years, Midsummer. Moderate.*

Kalmar **Stadshotellet.** Located in the city center, Stadshotellet is a fair-
Lodging ly large, Old World hotel. The main building dates from the

19th century. It features a fine restaurant. *Storgatan 14, tel. 0480/15180. 140 rooms with bath. Facilities: Jacuzzi, disco. AE, DC, MC, V. Closed Christmas and New Years. Expensive.*

Slottshotellet. Situated in a gracious old town house on a quiet street, Slottshotellet bears no resemblance to a hotel from the outside. But inside, it offers a host of modern facilities. Only breakfast is served. *Slottsvägen 7, tel. 0480/88260. 36 rooms with shower. AE, DC, MC, V. Closed Christmas. Moderate.*

Continental. Located about 100 yards (90 meters) from the train station, the Continental is a fairly basic but comfortable family hotel. Only breakfast is served. *Larmgatan 10, tel. 0480/15140. 39 rooms with bath. AE, MC, V. Closed Christmas. Inexpensive.*

Växjö
Dining and Lodging

Sara Statt. A conveniently located, traditional-style hotel, Sara Statt is popular with tour groups. The building dates from the early 19th century, but the rooms themselves are modern, and the hotel has a resident piano bar and à la carte restaurant. *Kungsgatan 6, tel. 04703/13400. 130 rooms with bath. AE, DC, MC, V. Closed Christmas and Midsummer. Moderate.*

Esplanad. Centrally located, Esplanad is a small, family hotel offering basic amenities; it has been recently renovated. Only breakfast is served. *Norra Esplanaden 21A, tel. 0470/22580. 27 rooms, most with shower. MC, V. Closed Christmas and New Years. Inexpensive.*

32 Switzerland

Introduction

Switzerland has most of the attractions of its larger European neighbors—mountain grandeur, gushing waterfalls, breathtaking scenery, sophisticated city life, and artistic excellence all around. Fine modern roads link towns and villages where old traditions are faithfully preserved. Landlocked Switzerland is a country of peace, yet it's strewn with castles that recall old battles for nationhood.

Since Switzerland is such a small country, you can see a lot of it during a relatively short stay: Public transportation is the best in Europe, and you can combine the delights of road, rail, and water travel. Within this small country, three cultures predominate: German in the north, French in the southwest, and Italian in the southeast, but English is spoken virtually everywhere.

Switzerland is a country of contrasts. If you stand on the peak of Rigi or walk the slopes of Klewenalp and listen to the cowbells tinkling in the valley below, it's hard to imagine that Zürich, one of the great financial centers of the world, is not so far away. Then take time, while enjoying the modern chic of Geneva, to reflect on the fact that in parts of Appenzell, women still don't have the right to vote in local elections.

The Swiss are a welcoming people, eager to smooth the way for the visitor. Swiss hotels are famous for their cleanliness and efficiency, and this applies as much to establishments in rural areas as to luxury ones in the cities. The cuisine mixes the best of French, Italian, and German with succulent Swiss specialties.

High living standards have earned Switzerland a reputation as expensive for visitors. This is true, but perhaps more than anywhere else, you'll get what you pay for, and that is, first and foremost, value for money. In the mountain areas, though, one of the main attractions is absolutely free—the air; it's exhilarating.

Before You Go

When to Go There's always something happening—it just depends on what you want. Winter sports begin around Christmas and last usually until mid-April, depending on the state of the snow. The countryside is a delight in spring when the wild flowers are in bloom, and the fall colors rival those in New England. In the Ticino (the Italian-speaking area) and around Lake Geneva (Lac Léman), summer stays late. There is often sparkling weather in September and October, and the popular resorts are less crowded then.

Climate Summer in Switzerland is generally warm and sunny, though the higher you go, of course, the cooler it gets, especially at night. Winter is cold everywhere: In low-lying areas the weather is frequently damp and overcast, while in the Alps there are often brilliantly clear days, but it is guaranteed to be very cold and very snowy.

Summer or winter, Switzerland is prone to an Alpine wind that blows from the south and is known as the Föhn. This gives rise

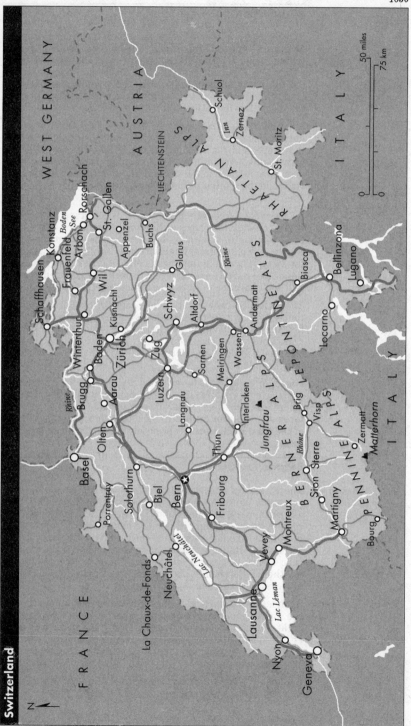

Switzerland

to clear but rather oppressive weather, which the Swiss claim causes headaches. The only exception to the general weather patterns is the Ticino. Here, protected by the Alps, the weather is positively Mediterranean; even in winter, it is significantly warmer than elsewhere.

The following are the average daily maximum and minimum temperatures for Zurich.

Jan.	36F	2C	May	67F	19C	Sept.	69F	20C
	26	– 3		47	8		51	11
Feb.	41F	5C	June	73F	23C	Oct.	57F	14C
	28	– 2		53	12		43	6
Mar.	51F	10C	July	76F	25C	Nov.	45F	7C
	34	1		56	14		35	2
Apr.	59F	15C	Aug.	75F	24C	Dec.	37F	3C
	40	4		56	13		29	-2

Currency The unit of currency is the Swiss franc, divided into 100 rappen (known as centimes in French-speaking areas). There are coins of 5, 10, 20, and 50 rappen, and of 1, 2, and 5 francs. The bills are of 10, 20, 50, 100, 500, and 1,000 francs.

At press time (fall 1988), the Swiss franc stood at 1.39 to the dollar and 2.42 to the pound.

All banks will change your money. Traveler's checks get a better exchange rate than cash. Main airports and train stations have exchange offices (*bureaux de change*) that are open longer hours than banks and often offer equally good rates of exchange. Most hotels and some restaurants will change money but usually at a far-less-favorable rate. Most major credit cards are generally, though not universally, accepted at hotels, restaurants, and shops.

What It Will Cost High standards of living mean that Switzerland is generally expensive: If it's luxury you're after, you'll pay more for it here than in almost any other European country. You'll find plenty of reasonably priced hotels and restaurants, however, if you look for them. Those who have visited Switzerland before will be surprised at how little prices have changed recently: Inflation has been less than 2% for years.

As in any other European country, the cities are more expensive than the smaller towns. Zürich and Geneva are the priciest; Basel, Bern, and Lugano are also quite expensive. Elsewhere, prices drop appreciably, particularly off the beaten track and in the northeast.

Sample Prices Cup of coffee, 2.20 Fr.; bottle of beer 2.50 Fr., Coca-Cola 2 Fr., ham sandwich 7 Fr.; a one-mile taxi ride, 5 Fr.

Customs on Arrival There are two levels of duty-free allowance for visitors to Switzerland. Residents of non-European countries may import 400 cigarettes or 100 cigars or 500 grams of tobacco, plus two liters of alcoholic beverage below 15% and one liter of alcoholic beverage in excess of 15%. Residents of European countries may import 200 cigarettes or 50 cigars or 250 grams of tobacco, plus two liters of alcoholic beverage below 15% and one liter of alcoholic beverage in excess of 15%. These allowances apply only to those aged 18 and above.

There are no restrictions on the import or export of any currency.

Language French is spoken in the southwest, around Lake Geneva, and in the cantons of Fribourg, Neuchâtel, Jura, and Vaud; Italian is spoken in the Ticino, and German is spoken everywhere else. English is also spoken everywhere: Most public signs are in English as well as in the regional language, and all hotels, restaurants, tourist offices, train stations, banks, and shops will have someone who can speak English fluently.

Getting Around

By Car
Road Conditions Swiss roads are usually well surfaced but are mostly winding and often mountainous. It's not really possible to achieve high average speeds. When estimating likely travel times, look carefully at the map: There may be only 20 miles between one point and another, but there could also be a mountain pass along the way. There is a well-developed highway network, though some notable gaps still exist in the south along an east-west line, roughly between Lugano and Lausanne. Under some mountain passes, there are tunnels through which cars can be transported by train while passengers remain in the cars—a curious experience and often a very cold one.

A combination of steep or winding routes and hazardous weather conditions means that some roads will be closed in winter. Dial 120 or 163 for bulletins and advance information on road conditions. For tourists, Swiss Radio 1 broadcasts information in English at around 7 PM.

Rules of the Road Driving is on the right. In built-up areas, the speed limit is 50 kph (30 mph) and on main highways, it's 120 kph (75 mph). On other roads outside built-up areas, the limit is 80 kph (50 mph).

Children under 12 are not permitted to sit in the front seat. Driving with parking lights is prohibited, and lights are compulsory in heavy rain or poor visibility; you *must* use headlights in road tunnels. Always carry your car registration papers and your valid license.

To use the main highways, you must display a disk, which you can buy from the Swiss National Tourist Office before you leave: It costs 30 Fr. Cars rented within Switzerland already have these disks.

Traffic going up a mountain has priority except for postal buses coming down. A sign with a yellow posthorn on a blue background means that postal buses have priority.

In winter, snow chains are advisable—sometimes compulsory. They can be rented in all areas, and snow-chain service stations have signs marked *Service de Chaînes à Neige.*

If you have an accident, even a minor one, you must call the police.

Parking Parking areas are clearly marked. Parking in public lots normally costs between 0.5 Fr. and 1 Fr. per hour.

Gasoline Lead-free gas costs 0.95 Fr. per liter, and regular gas costs 1 Fr. per liter.

Breakdowns Assistance is available through the telephone exchange: Ask for *Autohilfe.* Roadside repairs and towage are free to holders of international touring documents. The Touring Club Suisse has a 24-hour breakdown service. Useful organizations are the **Automobile Club de Suisse** (ACS), Wasserwerke 39, Bern, and the **Touring Club Suisse** (TCS), rue Pierre Fatio 9, Geneva 3, both of which have branches throughout Switzerland.

By Train Switzerland's trains are among Europe's finest. Generally, they are extremely fast, immaculately clean, and nearly always punctual. If you plan to use the trains extensively, get the official timetable (*Offizielles Kursbuch*), which costs 8.50 Fr.

Trains described as *Inter-City* or *Express* are the fastest, stopping only at principal towns. *Regionalzug* means a local train, often affording the most spectacular views. Meals, snacks, and drinks are provided on most main services; seat reservations are not necessary.

Fares There are numerous concessions for visitors. The **Swiss Holiday Card** is the best value, offering unlimited travel on Swiss Federal Railways, postal buses, lake steamers, and the local bus service of 24 cities. It also gives reductions on many privately owned railways, cable cars, and mountain railways. It's available from the Swiss National Tourist Office (SNTO) and from travel agents outside Switzerland. The card is valid for four days (cost 150 Fr.), eight days (180 Fr.), 15 days (220 Fr.), or one month (305 Fr.). Prices are for second-class travel; first-class travel costs about one-third more.

In some popular tourist areas, **Regional Holiday Season Tickets,** issued for seven or 15 days, give five days free travel by train, postal buses, steamers, and mountain railways, with half fare for the rest of the validity of the card. Increasingly popular with tourists is a card entitling the holder to half-fare travel for 30 days. For more information about train travel in Switzerland, get the free *Discover Switzerland* brochure from the SNTO.

By Bus Switzerland's famous yellow postal buses link main cities with villages off the beaten track. Free timetables can be picked up at any post office.

The **Holiday Card** (*see* Getting Around By Train) gives unlimited travel on the postal buses. If you prefer to do all your exploring by bus, get a **Postal Coach Season Ticket,** valid for one month, which allows three days free travel and half-price concessions for the rest of the validity of the ticket. The **Postal Coach Weekly Card** gives unlimited travel within certain regions. Both tickets can be bought at local post offices.

The postal buses pay special attention to hikers. You can get a free booklet, "The Best River and Lakeside Walks" from the SNTO. The booklet describes 28 walks you can enjoy by hopping on and off postal buses. Most walks take around three hours.

By Boat Drifting across a Swiss lake and stopping off here and there at picturesque villages nestling by the water makes a relaxing day's excursion, especially if you are lucky enough to catch one of the elegant old paddle steamers. Trips are scheduled on most of the lakes, with increased service in summer. Unlimited travel is free to holders of the **Swiss Holiday Card** (*see* Getting Around By Train). Most boats have refreshments, and several have restaurants with excellent food.

By Bicycle Bikes can be rented at all train stations and can be returned to any station. Rates are 12 Fr. per day, or 48 Fr. per week for a conventional bike; tandems cost 25 Fr. per day; 100 Fr. a week.

Families, regardless of size, are entitled to a special rate of 28 Fr. per day and 112 Fr. per week for all bikes. Groups get reductions according to the number of bikes involved. Reservations are necessary by 6 PM the day before use by individuals and a week ahead for groups.

Essential Information

Telephones
Local Calls
There is direct dialing to everywhere in Switzerland. For local and international codes, consult the pink pages at the front of the telephone book. It's cheapest to use the booths in train stations and post offices: Calls made from your hotel cost a great deal more. Rates are lower between 5 PM and 7 PM, after 9 PM, and on weekends. Calls to the United States cost 4 Fr. per minute, to the United Kingdom 1.80 Fr. per minute.

International Calls
You can dial most international numbers direct from Switzerland. If you want a number that cannot be reached directly, dial 114 for a connection. Dial 191 for international numbers and information.

Operators and Information
All telephone operators speak English, and there are instructions printed in English in all telephone booths.

Mail
Postal Rates
All mail goes by air. Current rates to the United States are 1.10 Fr. for letters under 10 grams; 1.70 Fr. for letters under 20 grams; and 1.10 Fr. for postcards. Letters to the United Kingdom under 20 grams cost 90 rappen, and postcards, 80 rappen.

Receiving Mail
If you're uncertain where you'll be staying, you can have your mail, marked *Poste Restante*, sent to any post office in Switzerland. It needs the sender's name and address on the back, and you'll need proof of identity to collect it. You can also have your mail sent to American Express for a small fee, payable when you collect it.

Shopping
Switzerland's city shops are among the most splendid in Europe. Don't be alarmed by the high prices in the most elegant shops—there are plenty of others that offer goods at lower prices. You'll find them mostly in the old quarters of the cities or in the smaller towns.

Try the food markets, which often give better value than the shops: Go early in the morning for the best buys.

Switzerland is famous for its watches; jewelry; embroidered articles, particularly blouses and tablecloths; and all kinds of wood carving. Specific regions have their characteristic crafts, such as ceramics. Swiss chocolates are among the finest in the world, and look for the famous Swiss all-purpose, multiblade pocket knife.

VAT Refunds
A 6.2% value-added tax on all goods is included in the price. Nonresidents may claim a VAT refund either at the time of purchase, or the shop will send the refund to your home. In order to qualify for a refund, you must sign a form at the time of purchase and present it to Swiss customs on departure.

Bargaining
Don't try bargaining: It just doesn't work. As with everything in Switzerland, prices are efficiently controlled.

Opening and Closing Times
Banks. Banks are open weekdays 8:30–4:30 or 5.
Museums. Museum times vary considerably, though many close on Monday. Check locally.
Shops. Shops are generally open 8–noon and 1:30–6:30. Some

will close at 4 on Saturday, and some are closed Monday morning. In cities, many large stores do not close for lunch.

National Holidays January 1 (New Year's Day); January 2 (Bank Holiday); March 24, 27 (Easter); May 1* (Labor Day); May 4 (Ascension); May 15 (Whit Monday); August 1* (National Day); December 25, 26. *Not throughout the country.

Dining Options range from luxury establishments to modest cafés or cellar restaurants and places that offer local specialties.

Because the Swiss are so good at preparing everyone else's cuisine, it is sometimes said that they have none of their own, but there definitely is a distinct and characteristic Swiss cuisine. Switzerland is the home of great cheeses—Gruyère, Emmentaler, Appenzell, and Vacherin—which form the basis of many dishes. *Raclette* is cheese fried over a fire; *rosti* are potatoes cooked in a fragrant herb cheese, and *fondue* is melted cheese, often flavored with kirsch, into which you dip chunks of bread. Other Swiss specialties to look for are *Geschnetzeltes Kalbsfleisch*, diced veal in cream sauce, and *stuffato alla Luganese*, beef stewed in marsala. Swiss sausages make both a filling and inexpensive meal.

Mealtimes At home, the main Swiss meal of the day is lunch, with a snack in the evening. Restaurants, however, are open at midday and in the evening; some are open all day.

Ratings Prices are per person, without wine or coffee, but including tip and taxes. Best bets are indicated by a star ★ . At press time, there were 1.39 Swiss francs to the dollar.

Category	Zürich	Other Areas
Very Expensive	over 80 Fr.	over 70 Fr.
Expensive	50 Fr.–80 Fr.	40 Fr.–70 Fr.
Moderate	20 Fr.–50 Fr.	20 Fr.–40 Fr.
Inexpensive	under 20 Fr.	under 20 Fr.

Credit Cards The following credit card abbreviations are used: AE, American Express; DC, Diners Club; MC, MasterCard; V, Visa.

Lodging Switzerland's accommodations span the gamut, from the most luxurious hotels to the more economical rooms in private homes. Pick up the "Schweizer Hotelführer" (Swiss Hotel Guide) from the SNTO before you leave home. The guide is free and lists all the members of the Swiss Hotel Association and nearly 90% of the nation's hotels, and sets out everything you will want to know.

Switzerland is justly proud of its hotels because of their emphasis on fast, friendly service. If you have a complaint, the manager will want to hear it. Equally, if you have a word of praise, go to the top as well. Any special requests, such as one concerning diet, should be made known as soon as you arrive.

Most hotel rooms today have private bath and shower; those that don't are usually two-thirds the price. Single rooms are generally about two-thirds the price of doubles, but this can vary considerably. Service charges and taxes are included in the price quoted and the bill you pay. Breakfast is included unless there is a clear notice to the contrary.

All major towns and train stations have hotel-finding services, which sometimes charge a small fee. Local tourist offices will also help.

Hotels Hotels are graded from one star (the lowest) to five stars. Always confirm what you are paying before you register. Major credit cards are generally accepted, but, again, make sure beforehand.

An important hotel chain is the **Romantik Hotels and Restaurants,** with premises that are generally either in historic houses or in houses that have some special character. Another chain with a good reputation is **Ambassador Hotels.** The **Check-In E and G Hotels** is a voluntary group of small hotels, boarding houses, and mountain lodges that offer accommodations at reasonable prices. Details are available from the SNTO. In addition to pamphlets recommending family hotels, it also has a list of hotels and restaurants catering specifically to Jewish travelers.

Country Inns Country inns offer clean, comfortable, and hospitable accommodations, often in areas of great scenic beauty. Most are in the inexpensive category and are a good value.

Rentals Switzerland has literally thousands of furnished châlets. Off-season, per-day prices are around 50 Fr. per person for four sharing a châlet. In peak season, prices would be at least twice as expensive. Deluxe chalets cost much more. For more information, pick up an illustrated brochure from the **Swiss Touring Club,** Wasserwerkegasse 39, 3000 Bern 13 or from Uto-Ring AG, Beethovenstr. 24, 8022 Zürich. In the United States, write to **Villa International,** 71 West 23rd St., New York, NY 10010. In Britain, contact **Interhome,** 383 Richmond Rd., Twickenham, Middlesex TW1 2EF.

Ratings Prices are for two people in a double room, including taxes, service charges, and breakfast. Best bets are indicated by a star ★. At press time, there were 1.39 Swiss francs to the dollar.

Category	Cost
Very Expensive	over 250 Fr.
Expensive	150 Fr.–250 Fr.
Moderate	70 Fr.–150 Fr.
Inexpensive	under 70 Fr.

Credit Cards The following credit card abbreviations are used: AE, American Express; DC, Diners Club; MC, MasterCard; V, Visa.

Tipping Generally speaking, there is no need to tip. With service charges of 15% and with taxes included in your hotel and restaurant bill, no one will expect or demand a tip, though if someone has been particularly helpful, a tip is appreciated. Elsewhere, give bathroom attendants 1 Fr. and hotel maids 2 Fr. Tip station porters well, especially for excessively heavy luggage. Theater and opera house ushers get 2 Fr. for showing you to your seat and selling you a program.

Zürich

Arriving and Departing

By Plane Kloten (tel. 01/8164081) is Switzerland's most important airport and is among the most sophisticated in the world. Several airlines fly directly to Zürich from major cities in the United States, Canada, and the United Kingdom.

Between the Airport and Downtown Beneath the air terminals, there's a train station with an efficient, direct service into the Hauptbahnhof (main station) in the center of Zürich. Fast trains run every 20 minutes, and the trip takes about 10 minutes. The fare is 4 Fr. and the ticket office is in the airport. There are express trains to most Swiss cities at least every hour. Trains run from 6 AM to midnight.

Taxis are very expensive and should be avoided, if possible. Some hotels provide their own bus service. Cars can be rented at the airport.

By Bus All bus services to Zürich will drop you at the Hauptbahnhof.

By Car There are direct highways from the border crossings with France, Germany, and Italy. The German frontier is the nearest.

Getting Around

Although Zürich is Switzerland's largest city, it has a population of less than 400,000 and is not large by European standards. That's one of its nicest features: You can explore it comfortably on foot. As in most cities, however, it's a good idea to take a guided bus tour first to get your bearings, then go alone at your leisure (*see* Guided Tours).

By Bus and Streetcar The city transit network is excellent. **VBZ Züri-Line** (Zürich Public Transport) buses run from 5:30 AM to midnight, every six minutes on all routes at peak hours, and about every 12 minutes at other times. Before you board the bus, you must buy your ticket from the automatic vending machines (instructions appear in English) found at every stop. A money-saving ticket for all travel for 24 hours is a good buy. Free route plans are available from VBZ offices.

By Taxi Taxis are very expensive and should be avoided unless you have no other means of getting around.

Important Addresses and Numbers

Tourist Information Bahnhofplatz 15 (Main Station), tel. 01/2114000. Open March–October, weekdays 8 AM–10 PM, weekends 8 AM–8:30 PM; November–February, Monday–Thursday 8–8, Friday 8 AM–10 PM, weekends 9–6.

Consulates U.S. Zollickerstr. 141, tel. 01/552566. **U.K.** Dufourstr. 56, tel. 01/471520.

Emergencies **Police,** tel. 117. **Ambulance,** tel. 01/3611661. **Doctor,** tel. 01/474700, poisoning cases, 01/2515151. **Dentist,** tel. 01/474700. **Pharmacy, Bellevue,** Theaterstr. 14, tel. 01/2424411, offers an all-night service.

English Bookstores   Payot, Bahnhofstr. 9. **Travel Book Shop,** Rindermarkt 20.

Travel Agencies   **American Express,** Bahnhofstr. 20, tel. 01/2118370. **Kuoni,** Bahnhofplatz 7, tel. 01/2213411. **Thomas Cook,** 22 Talacker, Sihlporteplatz, tel. 01/2118710.

Guided Tours

Orientation Tours   There are four bus tours available. The daily "Sights of Zürich" tour gives a good general idea of the city in two hours. "Zürich and the Vicinity" goes farther and includes an aerial cableway trip to Felsenegg. This is also a daily tour and takes 2½ hours. "Goldtimer," a one-hour tour of the center of Zürich by an old tram, operates between May and October. Another May-to-October tour is "Zürich by Night," which takes in everything from folklore to striptease in 3½ hours. All tours start from the main station. Contact the tourist office for reservations.

Special-Interest Tours   If you have a special interest, inquire at the tourist office for details about available tours.

Walking Tours   Conducted walking tours start from the tourist office and take roughly 2½ hours. Check times at the tourist office.

Excursions   There are many bus excursions to other areas, such as the Bernese Oberland, St. Gotthard, the Ticino, Lucerne, and Geneva. Since these depend on the season and weather, it's best to book them after you arrive and can check with the tourist office.

Personal Guides   The tourist office will recommend a personal guide.

Exploring Zürich

Zürich is not at all what you'd expect. Stroll around on a fine spring day and you'll ask yourself if this can really be one of the great business centers of the world: The lake glistening and blue in the sun, the sidewalk cafés, swans gliding in to land on the river, the hushed and haunted old squares of medieval guildhouses, and elegant shops. There's not a gnome (a mocking nickname for a Swiss banker) in sight, not a worried business frown to be seen. The point is that for all its economic importance, Zürich is a place where people enjoy life. Hardworking, inventive, serious when need be, the Swiss love the good things in life, and they have the money to enjoy them.

Zürich started as a Roman customs post on the Lindenhof overlooking the river Limmat. That was in 15 BC. Its growth really began around the 10th century AD. It became a free imperial city in 1336, a center of the Reformation in 1519, then gradually assumed commercial importance in the 19th century. Today there is peace as well as prosperity here, and since Zürich is so compact, you can take in its variety in a morning's stroll.

The Main Attractions

Collect your map (essential) from the **Tourist Office** (Bahnhofplatz 15), then start your walk from the nearby ❶ **Bahnhofstrasse,** famous for its shops and cafés and as the center of the banking network, though you'd be unlikely to guess it. Take Rennweg on your left, and then turn left again into the Fortunagasse, a quaint medieval street leading to the ❷ **Lindenhof,** where there are remains of Zürich's Roman origins.

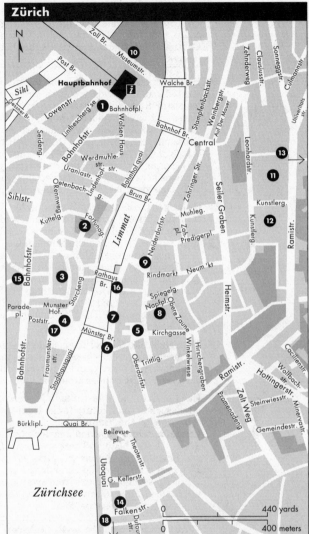

Main Attractions
Bahnhofstrasse, **1**
Fraumünster, **4**
Grossmünster, **5**
Limmatquai, **7**
Lindenhof, **2**
Niederdorf, **9**
Old Town, **8**
Peterskirche, **3**
Schweizerisches
Landesmuseum, **10**
Wasserkirche, **6**

Other Attractions
Centre Le Corbusier, **18**
Federal Institute of
Technology, **11**
Opernhaus, **14**
Rathaus, **16**
Stadthaus, **17**
University of Zürich, **12**
Wohnmuseum, **15**
Zoo, **13**

The **fountain** commemorates the ingenuity of the Zürich women who, when the city was besieged by the Hapsburgs in 1292, donned armor and marched around the walls. The invaders thought they were reinforcements and beat a hasty retreat.

③ An alley on the right leads to a picturesque square dating from the Middle Ages, with the **Peterskirche** (13th century), Zürich's oldest parish church, which also happens to have the largest clock face in Europe. Walk down to the river and follow **④** it to the 13th century **Fraumünster,** which has modern stained-glass windows by Chagall. There are two handsome guildhalls nearby: the **Zunfthaus zur Waag** hall of the linen weavers, built in 1637, and the **Zunfthaus zur Meise,** built in the 18th century for the wine merchants.

Time Out Backtrack to the Bahnhofstrasse, then the Paradeplatz, and visit **Sprüngli,** a café and famous meeting place of Zürich's socially conscious. Try the sinfully rich chocolate truffles. Continue to Bürkliplatz and cross the **Quai Bridge** to take in the impressive views of the lake and town.

❺ Having crossed the river, head for the **Grossmünster,** which started in the 11th century. In the 3rd century AD, St. Felix and his sister Regula were martyred by the Romans. Legend declares that having been beheaded, they then walked up the hill carrying their heads and collapsed on the spot where the Grossmünster now stands. On the south tower you can see a statue of Charlemagne (768–814), emperor of the West. In the 16th century, the Zürich reformer Huldrych Zwingli preached sermons here that were so threatening in their promise of fire and brimstone that Martin Luther himself was scared.

❻ Go back to the river to the **Wasserkirche** (Water Church), dating from the 15th century, a lovely example of late Gothic architecture. It is attached to the **Helmhaus,** originally an 18th-century
❼ cloth market. Here, on the **Limmatquai,** are some of Zürich's most enchanting old buildings. Today, most are restaurants. In the **Gesellschaftshaus zum Rüden,** a 13th-century noblemen's hall, you eat under a 300-year-old wooden ceiling. Other notable buildings here are the **Zunfthaus zur Saffran** (built in 1723 for haberdashers) and the **Zunfthaus zur Zimmerleuten** (built in 1708 for carpenters). The 17th-century baroque **Rathaus** (Town Hall) is nearby.

❽ Turn right into the **Old Town,** and you enter a maze of fascinating medieval streets where time seems to have stood still. The Rindmarkt, Napfplatz, and Kirchgasse all have their charming old houses. Just wander around at will.

❾ Head back to the river through **Niederdorf** (Zürich's red-light district), and you'll return to the Hauptbahnhof. On the north-
❿ ern edge of the Hauptbahnhof, go to the **Schweizerisches Landesmuseum,** housed in a curious 19th-century building, for a look at Swiss history. There are fascinating pre-Romanesque and Romanesque church art, glass paintings from the 15th to 17th centuries, splendid ceramic stoves, gold and silver from Celtic times, and weapons from many ages. *Museumstr. 2, tel. 01/2211010. Free. Open Tues.–Fri. 10–noon, 2–5, Sat. 10–noon, 2–4, Sun. 10–noon, 2–5.*

What to See and Do with Children

Most children are fascinated and intrigued by animals, and at Zürich's Zoo, one of Europe's best, there are more than 2,000 to keep them amused. Getting there on either streetcar 5 or 6 is also part of the fun. *Zürichbergstr. 222, tel. 01/2555411. Open daily 8–6; guided tour Sun. 10 AM.*

Zürich is called "the lakeside garden city" because of its parks, many of which have extensive facilities for energetic children. The most centrally located children's playgrounds are at **Lindenhof, Platzspitz,** and **Hohe Promenade.**

For a reminder of how things were before the advent of computer games, go to the **Zürich Toy Museum.** *Fortunagasse 15, tel. 01/2119305. Open Mon.–Fri. 2–5.*

There is a collection of puppets and dolls at the **Museum of Domestic Art.** *Bärengasse 22, tel. 01/2111716. Open Tues.-Fri. 10 -noon, 2-5, Sat. 10-noon, 2-4.*

Off the Beaten Track

The scheduled services of the steamers from the Bürkliplatz stop at several attractive villages on the lake shore. **Rapperswil** has a romantic-looking castle dating from the 12th century and an attractive Gothic Rathaus (town hall). This village also has many good fish restaurants. The **Forchbahn** train line from Stadelhofen station takes you to Forch with long views and good walking. A round-trip ticket costs 6.40 Fr. A 25-minute ride on the Uetlibergbahn from Selivau station provides a panoramic view of the city, lake, and far-off Alps. A round-trip ticket costs 8 Fr.

Shopping

Gift Ideas Typical Swiss products, all of the highest quality, include watches (not as expensive as you'd expect), clocks, jewelry, music boxes, embroidered goods, wood carvings, and the famous multiblade Swiss army pocket knife.

Shopping Districts The Bahnhofstrasse is as fine a shopping street as you'd come upon in Paris. Here you'll find **Jelmoli,** Switzerland's largest department store, carrying a wide range of tasteful Swiss goods. **Heimatwerk** specializes in handmade Swiss crafts, all of excellent quality. For high fashion, go to **Madame,** and for the finest porcelain, glass, and silverware, visit **Studio-Hag.** If you have a sweet tooth, head for **Sprüngli** for high-class chocolates: The truffles are out of this world.

In the Old Town and off the Limmatquai, you'll find boutiques, antiques shops, bookstores, and galleries in picturesque byways. The Löwenstrasse has such a diversity of shops it's been nicknamed "Shopville." The Langstrasse is another good shopping area and often has slightly lower prices.

Food and Flea Markets In many parts of town, there are lively markets where fruit, vegetables, and flowers are competitively priced. The best are at **Bürkliplatz, Helvetiaplatz, Milkbuckstrasse,** and **Marktplatz** (on the way to the airport). Get there early for the best buys. *Open Tues. 6 AM-11 AM.*

Burklialage is a flea market open May through October, and a curio market is held at **Rosenhof** every Thursday between April and Christmas.

Dining

Zürich's more than 1,000 restaurants offer everything from local specialties and fine French, Italian, and Spanish cuisine to Asian dishes. As with most other items in Switzerland, food will be of good quality and served with imagination and flair.

Ratings Prices are per person and include first course, main course, and dessert, but not wine or a tip. Best bets are indicated by a star ★ . At press time, there were 1.39 Swiss francs to the dollar.

Category	Cost
Very Expensive	over 80 Fr.
Expensive	50 Fr.–80 Fr.
Moderate	20 Fr.–50 Fr.
Inexpensive	under 20 Fr.

Credit Cards The following credit card abbreviations are used: AE, American Express; DC, Diners Club; MC, MasterCard; V, Visa.

Very Expensive **Agnes Amberg.** Some may find the decor at Agnes Amberg a bit overdone, but the exquisitely prepared dishes, made with the freshest ingredients, are beautifully presented. The service here is impeccable. *Hottingerstr. 5, tel. 01/2512626. Jacket and tie. Reservations essential. AE, DC, MC, V.*

★ **Chez Max.** Owner Max Kehl has earned a deserved reputation as one of the leading chefs of Switzerland. This elegant French restaurant is 2 miles (4 kilometers) out of the city on the road to Rapperswil and is worth the trip. This has been a gourmet's favorite for years. Kehl combines Japanese and French techniques to create unique and imaginative dishes. *Seestr. 53, Zollikon, tel. 01/3918877. Jacket and tie. Reservations essential. AE, DC, MC, V. Closed three weeks in July–Aug.*

Piccoli Accademia. The walls are decorated with photographs of personalities from the theater and the arts and their written appreciations of the fine food served them here. This is one of the best Italian restaurants outside Italy. The surroundings are very elegant—dark wood and crisp white tablecloths. Be sure to ask about the daily specials. *Rotwandstr.–48, tel. 01/2416243. Jacket and tie. Reservations essential. DC, MC.*

Expensive **Fluehgasse.** A charming 400-year-old half-timbered house stands on the outskirts of Zürich, on the road to Zollikon. This is Fluehgasse, which has been renovated with great sensitivity. The interior displays many fine Swiss antiques, warmed with abundant fresh flowers. The owner-chef, Robert Haupt, prepares the meals personally, basing his ever-changing menu on the fresh produce available at the daily market. *Zollikerstr. 214, tel. 01/531215. Jacket and tie. Reservations advised. AE, DC, MC, V.*

★ **Kronenhalle.** It's difficult to know whether to come here for the food (which is excellent) or for the superb art collection. Surrounded by the works of Picasso, Matisse, Utrillo, and Bonnard, you can savor traditional Swiss dishes as well as such French specialties as shoulder of lamb with garlic and Provençal herbs. Be sure to leave room for the famous chocolate mousse. This is a place to see and to be seen by *tout* Zürich. *Raemistr. 4, tel. 01/2510256. Jacket and tie. Reservations essential. AE, DC, MC, V.*

Moderate **Kindli Swiss Châlet.** Set in a Hollywood version of Heidi-land,
★ this is an absolute must for visitors to Zürich. Enjoy folk music and singing while sampling traditional Swiss dishes, such as fondue or sliced veal. *Rennweg/Pfalzgasse 1, tel. 01/2114282. Jacket and tie. Reservations advised. AE, DC, MC, V.*

Trattoria Toscana. Don't be put off by the pseudo-Italian decor, since this no-nonsense restaurant offers satisfying homemade cannelloni, ravioli, lasagna, and other Italian staples. At lunch, very reasonably priced set menus attract office workers. On sunny days, sit outside and be the envy of the busy passersby. *Fraumuestr. 14, tel. 01/2115751. Dress: casual. Reservations advised. AE, DC, MC, V.*

★ **Veltliner Keller.** This popular wine tavern, situated in one of the oldest parts of town, has quite a history. The house itself was built in 1325, and the tavern has been going strong since 1551. At the top of a flight of narrow steps is a wonderful carved wood interior with elegantly dressed tables. Specialties are local Swiss dishes, in particular the sliced veal in cream sauce and "Veltliner Pot," explained in full in the English menu. *Schluesselgass 8, tel. 01/2113228. Dress: casual. Reservations advised. AE, DC, MC, V.*

Zunfthaus Zur Saffran. Dine in Old World style beneath richly stuccoed ceilings and beside wide windows overlooking the Limmatquai. This guildhall restaurant dates back to 1723 and is the place for traditional Swiss dishes: veal and beef fillets, calf's liver, bacon and vegetables. *Limmatquai 54, tel. 01/476722. Dress: casual. Reservations advised. AE, DC, MC, V.*

Zunfthaus Zur Waag. Another guildhall tastefully converted into a restaurant, this one is decorated with antiques that evoke a bygone charm. From the second-floor dining room, you can look across the square to the Fraumünster. The food here is typically Swiss, but you'll be able to detect a French influence. Go with a hearty appetite to do justice to the generous portions. *Münsterhof 8, tel. 01/2110730. Dress: casual. Dinner reservations advised. AE, DC, MC, V.*

Inexpensive **Bierhalle Kropf.** Come to this old beer hall if you want to rub shoulders with students and the local arty set. Wherever they congregate, you can be sure of a good glass of beer and simple, wholesome Swiss meals. *In Gassen 16, tel. 01/211-1805. Dress: casual. Reservations not necessary. AE, DC, MC, V.*

Clipper. Located near the train station, this restaurant has an Oriental influence; it offers friendly service and the best dim sum in town. Try to get a table by the large window on the second floor and watch the world go by. *Lagerstr. 1, tel. 01/242-5320. Dress: casual. Reservations not necessary. AE, MC, V.*

Lodging

Zürich has an enormous range of hotels, from some of the most chic and prestigious in the country to modest guest houses. Standards of cleanliness and comfort, even at the lowest end of the scale, are high. Because this is Switzerland, prices tend to be higher than anywhere else in Europe, but you can be quite sure that you will get what you pay for: Quality and good service are guaranteed.

Ratings The following prices categories are for two people in a double room. Best bets are indicated by a star ★. At press time, there were 1.39 Swiss francs to the dollar.

Category	Cost
Very Expensive	over 250 Fr.
Expensive	150 Fr.–250 Fr.
Moderate	70 Fr.–150 Fr.
Inexpensive	under 70 Fr.

Credit Cards The following credit card abbreviations are used: AE, American Express; DC, Diners Club; MC, MasterCard; V, Visa.

Very Expensive
★

Hotel Baur Au Lac. This magnificent hotel is still owned by the family that built it in 1844, and it remains the choice of discerning travelers accustomed to the unrivaled quality of service offered here. Situated just a few steps from the Bahnhofstrasse and the lake, the Hotel Baur Au Lac has a splendid private park and wonderful views of the lake and the Alps. The luxuriously appointed rooms have every comfort you'd expect from a hotel of this standard. Meet for drinks in the expansive lounge decorated in Louis XVI and Empire style and muted, creamy shades. Service can be a bit slow here at times but is never less than friendly and courteous. The French restaurant sets high standards for its food, as does the famous grill room, where many of the rich and famous are to be seen. In summer, the wonderfully bright and fresh Garden Pavilion restaurant should not be missed. *Talstr. 1, tel. 01/2111650. 156 rooms with bath. Facilities: men's club, disco, bar. AE, DC, MC, V.*

Dolder Grand Hotel. A regular haunt of the super-rich, the Dolder Grand has long been recognized as one of the world's top hotels. It's 10 minutes from the center of the city in an elevated location with lovely views of the city and the lake. Its airy and spacious reception rooms have many attention-getting architectural features. The elegant restaurant has fine service and cuisine to match. *Kurhausstr. 65, tel. 01/2516231. 207 rooms with bath. Facilities: swimming pool, tennis courts. AE, DC, MC, V.*

Expensive

Hotel Glaernischhof. This pleasant hotel has an ideal location just off the Bahnhofstrasse shopping area and makes a fine sightseeing base. There is a good restaurant and a relaxing bar. Despite its central location, the Glaernischhof offers quiet, comfortable rooms. *Claridenstr. 30, tel. 01/2024747. 70 rooms with bath. AE, DC, MC, V.*

Moderate

Hotel Glockenhoff. Occupying the site of an old bell foundry gave this hotel its name. This centrally located establishment only recently completed a thorough renovation. The decor is best described as Nordic, and there's a choice of restaurants, one in an attractive garden terrace. *Sihlstr. 31, tel. 01/211–5650. 106 rooms with bath. AE, DC, MC, V.*

Hotel Limmathof. Set on the bustling thoroughfare that runs along the Limmat River and bordering the Old Town, this is a no-frills hotel, but in Switzerland that *doesn't* mean it isn't comfortable and welcoming. It makes an ideal base for exploring the city. *Limmatquai 142, tel. 01/474220. 55 rooms, some with bath. AE.*

★ **Hotel Sonnenberg.** If you don't mind staying a little ways out of town, try this hotel in a delightful residential area of the city. There are excellent views of the city, lake, and mountains from many of the rooms as well as the glassed-in restaurant. On sunny days, join the locals in the garden terrace for afternoon tea and pastry. *Am Dolder, tel. 01/470047. 40 rooms, some with bath. AE, DC, MC, V.*

Inexpensive

Hotel Linde. Near the university, this small hotel offers a handful of modest but agreeable rooms. There's only a communal bathroom on each floor, and if you want a quiet room, ask for one at the back. A streetcar stop is located across from the main entrance. *Universitaesstr. 91, tel. 01/3262109. 10 rooms, none with bath. AE, DC, V.*

Hotel Vorderer Sternen. On the edge of the Old Town and near the lake, this modest establishment gives you a feel of some of the bustle of the city. It's a short walk from the opera house, theaters, art galleries, and cinemas and is conveniently situated close to a main streetcar junction. All rooms are simple but perfectly adequate, and although there's no restaurant, breakfast is provided. *Theaterstr. 22, tel. 01/251–4949. 15 rooms, none with bath. AE, DC, MC, V.*

The Arts

Pick up *Zürich News*, published each week by the tourist office, to check what's on. Ticket reservations can be made through the **Billetzentrale.** *Werdmühleplatz, tel. 01/221–2283. Open Mon.–Fri. 10–6:30, Sat. 10–2.*

The **Zürich Tonhalle Orchestra** (Gotthardstr. 5, tel. 01/201–1580) ranks among Europe's best. The **Opernhaus** (Schillerstr., tel. 01/251–6922) is renowned for its adventurous opera, operetta, and ballet productions. The **Schauspielhaus** (Ramistr. 34, tel. 01/251–1111) is one of the finest German-speaking theaters in the world. Zurich has 40 movie theaters, with English-language films appearing regularly. The city boasts many art galleries of interest. Among them is **Sammlung E. G. Buhrle** (Zollikerstr. 172, tel. 01/550086), which specializes in 19th-century French masters. Take streetcar 2 or 4. *Open Tues. and Fri. 2–5, and the first Fri. of each month, 2–8.*

Entertainment and Nightlife

Zürich has a lively nightlife scene, mostly centered in the Niederdorf—the red-light district—parallel to the Limmat, across from the Hauptbahnhof. Many spots are short-lived, so check in advance. Informal dress is acceptable in most places, but again, check to make sure. The hotel porter is a good source of information.

Nightclubs Traditional nightclub atmosphere is to be found at the **Terrasse,** Limmatquai 3, tel. 01/251–1074; **Red House,** Marktgasse 17, tel. 01/252–1110; **Le Privé,** Helvetiaplatz, tel. 01/241–6487; **Moulin Rouge,** Mühlegasse 14, tel. 01/690730; and **Bali-Hari,** Langstr. 20, tel. 01/241–5985. All these nightclubs feature striptease shows.

Discos There's disco-dancing at the **Birdwatchers' Club,** Schutzengasse 16, tel. 01/211–5058; **City 5,** Limmastr. 195, tel. 01/422270; **Club of Clubs,** Nova Park Hotel, Badenstr., tel. 01/491–2222; **Evergreen,** Fraumünsterstr. 14, tel. 01/211–5750; and **Le Petit Prince,** Bleicherweg 21, tel. 01/201–1739.

Jazz Jazz can be heard at the **Casa Bar,** Münstergasse 30, tel. 01/472020.

Geneva

Arriving and Departing

By Plane Cointrin (tel. 0229/981122), Geneva's airport, is served by several airlines that fly directly to the city from New York, Toronto, or London. Check with individual airlines for their schedules.

Between the Airport and Downtown	Cointrin has a direct rail link with Cornavin, the city's main train station, which is located in the center of town. Trains run about every 10 minutes from 5:30 AM to midnight. The trip takes about six minutes, and the fare is 3 Fr.

There is regular bus service from the airport to the center of Geneva. The bus takes about 20 minutes, and the fare is 5 Fr. Some hotels have their own bus service.

Taxis, though plentiful, are very expensive; don't take one unless there's no alternative.

By Train	All services—domestic and international—use Cornavin Station in the center of the city. For information, dial 022/326100.
By Bus	Buses generally arrive at and depart from the bus station at place Dorcière, behind the English church, in the city center.
By Car	Since Geneva sits on France's doorstep, entry from France, just a few minutes away, is the most accessible.

Getting Around

By Bus and Streetcar	There are scheduled services by local buses and trains every few minutes on all routes. Before you board, you must buy your ticket from the machines at the stops (they have English instructions). Save money and buy a ticket covering six trips for 8 Fr. If you have a **Swiss Holiday Card,** you travel free (*see* Getting Around, By Train).
By Taxi	Taxis are extremely expensive; use them only if there's no alternative.

Guided Tours

Orientation Tours	Bus tours around Geneva are operated by **Key Tours** (tel. 022/314140). They leave from the bus station in place Dorcière, behind the English church, at 9:30, 10, 2, and 2:30. These tours last about two hours and cost 19 Fr.
Special-Interest Tours	The United Nations organizes tours around the Palais des Nations. Enter by the Pregny Gate in the avenue de la Paix. Tours, lasting about an hour, are given regularly from September to June, 10–noon and 2–4; July and August, 9–noon and 2–6. They cost 5 Fr.

The tourist office will provide you with an audio-guided tour (in English) of the Old Town that covers 26 points of interest, complete with map, cassette, and player; rental: 5 Fr.

Excursions	There are bus excursions from Geneva to Lausanne, Montreux, the Mont Blanc area, the Jura, and the Bernese Oberland. They vary considerably according to the weather and time of year, so inquire locally.

Boat excursions vary for the same reasons. When the weather is good, take one of the delightful day-long trips that stop at some of the waterside villages on the vineyard-fringed lake; pass (or perhaps call at) the 13th-century Château de Chillon, inspiration of Byron's *The Prisoner of Chillon.* Full details are available from **Mouettes Genevoises,** tel. 022/322944; **Swiss Boat,** tel. 022/324747; **Compagnie de Navigation,** tel. 022/212521; or from the tourist office. Boat trips vary in cost and duration, with some as low as 90 Fr. and lasting only two hours.

Tourist Information

Cornavin Station, tel. 022/455200. Open July–Sept. daily 8 AM–10 PM; Oct.–June Mon.–Fri. 8:15 AM–7:30 PM, Sat. 9–6, Sun. 4 PM–8 PM.

Exploring Geneva

Geneva is the headquarters of many international organizations—the World Health Organization and the International Red Cross, for example—and has a population of about 360,000; yet it's compact enough to explore in a single walk.

A city of humanity and enlightenment, Geneva provided a haven for the writers Voltaire, Hugo, Balzac, and Stendhal, as well as those religious refugees, Calvin and Knox. Byron arrived here from London in disgrace after being accused of incest with his half-sister; Shelley came here following the disintegration of his marriage to Harriet Westbrook; Wagner arrived with political police, creditors, and betrayed husbands hot on his heels; and Liszt sought refuge when his affair with the Countess of Agoult had shocked even Paris.

Geneva's history has always been troubled. The Romans controlled Geneva in 120 BC; the Franks in AD 534; the Dukes of Savoy threatened it with military and economic war; and Calvin gave it a very gloomy face. The French grabbed the city in 1798, but Napoleon had to give it back in 1814. The following year, Geneva joined the Swiss Confederation as a canton in its own right. In the 20th century, it became a city of elegance and style, where the hopes of international organizations are born and quite often realized.

The Main Attractions

① Start your walk from **Cornavin Station.** Go down the rue du Mont Blanc to the **lake.** On a fine day, it's worth going on to the **②** **Pont du Mont Blanc** to see the snow-clad peak of the mountain in the distance. From March to September, you'll have a fine view of the **Jet d'Eau,** Europe's highest fountain, gushing water 400 feet (122 meters) into the air.

Turn left when you come back from the bridge and walk down **③** the quai des Bergues. In the center of the river Rhône is **Rousseau Island,** with a statue of the Swiss-born philosopher. Turn **④** left onto **Pont de l'Ile,** right at the end, cross the road, turn left into rue de la Corraterie, and you are heading for Geneva's Vieille Ville—the old quarter. Cross the place Neuve with **⑤** Geneva's **Grand Théâtre** on your right, enter the park opposite, **⑥** and keep left. Here's Geneva's famous **Reformation Monument,** with statues of some pioneers of Protestant belief: Bèze, Calvin, Farel, and Knox. Leave the park by the exit on your left, and the peace of the Old Town gradually casts its spell. The charming place Bourg-de-Four is a characteristic square. The dreamy narrow streets meandering off to the left lead up to the **⑦** **Cathédrale St. Pierre,** with its odd mixture of architectural styles.

⑧ The **Hôtel de Ville** (town hall), also here, houses the Alabama Hall where on August 22, 1864, the Geneva Convention laid the

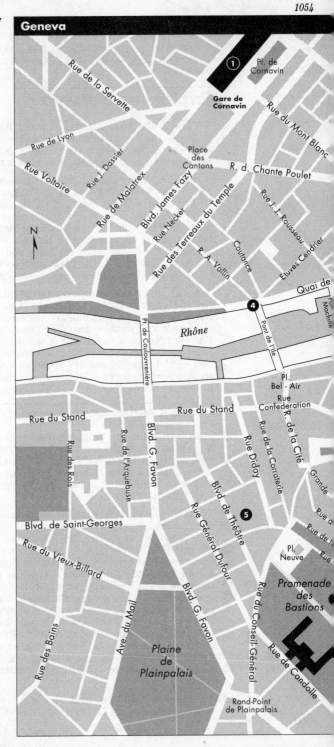

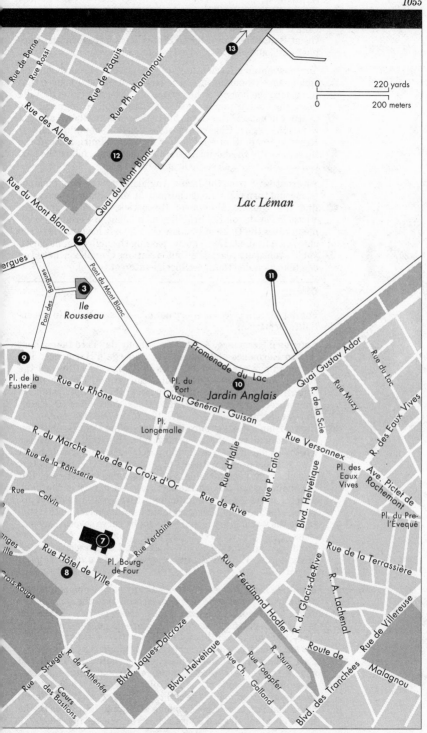

Rue de Berne
Rue Rossi
Rue de Pâquis
Rue Ph. Plantamour
Rue des Alpes
Rue du Mont Blanc
Quai du Mont Blanc

12

13

Lac Léman

0   220 yards
0   200 meters

2

ergues
Bergues
Pont des

3

*Ile
Rousseau*

Pont du Mont Blanc

11

Promenade du Lac

Quai Gustav Ador

Rue du Lac

9

Pl. de la
Fusterie

Rue du Rhône

Pl. du
Port

Quai Général - Guisan

10

Jardin Anglais

R. de la Scie

Rue Muzy

Rue des Eaux Vives

Pl.
Longemalle

R. du Marché

Rue de la Croix d'Or

Rue de la Rôtisserie

Rue d'Italie

Rue Versonnex

Rue P. Fatio

Pl. des
Eaux
Vives

Ave. Pictet de
Rochemont

Rue
Calvin

anges
ille

Rue de Rive

Blvd. Helvétique

Pl. du Pre-
l'Evequé

7

Rue Verdaine

Rue de la Terrassière

rois-Rouge

Rue Hôtel de Ville

8

Pl. Bourg-
de-Four

Rue
Ferdinand Hodler

R. d. Glacis-de-Rive

R. A. Lachenal

Rue de Villereuse

St-Léger

R. de l'Athénée

Blvd. Jaques-Dalcroze

Blvd. Helvétique

Rue Ch. Galland

Rue Toepffer

R. Sturm

Route de

Blvd. des Tranchées

Malagnou

Rue
des Bastions

Cours

foundations of the Red Cross. And in the same hall, in 1872, a Court of Arbitration settled the Alabama dispute between Great Britain and the United States arising from British support for Confederate ships in the Civil War.

You now enter a fascinating area of narrow, cobbled streets, small shops (though some have large prices), and houses that were once the homes of the aristocracy. The rue Hôtel de Ville (once the Italian quarter) has some beautifully designed 17th-century houses. Go down the hill to the **place du Rhône,** and you are on the edge of Geneva's most fashionable shopping quarter. Reserve temptation for another day and admire instead the flower clock of the **Jardin Anglais.** If time allows, follow the quai Gustav Ador for a closer look at the **Jet d'Eau.**

Alternatively, from the Jardin Anglais, cross the Pont du Mont Blanc and turn right along the quai du Mont Blanc. Here you'll find the unusual **Monument Brunswick,** modeled, in high-Victorian style, on the Scaglieri monument in Verona; it commemorates the Duke of Brunswick, who left his fortune to the city when he died. If you go on, passing through elegant parks, you'll eventually reach the **United Nations Complex,** where you can take a guided tour (*see* Special-Interest tours).

Dining

For details and price category definitions, *see* Dining in Essential Information.

Expensive **Auberge d'Hermance.** A treat on a sunny day is to take a boat trip to Hermance and dine at the Auberge d'Hermance. The surroundings are splendid, with stunning views toward the Jura. If the weather permits, eat in the garden. The fish at this superb restaurant is particularly good; the service, attentive but discreet. *Hermance, tel. 022/511368. Jacket and tie. Reservations essential. AE, DC, MC, V. Closed Dec. 15–Apr.*

★ **Cheval Blanc.** Ask a group of gourmets to list their favorite restaurants and you can be pretty sure they will each choose Cheval Blanc. It is all that a top-notch restaurant should be. It always looks pretty with lots of flowers and crisp tablecloths. The chairs are comfortable, and the service is first-rate. But the main reason this restaurant rates so highly is the food, which is never less than outstanding. Swiss restaurants are not famous for memorable desserts, but here is a selection to match any in the world; the waiters will happily serve several tiny portions per plate: Treat yourself. *Route de Meinier 1, Vandoeuvres, tel. 022/501401. Jacket and tie. Reservations essential. AE, V. Closed three weeks in July and 10 days at Christmas.*

Moderate **Brasserie Lipp.** Allegedly an exact copy of its famous counterpart in Paris, Brasserie Lipp has certainly got the atmosphere right. The food is excellent, typical brasserie fare. While the jet set does patronize the place, there's no guarantee of a film star, but you never know. *Confederation Center, tel. 022/293122. Dress: casual. Reservations advised. AE, DC, MC, V.*

★ **Cave Valaisanne et Chalet Suisse.** Every visitor to Switzerland should try *raclette, assiette valaisanne,* and *fondue* at least once, and this is one of the best places to do it. There's traditional Swiss food in just the right atmosphere, and the cheerful noise that frequently goes on long after midnight gives the lie to the idea that all good Swiss citizens are tucked into bed by 10

PM. *Blvd. Georges-Favon 23, tel. 022/281236. Dress: casual. Reservations advised. AE, DC, MC, V. Closed Christmas Eve.*

Cent Suisses. This is a restaurant of which one can truthfully say there is nothing quite like it. In winter, you eat surrounded by flags and emblems of the Swiss army (you're in Château de Penthes, which houses a museum devoted to Swiss mercenaries); in summer, you eat outside. The food ranges from good to better-than-average and the open pies for dessert—try the walnut—have to be among the best available. *Rue de Pregny 18, tel. 022/344865. Dress: casual. No credit cards. Closed two weeks at Christmas.*

Vieux Bois. Switzerland is renowned for its hotel schools, and the food and service at this one is beyond reproach. You'll dine in exquisite surroundings in the grounds of the Ariana Château at one of the entrances to the United Nations complex. The building has been modernized with tremendous discretion, and you'll pay a great deal less than you'd expect for the excellent meal, first-class service, and beautiful surroundings. *Av. de la Paix 12, tel. 022/330330 Dress: casual. Reservations advised. No credit cards.*

Inexpensive **Café Restaurant des Banques.** Popular with the locals, this restaurant has three things going for it: thoughtfully chosen, well-cooked food that is outstanding for the price; a warm, friendly atmosphere; and a flexible dinner hour that means you're welcome whether you eat impossibly early or horribly late. *Rue Hesse 6, tel. 022/214498. Dress: casual. Reservations advised. No credit cards.*

Chez Bouby. For as long as many of Geneva's old timers can remember, Chez Bouby was where those in the know dined, but in recent years, it's standards had declined. These days, with a change in chef-management, the food and atmosphere are much improved, while prices remain reasonable. It's handy for the shops and is certainly worth a try for its traditional French brasserie atmosphere. *Rue Grenus 1, tel. 022/310927. Dress: casual. Reservations advised. MC, V. Closed two weeks at Christmas.*

Lodging

For details and price category definitions, *see* Lodging in Essential Information.

Very Expensive **Beau-Rivage.** Its setting on the lake is so beautiful, each room so full of pretty things, and the entrance so grand and elegant that you'd think you're on a film set, not in a hotel run by the same family for four generations. This spot is one of the landmarks of Geneva. There are two restaurants: the Chât Botté, which many consider to be the best in Geneva, and the very upscale bistro, The Quai. *Quai du Mont-Blanc 13, tel. 022/310221. 115 rooms with bath. Facilities: terrace bar. AE, DC, MC, V.*

La Cicogne. This is a particular favorite with many people; it's very central, very pretty, and very quiet. At La Cicogne you'll know you're definitely *not* in a chain hotel. Each of the rooms is different; all the decorations are elegant, stylish, and individual. *Pl. Longemalle, tel. 022/214242. 50 rooms with bath. Facilities: restaurant, bar. AE, DC, MC, V.*

La Reserve. Were you to want a relaxing vacation within easy access of Geneva, it would be hard to think of a better place than La Reserve. The gardens are glorious, the view breathtaking, and the ambience everything you'd expect from a recently and very expensively refurbished hotel. *Rte. de Lausanne 301, 1293 Bellevue, tel. 022/41741. 114 rooms with bath. Facilities: pool, private harbor, water sports. AE, DC, MC, V.*

Expensive **The Epsom.** This is the flagship of the Swiss-owned Manotel group and claims to be the largest-capacity hotel in French-speaking Switzerland. It's situated near the lake, within easy walking distance of various international organizations and the train station. It's a functional, efficient hotel with good-size rooms and a loyal clientele that returns regularly. *Rue Richemont 18, tel. 022/320833. 330 rooms with bath. Facilities: restaurant, bar, conference room. AE, DC, MC, V.*

★ **The Metropole.** Once the Red Cross archives for prisoners of war, the Metropole has been thoroughly but imaginatively refurbished, though it retains its 1854 facade. It took a long time and greatly overran its budget, but the final effect is of elegant comfort. Its position is ideal, minutes away from Geneva's most enticing shops and across from the Jardin Anglais. It also has an excellent restaurant. *Quai General-Guisan 34, tel. 022/211344. 140 rooms with bath. Facilities: restaurant, bar, café.* AE, DC, MC, V.

Moderate **The Eden.** Though not particularly elegant, the Eden is comfortable and well situated, with pleasant views of the lake from many of the rooms. It's popular with U.N. types and is only a few minutes away from the Botanical Gardens. *Rue de Lausanne 135, tel. 022/326540. 80 rooms with bath. Facilities: restaurant, bar. AE, DC, MC, V.*

The Touring-Balance. The Swiss would say that a place like this is "correct," by which they mean it's very good in its category. It's well run, gives good value for money, and can't be faulted, though it may not be the most stunning hotel in town. *Pl. Longemalle 13, tel. 022/287122. 64 rooms, some with bath. Facilities: restaurant, café. AE, DC, MC, V.*

Inexpensive **Bernina.** You can't be more centrally placed than here at the Bernina, across from the station. It's a functional, well-run hotel that is good for its kind; other hotels in the area cost a lot more but haven't much more to offer. *22 pl. Cornavin, tel. 022/314950. 80 rooms with bath. AE, MC, V.*

St. Gervais. Somewhat basic and much cheaper than the Bernina, the St. Gervais is the nearest thing to a bargain in Geneva. There's no restaurant (though breakfast is provided) and little luxury, but it is clean, central, and many people return again and again. *Rue Corps Saints 20, tel. 022/324572. 26 rooms, 2 with bath. AE, MC, V.*

Lugano

Arriving and Departing

By Plane There are short connecting flights by Crossair—the Swiss domestic network—to Lugano Airport (tel. 091/505001) from Zürich, Geneva, Basel, and Bern. The nearest international airport is in Milan, Italy.

Between the Airport and Downtown There is regular bus service between the airport and central Lugano, four miles (seven kilometers) away. Taxis are available but are very expensive.

By Train There's a train from Zürich seven minutes past every hour, and the trip takes about three hours. If you're coming from Geneva, you can catch the Milan express at various times, changing at Domodossola and Bellinzona. There's a train 30 minutes past every hour from Milan's Centrale Station: The trip takes about an hour and a half. Always keep passports handy and confirm times with the SNTO. For train information in Lugano, tel. 091/229172.

By Car There are fast, direct highways from Milan and from Zürich. If you plan on coming from Geneva, check the weather conditions with the automobile associations beforehand: Advice will vary according to the season.

Getting Around

By Bus Well-integrated services run regularly on all local routes. You must buy your ticket from the machine at the stop before you board. Remember that with a **Swiss Holiday Card** you travel free (*see* Getting Around Switzerland By Train). If you don't have one of these cards, get a **Regional Holiday Season Ticket** for Lugano from the tourist office. This gives unlimited free travel for seven days on most routes from May to October and a 50% discount on longer trips. It costs 60 Fr. for adults and 30 Fr. for children 6–16.

By Taxi Though less expensive than in Zürich or Geneva, taxis are still not cheap. If you find this is the only way to get to your destination, call 091/512121 or 091/547722.

Guided Tours

The tourist office is the best source of information about any tours. Lugano has guided walks from April to October and horse-drawn carriage rides through the town, lasting either a whole or a half day, from June to October. There are bus trips to Locarno, Ascona, Lake Como, Lake Maggiore, Milan, Venice, St. Moritz, Florence, and the Alpine passes.

Tourist Information

Ente Turistico Lugano: riva Albertolli 5, tel. 091/214664. Open Mon.–Fri. 8–noon, 2–6 and, Easter–Oct., Sat 9–noon, 2–5.

Exploring Lugano

The largest city in the Ticino—the Italian-speaking corner of Switzerland—Lugano stands for sunshine, color, vitality, and warmth, which can be applied as much to the outgoing character of its people as to its weather. With 2,300 hours of sunshine a year, nearby Locarno has more than any other place in Switzerland, but Lugano isn't far behind. The view from the waterfront is unforgettable, its boulevards are fashionable, and its old quarter is reminiscent of sleepy old towns in Italy.

The Etruscans and Romans left their mark, as did the medieval Italian conflicts into which the city was drawn. From its incorporation into the Swiss Confederation in the early 19th century, Lugano grew to its present prosperity: A city that somehow blends the natural Italian *brio* with smooth Swiss efficiency.

❶ Start your walk at the **tourist office** (riva Albertolli) and enjoy the expansive view of the lake and its promenade. Visitors may be surprised to find a statue of George Washington on the promenade, particularly since Washington never visited Lugano. Angelo Brunere sculpted it in 1859 for a Swiss engineer who went to America, made his fortune, and presumably wanted to show his gratitude. Where the promenade becomes ❷ the **piazza R. Rezzonico,** leave the lake behind you, turning right into via G. Luvini, all vigorous Italian life, with the events of the day volubly disputed at characteristic outdoor cafés.

From here, you enter the Old Town, where steep, narrow ❸ streets fringed with colorful shops wind up at the **Cathedral of San Lorenzo.** It has a Renaissance exterior with noteworthy ❹ frescoes and sculptures inside. The **Church of Santa Maria degli Angioli** in piazza Luini, at the junction of via Nassa with the promenade, was started in 1455 and contains a fine example of the work of Bernardino Luini (1475–1532): a huge fresco depicting the Passion and Crucifixion.

❺ Lugano is justly proud of its parks. The **Parco Civico,** near the ❻ tourist office, has a lovely fragrant rose garden. The **Belvedere Gardens,** also by the lake on quai riva Caccia, is a little gem: Palms, camelias, oleanders, roses, and magnolias form the ❼ background for 12 modern sculptures. At the **Parco Tassino,** behind the train station, deer welcome you as you enter and there are 300 rose bushes of 80 varieties.

❽ The **Villa Favorita** at Castagnola, a short streetcar ride from the city center, will be high on the list of any art lover. It houses one of the world's finest private art collections, that of Baron Heinrich von Thyssen. Numerous masterpieces from the Middle Ages to the present day are displayed in 20 well-lit rooms. Note particularly van Eyck's *Annunciation* and Dürer's *Jesus Among the Scribes. Strada Castagnola, tel. 091/521741. Admission: 8 Fr. Open Tues.–Sun. 10–5.*

Dining

For details and price category definitions, *see* Dining in Essential Information.

Very Expensive **Al Portone.** There's always a warm welcome from the owner at this restaurant on the edge of town, toward Castagnola. You'll enjoy the refined ambience and the beautifully appointed tables (lace cloths and silver place settings). Superb dishes are cooked in the Italian style yet are light and creative. This is the type of place where it is safe to leave the selection of your meal to the chef. *Viale Cassarate 3, tel. 091/235995. Jacket and tie. Reservations advised. AE, DC, MC, V.*

★ **Veranda.** In the very grand and luxurious setting of the Hotel Splendide-Royal, the Veranda is decorated in blue and white, and with the ceiling is supported by four large columns. Notwithstanding such beautiful surroundings, make a point of reserving a window table to enjoy the splendid view. Fresh flowers adorn each table, setting the tone for a very special meal. Try the house specialty of *penne a la Ticinese. Riva Caccia 7, tel. 091/512001. Jacket and tie. Reservations advised. AE, DC, MC, V.*

Lugano

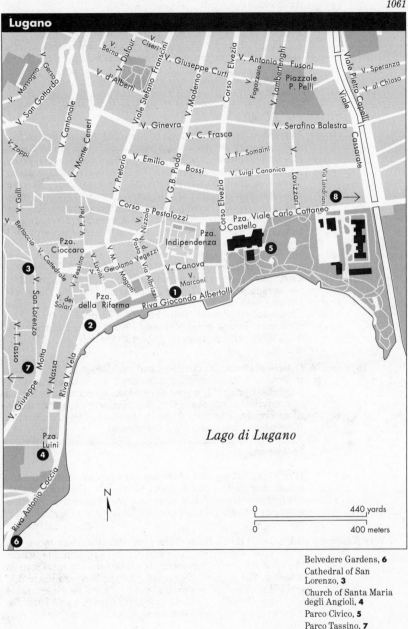

Lago di Lugano

N

| 0 | | 440 yards |
| 0 | | 400 meters |

Belvedere Gardens, **6**
Cathedral of San
Lorenzo, **3**
Church of Santa Maria
degli Angioli, **4**
Parco Civico, **5**
Parco Tassino, **7**
Piazza R. Rezzonico, **2**
Tourist Office, **1**
Villa Favorita, **8**

Expensive **Santabbondio.** The last thing you'd expect to find in this typical grotto building, circa 1860, on the road to Agno Airport is a classically elegant restaurant. A natural stone archway in the center of the dining area and windows overlooking a small pond add to the romantic charm of the place. You cannot fail to be impressed by the friendly service and the excellent food. Try the specialty—fillet of veal in an olive and breadcrumb crust. *Via ai Grotti, tel. 091/548535. Jacket and tie. Reservations essential. DC, MC, V.*

Moderate **Baron de la Mouette.** You can be sure of high-quality fresh food and dedicated service at this restaurant, part of the famous Moevenpick chain. It offers an elegant ambience, plush decor, and a warm welcome. Genuine U.S. beef is often on the menu. *Viale Cattaneo 25, tel. 091/232333. Dress: casual. Reservations advised. AE, DC, MC, V.*

Belmonte. When locals have a special occasion to celebrate, they come to the Belmonte, just 5 minutes out of town. It has a large terrace and a super view. On warm evenings, enjoy well-cooked and presented international cuisine in the quiet of a candle-lit atmosphere. *Via Serenella 29, tel. 091/514033. Jacket and tie. Reservations advised. AE, DC, MC, V.*

Cina. You'll have to look hard for the stairs to this second-floor restaurant, wedged between 2 popular candy shops. Those who succeed will be rewarded with the delights of a typical Cantonese-style meal, something of a surprise in this otherwise very Italian neighborhood. *Piazza della Riforma, tel. 091/235173. Dress: casual. Reservations advised. AE, DC, MC, V.*

Inexpensive **Osteria al Porto.** Windsurfers and yachtsmen have made this
★ their favorite meeting place. In summer you can dine under the huge chestnut trees, where hearty local specialties are served in a convivial atmosphere. Try the minestrone soup and mushroom risotto. *Via Foce 9, tel. 091/515035. Dress: informal. Reservations not needed. No credit cards.*

Lodging

It is worth noting that there are very few moderately priced hotels downtown, but a short drive into the surrounding countryside dramatically increases your choices. For details and price category definitions, *see* Lodging in Essential Information.

Very Expensive **Eden Grand Hotel.** Each of the glamorously modern rooms has a lake view. There's an American bar and 2 restaurants, where the wide windows overlooking the lake turn any meal into an occasion. The luxuriously pleasant atmosphere and the highly trained staff should ensure that your stay will be a memorable one. *Riva Paradiso 7, tel. 091/550121. 130 rooms with bath. Facilities: pool, sauna, fitness room, physiotherapy center. AE, DC, MC, V.*

★ **Villa Principe Leopoldo.** This breathtaking villa, the former residence of princes, perches high on the hills above the Old Town of Lugano. Set in lush green gardens, it epitomizes Old World sophistication and wealth. The lavishly appointed rooms are reminiscent of bygone days but have all the modern conveniences. *Via Montalbano 5, 6900, tel. 091/558855. 24 rooms with bath. Facilities: pool, tennis court, solarium, sauna, indoor golf. AE, DC, MC, V.*

Expensive **Belmonte.** This recently modernized hotel is just 5 minutes from the center of town. It's set on a hilltop, and each of the balconied rooms has spectacular views. Inside, the wide airy halls are complemented by comfortable public rooms. *Via Serenalla 29, tel. 091/514033. 43 rooms with bath. Facilities: pool, solarium, tennis court, golf, horseback riding. AE, DC, MC, V.*

★ **Du Lac Seehov.** Renovation of this 20-year-old building was completed recently, but the house proudly continues the service tradition of the Kneschaurek family, who has managed the hotel since 1920. The spacious, comfortable rooms feature elegantly modern furniture, the bar is decorated with tapestries, and the restaurant has lovely views of the lake. *Riva Paradiso 3, tel. 091/541921. 52 rooms with bath. Facilities: pool, private swimming area on lake, sauna, and massage room. AE, DC, MC, V.*

Moderate **Walter au Lac.** Just across the road from the boat-landing stage, this rather old-fashioned house offers simple rooms furnished with items from the last century. All rooms face the lake and some have a balcony. There's a small but reasonably priced restaurant on the second floor. *Piazza Rezzonico, tel. 091/227425. 35 rooms, some with bath. AE, DC, MC, V.*

Inexpensive **Lucerna Jura.** This hotel is most suited to those arriving or leaving by train, since it's just behind the station and has no parking. Its rooms are unpretentious but perfectly adequate. For the most part, you'll meet locals in the bar or, on summer days, outside in the garden in the shade of the large trees. *Via Basilea 22, tel. 091/561072. 28 rooms, some with bath. AE, V.*

Rex. If you're only in Lugano for a short stopover, this conveniently located hotel is a good choice. The rooms are quite large, and some even have balconies. It's only minutes from the center of town, across from a public park. There's parking close by. *Viale C. Cattaneo 11, tel. 091/227608. 25 rooms, some with bath. V.*

Northeast Switzerland— Schaffhausen to Appenzell

This itinerary has been chosen because it draws back the curtain on a Switzerland with a considerable diversity of interest. There are famous sights such as the Rhine Falls, as well as delightful corners relatively unexplored by tourists. Reminders of Switzerland's medieval past stand adjacent to stylish modern resorts: monasteries secluded on hilltops; castles haunted by the ghosts of the Hapsburgs and the counts of Kyburg; sleepy squares with half-timbered houses; agricultural villages; the Säntis range rising to 8,000 feet (2,450 meters); the remote country of Appenzell, and, stretching 40 miles (64 kilometers), Lake Konstanz, or the Bodensee, as it is also known.

This is an area best explored by car although a tour by public transportation is not difficult to plan. Start in Schaffhausen and end in the heights of Appenzell, making your bases in Schaffhausen and St. Gallen. If time allows, you may want to break your trip with a night or two at some of the lake resorts, in which case you'll find good hotels in Arbon, Romanhausen, and Rorschach. Remember that comfortable and usually inexpensive accommodations can often be found at short notice in private houses.

Getting Around

By Train There are hourly trains from Schaffhausen to Rorschach, at the eastern end of the Bodensee, that stop at most places mentioned in this itinerary. From Rorschach, there are trains to St. Gallen every hour. From Herisan, there's a twice hourly service to Appenzell. It's an itinerary on which the **Swiss Holiday Card** (*see* Getting Around, By Train) comes in handy.

By Bus The yellow postal buses have regular services along this route.

By Car Roads are generally good, and exploring the backroads is highly recommended. Good regional maps are available from gas stations and tourist offices. If you're worried about the weather, check with the local motoring organizations.

Guided Tours

There are bus tours from Schaffhausen, St. Gallen, and the principal lake towns, but these vary considerably according to the season and the weather, so check at the local tourist office.

Tourist Information

Appenzell. Verkehrsbuero, Hauptgasse 19, tel. 071/874141.
Arbon. Offizielles Verkehrsbuero, Bahnhofstr. 26, tel. 171/466577.
Heiden. Verkehrsbuero, Seeallee 813, tel. 071/911096.
Herisau. Verkehrsbuero, Obersorftsr. 1, tel. 071/574460.
Romanshorn. Verkehrsverein Bahnhofplatz, tel. 071/633232.
St. Gallen. Verkehrsbuero, Bahnhofplatz 1A, tel. 071/226262.
Schaffhausen. Verkehrsbuero, Vorstadt 12, tel. 053/55141.

Exploring

Before starting your tour to Bodensee and beyond, you must see the awe-inspiring **Rhine Falls** at Neuhaussen, a 15-minute bus ride from the town center. This is nature at its most magnificently untamed: Every second, more than 1,000 tons of water plunge 80 feet (24 meters) in three steps, spraying the countryside with a fine mist; take a raincoat! The noise is deafening, but the sunlight through the spray is magical.

Schaffhausen Schaffhausen was a free city before it joined the Swiss Confederation in 1501, after which it grew in prosperity and importance. Its handsome merchants' houses, with their oriel windows, and the guildhouses of the Vordergasse do much to shape the character of the place. The chief architectural feature of the town is the **Münster,** a Romanesque cathedral built in 1103. Follow Münstergasse to the shapely cloister archways of the former **zu Allerheiligen,** All Saints Monastery, which is now a museum of manuscripts, arts and crafts, costumes, and armor, uniforms, and flags. *Klosterplatz 1, tel. 053/54308. Free. Open Tues.–Sat. 2–4, Sun. 10–noon, 2–4.*

If you have the time, take a boat trip down the **Untersee,** an offshoot of the Bodensee, through charming countryside. The round-trip takes about eight hours.

Northeast Switzerland

Next head for Konstanz on Road 13 to the east, but stop at
Stein-am-Rhein, one of Switzerland's most enchanting little
towns, if you have time. Its cobbled streets are bordered by
medieval guildhouses and merchants' houses, many elaborately decorated, and the oriel windows of the Rathausplatz are as
varied as they are quaint. The **Rathaus** (1539), in the central
square, is a gem with a richly carved, half-timbered gallery
topping a facade of ornate murals. Everything conspires to recall the past: The statue of a fierce pike-holding soldier (so
heroic were the Swiss soldiers that the monarchs of Europe
vied to hire them as mercenaries), the coats of arms of the merchants of 400 years ago (you see them everywhere), the ancient
fountains.

Konstanz Follow the Konstanz road as before. Konstanz is one of those
frontier anomalies that occur regularly in Europe: a corner of
Germany jutting into Switzerland. If it were not for the frontier stations in the connecting streets, it would be difficult to
know where the German city of Konstanz ends and Swiss
Kreuzlingen begins. There is no difficulty in walking from one
to the other, but a valid passport is necessary. Here the Czech
reformers John Huss (1373–1415) and Jerome of Prague (d.
1416) were burned at the stake. Huss is remembered by an effigy on the house where he lived, on the street that is now named
after him. In the Romanesque **cathedral,** which dates from 1052
though it was rebuilt in 1452, you can see the spot on which
Huss stood defiantly while hearing his sentence.

The Renaissance **Town Hall** has elaborate frescoes, and the old
house where Frederick Barbarossa (Redbeard) signed the

treaty with the Lombards in 1183 still stands in the market square. The town's most famous statue celebrates airship pioneer Count Ferdinand von Zeppelin (1838–1917), who was born here and whose dirigibles were built at Friedrichshafen on the north shore of the lake.

From Konstanz, continue on the same road through Kreuzlingen (you're now back in Switzerland) to Bottighofen, increasingly well known for its beach, and on to Scherzingen, with its Baroque church and former Benedictine monastery. Then move on from Romanshorn, with its wealth of vacation facilities and good views of the Austrian mountains, to Arbon.

Arbon Arbon is characteristic of the Bodensee people's gift for marrying the dreamy past with the practical present. Beautiful gardens, sophisticated promenades, and water sports contrast with the stern gray castle, the half-timbered houses, the picturesque Rathaus (Town Hall) dating from 1791, and the fine stained-glass windows of the Church of St. Gallus.

Rorschach Continue on the same road to Rorschach. This is the largest port on the Swiss side of the lake, close to that corner of Europe where the borders of Switzerland, Austria, and Germany get tangled up. You might consider staying here for a while to take trips by train or car to Austria's Bregenz, a lively resort with Old World houses. Rorschach is the gateway to the woods and waterfalls of the Vorarlberg—home of a famous summer opera festivals on the lake. You can cross the lake by steamer to medieval Lindau in Germany. Swiss money is accepted everywhere, but keep your passport handy.

You can also take the mountain railway from Rorschach to enjoy the exhilarating air in Heiden, the little off-the-beaten-track town where Henri Dunant (1828–1910), founder of the Red Cross, was born. The house in which this occurred is now a museum dedicated to his memory. *Tel. 071/9110 for directions. Open daily 9–5.*

Rorschach is also the starting point for several mountain walks with spectacular views. From Rorschach, a road to the southeast brings the traveler quickly to St. Gallen, one of Switzerland's most important cities. It was founded in the 7th century when the Irish monk St. Gallus established a hermitage that later became a Benedictine abbey and a leading center of learning. The twin towers of the Baroque **cathedral** dominate the city. Approach it through the Marktgasse. From its square, there is a network of narrow streets made picturesque by buildings with old oriel windows, conical towers, and murals.

The **Siftsbibliothek** is St. Gallen's chief pride. This library of the former abbey is situated at the rear of the cathedral and has 100,000 old books and illuminated manuscripts, some dating from the 10th century. *Klosterhof 6D, tel. 021/247832. Open Tues.–Sat. 2–4, Sun. 10–noon, 2–4.*

Take the children to the **Peter and Paul Wildlife Park,** off the Dufourstrasse, to see wild boar, marmots, and chamois. Ask about shows at the **Puppentheater** in Lämmlisbrunnenstrasse.

St. Gallen has been famous for its textiles for centuries. To see specimens and get an idea of how the industry has developed down the ages, visit the Textile Museum. *Vadianstr. 2, tel. 071/221744. Open Mon.–Fri. 10–noon, 2–5.*

Appenzell Ascend to the Appenzell region, and you are really getting off the beaten track. From St. Gallen, the road climbs to Teufen. Continue to Glais, turn right and you come to Appenzell. Or if you are traveling by public transportation, take the narrow-gauge train from St. Gallen.

Appenzell is predominantly an agricultural area where traditions die hard. You'll see farmers smoking *lendauerlei*, a pipe with a wooden carved stem and a large decorated bowl topped with a lid. Men often wear a silver ring in their right ear. In some parts of Appenzell, women still don't have the vote in local elections. And there's no question of a private vote: Elections are held in public, and the result depends on how a show of hands looks to the official in charge.

Appenzell is a center of local craftsmen, many practicing skills that have been in their families for generations. The folk music so unique to this place has similarly been handed down and is played by a band of two violins, cello, string bass, and dulcimer. But Appenzell is most famous as the home of one of Switzerland's finest cheeses. You can see it being made at the Appenzell Showcase Cheese Dairy. *Stein, tel. 071/591733. Open daily 9–11, 1–3.*

The Appenzell mountain air is a tonic, the green meadows a delight, and the views exhilarating. From here, you can have a scenic drive back to Zürich via Waldstadt and Wattwil, joining the eastern end of Zürich's lake at Rapperswil. But if there's time, go on to Schwagalp and take the cable car from there to **Säntis** (8,000 feet, 2,450 meters), for wonderful views of the mountains of Switzerland, Austria, and Germany.

Dining and Lodging

For details and price category definitions, *see* Dining and Lodging in Essential Information.

Appenzell **Gasthaus Hof.** Mix with the locals at this restaurant; you'll be
Dining made to feel very welcome. The food is simple but hearty fare, and you can select from a variety of local cheese specialties. After your meal, if you have the energy, join in a game of skittles (bowling) or cards. *Landsgemeindeplatz, tel. 071/872210. Dress: casual. Reservations not necessary. No credit cards. Inexpensive.*

Lodging **Hotel Appenzell.** The central square in Appenzell is surrounded by hotels and restaurants including this one, built recently but in the traditional architectural style of the region. The rooms offer modern-day comforts and facilities. The hotel has its own pastry shop, which provides the hotel restaurant with delightful desserts. *Landsgemeindeplatz, tel. 071/874211. 15 rooms, with bath. AE, DC, MC, V. Moderate. Closed last 3 weeks Nov.*

★ **Hotel Saentis.** Also on the main square, the Saentis was first mentioned in records in 1800, and it typifies much of the local handiwork with a beautifully decorated facade. Sensitive renovation in recent years has retained the romantic charm of the place. The rooms are each decorated in a slightly different style; some have four-poster beds. The sunny terrace makes a delightful setting for lunches. *Landsgemeindeplatz, tel. 071/878722. 33 rooms with bath. AE, DC, MC, V. Moderate. Closed Jan., Feb.*

Arbon
Dining
★

Gasthof Brauefei Frohsinn. The atmosphere in this reconstructed old building is created by the tasteful use of lots of wood and pastel colors. The air is filled with the aroma of hops and malt, and you can enjoy delightful meals while looking over the master-brewer's shoulder as he supervises the making of the gasthof's own beer. The menu has many surprises, such as homemade noodles with mushroom sauce, delicate langouste with sherry sauce, a salmon ragout with wild rice, and an excellent veal steak in a cream sauce. Round off your meal with homemade hazelnut soufflé. *Romanshornerstr. 15, tel. 071/461046. Dress: casual. Reservations advised. DC, MC, V. Moderate.*

Lodging

Hotel Metropole. This 20-year-old hotel offers modern-style rooms: The better ones have views of the lake; the quiet ones are at the back. Relax with a drink in the roof-top garden, which offers glorious views over the Bodensee. *Bahnhofstr. 49, tel. 071/463535. 42 rooms with bath. AE, DC, MC, V. Moderate.*

Heiden
Lodging

Hotel Linde. In the center of the village, this fully restored 120-year-old building boasts a large banquet hall in Art Nouveau style. The extremely spacious rooms are more like suites and are finished in a modern Nordic decor. In warm weather enjoy your meals in the tranquility of the large terrace restaurant. *Poststr. 11, tel. 071/911414. 18 rooms, some with bath. DC, MC, V. Inexpensive.*

Herisau
Lodging

Hotel Landhaus. This recently renovated traditional Swiss landhaus is a local meeting spot with a warm and friendly atmosphere. The rotisserie, with its lead-framed glass windows, is especially charming. Next to the restaurant is a bowling alley. *Kasernenstr. 29, tel. 071/512082. 25 rooms, some with bath. AE, DC, MC, V. Moderate.*

Romanshorn
Lodging

Park Hotel Inseli. This attractive hotel is located in the park near the lake. All the rooms are well appointed; some of them have balconies. There's also a grill room, a main dining room, and a garden restaurant. *Inseliweg 6, tel. 071/635353. 35 rooms with bath. Facilities: pool, tennis, miniature golf. AE, DC, MC, V. Moderate.*

Hotel Bodan. The Hotel Bodan is just across the road from the train station. Its bright, modern rooms are comfortable, and you needn't worry about noise from the station; after nine there's hardly any traffic. The dining room can accommodate large groups, and there's a grill room too. *Bahnhofstr. 1, tel. 071/631502. 15 rooms with bath. AE, DC, MC, V. Inexpensive.*

St. Gallen
Dining

Schwarzer Baeren. This is an attractive country inn situated above St. Gallen. It has a warm and homey atmosphere that attracts locals and travelers alike. The restaurant is separate from the pub where the locals gather. The decision as to which of the creamy sauces to select—champagne, calvados, herb—will not be easy. *Speicherstr. 151, tel. 071/353055. Dress: casual. Reservations advised. V. Expensive.*

★

Zum Goldenen Schaefli. In a side street just off the market place, this restaurant is in a fine historic building and serves traditional Swiss food. Ancient, uneven floors lend charm to the place, but grandma's specialties such as veal liver with roesti and mocha mousse dessert are the main attractions. *Metzgergasse 5, tel. 071/233737. Dress: casual. Reservations advised. No credit cards. Moderate.*

Bistro. Food is served here until 11:30 at night, so this is an ideal spot for a post-theater meal. It's centrally located and serves European food with French and Italian touches. The variety of tortelloni is impressive, as are the salads. *Spisergasse 15, tel. 071/220088. Dress: casual. Reservations advised. No credit cards. Inexpensive.*

Lodging   **Einstein.** Once an embroidery factory, this centrally located hotel has been beautifully and thoughtfully restored. The large rooms are all well-appointed. The elegant interior is complimented by a fashionable bar, ideal for predinner drinks. *Berneggstr. 2, tel. 071/200033. 60 rooms with bath. AE, DC, MC, V. Expensive.*

Metropole. Don't be put off by the rather dark entrance hall here: The reception area is bright and cheerful, and the rooms are attractively decorated with flowered tapestries and antique furniture. It's ideally located just a few steps away from the station. *Bahnhofstr. 2, tel. 071/206161. 37 rooms with bath. AE, DC, MC, V. Moderate.*

Vadian. Though this hotel may be small, it's clean and comfortable, offering good value for your money. There's no restaurant, but a good breakfast is served. *Gallustr. 36, tel. 071/236080. AE, DC, MC, V. Inexpensive.*

Schaffhausen   **Fischerzunft.** You can't fail to be impressed by the delightful
Dining   surroundings of this restaurant, with its antique furniture and
★   fresh flower arrangements. The menu has a large selection of local fish dishes but is particularly noteworthy for its Chinese influence. It's in a beautiful building on the river. *Rheiquai 8, tel. 053/53281. Jacket and tie. Reservations advised. AE, DC, MC, V. Very expensive.*

Schloss Taverne. This is a remarkable restaurant, well worth the short trip out of town. It's located in a centuries-old castle and furnished throughout with antiques. The exquisitely prepared tables add to the romantic atmosphere. You can relax and enjoy the *menu gastronomique* with extensive ranges of courses: Discuss it with the helpful head waiter. *Schlosstr., 8207 Herblingen, tel. 053/21821. Jacket and tie. Reservations advised. MC, V. Expensive.*

Amadaeus. If you're yearning to try nouvelle cuisine Swiss-style, then head for Amadaeus. It's a centrally located, bright, modern restaurant, and the friendly staff will be pleased to advise you on seasonal specialties. Try the Roquefort mousse if it's available. *Bahnhofstr. 14, tel. 053/55727. Dress: informal. Reservations advised. AE, DC, MC, V. Moderate.*

Lodging   **Bellevue U.D. Rheinfall.** Located a little way out of town, the
★   Bellevue is in a very quiet location high above the Rhine Falls, and you can spend lazy hours on the large sunny terrace watching the water flow hundreds of feet below. All the comfortably furnished rooms are bright and sunny, and the views are some of the best of the Rhine. *Neuhausen B. Schaffhausen, tel. 053/22121. 27 rooms, 20 with bath. AE, DC, MC, V. Moderate.*

Park Villa. For a comfortable city-center hotel that doesn't charge high, city-center prices, try the Park Villa. It's across from the main park and close to the station. All the rooms are spacious and comfortable, with the conveniences you'd expect from a middle-range hotel. There's a pleasant garden restaurant, and if you're feeling energetic, there are tennis courts nearby. *Parkstr. 18, tel. 053/52737. 20 rooms with bath. AE, DC, MC, V. Moderate.*

33 Turkey

Introduction

Turkey is one place for which the term "East meets West" really applies, both literally and figuratively. It is in Turkey's largest city, Istanbul, where the continents of Europe and Asia meet, separated only by the Golden Horn, an inlet of the River Bosporous that flows 18 miles (28.8 kilometers) from the Black Sea to the Sea of Marmara.

Although most of Turkey's land mass is in Asia, Turkey has faced West politically since 1923, when Mustapha Kemal, better known as Atatürk, founded the modern republic. He transformed the remnants of the shattered Ottoman Empire into a secular state with a Western outlook. So thorough was this changeover, culturally, politically, and economically, that in 1988, 50 years after Atatürk's death, Turkey applied to join the European Economic Community (EEC). It has been a member of the North Atlantic Treaty Organization (NATO) since 1950.

For 16 centuries Istanbul, once known as Constantinople, played a major role in world politics, first as capital of the vast Byzantine Empire, and then as capital of the Ottoman Empire, the most powerful Islamic empire the world has ever known.

Turkey remains solidly Islamic. Of its 52 million people, 99% are Muslim, primarily rural people whose lives are deeply rooted in tradition. You can drive through areas where peasants still pick cotton by hand or collect hay with a pitch fork, while smoke rises from a nearby campsite—scenes that have barely changed over the centuries.

Before You Go

When to Go The height of the tourist season runs from April through October. July and August are the busiest and warmest months. They are also the best time to visit central and eastern Antolia in Asia Minor, which can be extremely cold in winter, with roads and mountain passes closed by snow. April through June and September and October are the best months to visit archaeological sites or Istanbul and the Marmara area because the days are cooler and the crowds are smaller. Istanbul is hot in the summer and cold in the winter.

Climate The Mediterranean and Aegean coasts have mild winters and hot summers. You can swim in the sea from late April through October. The Black Sea coast is mild and damp, with a rainfall of 90 inches (229 centimeters) a year. Summer brings hot and dry weather to eastern Anatolia, but evenings are cool.

The following are the average daily maximum and minimum temperatures for Istanbul.

Jan.	46F	8C	May	69F	21C	Sept.	76F	24C
	37	3		53	12		61	16
Feb.	47F	9C	June	77F	25C	Oct.	68F	20C
	36	2		60	16		55	13
Mar.	51F	11C	July	82F	28C	Nov.	59F	15C
	38	3		65	18		48	9
Apr.	60F	16C	Aug.	82F	28C	Dec.	51F	11C
	45	7		66	19		41	5

Currency The monetary unit is the Turkish lira (TL), which come in bank notes of 10, 20, 50, 100, 500, 1,000, and 10,000. Although there are coins of smaller denominations, they are seldom used. At press time (fall 1988), the exchange rate was 1,262 TL to the dollar and 2,300 TL to the pound sterling. Major credit cards and traveler's checks are widely accepted in hotels, shops, and expensive restaurants in cities and resorts, but rarely in villages and small shops and restaurants.

Be certain to retain your original exchange slips when you convert money into Turkish lira—you will need them to reconvert the money. Also, Turkish customs officials may ask you to show your currency-exchange receipts if you buy carpets or other high-ticket items. Because the Turkish lira is worth a lot less than the dollar or most foreign currencies, it's best to convert only what you plan to spend.

What It Will Cost Turkey is the least expensive of the Mediterranean countries. Although inflation hovers between 30% and 40%, frequent small devaluations of the lira keep prices fairly stable when measured against foreign currencies. Prices in this chapter are quoted in dollars, which indicate the real cost to the tourist more accurately than do the constantly increasing lira prices.

Sample Prices Coffee can range from about 30¢ to $2 a cup, depending on whether it's the less expensive Turkish coffee or American-style coffee and whether it's served in a luxury hotel or a café; tea, 15¢ to 30¢ a glass; local beer, 75¢ to $1; soft drinks, 30¢ to 70¢; lamb shish kebab, $1; taxi, $1 for one mile.

Customs Turkish customs officials rarely look through tourists' lug-
On Arrival gage on arrival. You are allowed to take in 400 cigarettes, 50 cigars, and five quarts of alcohol. Register all valuable personal items in your passport on entry. Turkey has duty-free shops in airports for international arrivals. Items are usually less expensive than in duty-free shops in European airports or than what's offered in-flight.

On Departure You must keep receipts of your purchases, especially items such as carpets, as proof that they were bought with legally exchanged currency. Also, it cannot be emphasized strongly enough that Turkey is extremely tough on anyone attempting to export antiques without authorization or on anyone caught with illegal drugs, regardless of the amount.

Language In 1928, Atatürk launched his sweeping language reforms that, over a period of six weeks, replaced Arabic script with the latin-based alphabet and eliminated many difficult and obtuse Arabic and Persian words from the Turkish language. The result has been dramatic: The literacy rate today is 75%, compared with 9% before the reforms.

English and German are widely spoken in hotels, restaurants, and shops in cities and resorts. In the villages or in remote areas, you'll have a hard time finding anyone who speaks anything but Turkish. Try learning a few basic Turkish words; the Turks will love you for it.

Getting Around

By Car Turkey has excellent roads—25,000 miles (40,000 kilometers)
Road Conditions of well-maintained, paved highways—but signposts are few and marked poorly, night lighting is scarce, and city traffic is

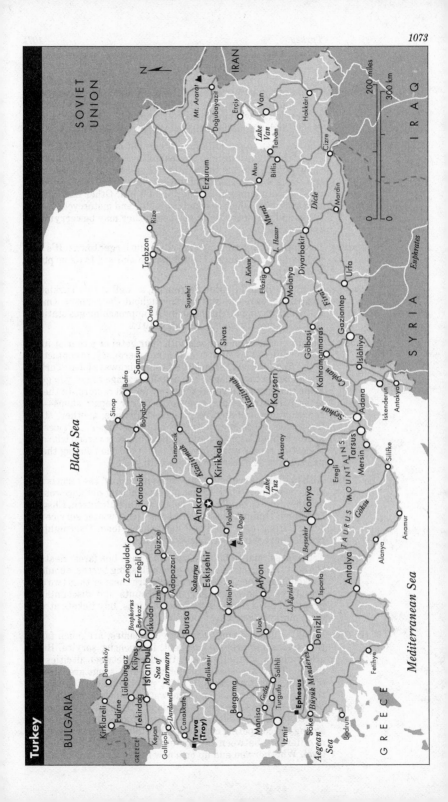

chaotic. City streets and highways are jammed with vehicles operated by high-speed lunatics and drivers who constantly blast their horns. In Istanbul, it's safer and faster to drive on the modern highways. Avoid the many small one-way streets, since you never know when someone is going to barrel down one of them in the wrong direction. Better yet, leave your car in a garage and use public transportation or take taxis.

Rules of the Road The best way to see Turkey is by car, but be warned that it has one of the highest accident rates in Europe. In general, Turkish driving conforms to Mediterranean customs, with driving on the right and passing on the left. But watch out for drivers passing on a curve or on the top of a hill. Other hazards are peasant carts, which are unlit at night, and motorcycles weaving in and out of traffic, even though they may be carrying an entire family.

Parking Parking is a big problem in the cities and larger towns. It's best to leave your car in your hotel garage and use taxis or public transportation.

Gasoline Mobil, Shell, and British Petroleum, as well as two Turkish oil companies, have gas stations throughout the country. On the main highways, billboards advertise approaching gas stations, which are usually open from 6 AM to 10 PM.

Breakdowns Before you start out, check with your hotel or a tourist information office about how, in case of an emergency, to contact one of the *Road Rescue Services* that some highways have. Turkish mechanics in the villages will usually manage to get you going again, at least until you reach a city for full repairs. In the cities, entire streets are given over to car repair shops—one repairs radiators; another, electrical fittings; another, steering wheels. Each shop is run by a team of experts. Prices are not high, but it's good to give a small tip to the person who does the actual repair work. If you're not in the shop during the repairs, take all the car documents with you.

By Train Although there are "express" trains in Turkey, the term is usually a misnomer. These trains ply several long-distance routes, but they tend to be slow. The best trains are **Mototren, Ekspres,** and **Mavi.** Dining cars on some trains have waiter service and serve surprisingly good and inexpensive food. Overnight expresses have sleeping cars and bunk beds.

Fares Train fares tend to be less expensive than bus fares. Seats on the best trains, as well as those with sleeping berths, should be booked in advance. Round-trip fares are cheaper than two one-way fares. There are student discounts and discounts for groups of 24 or more. In railroad stations, buy tickets at windows marked "Bilgisayer Giseleri."

By Bus Buses, which are run by private companies, are much faster than trains and provide excellent, inexpensive service. Buses are available, virtually around the clock, between all cities and towns. They are fairly comfortable and some are air-conditioned. Fares average about $1 per 120 miles (200 kilometers). *Su lutfen* (bottled mineral water) is included in the fare. You can purchase tickets at stands in a town's *Otogar* (central bus terminal). All seats are reserved. Fares don't vary much among the competing companies, but there's often a great deal of difference between the age of the buses and their comfort level. Whether you end up on a new bus or a rattling old one is simply a matter of luck. For very short trips, or getting around within a city, take minibuses or a *dolmuş* (shared taxi). Both are inexpensive and comfortable.

By Plane **Turkish Airlines (THY)** operates an extensive domestic network. There are eight flights daily on weekdays between Istanbul and Ankara. During the summer, many routes between the cities and coastal resorts are added. Try to arrive at the airport at least 45 minutes before your flight because security checks, which are rigidly enforced without exception, can be time consuming. Checked luggage is placed on trolleys on the tarmac and must be identified by boarding passengers before it is put on the plane. Unidentified luggage is left behind and checked for bombs or firearms.

THY offers several discounts on domestic flights: 10% for family members, including spouses; 10% for students; 50% for children aged 12 and under; 90% for children under two; and 50% for sports groups of five or more.

By Boat **Turkish Maritime Lines** operates car ferry and cruise services from Istanbul. Cruises are in great demand, so make your reservations well in advance, either through the head office in Istanbul (Rihtim Cad. 1, Karaköy, tel. 1/1440–207) or through **Sunquest Holidays** Ltd. in London (Aldine House, Aldine St., London W12 8AW, tel. 01/749–9933).

One of its cruises is the 10-day Mediterranean Cruise from Istanbul to Alanya, with ports of call at resorts along the way. The cruises, from June through September, depart every 15 days. Round-trip fares are about $900, including all meals and land tours.

The **Black Sea Ferry** sails year-round from Istanbul to Samsun and Trabzon and back, departing Monday evening from Sirkeci Dock in Istanbul. One-way fares to Trabzon are about $15 for a reclining seat, $20 to $55 for cabins, and $35 for cars.

Essential Information

Telephones Most pay phones are yellow, push-button models, although a few older, operator-controlled telephones are still in use. Multilingual directions are posted in phone booths.

Local Calls Public phones use *jetons* (tokens), which can be purchased for 50 TL at post offices and street booths. For a local call, deposit the token, wait until the light at the top of the phone goes off, then dial the number. If you need operator assistance for long-distance calls within Turkey, dial 031 or 091. Jetons are available for 250 TL and 750 TL for long-distance calls.

International Calls For direct-dial calls to the United States and Canada, dial 99, the country code, the area code, and the number. For calls to the United Kingdom, dial 44 first. You can use the higher-price jetons for this, or reach an international operator by dialing 528–23–03.

If you must make a call abroad, you're better off calling from a phone booth and using jetons or a telephone credit card; hotels in Turkey, as elsewhere, have hefty service charges for international calls.

Mail Post offices are painted bright yellow and have **"PPT"** signs on the front, which stand for Post, Phone, and Telegraph. The major ones are open Monday through Saturday, from 8 AM to midnight, and Sunday, 9 AM to 7 PM. Smaller branches close daily at 6 PM.

Postal Rates Because rates change constantly to keep up with inflation, check with your hotel desk for the latest rates.

Receiving Mail If you're uncertain where you'll be staying, have mail sent to *Posterestant, Merkez Postanesi* (central post office) in the town of your choice.

Shopping The best part of shopping in Turkey is visiting the *bedestans* (bazaars), all brimming with copper and brassware items, hand-painted ceramics, alabaster and onyx goods, fabrics, and richly colored carpets. The key word for shopping in the bazaars is "bargain." You must be willing to bargain, and bargain hard. It's great fun once you get the hang of it. As a rule of thumb, offer 50% less after you're given the initial price and be prepared to go up by about 25% to 30% of the first asking price. It's both bad manners and bad business to grossly underbid or to start bargaining if you're not serious about buying. Outside the bazaars, prices are usually fixed, although in resort areas some shopkeepers may be willing to bargain if you ask for a "better price." Part of the fun of roaming through the bazaars is having a free glass of *cay* (tea), which vendors will offer you whether you're a serious shopper or just browsing.

Carpets, cotton fabrics, and leather goods are excellent buys. Gold or silver jewelry is sold according to weight rather than design. Gold is a Turk's private insurance, and everyone wears some, whether it's in bracelets or on teeth. Beware of antiques. Chances are you will end up with an expensive fake, but even if you do find the genuine article, it's illegal to export antiques of any type.

VAT Refunds VAT (Value-Added Tax) is nearly always included in the price. If you want to claim back the VAT on expensive purchases, such as carpets or leather goods, ask before buying whether the shop offers VAT refund receipts, called *KDV Iade Ozel Fatura*. Not all shops participate in the service. The refunds are given at airports or port banks after you've cleared customs.

Opening and Closing Times **Banks.** Banks are open weekdays, 8:30 AM to noon and 1:30 PM to 5 PM.
Museums. Museums are generally open Tuesday through Sunday, 9:30 AM to 4:30 PM, and closed Monday. Palaces, open the same hours, are closed Thursday.
Shops. Most shops are closed daily from 1 PM to 2 PM and all day Sunday. Generally they're open Monday through Saturday, 9:30 AM to 1 PM and 2 PM to 7 PM. There are some exceptions in the resort areas, where shops stay open until 9 PM and are often open Sunday.

National Holidays January 1 (New Year's Day); April 23 (National Independence and Children's Day); May 7 (sunset) to May 9 (sunset): *Seker Bayrami* (sugar feast), three-day feast marking the end of Ramadan, a month-long Islamic observance that includes daytime fasting; Ramadan is based on the Muhammadan lunar calendar and varies yearly; May 19 (Youth and Sports Day); July 14 (sunset) to July 17 (sunset): *Kurban Bayrami* (sacrificial feast), Turkey's most important religious holiday celebrates Abraham's willingness to sacrifice his son to God; holiday varies yearly according to the lunar calendar; August 30 (Victory Day); October 29 (Republic Day).

Dining Turkish cuisine is one of the best in the world. The old cliché about it being hard to find a bad meal in Paris more aptly describes Istanbul, where the tiniest little hole-in-the-wall place serves delicious food. It's also an extremely healthful cuisine, full of fresh vegetables, yogurt, legumes, and grains, not to mention fresh seafood, roast lamb, and shish kebab made of lamb, beef, or chicken. Because Turkey is predominantly Muslim, pork is not readily available. But there's plenty of alcohol, including local beer and wine, which are excellent and inexpensive. Particularly good wines are Villa, Doluca, and Kavaklidere, available in *beyaz* (white) and *kirmizi* (red). The most popular local beer is Efes Pilsen. The national alcoholic drink, *raki*, is made from grapes and aniseed. Turks mix it with water or ice and sip it throughout their meal or serve it as an aperitif.

Hotel restaurants have English-language menus and usually serve a bland version of Continental cuisine. Far more adventurous and tasty are meals in *restorans* (Turkish restaurants) and in *lokantas* (cafés). Most lokantas do not have menus because they serve only what's fresh and in season, which varies daily. At lokantas, you simply sit back and let the waiter bring food to your table, beginning with a tray of *mezas* (appetizers). You point to the dishes that look inviting and take as many as you want. Then you select your main course from fresh meat or fish—displayed in glass-covered refrigerated units—which is then cooked to order, or from a steam table laden with casseroles and stews. For lighter meals, there are *kebabcıs*, tiny cafés specializing in kebabs served with salad and yogurt, and *pidecis*, selling *pides*, a pizzalike snack on flat bread, topped with butter, cheese, egg, or ground lamb, and baked in a wood-fired oven.

Mealtimes Lunch is generally served from 1 PM to 2 PM, and dinner from 8 PM to 9 PM. In the cities, you can find restaurants or cafés open virtually any time of day or night, but in the villages, finding a restaurant open at odd hours can be a problem.

Precautions Tap water is heavily chlorinated and supposedly safe to drink in cities and resorts. It's best to play it safe, however, and drink bottled mineral water *(maden suyu)*, which is better tasting and inexpensive.

Ratings Prices are per person and include an appetizer, main course, and dessert. Wine and gratuities are not included. A service charge of 15% is added to the bill; waiters expect another 10%. Best bets are indicated by a star ★. At press time, there were 1,262 Turkish lire to the dollar.

Category	Cost: Major Cities	Cost: Other Areas
Very Expensive	over 38,000 TL	over 32,000 TL
Expensive	22,000–38,000 TL	15,000–32,000 TL
Moderate	10,000–22,000 TL	6,500–12,500 TL
Inexpensive	under 10,000 TL	under 6,500 TL

Credit Cards The following credit card abbreviations are used: AE, American Express; DC, Diners Club; MC, MasterCard; V, Visa.

Lodging Hotels are officially classified in Turkey as HL (luxury), H1 to H5 (first- to fifth-class); motels, M1 to M2 (first- to second-class); and P, *pansiyons* (guest houses). The classification is arbitrary because the lack of a restaurant or a lounge automatically relegates the establishment to the bottom of the ratings. A lower-grade hotel may actually be far more charming and comfortable than one with a higher rating. There are also many local establishments that are licensed but not included in the official ratings list. You can obtain their names from local tourist offices.

Accommodations range from international luxury chains in Istanbul, Ankara, and Izmir to comfortable, family-run pansiyons. Plan ahead for the peak summer season, when resort hotels are often booked solid by tour companies. Turkey does not have central hotel reservations offices.

Rates vary from $7 to more than $240 a night for a double room. In the less expensive hotels, the plumbing and furnishings will probably leave much to be desired. You can find very acceptable, clean double rooms with bath for between $20 and $50, with breakfast included. Room rates are displayed in the reception area.

It is accepted practice in Turkey to ask to see the room in advance. Your room probably will be much more basic than the well-decorated reception area. Check for noise, especially if the room faces a street.

Ratings Prices are for double rooms. Best bets are indicated by a star ★ . At press time, there were 1,262 Turkish lire to the dollar.

Category	Cost: Major Cities	Cost: Other Areas
Very Expensive	over 100,000 TL	over 72,000 TL
Expensive	48,000–100,000 TL	38,000–72,000 TL
Moderate	25,000–48,000 TL	25,000 TL–30,000 TL
Inexpensive	under 25,000 TL	under 25,000 TL

Credit Cards The following credit card abbreviations are used: AE, American Express; DC, Diners Club; MC, MasterCard; V, Visa.

Tipping Except at inexpensive restaurants, a 10% to 15% charge is added to the bill. Since the money does not necessarily find its way to the waiter, leave an additional 10% on the table or hand it to the waiter. In the top restaurants, waiters expect tips of between 10% and 15%. Hotel porters expect about 30¢ to 40¢ per bag, and the chambermaid, about 50¢ a day. Taxi drivers don't expect tips, although they are becoming accustomed to foreigners giving them something. Round off the fare to the nearest 100 TL. At Turkish baths, the staff that attends you expects to share a tip of 30% to 35% of the bill. You won't miss them, they'll be lined up expectantly on your departure.

Istanbul

Arriving and Departing

By Plane   All international and domestic flights arrive at Istanbul's
Atatürk Airport. For information on times, call the individual
airline or the airport's information desk (tel. 1/573–29–20, ext.
864).

Between the   Shuttle buses run between the airport's international and do-
Airport and   mestic terminals to the Turkish Airlines (THY) terminal in
Downtown   downtown Istanbul, at Mesrutiyet Caddesi, near the Galata
Tower. Buses depart for the airport at the same address, every
half hour from 5 AM to 9 AM, every hour from 9 AM to 2 PM, and
every half hour from 2:30 PM to 7 PM. After that, departure time
depends on the number of passengers. Allow at least 45 minutes for the bus ride. Plan to be at the airport two hours before
your international flight because of the lengthy security and
check-in procedures. The ride from the airport into town takes
from 30 to 40 minutes, depending on traffic. Taxis charge about
$8.

By Train   Trains from the West arrive at Sirkeci Station (tel. 1/527–00–
51) in Old Istanbul. Eastbound trains to Anatolia depart from
Haydarpasa Station (tel. 1/336–04–75) on the Asian side.

By Bus   Buses arrive at Topkapı Terminal (not to be confused with the
area around the Topkapı Palace) just outside the city at the
Cannon Gate—at Trakya Otogari Terminal for buses from Europe and at Anadolu Otogari Terminal for buses going on to
other parts of Turkey. A few buses from Anatolia arrive at
Harem, on the eastern shore of the Bosporus. Some bus companies have minibus services (*servis arabasi*) to the hotel areas of
Taksim Square and Aksaray. There are local buses (No. 83 to
Taksim and No. 84 to Eminönü) as well as dolmuş. If you arrive
with baggage, it is much easier to take a taxi, which will cost
about $4 to Taksim from the bus terminals and about $3 to Old
Istanbul.

By Car   If you drive in from the West, the busy and often hair-raising
E5 highway, also called Londra Asfalti, leads from Edirne to
Atatürk Airport and on through the city walls at Cannon Gate.
E5 heading out of Istanbul leads into central Anatolia and on to
Iran and Syria. An alternative to E5, when leaving the city, is
to take one of the numerous car ferries that ply the Sea of Mar-
mara and the Dardanelles from Kabatas Dock, or try the
overnight ferry to Izmir, which leaves from Sirkeci.

Getting Around

The best way to get around all the magnificent monuments in
Sultanahmet in Old Istanbul is to walk. They're all within easy
distance of each other, along streets filled with peddlers, shoeshine boys, children playing, and craftsmen working. To get to
other areas, you can take a bus or one of the many ferries that
steam between the Asian and European continents. Dolmuş
and taxis are plentiful, inexpensive, and more comfortable than
city buses. There's no subway system, but there is the *Tünel*, a
tiny underground train that's handy for getting up the steep

hill from Karaköy to the bottom of Istiklal Caddesi. It runs every 10 minutes and costs about 15¢.

By Bus Buy a ticket before boarding a bus. You can buy them individually or in books of 10, at ticket stands around the city. Shoeshine boys or men on the street will also sell them to you, for a few cents more. Fares are about 15¢ per ride.

By Dolmuş These are shared taxis that stop at one of the red, black, and white dolmuş signs. The destination is shown either on a roof sign or a card in the front window. Many of them are classic American cars from the 50s.

By Taxi Taxis are inexpensive. Since most drivers do not speak English and may not know the street names, write down the street you want, the nearby main streets, and the name of the area. Taxis are metered. Although tipping is not expected, you should round off the fare to the nearest 100 TL.

By Boat For a fun and inexpensive ride, take the **Anadolu Kavaği** boat along the Bosporous to its mouth at the Black Sea. The boat leaves year-round from the Eminönü Docks, next to the Galata Bridge on the Old Istanbul side, at 10:30 AM and 1:30 PM, with extra trips in the summer. The fare is $2. The trip takes two hours and 45 minutes one way. You can disembark at any of the stops and return by land if you wish. Regular ferries depart from Kabataş Dock, near Dolmabahçe Palace on the European side, to Üsküdar on the Asian side; and also from Eminönü Docks 1 and 2, near Sirkeci Station.

Important Addresses and Numbers

Tourist Information Official tourist information offices are at **Atatürk Airport** (tel. 1/573-73-99 or 1/573-41-36); the **Hilton Hotel** (tel. 1/133-05-92); **Yolcu Salonu,** International Maritime Passenger Terminal (tel. 1/149-57-76); and in a pavilion in the Sultanamet district of **Old Istanbul** (Divan Yolu Cad. 3, tel. 1/522-49-03).

Consulates **U.S. Consulate,** Meşrutiyet Caddesi 106, Tepebaşı, Beyoğlu (tel. 1/151-36-02). **U.K.** Meşrutiyet Caddesi 34, Tepebaşı, Beyoğlu (tel. 1/144-75-40).

Emergencies **Doctors:** for an English-speaking doctor, call the American Hospital (Güzelbahçe Sokak 20, Nişantaşi, tel. 1/131-40-50) or ask your hotel for a recommendation. You may also find English-speaking doctors at the French Hospital on Taksim Square, behind the Divan Hotel (tel. 1/148-97-51). **Pharmacies:** There is one on duty 24 hours in every neighborhood. Consult the notice in the window of any pharmacy for the name and address of the nearest all-night shop. One that's centrally located is Pamuk in the Taksim district (Tak-i Zafer Cad. 1, tel. 1/149-12-68). **Ambulance:** Tel. 77. **Tourism Police:** Tel. 1/528-53-69 or 1/527-45-03.

English-Language Bookstores The most complete is **Redhouse,** near the Grand Bazaar (Riza Paşa Yokuşu 50, Sultanhamam, tel. 1/527-81-00). Others include **Haset Bookshop** (Istiklal Cad. 469); **Tünel,** with several branches, including one in the Hilton and the Sheraton hotels; and **Net,** publishers of tourism guides (Yerebatan Cad. 15/3, Sultanahmet, tel. 1/520-84-06).

Travel Agencies Most are concentrated along Cumhuriyet Caddesi, off Taksim Square, in the hotel area. They include **American Express** (Hilton Hotel, Cumhuriyet Cad. Harbiye, tel. 1/140-39-39); **Union**

of **Turkish Travel Agencies** (Elmadağ, Cumhuriyet Cad. 187, tel. 1/146–02–36); **Turkish Touring and Automobile Club** (Halaskargazi Cad. 364, Şişli, tel. 1/521–65–88); **Intra** (Halaskargazi Cad. 111, Harbiye, tel. 1/140–38–91); **Data Travel Services** (Cumhuriyet Cad. 243, Harbiye, tel. 1/140–82–90); **Tur Seyahat Koll** (Şti, Cumhuriyet Cad. 12/C, tel. 1/147–11–89); **Visitur Travel** (Cumhuriyet Cad. 129, Elmadağ, tel. 1/141–40–40); and **Vitur** (Cumhuriyet Cad. 259, Harbiye, tel. 1/146–57–83).

Guided Tours

There are guided tours for virtually every interest, from Islamic Arts, Religion, and Architecture to nightclub tours that include the Sound and Light Show at the Blue Mosque and full- or half-day tours that include lunch. You can also arrange for private tours with English-speaking guides.

Exploring Istanbul

Istanbul is a noisy, chaotic, and exciting city, where Asia meets Europe and spires and domes of mosques and medieval palaces dominate the skyline. At dawn, when the muzzeim's call to prayer rebounds from ancient minarets, many people are making their way home from the nightclubs and bars, while others are kneeling on their prayer rugs, facing Mecca.

Day and night, Istanbul has a schizophrenic air to it. Women in jeans, business suits, or elegant designer outfits pass women wearing the long skirts and head coverings that village women have worn for generations. Donkey-drawn carts vie with old Chevrolets and Pontiacs for dominance of the noisy, narrow streets, and the world's most fascinating Oriental bazaar competes with Western boutiques for the time and attention of both tourists and locals.

Ironically, Istanbul's Asian side is filled with Western-style sprawling suburbs, while its European side contains **Old Istanbul**—an Oriental wonderland of mosques, opulent palaces, and crowded bazaars. The Golden Horn, an inlet four miles long (6.4 kilometers), flows off the Bosporus on the European side, separating Old Istanbul from New Town. The center of New Town is **Beyoglu,** a modern district filled with hotels, banks, and shops grouped around Taksim Square. There are two bridges spanning the Golden Horn: the Atatürk and the Galata. The **Galata Bridge** is a central landmark and a good place to get your bearings. From it, you can see the city's layout and its seven hills. The bridge will also give you a taste of Istanbul's frenetic street life. It's filled with peddlers selling everything from pistachio nuts and spices to curly toed slippers fancy enough for a sultan; fishermen meanwhile grill their catch on coal braziers and sell them to passersby. None of this sits well with motorists, who blast their horns constantly, usually to no avail. If you want to orient yourself in a quieter way, take a boat trip from the docks on the Stamboul side of the Galata Bridge up the Bosporus.

The Main Attractions

❶ **Topkapı Palace,** which dates from the 15th century, was the residence of a number of sultans and their harems until the mid-19th century. In order to avoid the crowds, try to get there by 9:30 AM when the gates open. If you're arriving by taxi, tell the driver you want the Topkapı *Saray* (palace) in Sultanahmet, or you could end up at the Topkapı bus terminal on the outskirts of town.

Sultan Mehmet II built the first palace in the 1450s, shortly after the Ottoman conquest of Constantinople. Over the centuries, sultan after sultan added ever more elaborate architectural fantasies, until the palace eventually ended up with more than four courtyards and some 5,000 residents, many of them concubines and eunuchs. Topkapı was the residence and center of bloodshed and drama for the Ottoman rulers until the 1850s, when Sultan Abdül Mecit moved with his harem to the European-style **Dolmabaçhe Palace** farther up the Bosporous coast.

2 3 In Topkapı's outer courtyard is the **Church of St. Irene,** now used as a concert hall, and the **Court of the Janissaries,** members of the sultan's elite guard. Today, the area where the Janissaries once prepared their meals in giant soup kettles is occupied by the central ticket booth for entrance to the grounds, as well as a parking lot for taxis and buses.

4 To the left as you enter the outer courtyard, a lane slopes downhill to three museums grouped together: the **Archaeological Museum,** which houses a fine collection of Greek and Roman antiquities, including finds from Ephesus and Troy; the **Museum of the Ancient Orient,** with Sumerian, Babylonian, and Hittite treasures; and the **Çinili Köşkü (Tiled Pavilion),** which houses ceramics from the early Seljuk and Osmanli empires. *Gülhane Park 1. Admission: 500 TL. The Archaeological and Ancient Orient museums open daily 9:30–5; Çinili Ķöskü, Tues. only.*

Walk back up to the Court of the Janissaries to the ticket office, which is adjacent to the **Bab-i-Selam** (Gate of Salutation), built in 1524 by Süleyman the Magnificent, who was the only person allowed to pass through it. From the towers on either side, prisoners were kept until they were executed beside the fountain outside the gate in the first courtyard. In the second courtyard, amid the rose gardens, is the **Divan,** the Assembly Room of the Council of State, once presided over by the grand vizir (prime minister). The word *divan* in Turkish means a place of hard work. The sultan would sit behind a latticed window, hidden by a curtain so no one would know when he was listening, although occasionally he would pull the curtain aside to comment.

One of the most popular tours in Topkapı is the **Harem,** a maze of nearly 400 halls, terraces, rooms, wings, and apartments grouped around the sultan's private quarters. Forty have been meticulously restored and are open to the public. A small gate on the left opens onto the Harem. Next to the entrance are the quarters of the eunuchs and about 200 of the lesser concubines, who were lodged in tiny cubicles, as cramped and uncomfortable as the main rooms of the Harem are large and opulent. *Admission: 500 TL. Because only a limited number of visitors are allowed through the Harem each day, buy a ticket—at the entrance to the Harem—as soon as you enter the palace grounds. Tours begin about every half hour.*

In the third courtyard is the **Treasury,** four rooms filled with jewels, including two uncut emeralds each weighing 7.7 pounds

(3.5 kilos) that once hung from the ceiling. Here, too, you will be dazzled by the emerald dagger used in the movie *Topkapı* and the 84-carat "Spoonmaker" diamond that, according to legend, was found by a pauper and traded for three wooden spoons.

Time Out Just past the Treasury, on the right side of the courtyard, are steps leading to a 19th-century **Rococo Mecidiye pavilion,** now the **Konyali Restaurant** (tel. 1/526–27–27), which serves excellent Turkish food and has a magnificent view of the *seraglio* (sultan's household, including harem) and the Golden Horn. On a terrace below is an outdoor café, with an even better view. Go early or reserve a table to beat the tour-group crush. The restaurant and café are open for lunch only.

In the fourth and last courtyard are small, elegant summer houses, mosques, fountains, and reflecting pools scattered amid the gardens on different levels. Here, too, you will find the **Erivan Kiosk,** also known as the **Golden Cage,** where the closest relatives of the reigning sultan lived in strict confinement in what amounted to house arrest. The custom began in the 1800s after the old custom of murdering all possible rivals to the throne had been abandoned. The confinement of the heirs apparently helped keep the peace, but it deprived them of any chance to prepare themselves for the formidable task of ruling a great empire. *Seraglio Point. Admission: 1,000 TL. Open Sept.–June, Wed.–Mon. 9:30–5; July–Aug., 9:30–7. Closed Tues.*

⑤ Just outside the walls of Topkapı Palace is **Ayasofya** (St. Sophia), one of the world's greatest examples of Byzantine architecture. Built in AD 532 under the supervision of Emperor Justinian, it took 10,000 men and six years to complete. St. Sophia is made of ivory from Asia, marble from Egypt, and columns from the ruins of Ephesus. The dome, one of the most magnificent in the world, was also the world's largest until the dome at St. Peter's Basilica was built in Rome, 1,000 years later. St. Sophia was the cathedral of Constantinople for 900 years, surviving earthquakes and looting Crusaders until 1453, when it was converted into a mosque by Mehmet the Conqueror. Minarets were added by succeeding sultans. St. Sophia originally had many **mosaics** depicting Christian scenes, which were plastered over by Süleyman I, who felt they were inappropriate for a mosque. In 1935, Atatürk converted St. Sophia into a museum. Shortly after that, American archaeologists discovered the mosaics, which were restored and are now on display.

According to legend, the **Sacred Column,** in the north aisle of the mosque, "weeps water" that can work miracles. It's so popular that, over the centuries, believers have worn a hole through the marble and brass column. You can stick your finger in it and make a wish. *Ayasofya Meydani. Admission: 1,000 TL. Tickets are purchased separately for the galleries. Open Sept., Jan.–June, 9:30–4:30; July–Aug., 9:30–7. Closed Mon. and Oct.–Dec.*

⑥ Across from St. Sophia is the **Blue Mosque,** with its shimmering blue tile, 260 stained-glass windows, and six minarets, as grand and beautiful a monument to Islam as St. Sophia was to Christiandom. Sultan Ahmet I built the Blue Mosque in six years beginning in 1609, nearly 1,100 years after the comple-

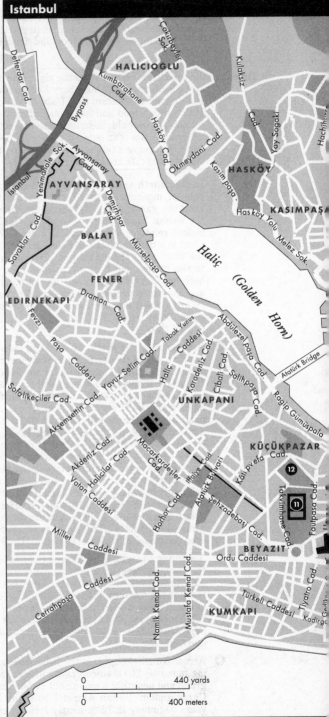

Istanbul

Archaeological Museum, **4**
Ayasofya (St. Sophia), **5**
Blue Mosque, **6**
Church of St. Irene, **2**
Court of the Janissaries, **3**
Dolmabahçe Mosque, **16**
Dolmabahçe Palace, **17**
Flower Market, **15**
Galata Tower, **14**
Hippodrome, **7**
Kapalı Carsı, **10**
Mısır Carsısı, **13**
Museum of Turkish and Islamic Arts, **8**
Süleymaniye Mosque, **12**
Topkapı Palace, **1**
University, **11**
Yerebatan Saray, **9**

HALICIOĞLU

Çakırbeyler Sok.

Kulaksız Cad.

Deftardar Cad.

Kumbarahane Cad.

Bypass

Hasköy Cad.

Okmeydanı Cad.

HASKÖY

Kasım paşa

KASIMPAŞA

Yeninahale Sok.
Ayvansaray Cad.

İstanbul

Savaklar Cad.

AYVANSARAY

Demirhisar Cad.

Haskö y Yolu Melez Sok.

BALAT

Mürselpaşa Cad.

Haliç (Golden Horn)

FENER

Draman Cad.

EDIRNEKAPI

Fevzi Paşa Caddesi

Sofalıkeçiler Cad.

Akşemsettin Cad.

Yavuz Selim Cad.

Tabak Yunus Caddesi

Haliç

Karadeniz Cad.

Abdülezel paşa Cad.

Cibali Cad.

Salihpaşa Cad.

Atatürk Bridge

Ragıp Gümüşpala

UNKAPANI

KÜÇÜKPAZAR Cad.

Akdeniz Cad.

Macarkardesler Cad.

İtfaiye Cad.

Atatürk Bulvarı

(12)

Vatan Caddesi

Haliclar Cad.

Horhor Cad.

Şehzadebaşı Cad.

Kâtip çelebi

Takvimhane Cad.

Fatih paşa Cad.

(11)

Millet Caddesi

Caddesi

Namık Kemal Cad.

Mustafa Kemal Cad.

BEYAZIT

Ordu Caddesi

Cerrahpaşa Caddesi

KUMPAPI

Türkeli Caddesi

Tiyatro Cad.

Kadirga

0   440 yards

0   400 meters

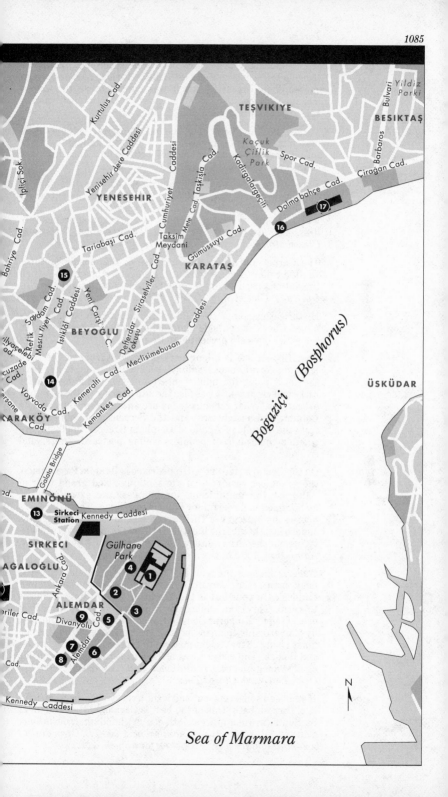

Yildiz Parki

TEŞVIKIYE

BESIKTAŞ

Bulvari

Kuruluş Cad.

Yenisehirdere Caddesi

İplici Sok.

YENESEHIR

Bahriye Cad.

Tariabaşi Cad.

Cumhuriyet Caddesi

Kaçuk Çiflik Park

Spor Cad.

Barbaros

Çiragan Cad.

Dolmabahçe Cad.

Mete Cad.

Taşkişla Cad.

Kadirgalargeçiti

Taksim Meydani

Gümussuyu Cad.

KARATAŞ

Caddesi

16

17

Saydam Cad.

Mesru'iyet Cad.

Refik

İstiklâl Caddesi

Yeni Çarşi

15

BEYOĞLU

Defterdar Yokuşu

Siraselviler Cad.

Meclisimebusan

rilyaçelebi ad.

cuzade Cad

Kemeralii Cad.

Kemankeş Cad.

14

ersane

Voyvoda Cad.

KARAKÖY Cad.

Galata Bridge

Boğaziçi (Bosphorus)

ÜSKÜDAR

ad.

EMINÖNÜ

13 Sirkeci Station

Kennedy Caddesi

SIRKECI

AGALOĞLU

Gülhane Park

4

1

Ankara Cad.

ALEMDAR

9

Divanyolu Cad.

2

3

5

eriler Cad.

7

Alemdar

6

8

Cad.

Kennedy Caddesi

N

Sea of Marmara

tion of St. Sophia. His goal was to surpass Justinian's master-piece, and many art critics believe he succeeded. The Blue Mosque is the only mosque in Turkey with six minarets, which caused some concern when it was built because the sacred mosque in Mecca also had six minarets at the time, although a seventh has since been added.

Turkey is one of the few Islamic countries that opens its mosques to tourists. If you hear the muzzeim calling the faith-ful to prayer, wait about a half hour before entering as a courtesy to the worshippers.

Enter the mosque at the side entrance that faces St. Sophia. You must remove your shoes and leave them at the entrance. Immodest clothing is not allowed, but an attendant at the door will lend you a robe if he feels you are not appropriately dressed. *Sultanahmet. Free; donations welcome. Open 9–5. Closed Mon.*

The **Carpet and Kilim museums** are in the mosque's stone-vaulted cellars and upstairs at the end of a stone ramp, which the sultans used to enter on horseback. *Admission: 500 TL. Open 9–5. Closed Mon.*

Historical pageants are held in the mosque on summer eve-nings. Check the outside bulletin boards for a schedule and to see which ones are presented in English.

❼ The **Hippodrome** is a long park directly in front of the Blue Mosque. As a Roman stadium with 100,000 seats, it was once the focal point for public entertainment, including chariot races and circuses. It was also the site of many riots and public executions. What remains today are an **Egyptian Obelisk,** the **Column of Constantinos,** and the **Serpentine Column** taken from the Temple of Apollo at Delphi in Greece. You'll also en-counter thousands of peddlers selling postcards, nuts, and trinkets.

On the western side of the Hippodrome is **Ibrahim Paşa Palace,** the grandiose residence of the son-in-law and grand vizir of Süleyman the Magnificent. Ibrahim Paşa was executed when he became too powerful for Süleyman's liking. The palace now
❽ houses the **Museum of Turkish and Islamic Arts,** which gives a superb insight into the lifestyles of Turks of every level of socie-ty, from the 8th century to the present. *Şifahane Sok. Admission: 300 TL. Open 10–5. Closed Mon.*

Walk back along the length of the Hippodrome and cross the busy main road, Divan Yolu. Turn left onto Hilaliahmer
❾ Caddesi. On your left is the **Yerebatan Saray** (Sunken Palace Cistern). This is an underground network of waterways first excavated by Emperor Constantine in the 3rd century and then by Emperor Justinian in the 6th century. It has 336 marble col-umns rising 26 feet (eight meters) to support Byzantine arches and domes. The cistern was always kept full as a precaution against long sieges. *Hilaliahmer Cad. Admission: 500 TL. Open 9:30–4:30. Closed Tues.*

If you need some time out and want a real treat, spend an hour in a Turkish bath. One of the best is **Cağaloğlu Hamami,** near St. Sophia in a magnificent 18th-century building. *Hilaliahmer Cad. 34, tel. 1/522–24–24. Admission: 1,000 TL. Open daily 7 AM–midnight for men; 7 AM–8 PM for women.*

❿ The next grand attraction is the **Kapalı Carsı** (Grand Bazaar), about a quarter-mile northwest of the Hippodrome. You can walk to it in about 15 minutes or take a five-minute taxi ride. The Grand Bazaar, also called the Covered Bazaar, is a maze of 65 winding, covered streets, with 4,000 shops, tiny cafés, and restaurants. Originally built by Mehmet the Conqueror in the 1450s, it was ravaged by two modern-day fires, one in 1954 that virtually destroyed it, and a smaller one in 1974. In both cases, the bazaar was quickly rebuilt. It's a shopper's paradise, filled with thousands of different types of items, including fabrics, clothing, brass candalabra, furniture, and jewelry.

It's extremely popular with locals as well as tourists. If you're thirsty or hungry, you can also shop for a place to eat, for there's an abundance of tea shops and small restaurants. The bazaar even has its own post office. *Yeniceriler Cad. and Fuatpasa Cad. Free. Open 8:30–6:30 in winter; 8:30–7, summer. Closed Sun.*

⓫ When you leave the bazaar, cross Fuatpasa Caddesi and walk around the grounds of the **university,** which has a magnificent gateway facing Takvimhane Caddesi. Follow Takvimhane Caddesi, the western border of the university, to the right to **⓬** the 16th-century **Süleymaniye Mosque.** The mosque was designed by Sinan, the architectural genius who masterminded more than 350 buildings and monuments under the direction of Süleyman the Magnificent. This is Sinan's grandest and most famous monument, and the burial site of both himself and his patron, Süleyman.

⓭ The Grand Bazaar isn't the only bazaar in Istanbul. Another one worth visiting is the **Mısır Carsısı** (Egyptian Bazaar). You reach it by walking down Uzuncarsi Caddesi to Firincilar Yok. Turn right at Firincilar Yok and left onto Sabun Caddesi, where you will see the back of the bazaar. It was built in the 17th century as a means of rental income for the upkeep of the Yeni Mosque. The bazaar was once a vast pharmacy, filled with burlap bags overflowing with herbs and spices for folk remedies. Today, you're more likely to see bags full of fruit, nuts, Royal Jelly from the bee hives of the Aegean coast, and white sacks spilling over with culinary spices. It's a lively, colorful scene. Nearby are the fruit and fish markets, which are equally colorful. *Yeni Cami. Open 8–7. Closed Sun.*

New Town

New Town is the area on the northern shore of the Golden Horn, the waterway that cuts through Istanbul and divides Europe from Asia. The area's most prominent landmark is the **⓮** **Galata Tower,** built by the Genoese in 1349 as part of their fortifications. In this century, it served as a fire lookout until 1960. Today it houses a restaurant and nightclub (*see* Dining), and a daytime viewing tower. *Galipdede Cad. Admission: 800 TL. Open daily 10–6.*

⓯ North of the tower is the **Flower Market** (Çiçek Pasaji), off Istiklal Caddesi, a lively blend of flower stalls, tiny restaurants, bars, and street musicians. Here you can eat inexpensively in scores of outdoor cafés and people-watch as you drink beer or sip tea.

16 17 Next head for **Dolmabahçe Mosque** and **Dolmabahçe Palace,** which are reached by following Istiklal Caddesi to Taksim Square and then taking Gümüssuyu Caddesi around the square to a junction. You will see the Dolmabahçe Mosque on your right and the clock tower and gateway to Dolmabahçe Palace on your left.

The palace was built in 1853 and, until the declaration of the modern Republic in 1923, was the residence of the last sultans of the Ottoman Empire. It was also the residence of Atatürk, who died here in 1938. The palace, flood-lit at night, is an extraordinary mixture of Hindu, Turkish, and European styles of architecture and interior design. Queen Victoria's contribution to the lavishness was a chandelier weighing 4½ tons. Guided tours of the palace take about 80 minutes. *Gümüssuyu Cad. Admission: 1,000 TL. Open Tues.–Sun. 9–11:30 and 1:30–4:30. Closed Mon.*

What to See and Do with Children

Visit **Princes' Islands,** where motor vehicles are banned, and take a leisurely *fayton* (horse and buggy ride). At the beach, you can rent a row boat. **Gülhane Park,** near Topkapı Palace, has a small zoo and playground. The best parks for picnics are **Yildiz** and the **Belgrade Forest** on the shores of the Bosporus. In the winter, the **Hilton Hotel** (tel. 1/146–70–50) has a Sunday brunch at which a clown usually shows up.

Off the Beaten Track

The views of the Istanbul skyline at sunset are enough to warrant a trip to this city. The best views are from **Çamlıca,** the highest hill on the Asian side of the city. The area has several pavilions, where you can order tea and sit on cushions at low brass tables, and outdoor booths, where you can buy such snacks as pancakes with honey or corn on the cob. At the Çamlıca café, you can dine by candlelight after the sun has set and be served by waiters in traditional Turkish garb. *Sefatepsesi, tel. 1/335–33–01. Dress: informal. Reservations not necessary. No credit cards. Open daily in summer 9:30 AM–midnight; winter, 9:30AM–10:30 PM. Moderate.*

Another great area for watching sunsets is **Salacak,** opposite Leander's Tower. You can reach it by ferry from Eminönü. The area has open-air cafés and *yalis* (old wooden houses) at water's edge.

In the cafés and restaurants along the waterfront, you can enjoy fish from the daily catch. A popular restaurant on the wharf, with an excellent view of the minaret-studded skyline, is **Huzur** (Iskele Cad. 20, tel. 1/333–31–57).

Shopping

Gift Ideas The **Grand Bazaar** (*see* Exploring Istanbul) is a treasure trove of all things Turkish—carpets, brass, copper, jewelry, textiles, and leather goods.

Stores Stores and boutiques are located in New Town on streets such as **Istiklal Caddesi,** which runs off Taksim Square, and **Rumeli,**

Halaskargezi, and **Valikonagi Caddleri,** north of the Hilton Hotel. Two streets in the Kadikoy area where there's good shopping are **Bagdat and Bahariye Caddleri.**

Markets **Balikpazari** (fish market) is in Beyoglu Caddesi, off Istiklal Caddesi. Despite its name, you will find anything connected with food at this market. A **flea market** is held in Beyazit Square, near the Grand Bazaar, every Sunday.

Dining

Istanbul has a wide range of eating establishments, with prices to match. Most of the major hotels have dining rooms serving rather bland international cuisine. It's far more rewarding to eat in Turkish restaurants.

Ratings Prices are per person and include appetizer, main course, and dessert, but not liquor or gratuities. Best bets are indicated by a star ★. At press time, there were 1,262 Turkish lire to the dollar.

Category	Cost
Expensive	over 22,000 TL
Moderate	10,000– 22,000 TL
Inexpensive	under 10,000 TL

Credit Cards The following credit card abbreviations are used: AE, American Express; DC, Diners Club; MC, MasterCard; V, Visa.

Expensive **Gelik.** This restaurant, located in a 2-story, 19th-century villa, is usually packed, often with people who want to savor its specialty: all types of meat cooked in deep wells. *Sahil Yolu 68–70, tel. 1/572–08–06. Dress: informal. Reservations advised. AE, DC, MC, V.*

Moderate **Borsa.** This unpretentious restaurant serves some of the best
★ food in Turkey. The baked lamb in eggplant puree and the stuffed artichokes are not to be missed. *Lokantasi, Yaliköskü Cad. Yaliköskü Han 60–62, Eminönü, tel. 1/522–41–73. Dress: informal. Reservations not necessary. No credit cards. Lunch only. Closed Sun.*
Cemal Balik. This is one of many excellent restaurants in the Kumkapi area that serves a wide variety of fish dishes. Try the fish kebabs or pickled fish. *Capariz Sok. 27, tel. 1/527–22–88. Dress: informal. Reservations not necessary. No credit cards.*
China. Established in the 1950s by the Wang family, China is extremely popular with Turks as well as tourists. Located near the international hotels, it's spacious, with 3 dining rooms and a Western-style bar. *Lamartin Cad. 17/1, Taksim, tel. 1/150–62–63. Dress: informal. Reservations advised. No credit cards. Closed Sun.*
Divan. You'll enjoy gourmet Turkish-French cuisine, elegant surroundings, and excellent service at this restaurant, located in the Divan Hotel. *Cumhuriyet Cad. 2, Elmadağ, tel. 1/146–40–30. Dress: informal. Reservations advised. AE, DC, MC.*
Dört Mevsim. Located in a large Victorian building, Dört Mevsim is noted for its blend of Turkish and French cuisine and for its owners, Gay and Musa, an Anglo-Turkish couple who opened it in 1965. On any given day, you'll find them in the

kitchen overseeing such delights as shrimp in cognac sauce or baked marinated lamb. *Istiklal Cad. 509, Beyoğlu, tel. 1/145-89-41. Dress: informal. Reservations advised. No credit cards. Closed Sun.*

Hacibaba. This is a large, cheerful-looking place, with a terrace overlooking the Greek Orthodox churchyard. Fish, meat, and a wide variety of vegetable dishes are on display for your selection. Before you choose your main course, you'll be offered a tray of appetizers that can be a meal in themselves. *Istiklal Cad. 49, Taksim, tel. 1/144-18-86. Dress: informal. Reservations advised. No credit cards.*

★ **Haci Salih.** A tiny, family-run restaurant, Haci Salih has only 10 tables, so you may have to line up and wait—but it's worth it. Traditional Turkish food is the fare here, with special emphasis on vegetable dishes and lamb. Alcohol is not served, but you can bring your own. *Anadolu Han 201, Alyon Sok, off Istklala Cad., tel. 1/143-45-28. Dress: informal. Reservations sometimes accepted. No credit cards.*

Lodging

The top hotels are located mainly around Taksim Square in New Town. All hotels add a 28.8% tax and service charge. Modern, middle-range hotels usually have a friendly staff, which compensates for the generally bland architecture and interiors. In Old Istanbul, the Aksaray, Laleli, Sultanahmet, and Beyazit areas have many conveniently located, inexpensive small hotels and family-run pansiyons. Istanbul has a chronic shortage of beds, so plan ahead.

Ratings The following price categories are for two people in a double room. They do not include the 28.8% service charge. At press time, there were 1,262 Turkish lire to the dollar.

Category	Cost
Very Expensive	over 100,000 TL
Expensive	48,000–100,000 TL
Moderate	25,000–48,000 TL
Inexpensive	under 25,000 TL

Credit Cards The following credit card abbreviations are used: AE, American Express; DC, Diners Club; MC, MasterCard; V, Visa.

Very Expensive **The Hilton.** Lavishly decorated with Turkish rugs and large brass urns, this is one of the best Hiltons in the chain, and worth a visit even if you don't plan to stay. Ask for a room with a view of the Bosporous. *Cumhuriyet Cad., Harbiye, tel. 1/131-46-46. 410 rooms with bath. Facilities: Turkish baths, beauty and health spa, pool, rooftop bar and restaurant, tennis, squash, shopping arcade. AE, DC, MC, V.*

The Sheraton. Taksim Park provides a splendid setting for this hotel. All rooms have views of the Bosporous or the square. For a night's spree, try the rooftop restaurant and nightclub. *Asker Ocaği Cad., Taksim, tel. 1/148-90-00. 437 rooms with bath. Facilities: restaurant, bar, nightclub and disco, pool, health and beauty spa. AE, DC, MC, V.*

Expensive **Ayasofia Pansiyons.** These guest houses are part of an imaginative project undertaken by the Touring and Automobile Club to restore a little street of historic wooden houses along the outer wall of Topkapı Palace. One of the houses has been converted into a library and two into pansiyons, furnished in late Osmanli style, with excellent dining rooms. During the summer, tea and refreshments are served in the gardens to guests and nonguests alike. *Soğukçesme Sokak, Sultanahmet, tel. 1/512–57–32, and 1/512–50–55. No credit cards.*

Divan. This is a quiet, small hotel with an excellent restaurant. *Cumhuriyet Cad. 2, Şisli, tel. 1/131–41–00. 98 rooms with bath. Facilities: restaurant, bar, tea shop, beauty salon. AE, DC, MC.*

Pera Palace. A grand hotel with a genuinely Turkish feel to it, the Pera Palace was built in 1892 to accommodate guests arriving on the *Orient Express*. Although it has been modernized, it has lost none of its original Victorian opulence. Ask to see the room where Atatürk used to stay—it's been maintained with some of his personal belongings and is a popular attraction. *Meşrutiyet Cad. 98, Tepebaşl, tel. 1/151–45–60. 116 rooms with bath. Facilities: bar. DC, V.*

Ramada. The first international chain hotel to open in Old Town, the Ramada is in a converted, four-story apartment block with courtyards leading into it. *Ordu Cad. 226, Laleli, tel. 1/519–40–50. 275 rooms with bath. Facilities: restaurant, bar, pool, casino. AE, DC, MC, V.*

Yeşil Ev (Green House). This hotel is decorated in old-fashioned Ottoman style with lace curtains and latticed shutters. In the summer, you can dine on marble tables in a high-walled garden. *Kalasakal Sok. 5, Sultanahmet, tel. 1/528–67–64. 20 rooms with bath. Facilities: restaurant and garden. V.*

Moderate **Barin.** Modern, clean, and comfortable, with good friendly service, the Barin caters to business travelers as well as tourists. *Fevziye Cad. 25, Sehzadebaşi, tel. 1/522–84–26. 30 rooms with bath. No credit cards.*

Barut's Guesthouse. Quiet and secluded and in the heart of Old Istanbul, Barut's has a roof terrace overlooking the Sea of Marmara. The owners, Hikmet and Fuson Barut, run this friendly, pleasant establishment. The foyer has a modern art gallery. *Ishakpaşa Cad. 8, Sultanahmet, tel. 1/520–12–27. 22 rooms with bath. No credit cards.*

Büyük Londra. This is another old Victorian hotel, similar to the Pera Palace, that has grown old gracefully. *Meşrutiyet Cad. 117, Tepebaşl, tel. 1/145–06–70. 42 rooms with bath. No credit cards.*

Inexpensive **Berk Guest House.** Clean and exceptionally comfortable, this is run by an English-speaking couple, Gungor and Nevin Evrensel. Two rooms have balconies overlooking a garden. *Kutluğün Sok. 27, Cankurtaran, Sultanahmet, tel. 1/511–07–37. 7 rooms with bath. No restaurant. No credit cards.*

Plaza. This is an older-style, well-run hotel overlooking the Bosporous. *Siraselviler Cad. Arslanyatağı Sok. 19, Taksim, tel. 1/145–32–73. 18 rooms with bath. No credit cards.*

The Arts

Entertainment in Istanbul ranges from the **Istanbul International Festival**—held late June through mid-July and attracting internationally renowned artists and performers—to local folklore and theatrical groups, some amateur, some professional. Because there is no central ticket agency, ask your hotel to help you. You may also pick up tickets at the box office or through a local tourist office.

For tickets to the Istanbul International Festival, apply to the **Istanbul Foundation for Culture and Arts** (Kültür ve Sanat Vakfı, Yildiz, Besiktas, tel. 1/160–45–33 and 1/160–90–72). Performances, which include modern and classical music, ballet, opera, and theater, are given throughout the city in historic buildings, such as St. Irene Church and Rumeli Castle. The highlight of the festival is the performance of Mozart's opera *Abduction from the Seraglio*, at Topkapı Palace, the site that inspired the opera.

Concerts Tickets for performances at the main concert hall, **Atatürk Kültür Merkezi,** are available from the box office at Taksim Square (tel. 1/143–54–00). From October through May, the **Istanbul State Symphony** gives performances here. It's also the location for ballet and dance companies. The Touring and Automobile Association organizes chamber music performances at **Beyaz Kösk** and **Hidiv Kasri,** two 19th-century mini-palaces. For information, contact the **Touring and Automobile Association** (Halaskargazi Cad. 364, Şişli, tel. 1/146–70–90).

Film The **Emek** (Istiklal Cad. 126, Beyoğlu, tel. 1/144–84–39) often shows English-language films.

Entertainment and Nightlife

Bars and Nightclubs **Kulis** (Cumhuriyet Cad. 117, tel. 1/146–93–45), an all-night hangout for actors and writers, offers good piano music. Open daily 10 PM to 5 AM. Local young professionals patronize **Zihni** (Bronz Sok. 21, Tesvikiye, Macka) for lunch or evening cocktails. Open daily noon to 10 PM.

A well-established nightclub, where you can dine, dance, and watch belly-dancing shows, is **Kervansaray** (Cumhuriyet Cad. 30, Elmadağ, tel. 1/147–16–30). Open daily 8 PM to midnight. Two other good places for floor shows are **Balim** (Kemerhatun Mah. Hamalbaşi Cad. 8, Beyoğlu, tel. 1/149–56–08), and **Olimpia** (Acar Sok. Tomtom Mah., off Istiklal Cad., tel. 1/144–94–56).

Jazz **Bilsak** (Soğanci Sok. 7, Siraselviler Cad., tel. 1/143–28–99) is an easygoing restaurant and jazz bar, where local groups and singers sometimes perform.

Discos A popular disco with a lively atmosphere is **Hydromel** (Cumhuriyet Cad. 12, Elmadağ, tel. 1/140–58–93). In the summer, it's open from 9 PM to 2 AM. **Club 29** (Iskele Cad. Fevit Tek Sok 1, Moda., tel. 1/338–10–88) is suitable for all ages and has a restaurant. **Regine** (Cumhuriyet Cad. 16, Elmadağ, tel. 1/146–74–49) is an upscale disco-nightclub that is open from 10 PM to 4 AM.

Central Anatolia——Cappadocia

Cappadocia, an area filled with ruins of ancient civilizations, is in the eastern part of Anatolia, the peninsula that comprises Asia Minor. Cappadocia has changed little over the centuries.

People travel between their farms and villages in horse-drawn carts, women drape their houses with strings of apricots and paprika for drying in the sun, and nomads pitch their black tents beside wheat and sunflower fields and cook on tiny fires that send smoke billowing through the tops of the tents. And in the distance, a minaret pierces the sky.

Getting Around

By Car There are good roads between Istanbul and the main cities of Anatolia—Ankara (the capital of Turkey), Konya, and Kyseri. The highways are generally well maintained and lead to all the major sites. Minor roads are full of potholes and are very rough. On narrow, winding roads, look out for oncoming trucks, whose drivers apparently don't believe in staying on their side of the road.

By Bus There is a good interlinking bus network between most towns and cities, and fares are reasonable.

By Train Though there are frequent trains between the main cities, they are almost nonexistent between small towns. It's much quicker to take a bus.

By Taxi Drivers are usually willing to take you to historical sites out of town, for reasonable fares.

By Bicycle Bicycling in cities and large towns is suicidal. It's less dangerous in remote areas and in small villages where there's little traffic. Even in remote areas, it's wise to get off the road at the sound of an approaching car.

Guided Tours

Since the Cappadocia area is so vast, you'll need at least two days to see the main sights. If you are driving, consider hiring a guide for about $20 a day. Local tourist offices and hotels will be able to recommend guides and excursions.

Tourist Information

Check with local tourist offices for names of travel agencies and English-speaking guides.

Aksaray. Hükümet Konagi, tel. 4811/2474).
Antalya. Cumhuriyet Cad. 91, tel. 311/117–47).
Nevsehir. Meteris Mah. Osmanli Cad. 37, tel. 4851/1137.
Ürgüp. Kayseri Cad. 37, tel. 4868/1059.

Exploring

The resort of **Antalya,** on the Mediterranean, is a good base for several worthwhile excursions. The city is on a beautifully restored harbor and filled with narrow streets lined with small houses, restaurants, and pansiyons. On the hilltop is a tea garden, where you can enjoy tea made in an old-fashioned samovar and look across the bay to the Taurus Mountains that parallel the coast. To the right of the port is the 13th-century **Fluted Minaret** (*Yivli Minare*).

An hour's drive from Antalya is **Termessos,** which has an almost complete Roman amphitheater built on a mountainside and the unexcavated remains of a Roman city on the other side of the

Central Anatolia and Cappadocia

Kızılırmak

Afyon

Lake Tuz

Avanos
Üçhisar — Kayseri
Nevşehir — Göreme
Ürgüp
Derinkuyu
Kaymaklı

Akşehir

Aksaray

Niğde

L. Eğridir

Sultan Han

Bor

L. Beyşehir

Konya

Egridir

Çatalhuyuk

Karapinar

Isparta

Behşehir

Eregli

Bucak

Cumra

Ayranci

Karaman

Bozkir

Kara Dag ▲

Termessos

Perge

T A U R U S

M O U N T A I N S

Aspendos

Antalya

Side

Manavgat

Göksu

Tarsus

Mersin

Adana

Kemer

*Gulf of
Anatolia*

Alanya

Ermenek

Mut

Erdemli

Karates

Gazipasa

Silifke

*Gulf of
Alexandretta*

Anamur

Aydinik

Ovacik

Seyhan

Mediterranean Sea

NORTHERN PORTION OF CYPRUS
OCCUPIED BY TURKEY

0 ——— 50 miles

0 ——— 75 km

N

CYPRUS

mountain. **Perge,** 11 miles (19 kilometers) east of Termessos, has many Roman ruins to explore. You can climb up a 22,000-seat ancient amphitheater, walk down a restored colonnaded street, visit well-preserved thermal baths and a Roman basilica, and see the spot where **St. Paul** preached his first sermon, in AD 45. Nearby, to the north, is **Aspendos,** which contains Anatolia's best-preserved amphitheater. The acoustics are so fine that modern-day performers don't need microphones or amplifiers.

Konya, home of the **Whirling Dervishes,** is reached by driving north from Antalya past **Lakes Eğridir and Beyşhir.** The Whirling Dervishes is a religious order founded in the 13th century by Melvana, a Muslim mystic, who said, "There are many ways of knowing God. I choose the dance and music." You can see the dervishes whirl to the sounds of a flute at the annual commemorative rites held in Konya in early December. Tickets are available from travel agencies or **Konya Turizm Vakfi** (tel. 331–162–55).

Sultan Han, 59 miles (95 kilometers) northeast of Konya, is Anatolia's largest and best-preserved caravansery, once a place of rest and shelter for travelers and their camels plying the ancient trade routes. Traditionally, caravanseries opened into vast courtyards from private and public rooms and had kitchens, a bathhouse, and a small mosque. Lodging was free because these were run by religious foundations funded by sultans. Caravanseries were built between 20 and 25 miles (32 and 40 kilometers) apart, a comfortable day's journey for a camel laden with goods.

Cappadocia roughly forms the triangular area between **Kayseri, Nevşehir,** and **Niğde.** Most of the main sights are within an even smaller triangular area linked by **Ürgup, Göreme,** and **Avanos.** Ürgup is the center from which to explore the villages and the best place to shop, as well as to arrange tours.

On the edge of Cappadocia is **Aksaray,** where the landscape is stark and lunarlike. It was formed by prehistoric volcanic eruptions that dumped layers of mud, ashes, and lava on the area. Eventually the ground turned to *tufa* (soft, porous rock). Rain, snow, and wind created a fantasyland of rock formations resembling chimneys, cones, needles, pillars, and pyramids, often topped by perfectly balanced gigantic slabs of rock. Then came earthquakes to add vast valleys, and oxidation to give the area the final artistic touch: rocks "painted" yellow, pink, red, russet, and gray-violet.

The softness of the rock in this area was ideal for hollowing out cave dwellings and forming defenses from invading armies. The Cappadocians carved out about 40 underground cities, with some structures as deep as 20 stories underground. The largest of these cities housed 20,000 people. Each had dormitories, dining halls, sewage disposal systems, ventilation chimneys, a cemetery, and a prison. Large millstones sealed off the entrances from enemies. Two of these cities are open to the public, one at **Derinkuyu,** 13 miles (21 kilometers) south of Nevsehir, and the other at **Kaymaklı,** 19 miles (30 kilometers) south of Nevsehir. *Admission: 400 TL. Open daily 8–noon and 1–5.*

The Christians also hid in these underground cities when the Islamic forces swept through Cappadocia in the 7th century. Some of the earliest relics of Christianity are to be found in the **Goreme Valley,** a few miles east of Nevsehir. There are dozens of old churches and monasteries covered by frescoes. For a history of the area, visit the **Aksaray Open-Air Museum.** *Admission: 600 TL. Open daily 8:30–5.*

Dining and Lodging

For details and price category definitions, *see* Dining and Lodging in Essential Information.

Antalya **Talya.** This is a luxurious resort hotel with its own beach that
Lodging you reach by taking an elevator down the side of a cliff. From every angle there's a view of the sea. It has a five-star rating and gets booked up quickly in high season. *Fevzi Cakmak Cad., tel 311/156–00. 150 rooms with bath. Facilities: disco, restaurant, pool, game room. AE, DC, MC, V. Very Expensive.*
Turban Adalya. Built in 1869 as a bank, Turban Adalya has been imaginatively transformed into a luxurious hotel overlooking the colorful fishing port. *Kaleici, tel. 311/180–66. 28 rooms with bath. Facilities: restaurant. AE, DC. Expensive.*
Altun Pansiyon. Near the Fluted Minaret and minutes from the seaport, this is a recent addition to Antalya's hotels. The staff is extremely helpful. It has a well-stocked bar and a pleasant courtyard. *Kaleici Mev., tel. 311/166–24. 15 rooms, some with showers. No credit cards. Inexpensive.*

Konya **Basak Palas.** An older but charming small hotel, Basak Palas
Lodging has all the comforts. *Hukumet Alani 3, tel. 331/113–38. 40 rooms, most with bath. No credit cards. Moderate.*

Ürgüp **Hanedan.** Located in the cellar of an old Greek house,
Dining Hanedan is on a hill a short distance from town. You can sit on
the terrace and watch the sunset across the plains toward the
mountains. The food is very good and presented with flair.
Nevsehir Yolu Uzen, tel. 4868/1266. Dress: informal. Reservations not necessary. No credit cards. Moderate.

Lodging **Buyuk.** Located in the center of town, this is a friendly hotel
that features folk dancing in the evenings—you're encouraged
to join in, but can just sit back and watch if you prefer. *Kayseri
Cad., tel. 4868/1060. 49 rooms with bath. No credit cards. Moderate.*

Hitit. The family-run Hitit is a comfortable, small hotel with a
restaurant serving basic but enjoyable food. *Dumlupinar Cad.
54, tel. 4868/1481. 15 rooms without bath. No credit cards. Inexpensive.*

Hotel Ozata. This is an ideal hotel if you're on a tight budget.
It's a clean, family-run place, just outside the center of town.
*Atatürk Bulvari 56, tel. 4868/1355. 32 rooms with bath. No
credit cards. Inexpensive.*

Mediterranean Turkey

Until the mid-1970s, Turkey's southwest coast was inaccessible
to all but the most determined travelers—those intrepid souls
in four-wheel-drive vehicles or on the backs of donkeys. Today,
well-maintained highways wind through the area and jets full
of tourists arrive at the new Dalaman Airport.

Thanks to strict developmental control, the area has not been
glutted with high-rise hotels and condos, but has maintained
its Turkish flavor, with low, whitewashed buildings and tiled
roofs. The beaches are clean, and you can swim and snorkel in
turquoise waters so clear that you can see fish 20 feet (6 meters)
below. There are excellent outdoor cafés and seafood restaurants in which to dine, and you won't find a shortage of bars,
discos, and nightclubs.

Getting Around

By Car Although the highways between towns are well maintained,
the smaller roads are usually unpaved and very rough.

By Boat There are lots of coves and picnic areas accessible only by boat.
For a small fee, local fishermen will take you to and from the
coves; also, you can take one of the many water taxis. Or charter a small yacht, with or without skipper, at the marinas of
Bodrum and Marmaris. Many people charter boats and join
small flotillas that leave the marinas daily for sightseeing in the
summer. One of the most enjoyable ways to see the coast is to
take a one- or two-week **Blue Voyage** cruise on a *gulet*, a wooden
craft with a full crew. There are also three-night **Mini Blue Voyage** trips for scuba divers and snorkelers.

Guided Tours and Tourist Information

Local tourist offices list all the guided tours for the area and
will also arrange for local guides.

Bodrum. Eylül Meyd. 12, tel. 6141/1091.
Dalaman. Dalaman Airport, tel. 1220.

Datca. Iskele Mah. Belediye Binasi, tel. 6145/1163.
Fethiye. Iskele Meyd. 1, tel. 6151/1527.
Kas. Cumhuriyet Meyd. 6, tel. 3226/1238.
Marmaris. Iskele Meyd. 39, tel. 6121/1035.

Exploring

Bodrum Bodrum, which sits between two crescent-shaped bays, has for years been the favorite haunt of the Turkish upper classes. Today, the elite are joined by thousands of foreign visitors, and the area is filling rapidly with hotels and guest houses, cafés, restaurants, and discos. Many compare it to St. Tropez on the French Riviera. Fortunately, it is still beautiful and unspoiled, with gleaming whitewashed buildings covered with bougainvillea and magnificent unfettered vistas of the bays.

People flock to Bodrum not for its beach, which is a disappointment, but for its fine dining and nightlife. You'll find beautiful beaches in the outlying villages on the peninsula—**Torba, Türkbükü, Yalikavak, Turgutreis, Akyarlar, Ortakent Bitez, and Gümbet.** Easy to reach by mini-bus or dolmuş, these villages are about an hour's drive away and have clean hotels and plenty of outdoor restaurants.

One of the outstanding sights in Bodrum is **Bodrum Castle,** known as the **Castle of St. Peter.** Located between the two bays, the castle was built by crusaders in the 11th century. It has beautiful gardens and a **Museum of Underwater Archaeology.** *Castle and museum open June–mid-Sept., daily 8:30–noon and 3–7; mid-Sept.–May, daily 8–noon and 1–5. Admission: 400 TL.*

The peninsula is downright littered with ancient Greek and Roman ruins, although getting to some of them involves driving over rough dirt roads. Three miles (5 kilometers) from Bodrum is **Halikarnas,** a well-preserved 10,000-seat Greek amphitheater, built in the 1st century BC and still used for town festivals.

Marmaris Another beach resort situated in the middle of two bays is Marmaris, which has some of the best sailing on the Mediterranean. Take Route 400 from Bodrum, first heading east, then south. You'll climb steep, winding mountain passes, with cliffs that drop straight into the sea. The final 19 miles (30 kilometers) into Marmaris is a broad boulevard lined with eucalyptus trees.

Marmaris, like Bodrum, is a sophisticated resort with boutiques, elegant restaurants, and plenty of nightlife. Nearby are quiet villages, easy to reach by boat or taxi. One of these is **Datca,** near **Knidos,** where you can see the ruins of Aphrodite's circular temple and an ancient theater. By road, Knidos is 21 very rough miles (34 kilometers) from Marmaris. It's easier and quicker to take a boat. Another town is **Turunc,** worth a day's visit, especially for its beaches and the restaurant at the **Turunc Bay Yacht Club,** where you can dine on a small terrace built into a hill above a sandy cove, surrounded by mountains and pine forests.

Boat excursions from Marmaris will take you to the **Dalyan delta,** breeding grounds of the loggerhead turtle. Smaller boats will take you farther upstream to the ruins of the acropolis at **Kaunus.** It's a steep climb to the top of the acropolis, but on the way down you can reward yourself with a soak in one of the hot springs that dot the hillside. The area is in a wildlife preserve,

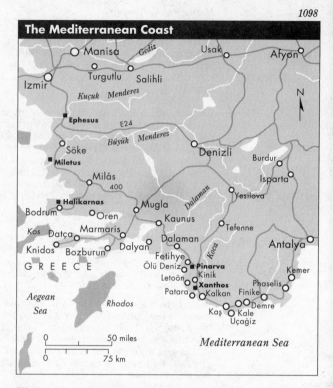

The Mediterranean Coast

filled with such birds as kingfishers, kestrels, egrets, and cranes.

Fetihye   Fetihye, 80 miles (130 kilometers) from Bodrum, was rebuilt after the original town was destroyed in an earthquake in 1957. The town is especially appealing at night, when residents promenade along the lighted harbor or relax in their gardens sipping tea. Although modern in appearance, it's still an old-fashioned agricultural community, where goats and sheep are herded along the main roads on their way to market.

Ölü Deniz   One of Turkey's greatest natural wonders is Ölü Deniz, an azure lagoon flanked by long, white beaches. The area is about 13 miles (15 kilometers) from Fetihye and can be reached by ferry. There are a few wooden chalets in camping grounds and one beachfront hotel. Opposite the beach, you'll find small restaurants with rooftop bars, many with live music that goes on all night. One of the beachside restaurants, **Ada Kamp,** serves excellent lobsters and barbecued jumbo shrimp. The area around the lagoon is a national park.

Southeast of Fetihye, near Route 400, are several ancient sites, including the ruins of **Pinara,** one of the most important cities of the former Roman province of Lycia. Near Pinara, up a steep and strenuous dirt road, you'll find nearly 200 Roman tombs cut honeycomb-fashion into the face of the cliffs.

Xanthos   Return to Route 400 and head south toward the village of Kinik. At Kinik leave the main highway and take a mile-long bumpy road to Xanthos, another major city of ancient Lycia. It was excavated in 1838 and much of what was found here is now in the

British Museum in London. What's left is still well worth the bumpy ride: the **acropolis,** the **Tomb of Harpies,** some plaster-cast reliefs, and ruins of some **Byzantine buildings.**

Patara and Kalkan Ten minutes from Xanthos is Patara, once the city's port. At Patara, you'll find ruins scattered around the marshes and sand dunes. The area's long, wide beaches remain beautiful and un-spoiled, despite the fact that they attract hundreds of Turkish families and tourists. You can find two small restaurants at the beach and some makeshift stalls with cold drinks for sale. The nearest place to stay is **Kalkan,** a fishing village 20 minutes away by minibus. Kalkan has plenty of small hotels, guest houses, and restaurants with roof terraces—ideal spots from which to watch sunsets across the bay. Its waterfront is lined with excellent seafood restaurants. From Kalkan, which has a small rocky beach, you can take a boat to nearby sandy coves and to the phosphorescent **Blue Caves,** where seals frolic.

Kaş Kaş, another fishing village that has become a popular resort, is also developing into a major yachting center. Although luxu-ry hotels have replaced many of the tiny houses on the hills, there are still plenty of old-fashioned pensiyons for those on a budget. One of the attractions here is the underwater city of **Kekova,** where you can look overboard and see ancient Roman and Greek columns that were once part of a thriving city before the area was flooded. Kekova is especially popular with scuba divers and snorkelers. Motorboats leave daily at 9:30 AM. Two interesting side trips from Kaş by boat include a visit to **Kale,** where you can roam through a Byzantine fortress at the top of a steep hill, and **Demre,** site of **St. Nicholas's Basilica,** built soon after the saint's death in the 4th century. His remains were stolen and taken to Bari, Italy, in 1087. St. Nicholas, the origi-nal Santa Claus, was a bishop of Myra in Asia Minor.

Dining and Lodging

For details and price category definitions, *see* Dining and Lodging in Essential Information.

Bodrum **Manzara Aparhotel.** On a hill looking across the bay toward
Lodging Bodrum Castle, the Manzara is a group of 20 small apartments, each with living room, kitchen, and terrace. At peak times, you may have to pay half-board. *Kumbahce Mah, Meteoroloji Yani, tel. 6141/1719. Facilities: restaurant, outdoor pool. AE, DC, MC, V. Expensive.*
Merhaba Pansiyon. Here, on the waterfront, you'll find a beau-tiful roof terrace and simply furnished but clean rooms. *Akasya Sok. 5, tel. 6141/2115. No credit cards. Inexpensive.*

Fetihye **Ülgen.** Travelers on a budget will find the Ülgen a pleasant,
Lodging simply furnished pansiyon. *Cumhuriyet Mah. Pasptir Mevki 3, Merdivenli Yokusu, tel. 6151/3491. No credit cards. Inexpen-sive.*

Kalkan **Kalkan Han.** A rambling old house in the back part of the vil-
Lodging lage, the Kalkan Han has a special treat for visitors: a roof terrace with sweeping views of the bay, a perfect place to enjoy breakfast. *Koyici Mev., tel 3215/151. 16 rooms with bath. No credit cards. Moderate. Closed Nov.–Apr.*

Ölü Deniz **Beyaz Yunus.** Wicker chairs and wooden floors fill this domed
Dining restaurant whose name means "white dolphin." The most ele-gant restaurant in the area, it's situated on a promontory near

Padirali and serves Continental and Turkish cuisine, imaginatively prepared and presented. *No telephone. Dress: informal. Reservations not necessary. No credit cards. Expensive.*

Kebapici Salonu. You can grill meat at your table in this outdoor restaurant, where tables and chairs are clustered around trees in a field. Meals are served with *meze* (appetizers), salad, and wine. *Behind Han Camp, no telephone. Dress: informal. Reservations not necessary. No credit cards. Inexpensive.*

Lodging **Meri Oteli.** Located on a steep incline above the lagoon, this is a series of bungalows, with rooms a bit down-at-the-heel but clean. These are the only accommodations at the lagoon. *Tel. 6151/1. 75 rooms with bath. Facilities: restaurant. AE, DC, MC, V. Moderate.*

Balikci Han. This delightful pansiyon is in a converted 19th-century inn, directly on the waterfront. *Tel. 3215/75. 7 rooms with bath. No credit cards. Inexpensive.*

Kaş **Mercan.** On the eastern side of the harbor, the Mercan serves
Dining good, basic Turkish food in an attractive open-air setting. The water is so close you can actually hear fish jumping. *Hukumet Cad. Dress: informal. Reservations not necessary. No credit cards. Moderate.*

Lodging **Kaş Oteli.** This hotel has wonderful views of the Greek island of Kastellorizo. There's good swimming off the rocks in front of the hotel, or you can laze in the sun with drinks and snacks from the bar or restaurant. *Hastana Cad. 15, tel. 3226/1271. No credit cards. Closed Nov.–Apr. Moderate.*

Mimosa. This is a new hotel conveniently located on a hill near the bus station, with plain but perfectly adequate rooms, all with balconies and views. *Elmali Cad., tel 3226/1272. 20 rooms with bath. No credit cards. Moderate.*

Çan Otel. Turkish carpets and antiques grace this village house that's been lovingly restored and turned into a pensiyon. It's on a tiny side street near the harbor. *Off Hukumet Cad., tel. 3226/1441. No credit cards. Inexpensive.*

Aegean Turkey

Some of the finest reconstructed Greek and Roman cities, including the fabled **Pergamum, Ephesus, Aphrodisias,** and **Troy,** are to be found in this region of Turkey. Bright yellow road signs pointing to historical sites or to those currently undergoing excavation are literally everywhere here. There are so many Greek and Roman ruins, in fact, that some haven't yet been excavated and others are going to seed.

Grand or small, all the sites are steeped in atmosphere and are best explored early in the morning or late in the afternoon when there are fewer crowds.

Getting Around

The E24 from Canakkale follows the coast until it turns inland at Kusadasi to meet the Mediterranean again at Antalya. All the towns on the itinerary are served by direct bus routes, and there are connecting services to the ancient sites.

Guided Tours

The travel agencies in all the major towns offer organized tours of the historical sites. **Troy-Anzac Tours** (tel. 1961/1447 or 1961/1449), in central Canakkale, has guided tours of the battlefields at Gallipoli. The tour takes about three hours and costs about 11,000 TL, per person. Travel agencies along Teyyare Caddesi in Kusadası offer escorted tours to Ephesus; Priene, Miletus, and Didyma; and Aphrodisias and Pamukkale.

Tourist Information

Contact the tourist office in each town for names of travel agencies and licensed tour guides.

Ayvalak. Yat Limani Karisi, tel. 6631/2122.
Bergama. Zafer Mah. Izmir Cad. 54, tel. 1862.
Bursa. Atatürk Cad., Ulu Cami Parki 64, tel. 241/123–59; and Cemal Nadir Cad., Tophane, tel. 241/133–68.
Canakkale. Iskele Meyd. 67, tel. 1961/1187.
Cesme. Iskele Meyd. 8, tel. 5492/6653.
Izmir. G.O.P. Bulv. Buyuk Efes Oteli Alti, tel. 51/142–147.
Kusadası. Iskele Meyd. tel. 6361/1103.

Exploring

Bursa Bursa, the first capital of the Ottoman Empire, is known as *Yeşil* (Green) Bursa, not only because of its many trees and parks but also because of its **Yeşil Cami** (Green Mosque) and **Yeşil Turbe** (Green Mausoleum). Both the mosque and mausoleum derive their names from the green tiles that line the interior of the buildings. They are located opposite each other on Yeşil Caddesi (Green Avenue). Bursa is also the site of **Ülüdag** (the Great Mountain), Turkey's most popular ski resort. To fully appreciate why the town is called Green Bursa, take a ride on the *teleferik* (cable car) up the mountain for a panoramic view.

The town square is called **Heykel,** which means statue, and is named for its statue of Atatürk. Off Heykel, along Atatürk Caddesi, is the **Ulu Cami** (Great Mosque) with its distinctive silhouette of 20 domes. Next to Ulu Cami, by the park, is **Koza Han,** a restored silk market in a two-story caravansery located within the town's covered bazaar.

A spa since Roman times, Bursa has thermal baths built on the slopes of Cekirge, a suburb with many hotels and guest houses that offer *celiks* (mineral baths) as part of the package.

Canakkale, at the northernmost tip of the Aegean coast, is 5½ hours west of Bursa by bus. This is a good stopping off point if you're heading for the battlefields of Gallipoli.

Troy The ruins of ancient Troy are 40 minutes southwest of Canakkale. Long thought to be simply an imaginary city from Homer's *Iliad*, Troy was excavated in the 1870s by Heinrich Schliemann, a German amateur archaeologist. While others laughed at him, he poured his considerable wealth into the excavations and had the last laugh: He found the remains not only of the fabled Troy but also of nine successive civilizations, one on top of the other, dating back 5,000 years. Considering Troy's fame, the site is surprisingly small. It's best to take a guided tour to appreciate fully the significance of this discovery and the unwavering passion of the man who proved that Troy was not just another ancient myth.

The E24 highway leads around the **Gulf of Edremit,** a glorious area of olive groves, pine forests, and small seaside resorts patronized more by Turks than by foreign visitors. Colorful tea gardens sprawl along the shores, and good seafood restaurants abound, most of them serving plates heaped with oysters.

Some worthwhile nearby villages include **Behram Kale** (a short detour off E24 at Ayvalik), where you'll find the ruins of **Assos,** an ancient Greek town; **Akcay,** with its hot springs and thermal baths; and **Oren,** which has camping grounds nearby.

Ayvalik, three miles (5 kilometers) off the main bus route, between Canakkale and Izmir, is an ideal place to stay while visiting the ruins of ancient **Pergamum,** 24 miles (40 kilometers) away. From Ayvalik you can take boats to **Ali Bey Adasi,** a tiny island with pleasant waterfront restaurants, and to the Greek island of Lesbos.

Pergamum

Pergamum is reached by driving southeast along E24 following the signs toward Bergama, the modern-day name of the ancient Greek-Roman site. If you're traveling by bus, be certain it is going all the way to Bergama, or you'll find yourself dropped off at the turn-in, five miles (8 kilometers) from the site.

Because the ruins of Pergamum are spread out over several miles, it's best to take a taxi from one site to the next. The most noteworthy places are the **Asklepieion,** the **Archaeological Museum,** the **Red Hall,** and the **Acropolis.**

Pergamum's glory peaked during the Greek Attalid dynasty (214–133 BC), when it was one of the world's most magnificent architectural and artistic centers—especially so under the rule of Eumenes II, who lavished his great wealth on the city. Greek rule continued until 133 BC, when the mad Attalus III died, bequeathing the entire kingdom to Rome.

The most famous building at the acropolis is the **library,** which once contained a collection of 200,000 books, all on papyrus. The library's collection was second only to the one in Alexandria, Egypt. When the troops of Julius Caesar burned down the library in Alexandria, Mark Antony consoled Cleopatra by shipping the entire collection of books from Pergamum to Alexandria. These, too, went up in flames 400 years later however, in wars between Muslims and Christians. *Library. Admission: 400 TL. Open daily 9–noon and 1–7.*

All that remains of the original **Temple of Zeus** are its foundations. It was excavated by German archaeologists who sent every unearthed stone to the Pergamum Museum in what is now East Berlin.

On the opposite side of Pergamum is **Kizil Avlu** (Red Hall), a huge basilica made of red brick. Farther up the hill is the **Ethnological Museum,** where you can see local costumes and carpets, and the **Archaeological Museum,** opposite the tourist office. *Admission: 500 TL. Both open summer, 9–noon and 1–7; winter, 9–noon and 1–5:30.*

The **Asklepieion** was the temple of Asklepios, god of medicine and forefather of many of today's holistic healing techniques,

The Aegean Coast

Samothrace • Gallipoli
• Lapseki
Imroz • Canakkale • Biga
Sea of Marmara
• Bandirma
Dardanelles E24
Gönen
• Gönen
Truva (Troy) ■
Ezine • *Kaz Dagi* (Mt. Ida) ▲
Ayvacik Akçay Ören • Susurluk
Behram Kale
Gulf of Edremit • Edremit • Balikesir
Kirmasti
Oraneli
Lesbos • Ayvalik
Bakir
Bursa • Ülüdag ▲
N
Gulf of Çandarli
■ Bergama (Pergamum)
• Sindirgi
Foça Akhisar
Karaburun *Gediz* • Manisa
Küçükbahçe *Gulf of Izmir* • Turgutlu
Khios Çeşme 300 Izmir (Smyrna) • Sahlihli
Usak
Seferihisar Tire • *Küçuk Menderes*
Colophon ■ Selçuk
Gulf of Kusada Ephesus ■
Ikaria Kuşadasi • Aydin • Nazili E24 • Pamukkale
Samos Priene *Büyük Menderes* Karacasu Sarayköy
Miletus ■ Söke Aphrodisias ■ Denizli
Didyma ■
Altinkum
0 ___ 50 miles
0 ___ 75 km

including massage, dream analysis, auto-suggestion, herbal
remedies, nutrition, and exercise. *Admission: 400 TL. Open
daily 9–noon and 1–7.*

Farther north are the scanty remains of a 50,000-seat **amphitheater,** which in ancient days was often partially flooded with
river water so people could be entertained by watching battles
between crocodiles and hippos.

Izmir The coastal area between Bergama and Izmir was once thick
with ancient Greek settlements. Today only Izmir remains.
Called Smyrna by the Greeks, it was a vital trading port that
was often ravaged by wars and earthquakes. Izmir was completely destroyed by a fire in 1922 following Turkey's War of
Independence against Greece. The war was a bloody battle to
win back the Aegean coast, which had been given to the Greeks
in the 1920 Treaty of Sevres. Atatürk was in Izmir helping to
celebrate the victory when celebrations soon turned to horror
as the fire engulfed the city.

After the city was rebuilt quickly, it became known by its
Turkish name, Izmir. It's a beautiful, modern city filled with
wide boulevards and apartment houses and office buildings.
The center of the city is **Kültürpark,** a large green park that is
the site of Izmir's industrial fair from late August to late September, a time when most hotels are full.

On top of Izmir's highest hill is the **Kadifekale (Velvet Fortress),**
built by Alexander the Great in 4 BC. It is easily reached by
dolmuş and is one of the few ancient ruins that was not destroyed in the fire. At the foot of the hill is the restored **Agora,**

the market of ancient Smyrna. The modern-day marketplace is in **Konak Square,** a maze of tiny streets filled with shops and covered stalls. *Open 8–8. Closed Sun.*

The road southwest of Konak Square leads to a coastal road and Route 300, lined with beaches and spas. Although the entire peninsula is filled with resorts, the area is too remote as a base for sightseeing.

Kusadası Kusadası, about 50 miles (80 kilometers) south of Izmir, has grown since the late 1970s from a fishing village into a sprawling, hyperactive town geared to serving thousands of tourists who visit the nearby ruins and beaches. Although it's packed with curio shops, Kusadası has managed to retain a pleasant atmosphere.

Ephesus The major attraction near Kusadası is Ephesus, a city created by the Ionians in the 11th century BC and now one of the grandest reconstructed ancient sites in the world. It is the showpiece of Aegean archaeology. Ephesus was a powerful trading port and the sacred center for the cult of Artemis, Greek goddess of chastity, the moon, and hunting. The Ionians built a temple in her honor, one of the Seven Wonders of the Ancient World. During the Roman period, it became a shrine for the Roman goddess Diana. Today, waterlogged foundations are all that remain of the temple.

Allow yourself at least one full day to tour Ephesus. It's especially appealing out of season, when it can seem like a ghost town with its shimmering, long, white marble road grooved by chariot wheels. In the summer it's packed with tourists, many of them coming off the Greek ships that cruise the Aegean and call at Kusadası. Two of the ancient city's most famous visitors were Mark Antony and Cleopatra.

Some of the splendors you can see here include the two-story **Library of Celsus,** filled with rolls of papyrus; houses of noblemen, with their terraces and courtyards; a 25,000-seat **amphitheater,** still used today during the Selçuk Ephesus Festival of Culture and Art; remains of the municipal baths; and a brothel. *Archaeological zone. Admission: 1,000 TL. Open daily 10–4.*

Selçuk On **Ayasoluk Hill** in Selçuk, 2½ miles (4 kilometers) from Ephesus, is the restored **Basilica of St. John,** containing the tomb of the apostle. Near the entrance to the Basilica is the **Ephesus Museum,** with two statues of Artemis. The museum also has marvelous frescoes and mosaics among its treasures. *Admission: 500 TL. Basilica and museum open daily 9:30–6:30.*

St. Paul and **St. John** preached in both Ephesus and Selçuk and changed the cult of Artemis into the cult of the **Virgin Mary. Meryemana,** three miles (5 kilometers) from Ephesus has the **House of Mary,** thought to have been the place where St. John took the mother of Jesus after the crucifixion and where some believe she ascended to heaven.

Priene and Miletus Priene and Miletus, 25 miles (40 kilometers) from Kusadasi, are sister cities, also founded by the Ionians in 11 BC. Nearby is **Didyma,** a holy sanctuary dedicated to Apollo.

Priene, on top of a steep hill, was an artistic and cultural center; **Miletus,** five miles (8 kilometers) from the sea, was a prosperous port city where commerce reigned supreme. You reach Priene by climbing up the hill and you go on from there to Miletus. Priene's main attraction is the **Temple of Athena,** a spectacular sight, with its five fluted columns and its backdrop of mountains and the fertile plains of the Meander River. You can also see the city's small amphitheater, gymnasium, council chambers, marketplace, and stadium.

Prosperous **Miletus,** a short walk away, was the first Greek city to use coins for money. It also became an Ionian intellectual center and home to such philosophers as Thales, Anaximander, and Anaximenes, all of whom made contributions to mathematics and the natural sciences.

The city's most magnificent building is the **Great Theater,** a remarkably intact 25,000-seat amphitheater built by the Ionians and kept up by the Romans. Climb to the highest seats in the amphitheater for a view across the city to the bay. *Admission: 400 TL. Priene and Miletus open daily 9–6.*

The temple of **Didyma** is reached by a 20-mile (32-kilometer) road called the **Sacred Way,** starting from Miletus at the bay. The temple's oracles were as revered as those of Delphi.

Under the courtyard is a network of corridors whose walls would throw the oracle's voice into deep and ghostly echoes. The messages would then be interpreted by the priests. Fragments of bas-relief include a gigantic **head of Medusa** and a small **statue of Poseidon** and his wife, **Amphitrite.** *Admission: 400 TL. Open daily 9–6.*

Pamukkale Seventy-five miles (120 kilometers) east of Kusadası is Pamukkale, which first appears as an enormous chalky white cliff rising some 330 feet (100 meters) from the plains. Mineral-rich volcanic spring water cascades over basins and natural terraces, crystallizing into white stalactites, curtains of solidified water seemingly suspended in air. The hot springs in the area were popular with the ancient Romans, who believed they had curative powers. You can see the remains of Roman baths among the ruins of nearby **Hierapolis.**

The village of Pamukkale has many small hotels surrounding the hot springs, which are used today by people who still believe that they can cure a variety of problems, including rheumatism. Farther down in the village are inexpensive pansiyons, some also with hot springs.

It's best to stay overnight in Pamukkale before heading on to the ruins of **Aphrodisias,** a city of 60,000 dedicated to Aphrodite, the Greek goddess of love and fertility. It thrived from 1 BC to AD 5. Aphrodisias is reached via **Karacasu,** a good place to stop for lunch at one of its many restaurants, where fresh trout is the local specialty.

Aphrodisias is filled with marble baths, temples, and theaters, all overrun with wild blackberries and pomegranates. Across a field sprinkled with poppies and sunflowers is a well-preserved **stadium,** which was built for 30,000 spectators.

Dining and Lodging

For details and price category definitions, *see* Dining and Lodging in Essential Information.

Ayvalik
Lodging

Buyuk Berk. This is a modern hotel on Ayvalik's best beach, about 2 miles (3 kilometers) from the center of town. *Sarimsakli Mev., tel. 661/2311. 97 rooms with bath. Facilities: outdoor pool, restaurant, disco. AE, DC, MC, V. Moderate.*

Ankara Oteli. Located on Sarimsakli beach, just a few feet from the surf, the Ankara Oteli gives excellent value for the money. *Sarimsakli Mev., tel. 661/1195. 57 rooms with bath. Facilities: café, bar, game room. No credit cards. Inexpensive.*

Bergama
Lodging

Tuscan Bergama Moteli. On the main road leading into Bergama, the Tuscan has a pool fed by hot springs. The rooms are simple and clean. *Izmir Yolu, Cati Mev., tel. 5411/1173. 42 rooms with bath. Facilities: outdoor pool. No credit cards. Moderate.*

Bursa
Dining

Özkent. Located in Kültür Park, the Özkent serves excellent Turkish food in a quiet setting. *Kültür Park, tel. 241/67-666. Dress: informal. Reservations advised. AE, DC, MC, V. Moderate.*

Pagağan. This is another typical Turkish restaurant, with excellent food and friendly service. *Murat Cad. 16, Çekirage, tel. 241/12-761. Dress: informal. Reservations advised. AE, DC, MC, V. Moderate.*

Lodging

Celik Palace. The main attraction of this luxurious five-star hotel is a domed, Roman-style pool fed by hot springs. *Çekirage Cad. 79, tel. 241/61-900. 173 rooms with bath. Facilities: restaurant, bar, pool. AE, DC, M, V. Expensive.*

Ada Pala. Located near Kültür Park, this hotel has an inviting thermal pool. *Murat Cad. 21, tel. 241/61-600. 11 rooms with bath. No credit cards. Moderate.*

Artic. In the center of town, the Artic is a good base for sightseeing. Ask for an inside room because the traffic noise can be fierce. *Fevzi Çakmak Cad. 123, tel. 241/19-500. 63 rooms with bath. No credit cards. Inexpensive.*

Huzur Oteli. Clean and tidy, this hotel is near the Hüdavendigâr Mosque and a good base for sightseeing. Another plus is its friendly staff. *Birinci Murat Camii Bitisgi, tel. 241/68-021. No credit cards. Inexpensive.*

Canakkale, Troy,
and Gallipoli
Lodging

Anafartalar. Located along the waterfront in Canakkale, this is a quiet, pleasant hotel. *Kayserili A. Paşa Cad., tel. 1961/4451. 69 rooms with bath. Facilities: restaurant. No credit cards. Moderate.*

Truva. Near the center of Canakkale, the Truva is an excellent base for sightseeing. *Yaliboyu, tel. 1961/1024. 66 rooms with bath. No credit cards. Moderate.*

Tusan-Truva. Surrounded by a pine forest on a beach at Intepe, north of Troy, the Tusan-Truva is one of the most popular hotels in the area. Be certain to reserve well in advance. *Intepe, E24, tel. 1961/1461. 64 rooms with bath. No credit cards. Closed Oct.–Feb. Moderate.*

Çesme
Lodging

Çesme Kervansaray. Built in 1528 during the reign of Sülyman the Magnificent, the Kervansaray is decorated in traditional Turkish style. It has an excellent restaurant, with outdoor dining in an ancient courtyard. Adjacent to the hotel is a medieval castle. *Cumhuriyet Mey, tel. 5492/6490. 32 rooms with bath. AE, DC, MC, V. Expensive.*

Izmir
Lodging

Büyük Efes. Elegant but showing its age, this hotel is distinguished by a beautiful and relaxing enclosed garden. *Cumhuriyet Mey., tel. 51/1443-00. 296 rooms with bath. Facilities:*

restaurant, outdoor pool, disco. AE, DC, MC, V. Very expensive.

Kismet. Tastefully decorated, the Kismet is a quiet, comfortable hotel with friendly service. *1377 Sok. 9, tel. 51/217–050. 68 rooms with bath. Facilities: restaurant. AE, DC, MC, V. Moderate.*

Kusadası Dining

Sultan Han. Full of atmosphere, with excellent food to boot, Sultan Han is an old house built around a courtyard, where the focal point is a gigantic tree. You can dine in the courtyard or upstairs in small rooms. One of the specialties is fresh seafood, which you select from platters piled high with fish and shellfish of every possible variety. Ask to have your after-dinner coffee served upstairs, where you can sit on cushions at low brass tables. *Bahar Sok. 8, tel. 6361/3849. Jacket and tie. Reservations necessary. No credit cards. Expensive.*

Lodging

Akman. One of the many reasonable priced, family-run pansiyons in and around Kusadasi, Akman is well located on a beach a few minutes from town. *Istiklal Cad. 13, tel. 6361/1501. 46 rooms with bath. No credit cards. Moderate.*

Aran. Although it's quite a climb up the steep hill to this hotel, it's worth it for the view from the roof terrace. *Kaya Aldogan Cad. 4, tel. 6361/1632. 22 rooms with bath. No credit cards. Inexpensive.*

Club Kervansaray. A refurbished, 300-year-old caravansery, this hotel is decorated in the Ottoman style and loaded with charm and atmosphere. It's in the center of town and features a restaurant with a floor show. There's dancing after dinner in the courtyard, where the camels were once kept. *Barbaros Cad., tel. 6361/4115. 38 rooms with bath. Facilities: restaurant, nightclub, bar. No credit cards. Expensive.*

Kismet. Although it's a small hotel, Kismet is run on a grand scale, surrounded by beautifully maintained gardens on a promontory overlooking the marina on one side and the Aegean on the other. Ask for rooms in the garden annex. Its popularity makes reservations a must. *Akyar Mev., tel. 6361/2005. 89 rooms with bath. Facilities: private beach, restaurant. MC, V. Closed Nov.–Mar. Expensive.*

Stella. Set atop a steep hillside outside town, Stella has a very pleasant bar and a beautiful roof terrace. *Bezirgan Sok. 44, tel. 6361/1632. 15 rooms with bath. No credit cards. Moderate.*

Pammukale Lodging

Tusan. The best feature of the Tusan is its pool, one of the most inviting in the area. The rooms are basic and comfortable. The one-story building is at the top of a steep hill. *Tel. 6218/1010. 47 rooms with bath. Facilities: restaurant, outdoor pool. AE, DC, MC, V. Moderate.*

Selçuk Lodging

Hulya. This is a pleasant, family-run pansiyon, where one of the family members is a fisherman who brings in some of his daily catch. You can enjoy a delicious fish meal cooked to order. *Atatürk Cad., Ozgur Sok. 15, tel. 5451/2120. No credit cards. Inexpensive.*

Kale Han. Located in a refurbished stone inn, Kale Han is also a pansiyon run by a warm, welcoming family. *Atatürk Cad. 49, tel. 5451/1154. 18 rooms with bath. No credit cards. Inexpensive.*

34 Yugoslavia

Introduction

"Never the twain shall meet," declared Rudyard Kipling, referring, of course, to East and West. Had modern Yugoslavia existed at the time, he might just have changed his mind.

The line that divided the Roman Empire into Byzantine East and Papal West in the 4th and 5th centuries ran straight through present-day Yugoslavia. A thousand years later, roughly the same boundary divided the Turkish Ottoman Empire from the rest of Europe.

It was along the coast that graceful Venetian Gothic and Italian Renaissance flourished, while Central European Baroque left its greatest imprint on the plains. And deep in the south, glorious medieval Orthodox monasteries survive alongside the slender minarets and domed *hamams* of Islam. The Roman and Cyrillic alphabets spell out more or less the same words, according to whether you're in the north and west or the center and south. And music, customs, costume, and architecture reflect influences that kept two halves of the country poles apart for centuries.

Yugoslavia (land of the South Slavs) first made it onto the map of Europe with the demise of the Hapsburg Empire in 1918, initially as a kingdom, subsequently as a Socialist Federal Republic. The West regards it as Communist rather than Socialist but finds this particular brand of Communism difficult to classify. Small-scale private business thrives; enterprises compete hotly with each other. They've even developed such Western economic ills as unemployment and inflation.

It is a beautiful country, replete with mountain massifs, river gorges, rugged coastline, hundreds of islands, and fertile plains. The biggest mistake anyone can make is to choose one resort and barely move away from it, though all too many visitors do just that. The freedom of your own four wheels is the best answer to Yugoslavia's staggering variety, but escorted bus tours radiate from most resorts, so you can see a lot with very little effort.

Since the tourist boom of the '60s and early '70s, when enthusiastic developers produced uninspired architecture, the Yugoslavs have graduated to much more attractive modern buildings. The plumbing can still be patchy, the service a bit frenetic (especially in high season), but resort facilities and service have acquired a polish that would have been hard to predict in the '50s. That was when the country was still piecing itself together after a war that destroyed 10% of its population, along with most of its industry and communications.

One country, two alphabets, three religions, four languages, five nationalities, six republics, and seven frontiers: That's the easy way to sum it up. But our simple arithmetic merely hints at the reality.

Before You Go

When to Go The tourist season runs from April or May through October. Outside this period, many resort hotels close, but you will find good bargains in those that don't. July and August are the hottest and most crowded months, to be avoided unless you've

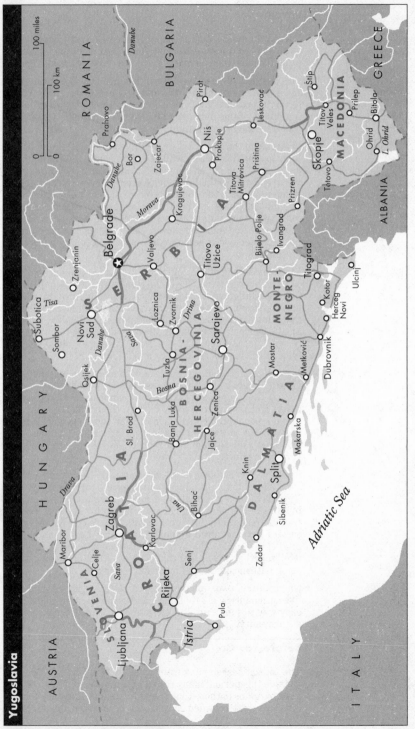

Yugoslavia

planned to attend one of the major festivals. Spring and fall have all the advantages of good weather and reduced rates for accommodations. If you must visit in summer, it's a good idea to split your stay between the coast and the mountains.

Climate Along the coast, winters are relatively mild, although rain can be heavy through April. Summers are hot. There can be strong winds: *bura* (dry, northerly, mainly in winter), *yugo* (humid, southerly, mainly in winter), and *maestral* (steady, generally westerly, and the most frequent). Summer storms are fierce but brief. Inland, summers are extremely hot and the mountains are your best bet; in winter it gets very cold. The main winter sports season is January through March or April, depending on altitude.

The following are the average daily maximum and minimum temperatures for Belgrade.

Jan.	37F	3C	May	73F	23C	Sept.	76F	24C
	26	−3		54	12		56	13
Feb.	42F	5C	June	79F	26C	Oct.	64F	18C
	29	−2		59	15		47	8
Mar.	52F	11C	July	83F	28C	Nov.	51F	11C
	36	2		62	17		39	4
Apr.	64F	18C	Aug.	83F	28C	Dec.	42F	5C
	45	7		62	17		32	0

Currency The unit of currency is the dinar. Bills are in denominations of 50, 100, 500, 1,000, 5,000, 10,000, and 20,000 dinars. Coins are 1, 2, 5, 10, 20, 50, and 100 dinars. Some of the newer coins are a different size and color from the older ones, which are gradually being phased out though they represent the same values. You are allowed to import or export up to 50,000 dinars.

At press time (fall 1988), the exchange rate was 1,400 dinars to the dollar and 2,400 dinars to the pound, but this is constantly changing to match the ferocious rate of inflation. *Don't* exchange more than enough to meet your immediate needs. Traveler's checks can be exchanged at banks, exchange bureaus, travel agencies, and many hotels. Major credit cards—American Express, Diners Club, MasterCard, and Visa—are widely accepted.

What It Will Cost The rate of inflation was running at 160% at press time (fall 1988) and the rate of exchange was constantly changing, so the approximate equivalents in dollars are given. For visitors, prices are very reasonable, but you will notice big variations, in the cost of accommodations for different parts of the country (*see* Lodging). Costs generally drop as you progress inland and south.

Hotel taxes are included in the rates quoted. There is no sales tax. The departure tax at airports for international flights at press time was 4,000 dinars, for domestic flights 1,500 dinars.

Sample Prices Cup of coffee, 40¢; bottle of beer, 60¢; Coca-Cola, 40¢; ham sandwich, 80¢; one-mile taxi ride, $1.30.

Visas U.S. and Canadian citizens require both a valid passport to enter Yugoslavia and a visa. A visa can be obtained free at Yugoslav embassies or, for a small fee, at Yugoslav entry points.

All British citizens need a passport to enter Yugoslavia; visas are not required. If your passport has less than three months' validity, however, you must obtain a Tourist Pass, valid for 30 days, at entry points; these are issued free.

Customs
On Arrival Visitors are permitted to bring in personal effects and normal amounts of photographic, recording, and sports equipment. All travelers 16 and older may also bring in 200 cigarettes or their equivalent in tobacco, one liter of wine, one liter of liquor, a quarter liter of eau de cologne, and small quantities of perfume.

On Departure When you leave, a special permit is needed if you have purchased goods of historical or cultural value. If you have any questions on this point, make sure to ask the seller for instructions while you make your purchase.

Language English is widely spoken among the young and those in the travel industry. Away from tourist areas, you're likely to have some communication problems, although German is understood by many of the older generation.

The main language is Serbo-Croat, an umbrella name for the similar Serbian and Croatian languages understood by most Yugoslavs. Slovene is spoken in Slovenia, Macedonian in Macedonia.

The Roman alphabet is used in the north, the west, and along the coast; the Cyrillic alphabet predominates in the center and south, though road signs and important notices are often in both alphabets. It's a good idea to get a working knowledge of Cyrillic, however, if only to recognize a PECTOPAH for the restaurant that it is.

Getting Around

By Car
Road Conditions Yugoslavia's network of major highways *(autoput)* is expanding, especially the network connecting Zagreb, Belgrade, Niš, and Skopje. Most main roads are good, but often twisting and narrow for the weight of traffic carried in summer. Take care because Yugoslavs are impetuous drivers, and so are many of their visitors. The dirt roads, marked in green on the free, annually revised map available from the Yugoslav National Tourist Office, are usually rough and often spectacular.

Rules of the Road Driving is on the right; at intersections, traffic from the right has priority, except on main highways or where otherwise indicated. The speed limit in cities and towns is 60 kph (37 mph); otherwise it's 80 kph (50 mph), 100 kph (62 mph), or 120 kph (75 mph) as indicated. Seat belts are compulsory. Penalties are severe for drunk driving.

Parking Drivers will have trouble finding parking spaces in summer resorts and larger towns. Facilities range from inexpensive meters, occasional multistory garages, and free areas. Cars parked illegally may be removed by a menacing machine known as the "spider," and retrieval is costly.

Gasoline The price of gasoline is about 55¢ per liter. At the border you can buy gas coupons that allow a 5% reduction, but it's not really worth the hassle.

Breakdowns The Yugoslav Automobile Association (AMSJ) runs a 24-hour breakdown service and a fleet of yellow patrol vehicles marked *Pomoć-Informacije*. To summon help, phone 987. In case of accident, you're legally obliged to call the police (tel. 92) and, in case of injury, ambulance (tel. 94).

By Train Lateral routes link the major inland cities with the coast. With so many mountains, journeys are often slow but scenically rewarding. Car trains are on routes linking Ljubljana, Zagreb, and Belgrade; and Ljubljana and Zagreb with Rijeka, Split, and Sarajevo-Kardeljevo.

By Plane Yugoslavia's national airline (**JAT**) has domestic service with links to 18 centers; **Adria Airways's** network links 12. In summer, you'll need to make reservations well in advance.

By Bus Express buses link main centers, slower ones serve the villages. Reserve a seat if you can (though this is possible only at main terminals) because buses are usually crowded.

By Boat **Jadrolinija** operates an extended network of express services, passenger and car ferries, and hydrofoils linking coastal and island centers. Try to take at least one boat trip during your stay. A hydrofoil trip on the Danube from Belgrade to the Iron Gates (gorge and dam) on the Yugoslav-Romanian border is a wonderful experience. Timetables are available from Yugoslav National Tourist Offices overseas and local travel agencies.

Essential Information

Telephones Pay phones work with 10, 50, and 100 dinar coins. Lift the re-
Local Calls ceiver, insert the coins, and dial: The money is returned if the connection is not made.

International Calls Direct dialing is in service to the United States and Britain, but during high season and in the south insufficient lines can cause long delays. The cheapest way is to call from a post office; you may do the dialing yourself or have the operator do it for you. Either way, you pay after your call. It can cost up to twice as much from your hotel.

Mail At press time, airmail letters to the United States cost 580 di-
Postal Rates nars, postcards 320; to the United Kingdom, airmail letters cost 450 dinars, postcards 240. Prices will certainly have increased by 1989. Make sure you use an airmail label; there are lower rates for surface mail, but it's very slow.

Receiving Mail If you are uncertain about your itinerary, you can collect mail "kept waiting" (Poste Restante) at any post office. There is no charge. American Express (*see* Important Addresses) also offers a free Clients' Mail service and will hold mail up to one month.

Shopping Artisan skills still thrive in Yugoslavia, whether in pottery, wood carving, textiles, embroidery, lace, silver filigree, copperware, leather, or Oriental-style carpets. Almost every district has its specialty. In many regions, companies market wares that have been produced in homes and small factories. The shops run by Narodna Radinost, Jugoexport, Dom, Bosna Folklore, Rukotvorine, and Minceta are all reliable, but it is also worth looking at the many small private boutiques and studios that have proliferated. Look, too, for the work of rising young graphic artists. Many of the better hotels now have duty-free shops (hard currency only) that sell tobacco, liquor, perfume, cameras, electronic goods, and souvenirs.

Opening and Closing Times

Banks. Banks are open weekdays 7–7, Saturday 7–1.
Museums. Museums are normally open 9–1, sometimes 10–12; also 2–6 or 4–7; normally closed one day a week, usually Sunday or Monday. Always check before going.
Shops. Most stores are open weekdays, 8–8, Saturday 8–3. Some close for three or four hours in the middle of the day, and some are open Sunday morning. Markets usually operate in the morning, 5:30–12:30.

National Holidays

January 1 (New Year's Day); January 2; May 1 (Labor Day); May 2; July 4 (Veterans); November 29, 30 (Republic). In addition, in *Serbia:* July 7; in *Macedonia:* August 2, October 11; in *Montenegro:* July 13; in *Slovenia:* July 22, 23; and in *Croatia* and *Bosnia-Herzegovina:* July 27.

Dining

There is a wide selection of restaurants, many of them now privately owned. There are also inexpensive cafeterias, cafés *(kafana)*, and ice cream parlors. If a restaurant name includes the word *riblji*, it specializes in fish. Charcoal-grilled dishes—you'll find them everywhere—are *čevapčiči* (small spiced ground beef or lamb rolls); *ražnjiči* (pieces of pork or veal on skewers); and *pleskavica* (a kind of hamburger with raw onions and red peppers). It is worth being adventurous. Yugoslavia's typically Balkan dishes include various vegetables or leaves (cabbage and grape) stuffed with spiced meats and rice. There are also a variety of savory stews *(čorba)* and extremely rich fish or chicken soups *(paprikaš)*.

Coffee in Slovenia and Croatia is Italian-style espresso and cappuccino; farther south it's more likely to be thick black Turkish coffee *(turska kava)*. Ask for it *bez šećera* if you don't like it sweet. The beer is fairly tasteless, but there are very good wines.

Mealtimes

The main meal is lunch, usually from 1 to 3. Dinner is normally from 7 to 10 PM.

Precautions

It is not necessary to be on your guard here, but if you're worried about the tap water, excellent mineral waters *(mineralni voda)* and concentrated fruit juices *(gusti sok)* are available.

Ratings

Prices are per person and include a first course, main course, and dessert, without wine and tip. The service charge is usually included in the bill, but you can add 5% to 7% if you're satisfied with the service. Best bets are indicated by a star ★. Due to the volatility of the dinar, prices are given in U.S. dollars.

Category	Belgrade and Major Resorts	Other Areas
Very Expensive	over $15	over $12
Expensive	$10–$15	$8–$12
Moderate	$5–$10	$4–$8
Inexpensive	under $5	under $4

Credit Cards

The following credit card abbreviations are used: AE, American Express; DC, Diners Club; MC, MasterCard; V, Visa.

Lodging The Yugoslavs saw the error of their ways before the building boom of the '60s and '70s got out of hand and have avoided the worst excesses of other coastal resorts. Among the newer hotels, tasteful design dominates, as well as the traditional grand or villa styles of the older resorts, although concrete hasn't been banned completely. Local travel agencies will make reservations for you, but you'll run into trouble along the coast in the peak season if you haven't made reservations in advance. Tourist complexes in some resorts can be several miles from the resort itself, so if you like to stroll out of your hotel and feel part of the local scene, make sure of its location.

Hotels Yugoslavian hotels are officially classified Deluxe, A, B, C, or D—all Bs and up, and some Cs, will have all or some rooms with bath or shower. It's difficult to generalize about standards. In main resorts they are generally good, but elsewhere service doesn't always match the amenities, especially as you travel inland and south. Despite a constant program of renovating, some of the newer B-classified hotels are better than some older establishments in the A category. If there's one piece of advice to take to heart, it is that you should *always* take a standard bath plug or rubber drain cover with you when traveling.

Guest Houses You'll find these mostly in Slovenia *(gostilna)* and Croatia *(gostioniča)*. They can be charming as well as inexpensive.

Private Homes Thousands of private rooms are available through local tourist offices and travel agencies. The Yugoslav National Tourist Office publishes a free booklet detailing price ranges and facilities.

Farmhouses Most of these are in Slovenia and offer deals where you have two or three meals, but a growing number are located in other areas. Local tourist offices will have details.

Apartments and Villas A growing number of new complexes along the coast give you the option of renting, with supermarkets, restaurants, and recreational amenities nearby.

Camping The Yugoslav National Tourist Office publishes an annually revised list of sites. These get packed in the summer, so start looking early.

Budget Accommodations During summer months, student hostels become inexpensive lodging for tourists in most main towns. Local tourist offices can advise.

Ratings Prices are for two people in a double room with bath; those at the low end of the scale are off-season rates. All prices include breakfast and tips. Best bets are indicated by a star ★. Due to the volatility of the dinar, prices are given in U.S. dollars.

Category	Belgrade and Major Resorts	Other Areas
Very Expensive	over $120	over $80
Expensive	$70–$120	$50–$80
Moderate	$45–$70	$30–$50
Inexpensive	under $45	under $30

Credit Cards The following credit card abbreviations are used: AE, American Express; DC, Diners Club; MC, MasterCard; V, Visa.

Tipping Yugoslavs are just like the rest of us: They appreciate being rewarded for good service. They'll especially appreciate hard currency, although it's not officially encouraged. *See* Dining, above, for hints on tipping in restaurants. For taxis, add 5%. Train and airport porters have a fixed charge, but check this in advance; you can add 50¢ per bag if they've been helpful. At top hotels, give doormen and bellhops 50¢ per bag; at moderate hotels 30¢. There is no need to tip theater ushers and service station attendants.

Belgrade

Arriving and Departing

By Plane All flights arrive at Belgrade airport at Surčin, 11 miles (18 kilometers) from the city along the highway. For information on arrivals and departures, phone 011/675992 or 011/601424.

Between the Regular JAT buses run from the airport to Trg Sveti Marko (on
Airport and Bulevar revolucije), the Jugoslavija hotel (New Belgrade), and
Downtown the Slavija hotel. The trip by bus will cost about 1,000 dinars; by taxi about 5,000 dinars (these prices may well have doubled by 1989).

By Train The main train station is Belgrade Central, Trg bratstva i jedinstva 2, tel. 011/645822.

By Bus The main bus station is at Železnička 4, tel. 011/624751 or 627049.

By Car Downtown exits off the highway are clearly marked *Centar*.

Getting Around

By Streetcar and You can buy an economical day ticket giving unlimited travel
Bus from ticket offices marked "Duvan," near tram and bus stops. A single ride costs about 850 dinars. Punch your ticket in a machine when you board the vehicle.

By Taxi Taxi meters start at 400 dinars, and rates are quite inexpensive. Taxis are easy to come by, but if you have any problems, phone 011/4443–443 or 011/457–277.

Important Addresses and Numbers

Tourist The main tourist information center is in Terozije's under-
Information ground pedestrian crossing, near the Albanija Palace (open daily 8–8, tel. 011/635343 or 011/635622). Tourist information offices are also at the central train station (open daily, 7 AM–9 PM, tel. 011/646240) and at Belgrade airport (open daily, 7 AM–9 PM, tel. 011/602326).

Embassies U.S. Kneza Miloša 50, tel. 011/645655; **Canadian.** Kneza Miloša 75, tel. 011/644666; **U.K.** Generala Ždanova 46, tel. 011/645055.

Emergencies Police, tel. 92. **Ambulance,** tel. 94. **Doctor,** Boris Kidrič Health Center, Pasterova 1, tel. 011/683755. **Dentist,** Dental Polyclinic, Ivana Milutinovića 15, tel. 011/4443491). **Pharmacies.** The following are open 24 hours: **Prvi Maj,** Maršala Tita 9; **Savski venac,** Nemanjina 2; **Zemun,** Maršala Tita 34.

English Bookstores English-language publications are not always available. You are most likely to find newspapers at the Hotel Moskva and other main hotels, at booths at the train station, the pedestrian subway by the Beograd cinema, or in front of the Beograd department store.

Travel Agencies **American Express,** Atlas Travel Agency, Moše Pijade 11, tel. 011/341471. **Thomas Cook,** KSR, Moše Pijade 21, tel. 011/335331.

Guided Tours

Orientation Tours One of the main agencies for sightseeing tours is **Putnik,** Dragoslava Jovanovića 1, Tel. 011/320697 or 011/332591. It has a three-hour tour, covering the main sights, as well as a museum treasures tour, a tour of Belgrade by night, and a shopping tour. Check with the tourist information office for details.

Excursions **Putnik** (*see* above) offers a range of day excursions and longer trips. A popular short one is to the hill of Avala (11 miles, 18 kilometers), with its lovely scenery and famous Memorial to the Unknown Soldier by Ivan Meštrović. Others are a long day trip by hydrofoil down the Danube and tours to some of the magnificent medieval monasteries of Serbia.

Personal Guides Contact the **Association of Tourist Guides,** Studentski trg 21, tel. 011/629811.

Exploring Belgrade

From the deck of a Danube passenger boat, British traveler Michael Quin described Belgrade as "a splendid collection of mosques, with their white tall minarets, palaces with their domes, gardens, cypresses, and shady groves." That was in the 1830s, with the end of Turkish rule just over the horizon. Today, you'll find just one mosque. The rest of the scene has been replaced by solid Central European architecture and the white high rises of New Belgrade, built on land that was still a swamp 40 years ago.

Poised at the meeting point of the rivers Danube and Sava, Belgrade—Beograde to the Yugoslavs—was destined for centuries to be on the edge of somebody's empire: Roman, Turkish, or Hapsburg. It has taken such an incredible battering over the past 2,000 years that its great age is far from obvious. Most of the more spectacular sights are in museums. But remember that this was also the first capital of a free South Slav state in modern times, the first to shake off both Ottoman Turk and Hapsburg rule and to struggle for its own identity.

The Main Attractions

① When you've collected a map and the latest information from the **Tourist Information Center,** head for one of the café terraces on nearby Trg Republike (Republic Square) where you can get your bearings over a Turkish coffee in this bustling hub of the city.

② The National Museum is right on the square, and its collections, from prehistory on, will keep history buffs happy for hours. Its main message is that some of Europe's earliest cultures—a number going back as far as 5000 BC—had their origins in these

Kalemegdan, **4**
Military Museum, **5**
National Museum, **2**
Orthodox Cathedral, **6**
Skadarlija, **3**
Tito Memorial Center, **7**
Tourist Information
Center, **1**
Zemun, **8**

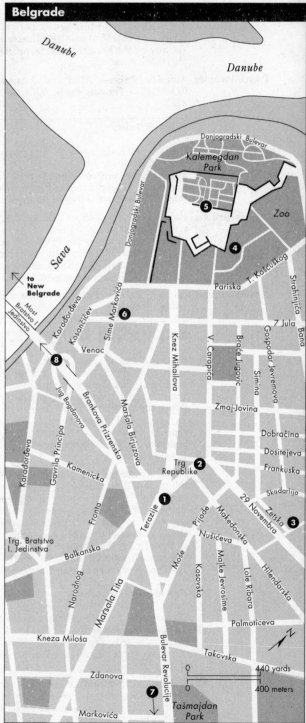

parts. Seek out the Bronze Age Duplja Chariot, borne by swamp birds and driven by an elegantly stylized charioteer, and the fine collection of gold jewelry from Greco-Roman times. *Admission: 2,000 dinars. Open 10–5, Thurs. 10–7, Sun. 10–2. Closed Mon.*

❸ Skadarlija is to Belgrade what Montmartre is to Paris, though in this case it's the name of a small district centered on the narrow street of Skadarska. The Bohemian set made it theirs in the 19th and early 20th centuries, filling its cafés with smoke and hot debate. It's best to return here in the evening, for restoration has made it a favorite area for dining out *(see* Dining), as well as for street entertainment based on national poetry, drama, and music.

Along Knez Mihailova, which you pass on your way to **❹ Kalemegdan,** you'll find some of the best shops in the city. The old fortifications of Kalemegdan are on the site of Belgrade's earliest roots. You'll understand why when you stand below Meštrović's Statue of Victory and look down on the meeting of the waters of the Sava and Danube, even less blue here than in Vienna! Until 1918, the opposite shores of both rivers were Hapsburg territory, from which the guns were turned on Belgrade for those first salvos of World War I. Nearly 2,000 years earlier, that same Danube had been the Romans's line of defense against invading barbarians. All in all, Kalemegdan Park **❺** is the right place for the **Military Museum,** which is infinitely more interesting than it sounds. Its excellent displays show how Yugoslavia came to exist—and survive. It is an intriguing story of Hapsburg assassination and Partisan courage against the Nazis. *Admission: 2,000 dinars. Open Tues.–Sun. 10–5.*

Time Out Znak? "Café of the Question Mark" offers respite and refreshment in one of Belgrade's oldest secular buildings. Its frame structure and bulging upper floor are typical of early 19th-century Balkan architecture. Znak? owes its name to the owner, who couldn't think of another after being admonished for "indecently" naming it Café of the Cathedral! Linger over a hearty soup or some strong coffee. *7 Jula 6.*

The **Orthodox Church Museum,** in the same block, has collections of paintings, manuscripts, vestments, and other ecclesiastic treasures. *Free. Open Sun. and Tues.–Fri. 8–1; Sat. 8–noon.*

❻ The **Orthodox Cathedral** across the street, built around 1840, isn't really worth a visit unless your visit coincides with choral practice or one of the concerts often held there.

The late President Tito spent many hours at the **House of Flowers.** It has now become his mausoleum, his tomb surrounded by banks of flowers. This, together with his residence and other **❼** buildings dedicated to his life and times, make up the **Tito Memorial Center.** The peaceful park setting is south of the city center in the Dedinje District. *Bulevar oktobarske revolucije. Free. Open Tues.–Sun. 9–4.*

Join strollers and fishermen along the banks of the Danube **❽** from New Belgrade to its elderly neighbor **Zemun.** You can eat inexpensive *paprikaš* (rich fish or chicken soup) and other Danube specialties at one of the waterside restaurants and watch the heavy traffic of barges and pleasure boats on Europe's most famous river.

Off the Beaten Track

If you're not able to visit any of southern Yugoslavia's famous medieval monasteries, you'll find good reproductions of the best frescoes and sculptures in the **Fresco Gallery.** *Cara Uroša 20. Admission: 2,000 dinars. Open Tues., Wed., and Fri., 10–5. Thurs. 10–7; Sun. 10–2.*

You'll find a restful oasis in **Topčider Park,** a favorite excursion spot for Belgrade's citizens, about 45 minutes away by bus. A number of early 19th-century buildings survive from the time of Prince Miloš Obrenović, including his elegant "cottage."

Shopping

Shopping Districts Belgrade's main shopping districts are in and around Terazie and Knez Mihailova. The city's largest department store is **Beogradjanka,** located in the high-rise block of the Beograd Palace on Maršala Tita. Another is **Beograd,** at Terazije 15–23, with a 24-hour drugstore *(Dragstor)* in Nušićeva's pedestrian subway.

Gift Ideas For exclusive (and expensive) fashions, look for the name **Jugoexport.** For traditional handcrafts, head for the reliable chain of **Narodna Radinost** stores. Don't forget about the major museums as a source, especially for replicas and prints. **Zadruga Pravoslong Svestenstva,** at Bulevar revolucije 24, is excellent for reproduction icons and jewelry.

Food and Flea Markets **Zeleni Venac,** in the city center, sells just about everything from just about every part of Yugoslavia—usually at the lowest prices you're likely to come across. *Open 5 AM, including Sun.*

Dining

Prices are per person and include first course, main course, and dessert, but no wine or tip. Figure on leaving around 5–7%. Best bets are indicated by a star ★. Due to the volatility of the dinar, prices are given in U.S. dollars.

Category	Cost
Very Expensive	over $15
Expensive	$10–$15
Moderate	$5–$10
Inexpensive	under $5

Very Expensive **Arhiv.** In the same building as the Metropol Hotel, Arhiv overlooks Tašmajdan Park. Its atmosphere is quiet and pleasant. The menu includes Serbian specialties. *Bulevar revolucije 69, tel. 011/330910. Dress: informal. Reservations accepted. AE, DC, V.*

Dva Jelena. This old favorite in the Skadarlija quarter spreads over several rooms in different styles. Hors d'oeuvres and grilled items are the specialties here, and there's music every evening. *Skadarska 32, tel. 011/334422. Dress: informal. Reservations accepted. AE, DC, V.*

Ima Dana. Another favorite in Skadarlija, Ima Dana goes in for steaks and other grilled meats. There is music each night in a late 19th-century atmosphere. *Skadarska 38, tel. 011/334422. Dress: informal. Reservations accepted. AE, DC, V.*

★ **Tri Šešira.** Diners here sometimes join in the nostalgic old songs that make for a very bohemian atmosphere. Spicy pork and lamb are the specialties. *Skadarska 29, tel. 011/347501. Dress: informal. Reservations accepted. AE, DC, V.*

Expensive **Dunavski Cvet.** It is worth getting here early for a table with fine views over the Danube. There are also performances of folk and popular music, and the specialties include Balkan grills and fresh fish. *Tadeuša Košćukog 63, tel. 011/186823. Dress: informal. Reservations accepted. AE.*

Zlatan Bokal. This is one of the less expensive Skadarlija establishments, matching the others for atmosphere and serving its own special "Skadarlija Supper," a fixed-price menu featuring grilled lamb or fish and lots of spices. *Skadarska 26, tel. 011/334834. Dress: informal. Reservations accepted. AE, DC, MC, V.*

Zlatna Ladja. You'll find this excellent restaurant, serving mainly freshwater fish, right in the center of town. The decor is suitably nautical, with nets and a feeling that you're in a Danube barge. *Kolarčeva 9, tel. 011/334018. Dress: informal. Reservations accepted. AE, DC, V.*

Moderate **Ali Baba.** As its name suggests, this restaurant goes in for Oriental specialties, with Ottomam decor to match. It's in the old town of Zemun, about 25 minutes by bus from the center of Belgrade. *Cara Dušana 128, Zemun, tel. 011/102302. Dress: informal. Reservations accepted. No credit cards.*

Klub Književnika. The Pen Club is the translation of the name of this intriguing restaurant, with some of the best food in the city and an interesting clientele. Its animated atmosphere—journalists love the place—spreads over several small rooms. Don't be put off by the shabby entrance. Specials change often so ask for the day's recommended meal. *Francuska 7, tel. 011/627931. Dress: informal. Reservations advisable. No credit cards.*

★ **Milošev Konak.** You'll find this popular restaurant in the pleasant setting of Topčider Park, about 45 minutes by bus from the center. The menu features Serbian specialties as well as more international fare. Be sure to include one of the hearty—and spicy—soups in your choice of meal. *Topčider 1, tel. 011/663146. Dress: informal. Reservations accepted. No credit cards.*

Inexpensive **Skala.** One of the best restaurants for vegetarian meals, Skala is located out in the old town of Zemun, about 25 minutes by bus from the center of Belgrade. *Bežanijska 3, Zemun, tel. 011/196605. Dress: informal. Reservations accepted. No credit cards.*

Atina. This popular pizzeria is good for a quick snack. It has a counter, opening onto the street, selling *piroški* (a kind of turnover). *Terazije 28. Dress: informal. No reservations. No credit cards.*

Koloseum. Another express restaurant, Koloseum serves fast food and Serbian specialties. *Terazije 40. Dress: informal. No reservations. No credit cards.*

Lodging

The hotels in the center of Belgrade are quite old, though most have been renovated. The best of the modern hotels are in New Belgrade, across the Sava River—less convenient but in a quieter location. Prices given here are for two people in a double room and include service charge. Best bets are indicated by a star ★. Due to the volatility of the dinar, prices are given in U.S. dollars.

Category	Cost
Very Expensive	over $120
Expensive	$70–$120
Moderate	$45–$70
Inexpensive	under $45

Very Expensive **Beograd Intercontinental.** Built in 1979, the Intercontinental is a high rise adjoining the glossy Sava Center, the main site for international conferences in New Belgrade. It's the most expensive—and best equipped—hotel in Belgrade, and the favorite among Americans. *Vladimira Popovića 10, tel. 011/ 134760, 011/138708. 420 rooms with bath and shower. Facilities: saunas, pool, tennis, nightclub. AE, DC, MC, V.*

Jugoslavija. On the banks of the Danube in New Belgrade, the Jugoslavija is about 15 minutes from the center. Rooms on the top 3 floors have the best views of the city and the Danube. *Bulevar Edvarda Kardelja 3, tel. 011/600222, 011/606433. 600 rooms with bath and shower. Facilities: saunas, pool, nightclub, casino. AE, DC, MC, V.*

Expensive **Excelsior.** A town house dating from the '20s and renovated in 1988, the Excelsior is centrally located near Tašmajdan Park. The room decor ranges from traditional, with high windows and heavy curtains, to more modern, with better soundproofing and chrome. *Kneza Miloša 5, tel. 011/331381. 81 rooms with bath. AE, DC, MC, V.*

★ **Metropol.** Looking out on Tašmajdan Park, the Metropol is the fanciest hotel in the center, sumptuous in a slightly old-fashioned way. Renovated in 1987, it attracts many Americans. *Bulevar revolucije 69, tel. 011/330911–19. 218 rooms with bath. Facilities: nightclub, casino. AE, DC, MC, V.*

Slavija. This is a comfortable and modern hotel, but a little less central and more impersonal than the others in this price range. Rooms in the annex are less expensive. *Svetosavska 1–3, tel. 011/450842. 536 rooms with bath or shower. AE, DC, MC, V.*

Moderate **Kasina.** This is a town house in the heart of the city. Some of the rooms can be noisy: It was last renovated in 1968 and the soundproofing needs some renewing. *Terazije 25. Tel. 011/335574. 96 rooms with bath. AE, DC, V.*

Splendid. Unlike most other Belgrade hotels, the Splendid has no restaurant, but it is in a quiet, central location near the Federal Assembly. This pre-World War II building was renovated in 1987 and the rooms are much brighter as a result. *Dragoslava Jovanovića 5, tel. 011/335443. 50 rooms with bath or shower. AE, DC, MC, V.*

Inexpensive **Taš.** Your money goes a long way at the quiet Taš, with its
★ pleasant location near the swimming stadium in Tašmajdan
Park. The facilities—and the low cost—make it a favorite for
families. *Borisa Kidrića 71, tel. 011/343507. 19 rooms with
bath. Facilities: saunas, pool, gymnasium. DC, V.*

The Arts

For listings of upcoming events, get the free magazine
Beogradscope from a hotel or travel agency. Belgrade has no
central ticket agency, so unless you have a guide or a helpful
hotel reception clerk, you'll have to get your own tickets.

Concerts On summer evenings, the **Skadarlija** district is the scene of lively street entertainment, including national music. You'll also
find open-air concerts in the parks, at **Kalemegdan** and in the
Fresco Gallery. Classical concerts are held in the **Zuzorić Art
Pavilion,** Kalemegdan and, in winter, **Kolorac Hall,** Studentski
trg.

Opera and Ballet The leading company is attached to the **National Theater;** the
main season is in winter.

Folklore If the **Kolo Company** is in town, don't miss one of its performances at Kolorac Hall, Studentski trg.

Entertainment and Nightlife

Again, the bohemian quarter of Skadarlija is where most
things happen.

Nightclubs In addition to the hotel nightclubs, try the **Lotos,** Zmaj jovina
4.

Discos Belgrade has no shortage of discos. Try **Amadeus,** Ćirila i
Metodija 2A; **Disko-Videoteka,** Bezistan, Terazije 27; **Dom
omladine** (Youth Center), Makedonska 18; **Italijanski Bistro,**
Masarikova 5.

Istria and the Julian Alps

On first impressions of scenery and architecture, Slovenia
might be an extension of Austria or Italy, depending on the direction from which you approach it. And, historically, so it was.
But listen closely and you'll hear the unmistakable Slav-ness of
the Slovene language. Look again and you'll notice the red star
over factory buildings. You'll become aware of countless differences in custom, dress, and food.

Most of Slovenia was ruled by the Austrian Hapsburgs until
1918. The Turks never got this far, and Hapsburg wealth, combined with Slovene intelligence and diligence, left a heritage
that still makes it the most affluent part of Yugoslavia. The
chalet-style houses of the mountains are neatly tended, as are
the villas on the coast, their gardens bright with flowers. Indeed, the well-organized Slovenes believe that they contribute
more than their fair share to the federal coffers, funds that, in
turn, are distributed to their less favored compatriots in the
south.

As you cross the invisible border into neighboring Croatia, the
more volatile Croats might echo similar sentiments. But with

accessible plains as well as mountains, the Croats have often been more active in both condoning and opposing oppression. The sinister pro-Nazi Ustaše movement, before and during World War II, was Croat, but, then, so were its fiercest and most dedicated opponent, Josip Broz Tito, and many of his partisan followers.

From Roman temples to Venetian Gothic to ornate Baroque, this is a region where you can pick your way through European cultural influences. This route is scenically glorious, too, and historically fascinating. A bonus is that some of the tourist amenities are as good as you'll find anywhere in Yugoslavia.

Getting Around

The whole of this itinerary is well served by bus, and this is the best way of seeing the countryside if you are not traveling by car. The main bus station in Ljubljana is by the Railroad Station at Trg osvobod fronte 4 (tel. 061/325885). The final leg from Rijeka (near Opatija) to Zagreb takes about five hours by train.

Guided Tours

Many travel agencies run guided tours from Ljubljana and the major resorts. The main operators for this region are **Kompas,** in Ljubljana (tel. 061/327761), and **Kvarner Express,** in Opatija (051/711111).

Tourist Information

Bled. Kompas, Ljubljanska 7, tel. 064/77245.
Ljubljana. Tourist Information Center, Titova 11, tel. 061/215412, 061/224222.
Opatija. Kvarner Express, Maršala Tita 186, tel. 051/711251.
Poreč. Adriatikturist, Trg Slobode 3, tel. 053/31244.
Zagreb. Tourist Information Center, Nikole Zrinjskog (Zrinjevac) 14, tel. 041/411883, 041/441880); Lotrščak Tower in the Upper Town.

Exploring

The descent from the Würzen Pass drops you more or less into **Kranjska Gora,** a winter sports resort as well as a border town jammed with traffic in the main season.

Bled   Lakeside Bled, a few miles off the main road to Ljubljana, is the oldest and best equipped resort. All have a spectacular backdrop: The towering Julian Alps, which include Triglav, Yugoslavia's highest mountain at 7,870 feet (2,400 meters). Bled is full of self-confident style and was much favored by the Hapsburg aristocracy, not to mention the late President Tito, whose villa is now a hotel. Bled has a craggy castle on a cliff, a church on an islet, and Yugoslavia's only (and very good) golf course: Yet it's basically a place for walking and climbing and just looking at stunning scenery. You can do this on a pleasant ride by horse-drawn carriage *(kočija)* to the **Vintgar Gorge,** three miles (five kilometers) away.

Ljubljana   Ljubljana sits astride the Ljubljanica river in the Ljubljana Gap, one of the few natural breaks in the mountains between inland Europe and the Mediterranean. That's why every empire builder passed this way and why the dominant building is the castle. The most interesting part of the city is at its feet, near the river around Mestni trg, medieval in origin but largely Baroque in decoration. Napoleon stayed in the Bishop's Palace, next to the cathedral, and must have looked out from those lovely arcaded balconies while he was busy re-creating the Roman province of Illyria, alas for him short-lived. You will come across traces of the Roman original (when Ljubljana was called Emona). Some can be found in the modern conference complex of Cankarjev in the downtown area west of the river. History buffs will get a fuller picture at the nearby **National Museum,** where treasures such as the magnificent bronze Vače urn predate the Romans by another half millenium. *National Museum, Trg Herojev 1. Admission: 2,500 dinars. Open Tues. –Sun. 9–1 and 4–7.*

Postojna Even if caves usually leave you cold, don't miss the ones at Postojna. Dress warmly. Guided tours start with a 1½-mile train ride, followed by a walk through some of the labyrinthine passages that link caves into a series of glittering art galleries, created over many eons by the stalactites and stalagmites. *Postojna. Admission: 5,000 dinars. Open 10–5, closed Mon.*

From Postojna take the main road in the direction of Koper and Portorož. To enjoy some lovely hill country that many of the sun seekers on the coast never see, take a left when you come upon signposts to **Buzet,** then head for the coast via **Istarske Toplice.** This was once border country between the territory of Venice and its Hapsburg rival, hence so many fortified hill villages. Buzet is one, **Motovun** another, and both are worth the detour.

Poreč Poreč is one of the largest resorts on the entire coast, but so widely scattered that you're unlikely to realize it. Most of the accommodations are in well-planned, self-contained modern complexes up to several miles out of town, near beaches of rock or pebble. (Again, it's a good idea to check on a hotel's location before making reservations.) The town itself clusters on a headland and is packed in summer. Poreč attracts a lot of day-trippers just because it is so charming and has many noteworthy aspects dating back to Roman times. The most important sight is the **Basilica of Euphrasius,** built in the 6th century, with fabulous Byzantine mosaics in the apse. And every evening you can count on the waterfront to become an animated mini-bazaar for souvenirs and handcrafts, with street artists ready to immortalize you with a few swift strokes on paper.

There's a direct route across the Istrian Peninsula to **Opatija,** but it's worth the longer run via Pula to see its huge oval 1st century AD amphitheater. Take in the hill villages of **Bale** and **Vodnjan** on the way.

Opatija In contrast to Poreč, Opatija is a much younger town but an older resort. It draws its Central European flavor from the nobles and notables of the Austrian and Hungarian courts who came in droves during the 19th century to take advantage of its balmy winter climate. Visitors included Emperor Franz Josef, who entertained his mistress in neighboring Volosko. Opatija still attracts a winter clientele, but it's much more of a summer center nowadays and the closest thing to a French Riviera resort you'll find in Yugoslavia. A pleasant if extensive walk along the beach is the eight-mile (13-kilometer) meander from Volosko through Opatija to Lovran.

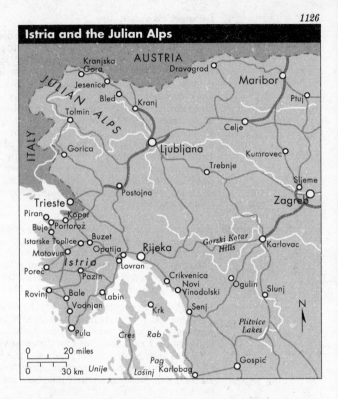

Istria and the Julian Alps

Zagreb Neighboring **Rijeka** is Yugoslavia's biggest port; from here, it's a pleasant drive through the hills of Gorski Kotar to Karlovac, where you join the highway to **Zagreb**. The capital of Croatia, this large, unpretentious, straightforward city has the benefit of some of the country's best museums, theaters, and sports amenities. Stand in **Trg Republike** and you're in the heart of the city, with most of the main sights within walking distance.

The first of these is the **cathedral.** It is remarkable not so much as a piece of architecture or house of worship but for the bustling humanity and varied wares on sale daily at Dolac Market, not far from its walls. This is the heart of Kaptol, the ecclesiastic community that for centuries developed separately from its secular neighbor, Gornji Grad, or Upper Town.

Gornji Grad is easily the most attractive part of Zagreb. If you're feeling lazy, take the venerable funicular up—the trip is less than a minute—from just off the main thoroughfare of Ilica. The cable railway will deposit you by Lotrščak Tower, where there's a tourist information center and small museum. But you would do better to climb up by steps through the narrow streets from Dolac to **Kamenita vrata** (Stone Gate). A devastating fire is said to have been miraculously halted here, and the gate now shelters a small shrine where those seeking solace have placed countless little plaques inscribed *hvala* (thank you), including one in English.

Gornji Grad is quite compact, so you can never really get lost. Browse through the old streets lined with the Baroque and neo-

classical palaces replacing much older predecessors that were
destroyed by earthquake or fire. Two churches here are worth
seeing: St. Catherine and, especially, St. Mark, in which modern sculptures and frescoes blend well with the 14th-century
Gothic sanctuary. The sculptures are by Ivan Meštrović,
Yugoslavia's best known sculptor, who spent his last years in
the United States. Not far away you'll find displays of his work
in the **Meštrović Studio.** *Mletačka 8. Admission: 2,000 dinars.
Open Tues.–Sat. 10–1 and 5–7; Sun. 10–1.*

Also nearby is one of the finest buildings in Zagreb—the **Arts
Center**—an old Jesuit monastery that has been beautifully restored to house world-class exhibits and is worth visiting for
the building alone. *Jesvitski trg. Admission: 2,000 dinars.
Open Tues.–Sun. 10–8, Mon. 2–8.*

Finally, try to make time to visit **Sljeme,** high above Zagreb.
Take the cable car from the Gračani district (or trams 14 and 21
from the center) or drive up. The views over Zagreb and its
hilly hinterland of Zagorje are memorable. Standing here, you
can contemplate the attraction of the region and realize that its
old churches, castles, spas, and way of life shelter the best
qualities of the past.

Dining and Lodging

For details and price category definitions, *see* Dining and
Lodging in Essential Information.

Bled   **Golf Club Restaurant.** This is attached to the splendid golf
Dining   course about 2 miles (3 kilometers) east of the resort. It's a glorious setting, and the food is good. Grilled pork and lamb are
always tasty here. *Tel. 064/78180. Dress: informal. Reservations advised. AE, DC, MC, V. Closed Jan.–Feb. Very
Expensive.*

Lodging   **Grand Hotel Toplice.** Built in the '30s and renovated in 1968, the
Grand Hotel is a pretty, vine-covered building, very much in
the old tradition. It's located by the lake and is a favorite among
Americans. *Lakefront, tel. 064/77222. 121 rooms with bath or
shower. Facilities: saunas, pool, gymnasium. AE, DC, MC, V.
Very Expensive.*
Vila Bled. Formerly a summer residence of President Tito, Villa Bled is an elegant villa set in gardens by the lake. It is a
lovely location, even if the rates are high. *Cesta Svobode 26, tel.
064/77436. 30 rooms with bath and shower. Facilities: lake
beach, tennis, golf (2 mi, 3 km), boats for rent. AE, DC, MC,
V. Closed Jan. 15–Mar. 15. Very Expensive.*
Jelovica. The Jelovica is modern, with gardens extending to the
lake shore. Extensive improvements were completed in 1987:
Rooms are comfortable and modern. Jelovica also has the unusual facility of a bowling alley. *Cesta Svobode 5, tel. 064/77316.
176 rooms with shower. AE, DC, MC. Closed Nov. 1–Dec. 15.
Moderate.*

Ljubljana   **Na Brinju.** This small restaurant goes in for good home cooking.
Dining   You can eat out in the pleasant small garden in summer, but either arrive early or make reservations for the best tables.
Start any meal with the soup of the day, which is almost a meal
in itself. *Vodovodna 44, tel. 061/342783. Dress: informal. Reservations advised. Closed weekends. Moderate.*
Pod Velbom. The in-house restaurant of the Hotel and Catering

School, Pod Velbom is located in the old town. Try the Slovene specialties, which include a type of wiener schnitzel *(Dumaiski Zrezek)* or the Austrian-influenced sausages. *Stari trg 3, tel. 061/222136. Dress: informal. Reservations advised. MC, V. Closed Sun. Moderate.*

Lodging **Holiday Inn.** Built in 1980, this is the best and most expensive hotel in Ljubljana. Most Americans who stay here are attracted by the location and services. This hotel is often busy with conferences, so it is best to make reservations. *Miklošičeva 3, tel. 061/211434. 133 rooms with bath. Facilities: saunas, pool. AE, DC, MC, V. Very Expensive.*

Slon. Right in the heart of the city, the Slon has the benefits and drawbacks of a central location. Rooms overlooking the main street will be noisy, but you are right in the middle of things. Its restaurant is good, specializing in national dishes: Try the *Štruklji*, a buckwheat and cheese pastry. *Titova 10. Tel. 061/211232. 185 rooms with bath or shower. AE, DC, MC, V. Moderate.*

Ilirja. A bit removed from it all on the city outskirts, Ilirja is worth considering if you're on a budget. This hotel is also a conference favorite, so try to make reservations. *Trg prekomorskih brigad 4, tel. 061/551162. 136 rooms, 129 with bath. AE, DC, MC. Inexpensive.*

Opatija **Ariston.** Spread over several rooms, the intimate Ariston res-
Dining taurant features regional specialties such as Adriatic prawns *(Skampa)*. It's about a mile from the resort center and is very popular. *Maršala Tita 243, tel. 051/711379. Dress: informal. Reservations advised. AE, DC, MC, V. Expensive.*

Bevanda. Priding itself on its fish dishes, Bevanda has a coastal setting that is appropriately maritime—about 1½ miles (2½ kilometers) from the resort center toward Volosko. Try the grilled fish or mussels cooked in wine *(ostrige)*. *Maršala Tita 62, tel. 051/712036. Dress: informal. Reservations advised. No credit cards. Closed Jan. 1–15, June 15–July 10. Expensive.*

Plavi Podrum. Seafood is the specialty at this restaurant, which is right by the water about 2 miles (3 kilometers) from the resort center. Try the fish soup *(brodet)*, which has a variety of fresh ingredients and winds up tasting like the French *bouillabaisse*. *Obala F. Supila 4, tel. 051/713629. Dress: informal. Reservations advised. AE, MC, V. Moderate.*

Lodging **Ambassador.** A high rise, dating from the '60s, the Ambassador is on the sea by a rock-and-pebble beach near the resort center. It is one of the most popular local hotels with Americans and does service as an attractive conference center. *Beachfront, tel. 051/712211. 280 rooms with bath and shower. Facilities: pools, sauna. AE, DC, V. Expensive.*

Kristal. The Kristal is an old hotel that was attractively modernized in 1970. It is also right by the sea and has separate beaches for sunning and swimming. Off-season rates drop dramatically. *Beachfront, tel. 051/711333. 136 rooms with bath or shower. Facilities: saunas, pool. AE, DC, V. Expensive.*

Kvarner. The *grande dame* of Opatija, the Kvarner was built in 1884 with spacious public rooms lit by glittering chandeliers. Even now, the atmosphere is reminiscent of the Hapsburg era and the heady days of the Orient Express. Rooms are comfortable and large, with good views of the hotel's rocky beach and the neighboring coastline. *Beachfront, tel. 051/711211. 86* *rooms with bath or shower. Facilities: saunas, pools. AE, DC, V. Expensive.*

Poreč **Parentium.** The main advantage of the Parentium is its quiet
Lodging location among gardens on a wooded headland, about 3 miles (5 kilometers) from the resort and just by a rock-and-pebble beach. Rooms are airy and bright, and the Taverna serves Istrian specialties. *Zelena Laguna, tel. 053/31144. 362 rooms with bath or shower. Facilities: saunas, pools, casino, nightclub, and facilities of nearby Zelena Laguna sports center. AE, DC, MC, V. Expensive.*

Neptun. This is one of the few hotels located within the resort center. It is about a 10-minute walk from a beach but overlooks the old harbor and is therefore ideal for those who want to feel part of the local scene. *Poreč center, tel. 053/31711. 143 rooms with bath or shower. AE, DC, MC, V. Moderate.*

Zagreb **Gradski Podrum.** Right in the center, on a corner of Republic
Dining Square, Gradski Podrum is one of Zagreb's best-known and most elegant eating places. It is probably the best place to try local specialties, such as *pohovano pile* (breaded chicken) and the flaky *štrudla* pastry. Wash it down with either *Zumberak* or *Moslavina:* Both are light local wines. *A. Cesarca 2, tel. 041/276597. Jacket and tie. Reservations advised. AE, DC, MC, V. Very Expensive.*

Pod mirnim krovovima. The specialties here are lamb-on-the-spit *(jagnje)* and freshwater fish dishes. It's fairly central, in the direction of Maksimir Park, and almost always crowded. *Fijanova 7, tel. 041/216269. Dress: informal. Reservations advised. AE, DC, MC, V. Expensive.*

Starogradski podrum. Set in the cellars of the old city hall in the Upper Town, this restaurant has a great atmosphere. It features unusual specialties taken from an early 19th-century recipe book. *Ćirila i Metoda 5, tel. 041/443639. Dress: informal. Reservations advised. AE, DC, MC, V. Closed lunch. Expensive.*

Lodging **Esplanade.** Opposite the main railroad station, the Esplanade is an imposing turn-of-the-century town house, last renovated in the mid '70s. The service is good and the hotel is generally very comfortable, but rooms overlooking the terrace (with dancing) can be noisy in summer. It is the first choice of most American visitors. *Mihanovićeva 1, tel. 041/534444. 236 rooms with bath or shower. Facilities: night club. AE, DC, MC, V. Very Expensive.*

Dvorac Brezovica If you have a car, it is worth going about 6 miles (10 kilometers) south of the city to this hotel in a quiet location. Once an old castle, it now offers cottage-style accommodations along with an elegant restaurant. *Brezovica bb, tel. 041/521880. 28 rooms with bath or shower. No credit cards. Moderate.*

Where East Meets West

This route starts from Sarajevo and heads south, through Mostar, to Korčula and the coast, ending up at Dubrovnik. There's nothing restful about the scenery you'll see. It is mountains all the way, some of them thick with forests, others rocky and arid. Most of them are rent by magnificent river gorges until you reach the Dalmatian Coast, when horizons open out to the island-studded Adriatic.

It would be difficult to find an itinerary with greater contrasts—scenically, culturally, even gastronomically. When Bosnia fell to the Turks in the 16th century, it became one of their most westerly provinces. Ivo Andrić's Nobel Prize-winning novel, *Bridge Over the Drina*, gives a gripping account of the uneasy and changing relationships between Muslim and Christian during those centuries. The story ends more than 400 years later, with Bosnia becoming a leading pawn in the chess game of Hapsburg power politics and eventually the scene of events leading to the horrors of World War I. As a result, few regions can boast a skyline shared by so many minarets, church domes, and spires, while plaintive Oriental music mingles with the latest pop blaring from modern apartment blocks a stone's throw from Oriental-style bazaars.

When you come to the coast, it's a totally different stage set. The medieval walled city of Dubrovnik never fell to anyone until Napoleon ended its status as independent republic in 1806. Farther south, the Montenegrins in the rugged fastness of their mountains were never wholly subjugated by the Turks. Their ferocious independence and bitter blood feuds had much in common with those of the Highland Scots! "Those are men who, when asked to pay tribute, offer stones," thundered British statesman William Gladstone in the House of Commons in the 19th century. "These are the men who dress cowards into women's clothes, and whose wives, when need requires, boldly get hold of the gun."

Getting Around

In order to see all the sights, you'll need a car. Otherwise, you have the choice of train or bus from Sarajevo to Kardeljevo on the coast. From Kardeljevo down to Dubrovnik and Budva, there are only buses. Alternatively, you can make use of the coastal services *(see* the section below about the stretch from Korčula to Dubrovnik). There are flights back to Belgrade from Tivat, Budva's nearest airport. For a much wider choice of flights (Belgrade, Zagreb, overseas), you will need to return to Dubrovnik.

Guided Tours

The mainland route from Sarajevo to Dubrovnik is a well-traveled trail featured in many tours marketed overseas, as well as by Yugoslav agencies. If you're staying in Dubrovnik and other main coastal areas, you'll also find local agencies arranging excursions inland to Mostar and Sarajevo. Regular runs by bus or boat are available to see most of the sights, too. Among the main agencies in these regions are **Unis-Turist,** in Sarajevo (tel. 071/534200), and **Atlas** in Dubrovnik (tel. 050/27333).

Tourist Information

Budva. Montenegroturist, tel. 086/41414.
Dubrovnik. Tourist Information Center, P. Miličevića 1, tel. 050/26354, 050/26355.
Korčula. HRO Korčula, tel. 050/711306.
Mostar. Helmosturist, Lacina 1, tel. 088/53344, 088/53345.
Sarajevo. Tourist Bureau, JNA 50, tel. 071/24844, 071/25151.

Exploring

Sarajevo   Sarajevo, the capital of Bosnia-Herzegovina, is a city engulfed by mountains. To find the most interesting sections of Sarajevo, you'll have to wend past its high-rise suburbs and industrial complexes because nature forced this city to grow up rather than out. But you will reach the solid Hapsburg structures, built between 1878 and World War I, and finally the old Turkish core of what was originally called Sarajovasi (Plain around the Palace) at the head of a narrow valley.

The tourist office is only a short stroll from the hub of the old town that is known as **Baščaršija** (the old bazaar), which, despite a lot of tidying up, is still a maze of alleys. They thread their way past tiny shops with double-shuttered doors, behind which craftsmen and merchants still work. Whole streets are dedicated to any one of a dozen crafts: There are saddlers, weavers, blacksmiths, coppersmiths, and goldsmiths. Among them are shops known as *aščinica*, serving spicy local specialties, as well as a growing number of café-discos.

A number of the most attention-getting buildings in this part of town date from the more enlightened rule of Gazi Husref-Bey in the 16th century, including the finest of the city's 73 mosques, **Begova Džamija** (Mosque of the Bey). Sightseers here often outnumber the faithful, and you will need to remove your shoes, as in all mosques. Other mosques have been converted for more mundane purposes, like the *hamam* (public baths that are now a restaurant) and *bezistan* (a covered market that's now commercial premises).

Close to Baščaršija you will find the **Orthodox church** (Maršala Tita 83), crouching behind a high wall to conform with a Turkish law that restricted the height of Christian places of worship. The magnificent iconostasis, a screen on which icons are placed, dates from its restoration in the 18th century. On the same street, there is also a restored **synagogue** commemorating the large Jewish community that flourished here from 1500, following the explusion of Sephardic Jews from Spain.

Several bridges span the little Miljacka river that flows through the city. On a street corner by **Princip Bridge,** you'll see two footsteps sunk into the sidewalk. They mark (more or less) the spot from which student Gavrilo Princip fired the fatal shots at Archduke Franz Ferdinand, the first of a series of sparks that exploded into World War I.

Pleasant excursions can be taken into the mountains of **Trebević, Jahorina,** and **Bjelašnica,** scene of the 1984 Winter Olympics. But your first choice should be an outing much closer to Sarajevo. Climb above the old town to the eastern slopes, scattered with ancient Jewish and Muslim cemeteries, and at one of the unpretentious cafés, sit over a Turkish coffee (Bosnians make the best) or *slivovica* (plum brandy). On a summer night, especially at soft twilight, the views from above the city are magical.

A few miles out of Sarajevo on your way to the coast, you pass the small spa of **Ilidža,** where Archduke Ferdinand spent the evening before his assassination. It is worth a short detour here, on foot or by horse and buggy, to see **Vrelo Bosne,** the

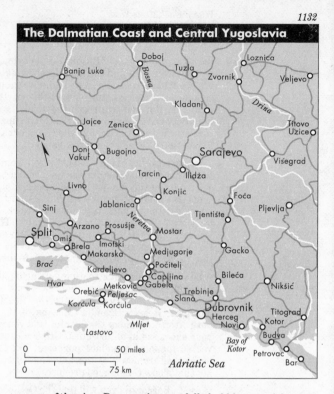

The Dalmatian Coast and Central Yugoslavia

Doboj

Banja Luka

Bosna

Tuzla

Loznica

Zvornik

Veljevo

Kladanj

Drina

Jajce

Zenica

Titovo Uzice

Doni Vakuf

Bugojno

Sarajevo

Višegrad

Tarcin

Ilidža

Livno

Konjic

Foča

Pljevlja

Sinj

Jablanica

Neretva

Tjentište

Split

Arzano

Prosušje

Mostar

Omiš

Brela

Imotski

Gacko

Makarska

Medjugorje

Brać

Kardeljevo

Počitelj

Bileća

Hvar

Metković

Capljina

Nikšić

Orebić

Gabela

Pelješac

Trebinje

Korčula

Korčula

Slano

Dubrovnik

Titograd

Mljet

Herceg Novi

Kotor

Lastovo

Bay of Kotor

Budva

Petrovac

Bar

0   50 miles

0   75 km

Adriatic Sea

source of the river Bosna as it peacefully bubbles out of the rock from several springs. Rivers are a major feature of Bosnia-Herzegovina's landscape, some now tamed into a series of reservoirs, such as lakelike **Neretva,** which you'll follow for much of the way to Mostar. The mountain scenery changes dramatically as you pass from the deeply wooded ranges of Bosnia into the pale, arid limestone ridges of **Herzegovina,** which, despite its thirsty look, produces excellent wines, olives, almonds, and tobacco.

Mostar Mostar is Herzegovina's main town. It has grown beyond recognition since its days as a backwoods halt in a remote Turkish province, but it is the Turkish-era Old Town that everyone wants to see. Its center is the slender steep-arched bridge built in 1556 and flanked by two watch towers—one of Yugoslavia's most photographed sights. You'll probably find some of Mostar's youth trying to prove their manhood by diving from its highest point into the fast green waters of the Neretva below. The most interesting of the town's many mosques is that of **Karadjoz Beg,** a few hundred yards away. A short walk uphill takes you to the little **Orthodox Church** on the east side of town. There is an unusual Muslim influence here: A wooden grill separates the women's gallery from male worshipers.

Stay with the river Neretva all the way to the coast. Apart from lovely scenery, there are three particular curiosities along the way. One is probably Europe's newest place of pilgrimage, the village of **Medjugorje.** It was catapulted out of obscurity in 1981 when visions of the Virgin Mary appeared to local schoolchildren. Hordes of believers and sightseers now throng to this spot, about 20 miles (30 kilometers) southwest of Mostar.

The second is **Počitelj**, an attractive fortified village, restored in recent years and now an active artists' colony. The third diversion is Gabela, south of Čapljina. According to a Mexican scholar, this is the true site of Homer's Troy—a claim dismissed by archaeologists but not by the recently formed Gabela Tourist Association.

Korčula If you're not traveling by car, it will be more practical to visit the island and town of **Korčula** by regular boat from Dubrovnik *(see* below), which takes just over three hours. If you are driving, you should now head down the long, narrow, and mountainous Pelješac Peninsula to **Orebić** for the ferry. It carries you across the strait to the exquisite old walled town of Korčula in about 20 minutes.

Korčula is attractive and charming. Narrow, crooked streets suddenly open out onto little squares bordered by old churches and former palaces, all bearing the imprint of long periods of Venetian rule. One of them is known as Marco Polo's house, where this formidable Venetian traveler of medieval times is said to have been born. Was he born here? No one can say for sure, but Polos are still in residence in Korčula.

Korčula offers a long list of art and architectural treasures. The most important is the Cathedral of **Sveti Marko** (St. Mark), a blend of Romanesque, Gothic, and Baroque. But at almost every turn, there's some unheralded feature to be observed: a Renaissance balcony or Gothic window, a family crest or elaborate cornice. If you try the good, sometimes powerful, local wines, beware of the amber-colored Grk—it goes straight to your knees!

Dubrovnik The next stop on the tour is Dubrovnik, and the best approach is from the south. You have to negotiate the harbor area of Gruž from the north, and that means missing the full visual impact of this walled city crowning a headland.

By means of sheer diplomatic guile, Dubrovnik survived until the 19th century as a tiny independent republic while every place around it fell to Turk, Venetian, or Hapsburg. (It was then called Ragusa, from which comes the word "argosy," meaning a great merchant ship.) The city also survived a number of earthquakes: The worst was in 1667, although the most recent, centered on Montenegro in 1979, also left its mark. Current restoration has led to new discoveries, but this is a long-term project and you may find a number of buildings still closed for restoration. The general effect of Gothic and Renaissance in pale Dalmatian stone is exquisite, however, and it will be very surprising if Dubrovnik disappoints you.

If you want to be within strolling distance of the old walled city, which is closed to traffic, choose your hotel carefully. Most of them are on the peninsula of **Lapad**, two or three miles (three to five kilometers) to the north, but the bus service is good.

The tourist information center is in the Old Town, near Pile (West) Gate. After collecting a map and the excellent free "Information Dubrovnik" booklet, get your bearings by following the main thoroughfare of **Placa** (also known as Stradun), which links Pile Gate with Ploče (East) Gate. You can climb up onto the walls (open summer 9–7) from either of these gates. The total circuit is about a mile (if you're short on time, at least do the landward side), and it's worth it for views of ancient tiled roofs, domes, and spires or glimpses into monastic courtyards and tiny rooftop gardens. In summer, you'll be accompanied by the tireless swoopings of swifts.

Allow time to wander up and down the maze of alleys and stairways that thread through the Old Town, which now has a large number of art studios, boutiques, and restaurants. In the course of your wanderings, you'll come across several small statues of **Sveti Vlaho** (St. Blaise), the city's patron saint, set into niches in the walls or adorning a church. The most famous is made of silver and shows the saint holding a model of the city: This is in the Baroque church of Sveti Vlaho at the eastern end of the Placa. Just around the corner in Pred Dvorom is one of the city's most beautiful buildings, the Rector's Palace. It houses the **Cultural and Historical Museum,** which tells of the life and times of the Ragusan Republic. It was from here that the rector ruled, a month at a time, during which time he was barred from leaving the confines of the Palace for fear that he would be distracted from his duties. *Pred Dvorom. Admission: 3,000 dinars. Open daily 9–1 and 2–6.*

For peace and quiet, seek out the lovely Gothic cloisters of the **Dominican Monastery,** near Ploče Gate. Try to make time for the short trip from the Old Town harbor to the green island of **Lokrum,** a protected nature reserve and favorite swimming place, from which you get wonderful views of the city.

The road from Dubrovnik to Budva features some of the finest coastal scenery in southern Europe. There are sweeping views back to Dubrovnik, while the magnificent Bay of Kotor in Montenegro is the closest you'll come to a Norwegian fjord this side of Oslo. Beneath towering mountains are a score of small communities, scattered along the shores of this contorted sea arm. Most share a seafaring history. The walled town of **Kotor** is the most attractive, although it is still being restored after major earthquake damage in 1979. The 12th-century cathedral, badly damaged in the earthquake, has been reopened and stands as the most important sight.

Budva South of the Bay of Kotor, the little homes of Budva cluster appealingly on a headland that was once an island. The Greeks and Romans were here for a time, but the Turks didn't quite get this far. Most of the buildings in the old walled town (again restored after the 1979 earthquake) date from the nearly four centuries of Venetian rule. Budva, in such a lovely setting, has considerable charm—not to mention its many modern tourist amenities. Most hotels are near the coarse sand or pebble beaches of **Slovenska Plaža,** about a mile from the town center or a little farther away in **Bečići.** Budva is an excellent base for excursions along the coast or into the Montenegrin mountains.

Dining and Lodging

For details and price category definitions, *see* Dining and Lodging in Essential Information.

Budva   **Avala.** The modern Avala, dating from the early '80s, is close to
Lodging   the Old Town and about 250 yards (230 meters) from a small
beach of coarse sand. Rooms are bright, well equipped, and
quiet. This hotel is particularly popular with young people—

many of whom are German—eager to get involved with the water sports. *Budva center, tel. 086/41022. 223 rooms with bath or shower. Facilities: pools, water skiing, boat rental, night club, casino. AE, DC, MC, V. Expensive.*

Slovenska Plaža. This plaza is a major new complex built in the early '80s, surrounded by landscaped gardens and close to a long, pebbled beach of coarse sand, about a mile from the Old Town. Accommodations, reception area, restaurants, and other amenities are in separate units to create a "village" atmosphere. *Slovenska Plaža, Budva, tel. 086/41044. 703 rooms with bath or shower, plus apartments. Facilities: pools, tennis, water skiing, wind surfing, table tennis, boat rental. AE, DC, MC, V. Closed Nov. 15–Mar. 15. Expensive.*

Dubrovnik **Amfora,** Located at Gruž Harbor, Amfora has a warm and casu-
Dining al atmosphere. Its wide-ranging menu features specialties using locally caught fish. Try the seafood risotto or any of the grilled fish specials. *Gruška obala 22, tel. 050/22919. Dress: informal. Reservations advised. V. Very Expensive.*

Dubravka. With an attractive location near Pile Gate, Dubravka has tables set under shady trees. The menu covers both local seafood specialties and more international fare. Squid and octopus—both regulars on the menu—are always good and fresh. *Brsalje 1, tel. 050/26319. Dress: informal. Reservations advised. AE, DC, MC, V. Closed Nov. 15–Apr. Expensive.*

Lodging **Belvedere.** One of the best coastal hotels in Yugoslavia, the Belvedere opened in 1985 with top-class facilities in a good location about a mile from the Old Town (boat service across the bay in summer). It's near a rocky beach and has dining terraces looking out over the sea. The combination of excellent facilities and first-class service makes it a favorite among Americans. *Frana Supila 28, tel. 050/28655. 200 rooms with bath and shower, plus suites. Facilities: saunas, pools, table tennis, gymnasium, solarium, billiards, night club, several bars and restaurants. AE, DC, MC, V. Very Expensive.*

Dubrovnik President. Built in 1976 and renovated annually, the President is on the Lapad Peninsula, 2½ miles (4 kilometers) from the Old Town. It rises 5 stories on streamlined tiers above a pebbled beach. Every room has its own balcony with a seaview. *Dubrava-Babin Kuk, tel. 050/22999, 050/20265. 163 rooms with bath, plus suites. Facilities: drugstore, pizzeria, saunas, pool, tennis, and sports facilities of nearby Dubrava Center. AE, DC, MC, V. Closed Jan. 4–Mar. Very Expensive.*

Dubrovnik Palace. In a quiet location on a wooded headland, 2½ miles (4 kilometers) from the Old Town in the Lapad district, the Dubrovnik Palace is popular with Americans. A modern hotel, renovated in 1985, it also has a rocky beach. Most of the well-equipped rooms have seaviews. *Masarykov put 18, tel. 050/28556. 270 rooms with bath, 47 with shower. Facilities: saunas, swimming pool, tennis, table tennis, disco nearby. AE, DC, V. Closed Nov. Expensive.*

Korčula **Adio Mare.** The specialties here are old Korčula and Venetian
Dining dishes, served on the vine-covered terrace of a fine late Gothic-Renaissance building in the Old Town. Try the fish soup, which is more like a chowder or stew, and then either lobster *(jastog)* or crayfish *(rak). Korčula Old Town, tel. 050/711253. Dress: informal. Reservations advised. AE, V. Closed Oct. 15–Apr. Moderate.*

Planjak. This is the favorite with the locals, who are likely to burst into Dalmation song while you enjoy the restaurant's good home cooking on its covered terrace by the sea. Follow their lead and accompany a meal of seafood with the locally produced *Grk* white wine. *Old Town, tel. 050/711015. Dress: informal. No reservations. AE, DC, MC, V. Moderate.*

Lodging **Liburna.** Located on a wooded promontory, Liburna is a short walk from the Old Town. It opened in 1985 and has the best facilities of any hotel in Korčula. It's by a rocky beach and has many choices for water sports fans. *Korčula, tel. 050/711026, 050/711006. 84 rooms, 25 apartments with bath or shower. Facilities: pool, tennis, miniature golf, windsurfing, boat and bicycle rental, table tennis, billiards. AE, DC, MC, V. Expensive.*

Korčula. Renovated in 1982 and a real favorite with regular visitors to Korčula, this hotel is by the sea in the heart of the Old Town. Two hundred yards (183 meters) from a beach, the Korčula is ideal if you want to feel part of the local scene or if you prefer accommodations on a smaller scale. Ask for a room *not* facing the street if you want to be spared late-night noise. *Old Town, tel. 050/711078. 24 rooms with bath. AE, DC, MC, V. Closed Nov.–Apr. Moderate.*

Mostar **Labirint.** The main attraction here is the setting in the Old
Dining Town, with a terrace overlooking the river and a fine view of the Old Bridge. Labirint is geared for tourists, so there is a choice of fixed-price menus as well as good explanations of à la carte items. *Kujundžiluk 12, tel. 088/32681. Dress: informal. Reservations advised. AE. Closed Dec.–Mar. Expensive.*

Stari Most. This restaurant takes its name from the Old Bridge, which is nearby. Roast lamb is the specialty here. Reserve or come early for one of the best tables in the garden. *Oneščukova 18, tel. 088/37215. Dress: informal. Reservations advised. AE. Expensive.*

Lodging **Neretva.** One of the oldest hotels in Yugoslavia, Neretva was built in the 1890s. It was renovated in 1950, but is showing its age today. Those with a taste for more traditional accommodations—which in some rooms means a bathroom down the hall—will see it as a break from the uniformity of many more modern hotels in Yugoslavia. The Neretva has a good central location by the river. *Trg Republike 7, tel. 088/32330, 088/21454. 42 rooms, 28 with bath. AE, DC, MC, V. Moderate.*

Sarajevo **Aeroplan.** Decorated in typical Bosnian style and located in the
Dining city center, Aeroplan has Bosnian specialties to match. Among them is *Bosanski lonac*, the delicious and hearty local stew. *Maršala Tita. Dress: informal. Reservations advised. AE, DC, MC. Expensive.*

Daire. Daire has been charmingly converted from a complex of 17th century storehouses. Again, the food and decor are typically Bosnian, reflecting the centuries of Turkish influence. Try the *musaka* or *sarma*, stuffed vine leaf. *Halaci 5, tel. 071/537614. Dress: informal. Reservations advised. AE, DC, MC. Expensive.*

Lodging **Holiday Inn Sarajevo.** Given its trial by fire when it was the base for many journalists covering the 1984 Olympics, the Holiday Inn remains the hotel most frequented by Americans. It is a modern, businesslike hotel, built in 1983, near the railroad station. There are no unpleasant surprises here. *Vojvode*

putnika 6a, tel. 071/215688. 330 rooms with shower. Facilities:
saunas, pool. AE, DC, MC. Expensive.

Europa. Here is a hotel that has been accommodating travelers
for more than 100 years; it was renovated and expanded in
1978. Service can be erratic, but it has style and is ideally
placed in the Old Town. *JNA bb, tel. 071/532722. 225 rooms*
with shower. AE, DC, MC. Moderate.

National. Across the river from the center, the National is an
older hotel, but worth considering if you're on a budget. Like
other inexpensive Yugoslav hotels, the National has fewer
comforts than its more modern counterparts, but the dark carpets and old wood everywhere combine to give it more of an
exotic feel. *Obala P. Komune 5, tel. 071/532266. 75 rooms, 43*
with bath. No credit cards. Inexpensive.

Macedonia

It is quite a trek to reach Macedonia, Yugoslavia's landlocked
southernmost republic. But it's worth it to experience one of
the least spoiled corners of Europe. At one time, of course,
Macedonia was the most powerful nation in the ancient world
and was even Alexander the Great's launchpad for a vast empire. Today, the original territory of Macedonia is fragmented
between Yugoslavia, Greece, and Bulgaria, although many
Macedonians share an intense feeling of nationality that tran-
scends any such boundaries.

It's not only the name that has survived centuries of Roman,
Byzantine, and Turkish rule, along with the more recent
games of power. The resemblance between some young Macedonians and the classical busts of their forefathers is really
quite startling.

In addition to fine scenery—mountains, fertile plains, and river gorges—Macedonia has a number of lakes skirting its
borders with Greece and Albania. These are good for the more
typical tourist pursuits of swimming and sailing.

Continuing excavations at Heraclea Lyncestis (near Bitola),
Lichnidos (Ohrid), Skupi (Skopje), and Stobi reveal ever more
evidence of the sophisticated lifestyles enjoyed in Greco-
Roman and Roman-Byzantine times. But above all, this was a
stronghold of the Orthodox faith, and you'll see dozens of
medieval monasteries—some of the earliest and finest examples of an architectural style that expressed a dynamism never
before seen in the Byzantine period. Some art historians claim
that this style foreshadowed the Renaissance of the 15th and
16th centuries, by which time Macedonia itself had been sub-
merged under Ottoman rule.

Modern industrialization and tourism have imposed their own
imprint, sometimes regrettable. But in the bazaars and mar-
ket-places and in scores of small communities, a profusion of
folklore is alive and well. The jet age still seems a world away.

Getting Around

Two or three flights a week are scheduled from Skopje to
Ohrid, taking 30 minutes. To see all the sights mentioned, you
need a car. Otherwise the main areas of the region are well

served by bus. The bus terminus in Skopje is in the center of town, near the Stone Bridge (tel. 091/236254).

Guided Tours

Tours around Macedonia are arranged in the main season from Skopje by **Interimpex** (tel. 091/239669 or 091/228604). Sightseeing tours from either Skopje or Ohrid take in all the main historic sights and places of natural beauty in their respective localities. Much of this itinerary also is featured in monastery tours around south Serbia.

Tourist Information

Ohrid. Turist bureau Biljana, Partizanska, tel. 096/22494.
Skopje. Gradski zid, blok III, tel. 091/233843; also at the entrance to Čaršija (Bazaar), near the Stone Bridge.

Exploring

Skopje   Skopje is in a beautiful setting at the foot of the mountain of Vodno, with views to the more distant range of Šar Planina. First impressions are of a thoroughly modern and fast-growing city. In fact, its roots are in prehistory. As the Roman town of Skupi, it prospered on a site about five miles (eight kilometers) northwest of the present center.

An earthquake destroyed ancient Skupi in AD 518, and nearly 1,500 years later, a similar disaster caused its rebirth as a modern city. If you arrive by train, you'll see, next to the new railroad station, the restored remnants of the old one (now housing the Skopje Town Museum), with its clock stopped at 5:17. That was the time on the morning of July 26, 1963, when the first of a series of tremors rumbled beneath Skopje. The earthquake ultimately destroyed 80% of the buildings and took more than 1,000 lives. The building of the new Skopje and restoration of the old are the result of a massive national effort with international support.

The city is divided by the winding river Vardar. The remains of the original fortified town rise above the north bank. The core of the **Old Town,** developed over 500 years of Turkish rule, is below: It is a maze of narrow alleys threading through the Čaršija, or Bazaar. From the modern center, you reach it by crossing the fine old **Stone Bridge.** You soon come to the Tourist Information Center, where you can get a map and the latest information. **Čaršija** is by far the most interesting quarter, with its workshops and boutiques offering slippers and other leather goods and items of gold and silver. You eventually come out into the lively marketplace near the largest of Skopje's several mosques.

Three main sights are not to be missed. The first is the little Orthodox church of **Sveti Spas** (St. Savior) on Samoilava Street. Its iconostasis—a magnificent carved screen separating nave from chancel—was completed in 1824. On the far right panel, you'll find self-portraits of the artists as they wield their tools at a workbench.

Kuršumli han is the second stop, a fine inn from the 16th century, now restored and housing the imposing archaeological

Macedonia

exhibits of the Museum of Macedonia. *Old Bazaar. Admission: 2,000 dinars. Open 10–6, closed Mon.*

For the third sight, you'll need to travel four miles (seven kilometers) up the slopes of Vodno mountain to the church of **Svati Pantelejmon** at Nerezi. It contains some of the most beautiful and best-known Byzantine frescoes in the country—among the first in the 12th century to demonstrate a new and powerful humanism. The grief on the face of Mary is almost tangible as she mourns over the body of Christ in *The Lamentation*. Just across the courtyard there is a good restaurant (*see* Dining).

Stobi About 50 miles (80 kilometers) southeast of Skopje, to the right of the main road, the ruins of the once great Roman city of Stobi lie scattered about the grassy plain of the Vardar valley. Its heyday extended from the 1st century until the Goths sacked it in the 5th; the earthquake of AD 518 completed the destruction. There's much more to be seen than first impressions might suggest, and guides are available to explain the site in meticulous detail. But there's a lot to be said for exploring alone and letting your imagination wander. Most of what you see is from the 4th and 5th centuries, including some of the most complete remains of early-Christian houses in the Mediterranean region. There are remains of churches, palaces, baths, and a fine amphitheater, but the highlights for most visitors are the outstanding mosaics totaling several thousand square yards (or meters). Time your trip for late April or after or you might miss out on them; they're protected by a covering of sand during the winter.

Just beyond Stobi, you turn right for the narrow, curving road over the Pletvor Pass 3,260 feet (994 meters). Somewhat clogged by trucks, it leads to the tobacco-growing center of **Prilep.** From here the main road to Bitola streaks across the fertile plains of Bitolska Polje, full of tobacco, wheat, poppies, and grapevines. There's an even prettier deviation via **Kruševo,** a marvelous mountain town that you'll see long before you reach it, perched high above in a vivid splash of red roofs.

Kruševo Kruševo was a hotbed of resistance against the Turks and even proclaimed itself a republic in 1903. Alas, the rebellion was short-lived, for after 12 da/s the populace was violently defeated. Not surprisingly, there isn't a mosque to be seen, but it's a living museum of urban architecture from the 19th and early 20th centuries, characterized by jutting upper stories, wood carving, and wrought ironwork.

Bitola Bitola was immensely important in Turkish times, as you might guess from some of the grand houses along Maršala Tita Street in the town center. Some are in need of spit and polish, but these were the houses of merchants who did business with the distant capitals of western Europe when Bitola was one of the most important centers in the Balkans. But its most famous sight lies just over one mile from the town. There are the ruins of the Greco-Roman settlement of **Heraclea Lyncestis,** which flourished up to the early Christian period. The setting against a mountainous backdrop is dramatic and, like Stobi, it has some superb mosaics. You'll find the most impressive in the vestibule of the Large Basilica: 120 square yards (100 square meters) representing the universe with all its forms of life, including such graphic details as a leopard tearing at a fallen stag.

Ohrid By the main road, it's 45 miles (72 kilometers) from Bitola to Ohrid. A short and worthwhile side trip is up into the **Pelister National Park,** nine miles (15 kilometers) west of Bitola. The highest point of the Pelister massif is 8,532 feet (2,600 meters), but the main attraction is its magnificent cloak of coniferous forests—one of the few habitats of the molica pine—as well as a great variety of plants, including rare crocuses. The combination of altitude and pinewoods makes for a heady cocktail of unpolluted air.

A rash of modern building has changed the outskirts of Ohrid beyond recognition in the past decade or so, but the lakeside core of this marvelous little town has been carefully protected. Of its complicated and often bloody history, the most important facts to remember are that it was on the famed Roman road, the Via Egnatia, linking the Adriatic and Aegean seas. In the 9th century, it became a major seat of Christian learning, drawing pilgrims and scholars from far and wide to study the new Slavonic script, culture, and art. Churches sprung up, and artists labored to cover almost every inch of their walls with frescoes of a wondrous vitality. During the 500 years of Turkish rule, most of the churches were turned into mosques or fell into disrepair, but a large proportion of the frescoes were covered with whitewash, thus conserving them for later generations to discover.

Start down at the harbor and work your way uphill, by the main thoroughfare of Car Samuil Street. Most of the houses, as opposed to the much older churches, are from the 19th and early 20th centuries, their jutting second and third stories all but meeting over your head. Very soon, on your left, you'll come to one of the greatest ecclesiastic monuments in Yugoslavia: the Cathedral of **Sveta Sofija** (St. Sofia). It has taken a major rescue operation to restore the shaky building and, mainly around the altar, its whitewashed frescoes, some of which date back to the 11th century and are among the best surviving examples of Byzantine art from that period. The *mimbar*, or pulpit, is a reminder of the cathedral's days as a mosque.

At the top of Car Samuil Street, turn right into **Ilindenska.** A Roman theater has recently been excavated on the left, and to the right is the way to **Sveti Kliment.** This was never a mosque and so became a repository for ecclesiastic treasures from many other places. Among the few named artists from the early 14th century were Mihailo and Eutihije; you'll find their initials in several places on the magnificent frescoes here, including on the bowl of *The Last Supper*.

Crowning the hill above old Ohrid are the imposing ruined fortress walls of Samuilo, emperor of the medieval Slav state of Macedonia. From the walls, paths lead down through the woods to an ancient complex, less visited than most but of particular significance. Though *St. Clement's Monastery* was later to be completely obliterated by a mosque, its original foundations have now been excavated, revealing the site of one of the world's first "universities," from which the earliest scholars of the new Slav alphabet went out to spread the message of Christianity. It's a peaceful spot, high on a bluff above the tiny fishing community of **Kaneo.** You can visit Kaneo by boat from Ohrid harbor and clamber up to the small 13th-century church of Sv. Jovan Kaneo, perched on the rocky bluff.

Struga About nine miles (15 kilometers) northwest of Ohrid is Struga, at the head of the lake. Saturday is the best day to visit. The market—one of the most colorful in the country—draws country folk in local costume from miles around with their rich variety of wares. Struga sits astride the fast-flowing river Crni Drim. On the return route to Skopje, you follow Crni Drim downstream toward Debar on the Albanian border. It's a dramatic road winding beneath the mountains, with villages clinging to steep slopes, some with baked-clay houses and slender minarets announcing their predominantly Albanian populations; others, with their square houses of rough and dressed stone, are typically Macedonian.

At Debar, the Crni Drim rushes off into Albania and the road turns away to follow the river Radika upstream between the Bistra and Korab mountain ranges. About 12 miles (20 kilometers) north of Debar, take a small road to the right and climb about a mile to the aptly named monastery of **Sveti Jovan Bigorski** (St. John of the Rocks). The views from here are stunning and the place itself enchanting, though mostly rebuilt in the early 19th century. The main sight is the iconostasis. If you've seen the one in Sveti Spas church in Skopje, you might recognize the masterly skill of the same craftsmen, the Filipovski brothers and Frčkovski from nearby Galičnik.

Galičnik Galičnik is the setting for famous wedding festivities each July. At 4,600 feet (1,400 meters), the village is cut off by snow for several months. Even nowadays it's all but deserted except in summer. The only way to reach it by road is from the summer lakeside resort of **Mavrovo,** just off the road to Skopje. Now begins a long winding descent to Gostivar for the final stretch across a plain watered by the upper Vardar river.

Tetovo The tobacco town of Tetovo is worth a halt for its 17th-century **Colored Mosque** (so-called because of the decorative painting on its outer walls) and the monastic complex of **Sersem Ali Baba**. The latter now houses a museum, a small hotel, and a restaurant from which you can look out over the gardens and ponder the frenetic rituals of the Whirling Dervishes whose home this was in the 18th and 19th centuries.

There are now only 24 miles (40 kilometers) to go, over the mountains and criss-crossing the river Vardar, before completing the Macedonian circuit.

Dining and Lodging

For details and price category definitions, *see* Dining and Lodging in Essential Information.

Kruševo **Montana.** A modern hotel built in 1974, the Montana stands on
Lodging a hillside with lovely views over this very attractive town. *Tel. 77121. 94 rooms with shower. Facilities: pool. AE. Moderate.*

Ohrid **Obridska Pastrmka.** Near the harbor and Old Town, this is the
Dining best place to try the special variety of salmon-trout found only in lake Ohrid. It's cooked with onions, tomato juice, parsley, and slices of lemon. *Ul. Petar Čaule, tel. 096/23827. Dress: informal. Reservations accepted. No credit cards. Moderate.*
Orient. A little outside the Old Town, Orient also serves local fish specialties as well as more international fare. *Tel. 096/22217. Dress: informal. Reservations accepted. AE, DC, V. Moderate.*

Lodging **Gorica.** This hotel is in a lovely wooded setting above its own pebbled beach, 3 miles (5 kilometers) south of the resort. Built in 1970, it was renovated in the early '80s and the rooms are bright and comfortable. *Ul. Naum Ohridski 57, tel. 096/22020. 131 rooms with bath. Facilities: pool, tennis. AE, DC, V. Expensive.*
Metropol. Five miles (8 kilometers) to the south of Ohrid, the Metropol is the best hotel in the area. A road separates it from the lakeshore and pebbled beach, but these are accessible by an underpass from the hotel that was built in 1975 and recently extended. *Dolnokonjsko bb, tel. 096/25000. More than 200 rooms with bath. Facilities: saunas, pool, tennis. AE, DC, MC, V. Expensive.*

Skopje **Sveti Pantelejmon.** It's well worth the 4-mile (6-kilometer) trek
Dining up the mountainside to Nerezi for the stunning views over the city and the well-prepared national dishes. Try one of the lamb or kebab specialties. The restaurant is part of the old monastery compound. *Nerezi, tel. 091/258045. Dress: informal. Reservations advised. No credit cards. Moderate.*

Lodging **Bristol.** A town house dating from the '20s, renovated in 1985, the Bristol is a small, comfortable hotel in the center of the city. *Maršala Tito, tel. 091/239821. 33 rooms with bath or shower. Facilities: nightclub. AE, DC, MC, V. Moderate.*
Grand Hotel Skopje. Centrally located, the Grand Hotel is by the river Vardar. Rooms are comfortable and some have river views. Its Ognjiste cellar restaurant is a better choice than the somewhat bleak main restaurant. *Moša Pijade 2, tel.*

091/239925. 180 rooms with bath or shower. Facilities: disco. AE, DC, V. Moderate.

Struga
Lodging

Biser. Here's a chance to get a real feel of Macedonian adventure. The Biser is built in attractive local style, set into a rock bluff adjoining Kalište Monastery, about 5 miles (8 kilometers) from Struga, near the Albanian border. Despite the atmospheric combination of history and mystery, the hotel is comfortable and well run. *KALišta, near Struga, tel. 72991. 51 rooms with bath or shower. Facilities: tennis. AE, DC, V. Expensive.*

Drim. Built in 1977 on the lakeshore near the Crni Drim river, Drim is a large and comfortable hotel. An attractive feature is its spacious, domed lobby with garden. *Kej. Boris Kidrić, tel. 72511. 325 rooms with bath or shower. Facilities: pool, tennis. AE, DC, V. Moderate.*

Conversion Tables

Distance

Kilometers/Miles To change kilometers to miles, multiply kilometers by .621.
To change miles to kilometers, multiply miles by 1.61.

Km to Mi	Mi to Km
1 = .62	1 = 1.6
2 = 1.2	2 = 3.2
3 = 1.9	3 = 4.8
4 = 2.5	4 = 6.4
5 = 3.1	5 = 8.1
6 = 3.7	6 = 9.7
7 = 4.3	7 = 11.3
8 = 5.0	8 = 12.9
9 = 5.6	9 = 14.5

Meters/Feet To change meters to feet, multiply meters by 3.28.
To change feet to meters, multiply feet by .305.

Meters to Feet	Feet to Meters
1 = 3.3	1 = .31
2 = 6.6	2 = .61
3 = 9.8	3 = .92
4 = 13.1	4 = 1.2
5 = 16.4	5 = 1.5
6 = 19.7	6 = 1.8
7 = 23.0	7 = 2.1
8 = 26.2	8 = 2.4
9 = 29.5	9 = 2.7

Weight

Kilograms/Pounds To change kilograms to pounds, multiply by 2.20.
To change pounds to kilograms, multiply by .453.

Kilos to Pounds	Pounds to Kilos
1 = 2.2	1 = .45
2 = 4.4	2 = .91
3 = 6.6	3 = 1.4
4 = 8.8	4 = 1.8
5 = 11.0	5 = 2.3
6 = 13.2	6 = 2.7

7 = 15.4	7 = 3.2
8 = 17.6	8 = 3.6
9 = 19.8	9 = 4.1

Grams/Ounces To change grams to ounces, multiply grams by .035.
To change ounces to grams, multiply ounces by 28.4.

Grams to Ounces	Ounces to Grams
1 = .04	1 = 28
2 = .07	2 = 57
3 = .11	3 = 85
4 = .14	4 = 114
5 = .18	5 = 142
6 = .21	6 = 170
7 = .25	7 = 199
8 = .28	8 = 227
9 = .32	9 = 256

Liquid Volume

Liters/U.S. Gallons To change liters to U.S. gallons, multiply liters by .264.
To change U.S. gallons to liters, multiply gallons by 3.79.

Liters to U.S. Gallons	U.S. Gallons to Liters
1 = .26	1 = 3.8
2 = .53	2 = 7.6
3 = .79	3 = 11.4
4 = 1.1	4 = 15.2
5 = 1.3	5 = 19.0
6 = 1.6	6 = 22.7
7 = 1.8	7 = 26.5
8 = 2.1	8 = 30.3
9 = 2.4	9 = 34.1

Clothing Sizes

Men Suits							
U.S./U.K.	36	38	40	42	44	46	48
Europe	46	48	50	52	54	56	58

Shirts	U.S./U.K.	14	14½	15	15½	16	16½	17	17½
	Europe	36	37	38	39	40	41	42	43

Shoes	U.S.	7½	8	8½/9	9½/10	10½/11	11½/12	12½
	Europe	40	41	42	43	44	45	46

Women Dresses and Coats	U.S.	4	6	8	10	12	14	16
	U.K.	28	30	32	34	36	38	40
	Europe	34	36	38	40	42	44	46

Blouses and Sweaters	U.S.	4	6	8	10	12	14	16
	U.K.	30	32	34	36	38	40	42
	Europe	36	38	40	42	44	46	48

Shoes	U.S.	5	6	7	8	9
	U.K.	3½	4½	5½	6½	7½
	Europe	35	37	38	39	40/41

Note that these sizes are not exact. You should *always* try on before buying.

Index

Introducing a new magazine for people who love to travel but don't care much for travel magazines

Condé Nast has done it.

If you yearn to travel *off* the beaten path—welcome to *Condé Nast Traveler,* a unique new magazine from the publishers of *Vogue, Gourmet, HG, GQ* and *Vanity Fair.*

Condé Nast Traveler brings you *real* inside information—the kind tourists never get—written by well-connected professional travelers.

From a hotel where you can feed giraffes from your bedroom window...to a room with a view that reveals the soul of Florence. From the best skiing in August to the best jazz joint in Dubrovnik. "Hot spots," great escapes, exciting adventures...

Act now, and get a full year of *Condé Nast Traveler* for only $1 an issue.

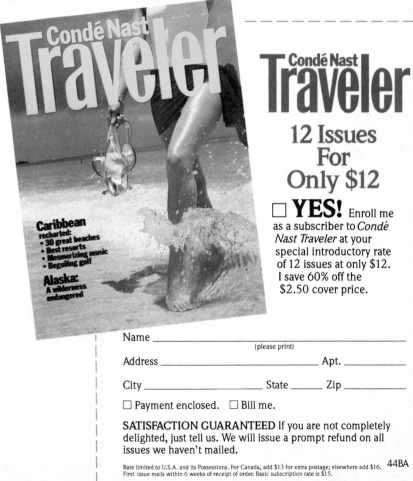

Condé Nast Traveler

12 Issues For Only $12

☐ **YES!** Enroll me as a subscriber to *Condé Nast Traveler* at your special introductory rate of 12 issues at only $12. I save 60% off the $2.50 cover price.

Name _____
(please print)

Address _____ Apt. _____

City _____ State _____ Zip _____

☐ Payment enclosed. ☐ Bill me.

SATISFACTION GUARANTEED If you are not completely delighted, just tell us. We will issue a prompt refund on all issues we haven't mailed.

Rate limited to U.S.A. and its Possessions. For Canada, add $13 for extra postage; elsewhere add $16. 44BA
First issue mails within 6 weeks of receipt of order. Basic subscription rate is $15.

Now street smarts around the world cost only $1 a month

Each issue of the exciting new *Condé Nast Traveler* brings you such uncommon guidance as...

Where to, How to, What to.
Where to find the best calypso and golf in the Caribbean; how to get a 30% food and booze discount at a posh Venice hotel; what to pack for India.

Travel secrets of the famous.
Shop where Princess Di shops; surf where Mick Jagger surfs; join two kings and a billionaire on a cruise up the Amazon.

Take-along Charts, Maps, Calendars.
30 great Caribbean beaches; an art-lover's map of Barcelona; a shoe-fetishist's map of Paris.

With *Condé Nast Traveler,* you will always have the insider's guide to the outside world.

NEW FROM CONDÉ NAST

Personal Itinerary

Departure *Date*

Time

Transportation

Arrival *Date* *Time*

Departure *Date* *Time*

Transportation

Accommodations

Arrival *Date* *Time*

Departure *Date* *Time*

Transportation

Accommodations

Arrival *Date* *Time*

Departure *Date* *Time*

Transportation

Accommodations

Personal Itinerary

Arrival *Date*   *Time*

Departure *Date*   *Time*

Transportation

Accommodations

Arrival *Date*   *Time*

Departure *Date*   *Time*

Transportation

Accommodations

Arrival *Date*   *Time*

Departure *Date*   *Time*

Transportation

Accommodations

Arrival *Date*   *Time*

Departure *Date*   *Time*

Transportation

Accommodations

Personal Itinerary

Arrival *Date*   *Time*

Departure *Date*   *Time*

Transportation

Accommodations

Arrival *Date*   *Time*

Departure *Date*   *Time*

Transportation

Accommodations

Arrival *Date*   *Time*

Departure *Date*   *Time*

Transportation

Accommodations

Arrival *Date*   *Time*

Departure *Date*   *Time*

Transportation

Accommodations

Personal Itinerary

Arrival	*Date*	*Time*
Departure	*Date*	*Time*
Transportation		
Accommodations		

Arrival	*Date*	*Time*
Departure	*Date*	*Time*
Transportation		
Accommodations		

Arrival	*Date*	*Time*
Departure	*Date*	*Time*
Transportation		
Accommodations		

Arrival	*Date*	*Time*
Departure	*Date*	*Time*
Transportation		
Accommodations		

Personal Itinerary

Arrival   *Date*   *Time*

Departure   *Date*   *Time*

Transportation

Accommodations

Arrival   *Date*   *Time*

Departure   *Date*   *Time*

Transportation

Accommodations

Arrival   *Date*   *Time*

Departure   *Date*   *Time*

Transportation

Accommodations

Arrival   *Date*   *Time*

Departure   *Date*   *Time*

Transportation

Accommodations

Personal Itinerary

Arrival *Date*   *Time*

Departure *Date*   *Time*

Transportation

Accommodations

Arrival *Date*   *Time*

Departure *Date*   *Time*

Transportation

Accommodations

Arrival *Date*   *Time*

Departure *Date*   *Time*

Transportation

Accommodations

Arrival *Date*   *Time*

Departure *Date*   *Time*

Transportation

Accommodations

Addresses

Name	*Name*
Address	*Address*
Telephone	*Telephone*
Name	*Name*
Address	*Address*
Telephone	*Telephone*
Name	*Name*
Address	*Address*
Telephone	*Telephone*
Name	*Name*
Address	*Address*
Telephone	*Telephone*
Name	*Name*
Address	*Address*
Telephone	*Telephone*
Name	*Name*
Address	*Address*
Telephone	*Telephone*
Name	*Name*
Address	*Address*
Telephone	*Telephone*
Name	*Name*
Address	*Address*
Telephone	*Telephone*

Addresses

Name	*Name*
Address	*Address*
Telephone	*Telephone*
Name	*Name*
Address	*Address*
Telephone	*Telephone*
Name	*Name*
Address	*Address*
Telephone	*Telephone*
Name	*Name*
Address	*Address*
Telephone	*Telephone*
Name	*Name*
Address	*Address*
Telephone	*Telephone*
Name	*Name*
Address	*Address*
Telephone	*Telephone*
Name	*Name*
Address	*Address*
Telephone	*Telephone*
Name	*Name*
Address	*Address*
Telephone	*Telephone*

Fodor's Travel Guides

U.S. Guides

Alaska
American Cities
The American South
Arizona
Atlantic City & the
  New Jersey Shore
Boston
California
Cape Cod
Carolinas & the
  Georgia Coast
Chesapeake
Chicago
Colorado
Dallas & Fort Worth
Disney World & the
  Orlando Area

The Far West
Florida
Greater Miami,
  Fort Lauderdale,
  Palm Beach
Hawaii
Hawaii (Great Travel
  Values)
Houston & Galveston
I-10: California to
  Florida
I-55: Chicago to New
  Orleans
I-75: Michigan to
  Florida
I-80: San Francisco to
  New York

I-95: Maine to Miami
Las Vegas
Los Angeles, Orange
  County, Palm Springs
Maui
New England
New Mexico
New Orleans
New Orleans (Pocket
  Guide)
New York City
New York City (Pocket
  Guide)
New York State
Pacific North Coast
Philadelphia
Puerto Rico (Fun in)

Rockies
San Diego
San Francisco
San Francisco (Pocket
  Guide)
Texas
United States of
  America
Virgin Islands
  (U.S. & British)
Virginia
Waikiki
Washington, DC
Williamsburg,
  Jamestown &
  Yorktown

Foreign Guides

Acapulco
Amsterdam
Australia, New Zealand
  & the South Pacific
Austria
The Bahamas
The Bahamas (Pocket
  Guide)
Barbados (Fun in)
Beijing, Guangzhou &
  Shanghai
Belgium & Luxembourg
Bermuda
Brazil
Britain (Great Travel
  Values)
Canada
Canada (Great Travel
  Values)
Canada's Maritime
  Provinces
Cancún, Cozumel,
  Mérida, The
  Yucatán
Caribbean
Caribbean (Great
  Travel Values)

Central America
Copenhagen,
  Stockholm, Oslo,
  Helsinki, Reykjavik
Eastern Europe
Egypt
Europe
Europe (Budget)
Florence & Venice
France
France (Great Travel
  Values)
Germany
Germany (Great Travel
  Values)
Great Britain
Greece
Holland
Hong Kong & Macau
Hungary
India
Ireland
Israel
Italy
Italy (Great Travel
  Values)
Jamaica (Fun in)

Japan
Japan (Great Travel
  Values)
Jordan & the Holy Land
Kenya
Korea
Lisbon
Loire Valley
London
London (Pocket Guide)
London (Great Travel
  Values)
Madrid
Mexico
Mexico (Great Travel
  Values)
Mexico City & Acapulco
Mexico's Baja & Puerto
  Vallarta, Mazatlán,
  Manzanillo, Copper
  Canyon
Montreal
Munich
New Zealand
North Africa
Paris
Paris (Pocket Guide)

People's Republic of
  China
Portugal
Province of Quebec
Rio de Janeiro
The Riviera (Fun on)
Rome
St. Martin/St. Maarten
Scandinavia
Scotland
Singapore
South America
South Pacific
Southeast Asia
Soviet Union
Spain
Spain (Great Travel
  Values)
Sweden
Switzerland
Sydney
Tokyo
Toronto
Turkey
Vienna
Yugoslavia

Special-Interest Guides

Bed & Breakfast
  Guide: North America
  1936...On the
  Continent

Royalty Watching
Selected Hotels of
  Europe

Selected Resorts
  and Hotels of the U.S.
Ski Resorts of North
  America

Views to Dine by
  around the World

Join us in updating the next edition of your Fodor's guide

Title of Guide:

1 Hotel ☐ Restaurant ☐ *(check one)*

Name

Number/Street

City/State/Country

Comments

2 Hotel ☐ Restaurant ☐ *(check one)*

Name

Number/Street

City/State/Country

Comments

3 Hotel ☐ Restaurant ☐ *(check one)*

Name

Number/Street

City/State/Country

Comments

Your Name *(optional)*

Address

General Comments

Business Reply Mail

First Class   Permit N⁰ 7775   New York, NY

Postage will be paid by addressee

Fodor's Travel Publications

201 East 50th Street

New York, NY 10022